Alternative Minimum Tax

If AMTI minus the exemption is:		The Tax Is:	
Over—	But Not Over—		Of the Amount Over—
$0	$175,000*	26%	$0
175,000*		$45,500* + 28%	175,000*

*$87,500 and $22,750 for married taxpayers filing separately.

Category		
OASDI		
Medicare	1.45%	None
Total	7.65%	

Self-Employment Tax

Category	Rate	Dollar Limit
OASDI	12.40%	$97,500
Medicare	2.90%	None
Total	15.30%	

STANDARD DEDUCTION

Filing Status	2007 Amount
Married individuals filing joint returns and surviving spouses	$10,700
Heads of households	7,850
Unmarried individuals (other than surviving spouses and heads of households)	5,350
Married individuals filing separate return	5,350
Additional standard deductions for the aged and the blind	
Individual who is married and surviving spouses	1,050*
Individual who is unmarried and not a surviving spouse	1,300*
Taxpayer claimed as dependent on another taxpayer's return	850

*These amounts are $2,100 and $2,600, respectively, for a taxpayer who is both aged and blind.

Personal Exemption 2007: $3,400 *Reduction in personal and dependency exemptions:* The personal and dependency exemption deductions are reduced or eliminated for certain high-income taxpayers. When a taxpayer's AGI exceeds the "phaseout begins after" amount described below, the deduction is reduced by 2% for each $2,500 (or fraction thereof) by which AGI exceeds such amount. For married persons filing separately, the exemption deduction is reduced by 2% for each $1,250 (or fraction thereof) by which AGI exceeds the "phaseout begins after" amount. The personal exemption deduction amount cannot be reduced below zero. Beginning in 2006, this phaseout is being gradually eliminated. In 2007, the full phaseout is decreased by one-third. The phaseout ranges for 2007 are:

Filing Status	*Phaseout Begins After*	*Phaseout Completed After*
Married individuals filing joint return and surviving spouses	$234,600	$357,100
Heads of households	195,500	318,000
Unmarried taxpayers (other than surviving spouses and heads of households)	156,400	278,900
Married individuals filing separate returns	117,300	178,550

Itemized Deductions

The itemized deductions that are otherwise deductible for the tax year are reduced by the lesser of (1) 3% of the excess of AGI over a threshold amount, or (2) 80% of the amount of itemized deductions otherwise deductible for the tax year excluding medical expenses, investment interest expense, casualty losses, and wagering losses to the extent of wagering gains. The threshold amount for the 2007 tax year is $156,400 (except for married individuals filing separate returns for which it is $78,200). Beginning in 2007, this reduction is being gradually eliminated. In 2007, the full reduction is decreased by one-third.

PRENTICE HALL'S FEDERAL TAXATION 2008

Corporations, Partnerships, Estates, and Trusts

EDITORS

KENNETH E. ANDERSON
University of Tennessee

THOMAS R. POPE
University of Kentucky

JOHN L. KRAMER
University of Florida

CONTRIBUTING AUTHORS

ANNA C. FOWLER
University of Texas at Austin (Emeritus)

DAVID S. HULSE
University of Kentucky

RICHARD J. JOSEPH
Hult International Business School

MICHAEL S. SCHADEWALD
University of Wisconsin—Milwaukee

Upper Saddle River, NJ 07458

AVP/Executive Editor: Steve Sartori
Development Manager: Ashley Santora
Project Manager: Susan Abraham
Editorial Assistant: Marybeth Ward
Associate Director, Production Editorial: Judy Leale
Managing Editor: Cynthia Zonneveld
Production Editor: Melissa Feimer
Permissions Coordinator: Charles Morris
Associate Director, Manufacturing: Vinnie Scelta
Manufacturing Buyer: Michelle Klein
Design/Composition Manager: Christy Mahon
Cover Design: Bruce Kenselaar
Manager, Cover Visual Research & Permissions: Karen Sanatar
Composition: Black Dot Group
Full-Service Project Management: Sandra Reinhard/Black Dot Group
Printer/Binder: Courier—Kendallville
Typeface: 10/12 Sabon

Credits and acknowledgments borrowed from other sources and reproduced, with permission, in this textbook appear on appropriate page within the text.

Pearson Education LTD.
Pearson Education Singapore, Pte. Ltd
Pearson Education, Canada, Ltd
Pearson Education–Japan
Pearson Education Australia PTY, Limited
Pearson Education North Asia Ltd
Pearson Educación de Mexico, S.A. de C.V.
Pearson Education Malaysia, Pte. Ltd.

10 9 8 7 6 5 4 3 2 1
ISBN-13: 978-0-13-615643-7
ISBN-10: 0-13-615643-6

CONTENTS

About the Editors

KENNETH E. ANDERSON

Kenneth E. Anderson is the Pugh & Company Professor of Accounting at the University of Tennessee. He earned a B.B.A. from the University of Wisconsin–Milwaukee and subsequently attained the level of tax manager with Arthur Young (now part of Ernst & Young). He then earned a Ph.D. from Indiana University. He teaches introductory taxation, corporate taxation, partnership taxation, tax research, and tax strategy, and has three times won the Beta Alpha Psi Outstanding Educator Award. Professor Anderson has published articles in *The Accounting Review, The Journal of the American Taxation Association,* the *Journal of Accountancy,* the *Journal of Financial Service Professionals,* and a number of other journals.

THOMAS R. POPE

Thomas R. Pope is the Ernst & Young Professor of Accounting at the University of Kentucky. He received a B.S. from the University of Louisville and an M.S. and D.B.A. in business administration from the University of Kentucky. He teaches international taxation, partnership and S corporation taxation, tax research and policy, and introductory taxation and has won outstanding teaching awards at the University, College, and School of Accountancy levels. He has published articles in *The Accounting Review,* the *Tax Adviser, Taxes,* and a number of other journals. Professor Pope's extensive professional experience includes eight years with Big Four accounting firms. Five of those years were with Ernst & Whinney (now part of Ernst & Young), including two years with their National Tax Department in Washington, D.C. He subsequently held the position of Senior Manager in charge of the Tax Department in Lexington, Kentucky. Professor Pope also has been a leader and speaker at professional tax conferences all over the United States and is active as a tax consultant.

JOHN L. KRAMER

John L. Kramer is a Professor of Accounting and the Randall Parks Professor at the University of Florida. He is a recipient of a Teaching Improvement Program award given by the University of Florida in 1994. He holds a Ph.D. in Business Administration and an M.B.A. from the University of Michigan (Ann Arbor), and a B.B.A. from the University of Michigan (Dearborn). He is a past president of the American Taxation Association and the Florida Association of Accounting Educators, as well as a past editor of *The Journal of the American Taxation Association.* In 2001, Professor Kramer received the Ray M. Sommerfeld Outstanding Tax Education Award, co-sponsored by the American Taxation Association and Ernst & Young. Professor Kramer has taught for the American Institute of CPAs, American Tax Institute of Europe, and a number of national and regional accounting firms. He is a frequent speaker at academic and professional conferences, as well as having served as an expert witness in a number of court cases. He has published over 50 articles in *The Accounting Review, The Journal of the American Taxation Association,* the *Tax Adviser,* the *Journal of Taxation,* and other academic and professional journals. Professor Kramer has been an editor on *The Prentice Hall Federal Tax* series since 1989.

About the Authors

Anna C. Fowler is the John Arch White Professor Emeritus in the Department of Accounting at the University of Texas at Austin. She received her B.S. in accounting from the University of Alabama and her M.B.A. and Ph.D. from the University of Texas at Austin. Active in the American Taxation Association throughout her academic career, she has served on the editorial board of its journal and held many positions, including president. She is a former member of the American Institute of CPA's Tax Executive Committee and currently chairs the AICPA's Regulation/Tax Subcommittee for the CPA exam. She has published a number of articles, most of which have dealt with estate planning or real estate transaction issues. In 2002, she received the Ray M. Sommerfeld Outstanding Educator Award, co-sponsored by the American Taxation Association and Ernst & Young.

David S. Hulse is the Deloitte & Touche Professor of Accountancy at the University of Kentucky. He received an undergraduate degree from Shippensburg University, an M.S. from Louisiana State University, and a Ph.D. from the Pennsylvania State University. He teaches introductory taxation and corporate taxation courses. Professor Hulse has published several articles on tax issues in academic and professional journals, including *The Journal of the American Taxation Association, Advances in Taxation,* the *Journal of Financial Service Professionals,* and *Tax Notes.*

Richard J. Joseph is the Academic Dean of Hult International Business School in Cambridge, Massachusetts. He is a current member of the Hult Accounting Faculty and a former member of the tax faculty of The University of Texas at Austin. A graduate *magna cum laude* of Harvard College (B.A.), Oxford University (M.Litt.), and the University of Texas at Austin School of Law (J.D.), he has taught individual, corporate, international, state and local taxation, tax research methods, and the fundamentals of financial and managerial accounting. A former adjunct professor at The University of Texas at Arlington, he also has taught contract, corporate, securities, agency, and partnership law. Before embarking on his academic career, Dean Joseph worked as an investment banker on Wall Street and as a mergers and acquisitions lawyer in Texas. His book, *The Origins of the American Income Tax*, explores the original intent, rationale, and effect of the early income tax.

Michael S. Schadewald, Ph.D., CPA, is on the faculty of the University of Wisconsin–Milwaukee, where he teaches graduate courses in multistate and international taxation. A graduate of the University of Minnesota, Professor Schadewald is a co-author of several books on multistate and international taxation, and has published more than 30 articles in academic and professional journals, including *The Accounting Review, The Journal of Accounting Research, Contemporary Accounting Research, The Journal of the American Taxation Association, The CPA Journal,* the *Journal of Taxation,* and the *Tax Adviser.* Professor Schadewald has also served on the editorial boards of *The Journal of the American Taxation Association, The International Journal of Accounting,* the *International Tax Journal, Issues in Accounting Education,* and the *Journal of Accounting Education.*

PREFACE

Why is the Pope/Anderson/Kramer series the best choice for your students?

The Pope/Anderson/Kramer 2008 Series in Federal Taxation includes three volumes and is appropriate for use in any first course in federal taxation:

Federal Taxation 2008: Individuals
Federal Taxation 2008: Corporations, Partnerships, Estates, and Trusts
(the companion book to *Individuals*)
Federal Taxation 2008: Comprehensive
(includes 29 chapters; 14 chapters from *Individuals* and 15 chapters from *Corporations*)

The 2008 Edition introduces a new feature: the financial statement implications of federal income taxes. In today's business environment of Sarbanes-Oxley and other oversight procedures, firms are paying increasing attention to how they account for income taxes in the financial statements. The primary document that dictates this treatment is *Statement of Financial Accounting Standards No. 109* (SFAS No. 109) issued by the Financial Accounting Standards Board (FASB). The increased scrutiny of the tax provision in financial statements compels tax and auditing professionals to have a strong working knowledge of this area. To help meet this need, the textbook includes a Financial Statement Implications section at the end of relevant chapters. Specifically, Chapter C:3 presents general coverage of the topic, and Chapters C:2, C:5, C:7, C:8, and C:16 describe the financial statement implications of specific transactions, for example, forming a corporation (Chapter C:2), the minimum tax credit (Chapter C:5), corporate acquisitions (Chapter C:7), intercompany transactions (Chapter C:8), and the foreign tax credit and deferred foreign earnings (Chapter C:16). Also, Problem C:3-64 provides a comprehensive tax return and financial accounting exercise to help students solidify their understanding of this important area.

We want to stress that *all* entities are covered in the *Individuals* volume although the treatment is often briefer than in the *Corporations* and *Comprehensive* volumes. The *Individuals* volume, therefore, is appropriate for colleges and universities that require only one semester of taxation as well as those that require more than one semester of taxation. Further, this volume adapts the suggestions of the Model Tax Curriculum as promulgated by the American Institute of Certified Public Accountants.

The 2008 series represents the highest level of publisher service, author expertise, and unique learning resources for students, innovative technology, and supplements:

- ***Blend of Technical Content and Readability***
  The Pope/Anderson/Kramer series is unsurpassed in blending the technical content of the tax law with a high level of readability for students. The authors continually refine this delicate balance to advance student learning.
- ***Problem Materials***
  The problem materials in the series are continually praised for enabling students to apply the tax principles in the chapters to real-life situations. Learning is enhanced with challenging problem materials and the Pope/Anderson/Kramer series offer outstanding materials for classroom use.
- ***JIT Custom Text***
  Now you can create your own tax book using content drawn from the Pope/Anderson/Kramer series. You can even include your own materials. Ask your Prentice Hall representative for specific information on custom text procedures and policies or log onto *www.prenhall.com/custombusiness* to learn more about your options.
- ***NEW TaxACT 2006 Software Packaged with the Text for a Nominal Price***
  This user-friendly tax preparation program includes more than 80 tax forms, schedules, and worksheets. TaxACT calculates returns and alerts the user to possible errors or entries.
- ***Commitment to Service***
  Faculty should log onto *www.prenhall.com/accounting* to locate their Prentice Hall representative using our unique "Rep Locator" search feature.

Expert Insights—Unique Student Learning Features

What Would You Do in This Situation? Boxes

Unique to the Pope/Anderson/Kramer series, these boxes place students in a decision-making role. The boxes include many *current controversies* that are as yet unresolved or are currently being considered by the courts.

These boxes make extensive use of **Ethical Material** as they represent choices that may put the practitioner at odds with the client.

> **WHAT WOULD YOU DO IN THIS SITUATION?**
>
> **INVENTORY VALUATION**
>
> **Jack is a new tax client. He says he and his previous accountant did not get along very well. Jack owns an automobile dealership with sales of $12 million. He has provided you with most of the information you need to prepare his tax return, but he has not yet given you the year-end inventory value. You have completed much of the work on his return, but cannot complete it without the inventory figure. You have called Jack three times about the inventory. Each time he has interrupted, and asked you what his tax liability will be at alternative inventory levels. What problem do you see?**

Stop & Think Boxes

These "speed bumps" encourage students to pause and apply what they have just learned. Solutions for each issue are provided in the box.

> **STOP & THINK** *Question:* When one company purchases the assets of another company, the purchasing company may acquire goodwill. Since purchased goodwill is a Sec. 197 intangible asset and may be amortized over 15 years, the determination of the cost of goodwill is important. How is the "cost" of goodwill determined when the purchasing company purchases many assets in the acquisition?
>
> *Solution:* The IRS requires that taxpayers use the "residual method" as prescribed in Sec. 1060. Under this method, all of the assets except for goodwill are valued. The total value of these assets are then subtracted from the total purchase price and the residual value is the amount of the purchase price that is allocated to goodwill.

Unique Margin Notes

These provide an extensive series of learning tips for students and faculty. No other text can match the quantity, quality, or variety of these resources:

- Additional Comment
- Key Points
- Real-World Examples
- Typical Misconceptions
- Ethical Points
- Self-Study Questions and Answers
- Book-to-Tax Accounting Comparisons
- Historical Notes
- Tax Strategy Tips

ETHICAL POINT

An employer must have a reasonable basis for treating a worker as an independent contractor or meet the general common law rules for determining whether an employer-employee relationship exists. Otherwise, the employer is liable for federal and state income tax withholding, FICA and FUTA taxes, interest, and penalties associated with the misclassification.

TAX STRATEGY TIP

Rather than having the corporation borrow money, an S corporation shareholder might consider borrowing money directly from the bank and then lending the loan proceeds to the corporation with the corporation guaranteeing the bank loan. In this way, the shareholder will obtain debt basis.

ADDITIONAL COMMENT

Stock purchased on which a dividend has been declared has an increased value. This value will drop when the corporation pays the dividend. If the dividend is eligible for a dividends-received deduction and the drop in value also creates a capital loss, corporate shareholders could use this event as a tax planning device. To avoid this result, no dividends-received deduction is available for stock held 45 days or less.

Innovative Technology and Supplements

For Instructors

- ***NEW TaxACT 2006 Software Packaged with the Text for a Nominal Price.*** This user-friendly tax preparation program includes more than 80 tax forms, schedules, and worksheets. TaxACT calculates, returns, and alerts the user to possible errors or entries.
- ***Instructor's Guide*** contains sample syllabi, instructor outlines, and notes on the end-of-chapter problems. It also contains solutions to the tax form/tax return preparation problems. It is available as a password-protected download from the Instructor Resource Center on *www.prenhall.com/phtax*. Ask your Prentice Hall representative for your password.
- ***Solutions Manual*** contains solutions to discussion questions, problems, and comprehensive and tax strategy problems. It also contains all solutions to the case study problems, research problems, and "What Would You Do in This Situation?" boxes. It is available as a password-protected download from the Instructor Resource Center on *www.prenhall.com/phtax* and also in hard copy. Upon written request, Prentice Hall may grant permission for faculty to post solutions on a student-accessible site, provided that this is password-protected at the school.
- ***Testing.*** The **printed Test Item File** contains a wealth of true/false, multiple-choice, and calculative problems. A computerized program is available to adopters.
- ***PowerPoint slides*** include over 300 full-color electronic transparencies available for *Individuals* and *Corporations*. These are available for download on the Instructor's Resource Center where students and faculty have access to them.

Text Companion Website for Faculty and Students Available at *www.prenhall.com/phtax*

The Web site provides a wealth of FREE material to help students study and help faculty prepare for class.

1. Free Student Resources include

- True/False and Multiple-Choice Questions
- Current Events
- Internet Resources
- Tax Law Updates
- PowerPoint Slides
- Multistate Income Taxation chapter with accompanying questions

2. Free Instructor Resources include

Supplements and PowerPoint slides are available for download at *www.prenhall.com/phtax.*

Online Tax Cases for *Individuals* and *Corporations*

- Computational questions
- Case Study Problems

ACKNOWLEDGMENTS

Our policy is to provide annual editions and to prepare timely updated supplements when major tax revisions occur. We are most appreciative of the suggestions made by outside reviewers because these extensive review procedures have been valuable to the authors and editors during the revision process.

We are also grateful to the various graduate assistants, doctoral students, and colleagues who have reviewed the text and supplementary materials and checked solutions to maintain a high level of technical accuracy. In particular, we would like to acknowledge the following colleagues who assisted in the preparation of supplemental materials for this text:

Priscilla Kenney (Supplements Coordinator)	University of Florida
Susan E. Anderson	North Carolina A&T State University
Arthur D. Cassill	Elon University
Ann Burstein Cohen	SUNY at Buffalo
Craig J. Langstraat	University of Memphis
Richard Newmark	University of Northern Colorado
Caroline Strobel	University of South Carolina

In addition, we want to thank Myron S. Scholes, Mark A. Wolfson, Merle Erickson, Edward L. Maydew, and Terry Shevlin for allowing us to use the model discussed in their text, *Taxes and Business Strategy: A Planning Approach*, as the basis for material in Chapter I:18.

Please send any comments to the editors:

Thomas R. Pope
Kenneth E. Anderson
John L. Kramer

1

CHAPTER

TAX RESEARCH

LEARNING OBJECTIVES

After studying this chapter, you should be able to

1. Describe the steps in the tax research process
2. Explain how the facts influence the tax consequences
3. Identify the sources of tax law and understand the authoritative value of each
4. Consult tax services to research an issue
5. Use a citator to assess tax authorities
6. Grasp the basics of computerized tax research
7. Understand guidelines that CPAs in tax practice should follow
8. Prepare work papers and communicate to clients

CHAPTER OUTLINE

This chapter introduces the reader to the tax research process. Its major focus is the sources of the tax law (i.e., the Internal Revenue Code and other tax authorities) and the relative weight given to each source. The chapter describes the steps in the tax research process and places particular emphasis on the importance of the facts to the tax consequences. It also describes the features of frequently used tax services and computer-based tax research resources. Finally, it explains how to use a citator.

The end product of the tax research process—the communication of results to the client—also is discussed. This text uses a hypothetical set of facts to provide a comprehensive illustration of the process. Sample work papers demonstrating how to document the results of research are included in Appendix A. In addition, a supplemental explanation of the computerized tax research process and related resources is available for download at *www.prenhall.com/phtax*. The text also discusses the American Institute of Certified Public Accountants' (AICPA's) *Statements on Standards for Tax Services,* which provide guidance for CPAs in tax practice. These statements are reproduced in Appendix E.

OVERVIEW OF TAX RESEARCH

Tax research is the process of solving tax-related problems by applying tax law to specific sets of facts. Sometimes it involves researching several issues and often is conducted to formulate tax policy. For example, policy-oriented research would determine how far the level of charitable contributions might decline if such contributions were no longer deductible. Economists usually conduct this type of tax research to assess the effects of government policy.

Tax research also is conducted to determine the tax consequences of transactions to specific taxpayers. For example, client-oriented research would determine whether Smith Corporation could deduct a particular expenditure as a trade or business expense. Accounting and law firms generally engage in this type of research on behalf of their clients.

This chapter deals only with client-oriented tax research, which occurs in two contexts:

ADDITIONAL COMMENT

Closed-fact situations afford the tax advisor the least amount of flexibility. Because the facts are already established, the tax advisor must develop the best solution possible within certain predetermined constraints.

1. **Closed-fact or tax compliance situations:** The client contacts the tax advisor after completing a transaction or while preparing a tax return. In such situations, the tax consequences are fairly straightforward because the facts cannot be modified to obtain different results. Consequently, tax savings opportunities may be lost.

EXAMPLE C:1-1 ▶ Tom informs Carol, his tax advisor, that on November 4 of the current year, he sold land held as an investment for $500,000 cash. His basis in the land was $50,000. On November 9, Tom reinvested the sales proceeds in another plot of investment property costing $500,000. This is a closed fact situation. Tom wants to know the amount and the character of the gain (if any) he must recognize. Because Tom solicits the tax advisor's advice after the sale and reinvestment, the opportunity for tax planning is limited. For example, the possibility of deferring taxes by using a like-kind exchange or an installment sale is lost. ◀

ADDITIONAL COMMENT

Open-fact or tax-planning situations give a tax advisor flexibility to structure transactions to accomplish the client's objectives. In this type of situation, a creative tax advisor can save taxpayers dollars through effective tax planning.

2. **Open-fact or tax-planning situations:** Before structuring or concluding a transaction, the client contacts the tax advisor to discuss tax planning opportunities. Tax-planning situations generally are more difficult and challenging because the tax advisor must consider the client's tax and nontax objectives. Most clients will not engage in a transaction if it is inconsistent with their nontax objectives, even though it produces tax savings.

EXAMPLE C:1-2 ▶ Diane is a widow with three children and five grandchildren and at present owns property valued at $10 million. She seeks advice from Carol, her tax advisor, about how to minimize her estate taxes while conveying the greatest value of property to her descendants. This is an open-fact situation. Carol could advise Diane to leave all but a few hundred thousand dollars of her property to a charitable organization so that her estate would owe no estate taxes. Although this recommendation would minimize Diane's estate taxes, Diane is likely to reject it because she wants her children or grandchildren to be her primary beneficiaries. Thus, reducing estate taxes to zero is inconsistent with her objective of allowing her descendants to receive as much after-tax wealth as possible. ◀

TAX STRATEGY TIP

Taxpayers should make investment decisions based on after-tax rates of return or after-tax cash flows.

When conducting research in a tax-planning context, the tax professional should keep a number of points in mind. First, the objective is not to minimize taxes per se but rather to maximize the after-tax return. For example, if the federal income tax rate is a constant 30%, an investor should not buy a tax-exempt bond yielding 5% when he or she could buy a corporate bond of equal risk that yields 9% before tax and 6.3% after tax. This is the case even though his or her explicit taxes (actual tax liability) would be minimized by investing in the tax-exempt bond.[1] Second, taxpayers typically do not engage in unilateral or self-dealing transactions; thus, the tax ramifications for all parties to the transaction should be considered. For example, in the executive compensation context, employees may prefer to receive incentive stock options (because they will not recognize income until they sell the stock), but the employer may prefer to grant a different type of option (because the employer cannot deduct the value of incentive stock options upon issuance). Thus, the employer might grant a different number of options if it uses one type of stock option versus another type as compensation. Third, taxes are but one cost of doing business. In deciding where to locate a manufacturing plant, for example, factors more important to some businesses than the amount of state and local taxes paid might be the proximity to raw materials, good transportation systems, the cost of labor, the quantity of available skilled labor, and the quality of life in the area. Fourth, the time for tax planning is not restricted to the beginning date of an investment, contract, or other arrangement. Instead, the time extends throughout the duration of the activity. As tax rules change or as business and economic environments change, the tax advisor must reevaluate whether the taxpayer should hold onto an investment and must consider the transaction costs of any alternatives.

ADDITIONAL COMMENT

It is important to consider nontax as well as tax objectives. In many situations, the nontax considerations outweigh the tax considerations. Thus, the plan eventually adopted by a taxpayer may not always be the best when viewed strictly from a tax perspective.

One final note: the tax advisor should always bear in mind the financial accounting implications of proposed transactions. An answer that may be desirable from a tax perspective may not always be desirable from a financial accounting perspective. Though interrelated, the two fields of accounting have different orientations and different objectives. Tax accounting is oriented primarily to the Internal Revenue Service (IRS). Its objectives include calculating, reporting, and predicting one's tax liability according to legal principles. Financial accounting is oriented primarily to shareholders, creditors, managers, and employees. Its objectives include determining, reporting, and predicting a business's financial position and operating results according to Generally Accepted Accounting Principles. Success in any tax practice, especially at the managerial level, requires consideration of both sets of objectives and orientations.

STEPS IN THE TAX RESEARCH PROCESS

OBJECTIVE 1

Describe the steps in the tax research process

In both open- and closed-fact situations, the tax research process involves six basic steps:

1. Determine the facts.
2. Identify the issues (questions).
3. Locate the applicable authorities.
4. Evaluate the authorities and choose those to follow where the authorities conflict.
5. Analyze the facts in terms of the applicable authorities.
6. Communicate conclusions and recommendations to the client.

[1] For an excellent discussion of explicit and implicit taxes and tax planning see M. S. Scholes, M. A. Wolfson, M. Erickson, L. Maydew, and T. Shevlin, *Taxes and Business Strategy: A Planning Approach,* third edition (Upper Saddle River, NJ: Pearson Prentice Hall, 2005). See also Chapter I:18 of the *Individuals* volume. An example of an implicit tax is the excess of the before-tax earnings on a taxable bond over the risk-adjusted before-tax earnings on a tax-favored investment (e.g., a municipal bond).

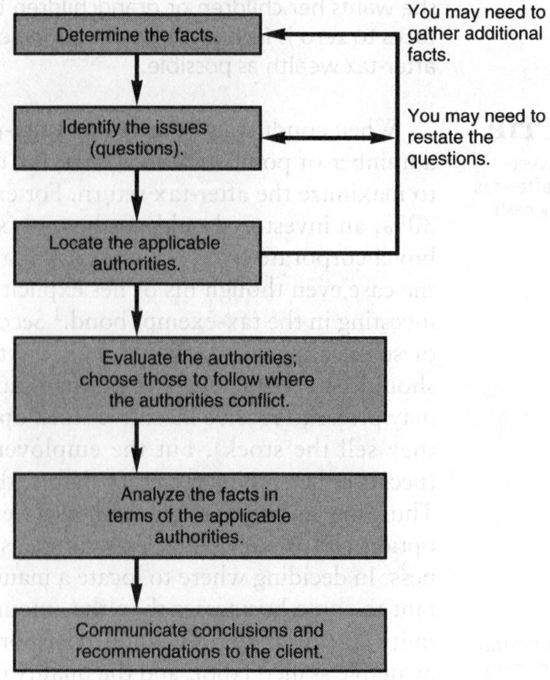

FIGURE C:1-1 ▶ STEPS IN THE TAX RESEARCH PROCESS

ADDITIONAL COMMENT

The steps of tax research provide an excellent format for a written tax communication. For example, a good format for a client memo includes (1) statement of facts, (2) list of issues, (3) discussion of relevant authority, (4) analysis, and (5) recommendations to the client of appropriate actions based on the research results.

Although the above outline suggests a lock-step approach, the tax research process often is circular. That is, it does not always proceed step-by-step. Figure C:1-1 illustrates a more accurate process, and Appendix A provides a comprehensive example of this process.

In a closed-fact situation, the facts have already occurred, and the tax advisor's task is to analyze them to determine the appropriate tax treatment. In an open-fact situation, by contrast, the facts have not yet occurred, and the tax advisor's task is to plan for them or shape them so as to produce a favorable tax result. The tax advisor performs the latter task by reviewing the relevant legal authorities, particularly court cases and IRS rulings, all the while bearing in mind the facts of those cases or rulings that produced favorable results compared with those that produced unfavorable results. For example, if a client wants to realize an ordinary loss (as opposed to a capital gain) on the sale of several plots of land, the tax advisor might consult cases involving similar land sales. The advisor might attempt to distinguish the facts of those cases in which the taxpayer realized an ordinary loss from the facts of those cases in which the taxpayer realized a capital gain. The advisor then might recommend that the client structure the transaction based on the fact pattern in the ordinary loss cases.

TYPICAL MISCONCEPTION

Many taxpayers think the tax law is all black and white. However, most tax research deals with gray areas. Ultimately, when confronted with tough issues, the ability to develop strategies that favor the taxpayer and then to find relevant authority to support those strategies will make a successful tax advisor.

Often, the research pertains to a gray area (i.e., it involves a question to which no clearcut, unequivocally correct answer exists). In such situations, probing a related issue might lead to a solution pertinent to the central question. For example, in researching whether the taxpayer may deduct a loss as ordinary instead of capital, the tax advisor might research the related issue of whether the presence of an investment motive precludes classifying a loss as ordinary. The solution to the latter issue might be relevant to the central question of whether the taxpayer may deduct the loss as ordinary.

Identifying the issue(s) to be researched often is the most difficult step in the tax research process. In some instances, the client defines the issue(s) for the tax advisor, such as where the client asks, "May I deduct the costs of a winter trip to Florida recommended by my physician?" In other instances, the tax advisor, after reviewing the documents submitted to him or her by the client, defines the issue(s) himself or herself. Doing so presupposes a firm grounding in tax law.[2]

[2] Often, in an employment context, supervisors define the questions to be researched and the authorities that might be relevant to the tax consequences.

Once the tax advisor locates the applicable legal authorities, he or she might have to obtain additional information from the client. Example C:1-3 illustrates the point. The example assumes that all relevant tax authorities are in agreement.

EXAMPLE C:1-3 ▶ Mark calls his tax advisor, Al, and states that he (1) incurred a loss on renting his beach cottage during the current year and (2) wonders whether he may deduct the loss. He also states that he, his wife, and their minor child occupied the cottage only eight days during the current year.

This is the first time Al has dealt with the Sec. 280A vacation home rules. On reading Sec. 280A, Al learns that a loss is *not* deductible if the taxpayer used the residence for personal purposes for longer than the greater of (1) 14 days or (2) 10% of the number of days the unit was rented at a fair rental value. He also learns that the property is *deemed* to be used by the taxpayer for personal purposes on any days on which it is used by any member of his or her family (as defined in Sec. 267(c)(4)). The Sec. 267(c)(4) definition of family members includes brothers, sisters, spouse, ancestors, or lineal descendants (i.e., children and grandchildren).

Mark's eight-day use is not long enough to make the rental loss nondeductible. However, Al must inquire about the number of days, if any, Mark's brothers, sisters, or parents used the property. (He already knows about use by Mark, his spouse, and his lineal descendants.) In addition, Al must find out how many days the cottage was rented to other persons at a fair rental value. Upon obtaining the additional information, Al proceeds to determine how to calculate the deductible expenses. Al then derives his conclusion concerning the deductible loss, if any, and communicates it to Mark. (This example assumes the passive activity and at-risk rules restricting a taxpayer's ability to deduct losses from real estate activities will not pose a problem for Mark. See Chapter I:8 of *Prentice Hall's Federal Taxation: Individuals* for a comprehensive discussion of these topics.) ◀

Many firms require that a researcher's conclusions be communicated to the client in writing. Members or employees of such firms may answer questions orally, but their oral conclusions should be followed by a written communication. According to the AICPA's *Statements on Standards for Tax Services* (reproduced in Appendix E),

> Although oral advice may serve a client's needs appropriately in routine matters or in well-defined areas, written communications are recommended in important, unusual, or complicated transactions. The member may use judgment about whether, subsequently, to document oral advice in writing.[3]

IMPORTANCE OF THE FACTS TO THE TAX CONSEQUENCES

OBJECTIVE 2

Explain how the facts influence the tax consequences

Many terms and phrases used in the Internal Revenue Code (IRC) and other tax authorities are vague or ambiguous. Some provisions conflict with others or are difficult to reconcile, creating for the researcher the dilemma of deciding which rules are applicable and which tax results are proper. For example, as a condition to claiming another person as a dependent, the taxpayer must provide more than half of such person's support.[4] Neither the IRC nor the Treasury Regulations define "support." This lack of definition could be problematic. For example, if the taxpayer purchased a used automobile costing $8,000 for an elderly parent whose only source of income is $7,800 in Social Security benefits, the question of whether the expenditure constitutes support would arise. The tax advisor would have to consult court opinions, revenue rulings, and other IRS pronouncements to ascertain the legal meaning of the term "support." Only after thorough research would the meaning of the term become clear.

In other instances, the legal language is quite clear, but a question arises as to whether the taxpayer's transaction conforms to a specific pattern of facts that gives rise to a particular tax result. Ultimately, the peculiar facts of a transaction or event determine its tax consequences. A change in the facts can significantly change the consequences. Consider the following illustrations:

[3] AICPA, *Statement on Standards for Tax Services,* No. 8, "Form and Content of Advice to Clients," 2000, Para. 6.

[4] Sec. 152(a).

Illustration One

Facts: A holds stock, a capital asset, that he purchased two years ago at a cost of $1,000. He sells the stock to B for $920. What are the tax consequences to A?

Result: Under Sec. 1001, A realizes an $80 capital loss. He recognizes this loss in the current year. A must offset the loss against any capital gains recognized during the year. Any excess loss is deductible from ordinary income up to a $3,000 annual limit.

Change of Facts: A is B's son.

New Result: Under Sec. 267, A and B are related parties. Therefore, A may not recognize the realized loss. However, B may use the loss if she subsequently sells the stock at a gain.

Illustration Two

Facts: C donates to State University ten acres of land that she purchased two years ago for $10,000. The fair market value (FMV) of the land on the date of the donation is $25,000. C's adjusted gross income is $100,000. What is C's charitable contribution deduction?

Result: Under Sec. 170, C is entitled to a $25,000 charitable contribution deduction (i.e., the FMV of the property unreduced by the unrealized long-term gain).

Change of Facts: C purchased the land 11 months ago.

New Result: Under the same IRC provision, C is entitled to only a $10,000 charitable contribution deduction (i.e., the FMV of the property reduced by the unrealized short-term gain).

Illustration Three

Facts: Acquiring Corporation pays Target Corporation's shareholders one million shares of Acquiring voting stock. In return, Target's shareholders tender 98% of their Target voting stock. The acquisition is for a bona fide business purpose. Acquiring continues Target's business. What are the tax consequences of the exchange to Target's shareholders?

Result: Under Sec. 368(a)(1)(B), Target's shareholders are not taxed on the exchange, which is solely for Acquiring voting stock.

Change of Facts: In the transaction, Acquiring purchases the remaining 2% of Target's shares with cash.

New Result: Under the same IRC provision, Target's shareholders are now taxed on the exchange, which is not solely for Acquiring voting stock.

CREATING A FACTUAL SITUATION FAVORABLE TO THE TAXPAYER

TYPICAL MISCONCEPTION

Many taxpayers believe tax practitioners spend most of their time preparing tax returns. In reality, providing tax advice that accomplishes the taxpayer's objectives is one of the most important responsibilities of a tax advisor. This latter activity is tax consulting as compared to tax compliance.

Based on his or her research, a tax advisor might recommend to a taxpayer how to structure a transaction or plan an event so as to increase the likelihood that related expenses will be deductible. For example, suppose a taxpayer is assigned a temporary task in a location (City Y) different from the location (City X) of his or her permanent employment. Suppose also that the taxpayer wants to deduct the meal and lodging expenses incurred in City Y as well as the cost of transportation thereto. To do so, the taxpayer must establish that City X is his or her tax home and that he or she temporarily works in City Y. (Section 162 provides that a taxpayer may deduct travel expenses while "away from home" on business. A taxpayer is deemed to be "away from home" if his or her employment at the new location does not exceed one year, i.e., it is "temporary.") Suppose the taxpayer wants to know the tax consequences of his or her working in City Y for ten months and then, within that ten-month period, finding permanent employment in City Y. What is tax research likely to reveal?

Tax research will lead to an IRS ruling stating that, in such circumstances, the employment will be deemed to be temporary until the date on which the realistic expectation about the temporary nature of the assignment changes.[5] After this date, the employment will be deemed to be permanent, and travel expenses relating to it will be nondeductible. Based on this finding, the tax advisor might advise the taxpayer to postpone his or her permanent job search in City Y until the end of the ten-month period and simply treat his or her assignment as temporary. So doing would lengthen the time he or she is deemed to be "away from home" on business and thus increase the amount of meal, lodging, and transportation costs deductible as travel expenses.

[5] Rev. Rul. 93-86, 1993-2 C.B. 71.

THE SOURCES OF TAX LAW

OBJECTIVE 3

Identify the sources of tax law and understand the authoritative value of each

The language of the IRC is general; that is, it prescribes the tax treatment of broad categories of transactions and events. The reason for the generality is that Congress can neither foresee nor provide for every detailed transaction or event. Even if it could, doing so would render the statute narrow in scope and inflexible in application. Accordingly, interpretations of the IRC—both administrative and judicial—are necessary. Administrative interpretations are provided in Treasury Regulations, revenue rulings, and revenue procedures. Judicial interpretations are presented in court opinions. The term *tax law* as used by most tax advisors encompasses administrative and judicial interpretations in addition to the IRC. It also includes the meaning conveyed in reports issued by Congressional committees involved in the legislative process.

THE LEGISLATIVE PROCESS

Tax legislation begins in the House of Representatives. Initially, a tax proposal is incorporated in a bill. The bill is referred to the House Ways and Means Committee, which is charged with reviewing all tax legislation. The Ways and Means Committee holds hearings in which interested parties, such as the Treasury Secretary and IRS Commissioner, testify. At the conclusion of the hearings, the Ways and Means Committee votes to approve or reject the measure. If approved, the bill goes to the House floor where it is debated by the full membership. If the House approves the measure, the bill moves to the Senate where it is taken up by the Senate Finance Committee. Like Ways and Means, the Finance Committee holds hearings in which Treasury officials, tax experts, and other interested parties testify. If the committee approves the measure, the bill goes to the Senate floor where it is debated by the full membership. Upon approval by the Senate, it is submitted to the President for his or her signature. If the President signs the measure, the bill becomes public law. If the President vetoes it, Congress can override the veto by at least a two-thirds majority vote in each chamber.

Generally, at each stage of the legislative process, the bill is subject to amendment. If amended, and if the House version differs from the Senate version, the bill is referred to a House-Senate conference committee.[6] This committee attempts to resolve the differences between the House and Senate versions. Ultimately, it submits a compromise version of the measure to each chamber for its approval. Such referrals are common. For example, in 1998 the House and Senate disagreed over what the taxpayer must do to shift the burden of proof to the IRS. The House proposed that the taxpayer assert a "reasonable dispute" regarding a taxable item. The Senate proposed that the taxpayer introduce "credible evidence" regarding the item. A conference committee was appointed to resolve the differences. This committee ultimately adopted the Senate proposal, which was later approved by both chambers.

ADDITIONAL COMMENT

Committee reports can be helpful in interpreting new legislation because they indicate the intent of Congress. With the proliferation of tax legislation, committee reports have become especially important because the Treasury Department often is unable to draft the needed regulations in a timely manner.

After approving major legislation, the Ways and Means Committee and Senate Finance Committee usually issue official reports. These reports, published by the U.S. Government Printing Office (GPO) as part of the *Cumulative Bulletin* and as separate documents, explain the committees' reasoning for approving (and/or amending) the legislation.[7] In addition, the GPO publishes both records of the committee hearings and transcripts of the floor debates. The records are published as separate House or Senate documents. The transcripts are incorporated in the *Congressional Record* for the day of the debate. In tax research, these records, reports, and transcripts are useful in deciphering the meaning of the statutory language. Where this language is ambiguous or vague, and the courts have not interpreted it, the documents can shed light on **Congressional intent**, i.e., what Congress *intended* by a particular term, phrase, or provision.

EXAMPLE C:1-4 ▶ As mentioned earlier, in 1998 Congress passed legislation concerning shifting the burden of proof to the IRS. This legislation was codified in Sec. 7491. The question arises as to what constitutes "credible evidence." (Remember, the taxpayer must introduce "credible evidence" to

---

[6] The size of a conference committee can vary. It is made up of an equal number of members from the House and the Senate.

[7] The *Cumulative Bulletin* is described in the discussion of revenue rulings on page C:1-12.

shift the burden of proof to the IRS). Section 7491 does not define the term. Because the provision was relatively new, few courts had an opportunity to interpret what "credible evidence" means. In the absence of relevant statutory or judicial authority, the researcher might have looked to the committee reports to ascertain what Congress intended by the term. Senate Report No. 105-174 states that "credible evidence" means evidence of a quality, which, "after critical analysis, the court would find sufficient upon which to base a decision on the issue if no contrary evidence were submitted."[8] This language suggests that Congress intended the term to mean evidence of a kind sufficient to withstand judicial scrutiny. Such a meaning should be regarded as conclusive in the absence of other authority. ◀

ADDITIONAL COMMENT
According to Sheldon S. Cohen, in *The Wall Street Journal's* weekly tax column, a bound volume of the Internal Revenue Code in 1952 measured three-fourths of an inch thick. Treasury Regulations could fit in one bound volume measuring one-half of an inch thick. Now, a bound volume of the Internal Revenue Code measures over four inches thick, and Treasury Regulations fit into five or six bound volumes measuring around ten inches thick.

THE INTERNAL REVENUE CODE

The IRC, which comprises Title 26 of the United States Code, is the foundation of all tax law. First codified (i.e., organized into a single compilation of revenue statutes) in 1939, the tax law was recodified in 1954. The IRC was known as the Internal Revenue Code of 1954 until 1986, when its name was changed to the Internal Revenue Code of 1986. Whenever changes to the IRC are approved, the old language is deleted and new language added. Thus, the IRC is organized as an integrated document, and a researcher need not read through the relevant parts of all previous tax bills to find the current version of the law.

The IRC contains provisions dealing with income taxes, estate and gift taxes, employment taxes, alcohol and tobacco taxes, and other excise taxes. Organizationally, the IRC is divided into subtitles, chapters, subchapters, parts, subparts, sections, subsections, paragraphs, subparagraphs, and clauses. Subtitle A contains rules relating to income taxes, and Subtitle B deals with estate and gift taxes. A set of provisions concerned with one general area constitutes a subchapter. For example, the topics of corporate distributions and adjustments appear in Subchapter C, and topics relating to partners and partnerships appear in Subchapter K. Figure C:1-2 presents the organizational scheme of the IRC.

An IRC section contains the operative provisions to which tax advisors most often refer. For example, they speak of "Sec. 351 transactions," "Sec. 306 stock," and "Sec. 1231 gains and losses." Although a tax advisor need not know all the IRC sections, paragraphs, and parts, he or she must be familiar with the IRC's organizational scheme to read and interpret it correctly. The language of the IRC is replete with cross-references to titles, paragraphs, subparagraphs, and so on.

EXAMPLE C:1-5 ▶ Section 7701, a definitional section, begins, "When used in this title . . ." and then provides a series of definitions. Because of this broad reference, a Sec. 7701 definition applies for all of Title 26; that is, it applies for purposes of the income tax, estate and gift tax, excise tax, and other taxes governed by Title 26. ◀

EXAMPLE C:1-6 ▶ Section 302(b)(3) allows taxpayers whose stock holdings are completely terminated in a redemption (a corporation's purchase of its stock from one or more of its shareholders) to receive capital gain treatment on the excess of the redemption proceeds over the stock's basis instead of ordinary income treatment on the entire proceeds. Section 302(c)(2)(A) states, "In the case of a distribution described in subsection (b)(3), section 318(a)(1) shall not apply if. . . ." Further, Sec. 302(c)(2)(C)(i) indicates "Subparagraph (A) shall not apply to a distribution to any entity unless. . . ." Thus, in determining whether a taxpayer will receive capital gain treatment in a stock redemption, a tax advisor must be able to locate and interpret various cross-referenced IRC sections, subsections, paragraphs, subparagraphs, and clauses. ◀

TREASURY REGULATIONS

The Treasury Department issues regulations that expound upon the IRC. Treasury Regulations often provide examples with computations that assist the reader in understanding how IRC provisions apply.[9]

[8] S. Rept. No. 105-174, 105th Cong., 1st Sess. (unpaginated) (1998).

[9] Treasury Regulations are formulated on the basis of Treasury Decisions (T.D.s). The numbers of the Treasury Decisions that form the basis of a Treasury Regulation usually are found in the notes at the end of the regulation.

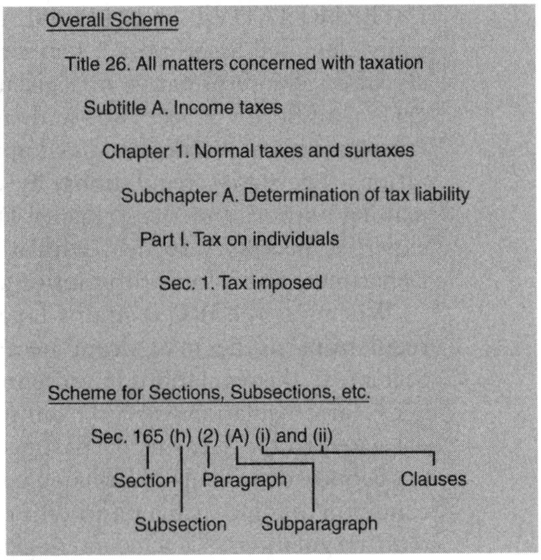

FIGURE C:1-2 ▶ ORGANIZATIONAL SCHEME OF THE INTERNAL REVENUE CODE

Because of frequent IRC changes, the Treasury Department does not always update the regulations in a timely manner. Consequently, when consulting a regulation, a tax advisor should check its introductory or end note to determine when the regulation was adopted. If the regulation was adopted before the most recent revision of the applicable IRC section, the regulation should be treated as authoritative to the extent consistent with the revision. Thus, for example, if a regulation issued before the passage of an IRC amendment specifies a dollar amount, and the amendment changed the dollar amount, the regulation should be regarded as authoritative in all respects except for the dollar amount.

PROPOSED, TEMPORARY, AND FINAL REGULATIONS. A Treasury Regulation is first issued in proposed form to the public, which is given an opportunity to comment on it. Parties most likely to comment are individual tax practitioners and representatives of organizations such as the American Bar Association, the Tax Division of the AICPA, and the American Taxation Association. The comments may suggest that the proposed rules could affect taxpayers more adversely than Congress had anticipated. In drafting a final regulation, the Treasury Department generally considers the comments and may modify the rules accordingly. If the comments are favorable, the Treasury Department usually finalizes the regulation with minor revisions. If the comments are unfavorable, it finalizes the regulation with major revisions or allows the proposed regulation to expire.

Proposed regulations are just that—proposed. Consequently, they carry no more authoritative weight than do the arguments of the IRS in a court brief. Nevertheless, they represent the Treasury Department's official interpretation of the IRC. By contrast, **temporary regulations** are binding on the taxpayer. Effective as of the date of their publication, they often are issued immediately after passage of a major tax act to guide taxpayers and their advisors on procedural or computational matters. Regulations issued as temporary are concurrently issued as proposed. Because their issuance is not preceded by a public comment period, they are regarded as somewhat less authoritative than final regulations.

Once finalized, regulations can be effective as of the date they were proposed or the date temporary regulations preceding them were first published in the *Federal Register*, a daily publication that contains federal government pronouncements. For changes to the IRC enacted after July 29, 1996, the Treasury Department generally cannot issue regulations with retroactive effect.

INTERPRETATIVE AND LEGISLATIVE REGULATIONS. In addition to being officially classified as proposed, temporary, or final, Treasury Regulations are unofficially classified as interpretative or legislative. **Interpretative regulations** are issued under the general authority of Sec. 7805 and, as the name implies, merely make the IRC's statutory language easier to understand and apply. In addition, they often illustrate various computations. **Legislative regulations**, by contrast, arise where Congress delegates its rule-making authority to the Treasury Department. Because Congress believes it lacks the expertise necessary to deal with a highly technical matter, it instructs the Treasury Department to set forth substantive tax rules relating to the matter.

Whenever the IRC contains language such as "The Secretary shall prescribe such regulations as he may deem necessary" or "under regulations prescribed by the Secretary," the regulations interpreting the IRC provision are legislative. The consolidated tax return regulations are an example of legislative regulations. In Sec. 1502, Congress delegated to the Treasury Department authority to issue regulations that determine the tax liability of a group of affiliated corporations filing a consolidated tax return. As a precondition to filing such a return, the corporations must consent to follow the consolidated return regulations.[10] Such consent generally precludes the corporations from later arguing in court that the regulatory provisions are invalid.

AUTHORITATIVE WEIGHT. Final regulations are presumed to be valid and have almost the same authoritative weight as the IRC. Despite this presumption, taxpayers occasionally argue that a regulation is invalid and, consequently, should not be followed. A court will not strike down an interpretative regulation unless, in its opinion, the regulation is "unreasonable and plainly inconsistent with the revenue statutes."[11] In other words, a court is unlikely to invalidate a legislative regulation because it recognizes that Congress has delegated to the Treasury Department authority to issue a specific set of rules. Nevertheless, courts have invalidated legislative regulations where, in their opinion, the regulations exceeded the scope of power delegated to the Treasury Department,[12] were contrary to the IRC,[13] or were unreasonable.[14]

KEY POINT

The older a Treasury Regulation becomes, the less likely a court is to invalidate the regulation. The legislative reenactment doctrine holds that if a regulation did not reflect the intent of Congress, lawmakers would have changed the statute in subsequent legislation to obtain their desired objectives.

In assessing the validity of Treasury Regulations, some courts apply the **legislative reenactment doctrine**. Under this doctrine, a regulation is deemed to receive Congressional approval whenever the IRC provision under which the regulation was issued is reenacted without amendment.[15] Underlying this doctrine is the rationale that, if Congress believed that the regulation offered an erroneous interpretation of the IRC, it would have amended the IRC to conform to its belief. Congress's failure to amend the IRC signifies approval of the regulation.[16] This doctrine is predicated on Congress's constitutional authority to levy taxes. This authority implies that, if Congress is dissatisfied with the manner in which either the executive or the judiciary have interpreted the IRC, it can invalidate these interpretations through new legislation.

STOP & THINK *Question:* You are researching the manner in which a deduction is calculated. You consult Treasury Regulations for guidance because the IRC states that the calculation is to be done "in a manner prescribed by the Secretary." After reviewing these authorities, you conclude that another way of doing the calculation arguably is correct under an intuitive approach. This approach would result in a lower tax liability for the client. Should you follow the Treasury Regulations or use the intuitive approach and argue that the regulations are invalid?

---

[10] Sec. 1501.

[11] *CIR v. South Texas Lumber Co.*, 36 AFTR 604, 48-1 USTC ¶5922 (USSC, 1948). In *U.S. v. Douglas B. Cartwright, Executor*, 31 AFTR 2d 73-1461, 73-1 USTC ¶12,926 (USSC, 1973), the Supreme Court concluded that a regulation dealing with the valuation of mutual fund shares for estate and gift tax purposes was invalid.

[12] *McDonald v. CIR*, 56 AFTR 2d 5318, 85-2 USTC ¶9494 (5th Cir., 1985).

[13] *Jeanese, Inc. v. U.S.*, 15 AFTR 2d 429, 65-1 USTC ¶9259 (9th Cir., 1965).

[14] *United States v. Vogel Fertilizer Co.*, 49 AFTR 2d 82-491, 82-1 USTC ¶9134 (USSC, 1982).

[15] *United States v. Homer O. Correll*, 20 AFTR 2d 5845, 68 USTC ¶9101 (USSC, 1967).

[16] One can rebut the presumption that Congress approved of the regulation by showing that Congress was unaware of the regulation when it reenacted the statute.

Solution: Because of the language "in a manner prescribed by the Secretary," the Treasury Regulations dealing with the calculation are legislative. Whenever Congress calls for legislative regulations, it explicitly authorizes the Treasury Department to write the "rules." As a consequence, such regulations are more difficult than interpretative regulations to be overturned by the courts. Thus, unless you intend to challenge the Treasury Regulations and believe you will prevail in court, you should follow them.

ADDITIONAL COMMENT

Citations serve two purposes in tax research: first, they substantiate propositions; second, they enable the reader to locate underlying authority.

CITATIONS. Citations to Treasury Regulations are relatively easy to understand. One or more numbers appear before a decimal place, and several numbers follow the decimal place. The numbers immediately following the decimal place indicate the IRC section being interpreted. The numbers preceding the decimal place indicate the general subject of the regulation. Numbers that often appear before the decimal place and their general subjects are as follows:

Number	*General Subject Matter*
1	Income tax
20	Estate tax
25	Gift tax
301	Administrative and procedural matters
601	Procedural rules

The number following the IRC section number indicates the numerical sequence of the regulation, such as the fifth regulation. No relationship exists between this number and the subsection of the IRC being interpreted. An example of a citation to a final regulation is as follows:

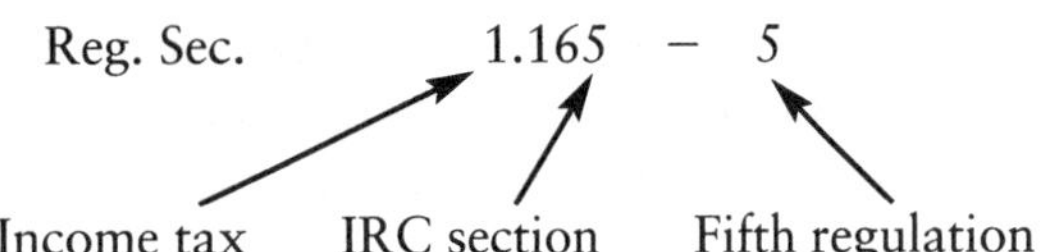

Citations to proposed or temporary regulations follow the same format. They are referenced as Prop. Reg. Sec. or Temp. Reg. Sec. For temporary regulations the numbering system following the IRC section number always begins with the number of the regulation and an upper case T (e.g., -1T).

Section 165 addresses the broad topic of losses and is interpreted by several regulations. According to its caption, the topic of Reg. Sec. 1.165-5 is worthless securities, which also is addressed in subsection (g) of IRC Sec. 165. Parenthetical information following the text of the Treasury Regulation indicates that the regulation was last revised on December 5, 1972, by Treasury Decision (T.D.) 7224. Section 165(g) was last amended on October 4, 2004. Thus, a researcher must be aware that some regulations may be outdated by subsequent IRC amendments.

When referencing a regulation, the researcher should fine-tune the citation to indicate the precise passage that supports his or her conclusion. An example of such a detailed citation is Reg. Sec. 1.165-5(i), Ex. 2(i), which refers to paragraph (i) of Example 2, found in paragraph (i) of the fifth regulation interpreting Sec. 165.

TYPICAL MISCONCEPTION

Even though revenue rulings do not have the same weight as Treasury Regulations or court cases, one should not underestimate their importance. Because a revenue ruling is the official published position of the IRS, in audits the examining agent will place considerable weight on any applicable revenue rulings.

ADMINISTRATIVE PRONOUNCEMENTS

The IRS interprets the IRC through **administrative pronouncements,** the most important of which are discussed below. After consulting the IRC and Treasury Regulations, tax advisors are likely next to consult these pronouncements.

REVENUE RULINGS. In **revenue rulings,** the IRS indicates the tax consequences of specific transactions encountered in practice. For example, in a revenue ruling, the IRS might indicate whether the exchange of stock for stock derivatives in a corporate acquisition is tax-free.

The IRS issues more than 50 revenue rulings a year. These rulings do not rank as high in the hierarchy of authorities as do Treasury Regulations or federal court cases. They simply represent the IRS's view of the tax law. Taxpayers who do not follow a revenue ruling will not incur a substantial understatement penalty if they have substantial authority for different treatment.[17] Nonetheless, the IRS presumes that the tax treatment specified in a revenue ruling is correct. Consequently, if an examining agent discovers in an audit that a taxpayer did not adopt the position prescribed in a revenue ruling, the agent will contend that the taxpayer's tax liability should be adjusted to reflect that position.

Soon after it is issued, a revenue ruling appears in the weekly *Internal Revenue Bulletin* (cited as I.R.B.), published by the U.S. Government Printing Office (GPO). Revenue rulings later appear in the *Cumulative Bulletin* (cited as C.B.), a bound volume issued semiannually by the GPO. An example of a citation to a revenue ruling appearing in the *Cumulative Bulletin* is as follows:

Rev. Rul. 97-4, 1997-1 C.B. 5.

This is the fourth ruling issued in 1997, and it appears on page 5 of Volume 1 of the 1997 *Cumulative Bulletin.* Before the GPO publishes the pertinent volume of the *Cumulative Bulletin,* researchers should use citations to the *Internal Revenue Bulletin.* An example of such a citation follows:

Rev. Rul. 2004-21, 2004-10 I.R.B. 544.

For revenue rulings (and other IRS pronouncements) issued after 1999, the full four digits of the year of issuance are set forth in the title. For revenue rulings (and other IRS pronouncements) issued before 2000, only the last two digits of the year of issuance are set forth in the title. The above citation represents the twenty-first ruling for 2004. This ruling is located on page 544 of the *Internal Revenue Bulletin* for the tenth week of 2004. Once a revenue ruling is published in the *Cumulative Bulletin,* only the citation to the *Cumulative Bulletin* should be used. Thus, a citation to the I.R.B. is temporary.

REVENUE PROCEDURES. As the name suggests, **revenue procedures** are IRS pronouncements that usually deal with the procedural aspects of tax practice. For example, one revenue procedure deals with the manner in which tip income should be reported. Another revenue procedure describes the requirements for reproducing paper substitutes for informational returns such as Form 1099.

As with revenue rulings, revenue procedures are published first in the *Internal Revenue Bulletin,* then in the *Cumulative Bulletin.* An example of a citation to a revenue procedure appearing in the *Cumulative Bulletin* is as follows:

Rev. Proc. 97-19, 1997-1 C.B. 644.

This pronouncement is found in Volume 1 of the 1997 *Cumulative Bulletin* on page 644. It is the nineteenth revenue procedure issued in 1997.

In addition to revenue rulings and revenue procedures, the *Cumulative Bulletin* contains IRS notices, as well as the texts of proposed regulations, tax treaties, committee reports, and U.S. Supreme Court decisions.

SELF-STUDY QUESTION

Are letter rulings of precedential value for third parties?

ANSWER

No. A letter ruling is binding only on the taxpayer to whom the ruling was issued. Nevertheless, letter rulings can be very useful to third parties because they provide insight as to the IRS's opinion about the tax consequences of various transactions.

LETTER RULINGS. **Letter rulings** are initiated by taxpayers who ask the IRS to explain the tax consequences of a particular transaction.[18] The IRS provides its explanation in the form of a letter ruling, that is, a response personal to the taxpayer requesting an answer. Only the taxpayer to whom the ruling is addressed may rely on it as authority. Nevertheless, letter rulings are relevant for other taxpayers and tax advisors because they offer insight into the IRS's position on the tax treatment of particular transactions.

[17] Chapter C:15 discusses the authoritative support taxpayers and tax advisors should have for positions they adopt on a tax return.

[18] Chapter C:15 further discusses letter rulings.

Originally the public did not have access to letter rulings issued to other taxpayers. As a result of Sec. 6110, enacted in 1976, letter rulings (with confidential information deleted) are accessible to the general public and have been reproduced by major tax services. An example of a citation to a letter ruling appears below:

Ltr. Rul. 200130006 (August 6, 2001).

The first four digits (two if issued before 2000) indicate the year in which the ruling was made public, in this case, 2001.[19] The next two digits denote the week in which the ruling was made public, here the thirtieth. The last three numbers indicate the numerical sequence of the ruling for the week, here the sixth. The date in parentheses denotes the date of the ruling.

ADDITIONAL COMMENT

A technical advice memorandum is published as a letter ruling. Whereas a taxpayer-requested letter ruling deals with prospective transactions, a technical advice memorandum deals with past or consummated transactions.

OTHER INTERPRETATIONS

Technical Advice Memoranda. When the IRS audits a taxpayer's return, the IRS agent might ask the IRS national office for advice on a complicated, technical matter. The national office will provide its advice in a **technical advice memorandum**, released to the public in the form of a letter ruling.[20] Researchers can identify which letter rulings are technical advice memoranda by introductory language such as, "In response to a request for technical advice. . . ." An example of a citation to a technical advice memorandum is as follows:

T.A.M. 9801001 (January 1, 1998).

This citation refers to the first technical advice memorandum issued in the first week of 1998. The memorandum is dated January 1, 1998.

Information Releases. If the IRS wants to disseminate information to the general public, it will issue an **information release**. Information releases are written in lay terms and are dispatched to thousands of newspapers throughout the country. The IRS, for example, may issue an information release to announce the standard mileage rate for business travel. An example of a citation to an information release is as follows:

I.R. 86-70 (June 12, 1986).

This citation is to the seventieth information release issued in 1986. The release is dated June 12, 1986.

ADDITIONAL COMMENT

Announcements are used to summarize new tax legislation or publicize procedural matters. Announcements generally are aimed at tax practitioners and are considered to be "substantial authority" [Rev. Rul. 90-91, 1990-2 C.B. 262].

Announcements and Notices. The IRS also disseminates information to tax practitioners in the form of **announcements** and **notices**. These pronouncements generally are more technical than information releases and frequently address current tax developments. After passage of a major tax act, and before the Treasury Department has had an opportunity to issue proposed or temporary regulations, the IRS may issue an announcement or notice to clarify the legislation. The IRS is bound to follow the announcement or notice just as it is bound to follow a revenue procedure or revenue ruling. Examples of citations to announcements and notices are as follows:

Announcement 2004-1, 2004-1 I.R.B. 254.
Notice 2004-3, 2004-5 I.R.B. 391.

The first citation is to the first announcement issued in 2004. It can be found on page 254 of the first *Internal Revenue Bulletin* for 2004. The second citation is to the third notice issued in 2004. It can be found on page 391 of the fifth *Internal Revenue Bulletin* for 2004. Notices and announcements appear in both the *Internal Revenue Bulletin* and the *Cumulative Bulletin*.

---

[19] Sometimes a letter ruling is cited as PLR (private letter ruling) instead of Ltr. Rul.

[20] Technical advice memoranda are discussed further in Chapter C:15.

JUDICIAL DECISIONS

Judicial decisions are an important source of tax law. Judges are reputed to be unbiased individuals who decide questions of fact (the existence of a fact or the occurrence of an event) or questions of law (the applicability of a legal principle or the proper interpretation of a legal term or provision). Judges do not always agree on the tax consequences of a particular transaction or event. Therefore, tax advisors often must derive conclusions against a background of conflicting judicial authorities. For example, a U.S. district court might disagree with the Tax Court on the deductibility of an expense. Likewise, one circuit court might disagree with another circuit court on the same issue.

OVERVIEW OF THE COURT SYSTEM. A taxpayer may begin tax litigation in any of three courts: the U.S. Tax Court, the U.S. Court of Federal Claims (formerly the U.S. Claims Court), or U.S. district courts. Court precedents are important in deciding where to begin such litigation (see page C:1-21 for a discussion of precedent). Also important is when the taxpayer must pay the deficiency the IRS contends is due. A taxpayer who wants to litigate either in a U.S. district court or in the U.S. Court of Federal Claims must first pay the deficiency. The taxpayer then files a claim for refund, which the IRS is likely to deny. Following this denial, the taxpayer must petition the court for a refund. If the court grants the taxpayer's petition, he or she receives a refund of the taxes in question plus accrued interest. If the taxpayer begins litigation in the Tax Court, on the other hand, he or she need not pay the deficiency unless and until the court decides the case against him or her. In that event, the taxpayer also must pay interest and penalties.[21] A taxpayer who believes that a jury would be sympathetic to his or her case should litigate in a U.S. district court, the only forum where a jury trial is possible.

SELF-STUDY QUESTION

What are some of the factors that a taxpayer should consider when deciding in which court to file a tax-related claim?

ANSWER

(1) Each court's published precedent pertaining to the issue, (2) desirability of a jury trial, (3) tax expertise of each court, and (4) when the deficiency must be paid.

If a party loses at the trial court level, it can appeal the decision to a higher court. Appeals of Tax Court and U.S. district court decisions are made to the court of appeals for the taxpayer's circuit. There are eleven geographical circuits designated by numbers, the District of Columbia Circuit, and the Federal Circuit. The map in Figure C:1-3 shows the states that lie in the various circuits. California, for example, lies in the Ninth Circuit. When referring to these appellate courts, instead of saying, for example, "the Court of Appeals for the Ninth Circuit," one generally says "the Ninth Circuit." All decisions of the U.S. Court of Federal Claims are appealable to one court—the Court of Appeals for the Federal Circuit—irrespective of where the taxpayer resides or does business.[22] The only cases the Federal Circuit hears are those that originate in the U.S. Court of Federal Claims.

The party losing at the appellate level can petition the U.S. Supreme Court to review the case under a **writ of certiorari**. If the Supreme Court agrees to hear the case, it grants certiorari.[23] If it refuses to hear the case, it denies certiorari. In recent years, the Court has granted certiorari in only about six to ten tax cases per year. Figure C:1-4 and Table C:1-1 provide an overview and summary of the court system with respect to tax matters.

THE U.S. TAX COURT. The U.S. Tax Court was created in 1942 as a successor to the Board of Tax Appeals. It is a court of national jurisdiction that hears only tax-related cases. All taxpayers, regardless of their state of residence or place of business, may litigate in the Tax Court. It has 19 judges, including one chief judge.[24] The President, with the consent of the Senate, appoints the judges for a 15-year term and may reappoint them for an additional term. The judges, specialists in tax-related matters, periodically travel to roughly 100 cities throughout the country to hear cases. In most instances, only one judge hears a case.

ADDITIONAL COMMENT

Because the Tax Court deals only with tax cases, it presumably has a higher level of tax expertise than do other courts. Tax Court judges are appointed by the President, in part, due to their considerable tax experience. In July 2006, the Tax Court judges faced a backlog of about 22,182 cases.

The Tax Court issues both regular and memorandum (memo) decisions. Generally, the first time the Tax Court decides a legal issue, its decision appears as a **regular decision**.

---

[21] Revenue Procedure 2005-18, 2005-13 I.R.B. 798, provides procedures for taxpayers to make remittances or apply overpayments to stop the accrual of interest on deficiencies.

[22] The Court of Claims was reconstituted as the United States Court of Claims in 1982. In 1992, this court was renamed the U.S. Court of Federal Claims.

[23] The granting of certiorari signifies that the Supreme Court is granting an appellate review. The denial of certiorari does not necessarily mean that the Supreme Court endorses the lower court's decision. It simply means the court has decided not to hear the case.

[24] The Tax Court also periodically appoints, depending on budgetary constraints, a number of trial judges and senior judges who hear cases and render decisions with the same authority as the regular Tax Court judges.

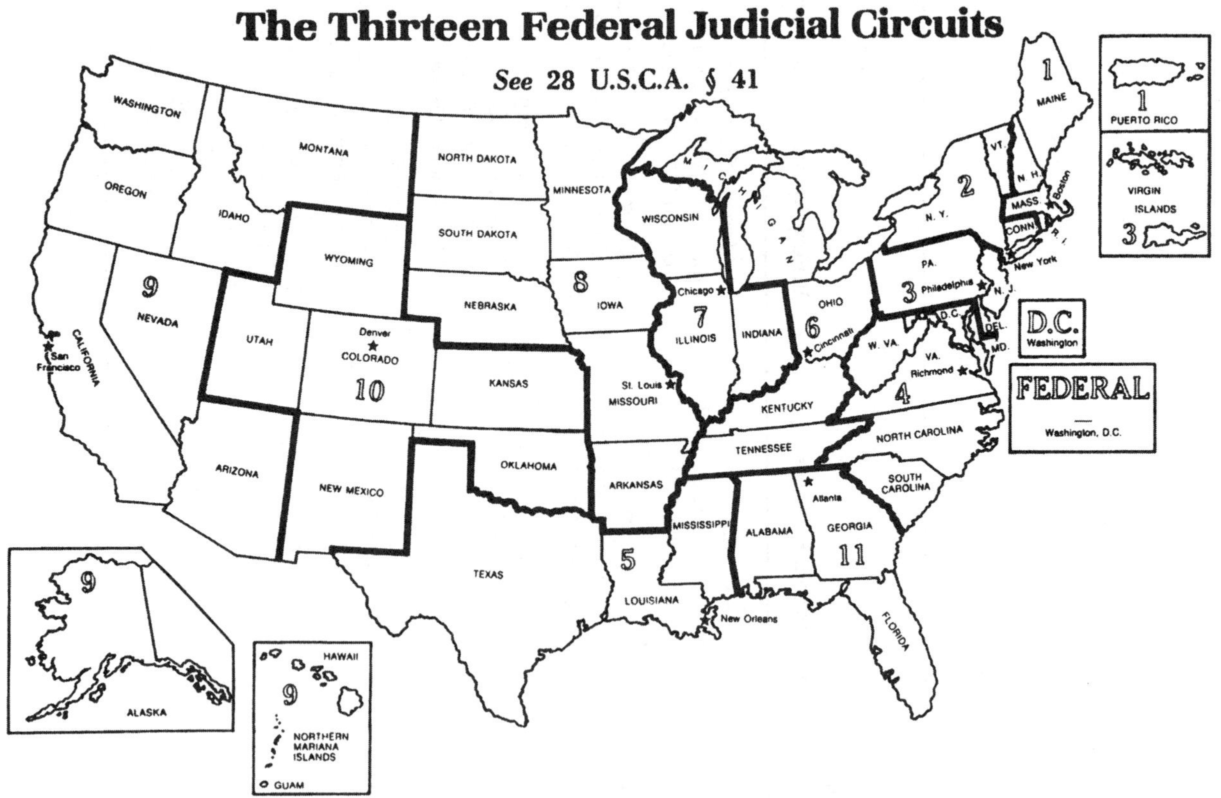

FIGURE C:1-3 ▶ MAP OF THE GEOGRAPHICAL BOUNDARIES OF THE CIRCUIT COURTS OF APPEALS

Source: Reprinted from *West's Federal Reporter,* with permission. © West, a Thomson business.

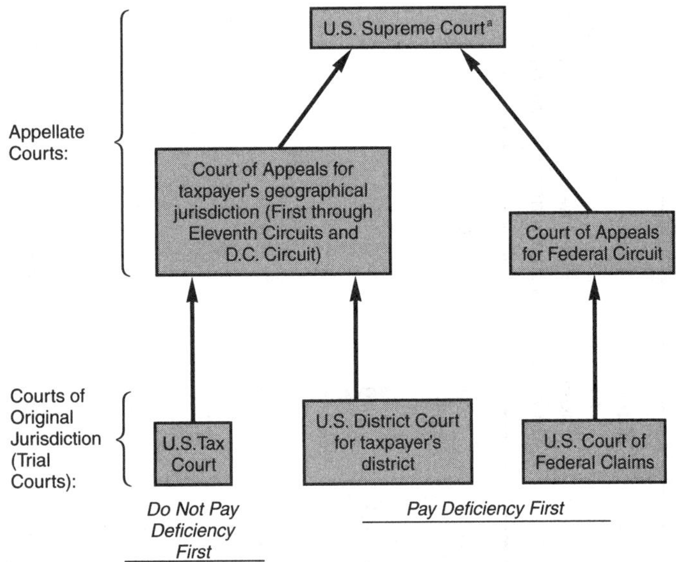

FIGURE C:1-4 ▶ OVERVIEW OF COURT SYSTEM—TAX MATTERS

▼ **TABLE C:1-1**
Summary of Court System—Tax Matters

Court(s) (Number of)	Number of Judges on Each	Personal Jurisdiction	Subject Matter Jurisdiction	Determines Questions of Fact	Trial by Jury	Precedents Followed	Where Opinions Published
U.S. district courts (over 95)	1–28*	Local	General	Yes	Yes	Same court Court for circuit where situated U.S. Supreme Court	*Federal Supplement* *American Federal Tax Reports* *United States Tax Cases*
U.S. Tax Court (1)	19	National	Tax	Yes	No	Same court Court for taxpayer's circuit U.S. Supreme Court	*Tax Court of the U.S. Reports* *CCH Tax Court Memorandum Decisions* *RIA Tax Court Memorandum Decisions*
U.S. Court of Federal Claims (1)	16	National	Claims against U.S. Government	Yes	No	Same court Federal Circuit Court U.S. Supreme Court	*Federal Reporter* (pre-1982) *U.S. Court of Federal Claims* *American Federal Tax Reports* *United States Tax Cases*
U.S. Courts of Appeals (13)	About 20	Regional	General	No	No	Same court U.S. Supreme Court	*Federal Reporter* *American Federal Tax Reports* *United States Tax Cases*
U.S. Supreme Court (1)	9	National	General	No	No	Same court	*U.S. Supreme Court Reports* *Supreme Court Reporter* *United States Reports, Lawyers' Edition* *American Federal Tax Reports* *United States Tax Cases*

*Although the number of judges assigned to each court varies, only one judge hears a case.

Memo decisions, on the other hand, usually deal with factual variations of previously decided cases. Nevertheless, regular and memo decisions carry the same authoritative weight.

At times, the chief judge determines that a particular case concerns an important issue that the entire Tax Court should consider. In such a situation, the words *reviewed by the court* appear at the end of the majority opinion. Any concurring or dissenting opinions follow the majority opinion.[25]

Another phrase sometimes appearing at the end of a Tax Court opinion is *Entered under Rule 155*. This phrase signifies that the court has reached a decision concerning the tax treatment of an item but has left computation of the deficiency to the two litigating parties.

SELF-STUDY QUESTION

What are some of the considerations for litigating under the small cases procedure of the Tax Court?

ANSWER

The small cases procedure gives the taxpayer the advantage of having his or her "day in court" without the expense of an attorney. But if the taxpayer loses, the decision cannot be appealed.

Small Cases Procedure. Taxpayers have the option of having their cases heard under the **small cases procedure** of the Tax Court if the amount in controversy on an annual basis does not exceed $50,000.[26] This procedure is less formal than the regular Tax Court procedure, and taxpayers can represent themselves without an attorney.[27] The cases are heard by special commissioners instead of by one of the 19 Tax Court judges. A disadvantage of the small cases procedure for the losing party is that the decision cannot be appealed. The opinions of the commissioners generally are not published and have no precedential value.

Acquiescence Policy. The IRS has adopted a policy of announcing whether, in future cases involving similar facts and similar issues, it will follow federal court decisions that are adverse to it. This policy is known as the IRS **acquiescence policy.** If the IRS wants taxpayers to know that it will follow an adverse decision in future cases involving similar facts and issues, it will announce its "acquiescence" in the decision. Conversely, if it wants taxpayers to know that it will not follow the decision in such future cases, it will announce its "nonacquiescence." The IRS does not announce its acquiescence or nonacquiescence in every decision it loses.

ADDITIONAL COMMENT

The only cases with respect to which the IRS will acquiesce or nonacquiesce are decisions that the government loses. Because the majority of cases, particularly Tax Court cases, are won by the government, the IRS will potentially acquiesce in only a small number of cases.

The IRS publishes its acquiescences and nonacquiescences as "Actions on Decision" first in the *Internal Revenue Bulletin,* then in the *Cumulative Bulletin*. Before 1991, the IRS acquiesced or nonacquiesced in regular Tax Court decisions only. In 1991, it broadened the scope of its policy to include adverse U.S. Claims Court, U.S. district court, and U.S. circuit court decisions.

In cases involving multiple issues, the IRS may acquiesce in some issues but not others. In decisions supported by extensive reasoning, it may acquiesce in the result but not the rationale (*acq. in result*). Furthermore, it may retroactively revoke an acquiescence or nonacquiescence. The footnotes to the relevant announcement in the *Internal Revenue Bulletin* and *Cumulative Bulletin* indicate the nature and extent of IRS acquiescences and nonacquiescences.

ADDITIONAL COMMENT

If a particular case is important, the chief judge will instruct the other judges to review the case. If a case is reviewed by the entire court, the phrase *reviewed by the court* is inserted immediately after the text of the majority opinion. A reviewed decision provides an opportunity for Tax Court judges to express their dissenting opinions.

These acquiescences and nonacquiescences have important implications for taxpayers. If a taxpayer bases his or her position on a decision in which the IRS has nonacquiesced, he or she can expect an IRS challenge in the event of an audit. In such circumstances, the taxpayer's only recourse may be litigation. On the other hand, if the taxpayer bases his or her position on a decision in which the IRS has acquiesced, he or she can expect little or no challenge. In either case, the examining agent will be bound by the IRS position.

Published Opinions and Citations. Regular Tax Court decisions are published by the U.S. Government Printing Office in a bound volume known as the *Tax Court of the United States Reports*. Soon after a decision is made public, Research Institute of America

---

[25] A judge who issues a concurring opinion agrees with the basic outcome of the majority's decision but not with its rationale. A judge who issues a dissenting opinion believes the majority reached an erroneous conclusion.

[26] Sec. 7463. The $50,000 amount includes penalties and additional taxes but excludes interest.

[27] Taxpayers can represent themselves in regular Tax Court proceedings also, even though they are not attorneys. Where taxpayers represent themselves, the words *pro se* appear in the opinion after the taxpayer's name. The Tax Court is the only federal court before which non-attorneys, including CPAs, may practice.

(RIA) and CCH Incorporated (CCH) each publish the decision in its respective reporter of Tax Court decisions. An official citation to a Tax Court decision is as follows:[28]

MedChem Products, Inc., 116 T.C. 308 (2001).

The citation indicates that this case appears on page 308 in Volume 116 of *Tax Court of the United States Reports* and that the case was decided in 2001.

From 1924 to 1942, regular decisions of the Board of Tax Appeals (predecessor of the Tax Court) were published by the U.S. Government Printing Office in the *United States Board of Tax Appeals Reports.* An example of a citation to a Board of Tax Appeals case is as follows:

J.W. Wells Lumber Co. Trust A., 44 B.T.A. 551 (1941).

This case is found in Volume 44 of the *United States Board of Tax Appeals Reports* on page 551. It is a 1941 decision.

ADDITIONAL COMMENT

Once the IRS has acquiesced in a federal court decision, other taxpayers generally will not need to litigate the same issue. However, the IRS can change its mind and revoke a previous acquiescence or nonacquiescence. References to acquiescences or nonacquiescences in federal court decisions can be found in the citators.

If the IRS has acquiesced or nonacquiesced in a federal court decision, the IRS's action should be denoted in the citation. At times, the IRS will not announce its acquiescence or nonacquiescence until several years after the date of the decision. An example of a citation to a decision in which the IRS has acquiesced is as follows:

Security State Bank, 111 T.C. 210 (1998), *acq.* 2001-1 C.B. xix.

The case appears on page 210 of Volume 111 of the *Tax Court of the United States Reports* and the acquiescence is reported on page xix of Volume 1 of the 2001 *Cumulative Bulletin.* In 2001, the IRS acquiesced in this 1998 decision. A citation to a decision in which the IRS has nonacquiesced is as follows:

Estate of Algerine Allen Smith, 108 T.C. 412 (1997), *nonacq.* 2000-1 C.B. xvi.

The case appears on page 412 of Volume 108 of the *Tax Court of the United States Reports.* The nonacquiescence is reported on page xvi of Volume 1 of the 2000 *Cumulative Bulletin.* In 2000, the IRS nonacquiesced in this 1997 decision.

Tax Court memo decisions are not published by the U.S. Government Printing Office. They are, however, published by RIA in *RIA T.C. Memorandum Decisions* and by CCH in *CCH Tax Court Memorandum Decisions.* In addition, shortly after its issuance, an opinion is made available electronically and in loose-leaf form by RIA and CCH in their respective tax services. The following citation is to a Tax Court memo decision:

KEY POINT

To access all Tax Court cases, a tax advisor must refer to two different publications. The regular opinions appear in the *Tax Court of the United States Reports,* published by the U.S. Government Printing Office, and the memo decisions are published by both RIA (formerly PH) and CCH in their own court reporters.

Edith G. McKinney, 1981 PH T.C. Memo ¶81,181, 41 TCM 1272.

McKinney is found at Paragraph 81,181 of Prentice Hall's (now RIA's)[29] 1981 *PH T.C. Memorandum Decisions* reporter, and in Volume 41, page 1272, of CCH's *Tax Court Memorandum Decisions.* The 181 in the PH citation indicates that the case is the Tax Court's 181st memo decision of the year. A more recent citation is formatted in the same way but refers to RIA memo decisions.

Paul F. Belloff, 1992 RIA T.C. Memo ¶92,346, 63 TCM 3150.

[28] In a citation to a case decided by the Tax Court, only the name of the plaintiff (taxpayer) is listed. The defendant is understood to be the Commissioner of Internal Revenue whose name usually is not shown in the citation. In cases decided by other courts, the name of the plaintiff is listed first and the name of the defendant second. For non-Tax Court cases, the Commissioner of Internal Revenue is referred to as *CIR* in our footnotes and text.

[29] For several years the Prentice Hall Information Services division published its *Federal Taxes 2nd* tax service and a number of related publications, such as the *PH T.C. Memorandum Decisions.* Changes in ownership occurred, and in late 1991 Thomson Professional Publishing added the former Prentice Hall tax materials to the product line of its RIA tax publishing division. Some print products such as the *PH T.C. Memorandum Decisions* still have the Prentice Hall name on the spine of older editions.

U.S. DISTRICT COURTS. Each state has at least one U.S. district court, and more populous states have more than one. Each district court is independent of the others and is thus free to issue its own decisions, subject to the precedential constraints discussed later in this chapter. Different types of cases—not just tax-related—are adjudicated in this forum. A district court is the only forum in which the taxpayer may have a jury decide questions of fact. Depending on the circumstances, a jury trial might be advantageous for the taxpayer.[30]

District court decisions are officially reported in the *Federal Supplement* (cited as F. Supp.) published by West Publishing Co. (West). Some decisions are not officially reported and are referred to as **unreported decisions**. Decisions by U.S. district courts on the topic of taxation also are published by RIA and CCH in secondary reporters that contain only tax-related opinions. RIA's reporter is *American Federal Tax Reports* (cited as AFTR).[31] CCH's reporter is *U.S. Tax Cases* (cited as USTC). A case not offically reported nevertheless might be published in the AFTR and USTC. An example of a complete citation to a U.S. district court decision is as follows:

> *Alfred Abdo, Jr. v. IRS,* 234 F. Supp. 2d 553, 90 AFTR 2d 2002-7484, 2003-1 USTC ¶50,107 (DC North Carolina, 2002).

ADDITIONAL COMMENT

A citation, at a minimum, should contain the following information: (1) the name of the case, (2) the reporter that publishes the case along with both a volume and page (or paragraph) number, (3) the year the case was decided, and (4) the court that decided the case.

In the example above, the **primary citation** is to the *Federal Supplement.* The case appears on page 553 of Volume 234 of the second series of this reporter. **Secondary citations** are to *American Federal Tax Reports* and *U.S. Tax Cases*. The same case is found in Volume 90 of the second series of the AFTR, page 2002-7484 (meaning page 7484 in the volume containing 2002 cases) and in Volume 1 of the 2003 USTC at Paragraph 50,107. The parenthetical information indicates that the case was decided in 2002 by the U.S. District Court for North Carolina. Because some judicial decisions have greater precedential weight than others (e.g., a Supreme Court decision versus a district court decision), information relating to the identity of the adjudicating court is useful in evaluating the authoritative value of the decision.

ADDITIONAL COMMENT

The U.S. Court of Federal Claims adjudicates claims (including suits to recover federal income taxes) against the U.S. Government. This court usually hears cases in Washington, D.C., but will hold sessions in other locations as the court deems necessary.

U.S. COURT OF FEDERAL CLAIMS. The U.S. Court of Federal Claims, another court of first instance that addresses tax matters, has nationwide jurisdiction. Originally, this court was called the U.S. Court of Claims (cited as Ct. Cl.), and its decisions were appealable to the U.S. Supreme Court only. In a reorganization, effective October 1, 1982, the reconstituted court was named the U.S. Claims Court (cited as Cl. Ct.), and its decisions became appealable to the Circuit Court of Appeals for the Federal Circuit. In October 1992, the court's name was again changed to the U.S. Court of Federal Claims (cited as Fed. Cl.).

Beginning in 1982, U.S. Claims Court decisions were reported officially in the *Claims Court Reporter,* published by West from 1982 to 1992.[32] An example of a citation to a U.S. Claims Court decision appears below:

> *Benjamin Raphan v. U.S.,* 3 Cl. Ct. 457, 52 AFTR 2d 83-5987, 83-2 USTC ¶9613 (1983).

The *Raphan* case appears on page 457 of Volume 3 of the *Claims Court Reporter*. Secondary citations are to Volume 52, page 83-5987 of the AFTR, Second Series, and to Volume 2 of the 1983 USTC at Paragraph 9613.

[30] Taxpayers might prefer to have a jury trial if they believe a jury will be sympathetic to their case.

[31] The *American Federal Tax Reports* (AFTR) is published in two series. The first series, which includes opinions issued up to 1957, is cited as AFTR. The second series, which includes opinions issued after 1957, is cited as AFTR 2d. The *Alfred Abdo, Jr.* decision cited as an illustration of a U.S. district court decision appears in the second *American Federal Tax Reports* series.

[32] Before the creation in 1982 of the U.S. Claims Court (and the *Claims Court Reporter*), the opinions of the U.S. Court of Claims were reported in either the *Federal Supplement* (F. Supp.) or the *Federal Reporter, Second Series* (F.2d). The *Federal Supplement* is the primary source of U.S. Court of Claims opinions from 1932 through January 19, 1960. Opinions issued from January 20, 1960, to October 1982 are reported in the *Federal Reporter, Second Series.*

Effective with the 1992 reorganization, decisions of the U.S. Court of Federal Claims are now reported in the *Federal Claims Reporter.* An example of a citation to an opinion published in this reporter is presented below:

Jeffrey G. Sharp v. U.S., 27 Fed. Cl. 52, 70 AFTR 2d 92-6040, 92-2 USTC ¶50,561 (1992).

The *Sharp* case appears on page 52 of Volume 27 of the *Federal Claims Reporter,* on page 6040 of the 70th volume of the AFTR, Second Series, and at Paragraph 50,561 of Volume 2 of the 1992 USTC reporter. Note that, even though the name of the reporter published by West has changed, the volume numbers continue in sequence as if no name change had occurred.

CIRCUIT COURTS OF APPEALS. Lower court decisions are appealable by the losing party to the court of appeals for the circuit in which the litigation originated. Generally, if the case began in the Tax Court or a U.S. district court, the case is appealable to the circuit for the individual's residence as of the appeal date. For a corporation, the case is appealable to the circuit for the corporation's principal place of business. The Federal Circuit hears all appeals of cases originating in the U.S. Court of Federal Claims.

As mentioned earlier, there are 11 geographical circuits designated by numbers, the District of Columbia Circuit, and the Federal Circuit. In October 1981, the Eleventh Circuit was created by moving Alabama, Georgia, and Florida from the Fifth to a new geographical circuit. The Eleventh Circuit has adopted the policy of following as precedent all decisions of the Fifth Circuit during the time the states currently constituting the Eleventh Circuit were part of the Fifth Circuit.[33]

EXAMPLE C:1-7 ▶ In the current year, the Eleventh Circuit first considered an issue in a case involving a Florida taxpayer. In 1980, the Fifth Circuit had ruled on the same issue in a case involving a Louisiana taxpayer. Because Florida was part of the Fifth Circuit in 1980, under the policy adopted by the Eleventh Circuit, it will follow the Fifth Circuit's earlier decision. Had the Fifth Circuit's decision been rendered in 1982—after the creation of the Eleventh Circuit—the Eleventh Circuit would not have been bound by the Fifth Circuit's decision. ◀

As the later discussion of precedent points out, different circuits may reach different conclusions concerning similar facts and issues.

Circuit court decisions—regardless of topic (e.g., civil rights, securities law, and taxation)—are now reported officially in the *Federal Reporter, Third Series* (cited as F.3d), published by West. The third series was created in October 1993 after the volume number for the second series reached 999. The primary citation to a circuit court opinion should be to the *Federal Reporter*. Tax decisions of the circuit courts also appear in the *American Federal Tax Reports* and *U.S. Tax Cases.* Below is an example of a citation to a 1994 circuit court decision:

Leonard Greene v. U.S., 13 F.3d 577, 73 AFTR 2d 94-746, 94-1 USTC ¶50,022 (2nd Cir., 1994).

The *Greene* case appears on page 577 of Volume 13 of the *Federal Reporter, Third Series.* It also is published in Volume 73, page 94-746 of the AFTR, Second Series, and in Volume 1, Paragraph 50,022, of the 1994 USTC. The parenthetical information indicates that the Second Circuit decided the case in 1994. (A *Federal Reporter, Second Series* reference is found in footnote 33 of this chapter.)

[33] *Bonner v. City of Prichard,* 661 F.2d 1206 (11th Cir., 1981).

ADDITIONAL COMMENT

A judge is not required to follow judicial precedent beyond his or her jurisdiction. Thus, the Tax Court, the U.S. district courts, and the U.S. Court of Federal Claims are not required to follow the others' decisions, nor is a circuit court required to follow the decision of a different circuit court.

U.S. SUPREME COURT. Whichever party loses at the appellate level can request that the U.S. Supreme Court hear the case. The Supreme Court, however, hears very few tax cases. Unless the circuits are divided on the tax treatment of an item, or the issue is deemed to be of great significance, the Supreme Court probably will not hear the case.[34] Supreme Court decisions are the law of the land and take precedence over all other court decisions, including the Supreme Court's earlier decisions. As a practical matter, a Supreme Court interpretation of the IRC is almost as authoritative as an act of Congress. If Congress does not agree with the Court's interpretation, it can amend the IRC to achieve a different result and has in fact done so on a number of occasions. If the Supreme Court declares a tax statute to be unconstitutional, the statute is invalid.

All Supreme Court decisions, regardless of subject, are published in the *United States Supreme Court Reports* (cited as U.S.) by the U.S. Government Printing Office, the *Supreme Court Reporter* (cited as S. Ct.) by West, and the *United States Reports, Lawyers' Edition* (cited as L. Ed.) by Lawyer's Co-operative Publishing Co. In addition, the AFTR and USTC reporters published by RIA and CCH, respectively, contain Supreme Court decisions concerned with taxation. An example of a citation to a Supreme Court opinion appears below:

> *Boeing Company v. U.S.,* 537 U.S. 437, 91 AFTR 2d 2003-1088, 2003-1 USTC ¶50,273 (USSC, 2003).

According to the primary citation, this case appears in Volume 537, page 437, of the *United States Supreme Court Reports*. According to the secondary citation, it also appears in Volume 91, page 2003-1088, of the AFTR, Second Series, and in Volume 1, Paragraph 50,273, of the 2003 USTC.

Table C:1-2 provides a summary of how the IRC, court decisions, revenue rulings, revenue procedures, and other administrative pronouncements should be cited. Primary citations are to the reporters published by West or the U.S. Government Printing Office, and secondary citations are to the AFTR and USTC.

SELF-STUDY QUESTION

Is it possible for the Tax Court to intentionally issue conflicting decisions?

ANSWER

Yes. If the Tax Court issues two decisions that are appealable to different circuit courts and these courts have previously reached different conclusions on the issue, the Tax Court follows the respective precedent in each circuit and issues conflicting decisions. This is a result of the *Golsen* Rule.

PRECEDENTIAL VALUE OF VARIOUS DECISIONS.

Tax Court. The Tax Court is a court of national jurisdiction. Consequently, it generally rules uniformly for all taxpayers, regardless of their residence or place of business. It follows U.S. Supreme Court decisions and its own earlier decisions. It is not bound by cases decided by the U.S. Court of Federal Claims or a U.S. district court, even if the district court has jurisdiction over the taxpayer.

In 1970, the Tax Court adopted what is known as the *Golsen* Rule.[35] Under this rule, the Tax Court departs from its general policy of adjudicating uniformly for all taxpayers and instead follows the decisions of the court of appeals to which the case in question is appealable. Stated differently, the *Golsen* Rule mandates that the Tax Court rule consistently with decisions of the court for the circuit where the taxpayer resides or does business.

EXAMPLE C:1-8 ▶ In the year in which an issue was first litigated, the Tax Court decided that an expenditure was deductible. The government appealed the decision to the Tenth Circuit Court of Appeals and won a reversal. This is the only appellate decision regarding the issue. If and when the Tax Court addresses this issue again, it will hold, with one exception, that the expenditure is deductible. The exception applies to taxpayers in the Tenth Circuit. Under the *Golsen* Rule, these taxpayers will be denied the deduction. ◀

---

[34] *Vogel Fertilizer Co. v. U.S.,* 49 AFTR 2d 82-491, 82-1 USTC ¶9134 (USSC, 1982), is an example of a case the Supreme Court heard to settle a split in judicial authority. The Fifth Circuit, the Tax Court, and the Court of Claims had reached one conclusion on an issue, while the Second, Fourth, and Eighth Circuits had reached another.

[35] The *Golsen* Rule is based on the decision in *Jack E. Golsen,* 54 T.C. 742 (1970).

▼ TABLE C:1-2
Summary of Tax-related Primary Sources—Statutory and Administrative

Source Name	Publisher	Materials Provided	Citation Example
U.S. Code, Title 26	Government Printing Office	Internal Revenue Code	Sec. 441(b)
Code of Federal Regulations, Title 26	Government Printing Office	Treasury Regulations (final)	Reg. Sec. 1.461-1(c)
		Treasury Regulations (temporary)	Temp. Reg. Sec. 1.62-1T(e)
Internal Revenue Bulletin	Government Printing Office	Treasury Regulations (proposed)	Prop. Reg. Sec. 1.671-1(h)
		Treasury decisions	T.D. 8756 (January 12, 1998)
		Revenue rulings	Rev. Rul. 2004-18, 2004-8 I.R.B. 509
		Revenue procedures	Rev. Proc. 2004-23, 2003-16 I.R.B. 785
		Committee reports	S.Rept. No. 105-33, 105th Cong., 1st Sess., p. 308 (1997)
		Public laws	P.L. 105-34, Sec. 224(a), enacted August 6, 1997
		Announcements	Announcement 2004-5, 2004-4 I.R.B. 362
		Notices	Notice 2004-14, 2004-9 I.R.B. 526
Cumulative Bulletin	Government Printing Office	Treasury Regulations (proposed)	Prop. Reg. Sec. 1.671-1(h)
		Treasury decisions	T.D. 8756 (January 12, 1998)
		Revenue rulings	Rev. Rul. 84-111, 1984-2 C.B. 88
		Revenue procedures	Rev. Proc. 77-28, 1977-2 C.B. 537
		Committee reports	S.Rept. No. 105-33, 105th Cong., 1st Sess., p. 308 (1997)
		Public laws	P.L. 105-34, Sec. 224(a), enacted August 6, 1997
		Announcements	Announcement 98-1, 1998-1 C.B. 282
		Notices	Notice 88-74, 1988-2 C.B. 385

Summary of Tax-related Primary and Secondary Sources—Judicial

Reporter Name	Publisher	Decisions Published	Citation Example
U.S. Supreme Court Reports	Government Printing Office	U.S. Supreme Court	*Boeing Company v. U.S.,* 537 U.S. 437 (2003)
Supreme Court Reports	West Publishing Company	U.S. Supreme Court	*Boeing Company v. U.S.,* 123 S. Ct. 1099 (2003)
Federal Reporter (1st–3rd Series)	West Publishing Company	U.S. Court of Appeal Pre-1982 Court of Claims	*Leonard Green v. U.S.,* 13 F.3d 577 (2nd Cir., 1994)
Federal Supplement Series	West Publishing Company	U.S. District Court	*Alfred Abdo, Jr. v. IRS,* 234 F. Supp. 2d 553 (DC North Carolina, 2002)
U.S. Court of Federal Claims	West Publishing Company	Court of Federal Claims	*Jeffery G. Sharp v. U.S.,* 27 Fed. Cl. 52 (1992)
Tax Court of the U.S. Reports	Government Printing Office	U.S. Tax Court regular	*Security State Bank,* 111 T.C. 210 (1998), acq. 2001-1 C.B. xix
Tax Court Memorandum Decisions	CCH Incorporated	U.S. Tax Court memo	*Paul F. Belloff,* 63 TCM 3150 (1992)
RIA Tax Court Memorandum Decisions	Research Institute of America	U.S. Tax Court memo	*Paul F. Belloff,* 1992 RIA T.C. Memo ¶92,346
American Federal Tax Reports	Research Institute of America	Tax: all federal courts except Tax Court	*Boeing Company v. U.S.,* 91 AFTR 2d 2003-1 (USSC, 2003)
U.S. Tax Cases	CCH Incorporated	Tax: all federal courts except Tax Court	*Ruddick Corp. v. U.S.,* 81-1 USTC ¶9343 (Ct. Cls., 1981)

U.S. District Court. Because each U.S. district court is independent of the other district courts, the decisions of each have precedential value only within its own jurisdiction (i.e., only with respect to subsequent cases brought before that court). District courts must follow decisions of the U.S. Supreme Court, the circuit court to which the case is appealable, and the district court's own earlier decisions regarding similar facts and issues.

EXAMPLE C:1-9 ▶ The U.S. District Court for Rhode Island, the Tax Court, and the Eleventh Circuit have decided cases involving similar facts and issues. Any U.S. district court within the Eleventh Circuit must follow that circuit's decision in future cases involving similar facts and issues. Likewise, the U.S. District Court for Rhode Island must decide such cases consistently with its previous decision. Tax Court decisions are not binding on the district courts. Thus, all district courts other than the one for Rhode Island and those within the Eleventh Circuit are free to decide such cases independently. ◀

U.S. Court of Federal Claims. In adjudicating a case, the U.S. Court of Federal Claims must rule consistently with U.S. Supreme Court decisions, decisions of the Circuit Court of Appeals for the Federal Circuit, and its own earlier decisions, including those rendered when the court had a different name. It need not follow decisions of other circuit courts, the Tax Court, or U.S. district courts.

EXAMPLE C:1-10 ▶ Assume the same facts as in Example C:1-9. In a later year, a case involving similar facts and issues is heard by the U.S. Court of Federal Claims. This court is not bound by precedents set by any of the other courts. Thus, it may reach a conclusion independently of the other courts. ◀

Circuit Courts of Appeals. A circuit court is bound by U.S. Supreme Court decisions and its own earlier decisions. If neither the Supreme Court nor the circuit in question has already decided an issue, the circuit court has no precedent that it must follow, regardless of whether other circuits have ruled on the issue. In such circumstances, the circuit court is said to be writing on a clean slate. In rendering a decision, the judges of that court may adopt another circuit's view, which they are likely to regard as relevant.

EXAMPLE C:1-11 ▶ Assume the same facts as in Example C:1-9. Any circuit other than the Eleventh would be writing on a clean slate if it adjudicated a case involving similar facts and issues. After reviewing the Eleventh Circuit's decision, another circuit might find it relevant and rule in the same way. ◀

In such a case of "first impression," when the court has had no precedent on which to base a decision, a tax practitioner might look at past opinions of the court to see which other judicial authority the court has found to be "persuasive."

Forum Shopping. Not surprisingly, courts often disagree on the tax treatment of the same item. This disagreement gives rise to differing precedents within the various jurisdictions (what is called a "split in judicial authority"). Because taxpayers have the flexibility of choosing where to file a lawsuit, these circumstances afford them the opportunity to **forum shop**. Forum-shopping involves choosing where among the courts to file a lawsuit based on differing precedents.

An example of a split in judicial authority concerned the issue of when it became too late for the IRS to question the tax treatment of items that "flowed through" an S corporation's return to a shareholder's return. The key question was this: if the time for assessing a deficiency (limitations period) with respect to the corporation's, but not the shareholder's, return had expired, was the IRS precluded from collecting additional taxes from the shareholder? In *Kelley,*[36] the Ninth Circuit Court of Appeals ruled that the IRS would be barred from collecting additional taxes from the shareholder if the limitations period for the *S corporation's* return had expired. In *Bufferd,*[37] *Fehlhaber,*[38] and *Green,*[39]

---

[36] *Daniel M. Kelley v. CIR,* 64 AFTR 2d 89-5025, 89-1 USTC ¶9360 (9th Cir., 1989).

[37] *Sheldon B. Bufferd v. CIR,* 69 AFTR 2d 92-465, 92-1 USTC ¶50,031 (2nd Cir., 1992).

[38] *Robert Fehlhaber v. CIR,* 69 AFTR 2d 92-850, 92-1 USTC ¶50,131 (11th Cir., 1992).

[39] *Charles T. Green v. CIR,* 70 AFTR 2d 92-5077, 92-2 USTC ¶50,340 (5th Cir., 1992).

three other circuit courts ruled that the IRS would be barred from collecting additional taxes from the shareholder if the limitations period for the *shareholder's* return had expired. The Supreme Court affirmed the *Bufferd* decision,[40] establishing that the statute of limitations for the shareholder's return governed. This action brought about certainty and uniformity within the judicial system.

Dictum. At times, a court may comment on an issue or a set of facts not central to the case under review. A court's remark not essential to the determination of a disputed issue, and therefore not binding authority, is called *dictum.* An example of dictum is found in *Central Illinois Public Service Co.*[41] In this case, the U.S. Supreme Court addressed whether lunch reimbursements received by employees constitute wages subject to withholding. Justice Blackman remarked in passing that earnings in the form of interest, rents, and dividends are not wages. This remark is dictum because it is not essential to the determination of whether lunch reimbursements are wages subject to withholding. Although not authoritative, dictum may be cited by taxpayers to bolster an argument in favor of a particular tax result.

STOP & THINK

Question: You have been researching whether an amount received by your new client can be excluded from her gross income. The IRS is auditing the client's prior year tax return, which another firm prepared. In a similar case decided a few years ago, the Tax Court allowed an exclusion, but the IRS nonacquiesced in the decision. The case involved a taxpayer in the Fourth Circuit. Your client is a resident of Maine, which is in the First Circuit. Twelve years ago, in a case involving another taxpayer, the federal court for the client's district ruled that this type of receipt is not excludable. No other precedent exists. To sustain an exclusion, must your client litigate? Explain. If your client litigates, in which court of first instance should she begin her litigation?

Solution: Because of its nonacquiescence, the IRS is likely to challenge your client's tax treatment. Thus, she may be compelled to litigate. She would not want to litigate in her U.S. district court because it would be bound by its earlier decision, which is unfavorable to taxpayers generally. A good place to begin would be the Tax Court because it is bound by appellate court, but not district court, decisions and because of its earlier pro-taxpayer position. No one can predict how the U.S. Court of Federal Claims would rule because no precedent that it must follow exists.

ADDITIONAL COMMENT
A tax treaty carries the same authoritative weight as a federal statute (IRC). A tax advisor should be aware of provisions in tax treaties that will affect a taxpayer's worldwide tax liability.

TAX TREATIES

The United States has concluded **tax treaties** with numerous foreign countries. These treaties address the alleviation of double taxation and other matters. A tax advisor exploring the U.S. tax consequences of a U.S. corporation's operations in another country should determine whether a treaty between that country and the United States exists. If one does, the tax advisor should ascertain the applicable provisions of the treaty. (See Chapter C:16 of this text for a more extensive discussion of treaties.)

KEY POINT
Tax articles can be used to help *find* answers to tax questions. Where possible, the underlying statutory, administrative, or judicial sources referenced in the tax article should be cited as authority and not the author of the article. The courts and the IRS will place little, if any, reliance on mere editorial opinion.

TAX PERIODICALS

Tax periodicals assist the researcher in tracing the development of, and analyzing tax law. These periodicals are especially useful when they discuss the legislative history of a recently enacted IRC statute that has little or no administrative or judicial authority on point.

Tax experts write articles on landmark court decisions, proposed regulations, new tax legislation, and other matters. Frequently, those who write articles of a highly technical nature are attorneys, accountants, or professors. Among the periodicals that provide in-depth coverage of tax-related matters are the following:

---

40 *Sheldon B. Bufferd v. CIR,* 71 AFTR 2d 93-573, 93-1 USTC ¶50,038 (USSC, 1993).

41 *Central Illinois Public Service Co. v. CIR,* 41 AFTR 2d 78-718, 78-1 USTC ¶9254 (USSC, 1978).

The Journal of Taxation
The Tax Adviser
Practical Tax Strategies
Taxes—The Tax Magazine
Tax Law Review
Tax Notes
Corporate Taxation
Business Entities
Real Estate Taxation
The Review of Taxation of Individuals
Estate Planning

The first six journals are generalized; that is, they deal with a variety of topics. As their titles suggest, the next five are specialized; they deal with specific subjects. All these publications (other than *Tax Notes,* which is published weekly) are published either monthly or quarterly. Daily newsletters, such as the *Daily Tax Report,* published by the Bureau of National Affairs (BNA), are used by tax professionals when they need updates more timely than can be provided by monthly or quarterly publications.

Tax periodicals and tax services are secondary authorities. The IRC, Treasury Regulations, IRS pronouncements, and court opinions are primary authorities. In presenting research results, the tax advisor should always cite primary authorities.

TAX SERVICES

OBJECTIVE 4

Consult tax services to research an issue

Various publishers provide multivolume commentaries on the tax law in what are familiarly referred to as **tax services.** These commentaries are available in print form and in electronic form via the Internet. While the organizational scheme of the print and Internet versions of each tax service is substantially the same (see "Computers as a Research Tool" below for a description of their salient differences), the organizational schemes of the various tax services differ significantly. Some are updated more frequently than others. Each has its own special features and editorial approach to tax issues. The best way to acquaint oneself with the various tax services is to use them in researching hypothetical or actual problems.

ADDITIONAL COMMENT

Tax services often are consulted at the beginning of the research process. A tax service helps identify the tax authorities pertaining to a particular tax issue. The actual tax authorities, and not the tax service, are generally cited as support for a particular tax position.

Organizationally, there are two types of tax services: "annotated" and "topical" (although this distinction has become somewhat blurred in the Internet version of these services). An **annotated tax service** is organized by IRC section. The IRC-arranged subdivisions of this service are likely to encompass several topics. A **topical tax service** is organized by broad topic. The topically arranged subdivisions of this service are likely to encompass several IRC sections. The principal annotated tax services are the *United States Tax Reporter* and *Standard Federal Tax Reporter.* The main topical services are the *Federal Tax Coordinator 2d, Law of Federal Income Taxation* (Mertens), *Tax Management Portfolios,* and *CCH Federal Tax Service.* Each of these services is discussed below.

KEY POINT

Both the *United States Tax Reporter* and the *Standard Federal Tax Reporter* services are organized by IRC section. Many tax advisors find both of these services easy to use. The other major tax services are organized by topic.

UNITED STATES TAX REPORTER

The *United States Tax Reporter* is a multivolume series published by RIA. It is devoted to income, estate, gift, and excise taxes and is organized by IRC section number. Accordingly, its commentary begins with Sec. 1 of the IRC and proceeds in numerical order through the last section of the IRC. Researchers who know the number of the IRC section applicable to their problem can turn directly to the paragraphs that discuss that section. Each organizational part presents an editorial commentary (with access to the text of the relevant IRC section), committee reports, Treasury Regulations, and IRS pronouncements, all indexed according to IRC section number. Separate volumes in the print version contain an index and finding lists that reference explanatory paragraphs respectively by topic and by case name or IRS pronouncement. These resources enable the researcher to access this service in one of three ways: first, by IRC section number; second, by topic; and third, by citation.

One of the more salient features of this service (as well as the CCH service discussed below) are the annotations accompanying the editorial commentaries. These annotations consist of digests or summaries of IRS pronouncements and court opinions that interpret a particular IRC section. They are classified by subtopic and cite pertinent primary authorities.

The print version of *United States Tax Reporter* is updated weekly. Information on recent developments is referenced in a table in Volume 16 and periodically moved into the main body of the text. To determine whether any recent developments impact a particular issue, the researcher should look in the table for references to the numbers of paragraphs that discuss the issue. The print service includes, in addition to the recent developments volume, several volumes on the IRC and Treasury Regulations, a compilation of newly issued *American Federal Tax Reports* decisions, and practical aids such as tax rate, interest rate, and per diem rate tables. The Internet version of the *United States Tax Reporter* is available on RIA CHECKPOINT™.

REAL-WORLD EXAMPLE

The 1913 CCH explanation of the federal tax law was a single 400-page volume. The current *Standard Federal Tax Reporter* is 25 volumes and over 100,000 pages in length.

STANDARD FEDERAL TAX REPORTER

CCH publishes the *Standard Federal Tax Reporter*, also organized by IRC section number. Separate services devoted to income taxes, estate and gift taxes, and excise taxes are available. Like RIA's *United States Tax Reporter*, the CCH service compiles in its main volumes editorial commentaries (with access to the text of the IRC), Treasury Regulations, and annotations. Also like the RIA service, the print version of the CCH service includes a topical index and finding lists that reference explanatory paragraphs respectively by topic and by authority. Thus, like the *United States Tax Reporter*, the CCH service can be accessed by IRC section number, topic, and citation.[42]

The IRC volumes of the CCH print version contain tables that cross-reference sections of the current IRC with other sections of the current IRC and with predecessor provisions of the 1954 IRC. The first of these tables enables the researcher to identify other sections of the current IRC that potentially impact a transaction or taxable event. The second table enables the researcher to trace the statutory history of particular IRC provisions. The IRC volumes of the CCH print version also contain a comprehensive listing of committee reports organized by IRC section number. This listing enables the researcher to locate sources that suggest the legislative intent behind a particular IRC provision.

The CCH service provides articles on current developments. Until the end of the calendar year, when CCH publishes a new reporter series, it supplies periodic updates of court opinions and revenue rulings. Throughout the year, information on major developments, such as new tax legislation and Supreme Court decisions, is incorporated in the main body of the text. The Internet version of the CCH service is available on the CCH Internet Tax Research NetWork™.

ADDITIONAL COMMENT

The RIA *Federal Tax Coordinator 2d* service is a more voluminous service than either the *United States Tax Reporter* or *Standard Federal Tax Reporter* services because it has more editorial commentary. The *Federal Tax Coordinator 2d* updates are integrated into the main body of the text. The service is not replaced each year. By contrast, both the *United States Tax Reporter* and *Standard Federal Tax Reporter* services compile their updates in one volume. CCH issues a new *Standard Federal Tax Reporter* service each year. The other services integrate the updates into the body of existing text at the beginning of each year.

FEDERAL TAX COORDINATOR 2d

The *Federal Tax Coordinator 2d* (FTC service), also published by RIA, is a multivolume publication organized by broad topic. It covers three major areas: income taxes, estate and gift taxes, and excise taxes. Unlike the print version of the annotated services, the print version of the FTC service presents its editorial commentary before excerpts of relevant IRC and Treasury Regulation sections. The latter excerpts are placed behind a tab titled Code & Regs within the same topical volume. The editorial commentary is heavily footnoted with references to court cases, revenue rulings, and other primary authorities that pertain to the topical discussion. An index volume references the numbers of paragraphs that discuss various topics. Cross-reference tables reference the numbers of paragraphs that discuss particular IRC sections, Treasury Regulations, IRS pronouncements, and court cases. Instead of providing a separate volume for new developments, the FTC service incorporates new developments information in the main body of the service.

A peculiar feature of the FTC service is its editorial notations, which suggest the practical implications of the tax principle under discussion. Among the notations are *illustration*, which offers examples of how the principle is applied; *caution*, which points to the

[42] Examples of citations to these tax services are as follows: (2006) 6 *United States Tax Reporter* (RIA) ¶3025 and (2006) 8 *Std. Fed. Tax Rep.* (CCH) ¶21,966.02, where 6 and 8 represent the volume numbers, and the paragraph numbers refer to the cited passages in the volume. Because citations should be to primary authorities, citations to secondary authorities are rarely used.

risks associated with application; *recommendation*, which suggests ways to minimize the risk; and *observation*, which offers an editorial analysis of the principle.

One part of the FTC service titled Practice Aids provides tools useful in tax practice. Other tax services provide similar tools. Such tools include Tax Savings Opportunity Checklists, designed to assist taxpayers in proceeding with business and personal transactions; a Current Legislation Table, which indicates the status of pending tax legislation; and an IRS Forms Table, which cross-references the numbers of IRS forms to those of paragraphs in the topical discussion; and tax calendars, tax schedules, sample client letters, and daily compound interest tables. Other segments of the FTC service present the text of tax treaties, revenue rulings, revenue procedures, and proposed Treasury Regulations. A separate part compiles issues of *Weekly Alert*, RIA's tax newsletter. The Internet version of the FTC service is available on RIA CHECKPOINT™.

LAW OF FEDERAL INCOME TAXATION (MERTENS)

The *Law of Federal Income Taxation,* published by West, originally was edited by Merten's and is called "Mertens" by tax practitioners and in this text. Legalistic in orientation, Mertens deals only with federal income taxation. Its commentary is narrative in form and reads like a treatise. Mertens is highly regarded by tax accountants and tax lawyers. It is the only tax service cited by the U.S. judiciary with any regularity. The text of Mertens is heavily footnoted. The footnotes contain a wealth of information relating to the IRC, Treasury Regulations, IRS pronouncements, and court opinions.

Mertens includes several parts devoted exclusively to Treasury Regulations and IRS pronouncements. These segments contain the full text of *current* Treasury Regulations and IRS pronouncements (this text does not appear in the main commentary volumes), as well as the full text of *old* Treasury Regulations and IRS pronouncements. The old versions enable the researcher to reconstruct the state of the tax law in any given year. Such reconstruction is useful in three contexts: first, where the IRS audits a taxpayer's return for a previous year; second, where the researcher evaluates the effects of a transaction beginning in a previous year; and third, where the researcher analyzes a court opinion issued in a previous year.

Like the annotated services, the print version of Mertens contains a topical index and finding lists cross-referenced to the IRC, Treasury Regulations, IRS pronouncements, and court opinions. Its *Current Rulings Materials* volume includes a Code-Rulings Table that lists by IRC section the numbers of all post-1954 revenue rulings that interpret a particular section. The same volume also includes a Rulings Status Table that indicates the status of every post-1954 revenue ruling (i.e., whether the ruling has been revoked, modified, amplified, or otherwise impacted by an IRS decision).[43] Its *Current Materials* volume compiles issues of *Development and Highlights*, Mertens' monthly periodical. The Internet version of Mertens is available on WESTLAW™.

TAX MANAGEMENT PORTFOLIOS

ADDITIONAL COMMENT

The *Tax Management Portfolios* are popular with many tax advisors because they are very readable yet still provide a comprehensive discussion of the pertinent tax issues. However, because the published portfolios do not cover all areas of the tax law, another service may be necessary to supplement the gaps in the portfolio coverage.

BNA publishes over 200 booklets of specialized tax materials called *Tax Management Portfolios* (referred to as BNA portfolios by many practitioners and in this text). BNA portfolios are issued in three series: U.S. income; foreign income; and estates, gifts, and trusts. Each portfolio is prepared by a specialized tax practitioner. Thus, the particular slant of BNA portfolios is practical application, as opposed to the theoretical. In each portfolio, the author's discussion of a particular topic is found in the Detailed Analysis section. Here, provisions of the IRC and Treasury Regulations are explained, court opinions are analyzed, and transactional structures are proposed. The text of the Detailed Analysis is heavily footnoted. The footnotes cite and summarize relevant primary and secondary sources.

A noteworthy feature of each BNA portfolio is its Working Papers, which are tools designed to aid the practitioner in tax planning and compliance. Among such tools are tax-related checklists, IRS forms and instructions, computational worksheets, and draft legal documents. The Bibliography and References section at the back of each print version

[43] RIA and CCH services provide essentially the same information in different formats.

volume lists primary and secondary sources used by the author to prepare the portfolio. In this section, the researcher will find a listing of IRC sections, Treasury Regulations, IRS pronouncements, and court opinions that support the Detailed Analysis, as well as references to pertinent law review articles and tax treatises.

Unlike the print version of the other services, the print version of BNA portfolios does not contain finding lists indexed to court opinions or IRS pronouncements. On the other hand, it does contain a topical index, an IRC reference table, and an IRS forms index that cross-references the numbers of IRS forms to pertinent pages in the portfolios. Like CCH and RIA, BNA publishes a weekly newsletter as part of its tax service. The Internet version of BNA portfolios is available in the BNA Tax Management Library and WESTLAW™.

CCH FEDERAL TAX SERVICE

The newest of the major tax services is the *CCH Federal Tax Service,* currently published by CCH and formerly published by Matthew Bender & Company. The print version of this service is a multivolume looseleaf publication that, like RIA's FTC service and Mertens, is organized by broad topic. Just like portfolios in the BNA service, chapters of the *CCH Federal Tax Service* are authored by tax practitioners and thus are practical in orientation.

The *CCH Federal Tax Service* does not compile sections of the IRC and Treasury Regulations in the same volumes in which the topical analysis appears. Rather, it publishes them in separate volumes devoted exclusively to the IRC and proposed, temporary, and final Treasury Regulations. A particular IRC section and its related Treasury Regulations are found in the same volume.

CCH periodically updates the *Federal Tax Service* to reflect current developments. As with its annotated tax service, CCH issues a weekly newsletter as part of this topical tax service. The Internet version of the *CCH Federal Tax Service* is available on the CCH Internet Tax Research NetWork™.

Figure C:1-5 provides an overview of one approach for using the tax services to research a tax question.

CITATORS

OBJECTIVE 5

Use a citator to assess tax authorities

Citators serve two functions: first, they trace the judicial history of a particular case (e.g., if the case under analysis is an appeals court decision, the citator indicates the lower court that heard the case and whether the Supreme Court reviewed the case); and second, they list other authorities (e.g., cases and IRS pronouncements) that cite the case in question. Two principal tax-related citators are the CCH citator and the *Research Institute of America Citator 2nd Series* (RIA citator).

CCH CITATOR

The print verison of the CCH citator consists of two loose-leaf volumes, one for cases with names beginning with the letters A through M and the other for cases with names starting with the letters N through Z. In the CCH Internet Tax Research NetWork™, this information is integrated into one citator service. The CCH citator analyzes every decision reported in CCH's *Standard Federal Tax Reporter,* its *Excise Tax Reporter,* and its *Federal Estate and Gift Tax Reporter* and selectively lists cases that cite the decision under analysis. (CCH editors decide which of these other cases influence the precedential weight of the decision under analysis.)

Although the CCH citator does not analyze IRS pronouncements, "status lists" found in the second citator volume of the CCH service does. (Comparable lists are found in the *United States Tax Reporter,* the FTC service, and Mertens.) These lists indicate the current status of revenue rulings, revenue procedures, private letter rulings, and other IRS pronouncements. They reveal whether these authorities have been cited in court cases, their impact on other IRS pronouncements, and whether they have been modified, superceded, or obsoleted. In the CCH Internet Tax Research NetWork™ and in RIA CHECKPOINT™, the status lists have been integrated in the main citator service. An excerpt from the CCH citator appears in Figure C:1-6.

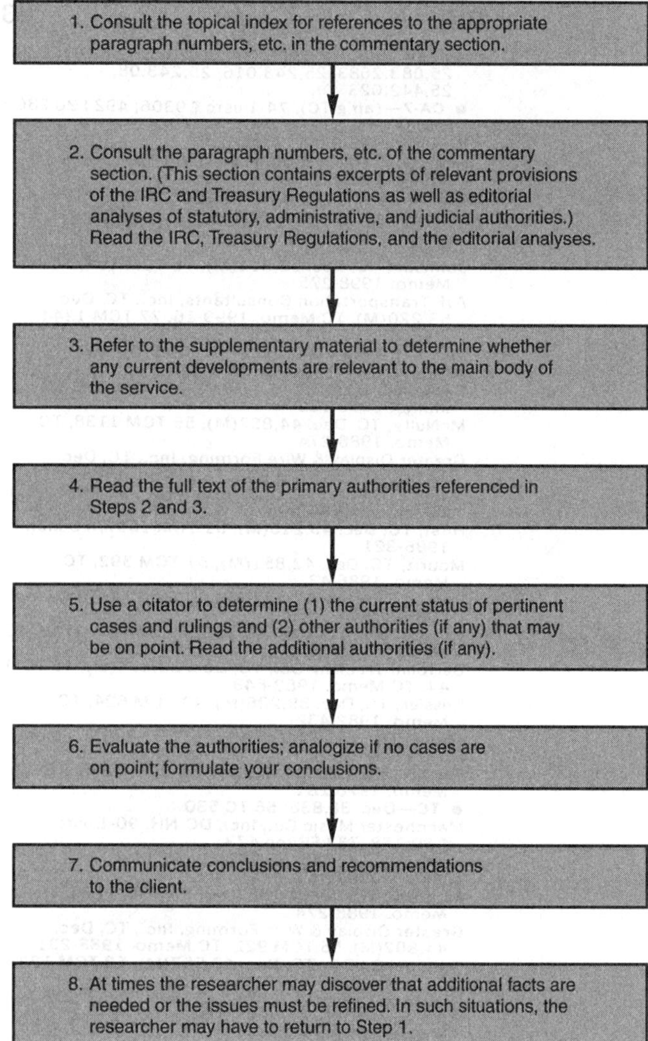

FIGURE C:1-5 ▶ USE OF TAX SERVICES TO RESEARCH A TAX QUESTION

Refer to Figure C:1-6 and find the *Leonarda C. Diaz* case. The information in bold print with bullets to the left denotes that *Diaz* was first decided by the Tax Court and then by the Second Circuit Court. It shows that the Second Circuit affirmed (upheld) the Tax Court's decision. The two cases listed beneath the Second Circuit decision (i.e., *Kuh* and *Damm*) cite the *Diaz* decision. The six cases listed beneath the Tax Court decision (i.e., *German, Jr., Orr, Zeidler, Schwerm, Wassenaar,* and *Toner*) cite the Tax Court's opinion in *Diaz*. The abbreviation *Dec.* appearing in some of the citations stands for *decision*. The CCH citator lists the decision numbers of the Tax Court cases.

The main CCH citator volumes are published once a year. The first of these volumes contains a "Current Citator Table," which lists court decisions recently cited, as well as additional citing cases for court decisions previously cited. Citator updates are issued quarterly. The *Diaz* decision has not been cited in any opinion issued since 2006, the year in which the CCH citator was last published. The applicable page from the main citator table for the *Diaz* decision is reproduced here.

The entry "¶5504.20" appearing to the right of *Alfonso Diaz* denotes the number of the *Standard Federal Tax Reporter* paragraph that discusses the case. Usually, before consulting the citator, a researcher already would have read about this case in the referenced paragraph and would have decided that it was relevant to his or her research. In such circumstances, the reference would not be particularly useful. In other circumstances, the reference would be useful. For example, if the researcher had heard about the case from a colleague and wanted to read more about it, he or she could readily locate the passage that discusses it.

DIA 93,302 ——CCH——

Diamond, Sol .. ¶5508.085, 8520.517, 21,005.123, 25,083.2683, 25,243.016, 25,243.08, 25,442.023
● **CA-7**—(aff'g TC), 74-1 USTC ¶9306; 492 F2d 286
Campbell, CA-8, 91-2 USTC ¶50,420
Rev. Proc. 93-27
Anderson, TC, Dec. 50,410(M), 69 TCM 1609, TC Memo. 1995-8
Banks, TC, Dec. 47,832(M), 62 TCM 1611, TC Memo. 1991-641
Arcia, TC, Dec. 52,701(M), 75 TCM 2287, TC Memo. 1998-178
Johnson, TC, Dec. 52,812(M), 76 TCM 194, TC Memo. 1998-275
AJF Transportation Consultants, Inc., TC, Dec. 53,220(M), TC Memo. 1999-16, 77 TCM 1244
Pacheco, CA-9, 90-2 USTC ¶50,458
Vestal, CA-8, 74-2 USTC ¶9501, 498 F2d 487
St. John, DC-III, 84-1 USTC ¶9158
Campbell, TC, Dec. 46,493(M), 59 TCM 236, TC Memo. 1990-162
McNulty, TC, Dec. 44,857(M), 55 TCM 1138, TC Memo. 1988-274
Greater Display & Wire Forming, Inc., TC, Dec. 44,802(M), 55 TCM 922, TC Memo. 1988-231
National Oil Co., TC, Dec. 43,557(M), 52 TCM 1223, TC Memo. 1986-596
Hirst, TC, Dec. 43,215(M), 51 TCM 1597, TC Memo. 1986-321
Mouriz, TC, Dec. 42,851(M), 51 TCM 392, TC Memo. 1986-43
Parker, TC, Dec. 42,129(M), 50 TCM 14, TC Memo. 1985-263
Kenroy, Inc., TC, Dec. 41,186(M), 47 TCM 1749, TC Memo. 1984-232
Bertolini Trucking Co., TC, Dec. 39,474(M), 45 TCM 44, TC Memo. 1982-643
Kessler, TC, Dec. 39,226(M), 44 TCM 624, TC Memo. 1982-432
Tooke, TC, Dec. 34,336(M), 36 TCM 396, TC Memo. 1977-91
Pierson, TC, Dec. 34,009(M), 35 TCM 1256, TC Memo. 1976-281
● **TC**—Dec. 30,838; 56 TC 530
Manchester Music Co., Inc., DC-NH, 90-1 USTC ¶50,168, 733 FSupp 473
Miller, Jr., TC, Dec. 45,977(M), 57 TCM 1419, TC Memo. 1989-461
McNulty, TC, Dec. 44,857(M), 55 TCM 1138, TC Memo. 1988-274
Greater Display & Wire Forming, Inc., TC, Dec. 44,802(M), 55 TCM 922, TC Memo. 1988-231
National Oil Co., TC, Dec. 43,557(M), 52 TCM 1223, TC Memo. 1986-596
Goodwin, David C., TC, Dec. 36,413, 73 TC 215
Schaevitz, TC, Dec. 30,925(M), 30 TCM 823, TC Memo. 1971-197

Diamond, Solomon .... ¶8632.68
● **TC**—Dec. 25,981(M); 22 TCM 229; TC Memo. 1963-57

Diamond T Motor Car Co.: Allen v. ..... ¶38,160.82
● **CA-10**—(rev'g DC), 61-1 USTC ¶9484; 291 F2d 115
Randall, CA-5, 76-2 USTC ¶9770, 542 F2d 270
Jefferson Bank and Trust, DC-Colo, 89-1 USTC ¶9221
Rodkey, DC-Okla, 87-1 USTC ¶9218
Nevada Rock & Sand Co., DC-Nev, 74-2 USTC ¶9617, 376 FSupp 161
Nomellini Construction Co., DC-Calif, 71-2 USTC ¶9510, 328 FSupp 1281
● **DC-Colo**—60-2 USTC ¶9557

Diamondhead Corp. v. Fort Hope Development, Inc. .... ¶40,720.1945
● **DC-Ga**—78-2 USTC ¶9718

Diamondstone, I. A. (See Kann, William L.)

DiAndre, Anthony F. .... ¶36,894.7255, 41,758.30
● **SCt**—Cert. denied, 3/19/93
● **CA-10**—(rev'g and rem'g unreported DC), 92-2 USTC ¶50,373; 968 F2d 1049
Stewart, DC-Ohio, 95-1 USTC ¶50,249
Russell, DC-Mich, 95-1 USTC ¶50,029
Jones, DC-Neb, 94-2 USTC ¶50,562, 869 FSupp 747
Schachter, DC-Calif, 94-1 USTC ¶50,242
Fostvedt, DC-Colo, 93-1 USTC ¶50,299, 824 FSupp 978
Jones, DC-Neb, 95-2 USTC ¶50,567, 898 FSupp 1360
May, DC-Mo, 95-2 USTC ¶50,605
Spence, DC-NM, 96-2 USTC ¶50,615
Spence, CA-10, 97-1 USTC ¶50,485
Roebuck, DC-NC, 99-2 USTC ¶50,627

DiAndrea, Inc. .. ¶16,233.25, 21,817.108, 44,507.09
● **TC**—Dec. 40,697(M); 47 TCM 731; TC Memo. 1983-768
Johnson, TC, Dec. 47,836(M), 62 TCM 1629, TC Memo. 1991-645

Diaz, Alfonso .... ¶5504.195
● **TC**—Dec. 31,442; 58 TC 560; A. 1972-2 CB 2
Marrone, TC, Dec. 50,424(M), 69 TCM 1684, TC Memo. 1995-22
Sloan, TC, Dec. 50,305(M), 68 TCM 1489, TC Memo. 1994-628
Muniz, TC, Dec. 49,775(M), 67 TCM 2625, TC Memo. 1994-151
Drabiuk, TC, Dec. 50,692(M), 69 TCM 2890, TC Memo. 1995-260
Jackson, TC, Dec. 50,736(M), TC Memo. 1995-300, 70 TCM 12
Levin, TC, Dec. 51,326(M), 71 TCM 2938, TC Memo. 1996-211
American Underwriters, Inc., TC, Dec. 51,694(M), TC Memo. 1996-548, 72 TCM 1511
Solaas, TC, Dec. 52,529(M), 75 TCM 1613, TC Memo. 1998-25
Arcia, TC, Dec. 52,701(M), 75 TCM 2287, TC Memo. 1998-178
Maslow, TC, Dec. 52,302(M), TC Memo. 1997-466, 74 TCM 910
Neff Est., TC, Dec. 51,999(M), TC Memo. 1997-186, 73 TCM 2606
Swiatek, TC, Dec. 53,485(M), 78 TCM 223, TC Memo. 1999-257
Schirle, TC, Dec. 52,398(M), TC Memo. 1997-552, 74 TCM 1379
Kong, TC, Dec. 46,090(M), 58 TCM 378, TC Memo. 1989-560
Caglia, E. Bonnie, TC, Dec. 45,585(M), 57 TCM 1, TC Memo. 1989-143
Ettig, TC, Dec. 44,736(M), 55 TCM 720, TC Memo. 1988-182
Heller, TC, Dec. 44,083(M), 53 TCM 1486, TC Memo. 1987-376
Anastasato, TC, Dec. 43,309(M), 52 TCM 293, TC Memo. 1986-400
Stevenson, TC, Dec. 43,068(M), 51 TCM 1050, TC Memo. 1986-207
Wilhelm, TC, Dec. 42,813(M), 51 TCM 261, TC Memo. 1986-12
Branson, TC, Dec. 38,026(M), 42 TCM 281, TC Memo. 1981-338
Calloway, TC, Dec. 37,019(M), 40 TCM 495, TC Memo. 1980-211
Greenfield, TC, Dec. 35,253(M), 37 TCM 1082, TC Memo. 1978-251
Leong, TC, Dec. 34,232(M), 36 TCM 89, TC Memo. 1977-19
Dougherty, TC, Dec. 32,138, 60 TC 917
Hernandez, TC, Dec. 52,552(M), TC Memo. 1998-46, 75 TCM 1714

Diaz, Antonio A. v. Southern Drilling Corp. .... ¶41,699.45
● **CA-5**—(aff'g unreported DC), 71-1 USTC ¶9236

Diaz, Enrique .. ¶33,538.43, 39,475.65, 39,585.63, 41,688.377
● **DC-Calif**—90-1 USTC ¶50,209
Van Camp & Bennion, P.S., DC-Wash, 96-2 USTC ¶50,438

Diaz, Frank .... ¶29,412.9911
● **TC**—Dec. 42,922(M); 51 TCM 594; TC Memo. 1986-98

Diaz, Greg, Acting County Recorder for the City and County of San Francisco (See Chase Manhattan Bank, N.A. v. City & County of San Francisco)

Diaz, Humberto (See Flicker, Marvin)

Diaz, Juan (See Setal, Manuel G.)

Diaz, Leonarda C. .... ¶8632.3876
● **CA-2**—(aff'g TC), 79-2 USTC ¶9473; 607 F2d 995
Kuh, TC, Dec. 40,461(M), 46 TCM 1405, TC Memo. 1983-572
Damm, TC, Dec. 37,861(M), 41 TCM 1359, TC Memo. 1981-203
● **TC**—Dec. 35,436; 70 TC 1067
German, Jr., TC, Dec. 48,867(M), 65 TCM 1931, TC Memo. 1993-59
Orr, TC, Dec. 48,532(M), 64 TCM 882, TC Memo. 1992-566
Zeidler, TC, Dec. 51,264(M), 71 TCM 2603, TC Memo. 1996-157
Schwerm, TC, Dec. 42,817(M), 51 TCM 270, TC Memo. 1986-16
Wassenaar, TC, Dec. 36,359, 72 TC 1195
Toner, TC, Dec. 35,877, 71 TC 772

Diaz, Miguel A. (See Powers (Belcher), Sandra L.)

Dibble, Leon N., Exr. .... ¶29,225.442
● **BTA**—Dec. 2320; 6 BTA 732; A. VI-2 CB 2

FIGURE C:1-6 ▶ EXCERPT FROM THE CCH CITATOR

The CCH citator lists cases even where they have not been cited in other cases. For example, refer to the entry for *Frank Diaz.* This Tax Court memo decision is listed among the cases analyzed, even though no other published decision has referred to it. Moreover, the citator indicates whether the IRS Commissioner has acquiesced or nonacquiesced in a court decision. For example, refer to the entry for *Alfonso Diaz.* Note that the first Tax Court citation is followed by a capital "A," then another citation. The "A" indicates that the IRS Commissioner acquiesced in the Tax Court decision. The second citation indicates that the Commissioner's acquiescence is found on page 2 of Volume 2 of the 1972 *Cumulative Bulletin.*

RESEARCH INSTITUTE OF AMERICA CITATOR 2nd SERIES

Like the CCH citator, the RIA citator[44] provides the history of each authority and lists the cases and pronouncements that have cited that authority. The RIA citator, however, conveys more information than does the CCH citator. This information includes the following:

- Whether the citing authorities comment favorably or unfavorably on the cited case, or whether they can be distinguished from the cited case[45]
- The specific issue(s) in the cited case that is (are) referenced by the citing authorities

ADDITIONAL COMMENT

The history of a case may be easier to find in CCH because each of the courts that tried the case is listed in a single volume in boldface print.

In print form, the RIA citator (formerly, the Prentice Hall citator) consists of seven hardbound volumes and several cumulative supplements. The first hardbound volume lists cases decided from 1919 through 1941; the second, cases decided from 1942 through September 30, 1948; the third, cases decided from October 1, 1948, through July 29, 1954; the fourth, cases decided from July 30, 1954, through December 15, 1977; the fifth, cases cited from December 15, 1977, through December 20, 1989; the sixth, cases decided from January 4, 1990, to December 26, 1996; and the seventh, cases decided from January 2, 1997, to December 19, 2002. A softback cumulative supplement lists cases decided from December 27, 2002, to January 5, 2006. Each year, a revised annual supplement is published. Each month, a revised monthly supplement is published. In analyzing a 1945 case, a researcher should consult every cumulative supplement and every main volume except the first. In analyzing a 1980 case, the researcher should consult every cumulative supplement and the last three bound volumes. The Internet version of the RIA citator (i.e., in RIA CHECKPOINT™) integrates this information, thus allowing the researcher to consult only one citator source.

As mentioned earlier, the RIA citator reveals the manner in which the citing authorities comment on the case under analysis. The nature of the comment is indicated by symbols that appear to the left of the citing authority. The RIA citator also reveals the history of the case under analysis (e.g., whether it was affirmed, reversed, etc.).[46] This history is indicated by symbols that appear to the left of citations to the same case heard at different appellate levels (parallel citations). Figure C:1-7 explains the meaning of the various symbols, which are spelled out in the Internet version.

The RIA citator is especially useful if the cited case deals with more than one issue. As previously pointed out, the citator reports the issue(s) addressed in the cited case that is (are) referenced in the citing authority. The numbers to the left of this authority denote the specific issue(s) referenced. These numbers correspond to headnotes published in *American Federal Tax Reports.* A **headnote** is an editorial summary of a particular point of case law. Headnotes appear in case reporters immediately before the text of the opinions authored by the judges.

An excerpt from the 1978–1989 citator volume appears in the first column of Figure C:1-8. Refer to it and locate the Tax Court decision for *Leonarda C. Diaz.* All the cases that cite the decision after 1977 and through 1989 are listed. (*Diaz* was decided by the

---

[44] The *Research Institute of America Citator 2nd Series* is published currently by RIA. It originally was published by Prentice Hall's Information Services Division, which was acquired in 1990 by Maxwell Macmillan. *Prentice Hall* and/or *Maxwell Macmillan* appears on the spines and title pages of the older citators and will remain there because, unlike the CCH citator, the RIA citator is not republished each year.

[45] When a court distinguishes the facts of one case from those of an earlier case, it suggests that its departure from the earlier decision is justified because the facts of the two cases are different.

[46] If a case is *affirmed,* the decision of the lower court is upheld. *Reversed* means the higher court invalidated the decision of the lower court because it reached a conclusion different from that derived by the lower court. *Remanded* signifies that the higher court sent the case back to the lower court with instructions to address matters not earlier addressed.

SYMBOLS USED IN CITATOR COURT DECISIONS
Judicial History

- **a** affirmed by a higher court (Note: When available, the official cite to the affirmance is provided; if the affirmance is by unpublished order or opinion, the date of the decision and the court deciding the case are provided.)
- **App auth** appeal authorized by the Treasury
- **adptd** magistrate judge's decision is accepted by district court
- **adptg** district court accepts magistrate judge's decision
- **App** appeal pending (Note: Later volumes may have to be consulted to determine if appeal was decided or dismissed.)
- **cert gr** petition for certiorari was granted by the U.S. Supreme Court
- **d** appeal dismissed by the court or withdrawn by the party filing the appeal
- **ep** citing case is an earlier proceeding of the cited case
- **(G)** following an appeal notation, this symbol indicates that it was the government filing the appeal
- **lp** citing case is a later proceeding of the cited case
- **m** the earlier decision has been modified by the higher court, or by a later decision.
- **o** decision has been overruled by legislation
- **r** the decision of the lower court has been reversed on appeal
- **rc** related case arising out of the same taxable event or concerning the same taxpayer
- **reh dend** rehearing of cited case has been denied by the citing case
- **reh deng** cited case has denied rehearing of citing case
- **reinst** a dismissed appeal has been reinstated by the appellate court and is under consideration again
- **remd** the case has been remanded for proceedings consistent with the higher court decision
- **remg** the cited case is remanding the earlier case
- **revg & remg** the decision of the lower court has been reversed and remanded by a higher court on appeal
- **revd & remd** a higher court has reversed and remanded to the lower court a decision of that lower court
- **s** same case or ruling
- **sa** the cited case is affirming the earlier case
- **sm** the cited case is modifying the earlier case
- **sr** the cited case is reversing the earlier case
- **sx** the cited case is an earlier proceeding in a case for which a petition for certiorari was denied
- **(T)** an appeal was filed from the lower court decision by the taxpayer
- **vacd** the lower court decision was vacated on appeal or by the original court on remand

v

- **vacg** a higher court or the original court on remand has vacated the lower court decision
- **widrn** the original opinion was withdrawn by the court
- **x** petition for certiorari was denied by the U.S. Supreme Court
- **•** Supreme Court cases are designated by a bold-faced bullet (•) before the case line for easy location

Certain notations appear at the end of the cited case line. These notations include:

- **(A) or acq** the government has acquiesced in the reasoning or the result of the cited case
- **(NA) or nonacq** the government has refused to acquiesce or to adopt the reasoning or the result of the cited case, and will challenge the position adopted if future proceedings arise on the same issue
- **on rem** the case has been remanded by a higher court and the case cited is the resulting decision

Evaluation of Cited Cases

- **c** the citing case court has adversely commented on the reasoning of the cited case, and has criticized the earlier decision
- **e** the cited case is used favorably by the citing case court
- **f** the reasoning of the court in the cited case is followed by the later decision
- **g** the cited and citing cases are distinguished from each other on either facts or law
- **inap** the citing case court has specifically indicated that the cited case does not apply to the situation stated in the citing case.
- **iv** on all fours (both the cited and citing cases are virtually identical)
- **k** the cited and citing case principles are reconciled
- ***l*** the rationale of the cited case is limited to the facts or circumstances surrounding that case (this can occur frequently in situations in which there has been an intervening higher court decision or law change)
- **n** the cited case was noted in a dissenting opinion
- **o** the later case directly overrules the cited case (use of the evaluation is generally limited to situations in which the court notes that it is specifically overturning the cited case, and that the case will no longer be of any value)
- **q** the decision of the cited case is questioned and its validity debated in relation to the citing case at issue

The evaluations used for the court decisions generally are followed by a number. That number refers to the headnoted issue in the American Federal Tax Reports (AFTR) or Tax Court decision to which the citing case relates. If the case is not directly on point with any headnote, a bracketed notation at the end of the citing case line directs the researcher to the page in the cited case on which the issue appears.

A blank may appear in the evaluation space. Generally, this means that the citing court didn't comment on any of the legal issues raised in the cited case.

vi

FIGURE C:1-7 ▶ ABBREVIATIONS USED IN RIA CITATOR 2ND SERIES

Source: Reprinted from Citator 2nd Series 2003–2005, ©2006 by RIA, 395 Hudson Street, New York, NY 10014

ADDITIONAL COMMENT

The RIA citator has the advantage of providing the most references for a cited case. This point is apparent when one compares RIA's six volumes plus supplements with CCH's two volumes. Also, RIA numbers each tax issue litigated in a court case. This coding allows the tax advisor to identify cases dealing with the specific issue being researched. For example, if the advisor is interested in the first issue in the *Leonarda C. Diaz* Tax Court decision, the citator reproduced in Figure C:1-8 denotes five cases that deal specifically with issue 1 of which three follow the *Diaz* reasoning.

1978–1989
Citator Volume

DiANDREA, YOLANDA, TRANSFEREE, 1983 PH TC Memo ¶ 83,768 See DiAndrea, Inc.)
DIAZ, ALFONSO & MARIA de JESUS, 58 TC 560, ¶ 58.57 PH TC
Reilly, Peter W., Est. of, 76 TC 374, 76 PH TC 201 [See 58 TC 565, n. 2]
e—Greenfield, Stuart & Eileen, 1978 PH TC Memo 78-1070 [See 58 TC 564]
e—Calloway, Johnny T., 1980 PH TC Memo 80-952 [See 58 TC 564]
e—Branson, David L., 1981 PH TC Memo 81-1199 [See 58 TC 564, 565]
e—Cohen, Robert B. & Marilyn W., 1983 PH TC Memo 83-1042 [See 58 TC 564]
e—Patton, Luther R., 1985 PH TC Memo 85-629 [See 58 TC 564]
e—Malek, Theresa M. & Edward J., Sr., 1985 PH TC Memo 85-1905 [See 58 TC 574]
e—Wilhelm, Mary R., 1986 PH TC Memo 86-39 [See 58 TC 564]
e—Stevenson, Wayne E. & Marilyn J., 1986 PH TC Memo 86-866, 86-873 [See 58 TC 564]
e—Anastasato, Pano & Janice, 1986 PH TC Memo 86-1811 [See 58 TC 564]
e—Shih-Hsieh, Marilan, 1986 PH TC Memo 86-2429 [See 58 TC 562]
e—Heller, Jacob W. & Esther R., 1987 PH TC Memo 87-1881 [See 58 TC 562]
e—Ettig, Tobin R., 1988 PH TC Memo 88-953 [See 58 TC 564]
e—Belli, Melia, 1989 PH TC Memo 89-1950 [See 58 TC 564]
f-Kong, Young E. & Jeen K., 1989 PH TC Memo 89-2781 [See 58 TC 564-565]
e-1—Caglia, E. Bonnie, 1989 PH TC Memo 89-689
DIAZ, FRANK & AMPARO R., 1986 PH TC Memo ¶ 86,098
DIAZ, LEONARDA C., 70 TC 1067, ¶ 70.95 PH TC
a—Diaz, Leonarda C. v Comm., 44 AFTR2d 79-6027 (USCA 2)
e—Stazer, Alan K. & Katalin V., 1981 PH TC Memo 81-505 [See 70 TC 1076]
e—Damm, Marvin V. & Nina M., 1981 PH TC Memo 81-673 [See 70 TC 1074-1075]
e—Stuart, Ian & Maria, 1981 PH TC Memo 81-1311, 81-1312 [See 70 TC 1076]
e—Olsen, Randy B. & Deborah R., 1981 PH TC Memo 81-2409 [See 70 TC 1076]
f—Kuh, Johannes L. & Adriana, 1983 PH TC Memo 83-2311 [See 70 TC 1075, 1076]
f-1—Wassenaar, Paul R., 72 TC 1200, 72 PH TC 659
f-1—Browne, Alice Pauline, 73 TC 726, 73 PH TC 402 [See 70 TC 1074]
f-1—Rehe, William G. & Suzanne M., 1980 PH TC Memo 80-1426
g-1—Schwerm, Gerald & Joyce J., 1986 PH TC Memo 86-54, 86-55
e-1—Baist, George A. & Janice, 1988 PH TC Memo 88-2859
f-2—Toner, Linda M. Liberi, 71 TC 778, 779, 781, 71 PH TC 435, 436, 437 [See 70 TC 1075]
2—Toner, Linda M. Liberi, 71 TC 782, 783, 71 PH TC 437, 438
n-2—Toner, Linda M. Liberi, 71 TC 790, 71 PH TC 441
f-2—Robinson, Charles A. & Elaine M., 78 TC 552, 78 PH TC 290 [See 70 TC 1074]
2—Gruman, David T., 1982 PH TC Memo 82-1700 [See 70 TC 1074]
DIAZ, LEONARDA C. v COMM., 44 AFTR2d 79-6027 (USCA 2, 6-25-79)
sa—Diaz, Leonarda C., 70 TC 1067, ¶ 70.95 PH TC
e—Stazer, Alan K. & Katalin V., 1981 PH TC Memo 81-505
e—Damm, Marvin V. & Nina M., 1981 PH TC Memo 81-673
e—Olsen, Randy B. & Deborah R., 1981 PH TC Memo 81-2409
f—Kuh, Johannes L. & Adriana, 1983 PH TC Memo 83-2311
e—Malek, Theresa M. & Edward J., Sr., 1985 PH TC Memo 85-1905
f-1—Rehe, William G. & Suzanne M., 1980 PH TC Memo 80-1426
g-1—Schwerm, Gerald & Joyce J., 1986 PH TC Memo 86-54, 86-55
e-1—Baist, George A. & Janice, 1988 PH TC Memo 88-2859
DIAZ, MIGUEL A. & FELICIA N., 1981 PH TC Memo ¶ 81,069 (See Powers, Sandra L.)

1990–1996
Citator Volume

DIANDRE, ANTHONY F. v U.S., 70 AFTR 2d 92-5190, 968 F2d 1049, 92-2 USTC ¶ 50,373, (CA10, 7-7-92)
x—Metro Denver Maintenance Cleaning, Inc. v. U.S., 507 US 1029, 113 S Ct 1843, 123 L Ed 2d 468, (US, 4-19-93), (T)
e-1—Barnes, William R. v U.S., 73 AFTR 2d 94-1161, (CA3)
e-1—Fostvedt, Robert J. v U.S., 71 AFTR 2d 93-1573, 824 F Supp 983, (DC CO)
e-1—Jones, Terry L., et al v. U.S., et al, 74 AFTR 2d 94-6706, 869 F Supp 753, (DC NE), [Cited at 71 AFTR2d 93-1573, 824 F Supp 983]
g-1—Russell, Orval D. v. U.S., 75 AFTR 2d 95-496, (DC MI)
e-1—Stewart, Daniel v. U.S., 75 AFTR 2d 95-2250, 95-2251, (DC OH)
e-1—Jones, Terry L., et al v. U.S., et al, 76 AFTR 2d 95-6607, 95-6615, 898 F Supp 1373, 1380, (DC NE), [Cited at 71 AFTR2d 93-1573, 824 F Supp 983]
e-1—May, Joseph A. v. U.S., 76 AFTR 2d 95-7228, (DC MO)
e-1—Cassity, James v. Great Western Bank, 76 AFTR 2d 95-8035, (DC CA)
e-1—Spence, Raymond v. U.S., 78 AFTR 2d 96-5777, (DC NM)
DIANDREA, INC., 1983 PH TC Memo ¶ 83,768
e-1—Johnson, Peter A., 1991 TC Memo 91-3185
DIAZ, ALFONSO & MARIA de JESUS, 58 TC 560, ¶ 58.57 PH TC, (A), 1972-2 CB 2
Sanai, Farhin, 1990 PH TC Memo 90-2459, [See 58 TC 564-565]
e—Hawkins, Robert Lavon & Pamela, 1993 RIA TC Memo 93-2734, [See 58 TC 564]
e—Muniz, Rolando, 1994 RIA TC Memo 94-760, [See 58 TC 564]
e—Sloan, Lorin G., 1994 RIA TC Memo 94-3427, [See 58 TC 564]
e—Marrone, Anthony & Carol, 1995 RIA TC Memo 95-145, [See 58 TC 564]
e—Wada, Takeshi & Young Sook, 1995 RIA TC Memo 95-1532, [See 58 TC 564]
e—Drabiuk, Stanislaw & Jeanette, 1995 RIA TC Memo 95-1649, [See 58 TC 565]
e—Jackson, Sammy Lee, 1995 RIA TC Memo 95-1875, [See 58 TC 564]
e—Levin, Harris & Gayle, 1996 RIA TC Memo 96-1557, [See 58 TC 564]
e—American Underwriters Inc, 1996 RIA TC Memo 96-3980, [See 58 TC 564]
DIAZ, BARBARA E., 1990 PH TC Memo ¶ 90,559, (See Taylor, Barbara E.)
DIAZ, ENRIQUE v. U.S., 71A AFTR 2d 93-3563, 90-1 USTC ¶ 50209, (DC CA, 3/19/90)
g-1—Van Camp & Bennion, P.S. v. U.S., 78 AFTR 2d 96-5847, (DC WA)
DIAZ, LEONARDA C., 70 TC 1067, ¶ 70.95 PH TC
a—Diaz, Leonarda C. v Comm., 44 AFTR 2d 79-6027, 607 F2d 995, (CA2)
f—Wiertzema, Vance v U.S., 66 AFTR 2d 90-5371, 747 F Supp 1365, (DC ND), [See 70 TC 1074-1075]
e—Barboza, David, 1991 TC Memo 91-1905, [See 70 TC 1074]
e—Orr, J. Thomas, 1992 RIA TC Memo 92-2912, [See 70 TC 1073]
e—German, Harry, Jr. & Carol, 1993 RIA TC Memo 93-261—93-262, [See 70 TC 1074—1075]
e—Meredith, Judith R., 1993 RIA TC Memo 93-1247, [See 70 TC 1074, cited at 73 TC 726]
e—Holmes, Lynn J., 1993 RIA TC Memo 93-1978, [See 70 TC 1072—1073]
e—Kersey, Robert C., 1993 RIA TC Memo 93-3396, [See 70 TC 1072-1073]
e—Zeidler, Gerald L. & Joy M., 1996 RIA TC Memo 96-1151, [See 70 TC 1074, cited at 73 TC 726]
DIAZ, LEONARDA C. v COMM., 44 AFTR 2d 79-6027, 607 F2d 995, (CA2, 6-25-79)
e—Wiertzema, Vance v U.S., 66 AFTR 2d 90-5371, 747 F Supp 1363, (DC ND)
e—Zeidler, Gerald L. & Joy M., 1996 RIA TC Memo 96-1151
DIBENEDETTO, FRANK R. v U.S., 35 AFTR 2d 75-1502, 75-1 USTC ¶ 9503, (DC RI, 11-7-74)
e-1—Seachrist, Craig v Riggs, C.W., 67 AFTR 2d 91-453, (DC VA)
e-1—Cook, Dean A. v U.S., 68 AFTR 2d 91-5053—91-5056, 765 F Supp 219, 221, (DC PA)
e-1—Carlucci, Joseph P. v U.S., 70 AFTR 2d 92-6002, 793 F Supp 484, (DC NY)
e-1—Padalino, Vincent v. U.S., 71A AFTR 2d 93-3016, (DC NJ)

FIGURE C:1-8 ▶ EXCERPTS FROM THE RIA CITATOR

Tax Court in 1978, so no earlier references will be found.) *Diaz* has been cited with respect to its first and second AFTR headnotes. If there are other AFTR headnotes, the case has not been cited with respect to them.

The "a" on the first line beneath the name of the case indicates that the Tax Court's decision was affirmed by the Second Circuit. The Tax Court's opinion has been explained and followed in various cases, but it has not been cited in an unfavorable manner. Thus, its authoritative weight is substantial.

The Second Circuit's decision appears as a separate entry. The letters "sa" signify that the circuit court affirmed the Tax Court decision in the *Diaz* case. The cases that have cited the circuit court's opinion are listed under the entry for such opinion. The appellate decision has not been questioned or criticized; thus, its authority is relatively strong.

More recent references to *Leonarda C. Diaz* are reported in the 1990–96 citator volume (see Figure C:1-8, Column 2). Nine additional cases cite the Tax Court decision[47]; two additional cases cite the Second Circuit Court decision. Recall that the CCH citator indicates that in 1972 the IRS Commissioner acquiesced in the Tax Court decision in *Alphonso Diaz*. This acquiescence is denoted by the capital "A," which appears after the citation to the same decision in the 1990–1996 citator volume.

Two additional cases citing the Leonarda C. Diaz Tax Court decision are listed in the 2003–2005 cumulative supplement.

COMPUTERS AS A RESEARCH TOOL

OBJECTIVE 6

Grasp the basics of computerized tax research

Tax professionals are increasingly using computers to conduct their tax-related research. Tax services have shifted most of their resources to media accessible by computer. With the technological advances in computer hardware and software, large databases are becoming more accessible and less costly. In the coming years, computer-assisted tax research will become an even more important tool for the tax advisor. A supplement to this chapter, which discusses this development, is available for download at *www.prenhall.com/phtax*. It also presents an overview of tax resources on the Internet.

In the major computerized tax services, most of the primary authorities discussed in this chapter appear as databases. Typically, each authority constitutes a separate database. Thus, the Internal Revenue Code comprises a separate database, as do Treasury Regulations, revenue rulings, revenue procedures, and other IRS pronouncements. Supreme Court opinions constitute a separate database, as do opinions of the Tax Court, the U.S. district courts, the Court of Federal Claims, and the circuit courts. Likewise, most of the secondary authorities discussed in this chapter appear as databases. Some authorities, however, are found exclusively in one service, while others are found in another. For example, the *Standard Federal Tax Reporter, Federal Tax Service,* and CCH citator are found exclusively in the CCH Internet Tax Research NetWork™. The *U.S. Tax Reporter, Federal Tax Coordinator 2d,* and RIA citator are found in RIA CHECKPOINT™. The basic features of the computerized and print sources generally are the same, with the following notable exceptions:

- Computerized sources have no finding lists. Cross referencing is facilitated through hyperlinks.
- Computerized sources have no cumulative supplements. New developments information is integrated into the main text.
- On computer, primary sources pertinent to explanatory paragraphs are accessible through hyperlink.
- On computer, citator symbols are explicitly spelled out.

[47] The first listing under the citation to the Tax Court decision in *Leonarda C. Diaz* refers to the same case decided at the Second Circuit Court level.

STATEMENTS ON STANDARDS FOR TAX SERVICES

OBJECTIVE 7

Understand guidelines that CPAs in tax practice should follow

Tax advisors confronted with ethical issues frequently turn to a professional organization for guidance. Although the guidelines set forth by such organizations are not *legally* enforceable, they carry significant moral weight, and may be cited in a negligence lawsuit as the proper "standard of care" for tax practitioners. They also may provide grounds for the termination or suspension of one's professional license. One such set of guidelines is the ***Statements on Standards for Tax Services*** (SSTSs),[48] issued by the American Institute of Certified Public Accountants (AICPA) and reproduced in Appendix E. Inspired by the principles of honesty and integrity, these guidelines define standards of ethical conduct for CPAs engaged in tax practice. In the words of the AICPA:

> In our view, practice standards are the hallmark of calling one's self a professional. Members should fulfill their responsibilities as professionals by instituting and maintaining standards against which their professional performance can be measured. The promulgation of practice standards also reinforces one of the core values of the AICPA Vision—that CPAs conduct themselves with honesty and integrity.[49]

The SSTSs differ in an important way from the AICPA's predecessor standards, *Statements on Responsibilites in Tax Practice,* in that the SSTSs are *professionally* enforceable; that is, they may be enforced through a disciplinary proceeding conducted by the AICPA, which may terminate or suspend a practitioner from AICPA membership.

Statement No. 1 defines the circumstances under which a CPA should (or should not) recommend a tax return position to a taxpayer. It also prescribes a course of conduct that the CPA should follow when making such a recommendation. Specifically,

- A member should not recommend that a tax return position be taken with respect to any item unless the member has a good-faith belief that the position has a realistic possibility of being sustained administratively or judicially on its merits if challenged . . .
- [A] member may recommend a tax return position that the member concludes is not frivolous so long as the member advises the taxpayer to appropriately disclose . . .
- When recommending tax return positions and when preparing or signing a return on which a tax return position is taken, a member should, when relevant, advise the taxpayer regarding potential penalty consequences of such tax return position and the opportunity, if any, to avoid such penalties through disclosure.

The "realistic possibility standard" set forth in Statement No. 1 parallels that of Sec. 6694. (For a discussion of the latter IRC section, see Chapter C:15.) However, it differs from the IRC standard in that it allows as support for a tax return position well-reasoned articles or treatises, in addition to primary tax authorities. The IRC standard allows as support for a tax return position only primary tax authorities.

Statement No. 3 addresses (1) whether tax practitioners can reasonably rely on information supplied to them by the taxpayer, (2) when they have a duty to examine or verify such information, (3) when they have a duty to make inquiries of the taxpayer, and (4) what information they should consider in preparing a tax return. Specifically,

- In preparing or signing a return, a member may in good faith rely, without verification, on information furnished by the taxpayer or by third parties. However, a member should make reasonable inquiries if the information furnished appears to be incorrect, incomplete, or inconsistent either on its face or on the basis of other facts known to a member . . .

---

[48] AICPA, *Statements on Standards for Tax Services*, 2000, effective October 31, 2000. The SSTSs supercede the AICPA's *Statements on Responsibilities in Tax Practice, 1991 Revision.*

[49] Letter to AICPA members by David A. Lifson, Chair, AICPA Tax Executive Committee, and Gerald W. Padwe, Vice President, AICPA Taxation Section (April 18, 2000).

WHAT WOULD YOU DO IN THIS SITUATION?

Regal Enterprises and Macon Industries, unaffiliated corporations, have hired you to prepare their respective income tax returns. In preparing Regal's return, you notice that Regal has claimed a depreciation deduction for equipment purchased from Macon on February 22 at a cost of $2 million. In preparing Macon's return, you notice that Macon has reported sales proceeds of $1.5 million from the sale of equipment to Regal on February 22. One of the two figures must be incorrect. How do you proceed to correct it?

- If the tax law or regulations impose a condition with respect to the deductibility or other tax treatment of an item . . . a member should make appropriate inquiries to determine to the member's satisfaction whether such condition has been met.
- When preparing a tax return, a member should consider information actually known to that member from the tax return of another taxpayer if the information is relevant to that tax return and its consideration is necessary to properly prepare that tax return . . .

Note that the duty to verify arises only when taxpayer-provided information appears "strange" on its face. Otherwise, the tax practitioner has no duty to investigate taxpayer facts and circumstances.

Statement No. 4 defines the circumstances in which a tax practitioner may use estimates in preparing a tax return. In addition, it cautions the practitioner as to the manner in which he or she may use estimates. Specifically,

- A member may advise on estimates used in the preparation of a tax return, but the taxpayer has the responsibility to provide the estimated data. Appraisals or valuations are not considered estimates . . .
- [A] member may use the taxpayer's estimates in the preparation of a tax return if it is not practical to obtain exact data and if the member determines that the estimates are reasonable based on the facts and circumstances known to the member. If the taxpayer's estimates are used, they should be presented in a manner that does not imply greater accuracy than exists.

Notwithstanding this statement, the tax practitioner may not use estimates when such use is implicitly prohibited by the IRC. For example, Sec. 274(d) disallows deductions for certain expenses (e.g., meals and entertainment) unless the taxpayer can substantiate the expenses with adequate records or sufficient corroborating information. The documentation requirement effectively precludes the taxpayer from estimating such expenses and the practitioner from using such estimates.

Statement No. 6 defines a tax practitioner's duty when he or she becomes aware of (1) an error in the taxpayer's return, (2) the taxpayer's failure to file a required return, or (3) the taxpayer's failure to correct an error in a prior year's return. Specifically,

- A member should inform the taxpayer promptly upon becoming aware of an error in a previously filed return or upon becoming aware of a taxpayer's failure to file a required return. A member should recommend the corrective measures to be taken . . . The member is not obligated to inform the taxing authority, and a member may not do so without the taxpayer's permission, except when required by law.
- If a member is requested to prepare the current year's return and the taxpayer has not taken appropriate action to correct an error in a prior year's return, the member should consider whether to withdraw from preparing the return and whether to continue a professional or employment relationship with the taxpayer . . .

This statement implies that the tax practitioner's primary duty is to the taxpayer, not the taxing authority. Furthermore, upon the taxpayer's failure to correct a tax-related error, the practitioner may exercise discretion in deciding whether or not to terminate the professional relationship.

Occasionally, the tax practitioner discovers a taxpayer error in the course of an administrative proceeding (e.g., an IRS audit or appeals conference). The practitioner may advise the client to disclose the error, and the taxpayer may refuse. Statement No. 7 provides guidance as to what to do in these situations. Specifically,

- If a member is representating a taxpayer in an administrative proceeding with respect to a return that contains an error of which the member is aware, the member should inform the taxpayer promptly upon becoming aware of the error. The member should recommend the corrective measures to be taken. . . . A member is neither obligated to inform the taxing authority nor allowed to do so without the taxpayer's permission, except where required by law.
- A member should request the taxpayer's agreement to disclose the error to the taxing authority. Lacking such agreement, the member should consider whether to withdraw from representing the taxpayer in the administrative proceeding and whether to continue a professional or employment relationship with the taxpayer.

Finally, Statement No. 8 addresses the quality of advice provided by the tax practitioner, what consequences presumably ensue from such advice, and whether the practitioner has a duty to update advice to reflect subsequent developments. Specifically,

- A member should use judgment to ensure that tax advice provided to a taxpayer reflect professional competence and appropriately serves the taxpayer's needs . . .
- A member should assume that tax advice provided to a taxpayer will affect the manner in which the matters or transactions considered would be reported on the taxpayer's tax returns . . .
- A member has no obligation to communicate with a taxpayer when subsequent developments affect advice previously provided with respect to significant matters except while assisting a taxpayer in implementing procedures or plans associated with the advice provided or when a member undertakes an obligation by specific agreement.

The statement implies that practitioner-taxpayer dealings should be neither casual nor nonconsensual nor open-ended; rather, they should be professional, contractual, and definite.

From the foregoing emerges the following picture of the normative relationship between the tax advisor and his or her client: unlike an auditor, a tax advisor is an advocate. His or her primary duty is to the client, not the IRS. In fullfilling this duty, the advisor is bound by the highest standards of care. These standards include a good-faith belief that a tax return position has a realistic possibility of being sustained on its merits and on quality advice based on professional competence and client needs. Encompassed under the advisor's duty is the obligation to inform the client of the potential adverse consequences of a tax return position, how the client can avoid a penalty through disclosure, errors in a previously filed tax return, and corrective measures to be taken. Also encompassed is the obligation to determine by inquiry that the client satisfies conditions for taking a deduction, and to obtain information when material provided by the client appears incorrect, incomplete, or inconsistent.

Excluded from the advisor's duty is the obligation to verify client-provided information when, based on the advisor's own knowledge, such information is not suspicious on its face. Also excluded is the obligation to update professional advice based on developments following its original conveyance. In preparing a tax return, the advisor may use estimates if obtaining concrete data is impractical and if the advisor determines that the estimates are reasonable. Although responsibility for providing the estimates resides with the client, responsibility for presenting them in a manner that does not imply undue accuracy resides with the advisor. Finally, the advisor may terminate a professional relationship if the client refuses to correct a tax-related error. On the other hand, unless legally bound, the advisor may not disclose the error to the IRS without the client's consent.

In addition to these obligations, the tax advisor has a strict duty of confidentiality to the client. Though not encompassed under the SSTSs, this duty is implied in the accountant-client privilege. (For a discussion of this privilege, see Chapter C:15.)

STOP & THINK *Question:* As described in the Stop & Think box on page C:1-10, you are researching the manner in which a deduction is calculated. The IRC states that the calculation is to be made "in a manner prescribed by the Secretary." After studying the IRC, Treasury Regulations, and committee reports, you conclude that another way of doing the calculation is arguably correct under an intuitive approach. This approach would result in a lower tax liability for the client. According to the *Statements on Standards for Tax Services,* may you take a position contrary to final Treasury Regulations based on the argument that the regulations are not valid?

Solution: You should not take a position contrary to the Treasury Regulations unless you have a "good-faith belief that the position has a realistic possibility of being sustained administratively or judicially on its merits." However, you can take a position that does not meet the above standard, provided you adequately disclose the position, and the position is not frivolous. Whether or not you have met the standard depends on all the facts and circumstances. Chapter C:15 discusses tax return preparer positions contrary to Treasury Regulations.

ADDITIONAL COMMENT

The underpayment penalty rules under Sec. 6662 impose a higher standard for disregarding a rule, such as a Treasury Regulation. Under these rules, the taxpayer must have a reasonable basis rather than a nonfrivolous position, in addition to disclosure.

SAMPLE WORK PAPERS AND CLIENT LETTER

OBJECTIVE 8

Prepare work papers and communicate to clients

Appendix A presents a set of sample work papers, including a draft of a client letter and a memo to the file. The work papers indicate the issues to be researched, the authorities addressing the issues, and the researcher's conclusions concerning the appropriate tax treatment, with rationale therefor.

The format and other details of work papers differ from firm to firm. The sample in this text offers general guidance concerning the content of work papers. In practice, work papers may include less detail.

PROBLEM MATERIALS

DISCUSSION QUESTIONS

C:1-1 Explain the difference between closed-fact and open-fact situations.

C:1-2 According to the AICPA's *Statements on Standards for Tax Services,* what duties does the tax practitioner owe the client?

C:1-3 Explain what is encompassed by the term *tax law* as used by tax advisors.

C:1-4 The U.S. Government Printing Office publishes both hearings on proposed legislation and committee reports. Distinguish between the two.

C:1-5 Explain how committee reports can be used in tax research. What do they indicate?

C:1-6 A friend notices that you are reading the Internal Revenue Code of 1986. Your friend inquires why you are consulting a 1986 publication, especially when tax laws change so frequently. What is your response?

C:1-7 Does Title 26 contain statutory provisions dealing only with income taxation? Explain.

C:1-8 Refer to IRC Sec. 301.
- a. Which subsection discusses the general rule for the tax treatment of a property distribution?
- b. Where should one look for exceptions to the general rule?
- c. What type of Treasury Regulations would relate to subsection (e)?

C:1-9 Why should tax researchers note the date on which a Treasury Regulation was adopted?

C:1-10 a. Distinguish between proposed, temporary, and final Treasury Regulations.

b. Distinguish between interpretative and legislative Treasury Regulations.

C:1-11 Which type of regulation is more difficult for a taxpayer to successfully challenge, and why?

C:1-12 Explain the legislative reenactment doctrine.

C:1-13 a. Discuss the authoritative weight of revenue rulings.
b. As a practical matter, what consequences are likely to ensue if a taxpayer does not follow a revenue ruling and the IRS audits his or her return?

C:1-14 a. In which courts may litigation dealing with tax matters begin?
b. Discuss the factors that might be considered in deciding where to litigate.
c. Describe the appeals process in tax litigation.

C:1-15 May a taxpayer appeal a case litigated under the Small Cases Procedure of the Tax Court?

C:1-16 Explain whether the following decisions are of the same precedential value: (1) Tax Court regular decisions, (2) Tax Court memo decisions, (3) decisions under the Small Cases Procedures of the Tax Court.

C:1-17 Does the IRS acquiesce in decisions of U.S. district courts?

C:1-18 The decisions of which courts are reported in the AFTR? In the USTC?

C:1-19 Who publishes regular decisions of the Tax Court? Memo decisions?

C:1-20 Explain the *Golsen* Rule. Give an example of its application.

C:1-21 Assume that the only precedents relating to a particular issue are as follows:
Tax Court—decided for the taxpayer
Eighth Circuit Court of Appeals—decided for the taxpayer (affirming the Tax Court)
U.S. District Court for Eastern Louisiana—decided for the taxpayer
Fifth Circuit Court of Appeals—decided for the government (reversing the U.S. District Court of Eastern Louisiana)
a. Discuss the precedential value of the foregoing decisions for your client, who is a California resident.
b. If your client, a Texas resident, litigates in the Tax Court, how will the court rule? Explain.

C:1-22 Which official publication(s) contain(s) the following:
a. Transcripts of Senate floor debates
b. IRS announcements
c. Tax Court regular opinions
d. Treasury decisions
e. U.S. district court opinions
f. Technical advice memoranda

C:1-23 Under what circumstances might a tax advisor find the provisions of a tax treaty useful?

C:1-24 Compare the print version of the tax services listed below (if they are found in your tax library) with respect to (a) how they are organized and (b) where current developments are reported.
a. *United States Tax Reporter*
b. *Standard Federal Tax Reporter*
c. *Federal Tax Coordinator 2d*
d. *Law of Federal Income Taxation* (Mertens)
e. BNA's *Tax Management Portfolios*
f. CCH's *Federal Tax Service*

C:1-25 Indicate (1) which Internet tax service provides each of the following secondary sources and (2) whether the source is annotated or topical.
a. *Federal Tax Coordinator 2d*
b. Mertens
c. *BNA Tax Management Portfolios*
d. *Standard Federal Tax Reporter*
e. *United States Tax Reporter*

C:1-26 What two functions does a citator serve?

C:1-27 Describe two types of information that can be gleaned from citing cases in the RIA citator but not those in the CCH citator.

C:1-28 Explain how your research approach might differ if you use the computerized version of a tax service instead of the print version (e.g., RIA or CCH).

C:1-29 Access the CCH Internet Tax Research NetWork™ at *http://tax.cch.com/network* and RIA CHECKPOINT™ at *http://checkpoint.riag.com*. Then answer the following questions:
a. What are the principal primary sources found in both Internet tax services?
b. What are the principal secondary sources found in each Internet tax service?
c. What citator is found in each Internet tax service?
(In answering these questions, consult the supplement to this chapter available for download at *www.prenhall.com/phtax*.)

C:1-30 Compare the features of the computerized tax services with those of Internet sites maintained by noncommercial institutions. What are the relative advantages and disadvantages of each? Could the latter sites serve as a substitute for a commercial tax service? (In answering these questions, consult the supplement to this chapter available for download at *www.prenhall.com/phtax*.)

C:1-31 According to the *Statements on Standards for Tax Services*, what belief should a CPA have before taking a pro-taxpayer position on a tax return?

C:1-32 Under the AICPA's *Statements on Standards for Tax Services*, what is the tax practitioner's professional duty in each of the following situations?
a. Client erroneously deducts $5,000 (instead of $500) on a previous year's tax return.
b. Client refuses to file an amended return to correct the deduction error.
c. Client informs tax practitioner that client incurred $200 in out-of-pocket office supplies expenses.

d. Client informs tax practitioner that client incurred $700 in business-related entertainment expenses.

e. Tax practitioner learns that the exemption amount for single taxpayers has been increased by $1,000. Client is a single taxpayer.

PROBLEMS

C:1-33 ***Interpreting the IRC.*** Under a divorce agreement executed in the current year, an ex-wife receives from her former husband cash of $25,000 per year for eight years. The agreement does not explicitly state that the payments are excludible from gross income.
a. Does the ex-wife have gross income? If so, how much?
b. Is the former husband entitled to a deduction? If so, is it for or from AGI?
Refer only to the IRC in answering this question. Start with Sec. 71.

C:1-34 ***Interpreting the IRC.*** Refer to Sec. 385 and answer the questions below.
a. Whenever Treasury Regulations are issued under this section, what type are they likely to be: legislative or interpretative? Explain.
b. Assume Treasury Regulations under Sec. 385 have been finalized. Will they be relevant to estate tax matters? Explain.

C:1-35 ***Using the Cumulative Bulletin.*** Consult any volume of the *Cumulative Bulletin*. In what order are revenue rulings arranged?

C:1-36 ***Using the Cumulative Bulletin.*** Which IRC section(s) does Rev. Rul. 2001-29 interpret? (Hint: consult the official publication of the IRS.)

C:1-37 ***Using the Cumulative Bulletin.*** Refer to the 1989-1 *Cumulative Bulletin.*
a. What time period does this bulletin cover?
b. What appears on page 1?
c. What items are found in Part I?
d. In what order are the items presented in Part I?
e. What items are found in Part II?
f. What items are found in Part III?

C:1-38 ***Using the Cumulative Bulletin.*** Refer to the 1990-1 *Cumulative Bulletin.*
a. For the time period covered by the bulletin, in which cases did the IRS nonacquiesce?
b. What is the topic of Rev. Rul. 90-10?
c. Does this bulletin contain a revenue ruling that interprets Sec. 162? If so, specify.

C:1-39 ***Determining Acquiescence.***
a. What official action (acquiescence or nonacquiescence) did the IRS Commissioner take regarding the 1986 Tax Court decision in *John McIntosh*? (Hint: Consult the 1986-1 *Cumulative Bulletin.*)
b. Did this action concern *all* issues in the case? If not, explain. (Before answering this question, consult the headnote to the court opinion.)

C:1-40 ***Determining Acquiescence.***
a. What original action (acquiescence or nonacquiescence) did the IRS Commissioner take regarding the 1952 Tax Court decision in *Streckfus Steamers, Inc.*?
b. Was the action complete or partial?
c. Did the IRS Commissioner subsequently change his mind? If so, when?

C:1-41 ***Determining Acquiescence.***
a. What original action (acquiescence or nonacquiescence) did the IRS Commissioner take regarding the 1956 Tax Court decision in *Pittsburgh Milk Co.*?
b. Did the IRS Commissioner subsequently change his mind? If so, when?

C:1-42 ***Evaluating a Case.*** Look up *James E. Threlkeld*, 87 T.C. 1294 (1988) either in print or in an Internet tax service, and answer the questions below.
a. Was the case reviewed by the court? If so, was the decision unanimous? Explain.
b. Was the decision entered under Rule 155?
c. Consult a citator. Was the case reviewed by an appellate court? If so, which one?

C:1-43 ***Evaluating a Case.*** Look up *Bush Brothers & Co.*, 73 T.C. 424 (1979) either in print or in an Internet tax service, and answer the questions below.
a. Was the case reviewed by the court? If so, was the decision unanimous? Explain.
b. Was the decision entered under Rule 155?
c. Consult a citator. Was the case reviewed by an appellate court? If so, which one?

C:1-44 ***Writing Citations.*** Provide the proper citations (including both primary and secondary citations where applicable) for the authorities listed below. (For secondary citations, reference both the AFTR and USTC.)

a. *National Cash Register Co.,* a 6th Circuit Court decision
b. *Thomas M. Dragoun v. CIR,* a Tax Court memo decision
c. *John M. Grabinski v. U.S.,* a U.S. district court decision
d. *John M. Grabinski v. U.S.,* an Eighth Circuit Court decision
e. *Rebekah Harkness,* a 1972 Court of Claims decision
f. *Hillsboro National Bank v. CIR,* a Supreme Court decision
g. Rev. Rul. 78-129

C:1-45 ***Writing Citations.*** Provide the proper citations (including both primary and secondary citations where applicable) for the authorities listed below. (For secondary citations, reference both the AFTR and USTC.)

a. Rev. Rul. 99-7
b. *Frank H. Sullivan,* a Board of Tax Appeals decision
c. *Tate & Lyle, Inc.,* a 1994 Tax Court decision
d. *Ralph L. Rogers v. U.S.,* a U.S. district court decision
e. *Norman Rodman v. CIR,* a Second Circuit Court decision

C:1-46 ***Interpreting Citations.*** Indicate which courts decided the cases cited below. Also indicate on which pages and in which publications the authority is reported.

a. *Lloyd M. Shumaker v. CIR,* 648 F.2d 1198, 48 AFTR 2d 81-5353 (9th Cir., 1981)
b. *Xerox Corp. v. U.S.,* 14 Cl. Ct. 455, 88-1 USTC ¶9231 (1988)
c. *Real Estate Land Title & Trust Co. v. U.S.,* 309 U.S. 13, 23 AFTR 816 (USSC, 1940)
d. *J. B. Morris v. U.S.,* 441 F. Supp. 76, 41 AFTR 2d 78-335 (DC TX, 1977)
e. Rev. Rul. 83-3, 1983-1 C.B. 72
f. *Malone & Hyde, Inc. v. U.S.,* 568 F.2d 474, 78-1 USTC ¶9199 (6th Cir., 1978)

C:1-47 ***Using a Tax Service.*** Use the topical index of the *United States Tax Reporter,* either in print or in RIA CHECKPOINT™, to locate authorities dealing with the deductibility of the cost of a facelift.

a. In which paragraph(s) does the *United States Tax Reporter* summarize and cite these authorities?
b. List the authorities.
c. May a taxpayer deduct the cost of a facelift paid in the current year? Explain.

C:1-48 ***Using a Tax Service.*** Refer to Reg. Sec. 1.302-1 at ¶3022 of the *United States Tax Reporter,* either in print or in RIA CHECKPOINT™. Does this Treasury Regulation reflect recent amendments to the IRC? Explain.

C:1-49 ***Using a Tax Service.*** Use the topical index of the *Standard Federal Tax Reporter,* either in print or in the CCH Internet Tax Research NetWork™, to locate authorities addressing whether termite damage constitutes a casualty loss.

a. In which paragraph(s) does the *Standard Federal Tax Reporter* summarize and cite these authorities?
b. List the authorities.
c. Have there been any recent developments concerning the tax consequences of termite damage? (*Recent* suggests authorities appearing in the cumulative index section of the print version or the current developments section of the Internet version.)

C:1-50 ***Using a Tax Service.***

a. Locate in the *Standard Federal Tax Reporter,* either in print or in the CCH Internet Tax Research NetWork™, where Sec. 303(b)(2)(A) appears. This provision states that Sec. 303(a) applies only if the stock in question meets a certain percentage test. What is the applicable percentage?
b. Locate Reg. Sec. 1.303-2(a) in the same service. Does this Treasury Regulation reflect recent amendments to the IRC with respect to the percentage test addressed in Part a? Explain.

C:1-51 ***Using a Tax Service.*** The questions below deal with BNA's *Tax Management Portfolios.*

a. What is the number of the main portfolio that deals with tax-free exchanges under Sec. 1031?
b. On which page does a discussion of "boot" begin?
c. What are the purposes of Worksheets 1 and 5 of this portfolio?
d. Refer to the bibliography and references at the end of the portfolio. Indicate the numbers of the IRC sections listed as "secondarily" relevant.

C:1-52 *Using a Tax Service.* This problem deals with Mertens' *Law of Federal Income Taxation.*
a. Refer to Volume 5. What general topics does it discuss?
b. Which section of Volume 5 discusses the principal methods for determining depreciation amounts?
c. In Volume 5, what is the purpose of the yellow and white sheets appearing before the tab labeled "Text"?
d. Refer to the Ruling Status Table in the Current Rulings Materials volume. What is the current status of Rev. Ruls. 79-433 and 75-335?
e. Refer to the Code-Rulings Tables in the same volume. List the numbers (e.g., Rev. Rul. 83-88) of all 1983 revenue rulings and revenue procedures that interpret Sec. 121.

C:1-53 *Using a Tax Service.* This problem deals with RIA's *Federal Tax Coordinator 2d.*
a. Use the topical index, either in print or in RIA CHECKPOINT™, to locate authorities dealing with the deductibility of the cost of work clothing by ministers (clergymen). List the authorities.
b. Where does this tax service report new developments?

C:1-54 *Using a Tax Service.* Refer to the print versions of the *United States Tax Reporter* and *Standard Federal Tax Reporter*. Then, for each tax reporter, answer the following questions.
a. In which volume is the index located?
b. Is the index arranged by topic or IRC section?
c. If you know an IRC section number, how do you locate additional authorities?
d. If you know the name of a court decision, how do you locate additional authorities?

C:1-55 *Using a Citator.* Trace *Biltmore Homes, Inc.,* a 1960 Tax Court memo decision, in both the CCH and RIA citators (either print or Internet form).
a. According to the RIA citator, how many times has the Tax Court decision been cited by other courts on Headnote Number 5?
b. How many issues did the lower court address in its opinion? (Hint: Refer to the case headnote numbers.)
c. Did an appellate court review the case? If so, which one?
d. According to the CCH citator, how many times has the Tax Court decision been cited by other courts?
e. According to the CCH citator, how many times has the circuit court decision been cited by other courts on Headnote Number 5?

C:1-56 *Using a Citator.* Trace *Stephen Bolaris,* 776 F.2d 1428, in both the CCH and RIA citators (either print or Internet form).
a. According to the RIA citator, how many times has the Ninth Circuit's decision been cited?
b. Did the decision address more than one issue? Explain.
c. Was the decision ever cited unfavorably? Explain.
d. According to the CCH citator, how many times has the Ninth Circuit's decision been cited?
e. According to the CCH citator, how many times has the Tax Court's decision been cited on Headnote Number 1?

C:1-57 *Interpreting a Case.* Refer to the *Holden Fuel Oil Company* case (31 TCM 184).
a. In which year was the case decided?
b. What controversy was litigated?
c. Who won the case?
d. Was the decision reviewed at the lower court level?
e. Was the decision appealed?
f. Has the decision been cited in other cases?

C:1-58 *Internet Research.* Access the IRS Internet site at *http://www.irs.gov* and answer the following questions: (In answering them, consult the supplement to this chapter available for download at *www.prenhall.com/phtax.*)
a. How does one file a tax return electronically?
b. How can the taxpayer transmit funds electronically?
c. What are the advantages of electronic filing?

C:1-59 *Internet Research.* Access the IRS Internet site at *http://www.irs.gov* and indicate the titles of the following IRS forms: (In so doing, consult the supplement to this chapter available for download at *www.prenhall.com/phtax.*)
a. Form 4506
b. Form 973
c. Form 8725

C:1-60 *Internet Research.* Access the Federation of Tax Administrators Internet site at *http://www.taxadmin.org/fta/link/forms.html* and indicate the titles of the following state tax forms and publications: (In so doing, consult the supplement to this chapter available for download at *www.prenhall.com/phtax.*)
a. Minnesota Form M-3
b. Illinois Schedule CR
c. New York State Form CT-3-C

C:1-61 *Internet Research.* Access Emory's *Federal Courts Finder* at *http://www.law.emory.edu/FEDCTS/* and answer the following questions: (In answering them, consult the supplement to this chapter available for download at *www.prenhall.com/phtax.*)
a. What is the historical timespan of the underlying databases?
b. In what ways can they be accessed?
c. What 1995 Eleventh Circuit Court decisions address the issue of the charitable deduction for estates?

COMPREHENSIVE PROBLEM

C:1-62 Your client, a physician, recently purchased a yacht on which he flies a pennant with a medical emblem on it. He recently informed you that he purchased the yacht and flies the pennant to advertise his occupation and thus attract new patients. He has asked you if he may deduct as ordinary and necessary business expenses the costs of insuring and maintaining the yacht. In search of an answer, consult either CCH's *Standard Federal Tax Reporter* or RIA's *United States Tax Reporter* first in print, and then on the Internet (i.e., the CCH Internet Tax Research NetWork or RIA CHECKPOINT). Then compare the steps taken on each to find your answer.

TAX STRATEGY PROBLEM

C:1-63 Your client, Home Products Universal (HPU), distributes home improvement products to independent retailers throughout the country. Its management wants to explore the possibility of opening its own home improvement centers. Accordingly, it commissions a consulting firm to conduct a feasibility study, which ultimately persuades HPU to expand into retail sales. The consulting firm bills HPU $150,000, which HPU deducts on its current year tax return. The IRS disputes the deduction, contending that, because the cost relates to entering a new business, it should be capitalized. HPU's management, on the other hand, firmly believes that, because the cost relates to expanding HPU's existing business, it should be deducted. In contemplating legal action against the IRS, HPU's management considers the state of judicial precedent: The federal court for HPU's district has ruled that the cost of expanding from distribution into retail sales should be capitalized. The appellate court for HPU's circuit has stated in *dictum* that, although in some circumstances switching from product distribution to product sales entails entering a new trade or business, improving customer access to one's existing products generally does not. The Federal Circuit Court has ruled that wholesale distribution and retail sales, even of the same product, constitute distinct businesses. In a case involving a taxpayer from another circuit, the Tax Court has ruled that such costs invariably should be capitalized. HPU's Chief Financial Officer approaches you with the question, "In which judicial forum should HPU file a lawsuit against the IRS: (1) U.S. district court, (2) the Tax Court, or (3) the U.S. Court of Federal Claims?" What do you tell her?

CASE STUDY PROBLEM

C:1-64 A client, Mal Manley, fills out his client questionnaire for the previous year and on it provides information for the preparation of his individual income tax return. The IRS has never audited Mal's returns. Mal reports that he made over 100 relatively small cash contributions totaling $24,785 to charitable organizations. In the last few years, Mal's charitable contributions have averaged about $15,000 per year. For the previous year, Mal's adjusted gross income was roughly $350,000, about a 10% increase from the year before.

Required: According to the *Statements on Standards for Tax Services,* may you accept at face value Mal's information concerning his charitable contributions? Now assume that the IRS recently audited Mal's tax return for two years ago and denied 75% of that year's charitable contribution deduction because the deduction was not substantiated. Assume also that Mal indicates that, in the previous year, he contributed $25,000 (instead of $24,785). How do these changes of fact affect your earlier decision?

TAX RESEARCH PROBLEMS

C:1-65 The purpose of this problem is to enhance your skills in interpreting the authorities that you locate in your research. In answering the questions that follow, refer only to *Thomas A. Curtis, M.D., Inc.*, 1994 RIA TC Memo ¶94,015.

a. What was the principal controversy litigated in this case?
b. Which party—the taxpayer or the IRS—won?
c. Why is the corporation instead of Dr. and/or Ms. Curtis listed as the plaintiff?
d. What is the relationship between Ellen Barnert Curtis and Dr. Thomas A. Curtis?
e. Approximately how many hours a week did Ms. Curtis work, and what were her credentials?
f. For the fiscal year ending in 1989, what salary did the corporation pay Ms. Curtis? What amount did the court decide was reasonable?
g. What dividends did the corporation pay for its fiscal years ending in 1988 and 1989?
h. To which circuit would this decision be appealable?
i. According to *Curtis*, what five factors did the Ninth Circuit mention in *Elliotts, Inc.* as relevant in determining reasonable compensation?

C:1-66 Josh contributes $5,000 toward the support of his widowed mother, aged 69, a U.S. citizen and resident. She earns gross income of $2,000 and spends it all for her own support. In addition, Medicare pays $3,200 of her medical expenses. She does not receive financial support from sources other than those described above. Must the Medicare payments be included in the support that Josh's mother is deemed to provide for herself?

Prepare work papers and a client letter (to Josh) dealing with the issue.

C:1-67 Amy owns a vacation cottage in Maine. She predicts that the time during which the cottage will be used in the current year is as follows:

By Amy, solely for vacation	12 days
By Amy, making repairs ten hours per day and vacationing the rest of the day	2 days
By her sister, who paid fair rental value	8 days
By her cousin, who paid fair rental value	4 days
By her friend, who paid a token amount of rent	2 days
By three families from the Northeast, who paid fair rental value for 40 days each	120 days
Not used	217 days

Calculate the ratio for allocating the following expenses to the rental income expected to be received from the cottage: interest, taxes, repairs, insurance, and depreciation. The ratio will be used to determine the amount of expenses that are deductible and, thus, Amy's taxable income for the year.

For the tax manager to whom you report, prepare work papers in which you discuss the calculation method. Also, draft a memo to the file dealing with the results of your research.

C:1-68 Look up *Summit Publishing Company*, 1990 PH T.C. Memo ¶90,288, 59 TCM 833, and *J.B.S. Enterprises*, 1991 PH T.C. Memo ¶91,254, 61 TCM 2829, and answer the following questions:

a. What was the principal issue in these cases?
b. What factors did the Tax Court consider in resolving the central issue?
c. How are the facts of these cases similar? How are they dissimilar?

C:1-69 Your supervisor would like to set up a single Sec. 401(k) plan exclusively for the managers of your organization. Concerned that this arrangement might not meet the requirements for a qualified plan, he has asked you to request a determination letter from the IRS. In a brief memorandum, address the following issues:

a. What IRS pronouncements govern requests for determination letters?
b. What IRS forms must be filed with the request?
c. What information must be provided in the request?
d. What actions must accompany the filing?
e. Where must the request be filed?

2

C H A P T E R

CORPORATE FORMATIONS AND CAPITAL STRUCTURE

LEARNING OBJECTIVES

After studying this chapter, you should be able to

1. Explain the tax advantages and disadvantages of alternative business forms
2. Apply the check-the-box regulations to partnerships, corporations, and trusts
3. Determine the legal requirements for forming a corporation
4. Explain the requirements for deferring gain or loss upon incorporation
5. Understand the tax implications of alternative capital structures
6. Determine the tax consequences of worthless stock or debt obligations
7. Understand the financial statement implications of forming a corporation

CHAPTER OUTLINE

When starting a business, entrepreneurs must decide whether to organize it as a sole proprietorship, partnership, corporation, limited liability company, or limited liability partnership. This chapter discusses the advantages and disadvantages of each form of business association. Because many entrepreneurs find organizing their business as a corporation advantageous, this chapter looks at the definition of a corporation for federal income tax purposes. It also discusses the tax consequences of incorporating a business. The chapter closes by examining the tax implications of capitalizing a corporation with equity and/or debt as well as the advantages and disadvantages of alternative capital structures.

This textbook takes a life-cycle approach to corporate taxation. The corporate life cycle starts with corporate formation, discussed in this chapter. Once formed and operating, the corporation's taxable income (or loss), federal income tax and other liabilities, and the tax consequences of distributions to its shareholders must be determined. Finally, at some point the corporation may outlive its usefulness and be dissolved. The corporate life cycle is too complex to discuss in one chapter. Therefore, additional coverage follows in Chapters C:3 through C:8.

ORGANIZATION FORMS AVAILABLE

OBJECTIVE 1

Explain the tax advantages and disadvantages of alternative business forms

Businesses can be organized in several forms including

- Sole proprietorships
- Partnerships
- Corporations
- Limited liability companies
- Limited liability partnerships

A discussion of the tax implications of each form is presented below.

ADDITIONAL COMMENT

The income/loss of a sole proprietorship reported on Schedule C carries to page 1 of Form 1040 and is included in the computation of the individual's taxable income. Net income, if any, also carries to Schedule SE of Form 1040 for computation of the sole proprietor's self-employment tax.

SOLE PROPRIETORSHIPS

A **sole proprietorship** is a business owned by one individual. It often is selected by entrepreneurs who are beginning a new business with a modest amount of capital. From a tax and legal perspective, a sole propriertorship is not a separate entity. Rather, it is a legal extension of its individual owner. Thus, the individual owns all the business assets and reports income or loss from the sole proprietorship directly on his or her individual tax return. Specifically, the individual owner (proprietor) reports all the business's income and expenses for the year on Schedule C (Profit or Loss from Business) or Schedule C-EZ (Net Profit from Business) of Form 1040. A completed Schedule C is included in Appendix B, where a common set of facts (with minor modifications) illustrates the similarities and differences in sole proprietorship, C corporation, partnership, and S corporation tax reporting.

If the business is profitable, the profit is added to the proprietor's other income.

EXAMPLE C:2-1 ▶ John, a single taxpayer, starts a new computer store, which he operates as a sole proprietorship. John reports a $15,000 profit from the store in its first year of operation. Assuming he has enough income from other sources to be taxed at a 35% marginal tax rate, John's tax on the $15,000 of profit from the store is $5,250 (0.35 × $15,000).[1] ◀

If the business is unprofitable, the loss reduces the proprietor's total taxable income, thereby providing tax savings.

EXAMPLE C:2-2 ▶ Assume the same facts as in Example C:2-1 except John reports a $15,000 loss instead of a $15,000 profit in the first year of operation. Assuming he still is taxed at a 35% marginal tax rate, the $15,000 loss on the new venture produces tax savings of $5,250 (0.35 × $15,000). ◀

---

[1] The $15,000 Schedule C profit in Example C:2-1 will increase adjusted gross income (AGI). The AGI level affects certain deduction calculations (e.g., medical, charitable contributions, and miscellaneous itemized) and may result in a taxable income increase different from the $15,000 AGI increase.

ADDITIONAL COMMENT

Although this chapter emphasizes the tax consequences of selecting the entity in which a business will be conducted, other issues also are important in making such a decision. For example, the amount of legal liability assumed by an owner is important and can vary substantially among the different business entities.

TAX ADVANTAGES. The tax advantages of conducting business as a sole proprietorship are as follows:

- The sole proprietorship, as a separate business, is not subject to taxation. Rather, the sole proprietor, as an individual, is taxed at his or her marginal tax rate on income earned by the business.
- The proprietor's marginal tax rate may be lower than the marginal tax rate that would have applied had the business been organized as a corporation.
- The owner may contribute cash to, or withdraw profits from, the business without tax consequences.
- Although the owner usually maintains separate books, records, and bank accounts for the business, the money in these accounts belongs to the owner personally.
- The owner may contribute property to, or withdraw property from, the business without recognizing gain or loss.
- Business losses may offset nonbusiness income, such as interest, dividends, and any salary earned by the sole proprietor or his or her spouse, subject to the passive activity loss rules.

TAX DISADVANTAGES. The tax disadvantages of conducting business as a sole proprietorship are as follows:

- The profits of a sole proprietorship are currently taxed to the individual owner, whether or not the profits are retained in the business or withdrawn for personal use. By contrast, the profits of a corporate business are taxed to its shareholders only when the corporation distributes the earnings as dividends.
- At times, corporate tax rates have been lower than individual tax rates. In such times, businesses conducted as sole proprietorships have been taxed more heavily than businesses organized as corporations.
- A sole proprietor must pay the full amount of Social Security taxes because he or she is not considered to be an employee of the business. By contrast, shareholder-employees must pay only half their Social Security taxes; the corporate employer pays the other half. (The employer, however, might pass this half onto employees in the form of lower wages.)
- Sole proprietorships may not deduct compensation paid to owner-employees. By contrast, corporations may deduct compensation paid to shareholder-employees.
- Certain tax-exempt benefits (e.g., premiums for group term life insurance) available to shareholder-employees are not available to owner-employees.[2]
- A sole proprietor must use the same accounting period for business and personal purposes. Thus, he or she cannot defer income by choosing a business fiscal year that differs from the individual's calendar year. By contrast, a corporation may choose a fiscal year that differs from the shareholders' calendar years.

REAL-WORLD EXAMPLE

The IRS estimates the following business entity returns to be filed for 2006:

Entity	Number
Partnership	2.61 million
C corporation	2.25 million
S corporation	3.76 million

PARTNERSHIPS

A **partnership** is an unincorporated business carried on by two or more individuals or other entities. The partnership form often is used by friends or relatives who engage in a business together and by groups of investors who want to share the profits, losses, and expenses of some type of investment such as a real estate project.

A partnership is a tax reporting, but not taxpaying, entity. The partnership acts as a conduit for its owners. Its income, expenses, losses, credits, and other tax-related items flow through to the partners who report these items on their separate tax returns.

Each year a partnership must file a tax return (Form 1065—U.S. Partnership Return of Income) to report the results of its operations. When the partnership return is filed, the preparer must send each partner a statement (Schedule K-1, Form 1065) that reports the

[2] Section 162(l) permits self-employed individuals to deduct as a trade or business expense all of the health insurance costs incurred on behalf of themselves, their spouses, and their dependents.

partner's allocable share of partnership income, expenses, losses, credits, and other tax-related items. The partner then must report these items on his or her separate tax return. As with a sole proprietorship, the partner's allocable share of business profits is added to the partner's other income and taxed at that partner's marginal tax rate. A completed Form 1065 appears in Appendix B.

EXAMPLE C:2-3 ▶ Bob is single and owns a 50% interest in the BT Partnership, a calendar year entity. The BT Partnership reports a $30,000 profit in its first year of operation. Bob's $15,000 share flows through from the partnership to Bob's individual tax return. Assuming Bob is taxed at a 35% marginal tax rate, his tax on the $15,000 is $5,250 (0.35 × $15,000). Bob must pay the $5,250 in taxes whether or not the BT Partnership distributes any of its profits to him. ◀

If a partnership reports a loss, the partner's allocable share of the loss reduces that partner's other income and provides tax savings based on the partner's marginal tax rate. The passive activity loss rules, however, may limit the amount of any loss deduction available to the partner. (For a discussion of these rules, see Chapter C:9 of this textbook.)

EXAMPLE C:2-4 ▶ Assume the same facts as in Example C:2-3 except that, instead of a profit, the BT Partnership reports a $30,000 loss for its first year of operation. Assuming Bob is taxed at a 35% marginal tax rate, his $15,000 share of the first year loss produces a $5,250 (0.35 × $15,000) tax savings. ◀

ADDITIONAL COMMENT
In some states, a limited partnership can operate as a limited liability limited partnership (LLLP) whereby the general partners obtain limited liability. See Chapter C:10 for additional discussion.

A partnership can be either general or limited. In a general partnership, the liability of each partner for partnership debts is unlimited. Thus, these partners are at risk for more than the amount of their capital investment in the partnership. In a limited partnership, at least one partner must be a general partner, and at least one partner must be a limited partner. As in a general partnership, the general partners are liable for all partnership debts, and the limited partners are liable only to the extent of their capital investment in the partnership, plus any amount they are obligated to contribute if called upon. Limited partners generally may not participate in the management of the partnership.

TAX ADVANTAGES. The tax advantages of doing business as a partnership are as follows:

- The partnership as an entity pays no tax. Rather, the income of the partnership passes through to the separate tax returns of the partners and is taxed directly to them.
- A partner's tax rate may be lower than a corporation's tax rate on the same level of taxable income.
- Partnership income is not subject to double taxation. Although partnership profits are accounted for at the partnership level, they are taxed only at the partner level.
- Additional taxes generally are not imposed on distributions to the partners. With limited exceptions, partners can contribute money or property to, or withdraw money or property from, the partnership without recognizing gain or loss.
- Subject to limitations, partners can use losses to offset income from other sources.
- A partner's basis in a partnership interest is increased by his or her share of partnership income. This basis adjustment reduces the amount of gain recognized when the partner sells his or her partnership interest, thereby preventing double taxation.

TAX DISADVANTAGES. The tax disadvantages of doing business as a partnership are as follows:

ADDITIONAL COMMENT
If two or more owners exist, a business cannot be conducted as a sole proprietorship. From a tax compliance and recordkeeping perspective, conducting a business as a partnership is more complicated than conducting the business as a sole proprietorship.

- All the partnership's profits are taxed to the partners when earned, even if reinvested in the business.
- A partner's tax rate could be higher than a corporation's tax rate on the same level of taxable income.
- A partner is not considered to be an employee of the partnership. Therefore, he or she must pay the full amount of self-employment taxes on his or her share of partnership

income. Some tax-exempt fringe benefits (e.g., premiums for group term life insurance) are not available to partners.[3]

- Partners generally cannot defer income by choosing a fiscal year for the partnership that differs from the tax year of the principal partner(s). However, if the partnership demonstrates a business purpose, or if it makes a special election, it may use a fiscal year.

Chapters C:9 and C:10 of this volume discuss partnerships in greater detail.

CORPORATIONS

Corporations can be divided into two categories: C corporations and S corporations. A C corporation is subject to double taxation. Its earnings are taxed first at the corporate level when earned, then again at the shareholder level when distributed as dividends. An S corporation, by contrast, is subject to single-level taxation, much like a partnership. Its earnings are accounted for at the corporate level but are taxed only at the shareholder level.

ADDITIONAL COMMENT

Unlike a sole proprietorship and a partnership, a C corporation is a separate taxpaying entity. This form can be an advantage because corporate rates start at 15%, which may be much lower than an individual shareholder's rate, which might be as high as 35%.

C CORPORATIONS. A **C corporation** is a separate entity taxed on its income at rates ranging from 15% to 35%.[4] A corporation must report all its income and expenses and compute its tax liability on Form 1120 (U.S. Corporation Income Tax Return). A completed Form 1120 appears in Appendix B. Shareholders are not taxed on the corporation's earnings unless these earnings are distributed as dividends. For years 2003 through 2010, dividends received by a noncorporate shareholder are taxed at the same rate that applies to net capital gains. This dividend rate is 15% for taxpayers whose tax bracket exceeds 15%. (See Chapter I:5 of the *Individuals* volume for details of this provision.)

EXAMPLE C:2-5 ▶

Jane owns 100% of York Corporation's stock. York reports taxable income of $50,000 for the current year. The first $50,000 of taxable income is taxed at a 15% rate, so York pays a corporate income tax of $7,500 (0.15 × $50,000). If the corporation distributes none of its earnings to Jane during the year, she pays no taxes on York's earnings. However, if York distributes its current after-tax earnings to Jane, she must pay tax on $42,500 ($50,000 − $7,500) of dividend income. Assuming she is in the 35% marginal tax bracket, the tax Jane pays on the dividend income is $6,375 (0.15 × $42,500). The total tax on York's $50,000 of profits is $13,875 ($7,500 paid by York + $6,375 paid by Jane). ◀

TAX STRATEGY TIP

If a shareholder is also an employee of the corporation, the corporation can avoid double taxation by paying a deductible salary instead of a dividend. The salary, however, must be reasonable in amount. See Tax Planning Considerations in Chapter C:3 for further discussion of this technique along with an example demonstrating how the reduced tax rate on dividends lessens the difference between salary and dividend payments.

Even when a corporation does not distribute its profits, double taxation may result. The profits are taxed to the corporation when they are earned. Then they may be taxed a second time (as capital gains) when the shareholder sells his or her stock or when the corporation liquidates.

EXAMPLE C:2-6 ▶

On January 2 of the current year, Carl purchases 100% of York Corporation stock for $60,000. In the same year, York reports taxable income of $50,000, on which it pays tax of $7,500. The corporation distributes none of the remaining $42,500 to Carl. On January 3 of the next year, Carl sells his stock to Mary for $102,500 (his initial investment plus the current year's accumulated earnings). Carl must report a capital gain of $42,500 ($102,500 − $60,000). Thus, York's profit is effectively taxed twice—first at the corporate level when earned and again at the shareholder level when Carl sells the stock. ◀

TAX STRATEGY TIP

By having a corporation accumulate earnings instead of paying dividends, the shareholder converts current ordinary income into deferred capital gains. The corporation, however, must avoid the accumulated earnings tax (see Chapter C:5).

Tax Advantages. The tax advantages of doing business as a C corporation are as follows:

- A corporation is an entity separate and distinct from its owners. Its marginal tax rate may be lower than its owners' marginal tax rates. So long as these earnings are not distributed and taxed to both the shareholders and the corporation, aggregate tax savings may result. If retained in the business, the earnings may be used for reinvestment and the retirement of debt. This advantage, however, may be limited by the accumulated earnings tax and the personal holding company tax. (See Chapter C:5 for a discussion of these two taxes.)

---

[3] Partners are eligible to deduct their health insurance costs in the same manner as a sole proprietor. See footnote 2 for details.

[4] As discussed in Chapter C:3, the corporate tax rate is 39% and 38% for certain levels of taxable income.

- Shareholders employed by the corporation are considered to be employees for tax purposes. Consequently, they are liable for only half their Social Security taxes, while their corporate employer is liable for the other half.
- Shareholder-employees are entitled to tax-free fringe benefits (e.g., premiums paid on group term life insurance and accident and health insurance). The corporation can provide these benefits with before-tax dollars (instead of after-tax dollars). By contrast, because sole proprietors and partners are not considered to be employees for tax purposes, they are ineligible for certain tax-free fringe benefits, although they are permitted to deduct their health insurance premiums.
- A corporation may deduct as an ordinary and necessary business expense compensation paid to shareholder-employees. Within reasonable limits, it may adjust this compensation upward to shelter corporate taxable income.
- A C corporation can use a fiscal instead of a calendar year as its reporting period. A fiscal year could permit a corporation to defer income to a later reporting period. (A personal service corporation, however, generally must use a calendar year as its tax year.[5])
- Special rules allow a shareholder to exclude 50% of the gain realized on the sale or exchange of stock held more than five years, provided the corporation meets certain requirements.

SELF-STUDY QUESTION

How are corporate earnings subject to double taxation?

ANSWER

Corporate earnings initially are taxed to the corporation. In addition, once these earnings are distributed to the shareholders (dividends), they are taxed again. Because the corporation does not receive a deduction for the distribution, these earnings have been taxed twice. Also, double taxation can occur when a shareholder sells his or her stock at a gain. Through 2010, qualified dividends and long-term capital gains both are subject to the 15% maximum tax rate.

Tax Disadvantages. The tax disadvantages of doing business as a C corporation are as follows:

- Double taxation of income results when the corporation distributes its earnings as dividends to shareholders or when shareholders sell or exchange their stock.
- Shareholders generally cannot withdraw money or property from the corporation without recognizing income. A distribution of cash or property to a shareholder generally is taxable as a dividend if the corporation has sufficient earnings and profits (E&P). (See Chapter C:4 for a discussion of E&P.)
- Net operating losses provide no tax benefit to the owners in the year the corporation incurs them. They can be carried back or carried forward to offset the corporation's income in other years. For start-up corporations, these losses provide no tax benefit until the corporation earns a profit in a subsequent year. Shareholders cannot use these losses to offset income from other sources.
- Capital losses provide no tax benefit to the owners in the year the corporation incurs them. They cannot offset the ordinary income of either the corporation or its shareholders. These losses must be carried back or carried forward to offset corporate capital gains realized in other years.

S CORPORATIONS. An **S corporation** is so designated because special rules governing its tax treatment are in Subchapter S of the IRC. Nevertheless, the general corporate tax rules apply unless overridden by the Subchapter S provisions. Like a partnership, an S corporation is a pass-through entity. Income, deductions, losses, and credits are accounted for by the S corporation, which generally is not subject to taxation. They flow through to the separate returns of its owners, who generally are subject to taxation. On the other hand, an S corporation offers its owners less flexibility than does a partnership. For example, the number and type of S corporation shareholders are limited, and the shareholders cannot allocate income, deductions, losses, and credits in a way that differs from their proportionate ownership. Like C corporation shareholders, S corporation shareholders enjoy limited liability.

To obtain S corporation status, a corporation must make a special election, and its shareholders must consent to that election. Each year, an S corporation files an information return, Form 1120S (U.S. Income Tax Return for an S Corporation), which reports the results of its operations and indicates the items of income, deduction, loss, and credit that pass through to the separate returns of its shareholders.

[5] Sec. 441. See Chapter C:3 for the special tax year restrictions applying to personal service corporations.

EXAMPLE C:2-7 ▶ Chuck owns 50% of the stock in Maine, an S corporation that uses the calendar year as its tax year. For its first year of operation, Maine reports $30,000 of taxable income, all ordinary in character. Maine pays no corporate income taxes. Chuck must pay taxes on his $15,000 (0.50 × $30,000) share of Maine's income whether or not the corporation distributes this income to him. If his marginal tax rate is 35%, Chuck pays $5,250 (0.35 × $15,000) of tax on this share. If Maine instead reports a $30,000 loss, Chuck's $15,000 share of the loss reduces his tax liability by $5,250 (0.35 × $15,000). ◀

TAX STRATEGY TIP

If a corporation anticipates losses in its early years, it might consider operating as an S corporation so that the losses pass through to the shareholders. When the corporation becomes profitable, it can revoke the S election if it wishes to accumulate earnings for growth.

Tax Advantages. The tax advantages of doing business as an S corporation are as follows:

- S corporations generally pay no tax. Corporate income passes through and is taxed to the shareholders.
- The shareholders' marginal tax rates may be lower than a C corporation's marginal tax rate, thereby producing overall tax savings.
- Corporate losses flow through to the separate returns of the shareholders and may be used to offset income earned from other sources. (Passive loss and basis rules, however, may limit loss deductions to shareholders. See Chapter C:11.) This treatment can be beneficial to owners of start-up corporations that generate losses in their early years of operation.
- Because capital gains, as well as other tax-related items, retain their character when they pass through to the separate returns of shareholders, the shareholders are taxed on these gains as though they directly realized them. Consequently, they can offset the gains with capital losses from other sources. Furthermore, they are taxed on these gains at their own capital gains rates.
- Shareholders generally can contribute money to or withdraw money from an S corporation without recognizing gain.
- Corporate profits are taxed only at the shareholder level in the year earned. Generally, the shareholders incur no additional tax liability when the corporation distributes the profits.
- A shareholder's basis in S corporation stock is increased by his or her share of corporate income. This basis adjustment reduces the shareholder's gain when he or she later sells the S corporation stock, thereby avoiding double taxation.

TAX STRATEGY TIP

Relatively low individual tax rates may increase the attractiveness of an S corporation relative to the C corporation form of doing business.

Tax Disadvantages. The tax disadvantages of doing business as an S corporation are as follows:

- Shareholders are taxed on all of an S corporation's current year profits whether or not these profits are distributed and whether or not the shareholders have the wherewithal to pay.
- If the shareholders' marginal tax rates exceed those for a C corporation, the overall tax burden may be heavier, and the after-tax earnings available for reinvestment and debt retirement may be reduced.
- Nontaxable fringe benefits generally are not available to S corporation shareholder-employees.[6] Ordinarily, fringe benefits provided by an S corporation are deductible by the corporation and taxable to the shareholder. On the other hand, S corporation shareholder-employees pay half of Social Security taxes while the S corporation employer pays the other half.
- S corporations generally cannot defer income by choosing a fiscal year other than a calendar year unless the S corporation can establish a legitimate business purpose for a fiscal year or unless it makes a special election.

Chapter C:11 discusses S corporations in greater detail. In addition, Appendix F compares the tax treatment of C corporations, partnerships, and S corporations.

---

[6] S corporation shareholders are eligible to deduct their health insurance costs in the same manner as sole proprietors and partners. See footnote 2 for details.

ADDITIONAL COMMENT
All 50 states have adopted statutes allowing LLCs.

LIMITED LIABILITY COMPANIES

A **limited liability company** (LLC) combines the best features of a partnership with those of a corporation even though, from a legal perspective, it is neither. An LLC with more than one owner generally is treated as a partnership while offering its owners the limited liability of a corporation. This limited liability extends to all the LLC's owners. In this respect, the LLC is similar to a limited partnership with no general partners. Unlike an S corporation, an LLC may have an unlimited number of owners who can be individuals, corporations, estates, and trusts. As discussed below, under the check-the-box regulations, the LLC may elect to be taxed as a corporation or be treated by default as a partnership. If treated by default as a partnership, the LLC files Form 1065 (U.S. Partnership Return of Income) with the IRS.

REAL-WORLD EXAMPLE
All the Big 4 accounting firms have converted general partnerships into LLPs.

LIMITED LIABILITY PARTNERSHIPS

Many states allow a business to operate as a **limited liability partnership** (LLP). This business form is attractive to professional service organizations, such as public accounting firms, that have adopted LLP status primarily to limit their legal liability. Under state LLP laws, partners are liable for their own acts and omissions as well as the acts and omissions of individuals under their direction. On the other hand, LLP partners are not liable for the negligence or misconduct of the other partners. Thus, from a liability perspective, an LLP partner is like a limited partner with respect to other partners' acts but like a general partner with respect to his or her own acts as well as the acts of his or her agents. Like a general partnership or LLC with more than one owner, an LLP can elect to be taxed as a corporation under the check-the-box regulations. If treated as a partnership by default, the LLP files Form 1065 (U.S. Partnership Return of Income) with the IRS.

CHECK-THE-BOX REGULATIONS

OBJECTIVE 2

Apply the check-the-box regulations to partnerships, corporations, and trusts

Most unincorporated businesses may choose whether to be taxed as a partnership or a corporation under rules commonly referred to as the **check-the-box regulations.** According to these regulations, an unincorporated business with two or more owners is treated as a partnership for tax purposes unless it elects to be taxed as a corporation. An unincorporated business with one owner is disregarded as a separate entity and thus treated as a sole proprietorship unless it elects to be taxed as a corporation.[7]

An eligible entity (i.e., an unincorporated business) may elect its classification by filing Form 8832 (Entity Classification Election) with the IRS. The form must be signed by each owner of the entity, or any officer, manager, or owner of the entity authorized to make the election. The signatures must specify the date on which the election will be effective. The effective date cannot be more than 75 days before or 12 months after the date the entity files Form 8832. A copy of the form must be attached to the entity's tax return for the election year.

TAX STRATEGY TIP
When applying the federal check-the-box regulations, taxpayers also must check to see whether or not their state will treat the entity in a consistent manner.

EXAMPLE C:2-8 ▶ On January 10 of the current year, a group of ten individuals organizes an LLC to conduct a bookbinding business in Texas. In the current year, the LLC is an eligible entity under the check-the-box regulations and thus may elect (with the owners' consent) to be taxed as a corporation. If the LLC does not make the election, it will be treated as a partnership for tax purposes by default. ◀

EXAMPLE C:2-9 ▶ Assume the same facts as in Example C:2-8 except only one individual organized the LLC. Unless the LLC elects to be taxed as a corporation, it will be disregarded for tax purposes by default. Consequently, its income will be taxed directly to the owner as if it were a sole proprietorship. ◀

[7] This rule does not apply to corporations, trusts, or certain special entities such as real estate investment trusts, real estate mortgage investment conduits, or publicly traded partnerships. Reg. Sec. 301.7701-2(b)(8). Publicly traded partnerships are discussed in Chapter C:10. Special check-the-box rules apply to foreign corporations. These rules are beyond the scope of this text.

If an entity elects to change its tax classification, it cannot make another election until 60 months following the effective date of the initial election. Following the election, certain tax consequences ensue. For example, following a partnership's election to be taxed as a corporation, the partnership is deemed to distribute its assets to the partners, who are then deemed to contribute the assets to a new corporation in a nontaxable exchange for stock. If an eligible entity that previously elected to be taxed as a corporation subsequently elects to be treated as a partnership or a disregarded entity, it is deemed to have distributed its assets and liabilities to its owners or owner in a liquidation as described in Chapter C:6. If a partnership, the deemed distribution is followed by a deemed contribution of assets and liabilities to a newly formed partnership.[8]

LEGAL REQUIREMENTS FOR FORMING A CORPORATION

OBJECTIVE 3

Determine the legal requirements for forming a corporation

The legal requirements for forming a corporation depend on state law. These requirements may include

- Investing a minimum amount of capital
- Filing articles of incorporation
- Issuing stock
- Paying state incorporation fees

One of the first decisions an entrepreneur must make when organizing a corporation is the state of incorporation. Although most entrepreneurs incorporate in the state where they conduct business, many incorporate in other states with favorable corporation laws. Such laws might provide for little or no income, sales, or use taxes; low minimum capital requirements; and modest incorporation fees. Regardless of the state of incorporation, the entrepreneur must follow the incorporation procedure set forth in the relevant state statute. Typically, under this procedure, the entrepreneur must file articles of incorporation with the appropriate state agency. The articles must specify certain information, such as the formal name of the corporation; its purpose; the par value, number of shares, and classes of stock it is authorized to issue; and the names of the individuals who will initially serve on the corporation's board of directors. The state usually charges a fee for incorporation or filing. In addition, it periodically may assess a franchise tax for the privilege of doing business in the state.

ADDITIONAL COMMENT

States are not consistent in how they tax corporations. Certain states have no state income taxes. Other states do not recognize an S election, thereby taxing an S corporation as a C corporation.

TAX CONSIDERATIONS IN FORMING A CORPORATION

Once the entrepreneur decides on the corporate form, he or she must transfer money, property (e.g., equipment, furniture, inventory, and receivables), or services (e.g., accounting, legal, or architectural services) to the corporation in exchange for its debt or equity. These transfers may have tax consequences for both the transferor investor and the transferee corporation. For instance, the sale of property for stock usually is taxable to the transferor.[9] However, if Sec. 351(a) (which treats an investor's interest in certain transferred business assets to be "changed in form" rather than "disposed of") applies, any gain or loss realized on the exchange may be deferred. In determining the tax consequences of incorporation, one must answer the following questions:

- What property should be transferred to the corporation?
- What services should the transferors or third parties provide for the corporation?

---

[8] Reg. Sec. 301.7701-3(g). An alternative way for a corporation to be taxed as a flow-through entity is to make an election to be taxed as an S corporation. See Chapter C:11.

[9] Sec. 1001.

► What liabilities, in addition to property, should be transferred?

► How should the property be transferred (e.g., sale, contribution to capital, or loan)?

Example C:2-10 and Table C:2-1 compare the tax consequences of taxable and nontaxable property transfers.

EXAMPLE C:2-10 ► For several years Brad has operated a successful manufacturing business as a sole proprietorship. To limit his liability, he decides to incorporate his business as Block Corporation. Immediately preceding the incorporation, he reports the following balance sheet for his sole proprietorship, which uses the accrual method of accounting:

BOOK-TO-TAX ACCOUNTING COMPARISON

The IRC treats most corporate formations as nontaxable transactions. Property received in a corporate formation transaction generally is recorded on the tax books using the carryover basis rules. Services are recorded at their FMV. The financial accounting rules, however, record services and noncash property received for stock at either the FMV of the stock issued or the FMV of the noncash consideration received, whichever is more readily determinable. Also see Financial Statement Implications later in this chapter.

		Adjusted Basis	*Fair Market Value*
Assets:			
Cash		$ 10,000	$ 10,000
Accounts receivable		15,000	15,000
Inventory		20,000	25,000
Equipment	$120,000		
Minus: Depreciation	(35,000)	85,000	100,000
Total		$130,000	$150,000
Liabilities and owner's equity:			
Accounts payable		$ 30,000	$ 30,000
Note payable on equipment		50,000	50,000
Owner's equity		50,000	70,000
Total		$130,000	$150,000

When Brad transfers the assets to Block in exchange for its stock, he realizes a gain because the value of the stock received exceeds his basis in the assets. If the exchange is taxable, Brad recognizes $5,000 of ordinary income on the transfer of the inventory ($25,000 FMV – $20,000 basis) and, because of depreciation recapture, $15,000 of ordinary income on the transfer of the equipment ($100,000 FMV – $85,000 basis). However, if the exchange meets the requirements of Sec. 351(a), it is tax-free. In other words, Brad recognizes none of the income or gain realized on the transfer of assets and liabilities to Block. ◄

STOP & THINK

Question: Joyce has conducted a business as a sole proprietorship for several years. She needs additional capital and wants to incorporate her business. The assets of her business (building, land, inventory, etc.) have a $400,000 adjusted basis and a $1.5 million FMV. Joyce is willing to exchange the assets for 1,500 shares of Ace Corporation stock each having a $1,000 fair market value. Bill and John are willing to invest $500,000 each in Joyce's business for 500 shares of stock. Why is Sec. 351 important to Joyce? Does it matter to Bill and John?

Solution: If not for Sec. 351, Joyce would recognize gain on the incorporation of her business. She realizes a gain of $1.1 million ($1,500,000 – $400,000) on her contribution of proprietorship assets to a new corporation in exchange for 60% of its outstanding shares (1,500 ÷ [1,500 + 500 + 500] = 0.60). However, she recognizes none of this gain because she meets the requirements of Sec. 351. Section 351 does not affect Bill or John because each is simply purchasing 20% of the new corporation's stock for $500,000 cash. They will not realize or recognize gain or loss unless they subsequently sell their stock at a price above or below the $500,000 cost.

If all exchanges of property for corporate stock were taxable, many entrepreneurs would find the tax cost of incorporating their business prohibitively high. In Example C:2-10, for example, Brad would recognize a $20,000 gain on the exchange of his assets for the corporate stock. Moreover, because losses also are realized in an exchange, without special rules, taxpayers could exchange loss property for stock and recognize the loss while maintaining an equity interest in the property transferred.

▼ **TABLE C:2-1**
Overview of Corporate Formation Rules

Tax Treatment for:	Taxable Property Transfer	Nontaxable Property Transfer
Transferors: 1. Gain realized	FMV of stock received Money received FMV of nonmoney boot property (including securities) received Amount of liabilities assumed by transferee corporation Minus: Adjusted basis of property transferred Realized gain (Sec. 1001(a))	Same as taxable transaction
2. Gain recognized	Transferors recognize the entire amount of realized gain (Sec. 1001(c)) Losses may be disallowed under related party rules (Sec. 267(a)(1)) Installment sale rules may apply to the realized gain (Sec. 453)	Transferors recognize none of the realized gain unless one of the following exceptions applies (Sec. 351(a)): a. Boot property is received (Sec. 351(b)) b. Liabilities are transferred to the corporation for a nonbusiness or tax avoidance purpose (Sec. 357(b)) c. Liabilities exceeding basis are transferred to the corporation (Sec. 357(c)) d. Services, certain corporate indebtednesses, and interest claims are transferred to the corporation (Sec. 351(d)) The installment method may defer recognition of gain when a shareholder receives a corporate note as boot (Sec. 453)
3. Basis of property received	FMV (Cost) (Sec. 1012)	Basis of property transferred to the corporation Plus: Gain recognized Minus: Money received (including liabilities treated as money) FMV of nonmoney boot property Total basis of stock received (Sec. 358(a)) Allocation of total stock basis is based on relative FMVs Basis of nonmoney boot property is its FMV
4. Holding period of property received	Day after the exchange date	Holding period of stock received includes holding period of Sec. 1231 property or capital assets transferred; otherwise it begins the day after the exchange date
Transferee Corporation: 1. Gain recognized	The corporation recognizes no gain or loss on the receipt of money or other property in exchange for its stock (including treasury stock) (Sec. 1032)	Same as taxable transaction except the corporation may recognize gain under Sec. 311 if it transfers appreciated nonmoney boot property (Sec. 351(f))
2. Basis	FMV (Cost) (Sec. 1012)	Generally, same as in transferor's hands plus any gain recognized by transferor (Sec. 362) If the total adjusted basis for all transferred property exceeds the total FMV of the property, the total basis to the transferor is limited to the property's total FMV
3. Holding period	Day after the exchange date	Transferor's carryover holding period for the property transferred regardless of the property's character (Sec. 1223(2)) Day after the exchange date if basis is reduced to FMV

To allow taxpayers to incorporate without incurring a high tax cost and to prevent taxpayers from recognizing losses while maintaining an equity claim to the loss assets, Congress enacted Sec. 351.

SECTION 351: DEFERRING GAIN OR LOSS UPON INCORPORATION

OBJECTIVE 4

Explain the requirements for deferring gain or loss upon incorporation

Section 351(a) provides that transferors recognize no gain or loss when they transfer property to a corporation solely in exchange for the corporation's stock provided that, immediately after the exchange, the transferors are in control of the corporation. Section 351 does not apply to a transfer of property to an investment company, nor does it apply in certain bankruptcy cases.

This rule is based on the premise that, when property is transferred to a controlled corporation, the transferors merely exchange direct ownership for indirect ownership through stock ownership of the transferee corporation, which gives them an equity claim to the underlying assets. In other words, the transferors maintain a continuity of interest in the transferred property. Furthermore, if the only consideration the shareholders receive is stock, they have not generated cash with which to pay their taxes. Therefore, they may not have the "wherewithal-to-pay." If the transferors of property receive other consideration in addition to stock, such as cash or debt instruments, they will have the wherewithal-to-pay and under Sec. 351(b) may have to recognize some or all of their realized gain.

TAX STRATEGY TIP

A transferor who wishes to recognize gain or loss must take steps to avoid Sec. 351 by failing at least one of its requirements or by engaging in sales transactions. See Tax Planning Considerations later in this chapter for details.

A transferor's realized gain or loss that is unrecognized for tax purposes, however, is not exempt from taxation. It is only *deferred* until the shareholder sells or exchanges the stock received in the Sec. 351 exchange. Shareholders who receive stock in such an exchange take a stock basis that reflects the deferred gain or loss. For example, if a shareholder receives stock in exchange for property and recognizes no gain or loss, the stock basis equals the basis of property transferred less liabilities assumed by the corporation (see Table C:2-1). Further discussion of this tax treatment appears later in this chapter. Under an alternative approach, the stock basis can be calculated as follows: FMV of qualified stock received minus any deferred gain (or plus any deferred loss). This latter approach highlights the deferral aspect of this type of transaction. If the shareholder later sells the stock, he or she will recognize the deferred gain or loss inherent in the basis adjustment.

EXAMPLE C:2-11 ▶ Assume the same facts as in Example C:2-10. If Brad satisfies the conditions of Sec. 351, he will not recognize the $20,000 realized gain ($15,000 gain on equipment + $5,000 gain on inventory) when he transfers the assets and liabilities of his sole proprietorship to Block Corporation. Under the alternative approach, Brad's basis for the Block stock is decreased to reflect the deferred gain. Thus, Brad's basis in the Block stock is $50,000 ($70,000 FMV − $20,000 deferred gain). If Brad later sells his stock for its $70,000 FMV, he will recognize the $20,000 gain at that time. ◀

The specific requirements for deferral of gain and loss under Sec. 351(a) are

- ▶ The transferors must transfer property to the corporation.
- ▶ The transferors must receive stock of the transferee corporation in exchange for their property.
- ▶ The transferors of the property must be in control of the corporation immediately after the exchange.

Each of these requirements is explained below.

THE PROPERTY REQUIREMENT

The rule of gain or loss nonrecognition applies only to transfers of property to a corporation in exchange for the corporation's stock. Section 351 does not define the term *property*. However, the courts and the IRS have defined *property* to include money and almost any other asset, including installment obligations, accounts receivable, inventory, equipment, patents and other intangibles representing know-how, trademarks, trade names, and computer software.[10]

Excluded from the statutory definition of property are[11]

- ▶ Services (such as legal or accounting services) rendered to the corporation in exchange for its stock
- ▶ Indebtedness of the transferee corporation not evidenced by a security
- ▶ Interest on transferee corporation debt that accrued on or after the beginning of the transferor's holding period for the debt

The first of these exclusions perhaps is the most important. A person receiving stock as compensation for services must recognize the stock's FMV as ordinary income for tax purposes. In other words, an exchange of services for stock is a taxable transaction even if Sec. 351 applies to other transfers.[12] A shareholder's basis in the stock received as compensation for services is the stock's FMV.

EXAMPLE C:2-12 ▶ Amy and Bill form West Corporation. Amy exchanges property for 90 shares (90% of the outstanding shares) of West stock. Amy's exchange is nontaxable because Amy has exchanged property for stock and controls West immediately after the exchange. Bill performs accounting services in exchange for ten shares of West stock worth $10,000. Bill's exchange is taxable because he has provided services in exchange for stock. Thus, Bill recognizes $10,000 of ordinary income—the FMV of the stock—as compensation for his services. Bill's basis in the stock is its $10,000 FMV. ◀

THE CONTROL REQUIREMENT

Section 351 requires the transferors, as a group, to be in control of the transferee corporation immediately after the exchange. A transferor may be an individual or any type of tax entity (such as a partnership, another corporation, or a trust). Section 368(c) defines *control* as ownership of at least 80% of the total combined voting power of all classes of stock entitled to vote and at least 80% of the total number of shares of all other classes of stock (e.g., nonvoting preferred stock).[13] The minimum ownership levels for nonvoting stock apply to each class of stock rather than to the nonvoting stock in total.[14]

EXAMPLE C:2-13 ▶ Dan exchanges property having a $22,000 adjusted basis and a $30,000 FMV for 60% of newly created Sun Corporation's single class of stock. Ed exchanges $20,000 cash for the remaining 40% of Sun stock. The transaction qualifies as a nontaxable exchange under Sec. 351 because the transferors, Dan and Ed, together own at least 80% of the Sun stock immediately after the exchange. Therefore, Dan defers recognition of his $8,000 ($30,000 − $22,000) realized gain. (Ed realizes no gain because he contributes cash.) ◀

Because services do not qualify as property, stock received by a person who exclusively provides services does not count toward the 80% control threshold. Unless transferors of property own at least 80% of the corporation's stock immediately after the exchange, the control requirement will not be met, and the entire transaction will be taxable.

EXAMPLE C:2-14 ▶ Dana transfers property having an $18,000 adjusted basis and a $35,000 FMV to newly created York Corporation for 70 shares of York stock. Ellen provides legal services worth $15,000 for the remaining 30 shares of York stock. Because Ellen does not transfer property to York, her stock is not counted toward the 80% ownership threshold. On the other hand, because Dana transfers property to York, his stock is counted toward this threshold. However, Dana is not in control of York immediately after the exchange because he owns only 70% of York stock. Therefore, Dana recognizes all $17,000 ($35,000 − $18,000) of his gain realized on the exchange. Dana's basis in his York stock is its $35,000 FMV. Ellen recognizes $15,000 of ordinary income, the FMV of stock received for her services. Ellen's basis in her York stock is $15,000. The tax consequences to Ellen are the same whether or not Dana meets the control requirement. ◀

---

[10] For an excellent discussion of the definition of *property*, see footnote 6 of *D.N. Stafford v. U.S.*, 45 AFTR 2d 80-785, 80-1 USTC ¶9218 (5th Cir., 1980).

[11] Sec. 351(d).

[12] Secs. 61 and 83.

[13] In determining whether the 80% requirements are satisfied, the constructive ownership rules of Sec. 318 do not apply (see Rev. Rul. 56-613, 1956-2 C.B. 212). See Chapter C:4 for an explanation of Sec. 318.

[14] Rev. Rul. 59-259, 1959-2 C.B. 115.

If the property transferors own at least 80% of the stock immediately after the exchange, they, but not the provider of services, will be in control of the transferee corporation.

EXAMPLE C:2-15 ▶ Assume the same facts as in Example C:2-14, except a third individual, Fred, contributes $35,000 in cash for 70 shares of York stock. Now Dana and Fred together own more than 80% of the York stock (140 ÷ 170 = 0.82) immediately after the exchange. Therefore, the Sec. 351 control requirement is met, and neither Dana nor Fred recognizes gain on the exchange. Ellen still must recognize $15,000 of ordinary income, the FMV of the stock she receives for her services. ◀

TRANSFERORS OF BOTH PROPERTY AND SERVICES. If a person transfers both services *and* property to a corporation in exchange for the corporation's stock, all the stock received by that person, including stock received in exchange for services, is counted toward the 80% control threshold.[15]

EXAMPLE C:2-16 ▶ Assume the same facts as in Example C:2-14 except that, in addition to providing legal services worth $15,000, Ellen contributes property worth at least $1,500. In this case, all of Ellen's stock counts toward the 80% ownership threshold. Because Dana and Ellen together own 100% of the York stock, the exchange meets the Sec. 351 control requirement. Therefore, Dana recognizes no gain on her property exchange. However, she still must recognize $15,000 of ordinary income, the FMV of the stock received as compensation for services. ◀

When a person transfers both property and services in exchange for a corporation's stock, the property must have more than nominal value for that person's stock to count toward the 80% control threshold.[16] The IRS generally requires that the FMV of the stock received for transferred property be at least 10% of the value of the stock received for services provided. If the value of the stock received for the property is less than 10% of the value of the stock received for the services, the IRS will not issue an advance ruling stating that the transaction meets the requirements of Sec. 351.[17]

EXAMPLE C:2-17 ▶ Assume the same facts as in Example C:2-16 except that Ellen contributes only $1,000 worth of property in addition to $15,000 of legal services. In this case, the IRS will not issue an advance ruling that the transaction meets the Sec. 351 requirements because the FMV of stock received for the property ($1,000) is less than 10% of the value of the stock received for the services ($1,500 = 0.10 × $15,000). Consequently, if the IRS audits her tax return for the year of transfer, it probably will challenge Dana's and Ellen's position that the transfer is nontaxable under Sec. 351. ◀

TRANSFERS TO EXISTING CORPORATIONS. Section 351 applies to transfers to an existing corporation as well as transfers to a newly created corporation. The same requirements must be met in both cases. Property must be transferred in exchange for stock, and the property transferors must be in control of the corporation immediately after the exchange.

EXAMPLE C:2-18 ▶ Jack and Karen own 75 and 25 shares, respectively, of Texas Corporation stock. Jack transfers property with a $15,000 adjusted basis and a $25,000 FMV to the corporation in exchange for an additional 25 shares of Texas stock. The Sec. 351 control requirement is met because, immediately after the exchange, Jack owns 80% (100 ÷ 125 = 0.80) of Texas stock. Therefore, Jack recognizes no gain. ◀

If a shareholder transfers property to an existing corporation for additional stock but does not own at least 80% of the stock after the exchange, the control requirement is not met. Thus, Sec. 351 denies tax-free treatment for many transfers of property to an existing corporation by a new shareholder. A new shareholder's transfer of property to an existing corporation is nontaxable only if that shareholder acquires at least 80% of the corporation's stock, or if enough existing shareholders also transfer additional property so that the transferors as a group, including the new shareholder, control the corporation immediately after the exchange.

[15] Reg. Sec. 1.351-1(a)(2), Ex. (3).
[16] Reg. Sec. 1.351-1(a)(1)(ii).
[17] Rev. Proc. 77-37, 1977-2 C.B. 568, Sec. 3.07.

EXAMPLE C:2-19 ▶ Alice owns all 100 shares of Local Corporation stock, valued at $100,000. Beth owns property with a $15,000 adjusted basis and a $100,000 FMV. Beth contributes the property to Local in exchange for 100 shares of newly issued Local stock. The Sec. 351 control requirement is not met because Beth owns only 50% of Local stock immediately after the exchange. Therefore, Beth recognizes an $85,000 ($100,000 – $15,000) gain. ◀

If an existing shareholder exchanges property for additional stock to enable another shareholder to qualify for tax-free treatment under Sec. 351, the stock received must be of more than nominal value.[18] For advance ruling purposes, the IRS requires that this value be at least 10% of the value of the stock already owned.[19]

EXAMPLE C:2-20 ▶ Assume the same facts as in Example C:2-19 except that Alice transfers additional property worth $10,000 for an additional ten shares of Local stock. Now both Alice and Beth are transferors, and the Sec. 351 control requirement is met. Consequently, neither Alice nor Beth recognizes gain on the exchange. If Alice receives fewer than ten shares, the IRS will not issue an advance ruling that the exchange is tax-free under Sec. 351. ◀

STOP & THINK

Question: Matthew and Michael each own 50 shares of Main Corporation stock having a $250,000 FMV. Matthew wants to transfer property with a $40,000 adjusted basis and a $100,000 FMV to Main in exchange for an additional 20 shares. Can Matthew avoid recognizing $60,000 ($100,000 – $40,000) of the gain realized on the transfer?

Solution: If Matthew simply exchanges the property for additional stock, he must recognize the gain. The Sec. 351 control requirement will not have been met because Matthew will own only 70 of the 120 outstanding shares (or 58.33%) immediately after the exchange.

Gain recognition can be avoided in two ways:

1. Matthew can transfer sufficient property (i.e., $750,000 worth) to Main to receive 150 additional shares so that, immediately after the exchange, he will own 80% (200 out of 250 shares) of Main stock.
2. Alternatively, Michael also can contribute additional property to qualify as a transferor. Specifically, he can contribute to the corporation at least $25,000, or 10% of the $250,000 value of the Main stock that he already owns so that together the two transferors will own 100% of Main stock immediately after the exchange.

DISPROPORTIONATE EXCHANGES OF PROPERTY AND STOCK. Section 351 does not require that the value of the stock received by the transferors be proportional to the value of the property transferred. However, if the value of the stock received is *not* proportional to the value of the property transferred, the exchange may be treated in accordance with its economic effect, that is, a proportional exchange followed by a gift, payment of compensation, or extinguishment of a liability owed by one shareholder to another.[20] If the deemed effect of the transaction is a gift from one transferor to another, for example, the "donor" will be treated as though he or she received stock equal in value to that of the property contributed and then gave some of the stock to the "donee."

EXAMPLE C:2-21 ▶ Don and his son John transfer property worth $75,000 (adjusted basis to Don of $42,000) and $25,000 (adjusted basis to John of $20,000), respectively, to newly formed Star Corporation in exchange for all 100 shares of Star stock. Don and John receive 25 and 75 shares of Star stock, respectively. Because Don and John are in control of Star Corporation immediately after the exchange, they recognize no gain or loss. However, because Don and John did not receive the stock in proportion to the FMV of their respective property contributions, Don might be deemed to have received 75 shares (worth $75,000), then to have given 50 shares (worth $50,000) to John. If the IRS deems such a gift, it might require Don to pay gift taxes. Don's basis in his remaining 25 shares is $14,000 [(25 ÷ 75) × $42,000 basis in the property transferred]. John's basis in the 75 shares is $48,000 [$20,000 basis in the property transferred by John + ($42,000 – $14,000) basis in the shares deemed to have been gifted by Don]. ◀

[18] Reg. Sec. 1.351-1(a)(1)(ii).
[19] Rev. Proc. 77-37, 1977-2 C.B. 568, Sec. 3.07.
[20] Reg. Sec. 1.351-1(b)(1).

IMMEDIATELY AFTER THE EXCHANGE. Section 351 requires that the transferors be in control of the transferee corporation "immediately after the exchange." This requirement does not mean that all transferors must simultaneously exchange their property for stock. It does mean, however, that all the exchanges must be agreed to beforehand, and the agreement must be executed in an expeditious and orderly manner.[21]

EXAMPLE C:2-22 ▶ Art, Beth, and Carlos form New Corporation. Art and Beth each transfer noncash property worth $25,000 in exchange for one-third of the New stock. Carlos contributes $25,000 cash for another one-third of the New stock. Art and Carlos transfer their property and cash, respectively, on January 10. Beth transfers her property on March 3. Because all three transfers are part of the same prearranged transaction, the transferors are deemed to be in control of the corporation immediately after the exchange. ◀

TAX STRATEGY TIP

If one shareholder has a prearranged plan to dispose of his or her stock, and the disposition drops the ownership of the transferor shareholders below the required 80% control, such disposition can disqualify the Sec. 351 transaction for all the shareholders. As a possible protection, all shareholders could provide a written representation that they do not currently have a plan to dispose of their stock.

Section 351 does not require the transferors to retain control of the transferee corporation for any specific length of time after the exchange. Control is required only "immediately after the exchange." The IRS has interpreted this phrase to mean that the transferors must not have a prearranged plan to dispose of their stock outside the control group. If they do have such a plan, they are not considered to be in control immediately after the exchange.[22]

EXAMPLE C:2-23 ▶ Amir, Bill, and Carl form White Corporation. Each contributes to White appreciated property worth $25,000 in exchange for one-third of White stock. Before the exchange, Amir arranges to sell his stock to Dana as soon as he receives it. This prearranged plan implies that Amir, Bill, and Carl do *not* have control immediately after the exchange. Therefore, each must recognize gain in the exchange. ◀

THE STOCK REQUIREMENT

Under Sec. 351, transferors who exchange property solely for transferee corporation stock recognize no gain or loss if they control the corporation immediately after the exchange. Stock for this purpose may be voting or nonvoting. However, nonqualified preferred stock is treated as boot. Preferred stock is stock with a preferred claim to dividends and liquidating distributions. Such stock is nonqualified if

- ▶ The shareholder can require the corporation to redeem it,
- ▶ The corporation is either required to redeem the stock or is likely to exercise a right to redeem it, or
- ▶ The dividend rate on the stock varies with interest rates, commodity prices, or other similar indices.

These features render the preferred stock more like cash or debt than like equity. Thus, it is treated as boot subject to the rules discussed below. In addition, stock rights or stock warrants are not considered stock for purposes of Sec. 351.[23]

Topic Review C:2-1 summarizes the major requirements for a tax-free exchange under Sec. 351.

EFFECT OF SEC. 351 ON THE TRANSFERORS

If all Sec. 351 requirements are met, the transferors recognize no gain or loss on the exchange of their property for stock in the transferee corporation. The receipt of property other than stock does not necessarily render the entire transaction taxable. Rather, it could result in the recognition of all or part of the transferors' realized gain.

RECEIPT OF BOOT. If a transferor receives any money or property other than stock in the transferee corporation, the additional money or property is considered to be **boot.** Boot may include cash, notes, securities, or stock in another corporation. Upon receiving boot, the transferor recognizes gain to the extent of the lesser of the transferor's realized

---

[21] Reg. Sec. 1.351-1(a)(1).

[22] Rev. Rul. 79-70, 1979-1 C.B. 144.

[23] Reg. Sec. 1.351-1(a)(1)(ii).

Topic Review C:2-1

Major Requirements of Sec. 351

1. The nonrecognition of gain or loss rule applies only to transfers of property in exchange for a corporation's stock. It does not apply to an exchange of services for stock.
2. The property transferors must be in control of the transferee corporation immediately after the exchange. Control means ownership of at least 80% of the voting power and at least 80% of the total number of shares of all other classes of stock. Stock disposed of after the exchange pursuant to a prearranged plan does not meet the "immediately after the exchange" requirement.
3. The nonrecognition rule applies only to the gain realized in an exchange of property for stock. If the transferor receives property other than stock, such property is considered to be boot. The transferor recognizes gain to the extent of the lesser of the FMV of any boot received or the realized gain.

gain or the FMV of the boot property received.[24] A transferor never recognizes a loss in an exchange qualifying under Sec. 351 whether or not he or she receives boot.

The character of the recognized gain depends on the type of property transferred. For example, if the shareholder transfers a capital asset such as stock in another corporation, the recognized gain is capital in character. If the shareholder transfers Sec. 1231 property, such as equipment or a building, the recognized gain is ordinary in character to the extent of any depreciation recaptured under Sec. 1245 or 1250.[25] Thus, depreciation is not recaptured unless the transferor receives boot and recognizes a gain on the depreciated property transferred.[26] If the shareholder transfers inventory, the recognized gain is entirely ordinary in character.

EXAMPLE C:2-24 ▶ **Pam, Rob, and Sam form East Corporation and transfer the following property:**

Transferor	*Asset*	*Transferor's Adj. Basis*	*FMV*	*Consideration Received*
Pam	Machinery	$10,000	$12,500	25 shares East stock
Rob	Land	18,000	25,000	40 shares East stock and $5,000 East note
Sam	Cash	17,500	17,500	35 shares East stock

The machinery and land are Sec. 1231 property and a capital asset, respectively. The exchange meets the requirements of Sec. 351 except that, in addition to East stock, Rob receives boot of $5,000 (the FMV of the note). Rob realizes a $7,000 ($25,000 − $18,000) gain, of which he recognizes $5,000—the lesser of the $7,000 realized gain or the $5,000 boot received. The gain is capital in character because the property transferred was a capital asset in Rob's hands. Pam realizes a $2,500 gain on her exchange of machinery. However, even though Pam would have been required to recapture depreciation had she sold or exchanged the machinery, she recognizes no gain because she received no boot. Sam neither realizes nor recognizes gain on his cash purchase of East stock. ◀

ADDITIONAL COMMENT

If multiple assets were aggregated into one computation, any built-in losses would be netted against the gains. Such a result is inappropriate because losses cannot be recognized in a Sec. 351 transaction.

COMPUTING GAIN WHEN SEVERAL ASSETS ARE TRANSFERRED. Revenue Ruling 68-55 adopts a "separate properties approach" for computing gain or loss when a shareholder transfers more than one asset to a corporation.[27] Under this approach, the gain or loss realized and recognized is computed separately for each property transferred. The transferor is deemed to have received a proportionate share of stock, securities, and boot in exchange for each property transferred, based on the assets' relative FMVs.

EXAMPLE C:2-25 ▶ **Joan transfers two assets to newly created North Corporation in a transaction qualifying in part for tax-free treatment under Sec. 351. The total FMV of the assets is $100,000. The consideration**

---

[24] Sec. 351(b).

[25] Section 1239 also may require some gain to be characterized as ordinary income. Section 1250 ordinary depreciation recapture will not apply to real property placed in service after 1986 because MACRS mandates straight-line depreciation.

[26] Secs. 1245(b)(3) and 1250(c)(3).

[27] 1968-1 C.B. 140.

received by Joan consists of $90,000 of North stock and $10,000 of North notes. The following data illustrate how Joan determines her realized and recognized gain under the procedure set forth in Rev. Rul. 68-55.

	Asset 1	*Asset 2*	*Total*
Asset's FMV	$40,000	$60,000	$100,000
Percent of total FMV	40%	60%	100%
Consideration received in exchange for asset:			
Stock (Stock × percent of total FMV)	$36,000	$54,000	$ 90,000
Notes (Notes × percent of total FMV)	4,000	6,000	10,000
Total proceeds	$40,000	$60,000	$100,000
Minus: Adjusted basis	(65,000)	(25,000)	(90,000)
Realized gain (loss)	($25,000)	$35,000	$ 10,000
Boot received	$ 4,000	$ 6,000	$ 10,000
Recognized gain (loss)	None	$ 6,000	$ 6,000

Under the separate properties approach, the loss realized on the transfer of Asset 1 does not offset the gain realized on the transfer of Asset 2. Therefore, Joan recognizes $6,000 of the total $10,000 realized gain, even though she receives $10,000 of boot. Joan's sale of Asset 1 to North so as to recognize the loss might be advisable. See, however, the Sec. 267 loss limitation rules that may apply to Joan if she is a controlling shareholder (pages C:2-34 and C:2-35). ◀

COMPUTING A SHAREHOLDER'S BASIS.

Boot Property. A transferor's basis for any boot property received is the property's FMV.[28]

Stock. A shareholder computes his or her adjusted basis in stock received in a Sec. 351 exchange as follows:[29]

Adjusted basis of property transferred to the corporation	
Plus:	Any gain recognized by the transferor
Minus:	FMV of boot received from the corporation
	Money received from the corporation
	Liabilities assumed by the transferee corporation
Adjusted basis of stock received	

ADDITIONAL COMMENT

Because Sec. 351 is a deferral provision, any unrecognized gain must be reflected in the basis of the stock received by the transferor shareholder and is accomplished by substituting the transferor's basis in the property given up for the basis of the stock received. This substituted basis may be further adjusted by gain recognized and boot received.

EXAMPLE C:2-26 ▶ Bob transfers a capital asset having a $50,000 adjusted basis and an $80,000 FMV to South Corporation. He acquired the property two years earlier. Bob receives all 100 shares of South stock, having a $70,000 FMV, plus a $10,000 90-day South note (boot property). Bob realizes a $30,000 gain on the exchange, computed as follows:

FMV of stock received	$70,000
Plus: FMV of 90-day note	10,000
Amount realized	$80,000
Minus: Adjusted basis of property transferred	(50,000)
Realized gain	$30,000

Bob's recognized gain is $10,000, i.e.,the lesser of the $30,000 realized gain or the $10,000 FMV of the boot property. This gain is long-term capital in character. The Sec. 351 rules effectively require Bob to defer $20,000 ($30,000 − $10,000) of his realized gain. Bob's basis for the South stock is $50,000, computed as follows:

Adjusted basis of property transferred	$50,000
Plus: Gain recognized by Bob	10,000
Minus: FMV of boot received	(10,000)
Adjusted basis of Bob's stock	$50,000 ◀

SELF-STUDY QUESTION

What is an alternative method for determining the basis of the assets received by the transferor shareholder? How is this method applied to Bob in Example C:2-26?

[28] Sec. 358(a)(2).

[29] Sec. 358(a)(1).

If a transferor receives more than one class of qualified stock, his or her basis must be allocated among the classes of stock according to their relative FMVs.[30]

EXAMPLE C:2-27 ▶ Assume the same facts as in Example C:2-26 except Bob receives 100 shares of South common stock with a $45,000 FMV, 50 shares of South qualified preferred stock with a $25,000 FMV, and a 90-day South note with a $10,000 FMV. The total adjusted basis of the stock is $50,000 ($50,000 basis of property transferred + $10,000 gain recognized − $10,000 FMV of boot received). This basis must be allocated between the common and qualified preferred stock according to their relative FMVs, as follows:

$$\text{Basis of common stock} = \frac{\$45{,}000}{\$45{,}000 + \$25{,}000} \times \$50{,}000 = \$32{,}143$$

$$\text{Basis of preferred stock} = \frac{\$25{,}000}{\$45{,}000 + \$25{,}000} \times \$50{,}000 = \$17{,}857$$

Bob's basis for the note is its $10,000 FMV. ◀

ANSWER

The basis of all boot property is its FMV, and the basis of stock received is the stock's FMV minus any deferred gain or plus any deferred loss. Bob's stock basis under the alternative method is $50,000 ($70,000 FMV of stock − $20,000 deferred gain).

TRANSFEROR'S HOLDING PERIOD. The transferor's holding period for any stock received in exchange for a capital asset or Sec. 1231 property includes the holding period of the property transferred.[31] If the transferor exchanged any other kind of property (e.g., inventory) for the stock, the transferor's holding period for the stock begins on the day after the exchange. Likewise, the holding period for boot property begins on the day after the exchange.

EXAMPLE C:2-28 ▶ Assume the same facts as in Example C:2-26. Bob's holding period for the stock includes the holding period of the capital asset transferred. His holding period for the note starts on the day after the exchange. ◀

STOP & THINK

Question: The holding period for stock received in exchange for a capital asset or Sec. 1231 property includes the holding period of the transferred item. The holding period for inventory or other assets begins on the day after the exchange. Why the difference?

Solution: Because stock received in a Sec. 351 exchange represents a "continuity of interest" in the property transferred, the stock should not only be valued and characterized in the same manner as the asset exchanged for the equity claim, but also accorded the same tax attributes. Because the holding period of a capital asset is relevant in determining the character of gain or loss realized (i.e., long-term or short-term) on the asset's subsequent sale, stock received in a tax-free exchange of the asset should be accorded the same holding period for the purpose of determining the character of gain or loss realized on the stock's subsequent sale. By the same token, because the holding period of a noncapital asset is less relevant in determining the character of gain or loss realized on the asset's subsequent sale, stock received in a tax-free exchange of the asset need not be accorded the same holding period for the purpose of determining the character of gain or loss realized on the stock's subsequent sale. Given the very nature of a noncapital asset, this gain or loss generally is ordinary in character, in any event. Moreover, if stock received in exchange for a noncapital asset were accorded a holding period that includes that of the transferred property, a transferor could sell the stock in a short time to realize a long-term capital gain, thereby converting ordinary income (potentially from the sale of the noncapital asset) to capital gain from the sale of stock.

Topic Review C:2-2 summarizes the tax consequences of a Sec. 351 exchange to the transferor and the transferee corporation. Also see financial statement implications of forming a corporation later in this chapter.

---

[30] Sec. 358(b)(1) and Reg. Sec. 1.358-2(b)(2).

[31] Sec. 1223(1). Revenue Ruling 85-164 (1985-2 C.B. 117) provides that a single share of stock may have two holding periods: a carryover holding period for the portion of such share received in exchange for a capital asset or Sec. 1231 property and a holding period that begins on the day after the exchange for the portion of such share received for inventory or other property. The split holding period is relevant only if the transferor sells the stock received within one year of the transfer date.

Topic Review C:2-2

Tax Consequences of a Sec. 351 Exchange

To Shareholders:

1. Transferors recognize no gain or loss when they exchange property for stock. Exception: A transferor recognizes gain equal to the lesser of the realized gain or the sum of any money received plus the FMV of any non-cash property received. The character of the gain depends on the type of property transferred.
2. The basis of the stock received equals the adjusted basis of the property transferred plus any gain recognized by the transferor minus the FMV of any boot property received minus any money received (including liabilities assumed or acquired by the transferee corporation).
3. The holding period of stock received in exchange for capital assets or Sec. 1231 property includes the holding period of the transferred property. The holding period of stock received in exchange for any other property begins on the day after the exchange.

To Transferee Corporation:

1. A corporation recognizes no gain or loss when it exchanges its own stock for property or services.
2. The corporation's basis in property received is the transferor's basis plus any gain recognized by the transferor. However, if the total adjusted basis of all transferred property exceeds the total FMV of the property, the total basis to the transferee is limited to the property's total FMV.
3. The corporation's holding period for property received includes the transferor's holding period.

ADDITIONAL COMMENT

The nonrecognition rule for corporations that issue stock for property applies whether or not the transaction qualifies the transferor shareholder for Sec. 351 treatment.

TAX CONSEQUENCES TO TRANSFEREE CORPORATION

A corporation that issues stock or debt for property or services is subject to various IRC rules for determining the tax consequences of that exchange.

GAIN OR LOSS RECOGNIZED BY THE TRANSFEREE CORPORATION. Corporations recognize no gain or loss when they issue their own stock in exchange for property or services.[32] This rule applies whether or not Sec. 351 governs the exchange and whether or not the corporation issues new stock or treasury stock.

EXAMPLE C:2-29 ▶ West Corporation pays $10,000 to acquire 100 shares of its own stock from existing shareholders. The next year, West reissues these 100 treasury shares for land having a $15,000 FMV. West realizes a $5,000 ($15,000 − $10,000) gain on the exchange but recognizes none of this gain. ◀

Corporations also recognize no gain or loss when they exchange their own debt instruments for property or services. On the other hand, a corporation recognizes gain (but not loss) if it transfers appreciated property to a transferor as part of a Sec. 351 exchange. The amount and character of the gain are determined as though the property had been sold by the corporation immediately before the transfer.

EXAMPLE C:2-30 ▶ Alice, who owns 100% of Ace Corporation stock, transfers to Ace land having a $100,000 FMV and a $60,000 adjusted basis. In exchange, Alice receives 75 additional shares of Ace common stock having a $75,000 FMV, and Zero Corporation common stock having a $25,000 FMV. Ace's basis in the Zero stock, a capital asset, is $10,000. Alice realizes a $40,000 gain [($75,000 + $25,000) − $60,000] on the land transfer, of which $25,000 (i.e., the FMV of the boot property received) must be recognized. In addition, Ace recognizes a $15,000 capital gain ($25,000 − $10,000) upon transferring the Zero stock to Alice. ◀

TRANSFEREE CORPORATION'S BASIS FOR PROPERTY RECEIVED. A corporation that acquires property in exchange for its stock in a transaction that is taxable to the transferor takes a cost (i.e., its FMV) basis in the property. On the other hand, if the

32 Sec. 1032.

ADDITIONAL COMMENT

If a shareholder transfers built-in gain property in a Sec. 351 transaction, the built-in gain actually is duplicated. This duplication occurs because the transferee corporation assumes the potential gain through its carryover basis in the assets it receives, and the transferor shareholder assumes the potential gain through its substituted basis in the transferee corporation stock. A similar duplication occurs for built-in loss property. This result reflects the double taxation characteristic of C corporations.

exchange qualifies for nonrecognition treatment under Sec. 351 and is wholly or partially tax-free to the transferor, the corporation's basis for the property is computed as follows:[33]

Transferor's adjusted basis in property transferred to the corporation
Plus: Gain recognized by transferor (if any)
Minus: Reduction for loss property (if applicable)
Transferee corporation's basis in property

The transferee corporation's holding period for property acquired in a transaction satisfying the Sec. 351 requirements includes the period during which the property was held by the transferor.[34] This general rule applies to all types of property without regard for their character in the transferor's hands or the amount of gain recognized by the transferor. However, if the corporation reduces a property's basis to its FMV under the loss property limitation rule discussed below, the holding period will begin the day after the exchange date because no part of the new basis refers to the transferor's basis.

EXAMPLE C:2-31 ▶ Top Corporation issues 100 shares of its stock for land having a $15,000 FMV. Tina, who transferred the land, had a $12,000 basis in the property. If the exchange satisfies the Sec. 351 requirements, Tina recognizes no gain on the exchange. Top's basis in the land is $12,000, the same as Tina's basis. Top's holding period includes Tina's holding period. However, if the exchange does *not* satisfy the Sec. 351 requirements, Tina recognizes $3,000 of gain. Top's basis in the land is its $15,000 acquisition cost, and its holding period begins on the day after the exchange date. ◀

REDUCTION FOR LOSS PROPERTY. Section 362(e)(2) prevents shareholders from creating double losses by transferring loss property to a corporation. The double loss potential exists because the corporation would hold property with a built-in loss, and the shareholders would hold stock with a built-in loss. Accordingly, if a corporation's total adjusted basis for all properties transferred by a shareholder exceeds their total FMV, the basis to the corporation of the properties is limited to their total FMV. The reduction in basis must be allocated among the properties in proportion to their respective built-in losses. The limitation applies on a shareholder-by-shareholder basis. In other words, the property values and built-in losses of all shareholders are not aggregated.

EXAMPLE C:2-32 ▶ John transfers the following assets to Pecan Corporation in exchange for all of Pecan's stock worth $26,000.

Assets	*Adjusted Basis to John*	*FMV*
Inventory	$ 5,000	$ 8,000
Equipment	15,000	11,000
Furniture	9,000	7,000
Total	$29,000	$26,000

Although the transaction meets the requirements of Sec. 351, the total basis of the assets transferred ($29,000) exceeds their total FMV. Consequently, the total basis to Pecan is limited to the assets' FMV ($26,000). The $3,000 ($29,000 − $26,000) reduction in basis must be allocated among the assets in proportion to their respective built-in losses as follows:

Assets	*Built-in Losses*	*Allocated Reduction*
Equipment	$4,000	$2,000
Furniture	2,000	1,000
Total	$6,000	$3,000

[33] Sec. 362.

[34] Sec. 1223(2).

Thus, Pecan's bases for the assets transferred by John are:

Inventory	$ 5,000
Equipment ($15,000 – $2,000)	13,000
Furniture ($9,000 – $1,000)	8,000
Total	$26,000

Because each property's basis was not reduced to the property's FMV, the holding period of each property includes the tranferor's holding period. ◀

A corporation subject to the basis reduction rules described above can avoid this result if the corporation and all its shareholders so elect. Under the election, the corporation need not reduce the bases of the assets received, but the affected shareholder's basis in stock received for the property is reduced by the amount the corporation would have reduced its basis absent the election.

EXAMPLE C:2-33 ▶ Assume the same facts as in Example C:2-32 except John and Pecan elect not to reduce the bases of the assets Pecan received. Under the election, John's basis in his Pecan stock is reduced to $26,000 ($29,000 – $3,000). ◀

A corporation and its shareholders can avoid the basis reduction rules altogether if each shareholder transfers enough appreciated property to offset any losses built into the value of other property transferred. This avoidance opportunity exists because in making the comparison, each shareholder aggregates the adjusted bases and FMVs of his or her property transferred.

EXAMPLE C:2-34 ▶ Assume the same facts as in Example C:2-32 except the inventory's FMV is $12,000. In this case, total basis equals $29,000 and total FMV equals $30,000. Because total basis does not exceed total FMV, the limitation does not apply. Consequently, the corporation takes a carryover basis in each asset even though some assets have built-in losses. ◀

ASSUMPTION OF THE TRANSFEROR'S LIABILITIES

When a shareholder transfers property to a controlled corporation, the corporation often assumes the transferor's liabilities. The question arises as to whether the transferee corporation's assumption of liabilities is equivalent to a cash (boot) payment to the transferor. In certain types of transactions, the transferee's assumption of a transferor's liability is treated as a payment of cash to the transferor. For example, in a like-kind exchange, if a transferee assumes a transferor's liability, the transferor is treated as though he or she received a cash payment equal to the amount of the liability assumed. In contrast, if a transaction satisfies the Sec. 351 requirements, Sec. 357 provides relief from such treatment.

GENERAL RULE—SEC. 357(a). For the purpose of determining gain recognition, the transferee corporation's assumption of liabilities in a property transfer qualifying under Sec. 351 is *not* considered equivalent to the transferor's receipt of money. Consequently, the transferee corporation's assumption of liabilities does not result in the transferor's recognizing part or all of his or her realized gain. For the purpose of calculating the transferor's stock basis, however, the transferee corporation's assumption of liabilities *is* treated as money received and thus decreases the transferor's stock basis. Moreover, for the purpose of calculating the transferor's *realized* gain, the transferee corporation's assumption of liabilities is treated as part of the transferor's amount realized.[35]

EXAMPLE C:2-35 ▶ Roy and Eduardo transfer the following assets and liabilities to newly formed Palm Corporation:

[35] Sec. 358(d)(1).

Transferor	Asset/ Liability	Transferor's Adj. Basis	FMV	Consideration Received
Roy	Machinery	$15,000	$32,000	50 shares Palm stock
	Mortgage	8,000	—	Assumed by Palm
Eduardo	Cash	24,000	24,000	50 shares Palm stock

The transaction meets the requirements of Sec. 351. Roy's recognized gain is determined as follows:

FMV of stock received	$24,000
Plus: Palm's assumption of the mortgage liability	8,000
Amount realized	$32,000
Minus: Basis of machinery	(15,000)
Realized gain	$17,000
Boot received	$ -0-
Recognized gain	$ -0-

Although Palm's assumption of the mortgage liability increases Roy's amount realized, Roy recognizes none of his realized gain because the mortgage assumption is not considered to be boot for this purpose. Eduardo recognizes no gain because he transferred only cash. Roy's stock basis is $7,000 ($15,000 basis of property transferred − $8,000 liability assumed by Palm). Eduardo's stock basis is $24,000. ◀

ADDITIONAL COMMENT

If any of the assumed liabilities are created for tax avoidance purposes, *all* the assumed liabilities are tainted.

The general rule of Sec. 357(a), however, has two exceptions. These exceptions, discussed below, are (1) transfers for the purpose of tax avoidance or without a bona fide business purpose and (2) transfers where the liabilities assumed by the corporation exceed the total basis of the property transferred.

ETHICAL POINT

Information about any transferor liabilities assumed by the transferee corporation must be reported with the transferee and transferor's tax returns for the year of transfer (see page C:2-36). Where a client asks a tax practitioner to ignore the fact that tax avoidance is the primary purpose for transferring a liability to a corporation, the tax practitioner must examine the ethical considerations of continuing to prepare returns and provide tax advice for the client.

TAX AVOIDANCE OR NO BONA FIDE BUSINESS PURPOSE—SEC. 357(b). All liabilities assumed by a controlled corporation *are* considered money received by the transferor, and therefore boot, if the principal purpose of the transfer of any portion of such liabilities is tax avoidance or if the liability transfer has no bona fide business purpose.

Liabilities whose transfer might be considered to be motivated principally by tax avoidance are those the transferor incurred shortly before transferring the property and liabilities to the corporation. Perhaps the most important factor in determining whether a tax avoidance purpose exists is the length of time between the incurrence of the liability and the transfer of the liability to the corporation.

The assumption of liabilities normally is considered to have a business purpose if the transferor incurred the liabilities in the normal course of business or in the course of acquiring business property. Examples of liabilities without a bona fide business purpose and whose transfer would cause *all* liabilities transferred to be considered boot are personal obligations of the transferor, including a home mortgage or any other loans of a personal nature.

EXAMPLE C:2-36 ▶ David owns land having a $100,000 FMV and a $60,000 adjusted basis. The land is not encumbered by any liabilities. To obtain cash for his personal use, David transfers the land to his wholly owned corporation in exchange for additional stock and $25,000 cash. Because the cash is considered boot, David must recognize $25,000 of gain. Assume instead that David mortgages the land for $25,000 to obtain the needed cash. If shortly thereafter David transfers the land and the mortgage to his corporation for additional stock, the $25,000 mortgage assumed by the corporation is considered boot because the transfer of the mortgage appears to have no business purpose. David's recognized gain is $25,000, i.e., the lesser of the boot received ($25,000) or his realized gain ($40,000). The special liability rule prevents David from obtaining cash without boot recognition. ◀

LIABILITIES IN EXCESS OF BASIS—SEC. 357(c). Under Sec. 357(c), if the total amount of liabilities transferred to a controlled corporation exceeds the total adjusted basis of all property transferred, the excess liability is taxed as a gain to the transferor.

This rule applies regardless of whether the transferor realizes any gain or loss. The rule recognizes that the transferor has received a benefit (in the form of a release from liabilities) that exceeds his or her original investment in the transferred property. Therefore, the transferor should be taxed on this benefit. The character of the recognized gain depends on the type of property transferred to the corporation. The transferor's basis in any stock received is zero.

EXAMPLE C:2-37 ▶ Judy transfers $10,000 cash and land, a capital asset, to Duke Corporation in exchange for all its stock. At the time of the exchange, the land has a $70,000 adjusted basis and a $125,000 FMV. Duke assumes a $100,000 mortgage on the land for a bona fide business purpose. Although Judy receives no boot, Judy must recognize a $20,000 ($100,000 − $80,000) capital gain, the amount by which the liabilities assumed by Duke exceed the basis of the land and the cash. Judy's basis in the Duke stock is zero, computed as follows:

Judy's basis in the land transferred		$ 70,000
Plus:	Cash transferred	10,000
	Gain recognized	20,000
Minus:	Liabilities assumed by Duke	(100,000)
Judy's basis in the Duke stock		$ −0−

Note that, without the recogniton of the $20,000 gain, Judy's basis in the Duke stock would be a negative $20,000 ($80,000 − $100,000). ◀

STOP & THINK *Question:* What are the fundamental differences between the liability exceptions of Sec. 357(b) and Sec. 357(c)?

Solution: Section 357(b) treats all "tainted" liabilities as boot so that gain recognition is the lesser of gain realized or the amount of boot. Excess liabilities under Sec. 357(c) are not treated as boot; they require gain recognition whether or not the transferor realizes any gain. Section 357(b) tends to be punitive in that the "tax avoidance" liabilities cause all the "offending" shareholder's transferred liabilities to be treated as boot even if the transfer of some liabilities do not have a tax avoidance purpose. Section 357(c) is not intended to be punitive. It recognizes that the shareholder has received an economic benefit to the extent of excess liabilities, and it prevents the occurrence of a negative stock basis. In short, Section 357(b) deters or punishes tax avoidance while Sec. 357(c) taxes an economic gain.

KEY POINT

Because of the "liabilities in excess of basis" exception, many cash basis transferor shareholders might inadvertently create recognized gain in a Sec. 351 transaction. However, a special exception exists that protects cash basis taxpayers. This exception provides that liabilities that would give rise to a deduction when paid are not treated as liabilities for purposes of Sec. 357(c).

LIABILITIES OF A CASH METHOD TAXPAYER—SEC. 357(c)(3). In a Sec. 351 tax-free exchange, special problems arise when a taxpayer using the cash or hybrid method of accounting transfers property and liabilities of an ongoing business to a corporation.[36] Often, the principal assets transferred are accounts receivable having a zero basis. Liabilities usually are transferred as well. Consequently, the amount of liabilities transferred may exceed the total basis (but not the FMV) of the property transferred.

Under the general rule of Sec. 357(c), the transferor recognizes gain equal to the amount by which the liabilities assumed exceed the total basis of the property transferred. Section 357(c)(3), however, provides that, in applying the general rule, the term *liabilities* does *not* include any amount that would give rise to a deduction when paid. These amounts also are not considered liabilities for the purpose of determining the shareholder's basis in stock received.[37] Therefore, they generally do not reduce this basis. However, if after all other adjustments the stock's basis exceeds its FMV, these liabilities could reduce stock basis, but not below the stock's FMV.[38]

EXAMPLE C:2-38 ▶ Tracy operates a cash basis accounting practice as a sole proprietorship. She transfers the assets of her practice to Prime Corporation in exchange for all the Prime stock. The balance sheet for the transfered practice is as follows:

[36] Sec. 357(c)(3).
[37] Sec. 358(d)(2).
[38] Sec. 358(h)(1).

Assets and Liabilities	Adjusted Basis	FMV
Cash	$ 5,000	$ 5,000
Furniture	5,000	8,000
Accounts receivable	-0-	50,000
Total	$10,000	$63,000
Accounts payable (expenses)	$ -0-	$25,000
Note payable (on office furniture)	2,000	2,000
Owner's equity	8,000	36,000
Total	$10,000	$63,000

If, for purposes of Sec. 357(c), the accounts payable were considered liabilities, the $27,000 of liabilities transferred (i.e., the $25,000 of accounts payable and the $2,000 note payable) would exceed the $10,000 total basis of assets transferred. Because paying the $25,000 of accounts payable gives rise to a deduction, however, they are not considered liabilities for purposes of Sec. 357(c). On the other hand, the $2,000 note payable *is* considered a liability for this purpose because paying it would not give rise to a deduction. Thus, the total liabilities transferred to Prime amount to $2,000. Because that amount does not exceed the $10,000 total basis of the assets transferred, Tracy recognizes no gain. Moreover, the accounts payable are not considered liabilities for purposes of computing Tracy's basis in her stock because the stock's basis ($8,000) does not exceed its FMV ($36,000). Thus, her basis in the Prime stock is $8,000 ($10,000 − $2,000). ◀

Topic Review C:2-3 summarizes the liability assumption and acquisition rules of Sec. 357.

OTHER CONSIDERATIONS IN A SEC. 351 EXCHANGE

RECAPTURE OF DEPRECIATION. If a Sec. 351 exchange is completely nontaxable (i.e., the transferor receives no boot), no depreciation is recaptured. Instead, the corporation inherits the entire amount of the transferor's recapture potential. Where the transferor recognizes some depreciation recapture as ordinary income (e.g., because of boot recognition), the transferee inherits the remaining recapture potential. If the transferee corporation subsequently disposes of the depreciated property, the corporation is subject to recapture rules on depreciation it claimed subsequent to the transfer, plus the recapture potential it inherited from the transferor.

EXAMPLE C:2-39 ▶ Azeem transfers machinery having a $25,000 original cost, an $18,000 adjusted basis, and a $35,000 FMV for all 100 shares of Wheel Corporation's stock. Before the transfer, Azeem used the machinery in his business and claimed $7,000 of depreciation. In the transfer, Azeem recaptures no depreciation, and Wheel inherits the $7,000 recapture potential. After claiming an additional $2,000 of depreciation, Wheel has a $16,000 adjusted basis in the machinery. If

Topic Review C:2-3

Liability Assumption and Acquisition Rules of Sec. 357

1. *General Rule (Sec. 357(a)):* A transferee corporation's assumption of liabilities in a Sec. 351 exchange is not treated as boot by the shareholder for gain recognition purposes. On the other hand, the assumption of liabilities is treated as the receipt of money for purposes of determining the transferor's stock basis.
2. *Exception 1 (Sec. 357(b)):* All liabilities assumed by a transferee corporation *are* considered money/boot received by the transferor if the principal purpose of the transfer of any of the liabilities is tax avoidance or if no bona fide business purpose exists for the transfer.
3. *Exception 2 (Sec. 357(c)):* If the total amount of liabilities assumed by a transferee corporation exceeds the total basis of property transferred, the transferor recognizes the excess as gain.
4. *Special Rule (Sec. 357(c)(3)):* For purposes of Exception 2, the term *liabilities* for a transferor using a cash or hybrid method of accounting does not include any amount that would give rise to a deduction when paid.

Wheel now sells the machinery for $33,000, it must recognize a $17,000 ($33,000 − $16,000) gain. Of this gain, $9,000 is ordinary income recaptured under Sec. 1245. The remaining $8,000 is a Sec. 1231 gain. ◀

COMPUTING DEPRECIATION. When a shareholder transfers depreciable property to a corporation in a nontaxable Sec. 351 exchange and the shareholder has not fully depreciated the property, the corporation must use the depreciation method and recovery period used by the transferor.[39] For the year of the transfer, the depreciation must be allocated between the transferor and the transferee corporation according to the number of months each party held the property. The transferee corporation is assumed to have held the property for the entire month in which the property was transferred.[40]

EXAMPLE C:2-40 ▶ On June 10, 2006, Carla paid $6,000 for a computer (five-year property for MACRS purposes), which she used in her sole proprietorship business. In 2006, she claimed $1,200 (0.20 × $6,000) of depreciation and did not elect Sec. 179 expensing. On February 10, 2007, she transfers the computer and other sole proprietorship assets to King Corporation in exchange for King stock. Because Sec. 351 applies, she recognizes no gain or loss. King must use the same MACRS recovery period and method that Carla used. Depreciation for 2007 is $1,920 (0.32 × $6,000). That amount must be allocated between Carla and King. The computer is considered to have been held by Carla for one month and by King for 11 months (including the month of transfer). The 2007 depreciation amounts claimed by Carla and King are calculated as follows:

Carla	$6,000 × 0.32 × 1/12 = $ 160
King Corporation	$6,000 × 0.32 × 11/12 = $1,760

King's basis in the computer is calculated as follows:

Original cost	$6,000
Minus: 2006 depreciation claimed by Carla	(1,200)
2007 depreciation claimed by Carla	(160)
Adjusted basis on transfer date	$4,640

King's depreciation for 2007 and subsequent years is as follows:

2007 (as computed above)	$1,760
2008 ($6,000 × 0.1920)	1,152
2009 ($6,000 × 0.1152)	691
2010 ($6,000 × 0.1152)	691
2011 ($6,000 × 0.0576)	346
Total	$4,640 ◀

If the transferee corporation's basis in the depreciable property exceeds the transferor's basis (e.g., as a result of an upward adjustment to reflect gain recognized by the transferor), the corporation treats the excess amount as newly purchased MACRS property and uses the recovery period and method applicable to the class of property transferred.[41]

EXAMPLE C:2-41 ▶ Assume the same facts as in Example C:2-40 except that, in addition to King stock, Carla receives a King note. Consequently, she must recognize $1,000 of gain on the transfer of the computer. King's basis in the computer is calculated as follows:

Original cost	$6,000
Depreciation claimed by Carla	(1,360)
Adjusted basis on transfer date	$4,640
Plus: Gain recognized by Carla	1,000
Basis to King on transfer date	$5,640

The additional $1,000 of basis is depreciated as though it were separate, newly purchased five-year MACRS property. Thus, King claims depreciation of $200 (0.20 × $1,000) on this portion of

[39] Sec. 168(i)(7).

[40] Prop. Reg. Secs. 1.168-5(b)(2)(i)(B), 1.168-5(b)(4)(i), and 1.168-5(b)(8).

[41] Prop. Reg. Sec. 1.168-5(b)(7).

ADDITIONAL COMMENT

Currently, we have no clear guidance on how the corporation depreciates transferred property that has a reduced basis under the loss property limitation rule discussed on page C:2-21. For now, taxpayers probably should rely on Prop. Reg. 1.168-2(d)(3), which provides a method for calculating depreciation when the transferee's basis is less than the transferor's basis.

the basis in addition to the $1,760 of depreciation on the $4,640 carryover basis. Alternatively, King could elect to expense the $1,000 "new" basis under Sec. 179. ◀

ASSIGNMENT OF INCOME DOCTRINE. The **assignment of income doctrine** holds that income be taxed to the person who earns it and that it may not be assigned to another for tax purposes.[42] The question arises as to whether the assignment of income doctrine applies where a cash method taxpayer transfers uncollected accounts receivable to a corporation in a Sec. 351 exchange. Specifically, who must recognize the income when it is collected—the taxpayer who transferred the receivable or the corporation that now owns and collects on the receivable? The IRS has ruled that the doctrine does *not* apply in a Sec. 351 exchange if the taxpayer transfers substantially all the business assets and liabilities, and a bona fide business purpose exists for the transfer. Instead, the accounts receivable take a zero basis in the corporation's hands, and the corporation includes their value in its income when it collects on the receivables.[43]

EXAMPLE C:2-42 ▶ For a bona fide business purpose, Ruth, a lawyer who uses the cash method, transfers all the assets and liabilities of her legal practice to Legal Services Corporation in exchange for all of Legal Services' stock. The assets include $30,000 of accounts receivable that will generate earnings that Ruth has not included in her gross income. The assignment of income doctrine does not apply to the receivables transfer, and Legal Services takes a zero basis in the receivables. Subsequently, Legal Services includes the value of the receivables in its income as it collects on them. ◀

The question of whether a transferee corporation can deduct the accounts payable transferred to it in a nontaxable transfer has frequently been litigated.[44] Most courts have held that ordinarily expenses are deductible only by the party that incurred those liabilities in the course of its trade or business. However, the IRS has ruled that in a nontaxable exchange the transferee corporation may deduct the payments it makes to satisfy the transferred accounts payable even though they arose in the transferor's business.[45]

CHOICE OF CAPITAL STRUCTURE

OBJECTIVE 5

Understand the tax implications of alternative capital structures

When a corporation is formed, decisions must be made as to its capital structure. The corporation may obtain capital from shareholders, nonshareholders, and creditors. In exchange for their capital, shareholders may receive common or preferred stock; nonshareholders may receive benefits such as employment or special rates on items produced by the corporation; and creditors may receive long- or short-term debt. Each of these alternatives has tax advantages and disadvantages for the shareholders, creditors, and corporation.

CHARACTERIZATION OF OBLIGATIONS AS DEBT OR EQUITY

The deductibility of interest payments provides an incentive for corporations to incur as much debt as possible. Because debt financing often resembles equity financing (e.g., preferred stock), the IRS and the courts have refused to accept the form of the obligation as controlling.[46] In some cases, debt obligations that possess equity characteristics have been treated as common or preferred stock for tax purposes. In determining the appropriate tax treatment, the courts have relied on no single factor.

---

42 See, for example, *Lucas v. Guy C. Earl,* 8 AFTR 10287, 2 USTC ¶496 (USSC, 1930).

43 Rev. Rul. 80-198, 1980-2 C.B. 113.

44 See, for example, *Wilford E. Thatcher v. CIR,* 37 AFTR 2d 76-1068, 76-1 USTC ¶9324 (9th Cir., 1976), and *John P. Bongiovanni v. CIR,* 31 AFTR 2d 73-409, 73-1 USTC ¶9133 (2nd Cir., 1972).

45 Rev. Rul. 80-198, 1980-2 C.B. 113.

46 See, for example, *Aqualane Shores, Inc. v. CIR,* 4 AFTR 2d 5346, 59-2 USTC ¶9632 (5th Cir., 1959) and *Sun Properties, Inc. v. U.S.,* 47 AFTR 273, 55-1 USTC ¶9261 (5th Cir., 1955).

In 1969, Congress enacted Sec. 385 to establish a workable standard for determining whether an obligation is debt or equity. Section 385 provides that the following factors be considered in the determination:

HISTORICAL NOTE

The Treasury Department at one time issued proposed and final regulations covering Sec. 385. These regulations were the subject of so much criticism that the Treasury Department eventually withdrew them. The 1989 amendment to Sec. 385 makes it clear that Congress wants the Treasury Department to make another attempt at clarifying the debt-equity issue. So far, the Treasury Department has issued no "new" proposed or final regulations.

- Whether there is a written unconditional promise to pay on demand or on a specified date a certain sum of money in return for adequate consideration in the form of money or money's worth, in addition to an unconditional promise to pay a fixed rate of interest
- Whether the debt is subordinate to, or preferred over, other indebtedness of the corporation
- The ratio of debt to equity of the corporation
- Whether the debt is convertible into stock of the corporation
- The relationship between holdings of stock in the corporation and holdings of the interest in question[47]

DEBT CAPITAL

Tax laws govern (1) the issuance of debt; (2) the payment of interest on debt; and (3) the extinguishment, retirement, or worthlessness of debt. The tax implications of each of these occurrences are examined below.

SELF-STUDY QUESTION

From a tax perspective, why is the distinction between debt and equity important?

ANSWER

Interest paid with respect to a debt instrument is deductible by the payor corporation. Dividends paid with respect to an equity instrument are not deductible by the payor corporation. Thus, the determination of whether an instrument is debt or equity can provide different results to the payor corporation. Different results apply to the payee as well. Qualified dividends are subject to the 15% maximum tax rate (through 2010) while interest is ordinary income.

ISSUANCE OF DEBT. Under Sec. 351, appreciated assets may be exchanged tax-free for stock, provided the transferors control the transferee corporation immediately after the exchange. On the other hand, if the transferor transfers assets for corporate debt instruments as part of a Sec. 351 exchange or independently of such an exchange, the FMV of the debt received is treated as taxable boot.

PAYMENT OF INTEREST. Interest paid on indebtedness is deductible by the corporation in deriving taxable income.[48] Moreover, a corporation is not subject to the limitations on interest deductions applicable to individual taxpayers (e.g., investment interest). In contrast, the corporation cannot deduct dividends paid on equity securities.

If a corporation issues a debt instrument at a discount, Sec. 1272 requires the holder to amortize the original issue discount over the term of the obligation and treat the accrual as interest income. The debtor corporation amortizes the original issue discount over the term of the obligation and treats the accrual as an additional cost of borrowing.[49] If the corporation repurchases the debt instrument for more than the issue price (plus any original issue discount deducted as interest), the corporation deducts the excess of the purchase price over the issue price (adjusted for any amortization of original issue discount) as interest expense.[50]

If a corporation issues a debt instrument at a premium, Sec. 171 permits the holder to elect to amortize the premium over the term of the obligation and treat the accrual as a reduction in interest income earned on the obligation. The debtor corporation must amortize the premium over the term of the obligation and treat the accrual as additional interest income.[51] If the corporation repurchases the debt instrument at a price greater than the issue price (minus any premium reported as income), the corporation deducts the excess of the purchase price over the issue price (adjusted for any amortization of premium) as interest expense.[52]

EXTINGUISHMENT OF DEBT. Generally, the retirement of debt is not a taxable event. Thus, a debtor corporation's extinguishing an obligation at face value does not result in the creditor's recognizing gain or loss. However, amounts received by the holder

---

[47] See also *O.H. Kruse Grain & Milling v. CIR*, 5 AFTR 2d 1544, 60-2 USTC ¶9490 (9th Cir., 1960), which lists additional factors that the courts might consider.

[48] Sec. 163(a).

[49] Sec. 163(e).

[50] Reg. Sec. 1.163-7(c).

[51] Reg. Sec. 1.61-12(c)(2).

[52] Reg. Sec. 1.163-7(c).

of a debt instrument (e.g., note, bond, or debenture) at the time of its retirement are deemed to be "in exchange for" the obligation. Thus, if the obligation is a capital asset in the holder's hands, the holder must recognize a capital gain or loss if the amount received differs from its face value or adjusted basis, unless the difference is due to original issue or market discount.

EXAMPLE C:2-43 ▶ Titan Corporation issues a ten-year note at its $1,000 face amount. On the date of issuance, Rick purchases the note for $1,000. Because of a decline in interest rates, Titan calls the note at a price of $1,050 payable to each note holder. Rick reports the premium as a $50 capital gain, and Titan deducts total premiums paid as interest expense. ◀

ADDITIONAL COMMENT

Even though debt often is thought of as a preferred instrument because of the deductibility of the interest paid, the debt must be repaid at its maturity, whereas stock has no specified maturity date. Also, interest usually must be paid at regular intervals, whereas dividends do not have to be declared if sufficient funds are not available.

Table C:2-2 presents a comparison of the tax advantages and disadvantages of using debt in the capital structure.

EQUITY CAPITAL

Corporations can raise equity capital through the issuance of various types of securities. Some corporations issue only a single class of stock, whereas others issue numerous classes of stock. Reasons for the use of multiple classes of stock include

- Permitting nonfamily employees of family owned corporations to obtain an equity interest in the business while keeping voting control in the hands of family members
- Financing a **closely held corporation** through the issuance of preferred stock to an outside investor or wealthy individual, while leaving voting control in the hands of existing common stockholders.

Table C:2-3 lists some of the major tax advantages and disadvantages of using common and preferred stock in a corporation's capital structure.

SELF-STUDY QUESTION

Does the transferee corporation recognize gain on the receipt of appreciated property from a shareholder?

ANSWER

No. A corporation does not recognize gain when it receives property from its shareholders, whether or not it exchanges its own stock. However, the transfer must qualify as a Sec. 351 exchange or the transaction will be taxable to the shareholders.

CAPITAL CONTRIBUTIONS BY SHAREHOLDERS

A corporation recognizes no income when it receives money or noncash property as a capital contribution from a shareholder.[53] If the shareholders make voluntary pro rata payments to a corporation but do not receive any additional stock, the payments are treated as additional consideration for the stock already owned.[54] The shareholders' respective bases in their stock are increased by the amount of money contributed, plus the basis of any noncash property contributed, and plus any gain recognized by the shareholders. The

▼ TABLE C:2-2

Tax Advantages and Disadvantages of Using Debt in a Corporation's Capital Structure

Advantages:

1. A corporation can deduct interest paid on a debt obligation.
2. Shareholders do not recognize income when they receive a debt repayment as they would in a stock redemption.

Disadvantages:

1. If at the time the corporation is formed or later when a shareholder makes a capital contribution, the shareholder receives a debt instrument in exchange for property, the debt is treated as boot, and the shareholder recognizes gain to the extent of the lesser of the boot received or the realized gain.
2. If debt becomes worthless or is sold at less than its face value, the loss generally is a nonbusiness bad debt (treated as a short-term capital loss) or a capital loss. Section 1244 ordinary loss treatment applies only to stock (see pages C:2-32 and C:2-33).

[53] Sec. 118(a).

[54] Reg. Sec. 1.118-1.

▼ **TABLE C:2-3**

Tax Advantages and Disadvantages of Using Equity in a Corporation's Capital Structure

Advantages:

1. A 70%, 80%, or 100% dividends-received deduction is available to a corporate shareholder who receives dividends. A similar deduction is not available for the receipt of interest (see Chapter C:3).
2. A shareholder can receive common and preferred stock in a tax-free corporate formation under Sec. 351 or a nontaxable reorganization under Sec. 368 without recognizing gain (see Chapters C:2 and C:7, respectively). Receipt of debt obligations in each of these two types of transactions generally results in the shareholder's recognizing gain.
3. Common and preferred stock can be distributed tax-free to the corporation's shareholders as a stock dividend. Some common and preferred stock distributions, however, may be taxable as dividends under Sec. 305(b). Distributions of debt obligations generally are taxable as a dividend (see Chapter C:4).
4. Common or preferred stock that the shareholder sells or exchanges or that becomes worthless is eligible for limited ordinary loss treatment under Sec. 1244 (see pages C:2-32 and C:2-33). The loss recognized on similar transactions involving debt obligations generally is treated as capital in character.
5. Section 1202 permits a 50% capital gains exclusion on the sale or exchange of qualified small business (C) corporation stock that has been held for more than five years.
6. For years 2003 through 2010, qualified dividends are taxed at a maximum 15% tax rate.

Disadvantages:

1. Dividends are not deductible in determining a corporation's taxable income.
2. Redemption of common or preferred stock generally is taxable to the shareholders as a dividend. Under the general rule, none of the redemption distribution offsets the shareholder's basis for the stock investment. Redemption of common and preferred stock by the issuing corporation is eligible for exchange treatment only in certain situations specified in Secs. 302 and 303 (see Chapter C:4).
3. Preferred stock received by a shareholder as a nontaxable stock dividend may be treated as Sec. 306 stock. Sale, exchange, or redemption of such stock can result in the recognition of ordinary income instead of capital gain (see Chapter C:4).

TYPICAL MISCONCEPTION

The characteristics of preferred stock can be similar to those of a debt security. Often, a regular dividend is required at a stated rate, much like what would be required with respect to a debt obligation. The holder of preferred stock, like a debt holder, may have preferred liquidation rights over holders of common stock. Also, preferred stock is not required to possess voting rights. However, differences remain. A corporation can deduct its interest expense but not dividends. Interest income is ordinary income to shareholders, but qualified dividends are subject to the 15% maximum tax rate (through 2010).

corporation's basis in any property received as a capital contribution from a shareholder equals the shareholder's basis plus any gain recognized by the shareholder.[55] Normally, the shareholders recognize no gain when they transfer property to a controlled corporation as a capital contribution.

EXAMPLE C:2-44 ▶ **Dot and Fred own equally all of Trail Corporation's stock, and each has a $50,000 basis in that stock. Later, as a voluntary contribution to Trail's capital, Dot contributes $40,000 in cash and Fred contributes property having a $25,000 basis and a $40,000 FMV. As a result of the contributions, Trail recognizes no income. Dot's basis in her stock is increased to $90,000 ($50,000 + $40,000), and Fred's basis in his stock is increased to $75,000 ($50,000 + $25,000). Trail's basis in the property contributed by Fred is $25,000—the same as Fred's basis in the property.** ◀

If a shareholder-lender gratuitously forgives corporate debt, the debt forgiveness might be treated as a capital contribution equal to the principal amount of the forgiven debt. A determination of whether debt forgiveness is a capital contribution is based on the facts and circumstances of the event.

[55] Sec. 362(a).

WHAT WOULD YOU DO IN THIS SITUATION?

You are a CPA who has a corporate client that wants to issue 100-year bonds. The corporation's CEO reads *The Wall Street Journal* regularly and has observed that similar bonds have been issued by several companies, including Coca-Cola and Disney. He touts the fact that the interest rate on these bonds is little more than 30-year U.S. Treasury bonds. In addition, he expresses the belief that interest on the bonds would be deductible, whereas dividends paid on preferred or common stock would be nondeductible. You are concerned that the IRS might treat the bonds as equity because of their extraordinarily long term. If the IRS does, it might recharacterize the "interest" as dividends and deny an interest deduction.

Your CPA firm is advising the client on the prospective bond issue. What advice would you give the client now and when preparing its tax return after the new bonds have been issued?

CAPITAL CONTRIBUTIONS BY NONSHAREHOLDERS

BOOK-TO-TAX ACCOUNTING COMPARISON

The IRC requires capital contributions of property other than money made by a nonshareholder to be reported at a zero basis. Financial accounting rules, however, require donated capital to be reported at the FMV of the asset on the financial accounting books. Neither set of rules requires the property's value to be included in income.

Nonshareholders sometimes contribute capital to a corporation in the form of money or other property. For example, a city government might contribute land to a corporation to induce the corporation to locate within the city and provide jobs for citizens of the municipality. Such contributions are excluded from the corporation's gross income if the money or property contributed is neither a payment for goods or services nor a subsidy to induce the corporation to limit production.[56]

If a nonshareholder contributes noncash property to a corporation, the corporation's basis in such property is zero.[57] The zero basis precludes the corporation from claiming either a depreciation deduction or capital recovery offset with respect to the contributed property.

If a nonshareholder contributes money, the basis of any property acquired with the money during a 12-month period beginning on the day the corporation received the contribution is reduced by the amount of the money. This rule limits the corporation's deduction to the amount of funds it invested in the property. The amount of any money received from nonshareholders that the corporation did not spend to purchase property during the 12-month period reduces the basis of any noncash property held by the corporation on the last day of the 12-month period.[58]

The basis reduction applies to the corporation's property in the following order:

1. Depreciable property
2. Amortizable property
3. Depletable property
4. All other property

As a result of these downward adjustments, a property's basis may not be reduced below zero.

EXAMPLE C:2-45 ▶ To induce the company to locate there, the City of San Antonio contributes to Circle Corporation $100,000 in cash and a tract of land having a $500,000 FMV. Because of a downturn in Circle's business, the company spends only $70,000 of the contributed funds over a 12-month period. Circle recognizes no income as a result of the contribution. Circle's bases in the land and other property purchased with the contributed funds are zero. The basis of Circle's remaining assets, starting with its depreciable property, must be reduced by the $30,000 ($100,000 − $70,000) contributed but not spent. ◀

[56] Reg. Sec. 1.118-1.

[57] Sec. 362(c)(1).

[58] Sec. 362(c)(2).

WORTHLESSNESS OF STOCK OR DEBT OBLIGATIONS

OBJECTIVE 6

Determine the tax consequences of worthless stock or debt obligations

Investors who purchase stock in, or lend money to, a corporation usually intend to earn a profit and recover their investment. Some investments, however, do not offer an adequate return on capital, and an investor may lose part or all of the investment. When this event occurs, the securities evidencing the investment become worthless. This section examines the tax consequences of stock or debt securities becoming worthless.

SECURITIES

A debt or equity security that becomes worthless results in a capital loss for the investor as of the last day of the tax year in which the security becomes worthless. For purposes of this rule, the term *security* includes (1) a share of stock in a corporation; (2) a right to subscribe for, or the right to receive, a share of stock in a corporation; or (3) a bond, debenture, note, or other evidence of indebtedness with interest coupons or in registered form issued by a corporation.[59]

TYPICAL MISCONCEPTION

Probably the most difficult aspect of deducting a loss on a worthless security is establishing that the security is actually worthless. A mere decline in value is not sufficient to create a loss. The burden of proof of establishing total worthlessness rests with the taxpayer.

In some situations, investors recognize an ordinary loss when a security becomes worthless. Investors who contribute capital, either in the form of equity or debt to a corporation that later fails, generally prefer ordinary losses because such losses are deductible against ordinary income. Ordinary losses that generate an NOL can be carried back two years or forward up to 20 years. Ordinary loss treatment generally is available in the following circumstances:

- *Securities that are noncapital assets.* An ordinary loss occurs when a security that is a noncapital asset in the hands of the taxpayer is sold or exchanged or becomes totally worthless. Securities in this category include those held as inventory by a securities dealer.
- *Affiliated corporations.* A domestic corporation can claim an ordinary loss for any security of an affiliated corporation that becomes worthless during the tax year. The domestic corporation must own at least 80% of the total voting power of all classes of stock entitled to vote, and at least 80% of each class of nonvoting stock (other than stock limited and preferred as to dividends). At least 90% of the aggregate gross receipts of the loss corporation for all tax years must have been derived from nonpassive income sources.
- *Section 1244 stock.* Section 1244 permits a shareholder to claim an ordinary loss if qualifying stock issued by a small business corporation is sold or exchanged or becomes worthless. This treatment is available only to an individual who was issued the qualifying stock or who was a partner in a partnership at the time the partnership acquired the qualifying stock. In the latter case, the partner's distributive share of partnership losses includes the loss sustained by the partnership on such stock. Ordinary loss treatment is not available for stock inherited, received as a gift, or purchased from another shareholder. The ordinary loss is limited to $50,000 per year (or $100,000 if the taxpayer is married and files a joint return). Losses exceeding the dollar ceiling in any given year are considered capital in character.

SELF-STUDY QUESTION

Why would a shareholder want his or her stock to qualify as Sec. 1244 stock?

ANSWER

Section 1244 is a provision that may help the taxpayer but that can never hurt. If the Sec. 1244 requirements are satisfied, the individual shareholders of a small business corporation may treat losses from the sale or worthlessness of their stock as ordinary rather than capital losses. If the Sec. 1244 requirements are not satisfied, such losses generally are capital losses.

EXAMPLE C:2-46 ▶

Tammy and her husband Cole purchased 25% of the initial offering of Minor Corporation's single class of stock for $175,000. Minor is a small business corporation, and the Minor stock satisfies all the Sec. 1244 requirements. On September 1 of the current year Minor filed for bankruptcy. Two years later, the bankruptcy court notifies shareholders that the Minor stock is worthless. In that year, Tammy and Cole can deduct $100,000 of their initial investment as an ordinary loss. The remaining $75,000 loss is capital in character. ◀

If a corporation issues Sec. 1244 stock for property whose adjusted basis exceeds its FMV immediately before the exchange, the stock's basis is reduced to the property's FMV for the purpose of determining the ordinary loss amount.

[59] Sec. 165(g).

EXAMPLE C:2-47 ▶ In a Sec. 351 nontaxable exchange, Penny transfers to Small Corporation property having a $40,000 adjusted basis and a $32,000 FMV for 100 shares of Sec. 1244 stock. Ordinarily, Penny's basis in the stock would be $40,000. However, for Sec. 1244 purposes, her stock basis is the property's FMV, or $32,000. If Penny sells the stock for $10,000, her recognized loss is $30,000 ($10,000 – $40,000). Her ordinary loss under Sec. 1244 is $22,000 ($10,000 – $32,000 Sec. 1244 basis). The remaining $8,000 loss is capital in character. (Note also that Small would reduce its basis in the transferred property to its $32,000 FMV under Sec. 362(e)(2).) ◀

Section 1244 loss treatment requires no special election. Investors, however, should be aware that, if they fail to satisfy certain requirements, ordinary loss treatment will be unavailable, and their loss will be capital in character. The requirements are as follows:

- ▶ The issuing corporation must be a small business corporation at the time it issues the stock. A small business corporation is a corporation that receives in the aggregate $1 million or less in money or noncash property (other than stock and securities) in exchange for its stock.[60]
- ▶ The issuing corporation must have derived more than 50% of its aggregate gross receipts from "active" sources (i.e., other than royalties, rents, dividends, interest, annuities, and gains on sales of stock and securities) during the five most recent tax years ending before the date on which the shareholder sells or exchanges the stock or the stock becomes worthless.

TAX STRATEGY TIP

If a shareholder contributes additional money or property to an existing corporation, he or she should be sure to receive additional stock in the exchange so that it will qualify for Sec. 1244 treatment if all requirements are met. If the shareholder does not receive additional stock, the increased basis of existing stock resulting from the capital contribution will not qualify for Sec. 1244 treatment.

If a shareholder contributes additional money or property to a corporation after acquiring Sec. 1244 stock, the amount of ordinary loss recognized on the sale, exchange, or worthlessness of the Sec. 1244 stock is limited to the shareholder's capital contribution at the time the corporation issued the stock.

UNSECURED DEBT OBLIGATIONS

In addition to holding an equity interest, shareholders may lend money to the corporation. The type of loss allowed if the corporation does not repay the borrowed funds depends on the nature of the loan or advance.

If the unpaid loan was not evidenced by a security (i.e., an unsecured debt obligation), it is considered to be either business or nonbusiness bad debt. Nonbusiness bad debts are treated less favorably than business bad debts. Under Sec. 166, nonbusiness bad debts are deductible as short-term capital losses (up to the $3,000 annual limit for net capital losses) when they become totally worthless. Business bad debts are deductible as ordinary losses without limitation when they become either partially or totally worthless. The IRS generally treats a loan made by a shareholder to a corporation in connection with his or her stock investment as a nonbusiness advance.[61] It is understandable why a shareholder might attempt to rebut this presumption with the argument that a business purpose exists for the loan.

An advance in connection with the shareholder's trade or business, such as a loan to protect the shareholder's employment at the corporation, may be treated as an ordinary loss under the business bad debt rules. Regulation Sec. 1.166-5(b) states that whether a bad debt is business or nonbusiness related depends on the taxpayer's motive for making the advance. The debt is business related if the necessary relationship between the loss and the conduct of the taxpayer's trade or business exists at the time the debt was incurred, acquired, or became worthless.

In *U.S. v. Edna Generes,* the U.S. Supreme Court held that where multiple motives exist for advancing funds to a corporation, such as where a shareholder-employee advances funds to protect his or her employment, determining whether the advance is business or nonbusiness related must be based on the "dominant motivation" for the

[60] Regulation Sec. 1.1244(c)-2 provides special rules for designating which shares of stock are eligible for Sec. 1244 treatment when the corporation has issued more than $1 million of stock.

[61] The assumption is made here that the loan is not considered to be an additional capital contribution. In such a case, the Sec. 165 worthless security rules apply instead of the Sec. 166 bad debt rules.

KEY POINT

In many closely held corporations, the shareholders are also employees. Thus, when a shareholder-employee makes a loan to the corporation, a question arises whether the loan is being made in the individual's capacity as an employee or a shareholder. The distinction is important because an employee loan that is worthless is entitled to ordinary loss treatment, whereas a shareholder loan that is worthless is treated as a nonbusiness bad debt (short-term capital loss).

advance.[62] If the advance is only "significantly motivated" by considerations relating to the taxpayer's trade or business, such motivation will not establish a proximate relationship between the bad debt and the taxpayer's trade or business. Therefore, it may result in a nonbusiness bad debt characterization. On the other hand, if the advance is dominantly motivated by considerations relating to the taxpayer's trade or business, such motivation usually is sufficient to establish such a proximate relationship. Therefore, it may result in a business bad debt characterization.

Factors deemed important in determining the character of bad debt include the taxpayer's equity in the corporation relative to compensation paid by the corporation. For example, a modest salary paid by the corporation relative to substantial stockholdings in the corporation suggests an investment motive for the advance. Conversely, a substantial salary paid by the corporation relative to modest stockholdings suggests a business motive for the advance. The business motive at issue is the protection of the employee-lender's employment because the advance may help save the business from failing. Reasonable minds may differ on what is substantial and what is modest, and monetary stakes often are quite high in these cases. Consequently, the determination frequently requires litigation.

EXAMPLE C:2-48 ▶ Top Corporation employs Mary as its legal counsel. It pays Mary an annual salary of $100,000. In March of the current year, Mary advances the corporation $50,000 to assist it financially. In October of the current year, Top declares bankruptcy and liquidates. In the liquidation, Mary and other investors receive 10 cents on every dollar advanced. If Mary can show that her advance was dominantly motivated by her employment, her $45,000 ($50,000 × 0.90) loss will be treated as business bad debt, ordinary in character, and fully deductible in the current year. On the other hand, if Mary shows only that the advance was significantly motivated by her employment, her $45,000 loss will be treated as nonbusiness bad debt, capital in character, and deductible in this year and in subsequent years only to the extent of $3,000 in excess of any capital gains she recognizes. ◀

ADDITIONAL COMMENT

For the act of lending money to a corporation to be considered the taxpayer's trade or business, the taxpayer must show that he or she was individually in the business of seeking out, promoting, organizing, and financing business ventures. *Ronald L. Farrington v. CIR*, 65 AFTR 2d 90-617, 90-1 USTC ¶50,125 (DC, OK, 1990).

A loss sustained by a shareholder who guarantees a loan made by a third party to the corporation generally is treated as a nonbusiness bad debt. The loss can be claimed only to the extent the shareholder actually pays the third party and is unable to recover the payment from the debtor corporation.[63] Occasionally, the IRS treats the amount of a shareholder advance as additional paid in capital. In such circumstances, any worthless security loss the shareholder claims for his or her equity investment may be increased by this amount.

TAX PLANNING CONSIDERATIONS

SELF-STUDY QUESTION

Which tax provisions may potentially limit a transferor shareholder from recognizing a loss on the transfer of property to a corporation?

ANSWER

Such transfer cannot be to a controlled corporation, or Sec. 351 will defer the loss. Even if Sec. 351 can be avoided, losses on sales between a corporation and a more than 50% shareholder are disallowed under Sec. 267. Thus, to recognize a loss on the sale of property, such shareholder must, directly or indirectly, own 50% or less of the transferee corporation's stock.

AVOIDING SEC. 351

Section 351 is not an elective provision. If its conditions are met, a corporate formation is tax-free, even if the taxpayer does not want it to be. Most often, taxpayers desire Sec. 351 treatment because it allows them to defer gains when transferring appreciated property to a corporation. In some cases, however, shareholders find such treatment disadvantageous because they would like to recognize gain or loss on the property transferred.

AVOIDING NONRECOGNITION OF LOSSES UNDER SEC. 351. If a shareholder transfers to a corporation property that has declined in value, the shareholder may want to recognize the loss so it can offset income from other sources. The shareholder can recognize the loss only if the Sec. 351 nonrecognition rules and the Sec. 267 related party rules do not apply to the exchange.

Avoiding Sec. 351 treatment requires that one or more of its requirements not be met. The simplest way to accomplish this objective is to ensure that the transferors of property do not receive 80% of the voting stock.

62 29 AFTR 2d 72-609, 72-1 USTC ¶9259 (USSC, 1972).

63 Reg. Sec. 1.166-8(a).

Even if a shareholder avoids Sec. 351 treatment, he or she still may not be able to recognize the losses because of the Sec. 267 related party transaction rules. Under Sec. 267(a)(1), if the shareholder owns more than 50% of the corporation's stock, directly or indirectly, he or she is a related party and therefore cannot recognize loss on an exchange of property for the corporation's stock or other property. If the transferors of property receive less than 80% of the corporation's voting stock and if the transferor of loss property does not own more than 50% of the stock, the transferor of loss property may recognize the loss.

EXAMPLE C:2-49 ▶ Lynn owns property having a $100,000 basis and a $60,000 FMV. If Lynn transfers the property to White Corporation in a tax-free exchange under Sec. 351, she will not recognize a loss, which will be deferred until she sells her White stock. If the Sec. 351 requirements are not met, she will recognize a $40,000 loss in the year she transfers the property. If Lynn receives 50% of the White stock in exchange for her property, Cathy, an unrelated individual, receives 25% of the stock in exchange for $30,000 cash, and John, another unrelated individual, receives the remaining 25% for services performed, the Sec. 351 control requirement will not be met because the transferors of property receive less than 80% of the White stock. Moreover, Lynn will not be a related party under Sec. 267 because she will not own more than 50% of the stock either directly or indirectly. Therefore, Lynn will recognize a $40,000 loss on the exchange. ◀

ADDITIONAL COMMENT

Any potential built-in gain on property transferred to the transferee corporation is duplicated because such gain may be recognized at the corporate level and at the shareholder level. This double taxation may be another reason for avoiding the nonrecognition of gain under Sec. 351.

AVOIDING NONRECOGNITION OF GAIN UNDER SEC. 351. Sometimes a transferor would like to recognize gain when he or she transfers appreciated property to a corporation so the transferee corporation can get a stepped-up basis in the transferred property. Some other reasons for recognizing gain are as follows:

- ▶ If the transferor's gain is capital in character, he or she can offset this gain with capital losses from other transactions.
- ▶ Individual long-term capital gains are taxed at a maximum 15% rate (for years 2003 through 2010). This rate is below the 35% top marginal tax rate applicable to corporate-level capital gains.
- ▶ The corporation's marginal tax rate may be higher than a noncorporate transferor's marginal tax rate. In such case, it might be beneficial for the transferor to recognize gain so the corporation can get a stepped-up basis in the property. A stepped-up basis would either reduce the corporation's gain when it later sells the property or allow the corporation to claim greater depreciation deductions when it uses the property.

A transferor who does not wish to recognize gain on the transfer of appreciated property to a corporation can avoid Sec. 351 treatment through one of the following planning techniques:

- ▶ The transferor can sell the property to the controlled corporation for cash.
- ▶ The transferor can sell the property to the controlled corporation for cash and debt. This transaction involves relatively less cash than the previous transaction. However, the sale may be treated as a nontaxable exchange if the IRS recharacterizes the debt as equity.[64]
- ▶ The transferor can sell the property to a third party for cash and have the third party contribute the property to the corporation for stock.
- ▶ The transferor can have the corporation distribute sufficient boot property so that, even if Sec. 351 applies to the transaction, he or she will recognize gain.
- ▶ The transferors can fail one or more of the Sec. 351 tests. For example, if the transferors do not own 80% of the voting stock immediately after the exchange, the Sec. 351 control requirement will not have been met, and they will recognize gain.
- ▶ To trigger gain recognition under Sec. 357(b) or (c), the transferors may transfer to the corporation either debt that exceeds the basis of all property transferred or debt that lacks a business purpose.

---

[64] See, for example, *Aqualane Shores, Inc. v. CIR*, 4 AFTR 2d 5346, 59-2 USTC ¶9632 (5th Cir., 1959) and *Sun Properties, Inc. v. U.S.*, 47 AFTR 273, 55-1 USTC ¶9261 (5th Cir., 1955).

EXAMPLE C:2-50 ▶ Ten years ago, Jaime purchased land as an investment for $100,000. The land is now worth $500,000. Jaime plans to transfer the land to Bell Corporation in exchange for all its stock. Bell will subdivide the land and sell individual tracts. Its gain on the land sales will be ordinary income. Jaime has realized a large capital loss in the current year and would like to recognize capital gain on the transfer of the land to Bell. One way for Jaime to accomplish this objective is to transfer the land to Bell in exchange for all the Bell stock plus a note for $400,000. Because the note is boot, Jaime will recognize $400,000 of gain even though Sec. 351 applies to the exchange. However, if the note is due in a subsequent year, Jaime's gain will be deferred until collection unless she elects out of the installment method. ◀

COMPLIANCE AND PROCEDURAL CONSIDERATIONS

REPORTING REQUIREMENTS UNDER SEC. 351

A taxpayer who receives stock or other property in a Sec. 351 exchange must attach a statement to his or her tax return for the period encompassing the date of the exchange.[65] The statement must include all facts pertinent to the exchange, including:

ADDITIONAL COMMENT

The required information provided to the IRS by both the transferor-shareholders and the transferee corporation should be consistent. For example, the FMVs assigned to the stock and other properties included in the exchange should be the same for both sides of the transaction.

- ▶ A description of the property transferred and its adjusted basis to the transferor
- ▶ A description of the stock received in the exchange, including its type, number of shares, and FMV
- ▶ A description of any other securities received in the exchange, including principal amount, terms, and FMV
- ▶ The amount of money received
- ▶ A description of any other property received, including its FMV
- ▶ A statement of the liabilities transferred to the corporation, including the nature of the liabilities, when and why they were incurred, and the business reason for their transfer

The transferee corporation must attach a statement to its tax return for the year in which the exchange took place. The statement must include

- ▶ A complete description of all property received from the transferors
- ▶ The transferors' adjusted bases in the property
- ▶ A description of the stock issued to the transferors
- ▶ A description of any other securities issued to the transferors
- ▶ The amount of money distributed to the transferors
- ▶ A description of any other property distributed to the transferors
- ▶ Information regarding the transferor's liabilities assumed by the corporation

FINANCIAL STATEMENT IMPLICATIONS

OBJECTIVE 7

Understand the financial statement implications of forming a corporation.

FORMING A CORPORATION

Formation of a corporation under Sec. 351 is similar to a nontaxable business combination in that the amounts recorded for financial statement purposes differ from the carryover tax basis of transferred assets. For business combinations, SFAS No. 109 prescribes that the corporation recognize a deferred tax asset or liability for differences between the assigned financial statement values and the tax bases of the transferred assets and liabili-

65 Reg. Sec. 1.351-3.

ties. Goodwill for which the corporation is not allowed an amortization deduction, however, does not give rise to a temporary difference.

For example: At the beginning of the current year, a shareholder forms Beta Corporation by transferring an asset having a $50,000 FMV and a $30,000 adjusted basis in exchange for stock having a $50,000 FMV. The exchange qualifies for nontaxable treatment under Sec. 351. For tax purposes, Beta takes a $30,000 carryover basis, but for financial statement purposes, Beta records the asset at its $50,000 FMV. Assuming a 35% corporate tax rate, this $20,000 difference between the book value and the tax basis creates a $7,000 ($20,000 × 0.35) deferrerd tax liability. Because the asset's net value is $43,000 ($50,000 − $7,000), the corporation also records $7,000 of goodwill for financial statement purposes. Accordingly, Beta makes the following book journal entry:

Asset	50,000	
Goodwill	7,000	
Deferred tax liability		7,000
Common stock		50,000

After the formation and for the current year, Beta's book net income after $10,000 of book depreciation and $1,400 of goodwill impairment (SFAS No. 142) but before federal income tax (FIT) expense is $88,600. For tax purposes, Beta takes $6,000 of depreciation but amortizes no goodwill. The difference between the $1,400 book goodwill impairment and the zero tax goodwill amortization produces a permanent difference. Beta's net income to taxable income reconciliation is as follows:

Net income before FIT expense	$88,600
Goodwill impairment (permanent difference)	1,400
Net income after permanent differences	$90,000
Depreciation (temporary difference)	4,000
Taxable income	$94,000

Thus, assuming a 35% tax rate, Beta's federal income tax expense is $31,500 ($90,000 × 0.35), and its federal tax liability is $32,900 ($94,000 × 0.35). Also, Beta reduces its deferred tax liability by $1,400 ($4,000 × 0.35). Accordingly, Beta makes the following book journal entry:

Federal income tax expense	31,500	
Deferred tax liability	1,400	
Federal taxes payable		32,900

See Chapter C:3 for a general discussion of financial implications of federal income taxes.

PROBLEM MATERIALS

DISCUSSION QUESTIONS

C:2-1 What entities or business forms are available for a new business? Explain the advantages and disadvantages of each.

C:2-2 Alice and Bill plan to go into business together. They anticipate losses in the first two or three years, which they would like to use to offset income from other sources. They also are concerned about exposing their personal assets to business liabilities. Advise Alice and Bill as to what business form would best meet their needs.

C:2-3 Bruce and Bob organize Black LLC on May 10 of the current year. What is the entity's default tax classification? Are any alternative classification(s) available? If so, (1) how do Bruce and Bob elect the alternative classification(s) and (2) what are the tax consequences of electing an alternative classification?

C:2-4 John and Wilbur form White Corporation on May 3 of the current year. What is the entity's default tax classification? Are any alternative classification(s) available? If so, (1) how do John and Wilbur elect the alternative classification(s) and (2) what are the tax consequences of electing an alternative classification?

C:2-5 Barbara organizes Blue LLC on May 17 of the current year. What is the entity's default tax classification? Are any alternative classification(s) available? If so, (1) how does Barbara elect the alternative classification(s) and (2) what are the tax consequences of electing an alternative classification?

C:2-6 Debate the following proposition: All corporate formation transactions should be treated as taxable events.

C:2-7 What are the tax consequences of Sec. 351 for the transferor and transferee when property is transferred to a newly created corporation?

C:2-8 What items are considered to be property for purposes of Sec. 351(a)? What items are not considered to be property?

C:2-9 How is control defined for purposes of Sec. 351(a)?

C:2-10 Explain how the IRS has interpreted the phrase "in control immediately after the exchange" for purposes of a Sec. 351 exchange.

C:2-11 John and Mary each exchange property worth \$50,000 for 100 shares of New Corporation stock. Peter exchanges services for 98 shares of New stock and \$1,000 in money for two shares of New stock. Are the Sec. 351 requirements met? Explain why or why not. What advice would you give the shareholders?

C:2-12 Does Sec. 351 require shareholders to receive stock equal in value to the property transferred? Suppose Fred and Susan each transfer property worth \$50,000 to Spade Corporation. In exchange, Fred receives 25 shares of Spade stock and Susan receives 75 shares. Are the Sec. 351 requirements met? Explain the tax consequences of the exchange.

C:2-13 Does Sec. 351 apply to property transfers to an existing corporation? Suppose Ken and Lynn each own 50 shares of North Corporation stock. Ken transfers property worth \$50,000 to North for an additional 25 shares. Does Sec. 351 apply? Explain why or why not. If not, what can be done to qualify the transaction?

C:2-14 How are a transferor's basis and holding period determined for stocks and other property (boot) received in a Sec. 351 exchange? How does the transferee corporation's assumption of liabilities affect the transferor's basis in the stock?

C:2-15 How are the transferee corporation's basis and holding period determined for property received in a Sec. 351 exchange?

C:2-16 Under what circumstances is a corporation's assumption of liabilities considered boot in a Sec. 351 exchange?

C:2-17 What factor(s) would the IRS likely consider to determine whether the transfer of a liability to a corporation in a Sec. 351 exchange was motivated by a business purpose?

C:2-18 Mark transfers all the property of his sole proprietorship to newly formed Utah Corporation in exchange for all the Utah stock. Mark has claimed depreciation on some of the property. Under what circumstances is Mark required to recapture previously claimed depreciation deductions? How is the depreciation deduction calculated for the year of transfer? What are the tax consequences if Utah sells the depreciable property?

C:2-19 How does the assignment of income doctrine apply to a Sec. 351 exchange?

C:2-20 What factors did Congress mandate should be considered in determining whether indebtedness is classified as debt or equity for tax purposes?

C:2-21 What are the advantages and disadvantages of using debt in a firm's capital structure?

C:2-22 How are capital contributions by shareholders and nonshareholders treated by the recipient corporation?

C:2-23 What are the advantages of Sec. 1244 loss treatment when a stock investment becomes worthless? What conditions must be met to obtain this treatment?

C:2-24 What are the advantages of business bad debt treatment when a shareholder's loan or advance to a corporation cannot be repaid? How can one avoid characterization of this loss as a nonbusiness bad debt?

C:2-25 Why might shareholders want to avoid Sec. 351 treatment? Explain three ways they can accomplish this end.

C:2-26 What are the Sec. 351 reporting requirements?

ISSUE IDENTIFICATION QUESTIONS

C:2-27 Peter Jones has owned all 100 shares of Trenton Corporation stock for the past five years. This year, Mary Smith contributes property with a \$50,000 basis and an \$80,000 FMV for 80 newly issued Trenton shares. At the same time, Peter contributes \$15,000 in cash for 15 newly issued Trenton shares. What tax issues regarding the exchanges should Mary and Peter consider?

C:2-28 Carl contributes equipment with a $50,000 adjusted basis and an $80,000 FMV to Cook Corporation for 50 of its 100 shares of stock. His son, Carl Jr., contributes $20,000 cash for the remaining 50 Cook shares. What tax issues regarding the exchanges should Carl and his son consider?

C:2-29 Several years ago, Bill acquired 100 shares of Bold Corporation stock directly from the corporation for $100,000 in cash. This year, he sold the stock to Sam for $35,000. What tax issues regarding the stock sale should Bill consider?

PROBLEMS

C:2-30 ***Transfer of Property and Services to a Controlled Corporation.*** In 2007, Dick, Evan, and Fran form Triton Corporation. Dick contributes land (a capital asset) having a $50,000 FMV in exchange for 50 shares of Triton stock. He purchased the land in 2005 for $60,000. Evan contributes machinery (Sec. 1231 property purchased in 2004) having a $45,000 adjusted basis and a $30,000 FMV in exchange for 30 shares of Triton stock. Fran contributes services worth $20,000 in exchange for 20 shares of Triton stock.

a. What is the amount of Dick's recognized gain or loss?
b. What is Dick's basis in his Triton shares? When does his holding period begin?
c. What is the amount of Evan's recognized gain or loss?
d. What is Evan's basis in his Triton shares? When does his holding period begin?
e. How much income, if any, does Fran recognize?
f. What is Fran's basis in her Triton shares? When does her holding period begin?
g. What is Triton's basis in the land and the machinery? When does its holding period begin? How does Triton treat the amount paid to Fran for her services?

C:2-31 ***Transfer of Property and Services to a Controlled Corporation.*** In 2007, Ed, Fran, and George form Jet Corporation. Ed contributes land having a $35,000 FMV purchased as an investment in 2003 for $15,000 in exchange for 35 shares of Jet stock. Fran contributes machinery (Sec. 1231 property) purchased in 2003 and used in her business in exchange for 35 shares of Jet stock. Immediately before the exchange, the machinery had a $45,000 adjusted basis and a $35,000 FMV. George contributes services worth $30,000 in exchange for 30 shares of Jet stock.

a. What is the amount of Ed's recognized gain or loss?
b. What is Ed's basis in his Jet shares? When does his holding period begin?
c. What is the amount of Fran's recognized gain or loss?
d. What is Fran's basis in her Jet shares? When does her holding period begin?
e. How much income, if any, does George recognize?
f. What is George's basis in his Jet shares? When does his holding period begin?
g. What is Jet's basis in the land and the machinery? When does its holding period begin? How does Jet treat the amount paid to George for his services?
h. How would your answers to Parts a through g change if George instead contributed $5,000 in cash and services worth $25,000 for his 30 shares of Jet stock?

C:2-32 ***Control Requirement.*** In which of the following independent situations is the Sec. 351 control requirement met?

a. Olive transfers property to Quick Corporation for 75% of Quick stock, and Mary provides services to Quick for the remaining 25% of Quick stock.
b. Pete transfers property to Target Corporation for 60% of Target stock, and Robert transfers property worth $15,000 and performs services worth $25,000 for the remaining 40% of Target stock.
c. Herb and his wife, Wilma, each have owned 50 of the 100 outstanding shares of Vast Corporation stock since it was formed three years ago. In the current year, their son, Sam, transfers property to Vast for 50 newly issued shares of Vast stock.
d. Charles and Ruth develop a plan to form Tiny Corporation. On June 3 of this year, Charles transfers property worth $50,000 for 50 shares of Tiny stock. On August 1, Ruth transfers $50,000 cash for 50 shares of Tiny stock.
e. Assume the same facts as in Part d except that Charles has a prearranged plan to sell 30 of his shares to Sam on October 1.

C:2-33 ***Control Requirement.*** In which of the following exchanges is the Sec. 351 control requirement met? If the transaction does not meet the Sec. 351 requirements, suggest ways in which the transaction can be structured so as to meet these requirements.

a. Fred exchanges property worth $50,000 and services worth $50,000 for 100 shares of New Corporation stock. Greta exchanges $100,000 cash for the remaining 100 shares of New stock.
b. Maureen exchanges property worth $2,000 and services worth $48,000 for 100 shares of Gemini Corporation stock. Norman exchanges property worth $50,000 for the remaining 100 shares of Gemini stock.

C:2-34 ***Sec. 351 Requirements.*** Al, Bob, and Carl form West Corporation and transfer the following items to West:

	Item Transferred			
Transferor	*Item*	*Transferor's Basis*	*FMV*	*Shares Received by Transferor*
Al	Patent	-0-	$25,000	1,000 common
Bob	Cash	$25,000	25,000	250 preferred
Carl	Services	-0-	7,500	300 common

The common stock has voting rights. The preferred stock does not.

a. Is the exchange nontaxable under Sec. 351? Explain the tax consequences of the exchange to Al, Bob, Carl, and West.
b. How would your answer to Part a change if Bob instead had received 200 shares of common stock and 200 shares of preferred stock?
c. How would your answer to Part a change if Carl instead had contributed $800 cash as well as services worth $6,700?

C:2-35 ***Incorporating a Sole Proprietorship.*** Tom incorporates his sole proprietorship as Total Corporation and transfers its assets to Total in exchange for all 100 shares of Total stock and four $10,000 interest-bearing notes. The stock has a $125,000 FMV. The notes mature consecutively on the first four anniversaries of the incorporation date. The assets transferred are as follows:

Assets		*Adjusted Basis*	*FMV*
Cash		$ 5,000	$ 5,000
Equipment	$130,000		
Minus: Accumulated depreciation	(70,000)	60,000	90,000
Building	$100,000		
Minus: Accumulated depreciation	(49,000)	51,000	40,000
Land		24,000	30,000
Total		$140,000	$165,000

a. What are the amounts and character of Tom's recognized gains or losses?
b. What is Tom's basis in the Total stock and notes?
c. What is Total's basis in the property received from Tom?

C:2-36 ***Transfer to an Existing Corporation.*** For the last five years, Ann and Fred each have owned 50 of the 100 outstanding shares of Zero Corporation stock. Ann transfers land having a $10,000 basis and a $25,000 FMV to Zero for an additional 25 shares of Zero stock. Fred transfers $1,000 cash to Zero for one additional share of Zero stock. What amount of the gain or loss must Ann recognize on the exchange? If the transaction does not meet the Sec. 351 requirements, suggest ways in which it can be structured so as to meet these requirements.

C:2-37 ***Transfer to an Existing Corporation.*** For the last three years, Lucy and Marvin each have owned 50 of the 100 outstanding shares of Lucky Corporation stock. Lucy transfers property having an $8,000 basis and a $12,000 FMV to Lucky for an additional ten shares of Lucky stock. How much gain or loss must Lucy recognize on the exchange? If the transaction does not meet the Sec. 351 requirements, suggest ways in which it can be structured so as to meet these requirements.

C:2-38 ***Disproportionate Receipt of Stock.*** Jerry transfers property with a $28,000 adjusted basis and a $50,000 FMV to Texas Corporation for 75 shares of Texas stock. Frank, Jerry's father, transfers property with a $32,000 adjusted basis and a $50,000 FMV to Texas for the remaining 25 shares of Texas stock.

a. What is the amount of each transferor's recognized gain or loss?
b. What is Jerry's basis in his Texas stock?
c. What is Frank's basis in his Texas stock?

C:2-39 ***Sec. 351: Boot Property Received.*** Sara transfers land (a capital asset) having a $30,000 adjusted basis to Temple Corporation in a Sec. 351 exchange. In return, Sara receives the following consideration:

Consideration	*FMV*
100 shares of Temple common stock	$100,000
50 shares of Temple qualified preferred stock	50,000
Temple note due in three years	20,000
Total	$170,000

a. What are the amount and character of Sara's recognized gain or loss?
b. What is Sara's basis in her common stock, preferred stock, and note?
c. What is Temple's basis in the land?

C:2-40 ***Receipt of Bonds for Property.*** Joe, Karen, and Larry form Gray Corporation. Joe contributes land (a capital asset) having an $8,000 adjusted basis and a $15,000 FMV to Gray in exchange for Gray ten-year bonds having a $15,000 face value. Karen contributes equipment (Sec. 1231 property) having an $18,000 adjusted basis and a $25,000 FMV on which she previously claimed $10,000 of depreciation, for 50 shares of Gray stock. Larry contributes $25,000 cash for 50 shares of Gray stock.
a. What are the amount and character of Joe's, Karen's, and Larry's recognized gains or losses?
b. What basis do Joe, Karen, and Larry take in the stock or bonds they receive?
c. What basis does Gray take in the land and equipment? What happens to the $10,000 of depreciation recapture potential on the equipment?

C:2-41 ***Transfer of Depreciable Property.*** Nora transfers to Needle Corporation depreciable machinery originally costing $18,000 and now having a $15,000 adjusted basis. In exchange, Nora receives all 100 shares of Needle stock having an $18,000 FMV and a three-year Needle note having a $4,000 FMV.
a. What are the amount and character of Nora's recognized gain or loss?
b. What are Nora's bases in the Needle stock and note?
c. What is Needle's basis in the machinery?

C:2-42 ***Transfer of Personal Liabilities.*** Jim owns 80% of Gold Corporation stock. He transfers a business automobile to Gold in exchange for additional Gold stock worth $5,000 and Gold's assumption of his $1,000 automobile debt and his $2,000 education loan. The automobile originally cost Jim $12,000 and, on the transfer date, has a $4,500 adjusted basis and an $8,000 FMV.
a. What are the amount and character of Jim's recognized gain or loss?
b. What is Jim's basis in his additional Gold shares?
c. When does Jim's holding period for the additional shares begin?
d. What basis does Gold take in the automobile?

C:2-43 ***Liabilities in Excess of Basis.*** Barbara transfers machinery having a $15,000 basis and a $35,000 FMV along with $10,000 cash to Moore Corporation in exchange for 50 shares of Moore stock. The machinery was used in Barbara's business, originally cost Barbara $50,000, and is subject to a $28,000 liability, which Moore assumes. Sam exchanges $17,000 cash for the remaining 50 shares of Moore stock.
a. What are the amount and character of Barbara's recognized gain or loss?
b. What is Barbara's basis in the Moore stock?
c. What is Moore's basis in the machinery?
d. What are the amount and character of Sam's recognized gain or loss?
e. What is Sam's basis in the Moore stock?
f. When do Barbara and Sam's holding periods for their stock begin?
g. How would your answers to Parts a through f change if Sam received $17,000 of Moore stock for legal services (instead of money)?

C:2-44 ***Transfer of Business Properties.*** Jerry transfers property having a $32,000 adjusted basis and a $50,000 FMV to Emerald Corporation in exchange for all of Emerald's stock worth $15,000 and Emerald's assumption of a $35,000 mortgage on the property.

a. What is the amount of Jerry's recognized gain or loss?
b. What is Jerry's basis in the Emerald stock?
c. What is Emerald's basis in the property?
d. How would your answers to Parts a through c change if the mortgage assumed by Emerald were $15,000 and the Emerald stock were worth $35,000?

C:2-45 ***Incorporating a Cash Basis Proprietorship.*** Ted decides to incorporate his medical practice. He uses the cash method of accounting. On the date of incorporation, the practice reports the following balance sheet:

	Basis	*FMV*
Assets:		
Cash	$ 5,000	$ 5,000
Accounts receivable	–0–	65,000
Equipment (net of $15,000 depreciation)	35,000	40,000
Total	$40,000	$110,000
Liabilities and Owner's Equity:		
Current liabilities	$ –0–	$ 35,000
Note payable on equipment	15,000	15,000
Owner's equity	25,000	60,000
Total	$40,000	$110,000

All the current liabilities would be deductible by Ted if he paid them. Ted transfers all the assets and liabilities to a professional corporation in exchange for all of its stock.
a. What are the amount and character of Ted's recognized gain or loss?
b. What is Ted's basis in the stock?
c. What is the corporation's basis in the property?
d. Who recognizes income on the receivables upon their collection? Can the corporation obtain a deduction for the liabilities when it pays them?

C:2-46 ***Transfer of Depreciable Property.*** On January 10, 2007, Mary transfers to Green Corporation a machine purchased on March 3, 2004, for $100,000. The machine has a $60,000 adjusted basis and a $110,000 FMV on the transfer date. Mary receives all 100 shares of Green stock, worth $100,000, and a two-year Green note worth $10,000.
a. What are the amount and character of Mary's recognized gain or loss?
b. What is Mary's basis in the stock and note? When does her holding period begin?
c. What are the amount and character of Green's gain or loss?
d. What is Green's basis in the machine? When does Green's holding period begin?

C:2-47 ***Contribution to Capital by a Nonshareholder.*** The City of San Antonio donates land worth $500,000 to Ace Corporation to induce it to locate in San Antonio and provide 2,000 jobs for its citizens.
a. How much income, if any, must Ace report because of the land contribution?
b. What basis does the land have to Ace?
c. Assume the same facts except the City of San Antonio also donated to Ace $100,000 cash, which the corporation used to pay a portion of the $250,000 cost of equipment that it purchased six months later. How much income, if any, must Ace report because of the cash contribution? What basis does Ace take in the equipment?

C:2-48 ***Choice of Capital Structure.*** Reggie transfers $500,000 in cash to newly formed Jackson Corporation for 100% of Jackson's stock. In the first year of operations, Jackson's taxable income before any payments to Reggie is $120,000. What total amount of taxable income must Reggie and Jackson each report in the following two scenarios?
a. Jackson pays a $70,000 dividend to Reggie.
b. Assume that when Jackson was formed, Reggie transferred his $500,000 to the corporation for $250,000 of Jackson stock and $250,000 in Jackson notes payable in five annual installments of $50,000 plus 8% annual interest on the unpaid balance. During the current year, Jackson pays Reggie $50,000 in repayment of the first note plus $20,000 interest.

C:2-49 ***Worthless Stock or Securities.*** Tom and Vicki, husband and wife who file a joint tax return, purchase for $75,000 each one-half the stock in Guest Corporation from Al. Tom is employed full-time by Guest and earns $100,000 in annual salary. Because of Guest's financial difficulties, Tom and Vicki each lend Guest an additional $25,000. The $25,000 is secured by registered bonds and must be repaid in five years, with interest accruing at the prevailing market rate. Guest's financial difficulties escalate, and it declares bankruptcy. Tom and Vicki receive nothing for their Guest stock or Guest bonds.

a. What are the amount and character of each shareholder's loss on the worthless stock and bonds?

b. How would your answer to Part a change if the liability were not secured by bonds?

c. How would your answer to Part a change if Tom and Vicki had purchased their stock for $75,000 each at the time Guest was formed?

C:2-50 ***Worthless Stock.*** Duck Corporation is owned equally by Harry, Susan, and Big Corporation. Harry and Susan are single. Harry, Tom, and Big, the original investors in Duck, each paid $125,000 for their Duck stock in 1999. Susan purchased her stock from Tom in 2002 for $175,000. No adjustments to basis occur after the stock acquisition date. Duck encounters financial difficulties as a result of losing a lawsuit brought by a person who suffered personal injuries from using a defective product. Duck files for bankruptcy, and uses all its assets to pay its creditors in 2007. What are the amount and character of each shareholder's loss?

C:2-51 ***Sale of Sec. 1244 Stock.*** Lois, who is single, transfers property with an $80,000 basis and a $120,000 FMV to Water Corporation in exchange for all 100 shares of Water stock. The shares qualify as Sec. 1244 stock. Two years later, Lois sells the stock for $28,000.

a. What are the amount and character of Lois's recognized gain or loss?

b. How would your answer to Part a change if the FMV of the property were $70,000?

C:2-52 ***Transfer of Sec. 1244 Stock.*** Assume the same facts as in Problem C:2-51 except that Lois gave the Water stock to her daughter, Sue, six months after she received it. The stock had a $120,000 FMV when Lois acquired it and when she made the gift. Sue sold the stock two years later for $28,000. How is the loss treated for tax purposes?

C:2-53 ***Avoiding Sec. 351 Treatment.*** Six years ago, Donna purchased land as an investment. The land cost her $150,000 and is now worth $480,000. Donna plans to transfer the land to Development Corporation, which will subdivide it and sell individual tracts. Development's income on the land sales will be ordinary in character.

a. What are the tax consequences of the asset transfer and land sales if Donna contributes the land to Development in exchange for all its stock?

b. In what alternative ways can the transaction be structured to achieve more favorable tax results? Assume Donna's marginal tax rate is 35%, and Development's marginal tax rate is 34%.

COMPREHENSIVE PROBLEMS

C:2-54 On March 1 of the current year, Alice, Bob, Carla, and Dick form Bear Corporation and transfer the following items:

Property Transferred

Transferor	*Asset*	*Basis to Transferor*	*FMV*	*Number of Common Shares Issued*
Alice	Land	$12,000	$30,000	
	Building	38,000	70,000	400
	Mortgage on the land and building	60,000	60,000	
Bob	Equipment	25,000	40,000	300
Carla	Van	15,000	10,000	50
Dick	Accounting services	–0–	10,000	100

Alice purchased the land and building several years ago for $12,000 and $50,000, respectively. Alice has claimed straight-line depreciation on the building. Bob also receives a Bear note for $10,000 due in three years. The note bears interest at the prevailing market rate. Bob purchased the equipment three years ago for $50,000. Carla also receives $5,000 cash. Carla purchased the van two years ago for $20,000.

a. Does the transaction satisfy the requirements of Sec. 351?

b. What are the amount and character of the gains or losses recognized by Alice, Bob, Carla, Dick, and Bear?

c. What is each shareholder's basis in his or her Bear stock? When does the holding period for the stock begin?
d. What is Bear's basis in its property and services? When does the holding period for each property begin?

C:2-55 On June 3 of the current year, Eric, Florence, and George form Wildcat Corporation and transfer the following items:

	Item Transferred			
Transferor	*Asset*	*Basis to Transferor*	*FMV*	*Number of Common Shares Issued*
Eric	Land	$200,000	$50,000	500
Florence	Equipment	–0–	25,000	250
George	Legal services	–0–	25,000	250

Eric purchased the land (a capital asset) five years ago for $200,000. Florence purchased the equipment three years ago for $48,000. The equipment has been fully depreciated.
a. Does the transaction meet the requirements of Sec. 351?
b. What are the amount and character of the gains or losses recognized by Eric, Florence, George, and Wildcat?
c. What is each shareholder's basis in his or her Wildcat stock? When does the holding period for the stock begin?
d. What is Wildcat's basis in the land, equipment, and services? When does the holding period for each property begin?

TAX STRATEGY PROBLEMS

C:2-56 Assume the same facts as in Problem C:2-55.
a. Under what circumstances is the tax result in Problem C:2-55 beneficial, and for which shareholders?
b. Can you suggest ways to enhance the tax benefit?

C:2-57 Paula Green owns and operates the Green Thumb Nursery as a sole proprietorship. The business has total assets with a $260,000 adjusted basis and a $500,000 FMV. Paula wants to expand into the landscaping business. She views this expansion as risky and therefore wants to incorporate so as not to put her personal assets at risk. Her friend, Mary Brown, is willing to invest $250,000 in the enterprise.

Although Green Thumb has earned approximately $55,000 per year, Paula and Mary expect that, when the landscaping business is launched, the new corporation will incur losses of $50,000 per year for the next two years. They expect profits of at least $80,000 annually, beginning in the third year. Paula and Mary earn approximately $50,000 from other sources. They are considering the following alternative capital structures and elections:
a. Green Thumb issues 50 shares of common stock to Paula and 25 shares of common stock to Mary.
b. Green Thumb issues 50 shares of common stock to Paula and a $250,000 ten-year bond bearing interest at 8% to Mary.
c. Green Thumb issues 40 shares of common stock to Paula plus a $100,000 ten-year bond bearing interest at 6% and 15 shares of common stock to Mary, plus a $100,000 ten-year bond bearing interest at 6%.
d. Green Thumb issues 50 shares of common stock to Paula and 25 shares of preferred stock to Mary. The preferred stock is nonparticipating but pays a cumulative preferred dividend at 8% of its $250,000 stated value.

What are the advantages and disadvantages of each of these alternatives? What considerations are relevant for determining the best alternative?

CASE STUDY PROBLEMS

C:2-58 Bob Jones has a small repair shop that he has run for several years as a sole proprietorship. The proprietorship uses the cash method of accounting and the calendar year as its tax year. Bob needs additional capital for expansion and knows two people who might be interested in investing in the business. One would like to work for the business. The other would only invest.

Bob wants to know the tax consequences of incorporating the business. His business assets include a building, equipment, accounts receivable, and cash. Liabilities include a mortgage on the building and a few accounts payable, which are deductible when paid.

Required: Write a memorandum to Bob explaining the tax consequences of the incorporation. As part of your memorandum examine the possibility of having the corporation issue common and preferred stock and debt for the shareholders' property and money.

C:2-59 Eric Wright conducts a dry cleaning business as a sole proprietorship. The business operates in a building that Eric owns. Last year, Eric mortgaged the building and the land on which the building sits for $150,000. He used the money for a down payment on his personal residence and college expenses for his two children. He now wants to incorporate his business and transfer the building and the mortgage to a new corporation, along with other assets and some accounts payable. The amount of the unpaid mortgage balance will not exceed Eric's adjusted basis in the land and building at the time he transfers them to the corporation. Eric is aware that Sec. 357(b) could impact the tax consequences of the transaction because no bona fide business purpose exists for the mortgage transfer, and the IRS might consider it to have been transferred for a tax avoidance purpose. However, Eric refuses to acknowledge this possibility when you confront him. He maintains that many taxpayers play the audit lottery and that, in the event of an audit, this issue can be used as a bargaining ploy.

Required: What information about the transaction must be provided with the transferor and transferee's tax returns for the year in which the transfer takes place? Discuss the ethical issues raised by the AICPA's *Statements on Standards for Tax Services No. 1, Tax Return Positions* (which can be found in Appendix E) as it relates to this situation. Should the tax practitioner act as an advocate for the client? Should the practitioner sign the return?

TAX RESEARCH PROBLEMS

C:2-60 Anne and Michael own and operate a successful mattress business. They have decided to take the business public. They contribute all the assets of the business to newly formed Spring Corporation each in exchange for 20% of the stock. The remaining 60% is issued to an underwriting company that will sell the stock to the public and charge 10% of the sales proceeds as a commission. Prepare a memorandum for your tax manager explaining whether or not this transaction meets the tax-free requirements of Sec. 351.

C:2-61 Bob and Carl transfer property to Stone Corporation for 90% and 10% of Stone stock, respectively. Pursuant to a binding agreement concluded before the transfer, Bob sells half of his stock to Carl. Prepare a memorandum for your tax manager explaining why the exchange does or does not meet the Sec. 351 control requirement. Your manager has suggested that, at a minimum, you consult the following authorities:

- IRC Sec. 351
- Reg. Sec. 1.351-1

C:2-62 In an exchange qualifying for Sec. 351 tax-free treatment, Greta receives 100 shares of White Corporation stock plus a right to receive another 25 shares. The right is contingent on the valuation of a patent contributed by Greta. Because the patent license is pending, the patent cannot be valued for several months. Prepare a memorandum for your tax manager explaining whether the underlying 25 shares are considered "stock" for purposes of Sec. 351 and what tax consequences ensue from Greta's receipt of the 100 shares now and 25 shares later upon exercise of the right.

TAX & FINANCIAL ACCOUNTING

C:2-63 Your clients, Lisa and Matthew, are planning to form Lima Corporation. Lisa will contribute $50,000 cash to Lima for 50 shares of its stock. Matthew will contribute land having a $35,000 adjusted basis and a $50,000 FMV for 50 shares of Lima stock. Lima will borrow additional capital from a bank and then will subdivide and sell the land. Prepare a memorandum for your tax manager outlining the tax treatment of the corporate formation. In your memorandum, compare tax and financial accounting for this transaction. References:

- IRC Sec. 351
- APB, *Opinions of the Accounting Principles Board No. 29* [Accounting for Nonmonetary Transactions]

C:2-64 John plans to transfer the assets and liabilities of his business to Newco in exchange for all of Newco's stock. The assets have a $250,000 basis and an $800,000 FMV. John also plans to transfer $475,000 of business related liabilities to Newco. Under Sec. 357(c), can John avoid recognizing a $175,000 gain (the excess of liabilities over the basis of assets tranferred) by transferring a $175,000 personal promissory note along with the assets and liabilities?

C:2-65 Six years ago, Leticia, Monica, and Nathaniel organized Lemona Corporation to develop and sell computer software. Each individual contributed $10,000 to Lemona in exchange for 1,000 shares of Lemona stock (for a total of 3,000 shares issued and outstanding). The corporation also borrowed $250,000 from Venture Capital Associates to finance operating costs and capital expenditures.

Because of intense competition, Lemona struggled in its early years of operation and sustained chronic losses. This year, Leticia, who serves as Lemona's president, decided to seek additional funds to finance Lemona's working capital.

Venture Capital Associates declined Leticia's request for additional capital because of the firm's already high credit exposure to the software corporation. Hi-Tech Bank proposed to lend Limona $100,000, but at a 10% premium over the prime rate. (Other software manufacturers in the same market can borrow at a 3% premium.) Investment Managers LLC proposed to inject $50,000 of equity capital into Lemona, but on condition that the investment firm be granted the right to elect five members to Lemona's board of directors. Discouraged by the "high cost" of external borrowing, Leticia turned to Monica and Nathaniel.

She proposed to Monica and Nathaniel that each of the three original investors contribute an additional $25,000 to Lemona, each in exchange for five 20-year debentures. The debentures would be unsecured and subordinated to Venture Capital Associates debt. Annual interest on the debentures would accrue at a floating 5% premium over the prime rate. The right to receive interest payments would be cumulative; that is, each debenture holder would be entitled to past and current interest payents before Lemona's board could declare a common stock dividend. The debentures would be both nontransferable and noncallable.

Leticia, Monica, and Nathaniel have asked you, their tax accountant, to advise them on the tax implications of the proposed financing arrangement. After researching the issue, set forth your advice in a client letter. At a minimum, you should consult the following authorities:

- IRC Sec. 385
- *Rudolph A. Hardman*, 60 AFTR 2d 87-5651, 82-7 USTC ¶9523 (9th Cir., 1987)
- *Tomlinson v. The 1661 Corporation*, 19 AFTR 2d 1413, 67-1 USTC ¶9438 (5th Cir., 1967)

3

CHAPTER

THE CORPORATE INCOME TAX

LEARNING OBJECTIVES

After studying this chapter, you should be able to

1. Apply the requirements for selecting tax years and accounting methods to various types of C corporations
2. Compute a corporation's taxable income
3. Compute a corporation's income tax liability
4. Understand what a controlled group is and the tax consequences of being a controlled group
5. Understand how compensation planning can reduce taxes for corporations and their shareholders
6. Determine the requirements for paying corporate income taxes and filing a corporate tax return
7. Determine the financial statement implications of federal income taxes

CHAPTER OUTLINE

A **corporation** is a separate taxpaying entity that must file an annual tax return even if it has no income or loss for the year. This chapter covers the tax rules for **domestic corporations** (i.e., corporations incorporated in one of the 50 states or under federal law) and other entities taxed as domestic corporations under the check-the-box regulations.[1] It explains the rules for determining a corporation's taxable income, loss, and tax liability and for filing corporate tax returns. See Table C:3-1 for the general formula for determining the corporate tax liability. It also discusses the financial implications of federal income taxes. Some of these implications appear briefly in the Book-to-Tax Accounting Comparisons, and a more detailed discussion appears at the end of this chapter.

The corporations discussed in this chapter are sometimes referred to as regular or C corporations because Subchapter C of the Internal Revenue Code (IRC) dictates much of their tax treatment. Corporations that have a special tax status include S corporations (see Chapter C:11) and affiliated groups of corporations that file consolidated returns (see Chapter C:8). A comparison of the tax treatments of C corporations, partnerships, and S corporations appears in Appendix F.

CORPORATE ELECTIONS

OBJECTIVE 1

Apply the requirements for selecting tax years and accounting methods to various types of C corporations

Once formed, a corporation must make certain elections, such as selecting its **tax year** and its accounting methods. The corporation makes these elections on its first tax return. They are important and should be considered carefully because, once made, they generally can be changed only with permission from the Internal Revenue Service (IRS).

CHOOSING A CALENDAR OR FISCAL YEAR

A new corporation may elect to use either a calendar year or a fiscal year as its accounting period. The corporation's tax year must be the same as the annual accounting period used for financial accounting purposes. The corporation makes the election by filing its first tax return for the selected period. A calendar year is a 12-month period ending on December 31. A fiscal year is a 12-month period ending on the last day of any month other than December. Examples of acceptable fiscal years are February 1, 2007, through January 31, 2008, and October 1, 2007, through September 30, 2008. A fiscal year that runs from September 16, 2007, through September 15, 2008, however, is not an acceptable tax year because it does not end on the last day of the month. The IRS requires that a corporation using an unacceptable tax year change to a calendar year.[2]

KEY POINT

Whereas partnerships and S corporations generally must adopt a calendar year, C corporations (other than personal service corporations) have the flexibility of adopting a fiscal year. The fiscal year must end on the last day of the month.

SHORT TAX PERIOD. A corporation's first tax year might not cover a full 12-month period. If, for example, a corporation begins business on March 10, 2007, and elects a fiscal year ending on September 30, its first tax year covers the period from March 10, 2007, through September 30, 2007. Its second tax year covers the period from October 1, 2007, through September 30, 2008. The corporation must file a **short-period tax return** for its first tax year.[3] From then on, its tax returns will cover a full 12-month period. The last year of a corporation's life, however, also may be a short period covering the period from the beginning of the last tax year through the date the corporation ceases to exist.

RESTRICTIONS ON ADOPTING A TAX YEAR. A corporation may be subject to restrictions in its choice of a tax year. An S corporation generally must use a calendar year (see Chapter C:11). All members of an affiliated group filing a consolidated return must use the same tax year as the group's parent corporation (see Chapter C:8).

A personal service corporation generally must use a calendar year as its tax year. This restriction prevents a personal service corporation with, for example, a January 31 year-end from distributing a large portion of its income earned during the February through December portion of 2007 to its calendar year shareholder-employees in January 2008,

[1] Sec. 7701(a)(4). Corporations that are not classified as domestic are **foreign corporations.** Foreign corporations are taxed like domestic corporations if they conduct a trade or business in the United States.

[2] Sec. 441. Section 441 also permits accounting periods of either 52 or 53 weeks that always end on the same day of the week (such as Friday).

[3] Sec. 443(a)(2).

▼ TABLE C:3-1
General Rules for Determining the Corporate Tax Liability

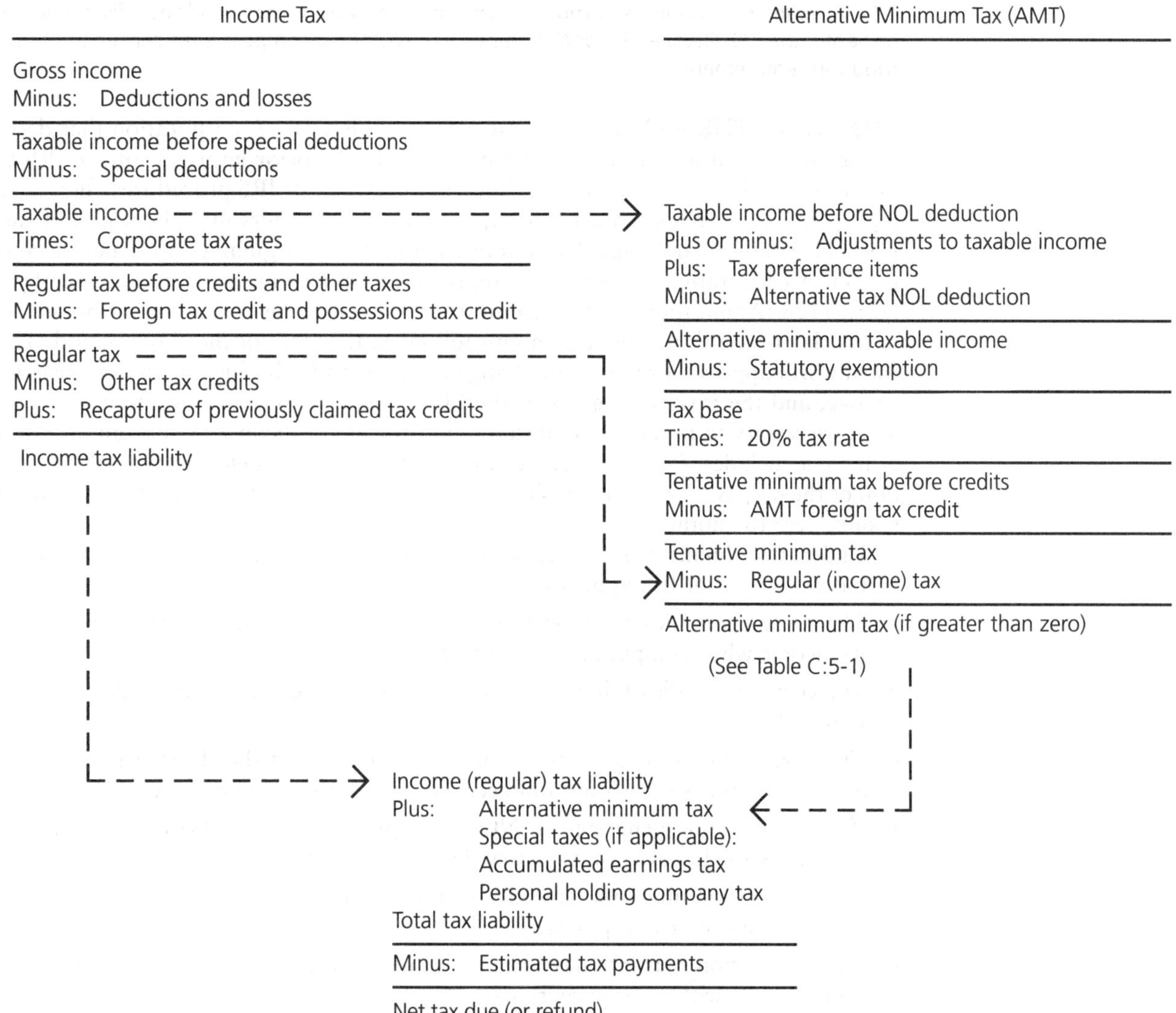

thereby deferring income largely earned in 2007 to 2008. For this purpose, the IRC defines a **personal service corporation** (PSC) as one whose principal activity is the performance of personal services by its employee-owners who own more than 10% of the stock (by value) on any day of the year.[4]

A PSC, however, may adopt a fiscal tax year if it can establish a business purpose for such a year. For example, it may be able to establish a natural business year and use that year as its tax year.[5] Deferral of income by shareholders is not an acceptable business purpose.

Even when no business purpose exists, a new PSC may elect to use a September 30, October 31, or November 30 year-end if it meets minimum distribution requirements to employee-owners during the deferral period.[6] If it fails to meet these distribution requirements, the PSC may have to defer to its next fiscal year the deduction for amounts paid to employee-owners.[7]

---

[4] Sec. 441(i).

[5] The natural business year rule requires that the year-end used for tax purposes coincide with the end of the taxpayer's peak business period. (See the partnership and S corporation chapters and Rev. Proc. 2006-46, 2006-45 I.R.B. 859, for a further explanation of this exception.)

[6] Sec. 444.

[7] Sec. 280H.

EXAMPLE C:3-1 ▶ Alice and Bob form Cole Corporation with each shareholder owning 50% of its stock. Alice and Bob use the calendar year as their tax year. Alice and Bob are both active in the business and are the corporation's primary employees. The new corporation performs engineering services for the automotive industry. Cole must use a calendar year as its tax year unless it qualifies for a fiscal year based on a business purpose exception. Alternatively, it may adopt a fiscal year ending on September 30, October 31, or November 30, provided it complies with certain minimum distribution requirements. ◀

CHANGING THE ANNUAL ACCOUNTING PERIOD. A corporation that desires to change its annual accounting period must obtain the prior approval of the IRS unless Treasury Regulations specifically authorized the change or IRS procedures allow an automatic change. A change in accounting period usually results in a short period running from the end of the old annual accounting period to the beginning of the new accounting period. A corporation must request approval of an accounting period change by filing Form 1128 (Application for Change in Annual Accounting Period) on or before the fifteenth day of the third calendar month following the close of the short period. The IRS usually will approve a request for change if a substantial business purpose exists for the change, and the taxpayer agrees to the IRS's prescribed terms, conditions, and adjustments necessary to prevent any substantial distortion of income. A substantial distortion of income includes, for example, a change that causes the "deferral of a substantial portion of the taxpayer's income, or shifting of a substantial portion of deductions, from one taxable year to another."[8]

Under IRS administrative procedures, a corporation may change its annual accounting period without prior IRS approval if it meets the following conditions:

- ▶ The corporation files a short-period tax return for the year of change and annualizes its income when computing its tax for the short period.
- ▶ The corporation files full 12-month returns for subsequent years ending on the new year-end.
- ▶ The corporation closes its books as of the last day of the short-period and subsequently computes its income and keeps its books using the new tax year.
- ▶ If the corporation generates an NOL or capital loss in the short period, it may not carry back the losses but must carry them over to future years.
- ▶ The corporation must not have changed its accounting period within the previous 48 months (with some exceptions).
- ▶ The corporation must not have an interest in a pass-through entity as of the end of the short period (with some exceptions).
- ▶ The corporation is not an S corporation, personal service corporation, tax-exempt organization, or other specialized corporation (however, see footnote 9 below).[9]

BOOK-TO-TAX ACCOUNTING COMPARISON

Treasury Regulations literally require taxpayers to use the same overall accounting method for book and tax purposes. However, the courts have allowed different methods if the taxpayer maintains adequate reconciling workpapers. The IRS has adopted the courts' position on this issue.

ACCOUNTING METHODS

A new corporation must select the overall **accounting method** it will use for tax purposes. The method chosen must be indicated on the corporation's initial return. The three possible accounting methods are: accrual, cash, and hybrid.[10]

ACCRUAL METHOD. Under the accrual method, a corporation reports income when it has been earned and reports expenses when they have been incurred. A corporation must use this method unless it qualifies under one of the following exceptions:

- ▶ A qualified family farming corporation.[11]

---

[8] Reg. Sec. 1.442-1(b)(3). Also see Rev. Proc. 2002-39, 2002-1 C.B. 1046.

[9] Rev. Proc. 2002-37, 2002-1 C.B. 1030. For automatic change procedures for S corporations and personal service corporations, see Rev. Proc. 2006-46, 2006-45 I.R.B. 859.

[10] Sec. 446.

[11] Sec. 448. Certain family farming corporations having gross receipts of less than $25 million may use the cash method of accounting. Section 447 requires farming corporations with gross receipts over $25 million to use the accrual method of accounting.

- A qualified personal service corporation, which is a corporation substantially all of whose activities involve the performance of services in the fields of health, law, engineering, architecture, accounting, actuarial science, performing arts, or consulting; and substantially all of whose stock is held by current (or retired) employees performing the services listed above, their estates, or (for two years only) persons who inherited their stock from such employees.[12]
- Corporations that meet a $5 million gross receipts test for all prior tax years beginning after December 31, 1985. A corporation meets this test for any prior tax year if its average gross receipts for the three-year period ending with that prior tax year do not exceed $5 million. If the corporation was not in existence for the entire three-year period, the period during which the corporation *was* in existence may be used.
- S corporations.

ADDITIONAL COMMENT

Whereas partnerships and S corporations are generally allowed to be cash method taxpayers, most C corporations must use the accrual method of accounting. This restriction can prove inconvenient for many small corporations (with more than $5 million of gross receipts) that would rather use the less complicated cash method of accounting.

If a corporation meets one of the exceptions listed above, it may use either the accrual method or one of the following two methods.

CASH METHOD. Under the cash method, a corporation reports income when it actually or constructively receives the income and reports expenses when it pays them. Corporations in service industries such as engineering, medicine, law, and accounting generally use this method because they prefer to defer recognition until they actually receive the income. This method may not be used if inventories are a material income-producing factor. In such case, the corporation must use either the *accrual* method or the *hybrid* method of accounting.

HYBRID METHOD. Under the hybrid method, a corporation uses the accrual method of accounting for sales, cost of goods sold, inventories, accounts receivable, and accounts payable, and the cash method of accounting for all other income and expense items. Small businesses with inventories (e.g., retail stores) often use this method. Although they must use the accrual method of accounting for sales-related income and expense items, they often find the cash method less burdensome to use for other income and expense items, such as utilities, rents, salaries, and taxes.

GENERAL FORMULA FOR DETERMINING THE CORPORATE TAX LIABILITY

Each year, C corporations must determine their corporate income (or regular) tax liability. In addition to the income tax, a C corporation may owe the corporate alternative minimum tax and possibly either the accumulated earnings tax or the personal holding company tax. A corporation's total tax liability equals the sum of its regular income tax liability plus any additional taxes that it owes.

This chapter explains how to compute a corporation's income (or regular) tax liability. Chapter C:5 explains the computation of the corporate alternative minimum tax, personal holding company tax, and accumulated earnings tax.

[12] The personal service corporation definition for the tax year election [Sec. 441(i)] is different from the personal service corporation definition for the cash accounting method election [Sec. 448].

COMPUTING A CORPORATION'S TAXABLE INCOME

OBJECTIVE 2

Compute a corporation's taxable income

Like an individual, a corporation is a taxpaying entity with gross income and deductions. However, a number of differences arise between individual and corporate taxation as summarized in Figure C:3-1. This section of the text expands on some of these items and discusses other tax aspects particular to corporations.

SALES AND EXCHANGES OF PROPERTY

Sales and exchanges of property generally are treated the same way for corporations as for an individual. However, special rules apply to capital gains and losses, and corporations are subject to an additional 20% depreciation recapture rule under Sec. 291 on sales of Sec. 1250 property.

1. **Gross income:** Generally, the same gross income definition applies to individuals and corporations. Certain exclusions are available to individuals but not to corporations (e.g, fringe benefits); other exclusions are available to corporations but not to individuals (e.g., capital contributions).
2. **Deductions:** Individuals have above-the-line deductions (*for* AGI), itemized deductions (*from* AGI), and personal exemptions. Corporations do not compute AGI, and their deductions are presumed to be ordinary and necessary business expenses.
3. **Charitable contributions:** (a) Individuals are limited to 50% of AGI (30% for capital gain property). Corporations are limited to 10% of taxable income computed without regard to the dividends-received deductions, the U.S. production activities deduction, NOL and capital loss carrybacks, and the contribution deduction itself. (b) Individuals deduct a contribution only in the year they pay it. Accrual basis corporations may deduct contributions in the year of accrual if the board of directors authorizes the contribution by year-end, and the corporation pays it by the fifteenth day of the third month of the next year.
4. **Depreciation on Sec. 1250 property:** Individuals generally do not recapture depreciation under the MACRS rules because straight-line depreciation applies to real property. Corporations must recapture 20% of the excess of the amount that would be recaptured under Sec. 1245. Individuals are subject to a 25% tax rate on Sec. 1250 gains. Corporations are not subject to this rate.
5. **Net capital gains:** Individuals usually are taxed at a maximum rate of 15% (however, 5%, 25%, and 28% apply in special cases). Corporate capital gains are taxed at the regular corporate tax rates.
6. **Capital losses:** Individuals can deduct $3,000 of net capital losses to offset ordinary income. Individual capital losses carry over indefinitely. Corporations cannot offset any ordinary income with capital losses. However, capital losses carry back three years and forward five years and offset capital gains in those years.
7. **Dividends-received deduction:** Not available for individuals. Corporations receive a 70%, 80%, or 100% special deduction depending on the percentage of stock ownership.
8. **NOLs:** Individuals must make many adjustments to arrive at the NOL they are allowed to carry back or forward. A corporation's NOL is simply the excess of its deductions over its income for the year. The NOL carries back two years and forward 20 years for individuals and corporations, or the taxpayer can elect to forgo the carryback and only carry the NOL forward.
9. For individuals, the U.S. production activities deduction is based on the lesser of qualified production activities income or AGI. For corporations, the deduction is based on the lesser of qualified production activities income or taxable income.
10. **Tax rates:** Individual's tax rates range from 10% to 35% (in 2007). Corporate tax rates range from 15% to 39%.
11. **AMT:** Individual AMT rates are 26% or 28%. The corporate AMT rate is 20%. Corporations are subject to a special AMTI adjustment, called adjusted current earnings (ACE), that does not apply to individuals.
12. **Passive Losses:** Passive loss rules apply to individuals, partners, S corporation shareholders, closely held C corporations, and PSCs. They do not apply to widely held C corporations.
13. **Casualty losses:** Casualty losses are deductible in full by a corporation because all corporate casualty losses are considered to be business related. Moreover, they are not reduced by a $100 offset, nor are they restricted to losses exceeding 10% of AGI, as are an individual's nonbusiness casualty losses.

FIGURE C:3-1 ▶ DIFFERENCES BETWEEN INDIVIDUAL AND CORPORATE TAXATION

CAPITAL GAINS AND LOSSES. A corporation has a capital gain or loss if it sells or exchanges a capital asset. As with individuals, a corporation must net all its capital gains and losses to obtain its net capital gain or loss position.

Net Capital Gain. A corporation includes all its net capital gains (net long-term capital gains in excess of net short-term capital losses) for the tax year in gross income. Unlike with individuals, a corporation's capital gains receive no special tax treatment and are taxed in the same manner as any other ordinary income item.

EXAMPLE C:3-2 ▶ Beta Corporation has a net capital gain of $40,000, gross profits on sales of $110,000, and deductible expenses of $28,000. Beta's gross income is $150,000 ($40,000 + $110,000). Its taxable income is $122,000 ($150,000 − $28,000). The $40,000 of net capital gain receives no special treatment and is taxed using the regular corporate tax rates described below. ◀

Net Capital Losses. If a corporation incurs a net capital loss, it cannot deduct the net loss in the current year. A corporation's capital losses can offset only capital gains. They never can offset the corporation's ordinary income.

A corporation must carry back a net capital loss as a short-term capital loss to the three previous tax years and offset capital gains in the earliest year possible (i.e., the losses carry back to the third previous year first). If the loss is not totally absorbed as a carryback, the remainder carries over as a short-term capital loss for five years. Any unused capital losses remaining at the end of the carryover period expire.

EXAMPLE C:3-3 ▶ In 2007, East Corporation reports gross profits of $150,000, deductible expenses of $28,000, and a net capital loss of $10,000. East reported the following capital gain net income (excess of gains from sales or exchanges of capital assets over losses from such sales or exchanges) during 2004 through 2006:

Year	*Capital Gain Net Income*
2004	$6,000
2005	–0–
2006	3,000

East has gross income of $150,000 and taxable income of $122,000 ($150,000 − $28,000) for 2007. East also has a $10,000 net capital loss that carries back to 2004 first and offsets the $6,000 capital gain net income reported in that year. East receives a refund for the taxes paid in 2004 on the $6,000 of capital gains. The $4,000 ($10,000 − $6,000) remainder of the loss carryback carries to 2006 and offsets East's $3,000 capital gain net income reported in that year. East still has a $1,000 net capital loss to carry over to 2008. ◀

SELF-STUDY QUESTION

How does the use of a net capital loss differ for individual and corporate taxpayers?

ANSWER

Individuals and corporations treat net capital losses differently. Individuals may use up to $3,000 per year of net capital losses to offset ordinary income. They cannot carry back net capital losses but can carry over net capital losses indefinitely. In contrast, corporations may not use any net capital losses to offset ordinary income, can carry net capital losses back three years, and can carry over net capital losses for only five years.

SEC. 291: TAX BENEFIT RECAPTURE RULE. If a taxpayer sells Sec. 1250 property at a gain, Sec. 1250 requires that the taxpayer report the recognized gain as ordinary income to the extent the depreciation taken exceeds the depreciation that would have been allowed had the taxpayer used the straight-line method. This ordinary income is known as Sec. 1250 depreciation recapture. For individuals, any remaining gain is characterized as a combination of Sec. 1250 gain and Sec. 1231 gain. However, corporations must recapture as ordinary income an additional amount equal to 20% of the additional ordinary income that would have been recognized had the property been Sec. 1245 property instead of Sec. 1250 property.

EXAMPLE C:3-4 ▶ Texas Corporation purchased residential real estate in January 2005 for $125,000, of which $25,000 was allocated to the land and $100,000 to the building. Texas took straight-line MACRS depreciation deductions of $10,606 on the building in the years 2005 through 2007. In December 2007, Texas sells the property for $155,000, of which $45,000 is allocated to the land and $110,000 to the building. Texas has a $20,000 ($45,000 − $25,000) gain on the land sale, all of which is Sec. 1231 gain. This gain is not affected by Sec. 291 because land is not Sec. 1250 property. Texas has a $20,606 [$110,000 sales price − ($100,000 original cost − $10,606 depreciation)] gain on the sale of the building. If Texas were an individual taxpayer, $10,606 would be a Sec. 1250 gain subject to a 25% tax rate, and the remaining $10,000 would be a Sec. 1231

ADDITIONAL COMMENT

Section 291 results in the recapture, as ordinary income, of an additional 20% of the gain on sales of Sec. 1250 property. This recapture requirement reduces the amount of net Sec.1231 gains that can be offset by corporate capital losses.

gain. However, a corporate taxpayer reports $2,121 of gain as ordinary income. These amounts are summarized below:

	Land	Building	Total
Amount of gain:			
Sales price	$45,000	$110,000	$155,000
Minus: adjusted basis	(25,000)	(89,394)	(114,394)
Recognized gain	$20,000	$ 20,606	$ 40,606
Character of gain:			
Ordinary income	$ -0-	$ 2,121[a]	$ 2,121
Sec. 1231 gain	20,000	18,485	38,485
Recognized gain	$20,000	$ 20,606	$ 40,606

[a]0.20 × lesser of $10,606 depreciation claimed or $20,606 recognized gain. ◀

BUSINESS EXPENSES

Corporations are allowed deductions for ordinary and necessary business expenses, including salaries paid to officers and other employees of the corporation, rent, repairs, insurance premiums, advertising, interest, taxes, losses on sales of inventory or other property, bad debts, and depreciation.[13] No deductions are allowed, however, for interest on amounts borrowed to purchase tax-exempt securities, illegal bribes or kickbacks, fines or penalties imposed by a government, or insurance premiums incurred to insure the lives of officers and employees when the corporation is the beneficiary.

TAX STRATEGY TIP

A corporation always should have a Sec. 248 election in place because, if the IRS later reclassifies deducted expenses as organizational expenditures, the corporation cannot make a retroactive election.

ORGANIZATIONAL EXPENDITURES. When formed, a corporation may incur some organizational expenditures such as legal fees and accounting fees incident to the incorporation process. These expenditures must be capitalized. Unless the corporation makes an election under Sec. 248, however, it cannot amortize these expenditures because they have an unlimited life. A Sec. 248 election allows a corporation to deduct the first $5,000 of organizational expenditures. However, the corporation must reduce the $5,000 by the amount by which cumulative organizational expenditures exceed $50,000 although the $5,000 cannot be reduced below zero. The corporation can amortize the remaining organizational expenditures over a 180-month period beginning in the month it begins business.

EXAMPLE C:3-5 ▶ Sigma Corporation incorporates on January 10 of the current year, and begins business on March 3. Sigma elects a September 30 year-end. Thus, it conducts business for seven months during its first tax year. During the period January 10 through September 30, Sigma incurs $52,000 of organizational expenditures. Because these expenditures exceed $50,000, Sigma must reduce the first $5,000 by $2,000 ($52,000 − $50,000), leaving $3,000. Sigma amortizes the

WHAT WOULD YOU DO IN THIS SITUATION?

You are a CPA with a medium-size accounting firm. One of your corporate clients is an electrical contractor in New York City. The client is successful and had $10 million of sales last year. The contracts involve private and government electrical work. Among the corporation's expenses are $400,000 of kickbacks paid to people working for general contractors who award electrical subcontracts to the corporation, and $100,000 of payments to individuals in the electricians' union. Technically, these payments are illegal. However, your client says that everyone in this business needs to pay kickbacks to obtain contracts and to have enough electricians to finish the projects in a timely manner. He maintains that it is impossible to stay in business without making these payments. In preparing its tax return, your client wants you to deduct these expenses. What is your option concerning the client's request?

[13] Sec. 162.

remaining $49,000 ($52,000 – $3,000) over 180 months beginning in March of its first year. This portion of the deduction equals $1,906 ($49,000/180 × 7 months). Accordingly, its total first-year deduction is $4,906 ($3,000 + $1,906). ◀

BOOK-TO-TAX ACCOUNTING COMPARISON

Most corporations amortize organizational expenditures for tax purposes over the specified period. For financial accounting purposes, they are expensed currently under SOP 98-5. Thus, the differential treatment creates a deferred tax asset.

This rule applies to organizational expenditures incurred after October 22, 2004. Prior to October 23, 2004, a corporation was not allowed an initial deduction but had to amortize its organizational expenditures over a period of at least 60 months beginning in the month it began business.

The corporation makes the Sec. 248 amortization election in a statement attached to its first tax return filed no later than the due date of the tax return (including permitted extensions). If the corporation does not make an amortization election, it cannot deduct organizational expenditures until the corporation liquidates.

The election applies only to expenditures incurred before the end of the tax year in which the corporation begins business regardless of whether the corporation uses the cash or accrual method of accounting. A corporation begins business when it starts the business operations for which it was organized. Expenditures incurred after the first tax year has ended (e.g., legal expenses incurred to modify the corporate charter) must be capitalized and cannot be deducted until the corporation liquidates.[14]

Organizational expenditures include expenditures incident to the corporation's creation; chargeable to the corporation's capital account; and of a character that, if expended incident to the creation of a corporation having a limited life, would be amortizable over that life.

Specific organizational expenditures include

- Legal services incident to the corporation's organization (e.g., drafting the corporate charter and bylaws, minutes of organizational meetings, and terms of original stock certificates)
- Accounting services necessary to create the corporation
- Expenses of temporary directors and of organizational meetings of directors and stockholders
- Fees paid to the state of incorporation.[15]

Organizational expenditures do not include expenditures connected with issuing or selling the corporation's stock or other securities (e.g., commissions, professional fees, and printing costs) and expenditures related to the transfer of assets to the corporation.

EXAMPLE C:3-6 ▶ Omega Corporation incorporates on July 12 of the current year, starts business operations on August 10, and elects a tax year ending on September 30. Omega incurs the following expenditures while organizing the corporation:

Date	*Type of Expenditure*	*Amount*
June 10	Legal expenses to draft charter	$ 2,000
July 17	Commission to stockbroker for issuing and selling stock	40,000
July 18	Accounting fees to set up corporate books	2,400
July 20	Temporary directors' fees	1,000
August 25	Directors' fees	1,500
October 9	Legal fees to modify corporate charter	1,000

Omega's first tax year begins July 12 and ends on September 30. Omega has organizational expenditures of $5,400 ($2,000 + $2,400 + $1,000). The legal expenses to modify the corporate charter do not qualify because Omega did not incur them during the tax year in which it began its business operations. The commission for selling the Omega stock is treated as a reduction in the amount of Omega's paid-in capital. Omega deducts the directors' fees incurred in August as a trade or business expense under Sec. 162 because Omega had begun business operations by that date. If Omega elects to amortize its organizational expenditures, it can deduct $5,000 in its first tax year and amortize the remaining $400 over 180 months. Thus, its first year deduction is $5,004 [$5,000 + ($400/180) × 2 months].

[14] Reg. Sec. 1.248-1(a).

[15] Reg. Sec. 1.248-1(b)(2).

The following table summarizes the classification of expenditures:

			Type of Expenditure		
Date	*Expenditure*	*Amount*	*Organizational*	*Capital*	*Business*
6/10	Legal	$ 2,000	$2,000		
7/17	Commission	40,000		$40,000	
7/18	Accounting	2,400	2,400		
7/20	Directors' fees	1,000	1,000		
8/25	Directors' fees	1,500			$1,500
10/9	Legal	1,000		1,000	
	Total	$47,900	$5,400	$41,000	$1,500 ◀

If a corporation discontinues or disposes of its business before the end of the amortization period, it may deduct any remaining organizational expenditures as a loss.

START-UP EXPENDITURES. A distinction must be made between a corporation's organizational expenditures and its start-up expenditures. Start-up expenditures are ordinary and necessary business expenses paid or incurred by an individual or corporate taxpayer

BOOK-TO-TAX ACCOUNTING COMPARISON

A corporation must capitalize start-up expenditures for tax purposes with amortization permitted over 180 months (after a $5,000 deduction). *Statement of Financial Accounting Standards No. 7* holds that the financial accounting practices and reporting standards used for development stage businesses should be no different for an established business. The two different sets of rules can lead to different reporting for tax and book purposes.

- To investigate the creation or acquisition of an active trade or business
- To create an active trade or business
- To conduct an activity engaged in for profit or the production of income before the time the activity becomes an active trade or business

Examples of start-up expenditures include the costs for a survey of potential markets; an analysis of available facilities; advertisements relating to opening the business; the training of employees; travel and other expenses for securing prospective distributors, suppliers, or customers; and the hiring of management personnel and outside consultants. The expenditures must be such that, if incurred in connection with the operation of an existing active trade or business, they would be allowable as a deduction in the year paid or incurred. However, under Sec. 195, they must be capitalized.

Under Sec. 195, a corporation may elect to deduct the first $5,000 of start-up expenditures. However, this amount is reduced (but not below zero) by the amount by which the cumulative start-up expenditures exceed $50,000. The corporation can amortize the remaining start-up expenditures over a 180-month period beginning in the month it begins business. This rule applies to start-up expenditures incurred after October 22, 2004.

Prior to October 23, 2004, a corporation could not deduct start-up expenditures currently but had to amortize them over a period of at least 60 months starting with the month in which its business began.

If the corporation makes no election, it must capitalize start-up expenditures and cannot deduct them until the corporation liquidates. If the corporation discontinues or disposes of the business before the end of the amortization period, it may deduct any remaining start-up expenditures as a loss.

STOP & THINK

Question: What is the difference between an organizational expenditure and a start-up expenditure?

Solution: Organizational expenditures are outlays made in forming a corporation, such as fees paid to the state of incorporation for the corporate chapter and fees paid to an attorney to draft the documents needed to form the corporation. Start-up expenditures are outlays that otherwise would be deductible as ordinary and necessary business expenses but that are capitalized because they were incurred prior to the start of the corporation's business activities.

A corporation may elect to deduct the first $5,000 of organizational expenditures and the first $5,000 of start-up expenditures. The corporation can amortize the remainder of each set of expenditures over 180 months. Like a corporation, a partnership can deduct and amortize its organizational and start-up expenditures. A sole proprietorship may incur start-up expenditures, but sole proprietorships do not incur organizational expenditures.

LIMITATION ON DEDUCTIONS FOR ACCRUED COMPENSATION. If a corporation accrues an obligation to pay compensation, the corporation must make the payment within 2½ months after the close of its tax year. Otherwise, the deduction cannot be taken until the year of payment.[16] The reason is that, if a payment is delayed beyond 2½ months, the IRS treats it as a deferred compensation plan. Deferred compensation cannot be deducted until the year the corporation pays it and the recipient includes the payment in income.[17]

EXAMPLE C:3-7 ▶ On December 10, 2007, Bell Corporation, a calendar year taxpayer, accrues an obligation for a $100,000 bonus to Marge, a sales representative who has had an outstanding year. Marge owns no Bell stock. Bell must make the payment by March 15, 2007. Otherwise, Bell Corporation cannot deduct the $100,000 in its 2007 tax return but must wait until the year it pays the bonus. ◀

CHARITABLE CONTRIBUTIONS. The treatment of charitable contributions by individual and corporate taxpayers differs in three ways: the timing of the deduction, the amount of the deduction permitted for the contribution of certain nonmoney property, and the maximum deduction permitted in any given year.

Timing of the Deduction. Corporations may deduct contributions to qualified charitable organizations. Generally, the contribution must have been *paid* during the year (not just pledged) for a deduction to be allowed for a given year. A special rule, however, applies to corporations using the accrual method of accounting (corporations using the cash or hybrid methods of accounting are not eligible).[18] These corporations may elect to treat part or all of a charitable contribution as having been made in the year it accrued (instead of the year paid) if

- The board of directors authorizes the contribution in the year it accrued
- The corporation pays the contribution on or before the fifteenth day of the third month following the end of the accrual year.

The corporation makes the election by deducting the contribution in its tax return for the accrual year and by attaching a copy of the board of director's resolution to the return. Any portion of the contribution for which the corporation does not make the election is deducted in the year paid.

EXAMPLE C:3-8 ▶ Echo Corporation is a calendar year taxpayer using the accrual method of accounting. In 2007, its board of directors authorizes a $10,000 contribution to the Girl Scouts. Echo pays the contribution on March 10, 2008. Echo may elect to treat part or all of the contribution as having been paid in 2007. If the corporation pays the contribution after March 17, 2008 (March 15 falls on a Saturday), it may not deduct the contribution in 2007 but may deduct it in 2008. ◀

TAX STRATEGY TIP

The tax laws do not require a corporation to recognize a gain when it contributes appreciated property to a charitable organization. Thus, except for inventory and limited other properties, a corporation can deduct the FMV of its donation without having to recognize any appreciation in its gross income. On the other hand, a decline in the value of donated property is not deductible. Thus, the corporation should sell the loss property to recognize the loss and then donate the sales proceeds to the chariable organization.

Deducting Contributions of Nonmonetary Property. If a taxpayer donates money to a qualified charitable organization, the amount of the charitable contribution deduction equals the amount of money donated. If the taxpayer donates property, the amount of the charitable contribution deduction generally equals the property's fair market value (FMV). However, special rules apply to donations of appreciated nonmonetary property known as ordinary income property and capital gain property.[19]

In this context, **ordinary income property** is property whose sale would have resulted in a gain other than a long-term capital gain (i.e., ordinary income or short-term capital gain). Examples of ordinary income property include investment property held for one year or less, inventory property, and property subject to depreciation recapture under Secs. 1245 and 1250. The deduction allowed for a donation of such property is limited to the property's FMV minus the amount of ordinary income or short-term capital gain the corporation would have recognized had it sold the property.

[16] Temp. Reg. Sec. 1.404(b)-1T.
[17] Sec. 404(b).
[18] Sec. 170(a).
[19] Sec. 170(e).

In three special cases, a corporation may deduct the donated property's adjusted basis plus one-half of the excess of the property's FMV over its adjusted basis (not to exceed twice the property's adjusted basis). This special rule applies to inventory if

1. The use of the property is related to the donee's exempt function, and it is used solely for the care of the ill, the needy, or infants;
2. The property is not transferred to the donee in exchange for money, other property, or services; and
3. The donor receives a statement from the charitable organization stating that conditions (1) and (2) will be complied with.

A similar rule applies to contributions of scientific research property if the corporation created the property and contributed it to a college, university, or tax-exempt scientific research organization for its use within two years of creating the property.

EXAMPLE C:3-9 ▶ King Corporation donates inventory having a $26,000 adjusted basis and a $40,000 FMV to a qualified public charity. A $33,000 [$26,000 + (0.50 × $14,000)] deduction is allowed for the contribution of the inventory if the charitable organization will use the inventory for the care of the ill, needy, or infants, or if the donee is an educational institution or research organization that will use the scientific research property for research or experimentation. Otherwise, the deduction is limited to the property's $26,000 adjusted basis. If instead the inventory's FMV is $100,000 and the donation meets either of the two sets of requirements outlined above, the charitable contribution deduction is limited to $52,000, the lesser of the property's adjusted basis plus one-half of the appreciation [$63,000 = $26,000 + (0.50 × $74,000)] or twice the property's adjusted basis ($52,000 = $26,000 × 2). ◀

ADDITIONAL COMMENT

A similar rule also applies in 2007 for computer technology donated for educational purposes.

When a corporation donates appreciated property whose sale would result in long-term capital gain (also known as **capital gain property**) to a charitable organization, the amount of the contribution deduction generally equals the property's FMV. However, special restrictions apply if

- ▶ The corporation donates a patent, copyright, trademark, trade name, trade secret, know-how, certain software, or other similar property;
- ▶ A corporation donates tangible personal property to a charitable organization and the organization's use of the property is unrelated to its tax-exempt purpose; or
- ▶ A corporation donates appreciated property to certain private nonoperating foundations.[20]

In these cases, the amount of the corporation's contribution is limited to the property's FMV minus the long-term capital gain that would have resulted from the property's sale.

EXAMPLE C:3-10 ▶ Fox Corporation donates artwork to the MacNay Museum. The artwork, purchased two years earlier for $15,000, is worth $38,000 on the date Fox donates it. At the time of the donation, the museum's directors intend to sell the work to raise funds to conduct museum activities. Fox's deduction for the gift is limited to $15,000. If the museum plans to display the artwork to the public, the entire $38,000 deduction is permitted. Fox can avoid losing a portion of its charitable contribution deduction by, as a condition of the donation, placing restrictions on the sale or use of the property. ◀

Substantiation Requirements. Section 170(f)(11) imposes substantiation requirements for noncash charitable contributions. If the corporation does not comply, it will lose the charitable contribution deduction. The requirements are as follows:

- ▶ If the contribution deduction exceeds $500, the corporation must include with its tax return a description of the property and any other information required by Treasury Regulations.

[20] Sec. 170(e)(5). The restriction on contributions of appreciated property to private nonoperating foundations does not apply to contributions of stock for which market quotations are readily available.

- If the contribution deduction exceeds $5,000, the corporation must obtain a qualified appraisal and include with its tax return any information and appraisal required by Treasury Regulations. (Current regulations require an appraisal summary.)
- If the contribution deduction exceeds $500,000, the corporation must attach a qualified appraisal to the tax return.

The second and third requirements, however, do not apply to contributions of cash; publicly traded securities; inventory; or certain motor vehicles, boats, or aircraft the donee organization sells without any intervening use or material improvement. With regard to these vehicles, the donor corporation's deduction is limited to the amount of gross proceeds the donee organization receives on the sale.

BOOK-TO-TAX ACCOUNTING COMPARISON

For financial accounting purposes, all charitable contributions can be claimed as an expense without regard to the amount of profits reported. Only the tax deduction for charitable contributions is limited. Thus, the charitable contribution carryover for tax purposes creates a deferred tax asset, possibly subject to a valuation allowance.

Maximum Deduction Permitted. A limit applies to the amount of charitable contributions a corporation can deduct in a given year. The limit is calculated differently for corporations than for individuals. Contribution deductions by corporations are limited to 10% of adjusted taxable income. Adjusted taxable income is the corporation's taxable income computed without regard to any of the following amounts:

- The charitable contribution deduction
- An NOL carryback
- A capital loss carryback
- The dividends-received deduction[21]
- The U.S. production activities deduction

Contributions that exceed the 10% limit are not deductible in the current year. Instead, they carry forward to the next five tax years. Any excess contributions not deducted within those five years expire. The corporation may deduct excess contributions in the carryover year only after it deducts any contributions made in that year. The total charitable contribution deduction (including any deduction for contribution carryovers) is limited to 10% of the corporation's adjusted taxable income in the carryover year.[22]

EXAMPLE C:3-11 ▶ Golf Corporation reports the following results in 2007 and 2008:

	2007	*2008*
Adjusted taxable income	$200,000	$300,000
Charitable contributions	35,000	25,000

Golf's 2007 contribution deduction is limited to $20,000 (0.10 × $200,000). Golf has a $15,000 ($35,000 − $20,000) contribution carryover to 2008. The 2008 contribution deduction is limited to $30,000 (0.10 × $300,000). Golf's deduction for 2008 is composed of the $25,000 donated in 2008 and $5,000 of the 2007 carryover. The remaining $10,000 carryover from 2007 carries over to 2009, 2010, 2011, and 2012. ◀

Topic Review C:3-1 summarizes the basic corporate charitable contribution deduction rules.

SPECIAL DEDUCTIONS

C corporations are allowed three special deductions: the U.S. production activities deduction, the dividends-received deduction, and the NOL deduction.

ADDITIONAL COMMENT

While discussed in this text under special deductions, the U.S. production activities deduction actually appears before Line 28 on Form 1120.

U.S. PRODUCTION ACTIVITIES DEDUCTION. Section 199 allows a **U.S. production activities deduction** equal to a percentage times the lesser of (1) qualified production activities income for the year or (2) taxable income before the U.S. production activities deduction. The phased-in percentages are as follows:

2005, 2006	3%
2007, 2008, 2009	6%
2010 and thereafter	9%

[21] Sec. 170(b)(2).

[22] Sec. 170(d)(2).

Topic Review C:3-1

Corporate Charitable Contribution Rules

1. Timing of the contribution deduction
   a. General rule: A deduction is allowed for contributions paid during the year.
   b. Accrual method corporations can accrue contributions approved by their board of directors prior to the end of the accrual year and paid within 2½ months of that year-end.
2. Amount of the contribution deduction
   a. General rule: A deduction is allowed for the amount of money and the FMV of other property donated.
   b. Exceptions for ordinary income property:
      1. If donated property would result in ordinary income or short-term capital gain if sold, the deduction is limited to the property's FMV minus this potential ordinary income or short-term capital gain. Thus, for gain property the deduction equals the property's cost or adjusted basis.
      2. Special rule: For donations of (1) inventory used for the care of the ill, needy, or infants or (2) scientific research property or computer technology and equipment to certain educational institutions, a corporate donor may deduct the property's basis plus one-half of the excess of the property's FMV over its adjusted basis. The deduction may not exceed twice the property's adjusted basis.
   c. Exceptions for capital gain property: If the corporation donates tangible personal property to a charitable organization for a use unrelated to its tax-exempt purpose, or the corporation donates appreciated property to a private nonoperating foundation, the corporation's contribution is limited to the property's FMV minus the long-term capital gain that would result if the corporation sold the property.
3. Limitation on contribution deduction
   a. The contribution deduction is limited to 10% of the corporation's taxable income computed without regard to the charitable contribution deduction, any NOL or capital loss carryback, the dividends-received deduction, and the U.S production activities deduction.
   b. Excess contributions carry forward for a five-year period.

The deduction, however, cannot exceed 50% of the corporation's W-2 wages for the year.

Qualified production activities income is the taxpayer's domestic production gross receipts less the following amounts:

- Cost of goods sold allocable to these receipts;
- Other deductions, expenses, and losses directly allocable to these receipts; and
- A ratable portion of other deductions, expenses, and losses not directly allocable to these receipts or to other classes of income.

BOOK-TO-TAX ACCOUNTING COMPARISON

The U.S. production activities deduction is not expensed for financial accounting purposes. Thus, it creates a permanent difference that affects the corporation's effective tax rate but not its deferred taxes.

Domestic production gross receipts include receipts from the following taxpayer activities:

- The lease, rental, license, sale, exchange, or other disposition of (1) qualified production property (tangible property, computer software, and sound recordings) manufactured, produced, grown, or extracted in whole or significant part within the United States; (2) qualified film production; or (3) electricity, natural gas, or potable water produced within the United States
- Construction performed in the United States
- Engineering or architectural services performed in the United States for construction projects in the United States

ADDITIONAL COMMENT

In addition to providing a benefit, the U.S. production activities deduction will increase a corporation's compliance costs because of the time necessary to determine what income and deductions pertain to U.S. production activities.

Domestic production gross receipts, however, do not include receipts from the sale of food and beverages the taxpayer prepares at a retail establishment and do not apply to the transmission of electricity, natural gas, or potable water.

The U.S. production activities deduction has the effect of reducing a corporation's marginal tax rate on qualifying taxable income. For example, a 3% deduction (in 2005–2006) for a corporation in the 35% tax bracket produces about a 1% decrease in the corporation's marginal tax rate ($0.03 \times 35\% = 1.05\%$). Similarly, a 6% deduction (in 2007–2009) will decrease the marginal tax rate by about 2% ($0.06 \times 35\% = 2.1\%$), and a 9% deduction (after 2009) will decrease the marginal tax rate by about 3% ($0.09 \times 35\% = 3.15\%$).

EXAMPLE C:3-12 ▶ In 2007, Gamma Corporation earns domestic production gross receipts of $1 million and incurs allocable expenses of $400,000. Thus, its qualified production activities income is $600,000. In addition, Gamma has $200,000 of income from other sources, resulting in taxable income of $800,000 before the U.S. production activities deduction. Its U.S. production activities deduction, therefore, is $36,000 ($600,000 × 0.06), and its taxable income is $764,000 ($800,000 – $36,000). ◀

EXAMPLE C:3-13 ▶ Assume the same facts as in Example C:3-12 except Gamma has $100,000 of losses from other sources rather than $200,000 of other income, resulting in taxable income of $500,000 before the U.S. production activities deduction. In this case, its U.S. production activities deduction is $30,000 ($500,000 × 0.06), and its taxable income is $470,000 ($500,000 – $30,000). ◀

DIVIDENDS-RECEIVED DEDUCTION. A corporation must include in its gross income any dividends received on stock it owns in another corporation. As described in Chapter C:2, the taxation of dividend payments to a shareholder generally results in double taxation. When a distributing corporation pays a dividend to a corporate shareholder and the recipient corporation subsequently distributes these earnings to its shareholders, potential triple taxation of the earnings can result.

EXAMPLE C:3-14 ▶ Adobe Corporation owns stock in Bell Corporation. Bell reports taxable income of $100,000 and pays federal income taxes on its income. Bell distributes its after-tax income to its shareholders. The dividend Adobe receives from Bell must be included in its gross income and, to the extent it reports a profit for the year, Adobe will pay taxes on the dividend. Adobe distributes its remaining after-tax income to its shareholders. The shareholders must include Adobe's dividends in their gross income and pay federal income taxes on the distribution. Thus, Bell's income in this example potentially is taxed three times. ◀

BOOK-TO-TAX ACCOUNTING COMPARISON

A corporation includes dividends in its financial accounting income but does not subtract a dividends-received deduction in determining its book net income. Thus, the dividends-received deduction creates a permanent difference that affects the corporation's effective tax rate but not its deferred taxes.

To partially mitigate the effects of multiple taxation, corporations are allowed a **dividends-received deduction** for dividends received from other domestic corporations and from certain foreign corporations.

General Rule for Dividends-Received Deduction. Corporations that own less than 20% of the distributing corporation's stock may deduct 70% of the dividends received. If the shareholder corporation owns 20% or more of the distributing corporation's stock (both voting power and value) but less than 80% of such stock, it may deduct 80% of the dividends received.[23]

EXAMPLE C:3-15 ▶ Hale Corporation reports the following results in the current year:

Gross income from operations	$300,000
Dividends from 15%-owned domestic corporation	100,000
Operating expenses	280,000

Gross income from operations and expenses both pertain to qualified production activities, so Hale's qualified production activities income is $20,000 ($300,000 – $280,000). Hale's dividends-received deduction is $70,000 (0.70 × $100,000). Thus, Hale's taxable income is computed as follows:

Gross income	$400,000
Minus: Operating expenses	(280,000)
Taxable income before special deductions	$120,000
Minus: Dividends-received deduction	(70,000)
Taxable income before the U.S. production activites deduction	$ 50,000
Minus: U.S. production activities deduction ($20,000 × 0.06)	(1,200)
Taxable income	$ 48,800

◀

Limitation on Dividends-Received Deduction. In the case of dividends received from corporations that are less than 20% owned, the deduction is limited to the lesser of 70% of dividends received or 70% of taxable income computed without regard to any NOL deduction, any capital loss carryback, the dividends-received deduction itself, or the U.S. production activities deduction.[24] In the case of dividends received from a 20% or more

[23] Secs. 243(a) and (c).

[24] Sec. 246(b).

owned corporation, the dividends-received deduction is limited to the lesser of 80% of dividends received or 80% of taxable income computed without regard to the same deductions.

EXAMPLE C:3-16 ▶ Assume the same facts as in Example C:3-15 except Hale Corporation's operating expenses for the year are $310,000 and that qualified production activities income is zero (or negative). Thus, the corporation cannot claim the U.S. production activities deduction. Hale's taxable income before the dividends-received deduction is $90,000 ($300,000 + $100,000 − $310,000). The dividends-received deduction is limited to the lesser of 70% of dividends received ($70,000 = $100,000 × 0.70) or 70% of taxable income before the dividends-received deduction ($63,000 = $90,000 × 0.70). Thus, the dividends-received deduction is $63,000. Hale's taxable income is $27,000 ($90,000 − $63,000). ◀

A corporation that receives dividends eligible for both the 80% dividends-received deduction and the 70% dividends-received deduction must compute the 80% dividends-received deduction first and then reduce taxable income by the aggregate amount of dividends eligible for the 80% deduction before computing the 70% deduction.

EXAMPLE C:3-17 ▶ Assume the same facts as in Example C:3-16 except Hale Corporation receives $75,000 of the dividends from a 25%-owned corporation and the remaining $25,000 from a 15%-owned corporation. The tentative dividends-received deduction from the 25%-owned corporation is $60,000 ($75,000 × 0.80), which is less than the $72,000 ($90,000 × 0.80) limitation. Thus, Hale can deduct the entire $60,000. The tentative dividends-received deduction from the 15%-owned corporation is $17,500 ($25,000 × .70). The limitation, however, is $10,500 [($90,000 − $75,000) × 0.70]. Note that, in computing this limitation, Hale reduces its taxable income by the entire $75,000 dividend received from the 25%-owned corporation. Thus, Hale can deduct only $10,500 of the $17,500 amount. Hale's taxable income is $19,500 ($90,000 − $60,000 − $10,500). ◀

Exception to the Limitation. The taxable income limitation on the dividends-received deduction does not apply if, after taking into account the full dividends-received deduction, the corporation has an NOL for the year.

EXAMPLE C:3-18 ▶ Assume the same facts as in Example C:3-16 except Hale Corporation's operating expenses for the year are $331,000. Hale's taxable income before the dividends-received deduction is $69,000 ($300,000 + $100,000 − $331,000). The tentative dividends-received deduction is $70,000 (0.70 × $100,000). Hale's dividends-received deduction is not restricted by the limitation of 70% of taxable income before the dividends-received deduction because, after taking into account the tentative $70,000 dividends-received deduction, the corporation has a $1,000 ($69,000 − $70,000) NOL for the year. ◀

ADDITIONAL COMMENT

When the dividends-received deduction creates (or increases) an NOL, the corporation gets the full benefit of the deduction because it can carry back or carry forward the NOL.

TAX STRATEGY TIP

A corporation can avoid the dividends-received deduction limitation either by (1) increasing its taxable income before the dividends-received deduction so the limitation exceeds the tentative dividends-received deduction or (2) decreasing its taxable income before the dividends-received deduction so the tentative dividends-received deduction creates an NOL.

The following table compares the results of Examples C:3-15, C:3-16, and C:3-18:

	Example C:3-15	*Example C:3-16*	*Example C:3-18*
Gross income	$400,000	$400,000	$400,000
Minus: Operating expenses	(280,000)	(310,000)	(331,000)
Taxable income before special deductions	$120,000	$ 90,000	$ 69,000
Minus: Dividends-received deduction	(70,000)	(63,000)	(70,000)
U.S. production activities deduction	(1,200)	–0–	–0–
Taxable income (NOL)	$ 48,800	$ 27,000	$ (1,000)

Of these three examples, the only case where the dividends-received deduction does not equal the full 70% of the $100,000 dividend is Example C:3-16. In that case, the deduction is limited to $63,000 because taxable income before special deductions is less than the $100,000 dividend *and* because the full $70,000 deduction would not create an NOL. The special exception to the dividends-received deduction can create interesting situations. For example, the additional $21,000 of deductions incurred in Example C:3-18 (as compared to Example C:3-16) resulted in a $28,000 reduction in taxable income. Corporate taxpayers should be aware of these rules and consider deferring income or recognizing expenses to ensure being able to deduct the full 70% or 80% dividends-received deduction. If the taxable income limitation applies, the corporation loses the unused dividends-received deduction.

Members of an Affiliated Group. Members of an affiliated group of corporations can claim a 100% dividends-received deduction with respect to dividends received from other group members.[25] A group of corporations is affiliated if a parent corporation owns at least 80% of the stock (both voting power and value) of at least one subsidiary corporation, and at least 80% of the stock (both voting power and value) of each other corporation is owned by other group members. The 100% dividends-received deduction is not subject to a taxable income limitation and is taken before the 80% or 70% dividends-received deduction.[26]

EXAMPLE C:3-19 ▶ Hardy Corporation reports the following results for the current year:

Gross income from operations	$520,000
Dividend received from an 80%-owned affiliated corporation	100,000
Dividend received from a 20%-owned corporation	250,000
Operating expenses	550,000

Because Hardy's qualified production activities income is negative, it cannot claim the U.S. production activities deduction. Hardy's taxable income before any dividends-received deduction is $320,000 ($520,000 + $100,000 + $250,000 − $550,000). Hardy can deduct the entire dividend received from the 80%-owned affiliate without limitation. The tentative dividends-received deduction from the 20%-owned corporation is $200,000 ($250,000 × 0.80). The limitation, however, is $176,000 [($320,000 − $100,000) × 0.80]. Note that, in computing this limitation, Hardy first reduces its taxable income by the $100,000 dividend received from the 80%-owned affiliate. Thus, Hardy can deduct only $176,000 of the $200,000 amount. Hardy's taxable income is $44,000 ($320,000 − $100,000 − $176,000). ◀

Dividends Received from Foreign Corporations. The dividends-received deduction applies primarily to dividends received from domestic corporations. The dividends-received deduction does not apply to dividends received from a foreign corporation because the U.S. Government does not tax its income. Thus, that income is not subject to the multiple taxation illustrated above.[27]

ADDITIONAL COMMENT

Stock purchased on which a dividend has been declared has an increased value. This value will drop when the corporation pays the dividend. If the dividend is eligible for a dividends-received deduction and the drop in value also creates a capital loss, corporate shareholders could use this event as a tax planning device. To avoid this result, no dividends-received deduction is available for stock held 45 days or less.

Stock Held 45 Days or Less. A corporation may not claim a dividends-received deduction if it holds the dividend paying stock for less than 46 days during the 91-day period that begins 45 days before the stock becomes ex-dividend with respect to the dividend.[28] This rule prevents a corporation from claiming a dividends-received deduction if it purchases stock shortly before an ex-dividend date and sells the stock shortly thereafter. (The ex-dividend date is the first day on which a purchaser of stock is not entitled to a previously declared dividend.) Absent this rule, such a purchase and sale would allow the corporation to receive dividends at a low tax rate—a maximum of a 10.5% [(100% − 70%) × 0.35] effective tax rate—and to recognize a capital loss on the sale of stock that could offset capital gains taxed at a 35% tax rate.

EXAMPLE C:3-20 ▶ Theta Corporation purchases 100 shares of Maine Corporation's stock for $100,000 one day before Maine's ex-dividend date. Theta receives a $5,000 dividend on the stock and then sells the stock for $95,000 on the forty-fifth day after the dividend payment date. Because the stock is worth $100,000 immediately before the $5,000 dividend payment, its value drops to $95,000 ($100,000 − $5,000) immediately after the dividend. The sale results in a $5,000 ($100,000 − $95,000) capital loss that may offset a $5,000 capital gain. Assuming a 35% corporate tax rate, the following table summarizes the profit (loss) to Theta with and without the 45-day rule.

[25] Sec. 243(a)(3).

[26] Secs. 243(b)(5) and 1504.

[27] Sec. 245. A limited dividends-received deduction is allowed on dividends received from a foreign corporation that earns income by conducting a trade or business in the United States and, therefore, is subject to U.S. taxes.

[28] Sec. 246(c)(1).

	If Deduction Is Allowed	If Deduction Is Not Allowed
Dividends	$5,000	$5,000
Minus: 35% tax on dividend	(525)[a]	(1,750)
Dividend (after taxes)	$4,475	$3,250
Capital loss	$5,000	$5,000
Minus: 35% tax savings on loss	(1,750)	(1,750)
Net loss on stock	$3,250	$3,250
Dividend (after taxes)	$4,475	$3,250
Minus: Net loss on stock	(3,250)	(3,250)
Net profit (loss)	$1,225	$ –0–

[a][$5,000 − (0.70 × $5,000)] × 0.35 = $525

ADDITIONAL COMMENT

Borrowing money with deductible interest to purchase a tax-advantaged asset, such as stock eligible for the dividends-received deduction, is an example of "tax arbitrage." Many provisions in the IRC, such as the limits on debt-financial stock, are aimed at curtailing tax arbitrage transactions.

The profit is not available if Theta sells the stock shortly after receiving the dividend because Theta must hold the Maine stock for at least 46 days to obtain the dividends-received deduction. ◀

Debt-Financed Stock. The dividends-received deduction is not allowed to the extent the corporation borrows money to acquire the dividend paying stock.[29] This rule prevents a corporation from deducting interest paid on money borrowed to purchase the stock, while paying little or no tax on the dividends received on the stock.

EXAMPLE C:3-21 ▶ **Palmer Corporation, whose marginal tax rate is 35%, borrows $100,000 at a 10% interest rate to purchase 30% of Sun Corporation's stock. The Sun stock pays an $8,000 annual dividend. If a dividends-received deduction were allowed for this investment, Palmer would have a net profit of $940 annually on owning the Sun stock even though the dividend received is less than the interest paid. The following table summarizes the profit (loss) to Palmer with and without the debt-financing rule.**

REAL-WORLD EXAMPLE

Although sound in theory, the debt-financed stock limitation may be difficult to apply in practice. This difficulty became particularly apparent in a recent district court case, *OBH, Inc. v. U.S.*, 96 AFTR 2d, 2005-6801, 2005-2 USTC ¶50,627 (DC NB, 2005), where the IRS failed to establish that a corporation's debt proceeds were directly traceable to the acquisition of dividend paying stock.

	If Deduction Is Allowed	If Deduction Is Not Allowed
Dividends	$ 8,000	$ 8,000
Minus: 35% tax on dividend	(560)[a]	(2,800)
Dividend (after taxes)	$ 7,440	$5,200
Interest paid	$10,000	$10,000
Minus: 35% tax savings on deduction	(3,500)	(3,500)
Net cost of borrowing	$ 6,500	$6,500
Dividend (after taxes)	$ 7,440	$ 5,200
Minus: Net cost of borrowing	(6,500)	(6,500)
Net profit (loss)	$ 940	$(1,300)

[a][$8,000 − (0.80 × $8,000)] × 0.35 = $560

This example illustrates how the rule disallowing the dividends-received deduction on debt-financed stock prevents corporations from making an after-tax profit by borrowing funds to purchase stocks paying dividends that are less than the cost of the borrowing. ◀

NET OPERATING LOSSES (NOLs). If a corporation's deductions exceed its gross income for the year, the corporation has a **net operating loss (NOL)**. The NOL is the amount by which the corporation's deductions (including any dividends-received deduction) exceed its gross income.[30] In computing an NOL for a given year, no deduction is

[29] Sec. 246A.

[30] Sec. 172(c).

KEY POINT

An individual must make many adjustments to his or her taxable income to calculate his or her NOL. A corporation's NOL is simply the excess of its current deductions over its income.

permitted for a carryover or carryback of an NOL from a preceding or succeeding year. However, unlike an individual's NOL, no other adjustments are required to compute a corporation's NOL. If the corporation has an NOL, it also would not be allowed a U.S. production activities deduction because it has no positive taxable income.

A corporation's NOL carries back two years and carries over 20 years. It carries to the earliest of the two preceding years first and offsets taxable income reported in that year. If the loss cannot be used in that year, it carries to the immediately preceding year, and then to the next 20 years in chronological order. The corporation may elect to forgo the carryback period entirely and instead carry over the entire loss to the next 20 years.[31]

EXAMPLE C:3-22 ▶ In 2007, Gray Corporation has gross income of $150,000 (including $100,000 from operations and $50,000 in dividends from a 30%-owned domestic corporation) and $180,000 of expenses. Gray has a $70,000 [$150,000 – $180,000 – (0.80 × $50,000)] NOL. The NOL carries back to 2005 unless Gray elects to forego the carryback period. If Gray had $20,000 of taxable income in 2005, $20,000 of Gray's 2007 NOL offsets that income. Gray receives a refund of all taxes paid in 2005. Gray carries the remaining $50,000 of the 2007 NOL to 2006. Any of the NOL not used in 2006 carries over to 2008. ◀

BOOK-TO-TAX ACCOUNTING COMPARISON

An NOL carryover for tax purposes creates a deferred tax asset, possibly subject to a valuation allowance.

A corporation might elect not to carry an NOL back because its income was taxed at a low marginal tax rate in the carryback period and the corporation anticipates income being taxed at a higher marginal tax rate in later years or because it used tax credit carryovers in the earlier year that were about to expire. The corporation must make this election for the entire carryback by the due date (including extensions) for filing the return for the year in which the corporation incurred the NOL. The corporation makes the election by checking a box on Form 1120 when it files the return. Once made for a tax year, the election is irrevocable.[32] However, if the corporation incurs an NOL in another year, the decision as to whether that NOL should be carried back is a separate decision. In other words, each year's NOL is treated separately and is subject to a separate election.

To obtain a refund due to carrying an NOL back to a preceding year, a corporation must file either Form 1120X (Amended U.S. Corporation Income Tax Return) or Form 1139 (Corporation Application for a Tentative Refund).

THE SEQUENCING OF THE DEDUCTION CALCULATIONS. The rules for charitable contributions, dividends-received, NOL, and U.S. production activities deductions require that these deductions be calculated in the following sequence:

1. All deductions other than the charitable contributions deduction, the dividends-received deduction, and the NOL deduction
2. The charitable contributions deduction
3. The dividends-received deduction
4. The NOL deduction
5. The U.S. production activities deduction

As stated previously, the charitable contributions deduction is limited to 10% of taxable income before the charitable contributions deduction, any NOL or capital loss carryback, the dividends-received deduction, or the U.S. production activities deduction, but *after* any NOL carryover deduction. Once the corporation determines its charitable contributions deduction, it adds back any NOL carryover deduction and subtracts the charitable contributions deduction before computing the dividends-received deduction. The corporation then subtracts the NOL deduction, if any, before determining its U.S. production activities deduction.

---

[31] The two year carryback and 20-year carryforward applies to NOLs incurred in tax years beginning after August 5, 1997. The change does not apply to NOLs carried forward from earlier years. These NOLs are, in general, carried back three years and carried forward 15 years. NOLs incurred in 2001 and 2002 were allowed a five-year carryback period.

[32] Sec. 172(b)(3)(C).

EXAMPLE C:3-23 ▶ East Corporation reports the following results for 2007:

Gross income from operations	$150,000
Dividends from 30%-owned domestic corporation	100,000
Operating expenses	100,000
Charitable contributions	35,000

In addition, East has $50,000 of qualified production activities income in the current year and a $40,000 NOL carryover from the previous year. East's charitable contributions deduction is computed as follows:

Gross income from operations	$150,000
Plus: Dividends	100,000
Gross income	$250,000
Minus: Operating expenses	(100,000)
NOL carryover	(40,000)
Base for calculation of the charitable contributions limitation	$110,000

East's charitable contributions deduction is limited to $11,000 (0.10 × $110,000). The $11,000 limitation means that East has a $24,000 ($35,000 − $11,000) excess contribution that carries forward for five years. East Corporation computes its taxable income as follows:

ADDITIONAL COMMENT

The U.S. production activities deduction is last in the ordering of deductions because it is limited to taxable income after all other deductions. However, on the corporate tax return, it appears after the charitable contributions deduction but before the dividends-received and NOL deductions. Specifically, it appears on Form 1120, Line 25, before Line 28.

Gross income	$250,000
Minus: Operating expenses	(100,000)
Charitable contributions deduction	(11,000)
Taxable income before special deductions	$139,000
Minus: Dividends-received deduction ($100,000 × 0.80)	(80,000)
NOL carryover deduction	(40,000)
Taxable income before the U.S. production activities deduction	$ 19,000
Minus: U.S. production activities deduction ($19,000 × 0.06)	(1,140)
Taxable income	$ 17,860 ◀

Note that, if an NOL is carried *back* from a later year, it is *not* taken into account in computing a corporation's charitable contributions limitation. In other words, the contribution deduction remains the same as in the year of the original return.

EXAMPLE C:3-24 ▶ Assume the same facts as in Example C:3-23, except the facts pertain to a prior year (e.g., 2005), and East carries back a $40,000 NOL to that year. East's base for calculation of the charitable contributions limitation was computed as follows when it filed the original return:

ADDITIONAL COMMENT

These computations in the carryback year are done on an amended return or an application for refund.

Gross income from operations	$150,000
Plus: Dividends	100,000
Gross income	$250,000
Minus: Operating expenses	(100,000)
Base for calculation of the charitable contributions limitation	$150,000

East's charitable contributions deduction was limited to $15,000 (0.10 × $150,000). The $15,000 limitation means that East had a $20,000 ($35,000 − $15,000) contribution carryover from the prior year. East Corporation computes its taxable income after the NOL carryback as follows:

Gross income ($150,000 + $100,000)	$250,000
Minus: Operating expenses	(100,000)
Charitable contributions deduction	(15,000)
Taxable income before special deductions	$135,000
Minus: Dividends-received deduction ($100,000 × 0.80)	(80,000)
NOL carryback deduction	(40,000)
Taxable income before the U.S. production activities deduction	$ 15,000
Minus: U.S. production activities deduction ($15,000 × 0.03)	(450)
Taxable income as recomputed	$ 14,550

Thus, East's prior-year charitable contributions deduction remains the same as originally claimed. ◀

STOP & THINK *Question:* Why does a corporation's NOL or capital loss carryback not affect its charitable contributions deduction, but yet the corporation must take into account an NOL or capital loss carryover when calculating its charitable contribution limitation?

Solution: A carryback affects a tax return already filed in a prior year. If a carryback had to be taken into account when calculating the charitable contribution deduction limitation in the prior year, it might change the amount of the allowable charitable contribution. This change in turn might affect other items such as the carryback year's dividends-received deduction and some later years' deductions as well. For example, assume Alpha Corporation has a $10,000 NOL in 2007 that it carries back to 2005. If the NOL were permitted to reduce Alpha's allowable charitable contribution for 2005 by $1,000, Alpha's dividends-received deduction for 2005 and its charitable contribution deductions for 2006 as well might change.

To avoid these complications, which might force Alpha to amend its tax returns from the carryback year (2005) to the current year (2007), the law states that carrybacks are not taken into account in calculating the charitable contribution deduction limitation. Also, in the prior year, management made its charitable contribution decisions without knowledge of future NOLs. Altering the result of those prior decisions with future events might be unfair.

EXCEPTIONS FOR CLOSELY HELD CORPORATIONS

Congress has placed limits on certain transactions to prevent abuse in situations where a corporation is closely held. Some of these restrictions are explained below.

TRANSACTIONS BETWEEN A CORPORATION AND ITS SHAREHOLDERS. Special rules apply to transactions between a corporation and a controlling shareholder. Section 1239 may convert a capital gain realized on the sale of depreciable property between a corporation and a controlling shareholder into ordinary income. Section 267(a)(1) denies a deduction for losses realized on property sales between a corporation and a controlling shareholder. Section 267(a)(2) defers a deduction for accrued expenses and interest on certain transactions involving a corporation and a controlling shareholder.

In all three of the preceding situations, a controlling shareholder is one who owns more than 50% (in value) of the corporation's stock.[33] In determining whether a shareholder owns more than 50% of a corporation's stock, certain constructive stock ownership rules apply.[34] Under these rules, a shareholder is considered to own not only his or her own stock, but stock owned by family members (e.g., brothers, sisters, spouse, ancestors, and lineal descendants) and entities in which the shareholder has an ownership or beneficial interest (e.g., corporations, partnerships, trusts, and estates).

Gains on Sale or Exchange Transactions. If a controlling shareholder sells depreciable property to a controlled corporation (or vice versa) and the property is depreciable in the purchaser's hands, any gain on the sale is treated as ordinary income under Sec. 1239(a).

EXAMPLE C:3-25 ▶ Ann owns all of Cape Corporation's stock. Ann sells a building to Cape and recognizes a $25,000 gain, which usually would be Sec. 1231 gain or Sec. 1250 gain (taxed at a maximum 15% or 25% capital gains tax rate, respectively). However, because Ann owns more than 50% of the Cape stock and the building is a depreciable property in Cape's hands, Sec. 1239 requires that Ann recognize the entire $25,000 gain as ordinary income. ◀

BOOK-TO-TAX ACCOUNTING COMPARISON

The denial of deductions for losses involving related party transactions is unique to the tax area. Financial accounting rules contain no such disallowance provision.

Losses on Sale or Exchange Transactions. Section 267(a)(1) denies a deduction for losses realized on a sale of property by a corporation to a controlling shareholder or on a sale of property by the controlling shareholder to the corporation. If the purchaser later sells the property to another party at a gain, that seller recognizes gain only to the extent it exceeds the previously disallowed loss.[35] Should the purchaser instead sell the property at a loss, the previously disallowed loss is never recognized.

[33] Sec. 267(b)(2).
[34] Sec. 267(e)(3).
[35] Sec. 267(d).

EXAMPLE C:3-26 ▶ Quattros Corporation sells an automobile to Juan, its sole shareholder, for $6,500. The corporation's adjusted basis for the automobile is $8,000. Quattros realizes a $1,500 ($6,500 – $8,000) loss on the sale. Section 267(a)(1), however, disallows the loss to the corporation. If Juan later sells the auto for $8,500, he realizes a $2,000 ($8,500 – $6,500) gain. He recognizes only $500 of that gain, the amount by which his $2,000 gain exceeds the $1,500 loss previously disallowed to Quattros. If Juan instead sells the auto for $7,500, he realizes a $1,000 ($7,500-$6,500) gain but recognizes no gain or loss. The previously disallowed loss reduces the gain to zero but may not create a loss. Finally, if Juan instead sells the auto for $4,000, he realizes and may be able to recognize a $2,500 ($4,000 – $6,500) loss. However, the $1,500 loss previously disallowed to Quattros is permanently lost. ◀

KEY POINT

Section 267(a)(2) is primarily aimed at the situation involving an accrual method corporation that accrues compensation to a cash method shareholder-employee. This provision forces a matching of the income and expense recognition by deferring the deduction to the year the shareholder recognizes the income.

Corporation and Controlling Shareholder Using Different Accounting Methods. Section 267(a)(2) defers a deduction for accrued expenses or interest owed by a corporation to a controlling shareholder or by a controlling shareholder to a corporation when the two parties use different accounting methods and the payee thereby includes the amount in gross income later than when the payer accrues the deduction. Under this rule, accrued expenses or interest owed by a corporation to a controlling shareholder may not be deducted until the shareholder includes the payment in gross income.

EXAMPLE C:3-27 ▶ Hill Corporation uses the accrual method of accounting. Hill's sole shareholder, Ruth, uses the cash method of accounting. Both taxpayers use the calendar year as their tax year. The corporation accrues a $25,000 interest payment to Ruth on December 20 of the current year. Hill makes the payment on March 20 of next year. Hill, however, cannot deduct the interest in the current year but must wait until Ruth reports the income next year. Thus, the expense and income are matched. ◀

LOSS LIMITATION RULES

At-Risk Rules If five or fewer shareholders own more than 50% (in value) of a C corporation's outstanding stock at any time during the last half of the corporation's tax year, the corporation is subject to the at-risk rules.[36] In such case, the corporation can deduct losses pertaining to an activity only to the extent the corporation is at risk for that activity at year-end. Any losses not deductible because of the at-risk rules must be carried over and deducted in a succeeding year when the corporation's risk with respect to the activity increases. (See Chapter C:9 for additional discussion of the at-risk rules.)

Passive Activity Limitation Rules. Personal service corporations (PSCs) and **closely held C corporations** (those subject to the at-risk rules described above) also may be subject to the **passive activity limitations.**[37] If a PSC does not meet the material participation requirements, its net **passive losses** and credits must be carried over to a year when it has **passive income.** In the case of closely held C corporations that do not meet material participation requirements, passive losses and credits are allowed to offset the corporation's net active income but not its portfolio income (i.e., interest, dividends, annuities, royalties, and capital gains on the sale of investment property).[38]

COMPUTING A CORPORATION'S INCOME TAX LIABILITY

OBJECTIVE 3

Compute a corporation's income tax liability

Once a corporation determines its taxable income, it then must compute its tax liability for the year. Table C:3-2 outlines the steps for computing a corporation's regular (income) tax liability. This section explains the steps involved in arriving at a corporation's income tax liability in detail.

[36] Sec. 465(a).
[37] Secs. 469(a)(2)(B) and (C).
[38] Sec. 469(e)(2).

▼ **TABLE C:3-2**
Computation of the Corporate Regular (Income) Tax Liability

Taxable income	
Times:	Income tax rates
Regular tax liability	
Minus:	Foreign tax credit (Sec. 27)
Regular tax	
Minus:	General business credit (Sec. 38)
	Minimum tax credit (Sec. 53)
	Other allowed credits
Plus:	Recapture of previously claimed tax credits
Income tax liability	

GENERAL RULES

REAL-WORLD EXAMPLE

In 2005, the IRS collected $307 billion from corporations, which was 13.5% of the $2.27 trillion collected by the IRS. This percentage is up from 11.5% in 2004.

All C corporations (other than members of controlled groups of corporations and personal service corporations) use the same tax rate schedule to compute their **regular tax** liability. The following table shows these rates, which also are reproduced on the inside back cover of this textbook.

Taxable Income Over	*But Not Over*	*The Tax Is*	*Of the Amount Over*
$ –0–	$ 50,000	15%	$ –0–
50,000	75,000	$ 7,500 + 25%	50,000
75,000	100,000	13,750 + 34%	75,000
100,000	335,000	22,250 + 39%	100,000
335,000	10,000,000	113,900 + 34%	335,000
10,000,000	15,000,000	3,400,000 + 35%	10,000,000
15,000,000	18,333,333	5,150,000 + 38%	15,000,000
18,333,333	—	6,416,667 + 35%	18,333,333

EXAMPLE C:3-28 ▶ Copper Corporation reports taxable income of $100,000. Copper's regular tax liability is computed as follows:

Tax on first $50,000:	0.15 × $50,000 =	$7,500
Tax on second $25,000:	0.25 × 25,000 =	6,250
Tax on remaining $25,000:	0.34 × 25,000 =	8,500
Regular tax liability		$22,250

This tax liability also can be determined from the above tax rate schedule. ◀

If taxable income exceeds $100,000, a 5% surcharge applies to the corporation's taxable income exceeding $100,000. The surcharge phases out the lower graduated tax rates that apply to the first $75,000 of taxable income for corporations earning between $100,000 and $335,000 of taxable income. The maximum surcharge is $11,750 [($335,000 − $100,000) × 0.05]. The above tax rate schedule incorporates the 5% surcharge by imposing a 39% (34% + 5%) rate on taxable income from $100,000 to $335,000.

EXAMPLE C:3-29 ▶ Delta Corporation reports taxable income of $200,000. Delta's regular tax liability is computed as follows:

Tax on first $50,000:	0.15 × $ 50,000 =	$ 7,500
Tax on next $25,000:	0.25 × 25,000 =	6,250
Tax on remaining $125,000:	0.34 × 125,000 =	42,500
Surcharge (income over $100,000):	0.05 × 100,000 =	5,000
Regular tax liability		$61,250

Alternatively, from the above tax rate schedule, the tax is $22,250 + [0.39 × ($200,000 − $100,000)] = $61,250. ◀

If taxable income is at least $335,000 but less than $10 million, the corporation pays a flat 34% tax rate on all of its taxable income. A corporation whose income is at least $10 million but less than $15 million pays $3.4 million plus 35% of the income above $10 million.

EXAMPLE C:3-30 ▶ Elgin Corporation reports taxable income of $350,000. Elgin's regular tax liability is $119,000 (0.34 × $350,000). If Elgin's taxable income is instead $12 million, its tax liability is $4.1 million [$3,400,000 + (0.35 × $2,000,000)]. ◀

If a corporation's taxable income exceeds $15 million, a 3% surcharge applies to the corporation's taxable income exceeding $15 million (but not exceeding $18,333,333). The surcharge phases out the one percentage point lower rate (34% vs. 35%) that applies to the first $10 million of taxable income. The maximum surcharge is $100,000 [($18,333,333 − $15,000,000) × 0.03]. A corporation whose taxable income exceeds $18,333,333 pays a flat 35% tax rate on all its taxable income.

STOP & THINK

Question: Planner Corporation has an opportunity to realize $50,000 of additional income in either the current year or next year. Planner has some discretion as to the timing of this additional income. Not counting the additional income, Planner's current year taxable income is $200,000, and it expects next year's taxable income to be $500,000. In what year should Planner recognize the additional $50,000?

Solution: Even though Planner's current year taxable income is lower than next year's expected taxable income, Planner will have a lower marginal tax rate next year. The current year's marginal tax rate is 39% because Planner's taxable income is in the 5% surtax range (or 39% "bubble"). Next year's taxable income is beyond the 39% bubble and is in the flat 34% range. Thus, Planner can save $2,500 (0.05 × $50,000) in taxes by deferring the $50,000 until next year.

PERSONAL SERVICE CORPORATIONS

Personal service corporations are denied the benefit of the graduated corporate tax rates. Thus, all the income of personal service corporations is taxed at a flat 35% rate.

Section 448(d) defines a personal service corporation as a corporation that meets the following two tests:

- Substantially all its activities involve the performance of services in the fields of health, law, engineering, architecture, accounting, actuarial science, performing arts, and consulting.
- Substantially all its stock (by value) is held directly or indirectly by employees performing the services or retired employees who performed the services in the past, their estates, or persons who hold stock in the corporation by reason of the death of an employee or retired employee within the past two years.

This rule encourages employee-owners of personal service corporations either to withdraw earnings from the corporation as deductible salary (rather than have the corporation retain them) or make an S election.

CONTROLLED GROUPS OF CORPORATIONS

Special tax rules apply to corporations under common control to prevent them from avoiding taxes that otherwise would be due. The rules apply to corporations that meet the definition of a controlled group. This section explains why special rules apply to controlled groups, how the IRC defines controlled groups, and what special rules apply to controlled groups.

OBJECTIVE 4

Understand what a controlled group is and the tax consequences of being a controlled group

WHY SPECIAL RULES ARE NEEDED

Special controlled group rules prevent shareholders from using multiple corporations to avoid having corporate income taxed at a 35% rate. If these rules were not in effect, the owners of a corporation could allocate the corporation's income among two or more corporations and take advantage of the lower 15%, 25%, and 34% rates on the first $10 million of corporate income for each corporation.

The following example demonstrates how a group of shareholders could obtain a significant tax advantage by dividing a business enterprise among several corporate entities. Each corporation then could take advantage of the graduated corporate tax rates. To prevent a group of shareholders from using multiple corporations to gain such tax advantages, Congress enacted laws that limit the tax benefits of multiple corporations.[39]

EXAMPLE C:3-31 ▶ Axle Corporation reports taxable income of $450,000. Axle's regular tax liability on that income is $153,000 (0.34 × $450,000). If Axle could divide its taxable income equally among six corporations ($75,000 apiece), each corporation's federal income tax liability would be $13,750 [(0.15 × $50,000) + (0.25 × $25,000)], or an $82,500 total regular tax liability for all the corporations. Thus, Axle could save $70,500 ($153,000 − $82,500) in federal income taxes. ◀

The law governing controlled corporations requires special treatment for two or more corporations controlled by the same shareholder or group of shareholders. The most important restrictions on a controlled group of corporations are that the group must share the benefits of the progressive corporate tax rate schedule and pay a 5% surcharge on the group's taxable income exceeding $100,000, up to a maximum surcharge of $11,750, and also pay a 3% surcharge on the group's taxable income exceeding $15 million, up to a maximum surcharge of $100,000.

EXAMPLE C:3-32 ▶ White, Blue, Yellow, and Green Corporations belong to a controlled group. Each corporation reports $100,000 of taxable income (a total of $400,000). Only one $50,000 amount is taxed at 15% and only one $25,000 amount is taxed at 25%. Furthermore, the group is subject to the maximum $11,750 surcharge because its total taxable income exceeds $335,000. This surcharge is levied on the group member(s) that received the benefit of the 15 and 25% rates. Therefore, the group's total regular tax liability is $136,000 (0.34 × $400,000), as though one corporation earned the entire $400,000. Each corporation would be allocated $34,000 of this tax liability. ◀

WHAT IS A CONTROLLED GROUP?

A **controlled group** is comprised of two or more corporations owned directly or indirectly by the same shareholder or group of shareholders. Controlled groups fall into three categories: a parent-subsidiary controlled group, a brother-sister controlled group, and a combined controlled group. Each of these groups is subject to the limitations described above.

PARENT-SUBSIDIARY CONTROLLED GROUPS. In a **parent-subsidiary controlled group**, one corporation (the parent corporation) must directly own at least 80% of the voting power of all classes of voting stock, or 80% of the total value of all classes of stock, of a second corporation (the subsidiary corporation).[40] The group can contain more than one subsidiary corporation. If the parent corporation, the subsidiary corporation, or any other members of the controlled group in total own at least 80% of the voting power of all classes of voting stock, or 80% of the total value of all classes of stock, of another corporation, that other corporation also is included in the parent-subsidiary controlled group.

EXAMPLE C:3-33 ▶ Parent Corporation owns 80% of Axle Corporation's single class of stock and 40% of Wheel Corporation's single class of stock. Axle also owns 40% of Wheel's stock. (See Figure C:3-2.)

---

[39] Secs. 1561 and 1563.

[40] Sec. 1563(a)(1). Section 1563(d)(1) requires that certain attribution rules apply to determine stock ownership for parent-subsidiary controlled groups. If any person has an option to acquire stock, such stock is considered owned by the person having the option. Section 1563(c) excludes certain types of stock from the controlled group definition of stock.

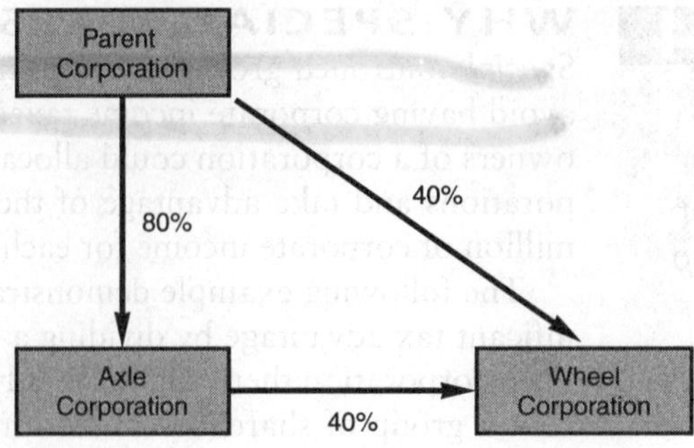

FIGURE C:3-2 ▶ PARENT-SUBSIDIARY CONTROLLED GROUP (EXAMPLE C:3-33)

Parent, Axle, and Wheel are members of the same parent-subsidiary controlled group because Parent directly owns 80% of Axle's stock and therefore is its parent corporation, and Wheel's stock is 80% owned by Parent (40%) and Axle (40%).

If Parent and Axle together owned only 70% of Wheel's stock and an unrelated shareholder owned the remaining 30%, Wheel would not be included in the parent-subsidiary group. The controlled group then would consist only of Parent and Axle. ◀

EXAMPLE C:3-34 ▶ Beta Corporation owns 70% of Spectrum Corporation's single class of stock and 60% of Red Corporation's single class of stock. Blue Corporation owns the remaining stock of Spectrum (30%) and Red (40%). No combination of these corporations forms a parent-subsidiary group because no corporation has direct stock ownership of at least 80% of any other corporation's stock. ◀

BROTHER-SISTER CONTROLLED GROUPS. The IRC contains two definitions of a brother-sister controlled group. This textbook will refer to them as the 80%-50% definition and the 50%-only definition. Under the 80%-50% definition, a group of two or more corporations is a brother-sister controlled group if five or fewer individuals, trusts, or estates own

- At least 80% of the voting power of all classes of voting stock (or at least 80% of the total value of the outstanding stock) of each corporation, and
- More than 50% of the voting power of all classes of stock (or more than 50% of the total value of the outstanding stock) of each corporation, taking into account only the stock ownership that is common with respect to each corporation.[41] A common ownership is the percentage of stock a shareholder owns that is common or identical in each of the corporations. For example, if a shareholder owns 30% of New Corporation and 70% of Old Corporation, his or her common ownership is 30%.

Thus, under the 50%-80% definition, the five or fewer shareholders not only must have more than 50% common ownership in the corporations, they also must own at least 80% of the stock of each corporation in the brother-sister group. This definition is narrow because the shareholders must meet two tests.

The 50%-only definition, on the other hand, is broader than the 50%-80% definition in that the five or fewer shareholders must satisfy only the 50% common ownership test described above. Consequently, in situations where the 50%-only definition applies, more corporations may be pulled into the controlled group than under the

[41] Sec. 1563(a)(2). Section 1563(d)(2) requires that certain attribution rules apply to determine stock ownership for brother-sister controlled groups. If any person has an option to acquire stock, such stock is considered to be owned by the person having the option. A proportionate amount of stock owned by a partnership, estate, or trust is attributed to partners having an interest of 5% or more in the capital or profits of the partnership or beneficiaries having a 5% or more actuarial interest in the estate or trust. A proportionate amount of stock owned by a corporation is attributed to shareholders owning 5% or more in value of the corporate stock. Family attribution rules also can cause an individual to be considered to own the stock of a spouse, child, grandchild, parent, or grandparent.

50%-80% definition. The list on page C:3-29 indicates which definition applies to specific situations.

EXAMPLE C:3-35 ▶ North and South Corporations have only one class of stock outstanding, owned by the following individuals:

	Stock Ownership Percentages		
Shareholder	*North Corp.*	*South Corp.*	*Common Ownership*
Walt	30%	70%	30%
Gail	70%	30%	30%
Total	100%	100%	60%

Five or fewer individuals (Walt and Gail) together own at least 80% (actually 100%) of each corporation's stock, and the same individuals own more than 50% (actually 60%) of the corporations' stock taking into account only their common ownership in each corporation. Because their ownership satisfies both tests, North and South are a brother-sister controlled group under the 50%-80% definition and under the 50%-only definition. (See Figure C:3-3.) ◀

EXAMPLE C:3-36 ▶ East and West Corporations have only one class of stock outstanding, owned by the following individuals:

	Stock Ownership Percentages		
Shareholder	*East Corp.*	*West Corp.*	*Common Ownership*
Javier	80%	25%	25%
Sara	20%	75%	20%
Total	100%	100%	45%

Five or fewer individuals (Javier and Sara) together own at least 80% (actually 100%) of each corporation's stock. However, those same individuals own only 45% of the corporations' stock taking into account only their common ownership. Because their ownership does not satisfy the more-than-50% test, East and West are not a brother-sister controlled group under either the 50%-80% or the 50%-only definition. Consequently, each corporation is taxed on its own income without regard to the earnings of the other. ◀

An individual's stock ownership can be counted for the 80% test only if that individual owns stock in each and every corporation in the controlled group.[42]

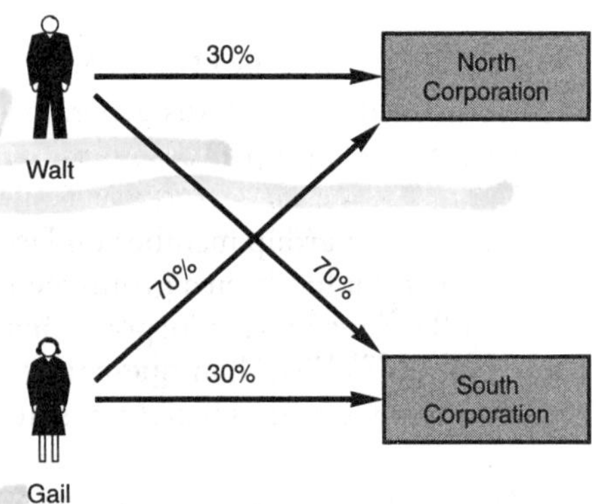

FIGURE C:3-3 ▶ BROTHER-SISTER CONTROLLED GROUP (EXAMPLE C:3-35)

[42] Reg. Sec. 1.1563-1(a)(3).

EXAMPLE C:3-37 ▶ Long and Short Corporations each have only a single class of stock outstanding, owned by the following individuals:

	Stock Ownership Percentages		
Shareholder	*Long Corp.*	*Short Corp.*	*Common Ownership*
Al	50%	40%	40%
Beth	20%	60%	20%
Carol	30%	—	—
Total	100%	100%	60%

Carol's stock does not count for purposes of Long's 80% stock ownership requirement because she owns no stock in Short. Only Al's and Beth's stock holdings count, and together they own only 70% of Long's stock. Thus, the 80% test fails. Consequently, Long and Short are not a brother-sister controlled group under the 50%-80% defintion, but they are a brother-sister controlled group under the 50%-only definition. ◀

COMBINED CONTROLLED GROUPS. A **combined controlled group** is comprised of three or more corporations meeting the following criteria:

- ▶ Each corporation is a member of a parent-subsidiary controlled group or a brother-sister controlled group
- ▶ At least one of the corporations is both the parent corporation of a parent-subsidiary controlled group and a member of a brother-sister controlled group.[43]

EXAMPLE C:3-38 ▶ Able, Best, and Coast Corporations each have a single class of stock outstanding, owned by the following shareholders:

KEY POINT

The combined controlled group definition does just what its name implies: It combines a parent-subsidiary controlled group and a brother-sister controlled group. Thus, instead of trying to apply the controlled group rules to two different groups, the combined group definition eliminates the issue by combining the groups into one controlled group.

	Stock Ownership Percentages		
Shareholder	*Able Corp.*	*Coast Corp.*	*Best Corp.*
Art	50%	50%	—
Barbara	50%	50%	—
Able Corp.	—	—	100%

Able and Coast are a brother-sister controlled group under the 50%-80% *and* 50%-only definitions because Art's and Barbara's ownership satisfy both the 80% and 50% tests. Able and Best are a parent-subsidiary controlled group because Able owns all of Best's stock. Each of the three corporations is a member of either the parent-subsidiary controlled group (Able and Best) or the brother-sister controlled group (Able and Coast), and the parent corporation (Able) of the parent-subsidiary controlled group also is a member of the brother-sister controlled group. Therefore, Able, Best, and Coast Corporations are members of a combined controlled group. (See Figure C:3-4.) ◀

APPLICATION OF THE CONTROLLED GROUP TEST

Controlled group status generally is tested on December 31. A corporation is included in a controlled group if it is a group member on December 31 and has been a group member on at least one-half of the days in its tax year that precede December 31. A corporation that is not a group member on December 31, nevertheless, is considered a member for the tax year if it has been a group member on at least one-half the days in its tax year that precede December 31. Corporations are excluded from the controlled group if they were members for less than one-half the days in their tax year that precede December 31 or if they retain certain special tax statuses such as being a tax-exempt corporation.

EXAMPLE C:3-39 ▶ Ace and Copper Corporations are members of a parent-subsidiary controlled group of which Ace is the common parent. Both corporations are calendar year taxpayers and have been group members for the entire year. They do not file a consolidated return. Bell Corporation, which has a fiscal year ending on August 31, becomes a group member on December 1 of the current year. Although Bell is a group member on December 31 of the current year, it has been a group

[43] Sec. 1563(a)(3).

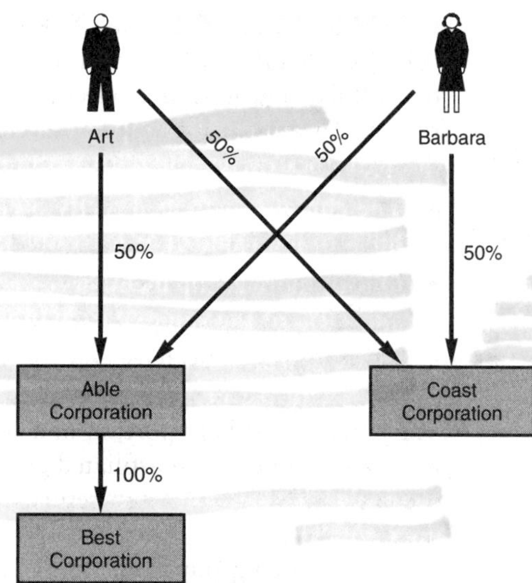

FIGURE C:3-4 ▶ COMBINED CONTROLLED GROUP (EXAMPLE C:3-38)

member for less than half the days in its tax year that precede December 31—only 30 of 121 days starting on September 1. Therefore, Bell is not a member of the Ace-Copper *controlled* group for its tax year beginning on September 1 of the current year. ◀

TAX STRATEGY TIP

A controlled group of corporations should elect to apportion the tax benefits in a manner that maximizes the tax savings from the tax benefits. See Tax Planning Considerations later in this chapter for details.

SPECIAL RULES APPLYING TO CONTROLLED GROUPS

As discussed earlier, if two or more corporations are members of a controlled group, the member corporations are limited to a total of $50,000 taxed at 15%, $25,000 being taxed at 25%, and $9,925,000 million being taxed at 34%. For brother-sister corporations, the broader 50%-only definition applies for limiting the reduced tax rates.

In addition, a controlled group must apportion certain other items among its group members, some of which are listed below. Notations in parentheses indicate which definition applies in the case of a brother-sister controlled group.

- The 5% and 3% surcharges (50%-only)
- The $40,000 exemption for the alternative minimum tax (50%-only)
- The $250,000 minimum accumulated earnings tax credit (50%-only)
- The $112,000 (in 2007) of depreciable assets that can be expensed annually (50%-80%)
- The $25,000 general business tax credit limitation (50%-80%)

ADDITIONAL COMMENT

One current proposal in Congress, if passed, would increase the Sec. 179 limitation in 2007 to $125,000.

Furthermore, Sec. 267(a)(1) allows no deduction for any loss on the sale or exchange of property between two members of the same controlled group. However, in contrast to losses between a corporation and controlling shareholder described earlier in this chapter, a loss realized on a transaction between members of a controlled group is deferred (instead of being disallowed). The original selling member recognizes the deferred loss when the property sold or exchanged in the intragroup transaction is sold outside the controlled group.

BOOK-TO-TAX ACCOUNTING COMPARISON

The disallowed tax loss on a sale to a controlling shareholder creates a permanent difference. The deferred loss between members of a controlled group, on the other hand, creates a deferred tax asset that reverses when the purchasing member sells the property to an outside party.

Section 267(a)(2) allows no deduction for certain accrued expenses or interest owed by one member of a controlled group to another member of the same controlled group when the two corporations use different accounting methods so that the payments would be reported in different tax years. (See page C:3-21 for a detailed discussion of Sec. 267.) The Sec. 1239 rules that convert capital gain into ordinary income on depreciable property sales between related parties also apply to sales or exchanges involving two members of the same controlled group. Sections 267 and 1239, however, provide special definitions of controlled groups that differ somewhat from those described above. These details are beyond the scope of this textbook.

TYPICAL MISCONCEPTION

The definitions of a parent-subsidiary controlled group and an affiliated group are similar, but not identical. For example, the 80% stock ownership test for controlled group purposes is satisfied if 80% of the voting power *or* 80% of the FMV of a corporation's stock is owned. For purposes of an affiliated group, 80% of both the voting power *and* the FMV of a corporation's stock must be owned.

CONSOLIDATED TAX RETURNS

WHO CAN FILE A CONSOLIDATED RETURN. Some groups of related corporations (i.e., affiliated groups) may elect to file a single income tax return called a **consolidated tax return.** An **affiliated group** is one or more chains of includible corporations connected through stock ownership with a common parent,[44] but only if the following criteria are met:

- The common parent directly owns stock with at least 80% of the voting power *and* 80% of the value of at least one includible corporation.
- One or more group members directly owns stock with at least 80% of the voting power *and* 80% of the value of each other corporation included in the affiliated group.[45]

Many parent-subsidiary controlled groups also qualify as affiliated groups and thus are eligible to file a consolidated return in place of separate tax returns for each corporation. The parent-subsidiary portion of a combined group also can file a consolidated tax return if it also qualifies as an affiliated group. Brother-sister controlled groups, however, are not eligible to file consolidated returns because the requisite parent-subsidiary relationship does not exist.

An affiliated group elects to file a consolidated tax return by filing Form 1120, which includes all the income and expenses of each of its members. Each corporate member of the affiliated group must consent to the original election. Thereafter, any new member of the affiliated group must join in the consolidated return.

SELF-STUDY QUESTION

What is probably the most common reason for making a consolidated return election?

ANSWER

Filing consolidated returns allows the group to offset losses of one corporation against the profits of other members of the group.

ADVANTAGES OF FILING A CONSOLIDATED RETURN. A consolidated return, in effect, is one tax return for the entire affiliated group of corporations. The main advantages of filing a consolidated return are

- Losses of one member of the group can offset profits of another member of the group.
- Capital losses of one member of the group can offset capital gains of another member of the group.
- Profits or gains realized on intercompany transactions are deferred until a sale outside the group occurs (i.e., if one member sells property to another member, the gain is postponed until the member sells the property to someone outside the affiliated group).

In contrast, if the group members file separate returns, members with NOLs or capital losses must either carry back these losses to earlier years or carry them over to future years rather than offset another member's profits or gains.

Although the losses of one group member can offset the profits of another group member when the group files a consolidated return, some important limitations apply to the use of a member corporation's NOL. These limitations prevent one corporation from purchasing another corporation's NOL carryovers to offset its own taxable income or purchasing a profitable corporation to facilitate the use of its own NOL carryovers. (See Chapters C:7 and C:8.)

The following example illustrates the advantage of a consolidated return election.

EXAMPLE C:3-40 ▶ Parent Corporation owns 100% of Subsidiary Corporation's stock. Parent reports $110,000 of taxable income, including a $10,000 capital gain. Subsidiary incurs a $100,000 NOL and a $10,000 capital loss. If Parent and Subsidiary file separate returns, Parent has a $26,150 [$22,250 + 0.39 × ($110,000 – $100,000)] tax liability. Subsidiary has no tax liability but may be able to use its $100,000 NOL and $10,000 capital loss to offset taxable income in other years. On the other hand, if Parent and Subsidiary file a consolidated return, the group's consolidated taxable income is zero and the group has no tax liability. By filing a consolidated return, the group saves $26,150 in taxes for the year. ◀

BOOK-TO-TAX ACCOUNTING COMPARISON

The corporations included in a consolidated tax return may differ from those included in consolidated financial statements. Page 1 of Schedule M-3 reconciles financial statement worldwide consolidated net income to financial statement net income (loss) of corporations included in the consolidated tax return.

DISADVANTAGES OF FILING A CONSOLIDATED RETURN. The main disadvantages of a consolidated return election are

- The election is binding on all subsequent tax years unless the IRS grants permission to discontinue filing consolidated returns or the affiliated group terminates.

---

44 Includible corporations are those eligible to join in the consolidated tax return election under Sec. 1504(b).

45 Sec. 1504(a).

ADDITIONAL COMMENT

Under Sec. 267 discussed earlier, intercompany losses may be deferred even if the corporations file separate tax returns.

- Losses on intercompany transactions are deferred until a sale outside the group takes place.
- One member's Sec. 1231 losses offset another member's Sec. 1231 gains instead of being reported as an ordinary loss.
- Losses of an unprofitable member of the group may reduce the deduction or credit limitations of the group below what would be available had the members filed separate tax returns.
- The group may incur additional administrative costs in maintaining the records needed to file a consolidated return.

Determining whether to make a consolidated tax return election is a complex decision because of the various advantages and disadvantages and because the election is so difficult to revoke once made. Chapter C:8 provides detailed coverage of the consolidated return rules.

TAX PLANNING CONSIDERATIONS

OBJECTIVE 5

Understand how compensation planning can reduce taxes for corporations and their shareholders

COMPENSATION PLANNING FOR SHAREHOLDER-EMPLOYEES

Compensation paid to a shareholder-employee in the form of salary has the advantage of single taxation because, while taxable to the employee, salary is deductible by the corporation. Dividend payments, on the other hand, are taxed twice. The corporation is taxed on its income when earned, and the shareholder is taxed on profits distributed as dividends. Double taxation occurs because the corporation may not deduct dividend payments. The reduced tax rate on dividends available through 2010, however, makes the difference between salary and dividends much less substantial than when dividends are taxed at ordinary rates.

EXAMPLE C:3-41 ▶ Delta Corporation earns $500,000 and wishes to distribute $100,000 or as much of the $100,000 as possible to Mary, its sole sharholder and CEO. Mary's ordinary tax rate is 35%, and the corporation's marginal tax rate is 34%. Ignoring payroll taxes, the following table compares salary and dividend payments to Mary with respect to the $100,000 of partial earnings:

	Salary	*Dividend at Ordinary Tax Rate*	*Dividend at Reduced Tax Rate*
1. Corporate earnings (partial)	$100,000	$100,000	$100,000
2. Minus: Salary deduction	(100,000)	-0-	-0-
3. Corporate taxable income (partial)	$ -0-	$100,000	$100,000
4. Times: Corporate tax rate	0.34	0.34	0.34
5. Corporate income tax (on partial income)	$ -0-	$ 34,000	$ 34,000
6. Dividend to Mary (Line 1 − Line 5)	$100,000	$ 66,000	$ 66,000
7. Times: Mary's tax rate	0.35	0.35	0.15
8. Mary's tax	$ 35,000	$ 23,100	$ 9,900
9. Total tax (Line 5 + Line 8)	$ 35,000	$ 57,100	$ 43,900
10. Overall tax rate (Line 9 ÷ Line 1)	35%	57.1%	43.9%

Thus, the preferential dividend rate reduces the overall tax rate on the corporate earnings from 57.1% to 43.9% and lessens the difference between salary and dividends from 22.1% (57.1% − 35%) to 8.9% (43.9% − 35%). This example demonstrates Congress's intent of reducing the double taxation of corporate earnings when the corporation pays dividends. ◀

To avoid double taxation, some owners of closely held corporations prefer to be taxed under the rules of Subchapter S (see Chapter C:11). Other owners of closely held corporations retain C corporation status to use the 15% and 25% marginal corporate tax rates and to benefit from tax-free fringe benefits such as health and accident insurance. These fringe benefits are nontaxable to the employee and deductible by the corporation. For both tax and nontax reasons, closely held corporations must determine the appropriate level of earnings to be withdrawn from the business in the form of salary and fringe benefits and the amount of earnings to be retained in the business.

ADDITIONAL COMMENT

Reasonableness of a salary payment is a question of fact to be determined in each case. No formula can be used to determine a reasonable amount.

ADVANTAGE OF SALARY PAYMENTS. If a corporation distributes all its profits as deductible salary and fringe benefit payments, it will eliminate double taxation. However, the following considerations limit such tax planning opportunities:

- Regulation Sec. 1.162-7(a) requires salary or fringe benefit payments to be reasonable in amount and to be paid for services rendered by the employee. If the IRS deems compensation to be unreasonable, it may disallow the portion of the salary it deems unreasonable while still requiring the employee to include all compensation in gross income (see Chapter C:4). This disallowance will result in double taxation. The reasonable compensation restriction primarily affects closely held corporations.
- A corporation may not deduct compensation paid to an executive of a publicly traded corporation that exceeds $1 million. However, this limitation does not apply to compensation paid to an executive other than the corporation's top five officers, or to performance-based compensation.[46]
- A corporation is a taxpaying entity independent of its owners. The first $75,000 of a corporation's earnings is taxed at 15% and 25% corporate tax rates. These rates are lower than the marginal tax rate that may apply to an individual taxpayer and provides an incentive to retain some earnings in the corporation instead of paying them out as salaries.
- A combined employee–employer social security tax rate of 15.3% applies in 2007. Employers and employees are each liable for 6.2% of old age security and disability insurance tax, or a total of 12.4% of the first $97,500 of wages in 2007. Employers and employees also are each liable for a 1.45% Medicare hospital insurance tax, for a total of 2.9% of all wages. In addition to these taxes, state and federal unemployment taxes may be imposed on a portion of wages paid.

TAX STRATEGY TIP

A fringe benefit probably is the most cost effective form of compensation because the amount of the benefit is deductible by the employer and never taxed to the employee. Thus, where possible, fringe benefits are an excellent compensation planning tool. For closely held corporations, however, the tax savings to shareholder-employees are reduced because the fringe benefit must be offered to all employees without discrimination.

ADVANTAGE OF FRINGE BENEFITS. Fringe benefits provide two types of tax advantages: a tax deferral or an exclusion. Qualified pension, profit-sharing, and stock bonus plans provide a tax deferral; that is, the corporation's contribution to such a plan is not taxable to the employees when the corporation makes the contribution. Instead, employees are taxed on the benefits when they receive them. Other common fringe benefits, such as group term life insurance, accident and health insurance, and disability insurance, are exempt from tax altogether; that is, the employee never is taxed on the value of these fringe benefits.

Because the employee excludes the value of fringe benefits from gross income, the marginal individual tax rate applicable to these benefits is zero. Thus, conversion of salary into a fringe benefit provides tax savings for the shareholder-employee equal to the amount of the converted salary times the employee's marginal tax rate, assuming the shareholder-employee could not purchase the same fringe benefit and deduct its cost on his or her individual tax return.

SPECIAL ELECTION TO ALLOCATE REDUCED TAX RATE BENEFITS

A controlled group may elect to apportion the tax benefits of the 15%, 25%, and 34% tax rates to the member corporations in any manner it chooses. If the corporations elect no special apportionment plan, the $50,000, $25,000, and $9,925,000 amounts allocated to the three reduced tax rate brackets are divided equally among all the corporations in the group.[47] If a controlled group has one or more group members that report little or no taxable income, the group should elect special apportionment of the reduced tax benefits to obtain the full tax savings resulting from the reduced rates.

---

46 Sec. 162(m).

47 Sec. 1561(a).

EXAMPLE C:3-42 ▶ North and South Corporations are members of a controlled group. The corporations file separate tax returns for the current year and report the following results:

Corporation	*Taxable Income (NOL)*
North	$(25,000)
South	100,000

If they elect no special apportionment plan, North and South are limited to $25,000 each taxed at a 15% rate and to $12,500 each taxed at a 25% rate. The tax liability for each corporation is determined as follows:

Corporation	*Calculation*	*Tax*
North		$ –0–
South	15% tax bracket: 0.15 × $25,000	$ 3,750
	25% tax bracket: 0.25 × $12,500	3,125
	34% tax bracket: 0.34 × $62,500	21,250
	Subtotal for South Corporation	$28,125
Total for North-South controlled group		$28,125

If the corporations elect a special apportionment plan, the group may apportion the full $50,000 and $25,000 amounts for each of the reduced tax rate brackets to South. The tax liability for each corporation is determined as follows:

Corporation	*Calculation*	*Tax*
North		$ –0–
South	15% tax bracket: 0.15 × $50,000	$ 7,500
	25% tax bracket: 0.25 × $25,000	6,250
	34% tax bracket: 0.34 × $25,000	8,500
	Subtotal for South Corporation	$22,250
Total for North-South controlled group		$22,250

By shifting the benefit of low tax brackets away from a corporation that cannot use it (North) to a corporation that can (South), the special apportionment election reduces the total tax liability for the North-South controlled group by $5,875 ($28,125 – $22,250). ◀

If a controlled group's total taxable income exceeds $100,000 ($15 million), a 5% (3%) surcharge recaptures the benefits of the reduced tax rates. The component member (or members) that took advantage of the lower tax rates pays this additional tax.

EXAMPLE C:3-43 ▶ Hill, Jet, and King Corporations are members of the Hill-Jet-King controlled group. The corporations file separate tax returns and report the following results:

Corporation	*Taxable Income*
Hill	$200,000
Jet	100,000
King	100,000
Total	$400,000

All the reduced tax rate benefits are allocated to Hill Corporation under a special apportionment plan. Hill's income tax is calculated as follows:

15% tax bracket: 0.15 × $50,000	$ 7,500
25% tax bracket: 0.25 × $25,000	6,250
34% tax bracket: 0.34 × $125,000	42,500
Surcharge	11,750
Hill's total tax liability	$68,000

Jet and King each have a regular tax liability of $34,000 (0.34 × $100,000). Thus, the group's total regular tax liability is $136,000 ($68,000 + $34,000 + $34,000). Because Hill, Jet, and King each report taxable income exceeding $75,000, the group would have the same total regular tax liability if the special apportionment plan apportioned all the tax benefit to Jet or King Corporation or divided them equally among the three corporations.[48] ◀

TAX STRATEGY TIP

A corporation may want to elect to forgo the NOL carryback when tax credit carryovers are being used in the earlier years. If the NOLs are carried back, the tax credits may expire. Thus, before deciding to carry back NOLs, the prior tax returns should be carefully examined to ensure that expiring tax credits do not exist.

USING NOL CARRYOVERS AND CARRYBACKS

When a corporation incurs an NOL for the year, it has two choices:

- ▶ Carry the NOL back to the second and first preceding years in that order, and then forward to the succeeding 20 years in chronological order until the NOL is exhausted.
- ▶ Forgo any carryback and just carry the NOL forward to the 20 succeeding years.

A corporation might elect to forgo an NOL carryback if it would offset income at a low tax rate, resulting in a small tax refund compared to a greater anticipated benefit if the NOL instead were carried over to a high tax rate year.

EXAMPLE C:3-44 ▶ Boyd Corporation incurs a $30,000 NOL in 2007. Boyd's 2005 taxable income was $50,000. If Boyd carries the NOL back to 2005, Boyd's tax refund is computed as follows:

Original tax on $50,000 (using 2005 rates)	$7,500
Minus: Recomputed tax on $20,000 [($50,000 − $30,000) × 0.15]	(3,000)
Tax refund	$4,500

If Boyd anticipates taxable income (after reduction for any NOL carryovers) of $75,000 or more in 2008, carrying over the NOL will result in the entire loss offsetting taxable income that otherwise would be taxed at a 34% or higher marginal tax rate. The tax savings is computed as follows:

Tax on $105,000 of expected taxable income	$24,200
Minus: Tax on $75,000 ($105,000 − $30,000)	(13,750)
Tax savings in 2008	$10,450

Thus, if Boyd expects taxable income to be $105,000 in 2008, it might elect to forgo the NOL carryback and obtain the additional $5,950 ($10,450 − $4,500) tax benefit. Of course, by carrying the NOL over to 2008, Boyd loses the value of having the funds immediately available. However, Boyd may use the NOL to reduce its estimated tax payments for 2008. If the corporation expects the NOL carryover benefit to occur at an appreciably distant point in the future, the corporation would have to determine the benefit's present value to make it comparable to a refund from an NOL carryback. This example ignores the effect the NOL carryover has on the U.S. production activities deduction in the carryover year. ◀

ETHICAL POINT

When tax practitioners take on a new client, they should review the client's prior year tax returns and tax elections for accuracy and completeness. Tax matters arising in the current year, such as an NOL, can affect prior year tax returns prepared by another tax practitioner. Positions taken or errors discovered in a prior year return may have ethical consequences for a practitioner who takes on a new client.

COMPLIANCE AND PROCEDURAL CONSIDERATIONS

ESTIMATED TAXES

Every corporation that expects to owe more than $500 in tax for the current year must pay four installments of estimated tax, each equal to 25% of its required annual payment.[49] For corporations that are not large corporations (defined below), the required annual payment is the lesser of 100% of the tax shown on the current year return or 100% of the tax shown on the preceding year return. A corporation may not base its required estimated tax amount on the tax shown on the preceding year return if the preceding year tax return showed a zero tax liability.[50] The estimated tax amount is the sum of the corporation's income tax and alternative minimum tax liabilities that exceeds its tax credits. The amount of estimated tax due may be computed on Schedule 1120-W (Corporation Estimated Tax).

[48] A 3% surcharge applies if the controlled group's total taxable income exceeds $15 million. The recapture rule applies in a fashion similar to Example C:3-42.

[49] Sec. 6655.

[50] Rev. Rul. 92-54, 1992-2 C.B. 320.

ESTIMATED TAX PAYMENT DATES. A calendar year corporation must deposit estimated tax payments in a Federal Reserve bank or authorized commercial bank on or before April 15, June 15, September 15, and December 15.[51] This schedule differs from that of an individual taxpayer. The final estimated tax installment for a calendar year corporation is due in December of the tax year rather than in January of the following tax year, as is the case for individual taxpayers. For a fiscal year corporation, the due dates are the fifteenth day of the fourth, sixth, ninth, and twelfth months of the tax year.

EXAMPLE C:3-45 ▶ Garden Corporation, a calendar year taxpayer, expects to report the following results for 2007:

Regular tax	$119,000
Alternative minimum tax	25,000

Garden's 2007 estimated tax liability is $144,000 ($119,000 regular tax liability + $25,000 AMT liability). Garden's 2006 tax liability was $120,000. Assuming Garden is not a large corporation, its required annual payment for 2007 is $120,000, the lesser of its 2006 liability ($120,000) or its 2007 tax return liability ($144,000). Garden will not incur a penalty if it deposits four equal installments of $30,000 ($120,000 ÷ 4) on or before April 16, June 15, September 17, and December 17, 2007 (April, September, and December 15 fall on weekends). ◀

TYPICAL MISCONCEPTION

The easiest method of determining a corporation's estimated tax payments is to pay 100% of last year's tax liability. Unfortunately, for "large corporations," other than for its first quarterly payment, last year's tax liability is not an acceptable method of determining the required estimated tax payments. Also, last year's tax liability cannot be used if no tax liability existed in the prior year or if the corporation filed a short-year return for the prior year.

Different estimated tax payment rules apply to large corporations. A large corporation's required annual payment is 100% of the tax shown on the current year return. A large corporation's estimated tax payments cannot be based on the prior year's tax liability except the first installment. If a large corporation bases its first estimated tax installment on the prior year's liability, any shortfall between the required payment based on the current year's tax liability and the actual payment must be made up with the second installment.[52] A large corporation is one whose taxable income was $1 million or more in any of its three immediately preceding tax years. Controlled groups of corporations must allocate the $1 million amount among its group members.

EXAMPLE C:3-46 ▶ Assume the same facts as in Example C:3-45 except Garden is a large corporation (i.e., it had more than $1 million of taxable income in one of its prior three years). Garden can base its first estimated tax payment on either 25% of its 2007 tax liability or 25% of its 2006 tax liability. Garden should elect to use its 2006 tax liability as the basis for its first installment because it can reduce the needed payment from $36,000 (0.25 × $144,000) to $30,000 (0.25 × $120,000). However, it must recapture the $6,000 ($36,000 − $30,000) shortfall when it pays its second installment. Therefore, the total second installment is $42,000 ($36,000 second installment + $6,000 recapture from first installment). ◀

KEY POINT

The amount of penalty depends on three factors: the applicable underpayment rate, the amount of the underpayment, and the amount of time that lapses until the corporation makes the payment.

PENALITES FOR UNDERPAYMENT OF ESTIMATED TAX. The IRS will assess a nondeductible penalty if a corporation does not deposit its required estimated tax installment on or before the due date for that installment. The penalty is the underpayment rate found in Sec. 6621 times the amount by which the installment due by a payment date exceeds the payment actually made.[53] The penalty accrues from the payment due date for the installment until the earlier of the actual date of the payment or the due date for the tax return (excluding extensions).

EXAMPLE C:3-47 ▶ Globe Corporation is a calendar year taxpayer that reported a $100,000 tax liability for 2006. Globe's tax liability for 2005 was $125,000. It should have made estimated tax payments of $25,000 ($100,000 ÷ 4) on or before April 17, June 15, September 15, and December 15, 2006 (April 15 falls on a Saturday). No penalty is assessed if Globe deposited the requisite amounts on or before each of the those dates. However, if Globe deposited only $16,000 ($9,000 less

---

[51] Sec. 6655(c)(2). Fiscal year corporations must deposit their taxes on or before the fifteenth day of the fourth, sixth, ninth, and twelfth month of their tax year. If the fifteenth falls on a weekend or holiday, the payment is due on the next business day.

[52] Sec. 6655(d)(2)(B). A revision to the required estimated tax payment amount also may be needed if the corporation is basing its quarterly payments on the current year's tax liability. Installments paid after the estimate of the current year's liability has been revised must take into account any shortage or excess in previous installment payments resulting from the change in the original estimate.

[53] Sec. 6621. This interest rate is the short-term federal rate as determined by the Secretary of the Treasury plus three percentage points. It is subject to change every three months. The interest rate for large corporations is the short-term federal rate plus five percentage points. This higher interest rate begins 30 days after the issuance of either a 30-day or 90-day deficiency notice.

than the required $25,000) on April 17, 2006, and did not deposit the remaining $9,000 before the due date for the 2006 return, the corporation must pay a penalty on the $9,000 underpayment for the period of time from April 17, 2006, through March 15, 2007. The completed Form 2220 in Appendix B calculates the penalty assuming Globe pays in $16,000 on each installment date. If Globe deposits $34,000 on the second installment date (June 15, 2006), so that it has paid a total of $50,000 by the second installment due date, the penalty runs only from April 17, 2006, through June 15, 2006. ◀

SPECIAL COMPUTATION METHODS. In lieu of the current year and prior year methods, corporations can use either of two special methods for calculating estimated tax installments:

- The annualized income method
- The adjusted seasonal income method

The Annualized Income Method. This method is useful if a corporation's income is likely to increase a great deal toward the end of the year. It allows a corporation to base its first and second quarterly estimated tax payments on its annualized taxable income for the first three months of the year. The corporation then bases its third payment on its annualized taxable income for the first six months of the year and its fourth payment on annualized taxable income for the first nine months of the year. (Two other options for the number of months used for each installment also are available.)

EXAMPLE C:3-48 ▶ Erratic Corporation, a calendar year taxpayer, reports taxable income of: $10,000 in each of January, February, and March; $20,000 in each of April, May, and June; and $50,000 in each of the last six months of the current year. Erratic's annualized taxable income and annualized tax are calculated as follows:

TAX STRATEGY TIP

Both the "annualized income exception" and the "adjusted seasonal income exception" are complicated computations. However, due to the large amounts of money involved in making corporate estimated tax payments along with the possible underpayment penalties, the time and effort spent in determining the least amount necessary for a required estimated tax payment are often worthwhile.

Through	*Cumulative Taxable Income*	*Annualization Factor*	*Annualized Taxable Income*	*Tax on Annualized Taxable Income*
Third month	$ 30,000	12/3	$120,000	$ 30,050
Sixth month	90,000	12/6	180,000	53,450
Ninth month	240,000	12/9	320,000	108,050

Assuming Erratic uses the annualized method for all four estimated tax payments, its installments will be as follows:

Installment Number	*Annualized Tax*	*Applicable Percentage*	*Installment Amount*	*Cumulative Installment*
One	$ 30,050	25%	$ 7,513[a]	$ 7,513
Two	30,050	50	7,512[b]	15,025
Three	53,450	75	25,063[c]	40,088
Four	108,050	100	67,962[d]	108,050

[a]$30,050 × 0.25
[b]($30,050 × 0.50) − $7,513
[c]$53,450 × 0.75) − $15,025
[d]($108,050 × 1.00) − $40,088 ◀

A corporation may use the annualized income method for an installment payment only if it is less than the regular required installment. It must recapture any reduction in an earlier required installment resulting from use of the annualized income method by increasing the amount of the next installment that does not qualify for the annualized income method.

For small corporations, the sure way to avoid a penalty for the underpayment of estimated tax is to base the current year's estimated tax payments on 100% of last year's tax. This approach is not possible, however, for large corporations or for corporations that owed no tax in the prior year or that filed a short period tax return for the prior year. This approach also is not advisable if the corporation had a high tax liability in the prior year and expects a low tax liability in the current year.

Adjusted Seasonal Income Method. A corporation may base its installments on its adjusted seasonal income. This method permits corporations that earn seasonal income to annualize their income by assuming income earned in the current year is earned in the same pattern as in preceding years. As in the case of the annualized income exception, a corporation can use the seasonal income exception only if the resulting installment payment is less than the regular required installment. Once the exception no longer applies, any savings resulting from its use for prior installments must be recaptured.

REPORTING THE UNDERPAYMENT. A corporation reports its underpayment of estimated taxes and the amount of any penalty on Form 2220 (Underpayment of Estimated Tax by Corporations). A completed Form 2220 using the facts from Example C:3-47 appears in Appendix B.

PAYING THE REMAINING TAX LIABILITY. A corporation must pay its remaining tax liability for the year when it files its corporate tax return. An extension of time to file the tax return does *not* extend the time to pay the tax liability. If any tax remains unpaid after the original due date for the tax return, the corporation must pay interest at the underpayment rate prescribed by Sec. 6621 from the due date until the corporation pays the tax. In addition to interest, the IRS assesses a penalty if the corporation does not pay the tax on time and cannot show reasonable cause for the failure to pay. The IRS presumes that reasonable cause exists if the corporation requests an extension of time to file its tax return and the amount of tax shown on the request for extension (Form 7004) or the amount of tax paid by the original due date of the return is at least 90% of the corporation's tax shown on its Form 1120.[54] A discussion of the failure-to-pay penalty and the interest calculation can be found in Chapter C:15.

STOP & THINK

Question: Why does the tax law permit a corporation to use special methods such as the annualized income method to calculate its required estimated tax installments?

Solution: A large corporation whose income varies widely may not be able to estimate its taxable income for the year until late in the year, and it is not allowed to base its estimates on last year's income. If, for example, a calendar year corporation earns income of $100,000 per month during the first six months of its year, it might estimate its first two installments on the assumption that it will earn a total taxable income of $1.2 million for the year. But if its income unexpectedly increases to $500,000 per month in the seventh month, it would need an annualized method to avoid an underpayment penalty for the first two installments. Were it not for the ability to use the annualized method, the corporation would have no way to avoid an underpayment penalty even though it could not predict its taxable income for the year when it made the first two installment payments.

OBJECTIVE 6

Determine the requirements for paying corporate incomes taxes and filing a corporate tax return

REQUIREMENTS FOR FILING AND PAYING TAXES

A corporation must file a tax return even if it has no taxable income for the year.[55] If the corporation did not exist for its entire annual accounting period (either calendar year or fiscal year), it must file a short period return for the part of the year it did exist. For tax purposes, a corporation's existence ends when it ceases business and dissolves, retaining no assets, even if state law treats the corporation as continuing for purposes of winding up its affairs.[56]

Corporations use Form 1120 (U.S. Corporation Income Tax Return) or Form 1120-A (U.S. Corporation Short-Form Income Tax Return) to file their tax returns. A corporation is eligible to use Form 1120-A if it satisfies the following requirements:[57]

---

[54] Reg. Sec. 301.6651-1(c)(4).
[55] Sec. 6012(a)(2).
[56] Reg. Sec. 1.6012-2(a)(2).
[57] See the instructions to Form 1120-A for a series of additional requirements (e.g., the corporation is not filing its final return).

REAL-WORLD EXAMPLE
The IRS estimates that, in 2006, 201,000 corporations will file Form 1120-A compared to 2.04 million corporations that will file the regular Form 1120.

- Its gross receipts are under $500,000.
- Its total income is under $500,000.
- Its total assets are under $500,000.

A completed Form 1120 corporate income tax return appears in Appendix B. A spreadsheet that converts book income into taxable income for the Johns and Lawrence business enterprise (introduced in Chapter C:2) is presented with the C corporation tax return.

WHEN THE RETURN MUST BE FILED

Corporations must file their tax returns by the fifteenth day of the third month following the close of their tax year.[58] A corporation can obtain an automatic six-month extension to file its tax return by filing Form 7004 (Application for Automatic 6-Month Extension of Time to File Certain Business Tax, Information, and Other Returns) by the original due date for the return. Corporations that fail to file a timely tax return are subject to the failure-to-file penalty. Chapter C:15 discusses this penalty in some detail.

EXAMPLE C:3-49 ▶ Palmer Corporation's fiscal tax year ends on September 30. Its corporate tax return for the year ending September 30, 2007, is due on or before December 17, 2007 (December 15 falls on a Saturday). If Palmer files Form 7004 by December 17, 2007, it can obtain an automatic extension of time to file until June 16, 2008 (June 15 falls on a Sunday). Assuming Palmer expects its 2007 tax liability to be $72,000 and it has paid $68,000 in estimated tax during the year, it must pay an additional $4,000 to the IRS by December 17, 2007. A completed Form 7004 appears in Appendix B. ◀

BOOK-TO-TAX ACCOUNTING COMPARISON
Schedule L requires a financial accounting balance sheet rather than a tax balance sheet. However, for many small corporations, the tax balance sheet is the same as the financial accounting balance sheet.

Additional extensions beyond the automatic six-month period are not available. The IRS can rescind the extension period by mailing a ten-day notice to the corporation before the end of the six-month period.[59]

TAX RETURN SCHEDULES

SCHEDULE L (OF FORM 1120): THE BALANCE SHEET. Schedule L of Form 1120 requires a balance sheet showing the financial accounting results at the beginning and end of the tax year.

RECONCILIATION SCHEDULES. The IRS also requires the reconciliation of the corporation's financial accounting income (also known as book income) and its taxable income (before special deductions). Book income is calculated according to generally accepted accounting principles (GAAP) including rules promulgated by the Financial Accounting Standards Board (FASB). On the other hand, taxable income must be calculated using tax rules. Therefore, book income and taxable income usually differ.

Some small corporations that do not require audited statements keep their books on a tax basis. For example, they may calculate depreciation for book purposes the same way they do for tax purposes. Income tax expense for book purposes may simply reflect the federal income tax liability. Most corporations, however, must use GAAP to calculate net income per books. For such corporations, taxable income and book income may differ significantly. The reconciliation of book income and taxable income provides the IRS with information that helps it audit a corporation's tax return.

For many corporations, the reconciliation must be provided on Schedule M-1 of Form 1120. Corporations with total assets of $10 million or more on the last day of the tax year, however, must complete Schedule M-3 instead of Schedule M-1. This schedule provides the IRS with much more detailed information on differences between book income and taxable income than does Schedule M-1. This additional transparency of corporate transactions will increase the IRS's ability to audit corporate tax returns. Form 1120 also requires an analysis of unappropriated retained earnings on Schedule M-2.

58 Sec. 6072(b).

59 Reg. Sec. 1.6081-3.

BOOK-TO-TAX ACCOUNTING COMPARISON

The Internal Revenue Code and related authorities determine the treatment of items in the tax return while *Statement of Financial Accounting Standard No. 109, Accounting for Income Taxes,* dictates the treatment of tax items in the financial statements.

SELF-STUDY QUESTION

Why might the IRS be interested in reviewing a corporation's Schedule M-1 or M-3?

ANSWER

Schedule M-1 or M-3 adjustments reconcile book income to taxable income. Thus, these schedules can prove illuminating to an IRS agent who is auditing a corporate return. Because Schedule M-1 or M-3 highlights each departure from the financial accounting rules, the schedules sometimes help the IRS identify tax issues it may want to examine further.

BOOK-TAX DIFFERENCES. A corporation's book income usually differs from its taxable income for a large number of transactions. Some of these differences are permanent. **Permanent differences** arise because:

- Some book income is never taxed. Examples include:
  1. Tax-exempt interest received on state and municipal obligations
  2. Proceeds of life insurance carried by the corporation on the lives of key officers or employees
- Some book expenses are never deductible for tax purposes. Examples include:
  1. Expenses incurred in earning tax-exempt interest
  2. Premiums paid for life insurance carried by the corporation on the lives of key officers or employees
  3. Fines and expenses resulting from a violation of law
  4. Disallowed travel and entertainment costs
  5. Political contributions
  6. Federal income taxes per books, which is based on GAAP (SFAS No. 109)
- Some tax deductions are never taken for book purposes. Examples include:
  1. The dividends-received deduction
  2. The U.S. production activities deduction
  3. Percentage depletion of natural resources in excess of their cost

Some of the differences are temporary. **Temporary differences** arise because:

- Some revenues or gains are recognized for book purposes in the current year but not reported for tax purposes until later years. Examples include:
  1. Installment sales reported in full for book purposes in the year of sale but reported over a period of years using the installment method for tax purposes
  2. Gains on involuntary conversions that are recognized for book purposes but deferred for tax purposes
- Some revenues or gains are taxable before they are reported for book purposes. These items are included in taxable income when received but are included in book income as they accrue. Examples include:
  1. Prepaid rent or interest income
  2. Advance subscription revenue
- Some expenses or losses are deductible for tax purposes after they are recognized for book purposes. Examples include:
  1. Excess of capital losses over capital gains, which are expensed for book purposes but carry back or over for tax purposes
  2. Book depreciation in excess of tax depreciation
  3. Charitable contributions exceeding the 10% of taxable income limitation, which are currently expensed for book purpose but carry over for tax purposes
  4. Bad debt accruals using the allowance method for book purposes and the direct write-off method for tax purposes
  5. Organizational and start-up expenditures, which are expensed currently for book purposes but partially deducted and amortized for tax purposes
  6. Product warranty liabilities expensed for book purposes when estimated but deducted for tax purposes when the liability becomes fixed
  7. Net operating losses (NOLs) that, for tax purposes, carry back two years and carry over 20 years
- Some expenses or losses are deductible for tax purposes before they are recognized for book purposes. Examples include:
  1. Tax depreciation in excess of book depreciation
  2. Prepaid expenses deducted on the tax return in the period paid but accrued over a period of years for book purposes

For book purposes, temporary differences listed under the first and fourth bullets create deferred tax liabilities while those listed under the second and third bullets create deferred tax assets. The Financial Statement Implications section later in this chapter discusses the financial accounting treatment of book-tax differences.

SCHEDULE M-1. The Schedule M-1 reconciliation of book to taxable income begins with net income per books and ends with taxable income before special deductions, which corresponds with Line 28 of Form 1120. Thus, some book-tax differences enumerated above do not appear in the reconciliation, for example, the dividends-received deduction and the net operating loss deduction.

The left side of Schedule M-1 contains items the corporation must add back to book income. These items include the following categories:

- ▶ Federal income tax expense (per books)
- ▶ Excess of capital losses over capital gains
- ▶ Income subject to tax but not recorded on the books in the current year
- ▶ Expenses recorded on the books but not deductible for tax purposes in the current year

The right side of the schedule contains items the corporation must deduct from book income and include the following categories:

- ▶ Income recorded on the books in the current year that is not taxable in the current year
- ▶ Deductions or losses claimed in the tax return that do not reduce book income in the current year

These categorizations, however, do not distinguish between permanent and temporary differences as does Schedule M-3 discussed below. The following example illustrates a Schedule M-1 reconciliation.

EXAMPLE C:3-50 ▶ Valley Corporation reports the following items for book and tax purposes in its first year of operations (2006):

	Book	*Tax*	*Difference*
Gross profit from operations	$900,000	$900,000	
Plus: Dividends from less than 20%-owned corporations	10,000	10,000	
Tax-exempt income	3,000	–0–	$ (3,000)
Prepaid rental income	–0–	8,000	8,000
Minus: Operating expenses	(300,000)	(300,000)	
Depreciation	(60,000)	(170,000)	(110,000)
Bad debt expense	(25,000)	(16,000)	9,000
Business interest expense	(75,000)	(75,000)	
Insurance premiums on life insurance for key employee (Valley is the beneficiary)	(2,800)	–0–	2,800
Net capital loss disallowed for tax purposes	(12,000)	–0–	12,000
U.S. production activities deduction	–0–	(10,170)	(10,170)
Net income before federal income taxes	$438,200		
Taxable income before special deductions		$346,830	
Minus: Federal income tax expense per books	(143,082)	–0–	143,082
Dividends-received deduction	–0–	(7,000)	(7,000)
Net income per books / Taxable income	$295,118	$339,830	
Federal tax liability ($339,830 × 0.34)		$115,542	
Effective tax rate ($143,082/$438,200)	32.65%		

Valley's Schedule M-1 reconciliation appears in Figure C:3-5.[60] ◀

BOOK-TO-TAX COMPARISON

Schedule M-1 and M-3 adjustments highlight the fact that financial accounting and tax accounting differ in many ways. A review of Schedule M-1 or M-3 is an excellent way to compare the financial accounting and tax accounting differences in a corporation.

SCHEDULE M-3. Schedule M-3 requires extensive detail in its reconciliation. Moreover, the schedule has the corporation distinguish between its permanent and temporary differences. The schedule contains three parts. Part I adjusts worldwide income per books to worldwide book income for only includible corporations. As described in

[60] A worksheet for converting book income to taxable income for a sample Form 1120 return is provided in Appendix B with that return.

1	Net income (loss) per books	295,118	7	Income recorded on books this year not included on this return (itemize): Tax-exempt interest $ 3,000	
2	Federal income tax	143,082			
3	Excess of capital losses over capital gains	12,000			3,000
4	Income subject to tax not recorded on books this year (itemize): Prepaid rent	8,000	8	Deductions on this return not charged against book income this year (itemize):	
5	Expenses recorded on books this year not deducted on this return (itemize):		a	Depreciation $110,000	
a	Depreciation $		b	Contributions carryover $	
b	Contributions carryover $			U.S. prod. act. ded. 10,170	
c	Travel and entertainment $ Premiums on life insurance 2,800 Bad debt expense 9,000	11,800			120,170
			9	Add lines 7 and 8	123,170
6	Add lines 1 through 5	470,000	10	Income (line 28, page 1)—line 6 less line 9	346,830

FIGURE C:3-5 ▶ VALLEY CORPORATION'S FORM 1120 SCHEDULE M-1 (EXAMPLE C:3-50)

Chapter C:8, some corporations may be included in the financial statement consolidation that might be excluded from the tax consolidated tax return. This resulting figure is then reconciled to taxable income before special deductions (again Line 28 of Form 1120). Part II enumerates the corporation's income and loss items, and Part III enumerates the expense and deduction items. The total items from Part III carry over to Part II for the final reconciliation. Both Parts II and III contain the following four columns: (a) book items, (b) temporary differences, (c) permanent differences, and (d) tax items.

Appendix B provides an example of Schedule M-3 using the data from Example C:3-50. Valley Corporation in that example is too small to be required to use Schedule M-3 although it may elect to do so. Nevertheless, that data is used to allow for comparison of Schedules M-1 and M-3. Note that Lines 1 and 2 of Schedule M-3, Part III, break the \$143,082 federal income tax expense into its current and deferred components. The current expense ties to the current tax liability (\$115,542), and the deferred expense ties to the change in net deferred tax liabilities and assets arising from temporary differences, specifically, depreciation, net capital loss, prepaid rent, and bad debt expense [$\$27,540 = 0.34 \times (\$110,000 - \$12,000 - \$8,000 - \$9,000)$]. These temporary differences appear in Column b of Schedule M-3, Parts II and III.

SCHEDULE M-2 (OF FORM 1120). Schedule M-2 of Form 1120 requires an analysis of changes in unappropriated retained earnings from the beginning of the year to the end of the year. The schedule supplies the IRS with information regarding dividends paid during the year and any special transactions that caused a change in retained earnings for the year.

Schedule M-2 starts with the balance in the unappropriated retained earnings account at the beginning of the year. The following items, which must be added to the beginning balance amount, are listed on the left side of the schedule:

- Net income per books
- Other increases (e.g., refund of federal income taxes paid in a prior year taken directly to the retained earnings account instead of used to reduce federal income tax expense)

The following items, which must be deducted from the beginning balance amount, are listed on the right side of the schedule:

- Dividends (e.g., cash or property)
- Other decreases (e.g., appropriation of retained earnings made during the tax year)

The result is the amount of unappropriated retained earnings at the end of the year.

ADDITIONAL COMMENT

Schedule M-2 requires an analysis of a corporation's retained earnings. Retained earnings is a financial accounting number that has little relevance to tax accounting. It would seem much more worthwhile for the IRS to require an analysis of a corporation's earnings and profits, which is an extremely important number in determining the taxation of a corporation and its shareholders.

EXAMPLE C:3-51 ▶ In the current year, Beta Corporation reports net income and other capital account items as follows:

Unappropriated retained earnings, January 1, current year	$400,000
Net income	350,000
Federal income tax refund for capital loss carryback	15,000
Cash dividends paid in the current year	250,000
Unappropriated retained earnings, December 31, current year	515,000

Beta Corporation's Schedule M-2 appears in Figure C:3-6. ◀

Topic Review C:3-2 summarizes the requirements for paying the taxes due and filing the corporate tax return.

FINANCIAL STATEMENT IMPLICATIONS

OBJECTIVE 7

Determine the financial statement implications of federal income taxes

The book-tax differences discussed on page C:3-39, have implications not only for preparing the reconciliation Schedules M-1 and M-3 but also affect how a firm's financial statements present income taxes. Income taxes impact both the income statement and balance sheet. For example, the tax section of the income statement might appear as follows:

Net income before federal income taxes
Minus: Federal income tax expense
Net income

Analysis of Unappropriated Retained Earnings per Books (Line 25, Schedule L)

1	Balance at beginning of year	400,000	5	Distributions: a Cash	250,000
2	Net income (loss) per books	350,000		b Stock	
3	Other increases (itemize):			c Property	
			6	Other decreases (itemize):	
	Federal tax refund	15,000	7	Add lines 5 and 6	250,000
4	Add lines 1, 2, and 3	765,000	8	Balance at end of year (line 4 less line 7)	515,000

FIGURE C:3-6 ▶ BETA CORPORATION'S FORM 1120 SCHEDULE M-2 (EXAMPLE C:3-51)

Topic Review C:3-2

Requirements for Paying Taxes Due and Filing Tax Returns

1. Estimated Tax Requirement
   a. Corporations that expect to owe more than $500 in tax for the current year must pay four installments of estimated tax, each equal to 25% of its required annual payment.
   b. Taxes for which estimated payments are required of a C corporation include regular tax and alternative minimum tax, minus any tax credits.
   c. If a corporation is not a large corporation, its required annual payment is the lesser of 100% of the tax shown on the current year's return or 100% of the tax shown on the preceding year's return.
   d. If a corporation is a large corporation, its required annual payment is 100% of the tax shown on the current year's return. Its first estimated tax payment may be based on the preceding year's tax liability, but any shortfall must be made up when the second installment is due.
   e. Special rules apply if the corporation bases its estimated tax payments on the annualized income or adjusted seasonal income method.
2. Filing Requirements
   a. The corporate tax return is due by the fifteenth day of the third month after the end of the tax year.
   b. A corporate taxpayer may request an automatic six-month extension to file its tax return (but not to pay its tax due).

Moreover, the **income tax expense** (also called the total tax provision) usually breaks down into a current component and a deferred component. The current component ties into the taxes payable for the current year, and the deferred component arises from book-tax temporary differences. The income tax expense also can contain a state tax component. For this textbook, however, we focus primarily on federal income taxes. Financial statements usually publish details concerning its tax provision in a footnote to the financial statements. Temporary differences also create **deferred tax liabilities** and **deferred tax assets**, which appear on the balance sheet.

The primary document that dictates financial statement treatment is *Statement of Financial Accounting Standards No. 109* (SFAS No. 109) issued by the Financial Accounting Standards Board (FASB). This section first describes the basic principles of SFAS No. 109 and then presents a comprehensive example to demonstrate its application.

SCOPE, OBJECTIVES, AND PRINCIPLES OF SFAS No. 109

SFAS No. 109 establishes principles of accounting for current income taxes and for deferred taxes arising from temporary differences. Specifically, SFAS No. 109 addresses the financial statement consequences of the following events:

- Revenues, expenses, gains, or losses recognized for tax purposes in an earlier or later year than recognized for financial statement purposes
- Other events that create differences between book and tax bases of assets and liabilities
- Operating loss and tax credit carrybacks or carryforwards

SFAS No. 109 sets out two objectives: (1) to recognize current year taxes payable or refundable and (2) to recognize deferred tax liabilities and assets for the future tax consequences of events recognized in a firm's financial statements or tax return. To implement these objectives, SFAS No. 109 applies the following principles:

- Recognize a current tax liability or asset for taxes payable or refundable on current year tax returns
- Recognize a deferred tax liability or asset for future tax effects attributable to temporary differences and carryforwards
- Measure current and deferred tax liabilities and assets using only enacted tax law, not anticipated future changes
- Reduce deferred tax assets by the amount of tax benefits the firm does not expect to realize, based on available evidence and adjusted via a valuation allowance

Interestingly, the only comment SFAS No. 109 makes about permanent differences is that "[s]ome events do not have tax consequences. Certain revenues are exempt from taxation and certain expenses are not deductible." In this context, SFAS No. 109 does not mention certain events that do have tax consequences but, nevertheless, create permanent differences, for example, the dividends-received deduction and the U.S. production activities deduction. As we show later, permanent differences do not affect deferred taxes, but they do impact the firm's effective tax rate.

TEMPORARY DIFFERENCES

Similarly to the discussion on page C:3-39, the following lists describe events that generate temporary differences and thus deferred tax liabilities and deferred tax assets. Deferred tax liabilities and assets appear on a firm's balance sheet.

Deferred tax liabilities occur when:

- Revenue or gains are recognized earlier for book purposes than for tax purposes
- Expenses or losses are deductible earlier for tax purposes than for book purposes
- Tax basis of an asset is less than its book basis
- Tax basis of a liability exceeds its book basis

Deferred tax assets occur when:

- Revenue or gains are recognized earlier for tax purposes than for book purposes
- Expenses or losses are deductible earlier for book purposes than for tax purposes

- Tax basis of an asset exceeds its book basis
- Tax basis of a liability is less than its book basis
- Operating loss or tax credit carryforwards exist

DEFERRED TAX ASSETS AND THE VALUATION ALLOWANCE

A deferred tax asset indicates that a firm will realize the tax benefit of an event some time in the future. For example, if the firm generates a net operating loss in the current year and, for tax purposes carries the loss forward, the firm will realize a tax benefit only if it earns sufficient future income to use the carryover before it expires. If the firm likely will not realize the entire tax benefit, it must record a **valuation allowance** to reflect the unrealizable portion. Thus, if the firm's NOL carryover is $200,000 and it expects to realize (deduct) the entire carryover at a 34% tax rate, the firm's deferred tax asset is $68,000 ($200,000 × 0.34). Accordingly, the firm makes the following book journal entry:

Deferred tax asset	68,000	
Federal income tax expense (benefit)		68,000

Thus, the deferred tax asset reduces the income tax expense or creates an income tax benefit.

If the firm determines that it likely will realize (deduct) only $150,000 of the NOL carryover, it must record a $17,000 ($50,000 × 0.34) valuation allowance. Accordingly, the firm makes the following book journal entry:

Deferred tax asset	68,000	
Valuation allowance		17,000
Federal income tax expense (benefit)		51,000

The valuation allowance is a contra-type account that reduces the deferred tax asset.

SFAS No. 109 specifically states that a deferred tax asset must be reduced by a valuation allowance if, based on the weight of evidence available, the firm *more likely than not* will fail to realize the benefit of the deferred tax asset. For this purpose, the term *more likely than not* means a greater than 50% likelihood. In assessing this likelihood, a firm must consider both negative and positive evidence, where negative evidence leads toward establishing a valuation allowance while positive evidence helps avoid a valuation allowance. SFAS No. 109 lists several examples of each type of evidence. Examples of negative evidence include the following items:

- Cumulative losses in recent years
- A history of expiring loss or credit carryforwards
- Expected losses in the near future
- Unfavorable contingencies with future adverse effects
- Short carryback or carryover periods that might limit realization of the deferred tax asset

Examples of positive evidence include the following items:

- Existing contracts or sales backlogs that will produce sufficient income to realize the deferred tax asset
- Excess of appreciated asset value over tax basis (i.e., built-in gain) sufficient to realize the deferred tax asset
- A strong earnings history aside from the event causing the deferred tax asset along with evidence that the event is an aberration

In essence, a firm can realize (deduct) a deferred tax asset if it has sufficient taxable income to offset the deduction. SFAS No. 109 suggests the following potential sources of such income:

- Future reversals of deferred tax liabilities
- Future taxable income other than reversing deferred tax liabilities

- Taxable income in carryback years assuming the tax law allows a carryback
- Taxable income from prudent and feasible tax planning strategies that a firm ordinarily would not take but nevertheless would pursue to realize an otherwise expiring deferred tax asset

BALANCE SHEET CLASSIFICATION

Deferred tax liabilities and assets must be classified as either current or noncurrent. If related to another asset or liability, the classification is the same as the related asset. For example, a deferred tax asset pertaining to a difference between book and tax bad debt expense is current because it relates to accounts receivable. On the other hand, a deferred tax liability pertaining to a difference between book and tax depreciation is noncurrent because it relates to fixed assets. If a deferred tax liability or asset does not relate to a particular asset or liability, it is classified as current or noncurrent depending on its expected reversal date. Once classified as current and noncurrent, all current deferred tax liabilities and assets must be netted and presented as one amount. Similarly, all noncurrent deferred tax liabilities and assets must be netted and presented as another amount.

TAX PROVISION PROCESS

The following steps outline the approach used in this chapter to provide for income taxes in the financial statements. This process addresses only federal income taxes.

1. Determine net income before federal income taxes (pretax book income).
2. Identify permanent differences, temporary differences, and carryforwards.
3. Adjust pretax book income for permanent differences.
4. Multiply the amount from step 3 by the appropriate statutory tax rate to derive the total federal income tax expense.
5. Adjust the amount from step 3 for temporary differences to derive taxable income or a net operating loss.
6. Multiply the amount from step 5 by the appropriate statutory tax rate to derive the current tax liability or the tax benefit of a net operating loss.
7. Calculate deferred tax liabilities and deferred tax assets using the applicable statutory tax rate.
8. Adjust deferred tax assets by a valuation allowance if necessary.
9. Check cumulative temporary differences against book-tax balance sheet differences.
10. Prepare and record tax related journal entries.
11. Prepare the tax rate reconciliation.
12. Prepare financial statements.

In practice, various firms may use slightly different approaches. For this chapter, however, the above steps provide a logical and systematic approach. The provision process also might contain a step to adjust the federal income tax expense for uncertain tax positions as dictated by *Financial Interpretation No. 48*.

COMPREHENSIVE EXAMPLE – YEAR 1

To provide comprehensiveness, this example continues with the facts set forth in Example C:3-50. Thus, when completed, the two examples together provide the financial statement implications of federal income taxes as well as the tax return reporting in Schedules M-1 and M-3 for 2006. We then continue the example with events occurring in Year 2 (2007).

In addition to the facts stated in Example C:3-50, Valley reports the following book and tax balance sheet items at the end of 2006, prior to adjustment for tax related items. Step 12 below presents the completed book balance sheet after making tax related journal entries.

Assets:	*Book*	*Tax*	*Difference*
Cash	$ 64,658	$ 64,658	
Accounts receivable	300,000	300,000	
Minus: Allowance for bad debts	(9,000)	–0–	
Net accounts receivable	291,000	300,000	$ 9,000

Investment in corporate stock	90,000	90,000	
Investment in tax-exempt bonds	50,000	50,000	
Inventory	500,000	500,000	
Fixed assets	1,200,000	1,200,000	
Minus: Accumulated depreciation	(60,000)	(170,000)	
Net fixed assets	1,140,000	1,030,000	110,000
Liabilities and stock equity:			
Accounts payable	225,000	225,000	
Unearned rental income	8,000	–0–	8,000
Long-term liabilities	930,000	930,000	
Common stock	650,000	650,000	

Step 1.
As provided in Example C:3-50, net income before federal income taxes equals $438,200.

Step 2.
Example C:3-50 identifies the various book-tax differences.

Steps 3 through 6.
The following schedule starts with net income before federal income taxes and performs Steps 3 through 6:

Net income before federal income taxes (FIT)	$438,200	
Permanent differences:		
Nondeductible insurance premiums	2,800	
Tax-exempt income	(3,000)	
U.S. production activities deduction	(10,170)	
Dividends-received deduction	(7,000)	
Net income after permanent differences	$420,830 × 0.34 =	$143,082 FIT expense
Temporary differences:		
Prepaid rental income	8,000	
Net capital loss disallowed for tax	12,000	
Bad debt expense	9,000	
Depreciation	(110,000)	
Taxable income	$339,830 × 0.34 =	$115,542 FIT liability

The above schedule confirms the taxable income and tax liability amounts determined in Example C:3-50. It also shows how Example C:3-50 arrived at the $143,082 total federal income tax expense.

Step 7.
The following three schedules calculate the deferred tax assets and deferred tax liability. In the first schedule, the prepaid rental income is current because Valley expects to earn that income next year. The bad debt expense is current because it relates to a current asset. Therefore, these items create current deferred assets. In the second schedule, the example assumes Valley does not expect to have sufficient capital gains to offset the capital loss carryover until two years from now. Therefore, this deferred tax asset will not reverse next year and is considered noncurrent. In the third schedule, the deferred tax liability pertaining to depreciation is noncurrent because it relates to a noncurrent asset.

Current deferred tax asset:	*End of 2006*
Prepaid rental income	$ 8,000
Bad debt expense	9,000
Total	$ 17,000
Times: Tax rate	0.34
Current deferred tax asset	$ 5,780

Noncurrent deferred tax asset:	*End of 2006*
Net capital loss	$ 12,000
Times: Tax rate	0.34
Noncurrent deferred tax asset	$ 4,080

Noncurrent deferred tax liability:	*End of 2006*
Depreciation	$110,000
Times: Tax rate	0.34
Noncurrent deferred tax liability	$ 37,400

Step 8.
Evidence suggests that Valley will realize its entire deferred tax asset. Therefore, Valley need not establish a valuation allowance.

Step 9.
Because this analysis pertains to Valley's first year, the temporary differences for the current year are the same as the cumulative amounts. Moreover, the cumulative temporary differences for prepaid rental income ($8,000), bad debt expense ($9,000), and depreciation ($110,000) tie to the book-tax balance sheet differences for unearned rental income, net accounts receivable, and net fixed assets (see schedule just before Step 1).

Step 10.
Given the amounts determined in Steps 3 through 7, Valley makes the following book journal entry:

Federal income tax expense	143,082	
Deferred tax assets (5,780 + 4,080)	9,860	
Deferred tax liability		37,400
Federal income taxes payable		115,542

Step 11.
A firm's **effective tax rate** is its federal income tax expense divided by its pretax book income. Because the federal income tax expense is based on net income after adjustment for permanent differences, these differences cause a firm's effective tax rate to differ from the statutory tax rate. In the footnotes to financial statements, firms reconcile the statutory tax rate to their effective tax rate. Accordingly, Valley's effective tax rate reconciliation is as follows:

Statutory tax rate	34.00%
Nondeductible insurance premiums [$2,800/$438,200 × 34%]	0.22%
Tax-exempt income [($3,000)/$438,200 × 34%]	(0.23)%
U.S. production activities deduction [($10,170)/$438,200 × 34%]	(0.79)%
Dividends-received deduction [($7,000)/$438,200 × 34%]	(0.55)%
Effective tax rate	32.65%

In practice, a firm would not disclose the detail shown here but would aggregate small percentage amounts into an "other" category.

Step 12.
At this point, Valley can complete its financial statements. The income statement appears in Example C:3-50, but the tax portion is repeated here.

Partial income statement:	
Net income before federal income taxes	$438,200
Minus: Federal income tax expense	(143,082)
Net income	$295,118
Effective tax rate ($143,082/$438,200)	32.65%

The federal income tax expense has two components as follows:

Current federal income tax expense	$115,542
Deferred income tax expense ($37,400 – $9,860)	27,540
Total federal income tax expense	$143,082

The book balance sheet for 2006 is as follows:

Assets:		
Cash		$ 64,658
Accounts receivable	$ 300,000	
Minus: Allowance for bad debts	(9,000)	291,000
Investment in corporate stock		90,000
Investment in tax-exempt bonds		50,000
Inventory		500,000
Current deferred tax asset		5,780
Fixed assets	$1,200,000	
Minus: Accumulated depreciation	(60,000)	1,140,000
Total assets		$2,141,438
Liabilities and equity:		
Accounts payable		$ 225,000
Unearned rental income		8,000
Noncurrent deferred liability ($37,400 – $4,080)		33,320
Long-term liabilities		930,000
Common stock		650,000
Retained earnings		295,118
Total liabilities and equity		$2,141,438

COMPREHENSIVE EXAMPLE – YEAR 2

Valley reports the following book and tax balance sheet items at the end of 2007, prior to adjustment for tax related items. Pertinent to the temporary differences, in 2007 Valley earned the rental income prepaid in 2006 and did not collect additional amounts. It also adjusted its allowance for bad debts and claimed additional depreciation on fixed assets. It did not recognize any capital gains to offset the capital loss carryover. Step 12 below presents the completed book balance sheet after making tax related journal entries.

	Book	*Tax*	*Difference*
Assets:			
Cash	$ 137,441	$ 137,441	
Accounts receivable	400,000	400,000	
Allowance for bad debts	(37,000)	–0–	
Net accounts receivable	363,000	400,000	$ 37,000
Investment in corporate stock	90,000	90,000	
Investment in tax-exempt bonds	50,000	50,000	
Inventory	600,000	600,000	
Fixed assets	1,200,000	1,200,000	
Accumulated depreciation	(180,000)	(465,000)	
Net fixed assets	1,020,000	735,000	285,000
Liabilities and stock equity:			
Accounts payable	295,000	295,000	
Unearned rental income	–0–	–0–	
Long-term liabilities	530,000	530,000	
Common stock	650,000	650,000	

Steps 1 and 2.

Valley also reports the following book income statement through net income before federal income taxes and tax return schedule through taxable income. The tax portion of the book income statement appears in Step 12.

	Book	*Tax*	*Difference*
Gross profit from operations	$1,300,000	$1,300,000	
Plus: Dividends from less than 20%-owned corporations	15,000	15,000	
Tax-exempt income	3,200	–0–	$ (3,200)
Prepaid rental income	8,000	–0–	(8,000)
Minus: Operating expenses	(500,000)	(500,000)	
Depreciation	(120,000)	(295,000)	(175,000)
Bad debt expense	(40,000)	(12,000)	28,000
Business interest expense	(60,000)	(60,000)	
Insurance premiums on life insurance for key employee (Valley is the beneficiary)	(3,500)	–0–	3,500
U.S. production activities deduction	–0–	(25,980)	(25,980)
Dividends-received deduction	–0–	(10,500)	(10,500)
Net income before federal income taxes / Taxable income	$ 602,700	$ 411,520	

Steps 3 through 6.
The following schedule starts with net income before federal income taxes and performs Steps 3 through 6:

Net income before federal income taxes (FIT)	$602,700	
Permanent differences:		
Nondeductible insurance premiums	3,500	
Tax-exempt income	(3,200)	
U.S. production activities deduction	(25,980)	
Dividends-received deduction	(10,500)	
Net income after permanent differences	$566,520 × 0.34 =	$192,617 FIT expense
Temporary differences:		
Prepaid rental income	(8,000)	
Bad debt expense	28,000	
Depreciation	(175,000)	
Taxable income	$411,520 × 0.34 =	$139,917 FIT liability

Step 7.
The following three schedules calculate the deferred tax assets and deferred tax liability. In the first schedule, the prepaid rental income item reverses, and the bad debt expense temporary difference increases. In the second schedule, Valley has not realized the deferred tax asset because it recognized no capital gains in 2007. Therefore, this deferred tax asset has not yet reversed. In the third schedule, the depreciation temporary difference increases.

Current deferred tax asset:	*End of 2006*	*Change*	*End of 2007*
Prepaid rent income	$ 8,000	($ 8,000)	$ –0–
Bad debt expense	9,000	28,000	37,000
Total	$ 17,000	$ 20,000	$ 37,000
Times: Tax rate	0.34	0.34	0.34
Current deferred tax asset	$ 5,780	$ 6,800	$ 12,580

Noncurrent deferred tax asset:	*End of 2006*	*Change*	*End of 2007*
Net capital loss	$ 12,000	$ –0–	$ 12,000
Times: Tax rate	0.34	0.34	0.34
Noncurrent deferred tax asset	$ 4,080	$ –0–	$ 4,080

Noncurrent deferred tax liability:	*End of 2006*	*Change*	*End of 2007*
Depreciation	$110,000	$175,000	$285,000
Times: Tax rate	0.34	0.34	0.34
Noncurrent deferred tax liability	$ 37,400	$ 59,500	$ 96,900

Step 8.
Evidence continues to suggest that Valley will realize its entire deferred tax asset. Therefore, Valley need not establish a valuation allowance.

Step 9.
From the schedule in Step 7, the cumulative (end of 2007) temporary differences for prepaid rental income ($0), bad debt expense ($37,000), and depreciation ($285,000) tie to the book-tax balance sheet differences for unearned rental income, net accounts receivable, and net fixed assets (see schedule just before Step 1).

Step 10.
Given the amounts determined in Steps 3 through 7, Valley makes the following book journal entry:

Federal income tax expense	192,617	
Deferred tax asset	6,800	
Deferred tax liability		59,500
Federal income taxes payable		139,917

Note that the deferred tax asset and liability amounts come from the change columns of the Step 7 schedules. Thus, the entries adjust the prior year balance sheet amounts up to the current year cumulative totals.

Step 11.
Valley's 2007 effective tax rate is its federal income tax expense divided by its pretax book income, or $192,617/$602,700 = 31.96%. Accordingly, Valley's effective tax rate reconciliation is as follows:

Statutory tax rate	34.00%
Nondeductible insurance premiums [$3,500/$602,700 × 34%]	0.20%
Tax-exempt income [($3,200)/$602,700 × 34%]	(0.18)%
U.S. production activities deduction [($25,980)/$602,700 x 34%]	(1.47)%
Dividends-received deduction [($10,500)/$602,700 x 34%]	(0.59)%
Effective tax rate	31.96%

Step 12.
At this point, Valley can complete its financial statements. The first part of the income statement appears in Steps 1 and 2, and the tax portion is as follows:

Partial income statement:	
Net income before federal income taxes	$602,700
Minus: Federal income tax expense	(192,617)
Net income	$410,083
Effective tax rate ($192,617/$602,700)	31.96%

The federal income tax expense has two components as follows:

Current federal income tax expense	$139,917
Deferred income tax expense ($59,500 − $6,800)	52,700
Total federal income tax expense	$192,617

The book balance sheet for 2007 is as follows:

Assets:		
Cash		$ 137,441
Accounts receivable	$ 400,000	
Minus: Allowance for bad debts	(37,000)	363,000
Investment in corporate stock		90,000
Investment in tax-exempt bonds		50,000
Inventory		600,000
Current deferred tax asset		12,580
Fixed assets	$1,200,000	
Minus: Accumulated depreciation	(120,000)	1,020,000
Total assets		$2,273,021
Liabilities and equity:		
Accounts payable		$ 295,000
Unearned rental income		–0–
Noncurrent deferred liability ($96,900 – $4,080)		92,820
Long-term liabilities		530,000
Common stock		650,000
Retained earnings		705,201
Total liabilities and equity		$2,273,021

OTHER TRANSACTIONS

Chapters C:2, C:5, C:7, C:8, and C:16 describe the financial statement implications of other transactions, for example, forming a corporation (Chapter C:2), the minimum tax credit (Chapter C:5), corporate acquisitions (Chapter C:7), intercompany transactions (Chapter C:8), and the foreign tax credit and deferred foreign earnings (Chapter C:16). Also, Problem C:3-64 provides a comprehensive tax return and financial accounting exercise.

PROBLEM MATERIALS

DISCUSSION QUESTIONS

C:3-1 High Corporation incorporates on May 1 and begins business on May 10 of the current year. What alternative tax years can High elect to report its initial year's income?

C:3-2 Port Corporation wants to change its tax year from a calendar year to a fiscal year ending June 30. Port is a C corporation owned by 100 shareholders, none of whom own more than 5% of the stock. Can Port change its tax year? If so, how can it accomplish the change?

C:3-3 Stan and Susan, two calendar year taxpayers, are starting a new business to manufacture and sell digital circuits. They intend to incorporate the business with $600,000 of their own capital and $2 million of equity capital obtained from other investors. The company expects to incur organizational and start-up expenditures of $100,000 in the first year. Inventories are a material income-producing factor. The company also expects to incur losses of $500,000 in the first two years of operations and substantial research and development expenses during the first three years. The company expects to break even in the third year and be profitable at the end of the fourth year, even though the nature of the digital circuit business will require continual research and development activities. What accounting methods and tax elections must Stan and Susan consider in their first year of operation? For each method and election, explain the possible alternatives and the advantages and disadvantages of each alternative.

C:3-4 Compare the tax treatment of capital gains and losses by a corporation and by an individual.

C:3-5 Explain the effect of the Sec. 291 recapture rule when a corporation sells depreciable real estate.

C:3-6 What are organizational expenditures? How are they treated for tax purposes?

C:3-7 What are start-up expenditures? How are they treated for tax purposes?

C:3-8 Describe three ways in which the treatment of charitable contributions by individual and corporate taxpayers differ.

C:3-9 Carver Corporation uses the accrual method of accounting and the calendar year as its tax year. Its board of directors authorizes a cash contribution on November 3, 2007 that the corporation pays on March 10, 2008. In what year(s) is it deductible? What happens if the corporation does not pay the contribution until April 20, 2008?

C:3-10 Zero Corporation contributes inventory (computers) to State University for use in its mathematics program. The computers have a $1,225 cost basis and an $2,800 FMV. How much is Zero's charitable contribution deduction for the computers? (Ignore the 10% limit.)

C:3-11 Why are corporations allowed a dividends-received deduction? What dividends qualify for this special deduction?

C:3-12 Why is a dividends-received deduction disallowed if the stock on which the corporation pays the dividend is debt-financed?

C:3-13 Crane Corporation incurs a $75,000 NOL in the current year. In which years can Crane use this NOL if it makes no special elections? When might a special election to forgo the carryback of the NOL be beneficial for Crane?

C:3-14 What special restrictions apply to the deduction of a loss realized on the sale of property between a corporation and a shareholder who owns 60% of the corporation's stock? What restrictions apply to the deduction of expenses accrued by a corporation at year-end and owed to a cash method shareholder who owns 60% of the corporation's stock?

C:3-15 Deer Corporation is a C corporation. Its taxable income for the current year is $200,000. What is Deer Corporation's income tax liability for the year?

C:3-16 Budget Corporation is a personal service corporation. Its taxable income for the current year is $75,000. What is Budget's income tax liability for the year?

C:3-17 Why do special restrictions on using the progressive corporate tax rates apply to controlled groups of corporations?

C:3-18 Describe the three types of controlled groups.

C:3-19 List five restrictions on claiming multiple tax benefits that apply to controlled groups of corporations.

C:3-20 What are the major advantages and disadvantages of filing a consolidated tax return?

C:3-21 What are the tax advantages of substituting fringe benefits for salary paid to a shareholder-employee?

C:3-22 Explain the tax consequences to both the corporation and a shareholder-employee if an IRS agent determines that a portion of the compensation paid in a prior tax year exceeds a reasonable compensation level.

C:3-23 What is the advantage of a special apportionment plan for the benefits of the 15%, 25%, and 34% tax rates to members of a controlled group?

C:3-24 What corporations must pay estimated taxes? When are the estimated tax payments due?

C:3-25 What is a "large" corporation for purposes of the estimated tax rules? What special rules apply to such large corporations?

C:3-26 What penalties apply to the underpayment of estimated taxes? The late payment of the remaining tax liability?

C:3-27 Describe the situations in which a corporation must file a tax return.

C:3-28 When is a corporate tax return due for a calendar-year taxpayer? What extension(s) of time in which to file the return are available?

C:3-29 List four types of differences that can cause a corporation's book income to differ from its taxable income.

ISSUE IDENTIFICATION QUESTIONS

C:3-30 X-Ray Corporation received a $100,000 dividend from Yancey Corporation this year. X-Ray owns 10% of the Yancey's single class of stock. What tax issues should X-Ray consider with respect to its dividend income?

C:3-31 Williams Corporation sold a truck with an adjusted basis of $100,000 to Barbara for $80,000. Barbara owns 25% of the Williams stock. What tax issues should Williams and Barbara consider with respect to the sale/purchase?

C:3-32 You are the CPA who prepares the tax returns for Don, his wife, Mary, and their two corporations. Don owns 100% of Pencil Corporation's stock. Pencil's current year taxable income is $100,000. Mary owns 100% of Eraser Corporation's stock. Eraser's current year taxable income is $150,000. Don and Mary file a joint federal income tax return. What issues should Don and Mary consider with respect to the calculation of the three tax return liabilities?

C:3-33 Rugby Corporation has a $50,000 NOL in the current year. Rugby's taxable income in each of the previous two years was $25,000. Rugby expects its taxable income for next year to exceed $400,000. What issues should Rugby consider with respect to the use of the NOL?

PROBLEMS

C:3-34 *Depreciation Recapture.* Young Corporation purchased residential real estate in 2003 for $225,000, of which $25,000 was allocated to the land and $200,000 was allocated to the building. Young took straight-line MACRS deductions of $30,000 during the years 2003–2007. In 2007, Young sells the property for $285,000, of which $60,000 is allocated to the land and $225,000 is allocated to the building. What are the amount and character of Young's recognized gain or loss on the sale?

C:3-35 *Organizational and Start-up Expenditures.* Delta Corporation incorporates on January 7, begins business on July 10, and elects to have its initial tax year end on October 31. Delta incurs the following expenses between January and October related to its organization during the current year:

Date	Expenditure	Amount
January 30	Travel to investigate potential business site	$2,000
May 15	Legal expenses to draft corporate charter	2,500
May 30	Commissions to stockbroker for issuing and selling stock	4,000
May 30	Temporary directors' fees	2,500
June 1	Expense of transferring building to Delta	3,000
June 5	Accounting fees to set up corporate books	1,500
June 10	Training expenses for employees	5,000
June 15	Rent expense for June	1,000
July 15	Rent expense for July	1,000

a. What alternative treatments are available for Delta's expenditures?
b. What amount of organizational expenditures can Delta Corporation deduct on its first tax return for the fiscal year ending October 31?
c. What amount of start-up costs can Delta Corporation deduct on its first tax return?

C:3-36 *Charitable Contribution of Property.* Yellow Corporation donates the following property to the State University:

- ABC Corporation stock purchased two years ago for $18,000. The stock, which trades on a regional stock exchange, has a $25,000 FMV on the contribution date.
- Inventory with a $17,000 adjusted basis and a $22,000 FMV. State will use the inventory for scientific research that qualifies under the special Sec. 170(e)(4) rules.
- An antique vase purchased two years ago for $10,000 and having an $18,000 FMV. State University plans to sell the vase to obtain funds for educational purposes.

Yellow Corporation's taxable income before any charitable contributions deduction, NOL or capital loss carryback, or dividends-received deduction is $250,000.
a. What is Yellow Corporation's charitable contributions deduction for the current year?
b. What is the amount of its charitable contributions carryover (if any)?

C:3-37 *Charitable Contributions of Property.* Blue Corporation donates the following property to Johnson Elementary School:

- XYZ Corporation stock purchased two years ago for $25,000. The stock has a $16,000 FMV on the contribution date.
- Computer equipment built one year ago at a cost of $16,000. The equipment has a $50,000 FMV on the contribution date. Blue is not in the business of manufacturing computer equipment.
- PQR Corporation stock purchased six months ago for $12,000. The stock has an $18,000 FMV on the contribution date.

The school will sell the stock and use the proceeds to renovate a classroom to be used as a computer laboratory. Blue's taxable income before any charitable contribution deduction, dividends-received deduction, or NOL or capital loss carryback is $400,000.

a. What is Blue's charitable contributions deduction for the current year?
b. What is Blue's charitable contribution carryback or carryover (if any)? In what years can it be used?
c. What would have been a better tax plan concerning the XYZ stock donation?

C:3-38 ***Charitable Contribution Deduction Limitation.*** Zeta Corporation reports the following results for 2007 and 2008:

	2007	*2008*
Adjusted taxable income	$180,000	$125,000
Charitable contributions (cash)	20,000	12,000

The adjusted taxable income is before Zeta claims any charitable contributions deduction, NOL or capital loss carryback, dividends-received deduction, or U.S. production activities deduction.

a. How much is Zeta's charitable contributions deduction in 2007? In 2008?
b. What is Zeta's contribution carryover to 2009, if any?

C:3-39 ***Taxable Income Computation.*** Omega Corporation reports the following results for the current year:

Gross profits on sales	$120,000
Dividends from less-than-20%-owned domestic corporations	40,000
Operating expenses	100,000
Charitable contributions (cash)	11,000

a. What is Omega's charitable contributions deduction for the current year and its charitable contributions carryover to next year, if any?
b. What is Omega's taxable income for the current year, assuming qualified production activities income is $20,000?

C:3-40 ***Dividends-Received Deduction.*** Theta Corporation reports the following results for the current year:

Gross profits on sales	$220,000
Dividends from less-than-20%-owned domestic corporations	100,000
Operating expenses	218,000

a. What is Theta's taxable income for the current year, assuming qualified production activities income is $2,000?
b. How would your answer to Part a change if Theta's operating expenses are instead $234,000, assuming qualified production activities income is zero or negative?
c. How would your answer to Part a change if Theta's operating expenses are instead $252,000, assuming qualified production activities income is zero or negative?
d. How would your answers to Parts a, b, and c change if Theta received $75,000 of the dividends from a 20%-owned corporation and the remaining $25,000 from a less-than-20%-owned corporation?

C:3-41 ***Stock Held 45 Days or Less.*** Beta Corporation purchased 100 shares of Gamma Corporation common stock (less than 5% of the outstanding stock) two days before the ex-dividend date for $200,000. Beta receives a $10,000 cash dividend from Gamma. Beta sells the Gamma stock one week after purchasing it for $190,000. What are the tax consequences of these three events?

C:3-42 ***Debt-financed Stock.*** Cheers Corporation purchased for $500,000 5,000 shares of Beer Corporation common stock (less than 5% of the outstanding Beer stock) at the beginning of the current year. It used $400,000 of borrowed money and $100,000 of its own cash to make this purchase. Cheers paid $50,000 of interest on the debt this year. Cheers received a $40,000 cash dividend on the Beer stock on September 1 of the current year.

a. What amount can Cheers deduct for the interest paid on the loan?
b. What dividends-received deduction can Cheers claim with respect to the dividend?

C:3-43 ***Net Operating Loss Carrybacks and Carryovers.*** In 2007, Ace Corporation reports gross income of $200,000 (including $150,000 of profit from its operations and $50,000 in dividends from less-than-20%-owned domestic corporations) and $220,000 of operating expenses. Ace's 2005 taxable income (all ordinary income) was $75,000, on which it paid taxes of $13,750.

a. What is Ace's NOL for 2007?
b. What is the amount of Ace's tax refund if Ace carries back the 2007 NOL to 2005?
c. Assume that Ace expects 2008's taxable income to be $400,000. Assume further that qualified production activities income is sufficiently less than taxable income so that the carryover will not affect the U.S. production activities deduction. What election could Ace make to increase the tax benefit from its NOL? What is the dollar amount of the expected benefit (if any)?

C:3-44 ***Ordering of Deductions.*** Beta Corporation reports the following results for the current year:

Gross income from operations	$180,000
Dividends from less-than-20%-owned domestic corporations	100,000
Operating expenses	150,000
Charitable contributions	20,000

In addition, Beta has a $50,000 NOL carryover from the preceding tax year, and its qualified production activities income is $30,000.

a. What is Beta's taxable income for the current year?
b. What carrybacks or carryovers are available to other tax years?

C:3-45 ***Sale to a Related Party.*** Union Corporation sells a truck for $18,000 to Jane, who owns 70% of its stock. The truck has a $24,000 adjusted basis on the sale date. Jane sells the truck to an unrelated party, Mike, for $28,000 two years later after claiming $5,000 in depreciation.

a. What is Union's realized and recognized gain or loss on selling the truck?
b. What is Jane's realized and recognized gain or loss on selling the truck to Mike?
c. How would your answers to Part b change if Jane instead sold the truck for $10,000?

C:3-46 ***Payment to a Cash Basis Employee-Shareholder.*** Value Corporation is a calendar year taxpayer that uses the accrual method of accounting. On December 10, 2007, Value accrues a bonus payment of $100,000 to Brett, its president and sole shareholder. Brett is a calendar year taxpayer who uses the cash method of accounting.

a. When can Value deduct the bonus if it pays it to Brett on March 11, 2008? On March 18, 2008?
b. How would your answers to Part a change if Brett were an employee of Value who owns no stock in the corporation?

C:3-47 ***Capital Gains and Losses.*** Western Corporation reports the following results for the current year:

Gross profits on sales	$150,000
Long-term capital gain	8,000
Long-term capital loss	15,000
Short-term capital gain	10,000
Short-term capital loss	2,000
Operating expenses	61,000

a. What are Western's taxable income and income tax liability for the current year, assuming qualified production activities income is $89,000?
b. How would your answers to Part a change if Western's short-term capital loss is $5,000 instead of $2,000?

C:3-48 ***Computing the Corporate Income Tax Liability.*** What is Beta Corporation's income tax liability assuming its taxable income is (a) $94,000, (b) $300,000, and (c) $600,000. How would your answers change if Beta were a personal service corporation?

C:3-49 ***Computing the Corporate Income Tax Liability.*** Fawn Corporation, a C corporation, paid no dividends and recognized no capital gains or losses in the current year. What is its income tax liability assuming its taxable income for the year is

a. $50,000
b. $14,000,000
c. $18,000,000
d. $34,000,000

C:3-50 ***Computing Taxable Income and Income Tax Liability.*** Pace Corporation reports the following results for the current year:

Gross profit on sales	$120,000
Long-term capital loss	10,000
Short-term capital loss	5,000
Dividends from 40%-owned domestic corporation	30,000
Operating expenses	65,000
Charitable contributions	10,000

a. What are Pace's taxable income and income tax liability, assuming qualified production activities income is $55,000?

b. What carrybacks and carryovers (if any) are available and to what years must they be carried?

C:3-51 ***Computing Taxable Income and Income Tax Liability.*** Roper Corporation reports the following results for the current year:

Gross profits on sales	$80,000
Short-term capital gain	40,000
Long-term capital gain	25,000
Dividends from 25%-owned domestic corporation	15,000
NOL carryover from the preceding tax year	9,000
Operating expenses	45,000

What are Roper's taxable income and income tax liability, assuming qualified production activities income is $35,000?

C:3-52 ***Controlled Groups.*** Which of the following groups constitute controlled groups? (Any stock not listed below is held by unrelated individuals each owning less than 1% of the outstanding stock.) For brother-sister corporations, which definition applies?

a. Judy owns 90% of the single classes of stock of Hot and Ice Corporations.

b. Jones and Kane Corporations each have only a single class of stock outstanding. The two controlling individual shareholders own the stock as follows:

	Stock Ownership Percentages	
Shareholder	*Jones Corp.*	*Kane Corp.*
Tom	60%	80%
Mary	30%	0%

c. Link, Model, and Name Corporations each have a single class of stock outstanding. The stock is owned as follows:

	Stock Ownership Percentages	
Shareholder	*Model Corp.*	*Name Corp.*
Link Corp.	80%	50%
Model Corp.		40%

Link Corporation's stock is widely held by over 1,000 shareholders, none of whom owns directly or indirectly more than 1% of Link's stock.

d. Oat, Peach, Rye, and Seed Corporations each have a single class of stock outstanding. The stock is owned as follows:

	Stock Ownership Percentages			
Shareholder	*Oat Corp.*	*Peach Corp.*	*Rye Corp.*	*Seed Corp.*
Bob	100%	90%		
Oat Corp.			80%	30%
Rye Corp.				60%

C:3-53 ***Controlled Groups of Corporations.*** Sally owns 100% of the outstanding stock of Eta, Theta, Phi, and Gamma Corporations, each of which files a separate return for the current year. During the current year, the corporations report taxable income as follows:

Corporation	*Taxable Income*
Eta	$40,000
Theta	(25,000)
Phi	50,000
Gamma	10,000

a. What is each corporation's separate tax liability, assuming the corporations do not elect a special apportionment plan for allocating the corporate tax rates?

b. What is each corporation's separate tax liability, assuming the corporations make a special election to apportion the reduced corporate tax rates in such a way that minimizes the group's total tax liability? Note: More than one plan can satisfy this goal.

C:3-54 ***Compensation Planning.*** Marilyn owns all of Bell Corporation's stock. Bell is a C corporation and employs 40 people. Marilyn is married, has two dependent children, and files a joint tax return with her husband. She projects that Bell will report $400,000 of pretax profits for 2007. Marilyn is considering five salary levels as shown below. Ignore the U.S. production activities deduction for this problem.

			Tax Liability		
Total Income	*Salary Paid to Marilyn*	*Earnings Retained by Bell Corporation*	*Marilyn*	*Bell Corporation*	*Total*
$400,000	$ –0–	$400,000			
400,000	$100,000	300,000			
400,000	200,000	200,000			
400,000	300,000	100,000			
400,000	400,000	–0–			

a. Determine the total tax liability for Marilyn and Bell for each of the five proposed salary levels. Assume no other income for Marilyn's family, and assume that Marilyn and her husband claim a combined itemized deduction and personal exemption of $25,000 regardless of AGI levels (i.e., ignore phase-outs). Also ignore employment taxes.

b. What recommendations can you make about a salary level for Marilyn that will minimize the total tax liability? Assume salaries paid up to $400,000 are considered reasonable compensation.

c. What is the possible disadvantage to Marilyn if Bell retains funds in the business and distributes some of the accumulated earnings as a dividend in a later tax year?

C:3-55 ***Fringe Benefits.*** Refer to the facts in Problem C:3-54. Marilyn has read an article explaining the advantages of paying tax-free fringe benefits (premiums on group term life insurance, accident and health insurance, etc.) and having deferred compensation plans (e.g., qualified pension and profit-sharing plans). Provide Marilyn with information on the tax savings associated with converting $3,000 of her salary into tax-free fringe benefits. What additional costs might Bell Corporation incur if it adopts a fringe benefit plan?

C:3-56 ***Estimated Tax Requirement.*** Zeta Corporation's taxable income for 2006 was $1.5 million, on which Zeta paid federal income taxes of $510,000. Zeta estimates calendar year 2007's taxable income to be $2 million, on which it will owe $680,000 in federal income taxes.

a. What are Zeta's minimum quarterly estimated tax payments for 2007 to avoid an underpayment penalty?

b. When is Zeta's 2007 tax return due?

c. When are any remaining taxes due? What amount of taxes are due when Zeta files its return assuming Zeta timely pays estimated tax payments equal to the amount determined in Part a?

d. If Zeta obtains an extension to file, when is its tax return due? Will the extension permit Zeta to delay making its final tax payments?

C:3-57 ***Filing the Tax Return and Paying the Tax Liability.*** Wright Corporation's taxable income for calendar years 2004, 2005, and 2006 was $120,000, $150,000, and $100,000, respectively. Its total tax liability for 2006 was $22,250. Wright estimates that its 2007 taxable income will be $500,000, on which it will owe federal income taxes of $170,000. Assume Wright earns its 2007 taxable income evenly throughout the year.

a. What are Wright's minimum quarterly estimated tax payments for 2007 to avoid an underpayment penalty?

b. When is Wright's 2007 tax return due?

c. When are any remaining taxes due? What amount of taxes are due when Wright files its return assuming it timely paid estimated tax payments equal to the amount determined in Part a?

d. How would your answer to Part a change if Wright's tax liability for 2006 had been $200,000?

C:3-58 ***Converting Book Income to Taxable Income.*** The following income and expense accounts appeared in the accounting records of Rocket Corporation, an accrual basis taxpayer, for the current calendar year.

	Book Income	
Account Title	*Debit*	*Credit*
Net sales		$ 3,000,000
Dividends		8,000 (1)
Interest		18,000 (2)
Gain on sale of stock		5,000 (3)
Key-person life insurance proceeds		100,000
Cost of goods sold	$2,000,000	
Salaries and wages	500,000	
Bad debts	13,000 (4)	
Payroll taxes	62,000	
Interest expense	12,000 (5)	
Charitable contributions	50,000 (6)	
Depreciation	60,000 (7)	
Other expenses	40,000 (8)	
Federal income taxes	96,000	
Net income	298,000	
Total	$3,131,000	$3,131,000

The following additional information applies.

1. Dividends were from Star Corporation, a 30%-owned domestic corporation.
2. Interest revenue consists of interest on corporate bonds, $15,000; and municipal bonds, $3,000.
3. The stock is a capital asset held for three years prior to sale.
4. Rocket uses the specific writeoff method of accounting for bad debts.
5. Interest expense consists of $11,000 interest incurred on funds borrowed for working capital and $1,000 interest on funds borrowed to purchase municipal bonds.
6. Rocket paid all contributions in cash during the current year to State University.
7. Rocket calculated depreciation per books using the straight-line method. For income tax purposes, depreciation amounted to $85,000.
8. Other expenses include premiums of $5,000 on the key-person life insurance policy covering Rocket's president, who died in December.
9. Qualified production activities income is $250,000.

Required: Prepare a worksheet reconciling Rocket's book income with its taxable income (before special deductions). Six columns should be used—two (one debit and one credit) for each of the following three major headings: book income, Schedule M-1 adjustments, and taxable income. (See the sample worksheet with Form 1120 in Appendix B if you need assistance).

C:3-59 ***Reconciling Book Income and Taxable Income.*** Zero Corporation reports the following results for the current year:

Net income per books (after taxes)	$33,000
Federal income tax per books	12,000
Tax-exempt interest income	6,000
Interest on loan to purchase tax-exempt bonds	8,000
MACRS depreciation exceeding book depreciation	3,000
Net capital loss	5,000
Insurance premium on life of corporate officer where Zero is the beneficiary	10,000
Excess charitable contributions carried over to next year	2,500
U.S. production activities deduction	2,000

Prepare a reconciliation of Zero's taxable income before special deductions with its book income.

C:3-60 ***Reconciling Unappropriated Retained Earnings.*** White Corporation's financial accounting records disclose the following results for the period ending December 31 of the current year:

Retained earnings balance on January 1	$246,500
Net income for year	259,574
Contingency reserve established on December 31	60,000
Cash dividend paid on July 23	23,000

What is White's unappropriated retained earnings balance on December 31 of the current year?

COMPREHENSIVE PROBLEM

C:3-61 Jackson Corporation prepared the following *book* income statement for its year ended December 31, 2007:

Sales			$765,000
Minus:	Cost of goods sold		(400,000)
Gross profit			$365,000
Plus:	Dividends received on Invest Corporation stock	$ 3,000	
	Gain on sale of Invest Corporation stock	30,000	
	Total dividends and gain		33,000
Minus:	Depreciation ($7,500 + $8,000)	$ 15,500	
	Charitable contributions	20,000	
	Other operating expenses	105,500	
	Loss on sale of Equipment 1	70,000	
	Federal income taxes per books	60,000	
	Total expenses and loss		(271,000)
Net income per books			$127,000

Information on equipment depreciation and sale:

Equipment 1:

- Acquired March 3, 2005 for $180,000
- For books: 12-year life; straight-line depreciation
- Sold February 17, 2007 for $80,000

Sales price				$ 80,000
Cost			$180,000	
Minus:	Depreciation for 2005 (½ year)	$ 7,500		
	Depreciation for 2006 ($180,000/12)	15,000		
	Depreciation for 2007 (½ year)	7,500		
	Total depreciation		(30,000)	
Book value at time of sale				(150,000)
Book loss on sale of Equipment 1				($70,000)

- For tax: 7-year MACRS property for which the corporation made no Sec. 179 election in the acquisition year.

Equipment 2:

- Acquired February 16, 2007 for $192,000
- For books: 12-year life; straight-line depreciation
- Book depreciation in 2007: $192,000/12 × 0.5 = $8,000
- For tax: 7-year MACRS property for which the corporation makes the Sec. 179 election.

Other information:

- Jackson has a $40,000 NOL carryover and a $6,000 capital loss carryover from last year.
- Jackson purchased the Invest Corporation stock (less than 20% owned) on June 21, 2005 for $25,000 and sold the stock on December 22, 2007 for $55,000.

- Jackson Corporation has qualified production activities income of $123,000. Its W-2 payroll wages equal $120,000.

Required:

a. For 2007, calculate Jackson's tax depreciation deduction for Equipment 1 and Equipment 2, and determine the tax loss on the sale of Equipment 1.

b. For 2007, calculate Jackson's taxable income and tax liability.

c. Prepare a schedule reconciling net income per books to taxable income before special deductions.

TAX STRATEGY PROBLEM

C:3-62 Mike Barton owns Barton Products, Inc. The corporation has 30 employees. Barton Corporation expects $500,000 of net income before taxes in 2007. Mike is married and files a joint return with his wife, Elaine, who has no earnings of her own. They have one dependent son, Robert, who is 16 years old. Mike and Elaine have no other income and do not itemize. Mike's salary is $230,000 per year (already deducted in computing Barton Corporation's $500,000 net income). Assume that variations in salaries will not affect the U.S. production activities deduction already reflected in taxable income.

a. Should Mike increase his salary from Barton to reduce the overall tax burden to himself and Barton Products? If so, by how much? Assume the corporation and Mike each would incur a 1.45% payroll tax with the corporate portion being deductible.

b. Should Barton employ Mike's wife for $50,000 rather than increase Mike's salary? Take into consideration employment taxes as well as federal income taxes.

c. How much would be saved in overall taxes if Barton employs Robert part-time for $20,000 per year? Assume the corporation and Robert each would incur a 7.65% payroll tax with the corporate portion being deductible.

TAX FORM/RETURN PREPARATION PROBLEM

C:3-63 Knoxville Musical Sales, Inc. is located at 5500 Kingston Pike, Knoxville, TN 37919. The corporation uses the calendar year and accrual basis for both book and tax purposes. It is engaged in the sale of musical instruments with an employer identification number (EIN) of 75-2008006. The company incorporated on December 31, 2002 and began business on January 2, 2003. Table C:3-3 contains balance sheet information at January 1, 2006, and December 31, 2006. Table C:3-4 presents an income statement for 2006. These schedules are presented on a book basis. Other information follows.

Estimated Tax Payments (Form 2220):
The corporation deposited estimated tax payments as follows:

April 17, 2006 (April 15 fell on a Sunday)	$118,000
June 15, 2006	243,000
September 15, 2006	285,000
December 15, 2006	285,000
Total	$931,000

Taxable income in 2005 was $2,200,000, and the 2005 tax was $748,000. The corporation earned its 2006 taxable income evenly throughout the year. Therefore, it does not use the annualization or seasonal methods.

Inventory and Cost of Goods Sold (Schedule A):
The corporation uses the periodic inventory method and prices its inventory using the lower of FIFO cost or market. Only beginning inventory, ending inventory, and purchases should be reflected in Schedule A. No other costs or expenses are allocated to cost of goods sold. Note: the corporation is exempt from the uniform capitalization (UNICAP) rules because average gross income for the previous three years was less than $10 million.

Line 9 (a)	Check (ii)
(b), (c) & (d)	Not applicable
(e) & (f)	No

▼ TABLE C:3-3
Knoxville Musical Sales, Inc.—Book Balance Sheet Information

Account	January 1, 2006 Debit	January 1, 2006 Credit	December 31, 2006 Debit	December 31, 2006 Credit
Cash	$ 254,567		$ 107,357	
Accounts receivable	417,960		486,000	
Allowance for doubtful accounts		$ 35,527		$ 41,310
Inventory	2,250,000		3,150,000	
Investment in corporate stock	180,000		37,000	
Investment in municipal bonds	30,000		30,000	
Cash surrender value of insurance policy	20,000		34,000	
Land	500,000		500,000	
Buildings	2,500,000		2,500,000	
Accumulated depreciation—Buildings		125,000		175,000
Equipment	600,000		840,000	
Accumulated depreciation—Equipment		100,000		115,333
Trucks	230,000		145,000	
Accumulated depreciation—Trucks		69,000		14,500
Accounts payable		1,500,000		550,000
Notes payable (short-term)		500,000		600,000
Accrued payroll taxes		25,000		28,000
Accrued state income taxes		8,000		11,000
Accrued federal income taxes				126,000
Bonds payable (long-term)		1,800,000		1,400,000
Deferred tax liability		70,000		75,000
Capital stock—Common		1,500,000		1,500,000
Retain earnings—Unappropriated		1,250,000		3,192,213
Totals	$6,982,527	$6,982,527	$7,829,357	$7,829,357

Compensation of Officers (Schedule E):

(a)	(b)	(c)	(d)	(f)
Mary Travis	345-82-7091	100%	50%	$265,000
John Willis	783-97-9105	100%	25%	160,000
Chris Parker	465-34-2245	100%	25%	160,000
Total				$585,000

Bad Debts:
For tax purposes, the corporation uses the direct writeoff method of deducting bad debts. For book purposes, the corporation uses an allowance for doubtful accounts. During 2006, the corporation charged $36,000 to the allowance account, such amount representing actual writeoffs for 2006.

Additional Information (Schedule K):

1 b	Accrual	6-7	No
2 a	451140	8	Do not check box
b	Retail sales	9	Fill in the correct amount
c	Musical instruments	10	3
3-4	No	11	Do not check box
5	Yes, 50%	12	Not applicable
		13	No

▼ TABLE C:3-4
Knoxville Musical Sales, Inc.—Book Income Statement 2006

Sales		$ 9,000,000
Returns		(225,000)
Net sales		$ 8,775,000
Beginning inventory	$2,250,000	
Purchases	4,950,000	
Ending inventory	(3,150,000)	
Cost of goods sold		(4,050,000)
Gross profit		$ 4,725,000
Expenses:		
Amortization	$ -0-	
Depreciation	142,833	
Repairs	18,720	
General insurance	49,500	
Premium–Officers' life insurance (net of cash buildup)	40,500	
Officer's compensation	585,000	
Other salaries	360,000	
Utilities	64,800	
Advertising	43,200	
Legal and accounting fees	45,000	
Charitable contributions	27,000	
Employment tax	56,250	
State tax	67,500	
Interest	189,000	
Bad debts	41,783	
Total expenses		(1,731,087)
Loss on exchange of trucks		(18,000)
Gain on sale of equipment		90,000
Interest on municipal bonds		4,500
Net gain on stock sales		14,000
Dividend income		10,800
Net income before FIT expense		$ 3,095,213
Federal income tax (FIT) expense		(1,063,000)
Net income per books		$ 2,032,213

Organizational Expenditures:
The corporation incurred $6,000 of organizational expenditures on January 2, 2003. For book purposes, the corporation expensed the entire expenditure pursuant to Statement of Position 98-5. For tax purposes, the corporation elected under Sec. 248 to amortize this amount over 60 months (the rule then in effect), with a full month's amortization taken for January 2003. The corporation reports this amortization in Part VI of Form 4562 and includes it in "Other Deductions" on Form 1120, Line 26.

Capital Gains and Losses:
The corporation sold 100 shares of PDQ Corp. common stock on March 7, 2006 for $95,000. The corporation acquired the stock on December 15, 2005 for $65,000. The corporation also sold 75 shares of JSB Corp. common stock on September 17, 2006 for $62,000. The corporation acquired this stock on September 18, 2003 for $78,000. The corporation has an $8,000 capital loss carryover from 2005.

Fixed Assets and Depreciation:
For book purposes: The corporation uses straight-line depreciation over the useful lives of assets as follows: Store building, 50 years; Equipment, 15 years (old) and ten years (new); and Trucks, five years (old and new). The corporation takes a half-year's depreciation in the year of acquisition and the year of disposition and assumes no salvage value. The

book financial statements in Tables C:3-3 and C:3-4 reflect these calculations. The designation "old" refers to property placed in service before 2006, and the designation "new" refers to property placed in service in 2006.

For tax purposes: All assets are MACRS property as follows: Store building, 39-year nonresidential real property; Equipment, seven-year property; and Trucks, five-year property. The corporation acquired the store building for $2.5 million and placed it in service on January 2, 2003. The corporation acquired two pieces of equipment for $200,000 (Equipment 1) and $400,000 (Equipment 2) and placed them in service on January 2, 2003. The corporation acquired the old trucks for $230,000 and placed them in service on July 18, 2004. The corporation did not make the expensing election under Sec. 179 on any property acquired before 2006 and elected not to claim bonus depreciation. Also, the corporation did not elect the straight-line option or the alternative depreciation system (ADS) under MACRS. Accumulated tax depreciation through December 31, 2005 on these properties is as follows:

Store building	$189,725
Equipment 1	112,540
Equipment 2	225,080
Trucks	119,600

On November 16, 2006, the corporation sold for $250,000 Equipment 1 that originally cost $200,000 on January 2, 2003. The corporation had no Sec. 1231 losses from prior years. In a separate transaction on November 17, 2006, the corporation acquired and placed in service a piece of equipment costing $440,000. These two transactions do *not* qualify as a like-kind exchange under Reg. Sec. 1.1031(k)-1(a). The new equipment is seven-year property. The corporation made the Sec. 179 expensing election with regard to the new equipment. The corporation relies on Sec. 179(d)(3) and Reg. Sec. 1.179-4(d) to determine the cost of its Sec. 179 property.

On May 15, 2006, the corporation exchanged its entire fleet of delivery trucks, which cost $230,000 on July 18, 2004 for similar trucks. On the date of exchange, the old trucks had a $120,000 FMV, and the new trucks had a $145,000 FMV. As part of the exchange, the corporation paid $25,000 cash in addition to the old trucks. For tax purposes, the exchange qualifies as a like-kind exchange. The new trucks are five-year property. Assume that neither the old nor new trucks are listed property according to Reg. Sec. 1.280F-6(c)(3)(iii) and Temp. Reg. Sec. 1.274-5T(k). The corporation relies on Temp. Reg. Sec. 1.168(i)-6T(e) to compute depreciation on the new trucks.

Where applicable, use published IRS depreciation tables to compute 2006 depreciation (reproduced in Appendix C of this text).

Other Information:

- The corporation's activities do not qualify for the U.S. production activities deduction.
- Ignore the AMT and accumulated earnings tax.
- The corporation received the $10,800 in dividends from taxable, domestic corporations, the stock of which Knoxville Musical Sales, Inc. owns less than 20%.
- The corporation paid $90,000 in cash dividends to its shareholders during the year and charged the payment directly to retained earnings.
- The corporation issued the bonds payable at par. Thus, no premium or discount need be amortized.
- The corporation is not entitled any credits.

Required: Prepare the 2006 corporate tax return for Knoxville Musical Sales, Inc. along with any necessary supporting schedules. Also, prepare Schedule M-3 as well as Schedule M-1 even though the IRS does not require both schedules.

C:3-64 Permtemp Corporation formed in 2005 and, for that year, reported the following book income statement and balance sheet, excluding the federal income tax expense, deferred tax assets, and deferred tax liabilities:

Sales	$20,000,000
Cost of goods sold	(15,000,000)
Gross profit	$ 5,000,000

Dividend income		50,000
Tax-exempt interest income		15,000
Total income		$ 5,065,000
Expenses:		
Depreciation	$ 800,000	
Bad debts	400,000	
Charitable contributions	100,000	
Interest	475,000	
Meals and entertainment	45,000	
Other	3,855,000	
Total expenses		(5,675,000)
Net loss before federal income taxes		$ (610,000)
Cash		$ 500,000
Accounts receivable	$ 2,000,000	
Allowance for doubtful accounts	(250,000)	1,750,000
Inventory		4,000,000
Fixed assets	$10,000,000	
Accumulated depreciation	(800,000)	9,200,000
Investment in corporate stock		1,000,000
Investment in tax-exempt bonds		50,000
Total assets		$16,500,000
Accounts payable		$2,610,000
Long-term debt		8,500,000
Common stock		6,000,000
Retained earnings		(610,000)
Total liabilities and equity		$16,500,000

Additional information for 2005:

- The investment in corporate stock is comprised of less-than-20%-owned corporations.
- Depreciation for tax purposes is $1.4 million under MACRS.
- Bad debt expense for tax purposes is $150,000 under the direct writeoff method.
- Limitations to charitable contribution deductions and meals and entertainment expenses must be tested and applied if necessary.
- Qualified production activities income is zero.

Required for 2005:

a. Prepare page 1 of the 2005 Form 1120, computing the corporation's NOL.

b. Determine the corporation's deferred tax asset and deferred tax liability situation, and then complete the income statement and balance sheet to reflect proper SFAS 109 accounting. Use the balance sheet information to prepare Schedule L of the 2005 Form 1120.

c. Prepare the 2005 Schedule M-3 for Form 1120.

d. Prepare a schedule that reconciles the corporation's effective tax rate to the statutory 34% tax rate.

Note: For 2005 forms, go to previous year forms at the IRS website, *www.irs.gov*.

For 2006, Permtemp reported the following book income statement and balance sheet, excluding the federal income tax expense, deferred tax assets, and deferred tax liabilities:

Sales	$33,000,000
Cost of goods sold	(22,000,000)
Gross profit	$11,000,000
Dividend income	55,000
Tax-exempt interest income	15,000
Total income	$11,070,000

Expenses:		
Depreciation	$ 800,000	
Bad debts	625,000	
Charitable contributions	40,000	
Interest	455,000	
Meals and entertainment	60,000	
Other	4,675,000	
Total expenses		(6,655,000)
Net income before federal income taxes		$ 4,415,000

Cash		$ 2,125,000
Accounts receivable	$ 3,300,000	
Allowance for doubtful accounts	(450,000)	2,850,000
Inventory		6,000,000
Fixed assets	$10,000,000	
Accumulated depreciation	(1,600,000)	8,400,000
Investment in corporate stock		1,000,000
Investment in tax-exempt bonds		50,000
Total assets		$20,425,000
Accounts payable		$ 2,120,000
Long-term debt		8,500,000
Common stock		6,000,000
Retained earnings		3,805,000
		$20,425,000

Additional information for 2006:

- Depreciation for tax purposes is $2.45 million under MACRS.
- Bad debt expense for tax purposes is $425,000 under the direct writeoff method.
- Qualified production activities income is $3 million.

Required for 2006:

a. Prepare page 1 of the 2006 Form 1120, computing the corporation's taxable income and tax liability.

b. Determine the corporation's deferred tax asset and deferred tax liability situation, and then complete the income statement and balance sheet to reflect proper SFAS 109 accounting. Use the balance sheet information to prepare Schedule L of the 2005 Form 1120.

c. Prepare the 2006 Schedule M-3 for Form 1120.

d. Prepare a schedule that reconciles the corporation's effective tax rate to the statutory 34% tax rate.

CASE STUDY PROBLEMS

C:3-65 Marquette Corporation, a tax client since its creation three years ago, has requested that you prepare a memorandum explaining its estimated tax requirements for 2008. The corporation is in the fabricated steel business. Its earnings have been growing each year. Marquette's taxable income for the last three tax years has been $500,000, $1.5 million, and $2.5 million, respectively. The Chief Financial Officer expects its taxable income in 2008 to be approximately $3 million.

Required: Prepare a one-page client memorandum explaining Marquette's estimated tax requirements for 2008, providing the necessary supporting authorities.

C:3-66 Susan Smith accepted a new corporate client, Winter Park Corporation. One of Susan's tax managers conducted a review of Winter Park's prior year tax returns. The review revealed that an NOL for a prior tax year was incorrectly computed, resulting in an overstatement of NOL carrybacks and carryovers to prior tax years.

a. Assume the incorrect NOL calculation does not affect the current year's tax liability. What recommendations (if any) should Susan make to the new client?

b. Assume the IRS is currently auditing a prior year. What are Susan's responsibilities in this situation?

c. Assume the NOL carryover is being carried to the current year, and Winter Park does not want to file amended tax returns to correct the error. What should Susan do in this situation?

C:3-67 The Chief Executive Officer of a client of your public accounting firm saw the following advertisement in *The Wall Street Journal:*

> DONATIONS WANTED
> The Center for Restoration of Waters
> A Nonprofit Research and Educational Organization
> Needs Donations—Autos, Boats, Real Estate, Etc.
> ALL DONATIONS ARE TAX-DEDUCTIBLE

Prepare a memorandum to your client Phil Nickelson explaining how the federal income tax laws regarding donations of cash, automobiles, boats, and real estate apply to corporate taxpayers.

TAX RESEARCH PROBLEMS

C:3-68 Wicker Corporation makes estimated tax payments of $6,000 in 2006. On March 15, 2007, it files its 2006 tax return showing a $20,000 tax liability, and it pays the $14,000 balance at that time. On April 18, 2007, it discovers an error and files an amended return for 2006 showing a reduced tax liability of $8,000. Prepare a memorandum for your tax manager explaining whether Wicker can base its estimated tax payments for 2007 on the $8,000 tax liability for 2006, or must it use the $20,000 tax liability reported on its original return. Your manager has suggested that, at a minimum, you consult the following resources:

- IRC Sec. 6655(d)(1)
- Rev. Rul. 86-58, 1986-1 C.B. 365

C:3-69 Alice, Bill, and Charles each received an equal number of shares when they formed King Corporation a number of years ago. King has used the cash method of accounting since its inception. Alice, Bill, and Charles, the shareholder-employees, operate King as an environmental engineering firm with 57 additional employees. King had gross receipts of $4.3 million last year. Gross receipts have grown by about 15% in each of the last three years and were just under $5 million in the current year. The owners expect the 15% growth rate to continue for at least five more years. Outstanding accounts receivable average about $600,000 at the end of each month. Forty-four employees (including Alice, Bill, and Charles) actively engage in providing engineering services on a full-time basis. The remaining 16 employees serve in a clerical and support capacity (secretarial staff, accountants, etc.). Bill has read about special restrictions on the use of the cash method of accounting and requests information from you about the impact these rules might have on King's continued use of that method. Prepare a memorandum for your tax manager addressing the following issues: (1) If the corporation changes to the accrual method of accounting, what adjustments must it make? (2) Would an S election relieve King from having to make a change? (3) If the S election relieves King from having to make a change, what factors should enter into the decision about whether King should make an S election?

Your manager has suggested that, at a minimum, you should consult the following resources:

- IRC Secs. 446 and 448
- Temp. Reg. Secs. 1.448-1T and -2T
- H. Rept. No. 99-841, 99th Cong., 2d Sess., pp. 285–289 (1986)

C:3-70 James Bowen owns 100% of Bowen Corporation stock. Bowen is a calendar year, accrual method taxpayer. During 2007, Bowen made three charitable contributions:

Donee	*Property Donated*	*FMV of Property*
State University	Bates Corporation stock	$110,000
Red Cross	Cash	5,000
Girl Scouts	Pledge to pay cash	25,000

Bowen purchased the Bates stock three years ago for $30,000. Bowen holds a 28% interest, which it accounts for under GAAP using the equity method of accounting. The current carrying value for the Bates stock for book purposes is $47,300. Bowen will pay the pledge to the Girl Scouts by check on March 3, 2008. Bowen's taxable income for the current year before the charitable contributions deduction, dividends-received deduction, NOL deduction, and U.S. production activities deduction is $600,000. Your tax manager has asked you to prepare a memorandum explaining how these transactions are to be treated for tax purposes and for accounting purposes. Your manager has suggested that, at a minimum, you should consult the following resources:

- IRC Sec. 170
- FASB, *Statement of Financial Accounting Standards No. 116*

C:3-71 Production Corporation owns 70% of Manufacturing Corporation's common stock and Rita Howard owns the remaining 30%. Each corporation operates and sells its product within the United States, and the corporations engaged in no intercompany transactions. Production's Chief Financial Officer (CFO) presents you with the following information pertaining to 2007 operations:

	Production Corporation	*Manufacturing Corporation*
Gross profit on sales	$500,000	$225,000
Minus: Operating expenses	(200,000)	(100,000)
Qualified production activities income	$300,000	$125,000
Plus: Dividends received from		
20%-owned corporations	20,000	-0-
Minus: Dividends-received deduction	(16,000)	-0-
NOL carryover deduction	-0-	(15,000)
Taxable income before the U.S. production activities deduction	$304,000	$110,000

Operating expenses include W-2 wages of $75,000 and $35,000 for Production and Manufacturing, respectively. Given this information, the CFO asks you to determine each corporation's qualified production activities deduction. At a minimum, you should consult the following resources:

- IRC Sec. 199
- Reg. Sec. 1.199-7

CHAPTER 4

CORPORATE NONLIQUIDATING DISTRIBUTIONS

LEARNING OBJECTIVES

After studying this chapter, you should be able to

1. Calculate corporate current earnings and profits (E&P)
2. Distinguish between current and accumulated E&P
3. Determine the tax consequences of nonliquidating distributions
4. Determine the tax consequences of stock dividends and the issuance of stock rights
5. Discern when a stock redemption should be treated as a sale and when it should be treated as a dividend
6. Explain the tax treatment of preferred stock bailouts
7. Determine the applicability and tax consequences of Sec. 304 to stock sales

CHAPTER OUTLINE

A corporation may distribute money, property, or stock to its shareholders. Shareholders who receive such distributions might recognize ordinary income, capital gain, or no taxable income at all. The distributing corporation may or may not be required to recognize gain or loss when making the distribution. How the corporation and its shareholders treat distributions for tax purposes depends on not only what the corporation distributes but also the circumstances surrounding the distribution. Was the corporation in the process of liquidating? Was the distribution made in exchange for some of the shareholder's stock?

This chapter addresses distributions made when a corporation is not in the process of liquidating. It discusses the tax consequences of the following types of distributions:

- Distributions of cash or other property where the shareholder does not surrender any stock
- Distributions of stock or rights to acquire stock of the distributing corporation
- Distributions of property in exchange for the corporation's own stock (i.e., stock redemptions)

Chapter C:6 discusses **liquidating distributions**, and Chapter C:7 discusses distributions associated with corporate reorganizations.

NONLIQUIDATING DISTRIBUTIONS IN GENERAL

SELF-STUDY QUESTION

How does a shareholder classify a distribution for tax purposes?

ANSWER

Distributions are treated as follows: (1) dividends to the extent of corporate E&P, (2) return of capital to the extent of the shareholder's stock basis, and (3) gain from the sale of stock.

Dividends → E&P
Capital → basis
Gain

When a corporation makes a nonliquidating distribution to a shareholder, the shareholder must answer the following three questions:

- What is the amount of the distribution?
- To what extent is this amount considered a dividend?
- What is the basis of the distributed property, and when does its holding period begin?

In addition, the distributing corporation must answer the following two questions:

- What are the amount and character of gain or loss the corporation must recognize?
- What effect does the distribution have on the distributing corporation's earnings and profits (E&P) account?

A brief summary of the rules for determining the taxability of a distribution follows, along with a simple example.

Section 301 requires a shareholder to include in gross income the amount of any corporate distribution to the extent it is a dividend. Qualified dividends received by a noncorporate shareholder in 2003 through 2010 are subject to a maximum 15% tax rate. Section 316(a) defines **dividend** as a distribution of property made by a corporation out of its E&P. Earnings and profits are discussed in the next section of this chapter. Section 317(a) defines **property** broadly to include money, securities, and any other property except stock or stock rights of the distributing corporation. Distributed amounts that exceed a corporation's E&P are treated as a return of capital that reduces the shareholder's basis in his or her stock (but not below zero). Distributions exceeding the shareholder's basis are treated as gain from the sale of the stock. If the stock is a capital asset in the shareholder's hands, the gain is capital in character.

EXAMPLE C:4-1 ▶ On March 1, Gamma Corporation distributes $60,000 in cash to each of its two equal shareholders, Ellen and Bob. At the time of the distribution, Gamma's E&P is $80,000. Ellen's basis in her stock is $25,000, and Bob's basis in his stock is $10,000. Ellen and Bob each recognize $40,000 (0.50 × $80,000) of dividend income. This portion of the distribution reduces Gamma's E&P to zero. The additional $20,000 that each shareholder receives is first treated as a return of capital and then as a capital gain. The following table summarizes the calculations:

	Ellen	Bob	Total
Distribution	$60,000	$60,000	$120,000
Dividend income[a]	(40,000)	(40,000)	(80,000)
Remaining distribution	$20,000	$20,000	$ 40,000
Return of capital[b]	(20,000)	(10,000)	(30,000)
Capital gain[c]	$ -0-	$10,000	$ 10,000

[a]Smaller of E&P allocable to the distribution or the amount of the distribution.
[b]Smaller of remaining distribution to shareholder or his or her stock basis.
[c]Any amount that exceeds the shareholder's basis in his or her stock. ◀

EARNINGS AND PROFITS (E&P)

TYPICAL MISCONCEPTION

Because E&P is such an important concept in many corporate transactions, one would assume that corporations know exactly what their E&P is. However, many corporations do not compute their E&P on a regular basis.

The term E&P is not specifically defined in the IRC. Its meaning must be gleaned from judicial opinions, Treasury Regulations, and IRC rules regarding how certain transactions affect E&P.

To some extent, E&P measures a corporation's economic ability to pay dividends to its shareholders. Distributions are presumed to be made out of the corporation's E&P unless the corporation reports no E&P.

CURRENT EARNINGS AND PROFITS

A corporation's E&P falls into one of two categories: current E&P or accumulated E&P. **Current E&P** is calculated annually as explained below. **Accumulated E&P** is the sum of undistributed current E&P balances for all previous years reduced by the sum of all previous current E&P deficits and any distributions the corporation made out of accumulated E&P. Distributions are deemed to have been made first out of current E&P and then out of accumulated E&P to the extent that current E&P is insufficient.

EXAMPLE C:4-2 ▶ Zeta Corporation formed in 2004. Its current E&P (or current E&P deficit) and distributions for each year through 2007 are as follows:

Year	Current E&P (Deficit)	Distributions
2004	$(10,000)	-0-
2005	15,000	-0-
2006	18,000	$9,000
2007	8,000	-0-

The corporation is deemed to have made the $9,000 distribution out of its 2006 current E&P account. At the beginning of 2007, Zeta's accumulated E&P balance is $14,000 (− $10,000 + $15,000 + $18,000 − $9,000). At the beginning of 2008, Zeta's accumulated E&P balance is $22,000 ($14,000 + $8,000). ◀

OBJECTIVE 1

Calculate corporate current earnings and profits (E&P)

COMPUTING CURRENT E&P. A corporation computes its current E&P on an annual basis at the end of each year. The starting point for computing current E&P is the corporation's taxable income or net operating loss (NOL) for the year. Taxable income or the NOL must be adjusted to derive the corporation's economic income or loss (current E&P) for the year. For example, federal income taxes must be deducted from taxable income to derive E&P. Because the corporation must pay these taxes to the U.S. government, they reduce the amount available to pay dividends to shareholders. On the other hand, tax-exempt income must be added to taxable income (or the NOL) because, even though not taxable, such income increases the corporation's ability to pay dividends.

Table C:4-1 lists some of the adjustments a corporation must make to taxable income (NOL) to derive current E&P. Some of these adjustments are explained below.[1]

[1] The adjustments are based on rules set forth in Sec. 312 and related Treasury Regulations.

▼ **TABLE C:4-1**
Computation of Current E&P

Taxable income

Plus: *Income excluded from taxable income but included in E&P*
- Tax-exempt interest
- Proceeds from a life insurance contract in which the corporation is named as the beneficiary
- Recoveries of bad debts and other deductions from which the corporation received no tax benefit
- Federal income tax refunds from prior years

Plus: *Income deferred to a later year when computing taxable income but included in E&P in the current year*
- Deferred gain on installment sales. Such gain is included in E&P in the year of sale.

Plus or minus: *Income and deduction items that must be recomputed when computing E&P*
- Income on long-term contracts must be based on the percentage of completion rather than the completed contract method
- Depreciation on personal and real property must be based on:
  - The straight-line method for other than MACRS property
  - The alternative depreciation system for MACRS property
- Excess of percentage depletion over cost depletion

Plus: *Deductions that reduce taxable income but are not allowed in computing E&P*
- Dividends-received deduction
- NOL carryovers, charitable contribution carryovers, and capital loss carryovers used in the current year
- U.S. production activities deduction

Minus: *Expenses and losses that are not deductible in computing taxable income but that reduce E&P*
- Federal income taxes
- Premiums on life insurance contracts in which the corporation is named as the beneficiary
- Excess capital losses that are not currently deductible
- Excess charitable contributions that are not currently deductible
- Expenses related to the production of tax-exempt income
- Nondeductible losses on sales to related parties
- Nondeductible penalties and fines
- Nondeductible political contributions and lobbying expenses

Current E&P balance (or deficit)

INCOME EXCLUDED FROM TAXABLE INCOME BUT INCLUDED IN E&P. Although certain items of income are specifically excluded from taxable income, these items must be included in E&P if they increase the corporation's ability to pay dividends. Thus, a corporation's current E&P includes both tax-exempt interest and life insurance proceeds. Current E&P also includes the recovery of an item deducted in a previous year if the deduction produced no tax benefit for the corporation and therefore was excluded from its taxable income.

EXAMPLE C:4-3 ▶ Ace Corporation deducted $10,000 of bad debts in 2006. Because Ace generated an NOL in 2006 that it was unable to carry back or forward, it derived no tax benefit from the deduction. In 2007, Ace recovers $8,000 of the debt owed to it. Ace excludes the $8,000 from its gross income for 2007 because it derived no tax benefit from the bad debt deduction in 2006. However, Ace must add the $8,000 to its taxable income when computing current E&P for 2007 because the NOL reduced current E&P in 2006. ◀

INCOME DEFERRED TO A LATER YEAR WHEN COMPUTING TAXABLE INCOME BUT INCLUDED IN E&P IN THE CURRENT YEAR. Gains and losses on property transactions generally are included in E&P in the same year they are recognized for taxable income purposes.

EXAMPLE C:4-4 ▶ Stone Corporation exchanges investment property with a $12,000 basis and an $18,000 fair market value (FMV) for $1,000 cash and investment property worth $17,000. Stone recognizes a $1,000 gain—the amount of boot received—on the like-kind exchange and defers the remaining $5,000 of realized gain. Stone includes the recognized gain in both taxable income and current E&P. It does not include the deferred gain in either taxable income or current E&P. ◀

In the case of an installment sale, however, the entire realized gain must be included in current E&P in the year of the sale. This rule applies to sales made by dealers and nondealers.

EXAMPLE C:4-5 ▶ In the current year, Tally Corporation sells land with a $12,000 basis and a $20,000 FMV to Rick, an unrelated individual. Rick makes a $5,000 down payment this year and promises to pay Tally an additional $5,000 in each of the next three years, plus interest on the unpaid balance at the prevailing market rate. Tally's realized gain is $8,000 ($20,000 − $12,000). For taxable income purposes, Tally currently recognizes $2,000 of gain [($8,000 ÷ $20,000) × $5,000] under the installment method for nondealers. For E&P purposes, Tally includes all $8,000 of its realized gain in current E&P. Thus, in computing current E&P, Tally increases taxable income by $6,000. As it receives the installments, Tally will recognize the remaining $6,000 of gain over the next three years ($2,000 per year) for taxable income purposes. It will reduce E&P by $2,000 in each of those years because it included in E&P all $8,000 in the current year. ◀

SELF-STUDY QUESTION

In computing taxable income and E&P, different depreciation methods are often used. What happens when the taxpayer sells such assets?

ANSWER

The taxpayer must calculate a gain/loss for taxable income and E&P purposes separately. This difference is an added complexity in making E&P calculations.

INCOME AND DEDUCTION ITEMS THAT MUST BE RECOMPUTED WHEN COMPUTING E&P. Some deductions are computed differently for E&P and taxable income purposes. Therefore, adjustments must be made to account for the differences.

- E&P must be computed under the percentage of completion method even if the corporation uses the completed contract method for taxable income purposes.
- Depreciation must be recomputed under the alternative depreciation system of Sec. 168(g). Also, the cost of property expensed under Sec. 179 must be recovered ratably over a five-year period starting with the month in which it is expensed. Other personal property must be depreciated over the property's class life under the half-year convention. Real property must be depreciated over a 40-year period under the straight-line method and mid-month convention.

EXAMPLE C:4-6 ▶ In January 2004, Radon Corporation paid $5,000 for equipment with a ten-year class life. In 2004, Radon expensed the cost of the equipment under Sec. 179. For E&P purposes, Radon's depreciation deduction is $1,000 ($5,000 ÷ 5) in each year from 2004 through 2008. ◀

- Cost depletion must be used for E&P purposes even if percentage depletion is used for taxable income purposes.
- Intangible drilling costs must be capitalized and amortized over 60 months.

BOOK-TO-TAX ACCOUNTING COMPARISION

Many corporations use retained earnings to measure the taxability of their dividend payments. However, because retained earnings are based on financial accounting concepts, E&P may represent a different amount and may provide a different measure of the corporation's economic ability to pay dividends.

DEDUCTIONS THAT REDUCE TAXABLE INCOME BUT ARE NOT ALLOWED IN COMPUTING E&P. Some deductions allowed for taxable income purposes are not allowed for E&P purposes.

- The dividends-received deduction is denied for E&P purposes because it does not reduce the corporation's ability to pay dividends. Therefore, in the computation of E&P, this deduction must be added back to taxable income.
- NOL, charitable contribution, and capital loss carryovers that reduce current taxable income cannot be deducted to derive E&P. These excess losses or deductions reduce E&P in the year they are incurred or taken.
- The U.S. production activities deduction is not permitted for E&P purposes because it does not reduce the corporation's ability to pay dividends. Therefore, it must be added back to taxable income to derive E&P.
- Amortization of organizational expenses is not permitted for E&P purposes.

XAMPLE C:4-7 ► Thames Corporation's taxable income is $500,000 after deductions for the following items: a $10,000 NOL carryover from two years ago, $20,000 for dividends received, and $8,000 for U.S. production activities. To compute current E&P, Thames must add $38,000 to its taxable income. Thus, current E&P is $538,000. ◄

EXPENSES AND LOSSES THAT ARE NOT DEDUCTIBLE IN COMPUTING TAXABLE INCOME BUT THAT REDUCE E&P. Some expenses and losses that are not deductible for taxable income purposes are deductible for E&P purposes.

- For taxable income purposes, federal income taxes are not deductible. For E&P purposes, however, federal income taxes are deductible in the year they accrue if the corporation uses the accrual method of accounting and in the year they are paid if the corporation uses the cash method of accounting.

EXAMPLE C:4-8 ► Perch Corporation, an accrual basis taxpayer, earns taxable income of $100,000 on which it owes $22,250 of federal income taxes. In computing current E&P, Perch reduces taxable income by $22,250. ◄

- For E&P purposes, charitable contributions are fully deductible. Thus, when current E&P is computed, taxable income must be reduced by any charitable contributions disallowed because of the 10% limitation.

EXAMPLE C:4-9 ► Dot Corporation computes $25,000 of taxable income before any charitable contribution deduction. Dot contributed $10,000 to the Red Cross. For taxable income purposes, Dot's charitable contribution deduction is limited to $2,500 because of the 10% limitation. However, Dot deducts the entire $10,000 in computing current E&P. Therefore, to compute current E&P, it must subtract the remaining $7,500 from taxable income of $22,500 ($25,000 − $2,500). In a later year, when the corporation deducts the $7,500 carryover to compute taxable income, it adds that amount to taxable income to derive current E&P. ◄

- Premiums paid on insurance policies covering the lives of key corporate personnel (net of any increase in the cash surrender value) are not deductible when computing taxable income but are deductible when computing E&P.
- Capital losses exceeding capital gains cannot be deducted when computing taxable income but can be deducted when computing current E&P.
- Nondeductible expenses related to the production of tax-exempt income (e.g., interest charges to borrow money to purchase tax-exempt securities) are deductible when computing E&P.
- Losses on related party sales that are disallowed under Sec. 267 are allowed when computing E&P.
- Fines, penalties, and political contributions that are nondeductible for taxable income purposes are deductible for E&P purposes.

The foregoing items constitute only a partial list of adjustments that must be made to taxable income to compute current E&P. The basic rule is that an adjustment to taxable income must be made so that current E&P reflects the corporation's economic ability to pay dividends.

OBJECTIVE 2

Distinguish between current and accumulated E&P

DISTINCTION BETWEEN CURRENT AND ACCUMULATED E&P

A distinction must be made between current and accumulated E&P. A nonliquidating distribution is taxed as a dividend if made out of either current or accumulated E&P. Corporate distributions are deemed to be made first out of current E&P and then out of accumulated E&P to the extent that current E&P is insufficient.[2] If current E&P is sufficient to cover all distributions during the year, each distribution is treated as a taxable div-

[2] The distinction between current and accumulated E&P is explained in Reg. Sec. 1.316-2.

idend. This rule applies even if the corporation reports a deficit in its beginning accumulated E&P account. Current E&P is computed as of the last day of the tax year without reduction for distributions during the year.

EXAMPLE C:4-10 ▶ At the beginning of the current year, Water Corporation has a $30,000 accumulated E&P deficit. For the entire year, Water generates current E&P of $15,000. During the year, Water distributes $10,000 in cash to its shareholders. The $10,000 distribution is a taxable dividend to the shareholders because it is deemed to be out of current E&P. At the beginning of the next tax year, Water's accumulated E&P deficit is $25,000 (– $30,000 E&P deficit + $5,000 undistributed current E&P). ◀

TAX STRATEGY TIP

A corporation with an accumulated deficit and current E&P may want to postpone distributions to a later year to avoid dividend treatment in the current year. See Example C:4-53 later in this chapter.

If distributions during the year exceed current E&P, current E&P is allocated on a pro rata basis regardless of when during the year the distributions occurred. Distributions exceeding current E&P are deemed to be made in chronological order out of accumulated E&P (if any). Distributions exceeding current and accumulated E&P are treated as a return of capital and reduce the shareholder's stock basis. However, such distributions cannot create an E&P deficit, which results only from losses. These rules are relevant if stock changes hands during the year and total E&P is insufficient to cover all distributions.

EXAMPLE C:4-11 ▶ At the beginning of the current year, Cole Corporation has $20,000 of accumulated E&P. For the entire year, Cole's current E&P is $30,000. On April 10, Cole distributes $20,000 in cash to Bob, its sole shareholder. On July 15, Cole distributes an additional $24,000 in cash to Bob. On August 1, Bob sells all of his Cole stock to Lynn. On September 15, Cole distributes $36,000 in cash to Lynn. Cole's current and accumulated E&P must be allocated among the three distributions as follows:

Date	*Distribution Amount*	*Current E&P*	*Accumulated E&P*	*Dividend Income*	*Return of Capital*
April 10	$20,000	$ 7,500	$12,500	$20,000	$ –0–
July 15	24,000	9,000	7,500	16,500	7,500
September 15	36,000	13,500	–0–	13,500	22,500
Total	$80,000	$30,000	$20,000	$50,000	$30,000

The current E&P allocated to the April 10 distribution is calculated as follows:

$$\$30{,}000 \text{ (Current E\&P)} \times \frac{\$20{,}000 \text{ (April 10 distribution)}}{\$80{,}000 \text{ (Total distributions)}}$$

Note that the total amount of dividends paid by Cole equals $50,000, the sum of $30,000 of current E&P and $20,000 of accumulated E&P. Current E&P is allocated among all three distributions on a pro rata basis, whereas accumulated E&P is allocated first to the April 10 distribution ($12,500), then to the July 15 distribution, so that no accumulated E&P is available for the September 15 distribution. Thus, Bob's dividend income from Cole is $36,500 ($20,000 + $16,500). He also receives a $7,500 return of capital that reduces his stock basis accordingly. Lynn's dividend income from Cole is $13,500. She also receives a $22,500 return of capital that reduces her stock basis accordingly. Bob cannot determine his gain on the stock sale until after the end of the year. He must wait until he knows the extent to which the April 10 and July 15 distributions reduce his stock basis. ◀

If the corporation generates both a current E&P deficit and an accumulated E&P deficit, none of the distributions is treated as a dividend. Instead, all distributions are treated as a return of capital to the extent of the shareholder's stock basis. Distributions exceeding this basis are taxed as a capital gain.

EXAMPLE C:4-12 ▶ At the beginning of the current year, Rose Corporation has a $15,000 accumulated E&P deficit. Rose's current E&P deficit is $20,000. Rose distributes $10,000 on July 1. The distribution is not treated as a dividend but rather as a return of capital to the extent of the shareholder's stock basis. Any amounts exceeding stock basis are taxed as a capital gain. Rose's accumulated E&P deficit on January 1 of next year is $35,000 because the distribution was not made out of E&P and because the negative balance in the current E&P account is transferred to the accumulated E&P account at the end of the current year. ◀

SELF-STUDY QUESTION

When is E&P measured for purposes of determining whether a distribution is a dividend?

ANSWER

Usually at year-end. However, if a current deficit exists, the E&P available for measuring dividend income is determined at the distribution date.

If the corporation has a current E&P deficit and a positive accumulated E&P balance, it must net the two accounts at the time of the distribution to determine the dividend amount.[3] The deficit in current E&P that has accrued up through the day before the distribution reduces the accumulated E&P balance on that date. If the balance remaining after the reduction is positive, the distribution is a dividend to the extent of the lesser of the distribution amount or the E&P balance. If the E&P balance is zero or negative, the distribution is treated as a return of capital. If the actual deficit in current E&P to the date of distribution cannot be determined, the current E&P deficit is prorated on a daily basis to the day before the distribution.

EXAMPLE C:4-13 ▶ Assume the same facts as in Example C:4-12 except that Rose Corporation has a $15,000 accumulated E&P balance. The current E&P deficit of $20,000 accrues on a daily basis unless information indicates otherwise. The amount of the July 1 distribution treated as a dividend is calculated as follows:

Date	Distribution Amount	Accumulated E&P	Dividend Income	Return of Capital
Jan. 1	$ -0-	$15,000		
July 1	10,000	(9,918)[a]	$5,082	$4,918
Total	$10,000	$ 5,082[b]	$5,082	$4,918

[a]181/365 × ($20,000) = ($9,918)—the current E&P deficit accrued up to the distribution date. (The 181/365 fraction assumes a nonleap year.)

[b]$15,000 − $9,918 = $5,082—accumulated E&P at beginning of year minus the current E&P deficit accrued up to the distribution date. ◀

STOP & THINK *Question:* Why is it necessary to keep separate balances for current and accumulated E&P?

Solution: If total current and accumulated E&P is less than the total distributions to the shareholders, E&P must be allocated to all distributions during the year to determine the amount of each distribution that should be treated as a dividend. When no change in the shareholder's stock ownership occurs during the year and all distributions are proportional to stock ownership, an E&P allocation is needed only to track each shareholder's stock basis. Tracking E&P to individual distributions is necessary to determine the taxability of a particular distribution when a change in a shareholder's stock ownership occurs because current E&P is allocated on a pro rata basis and accumulated E&P is allocated chronologically. As a result of the chronological allocation, a greater portion of distributions early in a tax year may be taxed as a dividend relative to distributions later in the year. On the other hand, because accrued current E&P deficits offset accumulated E&P balances, a smaller portion of distributions later in a tax year may be taxed as a dividend relative to distributions earlier in the year.

NONLIQUIDATING PROPERTY DISTRIBUTIONS

OBJECTIVE 3

Determine the tax consequences of nonliquidating distributions

CONSEQUENCES OF NONLIQUIDATING PROPERTY DISTRIBUTIONS TO THE SHAREHOLDERS

Property includes money, securities, and any other property except stock in the corporation making the distribution (or rights to acquire such stock).[4] When a corporation distributes property to its shareholders, the following three questions must be answered:

- ▶ What is the amount of the distribution?
- ▶ To what extent is this amount treated as a dividend?

[3] Reg. Sec. 1.316-2(b).

[4] Sec. 317(a).

KEY POINT

The amount of the distribution is measured by the FMV of the property less liabilities assumed (but not below zero) because this net amount represents the real economic value received by the shareholder.

- What is the basis of the property to the shareholder, and when does its holding period begin?

For cash distributions, these questions are easy to answer. The distribution amount is the cash distributed, which is treated as a dividend to the extent of the corporation's current and accumulated E&P. The E&P account is reduced by the amount distributed, and the shareholder's basis in the cash received is its face value. The distributing corporation recognizes no gain or loss on cash distributions.

When the corporation distributes property such as land or inventory these questions are more difficult to answer. Neither the distribution amount nor the shareholder's basis in the property is immediately apparent. The corporation must recognize gain (but not loss) on the distribution, and the impact of the distribution on the corporation's E&P, as well as the taxability of the distribution, must be ascertained. The following sections set forth rules that address these issues.

When the corporation distributes property to a shareholder, the distribution amount is the property's FMV, determined as of the distribution date.[5] The amount of any liability assumed by the shareholder in connection with the distribution, or to which the distributed property is subject, reduces the distribution amount, but never below zero. The distribution amount is treated as a dividend to the extent of the distributing corporation's E&P.

The shareholder takes a FMV basis in any property received. This basis is not reduced by any liabilities assumed by the shareholder or to which the property is subject.[6] The holding period for the property begins on the day after the distribution date and does not include the distributing corporation's holding period.

EXAMPLE C:4-14 ▶ Post Corporation has $100,000 of current and accumulated E&P. On March 1, Post distributes to Meg, its sole shareholder, land with a $60,000 FMV and a $35,000 adjusted basis. The land is subject to a $10,000 liability, which Meg assumes. The distribution amount is $50,000 ($60,000 − $10,000), all of which is a dividend to Meg because it does not exceed Post's E&P balance. Meg's basis in the property is its $60,000 FMV, and her holding period for the property begins on March 2. ◀

STOP & THINK

Question: When a corporation distributes property, why do liabilities reduce the amount of income realized by the shareholder but do not reduce the shareholder's adjusted basis in the property?

Solution: The amount of a distribution to a shareholder is the property's FMV on the distribution date. In Example C:4-14, Meg receives land worth $60,000 and also assumes the $10,000 debt, which she is obligated to pay. Therefore, the value of the distribution to Meg is the net amount that she receives, or $50,000 ($60,000 − $10,000). The adjusted basis of the land to Meg is its $60,000 FMV. This result is the same as Meg's purchasing the land for $60,000 and financing the purchase with a $10,000 loan. In the latter case, the basis of the land to Meg still would have been its $60,000 FMV.

Topic Review C:4-1 summarizes the tax consequences of a nonliquidating distribution to the shareholders.

CONSEQUENCES OF PROPERTY DISTRIBUTIONS TO THE DISTRIBUTING CORPORATION

KEY POINT

Property distributions may trigger income at both the shareholder and the distributing corporation level. This result is another example of the double taxation that exists in our corporate tax system.

Two questions must be answered with respect to a corporation that distributes property:

- What amount and character of gain or loss must the distributing corporation recognize?
- What effect does the distribution have on the corporation's E&P?

[5] Sec. 301(b).

[6] Sec. 301(d).

Topic Review C:4-1

Tax Consequences of a Nonliquidating Distribution to the Shareholders

1. The amount of a distribution is the amount of money received plus the FMV of any nonmoney property received reduced by any liabilities assumed or acquired by the shareholder.
2. The distribution is a dividend to the extent of the distributing corporation's current and accumulated E&P. Any excess distribution is treated as a return of capital that reduces the shareholder's stock basis (but not below zero). Any further excess distribution is treated as a capital gain.
3. The shareholder's basis in the property received is its FMV.
4. The shareholder's holding period for the property begins on the day after the distribution date.

CORPORATE GAIN OR LOSS ON PROPERTY DISTRIBUTIONS. When a corporation distributes property that has appreciated in value, the corporation must recognize gain as though the corporation had sold the property for its FMV. On the other hand, a corporation does not recognize loss when it distributes property that has depreciated in value even though the corporation would have recognized a loss upon selling the property.[7]

EXAMPLE C:4-15 ▶ Silver Corporation distributes to Mark, a shareholder, land (a capital asset) worth $60,000. Silver's adjusted basis in the land is $20,000. Upon distributing the land, Silver recognizes a $40,000 ($60,000 − $20,000) capital gain, as if Silver had sold the property. If the land instead had a $12,000 FMV, Silver would not have recognized a loss. ◀

TAX STRATEGY TIP

Rather than distribute loss property, the corporation should consider selling it and distributing the proceeds. The sale will allow the corporation to deduct the loss.

If the distributed property is subject to a liability or the shareholder assumes a liability in the distribution, for the purpose of calculating gain, the property's FMV is deemed to be no less than the amount of the liability.[8]

EXAMPLE C:4-16 ▶ Assume the same facts as in Example C:4-15 except the land's FMV is instead $25,000, and the land is subject to a $35,000 mortgage. For the purpose of calculating gain, the land's FMV is deemed to be $35,000 because this value cannot be less than the liability amount. Thus, Silver Corporation's gain is $15,000 ($35,000 − $20,000), the amount by which the land's deemed FMV exceeds its adjusted basis.[9] ◀

TAX STRATEGY TIP

If possible, a corporation should avoid distributing property subject to a liability exceeding the property's FMV because of the potential gain recognition caused by the excess liability.

EFFECT OF PROPERTY DISTRIBUTIONS ON THE DISTRIBUTING CORPORATION'S E&P. Distributions have two effects on E&P:[10]

- When a corporation distributes appreciated property to its shareholders, it must increase E&P by the **E&P gain**, which is the excess of the property's FMV over its adjusted basis for E&P purposes. Because a property's **E&P adjusted basis** may differ from its tax basis (as discussed earlier in this chapter), this E&P gain may differ from the corporation's recognized gain for taxable income purposes.
- If the E&P adjusted basis of the noncash asset distributed equals or exceeds its FMV, E&P is reduced by the asset's E&P adjusted basis. If the FMV of the asset distributed exceeds its E&P adjusted basis, E&P is reduced by the asset's FMV. In either case, the E&P reduction is net of any liability to which the asset is subject or that the shareholder assumes in the distribution. E&P also is reduced by the income tax liability incurred on any gain recognized.[11]

[7] Sec. 311(a).

[8] Sec. 311(b)(2).

[9] The tax treatment of the shareholder is not entirely clear. Section 336(b), which Sec. 311(b)(2) makes applicable to nonliquidating distributions, specifically states that this liability rule applies only for determining the corporation's gain or loss. Thus, its applicability does not seem to extend to Sec. 301(d), which gives the shareholder a FMV basis in the distributed property. Some commentators have suggested that a strict interpretation of the statutory provision that gives the shareholder an actual FMV basis, rather than the greater liability basis, produces an illogical result. (See B. C. Randall and D. N. Stewart, "Corporate Distributions: Handling Liabilities in Excess of the Fair Market Value of Property Remains Unresolved," *The Journal of Corporate Taxation*, 1992, pp. 55–64.) Also, given that the liability exceeds the distributed property's FMV, the shareholder's amount distributed should be zero, resulting in no dividend.

[10] Secs. 312(a) and (b).

[11] Secs. 312(a) and (c).

EXAMPLE C:4-17 ▶ Brass Corporation distributes to its shareholder, Joan, property with a $25,000 adjusted basis for taxable income purposes, a $22,000 adjusted basis for E&P purposes, and a $40,000 FMV. The property is subject to a $12,000 mortgage, which Joan assumes. In the distribution, Brass recognizes a $15,000 ($40,000 FMV − $25,000 tax adjusted basis) gain for taxable income purposes. For E&P purposes, Brass's E&P is increased by $18,000 ($40,000 FMV − $22,000 E&P adjusted basis) and is reduced by $28,000 ($40,000 FMV − $12,000 liability). E&P also is reduced by the amount of income taxes paid or accrued by Brass on the $15,000 gain. ◀

A special rule applies when a corporation distributes its own obligation (e.g., its notes, bonds, or debentures) to a shareholder. In such case, the distributing corporation's E&P is reduced by the principal amount, not the fair market value, of the obligation.[12]

Topic Review C:4-2 summarizes the tax consequences of a nonliquidating distribution to the distributing corporation.

BOOK-TO-TAX ACCOUNTING COMPARISON

The distributing corporation reports divdends-in-kind at their FMV for financial accounting (book) purposes. For book purposes, the distributing corporation recognizes the difference between the property's FMV and its carrying value as a gain or loss. For tax purposes, however, the corporation recognizes gains but not losses.

CONSTRUCTIVE DIVIDENDS

A **constructive dividend** (or deemed distribution) is the manner in which the IRS or the courts might recharacterize an excessive corporate payment to a shareholder to reflect the true economic benefit conferred upon the shareholder. As a result of the recharacterization, the IRS or courts usually recast a corporate-shareholder transaction as an E&P distribution, deny the corporation an offsetting deduction, and treat all or a portion of the income recognized by the shareholder as a dividend. Ordinarily, a corporate dividend involves a direct, pro rata distribution to all shareholders, which generally is declared by the board of directors. By contrast, a constructive dividend need not be direct or pro rata, nor be declared by the board of directors.

Constructive dividends are generally deemed to be paid in the context of a closely held corporation where the shareholders (or relatives of shareholders) and management groups overlap. In such situations, the dealings between the corporation and its shareholders are likely to be less structured and subject to closer review than dealings between a publicly held corporation and its shareholders. Constructive dividends also may occur in the context of a publicly held corporation.

ADDITIONAL COMMENT

The incentive to disguise dividends as salary, however, is somewhat diminished with the reduced tax rate on dividends.

INTENTIONAL EFFORTS TO AVOID DIVIDEND TREATMENT. The IRS's recharacterization of a payment as a constructive dividend often is in response to a shareholder's attempt either to bail out a corporation's E&P without subjecting it to taxation at the shareholder level or to obtain a deduction at the corporate level that otherwise would not be deductible. If a corporation generates sufficient E&P, dividend distributions are fully taxable to the shareholder but are not deductible by the distributing corporation.

Topic Review C:4-2

Tax Consequences of a Nonliquidating Distribution to the Distributing Corporation

1. When a corporation distributes appreciated property, it must recognize gain as if it sold the property for its FMV immediately before the distribution.
2. For gain recognition purposes, a property's FMV is deemed to be at least equal to any liability to which the property is subject or that the shareholder assumes in connection with the distribution.
3. A corporation recognizes no loss when it distributes to its shareholders property that has depreciated in value.
4. A corporation's E&P is increased by any E&P gain resulting from a distribution of appreciated property.
5. A corporation's E&P is reduced by (a) the amount of money distributed plus (b) the greater of the FMV or E&P adjusted basis of any nonmoney property distributed, minus (c) any liabilities to which the property is subject or that the shareholder assumes in connection with the distribution. E&P also is reduced by taxes paid or incurred on the corporation's recognized gain, if any.

---

[12] Sec. 312(a)(2).

Therefore, shareholders may try to disguise a dividend as a salary payment. Without recharacterization, the payment would be taxable to the shareholder-employee and deductible by the distributing corporation as long as the payment is reasonable in amount. Shareholders also may try to disguise dividends as loans to themselves. Without recharacterization, a loan would be neither deductible by the corporation nor taxable to the shareholder. If the IRS recharacterizes either payment as a dividend, the payment is taxable to the shareholder and nondeductible by the corporation.

ETHICAL POINT

A CPA should always be an advocate for his or her client if the question of whether a constructive dividend has been paid is in doubt (i.e., when the facts and the law are sufficiently gray and the taxpayer's position has reasonable support).

UNINTENTIONAL CONSTRUCTIVE DIVIDENDS. Some constructive dividends are inadvertent. Shareholders may not realize that the benefits they receive from the corporation are effectively taxable dividends until a tax consultant or the IRS examines the transactions. If a payment in the form of a salary, loan, lease, etc. is recast as a dividend, corresponding adjustments must be made at the corporate and shareholder levels. These adjustments may increase the shareholder's taxable income (e.g., because the distribution has been recharacterized as a dividend rather than a loan) or increase the distributing corporation's taxable income (i.e., because dividends are not deductible). Transactions most likely to be recast and treated as dividends are described below.

ADDITIONAL COMMENT

The government requires that, when loans exist between a corporation and its shareholders, the loans must bear a reasonable interest rate. If a "below-market" interest rate loan exists, the IRS will impute a reasonable rate of interest (Sec. 7872).

LOANS TO SHAREHOLDERS. Loans to shareholders may be viewed as disguised dividends unless the shareholders can prove that the loans are bona fide. Whether a loan is bona fide ordinarily depends on the shareholder's intent when he or she makes the loan. To prove that the loan is bona fide (and thus to avoid recharacterization of the loan as a dividend), the shareholder must show that he or she intends to repay the loan. Factors indicative of an intent to repay include

- Recording the loan on the corporate books
- Evidencing the loan by a written note
- Charging a reasonable rate of interest
- Scheduling regular payment of principal and interest

Factors that suggest the loan is *not* bona fide include

- Borrowing on "open account" (i.e., the shareholder borrows from the corporation with no fixed schedule for repayment, whenever he or she needs cash)
- Failing to charge a market rate of interest
- Failing to enforce the payment of interest and principal
- Paying advances in proportion to stockholdings
- Paying advances to a controlling shareholder

If the corporation lends money to a shareholder and then, after a period of time, cancels the loan, the amount cancelled might be treated as a dividend to the extent of the corporation's E&P. If the corporation charges a below market interest rate, the IRS could inpute interest on the loan. In such case, the corporation would be deemed to have earned interest income on the loan, and the shareholder would be allowed a deduction for interest deemed paid. The imputed interest would be treated as a dividend to the shareholder, thereby resulting in no offsetting corporate level deduction.

EXCESSIVE COMPENSATION PAID TO SHAREHOLDER-EMPLOYEES. Shareholders may be compensated for services in the form of salary, bonus, or fringe benefits. Ordinarily, the corporate employer may deduct such compensation as long as it represents an ordinary and necessary business expense and is reasonable in amount. However, if the IRS finds the compensation to be excessive, the excess amount will not be deductible by the corporation but still will be taxable to the shareholder. Depending upon the circumstances, this amount may be treated as a dividend or simply be included in the gross income of the recipient. No hard and fast rules offer guidance in determining when compensation is excessive. As a result, the issue frequently is litigated.

Before 2003, the IRS's main focus was the corporation's deducting the excess amount. The shareholder-employee recognized ordinary income regardless of whether the excess was characterized as compensation or a dividend. With the tax rate on dividends reduced to a maximum of 15% for 2003 through 2010, the corporation still will lose the deduction for excess compensation, but the IRS is unlikely to classify the excess as a dividend. Instead, the IRS probably will treat the excess as ordinary compensation income to the shareholder-employee even though the corporation is not allowed to deduct it.[13]

EXCESSIVE COMPENSATION PAID TO SHAREHOLDERS FOR THE USE OF SHAREHOLDER PROPERTY. As with compensation, corporate payments to shareholders for the use of property (i.e., rents, interest, and royalties) are deductible under Sec. 162(a) if they are ordinary, necessary, and reasonable in amount. The corporation may not deduct any amount exceeding what it would have paid to an unrelated party in an arm's-length transaction.

CORPORATE PAYMENTS FOR THE SHAREHOLDER'S BENEFIT. If a corporation pays the personal obligation of a shareholder, the corporate payment may result in gross income to the shareholder. Such a payment may cover the shareholder's personal debt obligation, expenses in connection with the shareholder's personal residence, expenses incurred for the improvement of the shareholder's real property, or a debt obligation personally guaranteed by the shareholder.

In addition, if the IRS denies a corporate deduction, the disallowed deduction may result in gross income to the shareholder if the expenditure associated with the deduction conferred an economic benefit upon the shareholder. Examples of such expenditures are unsubstantiated travel and entertainment expenses; club dues; and automobile, airplane, and yacht expenses related to the shareholder-employee's personal use.

BARGAIN PURCHASE OF CORPORATE PROPERTY. If a shareholder purchases corporate property at a discount relative to the property's FMV, the discount may be treated as a constructive dividend to the shareholder.

SHAREHOLDER USE OF CORPORATE PROPERTY. If a shareholder uses corporate property (such as a hunting lodge, yacht, or airplane) without paying adequate consideration to the corporation, the fair rental value of such property (minus any amounts paid) may be treated as a constructive dividend to the shareholder.

STOCK DIVIDENDS AND STOCK RIGHTS

OBJECTIVE 4

Determine the tax consequences of stock dividends and the issuance of stock rights

In 1919, the Supreme Court held in *Eisner v. Macomber* that a stock dividend is not income to the shareholder because it takes no property from the corporation and adds no property to the shareholder.[14] Subsequently, Congress enacted the Revenue Act of 1921, which provides that stock dividends are nontaxable. Although this general rule still applies today, Congress has carved out exceptions to prevent abuses.

Section 305(a) states, "Except as otherwise provided in this section, gross income does not include the amount of any distribution of the stock of a corporation made by such corporation to its shareholders with respect to its stock." Thus, a distribution of additional common stock with respect to a shareholder's pre-existing common stock holdings represents a nontaxable stock dividend. However, whenever a stock dividend changes or has the potential to change the shareholders' proportionate interests in the distributing corporation, the distribution will be taxable. Taxable stock distributions include those where

TYPICAL MISCONCEPTION

Stock dividends generally are nontaxable as long as a shareholder's proportionate interests in the corporation do not increase. If a shareholder's stock interest increases, Sec. 305(b) causes the dividend to be taxable.

- Any shareholder can elect to receive either stock of the distributing corporation or other property (e.g., money).
- Some shareholders receive property and other shareholders receive an increase in their proportionate interests in the distributing corporation's assets or E&P.

---

[13] *Sterno Sales Corp. v. U.S.*, 15 AFTR 2d 979, 65-1 USTC ¶9419 (Ct. Cl., 1965).

[14] *Eisner v. Myrtle H. Macomber*, 3 AFTR 3020, 1 USTC ¶32 (USSC, 1919).

- Some holders of common stock receive preferred stock and others receive additional common stock.
- The underlying stock is preferred unless the distribution involves a change in the conversion ratio of convertible preferred stock to take into account a common stock dividend or a common stock split.
- The distributed stock is convertible preferred, unless it can be established that the distribution will have no disproportionate effect.

The following example illustrates these exceptions.

EXAMPLE C:4-18 ▶ Two shareholders, Al and Beth, each own 100 of the 200 outstanding shares of Peach Corporation stock. Because Al's marginal tax rate is high, he does not want to recognize any additional income in the current year. Beth has a low marginal tax rate and needs additional cash. Peach, whose current E&P is $100,000, declares a dividend payable in stock or money. Each taxpayer can receive one share of Peach stock (valued at $100) or $100 in cash for each share of Peach stock already owned. Al, who elects to receive stock, receives 100 additional shares of Peach stock. Beth, who elects to receive cash, receives $10,000. Beth's distribution is taxable as a dividend. Absent any exceptions to Sec. 305, Al's dividend would be nontaxable because it was paid in Peach stock. After the distribution, however, Al owns two-thirds of the outstanding shares of Peach stock, whereas before the distribution he owned only one-half of Peach's outstanding shares. Therefore, an exception to the general rule of Sec. 305(a) applies so that Al is deemed to have received a taxable dividend equal to the value of the additional shares he received. Even if both shareholders elected a stock dividend, this dividend would be taxable because each shareholder had the option to receive cash. In this example, Al and Beth each recognize a $10,000 dividend. Al's basis in his new shares is their $10,000 FMV. His basis in his original shares is unchanged. Peach reduces its E&P by $20,000, the amount of the taxable dividend to Al and Beth. ◀

NONTAXABLE STOCK DIVIDENDS

If a stock dividend is nontaxable, the basis of the stock with respect to which the distribution was made must be allocated between the old and new shares.[15] The holding period of the new shares includes the holding period of the old shares.[16]

If the old and new shares are identical, the basis of each share is determined by dividing the basis of the old shares by the total number of shares held by the shareholder after the distribution.

EXAMPLE C:4-19 ▶ Barbara owns 1,000 shares of Axle Corporation common stock having a $66,000 basis ($66 per share). Barbara receives a nontaxable 10% common stock dividend and now owns 1,100 shares of Axle common stock. Her basis in each share of common stock becomes $60 ($66,000 ÷ 1,100). ◀

If the old and new shares are not identical, the basis of the old shares is allocated according to the relative FMVs of the old and new shares on the distribution date.

EXAMPLE C:4-20 ▶ Mark owns 1,000 shares of Axle Corporation common stock with a $60,000 basis. Mark receives 50 shares of Axle preferred stock as a nontaxable dividend. At the time of the distribution, the FMV of the common stock is $90,000 ($90 × 1,000 shares), and the FMV of the preferred stock is $10,000 ($200 × 50 shares). As a result of the distribution, $6,000 [($10,000 ÷ $100,000) × $60,000] of the common stock basis is allocated to the preferred stock, and the basis of the common stock is reduced from $60,000 to $54,000. ◀

REAL-WORLD EXAMPLE

Tracking the effects of nontaxable dividends, stock splits, stock dividends, and stock rights distributions on the basis of a stock investment can be difficult and time consuming. A number of publishers offer capital change reporters that provide a complete history of these four types of events for publicly traded companies. These reporters greatly simplify the making of stock basis calculations.

NONTAXABLE STOCK RIGHTS

Under Sec. 305, a distribution of stock rights is nontaxable unless it changes, or has the potential to change, the shareholders' proportionate interests in the distributing corporation. The same Sec. 305(b) exceptions to the nontaxable treatment of stock dividends also apply to distributions of stock rights.

---

[15] Sec. 307(a) and Reg. Secs. 1.307-1 and -2.

[16] Sec. 1223(5).

If the value of the stock rights is less than 15% of the value of the stock with respect to which the rights were distributed (i.e., the underlying stock), the basis of the rights is zero unless the shareholder elects to allocate stock basis to those rights.[17] If the taxpayer intends to sell the rights, an allocation of his or her stock basis to the rights might be advisable so as to minimize the amount of gain recognized on the sale. The election to allocate stock basis to the rights must be made in a statement attached to the shareholder's return for the year in which the rights are received. The allocation must be based on the relative FMVs of the stock and the stock rights. The holding period for the rights includes the holding period for the underlying stock.[18]

EXAMPLE C:4-21 ▶ Linda owns 100 shares of Yale Corporation common stock with a $27,000 basis and a $50,000 FMV. Linda receives 100 nontaxable stock rights with a $4,000 FMV. Because the FMV of the stock rights is less than 15% of the FMV of the underlying stock (0.15 × $50,000 = $7,500), the basis of the stock rights is zero unless Linda elects to allocate the $27,000 stock basis between the stock and the stock rights. If Linda makes the election, the basis of the rights is $2,000 [($4,000 ÷ $54,000) × $27,000], and the basis of the stock is $25,000 ($27,000 − $2,000). ◀

If the value of the stock rights is 15% or more of the value of the underlying stock, the shareholder must allocate the basis of the underlying stock between the stock and the stock rights. This provision is mandatory, not elective.

EXAMPLE C:4-22 ▶ Kay owns 100 shares of Minor Corporation common stock with a $14,000 basis and a $30,000 FMV. Kay receives 100 stock rights with a total FMV of $5,000. Because the FMV of the stock rights is at least 15% of the stock's FMV (0.15 × $30,000 = $4,500), the $14,000 basis must be allocated between the stock rights and the underlying stock based on their relative FMVs. The basis of the stock rights is $2,000 [($5,000 ÷ $35,000) × $14,000], and the basis of the underlying stock is $12,000 ($14,000 − $2,000). ◀

TYPICAL MISCONCEPTION

Taxpayers often get confused about what happens to a stock right. A stock right may be sold or exercised, which means the actual stock is acquired. If the rights are not sold or exercised, they eventually will lapse.

If the taxpayer sells the stock rights, he or she calculates gain or loss by subtracting the allocated basis of the rights (if any) from the sale price. A shareholder cannot claim a loss if the stock rights expire. If the stock rights do expire, the allocated rights basis is added back to the basis of the underlying stock. If the taxpayer exercises the rights before they expire, the allocated rights basis is added to the basis of the stock purchased through the exercise of those rights.[19] The holding period for the stock acquired through exercise of the rights begins on the exercise date.[20]

EXAMPLE C:4-23 ▶ In a nontaxable distribution, Jeff receives ten stock rights to which no stock basis is allocated. Each stock right entitles Jeff to acquire one share of Jackson stock for $20. If Jeff exercises all ten rights, the Jackson stock acquired will have a $200 (10 rights × $20) basis. If instead Jeff sells the ten rights for $30 each, he will recognize a gain of $300 [($30 × 10 rights) − 0 basis]. If the rights expire, Jeff can claim no loss. ◀

EFFECT OF NONTAXABLE STOCK DIVIDENDS ON THE DISTRIBUTING CORPORATION

BOOK-TO-TAX ACCOUNTING COMPARISON

For financial accounting purposes, stock dividends reduce retained earnings. However, for tax purposes, nontaxable stock dividends have no effect on a corporation's E&P.

From a tax perspective, nontaxable distributions of stock and stock rights have no effect on the distributing corporation. The corporation recognizes no gain or loss and does not reduce the balance in its E&P account.[21]

TAXABLE STOCK DIVIDENDS AND STOCK RIGHTS

If a distribution of stock or stock rights is taxable, the distribution amount equals the FMV of the stock or stock rights on the distribution date. The distribution is treated in the same way as any other property distribution. It is a dividend to the extent of the distributing corporation's E&P, and the recipient takes a FMV basis in the stock or stock rights

[17] Sec. 307(b)(1).
[18] Sec. 1223(5).
[19] Reg. Sec. 1.307-1(b).
[20] Sec. 1223(6).
[21] Secs. 311(a) and 312(d).

received.[22] The holding period for the stock or stock rights begins on the day after the distribution date. No adjustment is made to the basis of the underlying stock. The distributing corporation recognizes no gain or loss on the distribution,[23] and the corporation reduces its E&P by the FMV of the stock or stock rights on the distribution date.

STOCK REDEMPTIONS

OBJECTIVE 5

Discern when a stock redemption should be treated as a sale and when it should be treated as a dividend

A **stock redemption** is a corporation's acquisition of its own stock in exchange for corporate property. The property may be cash, securities of other corporations, or any other consideration the corporation wants to use to acquire its own stock.[24] The corporation may cancel the acquired stock, retire it, or retain it as treasury stock.

A stock redemption may be desirable for the following reasons:

- A shareholder may want to withdraw from the corporate business and sell his or her equity interest. In such a case, the shareholder may prefer that the corporation, rather than an outsider, purchase his or her stock so that the remaining shareholders (who may be family members) retain complete control and ownership of the corporation after his or her withdrawal from the business.
- A shareholder may be required to sell stock to the corporation under the terms of a stock purchase agreement with the issuing corporation.
- A shareholder may want to reduce his or her equity interest in a corporation but may be unwilling or unable to sell stock to outsiders. For example, no market may exist for the shares, or sales to outsiders may be restricted.
- A shareholder may want to withdraw assets from a corporation before a sale of the corporation's business. A potential purchaser may not be interested in acquiring all the assets or be able to pay the full value for all shares outstanding. A withdrawal of some assets by the seller in exchange for some of his or her shares allows the purchaser to acquire the remaining shares and business assets for a lower total price.
- After the death of a major shareholder, a corporation may agree to purchase the decedent's stock from either the estate or a beneficiary to provide sufficient funds to pay estate and inheritance taxes and funeral and administrative expenses.
- Management may believe that the corporation's stock is selling at a low price and that, to increase share value, the corporation should acquire some of this stock on the open market.

Whatever the reason for the redemption, the shareholder must answer the following questions:

- What are the amount and character of the income, gain, or loss recognized as a result of the redemption?
- What basis does the shareholder take in any property received in exchange for his or her stock?
- When does the holding period for the property begin?
- What basis does the shareholder take in any distributing corporation stock held after the redemption?

The distributing corporation must answer the following questions:

- What amount and character of gain or loss, if any, must the corporation recognize when it redeems stock with noncash property?
- What effect does the redemption have on the corporation's E&P?[25]

---

[22] Reg. Sec. 1.301-1(h)(2)(i).

[23] Sec. 311(a). Gain may be recognized when the shareholder can elect to receive either appreciated property or stock or stock rights of the distributing corporation.

[24] Sec. 317.

[25] The stock redemption discussion is for C corporation stock. Different rules apply if an S corporation redeems its stock.

TAX CONSEQUENCES OF THE REDEMPTION TO THE SHAREHOLDER

KEY POINT

As far as a shareholder is concerned, the basic issue in a stock redemption is whether the redemption is treated as a dividend or a sale.

As a general rule, when a shareholder sells or exchanges corporate stock, any gain or loss in the transaction is capital in character. In some cases, a redemption is treated as a stock sale. In other cases, a redemption is treated as a dividend. The reason for this difference is that some redemptions more closely resemble a stock sale to a third party, whereas others are essentially equivalent to a dividend. The following two examples illustrate the difference between a redemption resembling a dividend and a redemption resembling a sale. (The IRC refers to a "sale or exchange," but for simplicity in this chapter, we will use just the term "sale.")

EXAMPLE C:4-24 ▶ John owns all 100 outstanding shares of Tango Corporation stock. John's basis in his shares is $50,000, and Tango's E&P is $100,000. If Tango redeems 25 of John's shares for $85,000, John still owns 100% of Tango stock. Because John's proportionate ownership of Tango has not changed as a result of the redemption, the redemption resembles a dividend. Accordingly, for tax purposes, John is deemed to have received an $85,000 dividend. ◀

EXAMPLE C:4-25 ▶ Carol has owned three of the 1,000 outstanding shares of Water Corporation's stock for two years. Her basis in the shares is $1,000, and Water's E&P is $100,000. If Water redeems all three of Carol's shares for $5,000, Carol is in essentially the same position as a seller of stock to a third party. She has received $5,000 for her stock and has no further ownership interest in Water. This redemption resembles a sale because it terminates Carol's interest in the corporation. Thus, it is not essentially equivalent to a dividend. Consequently, Carol reports a $4,000 ($5,000 − $1,000) capital gain. ◀

Example C:4-24 is an extreme case involving a redemption that clearly should be treated as a dividend to the shareholder. Example C:4-25 is an extreme case involving a redemption that clearly should be treated as a sale of stock by the shareholder. Many cases, however, fall between the two extremes, and how the redemption should be treated is not immediately apparent. The problem for Congress and the courts has been distinguishing redemptions that should be treated as sales from those that should be treated as dividends. Under current law, a redemption qualifies for sale treatment only if it satisfies at least one of the following conditions:

- The redemption is substantially disproportionate.
- The redemption is a complete termination of the shareholder's interest.
- The redemption is not essentially equivalent to a dividend.
- The redemption involves a partial liquidation of the corporation in conjunction with its redeeming stock from noncorporate shareholders.
- The redemption provides funds for an estate to pay death taxes.

If a redemption qualifies as a sale, the shareholder is treated as though he or she sold the stock to an outside party. The shareholder recognizes gain or loss equal to the FMV of the property received less the shareholder's adjusted basis in the stock surrendered. The gain or loss is capital in character if the stock is a capital asset in the hands of the shareholder. The shareholder's basis for any property received is its FMV. The holding period for the property begins on the day following the exchange date.

A redemption that does not satisfy any of the five conditions necessary for sale treatment is regarded as a property distribution under Sec. 301. Accordingly, the entire amount of the distribution is treated as a dividend to the extent of the distributing corporation's E&P.[26] The shareholder's stock basis is not taken into account in determining the dividend amount. This basis is added to the basis of any remaining shares owned by the shareholder. If all the shareholder's stock has been redeemed, the basis of the redeemed shares is added to the basis of shares owned by those individuals whose ownership is attributed to the shareholder under the constructive stock ownership rules described below.[27]

---

[26] Sec. 302(d).

[27] Reg. Sec. 1.302-2(c).

EXAMPLE C:4-26 ▶ Amy and Rose each own 50 of the 100 outstanding shares of stock in York Corporation, which reports $100,000 of E&P. On May 10, York redeems 20 of Amy's shares with property worth $25,000. Amy's adjusted basis in those shares is $20,000. If the redemption satisfies one of the conditions necessary for sale treatment, Amy recognizes a capital gain of $5,000 ($25,000 – $20,000). Her basis in the property received is its $25,000 FMV, and its holding period begins on May 11. If the redemption does not satisfy any of the conditions necessary for sale treatment, Amy recognizes $25,000 of dividend income. Her $20,000 basis in the surrendered shares is added to the basis of her remaining 30 shares of York stock. ◀

ADDITIONAL COMMENT

Prior to 2003, sale or exchange treatment provided a third advantage, specifically, the capital gain received preferential tax treatment as compared to ordinary income treatment for dividends. As a result of the 2003 Act, however, dividends received by a noncorporate shareholder in 2003 through 2010 also obtain preferential treatment, thereby removing this advantage. Thus, because capital gains and qualified dividends are now taxed at the same rate, the difference in tax between exchange treatment and dividend treatment is solely a function of the taxpayer's basis in the redeemed stock.

Structuring a stock redemption as a sale offers two advantages. First, capital gains may be offset by capital losses. Second, in a sale, the basis of the shares redeemed reduces the amount of gain recognized. By constrast, if a redemption is treated as a dividend, the basis of the shares redeemed does not reduce the dividend amount. Instead, the basis shifts to the shareholder's remaining stock, which reduces the gain (or increases the loss) recognized on a later sale of this stock.

Topic Review C:4-3 summarizes the tax consequences of stock redemptions to both the shareholder and the distributing corporation.

ATTRIBUTION RULES

Three of the five tests for determining how a redemption should be treated (i.e., as a sale or dividend) are based on stock ownership before and after the redemption. The tests measure the extent to which the shareholder's proportionate interest in the corporation has been reduced. In general, if the shareholder's proportionate interest has been sufficiently reduced, the redemption is treated as a sale. On the other hand, if this interest remains essentially the same or increases, the redemption is treated as a dividend (assuming sufficient E&P).

Stock ownership for this purpose is determined under the constructive ownership or attribution rules of Sec. 318.[28] According to these rules, a shareholder owns not only the shares he or she directly owns but also shares owned by his or her spouse, other immediate family members, and related entities. In addition, corporations, partnerships, trusts, and estates are considered to constructively own shares owned by their shareholders, partners, and beneficiaries.

The attribution rules prevent shareholders from taking advantage of favorable tax rules or avoiding unfavorable rules by transferring to family members or related entities

Topic Review C:4-3

Tax Consequences of Stock Redemptions

Shareholders:

General Rule: The amount received by a shareholder in exchange for his or her stock is treated as a dividend to the extent of the distributing corporation's E&P. The basis of the surrendered stock is added to the basis of the shareholder's remaining stock.

Sale Exception: If the redemption meets specific requirements, the amount received by the shareholder is offset by the adjusted basis of the shares surrendered. The difference generally is treated as a capital gain or loss. No basis adjustment occurs.

Distributing Corporation:

Gain/Loss Recognition: Under either the general rule or sale exception, the corporation recognizes gain (but not loss) as though it had sold distributed noncash property for its FMV immediately before the redemption.

Earnings and Profits Adjustment: For a redemption treated as a dividend, E&P is reduced in the same manner as for a regular dividend (e.g., by the amount of money or FMV of property distributed). For a redemption treated as a sale, E&P is reduced by the portion of current and accumulated E&P attributable to the redeemed stock. Any distribution amount exceeding this portion reduces the corporation's paid-in capital.

---

[28] Sec. 302(c).

stock that the shareholder previously owned. The proportionate stock ownership tests would be subject to abuse if only direct ownership were considered.

Section 318(a) sets forth four types of attribution rules: attribution among family members, attribution from entities, attribution to entities, and option attribution. These rules are discussed below.

ADDITIONAL COMMENT

The family attribution rules of Sec. 318 are not as inclusive as the family attribution rules of Sec. 267 (covered in Chapter C:3). For example, siblings and grandparents are not considered family members by Sec. 318 but are included under Sec. 267.

FAMILY ATTRIBUTION. An individual is considered to own constructively all stock owned by or for a spouse, children, grandchildren, and parents. An individual is not considered to own stock owned by brothers, sisters, or grandparents.

Once attributed to an individual under one set of attribution rules, stock ownership may not be reattributed to another individual under the same set of rules. Thus, stock ownership attributed to one family member under the family attribution rules may not be reattributed to a second family member under the same set of rules. However, once attributed to an individual under one set of attribution rules, stock ownership may be reattributed to another individual under a different set of attribution rules. For example, stock ownership attributed from a corporation to its shareholder under the corporate attribution rules may be reattributed to the shareholder's spouse under the family attribution rules.

EXAMPLE C:4-27 ▶ Harry; his wife, Wilma; their son, Steve; and Harry's father, Frank, each own 25 of the 100 outstanding shares of Strong Corporation stock. Under the family attribution rules, Harry is considered to own all 100 Strong shares (25 directly plus constructively the shares owned by Wilma, Steve, and Frank). Wilma is considered to own 75 shares (25 directly plus constructively the 50 shares owned by Harry and Steve). Ownership of Frank's shares is neither directly attributed to Wilma nor reattributed to Wilma through Harry. Steve is considered to own 75 shares (25 directly plus constructively the 50 shares owned by his parents Harry and Wilma). Ownership of Frank's shares is neither directly attributed to Steve nor reattributed to Steve through Harry. Frank is considered to own 75 shares (25 directly plus constructively the shares owned by Harry and Steve (his grandson)). Ownership of Wilma's shares is neither directly attributed to Frank nor reattributed to Frank through Harry.

The diagram below illustrates the constructive stock ownership of the four shareholders. The arrows indicate the direction(s) of ownership attribution.

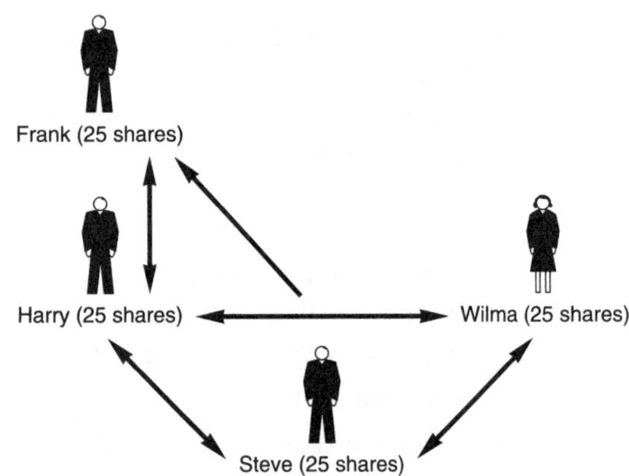

The table below shows each shareholder's direct and constructive stock ownership.

		Shares Owned via Constructive Ownership From:				
Shareholder	*Direct Ownership*	*Spouse*	*Child*	*Grandchild*	*Parent(s)*	*Total*
Frank	25		25	25		75
Harry	25	25	25		25	100
Wilma	25	25	25			75
Steve	25				50	75
	100					

◀

ATTRIBUTION FROM ENTITIES. Stock owned by or for a partnership is considered to be owned proportionately by the partners. Stock owned by or for an estate is considered to be owned proportionately by the beneficiaries. Stock owned by or for a trust is considered to be owned by the beneficiaries in proportion to their actuarial interests. Stock owned by or for a C corporation is considered to be owned proportionately only by shareholders owning (directly or indirectly) 50% or more of the corporation's stock value.[29]

EXAMPLE C:4-28 ▶ Bill, who is married, owns a 50% interest in Partnership A. Partnership A owns 40 of the 100 outstanding shares of Yellow Corporation stock, and Bill owns the remaining 60 shares. Under the entity attribution rules, Bill is considered to own 80 shares, 60 directly and 20 (0.50×40 shares) constructively. In addition, the stock ownership attributed to Bill under the entity attribution rules is reattributed to Bill's spouse under the family attribution rules. ◀

ATTRIBUTION TO ENTITIES. All stock owned by or for a partner is considered to be constructively owned by the partnership. All stock owned by or for a beneficiary of an estate or a trust is considered to be constructively owned by the estate or trust. All stock owned by or for a shareholder who owns (directly or indirectly) 50% or more of a C corporation's stock value is considered to be constructively owned by the corporation.

Stock ownership attributed to a partnership, estate, trust, or corporation from a partner, beneficiary, or shareholder is not reattributed from the entity to another partner, beneficiary, or shareholder.

EXAMPLE C:4-29 ▶ Assume the same facts as in Example C:4-28. The partnership in which Bill is a partner is considered to own all 100 shares of Yellow stock (40 directly and 60 constructively through Bill). Bill's stock ownership attributed to the partnership cannot be reattributed from the partnership to Bill's partners. ◀

OPTION ATTRIBUTION. A person who has an option to purchase stock is considered to own the underlying stock.

EXAMPLE C:4-30 ▶ John owns 25 of the 100 outstanding shares of Yard Corporation stock. He has an option to acquire an additional 50 shares. John is considered to own 75 Yard shares (25 directly plus 50 constructively through the option). ◀

SUBSTANTIALLY DISPROPORTIONATE REDEMPTIONS

Under Sec. 302(b)(2), if a stock redemption is substantially disproportionate with respect to a shareholder, it is treated as a sale and thus qualifies for capital gain as opposed to dividend treatment. A redemption is substantially disproportionate with respect to a shareholder if all the following conditions are met:

- After the redemption, the shareholder owns less than 50% of the total combined voting power of all classes of voting stock.
- After the redemption, the shareholder owns less than 80% of his or her percentage ownership of voting stock before the redemption.
- After the redemption, the shareholder owns less than 80% of his or her percentage ownership of common stock (whether voting or nonvoting) before the redemption.

TAX STRATEGY TIP

If possible, taxpayers should structure a redemption to meet the substantially disproportionate test rather than the subjective "not equivalent to a dividend" test (discussed on page C:4-23), thereby obtaining certainty of results rather than uncertainty.

These tests apply mechanically to each shareholder's ownership interest. The 50% test prevents shareholders from qualifying for capital gains treatment if they own a controlling interest in the distributing corporation after the redemption. The 80% tests indicate a degree of change in the shareholder's proportionate interest that makes the redemption substantially disproportionate. A redemption may be substantially disproportionate with respect to one shareholder but not another. If only one class of stock is outstanding, the second and third requirements are the same.

[29] For purposes of the attribution rules, S corporations are treated as partnerships, not as corporations. Thus, attribution occurs to and from shareholders owning less than 50% of the S corporation stock. Unless otherwise stated, all corporations in the examples are C corporations.

EXAMPLE C:4-31 ▶ Long Corporation has 400 shares of common stock issued and outstanding. It plans to redeem 100 of these shares. Before the redemption, Ann, Bob, Carl, and Dana (all unrelated) each owns 100 shares. Long redeems 55 shares from Ann, 25 shares from Bob, and 20 shares from Carl. The following table shows the ownership before and after the redemption.

ADDITIONAL COMMENT

In calculating the percentage of stock owned *after* a redemption note that the denominator used is the number of shares outstanding *after* the redemption.

	Before Redemption			*After Redemption*	
Shareholder	*No. of Shares Owned*	*Percentage of Ownership*	*Shares Redeemed*	*No. of Shares Owned*	*Percentage of Ownership*
	(1)	(1) ÷ 400	(2)	(1) − (2)	[(1) − (2)] ÷ 300
Ann	100	25%	55	45	15.00%
Bob	100	25%	25	75	25.00%
Carl	100	25%	20	80	26.67%
Dana	100	25%	—	100	33.33%
Total	400	100%	100	300	100.00%

The redemption is substantially disproportionate with respect to Ann because, after the redemption, she owns less than 50% of Long's stock, and her stock ownership percentage (15%) is less than 80% of her stock ownership percentage before the redemption (0.80 × 25% = 20%). The redemption is not substantially disproportionate with respect to Bob because the percentage reduction in his stock ownership is less than 80%. In fact, Bob owns the same percentage of stock (25%) after the redemption as he did before the redemption (25%). The redemption also is not substantially disproportionate with respect to Carl because his stock ownership percentage increases from 25% to 26.67%. Thus, only the redemption of Ann's shares is treated as a sale and qualifies for capital gains treatment. ◀

The constructive ownership rules of Sec. 318(a) apply in determining whether the shareholder has met the three conditions for a substantially disproportionate redemption.[30]

EXAMPLE C:4-32 ▶ Assume the same facts as in Example C:4-31 except that Ann is Bob's mother. In this case, the redemption is not substantially disproportionate with respect to either Ann or Bob because, before the redemption, each owns 200 shares, or 50% of the Long stock, and after the redemption each owns 120 shares, or 40% of the stock. Although the 50% test is met, neither Ann nor Bob satisfies the 80% test. After the redemption each owns *exactly* 80% of the percentage owned before the redemption (0.80 × 50% = 40%). ◀

COMPLETE TERMINATION OF THE SHAREHOLDER'S INTEREST

Under Sec. 302(b)(3), if a stock redemption completely terminates a shareholder's interest in the corporation, the redemption also is treated as a sale. At first glance, this rule does not offer a route to sale treatment that is not already provided by the other Sec. 302 rules. If a corporation redeems all of a shareholder's stock, in most cases the requirements for a substantially disproportionate redemption under Sec. 302(b)(2) would have been satisfied. However, the complete termination rule extends sale treatment to two redemptions not covered by the substantially disproportionate redemption rules:

- If a shareholder's interest in a corporation consists exclusively of nonvoting stock, a redemption of all the stock could not qualify as substantially disproportionate under Sec. 302(b)(2) because no reduction of voting power occurs. However, it could qualify as a complete termination of the shareholder's interest under Sec. 302(b)(3) because the interest does not have to consist of voting stock.
- If a shareholder owns some voting stock and the redemption terminates his or her entire interest in the corporation, the family attribution rules of Sec. 318(a)(1) may be waived. Consequently, the redemption could qualify for sale treatment even though other family members continue to own some or all of the corporation's stock.[31]

[30] Reg. Sec. 1.302-3(a).

[31] Section 302(c)(2) provides for the waiver of family attribution rules.

To have the family attribution rules waived, the shareholder must meet all of the following conditions:

- After the redemption, the shareholder must not retain any interest in the corporation except as a creditor. This restriction includes any interest as an officer, director, or employee.
- The shareholder must not acquire any such interest (other than by bequest or inheritance) for at least ten years from the date of the redemption.
- The shareholder must file a written agreement with the IRS that he or she will notify the IRS upon acquiring any prohibited interest.

The written agreement authorizes the IRS to assess additional taxes for the year of the redemption if the prohibited interest is acquired, even if the basic three-year limitations period has expired.

EXAMPLE C:4-33 ▶ Father and Son each own 50 of the 100 outstanding shares of Short Corporation stock. Short redeems all of Father's shares. Under the family attribution rules, Father is considered to own 100% of the Short stock both before and after the redemption. Thus, the redemption is not substantially disproportionate with respect to him. However, if Father agrees not to retain or acquire any interest in Short for ten years (except as a creditor, devisee, or heir), the family attribution rules may be waived. Consequently, the redemption will qualify as a complete termination of Father's interest and be treated as a stock sale. ◀

Waiver of the family attribution rules is not permitted in the following two situations involving related parties:

- Within the ten-year period ending on the distribution date, the distributee acquired, directly or indirectly, part or all of the redeemed stock from a person whose stock ownership would be attributable (at the time of the distribution) to the distributee under Sec. 318.
- Any person owns (at the time of the distribution) stock of the redeeming corporation the ownership of which is attributable to the distributee under Sec. 318, and such person acquired any stock in the redeeming corporation, directly or indirectly, from the distributee within the ten-year period ending on the distribution date.

The first restriction deters an individual from transferring stock to a related party (e.g., family member or controlled entity) so that the related party might use the complete termination provision to recognize a capital gain when the corporation redeems the transferred stock. The second restriction deters an individual from transferring a portion of his or her stock to a related party and then using the complete termination provision to recognize a capital gain when the corporation redeems his or her remaining stock. These prohibitions against waiving the family attribution rules do not apply if the shareholder transferred the stock more than ten years before the redemption or if the distributee can show that the acquisition or disposition of the stock did not have tax avoidance as one of its purposes. In the second situation above, the family attribution rules also can be waived if the corporation redeems as part of the same transaction stock previously transferred to the related party.

Note that only the family attribution rules can be waived. Entities are permitted to have the family attribution rules waived if both the entity and the individual whose stock is attributed to the entity agree not to acquire any prohibited interest in the corporation for at least ten years.

EXAMPLE C:4-34 ▶ Andrew created the A Trust, which owns 30% of Willow Corporation stock. Andrew's wife, Wanda, is the sole beneficiary of the trust. Their son, Steve, owns the remaining 70% of Willow stock. Willow redeems all of its stock owned by the A Trust. At first glance, the redemption does not qualify for sale treatment because the trust is deemed to own all the stock owned by Wanda, and Wanda is deemed to own all the stock owned by Steve. However, if both A Trust and Wanda agree not to acquire any interest in the corporation for ten years, the family attribution rules can be waived. Consequently, the redemption will be treated as a complete termination of the trust's interest in Willow and will be eligible for sale treatment. ◀

REDEMPTIONS NOT ESSENTIALLY EQUIVALENT TO A DIVIDEND

KEY POINT

Section 302(b)(1) has generally been interpreted to require that a shareholder incur a "meaningful reduction" of its stock interest. What constitutes a "meaningful reduction" is the subject of controversy.

Section 302(b)(1) provides that a redemption will be treated as a sale if it is not essentially equivalent to a dividend. The tax law sets forth no mechanical test for determining when a redemption is not essentially equivalent to a dividend. Instead, it implies that a determination should be based on the facts and circumstances of each case.[32] Sec. 302(b)(1) does not provide a safe harbor similar to the rules for substantially disproportionate redemptions or redemptions that are a complete termination of a shareholder's interest. On the other hand, the provision keeps the rules on redemptions from being too restrictive, especially in the case of transactions involving preferred stock.

The Supreme Court's decision in *Maclin P. Davis* defined criteria for determining when a redemption is not essentially equivalent to a dividend.[33] The Supreme Court held that (1) in this determination, a business purpose is irrelevant; (2) the Sec. 318 attribution rules must be applied to establish dividend equivalency; and (3) a redemption of part of a sole shareholder's stock is always essentially equivalent to a dividend. The Court further held that for Sec. 302(b)(1) purposes, there must be a "meaningful reduction" in the shareholder's proportionate interest in the corporation after taking into account the constructive ownership rules of Sec. 318(a). Despite this holding, the definition of "a meaningful reduction in interest" remains unclear.

Because of this lack of clarity, Sec. 302(b)(1) generally applies to a redemption of nonvoting preferred stock only when the shareholder does not own any common stock,[34] or to redemptions resulting in a substantial reduction in the shareholder's rights to vote and exercise control over the corporation, participate in earnings, and share in net assets upon liquidation. Generally, the IRS allows sale treatment if a controlling shareholder reduces his or her interest to a noncontrolling position,[35] or a noncontrolling shareholder further reduces his or her minority interest.[36] A shareholder does not qualify for sale treatment if he or she maintains control both before and after the redemption,[37] or if he or she assumes a controlling position.

EXAMPLE C:4-35 ▶ Four unrelated individuals own all of Thyme Corporation's single class of stock as follows: Alan, 27%; Betty, 24.33%; Clem, 24.33%, and David, 24.33%. Thyme redeems some of Alan's stock holdings, resulting in a reduction of Alan's interest to 22.27%. Betty, Clem, and David own equally the remaining 77.73% of Thyme stock. The redemption of Alan's stock does not qualify as substantially disproportionate because Alan's interest is not reduced below 21.6% (0.80 × 27% = 21.6%). Nor does the redemption qualify as a complete termination of Alan's interest because Alan still owns shares of Thyme stock. However, the redemption might be treated as a sale under Sec. 302(b)(1) because the transaction results in a meaningful reduction of Alan's noncontrolling interest in Thyme. ◀

PARTIAL LIQUIDATIONS

Under Sec. 302(b)(4), a redemption of a noncorporate shareholder's stock qualifies for sale treatment if the redemption is in **partial liquidation** of the corporation. A partial liquidation occurs when a corporation discontinues one line of business, distributes assets used in that business to its shareholders, and continues at least one other line of business.[38] A distribution in partial liquidation qualifies for sale treatment if it is not essentially equivalent to a dividend. The distribution must be made within the tax year in which a plan of partial liquidation has been adopted or within the succeeding tax year.

---

[32] Reg. Sec. 1.302-2(b).

[33] *U.S. v. Maclin P. Davis,* 25 AFTR 2d 70-827, 70-1 USTC ¶9289 (USSC, 1970).

[34] Reg. Sec. 1.302-2(a).

[35] In Rev. Rul. 75-502, 1975-2 C.B. 111, a reduction in stock ownership from 57% to 50% where the shareholder no longer had control was considered a meaningful reduction in interest.

[36] In Rev. Rul. 76-364, 1976-2 C.B. 91, a reduction in stock ownership from 27% to 22% was considered a meaningful reduction in interest.

[37] See *Jack Paparo,* 71 T.C. 692 (1979), where reductions in stock ownership from 100% to 81.17% and from 100% to 74.15% were not considered meaningful reductions in interest.

[38] A partial liquidation also can occur when a corporation sells one line of business, distributes the sales proceeds (after paying taxes on any gain from the sale), and continues at least one other line of business. See Rev. Rul. 79-275, 1979-2 C.B. 137.

DETERMINATION MADE AT THE CORPORATE LEVEL. For purposes of Sec. 302(b)(4), whether a distribution is not essentially equivalent to a dividend is determined at the corporate level.[39] The distribution must result from a bona fide contraction of the corporate business. In relevant Treasury Regulations and revenue rulings, the government provides guidance as to what constitutes a bona fide business contraction. Some examples involve

- The distribution of insurance proceeds received as a result of a fire that destroys part of a business.[40]
- Termination of a contract representing 95% of a domestic corporation's gross income.[41]
- Change in a corporation's business from a full-line department store to a discount apparel store, which results in the elimination of certain units; the elimination of most forms of credit; and a reduction in inventory, floor space, and employees.[42]

SAFE HARBOR RULE. Under Sec. 302(e)(2), a distribution satisfies the not essentially equivalent to a dividend requirement and qualifies as a partial liquidation if

- The distribution is attributable to the distributing corporation's ceasing to conduct a qualified trade or business, or consists of the assets of a qualified trade or business; and
- Immediately after the distribution, the distributing corporation is engaged in the active conduct of at least one qualified trade or business.

A qualified trade or business is any trade or business that

- Has been actively conducted throughout the five-year period ending on the date of the redemption; and
- Was not acquired by the corporation within such five-year period in a partially or wholly taxable transaction.

The definition of an active trade or business is the same as that used for Sec. 355 (corporate division) purposes as set forth in Chapter C:7.

EXAMPLE C:4-36 ▶ Sage Corporation has manufactured hats and gloves for the past five years. In the current year, Sage discontinues hat manufacturing, sells all of its hat-making machinery, and distributes the proceeds to its shareholders in redemption of some of their Sage shares. The corporation continues glove manufacturing. The distribution is pursuant to a partial liquidation and thus qualifies for sale treatment. ◀

TAX CONSEQUENCES OF A PARTIAL LIQUIDATION TO THE SHAREHOLDERS. If a distribution is in partial liquidation of the corporation, a noncorporate shareholder treats the redemption of his or her stock as a sale, whether or not the distribution is pro rata. In contrast, a corporate shareholder treats the redemption distribution as a dividend unless the corporation meets one of the other tests for sale treatment (i.e., Sec. 302(b)(1)-(3) or Sec. 303). For a corporate shareholder, dividend treatment may be more advantageous than sale treatment because a corporation receives no preferential tax rate on capital gains, but the dividend is eligible for a 70%, 80%, or 100% dividends-received deduction. In determining whether stock is owned by a corporate or noncorporate shareholder, stock held by a partnership, trust, or estate is considered to be held proportionately by its partners or beneficiaries.

EXAMPLE C:4-37 ▶ Assume the same facts as in Example C:4-36 except Sage Corporation is owned by Ted and Jolly Corporation. Each shareholder owns 50 shares of Sage stock with a $20,000 basis. Sage reports $100,000 of current and accumulated E&P. Sage distributes $18,000 to each shareholder in redemption of ten shares of stock worth $18,000. Because the redemption involves a partial liquidation, Ted treats the transaction as a sale and recognizes a capital gain of $14,000 ($18,000 – $4,000). Jolly, however, cannot treat the transaction as a sale because Jolly is a corporate

[39] Sec. 302(e)(1)(A).
[40] Reg. Sec. 1.346-1.
[41] Rev. Rul. 75-3, 1975-1 C.B. 108.
[42] Rev. Rul. 74-296, 1974-1 C.B. 80.

shareholder and thus recognizes $18,000 of dividend income. As a corporation, Jolly is eligible for a $14,400 (0.80 × $18,000) dividends-received deduction. Jolly's $4,000 basis in the ten redeemed shares is added to the basis of its 40 remaining shares, resulting in a $20,000 basis in the Sage shares. (If Jolly owned the Sage stock since Sage's inception, Jolly makes no further basis adjustments. However, if Jolly did not own the Sage stock since inception, Sec 1059(e) applies to reduce Jolly's basis in the Sage stock to $5,600 ($20,000 − $14,400) because the dividend is considered extraordinary.) ◀

STOP & THINK

Question: Why is a distribution in partial liquidation of a corporation treated as a sale by its noncorporate shareholders and as a dividend by its corporate shareholders?

Solution: The different tax treatment reflects different tax advantages. Noncorporate shareholders benefit most from sale treatment because they can offset their stock basis against any amount realized in the distribution. Corporate shareholders benefit most from dividend treatment because they can take the dividends-received deduction, thereby reducing the impact of the dividend income. These disparate advantages stem from the different tax status of corporations, other entities, and individuals.

TAX STRATEGY TIP

An estate with liquidity problems owing to large holdings of a closely held business also may want to consider installment payment of the estate tax under Sec. 6166. See Chapter C:13 for further details.

REDEMPTIONS TO PAY DEATH TAXES

If corporate stock represents a substantial portion of a decedent's gross estate, a redemption of the stock from the estate or its beneficiaries may be eligible for sale treatment under Sec. 303. This IRC section helps shareholders who inherit stock in a closely held corporation pay estate and inheritance taxes and funeral and administrative expenses. If the stock is not readily marketable, a stock redemption may be the only way to provide the estate and its beneficiaries with sufficient liquidity to defray the costs of estate administration. Under the substantially disproportionate or complete termination rules, ownership attribution would disqualify the redemption from sale treatment. Thus, the redemption would be treated as a dividend. Under Sec. 303, ownership attribution does not apply to the portion of a stock redemption that meets certain requirements.

Section 303 provides that a redemption of stock that was included in a decedent's gross estate is treated as a stock sale by the shareholder (i.e., either the estate or the beneficiary of the estate) if the following conditions are met:

1. The value of the redeeming corporation's stock included in the decedent's gross estate is more than 35% of the adjusted gross estate. The adjusted gross estate consists of the FMV of all property on the date of the decedent's death less allowable deductions for funeral and administrative expenses, claims against the estate, debts, and casualty and other losses.

EXAMPLE C:4-38 ▶ A decedent's gross estate, valued at $5.8 million, includes $3.4 million in cash and Pepper Corporation stock worth $2.4 million. Funeral and other deductible estate expenses amount to $1.8 million. Thus, the decedent's adjusted gross estate is $4 million ($5,800,000 − $1,800,000). Because the $2.4 million value of the Pepper stock included in the gross estate exceeds 35% of the adjusted gross estate ($1.4 million = 0.35 × $4,000,000), a redemption of this stock qualifies for sale treatment under Sec. 303. ◀

2. The maximum amount of the redemption distribution that can qualify for sale treatment is the sum of all federal and state estate and inheritance taxes, plus any interest due on those taxes, and all funeral and administrative expenses allowable as deductions in computing the federal estate tax. The redemption must be of stock held by the estate or by the decedent's heirs who are liable for estate taxes and other administrative expenses.

3. Section 303 applies to a redemption distribution only to the extent the shareholder's interest in the estate is reduced by the payment of death taxes and funeral and administration expenses. The maximum distribution eligible for sale treatment is the amount of estate taxes and expenses the shareholder is obligated to bear.

EXAMPLE C:4-39 ▶ Assume the same facts as in Example C:4-38 except that, before the decedent's death, all the stock was gifted to the decedent's son, Sam. The remaining assets were bequeathed to the decedent's wife, Wilma, who as beneficiary is indirectly liable for all estate taxes and administrative expenses. Section 303 sale treatment is not available to Sam because he is not liable for estate taxes or administrative expenses. If instead $1.6 million in nonstock assets had been gifted to Wilma before the decedent's death, and the remaining assets bequeathed to Sam, Sam as beneficiary would be indirectly liable for all estate taxes and administrative expenses. In such case, he could use Sec. 303 to obtain sale treatment for the redemption of enough of his stock to pay estate taxes and administrative expenses. ◀

4. Section 303 applies only to distributions within certain time limits.

a. In general, the redemption must occur not later than 90 days after the expiration of the period for assessment of the federal estate tax. Because the limitations period for the federal estate tax expires three years after the estate tax return is due and because the return is due nine months after the date of death, the redemption generally must occur within four years after the date of death.

b. If a petition for redetermination of an estate tax deficiency is filed with the Tax Court, the distribution period is extended to 60 days after the Tax Court's decision becomes final.

c. If the taxpayer made a valid election under Sec. 6166 to defer payment of federal estate taxes under an installment plan, the distribution period is extended to the time the installment payments are due.

5. The stock of two or more corporations may be aggregated to satisfy the 35% threshold, provided that 20% or more of the value of each corporation's outstanding stock is included in the gross estate.

EXAMPLE C:4-40 ▶ A decedent's gross estate, valued at $5.8 million, includes 80% of the stock of Curry Corporation, valued at $800,000, and 90% of the stock of Brodie Corporation, valued at $900,000. Deductible funeral and administrative expenses amount to $1.8 million. Thus, the decedent's adjusted gross estate is $4 million. Although the value of neither the Curry stock nor the Brodie stock exceeds 35% of the $4 million adjusted gross estate, the total value of both corporations' stock ($1.7 million = $800,000 + $900,000) exceeds 35% of the adjusted gross estate ($1.4 million = 0.35 × $4,000,000). Therefore, a redemption of sufficient Curry stock and/or Brodie stock to pay estate taxes and funeral and administrative expenses qualifies for sale treatment under Sec. 303. ◀

Although the legislative intent behind Sec. 303 is to provide liquidity for the payment of estate taxes and administrative expenses when a significant portion of the estate consists of stock in a closely held corporation, a redemption can qualify for Sec. 303 sale treatment even when the estate includes sufficient liquid assets to pay estate taxes and other expenses. The redemption proceeds need not be used for this purpose.

The advantage of a Sec. 303 redemption is that the redeeming shareholder usually realizes little or no capital gain because his or her basis in the redeemed stock is the stock's FMV on date of the decedent's death (or an alternate valuation date, if applicable). If the redemption does *not* qualify as a sale, the redeeming shareholder recognizes dividend income equal to the distribution proceeds received in redemption of the stock.

EXAMPLE C:4-41 ▶ Chili Corporation redeems 100 shares of stock for $105,000 from Art, who inherited the stock from his father, Fred. The stock's FMV on Fred's date of death was $100,000. Chili reports an E&P balance of $500,000. If the redemption qualifies as a sale under Sec. 303, Art recognizes a $5,000 ($105,000 – $100,000) capital gain. On the other hand, if the redemption does not qualify as a sale under Sec. 303 or one of the other redemption provisions, Art recognizes $105,000 of dividend income. Both the capital gain and the dividend income are subject to a maximum 15% tax rate. However, the dividend amount significantly exceeds the capital gain amount. ◀

SELF-STUDY QUESTION

How much gain is the redeeming shareholder likely to recognize in a qualifying Sec. 303 redemption?

ANSWER

Probably little or none. The basis in the redeemed stock equals its FMV at the decedent's date of death (or an alternate valuation date). The recognized gain generally is only the post-death appreciation.

EFFECT OF REDEMPTIONS ON THE DISTRIBUTING CORPORATION

As in the case of property distributions that are not in redemption of a shareholder's stock, two questions must be answered with respect to distributions in redemption of stock:

- What amount and character of gain or loss must the distributing corporation recognize?
- What effect does the distribution have on the corporation's E&P?

Each of these questions is addressed below.

CORPORATE GAIN OR LOSS ON PROPERTY DISTRIBUTIONS. The rules for gain or loss recognition for a corporation that distributes property in redemption of its stock are the same as the Sec. 311 rules pertaining to property distributions not in redemption of stock.

- The corporation recognizes gain when it redeems its stock by distributing property that has appreciated in value. The character of the gain depends on the character of the property distributed.
- The corporation recognizes no loss when it redeems its stock by distributing property that has declined in value.

EFFECT OF REDEMPTIONS ON E&P. A stock redemption affects a corporation's E&P in two ways. First, if the corporation distributes appreciated property, the excess of the property's FMV over its E&P adjusted basis increases the balance in the E&P account. Second, if the corporation distributes cash, or property, the corporation's E&P balance is reduced to reflect the amount of the distribution. This amount depends on whether the redemption is treated as a sale or a dividend by the shareholder.

If the redemption is a dividend, the corporation reduces its E&P by the face amount of any cash, the principal amount of any obligations, and the greater of the adjusted basis or FMV of any other property distributed, in the same way as it does for a property distribution not in redemption of stock.

If the redemption qualifies for sale treatment, the corporation reduces its E&P by the portion of its current and accumulated E&P attributable to the redeemed stock. In other words, E&P is reduced by a percentage equal to the percentage of the total outstanding shares redeemed, not to exceed the actual distribution amount. Any distribution amount exceeding this percentage reduces the corporation's tax basis paid-in capital.[43] Ordinary dividend amounts are subtracted from current E&P before the subtraction of stock redemption amounts. No such sequencing exists for accumulated E&P. Both ordinary dividend distributions and redemption distributions reduce accumulated E&P in chronological order.

EXAMPLE C:4-42 ▶ Apex Corporation has 100 shares of stock outstanding, 30 of which are owned by Mona. On December 31, Apex redeems all 30 of Mona's shares for $36,000 in a redemption qualifying as a sale under Sec. 302(b)(3). At the time of the redemption, Apex has $60,000 in paid-in capital and $40,000 of E&P. Because Apex redeemed 30% of its outstanding stock, the distribution reduces Apex's E&P by $12,000 (0.30 × $40,000). The remaining $24,000 ($36,000 − $12,000) reduces Apex's paid-in capital to $36,000 ($60,000 − $24,000).[44] ◀

PREFERRED STOCK BAILOUTS

OBJECTIVE 6

Explain the tax treatment of preferred stock bailouts

The stock redemption rules permit sale treatment in certain situations and require dividend treatment in all others. Generally, taxpayers prefer sale treatment for two reasons. First, sale treatment allows taxpayers to offset their stock basis against distribution proceeds. Second, gain on a stock sale generally is long-term and capital in character. Such gain may be entirely offset by the taxpayer's capital losses and thus not taxed at all. With these results in mind, taxpayers have devised methods to obtain sale rather than dividend treatment.

---

[43] Sec. 312(n)(7). This adjustment to paid-in capital might be necessary for companies that maintain tax basis balance sheets, for example, to determine book-tax differences in complying with *SFAS No. 109, Accounting for Income Taxes.*

[44] Distributions during the year require a different calculation, which is beyond the scope of this text.

ADDITIONAL COMMENT

When the term *bailout* is used in the corporate context, it generally refers to a scheme that allows a corporation to make a dividend distribution that for tax purposes is treated as a sale of a capital asset.

One such method is a **preferred stock bailout.** Prior to Congress' enacting anti-tax avoidance measures, a preferred stock bailout typically proceeded as follows:

1. A corporation issued a nontaxable dividend of nonvoting preferred stock to its common shareholders. Under the rules relating to nontaxable stock dividends, a portion of the common stock basis was allocated to the preferred stock. Its holding period included the holding period for the common stock.

2. The recipient shareholder then sold the preferred stock for FMV to an unrelated third party. As a result of the sale, the shareholder recognized a capital gain equal to the difference between the preferred stock's sale price and its allocated basis.

3. Next, the corporation redeemed the preferred stock from the third-party (usually at a small premium to reward the third party for his or her cooperation in the scheme).

4. As an alternative to steps 2 and 3, the corporation redeemed the preferred stock directly from the shareholder.

As a result of this preferred stock bailout, the shareholder extracted the corporation's E&P and converted what otherwise would have been a dividend into a long-term capital gain without changing his or her equity position in the company. To deter this tax-avoidance scheme, Congress enacted Sec. 306, which "taints" certain stock (usually preferred stock) when distributed to the shareholder in a nontaxable stock dividend. Section 306 treats the distribution proceeds as a dividend if the corporation redeems the tainted stock directly from the shareholder and treats the amount realized as ordinary income if the shareholder sells the stock to a third party. Either way, Sec. 306 prevents shareholders from using a preferred stock bailout to convert ordinary income into capital gain.

The 2003 Act, however, took the "sting" out of Sec. 306 by reducing the tax rate on dividends to a maximum of 15%. Thus, for 2003 through 2010, the dividend recognized on a direct redemption of Sec. 306 stock is taxed at 15%, and the amount realized on a third party sale of the stock is treated as a "deemed" dividend, also taxed at 15%. Nevertheless, the Sec. 306 taint is still disadvantageous because even though subject to the preferential capital gains tax rate, dividends cannot offset capital losses as can "real" capital gains. Also, if Sec. 306 recasts the redemption as a dividend, the shareholder is taxed on the entire amount of distribution proceeds rather than just the net gain.

SEC. 306 STOCK DEFINED

Section 306 stock is defined as follows:[45]

1. Stock (other than common issued with respect to common) received in a nontaxable stock dividend
2. Stock (other than common) received in a nontaxable corporate reorganization or corporate division if the effect of the transaction was substantially the same as the receipt of a stock dividend, or if the stock was received in exchange for Sec. 306 stock
3. Stock that has a basis determined by reference to the basis of Sec. 306 stock (i.e., a substituted or transferred basis)
4. Stock (other than common) acquired in an exchange to which Sec. 351 applies if the receipt of money (in lieu of the stock) would have been treated as a dividend

Preferred stock issued by a corporation with no current or accumulated E&P in the year the stock is issued is not Sec. 306 stock. Also, inherited stock is not Sec. 306 stock because the basis of such stock is its FMV on the date of the decedent's death (or alternate valuation date) and, therefore, is not determined by reference to the decedent's basis.[46]

TYPICAL MISCONCEPTION

Although the amount of deemed dividend income recognized on a sale of Sec. 306 stock is measured by the E&P existing in the year the Sec. 306 stock was distributed, the E&P of the distributing corporation is not reduced by the amount of the deemed dividend.

DISPOSITIONS OF SEC. 306 STOCK

If a shareholder sells or otherwise disposes of Sec. 306 stock (except in a redemption), the amount realized is treated as a deemed dividend to the extent the shareholder would have recognized a dividend at the time of the distribution had money equal to the stock's FMV been distributed instead of the stock itself. The shareholder's deemed dividend is mea-

[45] Sec. 306(c).

[46] Reg. Sec. 1.306-3(e).

sured by reference to the corporation's E&P in the year the Sec. 306 stock was issued, although the corporation does not reduce its E&P upon the sale. Any additional amount received for the Sec. 306 stock generally is treated as a return of capital. If the additional amount exceeds the shareholder's basis in the Sec. 306 stock, the excess is treated as a capital gain. If the additional amount is less than the shareholder's basis, the unrecovered basis is not treated as a loss. Rather, it is added back to the shareholder's basis in his or her common shares.

EXAMPLE C:4-43 ▶ Carlos owns all 100 outstanding shares of Adobe Corporation common stock. His basis in the shares is $100,000. Adobe, which has $150,000 of E&P, distributes 50 shares of nonvoting preferred to Carlos in a nontaxable stock dividend. On the distribution date, the FMV of the preferred stock is $50,000, and the FMV of the common stock is $200,000. Carlos must allocate his $100,000 common stock basis between the common and preferred stock according to their relative FMVs as follows:

	FMV	*Basis*
Common stock	$200,000	$ 80,000[a]
Preferred stock	50,000	20,000[b]
Total	$250,000	$100,000

[a] $\frac{\$200,000}{\$250,000} \times \$100,000$ [b] $\frac{\$50,000}{\$250,000} \times \$100,000$

Carlos subsequently sells the preferred stock to Dillon for $50,000. The $50,000 sales proceeds are treated as a deemed dividend because Adobe's E&P in the year the corporation distributed the preferred stock exceeded the stock's FMV. Carlos's $20,000 basis in the preferred stock is added back to the basis of his common stock, thereby restoring his common stock basis to $100,000. If instead Carlos sells the preferred stock for $80,000, he recognizes a $50,000 deemed dividend, a $20,000 return of capital, and a $10,000 capital gain computed as follows:

Sales proceeds	$80,000
Minus: Deemed dividend income[a]	(50,000)
Remaining sales proceeds	$30,000
Minus: Return of capital[b]	(20,000)
Capital gain[c]	$10,000

[a]Smaller of E&P in year stock was issued or stock's FMV on the distribution date.
[b]Smaller of remaining sales proceeds or stock adjusted basis.
[c]Sales proceeds received in excess of stock adjusted basis. ◀

REDEMPTIONS OF SEC. 306 STOCK

KEY POINT

The amount realized in a redemption of Sec. 306 stock is a dividend to the extent of E&P existing in the year of redemption. Unlike a sale of Sec. 306 stock, E&P is reduced as a result of a redemption.

If the issuing corporation redeems Sec. 306 stock, the shareholder's total amount realized is treated as a distribution to which the Sec. 301 dividend rules apply. Specifically, it is a dividend to the extent of the redeeming corporation's current and accumulated E&P measured *in the year of the redemption* and reduces corporate E&P accordingly. Amounts received in excess of the corporation's E&P are treated as a recovery of the shareholder's basis in his or her Sec. 306 stock, and then as a capital gain to the extent such amounts exceed basis. If all or a portion of the shareholder's basis in the redeemed stock is not recovered, the unrecovered amount increases the basis of the shareholder's common stock.

EXAMPLE C:4-44 ▶ Don owns all 100 shares of Brigham Corporation's common stock with a total $300,000 adjusted basis. On January 1, 2003, Brigham issued 50 shares of preferred stock to Don. On the distribution date, the FMVs of the preferred stock and common stock were $100,000 and $400,000, respectively. Brigham's E&P for 2003 was $200,000. Don's allocated basis in the preferred stock was $60,000 {[$100,000 ÷ ($100,000 + $400,000)] × $300,000}. The basis of Don's common stock was reduced to $240,000 ($300,000 − $60,000) as a result of this allocation. On January 2, 2007, Brigham redeems the preferred shares for $250,000. In the year of the redemption, Brigham's total E&P is $400,000. Thus, Don recognizes dividend income of $250,000. If Brigham's total E&P instead had been $200,000 in the year of the redemption, Don would have recognized $200,000 of dividend income and a $50,000 nontaxable return of capital. Because

Don's basis in his preferred stock is $60,000, the $10,000 unrecovered basis would have increased his basis in the common stock to $250,000 ($240,000 + $10,000). ◀

EXCEPTIONS TO SEC. 306 TREATMENT

Section 306 does not apply in the following situations.

- A shareholder sells all of his or her common and preferred stock, thereby completely terminating his or her interest in the issuing corporation.
- The corporation redeems all the shareholder's common and preferred stock, completely terminating the shareholder's interest in the corporation.
- The corporation redeems an individual shareholder's stock in a partial liquidation qualifying as a sale under Sec. 302(b)(4).
- A shareholder disposes of Sec. 306 stock in a way that triggers no gain or loss recognition (e.g., a gift). Although the donor recognizes no income when he or she disposes of Sec. 306 stock by gift, the stock retains its taint and remains Sec. 306 stock in the donee's hands. On the other hand, because heirs and devisees take a FMV basis in estate assets, the taint disappears when they inherit the stock.
- Section 306 does not apply if the taxpayer demonstrates to the IRS's satisfaction that the distribution and subsequent disposition of Sec. 306 stock did not have tax avoidance as a principal purpose.

TAX STRATEGY TIP

A taxpayer owning a portfolio of stock that includes Sec. 306 stock may want to retain the Sec. 306 stock and pass it on to his or her heirs, thereby eliminating the Sec. 306 taint, which again will have onerous effects after 2010. Market conditions, however, will dictate whether retaining the stock is a good investment strategy.

STOCK REDEMPTIONS BY RELATED CORPORATIONS

OBJECTIVE 7

Determine the applicability and tax consequences Sec. 304 to stock sales

If a shareholder sells stock in one corporation (the issuing corporation) to a second corporation (the acquiring corporation), the shareholder usually recognizes a capital gain or loss. However, if the shareholder controls both corporations, he or she may have to recognize dividend income because the net result may resemble a dividend more than a sale.

To prevent shareholders from using two corporations they commonly control to convert what is essentially a dividend into a capital gain, Sec. 304 requires that a sale of stock of one controlled corporation to a second controlled corporation be treated as a stock redemption. If the redemption meets the requirements for sale treatment (e.g., if the redemption is substantially disproportionate), the transaction will be treated as a sale. Otherwise, the redemption will be treated as a dividend to the extent of E&P. As in the case of Sec. 306 preferred stock bailouts, now that individuals pay a maximum tax rate of 15% on dividends and capital gains, Sec. 304 no longer delivers the "sting" it had before 2003. Nevertheless, Sec. 304 still is in effect. When it does apply, shareholders may have to recognize dividend income rather than capital gain and cannot offset either stock basis or capital losses against this income.

Section 304 applies to two types of sales. The first is a sale of stock involving two brother-sister corporations. The second is a sale of a parent corporation's stock to one of its subsidiaries. The following sections define brother-sister and parent-subsidiary corporations and explain how Sec. 304 applies to each group.

ADDITIONAL COMMENT

The definition of brother-sister corporations for Sec. 304 differs from the definition for controlled groups discussed in Chapter C:3.

BROTHER-SISTER CORPORATIONS

Two corporations are called brother-sister corporations when one or more shareholders control each of the corporations and a parent-subsidiary relationship does not exist. Control means ownership of at least 50% of the voting power or 50% of the total value of all the corporation's stock. The shareholder(s) who acquired such ownership are called controlling shareholders. If a controlling shareholder (or shareholders) transfers stock in one corporation to the other corporation in exchange for property, the exchange must be recast as a redemption.

To determine whether the redemption is a sale or a dividend, reference is made to the shareholder's stock ownership in the issuing corporation. For purposes of this determination, the attribution rules of Sec. 318(a) apply.[47]

REDEMPTION TREATED AS A DISTRIBUTION. If the redemption does not qualify for sale treatment, it is treated as a dividend paid first by the acquiring corporation to the extent of its E&P, and then by the issuing corporation to the extent of its E&P. The shareholder's basis in the issuing corporation's stock sold is added to his or her basis in the acquiring corporation's stock. The acquiring corporation takes the same basis in the issuing corporation's stock as the shareholder's.

EXAMPLE C:4-45 ▶ Bert owns 60 of the 100 outstanding shares of Frog Corporation stock and 60 of the 100 outstanding shares of Tree Corporation stock. Frog and Tree have \$50,000 and \$20,000 of E&P, respectively. Bert sells to Tree for \$20,000 20 shares of Frog stock with an adjusted basis of \$10,000. Because Bert owns at least 50% of each corporation's stock, Bert is deemed to control both Frog and Tree, and Sec. 304 governs the transaction. Accordingly, the sale is recast as a redemption. To determine whether the redemption qualifies for capital gains treatment, reference is made to Bert's percentage ownership of Frog stock. Before the redemption, Bert owned 60% of Frog stock. After the redemption, Bert owns 52% of Frog stock (40 shares directly and 12 [0.60 × 20] shares constructively through Tree). Because the redempton satisfies none of the Sec. 302 tests for capital gains treatment, it is treated as a distribution subject to Sec. 301. Under this provision, the entire distribution is treated as a dividend because it does not exceed Frog and Tree's total E&P of \$70,000. All \$20,000 of the distribution is deemed to have been made out of Tree's E&P because it is sufficient to cover the distribution amount. Tree's basis in the Frog stock is \$10,000, the same as Bert's. Bert increases his basis in Tree stock by \$10,000, his basis in the Frog stock that he is deemed to have contributed to Tree. ◀

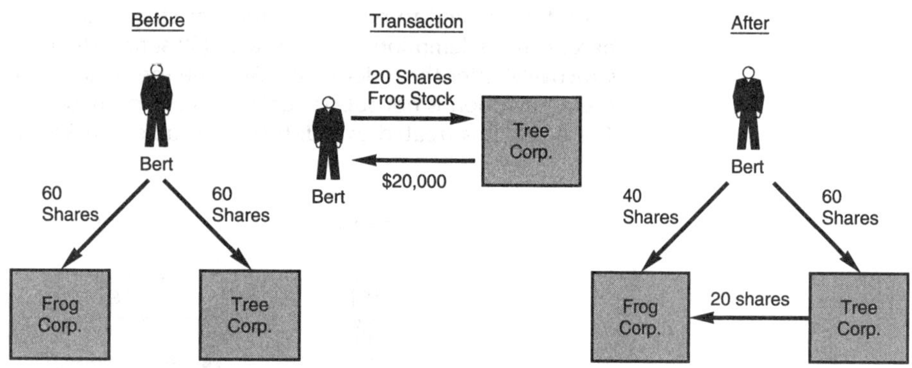

Bert's Ownership of Frog Corporation Stock:
Before: 60 shares (60%) directly
After: 52 shares [40 shares directly + 12 shares (60% x 20 shares) constructively]

FIGURE C:4-1 ▶ ILLUSTRATION OF A BROTHER-SISTER REDEMPTION (EXAMPLE C:4-45)

REDEMPTION TREATED AS A SALE. If the redemption qualifies for sale treatment, the shareholder's recognized gain or loss equals the difference between the amount received from the acquiring corporation and the shareholder's basis in the surrendered shares. The acquiring corporation is treated as having purchased the issuing corporation's shares and thus takes a cost basis in such shares.

EXAMPLE C:4-46 ▶ Assume the same facts as in Example C:4-45 except Bert sells 40 shares of Frog stock with an adjusted basis of \$20,000 to Tree Corporation for \$40,000. After the redemption, Bert owns

[47] For Sec. 304 purposes, the attribution rules of Sec. 318(a) are modified so that a shareholder is considered to own an amount of stock proportionate to that owned by any corporation of which he or she owns 5% or more (instead of 50% or more) of the value of the stock.

44 shares of Frog stock (20 shares directly and 24 [0.60 × 40] shares constructively through Tree). Therefore, he meets both the 50% and the 80% tests for substantially disproportionate redemptions, treats the redemption as a sale, and recognizes a capital gain of $20,000 ($40,000 received from Tree − $20,000 adjusted basis in the Frog shares). Tree's basis in the Frog shares acquired from Bert equals their $40,000 purchase price. ◀

ADDITIONAL COMMENT
The definition of a parent-subsidiary relationship for Sec. 304 differs from the definition for controlled groups or affiliated corporations discussed in Chapter C:3.

PARENT-SUBSIDIARY CORPORATIONS

If a shareholder sells stock in a parent corporation to a subsidiary of the parent, the sale is treated as a distribution in redemption of part or all of the shareholder's parent stock. A parent-subsidiary relationship exists if one corporation owns at least 50% of the voting power or 50% of the total value of all stock in another corporation.

To determine whether the redemption is treated as a sale or a dividend, reference is made to the shareholder's ownership of parent stock before and after the redemption. The constructive ownership rules of Sec. 318 apply for the purpose of this determination.

REDEMPTION TREATED AS A DIVIDEND. If the redemption does not qualify for sale treatment, the distribution is treated as a dividend, first from the subsidiary to the extent of its E&P and then from the parent to the extent of its E&P. This rule efffectively sets the combined E&P of both corporations as the standard for measuring the amount of the distribution that constitutes a dividend. The shareholder's basis in his or her remaining parent shares is increased by his or her basis in the shares transferred to the subsidiary. The subsidiary's basis in the parent stock is the amount the subsidiary paid for the stock.[48]

EXAMPLE C:4-47 ▶ Of the 100 shares of Parent Corporation stock, Brian owns 60 with a $15,000 basis. Parent owns 60 of the 100 shares of Subsidiary stock. Parent and Subsidiary have $10,000 and $30,000 of E&P, respectively. Brian sells ten of his Parent shares to Subsidiary for $12,000. (See Figure C:4-2.) Parent is deemed to have redeemed its stock from Brian, who owned 60% of Parent stock before the redemption and 53 shares (50 shares directly and 3 [0.60 × 0.50 × 10] shares constructively) after the redemption. Because the 50% and 80% tests of Sec. 302(b)(2) are not met, the redemption is not substantially disproportionate and does not qualify for sale treatment. Therefore, it is treated as a distribution subject to Sec. 301. Under this provision, Brian recog-

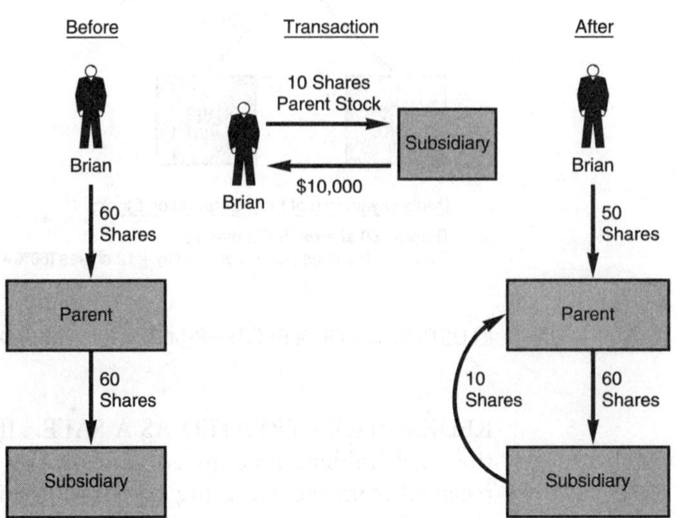

FIGURE C:4-2 ▶ ILLUSTRATION OF A PARENT-SUBSIDIARY REDEMPTION (EXAMPLE C:4-47)

[48] Rev. Rul. 80-189, 1980-2 C.B. 106.

nizes a $12,000 dividend. This dividend is deemed to have been paid out of Subsidiary's E&P, which is sufficient to cover the entire distribution amount. Brian's $2,500 basis in the redeemed shares increases his $12,500 basis in his remaining Parent shares, so that his total basis in those shares remains $15,000. Subsidiary's basis in the ten Parent shares acquired from Brian is $12,000, the amount that Subsidiary paid for the shares. ◀

REDEMPTION TREATED AS A SALE. If redemption of the parent's stock qualifies for sale treatment, the basis of the stock transferred to the subsidiary is subtracted from the amount realized in the distribution to derive the shareholder's recognized gain or loss.

EXAMPLE C:4-48 ▶ Assume the same facts as in Example C:4-47 except Brian sells 40 shares of Parent stock to Subsidiary for $48,000. Because Brian owns 60% of Parent stock before the redemption and 24.8% (20 shares directly and 4.8 [0.60 × 0.20 × 40] shares constructively) after the redemption, the redemption meets the Sec. 302(b)(2) 50% and 80% tests for a substantially disproportionate redemption. Consequently, Brian recognizes a capital gain of $38,000 ($48,000 − $10,000 adjusted basis in the 40 shares sold). Brian's adjusted basis for his remaining 20 shares of Parent stock is $5,000. Subsidiary's basis in the 40 Parent shares purchased from Brian is $48,000, the amount that Subsidiary paid for the shares. ◀

Topic Review C:4-4 summarizes the tax treatment of redemptions, as well as special redemption rules.

Topic Review C:4-4

Alternative Treatments of Stock Redemptions

General Rule: A distribution in redemption of stock generally is treated as a dividend (Secs. 302(d) and 301).
Exception: The following transactions qualify for sale (i.e., capital gains) treatment:

1. Redemptions that are not essentially equivalent to a dividend (Sec. 302(b)(1))
2. Substantially disproportionate redemptions (Sec. 302(b)(2))
3. Complete terminations of a shareholder's interest (Sec. 302(b)(3))
4. Partial liquidations in redemption of a noncorporate shareholder's stock (Sec. 302(b)(4))
5. Redemptions to pay death taxes (Sec. 303)

Special Redemption Rules

1. Redemptions of Sec. 306 stock generally are taxed as dividends to the shareholder (Sec. 306).
2. A sale of stock in one controlled corporation to another controlled corporation is treated in the same way as a redemption (Sec. 304).

TAX PLANNING CONSIDERATIONS

AVOIDING UNREASONABLE COMPENSATION

Chapter C:3 discussed the use of salary payments and fringe benefits to permit a shareholder of a closely held corporation to withdraw funds from the corporation and be subject to a single level of taxation. If a corporation pays too large a salary to a shareholder-employee, some of the salary may be disallowed as a corporate deduction while still being taxed to the shareholder-employee. In such case, double taxation of the disallowed portion results.

Corporations can avoid this result by entering into a **hedge agreement** with a shareholder-employee. The agreement obligates the shareholder-employee to repay any portion of salary the IRS disallows as a corporate deduction. Under Sec. 162, the shareholder-employee may deduct this amount in the year he or she repays it, provided a legal obligation to repay exists under state law.[49] If a hedge agreement is not in effect, voluntary repayment of the salary is not deductible by the shareholder-employee.[50]

EXAMPLE C:4-49 ▶ Theresa owns one-half the stock of Marine Corporation and serves as its president. The remaining Marine stock is owned by eight investors, none of whom owns more than 10% of the outstanding shares. In 2002, Theresa and Marine conclude a hedge agreement requiring Theresa to repay all compensation the IRS declares unreasonable. In 2004, Marine pays Theresa a salary and bonus of $750,000. The IRS subsequently claims that $300,000 of the salary is unreasonable and thus nondeductible by Marine. After protracted negotiations, Marine and the IRS settle for $180,000 as unreasonable and nondeductible by Marine. Theresa repays the $180,000 in 2007. The entire $750,000 is taxable to Theresa in 2004. However, she can deduct the $180,000 as a trade or business expense in 2007. ◀

Hedge agreements also have been used in connection with other payments between a corporation and its shareholders (e.g., travel and entertainment expenses). Some employers shy away from hedge agreements because the IRS might consider the very existence of such an agreement as evidence of unreasonable compensation.

BOOTSTRAP ACQUISITIONS

A prospective purchaser who wants to acquire the stock of a corporation may not have sufficient cash to do so. To facilitate the purchase, corporate funds could be used in the following way: a shareholder sells part of his or her stock to the purchaser and then causes the corporation to redeem the shareholder's remaining shares. Such an arrangement is called a **bootstrap acquisition.**

EXAMPLE C:4-50 ▶ Ted owns all 100 shares of Dragon Corporation stock having a $100,000 FMV. Vickie wants to purchase the stock from Ted but has only $60,000 of cash. Dragon has a large cash balance, which it does not need for its operations. Ted sells Vickie 60 shares of Dragon stock for $60,000 and then causes Dragon to redeem his remaining shares for $40,000. The redemption qualifies as a complete termination of Ted's interest under Sec. 302(b)(3) and, therefore, is eligible for capital gains treatment. ◀

Court cases have held that such redemptions qualify for sale treatment as long as the third-party sale and redemption are part of an integral plan to terminate the seller's entire corporate interest. Whether the redemption precedes the sale is immaterial.[51] The purchaser, however, must carefully avoid generating a dividend, actual or constructive. For example, a purchaser who contracts to acquire all the stock in a corporation on an installment plan and then causes the corporation to pay the installment obligations will recognize dividend income. The use of corporate funds constitutes a constructive dividend to the purchaser where the corporation discharges the purchaser's legal obligation. Even if the corporation uses its own funds to redeem the seller's shares, a purchaser who was legally obligated to purchase the shares is considered to have received a constructive dividend.[52]

EXAMPLE C:4-51 ▶ Assume the same facts as in Example C:4-50 except that, after Vickie purchases the 60 shares from Ted, she becomes legally obligated to purchase Ted's remaining 40 shares. After entering into the contract, Vickie causes Dragon Corporation to redeem the 40 shares. Because Dragon has extinguished Vickie's legal obligation, the corporation is deemed to have paid Vickie a $40,000 constructive dividend. No constructive dividend would have resulted had Vickie been legally obligated to purchase only 60 shares from Ted. ◀

Rev. Rul. 69-608 provides guidance to a bootstrap acquirer on how to avoid constructive dividend treatment.[53] According to this ruling, when the corporation redeems some of the seller's shares, the buyer will not be deemed to have received a constructive dividend as

---

[49] Rev. Rul. 69-115, 1969-1 C.B. 50, and *Vincent E. Oswald*, 49 T.C. 645 (1968), *acq.* 1968-2 C.B. 2.

[50] *Ernest H. Berger*, 37 T.C. 1026 (1962), and *John G. Pahl*, 67 T.C. 286 (1976).

[51] See, for example, *U.S. v. Gerald Carey*, 7 AFTR 2d 1301, 61-1 USTC ¶9428 (8th Cir., 1961).

[52] *H. F. Wall v. U.S.*, 36 AFTR 423, 47-2 USTC ¶9395 (4th Cir., 1947).

[53] Rev. Rul. 69-608, 1969-2 C.B. 42.

WHAT WOULD YOU DO IN THIS SITUATION?

One of the most cherished traditions observed by many professional firms involves the year-end bonus. Legal, medical, business, and accounting administrators often use bonus compensation to clear the books at the end of the year. In partnerships, bonuses are characterized as distributive shares or a form of compensation. As such, they are taxed only once as income paid to professionals for services rendered, net of appropriate accounting adjustments.

With the advent of the professional corporation, an entity designed to limit personal liability, many professionals have opted to do business as shareholders. The continued use of the year-end bonus in the professional corporation has come under close IRS scrutiny. The position taken by the IRS is clear. If the payments to the shareholder-professional are in exchange for his or her services rendered to the firm, the corporation may deduct them as salaries (assuming they are reasonable in amount). On the other hand, if they are a disguised payout of owners' profits, the corporation cannot deduct them. As a result, the corporation's taxable income will be increased by the amount of the disallowed deduction. The shareholder who receives the bonus must treat the receipt as a dividend rather than salary. However, treating the bonus as a dividend generally results in less tax paid by the shareholder because dividends are taxed at a maximum rate of 15% as opposed to 35% for salary. The consequences are negative only to the corporation, which may not deduct the dividend payment.

This principle is illustrated in a case, *Rapco, Inc. v. CIR,* 77 AFTR 2d 2405, 96-1 USTC ¶50,297 (CA-2, 1996), decided by the Second Circuit. In *Rapco,* the court denied a deduction for bonus payments to the president of the company, even though he played a significant role in the company's rapid growth and had guaranteed third party loans to Rapco. Reasons cited by the court were that Rapco's compensation scheme was "bonus-heavy and salary light," suggesting dividend avoidance; Rapco had ignored its own bonus policy set forth in its preincorporation minutes; the corporation had a history of never paying dividends; the shareholder who determined the amount of his own salary owned 95% of the corporation's stock; and Rapco's own expert testified that $400,000 to $500,000 was fair compensation for the president's services. (The IRS allowed a salary deduction of $405,000).

Assuming your CPA firm is acting as a tax advisor to several similarly situated professional corporations, what advice that complies with the IRC, Treasury Regulations, and the AICPA's *Statements on Standards for Tax Services* would you give?

long as he or she does not have a primary and unconditional obligation to purchase the shares, and as long as the corporation pays no more for the redeemed shares than their FMV. Furthermore, a purchaser who has an option—not a legal obligation—to purchase the seller's remaining shares, and who assigns the option to the redeeming corporation, is unlikely to generate a constructive dividend.[54]

TIMING OF DISTRIBUTIONS

Dividends can be paid only out of a corporation's E&P. Therefore, if distributions can be timed to be made when the corporation has little or no E&P, the distributions are treated as a return of capital rather than as a dividend.

If a corporation generates a current E&P deficit, the deficit reduces accumulated E&P evenly throughout the year unless the corporation can demonstrate that it incurred the deficits on particular dates. Thus, if a corporation with a current E&P deficit, but a positive accumulated E&P balance, makes a distribution in the current year, the timing of the distribution may determine whether the distribution will be treated as a dividend or a return of capital.

EXAMPLE C:4-52 ▶ Major Corporation has a $30,000 accumulated E&P balance at the beginning of the year and incurs a $50,000 deficit during the year. Because of its poor operating performance, Major pays to its sole shareholder only two of its four $5,000 quarterly dividends, the two being those ordinarily paid on March 31 and June 30. The tax treatment of the two distributions is determined as follows:

[54] *Joseph R. Holsey v. CIR,* 2 AFTR 2d 5660, 58-2 USTC ¶9816 (3rd Cir., 1958).

E&P balance, January 1	$30,000
Minus: Reduction for first quarter loss	(12,500)
Reduction for March 31 distribution	(5,000)
E&P balance, April 1	$12,500
Minus: Reduction for second quarter loss	(12,500)
E&P balance, June 30	$ –0–

The first and second quarter losses each are $12,500 [($50,000) × 0.25 = ($12,500)].

The operating loss reduces the accumulated E&P balance evenly throughout the year. All of the March 31 distribution is taxable because the corporation did not incur sufficient losses to offset the positive accumulated E&P balance at the beginning of the year. The second quarter loss results in the treatment of the June 30 distribution and any other distributions before year-end as tax-free returns of capital (assuming that the shareholder's basis in his or her stock exceeds the distribution amount). Delaying all the distributions until late in the year could result in the tax-free return of capital. ◀

The timing of a distribution also can be critical if the distributing corporation has an accumulated E&P deficit and a positive current E&P balance.

EXAMPLE C:4-53 ▶ At the beginning of 2006, Yankee Corporation has an accumulated E&P deficit of $250,000. During 2006 and 2007, Yankee reports the following current E&P balances and makes the following distributions to Joe, its sole shareholder:

Year	*Current E&P*	*Distributions*	*Distribution Date*
2006	$100,000	$75,000	December 31
2007	–0–	–0–	None

The $75,000 distribution in 2006 is taxable as a dividend. The $25,000 of current E&P that is not distributed reduces Yankee's accumulated E&P deficit to $225,000. Had Yankee delayed distributing the $75,000 until sometime in 2007, the distribution would have been treated as a nontaxable return of Joe's investment. ◀

COMPLIANCE AND PROCEDURAL CONSIDERATIONS

CORPORATE REPORTING OF NONDIVIDEND DISTRIBUTIONS

ADDITIONAL COMMENT

Information on basis adjustments for nontaxable dividends, stock splits, stock dividends, etc. for individual firms can be found in special tax services.

A corporation that makes a nondividend distribution to its shareholders must file with its income tax return Form 5452 (Corporate Report of Nondividend Distributions), along with supporting computations. Form 5452 reports the distributing corporation's E&P so as to enable the IRS to verify the nontaxability of the distribution. Form 5452 requires the following information: current and accumulated E&P, distribution amounts paid to shareholders during the tax year, the percentage of each payment that is taxable and nontaxable, and a detailed computation of E&P from the date of incorporation.

AGREEMENT TO TERMINATE INTEREST UNDER SEC. 302(b)(3)

KEY POINT

The statute of limitation extends to one year beyond the date a shareholder notifies the IRS that a forbidden interest has been acquired. Otherwise, it would be almost impossible for the IRS to administer this provision.

As mentioned earlier, if a redemption completely terminates a shareholder's interest in a corporation, the family attribution rules of Sec. 318(a)(1) may be waived. To have the rules waived, the shareholder must agree in writing that he or she will notify the IRS upon acquiring any prohibited interest within the ten-year period following the redemption. A copy of this agreement (in the form of a signed statement in duplicate) must be attached to the first return filed by the shareholder for the tax year in which the redemption occurs. If the agreement cannot be filed on time, the IRS may grant an extension. Regulation Sec. 1.302-4(a) provides that an extension will be granted only if reasonable cause exists for failure to timely file the agreement and if the request for such an extension is filed within such time as the appropriate IRS official considers reasonable in the circumstances.

Treasury Regulations do not indicate what constitutes reasonable cause for failure to file or what constitutes a reasonable extension of time. In *Edward J. Fehrs* the U.S. Court of Claims held that late filing of a ten-year agreement was permissible where a taxpayer could not reasonably have expected that a filing would be necessary, where the taxpayer filed the agreement promptly after receiving notice that it was required, and where the agreement was filed before the issues in question were presented for trial.[55] However, in *Robin Haft Trust,* an agreement was filed *after* an adverse court ruling. In an appeal for a rehearing, the judge ruled that the filing of the agreement after the case was brought to trial was too late. Consequently, the judge denied the appeal for a rehearing.[56]

If the shareholder acquires a prohibited interest within the ten-year period following the redemption, the IRS may assess additional taxes. Such an acquisition ordinarily results in recasting the redemption as a dividend rather than a sale. The limitations period for assessing additional taxes extends to one year after the date the shareholder files with the IRS notice of acquiring the prohibited interest.[57]

PROBLEM MATERIALS

DISCUSSION QUESTIONS

C:4-1 Explain how a corporation computes its current and accumulated E&P balances.

C:4-2 Why is it necessary to distinguish between current and accumulated E&P?

C:4-3 Describe the effect of a $100,000 cash distribution paid on January 1 to the sole shareholder of a calendar year corporation whose stock basis is $25,000 when the corporation has

a. $100,000 of current E&P and $100,000 of accumulated E&P
b. A $50,000 accumulated E&P deficit and $60,000 of current E&P
c. A $60,000 accumulated E&P deficit and a $60,000 current E&P deficit
d. An $80,000 current E&P deficit and $100,000 of accumulated E&P

Answer Parts a through d again, assuming instead that the corporation makes the distribution on October 1 in a nonleap year.

C:4-4 Pecan Corporation distributes land to a noncorporate shareholder. Explain how the following items are computed:

a. The amount of the distribution
b. The amount of the dividend
c. The shareholder's basis in the land
d. When the holding period for the land begins.

How would your answers change if the distribution were made to a corporate shareholder?

C:4-5 What effect do the following transactions have on the calculation of Young Corporation's current E&P? Assume that the starting point for the calculation is Young's taxable income for the current year.

a. The corporation earns tax-exempt interest income of $10,000.
b. Taxable income includes a $10,000 dividend and is reduced by a $7,000 dividends-received deduction.
c. A $5,000 capital loss carryover from the preceding tax year offsets $5,000 of capital gains.
d. The corporation accrued federal income taxes of $25,280.
e. The corporation took a U.S. production activities deduction of $3,000.

C:4-6 Badger Corporation was incorporated in the current year. It reports an $8,000 NOL on its initial tax return. Badger distributed $2,500 to its shareholders. Is it possible for this distribution to be taxed as a dividend to Badger's shareholders? Explain.

C:4-7 Does the timing of a distribution matter as to whether it is taxed as a dividend or as a return of capital? Explain.

C:4-8 Hickory Corporation owns a building with a $160,000 adjusted basis and a $120,000 FMV. Hickory's E&P is $200,000. Should the

[55] *Edward J. Fehrs v. U.S.*, 40 AFTR 2d 77-5040, 77-1 USTC ¶9423 (Ct. Cl., 1977).

[56] *Robin Haft Trust*, 62 T.C. 145 (1974).

[57] Sec. 302(c)(2)(A).

corporation sell the property and distribute the sale proceeds to its shareholders or distribute the property to its shareholders and let them sell the property? Why?

C:4-9 Walnut Corporation owns a building with a $120,000 adjusted basis and a $160,000 FMV. Walnut's E&P is $200,000. Should the corporation sell the property and distribute the sale proceeds to its shareholders or distribute the property to its shareholders and let them sell the property? Why?

C:4-10 What is a constructive dividend? Under what circumstances is the IRS likely to argue that a constructive dividend has been paid?

C:4-11 Why are stock dividends generally nontaxable? Under what circumstances are stock dividends taxable?

C:4-12 For tax purposes, how is a distribution of stock rights treated by a shareholder? By the distributing corporation?

C:4-13 What is a stock redemption? What are some reasons for redeeming stock? Why are some redemptions treated as sales and others as dividends?

C:4-14 Field Corporation redeems 100 shares of its stock from Andrew for $10,000. Andrew's basis in those shares is $8,000. Explain the possible tax treatments of Andrew's receiving the $10,000.

C:4-15 What conditions must be met for a redemption to be treated as a sale by the redeeming shareholder?

C:4-16 Explain the purpose of the attribution rules in determining stock ownership in a redemption. Describe the four types of attribution rules that apply to redemptions.

C:4-17 Abel, the sole shareholder of Ace Corporation, has an opporunity to purchase the assets of a sole proprietorship for $50,000 in cash. Ace has a substantial E&P balance. Abel does not have sufficient cash to personally make the purchase. If Abel obtains the needed $50,000 from Ace via a nonliquidating distribution, Abel will have to recognize dividend income. Alternatively, would Ace's purchase of the assets of the sole proprietorship followed by their distribution to Abel in redemption of part of his stock holdings constitute a partial liquidation? Explain.

C:4-18 Why does a redemption that qualifies for sale treatment under Sec. 303 usually result in the shareholder's recognizing little or no gain or loss?

C:4-19 Under what circumstances does a corporation recognize gain or loss when it distributes noncash property in redemption of its stock? What effect does a redemption distribution have on the distributing corporation's E&P?

C:4-20 What is a preferred stock bailout? How does Sec. 306 operate to prevent a shareholder from realizing the otherwise available tax benefits of a preferred stock bailout?

C:4-21 Bill owns all 100 of the outstanding shares of Plum Corporation stock and 80 of the 100 outstanding shares of Cherry Corporation stock. He sells 20 Plum shares to Cherry for $80,000. Explain why this transaction is treated as a stock redemption, and determine the tax consequences of the transaction.

C:4-22 Explain the tax consequences, to both the corporation and a shareholder-employee, of an IRS determination that a portion of the compensation paid in a prior tax year is unreasonable. What steps can the corporation and shareholder-employee take to avoid the double taxation usually associated with such a determination?

C:4-23 What is a bootstrap acquisition? What are the tax consequences of such a transaction?

ISSUE IDENTIFICATION QUESTIONS

C:4-24 Marsha receives a $10,000 cash distribution from Dye Corporation in April of the current year. Dye has $4,000 of accumulated E&P at the beginning of the year and $8,000 of current E&P. Dye also distributed $10,000 in cash to Barbara, who purchased all 200 shares of Dye stock from Marsha in June of the current year. What tax issues should be considered with respect to the distributions made to Marsha and Barbara?

C:4-25 Neil purchased land from Spring Harbor, his 100%-owned corporation, for $275,000. The corporation purchased the land three years ago for $300,000. Similar tracts of land located nearby have sold for $400,000 in recent months. What tax issues should be considered with respect to the corporation's sale of the land?

C:4-26 Price Corporation has 100 shares of common stock outstanding. Price repurchased all of Penny's 30 shares for $35,000 cash during the current year. Three years ago, Penny received the shares as a gift from her mother. They have a basis to her of $16,000. Price has $100,000 of current and accumulated E&P. Penny's mother owns 40 of the remaining shares; unrelated individuals own the other 30 shares. What tax issues should be considered with respect to the corporation's purchase of Penny's shares?

C:4-27 George owns all 100 shares of Gumby's Pizza Corporation. The shares are worth $200,000, but George's basis is only $70,000. Mary and George have reached a tentative agreement for George to sell all his shares to Mary. However, Mary is unwilling to pay more than

$150,000 for the stock because the corporation currently has excess cash balances. They have agreed that George can withdraw $50,000 in cash from Gumby's before the stock sale. What tax issues should be considered with respect to George and Mary's agreement?

PROBLEMS

C:4-28 ***Current E&P Calculation.*** Beach Corporation, an accrual basis taxpayer, reports the following results for the current year:

Income:	
Gross profit from manufacturing operations	$250,000
Dividends received from 25%-owned domestic corporation	20,000
Interest income: Corporate bonds	10,000
Municipal bonds	12,000
Proceeds from life insurance policy on key employee	100,000
Section 1231 gain on sale of land	8,000
Expenses:	
Administrative expenses	110,000
Bad debt expense	5,000
Depreciation:	
Financial accounting	68,000
Taxable income	86,000
Alternative depreciation system (Sec. 168(g))	42,000
NOL carryover	40,000
Charitable contributions: Current year	8,000
Carryover from last year	3,500
Capital loss on sale of stock	1,200
U.S. production activities deduction	1,500
Penalty on late payment of federal taxes	450

a. What is Beach's taxable income?
b. What is Beach's current E&P?

C:4-29 ***Current E&P Computation.*** Water Corporation reports $500,000 of taxable income for the current year. The following additional information is available:

- For the current year, Water reports an $80,000 long-term capital loss and no capital gains.
- Taxable income includes $80,000 of dividends from a 10%-owned domestic corporation.
- Water paid fines and penalties of $6,000 that were not deducted in computing taxable income.
- In computing this year's taxable income, Water deducted a $20,000 NOL carryover from a prior tax year.
- Water claimed a $10,000 U.S. production activities deduction.
- Taxable income includes a deduction for $40,000 of depreciation that exceeds the depreciation allowed for E&P purposes.

Assume a 34% corporate tax rate. What is Water's current E&P for this year?

C:4-30 ***Calculating Accumulated E&P.*** Investors formed Peach Corporation in 2004. Its current E&P (or current E&P deficit) and distributions for the period 2004–2007 are as follows:

Year	*Current E&P (Deficit)*	*Distributions*
2004	$ (8,000)	$ 2,000
2005	(12,000)	–0–
2006	10,000	5,000
2007	14,000	17,000

What is Peach's accumulated E&P at the beginning of 2005, 2006, 2007, and 2008?

C:4-31 ***Consequences of a Single Cash Distribution.*** Clover Corporation is a calendar year taxpayer. Connie owns all of its stock. Her basis for the stock is $10,000. On April 1 of the current (non-leap) year Clover distributes $52,000 to Connie. Determine the tax consequences of the cash distribution in each of the following independent situations:

a. Current E&P of $15,000; accumulated E&P of $25,000.
b. Current E&P of $30,000; accumulated E&P of ($20,000).

c. Current E&P of ($73,000); accumulated E&P of $50,000.
d. Current E&P of ($20,000); accumulated E&P of ($15,000).

C:4-32 ***Consequences of a Single Cash Distribution.*** Pink Corporation is a calendar year taxpayer. Pete owns one third of Pink stock (100 shares). His basis in the stock is $25,000. Cheryl owns two-thirds of Pink stock (200 shares). Her basis in the stock is $40,000. On June 10 of the current year, Pink distributes $40,000 to Pete and $80,000 to Cheryl. Determine the tax consequences of the cash distributions to Pete and Cheryl in each of the following independent situations:
a. Current E&P of $60,000; accumulated E&P of $100,000.
b. Current E&P of $36,000; accumulated E&P of $30,000.

C:4-33 ***Consequences of Multiple Cash Distributions.*** At the beginning of the current (non-leap) year, Charles owns all of Pearl Corporation's outstanding stock. His basis in the stock is $80,000. On July 1, he sells all his stock to Donald for $125,000. During the year, Pearl, a calendar year taxpayer, makes two cash distributions: $60,000 on March 1 to Charles and $90,000 on September 1 to Donald. How are these distributions treated in the following independent situations? What are the amount and character of Charles' gain on his sale of stock to Donald? What is Donald's basis in his Pearl stock at the end of the year?
a. Current E&P of $40,000; accumulated E&P of $30,000.
b. Current E&P of $100,000; accumulated E&P (deficit) of ($50,000).
c. Current E&P (deficit) of ($36,500); accumulated E&P of $120,000.

C:4-34 ***Distribution of Appreciated Property.*** In the current year, Sedgwick Corporation has $100,000 of current and accumulated E&P. On March 3, Sedgwick distributes to its shareholder Dina a parcel of land (a capital asset) having a $56,000 FMV. The land has a $40,000 adjusted basis (for both taxable income and E&P purposes) to Sedgwick and is subject to an $8,000 mortgage, which Dina assumes. Assume a 34% marginal corporate tax rate.
a. What are the amount and character of the income Dina recognizes as a result of the distribution?
b. What is Dina's basis in the land?
c. What are the amount and character of Sedgwick's gain or loss as a result of the distribution?
d. What effect does the distribution have on Sedgwick's E&P?

C:4-35 ***Distribution of Property Subject to a Liability.*** On May 10 of the current year, Stowe Corporation distributes to its shareholder Arlene $20,000 in cash and land (a capital asset) having a $50,000 FMV. The land has a $15,000 adjusted basis (for both taxable income and E&P purposes) and is subject to a $60,000 mortgage, which Arlene assumes. Stowe has an E&P balance exceeding the amount distributed and is subject to a 34% marginal corporate tax rate.
a. What are the amount and character of the income Arlene recognizes as a result of the distribution?
b. What is Arlene's basis in the land?
c. What are the amount and character of Stowe's gain or loss as a result of the distribution?

C:4-36 ***Distribution of Depreciable Property.*** On May 15 of the current year, Quick Corporation distributes to its shareholder Calvin a building having a $250,000 FMV and used in its business. The building originally cost $180,000. Quick claimed $30,000 of straight-line depreciation, so that the adjusted basis of the building on the date of distribution for taxable income purposes is $150,000. The adjusted basis of the building for E&P purposes is $160,000. The building is subject to an $80,000 mortgage, which Calvin assumes. Quick has an E&P balance exceeding the amount distributed and is subject to a 34% marginal corporate tax rate.
a. What are the amount and character of the income Calvin recognizes as a result of the distribution?
b. What is Calvin's basis in the building?
c. What are the amount and character of Quick's gain or loss as a result of the distribution?
d. What effect does the distribution have on Quick's E&P?

C:4-37 ***Distribution of Various Types of Property.*** During the current year, Zeta Corporation distributes the assets listed below to its sole shareholder, Susan. For each asset listed, determine the gross income recognized by Susan, her basis in the asset, the amount of gain or loss recognized by Zeta, and the effect of the distribution on Zeta's E&P. Assume that Zeta has an E&P balance exceeding the amount distributed and is subject to a 34% marginal tax rate. Unless stated otherwise, adjusted bases for taxable income and E&P purposes are the same.

a. A parcel of land used in Zeta's business that has a $200,000 FMV and a $125,000 adjusted basis.
b. Assume the same facts as in Part a except that the land is subject to a $140,000 mortgage.
c. FIFO inventory having a $25,000 FMV and an $18,000 adjusted basis.
d. A building used in Zeta's business having an original cost of $225,000, a $450,000 FMV, and a $150,000 adjusted basis for taxable income purposes. Zeta has claimed $75,000 of depreciation for taxable income purposes under the straight-line method. Depreciation for E&P purposes is $60,000.
e. An automobile used in Zeta's business having an original cost of $12,000, an $8,000 FMV, and a $5,760 adjusted basis, on which Zeta has claimed $6,240 of MACRS depreciation for taxable income purposes. For E&P purposes, depreciation was $5,200.
f. Installment obligations having a $35,000 face amount (and FMV) and a $24,500 adjusted basis. The obligations were created when Zeta sold a Sec. 1231 asset.

C:4-38 ***Disguised Dividends.*** King Corporation is a profitable manufacturing concern with $800,000 of E&P. It is owned in equal shares by Harry and Wilma, husband and wife. Both individuals are actively involved in the business. Determine the tax consequences of the following independent events:

a. In reviewing a prior year tax return for King, the IRS determines that the $500,000 of salary and bonuses paid to Wilma is unreasonable and that reasonable compensation is $280,000.
b. King loaned Harry $400,000 over the past three years. None of the money has been repaid. Harry does not pay interest on the loans.
c. King sells a building to Wilma for $150,000 in cash. The property has an adjusted basis of $90,000 and is subject to a $60,000 mortgage, which Wilma assumes. The FMV of the building is $350,000.
d. Harry leases a warehouse to King for $50,000 per year. According to an IRS auditor, similar warehouses can be leased for $35,000 per year.
e. Wilma sells to King for $250,000 land on which King intends to build a factory. According to a recent appraisal, the FMV of the land is $185,000.
f. The corporation owns an airplane that it uses to fly executives to business meetings. When the airplane is not being used for business, Harry and Wilma use it to travel to their ranch in Idaho for short vacations. The approximate cost of their trips to the ranch in the current year is $8,000.

C:4-39 ***Unreasonable Compensation.*** Forward Corporation is owned by a group of 15 shareholders. During the current year, Forward pays $550,000 in salary and bonuses to Alvin, its president and controlling shareholder. The corporation's marginal tax rate is 34%, and Alvin's marginal tax rate is 35%. The IRS audits Forward's tax return and determines that reasonable compensation for Alvin is $350,000. Forward agrees to the adjustment. What effect does the disallowance of part of the salary and bonus deduction have on Forward's and Alvin's respective tax positions? Ignore payroll taxes, such as FICA.

C:4-40 ***Stock Dividend Distribution.*** Wilton Corporation has a single class of common stock outstanding. Robert owns 100 shares, which he purchased in 2001 for $100,000. In 2007, when the stock is worth $1,200 per share, Wilton declares a 10% dividend payable in common stock. On December 10, 2007, Robert receives ten additional shares. On January 30, 2008, he sells five of the ten shares for $7,000.

a. How much income must Robert recognize when he receives the stock dividend?
b. How much gain or loss must Robert recognize when he sells the common stock?
c. What is Robert's basis in his remaining common shares? When does his holding period in the new common shares begin?

C:4-41 ***Stock Dividend Distribution.*** Moss Corporation has a single class of common stock outstanding. Tillie owns 1,000 shares, which she purchased in 2003 for $100,000. Moss declares a stock dividend payable in 8% preferred stock having a $100 par value. Each shareholder receives one share of preferred stock for ten shares of common stock. On the distribution date—December 10, 2007—the common stock was worth $180 per share, and the preferred stock was worth $100 per share. On April 1, 2007, Tillie sells half of her preferred stock for $5,000.

a. How much income must Tillie recognize when she receives the stock dividend?
b. How much gain or loss must Tillie recognize when she sells the preferred stock? (Ignore the implications of Sec. 306.)
c. What is Tillie's basis in her remaining common and preferred shares after the sale? When does her holding period for the preferred shares begin?

C:4-42 ***Stock Rights Distribution.*** Trusty Corporation has a single class of common stock outstanding. Jim owns 200 shares, which he purchased for $50 per share two years ago. On April 10 of the current year, Trusty distributes to its common shareholders one right to purchase for $60 one common share for each common share owned. At the time of the distribution, each common share is worth $75, and each right is worth $15. On September 10, Jim sells 100 rights for $2,000 and exercises the remaining 100 rights. On November 10, he sells for $80 each 60 of the shares acquired through exercise of the rights.

a. What are the amount and character of income Jim recognizes upon receiving the rights?
b. What are the amount and character of gain or loss Jim recognizes upon selling the rights?
c. What are the amount and character of gain or loss Jim recognizes upon exercising the rights?
d. What are the amount and character of gain or loss Jim recognizes upon selling the newly acquired common shares?
e. What basis does Jim have in his remaining shares?

C:4-43 ***Attribution Rules.*** George owns 100 of the 1,000 outstanding shares of Polar Corporation common stock. Under the Sec. 318 family attribution rules, to which of the following individuals will ownership of George's stock be attributed?

a. George's wife
b. George's father
c. George's brother
d. George's mother-in-law
e. George's daughter
f. George's son-in law
g. George's grandfather
h. George's grandson
i. George's mother's brother (his uncle)

C:4-44 ***Attribution Rules.*** Moose Corporation's 400 shares of outstanding stock are owned as follows:

Name	*Shares*
Lara (an individual)	60
LMN Partnership (Lara is a 20% partner)	50
LST Partnership (Lara is a 70% partner)	100
Lemon Corporation (Lara is a 30% shareholder)	100
Lime Corporation (Lara is a 60% shareholder)	90
Total	400

How many shares is Lara deemed to own under the Sec. 318 attribution rules?

C:4-45 ***Redemption from a Sole Shareholder.*** Paul owns all 100 shares of Presto Corporation stock. His basis in the stock is $10,000. Presto has $100,000 of E&P. Presto redeems 25 of Paul's shares for $30,000. What are the tax consequences of the redemption to Paul and to Presto?

C:4-46 ***Multiple Redemptions.*** Four unrelated shareholders own Benton Corporation's 400 shares of outstanding stock. Benton redeems 100 shares for $500 per share from the shareholders as shown below. Each shareholder has a $230 per share basis in his or her stock. Benton's current and accumulated E&P at the end of the tax year is $150,000.

Shareholder	*Shares Held Before the Redemption*	*Shares Redeemed*
Ethel	200	40
Fran	100	30
Georgia	50	30
Henry	50	-0-
Total	400	100

a. What are the tax consequences (e.g., basis of remaining shares and amount and character of recognized income, gain, or loss) of the redemptions to Ethel, Fran, and Georgia?
b. How would your answer to Part a change if Ethel is Georgia's mother?

C:4-47 ***Partial Liquidation.*** Unrelated individuals Amy, Beth, and Carla, and Delta Corporation each own 25 of the 100 outstanding shares of Axle Corporation stock. Axle distributes $20,000 cash to each shareholder in exchange for five Axle shares in a transaction that qualifies as a partial liquidation. Each share redeemed has a $1,000 basis to the shareholder and a $4,000 FMV. How does each shareholder treat the distribution for tax purposes?

C:4-48 ***Redemption to Pay Death Taxes.*** John died on March 3. His gross estate of $2.5 million includes First Corporation stock (400 of the 1,000 outstanding shares) worth $1.5 million. John's wife, Myra, owns the remaining 600 shares. Deductible funeral and administrative expenses amount to $250,000. John, Jr. is the sole beneficiary of John's estate. Estate taxes amount to $350,000.
a. Does a redemption of First stock from John's estate, John, Jr., or John's wife qualify for sale treatment under Sec. 303?
b. On September 10, First Corporation redeems 200 shares of its stock from John's estate for $800,000. How does the estate treat this redemption for tax purposes?

C:4-49 ***Effect of Redemption on E&P.*** White Corporation has 100 shares of stock outstanding. Ann owns 40 of these shares, and unrelated shareholders own the remaining 60 shares. White redeems 30 of Ann's shares for $30,000. In the year of the redemption, White has $30,000 of paid-in capital and $80,000 of E&P.
a. How does the redemption affect White's E&P balance if the redemption qualifies for sale treatment?
b. How does the redemption affect White's E&P balance if the redemption does *not* qualify for sale treatment?

C:4-50 ***Various Redemption Issues.*** Alan, Barbara, and Dave are unrelated. Each has owned 100 shares of Time Corporation stock for five years and each has a $60,000 basis in those shares. Time's E&P is $240,000. Time redeems all 100 of Alan's shares for their $100,000 FMV.
a. What are the amount and character of Alan's recognized gain or loss? What basis do Barbara and Dave take in their remaining shares? What effect does the redemption have on Time's E&P?
b. If Alan is Barbara's son, how would your answers to the questions in Part a change?
c. Assume the same facts as in Part b except Alan agrees with the IRS to waive the family attribution rules. Based on this assumption, how would your answers to the questions in Part a again change?

C:4-51 ***Various Redemption Issues.*** Andrew, Bea, Carl, and Carl, Jr. (Carl's son), and Tetra Corporation own all of the single class of Excel Corporation stock as follows:

Shareholder	*Shares Held*	*Adjusted Basis*
Andrew	20	$3,000
Bea	30	6,000
Carl	25	4,000
Carl, Jr.	15	3,000
Tetra Corporation	10	2,000
Total	100	

Andrew, Bea, and Carl are unrelated. Bea owns 75% of the Tetra stock, and Andrew owns the remaining 25%. Excel's E&P is $100,000. Determine the tax consequences of the following independent transactions to the shareholders and Excel:
a. Excel redeems 25 of Bea's shares for $30,000.
b. Excel redeems 10 of Bea's shares for $12,000.
c. Excel redeems all of Carl's shares for $30,000.
d. Assume the same facts as in Part c except the stock is redeemed from Carl's estate to pay death taxes, and the entire redemption qualifies for sale treatment under Sec. 303. The stock has a $28,000 FMV on the date of Carl's death. The alternate valuation date is not elected.
e. Excel redeems all of Andrew's shares for Excel land having a $6,000 basis for both taxable income and E&P purposes and a $24,000 FMV. Assume a 34% marginal corporate tax rate.

f. Assume that Carl owns 25 shares of Excel stock and that Carl, Jr. owns the remaining 75 shares. Determine the tax consequences to Carl and Excel if Excel redeems all 25 of Carl's shares for $30,000.

C:4-52 ***Comparison of Dividends and Redemptions.*** Bailey is one of four equal unrelated shareholders of Checker Corporation. Bailey has held Checker stock for four years and has a basis in her stock of $40,000. Checker has $280,000 of current and accumulated E&P and distributes $100,000 to Bailey.

a. What are the tax consequences to Checker and to Bailey if Bailey is an individual and the distribution is treated as a dividend?
b. In Part a, what would be the tax consequences if Bailey were a corporation?
c. What are the tax consequences to Checker and to Bailey (an individual) if Bailey surrenders all her stock in a redemption qualifying for sale treatment?
d. In Part c, what would be the tax consequences if Bailey were a corporation?
e. Which treatment would Bailey prefer if Bailey were an individual? Which treatment would Bailey Corporation prefer?

C:4-53 ***Preferred Stock Bailout.*** Does Sec. 306 apply in each of the following independent situations? If so, what is its effect?

a. Beth sells her Sec. 306 stock to Marvin in a year in which the issuing corporation has no E&P.
b. Zero Corporation redeems Sec. 306 stock from Jim in a year in which it has no E&P.
c. Zero Corporation redeems Sec. 306 stock from Ruth in a year in which it has a large E&P balance.
d. Joan gives 100 shares of her Sec. 306 stock to her nephew, Barry.
e. Ed completely terminates his interest in Zero Corporation by having Zero redeem all his common and Sec. 306 preferred stock.
f. Carl inherits 100 shares of Sec. 306 stock from his uncle Ted.

C:4-54 ***Preferred Stock Bailout.*** Fran owns all 100 shares of Star Corporation stock. Her stock basis is $60,000. On December 1 of the current year, Star distributes 50 shares of preferred stock to Fran in a nontaxable dividend. In the year of the distribution, Star's total E&P is $100,000, the preferred shares are worth $150,000, and the common shares are worth $300,000.

a. What are the tax consequences to Fran and to Star if Fran sells her preferred stock to Ken for $200,000 on January 10 of the following year? In that year, Star's current E&P is $75,000 (in addition to the $100,000 from the prior year).
b. How would your answer to Part a change if Fran sells her preferred stock to Ken for $110,000 instead of $200,000?
c. How would your answer to Part a change if Star redeems Fran's preferred stock for $200,000 on January 10 of the following year?

C:4-55 ***Brother-Sister Redemptions.*** Bob owns 60 of the 100 outstanding shares of Dazzle Corporation stock and 80 of the 100 outstanding shares of Razzle Corporation stock. Bob's basis in his Dazzle shares is $12,000, and his basis in his Razzle shares is $8,000. Bob sells 30 of his Dazzle shares to Razzle for $50,000. At the end of the year of sale, Dazzle and Razzle have E&P of $25,000 and $40,000, respectively.

a. What are the amount and character of Bob's recognized gain or loss on the sale?
b. What is Bob's basis in his remaining shares of the Dazzle and Razzle stock?
c. How does the sale affect the E&P of Dazzle and Razzle?
d. What basis does Razzle take in the Dazzle shares it purchases?
e. How would your answer to Part a change if Bob owns only 50 of the 100 outstanding shares of Razzle stock?

C:4-56 ***Parent-Subsidiary Redemptions.*** Jane owns 150 of the 200 outstanding shares of Parent Corporation stock. Parent owns 160 of the 200 outstanding shares of Subsidiary Corporation stock. Jane sells 50 shares of her Parent stock to Subsidiary for $40,000. Jane's basis in her Parent shares is $15,000 ($100 per share). At the end of the year of sale, Subsidiary and Parent have E&P of $60,000 and $25,000, respectively.

a. What are the amount and character of Jane's recognized gain or loss on the sale?
b. What is Jane's basis in her remaining shares of Parent stock?
c. How does the sale affect the E&P of Parent and Subsidiary?
d. What basis does Subsidiary take in the Parent shares it purchases?
e. How would your answer to Part a change if Jane instead sells 100 of her Parent shares to Subsidiary for $80,000?

C:4-57 *Bootstrap Acquisition.* Jana owns all 100 shares of Stone Corporation stock having a $1 million FMV. Her basis in the stock is $400,000. Stone's E&P balance is $600,000. Michael would like to purchase the stock but wants only the corporation's non-cash assets valued at $750,000. Michael is willing to pay $750,000 for these assets.

a. What are the tax consequences to Jana, Michael, and Stone if Michael purchases 75 shares of Stone stock for $750,000 and Stone redeems Jana's remaining 25 shares for $250,000 cash?
b. How would your answer to Part a change (if at all) if Stone first redeems 25 shares of Jana's stock for $250,000 and then Michael purchases the remaining 75 shares from Jana for $750,000?

COMPREHENSIVE PROBLEM

C:4-58 Several years ago, Brian formed Sigma Corporation, a retail company ineligible for the U.S. production activities deduction. Sigma uses the accrual method of accounting. In 2007, the corporation reported the following items:

Gross profit	$290,000
Long-term capital gain	20,000
Tax-exempt interest received	7,000
Salary paid to Brian	80,000
Payroll tax on Brian's salary (Sigma's share)	6,000
Depreciation	25,000 ($21,000 for E&P purposes)
Other operation expenses	89,000
Dividend distribution to Brian	60,000

In addition to owning 100% of Sigma's stock, Brian manages Sigma's business and earns the $80,000 salary listed above. This salary is an ordinary and necessary business expense of the corporation and is reasonable in amount. The payroll tax on Brian's $80,000 salary is $12,000, $6,000 of which Sigma pays and deducts, and the other $6,000 of which Brian pays through Social Security (FICA) withholding. Brian is single with no dependents and claims the standard deduction.

a. Compute Sigma's and Brian's 2007 taxable income and total tax liability, as well as their combined tax liability. Also, calculate the corporation's current E&P after the dividend distribution.
b. Assume instead that Brian operates Sigma as a sole proprietorship. In the current year, the business reports the same operating results as above, and Brian withdraws $140,000 in lieu of the salary and dividend. Assume Brian's self-employment tax is $17,000. Compute Brian's total tax liability for 2007.
c. Assume a C corporation such as in Part a distributes all of its after-tax earnings. Compare the tax treatment of long-term capital gains, tax-exempt interest, and operating profits if earned by a C corporation with the tax treatment of these items if earned by a sole proprietorship.

TAX STRATEGY PROBLEM

C:4-59 John owns all 100 shares of stock in Jamaica Corporation, which has $100,000 of current E&P. John would like to receive a $50,000 distribution from the corporation. Jamaica owns the following assets that it could distribute to John. What are the tax consequences of Jamaica's distributing each of the following assets? Assume Jamaica has a 34% marginal tax rate and, unless stated otherwise, its bases for E&P and taxable income purposes are the same.

a. $50,000 cash.
b. 100 shares of XYZ stock purchased two years ago for $10,000 and now worth $50,000.
c. 100 shares of ABC stock purchased one year ago for $72,000 and now worth $50,000.
d. Equipment purchased four years ago for $120,000 that now has a tax adjusted basis of $22,000 and an E&P adjusted basis of $40,000. John would assume a liability of $31,000 on the equipment. The equipment is now worth $81,000.
e. An installment obligation with a face value of $50,000 and a basis of $32,000. Jamaica acquired this obligation three years ago when it sold land held as an investment.
f. Would your answers in Parts a–e change if Jamaica redeems 50 of John's shares for each of the properties listed?
g. Which distribution would you recommend? Which distribution(s) should be avoided?

CASE STUDY PROBLEMS

C:4-60 Amy, Beth, and Meg each own 100 of the 300 outstanding shares of Theta Corporation stock. Amy wants to sell her shares, which have a $40,000 basis and a $100,000 FMV. Either Beth and/or Meg can purchase Amy's shares (50 shares each) or Theta can redeem all of them. Theta has a $150,000 E&P balance.

Required: Write a memorandum comparing the tax consequences of the two options to the three sisters, who are active in managing Theta.

C:4-61 Maria Garcia is a CPA whose firm has for many years prepared the tax returns of Stanley Corporation. A review of Stanley's last three tax returns by a new staff accountant, who has been assigned to the client for the first time, reveals that the corporation may be paying to one of its key officers excessive compensation that the IRS might deem to be a constructive dividend. The staff accountant feels that the firm should inform the IRS and/or report the excess amount as a nondeductible dividend. The facts are sufficiently gray, i.e., reasonable support exists for the assertion that the compensation paid in the current year and prior years is reasonable.

Required: Discuss Maria's role as an advocate for Stanley, and discuss the possible consequences of a subsequent audit.

TAX RESEARCH PROBLEMS

C:4-62 Fifteen years ago, husband and wife Stuart and Marsha Widell organized Widell Engineering Associates (WEA), a Delaware corporation that builds, repairs, and manages waste treatment plants throughout the Southwest. The Widells capitalized WEA with cash of $500,000 and industrial equipment having an adjusted basis of $4.5 million, each in exchange for 2,500 shares of WEA common stock. Three years later, Stuart and Marsha each gifted 500 shares of their WEA stock to their son Weymouth.

As a result of a sharp upswing in the economy, WEA's profits swelled under the joint management of Stuart and Weymouth. After ten years of joint control, however, and because of irreconcilable differences with his father, Weymouth decided to leave WEA and organize his own engineering firm, Fortunelle.

To keep WEA's business in the family and to give Stuart complete WEA management control, Stuart, Marsha, and Weymouth agreed that WEA would redeem all of Weymouth's 1,000 shares with waste treatment property worth $8.5 million. To ensure capital gains treatment, Weymouth obtained a waiver of the family attribution rules in return for an agreement with the IRS not to acquire an equity interest in WEA for ten years and to notify the IRS if he does so. Following the redemption, Weymouth transferred the property to Fortunelle in exchange for all 8,500 shares of Fortunelle common stock.

Last year, Stuart suffered a heart attack. He now has proceeded to reconcile his differences with Weymouth. To retain Widell family control of WEA's business, Stuart, Marsha, and Weymouth propose that WEA and Fortunelle conclude an "arms length" agreement under which Fortunelle would manage WEA's waste treatment plants in return annually for 20% of WEA's gross rental revenues, but no equity interest. The Widells are convinced that the proposed arrangement does not violate either the Sec. 302 waiver rules or Weymouth's agreement with the IRS. They have asked you to draft a letter that confirms this understanding. In researching the issue, consult at a minimum the following authorities:

- IRC Sec. 302(c)(2)
- Rev. Rul. 70-104, 1970 C.B. 66
- *Chertkof v. Commissioner*, 48 AFTR 2d 81-5194, 81-1 USTC ¶9462 (4th Cir, 1981)

C:4-63 When the IRS audited Winter Corporation's 2004 tax return, the IRS disallowed $10,000 of travel and entertainment expenses incurred by Charles, an officer-shareholder, because of inadequate documentation. The IRS asserted that the $10,000 expenditure was a constructive dividend to Charles, who maintained that the expense was business related. Charles argued that he derived no personal benefit from the expenditure and therefore received no constructive dividend. Prepare a memorandum for your tax manager explaining whether the IRS's assertion or Charles's assertion is correct. Your manager has suggested that, at a minimum, you consult the following resources:

- IRC Secs. 162 and 274
- Reg. Secs. 1.274-1 and -2

C:4-64 Scott and Lynn Brown each own 50% of Benson Corporation stock. During the current year, Benson made the following distribution to the shareholders:

Shareholder	*Property Distributed*	*Adjusted Basis to Corporation*	*Property's FMV*
Scott Brown	Land parcel A	$ 40,000	$75,000
Lynn Brown	Land parcel B	120,000	75,000

Benson had E&P of $250,000 immediately before the distribution. Prepare a memorandum for your tax manager explaining how Benson should treat these transactions for tax and financial accounting purposes. How will the two shareholders report the distributions? Assume Benson's marginal tax rate is 34%. Your manager has suggested that, at a minimum, you should consult the following resources:

- IRC Sec 301
- IRC Sec. 311
- IRC Sec. 312
- *Accounting Principles Board Opinion No. 29*

C:4-65 John and Jean own 80% and 20%, respectively, of Plum Corporation stock. Thanks to their hard work, Plum's software sales have sky rocketed. In 2003, Plum's earnings were minimal, but by 2007, Plum grossed $10 million. Plum compensated John and Jean as follows: John received a bonus of 76% of net profits and Jean received a bonus of 19% of net profits at the end of each year. Plum never paid any dividends. Can Plum deduct any or all of the "salaries" paid to John and Jean?

C:4-66 Sara owns 60% of Mayfield Corporation's single class of stock. A group of five family members and three key employees own the remaining 40% of Mayfield stock. Mayfield is a calendar year taxpayer that uses the accrual method of accounting. Sara is a Mayfield officer and director and uses the cash method of accounting. During the period 2004–2006, Sara received the following amounts as salary and tax-free fringe benefits from Mayfield: 2004, $160,000; 2005, $240,000; and 2006, $290,000. She earned these amounts evenly throughout the tax years in question. In 2007, upon auditing Mayfield's tax returns for 2004–2006, a revenue agent determined that reasonable compensation for Sara's services for the three years in question is $110,000, $165,000, and $175,000, respectively. The bylaws of Mayfield were amended on December 15, 2005 to provide that:

> Any payments made to an officer of the corporation, including salary, commissions, bonuses, other forms of compensation, interest, rent, or travel and entertainment expenses incurred, and which shall be disallowed in whole or in part as a deductible expense by the Internal Revenue Service, shall be reimbursed by such officer to the corporation to the full extent of such disallowance.

Following the disallowance of $240,000 of the total salary expense, the board of directors met and requested that Sara reimburse Mayfield for the portion of her salary deemed to be excessive. Because of the large amount of money involved, the board of directors approved an installment plan whereby Sara would repay the $240,000 in five annual installments of $48,000 each over the period 2008–2012. The corporation would not charge Sara interest on the unpaid balance of $240,000. Prepare a memorandum for your tax manager explaining what salary and fringe benefits are taxable to Sara in the period 2004–2006 and what reimbursements Sara can deduct during the period 2008–2012.

5

CHAPTER

OTHER CORPORATE TAX LEVIES

LEARNING OBJECTIVES

After studying this chapter, you should be able to

1. Calculate the corporation's alternative minimum tax liability (if any)
2. Determine whether a corporation is a personal holding company (PHC)
3. Calculate the corporation's PHC tax
4. Determine whether a corporation is liable for the accumulated earnings tax
5. Calculate the corporation's accumulated earnings tax
6. Explain how a corporation can avoid the personal holding company tax
7. Explain how a corporation can avoid the accumulated earnings tax
8. Understand the financial statement implications of the minimum tax credit

CHAPTER OUTLINE

Chapter C:3 examined the corporate income tax and the procedures for calculating, reporting, and paying this tax. Chapter C:5 focuses on the following three additional taxes that may be imposed on a C corporation: (1) the corporate alternative minimum tax, (2) the personal holding company tax, and (3) the accumulated earnings tax. Each additional tax may apply in different situations. A corporation's total tax liability equals the sum of its corporate income tax, alternative minimum tax, and either the accumulated earnings tax or the personal holding company tax (if any). This chapter examines when the additional taxes are likely to be assessed and measures a corporation can take to avoid them.

THE CORPORATE ALTERNATIVE MINIMUM TAX

OBJECTIVE 1

Calculate the corporation's alternative minimum tax liability (if any)

THE GENERAL FORMULA

The purpose of the corporate **alternative minimum tax (AMT)** is similar to that of the individual AMT.[1] It is to ensure that every taxpayer with substantial economic income pays a minimum tax despite its use of exclusions, deductions, and credits to reduce its income tax liability.

The starting point for computing a corporation's AMT is its regular taxable income. Taxable income is increased by tax preference items, modified by adjustments, and reduced by a statutory exemption amount. The resulting tax base is multiplied by 20% to yield the **tentative minimum tax (TMT)**. If the TMT exceeds the corporation's regular tax liability, the excess is the corporation's AMT liability. If the TMT does not exceed the corporation's regular tax, the AMT is zero. Even if a corporation pays no AMT, the AMT nevertheless may restrict its ability to claim certain business credits (see pages C:5-14 and C:5-15). The computation of a corporation's AMT is set forth in Table C:5-1.

REAL-WORLD EXAMPLE

The small corporation AMT exemption will exempt 95% of incorporated businesses from the AMT. The expected tax savings for small corporations are $762 million over the period 1998 to 2007.

For tax years beginning after 1997, the AMT does not apply to small business corporations. A small business corporation is an entity whose average gross receipts are $7.5 million or less for all three-year periods ending before the year for which the corporation claims the exemption.[2] This moving average gross receipts calculation includes only tax years beginning after December 31, 1993 and is reduced to $5 million for the corporation's first three-year period (or portion thereof) that begins after 1993.

EXAMPLE C:5-1 ▶ Ramirez Corporation began business in 1993 and had gross receipts as shown below:

Year	*Gross Receipts*
1993	$2,000,000
1994	$3,000,000
1995	4,000,000
1996	5,000,000
1997	6,000,000
1998	12,000,000

Because Ramirez existed before 1994, its relevant gross receipts begin in 1994. Accordingly, its average gross receipts are as follows:

1994–1996: $4,000,000 = [($3,000,000 + $4,000,000 + $5,000,000) ÷ 3]
1995–1997: $5,000,000 = [($4,000,000 + $5,000,000 + $6,000,000) ÷ 3]
1996–1998: $7,666,667 = [($5,000,000 + $6,000,000 + $12,000,000) ÷ 3]

[1] S corporations are not subject to the corporate AMT. These entities pass their tax adjustments and preferences through to their shareholders.

[2] Sec. 55(e). The exemption also applies to a noncorporate entity that elects to be taxed as a C corporation under the check-the-box regulations. Gross receipts are calculated using the entity's tax year.

▼ TABLE C:5-1
Determination of the Corporate Alternative Minimum Tax Liability

Regular taxable income or loss before NOL deduction	
Plus:	Tax preference items
Plus or minus:	Adjustments to taxable income other than the ACE adjustment, the alternative tax NOL deduction, and the adjustment for the U.S. production activities deduction
Preadjustment AMTI	
Plus or minus:	75% of the difference between pre-adjustment AMTI and adjusted current earnings (ACE)
Minus:	Alternative tax NOL deduction
AMTI before adjustment for the U.S. production activities deduction	
Minus:	Adjustment for the U.S. production activities deduction (if any)
Alternative minimum taxable income (AMTI)	
Minus:	Statutory exemption
Tax base	
Times:	0.20 tax rate
Tentative minimum tax before credits	
Minus:	AMT foreign tax credit (AMT FTC)
Tentative minimum tax (TMT)	
Minus:	Regular (income) tax
Alternative minimum tax (if any) owed (AMT)	

ADDITIONAL COMMENT

The corporate AMT produces little tax revenue. In 2003, AMT collections were $2.3 billion compared to $177 billion for the corporate income tax net of tax credits. Only 9,564 corporations paid the AMT in 2003.

Ramirez qualified as a small corporation in 1998 because its average gross receipts for 1994–1996 did not exceed $5 million and because its average gross receipts for 1995–1997 did not exceed $7.5 million. In 1999, however, Ramirez lost its AMT exemption because average gross receipts for 1996–1998 exceeded $7.5 million. Ramirez cannot reacquire its AMT exemption in later years even if its average gross receipts for a three-year period drop below $7.5 million. ◀

Section 55(e), which provides for the small corporation AMT exemption, references the following Sec. 448(c) operating rules relating to the average gross receipts calculation:

- Gross receipts for any short tax year (for example, an initial year) must be annualized.
- A corporation not in existence for a full three-year period determines average gross receipts for the period it was in existence.
- A controlled group of corporations must be treated as one entity.
- A successor corporation must include the gross receipts of its predecessor. (For example, a newly created subsidiary's gross receipts would include those of its parent corporation).

A corporation created after 1997 is exempt from the corporate AMT for its initial tax year regardless of its gross receipts for that year unless the corporation is aggregated with one or more other corporations under bullet point three above or is considered to be a successor to another corporation. To qualify for the second year, the corporation's gross receipts for the first year must be less than $5 million. To qualify for the third year, the corporation's average gross receipts for the first two years must be less than $7.5 million. To qualify for the fourth year, the corporation's average gross receipts for the first three years must be less than $7.5 million.

EXAMPLE C:5-2 ▶ Rubio Corporation, a calendar year corporation formed on January 1, 2003, has gross receipts as follows:

Year	*Gross Receipts*
2003	$3,000,000
2004	4,000,000
2005	5,000,000
2006	8,000,000
2007	9,000,000

Rubio does not succeed to a pre-existing corporation. In 2003, Rubio is automatically exempt from the corporate AMT under the small corporation rules without regard to its gross receipts. Rubio is exempt from the corporate AMT in 2004 because the gross receipts for its first tax year (2003) did not exceed $5 million.

Rubio must calculate its average gross receipts in subsequent tax years to see whether the small business exemption remains available. Rubio's average gross receipts calculations for subsequent tax years are as follows:

2003–2004: $3,500,000 = [($3,000,000 + $4,000,000) ÷ 2]
2003–2005: $4,000,000 = [($3,000,000 + $4,000,000 + $5,000,000) ÷ 3]
2004–2006: $5,666,667 = [($4,000,000 + $5,000,000 + $8,000,000) ÷ 3]
2005–2007: $7,333,333 = [($5,000,000 + $8,000,000 + $9,000,000) ÷ 3]

Rubio maintains its exemption in 2005 because its average gross receipts for 2003–2004 do not exceed $7.5 million. Similarly, Rubio continues to qualify in 2006, 2007, and 2008 because its average gross receipts for each preceding three-year period (2003–2005, 2004–2006, and 2005–2007, respectively) do not exceed $7.5 million. The consistent increase in gross receipts, however, makes it unlikely that Rubio will retain its exemption after 2008. ◀

Note that the moving average test is based on gross receipts, not gross income or taxable income. Gross receipts is not reduced by cost of goods sold and includes services income, investment income, and gains and losses (net of the property's adjusted basis). Thus, a corporation with substantial gross receipts and substantial expenses could be subject to the AMT even though it might have a low level of taxable income.

Firms not eligible for the small corporation AMT exemption because their gross receipts exceed the $5 or $7.5 million threshold nevertheless can take advantage of the $40,000 statutory exemption discussed in the Definitions section below.

A corporation that loses its small corporation status because its average gross receipts exceed the statutory ceiling becomes liable for the AMT. The AMT for such a corporation includes only tax preference items and adjustments reflecting transactions conducted and investments made after the corporation lost its small corporation status. The calculation of this AMT, as well as a special AMT credit available for such corporations, is beyond the scope of this chapter.

ADDITIONAL COMMENT

Relative to the regular tax, the AMT results in an acceleration of income recognition. This acceleration is accomplished by adding back tax preference items and making other adjustments to taxable income in deriving AMTI. Even though the AMT rate (20%) is lower than the top corporate income tax rate (35%), the AMT results in a higher tax liability for some corporations because their AMT base is larger than their regular tax base.

DEFINITIONS

This section defines the terms used in the AMT computation.[3]

ALTERNATIVE MINIMUM TAXABLE INCOME (AMTI). **Alternative minimum taxable income** is the corporation's taxable income (1) increased by tax preference items, (2) adjusted (either upward or downward) for income, gain, deduction, and loss items that must be recomputed under the AMT, (3) increased or decreased by 75% of the difference between pre-adjustment AMTI and adjusted current earnings (ACE), and (4) reduced by the alternative tax NOL deduction.

[3] Sec. 55.

STATUTORY EXEMPTION AMOUNT. AMTI is reduced by a statutory exemption amount to derive the AMT tax base. This amount is $40,000, reduced by 25% of the amount (if any) by which AMTI exceeds $150,000. The statutory exemption is phased out when AMTI reaches $310,000.

EXAMPLE C:5-3 ▶ Yellow Corporation's AMTI is $200,000. Because its AMTI exceeds $150,000, its exemption amount is reduced to $27,500 {$40,000 − [0.25 × ($200,000 − $150,000)]}.[4] ◀

TENTATIVE MINIMUM TAX (TMT). The tentative minimum tax is calculated by multiplying the corporation's AMTI, less the statutory exemption amount, by 20%. The corporation then applies foreign tax credits allowable under the AMT (AMT FTCs).[5]

REGULAR TAX. The corporation's **regular tax** is its tax liability for income tax purposes, reduced by foreign tax credits and possession tax credits, but not by other tax credits.

ALTERNATIVE MINIMUM TAX. The AMT equals the amount by which a corporation's TMT exceeds its regular tax for the year.

The following example illustrates the AMT computation.

EXAMPLE C:5-4 ▶ Badger Corporation has $400,000 of taxable income. It also has $350,000 of tax preference items and $250,000 of positive AMT adjustments. It has no available tax credits. Badger's regular tax liability is $136,000 (0.34 × $400,000). Badger's AMTI is $1 million ($400,000 taxable income + $250,000 AMT adjustments + $350,000 tax preferences). Its statutory exemption is zero because AMTI exceeds $310,000 (i.e., the complete phase-out threshold). Therefore, its AMT tax base (i.e., AMTI minus the zero statutory exemption) also is $1 million. The corporation's TMT is $200,000 (0.20 × $1,000,000). Badger's AMT liability is $64,000 ($200,000 − $136,000 regular tax liability). Thus, Badger must pay a total federal tax of $200,000 ($136,000 + $64,000). ◀

STOP & THINK

Question: In the preceding example, Badger Corporation pays both the regular tax and the AMT. How is this result possible if the regular tax rate for corporations with less than $10 million of taxable income is 34% while the AMT rate is a flat 20%?

Solution: The result is possible because different tax bases are used to calculate the two tax amounts. The regular tax calculation is based on regular taxable income while the AMT calculation is based on alternative minimum taxable income less a statutory exemption. A corporation owes the AMT when its TMT exceeds its regular tax liability. The circumstance in which a corporation will owe the AMT can be expressed as follows:

$$[\text{Taxable Income (TI)} + \text{Preferences (P)} \pm \text{Adjustments (A)}] \times 0.20 > \text{TI} \times 0.34$$

Both sides of the inequality can be reformulated as follows:

$$0.20\,(\text{P} \pm \text{A}) > 0.14\ \text{TI}$$

$$(\text{P} \pm \text{A}) > 0.70\ \text{TI}$$

In Example C:5-4, where Badger is liable for the AMT, its preference items and positive adjustments are $350,000 and $250,000, respectively, or $600,000 in total. Seventy percent of taxable income equals $280,000 (0.70 × $400,000). Thus, the general relationship between (P ± A) and TI holds in our example.[a]

[a] The relationship between (P ± A) and TI may be different if the corporation is subject to a marginal income tax rate lower (e.g., 15% or 25%) or higher (e.g., 35%, 38%, or 39%) than the 34% marginal income tax rate used above.

[4] In the examples, assume that all corporations are C corporations that do not qualify as small corporations for AMT purposes.

[5] Sec. 55(b).

TYPICAL MISCONCEPTION

Tax preference items always increase AMTI. As noted in the text below, adjustments can increase or decrease AMTI.

TAX PREFERENCE ITEMS

Tax preference items that must be added to a corporation's regular taxable income to derive its AMTI include[6]

- The excess of the depletion deduction allowable for the tax year over the adjusted basis of the depletable property at the end of the tax year (excluding the current year's depletion deduction).[7]
- The amount by which excess intangible drilling and development costs (IDCs) incurred in connection with oil, gas, and geothermal wells exceeds 65% of the net income from such property.[8]
- Tax-exempt interest on certain private activity bonds issued after August 8, 1986. Although the interest on private activity bonds is tax-exempt for regular tax purposes, it is not exempt for AMT purposes.[9]
- The excess of accelerated depreciation on real property for the tax year over a straight-line depreciation amount based on either the property's useful life or a special ACRS recovery period. This preference item applies only to real property placed in service before 1987.

ADDITIONAL COMMENT

Each year, the amount of real property tax preference due to accelerated depreciation declines as the property ages. For most pre-1987 properties, this amount is zero in 2006.

EXAMPLE C:5-5 ▶ Duffy Corporation mines iron ore in the upper peninsula of Michigan. The adjusted basis in one of its properties has been fully recovered by depletion deductions claimed in previous years. Current year gross income and regular taxable income earned from the sale of ore extracted from this property are $125,000, and $45,000, respectively. The iron ore depletion percentage is 15%. Percentage depletion is $18,750 ($125,000 × 0.15) because it is less than the 50% of taxable income ceiling ($22,500 = $45,000 × 0.50). All the percentage depletion is deductible for regular tax purposes. For AMT purposes, however, the entire percentage depletion amount is a tax preference item because the property's basis already has been reduced to zero. Including this item in the AMTI calculation reduces the depletion deduction to zero. ◀

EXAMPLE C:5-6 ▶ Salek Corporation earns the following interest income in the current year:

Source	*Amount*
IBM corporate bonds	$25,000
Wayne County School District bonds	30,000
City of Detroit bonds	15,000

The City of Detroit bonds were issued several years ago to finance a parking garage, where 35% of the space is leased exclusively to a nonexempt corporation. Thus, the bonds are considered to be private activity bonds. The Wayne County bonds were issued to renovate existing school facilities. Interest earned on the IBM bonds is taxable because the bonds are obligations of a private corporation. Only interest earned on the City of Detroit bonds is a tax preference item because, in contrast to the school district bond proceeds, the municipal bond proceeds were used to finance a private activity. ◀

ADJUSTMENTS TO TAXABLE INCOME

While tax preference items always *increase* taxable income, adjustments may either *increase* or *decrease* taxable income because they require a recomputation of certain income, gain, loss, and deduction items. Common adjustments are presented below.[10]

---

[6] Sec. 57(a).

[7] The percentage depletion preference was repealed for oil and gas depletion claimed by independent producers and royalty owners for 1993 and later tax years. The oil and gas percentage depletion preference applies almost exclusively to integrated oil companies.

[8] The oil and gas excess IDC preference was repealed for independent producers for 1993 and later years but continues to apply to integrated oil companies. Excess IDCs are the amount by which IDCs arising in the tax year exceed the deduction that would have been allowable if the IDCs had been capitalized and amortized under the straight-line method over a ten-year period.

[9] A private activity bond is a debt obligation the proceeds of which are used wholly or partially for activities unrelated to a governmental use (for example, bond proceeds to construct a sports facility used by professional football and other sports teams for their at-home games).

[10] Sec. 56(a).

DEPRECIATION. Different depreciation rules are used for computing taxable income and for computing AMTI.

- *Depreciation on real property placed in service after 1986 and before 1999*. For AMT purposes, the taxpayer must use the alternative depreciation system under Sec. 168(g). Annually, taxable income is increased by the excess of regular tax depreciation over AMT depreciation and is decreased by the excess of AMT depreciation over regular tax depreciation. See depreciation Tables 7–9 in Appendix C for regular tax depreciation rates and Table 12 for AMT depreciation rates.
- *Depreciation on real property placed in service after 1998*. No adjustments are required for this class of property because regular tax depreciation and AMT depreciation are the same.
- *Depreciation on personal property placed in service after 1986 and before 1999*. For AMT purposes, the taxpayer must use the alternative depreciation system under Sec. 168(g). While regular tax depreciation ordinarily is calculated under a 200% declining balance method (with a switch to straight-line) over the property's general depreciation recovery period, AMT depreciation requires a 150% declining balance method (with a switch to straight-line) over the property's class life, as determined under Sec. 168(g)(3) and related IRS pronouncements. If these authorities do not specify a class life for an item of personal property, its class life is deemed to be 12 years. If the taxpayer elected the straight-line method or the alternative depreciation system for regular tax purposes, no AMT adjustments are required. For property depreciated under the half-year convention, see depreciation Table 1 in Appendix C for regular tax rates and depreciation Table 10 for AMT rates.
- *Depreciation on personal property placed in service after 1998 but before September 11, 2001, or placed in service after 2004*. For AMT purposes, the taxpayer must use the 150% declining balance method (with a switch to straight-line) over the property's general depreciation recovery period. Thus, the taxpayer uses the same recovery period for both regular tax and AMT purposes. However, the taxpayer uses the 200% declining balance method to calculate regular tax depreciation and the 150% declining balance method to calculate AMT depreciation. If the taxpayer elects the straight-line method or 150% declining balance method for regular tax purposes, no AMT adjustments are required. For property depreciated under the half-year convention, see depreciation Table 1 in Appendix C for regular tax rates and depreciation Table 10 for AMT rates.
- *Depreciation on qualified personal property placed in service after September 10, 2001, and before January 1, 2005*. Depreciation on *new* personal property with a MACRS class life of 20 years or less is calculated under the 200% declining balance method (with a switch to straight-line). No adjustments to the general MACRS cost recovery period and cost recovery method are required for AMT purposes. This "AMT relief rule" applied to all property eligible for the additional first-year 50% (or 30%) bonus depreciation allowance (discussed below).[11]

EXAMPLE C:5-7 ▶ Early in 2005, Bulldog Corporation placed into service new office furniture costing $3,000 and having a ten-year class life. The corporation did not elect Sec. 179 expensing for this property. Even though the furniture's class life is ten years, the property's tax recovery period is seven years under both the MACRS General Depreciation System for regular tax purposes and the MACRS Alternative Depreciation System for AMTI purposes. Regular tax depreciation was $429 [$3,000 × 0.1429 (Table 1, Appendix C)] in the first year under the half-year convention, and AMTI depreciation was $321 [$3,000 × 0.1071 (Table 10, Appendix C)]. The smaller AMTI depreciation resulted in a $108 ($429 – $321) positive adjustment to taxable income. Toward the end of the recovery period, the depreciation adjustment becomes negative. For example, in 2010, regular tax depreciation is $268 ($3,000 × 0.0892) while AMTI depreciation is $368 ($3,000 × 0.1225). Thus, a negative $100 ($268 – $368) adjustment results. ◀

---

[11] Sec. 168(k)(2)(F).

Depreciation on certain classes of "qualified property" (primarily computer software and personal property with a MACRS class life of 20 years or less) acquired after May 5, 2003, and before January 1, 2005, included a special 50% initial year depreciation allowance. (The percentage was 30% for qualified property placed in service after September 10, 2001, but before May 6, 2003.) This "bonus depreciation" provision applied only to *new* MACRS property acquired between the above dates and placed in service before January 1, 2005. The 50% bonus depreciation could be used even if the taxpayer did not elect Sec. 179 expensing. If both the 50% bonus depreciation rule and Sec. 179 expensing provision applied to an item of personal property, the Sec. 179 expensing provision applied first. Then, the 50% bonus depreciation rule applied to cost minus the Sec. 179 expense. Finally, the regular MACRS depreciation percentages applied to the remaining adjusted basis. For these classes of property, the Sec. 179 expensing rule, 50% bonus depreciation provision, and general MACRS cost recovery periods and methods also applied for AMT purposes.

EXAMPLE C:5-8 ▶ On April 3, 2004, Brighton Corporation purchased $252,000 of new MACRS five-year property. It placed the property in service on May 7, 2004. In 2004, Brighton could expense $102,000 under Sec. 179. In addition, it could claim an additional 50% bonus depreciation, or $75,000 ($150,000 × 0.50), on the adjusted basis that remained after expensing. Also in 2004, the corporation could claim regular MACRS depreciation on the $75,000 ($252,000 − $102,000 − $75,000) that remained after subtracting the 50% bonus depreciation. Thus, for regular tax purposes, first-year MACRS depreciation was $15,000 ($75,000 × 0.20), and total first-year depreciation and expensing was $192,000 ($102,000 + $75,000 + $15,000). Because the property was "qualified property" placed in service after September 10, 2001, total depreciation and expensing for AMT purposes also was $192,000. Thus, in 2004 the corporation had no AMT adjustment for depreciation on this property and will have no adjustment for this property in subsequent years. ◀

BASIS CALCULATIONS. For property depreciated under different methods for regular tax and AMT purposes, separate regular tax and AMT gain or loss calculations are necessary when the taxpayer disposes the property. A depreciable property's basis for regular tax purposes is adjusted downward by the regular tax depreciation allowance. A depreciable property's basis for AMT purposes is adjusted downward by the AMT depreciation allowance. Therefore, an asset may have different bases for regular tax and AMT purposes. An adjustment is made to reflect the difference between the amount of gain or loss recognized for taxable income purposes and for AMTI purposes. The adjustment calculation is illustrated in the following example.

EXAMPLE C:5-9 ▶ Assume the same facts as in Example C:5-7 except that on April 1 of the fourth year Bulldog Corporation sells the property for $2,000. The depreciation allowances claimed for regular tax and AMT purposes, adjusted bases of the property at the beginning of the year, and the positive or negative adjustment to taxable income in deriving AMTI for each of the four years are presented below.

	Regular Tax			AMT			
Year	*1/1 Adj. Basis (1)*	*Depr. (2)*	*12/31 Adj. Basis (3)*[a]	*1/1 Adj. Basis (4)*	*Depr. (5)*	*12/31 Adj. Basis (6)*[b]	*Taxable Income Adjustment(7)*[c]
1	$3,000	$ 429	$2,571	$3,000	$ 321	$2,679	$108
2	2,571	735	1,836	2,679	574	2,105	161
3	1,836	525	1,311	2,105	451	1,654	74
4	1,311	187	1,124	1,654	184	1,470	3
		$1,876			$1,714		$346

[a] (3) = (1) − (2) Adjusted basis for sale date is reduced for the depreciation claimed in Year 4.
[b] (6) = (4) − (5) Six months of depreciation is claimed in years 1 and 4.
[c] (7) = (2) − (5)

Bulldog recognizes an $876 ($2,000 proceeds − $1,124 adjusted basis) gain in Year 4 for regular tax purposes and a $530 ($2,000 proceeds − $1,470 adjusted basis) gain for AMT purposes.

This difference necessitates a $346 negative adjustment to taxable income when computing AMTI to take into account the different depreciation allowances claimed in the four years. The basis adjustment is the net of the aggregate positive and negative depreciation adjustments for the four years. ◀

INSTALLMENT SALES. When calculating taxable income and AMTI, the corporation may use the installment method to report sales of noninventory property.

LONG-TERM CONTRACTS ENTERED INTO AFTER MARCH 1, 1986. These contracts must be accounted for under the percentage of completion method. When determining AMTI, corporations using the percentage of completion-capitalized cost or cash methods of accounting for regular tax purposes must make adjustments.

LOSS LIMITATIONS. Closely held corporations and personal service corporations must recalculate at-risk and passive activity losses, taking into account the corporation's AMTI adjustments and tax preference items.

NOL DEDUCTIONS. The regular tax NOL deduction is replaced with the alternative tax NOL deduction. To compute the alternative tax NOL deduction, the regular tax NOL deduction is adjusted in the same way that regular taxable income is adjusted to derive AMTI. The regular tax NOL is reduced by adding back any tax preference items and any losses disallowed under the passive activity and at-risk rules. Adjustments may either increase or decrease the regular tax NOL in deriving the alternative tax NOL. Generally, the amount of the alternative tax NOL differs from that of the regular tax NOL because of these adjustments. The resulting alternative tax NOL carries back two years and forward 20 years. The alternative tax NOL deduction cannot exceed 90% of AMTI before the alternative tax NOL deduction.

U.S. PRODUCTION ACTIVITIES DEDUCTION. Taxable income (the starting point for calculating AMTI) is net of the U.S. production activities deduction. For regular tax purposes, the deduction is 6% (in 2007) times the lesser of qualified production activities income or taxable income before the deduction (see Chapter C:3). For AMTI purposes, however, the computation is based on the lesser of qualified production activities income or AMTI before the deduction.[12] Thus, if qualified production activities income is less than regular taxable income and regular taxable income is less than AMTI, no adjustment will apply because the deduction will be the same for both purposes. On the other hand, an AMT adjustment could apply if regular taxable income is less than qualified production activities income because the smaller regular taxable income amount would be the base for regular tax purposes while either AMTI or qualified production activities income would be the base for AMTI purposes. For example, if AMTI exceeds regular taxable income (both before the deduction) and qualified production activities income falls between these two amounts, the U.S. production activities deduction is 6% of regular taxable income and 6% of qualified production activities income for AMTI purposes, thereby leading to a negative AMT adjustment.

The following example illustrates the computation of **preadjustment AMTI** (see Table C:5-1). Preadjustment AMTI will be a component of the ACE and AMTI calculations presented later.

EXAMPLE C:5-10 ▶ Marion Corporation engages in copper mining activities. In the current year, it reports $300,000 of regular taxable income, which takes into account deductions of $70,000 for percentage depletion and $80,000 for MACRS depreciation. Of the percentage depletion claimed, $30,000 exceeded the adjusted basis of the depletable property. The hypothetical AMT depreciation deduction under the alternative depreciation system would have been only $55,000. Preadjustment AMTI is calculated as follows:

[12] Sec. 199(d)(6).

Regular taxable income		$300,000
Plus:	Percentage depletion in excess of basis	30,000
	MACRS depreciation	80,000
Minus:	AMTI depreciation	(55,000)
Preadjustment AMTI		$355,000

The depreciation adjustment results in an AMTI increase of $25,000 ($80,000 − $55,000). ◀

HISTORICAL NOTE

The ACE adjustment involves a complex computation. It was added in an attempt to further adjust the AMT tax base toward the corporation's economic income. However, the ACE adjustment, as initially enacted by the Tax Reform Act of 1986, would have been much more complicated. The single most important simplification is that depreciation based on ACE does not include the present value depreciation computations required by the 1986 Act.

ADJUSTED CURRENT EARNINGS (ACE) ADJUSTMENT

A corporation makes a positive adjustment equal to 75% of preadjustment AMTI, which is the excess of ACE over AMTI (before this adjustment and the alternative tax NOL deduction). ACE is based on a concept of earnings and profits (E&P) used to determine whether a corporate distribution is a dividend or a return of capital (see Chapter C:4). ACE equals preadjustment AMTI for the tax year plus or minus a series of special adjustments described below. However, ACE is not the same as E&P even though many items are treated in the same manner for both purposes. The ACE adjustment is not required of S corporations since the AMT tax preferences and adjustments flow through to their noncorporate shareholders.[13] A $1 positive ACE adjustment results in a 15% (0.20 statutory rate × 0.75 inclusion ratio) effective tax rate if the corporation's TMT (before the ACE adjustment) exceeds its regular tax amount.

A negative adjustment equal to 75% of the excess of the corporation's preadjustment AMTI over its ACE also is permitted. This adjustment, however, cannot exceed the cumulative net amount of the corporation's positive and negative ACE adjustments in all post-1989 tax years.[14] Any excess of preadjustment AMTI over ACE not allowed as a negative adjustment because of the limitation cannot be carried over to a later year to reduce a required positive ACE adjustment.

EXAMPLE C:5-11 ▶ Bravo Corporation, which was formed in 2005, reports the following ACE and preadjustment AMTI amounts for 2005–2007.

	2005	*2006*	*2007*
ACE	$2,000	$1,500	$1,000
Preadjustment AMTI	1,500	1,500	1,500

The corporation makes a $375 [($2,000 − $1,500) × 0.75] positive ACE adjustment in 2005. It makes no ACE adjustment in 2006 because ACE and preadjustment AMTI are the same. It makes a $375 [($1,000 − $1,500) × 0.75] negative ACE adjustment in 2007. The total ACE adjustments over the three years is zero. ◀

EXAMPLE C:5-12 ▶ Assume the same facts as in Example C:5-11 except the preadjustment AMTI amount in 2007 is $2,000. The tentative negative ACE adjustment is $750 [($1,000 − $2,000) × 0.75]. Only a $375 negative ACE adjustment can be made because the negative ACE adjustment may not exceed the $375 ($375 + $0) total cumulative net positive ACE adjustments made in prior years. ◀

Four general rules provide a framework for the ACE calculation:

- Any amount that is permanently excluded from gross income when computing AMTI, but which is taken into account in determining E&P, is included in gross income for ACE purposes (e.g., interest on tax-exempt bonds other than private activity bonds, and life insurance proceeds). The adjustment is reduced by any deduction that would have been allowable in computing AMTI had the excluded income amount been included in gross income for AMTI purposes. No adjustment is made for timing differences. Thus, any item that is, has been, or will be included in preadjustment AMTI will not be included in the ACE adjustment.

[13] Sec. 56(g)(6).

[14] Sec. 56(g)(2).

TYPICAL MISCONCEPTION

Interest on certain state and local government obligations has traditionally not been subject to the federal income tax. However, to the extent that a corporation's tax-exempt income is not already included in AMTI as a preference item (e.g., interest income on private activity bonds), 75% of such income is subjected to the AMT through the ACE adjustment. If the corporation's TMT exceeds its regular tax before the ACE adjustment, a 15% (20% × 75%) effective tax rate is imposed on the otherwise tax-exempt bond interest income. State and local governments have expressed concern over this aspect of the ACE adjustment, which they view as an impediment to their ability to raise capital.

- A deduction for any expense, loss, or other item not deductible in the tax year when computing E&P cannot be claimed when computing ACE even if such item already has been deducted in determining preadjustment AMTI. These items result in a positive adjustment to ACE to the extent they already have been deducted in determining pre-adjustment AMTI.[15] Special rules apply for the dividends-received deduction. The 80% and 100% dividends-received deductions are allowed for ACE purposes although they cannot be claimed when computing E&P. The 70% dividends-received deduction, however, is not allowed for either ACE or E&P purposes. Also, the U.S. production activities deduction is allowed for ACE purposes even though not allowed for E&P purposes. Thus, like the 80% and 100% dividends-received deduction, this deduction results in no ACE adjustment.
- Income items included in preadjustment AMTI are included in ACE even if the items are excluded from E&P.
- Items not deductible in determining preadjustment AMTI are not deducted when computing ACE even if the items are deductible in deriving E&P. Examples include federal income taxes and capital losses that exceed capital gains.[16]

In addition to the four general rules, a series of specific adjustments mandated by Sec. 56(g) must be made to AMTI to derive ACE. The more common adjustments are discussed below. As with the general AMT adjustments set forth above, these items require a recomputation of certain income, gain, loss, and deduction items and may either increase or decrease AMTI. Unless otherwise indicated, these changes are effective for tax years beginning after 1989.

ADDITIONAL COMMENT

The ACE depreciation adjustment was the single largest ACE adjustment for tax years 1990–1993. Elimination of the need to make such an adjustment for property placed in service in 1994 and later tax years reduces both the taxpayer's expense incurred in calculating the adjustment and the government's revenues from the AMT.

- Depreciation on property placed in service in a tax year after 1989 and before January 1, 1994, is determined under the alternative depreciation system. All property is depreciated under the straight-line method, the appropriate recovery period, and averaging convention prescribed in the alternative depreciation system.[17] Elimination of the ACE depreciation adjustment for property placed in service after December 31, 1993, does not preclude a corporation from having to make the adjustment for property placed in service before 1994. Special transitional rules apply for property placed in service before 1990.
- An asset's adjusted basis is determined according to the depreciation, depletion, or amortization rules applicable in the ACE calculation. As a result, a basis adjustment similar to that described above for the AMTI calculation may be required when an asset is sold, exchanged, or otherwise disposed of.[18]
- When calculating ACE, the gain realized on an installment sale of noninventory property is fully recognized in the year of sale.[19]

ADDITIONAL COMMENT

Even if a corporation is not currently subject to the AMT, the AMT depreciation amounts should be calculated annually. A less efficient and more costly approach is to wait until the AMT applies and then try to compute the appropriate depreciation numbers for past years.

- Organizational expenditures otherwise amortizable under Sec. 248 are not amortized for ACE purposes if made after December 31, 1989.[20]
- The increase or decrease in the annual LIFO recapture amount increases or decreases ACE. LIFO recapture is the amount by which ending inventory under the first-in, first-out (FIFO) method exceeds ending inventory under the last-in, first-out (LIFO) method.[21] This adjustment effectively converts the corporation's inventory method from LIFO to FIFO for ACE purposes.
- Depletion on property placed in service after 1989 is determined under the cost method.[22] Intangible drilling costs must be amortized over 60 months beginning with the month in which they are paid or incurred.
- Taxpayers must recalculate charitable contribution and percentage depletion deduction limits to take into account AMT adjustment and preference items.[23] They also

---

[15] Secs. 56(g)(4)(C)(i) and (ii). A partial list of items falling into this category is presented in Reg. Sec. 1.56(g)-1(d)(3) and (4).
[16] Reg. Sec. 1.56(g)-1(e).
[17] Sec. 56(g)(4)(A).
[18] Sec. 56(g)(4)(I).
[19] Sec. 56(g)(4)(D)(iv).
[20] Sec. 56(g)(4)(D)(ii).
[21] Secs. 56(g)(4)(D)(iii) and 312(n)(4).
[22] Sec. 56(g)(4)(G).
[23] Ltr. Rul. 9320003 (February 1, 1993). Because the IRS treats the AMT as a parallel tax system independent of the regular tax system, any deduction expressed as a percentage of regular taxable income must be recalculated for AMT purposes.

must separately account for carryovers for regular tax and AMT purposes. Corporations, in particular, must determine separate charitable contribution limits and carryovers for AMTI and ACE purposes. For many corporations, the AMTI and ACE charitable contribution limits will be higher than the regular tax limit because their ACE and AMT adjusted taxable income counterparts are usually larger.

Topic Review C:5-1 summarizes the ACE calculation.

STOP & THINK *Question:* Flair Corporation was considering investing in state government obligations. Flair's Chief Financial Officer (CFO) knew that the interest earned on these obligations is exempt from federal income tax. She also knew that the state in which Flair operates exempts from the state income tax interest earned on state and local bonds issued by the state. The CFO was surprised to discover that the so-called tax-exempt interest could be taxed by the federal government at a rate of up to 20% if earned by a corporation. She called her CPA to find out how this could occur. What did the CPA say?

Solution: If the debt obligation is a private activity bond issued after 1986, the interest income constitutes a tax preference item. One would expect $1 of interest income to increase the AMT tax base by $1 and the AMT by $0.20. However, under the corporate alternative minimum tax scheme, $1 of interest income that is a tax preference item can produce one of the following results:

Tenative Minimum Tax		
Excluding Tax-Exempt Interest Income	*Including Tax-Exempt Interest Income*	*Additional Tax on $1 of Tax-Exempt Interest Income*
TMT > regular tax	TMT > regular tax	$0.20
TMT < regular tax	TMT < regular tax	$0.00
TMT < regular tax	TMT > regular tax	$0.00 to $0.20

Topic Review C:5-1

Summary of Common Alternative Minimum Tax Adjustments

Income/Expense Item	Most Common Adjustment To:[a] Regular Taxable Income to Derive AMTI	Preadjustment AMTI to Derive ACE
Tax-exempt interest:		
Private activity bonds	Increase	None
Other bonds	None	Increase
Life insurance proceeds	None	Increase
Deferred gain on nondealer installment sales	None	Increase
LIFO inventory adjustment	None	Increase
"Basis adjustment" on asset sale	Decrease	Decrease
Depreciation	Increase	Increase
Excess charitable contributions	Decrease	Decrease
Excess capital losses	None	None
Dividends-received deduction:		
80% and 100% DRD	None	None
70% DRD	None	Increase
U.S. production activities deduction	None or Decrease	None
Organizational expenditure amortization	None	Increase
Federal income taxes	None	None
Penalties and fines	None	None
Disallowed travel and entertainment expenses and club dues	None	None

[a] Adjustments such as depreciation may increase or decrease taxable income in deriving AMTI and ACE.

If the interest income is not a tax preference item, only 75% of the interest is included in the ACE adjustment. The \$0.20 additional tax ceiling on \$1 of interest from private activity obligations is reduced to \$0.15 (0.75 × \$0.20) for tax-exempt interest earned on debt obligations other than private activity obligations.

COMPREHENSIVE EXAMPLE. Glidden Corporation is not eligible for the small corporation AMT exemption. Using the accrual method, Glidden reported the following taxable income and tax liability data for 2006:

Gross profit from sales	\$300,000
Dividends: From 20%-owned corporation	10,000
From 10%-owned corporation	20,000
Gain on sale of depreciable property	12,778
Gain on installment sale of land	25,000
Gross income	\$367,778
Operating expenses	(175,000)
Depreciation	(40,000)
Amortization of organizational expenditures	(2,500)
Dividends-received deduction	(22,000)
Total deductions	(\$239,500)
Taxable income	\$128,278
Regular tax	\$ 33,278

REAL-WORLD EXAMPLE

An interesting Web site devoted to the AMT is *http://www.reformamt.org.*

Assume the following additional facts:

- The corporation earned tax-exempt bond interest of \$15,000. The bonds are not private activity obligations.
- Upon the death of an executive, the corporation received life insurance proceeds of \$100,000.
- On January 30 of the current year, the corporation sold the land for a total gain of \$77,000, of which it reported \$25,000 under the installment method for regular tax purposes. Glidden is not a dealer, and it pays no interest on the taxes owed on the deferred gain.
- The gain reported for AMTI and ACE purposes on the sale of depreciable property is \$5,860.
- Depreciation for AMTI and ACE purposes is \$32,500. All of Glidden's depreciable assets were placed in service between 1998 and 2003. Some of the assets were used in a predecessor proprietorship incorporated in 2001.
- The corporation incurred organizational expenditures in 2002, which are amortized over a 60-month period for regular tax purposes because they occurred before October 23, 2004.

Preadjustment AMTI is calculated as follows:

Taxable income	\$128,278
Plus: Depreciation adjustment	7,500[a]
Minus: Basis adjustment on machine sale	(6,918)[b]
Preadjustment AMTI	\$128,860

[a] \$40,000 − \$32,500 = \$7,500.
[b] \$12,778 − \$5,860 = \$6,918.

AMTI depreciation is less than regular taxable income depreciation because of different depreciation methods. The gain on the depreciable property sale is smaller for preadjustment AMTI and ACE purposes than for regular taxable income purposes because depreciation claimed for AMTI and ACE purposes was calculated under the alternative depreciation system. The corporation makes no adjustment for the \$52,000 deferred gain on the installment sale because it can use the installment method to report sales of noninventory property when calculating both regular taxable income and AMTI.

Adjusted current earnings (ACE) is calculated as follows:

Preadjustment AMTI	$128,860
Plus: Tax-exempt bond interest	15,000
Life insurance proceeds	100,000
Deferred gain on land sale	52,000
Organizational expenditures adjustment	2,500
Dividends-received deduction adjustment	14,000
Adjusted current earnings	$312,360

The life insurance proceeds and the tax-exempt bond interest are included only in the ACE calculation. Part of the gain on the land sale under the installment method is included in taxable income and preadjustment AMTI. The entire gain is reported for ACE purposes in the year of sale because dealers or nondealers may not use the installment method for ACE purposes except where interest is charged for the tax deferral privilege. No deduction is allowed for ACE purposes for either the amortization of the organizational expenditures or the 70% deduction otherwise allowed for dividends received from a 10%-owned corporation.

The AMT liability is calculated as follows:

Preadjustment AMTI		$128,860
Plus: ACE	$312,360	
Minus: Preadjustment AMTI	(128,860)	
Difference	$183,500	
Times: 75% inclusion ratio	× 0.75	137,625
Alternative minimum taxable income		$266,485
Minus: Statutory exemption		(10,879)[a]
AMT base		$255,606
Times: 20% tax rate		× 0.20
Tentative minimum tax		$ 51,121
Minus: Regular tax		(33,278)
Alternative minimum tax		$ 17,843

[a] $40,000 – [0.25 × ($266,485 – $150,000)] = $10,879.

The statutory exemption is reduced because AMTI exceeds $150,000. The AMT liability is the excess of the tentative minimum tax over the regular tax. A completed Form 4626 for this comprehensive example appears in Appendix B.

MINIMUM TAX CREDIT

When a corporation pays an AMT, it may be eligible for a **minimum tax credit** that can offset its future regular tax liabilities. The minimum tax credit prevents the same item of income from being taxed twice: once under the AMT rules and second under the regular tax rules. Thus, because of the minimum tax credit, the AMT effectively becomes a prepaid tax that accelerates the payment of a corporation's income taxes.

The entire corporate AMT may be claimed as a credit. The amount creditable includes the portion of the AMT attributable to deferral adjustments and preference items that reflect timing differences that will reverse in future tax years. It also includes the portion of the AMT attributable to permanent adjustments and preference items that never will reverse.[24]

The minimum tax credit that a corporation can use in a tax year equals the total of the net minimum taxes paid in all prior post-1986 tax years minus the amount claimed as a

[24] Sec. 53. Most AMT adjustments and preference items accelerate the tax consequences of transactions that are deferred for regular tax purposes, i.e., timing differences. However, two preference items that reflect permanent differences are percentage depletion and tax-exempt private activity bond interest. Also, ACE adjustments that reflect permanent differences include life insurance proceeds and tax-exempt interest on bonds other than private activity bonds.

minimum tax credit in those years. Use of available minimum tax credits in the current year is limited to the excess of the corporation's regular tax (minus all credits other than refundable credits) over its tentative minimum tax.

EXAMPLE C:5-13 ▶ In the current year, Seminole Corporation generates $400,000 of taxable income. It also incurs $250,000 of positive AMT adjustments and $350,000 of tax preference items. Its regular tax is $136,000 (0.34 × $400,000), and its AMT is $64,000 [(0.20 × $1,000,000) − $136,000]. Seminole's minimum tax credit is the entire amount of its AMT, or $64,000. ◀

The minimum tax credit carries forward indefinitely and offsets regular taxes in future years, but only to the extent the regular tax exceeds the corporation's TMT in the carryforward year. The minimum tax credit cannot be carried back to an earlier tax year.

TAX CREDITS AND THE AMT

ADDITIONAL COMMENT

Because the general business credit limitation is tied to the TMT, *every* corporation with excess general business credits will have to compute its TMT even though the corporation may not be liable for the AMT.

As illustrated in Table C:3-2, a corporation can reduce its regular tax by any available tax credits. Special rules restrict the use of tax credits to offset the corporate AMT. These rules are explained below.

AMT AND THE GENERAL BUSINESS CREDIT. The general business credit may not be used to offset the alternative minimum tax, the accumulated earnings tax, the personal holding company (PHC) tax, or all of a corporation's regular tax.

Under Sec. 38(c), the general business credit for a tax year is limited to the excess (if any) of the corporation's net income tax (reduced by certain other credits) over the greater of its tentative minimum tax or 25% of the corporation's net regular tax that exceeds $25,000.

KEY POINT

Because the purpose of the AMT is to ensure that all profitable corporations pay a minimum amount of tax, the use of tax credits also is limited. For example, the general business credit cannot reduce the regular tax below the TMT.

A corporation's net income tax is the sum of its regular tax and AMT reduced by the foreign tax credit, possessions tax credit, and Puerto Rico economic activity credit. Any general business credits that cannot be used in the current year because of credit limitations carry back one year and forward 20 years.[25] The result of this limitation is that the general business credit can offset only the portion of the regular tax that exceeds the TMT, not all of a corporation's regular tax.

EXAMPLE C:5-14 ▶ In the current year, Scientific Corporation's regular tax before credits is $125,000. Its TMT is $50,000. Scientific's only available credit for the year is a general business credit of $140,000. Scientific's net income tax is $125,000 because its regular tax ($125,000) is greater than its TMT ($50,000). As computed below, Scientific's general business credit is limited to the smaller of its $75,000 credit limitation or the $140,000 credit earned.

Net income tax		$125,000
Minus: Greater of:		
(1) 25% of regular tax (reduced by other credits) exceeding $25,000 [0.25 × ($125,000 − $25,000)]	$25,000	
OR		
(2) Tentative minimum tax	$50,000	(50,000)
General business credit limitation		$ 75,000

Scientific incurs a regular tax of $50,000 ($125,000 − $75,000 credit) but no AMT. Its general business credit carryback or carryover is $65,000 ($140,000 − $75,000), which can be carried back one year and forward 20 years. ◀

The AMT credit for small corporations is limited by the amount the corporation's regular tax (reduced by other credits) exceeds 25% times the excess (if any) of (a) the corporation's regular tax (reduced by other credits) minus (b) $25,000.[26]

[25] Sec. 38(c)(2). Special rules apply to the empowerment zone employment credit, which can offset up to 25% of a taxpayer's AMT liability.

[26] Sec. 55(e)(5).

Topic Review C:5-2

Alternative Minimum Tax (AMT)

1. The AMT is levied in addition to the regular income tax.
2. Special AMT exemptions are available for small corporations with gross receipts generally of $7.5 million or less and for any corporation with a low level of alternative minimum taxable income (AMTI) (generally less than $310,000).
3. The starting point for the AMT calculation is regular taxable income before NOLs. Regular taxable income is increased by tax preference items and then adjusted to derive AMTI.
4. AMTI is reduced by a statutory exemption to derive the AMT base. The $40,000 statutory exemption is phased out when AMTI falls between $150,000 and $310,000.
5. A 20% rate applies to the AMT base to derive the tentative minimum tax.
6. The tentative minimum tax is reduced by the AMT foreign tax credit. Other tax credits, such as the general business credit, do not reduce the tentative minimum tax.
7. The excess of a corporation's tentative minimum tax over its regular tax may be claimed as a minimum tax credit. This credit carries over to a later year to offset the excess of the regular tax over the tentative minimum tax.
8. The AMT, as well as the regular tax, must be estimated and paid quarterly.

AMT AND THE FOREIGN TAX CREDIT. For purposes of computing the AMT, the full amount of foreign tax credits (AMT FTCs) can offset the TMT, computed without the alternative tax NOL deduction. Credits that cannot be used in the current year carry back two years and forward five years to offset the TMT in those years.[27] A simplified AMT foreign tax credit limitation election is available under Sec. 59(a), which bases the limit on the ratio of foreign source taxable income to worldwide AMTI.

Topic Review C:5-2 presents an overview of the alternative minimum tax. Also see financial statement implication of the minimum tax credit later in this chapter.

Personal Holding Company Tax

OBJECTIVE 2

Determine whether a corporation is a personal holding company (PHC)

A corporation that meets both a stock ownership test and a passive income test is classified as a **personal holding company (PHC)** for the tax year. Congress enacted the PHC tax to prevent taxpayers from using closely held corporations to shelter passive income from the higher individual tax rates. In tax years 2003 through 2010, this penalty tax will be levied at a 15% rate on the PHC's undistributed personal holding company income (UPHCI). After 2010, the PHC tax rate will revert to the highest marginal tax rate for individuals. A corporation subject to the PHC tax pays this tax in addition to the regular corporate tax and the corporate alternative minimum tax. Corporations, however, can escape the PHC tax by intentionally failing either the stock ownership test or passive income test or through dividend distributions that reduce UPHCI to zero.

The significance of the PHC tax has diminished in the aftermath of the 2003 Act. This act lowered the highest marginal rate for individuals to the same level as that for corporations (35%). In so doing, it has reduced the attractiveness of using the C corporation as a vehicle for sheltering what are essentially individual earnings. Even with a narrowing or elimination of the individual-corporate tax rate gap, however, the PHC tax remains an important anti-tax avoidance tool, particularly where wealthy individuals in the 35% marginal tax bracket control corporations with effective tax rates less than 35%.

---

[27] Sec. 59(a)(2).

ADDITIONAL COMMENT

The Congressional intent behind enacting the personal holding company and accumulated earnings penalty taxes was not to produce large amounts of tax revenues. However, the presence of these taxes in the IRS's arsenal prevents substantial revenue losses from certain tax-motivated transactions involving closely held corporations.

PERSONAL HOLDING COMPANY DEFINED

A personal holding company is any corporation that (1) has five or fewer individual shareholders who own more than 50% of the corporation's outstanding stock at any time during the last half of its tax year and (2) has personal holding company income that is at least 60% of its adjusted ordinary gross income for the tax year.[28]

Corporations with special tax status generally are excluded from the PHC definition. Among these are S corporations and tax-exempt organizations.

STOCK OWNERSHIP REQUIREMENT

Section 542(a)(2) provides that a corporation satisfies the PHC stock ownership requirement if more than 50% of the value of its outstanding stock is directly or indirectly owned by five or fewer individuals at any time during the last half of its tax year.[29] Any corporation with fewer than ten individual shareholders at any time during the last half of its tax year, which is not an excluded corporation, will meet the stock ownership requirement.[30]

For purposes of determining whether the 50% requirement is satisfied, stock owned directly or indirectly by or for an individual is considered to be owned by that individual. The Sec. 544 stock attribution rules provide that

TYPICAL MISCONCEPTION

The PHC penalty tax applies to any corporation deemed to be a personal holding company based on objective criteria. No improper intent is necessary. Thus, the PHC tax truly fits into the category of "a trap for the unwary."

- Stock owned by a family member is considered to be owned by the other members of his or her family. Family members include a spouse, brothers and sisters, ancestors, and lineal descendants.
- Stock owned directly or indirectly by or for a corporation, partnership, estate, or trust is considered to be owned proportionately by its shareholders, partners, or beneficiaries.
- A person who holds an option to acquire stock is considered to own such stock whether or not the individual intends to exercise the option.
- Stock owned by a partner is considered to be owned by his or her partners.
- The family, partnership, and option rules can be used only to make a corporation a PHC. They cannot be used to prevent a corporation from acquiring PHC status.[31]

PASSIVE INCOME REQUIREMENT

A corporation whose shareholders satisfy the stock ownership requirement is not a PHC unless the corporation also earns predominantly passive income. The passive income requirement is met if at least 60% of the corporation's **adjusted ordinary gross income (AOGI)** for the tax year is personal holding company income (PHCI). The following text sections define AOGI and PHCI and outline ways in which a corporation can sidestep the passive income requirements.

KEY POINT

To be deemed a PHC, a corporation must satisfy two tests: a stock ownership test and a passive income test. Because most closely held corporations satisfy the stock ownership test, the passive income test usually is decisive.

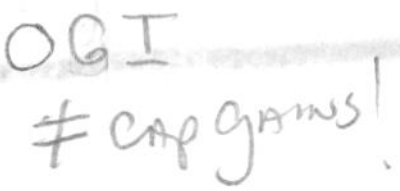

ADJUSTED ORDINARY GROSS INCOME DEFINED. The first step toward determining AOGI is calculating the corporation's gross income (see Figure C:5-1). Gross income is determined under the same accounting method used to compute taxable income. Thus, an income item excluded from gross income also is excluded from AOGI. Gross receipts from sales are reduced by the corporation's cost of goods sold.

The next step toward determining AOGI is calculating the corporation's **ordinary gross income (OGI)**. To do this, the corporation's gross income is reduced by the amount of its capital gains and Sec. 1231 gains.[32] These items are neutral in determining whether a corporation is a PHC; that is, the realization and recognition of a large Sec. 1231 or capital gain cannot make a corporation a PHC.

---

[28] Sec. 542(a).

[29] The PHC stock ownership test also is used to determine whether a closely held C corporation is subject to the at-risk rules (Sec. 465) or the passive activity loss and credit limitation rules (Sec. 469). Thus, a closely held corporation that is not a PHC may be subject to certain restrictions because of the PHC stock ownership rules.

[30] This statement may not be valid if entities own stock that might be attributed to the individual owners.

[31] Sec. 544(a)(4)(A).

[32] Sec. 543(b)(1).

▼ **FIGURE C:5-1**
Determining Adjusted Ordinary Gross Income

Gross income (GI) reported for taxable income and PHC purposes
Minus: Gross gains on the sale of capital assets
Gross gains on the sale of Sec. 1231 property

Ordinary gross income (OGI)
Minus: Certain expenses relating to gross income from rents; mineral, oil, and gas royalties; and working interests in oil or gas wells
Interest earned on certain U.S. obligations held for sale to customers by dealers
Interest on condemnation awards, judgments, or tax refunds
Certain expenses relating to rents from tangible personal property manufactured or produced by the corporation, provided it has engaged in substantial manufacturing or production of the same type of personal property in the current tax year

Adjusted ordinary gross income (AOGI)

Next, OGI is reduced by certain expenses. These expenses relate to the generation of rental income; mineral, oil, and gas (M, O, & G) royalties; and income from working interests in oil or gas wells.[33] The rental income adjustment is described below.

Reduction by Rental Income Expenses. Gross income from rents is reduced by deductions for depreciation or amortization, property taxes, interest, and rental payments. This net amount is known as **adjusted income from rents (AIR)**.[34] No other Sec. 162 expenses incurred in the generation of rental income reduce OGI. The expense adjustment cannot exceed total gross rental income.

EXAMPLE C:5-15 ▶ Ingrid owns all of Keno Corporation's single class of stock. Both Ingrid and Keno use the calendar year as their tax year. Keno reports the following results for the current year:

Rental income	$100,000
Depreciation	15,000
Interest expense	9,000
Real estate taxes	4,000
Maintenance expenses	8,000
Administrative expenses	12,000

Keno's AIR is $72,000 [$100,000 − ($15,000 + $9,000 + $4,000)]. The maintenance and administrative expenses are deductible in determining taxable income and, consequently, UPHCI, but do not reduce the AIR amount. ◀

ADDITIONAL COMMENT
Income not included in AOGI cannot be PHCI. In calculating the 60% passive income test, PHCI is the numerator and AOGI is the denominator. Because the passive income test is purely objective, both the numerator and denominator can be manipulated. When the ratio is close to 60%, one planning opportunity is to accelerate the recognition of income that is AOGI but not PHCI.

PERSONAL HOLDING COMPANY INCOME DEFINED. **Personal holding company income** includes dividends, interest, annuities, adjusted income from rents, royalties, produced film rents, income from personal service contracts involving a 25% or more shareholder, rental income from corporate property used by a 25% or more shareholder, and distributions from estates or trusts.

PHCI is determined according to the following general rules:

▶ *Dividends:* Includes only distributions out of E&P. Any amounts that are tax exempt (e.g., return of capital distributions) or eligible for capital gain treatment (e.g., liquidating distributions) are excluded from PHCI.[35]

▶ *Interest income:* Includes interest included in gross income. Interest excluded from gross income also is excluded from PHCI.[36]

[33] Sec. 543(b)(2).
[34] Sec. 543(b)(3).
[35] Reg. Sec. 1.543-1(b)(1).
[36] Reg. Sec. 1.543-1(b)(2).

HISTORICAL NOTE

The exception for royalties on computer software was added by the Tax Reform Act of 1986. Without this exception, many computer software companies would almost certainly be deemed to be PHCs.

SELF-STUDY QUESTION

What is the effect of the two-pronged test that allows the exclusion from PHCI of certain AIR?

ANSWER

This two-pronged test makes it difficult to use rents to shelter other passive income. For example, the 50% test would require at least $100 of AIR to shelter $100 of interest income. The 10% test is even more restrictive. To satisfy this test, it would be necessary to generate $900 of OGI (AIR and other items) to shelter the same $100 of interest income.

- *Annuity proceeds:* Includes only annuity amounts included in gross income. Annuity amounts excluded from gross income (for example, as a return of capital) also are excluded from PHCI.[37]
- *Royalty income:* Includes amounts received for the use of intangible property (e.g., patents, copyrights, and trademarks). Special rules apply to copyright royalties, mineral, oil, and gas royalties, active business computer software royalties, and produced film rents. Each of these four types of income constitutes a separate PHCI category that may be excluded under one of the exceptions discussed below and set forth in Table C:5-2.[38]
- *Distributions from an estate or trust:* Included in PHCI.[39]

In the calculation of PHCI, special rules apply that could result in the exclusion of rents; mineral, oil, and gas royalties; copyright royalties; produced film rents; rental income from the use of property by a 25% or more shareholder; and active business computer software royalties from PHCI. These rules, summarized in Table C:5-2, reduce the likelihood that a corporation will be deemed a PHC. The two most frequently encountered exclusions, for rental income and personal service contract income, are explained in the next two sections.

Exclusion for Rents. Adjusted income from rents (AIR) is included in PHCI unless a special exception applies for corporations earning predominantly rental income. PHCI does not include rents if (1) AIR is at least 50% of AOGI and (2) the dividends-paid deduction equals or exceeds the amount by which nonrental PHCI exceeds 10% of OGI.[40] The special exception permits corporations earning predominantly rental income and very little nonrental PHCI to avoid PHC status. The dividends-paid deduction is available for (1) dividends paid during the tax year, (2) dividends paid within 2½ months of the end of the tax year for which the PHC makes a special throwback election to treat the distribution as

TAX STRATEGY TIP

Taxpayers potentially liable for the PHC should carefully monitor the PHC exclusion requirements to avoid having to pay the tax or having to make a deficiency dividend payment.

▼ TABLE C:5-2
Tests to Determine Exclusions from Personal Holding Company Income

PHCI Category	A PHCI Category Is Excluded If: Income in the Category Is:	Other PHCI Is:	Business Expenses Are:
Rents – AIR	≥50% of AOGI[a]	≤10% of OGI (unless reduced by distributions)	—
Mineral, oil, and gas royalties	≥50% of AOGI[a]	≤10% of OGI	≥15% of AOGI
Copyright royalties	≥50% of OGI	≤10% of OGI	≥25% of OGI
Produced film rents	≥50% of OGI	—	—
Compensation for use of property by a shareholder owning at least 25% of the outstanding stock	—	≤10% of OGI	—
Active business computer software royalties	≥50% of OGI	≤10% of OGI (unless reduced by distributions)	≥25% of OGI[b]
Personal services contract income	—[c]	—	—

[a] Measured in terms of adjusted income from rents or mineral, oil, and gas royalties, respectively.
[b] The deduction test can apply to either the single tax year in question or the five-year period ending with the tax year in question.
[c] Personal services income is excluded from PHCI if the corporation has the right to designate the person who is to perform the services or if the person performing the services owns less than 25% of the corporation's outstanding stock.

---

[37] Reg. Sec. 1.543-1(b)(4).
[38] Reg. Sec. 1.543-1(b)(3). Royalties include mineral, oil, and gas royalties, royalties on working interests in oil or gas wells, computer software royalties, copyright royalties, and all other royalties.
[39] Sec. 543(a)(8).
[40] Sec. 543(a)(2). AIR excludes rental income earned from leasing property to a shareholder owning 25% or more of the corporation's stock. Such income is included in PHCI as a separate category.

having been paid on the last day of the preceding tax year, and (3) consent dividends (see page C:5-23). Nonrental PHCI includes all PHCI (determined without regard to the exclusions for copyright royalties and mineral, oil, and gas royalties) *other than* adjusted income from rents and rental income earned from leasing property to a shareholder owning 25% or more of the corporation's stock.

EXAMPLE C:5-16 ▶ Karen owns all of Texas Corporation's single class of stock. Both Karen and Texas use the calendar year as their tax year. Texas reports the following results for the current year:

Rental income	$100,000
Operating profit from sales	40,000
Dividend income	15,000
Interest income on corporate bonds	10,000
Rental expenses:	
Depreciation	15,000
Interest	9,000
Real estate taxes	4,000
Other expenses	20,000

Texas pays no dividends during the current year or during the 2½ month throwback period following year-end. Because one shareholder owns all the Texas stock, Texas satisfies the stock ownership requirement. Texas's AOGI is calculated as follows:

Rental income			$100,000
Operating profit from sales			40,000
Dividends			15,000
Interest income			10,000
Gross income and OGI			$165,000
Minus:	Depreciation	$15,000	
	Interest expense	9,000	
	Real estate taxes	4,000	(28,000)
AOGI			$137,000

The two AIR tests are illustrated as follows:

Test 1:	Rental income		$100,000
	Minus:	Depreciation	(15,000)
		Interest expense	(9,000)
		Real estate taxes	(4,000)
	AIR		$ 72,000
	50% of AOGI (0.50 × $137,000 AOGI) [Test passed]		$ 68,500
Test 2:	Dividends		$ 15,000
	Interest income		10,000
	Nonrental income		$ 25,000
	Minus: 10% of OGI (0.10 × $165,000)		(16,500)
	Minimum amount of distributions		$8,500
	Actual dividends paid [Test failed]		$ –0–

AIR exceeds the 50% threshold, so Texas passes Test 1. Because Texas paid no dividends, its dividends-paid deduction is less than the nonrental income ceiling, and Texas fails Test 2. AIR is included in PHCI because Texas passed only one of the two tests. Application of the 60% PHC income test is illustrated below:

AIR	$ 72,000
Dividends	15,000
Interest income	10,000
PHCI	$ 97,000
AOGI	$137,000
Times: AOGI threshold	× 0.60
AOGI ceiling [Test passed]	$ 82,200

Texas is a PHC because PHCI exceeds 60% of AOGI.

Texas could have avoided PHC status by paying sufficient cash dividends during the current year or a consent dividend following year-end. The amount of dividends required to avoid PHC status is the excess of nonrental PHCI ($25,000) over 10% of OGI ($16,500), or $8,500. Thus, an $8,500 cash dividend paid during the current year or consent dividend paid after year-end would have permitted Texas to exclude the $72,000 of AIR from PHCI. PHCI then would have been $25,000 ($15,000 + $10,000), which is less than 60% of AOGI ($82,200). (Consent dividends are discussed on page C:5-23.) ◀

ADDITIONAL COMMENT

Congress enacted the provision for personal service contracts to prevent entertainers, athletes, and other highly compensated professionals from incorporating their activities and, after paying themselves a below-normal salary, having the rest of the income taxed at the corporate rates. Even if it is apparent that a 25%-shareholder will perform the services, as long as no one other than the corporation has the right to designate who performs the services, the income is not PHCI. Thus, the careful drafting of contracts is important.

Exclusion for Personal Service Contracts. Income earned from contracts under which the corporation is obligated to perform personal services, as well as income earned on the sale of such contracts, is included in PHCI if the following two conditions are met:

- ▶ A person other than the corporation has the right to designate (by name or by description) the individual who is to perform the services, or the individual who is to perform the services is designated (by name or by description) in the contract.
- ▶ 25% or more of the value of the corporation's outstanding stock is directly or indirectly owned by the person who has performed, is to perform, or may be designated as the person to perform the services.[41]

The 25% or more requirement must be satisfied at some point during the tax year and is determined under the Sec. 544 constructive stock ownership rules. Congress enacted this provision to prevent professionals, entertainers, and sports figures from incorporating their activities, paying themselves a substandard salary, and sheltering at the lower corporate tax rates the difference between their actual earnings and their substandard salary.

EXAMPLE C:5-17 ▶

Dr. Kellner owns all the stock in a professional corporation that provides medical services. The professional corporation concludes with Dr. Kellner an exclusive employment contract that specifies the terms of his employment and that provides for the hiring of a qualified substitute when Dr. Kellner is off duty. The corporation provides office space for Dr. Kellner and employs office staff to enable Dr. Kellner to perform medical services. The income earned by Dr. Kellner does not constitute PHCI because (1) the normal patient–physician relationship generally does not involve a contract that designates a doctor who will perform the services, nor will the patient generally be permitted to designate a doctor who will perform the services, and (2) the professional corporation will be able to appoint a qualified substitute when Dr. Kellner is not on duty (for example, when he is on vacation or not on call).[42]

The income earned by the corporation in connection with Dr. Kellner's services would constitute PHCI if the contract with the patient specified that only Dr. Kellner would provide the services or if the services provided by Dr. Kellner were so unique that only he could provide them. Any portion of the corporation's income from the personal service contract attributable to "important and essential" services provided by persons other than Dr. Kellner is not included in PHCI.[43] ◀

OBJECTIVE 3

Calculate the corporation's PHC tax

CALCULATING THE PHC TAX

The PHC tax is calculated in two basic steps. First, the corporation determines the amount of its undistributed personal holding company income (UPHCI). It then applies the 15% PHC tax rate (in 2003–2010) to UPHCI. If the corporation owes the PHC tax, it can avoid paying the tax by making a timely consent or deficiency dividend distribution.

CALCULATING UPHCI. The starting point for calculating UPHCI is the corporation's taxable income. A series of adjustments are made to taxable income to derive UPHCI. The most important of these adjustments are discussed below.

---

[41] Sec. 543(a)(7).

[42] Rev. Rul. 75-67, 1975-1 C.B. 169. See also Rev. Ruls. 75-249, 1975-1 C.B. 171 (relating to a composer), and 75-250, 1975-1 C.B. 172 (relating to an accountant).

[43] Reg. Sec. 1.543-1(b)(8)(ii).

▼ **FIGURE C:5-2**
Calculating the Personal Holding Company Tax

UPHCI =

Taxable income
Plus: Positive adjustments
1. Dividends-received deduction
2. NOL deduction
3. Excess charitable contributions carried over from a preceding tax year and deducted in determining taxable income
4. Net loss attributable to the operation or maintenance of property leased by the corporation
5. Rental expenses that exceed rental income

Minus: Negative adjustments
1. Accrued U.S. and foreign income taxes
2. Charitable contributions that exceed the 10% corporate limitation
3. NOL (computed without regard to the dividends-received deduction) incurred in the immediately preceding tax year
4. Net capital gain minus the amount of any income taxes attributed to it

Minus: Dividends-paid deduction

Undistributed personal holding company income (UPHCI)
Times: 0.15 (in 2003–2010)

Personal holding company tax

KEY POINT

The PHC tax is assessed at a 15% rate in 2003–2010. This tax is in addition to the corporate income tax. Thus, the existence of both taxes eliminates any advantage obtained by interposing a corporation between the taxpayer and his or her income-producing assets.

Positive Adjustments to Taxable Income. A PHC may not claim a dividends-received deduction. Thus, its taxable income must be increased by the amount of any dividends-received deductions claimed.[44] Rental expenses that exceed rental income also are added back to taxable income to derive UPHCI.

Because PHCs may deduct only the NOL for the immediately preceding tax year, two NOL compensating adjustments must be made. First, the amount of the NOL deduction claimed in determining taxable income must be added back to taxable income. Second, the entire amount of the corporation's NOL (computed without regard to the dividends-received deduction) for the immediately preceding tax year must be subtracted from taxable income.[45] The U.S. production activities deduction, however, is not added back to taxable income.

KEY POINT

The negative adjustments made to taxable income in deriving UPHCI (e.g., federal income taxes) represent items that do not reduce taxable income but reduce the earnings available for distribution to the shareholders. In contrast, positive adjustments made to taxable income (e.g., the dividends-received deduction) are not allowed in deriving UPHCI because they do not represent a reduction in earnings available for distribution to the shareholders.

Negative Adjustments to Taxable Income. Charitable contributions made by individuals are deductible up to 20%, 30%, or 50% of adjusted gross income, depending on the type of contribution and type of donee. Thus, two adjustments to the deductions claimed by individuals may be required: (1) subtracting the amount of charitable contributions exceeding the 10% corporate limitation, but not exceeding the individual limitations, and (2) adding back charitable contribution carryovers deducted in the current year for regular tax purposes, but in an earlier year for PHC tax purposes.[46]

Income taxes (i.e., federal income taxes, the corporate AMT, foreign income taxes, and U.S. possessions' income taxes) accrued by the corporation reduce UPHCI.[47]

A PHC is allowed a deduction for its net capital gain (i.e., net long-term capital gain over net short-term capital loss) minus income taxes attributable to the net capital gain.[48] The portion of federal income taxes attributable to the net capital gain equals the tax imposed on the corporation's taxable income minus the tax imposed on the corporation's taxable income excluding the net capital gain. The tax offset eliminates the possibility of a double benefit for federal income taxes, which are deductible in determining UPHCI.

44 Sec. 545(b)(3).
45 Sec. 545(b)(4) and Rev. Rul. 79-59, 1979-1 C.B. 209.
46 Sec. 545(b)(2).
47 Sec. 545(b)(1).
48 Sec. 545(b)(5).

The capital gains adjustment precludes a corporation from being classified as a PHC because of a large capital gain. Even where the corporation is classified as a PHC, the capital gains adjustment allows it to avoid the PHC tax on its long-term (but not short-term) capital gains.

AVOIDING THE PHC DESIGNATION AND TAX LIABILITY BY MAKING DIVIDEND DISTRIBUTIONS

ADDITIONAL COMMENT

The intent behind the PHC rules is not to collect taxes from a corporation. Instead, the rules are meant to compel the distribution of income by a closely held corporation so that such income will be taxed at the shareholders' individual tax rates. This purpose is evidenced by the flexibility of the dividends-paid deduction.

The PHC can claim a **dividends-paid deduction** for distributions made during the current year if they are made out of the corporation's current or accumulated E&P.[49] A dividends-paid deduction is not available for **preferential dividends**. A dividend is preferential when (1) the amount distributed to a shareholder exceeds his or her ratable share of the distribution as determined by the number of shares of stock owned or (2) the amount received by a class of stock is greater or less than its rightful amount.[50] In either case, the entire distribution (and not just any excess distributions) is considered to be a preferential dividend.

Throwback dividends are distributions made in the first 2½ months after the close of the tax year. A dividend paid in the first 2½ months of the next tax year is treated as a throwback distribution in the preceding tax year only if the PHC makes the appropriate election.[51] Otherwise, the dividends-paid deduction is allowable only in the tax year in which the PHC actually makes the distribution. Throwback dividends paid by a PHC are limited to the lesser of the PHC's UPHCI or 20% of the amount of any dividends (other than consent dividends) paid during the tax year. Thus, a PHC that fails to make any dividend distributions during its tax year is precluded from paying a throwback dividend.

TAX STRATEGY TIP

If the corporation does not have the cash to pay a throwback dividend, it should consider a consent dividend. The consent dividend is not subject to the 20% limitation on throwback dividends and may be paid up to the extended due date for the corporation's tax return.

Consent dividends are hypothetical dividends deemed to have been paid to shareholders on the last day of the corporation's tax year. Consent dividends permit a corporation to reduce its PHC tax liability when it cannot make an actual dividend distribution because of a lack of cash, a restrictive loan covenant, or other financial or legal constraints. Any shareholder who owns stock on the last day of the corporation's tax year can elect to pay a consent dividend.[52] For PHC tax purposes, the election results in the payment of a hypothetical cash dividend on the last day of the PHC's tax year for which the dividends-paid deduction is claimed. The shareholder treats the consent dividend as received on the distribution date and then immediately contributed by the shareholder to the distributing corporation's capital account. The contribution increases the shareholder's stock basis. The shareholder can make the consent dividend election through the due date for the corporation's income tax return (including any permitted extensions).

Dividend Carryovers. Dividends paid in the preceding two tax years may be used as a dividend carryover to reduce the amount of the current year's PHC tax liability.[53] Section 564 permits a PHC to deduct the amount by which its dividend distributions eligible for a dividends-paid deduction in each of the two preceding tax years exceed the corporation's UPHCI for such year.

TAX STRATEGY TIP

A deficiency dividend can be beneficial if a corporation fails to eliminate its UPHCI, either under the erroneous assumption that it was not a PHC or due to a miscalculation of its UPHCI. If certain requirements are satisfied, a deficiency dividend can be retroactively paid and thus be deductible from UPHCI earned in a previous year.

Liquidating Dividends. Section 562 allows a dividends-paid deduction for liquidating distributions made by a PHC within 24 months of adopting a plan of liquidation.[54]

Deficiency Dividends. Under Sec. 547, a corporation liable for the PHC tax can avoid paying the tax by electing to pay a **deficiency dividend**. The deficiency dividend provisions substitute a tax on the dividend at the shareholder level for the PHC tax at the corporate level. The distributing corporation's shareholders must include the deficiency dividend in their gross income in the tax year in which it is received, not the tax year for which the PHC claims a dividends-paid deduction. Payment of a deficiency dividend does not relieve the PHC from liability for interest and penalties relating to the PHC tax.

---

[49] Secs. 561(a) and 562(a).
[50] Sec. 562(c).
[51] Sec. 563(b).
[52] Sec. 565.
[53] Sec. 561(a)(3).
[54] Sec. 562(b).

To claim a dividends-paid deduction for a deficiency dividend, a PHC must meet the following requirements:

- ▶ Obtain a determination (e.g., judicial decision or IRS agreement) that establishes the amount of the PHC tax liability.
- ▶ Pay a dividend within 90 days after this determination.
- ▶ File a claim for a dividends-paid deduction within 120 days of the determination date.[55]

EXAMPLE C:5-18 ▶ On its current year return, Boston Corporation characterizes a $200,000 distribution received pursuant to a stock redemption as a capital gain. Upon audit, the IRS and Boston agree that the distribution should be recharacterized as a dividend and that Boston is liable for the PHC tax. Boston can extinguish its PHC tax liability if it pays a deficiency dividend within 90 days after signing the agreement and if Boston files a timely claim. ◀

PHC TAX CALCULATION

The following example illustrates how UPHCI is calculated and how a corporation's regular tax and PHC tax liabilities are determined.

EXAMPLE C:5-19 ▶ Marlo Corporation is deemed to be a PHC for 2007, and reports $226,000 of taxable income on its federal income tax return as follows:

Operating profit	$100,000
Long-term capital gain	60,000
Short-term capital gain	30,000
Dividends (20%-owned corporation)	200,000
Interest	100,000
Gross income	$490,000
Salaries	(40,000)
General and administrative expenses	(20,000)
Charitable contributions	(43,000)[a]
Dividends-received deduction	(160,000)
U.S. production activities deduction	(1,000)
Taxable income	$226,000

[a] $43,000 limit = 0.10 × ($490,000 − $40,000 − $20,000).

Ignoring any AMT liability, Marlo determines its federal income tax liability to be $71,390 [$22,250 + (0.39 × $126,000)]. Marlo contributed $60,000 to charities in the current year and paid $50,000 in dividends in August.

Marlo's PHC tax liability is calculated as follows:

Taxable income			$226,000
Plus:	Dividends-received deduction		160,000
Minus:	Excess charitable contributions		(17,000)[b]
	Federal income taxes		(71,390)
	Dividends-paid deduction		(50,000)
	Long-term capital gain	$60,000	
	Minus: Federal income taxes	(23,400)[c]	
	LTCG adjustment		(36,600)
Undistributed personal holding company income			$211,010
Times:	Tax rate		× 0.15
Personal holding company tax			$ 31,652

[b] $60,000 total contributions − $43,000 limitation = $17,000 excess contributions.

[c] Because Marlo is in the 39% tax bracket with and without the LTCG, it can calculate the applicable federal income tax as 0.39 × $60,000 = $23,400.

[55] Secs. 547(c) through (e).

Marlo's total federal tax liability is $103,042 ($71,390 + $31,652). Marlo can avoid the $31,652 PHC tax by timely paying a deficiency dividend of $211,010, which equals the amount of UPHCI in 2007. ◀

Topic Review C:5-3 presents an overview of the personal holding company tax.

ACCUMULATED EARNINGS TAX

ADDITIONAL COMMENT

The accumulated earnings tax is a penalty imposed on corporations that accumulate unreasonable amounts of earnings for the purpose of avoiding shareholder-level taxes. When corporate tax rates are lower than individual rates, tax incentives exist for accumulating earnings inside a corporation. These opportunities should lead to the IRS imposing the accumulated earnings tax.

Corporations not subject to the personal holding company tax may be subject to the accumulated earnings tax. The **accumulated earnings tax** attempts "to compel the company to distribute any profits not needed for the conduct of its business so that, when so distributed, individual stockholders will become liable" for taxes on the dividends received.[56] Unlike its name, the tax is not levied on the corporation's total accumulated earnings balance but only on its current year addition to the balance. In other words, the tax is levied on current earnings that are not needed for a reasonable business purpose, such as excessive earnings invested by a corporation in speculative securities. Note, however, that the 15% maximum tax rate on dividends through 2010 reduces the negative effect of double taxation.

CORPORATIONS SUBJECT TO THE PENALTY TAX

Section 532(a) states that the accumulated earnings tax applies "to every corporation . . . formed or availed of for the purpose of avoiding the income tax with respect to its shareholders . . . by permitting earnings and profits to accumulate instead of being divided or distributed." Three corporate forms are excluded from the accumulated earnings tax:

- Domestic and foreign personal holding companies
- Corporations exempt from tax under Secs. 501-505
- S corporations[57]

Topic Review C:5-3

Personal Holding Company (PHC) Tax

1. The PHC tax applies only to corporations deemed to be PHCs. A PHC has (1) five or fewer individual shareholders owning more than 50% in value of the corporation's stock at any time during the last half of the tax year and (2) PHCI that is at least 60% of its adjusted ordinary gross income for the tax year.
2. Two special exceptions to the PHC test may apply. First, certain types of corporations (e.g., S corporations) are excluded from the tax. Second, certain categories of income (e.g., rents and active business computer software royalties) are excluded if conditions relating to percentage of income, maximum level of other PHC income, and minimum level of business expenses are met. Table C:5-2 on page C:5-19 summarizes the excludable categories of income and related requirements.
3. The PHC tax equals 15% (in 2003–2010) times UPHCI. UPHCI equals taxable income plus certain positive adjustments (e.g., dividends-received deduction) and minus certain negative adjustments (e.g., federal income taxes, excess charitable contributions, and net capital gain reduced by federal income taxes attributable to the gain).
4. UPHCI can be reduced by a deduction for cash and property dividends paid during the tax year, as well as consent and throwback dividends distributed after year-end.
5. A PHC tax liability (but not liability for related interest and penalties) can be extinguished through payment of a deficiency dividend. Deficiency dividend provisions effectively substitute an income tax levy at the shareholder level for the corporate-level PHC tax.

[56] *Helvering v. Chicago Stock Yards Co.*, 30 AFTR 1091, 43-1 USTC ¶9379 (USSC, 1943).

[57] Secs. 532(b) and 1363(a).

WHAT WOULD YOU DO IN THIS SITUATION?

In 2006, shareholders formed Taylor Corporation and on July 1 of that year contributed $1 million of capital to the corporation. Because of delays in procuring manufacturing equipment, Taylor did not begin business until January 2007. During the last six months of 2006, the corporation earned $50,000 of taxable interest and incurred $20,000 of deductible expenses. A second-year accountant in a small accounting firm was assigned to prepare the Taylor corporate tax return. All of his previous assignments were for individual tax returns. The senior accountant responsible for the assignment told him that the return "would be simple and that all you need to do is input the interest and expense information into the Form 1120 software." Because of the rush to finish and deliver the return to the client by March 15, no one in the office noticed during the review process that Taylor might be deemed to be a personal holding company (PHC) in 2006. The corporation filed its return on March 15 without paying any PHC tax. Another Taylor corporate issue arose in August 2007 and was assigned to you. When you considered the issue, you asked yourself, "Does Taylor have a PHC tax problem?" If so, what can Taylor and/or you do to resolve the problem?

In principle, the accumulated earnings tax applies to both large and small corporations.[58] In practice, however, it applies primarily to closely held corporations where management can implement a corporate dividend policy to reduce the tax liability of the shareholder group.

OBJECTIVE 4

Determine whether a corporation is liable for the accumulated earnings tax

PROVING A TAX-AVOIDANCE PURPOSE

Section 533(a) provides that the accumulation of E&P by a corporation beyond the reasonable needs of the business indicates a tax-avoidance purpose unless the corporation can prove that it is not accumulating the earnings merely to avoid taxes. In limited circumstances, this burden of proof may be shifted to the IRS under rules set forth in Sec. 534.

The existence of a tax-avoidance purpose may be inferred from all pertinent facts and circumstances. Regulation Sec. 1.533-1(a)(2) lists the following specific circumstances that suggest a tax-avoidance purpose:

- Dealings between the corporation and its shareholders (e.g., loans made by the corporation to its shareholders or funds expended by the corporation for the shareholders' personal benefit).
- Investments of undistributed earnings in assets having no reasonable connection to the corporation's business.
- The extent to which the corporation has distributed its E&P (e.g., a low dividend payout rate, low salaries, and substantial earnings accumulation may indicate a tax-avoidance purpose).

TAX STRATEGY TIP

When the IRS determines that the accumulation of earnings is unreasonable, it presumes that its determination is correct. To rebut this presumption, the taxpayer must show by a preponderance of the evidence that the IRS's determination is improper. Thus, periodic updating of the plans to use corporate earnings should be undertaken to reduce accumulated earnings tax problems.

Holding or investment companies are held to a standard different from that which applies to operating companies. Section 533(b) provides that holding or investment company status is prima facie evidence of a tax-avoidance purpose.[59] A holding company, like an operating company, can rebut this presumption by showing that it was neither formed nor availed of to avoid shareholder income taxes.

A tax-avoidance purpose may be only one of several reasons for the corporation's accumulation of earnings. In *U.S. v. The Donruss Company*, the Supreme Court held that tax avoidance does not have to be the dominant motive for the accumulation of earnings, which could lead to imposition of the accumulated earnings tax. According to the court,

[58] Sec. 532(c). See, however, *Technalysis Corporation v. CIR* [101 T.C. 397 (1993)] where the Tax Court held that the accumulated earnings tax can be imposed on a publicly held corporation regardless of the concentration of ownership or whether the shareholders are actively involved in corporate operations.

[59] Regulation Sec. 1.533-1(c) defines a holding or investment company as "a corporation having no activities except holding property and collecting income therefrom or investing therein."

for a tax avoidance purpose to exist, the corporation must know about the tax consequences of accumulating earnings.[60] Such knowledge need not be the dominant motive or purpose for the accumulation of the earnings.

EVIDENCE CONCERNING THE REASONABLENESS OF AN EARNINGS ACCUMULATION

The courts have not specified any single factor that indicates an unreasonable level of accumulated earnings. Instead, they have alluded to several factors that suggest a tax-avoidance motive. The IRS and the courts have cited other factors that indicate reasonable business needs for the legitimate accumulation of earnings and profits.

TYPICAL MISCONCEPTION

The IRC refers to the existence of a tax-avoidance purpose, which would appear to involve a subjective test. However, the existence of the tax-avoidance purpose really hinges on the objective determination of whether a corporation has accumulated earnings beyond the reasonable needs of the business.

EVIDENCE OF A TAX-AVOIDANCE MOTIVE. A corporation that wants to avoid liability for the accumulated earnings tax should act defensively. It can minimize this liability by avoiding or restricting the following transactions:

- Loans to shareholders
- Corporate expenditures for the personal benefit of shareholders
- Loans having no reasonable relation to the conduct of business (e.g., loans to relatives or friends of shareholders)
- Loans to a corporation controlled by the same shareholders that control the lending corporation
- Investments in property or securities unrelated to the activities of the corporation
- Insuring against unrealistic hazards[61]

Loans to shareholders or corporate expenditures for the personal benefit of shareholders are viewed as as substitutes for dividend payments to shareholders. Similarly, corporate loans made to relatives or friends of shareholders are viewed as substitutes for dividend payments to shareholders, who then make personal loans to their friends and relatives. All three measures suggest an unreasonable accumulation of corporate earnings, which should have been distributed as dividends.

Likewise, loans or corporate expenditures made for the benefit of a second corporation controlled by the shareholder (or the shareholder group) who also controls the first corporation may be considered to have a tax-avoidance purpose. Theoretically, the first corporation instead could have paid a dividend to the shareholder who in turn could have paid income taxes on the dividend and then contributed after-tax funds to the second corporation.

Another factor indicative of a tax-avoidance motive, but not mentioned in Treasury Regulations, is operating a corporation as a holding or investment company that pays little or no dividends.

STOP & THINK

Question: In 2007, an IRS auditor examines Baylor Corporation's 2004 C corporation tax return. What items might the auditor scrutinize to assertain excess accumulated earnings?

Solution: The auditor might look first at the retained earnings accounts in the beginning and year-end balance sheets (Schedule L, Page 4 of Form 1120). Then, the auditor might review Schedule M-2 (Analysis of Unappropriated Retained Earnings per Books) for current year earnings, the amount of earnings distributed as dividends, and the manner in which the corporation used the undistributed earnings. Next, the auditor might examine the beginning and year-end balance sheets for evidence of transactions suggesting a tax-avoidance motive. Such transactions might include loans to stockholders (Schedule L, Line 7), loans to persons other than stockholders (Schedule L, Line 6), and portfolio

---

[60] *U.S. v. The Donruss Company,* 23 AFTR 2d 69-418, 69-1 USTC ¶9167 (USSC, 1969).

[61] Reg. Sec. 1.537-2(c).

investments (Schedule L, Lines 4, 5, 6, and 9). Information about expenditures of corporate funds made for the personal benefit of shareholders might be found in the noncurrent asset section of the balance sheets (e.g., corporate ownership of a boat, airplane, or second home of a major stockholder).

KEY POINT

In determining whether an accumulation of earnings is reasonable, the IRS applies the "prudent businessman" standard set forth in the Treasury Regulations. In applying this standard, the courts are reluctant to substitute their judgment for that of corporate management unless the facts and circumstances clearly suggest that the accumulation of earnings are not for reasonable business needs.

REASONABLE BUSINESS NEEDS. Section 537 defines **reasonable business needs** as

- Reasonably anticipated needs of the business
- Section 303 (death tax) redemption needs
- Excess business holdings redemption needs
- Product liability loss reserves

Regulation Sec. 1.537-1(a) sets forth the following relevant standard of reasonableness:

> An accumulation of the earnings and profits . . . is in excess of reasonable needs of the business if it exceeds the amount that a prudent businessman would consider appropriate for the present business purposes and for the reasonably anticipated future needs of the business. The need to retain earnings and profits must be directly connected with the needs of the corporation itself and must be for bona fide business purposes.

Specific, Definite, and Feasible Plans. A corporation's accumulation of earnings is justified only if facts and circumstances indicate that the future needs of the business require such an accumulation. The corporation usually must have specific, definite, and feasible plans for the use of the accumulation.

No Specific Time Limitations. The earnings accumulation need not be used within a short period of time after the close of the tax year. However, the plans must provide that, based on all the facts and circumstances associated with the future needs of the business, the corporation will use the accumulation within a reasonable period of time after the close of the tax year.

Impact of Subsequent Events. A determination of the reasonably anticipated needs of the business is based on all relevant facts and circumstances that exist at the end of the tax year. Regulation Sec. 1.537-1(b)(2) provides that subsequent events may not be used to show that an earnings accumulation is unreasonable if all the elements of reasonable anticipation are present at the close of the tax year. However, subsequent events may be used to ascertain whether the taxpayer actually intended to consummate the plans for which the earnings were accumulated.

Treasury Regulations and the courts have cited as determinative or relevant a number of factors that represent reasonable needs for accumulating earnings. These factors include:

- Expansion of a business or replacement of plant
- Acquisition of a business enterprise
- Debt retirement
- Working capital build-up
- Loans to suppliers or customers
- Product liability losses
- Stock redemptions
- Business contingencies

Expansion of a Business or Replacement of Plant. The IRS and the courts generally have viewed the expansion of a corporation's present business facilities or the replacement of existing plant and equipment as involving a reasonable need of a business. Taxpayers have encountered problems only when the plans are undocumented, indefinite, vague, or unfeasible.[62] Although the plans need not be reduced to writing, adequate documentation is advisable.

Acquisition of a Business Enterprise. The acquisition of a business enterprise might involve extension of the same business or expansion into a new business through the purchase of either the stock or the assets of a corporation conducting the new business. Taxpayers should be careful to acquire a sufficient interest in the new business so that it will not be considered a passive investment.

Working Capital: The Bardahl Formula. Working capital is defined generally as the excess of current assets over current liabilities.The *Bardahl* formula attempts to measure the amount of working capital necessary for an operating cycle. The operating cycle encompasses a period of time necessary for the corporation to acquire inventory, sell the inventory, generate accounts receivable, and collect on the receivables. Acquiring working capital for one operating cycle is considered a reasonable need of a business. Accordingly, accumulated earnings sufficient to finance such working capital is considered reasonable.

At one time, the courts used certain rules of thumb (e.g., a current ratio of 2 to 1 or 3 to 1 or the accumulation of funds to cover a single year's operating expenses) to establish adequate working capital. Later, in the first of two *Bardahl* cases, the Tax Court endorsed a mathematical formula for measuring an operating cycle. This formula is now used to ascertain the amount of working capital required for the reasonable needs of the business.

The working capital needs of a manufacturing business differ from those of a service business. For a manufacturing business, an operating cycle is the "period of time required to convert cash into raw materials, raw materials into an inventory of marketable . . . products, the inventory into sales and accounts receivable, and the period of time to collect its outstanding accounts."[63]

In the second *Bardahl* case, the Tax Court ruled that amounts advanced to a corporation by its suppliers in the form of short-term credit (e.g., trade payables) reduce the required amount of working capital.[64] Based on this ruling, the ***Bardahl* formula** for determining average operating cycle has become

$$\begin{array}{c}\text{Average}\\\text{operating}\\\text{cycle}\end{array} = \begin{array}{c}\text{Inventory}\\\text{period}\end{array} + \begin{array}{c}\text{Accounts}\\\text{receivable}\\\text{period}\end{array} - \begin{array}{c}\text{Credit}\\\text{period}\end{array}$$

In this formula, the *inventory period* is the time (expressed as a percentage of a year) spanning the acquisition of raw materials inventory to the sale of finished goods inventory. The *accounts receivable period* is the time (expressed as a percentage of a year) spanning the sale date to the date on which accounts receivable are collected. The *credit period* is the time (expressed as a percentage of a year) from which the corporation incurs an expense or purchases inventory to the time at which it pays the liability.

The *Bardahl* formula can be expanded to include financial and operating data as follows:

$$\begin{array}{c}\text{Average operating cycle}\\\text{(as a percentage of a year)}\end{array} =$$

$$\left[\frac{\begin{array}{c}\text{Inventory}\\\text{amount}\end{array}}{\begin{array}{c}\text{Annual cost of}\\\text{goods sold}\end{array}} + \frac{\begin{array}{c}\text{Accounts receivable}\\\text{amount}\end{array}}{\text{Annual sales}} - \frac{\begin{array}{c}\text{Accounts payable}\\\text{amount}\end{array}}{\begin{array}{c}\text{Annual operating}\\\text{expenses and purchases}\\\text{(less noncash expenses)}\end{array}}\right] \times 100$$

[62] See, for example, *Myron's Enterprises v. U.S.*, 39 AFTR 2d 77-693, 77-1 USTC ¶9253 (9th Cir., 1977) and *Atlas Tool Co., Inc. v. CIR*, 45 AFTR 2d 80-645, 80-1 USTC ¶9177 (3rd Cir., 1980).

[63] *Bardahl Manufacturing Corp.*, 1965 PH T.C. Memo ¶65,200, 24 TCM 1030, at 1044.

[64] *Bardahl International Corp.*, 1966 PH T.C. Memo ¶66,182, 25 TCM 935.

This formula is linked to the working capital requirements of the business through the following equation:

$$\begin{matrix}\text{Average operating} \\ \text{cycle (as a} \\ \text{percentage of a year)}\end{matrix} \times \left[\begin{matrix}\text{Cost of goods} \\ \text{sold}\end{matrix} + \begin{matrix}\text{Operating} \\ \text{expenses}\end{matrix} \right] = \begin{matrix}\text{Working} \\ \text{capital} \\ \text{requirements}\end{matrix}$$

Cost of goods sold is determined on a full-cost basis (i.e., including both direct and indirect expenses). Operating expenses exclude noncash expenses such as depreciation, amortization, and depletion, as well as capital expenditures and charitable contributions. The Tax Court has allowed federal income taxes (e.g., quarterly estimated tax payments) to be included as an operating expense.[65]

The working capital requirement for one operating cycle is compared with actual working capital employed at year-end. If the working capital requirement exceeds actual working capital, the excess, along with amounts required for specific needs of the business, is deemed to justify accumulating a portion of the corporation's earnings. If the working capital requirement is less than the corporation's actual working capital, the excess generally is deemed to reflect an unreasonable accumulation unless the corporation can somehow justify the excess (e.g., for plant replacement).

TYPICAL MISCONCEPTION

No exact method exists for determining the working capital needs of a corporation. The *Bardahl* formula is merely a rule of thumb adopted by the Tax Court. The basic approaches (peak cycle approach versus the average cycle approach) sanctioned by the *Bardahl* formula are subject to dispute among the courts.

In establishing "adequate" working capital, the *Bardahl* formula may provide a false sense of mathematical precision because the IRS and the courts have interpreted it differently. Some courts have used peak month inventory, accounts receivable, and trade payables turnover (instead of an annual average) to measure an operating cycle.[66] Relative to the annual average method, the peak month method generally lengthens the corporation's operating cycle. Use of these two methods can lead to very different estimates of working capital requirements. As a result, significant disputes have arisen between the IRS and taxpayers over what constitutes "adequate" working capital.

EXAMPLE C:5-20 ▶ Austin Corporation's managers believe that Austin may be liable for the accumulated earnings tax. They ask their tax advisor to determine the corporation's working capital requirement as of December 31 of the current year under the *Bardahl* formula. The following information from Austin's records for the current year is available:

Cost of goods sold	$2,700,000
Average inventory	675,000
Purchases	3,000,000
Sales (all on account)	6,000,000
Average accounts receivable	750,000
Operating expenses (including depreciation and other noncash charges)	875,000
Depreciation and other noncash charges	75,000
Average trade payables	350,000
Estimated federal income tax payments	100,000
Working capital on December 31	825,000

The operating cycle based on the annual average method is calculated as follows (assuming a nonleap year):

$$\text{Inventory turnover} = (\$675{,}000 \div \$2{,}700{,}000) \times 365 = 91.25 \text{ days}$$

$$\text{Receivables turnover} = (\$750{,}000 \div \$6{,}000{,}000) \times 365 = 45.625 \text{ days}$$

$$\text{Payables turnover} = \frac{\$350{,}000}{\$3{,}000{,}000 + \$800{,}000} \times 365 = 33.62 \text{ days}$$

$$\text{Operating cycle} = \frac{91.25 + 45.625 - 33.62}{365} \times 100 = 28.3\% \text{ of a year}$$

---

[65] *Doug-Long, Inc.*, 72 T.C. 158 (1979).

[66] *State Office Supply, Inc.*, 1982 PH T.C. Memo ¶82,292, 43 TCM 1481.

Based on this operating cycle, the tax advisor estimates Austin's working capital requirement as follows:

Annual operating expenses = $2,700,000 + $875,000 − $75,000 + $100,000 = $3,600,000
Working capital requirement = $3,600,000 × 0.283 = $1,018,800

The estimated $1,018,800 working capital requirement is $193,800 more than the $825,000 of actual working capital recorded on December 31. This excess justifies accumulating additional current earnings for working capital needs. ◄

The *Bardahl* formula also is used to estimate the working capital requirements of service companies. A different calculation is used because service companies generally hold little inventory. For service companies, one looks primarily at the financing of accounts receivables. Because their principal asset is key personnel, these companies must maintain adequate working capital to retain employees when a below-normal level of business is expected. Therefore, some amount may be added to actual working capital to cover the cost of retaining personnel for a period of time.[67]

REAL-WORLD EXAMPLE

Apparently, an accumulation of funds to redeem stock under a buy–sell agreement is not a reasonable business need. Even though a 50% shareholder was killed in a plane crash shortly after year-end, the Tax Court refused to recognize the validity of an accumulation to redeem such shareholder's stock (*Technalysis Corp.*, 101 T.C. 397 (1993).

Stock Redemptions. Section 537(a) permits corporations to accumulate earnings for two types of stock redemptions: Sec. 303 (death tax) redemptions and excess business holdings redemptions. In the first case, after the death of a shareholder, a corporation can accumulate earnings to redeem stock from the shareholder's estate or a beneficiary of the estate. These earnings cannot exceed the amount of stock redeemable under Sec. 303. In the second case, a corporation can accumulate earnings to redeem stock held by a private foundation to the extent the stock exceeds the business holdings limit imposed on such foundations.

Business Contingencies. The courts and IRS have sanctioned the accumulation of earnings for business contingencies not specifically mentioned in the Sec. 537 Treasury Regulations. Among these contingencies are actual or potential litigation, a likely decline in business activities following the loss of a major customer, insuring against a potential loss, providing for a threatened strike, and funding an employee retirement plan.

OBJECTIVE 5

Calculate the corporation's accumulated earnings tax

CALCULATING THE ACCUMULATED EARNINGS TAX

The accumulated earnings tax calculation is set forth in Figure C:5-3. The tax is levied at a 15% rate in 2003 through 2010. After 2010, the rate will revert to the highest marginal tax rate for individuals. As with the PHC penalty tax, a corporation can reduce its tax liability by making dividend distributions. However, corporations generally do not avail themselves of this tax planning device because they often pay only a nominal dividend or no dividend at all. Also, IRS auditors generally do not raise the accumulated earnings tax issue until one or more years after the corporation has filed its tax return. Unlike the PHC tax liability, the accumulated earnings tax liability cannot be extinguished through the payment of deficiency dividends.

ADDITIONAL COMMENT

Accumulated taxable income should not be confused with current E&P. In fact, the accumulated earnings tax has been assessed in years where no increase in the corporation's E&P had occurred.

ACCUMULATED TAXABLE INCOME.

The starting point for calculating **accumulated taxable income** is the corporation's regular taxable income. A series of positive and negative adjustments to regular taxable income are made to derive accumulated taxable income.

ADDITIONAL COMMENT

The accumulated earnings tax adjustments derive an amount that more closely corresponds to the corporation's economic income and thus better measures the dividend-paying capability of the corporation than does taxable income.

Positive Adjustments to Regular Taxable Income. A corporation may not claim a dividends-received deduction. Thus, regular taxable income must be increased by the amount of this deduction in a manner similar to that under the PHC tax rules.[68] The U.S. production activities deduction, however, is not added back to regular taxable income to

[67] See, for example, *Simons-Eastern Co. v. U.S.*, 31 AFTR 2d 73-640, 73-1 USTC ¶9279 (D.C. GA, 1972).

[68] Sec. 535(b).

▼ **FIGURE C:5-3**
Calculating the Accumulated Earnings Tax

Regular taxable income
Plus: Positive adjustments
1. Dividends-received deduction
2. NOL deduction
3. Excess charitable contributions carried over from a preceding tax year and deducted in determining taxable income
4. Capital loss carryover deduction
Minus: Negative adjustments
1. Accrued U.S. and foreign income taxes
2. Charitable contributions that exceed the 10% corporate limitation
3. Net capital losses (where capital losses for the year exceed capital gains)
4. Net capital gain minus the amount of any associated income taxes
Minus: Dividends-paid deduction
Minus: Accumulated earnings credit

Accumulated taxable income
Times: 0.15 (in 2003–2010)

Accumulated earnings tax

derive accumulated taxable income. Any NOL deduction claimed must be added back to regular taxable income. The IRC allows no special deduction for an NOL incurred in the immediately preceding year, as it does under the PHC tax rules.

Negative Adjustments to Taxable Income. Charitable contributions are deductible without regard to either the 10% corporate limitation or the individual limitations. The same adjustments required for PHC tax purposes are required for accumulated earnings tax purposes.

U.S. and foreign income taxes accrued by the corporation reduce accumulated taxable income whether the corporation uses the accrual or cash method of accounting. A corporation may deduct the amount of its net capital gain, minus income taxes attributable to this gain. The capital gains adjustment prevents a corporation with substantial capital gains from paying the accumulated earnings tax on that portion of the gains retained in the business. Net capital losses (the excess of capital losses over capital gains for the year) represent a negative adjustment to regular taxable income.

WHAT WOULD YOU DO IN THIS SITUATION?

Magnum Corporation, your client, has manufactured handguns and rifles for years. Because of competition from foreign manufacturers, demand for U.S. manufactured guns has recently declined. The total historical cost of Magnum's operating assets at the end of its most recent fiscal year is $10 million. Total gross operating revenues are $18 million. Over the years, the company accumulated $2.5 million of earnings that Magnum's CEO Allen Blay invested in securities. The investment portfolio consists primarily of growth stocks, debt instruments, and Internet stocks. Along with his other duties as CEO, Allen manages this portfolio. With the recent surge in the stock market, the value of Magnum's investment securities have increased to more than $12 million. The portfolio took a small "hit" in Fall 2006. The dividend and interest income earned on the portfolio represents only a small portion of Magnum's gross income. During a meeting with you, Allen brings to your attention this investment and its stellar performance. Is Magnum liable for the accumulated earnings tax? What action(s) do you recommend that the corporation take?

Dividends-Paid Deduction. A deduction is allowed for four types of dividends paid:

- Regular dividends
- Throwback dividends
- Consent dividends
- Liquidating distributions

With minor exceptions, the rules for the dividends-paid deduction are the same in the PHC tax calculation as in the regular tax calculation. Nonliquidating distributions paid during the tax year are eligible for the dividends-paid deduction only if paid out of the corporation's E&P. A dividends-paid deduction is not available for preferential dividends.[69]

Throwback dividends are distributions made out of E&P in the first 2½ months following the close of the tax year. The accumulated earnings tax rules require that any distribution made in the first 2½ months following the close of the tax year be treated as if paid on the last day of the preceding tax year without regard to the amount of dividends actually paid during the preceding tax year.[70] Because the IRS generally does not raise the accumulated earnings tax issue until after it has audited a corporation's tax return, throwback and consent dividends are of limited use in avoiding the accumulated earnings tax. Liquidating distributions eligible for the dividends-paid deduction include those made in connection with a complete liquidation, a partial liquidation, or a stock redemption.[71]

ADDITIONAL COMMENT

The minimum accumulated earnings credit is $250,000 ($150,000 for certain personal service corporations) reduced by accumulated E&P at the close of the preceding year. In many situations, corporations that have been in existence for some time have accumulated E&P exceeding $250,000. Thus, the minimum credit is of little practical significance for them.

Accumulated Earnings Credit. The accumulated earnings credit permits a corporation to accumulate E&P up to either a minimum amount ($250,000 for most C corporations) or the level of its earnings accumulated for the reasonable needs of the business. Unlike other credits, the **accumulated earnings credit** does not offset the accumulated earnings tax liability on a dollar-for-dollar basis. Instead, it serves to reduce accumulated taxable income. Different rules for the accumulated earnings credit exist for operating companies, service companies, and holding or investment companies.[72]

TYPICAL MISCONCEPTION

The maximum accumulated earnings credit is the amount of current E&P retained to meet the reasonable needs of the business minus an adjustment for net capital gains. This amount does not include the entire accumulation for business needs but only the accumulation in the current tax year. Thus, to calculate the maximum credit, it is necessary to determine how much of prior accumulations are retained for reasonable business needs.

- Operating companies can claim a credit equal to the greater of (1) $250,000 minus accumulated E&P at the end of the preceding tax year[73] or (2) current E&P retained to meet the reasonable needs of the business.
- The accumulated E&P balance mentioned in the previous bullet point is reduced by the amount of any current year throwback distributions treated as having been made out of the preceding year's E&P.
- Current E&P is reduced by the dividends-paid deduction. Any net capital gains (reduced by federal taxes attributable to the gains) reduce the amount of current E&P retained for business needs.
- Special rules apply to personal service companies operating primary in the fields of health, law, engineering, architecture, accounting, actuarial science, performing arts, and consulting. For these companies, the basic calculation set forth above applies, but the $250,000 minimum credit is reduced to $150,000.
- Holding and investment companies may claim a credit equal to $250,000 minus accumulated E&P at the end of the preceding tax year. An increased credit based on the reasonable needs of the business is not available to a holding or investment company.

EXAMPLE C:5-21 ▶ Midway Corporation reports accumulated E&P, current E&P, and current E&P retained for business needs as shown in the table below. The corporation paid no dividends during the current year. Midway is a C corporation that is not a personal service or investment company. Its minimum credit is $250,000.

---

[69] Sec. 562(c). See page C:5-23 for a more detailed discussion.

[70] Sec. 563(a). Personal holding companies, on the other hand, must elect throwback treatment for dividends paid in the 2½ month period following the end of the tax year.

[71] Sec. 562(b)(1)(B).

[72] Sec. 535(c).

[73] Section 1561(a)(2) limits a controlled group of corporations to a single statutory exemption.

TYPICAL MISCONCEPTION

Although called a *credit*, the accumulated earnings credit actually is a *deduction* in deriving accumulated taxable income.

Tax Items	*Scenario One*	*Scenario Two*
1. Accumulated E&P	$ 75,000	$ 75,000
2. Lifetime minimum credit	250,000	250,000
2a. Current year minimum credit (2a = 2 − 1)	175,000	175,000
3. Current E&P	400,000	400,000
3a. Current E&P retained for business needs	300,000	50,000
3b. Current E&P exceeding business needs (3b = 3 − 3a)	100,000	350,000
4. Accumulated earnings credit (Greater of 2a or 3a)	300,000	175,000

In both scenarios, $175,000 of the minimum credit is available. In Scenario One, because the available $175,000 minimum credit is less than $300,000 of E&P retained for business needs, the accumulated earnings credit is $300,000. In Scenario Two, because the available $175,000 minimum credit is greater than the $50,000 of E&P retained for business needs, the accumulated earnings credit is $175,000. In both scenarios, no minimum credit is available in future years. All future accumulated earnings credits are based on E&P retained for business needs. ◀

COMPREHENSIVE EXAMPLE

The following example illustrates the calculation of accumulated taxable income and the accumulated earnings tax liability.

EXAMPLE C:5-22 ▶ Pasadena is a closely held family corporation that has conducted a successful manufacturing business for several years. On January 1 of the current year, Pasadena reports a $750,000 accumulated E&P balance. The following information pertains to current year operations:

Operating profit	$650,000
Long-term capital gain	30,000
Dividends received from a 20%-owned corporation	150,000
Interest	70,000
Gross income	$900,000
Dividends-received deduction	(120,000)
Salaries	(100,000)
General and administrative expenses	(200,000)
Charitable contributions	(60,000)[a]
U.S. production activities deduction	(10,000)
Regular taxable income	$410,000

[a] $60,000 = 0.10 × [$900,000 − ($100,000 + $200,000)].

Federal income taxes (based on current rates and assuming no alternative minimum tax liability) accrued by Pasadena are $139,400. Actual charitable contributions are $75,000. On June 30, the corporation paid cash dividends of $20,000. Pasadena's current E&P retained for the reasonable needs of the business (after the dividends-paid deduction) is $160,000.

If the IRS determines that Pasadena has accumulated earnings exceeding the reasonable needs of its business, Pasadena's accumulated earnings tax liability would be calculated as follows:

Regular taxable income			$410,000
Plus:	Dividends-received deduction		120,000
Minus:	Excess charitable contributions		(15,000)[a]
	Federal income taxes		(139,400)
	Long-term capital gain	$ 30,000	
	Minus: Federal income taxes	(10,200)[b]	(19,800)
	Dividends-paid deduction		(20,000)
	Accumulated earnings credit:		
	Increase in current year reasonable needs	$160,000	
	Minus: Long-term capital gain (net of taxes)	(19,800)	(140,200)

Accumulated taxable income	$195,600
Times: Tax rate	× 0.15
Accumulated earnings tax liability	$ 29,340

[a] $75,000 total contributions − $60,000 limitation = $15,000 excess contributions.
[b] $10,200 = $30,000 × 0.34

Assuming the corporation owes no AMT liability, Pasadena's total federal tax liability for the current year would be $168,740 ($139,400 + $29,340). ◀

Topic Review C:5-4 presents an overview of the accumulated earnings tax.

TAX PLANNING CONSIDERATIONS

This section examines three areas of tax planning: special accounting method elections for AMT purposes, avoiding the PHC tax, and avoiding the accumulated earnings tax.

SPECIAL AMT ELECTIONS

Under the AMT rules, two special elections permit taxpayers to defer certain deductions for regular tax purposes. Although deferral of these deductions will increase the taxpayer's regular tax liability, it will decrease the taxpayer's AMT liability.

Section 59(e) permits an extended writeoff period for certain expenditures that otherwise would be tax preference items or AMT adjustments. If the corporation so elects, each expenditure to which the extended writeoff period applies will not be a Sec. 57 tax preference item, nor will the corporation have to make an adjustment for the expenditure under Sec. 56. The expenditures for which the special election can be made and the extended writeoff periods that apply are as follows:

ADDITIONAL COMMENT

Not only can special AMT elections reduce a taxpayer's AMT liability, but they also can reduce compliance costs by eliminating the need to keep an additional set of depreciation or amortization records.

Topic Review C:5-4

Accumulated Earnings Tax

1. The accumulated earnings tax rules apply to all but certain types of corporations. As a practical matter, the tax is assessed primarily on closely held corporations (other than S corporations).
2. Certain transactions generally lead IRS auditors to believe that an accumulated earnings tax problem exists. These transactions include loans made by the corporation to its shareholders, the expenditure of corporate funds for the personal benefit of shareholders, and investments in property or securities unrelated to the corporation's principal activities.
3. Earnings accumulated for the reasonable needs of the business are exempt from the accumulated earnings tax. Among such needs are a business acquisition, debt retirement, and the build up of working capital. A $250,000 minimum credit is available to reduce accumulated taxable income. The credit amount declines to $150,000 for certain personal service corporations.
4. The accumulated earnings tax is 15% (in 2003–2010) of accumulated taxable income. Accumulated taxable income is regular taxable income plus certain positive adjustments (e.g., dividends-received deduction) and minus certain negative adjustments (e.g., federal income taxes, excess charitable contributions, and a portion of net capital gains). An accumulated earnings credit equal to the greater of a fixed dollar amount or earnings accumulated during the year for the reasonable needs of the business also is available.
5. Accumulated taxable income can be reduced by cash and property dividends paid during the year as well as consent and throwback dividends paid after year-end. Deficiency dividends, available for PHC tax purposes, are not available for accumulated earnings tax purposes.

IRC Section	*Type of Expenditure*	*Writeoff Period (Years)*
173	Circulation	3
174	Research and experimental	10
263	Intangible drilling and development	5
616	Mining and natural resource development	10
617	Mining exploration	10

A corporation can make this election for any portion of a qualified expenditure and can revoke it only with IRS consent.[74]

The second election permits taxpayers to elect for regular tax purposes the depreciation method generally required for AMT purposes. Such an election allows the taxpayer to change the depreciation method for personal property placed in service after 1998 from the 200% declining balance method normally used for regular tax purposes to the 150% declining balance method as used for AMT purposes. The election is not relevant for nonresidential real property or residential rental property because AMT depreciation for such property placed in service after 1998 is the same as regular tax depreciation. Through this election, the taxpayer reduces or eliminates the amount of annual AMT depreciation and basis adjustments. For any tax year, the taxpayer may make this election with respect to one or more classes of property. Once made, the election applies to all property in such class placed in service during the tax year. The taxpayer must make the election by the due date for its annual return (including any permissible extensions).[75]

ELIMINATING THE ACE ADJUSTMENT

C corporations must increase their AMTI by the amount of the ACE adjustment. For some C corporations this adjustment can be substantial. If the corporation is closely held, it can elect to be taxed as an S corporation and thereby avoid the ACE adjustment.[76] S corporations are not subject to the corporate AMT. They pass their AMT adjustments and preference items through to their shareholders.

OBJECTIVE 6

Explain how a corporation can avoid the personal holding company tax

AVOIDING THE PERSONAL HOLDING COMPANY TAX

Five tax planning techniques can be used to avoid the PHC tax.

CHANGES IN THE CORPORATION'S STOCK OWNERSHIP. To circumvent the stock ownership rules, a potential PHC can issue additional stock to unrelated parties. The stock may be either common or preferred. The issuance of nonvoting preferred stock to unrelated parties permits the corporation to spread out stock ownership among a larger number of individuals without diluting the voting power of the current common shareholder group.

CHANGING THE AMOUNT AND TYPE OF INCOME EARNED BY THE CORPORATION. A corporation can change the amount and type of its income in the following ways:

- Adding "operating" activities to its business to decrease the proportion of passive or investment income in its total income.
- Converting taxable interest or dividends earned on an investment portfolio into nontaxable interest or long-term capital gains. Nontaxable interest and long-term capital gains are excluded from PHCI.
- Generating passive income of a type that is excludible from PHCI or in an amount that diminishes the proportion of other items includible in PHCI. For example, a corporation might attempt to increase the proportion of its rental income to more than 50% of AOGI so as to exclude from PHCI adjusted income from rents.

[74] Secs. 59(e)(4)(A) and (B).
[75] Secs. 168(b)(2) and (5).
[76] Sec. 56(g)(6).

KEY POINT

One of the easiest ways to avoid the PHC penalty tax is a dividend distribution. If a corporation lacks the funds to pay a cash dividend, it can pay a consent dividend (which is a hypothetical dividend). In addition, throwback, consent, and deficiency dividends can be declared after year-end in after-the-fact tax planning.

DIVIDEND DISTRIBUTIONS. Dividend payments reduce the PHC tax base. A corporation can exclude certain categories of income (e.g., adjusted income from rents) from PHCI through the payment of dividends sufficient to reduce the amount of other PHCI to 10% or less of OGI. Some of these dividends (e.g., throwback, consent, and deficiency) can be paid after year-end, thereby allowing last-minute tax planning.

MAKING AN S CORPORATION ELECTION. As mentioned earlier, an S corporation election eliminates liability for the PHC tax because S corporations are exempt from this tax. The election also eliminates the double taxation of corporate earnings distributed as dividends (see Chapter C:11). Such an election is advantageous where corporate tax rates exceed individual tax rates. The LLC form offers many of the same tax and nontax benefits offered by the S corporation form.

LIQUIDATING THE CORPORATION. A PHC could liquidate and distribute its assets to the shareholders. Liquidating distributions made out of E&P are eligible for the dividends-paid deduction and thus can reduce UPHCI. This alternative, however, may be unattractive where top individual tax rates exceed corporate tax rates.

OBJECTIVE 7

Explain how a corporation can avoid the accumulated earnings tax

AVOIDING THE ACCUMULATED EARNINGS TAX

The primary defense against an IRS argument that the corporation has accumulated an unreasonable amount of earnings is that the earnings accumulations are necessary to meet the future needs of the business. Business plans in support of this defense should be documented and revised periodically. The plans should describe completed, but not abandoned, projects in sufficient detail. In the event of an IRS challenge, a tentative timetable for the completion of current projects should be set forth. Such plans might be incorporated into the minutes of one or more board meetings.

Transactions suggesting an unreasonable earnings accumulation (e.g., loans to shareholders or large investment portfolios) should be avoided. The business purpose for major transactions should be thoroughly documented.

Corporations potentially liable for the accumulated earnings tax should consider making an S corporation election. S corporations avoid accumulated earnings tax liability on a prospective basis. By implication, an S corporation election will not eliminate potential exposure to the accumulated earnings tax for tax years prior to the year in which the election becomes effective.

COMPLIANCE AND PROCEDURAL CONSIDERATIONS

ALTERNATIVE MINIMUM TAX

A corporation reports the AMT calculation on Form 4626 (Alternative Minimum Tax—Corporations). A completed Form 4626, based on the facts in the comprehensive example on pages C:5-13 and C:5-14, appears in Appendix B.

Chapter C:3 discussed the corporate estimated income tax. Section 6655(g) provides that the corporate AMT be included in the required estimated tax payments. Failure to do so will subject a corporation to underpayment penalties, which are discussed in Chapter C:3.

ETHICAL POINT

A tax practitioner has a responsibility to advise his or her client early in the year about potential PHC problems and steps that can be taken to avoid the penalty tax. Because the PHC tax is self-assessed, a Schedule PH must be filed with Form 1120 even if the corporation owes no PHC tax.

PERSONAL HOLDING COMPANY TAX

FILING REQUIREMENTS FOR TAX RETURNS. A PHC must file a corporate income tax return (Form 1120). Schedule PH must accompany the return. Schedule PH incorporates the tests for determining whether a corporation is a PHC as well as the UPHCI and PHC tax calculations. Regulation Sec. 301.6501(f)-1 extends from three to six years the limitations period for the PHC tax if a PHC fails to file Schedule PH, even if the corporation owes no additional tax.

ETHICAL POINT

Notwithstanding the tax practitioner's responsibility to advise his or her client about potential accumulated earnings tax problems, because the tax is not self-assessed, the CPA or the client are under no duty to notify the IRS of the tax problem.

PAYMENT OF THE TAX, INTEREST, AND PENALTIES. Corporations ordinarily pay the PHC tax when they file Form 1120 and Schedule PH, or when the IRS or the courts determine that the corporation owes the tax. Unlike the AMT, the PHC tax is not included in the corporation's required estimated tax payments. Corporations that pay the PHC tax after the due date for filing their return (without regard to extensions) generally will also owe interest and penalties on the unpaid PHC tax balance. Interest will accrue from the date the return is originally due (without regard to extensions) until the entire tax is paid.[77]

ACCUMULATED EARNINGS TAX

No schedule or return is required for reporting the accumulated earnings tax. Because of the ad hoc nature of this tax, a corporation generally will not pay it until some time after the IRS has audited its tax return. Sec. 6601(b) requires the charging of interest on the accumulated earnings tax balance from the original due date for the return (without regard to extensions) until the date the IRS receives full tax payment.[78] The IRS also may impose a penalty for negligent underpayment of an accumulated earnings tax.[79]

FINANCIAL STATEMENT IMPLICATIONS

OBJECTIVE 8

Understand the financial statement implications of the minimum tax credit.

MINIMUM TAX CREDIT

SFAS No. 109 prescribes the following requirements for accounting for the AMT in financial statements:

- Measure the total deferred tax liability and asset for regular tax temporary differences and carryforwards using the regular tax rate.
- Measure the total deferred tax asset for the minimum tax credit arising from the AMT.
- Reduce the deferred tax asset for the minimum tax credit by a valuation allowance if, based on available evidence, it is more likely than not (i.e., greater than 50%) that all or some of the deferred asset will not be realized.

For example: In the current year, Alpha Corporation incurs a $40,000 regular tax liability and a $10,000 AMT liability, which also creates a $10,000 minimum tax credit carryforward. Alpha determines that it will realize (use) the entire credit in a future year. Therefore, it need not establish a valuation allowance. Alpha has no regular tax temporary differences, resulting in the minimum tax credit carryover being the only deferred tax asset or liability item. Accordingly, Alpha makes the following book journal entry:

Federal income tax expense	40,000	
Deferred tax asset	10,000	
Taxes payable		50,000

In a subsequent year, Alpha's regular tax is $90,000, and its tentative minimum tax is $70,000. Thus, it can realize (use) the entire $10,000 minimum tax credit for a net tax liability of $80,000. Accordingly, it will make the following book journal entry:

Federal income tax expense	90,000	
Deferred tax asset		10,000
Taxes payable		80,000

See Chapter C:3 for a general discussion of financial implications of federal income taxes.

[77] *Hart Metal Products Corp. v. U.S.*, 38 AFTR 2d 76-6118, 76-2 USTC ¶9781 (Ct. Cls., 1976).

[78] Rev. Rul. 87-54, 1987-1 C.B. 349.

[79] Rev. Rul. 75-330, 1975-2 C.B. 496.

PROBLEM MATERIALS

DISCUSSION QUESTIONS

C:5-1 Explain the legislative intent behind the enactment of the corporate alternative minimum tax (AMT).

C:5-2 Define the following terms relating to the corporate AMT:
a. Tax preference item
b. AMT adjustment
c. Alternative minimum taxable income
d. Statutory exemption amount
e. Tentative minimum tax
f. Minimum tax credit

C:5-3 What special rules (if any) apply to the calculation of the AMT for the following entities:
a. Small corporations
b. Closely held corporations
c. S corporations
d. Limited liability companies (LLCs)

C:5-4 Agnew Corporation operates a small manufacturing business. During its first tax year (2007), the company reported gross income of $1 million. The gross income originated from sales of small toys that Agnew manufactured and sold for $3.8 million. Agnew's cost of goods sold was $2.8 million. Taxable income was $125,000. The corporation's owner estimates that future sales will grow at 25% per year. Agnew is not related to any other C corporations. Does Agnew's CPA need to calculate the corporation's alternative minimum tax in the initial year? In any of the next five years? Explain.

C:5-5 Seminole Corporation began conducting business in the current year. Its gross receipts for the first year were less than $1 million. Austin and Frank each own 50% of the Seminole stock. The same two individuals also own equally three other corporations that have had gross receipts totaling $10 million or more in the current year and in the three preceding years. Explain to Austin and Frank whether Seminole and its sister corporations will be exempt from the corporate AMT in the current year.

C:5-6 Dunn Corporation's taxable income is less than $40,000. The corporation is not eligible for the AMT small corporation exemption. The CPA preparing the corporate tax return does not calculate the AMT because he knows that taxable income is less than the AMT statutory exemption amount. Is he correct in his belief? Explain.

C:5-7 Determine whether the following statements relating to the corporate AMT are true or false. If false, explain why.
a. Tax preference items may either increase or decrease AMTI.
b. The same NOL carryover amount is used for regular tax and AMT purposes.
c. The amount by which the tentative minimum tax exceeds the regular tax generates a minimum tax credit.
d. A corporate taxpayer's general business credit can offset not only its regular tax liability but also its AMT liability.
e. The ACE adjustment can only increase preadjustment AMTI.
f. The corporate AMT is levied on and paid by both C corporations and S corporations.
g. The minimum tax credit can be carried back as well as forward.

C:5-8 Identify the following items as an AMT adjustment to taxable income (A), a tax preference item (P), or neither (N):
a. Percentage depletion in excess of a property's adjusted basis at the end of the tax year.
b. The Sec. 179 expense and first-year MACRS depreciation claimed on a machine costing $200,000 and placed in service in the current year.
c. The difference between gain on the sale of the asset in Part b for taxable income purposes and alternative minimum taxable income purposes.
d. Tax-exempt interest earned on State of Michigan private activity bonds.
e. Tax-exempt interest earned on State of Michigan general revenue bonds.
f. 75% of the excess of adjusted current earnings (ACE) over preadjustment AMTI.

C:5-9 What adjustment must be made if ACE exceeds preadjustment AMTI? If ACE is less than preadjustment AMTI? What restrictions on negative ACE adjustments apply?

C:5-10 Florida Corporation encounters an AMT problem for the first time in the current year. The problem is due to a $2 million gain on a nondealer installment sale recognized over a ten-year period for financial accounting and taxable income purposes. The gain is fully includible in current year ACE. Explain to Florida's president the ACE adjustment, how the adjustment is similar to and different from E&P adjustments with which he is familiar, and whether the adjustment will partially or completely reverse in future years.

C:5-11 Some tax authorities say a positive ACE adjustment can produce three different effective tax rates depending on the corporation's tax situation: (1) a 0% effective tax rate, (2) a 15% effective tax rate, or (3) between a 0% and 15% effective tax rate. Explain what the tax authorities mean.

C:5-12 Indicate whether the following items are includible in taxable income, preadjustment AMTI, and/or ACE.
a. Tax-exempt interest on private activity bonds
b. Proceeds from an insurance policy (with no cash surrender value) on the life of a corporate officer
c. Gain on a current year sale of Sec. 1231 property that a nondealer reports under the installment method of accounting
d. Interest earned on State of Michigan general revenue bonds
e. Intangible drilling costs incurred and deducted in the current year
f. Amortization of organizational expenditures made last year
g. Deduction for a dividend received from a 25%-owned domestic corporation

C:5-13 Discuss the taxable income, AMTI, and ACE depreciation rules applicable to the following types of new property acquired in the current year and later tax years.
a. Section 1250 property—a factory building
b. Section 1245 property—a drill press

C:5-14 In the current year, Burbank Corporation incurs an AMT liability for the first time. The liability is due entirely to an ACE adjustment resulting from the receipt of $4 million of life insurance proceeds paid upon the death of the firm's chief executive officer. The policy had no cash surrender value. Explain to Burbank's director of taxes whether Burbank can reduce future regular tax liabilities by the AMT paid in the current year.

C:5-15 The personal holding company tax and the accumulated earnings tax reflect efforts to prevent use of the corporate entity to avoid taxation. Explain the congressional intent behind these two tax measures.

C:5-16 Which of the following corporate forms are exempt from the PHC tax? The accumulated earnings tax?
a. Closely held corporations
b. S corporations
c. Professional corporations
d. Tax-exempt organizations
e. Publicly held corporations
f. Corporations filing a consolidated tax return
g. Limited liability companies

C:5-17 Because of its quality investments, Carolina Corporation has always generated 30% to 40% of its gross income from passive sources. For years, the corporation held a block of stock in a company that was recently acquired. As a result of the acquisition, the corporation realized a substantial long-term capital gain that will increase this year's investment income from 40% to 70% of gross income. Explain to Carolina's president why she should or should not be worried about the personal holding company tax.

C:5-18 Which of the following income items, when received by a corporation, are included in personal holding company income (PHCI)? Indicate whether any special circumstances would exclude an income item that is generally includible in PHCI.
a. Dividends
b. Interest on a corporate bond
c. Interest on a general revenue bond issued by a state government
d. Rental income from a warehouse leased to a third party
e. Rental income from a warehouse leased to the corporation's sole shareholder
f. Royalty income on a book whose copyright is owned by the corporation
g. Royalty income on a computer software copyright developed by the corporation and leased to a software marketing firm
h. Accounting fees earned by a professional corporation owned by three equal shareholders, which offers public accounting services to various clients
i. Long-term capital gain on the sale of a stock investment

C:5-19 Which of the following dividends are eligible for the dividends-paid deduction in computing the PHC tax? The accumulated earnings tax?
a. Cash dividend paid on common stock during the tax year
b. Annual cash dividend paid on preferred stock where no dividend is paid to the common shareholders
c. Dividend payable in the stock of an unrelated corporation
d. Stock dividend payable in the single class of stock of the distributing corporation
e. Cash dividend paid two months after the close of the tax year

C:5-20 Define the term *consent dividend*. How can a consent dividend be used to avoid the PHC and accumulated earnings taxes? In each case, what requirements must be met by the distributing corporation and/or its shareholders to qualify a consent dividend for the dividends-paid deduction? What are the tax consequences of a consent dividend to the shareholders and the distributing corporation?

C:5-21 Explain the advantages of a deficiency dividend. What requirements must a PHC and its shareholders meet to use a deficiency dividend to reduce or eliminate the PHC tax liability? Can a deficiency dividend eliminate interest and penalties, in addition to the PHC tax liability?

C:5-22 Determine whether the following statements regarding the PHC tax are true or false:

a. In a given tax year, a corporation might not owe the PHC tax even though it is deemed to be a PHC.
b. A sale of a large tract of land held for investment can make a manufacturing corporation a PHC.
c. Federal income taxes (including the alternative minimum tax) accrued by the PHC reduce UPHCI for the tax year.
d. To reduce UPHCI, the corporation can pay consent dividends any time from the first day of the tax year through the due date for the corporation's tax return (including extensions).
e. The payment of a deficiency dividend permits a PHC to eliminate its PHC tax liability, as well as related interest and penalties.
f. A corporation deemed to be a PHC for a particular tax year also can be liable for the accumulated earnings tax for that year.
g. A PHC can be subject to the alternative minimum tax.

C:5-23 Explain the implication of the following statement: "Like many dogs, the threat (bark) of the PHC tax is much worse than the actual penalties assessed in connection with its (bite)."

C:5-24 Explain the following statement: "Although the accumulated earnings tax can be imposed on both publicly held and closely held corporations, the tax is likely to be imposed primarily on closely held corporations."

C:5-25 The accumulated earnings tax is imposed only when the corporation is "formed or availed of for the purpose of avoiding the income tax." Does tax avoidance have to occur at the corporate or the shareholder level for the accumulated earnings tax to be imposed? Does tax avoidance have to be the sole motive for earnings accumulation before such imposition?

C:5-26 How, in its first year of operation, can a newly formed corporation be subject to the PHC tax but not the AMT and the accumulated earnings tax?

C:5-27 Gamma Corporation has generated substantial cash flows from its manufacturing activities. It has only a moderate need to reinvest its earnings in existing facilities or for expansion. In recent years, the corporation has amassed a large investment portfolio due to management's unwillingness to pay dividends. The corporation is unlikely to be deemed a PHC but is concerned about its exposure to the accumulated earnings tax. Explain to Gamma's president what steps he can take to avoid liability for the accumulated earnings tax in the current year? In future tax years? Do these steps require the payment of a cash dividend?

C:5-28 Explain the *Bardahl* formula. Why have some tax authorities said that this formula implies a greater degree of mathematical precision than is actually the case? Does the *Bardahl* formula apply to service companies?

C:5-29 Different rules for calculating the accumulated earnings credit apply to operating companies, holding and investment companies, and service companies. Explain the differences.

C:5-30 Determine whether the following statements about the accumulated earnings tax are true or false:

a. Before the IRS can impose the accumulated earnings tax, it need only show that tax avoidance was one of the motives for the corporation's unreasonable accumulation of earnings.
b. Long-term capital gains are included in the accumulated earnings tax base.
c. Each corporate member of a controlled group can claim a separate \$150,000 or \$250,000 accumulated earnings credit.
d. A dividends-paid deduction can be claimed for both cash and property distributions (other than nontaxable stock dividends) made by a corporation. This deduction reduces both regular taxable income and accumulated taxable income.
e. The accumulated earnings tax liability cannot be eliminated by paying a deficiency dividend.
f. Interest and penalties on the accumulated earnings tax deficiency accrue only from the date the IRS or the courts determine that the tax is owed.
g. The accumulated earnings tax is self-reported on Form 1120-AET that is filed along with the corporate tax return.

C:5-31 For each of the following statements, indicate whether the statement is true for the PHC tax only (P), the accumulated earnings tax only (A), both taxes (B), or neither tax (N).

a. The tax is imposed only if the corporation satisfies certain stock ownership and income requirements.
b. The tax applies to both closely held and publicly traded corporations.
c. The tax is ad hoc in nature (i.e., assessed in the course of an audit).
d. Long-term capital gains are a neutral factor in determining the amount of the tax liability.
e. Tax-exempt interest income is excluded from the tax base.
f. A credit that reduces the tax liability on a dollar-for-dollar basis is available.
g. Throwback dividends may be paid without limit.
h. Consent dividends are eligible for a dividends-paid deduction.
i. Throwback and consent dividends are effective in reducing or eliminating the tax liability.
j. The tax can be avoided by paying a deficiency dividend.
k. The tax applies to S corporations.

ISSUE IDENTIFICATION QUESTIONS

C:5-32 Bird Corporation purchases for its manufacturing facility a new precision casting machine costing $1 million. Installation costs are $75,000. The machine is placed in service in June 2007. The old casting machine, which was placed in service in 1998, was sold to an unrelated party at a $125,000 financial accounting profit. What asset disposition and capital recovery issues must you, as Bird's director of federal taxes, address when accounting for removing the old machine from, and placing the new machine in service and in calculating the 2007 tax depreciation?

C:5-33 Parrish is a closely held C corporation. Robert and Kim Parrish own all its stock. The corporation, now in its second month of operation, expects to earn $200,000 of gross income in the current tax year. This income is expected to consist of approximately 40% dividends, 30% corporate bond interest, and 30% net real estate rentals (after interest expense, property taxes, and depreciation). Administrative expenses are estimated to be $40,000. What special problems does the substantial passive income that Parrish Corporation expects to earn present to you as its CPA?

C:5-34 McHale is a C corporation owned by eight individuals, three of whom own 51% of the stock and comprise the board of directors. The corporation operates a successful automobile repair parts manufacturing business. It has accumulated $2 million of E&P and expects to accumulate another $300,000 annually. Annual dividends are $30,000. Because Americans retain their vehicles longer than they did 20 years ago, demand for McHale's repair parts has been strong for the past five years. However, little expansion or replacement of the current plant is projected for three to five years. Management has invested $200,000 annually in growth stocks. Its current investment portfolio, which is held primarily as protection against a business downturn, is valued at $1.2 million. Loans to shareholder-employees currently amount to $400,000. As McHale Corporation's tax return preparer, what tax issues should you have your client consider?

PROBLEMS

C:5-35 ***Small Corporation AMT Exemption.*** Willis Corporation reports the following gross receipts for its initial years of operation.

Year	*Gross Receipts*
2007	$ 2,750,000
2008	3,987,500
2009	5,682,188
2010	8,097,117
2011	11,538,392
2012	16,442,209

For purposes of applying the gross receipts test, Willis is not related to any other corporations, nor is it a successor to another corporation. Year 2007 gross receipts have been annualized. Is Willis exempt from the corporate alternative minimum tax if it was formed in 2007? Explain.

C:5-36 ***Alternative Minimum Tax Calculation.*** In the current year, Whitaker Corporation reports taxable income of $700,000. It has net positive AMT adjustments of $600,000 and tax preference items of $100,000. Adjusted current earnings for the year are $2 million. Whitaker is not eligible for the small corporation exemption.

a. What is Whitaker's AMTI?
b. What is Whitaker's tentative minimum tax?
c. What is Whitaker's regular tax liability?
d. What is Whitaker's AMT liability?
e. What is Whitaker's minimum tax credit?
f. By what amount would Whitaker have to reduce its AMT adjustment to avoid paying the AMT?

C:5-37 ***Depreciation Calculations.*** On June 1, 2004, Water Corporation placed a machine costing $10,000 in service. The machine is seven-year property under the MACRS rules. The machine has a 12-year class life. The corporation claimed bonus depreciation in 2004 but did not elect Sec. 179 expensing. Based on the half-year convention, calculate the annual depreciation deductions for purposes of determining

a. Taxable income
b. Alternative minimum taxable income
c. Are separate depreciation calculations necessary to compute adjusted current earnings?
d. How would your answers to Parts a–c change if the machine were instead purchased and placed in service on June 1, 2007?

C:5-38 ***Basis Adjustment.*** Assume the same basic facts as in Part d of Problem C:5-37. Water Corporation sells the machine for $9,000 on August 31, 2009.
a. What gain does Water report for purposes of determining regular taxable income, AMTI, and adjusted current earnings?
b. If you were using regular taxable income as the starting point for calculating AMTI, what type of adjustment would you need to report the transaction in 2009 for AMTI purposes?

C:5-39 ***ACE Adjustment.*** Calculate the ACE adjustment for Towne Corporation for each year since its incorporation in 2003.

	2003	*2004*	*2005*	*2006*	*2007*
ACE	$500	$500	$500	$500	$(500)
Preadjustment AMTI	(100)	600	900	–0–	(300)
ACE adjustment	?	?	?	?	?

C:5-40 ***Regular Tax and AMT Calculations.*** Bronze Corporation, an accrual method taxpayer, reports the following data relating to its year 2007 operations:

Taxable income from recurring operations	$278,000
Other income and expense items not included in the $278,000 figure:	
Dividend from 10%-owned corporation	40,000
Life insurance proceeds received upon the death of a corporate officer	500,000
Tax-exempt bond interest on private activity bonds	25,000
Tax-exempt bond interest (on general revenue bonds)	30,000
Installment sale of land (a capital asset) in June:	
Total realized gain	400,000
Portion of gain on installment collections in 2007	32,000
Depreciation:	
For regular tax purposes	120,000
For AMTI purposes	85,000
For ACE purposes	60,000
Sec. 1245 property sold in current year:	
Recognized gain for regular tax purposes	30,000
Basis for regular tax purposes	54,000
Basis for AMTI purposes 30 − 6 = 24 gain	6K 60,000
Basis for ACE purposes	4K 64,000

Bronze is not eligible for the small corporation exemption and has no AMT adjustment for the U.S. production activities deduction.
a. What is Bronze's ACE adjustment?
b. What is Bronze's AMTI?
c. What is Bronze's AMT liability?
d. What is Bronze's available minimum tax credit (if any)?
e. In what years can the minimum tax credit be used?
f. Does Bronze have to include the amount of its projected minimum tax liability in its 2007 estimated tax calculation?
g. Does Bronze have to include the amount of its minimum tax liability in the determination of its tax underpayment penalty (if any) for 2007?

C:5-41 ***Regular Tax and AMT Calculations.*** Campbell Corporation reports regular taxable income of $210,000 in 2007. Campbell is not eligible for the small corporation exemption and has no AMT adjustment for the U.S. production activities deduction. The following facts were taken into account in deriving regular taxable income.
1. Equipment acquired in 2001–2007 was depreciated under MACRS. For 2007, MACRS depreciation on this equipment is $100,000. Depreciation for AMT purposes is $75,000.
2. Campbell recognizes a Sec. 1245 gain of $12,000 for regular tax purposes on the sale of an asset. The asset's income tax basis is $9,000 less than its AMT basis.

3. Campbell's adjusted current earnings for 2007 is $480,000.
a. What is Campbell's AMTI?
b. What is Campbell's AMT liability?
c. What is the amount (if any) of Campbell's minimum tax credit? To what years can this credit be carried over?
d. Does Campbell have to include the amount of its projected minimum tax liability in its 2007 estimated tax calculation?
e. Does Campbell have to include the amount of its minimum tax liability in the determination of its tax underpayment penalty (if any) for 2007?
f. Does Campbell have to include the amount of a projected AMT liability in its quarterly estimated tax payments for 2008?

C:5-42 ***Regular Tax and AMT Calculations.*** Sheldon Corporation reports taxable income of $150,000 for its second tax year (2007). Its regular tax liability is $41,750. The following facts were taken into account in deriving taxable income.

- Used equipment is depreciated under MACRS. The amount of MACRS depreciation claimed is $90,000. Depreciation for AMT purposes in 2007 is $60,000.
- The corporation includes in taxable income a $12,000 gain on the sale of equipment. The asset's regular tax basis at the time of sale is $9,000 less than its AMT basis.
- Sheldon's adjusted current earnings is $340,000.
- Sheldon has no AMT adjustment for the U.S. production activities deduction.

No NOL, capital loss, tax credit, or negative ACE carryovers from the first year of operations are available for use in the second year.
a. What is Sheldon's AMT liability?
b. Is any minimum tax credit carryback or carryover available? If so, to what years?

C:5-43 ***Regular Tax and AMT Calculations.*** Subach Corporation, organized in 1999, reports the following results for 2007:

Taxable income	$600,000
Preadjustment AMTI	630,000
Adjusted current earnings, excluding the following transactions:	900,000
• Tax-exempt bond interest (on general revenue bonds)	100,000
• Recognized gain on a capital asset installment sale concluded this year. No collections were made this year.	150,000
• Life insurance proceeds received upon the death of a corporate executive	500,000
• Amortization of organizational expenditures	5,000

Subach uses the accrual method of accounting. The only adjustment the corporation makes to taxable income to derive preadjustment AMTI is a $30,000 addition to reflect a different depreciation method used in calculating AMTI. Taxable income, preadjustment AMTI, and the beginning ACE amounts all include an $80,000 deduction for a dividend received from a 25%-owned corporation. No NOL, capital loss, tax credit, or negative ACE adjustment carryovers from prior years are available in the current year. What is Subach's current year federal tax liability?

C:5-44 ***AMTI Calculation.*** Alabama Corporation conducts a copper mining business. During the current year, it reports taxable income of $400,000, which includes a $100,000 deduction for percentage depletion. The depletable property's adjusted basis at year-end (before reduction for current year depletion) is $40,000. Cost depletion, had it been deducted, would have been $30,000. Depreciation under MACRS is $140,000 for regular tax purposes and $90,000 for AMTI purposes. Alabama sold an asset at a $12,000 gain that is included in taxable income. The asset's adjusted basis is $10,000 higher for AMT purposes than for regular tax purposes. Alabama's adjusted current earnings is $800,000. Alabama is not eligible for the small corporation exemption and has no AMT adjustment for the U.S. production activities deduction.
a. What is Alabama's AMTI?
b. What is Alabama's AMT liability?
c. What is the amount (if any) of Alabama's minimum tax credit? To what years can it be carried over?

C:5-45 *Regular Tax and AMT Calculations.* What is Middle Corporation's regular tax liability, AMT liability, and minimum tax credit (if any) in the following three scenarios? Assume that, in prior years, Middle has had $120,000 of positive ACE adjustments. Middle is not eligible for the small corporation exemption.

	Scenario 1	*Scenario 2*	*Scenario 3*
Taxable income	$200,000	$ 50,000	$300,000
Tax preference items and positive AMTI adjustments (other than the ACE adjustment)	100,000	25,000	160,000
Adjusted current earnings	500,000	150,000	400,000

C:5-46 *Regular Tax and AMT Calculations.* Delta Corporation reports taxable income of $2 million, tax preference items of $100,000, net positive AMTI adjustments of $600,000 before the ACE adjustment, and adjusted current earnings of $4 million. Delta is not eligible for the small corporation exception and has no AMT adjustment for the U.S. production activities deduction.

a. What is Delta's regular tax liability?
b. What is Delta's AMT liability?
c. What is the amount (if any) of Delta 's minimum tax credit? To what years can it be carried over?

C:5-47 *Minimum Tax Credit.* Jones Corporation has $600,000 of taxable income plus $400,000 of positive AMTI adjustments and $200,000 of tax preference items. Jones is not eligible for the small corporation exemption.

a. What is Jones' regular tax liability and AMT liability?
b. What is Jones' minimum tax credit (if any)? To what years can it be carried over?

C:5-48 *Minimum Tax Credit.* Gulf Corporation reports the following tax amounts for the period 2005–2007:

Tax Amounts	*2005*	*2006*	*2007*
Regular tax	$75,000	$100,000	$210,000
Tentative minimum tax	40,000	150,000	170,000

In what years does a minimum tax credit arise? To what years can the credit be carried over? Do any credit carryovers remain in 2008?

C:5-49 *Minimum Tax Analysis.* Duncan Manufacturing Corporation, an accrual method taxpayer, sold a parcel of land on July 1, 2007. Duncan had planned to use the land to expand its manufacturing facilities. The land (a Sec. 1231 asset) had a $3 million market value and a $1.2 million adjusted basis. As partial consideration for the sale, Duncan received a $300,000 cash down payment on July 1, 2007. In addition, the purchaser will pay annual payments of $540,000 [0.20 × ($3,000,000 − $300,000)] over the next five years on July 1 of each year. Duncan charges a market interest rate on the unpaid balance. The CEO has asked you to prepare a year-by-year analysis of the impact of this land sale on the firm's tax position. In your calculation, you can ignore interest earned on the sale. On a year-by-year basis, what are the expected effects of the installment sale on the corporation's regular tax and AMT liabilities? Assume for AMT purposes that Duncan is not a small corporation and has no AMT adjustment for the U.S. production activities deduction. Also assume a 34% regular tax rate.

C:5-50 *General Business Credit.* In the current year, Edge Corporation's regular tax before credits is $165,000. Its tentative minimum tax is $100,000. Its only credit in the current year is a $200,000 general business credit relating to research expenditures.

a. What amount of this credit may Edge use to reduce its current year tax liability?

b. What carryovers and carrybacks are available, and to what years may they be carried?

C:5-51 *Estimated Tax Requirement.* Ajax Corporation expects to owe a $100,000 regular tax liability and a $70,000 AMT liability for the current year. Last year, it owed a $200,000 regular tax liability and no AMT liability. What is Ajax's minimum estimated tax payment for the current year?

C:5-52 *Estimated Tax Payments.* Dallas Corporation reports the following 2006 and 2007 tax liabilities:

Type of Liability	*2006*	*2007*
Regular tax	$100,000	$150,000
AMT	–0–	25,000

Each tax year covers a 12-month period. Dallas is a small corporation. It made $23,000 of estimated tax payments for each quarter of 2007.

a. How much tax will Dallas owe when it files its 2007 tax return?

b. Is Dallas liable for any estimated tax underpayment penalties? If so, how much did it underpay in each quarter?

C:5-53 ***PHC Definition.*** In which of the following situations will Small Corporation be deemed to be a PHC? Assume that personal holding company income comprises more than 60% of Small's adjusted ordinary gross income.

a. Art owns 100% of Parent Corporation stock, and Parent owns 100% of Small stock. Parent and Small file separate tax returns.

b. Art owns one-third of Small stock. The PRS Partnership, of which Phil, Robert, and Sue each have a one-third capital and profits interest, also own one-third of Small stock. The remaining shares of Small stock are owned by 50 individuals unrelated to Art, Phil, Robert, and Sue.

c. Art and his wife, Becky, each own 20% of Small stock. The remaining shares of Small stock are owned by the Whitaker Family Trust. Becky and her three sisters each have a one-fourth beneficial interest in the trust.

C:5-54 ***Personal Holding Company Status.*** In each of the following four scenarios, determine whether the corporation is a personal holding company. Assume the corporation's outstanding stock is owned equally by three shareholders.

Item	*Scenario 1*	*Scenario 2*	*Scenario 3*	*Scenario 4*
Gross profit from sales	$40,000	$ 80,000	$40,000	$ 60,000
Capital gains	–0–	10,000	5,000	10,000
Interest income	15,000	15,000	10,000	20,000
Dividends	10,000	10,000	2,000	–0–
Rental income	80,000	150,000	–0–	–0–
Copyright royalties	–0–	5,000	80,000	–0–
Personal service income	–0–	–0–	–0–	100,000
Rent-related expenses	20,000	30,000	–0–	–0–
Copyright-related expenses	–0–	–0–	25,000	–0–
Dividends paid	8,000	10,000	5,000	10,000

C:5-55 ***PHC Tax.*** In the current year, Moore Corporation is deemed to be a PHC and reports the following results:

Taxable income	$200,000
Dividend received from an 18%-owned domestic corporation	50,000
Dividends paid	75,000

a. What is Moore's regular tax liability (ignoring any AMT implications)?

b. What is Moore's PHC tax liability?

c. What measures can Moore take to eliminate its PHC tax liability after year-end and before it files its tax return? After it files its tax return?

C:5-56 ***PHC Tax.*** In the current year, Kennedy Corporation is deemed to be a PHC and reports the following results:

Taxable income	$400,000
Federal income taxes	136,000
Dividends paid to Marlene, Kennedy's sole shareholder	75,000

The following information is available:

- The corporation received $100,000 of dividends from a 25%-owned domestic corporation.
- The corporation received $30,000 of tax-exempt interest income.
- The corporation recognized a $175,000 Sec. 1231 gain on the sale of land.

a. What is Kennedy's PHC tax liability?

b. What measures can Kennedy take to eliminate the PHC tax liability after year-end and before Kennedy files its tax return? After Kennedy files its tax return?

C:5-57 *PHC Tax.* Alice and Barry each own shares of Alpha Corporation. For 2007, the corporation reports the following income and expenses:

Rental income		$ 750,000
Dividend income from less than 20%-owned corporations		200,000
Tax-exempt interest income		40,000
Gross profit on sale of merchandise		50,000
Long-term capital gain on the sale of stocks		200,000
Total income		$1,240,000
Minus: Rent related expenses:		
Interest expense	$140,000	
Depreciation expense	150,000	
Property taxes	175,000	
Other Sec. 162 expenses	165,000	(630,000)
Minus: Administrative expenses		(90,000)
Pre-tax profit		$ 520,000

During 2007, Alpha Corporation paid $50,000 in dividends to its shareholders. Assume Alpha is not eligible for the U.S. production activities deduction.

a. Is Alpha a personal holding company?
b. What is Alpha's regular tax liability?
c. What is Alpha's personal holding company tax liability (if any)?

C:5-58 ***Unreasonable Accumulation of Earnings.*** In each of the following scenarios, indicate why Adobe Corporation's accumulation of earnings might be unreasonable relative to its business needs. Provide one or more arguments the corporation might put forth to support its positon that the accumulation is reasonable. Assume that Tess owns all the Adobe stock.

a. Ten years ago, Adobe established a sinking fund to retire its ten-year notes and has added cash to the fund annually. Six months ago, the corporation decided to refinance the notes at maturity at a lower interest rate through the issuance of a new series of bonds sold to an insurance company. The sinking fund balance is invested in stocks and commercial paper. A general plan exists to use the balance to purchase operating assets. No definite plans have been established by year-end.
b. Adobe regularly lends money to Tess at a rate slightly below the rate charged by a commercial bank. Tess has repaid about 20% of these loans. The current balance on the loans is $500,000, which approximates one year's net income for Adobe.
c. Adobe has heavily invested in stocks and bonds. The current market value of its investments is $2 million. The investment portfolio comprises approximately one-half of Adobe's assets.
d. Tess owns three other corporations, which, together with Adobe, form a brother-sister controlled group. Adobe regularly lends funds to Tess's three other corporations. Current loans amount to $500,000. The interest rate charged approximates the commercial rate for similar loans.

C:5-59 ***Bardahl Formula.*** Lion Corporation is concerned about a potential accumulated earnings tax liability. It accumulates E&P for working capital necessary to conduct its manufacturing business. The following data appear in its current year balance sheets.

Account	*Beginning Balance*	*Ending Balance*	*Peak Balance for the Year*
Accounts receivable	$300,000	$400,000	$400,000
Inventory	240,000	300,000	375,000
Accounts payable	150,000	200,000	220,000

The following data appear in Lion's current year income statement:

Sales	$3,200,000
Cost of goods sold	1,500,000
Purchases	1,200,000
Operating expenses (other than cost of goods sold)	1,000,000

Included in operating expenses are depreciation of $150,000 and federal income taxes of $100,000.

a. What is Lion's operating cycle in days? As a decimal?
b. What is Lion's reasonable working capital amount as determined under the *Bardahl* formula?
c. What steps must Lion take to justify accumulating earnings that exceed the amount sanctioned under the *Bardahl* formula?

C:5-60 ***Accumulated Earnings Credit.*** In each of the following scenarios, calculate the accumulated earnings credit. Assume the corporation uses a calendar year as its tax year. Also assume that it realizes no current year capital gains.

a. Frank Corporation, a manufacturer of plastic toys, started business last year and reported E&P of $50,000. In the current year, the corporation reports E&P of $150,000 and pays no dividends. Of the $150,000 current E&P, the corporation retains $130,000 to meet its business needs.
b. How would your answer to Part a change if Frank were a service company that provides accounting services?
c. Hall Corporation's accumulated E&P balance at January 1 of the current year is $200,000. During the year, Hall, a glass container manufacturer, reports $100,000 of current E&P, all of which is retained to meet the reasonable needs of the business. Hall pays no dividends.

C:5-61 ***Accumulated Earnings Tax.*** Twentieth Century Cleaning Services, Inc. provides cleaning services in Atlanta, Georgia. It is not a member of a controlled or an affiliated group. Twentieth Century reports the following results for the current year:

Taxable income	$500,000
Federal income taxes (at 34%)	170,000
Dividends paid in August of the current year	75,000

Included in taxable income are the following items that may require special treatment:

Long-term capital gains	$ 30,000
Short-term capital gains	10,000
Dividends from 21%-owned domestic corporation	100,000
Excess charitable contributions from last year that are deductible in the current year	25,000

Twentieth Century's accumulated E&P balance and its reasonable business needs on January 1 of the current year, were $125,000. The firm can justify the retention of $90,000 of current E&P to meet its reasonable business needs. Assume the corporation is not eligible for the U.S. production activities deduction.

a. What is Twentieth Century's accumulated taxable income?
b. What is Twentieth Century's accumulated earnings tax liability?

C:5-62 ***Accumulated Earnings Tax.*** Howard Corporation conducts a manufacturing business and has a compelling need to accumulate earnings. Its January 1, E&P balance is $600,000. It reports the following operating results for the current year:

Taxable income		$700,000
Federal income taxes		238,000
Dividends paid:	July 15 of the current year	50,000
	February 10 of the following year	100,000

Other information relating to Howard's current year operations is as follows:

NOL carryover from last year deducted in the current year	$100,000
Net capital gain	100,000
Dividends received from 10%-owned domestic corporation	75,000

Current year E&P before dividend payments is $400,000. Howard can justify the retention of $120,000 of current E&P to meet the reasonable needs of its business.

a. What is Howard's accumulated taxable income?
b. What is Howard's accumulated earnings tax liability?

COMPREHENSIVE PROBLEM

C:5-63 Stock in Random Corporation is owned equally by two individual shareholders. During the current year, Random reports the following results:

Income: Rentals	$200,000
Dividend (from a 25%-owned domestic corporation)	30,000
Interest	15,000
Short-term capital gains	3,000
Long-term capital gains	17,000
Expenses related to rental income:	
Interest	30,000
Depreciation	32,000
Property taxes	11,000
Other Sec. 162 expenses	50,000
General and administrative expenses	10,000
Dividend paid on June 30	15,000

a. What is Random's gross income?
b. What is Random's ordinary gross income?
c. What is Random's adjusted income from rents?
d. What is Random's adjusted ordinary gross income?
e. What is Random's personal holding company income?
f. Is Random a PHC?
g. What is Random's regular taxable income and regular tax liability?
h. What is Random's undistributed PHC income (UPHCI) and PHC tax liability?
i. What measures can Random take before year-end to avoid the PHC tax? Alternatively, what can Random do after year-end but before the corporation files its tax return? If the corporation takes no action before or after filing its return, what remedy does it have after filing?
j. Assume that Random's income and expense items will be similar in future years unless management changes Random's asset mix. What changes can management make to reduce the corporation's PHC exposure in future years?
k. If Random is a PHC, can it also be subject to the accumulated earnings tax?

TAX STRATEGY PROBLEMS

C:5-64 Galadriel and John, married with no children, own all the stock in Marietta Horse Supplies. The couple's C corporation has been in business for ten years. The business has been successful, permitting both owners to pay themselves a reasonable salary from its revenues. Although the salaries cover life's necessities, a review of industry statistics shows that the salary of each owner is about one-half or two-thirds of salaries paid by similar-sized horse supply businesses. The reason for the low salaries is that, for a number of years, the owners had felt continual pressure to retain as much of the profits in the business as possible to have sufficient working capital to finance inventories and other business needs. In the past two years, the firm has established lines of credit with two local banks that have alleviated much of this pressure. However, the couple has never had time to review the amount of their compensation. Recently, an IRS agent asked the couple about items reported in a previously filed tax return. The agent reviewed all three open years and proposed a settlement for the items in question. While in the office, the IRS agent indicated to you as the couple's CPA that, in her opinion, the company had unreasonably accumulated earnings and that she would be investigating the issue before closing the audit. What advice can you give the couple about their salaries and potential liability for the accumulated earnings tax?

C:5-65 Steve and Andrew write music and lyrics for popular songs. In 2004, they organized S&A Music Corporation, each brother owning one-half of its stock. Through the end of 2006, they contributed a total of $250,000 in capital to the business. The songs that Steve and Andrew write and promote have been successful. Annually, the firm earns $300,000 of royalties from the copyrights that it owns. With the aid of their aunt who operates a local bookkeeping service, Steve and Andrew organized their business as a C corporation. The brothers decide that, with the success of their music business, perhaps they should move their accounting services to an accounting firm that specializes in providing tax advice for small- or medium-sized businesses. As a staff member of this accounting firm, what advice can you provide the brothers about possible tax problems and potential tax strategies?

TAX FORM/RETURN PREPARATION PROBLEM

C:5-66 King Corporation, I.D. No. 38-1534789, an accrual method taxpayer, reports the following results for 2006:

Taxable income	$ 800,000
Regular tax (before credits)	272,000
Alternative tax NOL deduction	175,000
Depreciation adjustment for personal property placed in service after 1986	148,000
Personal property acquired in 1998 sold this year:	
Acquisition cost	50,000
Regular tax depreciation	38,845
AMT depreciation	26,845
Increase in LIFO recapture amount	75,000
Tax-exempt interest income:	
Private activity bonds	15,000
Other bonds	5,000
Adjusted current earnings	2,000,000
General business credit (targeted jobs credit)	10,000
Dividends paid	120,000

King is not eligible for the small corporation exemption and has no AMT adjustment for the U.S. production activities deduction. Taxable income includes $95,000 of Sec. 1231 gain from a payment received in 2006 relating to an installment sale of land that King made in 2005. King realized a $950,000 gain on the sale in 2005 and is recognizing gain over a ten-year period as the purchaser makes equal annual payments. King reported the transaction properly in 2005. Prepare Form 4626 for King Corporation to report its AMT liability (if any) for 2006.

CASE STUDY PROBLEMS

C:5-67 Eagle Corporation operates a family business established by Edward Eagle, Sr. ten years ago. Edward Eagle, Sr. died, and the Eagle stock passed to his children and grandchildren. The corporation operates rental property and also invests in dividend paying stock and corporate bonds. Eagle's tax advisor made the following profit projection for the current year:

Rentals	$260,000
Dividend income (from a 40%-owned domestic corporation)	90,000
Interest income	20,000
Gross income	$370,000
Rental expenses:	
Depreciation expense	$ 70,000
Interest expense	100,000
Property taxes	10,000
Other Sec. 162 expenses	20,000
General and administrative expenses	15,000
Total expenses	$215,000
Net profit	$155,000

Eagle paid dividends of $40,000 in each of the past three years. Eagle was not a PHC in prior years.

Required: Prepare a memorandum to Edward Eagle, Jr. regarding potential liability for the PHC tax. In your memorandum, discuss the following two questions:

a. Is Eagle likely to be deemed a PHC for the current year?
b. If Eagle is likely to be deemed a PHC for the current year, what measures (if any) should be taken before year-end to eliminate the PHC tax liability? After year-end?

C:5-68 Goss Corporation is a leading manufacturer of hangers for the laundry and dry cleaning industry. The family-owned business has prospered for many years and has generated approximately $100 million of sales and $8 million in after-tax profits. Your accounting firm has performed the audit and tax work for Goss and its executives since the company was created in 1948. Little technological change in the manufacturing of hangers has occurred, and much of the equipment currently used dates back to the 1950s and 1960s. The advent of plastic hangers and improved fabrics has kept the company's market share constant, and the corporation plans no major plant expansions or additions. Salaries paid to corporate executives, most of whom are family members, are above the national averages for similar officers. Dividend payments in recent years have not exceeded 10% of the after-tax profits. On December 1, 2007, you were assigned to oversee the preparation of the 2007 Goss tax return. In undertaking the assignment, you review the 2004–2006 Goss tax returns. You note from Schedule L (the balance sheet) that the corporation made about $1.5 million in loans to three executives and regularly increased the size of its stock portfolio between 2004 and 2006. This increase leads you to believe that Goss may be liable for the accumulated earnings tax in 2007 and prior years.

Required:

a. What responsibility do you have to make Goss or the partner in charge of the Goss account aware of the potential accumulated earnings tax liability?
b. Should you advise the IRS of the potential liability for prior years? Should you disclose the potential liability on the current year return?
c. Prepare a list of measures that can be taken to reduce or eliminate Goss' liability for the accumulated earnings tax.

TAX RESEARCH PROBLEMS

C:5-69 Brown Corporation purchased (and placed in service) two assets in January 2004, its initial year of operation. The first asset, a commercial factory building, cost $200,000, with $40,000 of the acquisition price allocated to the land. The second, a used machine that is seven-year MACRS property, cost $80,000. The class life for the machine is ten years. In March 2007, Brown sold both assets in connection with the relocation of its manufacturing activities. The sale price for the factory building was $225,000, with $45,000 of the sale price allocated to the land. The sale price for the machine was $70,000. Brown used MACRS depreciation on each asset for regular tax purposes but did not make a Sec. 179 election or claim bonus depreciation. Assume the machine was depreciated under the half-year convention, and the building was depreciated under the mid-month convention. What are the amount and character of the gains reported by Brown for regular tax and alternative minimum tax purposes?

C:5-70 Camp Corporation is owned by Hal and Ruthie, who have owned their stock since the corporation was formed in 1992. The corporation uses the calendar year as its tax year and the accrual method of accounting. In 2006, Camp borrowed $4 million from a local bank. The loan is secured by a lien on its machinery. Camp loaned 90% of the borrowings to Vickers Corporation at the same annual rate as the rate on the bank loan. Vickers also is owned equally by Hal and Ruthie. Vickers sells to the automobile industry parts that are manufactured by Camp and unrelated companies. Camp's operating results suffered as a result of a slowdown in the automobile industry. The gross margin on its sales declined from $1 million in 2006 to $200,000 in 2007. Interest earned by Camp on the loan to Vickers is $432,000 in 2007. Other passive income earned by Camp is $40,000. Camp's accountant believes that the corporation is not a PHC because the interest income Camp earns can be netted against the $432,000 interest expense paid to the bank for the loan to Vickers. Is he correct in his belief?

A partial list of sources is

- IRC Secs. 542(a) and 543(a)(1)
- Reg. Sec. 1.543-1(b)(2)
- *Bell Realty Trust,* 65 T.C. 766 (1976)
- *Blair Holding Co., Inc.,* 1980 PH T.C. Memo ¶80,079, 39 TCM 1255

C:5-71 William Queen owns all the stock in Able and Baker Corporations. Able, a successful enterprise, has generated excess working capital of $3 million. Baker is still in its developmental stages and has had substantial capital needs. To meet some of these needs, William has had Able lend Baker $2 million during 2005 and 2006. These loans are secured by

Baker notes, but not other Baker property. Able has charged Baker interest at a rate ordinarily charged by a commercial lender. Upon reviewing Able's 2007 books in the audit of its 2005 tax return, an IRS agent indicates that Able is liable for the accumulated earnings tax because of its build up of excess working capital and its loans to Baker. Later this week, you will meet with the agent for a third time. Before this meeting, you must research whether loans to a related corporation to finance its working capital meet a reasonable need of the business. At a meeting to discuss this problem, William asks whether filing a consolidated tax return would eliminate this potential problem and, if so, how must the ownership structure change to accomplish this objective.

A partial list of research sources is

- IRC Secs. 532 and 537
- Reg. Secs. 1.537-2(c) and -3(b) and 1.1502-43
- *Latchis Theatres of Keene, Inc. v. CIR*, 45 AFTR 1836, 54-2 USTC ¶9544 (1st Cir., 1954)
- *Bremerton Sun Publishing Co.*, 44 T.C. 566 (1965)

C:5-72 Three years ago, Sadaka Oil Company filed a Form 1120 corporate tax return on which it reported $9,284,000 of gross income. Because the corporation incurred extraordinary drilling and depletion costs and sustained substantial partnership investment losses, Sadaka reported negative taxable income of $1,691,400. The company filed a Form 4626 alternative minimum tax return, on which it included in its gross income $5,719,400 of tax preference items. As a result of this inclusion, Sadaka reported alternative minimum taxable income of $2,533,300 and an alternative minimum tax liability of $506,660.

The corporation paid the $506,660 alternative minimum tax under protest. Now, it plans to petition the IRS for a refund of $338,280. In its petition, Sadaka will argue that the tax preference items, which had been reported as regular tax deductions on its Form 1120, conferred a regular tax benefit of only $4,028,000. Therefore, the company should have incurred an alternative minimum tax liability of $168,380, based on the extent to which Sadaka derived a regular tax benefit from the tax preference items. Sadaka's accountants calculated this alternative minimum tax amount as follows:

Gross income reported on Form 1120	$9,284,000
Less: Regular tax deductions reported on Form 1120	(5,256,000)
Subtotal	$4,028,000
Less: Tax preference items reported on Form 4626	(5,719,400
Tax preference items producing no regular tax benefit	($1,691,400)
AMTI reported on Form 4626	$2,533,300
Less: Tax preference items producing no regular tax benefit	(1,691,400)
Adjusted AMTI reflecting regular tax benefit	$ 841,900
Times: AMT rate	× 20%
AMT reflecting regular tax benefit	$ 168,380

Sadaka's chief tax officer has asked you to evaluate the merits of this argument. After reviewing the calculation and researching the issue, what do you advise him? At a minimum consult the following authorities:

- IRC Sec. 56
- *Weiser v. U.S.*, 69 AFTR 2d 92-934, 92-1 USTC ¶50,169 (9th Cir., 1992)

CHAPTER 6

CORPORATE LIQUIDATING DISTRIBUTIONS

LEARNING OBJECTIVES

After studying this chapter, you should be able to

1. Understand the difference between a complete liquidation and a dissolution
2. Apply the general shareholder gain and loss recognition rules for a corporate liquidation
3. Determine when the liquidating corporation recognizes gains and losses on making a liquidating distribution
4. Determine when the Sec. 332 and Sec. 337 nonrecognition rules apply to the liquidation of a subsidiary corporation
5. Determine the effect of a liquidation on the liquidating corporation's tax attributes
6. Understand the different tax treatments for open and closed liquidation transactions
7. Determine when a liquidating corporation recognizes gains and losses on the retirement of debt

CHAPTER OUTLINE

As part of the corporate life cycle, management may decide to discontinue the operations of a profitable or unprofitable corporation by liquidating it. As a result of this decision, the shareholders may receive liquidating distributions of the corporation's assets. Preceding the formal liquidation of the corporation, management may sell part or all the corporation's assets. The sale may be undertaken to dispose of assets the shareholders may not want to receive in a liquidating distribution or to obtain cash that can be used to pay the corporation's liabilities (including federal income taxes incurred on the liquidation).

Ordinarily, the liquidation transaction is motivated by a combination of tax and business reasons. However, sometimes it is undertaken principally for tax reasons.

- If the corporation liquidates and its shareholders hold the assets in an unincorporated form (e.g., sole proprietorship or partnership), the marginal tax rate may be reduced from the 35% top corporate rate to a lower 10%, 15%, 25%, 28%, or 33% individual rate (in 2007). For example, even low amounts of taxable income are taxed at 35% in a personal service corporation.
- If the assets are producing losses, the shareholders may prefer to hold them in an unincorporated form and deduct the losses on their personal tax returns.
- Corporate earnings are taxed once under the corporate income tax rules and a second time when the corporation distributes the earnings as dividends or when the shareholder sells or exchanges the corporate stock at a gain. Liquidation of the corporation permits the assets to be held in an unincorporated form, thereby avoiding double taxation of subsequent earnings.

ADDITIONAL COMMENT

Capital gains recognized after May 5, 2003, through 2010 are taxed at a maximum 15% rate as are qualified dividends received in tax years 2003 through 2010. Thus, dividends and capital gains receive comparable tax rate treatment except that capital gain taxation is deferred until sale of the stock or liquidation of the corporation.

Liquidating a corporation carries a tax cost, however. The liquidating corporation is taxed as though it sold its assets, and the shareholders receiving liquidating distributions are taxed as though they sold their stock. A C corporation cannot simply elect to be treated as a flow-through entity under the check-the-box regulations (see Chapter C:2). Thus, the only route to converting a C corporation into a sole proprietorship, partnership, limited liability company, or limited liability partnership is via a taxable corporate liquidation followed by formation of the desired entity. Alternatively, a C corporation could obtain flow-through status without liquidating if it elects S corporation status. Even with this approach, the S corporation faces potential taxation on its built-in gains (see Chapter C:11).

This chapter explains the tax consequences of corporate liquidations to both the liquidating corporation and its shareholders. In so doing, the chapter presents two sets of liquidation rules. The general liquidation rules apply to liquidations of corporations not controlled by a parent corporation. Special rules apply to the liquidation of a controlled subsidiary.

OVERVIEW OF CORPORATE LIQUIDATIONS

This chapter initially presents an overview of the tax and nontax consequences of a corporate liquidation to both the shareholders and the distributing corporation.

THE SHAREHOLDER

Determining the tax consequences of the liquidation to each of the liquidating corporation's shareholders entails several questions:

- What are the amount, timing, and character of the shareholder's recognized gain or loss?
- What is the shareholder's adjusted basis of each property received?
- When does the holding period begin for each property received by the shareholder?

When a corporation liquidates under the general rules, a shareholder treats the liquidating distribution as an amount received in exchange for his or her stock. The shareholder recognizes a capital gain or loss equal to the excess of any money received plus the FMV of any nonmoney property received over the adjusted basis of his or her stock. The basis of each property received is stepped-up or stepped-down to the property's FMV on the liquidation date. The holding period for the asset begins the day after the liquidation date.

If a parent corporation liquidates a controlled subsidiary under special rules, however, the parent corporation (shareholder) recognizes no gain or loss. In addition, the bases and holding periods of the subsidiary's assets carry over to the parent.

THE CORPORATION

TAX STRATEGY TIP

Although the shareholders and corporation usually incur no tax cost upon forming a corporation, the tax costs of liquidating a corporation (other than a controlled subsidiary) may be substantial. The tax consequences of liquidating a corporation should be a consideration in the initial decision to use the corporate form. For example, assuming a 34% corporate tax rate and a 15% capital gains rate at the shareholder level, the effective tax cost of a complete liquidation is approximately 43.9% {34% + [(1 − 0.34) × 15%]}.

Two questions must be answered to determine the tax consequences of the liquidation transaction for the liquiding corporation:

- What are the amount and character of the corporation's recognized gain or loss?
- What happens to the corporation's tax attributes upon liquidation?

When a liquidation occurs under the general rules, the liquidating corporation recognizes gain or loss on the distribution of property to its shareholders. The recognized gain or loss is the same as what the corporation would recognize had it sold the distributed property to its shareholders. Some restrictions (discussed later in the chapter) limit loss recognition in certain potentially abusive situations. Also, tax attributions, such as net operating loss (NOL) carryovers and earnings and profits, disappear when the corporation liquidates under the general rules.

If the liquidating corporation is an 80%-controlled subsidiary of the parent corporation, the liquidating corporation recognizes no gain or loss under special rules. In this case, the subsidiary's tax attributes carry over to the parent corporation.

EXAMPLE C:6-1 ▶ Randy Jones owns Able Corporation, a C corporation. Randy's basis for his Able stock is $100,000. The corporation's assets are summarized below:

Assets	*Adjusted Basis*	*Fair Market Value*
Cash	$ 50,000	$ 50,000
General Cable stock	75,000	125,000
Machinery	115,000	200,000
Total	$240,000	$375,000

Able Corporation owes $60,000 to its creditors. In step 1, Able sells its machinery to an unrelated purchaser for $200,000 cash. The machinery originally cost $250,000, and Able has claimed $135,000 of depreciation on the machinery. Able recognizes a total gain on the machinery sale of $85,000 ($200,000 − $115,000). In step 2, Able uses $60,000 in cash to pay its creditors. In step 3, Able distributes the General Cable stock, a capital asset, to Randy Jones. Able recognizes a $50,000 ($125,000 − $75,000) capital gain on the distribution. Assuming a 34% marginal tax rate, Able must pay $45,900 [($85,000 + $50,000) × 0.34] in federal income taxes on the distribution of the General Cable stock and the sale of the machinery (step 4). The tax payment reduces Able's remaining assets to $144,100 in cash [($50,000 + $200,000) − $60,000 paid to creditors − $45,900 paid in federal income taxes]. Randy Jones recognizes a $169,100 ($144,100 cash + $125,000 securities − $100,000 basis for stock) long-term capital gain on the liquidating distribution. The same federal income taxes would have occurred had Able sold both the stock and machinery to unrelated purchasers, or had Able distributed both the stock and machinery to Randy Jones because each of Able's noncash assets have FMVs exceeding their adjusted bases.[1] (See Figure C:6-1 for an illustration of the corporate liquidation.) ◀

OBJECTIVE 1

Understand the difference between a complete liquidation and a dissolution

DEFINITION OF A COMPLETE LIQUIDATION

The term *complete liquidation* is not defined in the IRC, but Reg. Sec. 1.332-2(c) indicates that distributions made by a liquidating corporation must either completely cancel or redeem all its stock in accordance with a plan of liquidation or be one of a series of distributions that completely cancels or redeems all its stock in accordance with a plan of liquidation (see page C:6-21 for a discussion of plans of liquidation). When more than one distribution occurs, the corporation must be in a liquidation status when it makes the first

[1] The corporation's recognized gains and losses might be different if one or more of the properties had declined in value. The loss might be disallowed if the property were distributed to Randy Jones, where it would be recognized if the property had been sold to an unrelated purchaser.

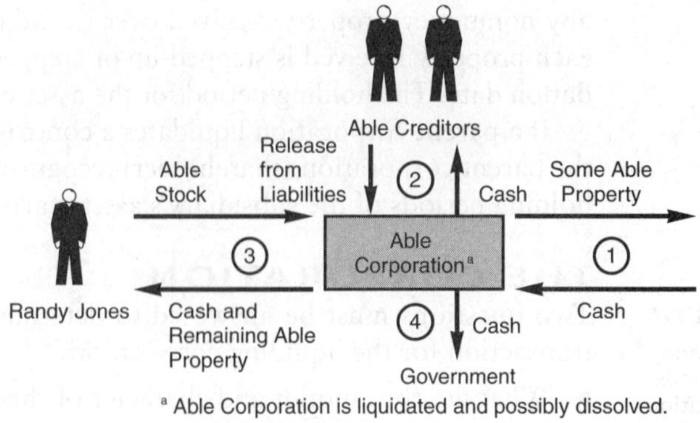

Able Creditors
Release from Liabilities (2) Cash
Able Stock
Some Able Property
Able Corporation[a]
(3) Randy Jones — Cash and Remaining Able Property
(1) Cash — Unrelated Purchaser
(4) Cash — Government

[a] Able Corporation is liquidated and possibly dissolved.

FIGURE C:6-1 ▶ ILLUSTRATION OF CORPORATE LIQUIDATION (EXAMPLE C:6-1)

liquidating distribution under the plan, and such status must continue until the liquidation is completed. A distribution made before the corporation adopts a plan of liquidation is taxed to the shareholders as a dividend distribution or stock redemption (see Chapter C:4).

Liquidation status exists when the corporation ceases to be a going concern and its activities are for the purpose of winding up its affairs, paying its debts, and distributing any remaining property to its shareholders. A liquidation is completed when the liquidating corporation has divested itself of substantially all property. Retention of a nominal amount of assets (e.g., to retain the corporation's name) does not prevent a liquidation from occurring under the tax rules.

The liquidation of a corporation does not mean the corporation has undergone dissolution. **Dissolution** is a legal term that implies the corporation has surrendered the charter it received from the state. A corporation may complete its liquidation before surrendering its charter to the state and undergoing dissolution. Dissolution may never occur if the corporation retains its charter to protect the corporate name from being acquired by another party.

EXAMPLE C:6-2 ▶ Thompson Corporation adopts a plan of liquidation in December of the current year. The corporation distributes all but a nominal amount of its assets to its shareholders in January of the next year. The nominal assets retained are the minimum amount needed to preserve the corporation's existence under state law and to prevent others from acquiring its name. Despite the retention of a nominal amount of assets, Thompson Corporation has liquidated for tax purposes even though it has not dissolved. ◀

STOP & THINK

Question: Peter Jenkins, age 58, is considering forming a new business entity to operate the rental real estate activities that he and his wife have owned personally for a number of years. He has heard about corporations and limited liability companies from reading various real estate journals. Because of their level of personal wealth and the liability protection afforded by the corporate form of doing business, Peter wants to use a corporation to own and operate their real estate. The assets Peter and his wife plan to transfer to the corporation have a $600,000 FMV and a $420,000 adjusted basis. As Peter's CPA, why should you consider the tax cost of liquidating the corporation as part of the overall analysis of the business entity selection decision?

Solution: A transfer of real estate by Peter and his wife to a corporation is tax-free. A subsequent liquidation of the corporation is not tax-free because both the corporation and the shareholder may recognize gain or loss. Peter and his wife have $180,000 ($600,000 − $420,000) of appreciation in their real estate. Even if no change in value occurs, liquidation of the real estate corporation at a later date will cause $180,000 to be taxed twice, once at the corporate level and again at the shareholder level. On the other hand, creation and liquidation of a limited liability company are not taxable events to the entity or its owners. Thus, the difference in liquidation treatment at a future date is one of many differences the owners must consider when forming an entity. More information on liquidating a limited liability company can be found in Chapter C:10.

GENERAL LIQUIDATION RULES

This chapter section presents the general liquidation rules. These rules are considered in two parts: the effects of liquidating on the shareholders and the effects of liquidating on the corporation.

OBJECTIVE 2

Apply the general shareholder gain and loss recognition rules for a corporate liquidation

EFFECTS OF LIQUIDATING ON THE SHAREHOLDERS

Three aspects of the general liquidation rules are discussed below: amount and timing of gain or loss recognition, character of the recognized gain or loss, and basis and holding period of property received in the liquidation. Table C:6-1 summarizes the liquidation rules applying to shareholders under both the general liquidation rules and the controlled subsidiary corporation exception.

AMOUNT OF RECOGNIZED GAIN OR LOSS. Section 331(a) requires that liquidating distributions received by a shareholder be treated as full payment in exchange for his or her stock. The shareholder's recognized gain or loss equals the difference between the amount realized (the FMV of the assets received from the corporation plus any money) and his or her basis in the stock. If a shareholder assumes or acquires liabilities of the liquidating corporation, the amount of these liabilities reduces the shareholder's amount realized.

EXAMPLE C:6-3 ▶ Gamma Corporation liquidates, with Joseph receiving $10,000 in cash plus other property having a $12,000 FMV. Joseph's basis in his Gamma stock is $16,000. Joseph's amount realized is $22,000 ($12,000 + $10,000). Therefore, he recognizes a $6,000 ($22,000 − $16,000) gain on the liquidation. ◀

EXAMPLE C:6-4 ▶ Assume the same facts as in Example C:6-3 except Joseph also assumes a $2,000 mortgage attaching to the other property. Joseph's amount realized is reduced by the $2,000 liability assumed and is $20,000 ($22,000 − $2,000). His recognized gain on the liquidation is $4,000 ($20,000 − $16,000). ◀

▼ TABLE C:6-1
Tax Consequences of a Liquidation to the Shareholders

	Amount of Gain or Loss Recognized	Character of Gain or Loss Recognized	Adjusted Basis of Property Received	Holding Period of Property Received
General rule	Shareholders recognize gain or loss (money + FMV of nonmoney property received − adjusted basis of stock) upon liquidation (Sec. 331).	Long-term or short-term capital gain or loss (Sec. 1222). Ordinary loss treatment available (Sec. 1244).	FMV of the property (Sec. 334(a)).	Begins on the day after the liquidation date (Sec. 1223(1)).
Controlled subsidiary corporation rule	Parent corporation recognizes no gain or loss when an 80% controlled subsidiary corporation liquidates into the parent corporation (Sec. 332).[a]	Not applicable.[a]	Carryover basis for property received from subsidiary corporation (Sec. 334(b)).[a]	Includes subsidiary corporation's holding period for the assets (Sec. 1223(2)).[a]

[a] Minority shareholders use the general rule.

Impact of Accounting Method. Shareholders who use the accrual method of accounting recognize gain or loss when all events have occurred that fix the amount of the liquidating distribution and the time the shareholders are entitled to receive the distribution upon surrender of their shares. Shareholders who use the cash method of accounting report the gain or loss when they have actual or constructive receipt of the liquidating distribution(s).[2]

ADDITIONAL COMMENT

Calculating the gain/loss separately on each block may result in (1) both gains and losses existing in the same liquidating distribution and (2) the character of the various gains/losses being different.

When Stock Is Acquired. A shareholder may have acquired his or her stock at different times or for different per-share amounts. In this case, the shareholder must compute the gain or loss separately for each share or block of stock owned.[3]

CHARACTER OF THE RECOGNIZED GAIN OR LOSS. Generally, the liquidating corporation's stock is a capital asset in the shareholder's hands. The gain or loss recognized, therefore, is a capital gain or loss for most shareholders. Two exceptions to these rules are indicated below.

- Loss recognized by an individual shareholder on Sec. 1244 stock is an ordinary loss, within limits (see Chapter C:2).
- Loss recognized by a corporate shareholder on the worthlessness of the controlled subsidiary's stock is an ordinary loss under Sec. 165(g)(3) (see Chapter C:2).

BASIS AND HOLDING PERIOD OF PROPERTY RECEIVED IN THE LIQUIDATION. Section 334(a) provides that the shareholder's basis of property received under the general liquidation rules is its FMV on the distribution date. The holding period for the property starts on the day after the distribution date.

OBJECTIVE 3

Determine when the liquidating corporation recognizes gains and losses on making a liquidating distribution

EFFECTS OF LIQUIDATING ON THE LIQUIDATING CORPORATION

Two aspects of the general liquidation rules are discussed below: (1) the recognition of gain or loss by the liquidating corporation when it distributes property in redemption of its stock and (2) the special valuation rules used when the liabilities assumed or acquired by the shareholder exceed the property's adjusted basis in the liquidating corporation's hands. Table C:6-2 summarizes rules applying to the liquidating corporation.

RECOGNITION OF GAIN OR LOSS WHEN CORPORATION DISTRIBUTES PROPERTY IN REDEMPTION OF STOCK. Section 336(a) provides that the liquidating corporation must recognize gain or loss when it distributes property in a complete liquidation. The amount and character of the gain or loss are determined as if the corporation sold the property to the shareholder at its FMV.

EXAMPLE C:6-5 ▶ Under West Corporation's plan of liquidation, the corporation distributes land to one of its shareholders, Arnie. The land, which is used in West's trade or business, has a $40,000 adjusted basis and a $120,000 FMV on the distribution date. West recognizes an $80,000 ($120,000 − $40,000) Sec. 1231 gain when it makes the liquidating distribution. Arnie recognizes a capital gain to the extent the land's FMV exceeds his basis in the West stock. Arnie's basis for the land is its $120,000 FMV. A nonliquidating distribution would have produced similar results for the corporation. However, for the shareholder, the entire FMV would have been a dividend instead of a capital gain assuming sufficient E&P. Thus, both liquidating and nonliquidating distributions produce double taxation although the amount and character of the shareholder's gain or income differ. ◀

ADDITIONAL COMMENT

Through 2010, both capital gains and qualified dividends are taxed at the maximum 15% tax rate.

With limited exceptions, the liquidating corporation can recognize a loss when it distributes property that has declined in value to its shareholders. This rule eliminates the need for a liquidating corporation to sell property that has declined in value to recognize its losses.

EXAMPLE C:6-6 ▶ Assume the same facts as in Example C:6-5 except the land's FMV is instead $10,000. West recognizes a $30,000 ($10,000 − $40,000) Sec. 1231 loss when it distributes the land to Arnie. Arnie's basis for the land is $10,000. ◀

---

[2] Rev. Rul. 80-177, 1980-2 C.B. 109.

[3] Reg. Sec. 1.331-1(e).

▼ TABLE C:6-2
Tax Consequences of a Liquidation to the Liquidating Corporation

	Amount and Character of Gain, Loss, or Income Recognized	Treatment of the Liquidating Corporation's Tax Attributes
General rule	The liquidating corporation recognizes gain or loss when it distributes property as part of a complete liquidation (Sec. 336(a)).	Tax attributes disappear when the liquidation is completed.
Controlled subsidiary corporation rules	1. The liquidating subsidiary corporation recognizes no gain or loss upon a distribution of property to its parent corporation when the Sec. 332 nonrecognition rules apply to the parent corporation (Sec. 337(a)). 2. The liquidating subsidiary corporation recognizes no loss upon a distribution of property to minority shareholders when the Sec. 332 nonrecognition rules apply to the parent corporation (Sec. 336(d)(3)). It does recognize gains, however.	Tax attributes of a subsidiary corporation carry over to the parent corporation when the Sec. 332 rules apply (Sec. 381(a)).
Related party rule	The liquidating subsidiary corporation recognizes no loss upon a distribution of property to a related person unless the corporation distributes such property ratably to all shareholders *and* the liquidating corporation did not acquire the property in a Sec. 351 transaction or as a capital contribution during the five years preceding the distribution (Sec. 336(d)(1)).	
Tax avoidance rule	The liquidating subsidiary corporation recognizes no loss when a sale, exchange, or distribution of property occurs and the liquidating corporation acquired such property in a Sec. 351 transaction or as a capital contribution having as a principal purpose the recognition of loss (Sec. 336(d)(2)).	

The Sec. 336 rules apply only to property distributed in exchange for the liquidating corporation's stock as part of a complete liquidation. These rules do not apply to distributions of appreciated property as part of a partial liquidation, or when a debt of the liquidating corporation is retired in exchange for appreciated property.

TAX STRATEGY TIP

If possible, a corporation should avoid distributing property subject to a mortgage that exceeds the property's FMV. Such distributions cause excessive corporate gain recognition and uncertainty of results at the shareholder level.

LIABILITIES ASSUMED OR ACQUIRED BY THE SHAREHOLDERS. For purposes of determining the amount of gain or loss recognized under Sec. 336, property distributed by the liquidating corporation is treated as having been sold to the distributee for its FMV on the distribution date. Section 336(b) contains a special restriction on valuing a liquidating property distribution when the shareholders assume or acquire liabilities. According to this rule, the FMV of the distributed property cannot be less than the amount of the liability assumed or acquired. Congress enacted Sec. 336(b) because the corporation realizes an economic gain or benefit equal to the amount of the liability the shareholder assumes or acquires (and not just the lower FMV of the property distributed) as part of the liquidation. Treatment at the shareholder level is not completely clear. Section 336(b) specifically states that this liability rule applies only for determining the corporation's gain or loss. Thus, it does not seem to extend to Sec. 334(a), which requires the shareholder to take a FMV basis in the distributed property. Some commentators have suggested that the strict statutory interpretation of giving the shareholders the actual FMV basis, rather than the greater liability basis, produces an illogical result.[4] Also, given that the liability exceeds the distributed property's FMV, the shareholder's amount realized should be zero, resulting in a capital loss equal to the shareholder's stock basis.

[4] For a detailed discussion, see B. C. Randall and D. N. Stewart, "Corporate Distributions: Handling Liabilities in Excess of the Fair Market Value of Property Remains Unresolved," *The Journal of Corporate Taxation*, Spring 1992, pp. 55–64.

EXAMPLE C:6-7 ▶ Jersey Corporation owns an apartment complex costing $3 million that has been depreciated so that its adjusted basis is $2.4 million. The property is secured by a $2.7 million mortgage. Pursuant to a plan of liquidation, Jersey distributes the property and the mortgage to Rex, Jersey's sole shareholder, at a time when the property's FMV is $2.2 million. Rex's stock basis is $500,000. Jersey recognizes a $300,000 ($2,700,000 – $2,400,000) gain on distributing the property because its FMV cannot be less than the $2.7 million mortgage. The shareholder recognizes a $500,000 capital loss on the corporate stock and takes either a $2.2 million or $2.7 million basis in the property, depending on which interpretation applies. ◀

EXCEPTIONS TO THE GENERAL GAIN OR LOSS RECOGNITION RULE. The IRC provides four exceptions to the general recognition rule of Sec. 336(a). Two of these exceptions apply to liquidations of controlled subsidiary corporations and are covered later. The other two exceptions prevent certain abusive practices (e.g., the manufacturing of losses) from being accomplished and are examined below. Also, Sec 362(e)(2) may reduce a liquidating corporation's loss recognition. Specifically, for property contributed to a controlled corporation after October 22, 2004, the corporation must reduce the basis of loss property if the total adjusted basis of property contributed by a shareholder exceeds the total FMV of that property (see Chapter C:2 for details). Consequently, upon a later liquidating distribution, the corporation will realized a smaller loss or no loss at all.[5]

ADDITIONAL COMMENT

The disqualified property rule prohibits a shareholder from infusing loss property into the liquidating corporation and generating losses at both the corporate and shareholder levels by liquidating the corporation.

Distributions to Related Persons. Section 336(d)(1)(A) prevents loss recognition in connection with property distributions to a related person if (1) the distribution of loss property is other than pro rata to all shareholders based on their stock ownership or (2) the distributed property is disqualified property. Section 267(b) defines a related person as including, for example, an individual and a corporation whose stock is more than 50% owned (in terms of value) by such individual, as well as two corporations that are members of the same controlled group. Section 336(d)(1)(B) defines disqualified property as (1) any property acquired by the liquidating corporation in a transaction to which Sec. 351 applies, or as a contribution to capital, during the five-year period ending on the distribution date or (2) any property having an adjusted basis that carries over from disqualified property.

EXAMPLE C:6-8 ▶ Lei owns 60% and Betty owns 40% of Mesa Corporation's stock. Mesa adopts a plan of liquidation. Pursuant to the plan, Mesa distributes to Lei Beta stock that Mesa purchased two years ago. The Beta stock, which is not disqualified property, has a $40,000 FMV and a $100,000 adjusted basis. Betty receives only cash in the liquidation. The non–pro rata distribution of the Beta stock (the loss property), however, prevents Mesa from claiming a $60,000 capital loss when it makes the distribution. If Mesa instead distributes the Beta stock 60% to Lei and 40% to Betty, Mesa deducts the entire capital loss, assuming Mesa has offsetting capital gains. ◀

EXAMPLE C:6-9 ▶ Assume the same facts as in Example C:6-8 except Mesa acquired the Beta stock two years ago as a capital contribution from Lei when the Beta stock basis was $100,000 and its FMV was $105,000. Thus, the stock was not subject to the Sec. 362(e)(2) basis reduction rule when contributed, and Mesa took a $100,000 carryover basis in the stock. The stock's FMV now is $40,000, and the corporation distributes it to Lei upon liquidation of the corporation. The Beta stock in this case is disqualified property. The $60,000 realized loss is disallowed because Lei is a related party under Sec. 267(b). If Mesa instead distributes the Beta stock 60% to Lei and 40% to Betty, Mesa still is prohibited from deducting the portion of the $60,000 capital loss attributable to the stock distributed to the related party even though Mesa distributed it ratably to Lei and Betty. Mesa can deduct only the $24,000 ($60,000 × 0.40) capital loss attributable to the Beta stock distributed to Betty because she is not a related party. Alternatively, a sale of the disqualified property to an unrelated purchaser permits Mesa to recognize the entire $60,000 loss, again assuming offsetting capital gains exist. ◀

EXAMPLE C:6-10 ▶ Assume the same facts as in Example C:6-9 except the Beta stock had an $85,000 FMV when contributed, and Mesa had to reduce its basis in the stock to $85,000 at that time. Upon liqui-

[5] For a detailed discussion, see B. C. Randall, B. C. Spilker, and J. M. Werlhof, "The Interaction of New Section 362(e)(2) With the Loss Disallowance Rules in Corporate Liquidations," *Corporate Taxation*, September/October 2005.

dation and distribution to Lei, Mesa realizes a $45,000 ($40,000 − $85,000) loss, which is disallowed under the related person, disqualified property rule. If instead Mesa distributes the Beta stock ratably to Lei and Betty, Mesa can deduct $18,000 ($45,000 × 0.40) of the loss attributable to the stock distributed to Betty, again assuming Mesa recognizes offsetting gains on other property. ◀

Sales Having a Tax-Avoidance Purpose. Section 336(d)(2) restricts loss recognition with respect to the sale, exchange, or distribution of property acquired in a Sec. 351 transaction, or as a contribution to capital, where the liquidating corporation acquired the property as part of a plan having the principal purpose of loss recognition by the corporation in connection with its liquidation. This loss limitation prevents a shareholder from transferring loss property into a corporation to reduce or eliminate the gain the liquidating corporation otherwise would have recognized from the distribution of other appreciated property.

TAX STRATEGY TIP

To avoid loss disallowance under Sec. 336(d)(2), a corporation should delay adopting a plan of liquidation until two years after receiving loss property in a Sec. 351 transaction.

TAX STRATEGY TIP

If the corporation made a basis reduction for contributed loss property under Sec. 362(e)(2), it might argue that no tax avoidance purpose existed, thereby making a Sec. 336(d) disallowance inapplicable. See article referenced in footnote 5.

Property acquired by the liquidating corporation in any Sec. 351 transaction or as a contribution to capital within two years of the date on which a plan of complete liquidation is adopted are treated as part of a plan having a tax-avoidance purpose unless exempted by forthcoming regulations. Treasury Regulations, when issued, should not prevent corporations from deducting losses associated with dispositions of assets that are contributed to the corporation and used in a trade or business (or a line of business), or dispositions occurring during the first two years of a corporation's existence.[6]

The basis of the contributed property for loss purposes equals its adjusted basis to the corporation at the time of liquidation reduced (but not below zero) by the excess (if any) of the property's adjusted basis over its FMV immediately after its contribution to the corporation. This adjusted basis already may include a reduction under Sec. 362(e)(2) for contributed loss property. No adjustment occurs to the contributed property's adjusted basis when determining the corporation's recognized gain.

EXAMPLE C:6-11 ▶ Terry contributed a widget maker having a $1,000 adjusted basis and a $100 FMV to Pirate Corporation in exchange for additional stock on January 10, 2006. At the same time, Terry contributed a second property having a $2,000 FMV and a $900 adjusted basis. Because the total FMV of Terry's contributed property ($2,100) exceeded the total adjusted basis of that property ($1,900), the corporation did not reduce the loss property's basis under Sec. 362(e)(2) at that time. On April 1, 2007, Pirate adopts a plan of liquidation. Between January 10, 2006, and April 1, 2007, Pirate does not use the widget maker in its trade or business. Liquidation occurs on July 1, 2007, and Pirate distributes the widget maker and a second property that has a $2,500 FMV and a $900 adjusted basis. Because Terry contributed the widget maker to Pirate after April 1, 2005 (two years before Pirate adopted its plan of liquidation), and the widget maker is not used in Pirate's trade or business, its acquisition and distribution are presumed to be motivated by a desire to recognize the $900 loss. Unless Pirate can establish otherwise (e.g., by arguing that Sec. 362(e)(2) precludes a tax avoidance purpose), Sec. 336(d)(2) will apply to the distribution of the widget maker. Pirate's basis for determining its loss will be $100 [$1,000 − ($1,000 − $100)]. Thus, Pirate cannot claim a loss upon distributing the widget maker. This rule prevents Pirate from offsetting the $1,600 ($2,500 − $900) gain recognized on distributing the second property by the $900 loss realized on distributing the widget maker. ◀

The basis adjustment also affects sales, exchanges, or distributions of property made before the adoption of the plan of liquidation or in connection with the liquidation. Thus, losses claimed in a tax return filed before the adoption of the plan of liquidation may be restricted by Sec. 336(d)(2). The liquidating corporation may recapture these losses in the tax return for the tax year in which the plan of liquidation is adopted, or it can file an amended tax return for the tax year in which it originally claimed the loss.

EXAMPLE C:6-12 ▶ Assume the same facts as in Example C:6-11 except Pirate sells the widget maker for $200 on July 10, 2006. Pirate reports an $800 loss ($200 − $1,000) on its 2006 tax return. The adoption of the plan of liquidation on April 1, 2007, causes the loss on the sale of the widget maker to be

[6] H. Rept. No. 99-841, 99th Cong., 2d Sess., p. II-201 (1986). The Conference Committee Report for the 1986 Tax Act indicates that property transactions occurring more than two years in advance of the adoption of the plan of liquidation will be disregarded unless no clear and substantial relationship exists between the contributed property and the conduct of the corporation's current or future business enterprises.

covered by the Sec. 336(d)(2) rules, again assuming a tax avoidance purpose exists. Pirate can file an amended 2006 tax return showing the $800 loss being disallowed, or it can file its 2007 tax return reporting $800 of income under the loss recapture rules.[7] ◀

Topic Review C:6-1 summarizes the general corporate liquidation rules.

Topic Review C:6-1

Tax Consequences of a Corporate Liquidation

General Corporate Liquidation Rules

1. The shareholder's recognized gain or loss equals the amount of cash plus the FMV of the other property received minus the adjusted basis of the stock surrendered. Corporate liabilities assumed or acquired by the shareholder reduce the amount realized.
2. The gain or loss is capital if the stock investment is a capital asset. If the shareholder recognizes a loss on the liquidation, Sec. 1244 permits ordinary loss treatment (within limits) for qualifying individual shareholders.
3. The adjusted basis of the property received is its FMV on the distribution date.
4. The shareholder's holding period for the property begins the day after the distribution date.
5. With certain limited exceptions, the distributing corporation recognizes gain or loss when making the distribution. The amount and character of the gain or loss are determined as if the corporation sold the property for its FMV immediately before the distribution. Special rules apply when the shareholders assume or acquire corporate liabilities and the amount of such liabilities exceeds the property's FMV.
6. The liquidated corporation's tax attributes disappear upon liquidation.

Liquidation of a Controlled Subsidiary Corporation

OBJECTIVE 4

Determine when the Sec. 332 and Sec. 337 nonrecognition rules apply to the liquidation of a subsidiary corporation

The following discussion of the controlled subsidiary exception is divided into three parts: the requirements for using the exception, the effects of liquidating on the parent corporation, and the effects of liquidating on the subsidiary corporation.

Section 332(a) provides that the parent corporation recognizes no gain or loss when a controlled subsidiary corporation liquidates into its parent corporation. This liquidation rule permits a corporation to modify its corporate structure without incurring any adverse tax consequences. Section 332 applies only to the parent corporation. Other shareholders owning a minority interest are taxed under the general liquidation rules of Sec. 331. When Sec. 332 applies to the parent corporation, Sec. 337 permits the liquidating corporation to recognize no gains or losses on the assets distributed to the parent corporation. The liquidating corporation, however, recognizes gains (but not losses) on distributions made to shareholders holding a minority interest. The nonrecognition of gain or loss rule is logical for the distribution to the parent corporation because the assets remain within the corporate group following the distribution. Thus, the subsidiary corporation can be liquidated and operated as a division of its parent corporation without gain or loss recognition.

EXAMPLE C:6-13 ▶ Parent Corporation owns all of Subsidiary Corporation's stock. Subsidiary's assets have a $1 million FMV and a $400,000 adjusted basis. Parent's basis for its Subsidiary stock is $250,000. The liquidation of Subsidiary results in a $600,000 ($1,000,000 – $400,000) realized gain for Subsidiary on the distribution of its assets, none of which is recognized. Parent has a $750,000 ($1,000,000 – $250,000) realized gain on surrendering its Subsidiary stock, none of which is recognized. If Secs. 332 and 337 were not available, both Subsidiary and

[7] The property has a $1,000 basis when determining Pirate's gain on the sale and a $100 ($1,000 – $900) basis when determining its loss on the sale. Therefore, Pirate recognizes no gain or loss because the $200 sale price lies between the gain and loss basis amounts.

Parent would recognize their realized gains. In this case, Parent's gain would be reduced by the taxes paid by Subsidiary on its gain because Subsidiary's taxes reduce the amount available for distribution to Parent. ◀

REQUIREMENTS

TAX STRATEGY TIP

A parent corporation that does not own the requisite 80% should consider purchasing additional subsidiary stock from minority shareholders or consider having the subsidiary redeem shares from its minority shareholders. In either case, the strategy to attain 80% ownership must be applied before the corporations adopt a plan of liquidation. See Tax Planning Considerations for further details.

All the following requirements must be met for a liquidation to qualify for the Sec. 332 nonrecognition rules:

- The parent corporation must own at least 80% of the total combined voting power of all classes of stock entitled to vote and 80% of the total value of all classes of stock (other than certain nonvoting preferred stock) from the date on which the plan of liquidation is adopted until receipt of the subsidiary corporation's property.[8]
- The property distribution must be in complete cancellation or redemption of all the subsidiary corporation's stock.
- Distribution of the property must occur within a single tax year or be one of a series of distributions completed within three years of the close of the tax year during which the subsidiary makes the first of the series of liquidating distributions.

If the corporations meet all these requirements, the Sec. 332 nonrecognition rules are mandatory. If one or more of the conditions listed above are not met, the parent corporation is taxed under the previously discussed general liquidation rules.

TYPICAL MISCONCEPTION

The 80% stock ownership requirement of Sec. 332 is not the same stock ownership requirement for corporate formations in Chapter C:2. Instead, the Sec. 332 ownership requirement is the same one used for affiliated groups filing consolidated tax returns (see Chapter C:8).

STOCK OWNERSHIP. For Sec. 332 to apply, the parent corporation must own the requisite amount of voting and nonvoting stock. In applying this requirement, the Sec. 318 attribution rules for stock ownership do not apply (see Chapter C:4).[9] The parent corporation must own the requisite 80% of voting and nonvoting stock from the date on which the plan of liquidation is adopted until the liquidation is completed. Failure to satisfy this requirement denies the transaction the benefits of Secs. 332 and 337. (See page C:6-19 for further discussion of the stock ownership question.)

CANCELLATION OF THE STOCK. The subsidiary corporation must distribute its property in complete cancellation or redemption of all its stock in accordance with a plan of liquidation. When more than one liquidating distribution occurs, the subsidiary corporation must have adopted a plan of liquidation and be in a status of liquidation when it makes the first distribution. This status must continue until the liquidation is completed. Regulation Sec. 1.332-2(c) indicates that a liquidation is completed when the liquidating corporation has divested itself of all its property. The liquidating corporation, however, may retain a nominal amount of property to permit retention or sale of the corporate name.

TIMING OF THE DISTRIBUTIONS. The distribution of all the subsidiary corporation's assets within one subsidiary tax year in complete cancellation or redemption of all its stock is considered a complete liquidation.[10] Although a formal plan of liquidation can be adopted, the shareholders' adoption of a resolution authorizing the distribution of the corporation's assets in complete cancellation or redemption of its stock is considered to be the adoption of a plan of liquidation when the distribution occurs within a single tax year. The tax year in which the liquidating distribution occurs does not have to be the same as the one in which the plan of liquidation is adopted.[11]

The subsidiary corporation can carry out the plan of liquidation by making a series of distributions that extend over a period of more than one tax year to cancel or redeem its stock. A formal plan of liquidation must be adopted when the liquidating distributions extend beyond a single tax year of the liquidating corporation. The liquidating distributions must include all the corporation's property and must be completed within three years of the close of the tax year during which the subsidiary makes the first distribution under the plan.[12]

---

[8] The stock definition used for Sec. 332 purposes excludes any stock that is not entitled to vote, is limited and preferred as to dividends and does not participate in corporate growth to any significant extent, has redemption and liquidation rights that do not exceed its issue price (except for a reasonable redemption or liquidation premium), and is not convertible into another class of stock.

[9] Sec. 332(b)(1).

[10] Sec. 332(b)(2) and Reg. Sec. 1.332-3.

[11] Rev. Rul. 76-317, 1976-2 C.B. 98.

[12] Sec. 332(b)(3) and Reg. Sec. 1.332-4.

EFFECTS OF LIQUIDATING ON THE SHAREHOLDERS

RECOGNITION OF GAIN OR LOSS.

SELF-STUDY QUESTION

What are the tax consequences if the liquidating subsidiary is insolvent?

ANSWER

The parent generally is entitled to an ordinary loss deduction under Sec. 165(g)(3) when it fails to receive any liquidation proceeds because the subsidiary is insolvent. The parent also may have a bad debt deduction under Sec. 166.

Parent Corporation. The Sec. 332(a) nonrecognition rules apply only to a parent corporation that receives a liquidating distribution from a solvent subsidiary. Section 332(a) does not apply to a parent corporation that receives a liquidating distribution from an insolvent subsidiary, to minority shareholders who receive liquidating distributions, or to a parent corporation that receives a payment to satisfy the subsidiary's indebtedness to the parent. All of these exceptions are discussed below.

Section 332 does not apply if the subsidiary corporation is insolvent at the time of the liquidation because the parent corporation does not receive the distributions in exchange for its stock investment. An insolvent subsidiary is one whose liabilities exceed the FMV of its assets. Regulation Sec. 1.332-2(b) requires the parent corporation to receive at least partial payment for the stock it owns in the subsidiary corporation to qualify for nonrecognition under Sec. 332. If the subsidiary is insolvent, however, the special worthless security rules of Sec. 165(g)(3) for affiliated corporations and the bad debt rules of Sec. 166 permit the parent corporation to recognize an ordinary loss with respect to its investment in the subsidiary's stock or debt obligations (see Chapter C:2).

EXAMPLE C:6-14 ▶ Parent Corporation owns all of Subsidiary Corporation's stock. Parent established Subsidiary to produce and market a product that proved unsuccessful. Parent has a $1.5 million basis in its Subsidiary stock. In addition, it made a $1 million advance to Subsidiary that is not secured by a note. Under a plan of liquidation, Subsidiary distributes all its assets, having a $750,000 FMV, to Parent in partial satisfaction of the advance after having paid all third-party creditors. No assets remain to pay the remainder of the advance or to redeem the outstanding stock. Because Subsidiary is insolvent immediately before the liquidating distribution, it distributes none of its assets in redemption of the Subsidiary stock. Therefore, the liquidation cannot qualify under the Sec. 332 rules. Parent, therefore, claims a $250,000 business bad debt with respect to the unpaid portion of the advance and a $1.5 million ordinary loss for its stock investment. ◀

TYPICAL MISCONCEPTION

Section 332 applies only to the parent corporation. If a minority interest exists, the general liquidation rules of Sec. 331 apply to the minority shareholders.

STOP & THINK

Question: In Example C:6-14, assume Subsidiary Corporation had a $3 million net operating loss (NOL) carryover, which would disappear upon liquidation because Sec. 332 did not apply. To prevent this disappearance, Parent Corporation proposes to cancel the $1 million advance as a contribution to Subsidiary's capital. Thus, Parent would have a $2.5 million basis in its Subsidiary stock prior to the liquidation and no advances receivable. Now when Parent liquidates Subsidiary, all of Subsidiary's assets redeem its outstanding stock, and the transaction seems to qualify for Sec. 332 treatment. Under these circumstances, the $3 million NOL would carry over to Parent under Sec. 381, giving Parent $3 million worth of NOL deductions rather than $1.75 million worth of bad debt and worthless stock deductions under the original transaction. Do you think the IRS would condone this proposed transaction?

Solution: No. In Rev. Rul. 68-602, 1968-2 C.B. 135, the IRS held under similar circumstances that, because the cancellation "was an integral part of the liquidation and had no independent significance other than to secure the tax benefits of [Subsidiary's] net operating loss carryover, such step will be considered transitory and, therefore, disregarded." Thus, if Parent proceeded with the proposed transaction, the IRS would ignore it and treat the liquidation the same as originally done in Example C:6-14.

The 2004 Jobs Act added a special rule to prevent the importation of built-in losses from foreign corporations. Specifically, the parent takes a FMV basis in each transferred property if the following three conditions prevail: (1) the parent is a U.S. corporation, (2) the liquidating subsidiary is a foreign corporation, and (3) the aggregate adjusted basis of the transferred property exceeds the aggregate FMV.

Minority Shareholders. Liquidating distributions made to minority shareholders are taxed under the Sec. 331 general liquidation rules. These rules require the minority shareholders to recognize gain or loss—which generally is capital—upon the redemption of their stock in the subsidiary corporation.

EXAMPLE C:6-15 ▶ Parent Corporation and Jane own 80% and 20%, respectively, of Subsidiary Corporation's single class of stock. Parent and Jane have adjusted bases of $100,000 and $15,000, respectively, for their stock interests. Subsidiary adopts a plan of liquidation on May 30 and makes liquidating distributions of two parcels of land having $250,000 and $62,500 FMVs to Parent and Jane, respectively, on November 1 in exchange for their stock. Parent does not recognize its $150,000 ($250,000 − $100,000) gain because of Sec. 332. Jane recognizes a $47,500 ($62,500 − $15,000) capital gain under Sec. 331. (Subsidiary also faces gain recognition on the distribution to its minority shareholder as demonstrated in Example C:6-18.) ◀

SELF-STUDY QUESTION

What bases do both the parent and minority shareholders take in the assets received in a Sec. 332 liquidation?

ANSWER

Because the parent corporation recognizes no gain or loss in the transaction, the parent corporation takes a carryover basis in its assets. However, because the minority shareholders are involved in a taxable exchange, they take a FMV basis in their assets.

BASIS OF PROPERTY RECEIVED. Under Sec. 334(b)(1), the parent corporation's basis for property received in the liquidating distribution is the same as the subsidiary corporation's basis prior to the distribution. This carryover basis rule reflects the principle that the liquidating corporation recognizes no gain or loss when it distributes the property and that the property's tax attributes (e.g., the depreciation recapture potential) carry over from the subsidiary corporation to the parent corporation. The parent corporation's basis for its stock investment in the subsidiary corporation is ignored in determining the basis for the distributed property and disappears once the parent surrenders its stock in the subsidiary. Property received by minority shareholders takes a basis equal to its FMV.

EXAMPLE C:6-16 ▶ Assume the same facts as in Example C:6-15 and that the two parcels of land received by Parent Corporation and Jane have adjusted bases of $175,000 and $40,000, respectively, to Subsidiary. Parent takes a $175,000 carryover basis for its land, and Jane takes a $62,500 FMV basis for her land. ◀

STOP & THINK

Question: Why should a corporation that is 100%-owned by another corporation be treated differently when it liquidates than a corporation that is 100%-owned by an individual?

Solution: A corporation that is 100%-owned by another corporation can file a consolidated tax return (see Chapters C:3 and C:8). As a result, the parent and its subsidiary corporations are treated as a single entity. This result is the same as if the subsidiary were one of a number of divisions of a single corporation. An extension of the single-entity concept is that a subsidiary corporation can be liquidated tax-free into its parent corporation. An individual and his or her corporation are treated as two separate tax entities when calculating their annual tax liabilities. As separate entities, nonliquidating distributions (e.g., ordinary distributions and stock redemptions) from the corporation to its shareholder(s) are taxable. The same principle applies to liquidating distributions.

EFFECTS OF LIQUIDATING ON THE SUBSIDIARY CORPORATION

RECOGNITION OF GAIN OR LOSS. Section 337(a) provides that the liquidating corporation recognizes no gain or loss on the distribution of property to the 80% distributee in a complete liquidation to which Sec. 332 applies.[13] Section 337(c) defines the term 80% distributee as a corporation that meets the 80% stock ownership requirement specified in Sec. 332 (see page C:6-11).

EXAMPLE C:6-17 ▶ Parent Corporation owns all the stock of Subsidiary Corporation. Pursuant to a plan of complete liquidation, Subsidiary distributes land having a $200,000 FMV and a $60,000 basis to Parent. Subsidiary recognizes no gain with respect to the distribution. Parent takes a $60,000 basis for the land. ◀

The depreciation recapture provisions in Secs. 1245, 1250, and 291 do not override the Sec. 337(a) nonrecognition rule if a controlled subsidiary corporation liquidates into its parent corporation. Instead, the parent corporation assumes the depreciation recapture

[13] Section 336(e) permits a corporation to sell, exchange, or distribute the stock of a subsidiary corporation and to elect to treat such a transaction as a disposition of all the subsidiary corporation's assets. The parent corporation recognizes no gain or loss on the sale, exchange, or distribution of the stock. The economic consequences of making this election for a stock sale are essentially the same as if the parent corporation instead liquidates the subsidiary in a transaction to which Sec. 332 applies and then immediately sells the properties to the purchaser.

TAX STRATEGY TIP

A corporation that sells, exchanges, or distributes the stock of a subsidiary may elect to treat the sale of the stock as a sale of the subsidiary's assets. This election could prove beneficial when a sale of the subsidiary stock occurs and the assets of the subsidiary corporation are substantially less appreciated than the subsidiary stock itself.

potential associated with the distributed property, and recapture occurs when the parent corporation sells or exchanges the property.[14]

The Sec. 337(a) nonrecognition rule applies only to distributions to the parent corporation. Liquidating distributions to minority shareholders are not eligible for nonrecognition under Sec. 337(a). Consequently, the liquidating corporation must recognize gain under Sec. 336(a) when it distributes appreciated property to the minority shareholders. Section 336(d)(3), however, prevents the subsidiary corporation from recognizing loss on distributions made to minority shareholders. Thus, for the subsidiary, liquidating distributions made to minority shareholders are treated the same way as nonliquidating distributions.

EXAMPLE C:6-18 ▶ Assume the same facts as in Example C:6-17 except Parent Corporation owns 80% of the Subsidiary stock, Chuck owns the remaining 20% of such stock, and Subsidiary distributes two parcels of land to Parent and Chuck. The parcels have FMVs of $160,000 and $40,000, and adjusted bases of $50,000 and $10,000, respectively. Subsidiary does not recognize the $110,000 ($160,000 – $50,000) gain realized on the distribution to Parent. However, Subsidiary does recognize the $30,000 ($40,000 – $10,000) gain realized on the distribution to Chuck because the Sec. 337(a) nonrecognition rule applies only to distributions to the 80% distributee. Assume that the land distributed to Chuck instead has a $40,000 FMV and a $50,000 adjusted basis. Subsidiary can deduct none of the $10,000 loss because it distributed the land to a minority shareholder. ◀

OBJECTIVE 5

Determine the effect of a liquidation on the liquidating corporation's tax attributes

TAX ATTRIBUTE CARRYOVERS. The **tax attributes** of the liquidating corporation disappear when the liquidation is completed under the general rules. They carry over, however, in the case of a controlled subsidiary corporation liquidated into its parent corporation under Sec. 332.[15] The following items are included among the carried-over attributes:

- ▶ NOL carryovers
- ▶ Earnings and profits
- ▶ Capital loss carryovers
- ▶ General business and other tax credit carryovers

The carryover amount is determined as of the close of the day on which the subsidiary corporation completes the distribution of all its property. Chapter C:7 contains further discussion of these rules.

Topic Review C:6-2 summarizes the special rules applicable to the liquidation of a controlled subsidiary corporation.

Topic Review C:6-2

Tax Consequences of a Corporate Liquidation

Tax Consequences of Liquidating a Controlled Subsidiary Corporation

1. Specific requirements must be met with respect to (a) stock ownership, (b) distribution of the property in complete cancellation or redemption of all the subsidiary's stock, and (c) distribution of all property within a single tax year or a three-year period. To satisfy the stock ownership requirement, the parent corporation must own at least 80% of the total voting power of all voting stock and at least 80% of the total value of all stock.
2. The parent corporation recognizes no gain or loss when it receives distributed property from the liquidating subsidiary. Section 332 does not apply to liquidations of insolvent subsidiaries and distributions to minority shareholders.
3. The basis of the distributed property carries over from the subsidiary corporation to the parent corporation.
4. The parent corporation's holding period for the assets includes the subsidiary corporation's holding period.
5. The subsidiary corporation recognizes no gain or loss when making a distribution to an 80% distributee (parent). The liquidating subsidiary recognizes gain (but not loss) on distributions to minority shareholders. Also, the liquidating subsidiary recognizes no gain when it distributes appreciated property to satisfy certain subsidiary debts owed to the parent corporation.
6. The subsidiary corporation's tax attributes carry over to the parent corporation as part of the liquidation.

[14] Secs. 1245(b)(3) and 1250(d)(3).

[15] Sec. 381(a).

SPECIAL SHAREHOLDER REPORTING ISSUES

Four special shareholder reporting rules apply to liquidation transactions described below. These rules add different degrees of complexity to the general liquidation rules outlined above.

PARTIALLY LIQUIDATING DISTRIBUTIONS

Shareholders often receive a series of partially liquidating distributions that culminate in complete liquidation. Section 346(a) indicates that a series of partially liquidating distributions received in complete liquidation of the corporation are taxed under the Sec. 331 liquidation rules instead of under the Sec. 302 rules applying to redemptions in partial liquidation. The IRS permits the shareholder's basis to be recovered first and requires the recognition of gain once the shareholder fully recovers the basis of a particular share or block of stock. The shareholder cannot recognize a loss with respect to a share or block of stock until he or she receives the final liquidating distribution, or until it becomes clear that no more liquidating distributions will occur.[16]

EXAMPLE C:6-19 ▶ Diane owns 1,000 shares of Adobe Corporation stock purchased for $40,000 in 2002. Diane receives the following liquidating distributions: July 23, 2005, $25,000; March 12, 2006, $17,000; and April 5, 2007, $10,000. Diane recognizes no gain in 2005 because her $40,000 basis is not fully recovered by year-end. The $15,000 ($40,000 – $25,000) unrecovered basis that exists after the first distribution is less than the $17,000 liquidating distribution received on March 12, 2006, so Diane recognizes a $2,000 gain at this time. She recognizes an additional $10,000 gain in 2007 when she receives the final liquidating distribution. ◀

EXAMPLE C:6-20 ▶ Assume the same facts as in Example C:6-19 except Diane paid $60,000 for her Adobe stock. The receipt of each of the liquidating distributions is tax-free because Diane's $60,000 basis exceeds the $52,000 ($25,000 + $17,000 + $10,000) total of the distributions. Diane recognizes an $8,000 ($52,000 – $60,000) loss in 2007 when she receives the final liquidating distribution. ◀

SELF-STUDY QUESTION

If a cash method shareholder is subsequently obligated to pay a contingent liability of the liquidated corporation, what are the tax consequences of such a payment?

ANSWER

First, the prior tax year return is not amended. The additional payment results in a loss recognized in the year of payment. The character of the loss depends on the nature of the gain or loss recognized by the shareholder in the year of liquidation.

SUBSEQUENT ASSESSMENTS AGAINST THE SHAREHOLDERS

At some date after the liquidation, the shareholders may be required to pay a contingent liability of the corporation or a liability not anticipated at the time of the liquidating distribution (e.g., an income tax deficiency determined after the liquidation is completed or a judgment that is contingent when the corporation makes the final liquidating distribution). The additional payment does not affect the reporting of the initial liquidating transaction. The tax treatment for the additional payment depends on the nature of the gain or loss originally reported by the shareholder and not on the type of loss or deduction the liquidating corporation would have reported had it paid the liability.[17] If the liquidation results in a recognized capital gain or loss, a cash method shareholder treats the additional payment as a capital loss in the year of payment (i.e., the shareholder does not file an amended tax return for the year in which he or she originally reported the gain or loss from the liquidation). An accrual method shareholder recognizes the capital loss when he or she incurs the liability.

EXAMPLE C:6-21 ▶ Coastal Corporation liquidated three years ago with Tammy, a cash method taxpayer, reporting a $30,000 long-term capital gain on the exchange of her Coastal stock. In the current year, Tammy pays $5,000 as her part of the settlement of a lawsuit against Coastal. All shareholders pay an additional amount because the settlement exceeds the amount of funds that Coastal placed into an escrow account as a result of the litigation. The amount placed into the escrow account was not included in the amount Tammy realized from the liquidating distribution

---

16 Rev. Ruls. 68-348, 1968-2 C.B. 141, 79-10, 1979-1 C.B. 140, and 85-48, 1985-1 C.B. 126.

17 *F. Donald Arrowsmith v. CIR*, 42 AFTR 649, 52-2 USTC ¶9527 (USSC, 1952).

three years ago. Because Tammy had not been taxed on the cash placed in the escrow account, she cannot deduct the amount of the payment made from the escrow account in the current year. Nevertheless, Tammy treats the $5,000 paid from her personal funds as a long-term capital loss in the current year. ◀

OBJECTIVE 6

Understand the different tax treatments for open and closed liquidation transactions

OPEN VERSUS CLOSED TRANSACTIONS

Sometimes the value of property received in a corporate liquidation cannot be determined by the usual valuation techniques. Property that can be valued only on the basis of uncertain future payments falls into this category. In such a case, the shareholders may attempt to rely on the **open transaction doctrine** of *Burnet v. Logan* and treat the liquidation as an open transaction.[18] Under this doctrine, the shareholder's gain or loss from the liquidation is not determined until the assets that cannot be valued are subsequently sold, collected, or able to be valued. Any assets that cannot be valued are assigned a zero value. The IRS's position is that the FMV of almost any asset should be ascertainable. Thus, the IRS assumes that the open transaction method should be used only in extraordinary circumstances. For example, an open transaction cannot be used merely because a market valuation for an investment in a closely held corporation is not readily available through market quotations for the stock.

ETHICAL POINT

A tax practitioner needs to ensure that the client obtains appropriate appraisals to support the values assigned to property distributed to shareholders in a corporate liquidation. A 20% substantial underpayment penalty may be imposed on corporations and shareholders that substantially understate their income tax liabilities.

INSTALLMENT OBLIGATIONS RECEIVED BY A SHAREHOLDER

Shareholders who receive an installment obligation as part of their liquidating distribution ordinarily report the FMV of their obligation as part of the consideration received to calculate the amount of the recognized gain or loss. Shareholders who receive an installment obligation that was acquired by the liquidating corporation in connection with the sale or exchange of its property are eligible for special treatment in reporting their gain on the liquidating transaction if the sale or exchange takes place during the 12-month period beginning on the date a plan of complete liquidation is adopted and the liquidation is completed during such 12-month period. These shareholders may report their gain as they receive the installment payments.[19]

SPECIAL CORPORATE REPORTING ISSUES

EXPENSES OF THE LIQUIDATION

The corporation can deduct the expenses incurred in connection with the liquidation transaction. These expenses include attorneys' and accountants' fees, costs incurred in drafting the plan of liquidation and obtaining shareholder approval, and so on.[20] Such amounts ordinarily are deductible in the liquidating corporation's final tax return.

A liquidating corporation treats expenses associated with selling its property as an offset against the sales proceeds. When a corporation sells an asset pursuant to its liquidation, the selling expenses reduce the amount of gain or increase the amount of loss reported by the corporation.[21]

EXAMPLE C:6-22 ▶ Madison Corporation adopts a plan of liquidation on July 15 and shortly thereafter sells a parcel of land on which it realizes a $60,000 gain (excluding the effects of a $6,000 sales commission). Madison pays its legal counsel $1,500 to draft the plan of liquidation. Madison distributes all its remaining properties to its shareholders on December 15. The $1,500 paid to legal counsel is deductible as a liquidation expense in Madison's current year income tax return. The sales commission reduces the $60,000 gain realized on the land sale, so that Madison's recognized gain is $54,000 ($60,000 – $6,000). ◀

---

[18] *Burnet v. Edith A. Logan*, 9 AFTR 1453, 2 USTC ¶736 (USSC, 1931).

[19] Sec. 453(h)(1)(A). A tax deferral is available only with respect to the gain realized by the shareholder. The liquidating corporation must recognize the deferred gain when it distributes the installment obligation to the shareholder as if it had sold the obligation immediately before the distribution.

[20] *Pridemark, Inc. v. CIR*, 15 AFTR 2d 853, 65-1 USTC ¶9388 (4th Cir., 1965).

[21] See, for example, *J. T. Stewart III Trust*, 63 T.C. 682 (1975), *acq.* 1977-1 C.B. 1.

Any capitalized expenditures unamortized at the time of liquidation should be deducted if they have no further value to the corporation (e.g., unamortized organizational costs).[22] Capitalized expenditures that have value must be allocated to the shareholders receiving the benefit of such an outlay (e.g., prepaid insurance and prepaid rent).[23] Expenses related to issuing the corporation's stock are nondeductible, even at the time of liquidation, because they are treated as a reduction of paid-in capital. Unamortized bond premiums, however, are deductible at the time the corporation retires the bonds.

TREATMENT OF NET OPERATING LOSSES

TAX STRATEGY TIP

If a liquidating corporation creates an NOL in the year of liquidation or already has NOL carryovers, these losses may disappear with the liquidated corporation. If the liquidation is a Sec. 332 liquidation, the parent corporation acquires the NOL. If the liquidation is taxed under Sec. 331, the liquidating corporation may want to consider an S election for the liquidation year so any NOLs created in that year can pass through to the shareholders.

If the liquidating corporation reports little or no income in its final income tax return, the corporation may create an NOL when it deducts its liquidating expenses and any remaining capitalized expenditures. The NOL carries back to reduce corporate taxes paid in prior years. The resultant federal income tax refund increases (decreases) the gain (loss) previously reported by the shareholder. Alternatively, the shareholders might consider having the corporation make an S election for the liquidation year and have the flow-through loss reported on the shareholders' tax returns. (See Chapter C:11 for the tax treatment of S corporations.)

The need for a liquidating corporation to recognize gains when distributing appreciated property can be partially or fully offset by expenses incurred in carrying out the liquidation or by any available NOL carryovers. Losses recognized by the liquidating corporation when distributing property that has declined in value can offset operating profits or capital gains earned in the liquidation year. Should such losses produce an NOL or net capital loss, the losses may be carried back to provide a refund of taxes paid in a prior year, or they may be passed through to the corporation's shareholders if the corporation makes an S corporation election for the tax year.

RECOGNITION OF GAIN OR LOSS WHEN PROPERTY IS DISTRIBUTED IN RETIREMENT OF DEBT

OBJECTIVE 7

Determine when a liquidating corporation recognizes gains and losses on the retirement of debt

GENERAL RULE

A shareholder recognizes no gain or loss when the liquidating corporation pays off an unsecured debt obligation it owes to the shareholder. However, when the corporation retires a security at an amount different from the shareholder's adjusted basis for the obligation, the shareholder recognizes gain or loss for the difference. These rules apply whether the debtor corporation pays or retires the debt as part of its operations or as part of its liquidation. The debtor corporation recognizes no gain or loss when it uses cash to satisfy its debt obligations. However, the debtor corporation recognizes gain when it uses appreciated noncash property to satisfy its debt obligations. Similarly, a debtor corporation recognizes a loss when it uses noncash property that has declined in value to satisfy its debt obligations.

SATISFACTION OF THE SUBSIDIARY'S DEBT OBLIGATIONS

The Sec. 332(a) nonrecognition rules apply only to amounts received by the parent corporation in its role as a shareholder. The parent corporation, however, does recognize gain or loss upon receipt of property in payment of a subsidiary corporation indebtedness if the payment differs from the parent's basis in the debt.[24]

As mentioned above, the use of property to satisfy an indebtedness generally results in the debtor recognizing gain or loss at the time it transfers the property.[25] Section 337(b), however, prevents a liquidating subsidiary corporation from recognizing gain or loss

---

[22] Reg. Sec. 1.248-1(b)(3).

[23] *Koppers Co., Inc. v. U.S.*, 5 AFTR 2d 1597, 60-2 USTC ¶9505 (Ct. Cls., 1960).

[24] Sec. 1001(c).

[25] Ibid.

WHAT WOULD YOU DO IN THIS SITUATION?

Andrea has operated her trendy, upscale clothing store as a C corporation for a number of years. Annually, the corporation earns $200,000 in pretax profits. Andrea's stock is worth about $800,000. Her stock basis is $125,000. One of her good friends, Jenna, has opened a clothing store as a limited liability company and has been telling Andrea about the advantage of not having to pay the corporate income tax. She also hears about the check-the-box regulations that permit corporations to elect to be taxed as partnerships and limited liability companies. She calls and tells you that she wants you to file the necessary paperwork with the IRS to make the change from being taxed as a C corporation to being taxed as a flow-through entity. What advice should you provide Andrea in this situation?

when it transfers noncash property to its parent corporation in satisfaction of an indebtedness. The IRC provides this exception because the property remains within the economic unit of the parent-subsidiary group.

Section 337(b) applies only to the subsidiary's indebtedness owed to the parent corporation on the date the plan of liquidation is adopted and that is satisfied by the transfer of property pursuant to a complete liquidation of the subsidiary corporation. It does not apply to liabilities owed to other shareholders or third-party creditors, or to liabilities incurred after the plan of liquidation is adopted. In addition, if the subsidiary corporation satisfies the indebtedness for less than its face amount, it may have to recognize income from the discharge of an indebtedness.

EXAMPLE C:6-23 ▶ Parent Corporation owns all of Subsidiary Corporation's single class of stock. At the time of its acquisition of the Subsidiary stock, Parent purchased $1 million of Subsidiary bonds at their face amount. Subsequently, Parent and Subsidiary adopt a plan of liquidation, and Subsidiary distributes to Parent property having a $1 million FMV and a $400,000 adjusted basis in cancellation of the bonds. Subsidiary also distributes its remaining property to Parent in exchange for all of its outstanding stock. Subsidiary recognizes no gain on the transfer of the property in cancellation of its bonds. Parent recognizes no gain on receipt of the property because the property's FMV equals Parent's adjusted basis of the bonds. Parent takes a $400,000 carryover basis for the noncash property it receives in cancellation of the bonds. ◀

TAX PLANNING CONSIDERATIONS

TIMING THE LIQUIDATION TRANSACTION

TAX STRATEGY TIP

Timing the distribution of loss property so that the losses may be used to offset high-bracket taxable income at the corporate level makes good tax sense if the general liquidation rules are applicable. However, this planning opportunity would not exist in a Sec. 332 parent-subsidiary liquidation because the liquidating subsidiary does not recognize losses.

Sometimes corporations adopt a plan of liquidation in one year but do not complete the liquidation until a subsequent year. Corporations planning to distribute properties that have both increased in value and decreased in value may find it advantageous to sell or distribute property that has declined in value in a tax year in which they also conducted business activities. As such, the loss recognized when selling or distributing the property can offset profits that are taxed at higher rates. Deferring the sale or distribution of property that has appreciated in value may delay the recognition of gain for one tax year and also place the gain in a year in which the marginal tax rate is lower.

EXAMPLE C:6-24 ▶ Miami Corporation adopts a plan of liquidation in November of the current year, a tax year in which it earns $150,000 in operating profits. Miami discontinues its operating activities before the end of the current year. Pursuant to the liquidation, it distributes assets, producing $40,000 of recognized ordinary losses. In January of next year, Miami distributes assets that have appreciated in value, producing $40,000 of recognized ordinary income. Distributing the loss property in the current year results in a $15,600 tax savings ($40,000 × 0.39). Only $6,000 ($40,000 × 0.15) in taxes result from distributing the appreciated property next year. The rate differential provides a $9,600 ($15,600 − $6,000) net savings to Miami. ◀

Timing the liquidating distributions should not proceed without the planner also considering the tax position of the various shareholders. Taxpayers should be careful about timing the liquidating distributions to avoid creating a short-term capital gain taxed at ordinary rates rather than long-term capital gains taxed at 15% or 5%. If the liquidation results in a recognized loss, shareholders should take advantage of the opportunity to offset the loss against capital gains plus $3,000 of ordinary income, as well as attempt to increase the portion of the loss eligible for ordinary loss treatment under Sec. 1244 (See next section).

RECOGNITION OF ORDINARY LOSSES WHEN A LIQUIDATION OCCURS

Shareholders sometimes recognize losses when a liquidation occurs. Individual shareholders should be aware that, because a complete liquidation is treated as an exchange transaction, Sec. 1244 ordinary loss treatment is available when a small business corporation liquidates. This treatment permits the shareholder to claim $50,000 of ordinary loss when he or she surrenders the stock ($100,000 if the taxpayer is married and files a joint return).

Ordinary loss treatment also is available for a domestic corporation that owns stock or debt securities in a subsidiary corporation. Because the rules in Sec. 332 regarding nonrecognition of gain or loss do not apply when a subsidiary corporation is insolvent (see page C:6-12), the parent corporation can recognize a loss when the subsidiary corporation's stocks and debt securities are determined to be worthless. This loss is an ordinary loss (instead of a capital loss) if the domestic corporation owns at least 80% of the voting stock and 80% of each class of nonvoting stock and more than 90% of the liquidating corporation's gross income for all tax years has been other than passive income.[26]

OBTAINING 80% OWNERSHIP TO ACHIEVE SEC. 332 BENEFITS

The 80% stock ownership requirement provides tax planning opportunities when a subsidiary corporation liquidates. A parent corporation seeking nonrecognition under Sec. 332 may acquire additional shares of the subsidiary corporation's stock *before* the adoption of the plan of liquidation. This acquisition helps the parent corporation meet the 80% minimum and avoids gain recognition on the liquidation. If the parent corporation purchases these additional shares of stock from other shareholders to satisfy the 80% minimum *after* adopting the plan of liquidation, Sec. 332 will not apply.[27]

EXAMPLE C:6-25 ▶ Parent Corporation owns 75% of Subsidiary Corporation's single class of stock. On March 12, Parent purchases for cash the remaining 25% of the Subsidiary stock from three individual shareholders pursuant to a tender offer. Parent and Subsidiary adopt a plan of liquidation on October 1, and Subsidiary distributes its assets to Parent on December 1 in exchange for all of Subsidiary's outstanding stock. Parent recognizes no gain or loss on the redemption of its Subsidiary stock in the liquidation because all the Sec. 332 requirements had been satisfied prior to adoption of the plan of liquidation. ◀

Alternatively, the parent corporation might cause the subsidiary corporation to redeem some of its shares held by minority shareholders before the plan of liquidation is adopted. The IRS originally held that the intention to liquidate is present once the subsidiary corporation agrees to redeem the shares of the minority shareholders. Thus, redemption of a 25% minority interest did not permit Sec. 332 to be used even though the parent corporation owned 100% of the outstanding stock after the redemption.[28]

In *George L. Riggs, Inc.*, however, the Tax Court held that a parent corporation's tender offer to minority shareholders and the calling of the subsidiary's preferred stock do not invalidate the Sec. 332 liquidation because "the formation of a conditional intention to liquidate in the future is not the adoption of a plan of liquidation."[29] The IRS has acquiesced to the *Riggs* decision.

Thus, careful planning can help both the parent corporation and subsidiary corpora-

---

[26] Sec. 165(g)(3).

[27] Rev. Rul. 75-521, 1975-2 C.B. 120.

[28] Rev. Rul. 70-106, 1970-1 C.B. 70.

[29] *George L. Riggs, Inc.*, 64 T.C. 474 (1975), *acq.* 1976-2 C.B. 2.

tion avoid gain recognition under Secs. 332 and 337. Nonrecognition, however, does not extend to minority shareholders as discussed earlier.

EXAMPLE C:6-26 ▶ Parent Corporation owns 80% of Subsidiary Corporation's stock. Anthony owns the remaining 20% of Subsidiary stock. Parent and Anthony have adjusted bases of $200,000 and $60,000, respectively, for their Subsidiary stock. Subsidiary distributes land having a $250,000 adjusted basis and a $400,000 FMV to Parent and $100,000 in cash to Anthony. Subsidiary recognizes no gain or loss on the distribution of the land or the cash. Parent recognizes no gain on the liquidation and takes a $250,000 basis for the land. Anthony recognizes a $40,000 ($100,000 − $60,000) capital gain on the receipt of the money. Alternatively, distribution of the land and cash ratably to Parent and Anthony would require Subsidiary to recognize as gain the appreciation on the portion of land distributed to Anthony. ◀

AVOIDING SEC. 332 TO RECOGNIZE LOSSES

A parent corporation may want to avoid the Sec. 332 nonrecognition rules to recognize a loss when a solvent subsidiary corporation liquidates. Because the stock ownership requirement must be met during the entire liquidation process, the parent corporation apparently can sell some of its stock in the subsidiary corporation to reduce its stock ownership below the 80% level at any time during the liquidation process and be able to recognize the loss.[30] Such a sale permits the parent corporation to recognize a capital loss when it surrenders its stock interest in the subsidiary corporation. The parent corporation may desire this capital loss if it has offsetting capital gains.

ADDITIONAL COMMENT

The parent corporation, however, would not acquire the subsidiary's tax attributes if a taxable liquidation occurs.

The sale of a portion of the subsidiary's stock after the plan of liquidation is adopted prevents Sec. 332 from applying to the parent corporation. The Sec. 337 rules, which prevent the subsidiary corporation from recognizing gain or loss when making a liquidating distribution to an 80% distributee, also do not apply because nonrecognition is contingent on Sec. 332 applying to the distributee. Thus, the subsidiary corporation also can recognize a loss when it distributes property that has declined in value.

COMPLIANCE AND PROCEDURAL CONSIDERATIONS

GENERAL LIQUIDATION PROCEDURES

Section 6043(a) requires a liquidating corporation to file Form 966 (Corporate Dissolution or Liquidation) within 30 days after the adoption of any resolution or plan calling for the liquidation or dissolution of the corporation. The liquidating corporation files this form with the District Director of the IRS for the district in which it files its income tax return. Any amendment or supplement to the resolution or plan must be filed on an additional Form 966 within 30 days of making the amendment or supplement. The liquidating corporation must file Form 966 whether the shareholders' realized gain is recognized or not. The information included with Form 966 is described in Reg. Sec. 1.6043-1(b).

Regulation Sec. 1.6043-2(a) requires every corporation that makes a distribution of $600 or more during a calendar year to any shareholder in liquidation of part or all of its capital stock to file Form 1099-DIV (U.S. Information Return for Recipients of Dividends and Distributions). A separate Form 1099-DIV is required for each shareholder. The information that must be included with the Form 1099-DIV is described in Reg. Secs. 1.6043-2(a) and (b).

Regulation Sec. 1.6012-2(a)(2) requires a corporation that exists for part of a year to file a corporate tax return for the portion of the tax year that it existed. A corporation that ceases business and dissolves, while retaining no assets, is not considered to be in existence for federal tax purposes even though under state law it may be considered for certain purposes to be continuing its affairs (e.g., for purposes of suing or being sued).

---

[30] *CIR v. Day & Zimmerman, Inc.*, 34 AFTR 343, 45-2 USTC ¶9403 (3rd Cir., 1945).

ADDITIONAL COMMENT

As evidenced in this chapter, the compliance and procedural requirements of complete liquidations are formidable. Any taxpayer contemplating this type of corporate transactions should consult competent tax and legal advisors to ensure that the technical requirements of the proposed transaction are satisfied.

SECTION 332 LIQUIDATIONS

Regulation Sec. 1.332-6 requires every corporation receiving distributions in a Sec. 332 complete liquidation to maintain permanent records. A complete statement of all facts pertinent to the nonrecognition of gain or loss must be included in the corporate distributee's return for the tax year in which it receives a liquidating distribution. This statement includes the following: a certified copy of the plan of liquidation, a list of all property received upon the distribution, a statement of any indebtedness of the liquidating corporation to the recipient corporation, and a statement of stock ownership.

Treasury Regulations require a special waiver of the general three-year statute of limitations when the liquidation covers more than one tax year.[31] The distributee corporation must file a waiver of the limitations period on assessment for each of its tax years that falls partially or wholly within the liquidation period. The distributee corporation files this waiver at the time it files its income tax return. This waiver must extend the assessment period to a date at least one year after the last date of the period for assessment of such taxes for the last tax year in which the liquidation may be completed under Sec. 332.

PLAN OF LIQUIDATION

A **plan of liquidation** is a written document detailing the steps to be undertaken while carrying out the complete liquidation of the corporation. Although a formal plan of liquidation is not required, it may assist the corporation in determining when it enters a liquidation status and, therefore, when distributions to the shareholders qualify for exchange treatment under Sec. 331 (instead of possibly being treated as a dividend under Sec. 301). The adoption of a formal plan of liquidation can provide the liquidating corporation or its shareholders additional benefits under the tax laws. For example, the adoption of a plan of liquidation permits a parent corporation to have a three-year time period (instead of one tax year) to carry out the complete liquidation of a subsidiary corporation.

PROBLEM MATERIALS

DISCUSSION QUESTIONS

C:6-1 What is a complete liquidation? A partial liquidation? Explain the difference in the tax treatment accorded these two different events.

C:6-2 Summitt Corporation has manufactured and distributed basketball equipment for 20 years. Its owners would like to avoid the corporate income tax and are considering becoming a limited liability company (LLC). What tax savings may result from electing to be taxed as an LLC? What federal tax costs will be incurred to make the change from a C corporation to an LLC? Would the same transaction costs be incurred if instead the corporation made an S election? Would the transaction costs be incurred had LLC status been adopted when the entity was initially organized?

C:6-3 Explain why tax advisors caution people who are starting a new business that the tax costs of incorporating a business may be low while the tax costs of liquidating a business may be high.

C:6-4 Explain the following statement: A corporation may be liquidated for tax purposes even though dissolution has not occurred under state corporation law.

C:6-5 Compare the tax consequences to the shareholder and the distributing corporation of the following three kinds of corporate distributions: ordinary dividends, stock redemptions, and complete liquidations.

C:6-6 What event or occurrence determines when a cash or accrual method of accounting taxpayer reports a liquidating distribution?

C:6-7 Explain why a shareholder receiving a liquidating distribution would prefer to receive either capital gain treatment or ordinary loss treatment.

C:6-8 A liquidating corporation could either (1) sell its assets and then distribute remaining cash to its shareholders or (2) distribute its assets directly to

[31] Reg. Sec. 1.332-4(a)(2).

the shareholders who then sell the distributed assets. Do the tax consequences of these alternatives differ?

C:6-9 Explain the circumstances in which a liquidating corporation does not recognize gain and/or loss when making a liquidating distribution.

C:6-10 Kelly Corporation makes a liquidating distribution. Among other property, it distributes land subject to a mortgage. The mortgage amount exceeds both the adjusted basis and FMV for the land. Explain to Kelly Corporation's president how the amount of its recognized gain or loss on the distribution and the shareholder's basis for the land are determined.

C:6-11 Explain the congressional intent behind the enactment of the Sec. 332 rules regarding the liquidation of a subsidiary corporation.

C:6-12 What requirements must be satisfied for the Sec. 332 rules to apply to a corporate shareholder?

C:6-13 Compare the general liquidation rules with the Sec. 332 rules for liquidation of a subsidiary corporation with respect to the following items:

a. Recognition of gain or loss by the distributee corporation
b. Recognition of gain or loss by the liquidating corporation
c. Basis of assets in the distributee corporation's hands
d. Treatment of the liquidating corporation's tax attributes

C:6-14 Parent Corporation owns 80% of the stock of Subsidiary Corporation, which is insolvent. Tracy owns the remaining 20% of the stock. The courts determine Subsidiary to be bankrupt. The shareholders receive nothing for their investment. How do they report their losses for tax purposes?

C:6-15 Parent Corporation owns all the stock of Subsidiary Corporation and a substantial amount of Subsidiary Corporation bonds. Subsidiary proposes to transfer appreciated property to Parent in redemption of its bonds pursuant to the liquidation of Subsidiary. Explain the tax consequences of the redemption of the stock and bonds to Parent and Subsidiary.

C:6-16 Explain the differences in the tax rules applying to distributions made to the parent corporation and a minority shareholder when a controlled subsidiary corporation liquidates.

C:6-17 Parent Corporation owns 80% of Subsidiary Corporation's stock. Sally owns the remaining 20% of the Subsidiary stock. Subsidiary plans to distribute cash and appreciated property pursuant to its liquidation. It has more than enough cash to redeem all of Sally's stock. What strategy for distributing the cash and appreciated property would minimize the gain recognized by Subsidiary on the distribution? Does the substitution of appreciated property for cash change the tax consequences of the liquidating distribution for Sally?

C:6-18 Parent Corporation owns 70% of Subsidiary Corporation's stock. The FMV of Subsidiary's assets is significantly greater than their basis to Subsidiary. The FMV of Parent's interest in the assets also substantially exceeds Parent's basis for the Subsidiary stock. Also, Parent's basis in its Subsidiary stock exceeds Subsidiary's basis in its assets. On January 30, Parent acquired an additional 15% of Subsidiary stock from one of Subsidiary's shareholders who owns none of the Parent stock. Subsidiary adopts a plan of liquidation on March 12. The liquidation is completed before year-end. What advantages accrue to Parent with respect to the liquidation by acquiring the additional Subsidiary stock?

C:6-19 Texas Corporation liquidates through a series of distributions to its shareholders after a plan of liquidation has been adopted. How are these distributions taxed?

C:6-20 Hill Corporation's shareholders are called on to pay an assessment that was levied against them as a result of a liability not anticipated at the time of liquidation. When will the shareholders claim the deduction for the additional payment, assuming they all use the cash method of accounting? What factors determine the character of the deduction claimed?

C:6-21 Able Corporation adopts a plan of liquidation. Under the plan, Robert, who owns 60% of the Able stock, is to receive 2,000 acres of land in an area where a number of producing oil wells have been drilled. No wells have been drilled on Able's land. Discussions with two appraisers have produced widely differing market values for the land, both of which are above Able's basis for the land and Robert's basis for the Able stock. Explain the alternatives available to Able and Robert for reporting the liquidating distribution.

C:6-22 Explain the IRS's position regarding whether a liquidation transaction will be considered open or closed.

C:6-23 For a corporation that intends to liquidate, explain the tax advantages to the shareholders of having the corporation (1) adopt a plan of liquidation, (2) sell its assets in an installment sale, and then (3) distribute the installment obligations to its shareholders.

C:6-24 Cable Corporation is 60% owned by Anna and 40% owned by Jim, who are unrelated. It has noncash assets, which it sells to an unrelated purchaser for $100,000 in cash and $900,000 in installment obligations due 50% in the current year and 50% in the following year. Cable will distribute its remaining cash, after payment of the federal income taxes on the sale and other corporate obligations, to Jim and Anna along with the installment obligations. Explain to the two shareholders the alternatives for reporting the gain realized on their receipt of the installment obligations.

C:6-25 Describe the tax treatment accorded the following expenses associated with a liquidation:

a. Commissions paid on the sale of the liquidating corporation's assets
b. Accounting fees paid to prepare the corporation's final income tax return
c. Unamortized organizational expenditures
d. Prepaid rent for office space occupied by one of the shareholders following the liquidation (Assume the prepaid rent was deducted in the preceding year's corporate tax return.)

C:6-26 Yancy owns 70% of Andover Corporation stock. At the beginning of the current year, the corporation has $400,000 of NOLs. Yancy plans to liquidate the corporation and have it distribute assets having a $600,000 FMV and a $350,000 adjusted basis to its shareholders. Explain to Yancy the tax consequences of the liquidation to Andover Corporation.

C:6-27 Nils Corporation, a calendar year taxpayer, adopts a plan of liquidation on April 1 of the current year. The final liquidating distribution occurs on January 5 of next year. Must Nils Corporation file a tax return for the current year? For next year?

C:6-28 What is a plan of liquidation? Why is it advisable for a corporation to adopt a formal plan of liquidation?

C:6-29 Indicate whether each of the following statements about a liquidation is true or false. If the statement is false, explain why.

a. Liabilities assumed by a shareholder when a corporation liquidates reduce the amount realized by the shareholder on the surrender of his or her stock.
b. The loss recognized by a shareholder on a liquidation generally is characterized as an ordinary loss.
c. A shareholder's basis for property received in a liquidation is the same as the property's basis in the liquidating corporation's hands.
d. The holding period for property received in a liquidation includes the period of time it is held by the liquidating corporation.
e. The tax attributes of a liquidating corporation are assumed ratably by its shareholders.
f. A parent corporation can elect to recognize gain or loss when it liquidates a controlled subsidiary corporation.
g. A liquidating subsidiary recognizes no gain or loss when it distributes its property to its parent corporation.
h. A parent corporation's basis for the assets received in a liquidation where gain is not recognized remains the same as it was to the liquidating subsidiary corporation.

ISSUE IDENTIFICATION QUESTIONS

C:6-30 Cable Corporation, which operates a fleet of motorized trolley cars in a resort city, is undergoing a complete liquidation. John, who owns 80% of the Cable stock, plans to continue the business in another city, and will receive the cable cars, two support vehicles, the repair parts inventory, and other tools and equipment. Peter, who owns the remaining 20% of the Cable stock, will receive a cash distribution. The corporation will incur $15,000 of liquidation expenses to break its lease on its office and garage space and cancel other contracts. What tax issues should Cable, John, and Peter consider with respect to the liquidation?

C:6-31 Parent Corporation, which operates an electric utility, created a 100%-owned corporation, Subsidiary, that built and managed an office building. Assume the two corporations have filed separate tax returns for a number of years. The utility occupied two floors of the office building, and Subsidiary offered the other ten floors for lease. Only 25% of the total rental space was leased because of the high crime rate in the area surrounding the building. Rental income was insufficient to cover the mortgage payments, and Subsidiary filed for bankruptcy because of the poor prospects. Subsidiary's assets were taken over by the mortgage lender. Parent lost its entire $500,000 investment. Another $100,000 of debts remained unpaid for the general creditors, which included a $35,000 account payable to Parent, at the time Subsidiary was liquidated. What tax issues should Parent and Subsidiary consider with respect to the bankruptcy and liquidation of Subsidiary?

C:6-32 Alpha Corporation is a holding company owned equally by Harry and Rita. They acquired the Alpha stock many years ago when the corporation was formed. Alpha has its money invested almost entirely in stocks, bonds, rental real estate, and land. Market quotations are available for all of its stock and bond investments except for 10,000 shares of Mayfair Manufacturing Corporation stock. Mayfair is privately held with 40 individuals owning all 100,000 outstanding shares. Last year, Mayfair reported slightly more than $3 million in net income. In a discussion with Harry and Rita, you find that they plan to liquidate Alpha Corporation in the next six months to avoid the personal holding company tax. What tax issues should Harry and Rita consider with respect to this pending liquidation?

PROBLEMS

C:6-33 ***Shareholder Gain or Loss Calculation.*** For seven years, Monaco Corporation has been owned entirely by Stacy and Monique, who are husband and wife. Stacy and Monique have a $165,000 basis in their jointly owned Monaco stock. The Monaco stock is Sec. 1244 stock. They receive the following assets in liquidation of their corporation: accounts receivable, $25,000 FMV; a car, $16,000 FMV; office furniture, $6,000 FMV; and $5,000 cash.

a. What are the amount and character of their gain or loss?

b. How would your answer change if the accounts receivable instead had a $140,000 FMV?

c. What is the Monaco's basis for each property received in the liquidation in Parts a and b?

C:6-34 ***Shareholder Gain or Loss Calculation.*** For three years, Diamond Corporation has been owned equally by Arlene and Billy. Arlene and Billy have $40,000 and $20,000 adjusted bases, respectively, in their Diamond stock. Arlene receives a $30,000 cash liquidating distribution in exchange for her Diamond stock. Billy receives as a liquidating distribution a parcel of land having a $70,000 FMV and subject to a $45,000 mortgage, which he assumes, and $5,000 of cash in exchange for his Diamond stock.

a. What are the amount and character of each shareholder's gain or loss?

b. What is each shareholder's basis for the property received in the liquidation?

C:6-35 ***Timing of Gain/Loss Recognition.*** Peter owns 25% of Crosstown Corporation stock in which he has a $200,000 adjusted basis. In each of the following situations, what amount of gain/loss will Peter report in the current year? In the next year?

a. Peter is a cash method of accounting taxpayer. Crosstown determines on December 24 of the current year that it will make a $260,000 liquidating distribution to Peter. Crosstown pays the liquidating distribution on January 3 of the next year.

b. Assume the same facts as in Part a except that Peter is an accrual method of accounting taxpayer.

C:6-36 ***Corporate Formation/Corporate Liquidation.*** Ken Wallace contributed assets with a $100,000 adjusted basis and a $400,000 FMV to Ace Corporation in exchange for all of its single class of stock. The corporation conducted operations for five years and was liquidated. Ken Wallace received a liquidating distribution of $500,000 cash (less federal income taxes owed on the liquidation by the corporation) and the assets that he had contributed, which now have a $100,000 adjusted basis and a $500,000 FMV. Assume a 34% corporate tax rate.

a. What are the tax consequences of the corporate formation transaction?

b. What are the tax consequences of the corporate liquidation transaction?

c. Would your answers to Parts a and b remain the same if instead the assets had been contributed by Wallace Corporation to Ace Corporation? If not, explain how your answer(s) would change?

C:6-37 ***Gain or Loss on Making a Liquidating Distribution.*** What are the amount and character of the gain or loss recognized by the distributing corporation when making liquidating distributions in the following situations? What is the shareholder's basis for the property received? In any situation where a loss is disallowed, indicate what changes would be necessary to improve the tax consequences of the transaction.

a. Best Corporation distributes land having a $200,000 FMV and a $90,000 adjusted basis to Tanya, its sole shareholder. The land, a capital asset, is subject to a $40,000 mortgage, which Tanya assumes.

b. Wilkins Corporation distributes depreciable property to its two equal shareholders. Robert receives a milling machine having a $50,000 adjusted basis and a $75,000 FMV. The corporation claimed $30,000 depreciation on the machine. The corporation purchased the milling machine from an unrelated seller four years ago. Sharon receives an automobile that originally cost $40,000 two years earlier and has a $26,000 FMV. The corporation claimed $25,000 depreciation on the automobile.

c. Jordan Corporation distributes marketable securities having a $100,000 FMV and a $175,000 adjusted basis to Brad, a 66.67% shareholder. Jordan purchased the marketable securities three years ago. Jordan distributes $50,000 cash to Ann, a 33.33% shareholder.

d. Assume the same facts as in Part c except the securities and cash are instead each distributed two-thirds to Brad and one-third to Ann.

C:6-38 ***Gain or Loss Recognition by a Distributing Corporation.*** Melon Corporation, which is owned equally by four individual shareholders, adopts a plan of liquidation for distributing the following property:

- Land (a capital asset) having a $30,000 FMV and a $12,000 adjusted basis.
- Depreciable personal property having a $15,000 FMV and a $9,000 adjusted basis. Melon has claimed depreciation of $10,000 on the property during the three years since its acquisition.
- Installment obligations having a $30,000 FMV and face amount and a $21,000 adjusted basis, acquired when Melon sold a Sec. 1231 property.
- Supplies that cost $6,000 and were expensed in the preceding tax year. The supplies have a $7,500 FMV.
- Marketable securities having a $15,000 FMV and an $18,000 adjusted basis. Melon purchased the marketable securities from a broker 12 months ago.

a. Which property, when distributed by Melon Corporation to one of its shareholders, will require the distributing corporation to recognize gain or loss?
b. How will your answer to Part a change if the distribution instead is made to Melon's parent corporation as part of a complete liquidation meeting the Sec. 332 requirements?
c. How will your answer to Part b change if the distribution instead is made to a minority shareholder?

C:6-39 ***Distribution of Property Subject to a Mortgage.*** Titan Corporation adopts a plan of liquidation. It distributes an apartment building having a $3 million FMV and a $1.8 million adjusted basis, and land having a $1 million FMV and a $600,000 adjusted basis, to MNO Partnership in exchange for all the outstanding Titan stock. MNO Partnership has an $800,000 basis in its Titan stock. Titan has claimed $600,000 of MACRS depreciation on the building. MNO Partnership agrees to assume the $3 million mortgage on the land and building. All of Titan's assets other than the building and land are used to pay its federal income tax liability.

a. What are the amount and character of Titan's recognized gain or loss on the distribution?
b. What are the amount and character of MNO Partnership's gain or loss on the liquidation? What is its basis for the land and building?
c. How would your answer to Parts a and b change if the mortgage instead was $4.5 million?

C:6-40 ***Sale of Loss Property by a Liquidating Corporation.*** In March 2006, Mike contributed the following two properties, which he acquired in February 2005, to Kansas Corporation in exchange for additional Kansas stock: (1) land having a $50,000 FMV and a $75,000 basis and (2) another property having an $85,000 FMV and a $70,000 adjusted basis. Kansas' employees uses the land as a parking lot until Kansas sells it in March 2007 for $45,000. One month after the sale, in April 2007, Kansas adopts a plan of liquidation.

a. What is Kansas' adjusted basis in the land immediately after the March 2006 contribution?
b. What is Kansas' recognized gain or loss on the subsequent land sale?
c. How would your answer to Part b change if the land were not used in Kansas' trade or business?
d. How would you answer to Part c change if Mike contributed the land and other property in March 2005 instead of March 2006?
e. How would your answer to Part c change if the corporation sold the land (contributed in March 2006) for $80,000 instead of $45,000?

C:6-41 ***Tax Consequences of a Corporate Liquidation.*** Marsha owns 100% of Gamma Corporation's common stock. Gamma is an accrual basis, calendar year corporation. Marsha formed the corporation six years ago by transferring $250,000 of cash in exchange for the Gamma stock. Thus, she has held the stock for six years and has a $250,000 adjusted basis in the stock. Gamma's balance sheet at January 1 of the current year is as follows:

Assets	*Basis*	*FMV*
Cash	$ 400,000	$ 400,000
Marketable securities	50,000	125,000
Inventory	300,000	350,000
Equipment	200,000	275,000
Building	500,000	750,000
Total	$1,450,000	$1,900,000

Liabilities and Equity		
Accounts payable	$ 175,000	$ 175,000
Common stock	250,000	1,725,000
Retained earnings (and E&P)	1,025,000	
Total	$1,450,000	$1,900,000

Gamma has held the marketable securities for two years. In addition, Gamma has claimed $60,000 of MACRS depreciation on the machinery and $90,000 of straight-line depreciation on the building. On January 2 of the current year, Gamma liquidates and distributes all property to Marsha except that Gamma retains cash to pay the accounts payable and any tax liability resulting from Gamma's liquidation. Assume that Gamma has no other taxable income or loss. Determine the tax consequences to Gamma and Marsha.

C:6-42 ***Sale of Assets Followed by a Corporation Liquidation.*** Assume the same facts as in Problem C:6-41 except, on January 2 of the current year, Gamma Corporation sells all property other than cash to Acquiring Corporation for FMV. Gamma pays off the accounts payable and retains cash to pay any tax liability resulting from Gamma's liquidation. Gamma then liquidates and distributes all remaining cash to Marsha. Assume that Gamma has no other taxable income or loss. Determine the tax consequence to Gamma, Acquiring, and Marsha. How do these results compare to those in Problem C:6-41?

C:6-43 ***Tax Consequences of a Corporate Liquidation.*** Pamela owns 100% of Sigma Corporation's stock. She purchased her stock ten years ago, and her current basis for the stock is $300,000. On June 10, Pamela decided to liquidate Sigma. Sigma's balance sheet prior to the sale of the assets, payment of the liquidation expenses, and payment of federal income taxes is as follows:

Assets	*Basis*	*FMV*
Cash	$240,000	$ 240,000
Marketable securities	90,000	80,000
Equipment	150,000	200,000
Land	320,000	680,000
Total	$800,000	$1,200,000
Equity		
Common stock	$300,000	$1,200,000
Retained earnings (and E&P)	500,000	
Total	$800,000	$1,200,000

- The corporation has claimed depreciation of $150,000 on the equipment.
- The corporation received the marketable securities as a capital contribution from Pamela three years earlier at a time when their adjusted basis was $90,000 and their FMV was $70,000.
- Sigma incurred $20,000 in liquidation expenses in its final tax year.

a. What are the tax consequences of the liquidation to Pamela and Sigma Corporation? Assume a 34% corporate tax rate.

b. How would your answer change if Pamela contributed the marketable securities six years ago?

C:6-44 ***Liquidation of a Subsidiary Corporation.*** Parent Corporation owns 100% of Subsidiary Corporation's stock. The adjusted basis of its stock investment is $175,000. A plan of liquidation is adopted, and Subsidiary distributes to Parent assets having a $400,000 FMV and a $300,000 adjusted basis (to Subsidiary), and liabilities in the amount of $60,000. Subsidiary has a $150,000 E&P balance.

a. What are the amount and character of Subsidiary's recognized gain or loss on the distribution?

b. What are the amount and character of Parent's recognized gain or loss on the surrender of the Subsidiary stock?

c. What basis does Parent take in the assets?

d. What happens to Parent's basis in the Subsidiary stock and to Subsidiary's tax attributes?

C:6-45 ***Liquidation of a Subsidiary Corporation.*** Parent Corporation owns 100% of Subsidiary Corporation's single class of stock. Its adjusted basis for the stock is $175,000. After adopting a plan of liquidation, Subsidiary distributes the following property to Parent: money, $20,000; LIFO inventory, $200,000 FMV; and equipment, $150,000 FMV. The inventory has a $125,000 adjusted basis. The equipment originally cost $280,000. Subsidiary has claimed depreciation of $160,000 on the equipment. Subsidiary has a $150,000 E&P balance and a $40,000 NOL carryover on the liquidation date.

a. What are the amount and character of Subsidiary's recognized gain or loss when it makes the liquidating distributions?

b. What are the amount and character of Parent's recognized gain or loss on its surrender of the Subsidiary stock?

c. What is Parent's basis in each nonmoney property?

d. What happens to Subsidiary's E&P balance and NOL carryover following the liquidation?

e. What happens to Parent's $175,000 basis in the Subsidiary stock?

C:6-46 ***Liquidation of a Subsidiary Corporation.*** Parent Corporation owns 100% of Subsidiary Corporation's single class of stock and $2 million of Subsidiary debentures. Parent purchased the debentures in small blocks from various unrelated parties at a $100,000 discount from their face amount. Parent has a $1.3 million basis in the Subsidiary stock. Subsidiary adopts a plan of liquidation whereby it distributes property having a $4 million FMV and a $2.4 million adjusted basis in redemption of the Subsidiary stock. The debentures are redeemed for Subsidiary property having a $2 million FMV and a $2.2 million adjusted basis.

a. What income or gain does Subsidiary recognize as a result of making the liquidating distributions?

b. What gain or loss does Parent recognize on the surrender of the Subsidiary stock? The Subsidiary debentures?

c. What is Parent's basis for the property received from Subsidiary?

C:6-47 ***Liquidation of an Insolvent Subsidiary.*** Subsidiary Corporation is a wholly-owned subsidiary of Parent Corporation. The two corporations have the following balance sheets:

Assets	*Parent*	*Subsidiary*
General assets	$1,500,000	$ 750,000
Investment in Subsidiary stock	200,000	
Note receivable from Subsidiary	1,000,000	
Total	$2,700,000	$ 750,000
Liabilities & Equity		
General liabilities	$1,500,000	$ 150,000
Note payable to Parent		1,000,000
Common Stock	300,000	200,000
Retained earnings (deficit)	900,000	(600,000)
Total	$2,700,000	$ 750,000

Other Facts:

- Parent's basis in its Subsidiary stock is $200,000, which corresponds to the $200,000 common stock on Subsidiary's balance sheet.
- The $1 million note payable on Subsidiary's balance sheet is payable to Parent and corresponds to the note receivable on Parent's balance sheet.
- The corporations do not file consolidated tax returns.
- Subsidiary has $600,000 of net operating loss (NOL) carryovers.
- The FMV and adjusted basis of Subsidiary's assets are the same amount.
- Just prior to the liquidation, Subsidiary uses $150,000 of its assets to pay off its general liabilities.
- Subsidiary transfers all its assets and liabilities to Parent upon a complete liquidation.

Determine the tax consequences to Parent and Subsidiary upon Subsidiary's liquidation.

C:6-48 ***Liquidation of a Subsidiary Corporation.*** Majority Corporation owns 90% of Subsidiary Corporation's stock and has a $45,000 basis in that stock. Mindy owns the other 10% and has a $5,000 basis in her stock. Subsidiary holds $20,000 cash and other assets having a $110,000 FMV and a $40,000 adjusted basis. Pursuant to a plan of liquidation, Subsidiary (1) distributes to Mindy assets having an $11,000 FMV and a $4,000 adjusted basis prior to the liquidation, (2) distributes to Majority assets having a $99,000 FMV and a $36,000 adjusted basis prior to the liquidation, and (3) distributes ratably to the two shareholders any cash remaining after taxes. Assume a 34% corporate tax rate and a 15% capital gains tax rate.

a. What are the tax consequences of the liquidation to Majority Corporation, Subsidiary Corporation, and Mindy?
b. Can you recommend a different distribution of assets that will produce better tax results than in Part a?

C:6-49 *Tax Consequences of a Corporate Liquidation.* Gabriel Corporation is owned 90% by Zeier Corporation and 10% by Ray Goff, a Gabriel employee. A preliquidation balance sheet for Gabriel is presented below:

Assets	*Basis*	*FMV*
Cash	$ 100,000	$ 100,000
Inventory	420,000	700,000
Equipment	80,000	100,000
Land	400,000	300,000
Total	$1,000,000	$1,200,000
Equity		
Accounts payable	$ 100,000	$ 100,000
Bonds payable	500,000	500,000
Common stock	100,000	600,000
Retained earnings (and E&P)	300,000	
Total	$1,000,000	$1,200,000

Gabriel has claimed $150,000 of MACRS depreciation on the equipment. Gabriel purchased the land three years ago as a potential plant site. Plans to build the plant never were consummated, and Gabriel has held the land since then as an investment. Zeier and Ray Goff have $90,000 and $10,000 bases, respectively, in their Gabriel stock. Both shareholders have held their stock since the corporation's inception ten years ago. Zeier purchased the Gabriel bonds from an insurance company two years ago for $20,000 above their face amount. Gabriel adopts a plan of liquidation. Gabriel transfers $500,000 of inventory to Zeier to retire the bonds. The shareholders receive their share of Gabriel's remaining assets and assume their share of Gabriel's liabilities (other than federal income taxes). Gabriel pays federal income taxes owed on the liquidation. Assume a 34% corporate tax rate. What are the tax consequences of the liquidation to Ray Goff, Zeier Corporation, and Gabriel Corporation?

C:6-50 *Tax Consequences of a Corporate Liquidation.* Art owns 80% of Pueblo Corporation stock, and Peggy owns the remaining 20%. Art and Peggy have $320,000 and $80,000 adjusted bases, respectively, for their Pueblo stock. Pueblo owns the following assets: cash, $25,000; inventory, $150,000 FMV and $100,000 adjusted basis; marketable securities, $100,000 FMV and $125,000 adjusted basis; and equipment, $325,000 FMV and $185,000 adjusted basis. Pueblo purchased the equipment four years ago and subsequently claimed $215,000 of MACRS depreciation. The securities are not disqualified property. On July 1 of the current year, Pueblo adopts a plan of liquidation at a time when it has $250,000 of E&P and no liabilities. Pueblo distributes the equipment, $50,000 of inventory, the marketable securities, and $5,000 of money to Art before year-end as a liquidating distribution. Pueblo also distributes $20,000 of cash and $100,000 of inventory to Peggy before year-end as a liquidating distribution.

a. What are the gain and loss tax consequences of the liquidation to Pueblo Corporation and to Art and Peggy?
b. Can you offer any suggestions to Pueblo's management that could improve the tax consequences of the liquidation? Explain.
c. How would your answers to Parts a and b change if Art and Peggy instead were domestic corporations rather than individuals?

C:6-51 *Tax Attribute Carryovers.* Bell Corporation is 100% owned by George, who has a $400,000 basis in his Bell stock. Bell's operations have been unprofitable in recent years, and it has incurred small NOLs. Its operating assets currently have a $300,000 FMV and a $500,000 adjusted basis. George is approached by Time Corporation, which wants to purchase Bell's assets for $300,000. Bell expects to have approximately $200,000 in cash after the payment of its liabilities.

a. What are the tax consequences of the transaction if Bell adopts a plan of liquidation, sells the assets, and distributes the cash in redemption of the Bell stock within a 12-month period?

b. What advantages (if any) would accrue to Bell and George if the corporation remains in existence and uses the $200,000 of cash that remains after payment of the liabilities to conduct a new trade or business?

C:6-52 *Series of Liquidating Distributions.* Union Corporation is owned equally by Ron and Steve. Ron and Steve purchased their stock several years ago and have adjusted bases for their Union stock of $15,000 and $27,500, respectively. Each shareholder receives two liquidating distributions. The first liquidating distribution, made in the current year, results in each shareholder receiving a one-half interest in a parcel of land that has a $40,000 FMV and an $18,000 adjusted basis to Union Corporation. The second liquidating distribution, made in the next year, results in each shareholder receiving $20,000 in cash.

a. What are the amount and character of Ron and Steve's recognized gain or loss for the current year? For the next year?

b. What is the basis of the land in Ron and Steve's hands?

c. How would your answers to Parts a and b change if the land has a $12,000 FMV instead of a $40,000 FMV?

C:6-53 *Subsequent Assessment on the Shareholders.* Meridian Corporation originally was owned equally by five individual shareholders. Four years ago, Meridian adopted a plan of liquidation, and each shareholder received a liquidating distribution. Tina, a cash method taxpayer, reported a $30,000 long-term capital gain in the prior liquidation year on the redemption of her stock. Pending the outcome of a lawsuit in which Meridian is one of the defendents, $5,000 of Tina's liquidating distribution was held back and placed in escrow. Settlement of the lawsuit in the current year requires that the escrowed funds plus the interest earned on these funds be paid out to the plaintiff and that each shareholder pay an additional $2,500. Tina pays the amount due in the next year. How does Tina report the settlement of the lawsuit and the payment of the additional amount?

COMPREHENSIVE PROBLEM

C:6-54 The following facts pertain to Lifecycle Corporation:

- Able owns a parcel of land (Land A) having a $30,000 FMV and $16,000 adjusted basis. Baker owns an adjacent parcel of land (Land B) having a $20,000 FMV and $22,000 adjusted basis. On January 2, 2007, Able and Baker contribute their parcels of land to newly formed Lifecycle Corporation in exchange for 60% of the corporation's stock for Able and 40% of the corporation's stock for Baker. The corporation elects a calendar tax year and the accrual method of accounting.
- On January 2, 2007, the corporation borrows $2 million and uses the loan proceeds to build a factory ($1 million), purchase equipment ($500,000), produce inventory ($450,000), pay other operating expenses ($30,000), and retain working cash ($20,000). Assume the corporation sells all inventory produced and collects on all sales immediately so that, at the end of any year, the corporation has no accounts receivable or inventory balances.
- Operating results for 2007 are as follows:

Sales	$964,000	
Cost of goods sold	450,000	
Interest paid on loan	140,000	
Depreciation:		
Equipment	70,000	($25,000 for E&P)
Building	24,000	($24,000 for E&P)
Operating expenses	30,000	

Of these amounts, $250,000 is qualified production activities income. The deduction percentage is 6% in 2007.

- In 2008, Lifecycle Corporation invests $10,000 of excess cash in Macro Corporation stock (less than 20% owned) and $20,000 in tax-exempt bonds. In addition, the corporation pays Able a $12,000 salary and distributes an additional $42,000 to Able and $28,000 to Baker. The corporation also makes a $100,000 principal payment on the loan.
- Results for 2008 are as follows:

Sales	$990,000	
Cost of goods sold	500,000	
Interest paid on loan	130,000	
Depreciation:		
Equipment	125,000	($50,000 for E&P)
Building	25,000	($25,000 for E&P)
Operating expenses	40,000	
Salary paid to Able	12,000	
Dividend received on Macro Corporation stock	2,000	
Short-term capital gain on sale of portion of Macro Corporation stock holdings ($4,000 – $3,000)	1,000	
Tax-exempt interest received	1,500	
Charitable contributions	500	

Of these amounts, $158,000 is qualified production activities income. The deduction percentage is 6% in 2008.

- In 2009, the corporation did not pay a salary to Able and made no distributions to the shareholders. The corporation, however, made a $30,000 principal payment on the loan.
- Results for 2009 are as follows:

Sales	$500,000	
Cost of goods sold	280,000	
Interest paid on loan	125,000	
Depreciation:		
Equipment	90,000	($50,000 for E&P)
Building	25,000	($25,000 for E&P)
Operating expenses	60,000	
Long-term capital gain on sale of remaining Macro Corporation stock ($9,000 – $7,000)	2,000	
Long-term capital gain on sale of tax-exempt bond ($21,000 – $20,000)	1,000	

Of these amounts, qualified production activities income is zero (because it is negative).

- On January 2, 2010, the corporation receives a refund for the 2009 NOL carried back to 2007. When carrying back the NOL, remember to recalculate the U.S. production activities deduction in the carryback year because of the reduced taxable income resulting from carryback. In addition, the corporation sells its assets, pays taxes on the gain, and pays off the $1.87 million remaining debt.

	Sales Price	*Tax Adj. Basis**	*E&P Adj. Basis*
Equipment	$ 250,000	$ 215,000	$ 375,000
Building	986,000	926,000	926,000
Land A	80,000	16,000	16,000
Land B	50,000	20,000	20,000
Total	$1,366,000	$1,177,000	$1,337,000

*Note: Technically, the equipment should be depreciated for ½ year in the year of disposition, and the building should be depreciated for ½ month (because of the January disposition). However, for simplicity, the above calculations ignore depreciation deductions in the disposition year, which creates an offsetting overstatement of adjusted basis. Section 362(e)(2) limits Land B basis to the FMV.

Immediately after these transactions, the corporation makes a liquidating distribution of the remaining cash to Able and Baker. The remaining cash is $344,766, which the corporation distributes in proportion to the shareholders' ownership (60% and 40%). Long-term capital gains are taxed at 15% in 2010.

Required:

a. Determine the tax consequences of the corporate formation to Able, Baker, and Lifecycle Corporation.
b. For 2007–2009, prepare schedules showing corporate taxable income, taxes, and E&P activity. Assume that Lifecycle pays its taxes in the same year they accrue.
c. For 2010, prepare a schedule showing the results of this year's transactions on Lifecycle Corporation, Able, and Baker.

TAX STRATEGY PROBLEMS

C:6-55 Sarah plans to invest $1 million in a business venture that will last five years. She is debating whether to operate the business as a C corporation or a sole proprietorship. If a C corporation, she will liquidate the corporation at the end of the five-year period. She expects the business to generate taxable income as follows:

Year	Taxable Income
1	$ 40,000
2	70,000
3	90,000
4	150,000
5	350,000

If incurred in corporate form, these taxable income amounts will be subject to the corporate tax rate schedule. If in proprietorship form, they will be subject to Sarah's 35% marginal tax rate. Assume that any capital gain upon corporate liquidation will be taxed at a 15% capital gains rate and that Sec. 1202 does not apply.

Required: Determine the after-tax amount Sarah will have at the end of five years under each alternative. Which alternative do you recommend?

C:6-56 One way to compare the accumulation of income by alternative business entity forms is to use mathematical models. The following models express the investment after-tax accumulation calculation for a particular entity form:

Flow-through entities and sole proprietorships: Contribution $\times$ $[1 + R(1 - t_p)]^n$
C corporation: Contribution $\times$ $\{[1 + R(1 - t_c)]^n(1 - t_g) + t_g\}$

Where: ATA = after-tax accumulation in n years
R = before-tax rate of return for the business entity
t_p = owner's marginal tax rate on ordinary income
t_c = corporation's marginal tax rate
t_g = owner's tax rate on capital gains
n = number of periods

In the C corporation model, the corporation operates for n years, paying taxes currently and distributing no dividends. At the end of its existence, the corporation liquidates, causing the shareholder to recognize a capital gain. In the flow-through model, the entity or sole proprietorship distributes just enough cash for the owner or owners to pay individual taxes, and the entity reinvests the remaining after-tax earnings in the business. (See Chapter I:18 of the *Individuals* volume for a detailed explanation of these models.)

Now consider the following facts. Twelve years ago, your client formed a C corporation with a $100,000 investment (contribution). The corporation's before-tax rate of return (R) has been and will continue to be 10%. The corporate tax rate (t_c) has been and will continue to be 35%. The corporation pays no dividends and reinvests all after-tax earnings in its business. Thus, the corporation's value grows at its after-tax rate of return. Your client's marginal ordinary tax rate (t_p) has been 33%, and her capital gains rate (t_g) has been 15%. Your client expects her ordinary tax rate to drop to 25% at the beginning of this year and stay at that level indefinitely. Her capital gains tax rate will remain at 15%. Assume the corporate stock does not qualify for the Sec. 1202 exclusion.

Your client wants you to consider two alternatives:

(1) Continue the business in C corporation form for the next 20 years and liquidate at that time (32 years in total).

(2) Liquidate the C corporation at the beginning of this year, invest the after-tax proceeds in a sole proprietorship, and operate as a sole proprietorship for the next 20 years.

The sole proprietorship's before-tax rate of return (R) also will be 10% for the next 20 years. Earnings from the sole proprietorship will be taxed currently at your client's ordinary tax rate, and your client will withdraw just enough earnings from the business to pay her taxes on the business's income. The remaining after-tax earnings will remain in the business until the end of the investment horizon (20 years from now).

Required: Show the results of each alternative along with supporting models and calculations. Ignore self employment taxes and the accumulated earnings tax. Which alternative should your client adopt?

Note: See Problem C:11-61 for a third alternative to consider.

CASE STUDY PROBLEMS

C:6-57 Paul, a long-time client of yours, has operated an automobile repair shop (as a C corporation) for most of his life. The shop has been fairly successful in recent years. His children are not interested in continuing the business. Paul is age 62 and has accumulated approximately $500,000 in assets outside of his business, most of which are in his personal residence and retirement plan. A recent balance sheet for the business shows the following amounts:

Assets	*Adjusted Basis*	*FMV*	*Liabilities & Equity*	*Amount*
Cash	$ 25,000	$ 25,000	Accounts payable	$ 30,000
Inventory	60,000	75,000	Mortgage payable	70,000
Equipment	200,000	350,000	Paid-in capital	120,000
Building	100,000	160,000	Retain earnings	205,000
Land	40,000	60,000		
Goodwill	–0–	100,000		
Total	$425,000	$770,000	Total	$425,000

The inventory is accounted for using the first-in, first-out inventory method. The corporation has claimed depreciation of $250,000 on the equipment. The corporation acquired the building 11 years ago and has claimed $25,000 of depreciation under the MACRS rules. The goodwill is an estimate that Paul feels reflects the value of his business over and above the other tangible assets.

Paul has received an offer of $775,000 from a competing automobile repair company for the noncash assets of his business, which will be used to establish a second location for the competing company. The corporation will sell the assets within 60 days and distribute remaining cash to Paul in liquidation of the corporation. The purchaser has obtained the necessary bank financing to make the acquisition. Paul's basis in his stock is $300,000.

Required: Prepare a memorandum for Paul outlining the tax consequences of the sale transaction and liquidation of the corporation.

C:6-58 Your accounting firm has done the audit and tax work for the Peerless family and their business entities for 20 years. Approximately 25% of your accounting and tax practice billings come from Peerless family work. Peerless Real Estate Corporation owns land and a building (MACRS property) having a $4.5 million FMV and a $1.0 million adjusted basis. The corporation owes a $1.3 million mortgage balance on the building. The corporation used substantial leverage to acquire the building so Myron Peerless and his brother Mark Peerless, who are equal shareholders in Peerless Real Estate, each have only $200,000 adjusted bases in their stock. Cash flows are good from the building, and only a small portion of the annual profits is needed for reinvestment in the building. Myron and Mark have decided to liquidate the corporation to avoid the federal and state corporate income taxes and continue to operate the business as a partnership. They want the MM Partnership, which has Mark and Myron equally sharing profits, losses, and liabilities, to purchase the building from the corporation for $400,000 cash plus their assumption of the $1.3 million mortgage. Mark knows a real estate appraiser who, for the right price, will provide a $1.7 million appraisal. Current corporate cash balances are sufficient to pay any federal and state income taxes owed on the sale of the building. Mark and Myron each would receive $200,000 from the corporation in cancellation of their stock.

Required: Prepare notes on the points you will want to cover with Myron and Mark Peerless about the corporate liquidation and the Peerless' desire to avoid federal and state corporate income taxes at your meeting tomorrow.

TAX RESEARCH PROBLEMS

C:6-59 Parent Corporation owns 85% of the common stock and 100% of the preferred stock of Subsidiary Corporation. The common stock and preferred stock have adjusted bases of $500,000 and $200,000, respectively, to Parent. Subsidiary adopts a plan of liquidation on July 3 of the current year, when its assets have a $1 million FMV. Liabilities on that date amount to $850,000. On November 9, Subsidiary pays off its creditors and distributes $150,000 to Parent with respect to its preferred stock. No cash remains to be paid to Parent with respect to the remaining $50,000 of its liquidation preference for the preferred stock, or with respect to any of the common stock. In each of Subsidiary's tax years, less than 10% of its gross income has been passive income. What are the amount and character of Parent's loss on the preferred stock? The common stock?

A partial list of research sources is

- IRC Secs. 165(g)(3) and 332(a)
- Reg. Sec. 1.332-2(b)
- *Spaulding Bakeries, Inc.*, 27 T.C. 684 (1957)
- *H. K. Porter Co., Inc.*, 87 T.C. 689 (1986)

C:6-60 Parent Corporation has owned 60% of Subsidiary Corporation's single class of stock for a number of years. Tyrone owns the remaining 40% of the Subsidiary stock. On August 10 of the current year, Parent purchases Tyrone's Subsidiary stock for cash. On September 15, Subsidiary adopts a plan of liquidation. Subsidiary then makes a single liquidating distribution on October 1. The activities of Subsidiary continue as a separate division of Parent. Does the liquidation of Subsidiary qualify for nonrecognition treatment under Secs. 332 and 337? Must Parent assume Subsidiary's E&P balance?

A partial list of research sources is

- IRC Secs. 332(b) and 381
- Reg. Sec. 1.332-2(a)

7

CHAPTER

CORPORATE ACQUISITIONS AND REORGANIZATIONS

LEARNING OBJECTIVES

After studying this chapter, you should be able to

1. Identify the types of taxable acquisition transactions.
2. Distinguish between taxable and nontaxable acquisitions.
3. Explain the types of nontaxable reorganizations and their requirements.
4. Determine the tax consequences of a nontaxable reorganization to the target corporation.
5. Determine the tax consequences of a nontaxable reorganization to the acquiring corporation.
6. Determine the tax consequences of a nontaxable reorganization to target corporation shareholders and security holders.
7. Understand judicial doctrines that govern the tax treatment of corporate reorganizations.
8. Explain what happens to tax attributes in a reorganization.
9. Explain restrictions on the use of NOL carryovers following an acquisition.
10. Understand the financial statement implications of corporate acquisitions.

CHAPTER OUTLINE

A corporation's directors or shareholders may decide to have that corporation acquire a second corporation (the target). Alternatively, they may decide to divest the corporation of part or all of its assets, such as the assets of an operating division or stock in a subsidiary. These acquisitions or divestitures can be either taxable or nontaxable. In a taxable transaction, the entire realized gain or loss is recognized. To qualify as nontaxable, the transaction must meet certain statutory and judicial requirements. If the transaction meets these requirements, part or all of the realized gain or loss generally goes unrecognized. This unrecognized gain or loss is deferred until the assets or stock exchanged are sold or disposed of in a taxable transaction. The nontaxable reorganization rules are an example of the wherewithal to pay concept, which holds that no tax is imposed if the taxpayer retains a continuing equity interest. A tax is imposed, however, where the taxpayer receives property other than stock or securities (e.g., money).[1] On the other hand, taxpayers are likely to engage in a taxable transaction (instead of a nontaxable reorganization) where they prefer to recognize loss on an asset sale or stock disposition.

This chapter presents an overview of taxable and nontaxable acquisitions and divestitures. It also examines the statutory provisions and judicial doctrines that determine the tax consequences of acquisitions and divestitures.

TAXABLE ACQUISITION TRANSACTIONS

OBJECTIVE 1

Identify the types of taxable acquisition transactions

In taxable acquisitions, corporations can acquire a **target corporation** in two principal ways.[2] First, they can purchase the assets directly from the target corporation. Second, they can acquire an equity claim to the assets by purchasing a controlling interest in the target corporation's stock. Three options exist once the acquiring corporation has purchased the target stock.

- The acquiring corporation and its new subsidiary can exist as separate entities.
- The acquiring corporation can liquidate its new subsidiary corporation in a nontaxable transaction. Following the liquidation, the parent corporation retains a direct interest in the target corporation assets.
- The acquiring corporation can make a Sec. 338 election, which adjusts the basis of subsidiary assets to the price the acquiring corporation paid for the subsidiary stock, plus the amount of any subsidiary liabilities.

The principal asset and stock acquisition transactions are examined below. Table C:7-1 summarizes the tax consequences of these transactions.

ASSET ACQUISITIONS

From a tax perspective, accounting for an asset purchase is not difficult. The selling corporation calculates the gain or loss recognized on the sale of each asset. Sales of depreciable assets (e.g., Sec. 1245 and 1250 property) may result in the recapture of previously claimed depreciation.

TAX STRATEGY TIP

Three types of state taxes may arise in an *asset* sale—transfer taxes, state income taxes, and sales taxes (some state sales tax laws allow certain bulk-sale exceptions). These taxes need to be taken into account by both the buyer and seller when drafting the sales agreement. When a *stock* sale occurs, these taxes can be avoided because the assets remain inside the same entity before and after the stock sale.

The purchaser's bases in the acquired assets equal their acquisition cost.[3] The purchaser can claim depreciation based on the total acquisition cost of depreciable property.

A taxable asset acquisition provides the purchaser with two major advantages. First, a significant portion of the acquisition cost can be debt-financed. Interest accruing on the debt is deductible for federal income tax purposes. By contrast, in a nontaxable acquisition, the use of debt is either prohibited or restricted. Second, only assets and liabilities specified in the purchase-sale agreement are acquired. The purchaser need not acquire all or substantially all the target corporation's assets, as in the case of a taxable or nontax-

[1] The tax deferral can be permanent if the stock and securities are held until death. At death, the carryover or substituted basis is stepped-up to its fair market value (FMV) without incurring any income tax liability.

[2] The terms *target* and *acquired corporation* are used interchangeably here.

[3] Sec. 1012.

▼ **TABLE C:7-1**
Comparison of Taxable Acquisition Transactions

	Taxable Asset Acquisition	Taxable Stock Acquisition with: No Liquidation of Target	Nontaxable Liquidation of Target	Sec. 338 Election for Target
Acquiring corporation's basis in stock	N/A	Cost basis	Cost basis initially; disappears upon liquidation of target corporation	Cost basis
Parent-subsidiary relationship created	No	Yes	Yes, until liquidation occurs	Yes
Consolidated tax return election available	No	Yes	Yes, until liquidation occurs	Yes
Gain/loss recognized by target corporation on asset sale	Yes	No	No	Yes, on deemed sale of assets from old target corporation to new target corporation.
Gain/loss recognized by target corporation upon liquidating	Yes, if target elects to liquidate before or after the asset sale.	N/A	No	No
Gain recognized by acquiring corporation in liquidating distribution	N/A	N/A	No	No
Acquiring corporation's basis in assets acquired	Cost basis to acquiring corporation	No change in basis of target corporation's assets	Carryover basis upon liquidation	Cost basis in target stock acquired plus amount of target's liabilities
Transfer of tax attributes to acquiring corporation	Remain with target corporation	Remain with target corporation	Carryover to acquiring corporation upon liquidation	Disappear upon deemed sale of assets by old target corporation

N/A = Not applicable.

able stock acquistion or a nontaxable asset acquistion. Similarly, the purchaser assumes only liabilities specified in the purchase-sale agreement. Contingent or unknown liabilities remain the responsibility of the seller.

The target (acquired) corporation recognizes gain or loss on the sale of assets and may subsequently liquidate. If it liquidates, any property retained by the target corporation is distributed to the shareholders as part of the liquidation. The liquidating corporation recognizes gain or loss on the distribution as if such property had been sold. Upon receiving the liquidating distribution, the target corporation's shareholders recognize capital gain or loss (see Chapter C:6).

EXAMPLE C:7-1 ▶ Six years ago, Ann, Bob, and Cathy each acquired one-third of Target Corporation stock. Each shareholder has a $20,000 basis in his or her stock. Acquiring Corporation purchases Target's noncash assets for $100,000 in cash and $300,000 in Acquiring debt obligations. Target retains its $50,000 of cash. On the sale date, Target's noncash assets have a $280,000 adjusted basis and a $400,000 FMV. Its liabilities total $100,000 on the sale date. Target recognizes a $120,000 aggregate gain [($100,000 + $300,000) – $280,000]. The character of its separate asset gains and losses depends on the particular properties sold. Based on a 34% corporate tax rate, Target's tax liability on the sale is $40,800 ($120,000 × 0.34). Acquiring takes a $400,000 basis in the noncash assets acquired. After Target pays its income tax and other liabilities, Ann, Bob, and Cathy each receive a liquidating distribution on which they report a capital gain. ◀

Sometimes a target corporation liquidates before it sells its assets. In this case the target corporation distributes the assets to the shareholders who then sell them. The tax consequences of the liquidation are set forth in Chapter C:6. In general, the total tax liability of the corporation and its shareholders are the same whether the liquidation of the target corporation precedes or follows the asset sale.

STOCK ACQUISITIONS

KEY POINT

In a stock acquisition, only the shareholders of the target corporation recognize gain. In an asset acquisition, both the target corporation and its shareholders may recognize gain.

STOCK ACQUISITION WITH NO LIQUIDATION. A stock purchase is the simplest of acquisition transactions. Gain recognized on the sale is capital in character if the stock is a capital asset in the seller's hands. If payment of part or all of the consideration is deferred to a later year, the seller can defer gain recognition using the installment method of accounting.[4] If part of the total amount received by the seller represents consideration for a promise not to compete with the purchaser, this portion is taxed as ordinary income.[5]

The purchaser's basis in the stock is its acquisition cost.[6] The target corporation's basis in its assets ordinarily does not change as a result of the stock sale. Any potential for depreciation recapture that exists on the transaction date remains with the target corporation's assets and, therefore, is assumed by the purchaser. If the target corporation has loss or credit carryovers, these carryovers can be subject to special limitations in the post-acquisition tax years (see pages C:7-43 through C:7-46).

ADDITIONAL COMMENT

A shareholder's basis in stock sometimes is referred to as "outside basis" as opposed to "inside basis," which is the corporation's basis in its assets.

Stock sales are popular with sellers because they often are less costly than asset sales due to a single level of taxation. No adjustment to the bases of the target corporation's assets is made after a stock sale even though the basis of the stock acquired may be substantially higher than the aggregate basis of these assets. Thus, one of the tax advantages of purchasing target corporation assets—a higher asset basis—is not available in a stock purchase unless the purchasing corporation makes a Sec. 338 deemed sale election (discussed later in this chapter).

EXAMPLE C:7-2 ▶ Assume the same facts as in Example C:7-1 except Acquiring offers to purchase Target stock for $50 per share. Ann, Bob, and Cathy tender their 7,000 Target shares in response to Acquiring's offer. Acquiring's $350,000 (7,000 shares × $50/share) purchase price equals Target's net asset value ($450,000 − $100,000 liabilities). Ann, Bob, and Cathy each recognize a long-term capital gain on the sale of their stock. Target becomes a wholly-owned subsidiary of Acquiring and, without a Sec. 338 election, does not adjust the bases of its assets. ◀

KEY POINT

In Example C:7-2, the built-in gain in Target's assets is not recognized in a stock acquisition. Likewise, Target's assets are not stepped-up in basis even though Acquiring pays their full $350,000 FMV for the Target stock.

If the purchasing corporation is a member of an affiliated group that files a consolidated tax return, the new subsidiary must join in the consolidated return election if the purchasing corporation owns at least 80% of the subsidiary's stock and if the subsidiary is an includible corporation (see Chapter C:8). Otherwise, the parent and subsidiary corporations may make an initial consolidated return election.

TYPICAL MISCONCEPTION

Taxpayers often do not understand that the parent's basis in its subsidiary's stock disappears in a Sec. 332 liquidation. Instead, the subsidiary's bases in the liquidated assets carry over to the parent.

STOCK ACQUISITION FOLLOWED BY A LIQUIDATION. The type of stock acquisition discussed in the preceding section can be followed by a liquidation of the acquired (subsidiary) corporation into its acquiring (parent) corporation. If the parent corporation owns at least 80% of subsidiary corporation stock, the liquidation is nontaxable under the Sec. 332 and 337 rules outlined in Chapter C:6.[7] The bases of the subsidiary's assets carry over to the parent corporation. If the parent corporation paid a premium for the assets (i.e., an amount exceeding the aggregate asset adjusted basis), this premium is lost upon liquidation because the parent corporation's basis in the stock disappears. The stock basis "loss" cannot be deducted and provides no tax benefit. If the parent corporation

---

[4] Sec. 453(a).

[5] The purchaser can amortize over a 15-year period any amounts paid to the seller with respect to the agreement not to compete (Sec. 197).

[6] Sec. 1012.

[7] The liquidation may be taxable to any minority shareholders and to the subsidiary corporation on distributions made to the minority shareholders.

paid less than the aggregate asset adjusted basis, the "excess" asset basis is included in the asset carryover basis, which can provide additional tax benefits.

EXAMPLE C:7-3 ▶ Assume the same facts as in Example C:7-2 except, following the stock acquisition, Acquiring and Target Corporations continue to file separate tax returns, and Target liquidates into Acquiring shortly after the acquisition. Target's assets have the following adjusted bases and FMVs immediately before the sale:

Assets	*Adjusted Basis*	*FMV*
Cash	$ 50,000	$ 50,000
Marketable securities	49,000	55,000
Accounts receivable	60,000	60,000
Inventory	60,000	90,000
Building	27,000	44,000
Land	10,000	26,000
Machinery and equipment[a]	74,000	125,000
Total	$330,000	$450,000

[a]The machinery and equipment are Sec. 1245 property. Recapture potential of the machinery and equipment is $107,000.

Target and Acquiring recognize no gain or loss on the liquidation. Acquiring assumes Target's $100,000 in liabilities and takes a $330,000 total basis in Target assets, the basis of each asset carrying over. In addition, Acquiring inherits all of Target's tax attributes, including any NOL carryovers, E&P, and the $107,000 depreciation recapture potential of the machinery and equipment. ◀

ADDITIONAL COMMENT

A Sec. 338 election triggers immediate taxation to the target corporation. Therefore, in most situations it makes little sense to pay an immediate tax to obtain a step-up in basis when such additional basis can be recovered only in future years. The election can be beneficial, however, if the target corporation has enough NOLs to offset most or all of the gain recognized on the deemed asset sale. The election also can be beneficial if Sec. 338(h)(10) applies (see footnote 9).

SECTION 338 DEEMED SALE ELECTION. The Sec. 338 **deemed sale election** operates as follows: First target corporation's shareholders sell their stock to the acquiring corporation. Then the acquiring corporation makes a Sec. 338 deemed sale election with respect to the purchased stock. This election results in a hypothetical sale of the "old" target corporation's assets to a "new" target corporation for their **aggregate deemed sale price (ADSP)** in a transaction that requires the seller ("old" target) to recognize gains and losses on its final tax return. The "old" target corporation goes out of existence for tax purposes only.[8] The "new" target corporation is treated as a new entity for tax purposes (i.e., it makes new accounting method and tax year elections). The bases of the old target corporation's assets are stepped-up or stepped-down to the price paid by the acquiring corporation for target corporation stock plus the amount of target corporation liabilities (including any federal income taxes owed on the hypothetical sale). Corporate purchasers generally do not find the Sec. 338[9] election appealing because, in the year of the election, the target corporation usually incurs a significant tax liability.

PRACTICAL APPLICATION

The purchasing corporation most likely would not make a Sec. 338 election if it resulted in the target corporation's asset tax bases being stepped-down.

Eligible Stock Acquisitions. Section 338 requires the acquiring corporation to purchase 80% or more of target corporation voting stock and 80% or more of the total value of all classes of target stock except certain nonvoting preferred stock during a continuous 12-month (or shorter) qualified stock acquistion period.[10] The acquistion period begins on the date the acquiring corporation first purchases target stock and ends on the date the qualified stock purchase is completed. If the acquiring corporation does not acquire the necessary 80% minimum within the 12-month acquisition period, it cannot make a Sec. 338 election.

[8] The target corporation's legal existence does not change under the applicable corporation laws. For federal income tax purposes, the target corporation (commonly referred to as "old" target) goes out of existence. A "new" target corporation is created. This new corporation acquires for tax purposes all the assets of the "old" corporation.

[9] An alternative Sec. 338 election is permitted under Sec. 338(h)(10) for members of an affiliated group. This election generally is used by affiliated groups that file consolidated tax returns. The Sec. 338(h)(10) election permits the target corporation (e.g., a subsidiary) to recognize gain or loss as if it had sold its assets in a single transaction. The corporation selling the stock (e.g., a parent corporation) does not recognize gain on the stock sale, thereby resulting in a single level of taxation. This special Sec. 338 election has become popular in recent years.

[10] The basic Sec. 332 liquidation of a controlled subsidiary stock definition outlined in Chapter C:6 also is used for Sec. 338 purposes.

EXAMPLE C:7-4 ▶ Missouri Corporation purchases a 25% block of Target Corporation's single class of stock on each of four dates: April 1, 2006; July 1, 2006; December 1, 2006; and February 1, 2007. Because Missouri acquires at least 80% of Target stock within a 12-month period (April 1, 2006, through February 1, 2007), it can make a Sec. 338 deemed sale election. ◀

EXAMPLE C:7-5 ▶ Assume the same facts as in Example C:7-4 except Missouri Corporation instead purchases the final 25% block on May 15, 2007. In this case, Missouri acquires only 75% of the Target stock during a 12-month period. Two possible 12-month periods may occur—April 1, 2006, through March 31, 2007, and May 16, 2006, through May 15, 2007. The 80% stock ownership minimum is not achieved in either period. Thus, Missouri cannot make a Sec. 338 election. ◀

For the purpose of the 80% requirement, the following stock acquisitions are not treated as purchases:

- Stock whose adjusted basis is determined in whole or part by its basis in the hands of the person from whom it was acquired (e.g., stock acquired as a capital contribution)
- Stock whose basis is determined under Sec. 1014(a) (i.e., FMV on the date of decedent's death or alternative valuation date)
- Stock acquired in a nontaxable transaction under Sec. 351, 354, 355, or 356 (e.g., corporate formations, divisions, or reorganizations)
- Stock acquired from a related party where stock ownership may be attributed to the purchaser under Secs. 318(a)(1) through (3)

The Election. A Sec. 338 election must be made no later than the fifteenth day of the ninth month beginning after the month in which the acquisition date falls. The acquisition date is the first date during the 12-month acquisition period on which the 80% stock ownership requirement is met.[11]

EXAMPLE C:7-6 ▶ On April 1, 2007, Arizona Corporation purchased 40% of Target Corporation's single class of stock. On October 20, 2007, it purchases an additional 50% of Target stock. The acquisition date is October 20, 2007. Arizona must make a Sec. 338 election on or before July 15, 2008. ◀

Deemed Sale Transaction. When the acquiring corporation makes a Sec. 338 election, the target corporation is treated as having sold all its assets at their aggregate deemed sale price (ADSP) in a single transaction at the close of the acquisition date. The asset sale is a taxable transaction, with gain or loss recognized by the target corporation. ADSP is calculated as follows:[12]

$$ADSP = \frac{G + L - (T_R \times B)}{(1 - T_R)}$$

Where: G = Acquiring's grossed-up basis in recently purchased target corporation stock;
L = Target liabilities other than its tax liability for the deemed sale gain determined by reference to the ADSP;
T_R = the applicable federal income tax rate; and
B = the adjusted basis of the asset(s) deemed sold.

EXAMPLE C:7-7 ▶ Assume the same facts as in Examples C:7-2 and C:7-3 except Acquiring makes a timely Sec. 338 election. Also assume that Target's marginal tax rate is 34%. The aggregate deemed sale price is calculated as follows:

$$ADSP = \frac{G + L - (T_R \times B)}{(1 - T_R)}$$

[11] Secs. 338(g) and 338(h)(2).

[12] This equation is derived as follows:

$$ADSP = G + L + [T_R \times (ADSP - B)]$$
$$ADSP = G + L + (T_R \times ADSP) - (T_R \times B)$$
$$ADSP - (T_R \times ADSP) = G + L - (T_R \times B)$$
$$ADSP \times (1 - T_R) = G + L - (T_R \times B)$$
$$ADSP = \frac{G + L - (T_R \times B)}{(1 - T_R)}$$

$$\text{ADSP} = \frac{\$350{,}000 + \$100{,}000 - (0.34 \times \$330{,}000)}{(1 - 0.34)}$$

$$0.66\ \text{ADSP} = \$337{,}800$$

$$\text{ADSP} = \$511{,}818$$

Thus, Target recognizes a gain of $181,818 ($511,818 – $330,000) and pays taxes of $61,818 (0.34 × $181,818) on the gain. ◀

TAX STRATEGY TIP

Many taxpayers avoid Sec. 338 because it requires an advance payment of taxes to achieve a step-up in basis of target corporation's assets. A Sec. 338 election becomes more viable, however, when the target corporation has NOLs that can offset its gain on the deemed sale of its assets, thereby reducing the cost of making the election.

The Sec. 338 election was intended for transactions in which the acquisition price of the target stock exceeds the adjusted basis of target assets. In many of these transactions, the amount of gain recognized by the target corporation, as well as the associated tax liability, could be substantial. This potential tax cost might induce companies to forego the Sec. 338 election or lower the price they are willing to pay for target stock if they intend to make a Sec. 338 election.

Tax Basis of the Assets After the Deemed Sale. Similarly to the ADSP, the tax basis in the assets of the new target corporation is based on the amount paid by the acquiring corporation for target corporation stock. This amount is called the **adjusted grossed-up basis** in the target corporation stock. The adjusted grossed-up basis equals the sum of

- The purchasing corporation's grossed-up basis in recently purchased target corporation stock;
- The purchasing corporation's basis in nonrecently purchased target corporation stock;
- The liabilities of the new target corporation; and
- Other relevant items.[13]

The adjusted grossed-up basis is determined as of the beginning of the day following the acquisition date. Example C:7-10 illustrates the calculation of the adjusted grossed-up basis.

The target corporation stock owned by the acquiring corporation falls into two categories: recently purchased stock and nonrecently purchased stock. This categorization is necessary because only the recently purchased stock is treated as consideration used in a deemed purchase of the target corporation assets. Recently purchased stock includes any target corporation stock held on the acquisition date that the acquiring corporation purchased during the 12-month (or shorter) acquisition period. Nonrecently purchased stock includes all other target corporation stock acquired before the acquisition period and held by the acquiring corporation on the acquisition date.[14] The basis of the purchasing corporation's ownership interest equals the grossed-up basis of the recently purchased stock plus the basis of the nonrecently purchased stock.

EXAMPLE C:7-8 ▶ On July 23 of the current year, Apple Corporation purchases all of Target Corporation's single class of stock. All the Target stock is considered to be recently purchased because it is purchased in a single transaction. The acquisition date is July 23 of the current year. ◀

EXAMPLE C:7-9 ▶ Assume the same facts as in Example C:7-8 except Apple already owns 10% of Target stock (purchased five years ago) and purchases the remaining 90% of Target stock. The original block of Target stock is not considered to be recently purchased because it was acquired more than 12 months before the acquisition date (July 23 of the current year). ◀

When the acquiring corporation does not own all the target's outstanding stock, the basis of the acquiring corporation's recently purchased stock must be increased or grossed-up to a hypothetical value that reflects ownership of all the stock.[15]

---

[13] Secs. 338(b)(1) and (2). The IRS has indicated that other relevant items include only items that arise from adjustment events that occur after the close of the new target's first tax year and items discovered as a result of an IRS examination of a tax return (e.g., the payment of contingent amounts for recently or nonrecently purchased stock).

[14] Sec. 338(b)(6). A special gain recognition election is available to adjust the basis of nonrecently purchased stock. This election, which is found in Sec. 338(b)(3), is beyond the scope of this text.

[15] Sec. 338(b)(4). The gross-up operation involves taking the purchasing corporation's basis for the recently purchased target stock and dividing it by the percentage (by value) of recently purchased target stock owned (expressed as a decimal).

Specifically, the basis of the recently purchased stock must be increased by the face amount of any target liabilities outstanding on the day following the acquisition date, plus the tax liability incurred on any gain realized in the deemed sale.[16] This liability adjustment embodies the notion that, if the acquisition had been structured as an asset purchase, the assumption of liabilities would have been reflected in the total purchase price.

Allocation of Basis to Individual Assets. The adjusted grossed-up basis of the stock is allocated among seven classes of assets under the residual method.[17] The residual method requires that the adjusted grossed-up basis be allocated to the corporation's tangible and intangible property (other than goodwill and going concern value) on a priority basis. Any amount exceeding the aggregate FMVs of this property is allocated to target corporation goodwill and going concern value.

PRACTICAL APPLICATION

Because goodwill now can be amortized, the fact that the residual purchase price is allocated to goodwill may be a desirable tax result. Goodwill was not amortized under pre-Sec. 197 law because it had an indefinite life. On the negative side, however, the required 15-year amortization period under Sec. 197 is longer than the time period used by many taxpayers under pre-Sec. 197 law to amortize intangible assets that had a shorter determinable life.

The seven classes of assets to which the adjusted grossed-up basis is allocated are as follows:

- Class I: cash and general deposit accounts, including demand deposit and similar accounts in banks, savings and loan associations, and other financial institutions.
- Class II: actively traded personal property (as defined in Sec. 1092(d)(1)), such as U.S. government obligations and publicly traded securities.
- Class III: accounts receivable, mortgages, and credit card receivables that arise in the ordinary course of business.
- Class IV: inventory or other property held primarily for sale to customers in the ordinary course of business.
- Class V: all assets other than Class I, II, III, IV, VI, and VII assets. Included in this category are tangible and intangible property without regard to whether such property is depreciable, depletable, or amortizable.
- Class VI: all amortizable Sec. 197 intangible assets except goodwill and going concern value.
- Class VII: Sec. 197 intangible assets in the nature of goodwill and going concern value.[18]

ADDITIONAL COMMENT

The residual method ensures that any premium paid for the target stock is reflected in goodwill. Because the residual method is the only acceptable allocation method, the only uncertainty that remains is to determine the FMVs of the assets listed in Classes II through VI.

Class VI and VII intangible assets are amortizable over a 15-year period if they are used in the active conduct of a trade or business. Among such assets are goodwill, going concern value, and covenants not to compete.

The adjusted grossed-up basis is first allocated to individual Class I assets based on their actual dollar amounts.[19] Any excess is allocated to Class II assets based on, and to the extent of, their relative gross FMVs. Similar allocations are made to Class III through VI assets based on, and to the extent of, the relative gross FMVs of individual assets within each class. The intraclass allocation is based on the asset's total gross FMV, not its net FMV (gross FMV minus liens on the property). Any remaining adjusted grossed-up basis is allocated to Class VII (goodwill).

EXAMPLE C:7-10 ▶ Assume the same facts as in Example C:7-7, with assets classified as follows:

Asset Class	*Assets*	*FMV*
I	Cash	$ 50,000
II	Marketable securities	55,000
III	Accounts receivable	60,000
IV	Inventory	90,000
V	Building	44,000
V	Land	26,000
V	Machinery and equipment	125,000
	Total	$450,000

[16] Sec. 338(b)(2) and Reg. Secs. 1.338(b)-1(f)(1) and (2).
[17] Reg. Sec. 1.338-6(a).
[18] Reg. Sec. 1.338(b)-6(b).
[19] Ibid.

The adjusted grossed-up basis of Acquiring's interest in Target stock is calculated as follows:

Recently purchased stock	$350,000
Plus: Target corporation's nontax liabilities	100,000
Target corporation's tax liability [($511,818 − $330,000) × 0.34]	61,818
Adjusted grossed-up basis	$511,818

ADDITIONAL COMMENT

Occasionally, a firm will purchase a target corporation's stock for a price below the total FMV of its tangible assets. In such a case, the adjusted grossed-up basis to be allocated to the Class I through V assets is less than their total FMV. Class I through IV assets will receive a basis equal to their individual FMVs. Any basis remaining after making the allocation to the Class IV assets is allocated to the Class V assets using their relative FMVs.

The adjusted grossed-up basis is allocated to Target's seven asset classes as follows:

Step 1: Allocate $50,000 to cash (Class I asset).

Step 2: Allocate $55,000 to marketable securities (Class II asset).

Step 3: Allocate $60,000 to accounts receivable (Class III asset).

Step 4: Allocate $90,000 to inventory (Class IV asset).

Step 5: Allocate $195,000 to the building, land, and machinery and equipment (Class V assets). Because the total basis that remains after the Step 4 allocation ($256,818) exceeds the aggregate FMV of the Class V assets ($195,000), each asset will take a basis exactly equal to its FMV.

Step 6: No allocation to Class VI assets.

Step 7: Allocate the residual $61,818 [$511,818 − ($50,000 + $55,000 + $60,000 + $90,000 + $195,000)] to goodwill (Class VII asset). The $61,818 is amortizable under Sec. 197. ◀

STOP & THINK

Question: In Example C:7-10, Target Corporation is considering changing from the FIFO to the LIFO inventory method after all the Sec. 338 adjustments have been made. How and when will the $30,000 ($90,000 FMV − $60,000 cost) upward adjustment to the inventory's basis be recovered if Target makes the LIFO election?

Solution: The basis step-up will be recovered only if Target sells the LIFO inventory layers in existence on the acquisition date. In general, such sales will not be made unless inventory levels are reduced below the amount held on the acquisition date. If Target retains the FIFO inventory method, the step-up in the inventory's basis will be included in cost of goods sold in the first post-election tax year. Some reasons for not making the Sec. 338 election include the lengthy capital recovery periods for the building and goodwill adjustments, and the inability to recover the adjustment made to the basis of the land through depreciation or amortization.

SELF-STUDY QUESTION

What are some of the tax consequences of a Sec. 338 election?

ANSWER

The effects of a Sec. 338 election include termination of the "old" target corporation, creation of a "new" target corporation with the option of a new tax year and different accounting methods, new depreciation elections without regard to anti-churning rules, and elimination of the old target's tax attributes (i.e., NOL carryforwards).

Tax Accounting Elections for the New Corporation. Because it is a separate legal entity, the "new" target corporation files a tax return separate from that of the acquiring corporation (unless the group files a consolidated return). For tax purposes, the "new" target corporation is a new entity.[20] For example, without obtaining prior approval from the IRS, the target corporation may adopt any tax year that meets the requirements of Sec. 441 and any accounting method that meets the requirements of Sec. 446.

The new target corporation can claim depreciation under the MACRS rules without regard to the elections made by the old target corporation and without regard to the anti-churning rules.[21] The holding period for the new target corporation's assets begins on the day after the acquisition date.

For purposes of the tax attribute carryover rules, the new target corporation is not a continuation of the old target corporation.[22] As a result, when the purchasing corporation makes a Sec. 338 deemed sale election, tax attribute carryovers that exist on the acquisition date are permanently lost. Gain recognized on the deemed sale, however, may be offset by target corporation loss and credit carryovers that otherwise might be forfeited. Thus, if Target in Examples C:7-7 and C:7-10 had a $200,000 NOL on the acquisition

[20] The "old" target also files a separate tax return that includes the gains from the Sec. 338 deemed sale. The "old" target may not file a consolidated tax return with the acquiring corporation.

[21] Reg. Sec. 1.338-2(d)(1)(i).

[22] Sec. 381(a)(1).

Topic Review C:7-1

Section 338 Deemed Sale

Election Requirements

1. The acquiring corporation must make a qualified stock purchase (i.e., within a 12-month period purchase 80% or more of target voting stock and 80% or more of the total value of all target stock).
2. Stock received in transactions that result in a substituted basis (e.g., nontaxable reorganizations, corporate formations, and gifts), transfers at death, or related party exchanges do not count toward the 80% minimum.
3. The acquiring corporation must make the election not later than the fifteenth day of the ninth month beginning after the month in which the acquisition date falls. The acquisition date is the first date on which the 80% stock ownership requirement is met.

Tax Consequences of a Sec. 338 Election

1. The old target corporation is treated as having sold all its assets to the new target corporation at their aggregate deemed sales price in a single transaction at the close of the acquisition date. The old target corporation recognizes gain or loss on the deemed sale.
2. The new target corporation takes an aggregate asset basis equal to the acquiring corporation's adjusted grossed-up basis in the target stock, that is, the sum of the acquiring corporation's basis in the target corporation stock on the day following the acquisition date, the target corporation's liabilities on the day after the acquisition date, and other relevant items (e.g., contingent liabilities that become fixed).
3. The total adjusted grossed-up basis is allocated to individual assets under the residual method. This method requires allocation of basis first to cash and near-cash items, then to other tangible and intangible assets, and finally to goodwill and going concern value.
4. After the Sec. 338 deemed asset sale, the tax attributes of the old target corporation disappear.
5. The new target corporation makes new tax year and accounting method elections.

date, the asset gain resulting from the Sec. 338 election would have been entirely offset. Consequently, only a small portion of Target's $200,000 NOL would have been lost. The acquiring corporation must carefully consider the relative benefit of obtaining a stepped-up basis in target assets versus the economic value of target tax attributes (e.g., NOL carryovers).

Topic Review C:7-1 summarizes the requirements for, and tax consequences of, a Sec. 338 deemed sale election.

Comparison of Taxable and Nontaxable Acquisitions

OBJECTIVE 2

Distinguish between taxable and nontaxable acquisitions

KEY POINT

Determining whether a transaction is taxable or nontaxable is doubly important to the target corporation because it is involved in two potentially taxable exchanges: the exchange between the target corporation and the acquiring corporation and the exchange between the acquiring corporation and its shareholders.

Taxable and Nontaxable Asset Acquisitions

One way to illustrate the difference between taxable and nontaxable asset acquisitions is to define the type of consideration used to acquire the assets and to compare the tax consequences of the transactions. For this discussion, we assume that the acquiring corporation acquires all the target corporation's assets and liabilities and that the target corporation liquidates immediately after the acquisition. If the acquiring corporation uses cash and/or other property to purchase the assets, the target corporation is taxed on the sale and its shareholders are taxed on the liquidation. On the other hand, if the acquiring corporation uses its own stock, the asset acquisition may qualify as a reorganization that is nontaxable to the target corporation and its shareholders. If the acquiring corporation supplements its stock with a limited amount of cash and/or other property, the transaction still may qualify as a reorganization but may be partially taxable.

TAX CONSEQUENCES TO THE TARGET CORPORATION. Section 1001(c) requires that, with certain exceptions, the entire gain or loss realized on a sale or exchange of property be recognized. Thus, the target corporation recognizes all gains and losses realized on selling its assets.

A reorganization is one exception to the general rule. The target corporation generally recognizes no gain or loss when it exchanges its assets for acquiring corporation stock. It also recognizes no gain or loss when it distributes the acquiring corporation stock to its shareholders. The target corporation, however, could recognize gain if it receives boot and does not distribute the boot to its shareholders or if it distributes boot or retained property whose FMV exceeds its adjusted basis. The term *retained property* refers to property not transferred to the acquiring corporation as part of the acquisition.

SELF-STUDY QUESTION

Why would an acquiring corporation want an acquisition to be nontaxable if it gets only a substituted basis rather than a FMV basis in the acquired assets?

ANSWER

Usually the motivation for an acquisition to be nontaxable comes from the target corporation and its shareholders. However, two reasons why the acquiring corporation may desire a nontaxable acquisition are (1) the acquiring corporation has no cash to acquire the assets, so it must use stock as the consideration for the purchase and (2) the target corporation may have favorable tax attributes (e.g., an NOL) that the acquiring corporation would like to use.

TAX CONSEQUENCES TO THE ACQUIRING CORPORATION. The acquiring corporation recognizes no gain or loss when it issues its stock in exchange for property in either a taxable or nontaxable acquisition. In a taxable acquisition, the acquiring corporation takes a cost (FMV) basis in the assets received, and the holding period for the acquired assets begins the day after the acquisition. In a reorganization, the acquiring corporation takes a carryover basis equal to target's basis before the transfer. If the target corporation recognizes a gain because it does not distribute boot property to its shareholders, the carryover basis is adjusted upward to reflect this recognized gain. The acquiring corporation's holding period includes the target corporation's holding period.

In a taxable acquisition all the target corporation's tax attributes (e.g., an NOL carryover) disappear when it liquidates, while in a nontaxable reorganization, the acquiring corporation inherits the target's tax attributes.

TAX CONSEQUENCES TO TARGET CORPORATION SHAREHOLDERS. If the target corporation liquidates as part of a taxable acquisition, its shareholders recognize gain or loss on the surrender of their stock. The target assets they receive take a basis equal to their FMV. A reorganization requires the shareholders to recognize gain only to the extent they receive boot. The gain generally is capital in character. In some circumstances, however, target shareholders could recognize dividend income. The stock and securities they receive take a substituted basis that references the basis of the target stock and securities surrendered. Their basis in any boot property received is its FMV.

ACCOUNTING FOR THE ACQUISITION. For financial reporting purposes, only the purchase method is available to account for acquisitions. Thus, the acquired assets must be recorded at their fair market values. Any goodwill created in the acquisition cannot be amortized, but rather must be tested for impairment. Any impairment of an indefinite-life intangible asset must be reported in the acquiring corporation's financial statements as a loss from continuing operations. Also, see Financial Statement Implications at the end of this chapter.

Topic Review C:7-2 compares taxable and nontaxable asset acquisitions.

TAX STRATEGY TIP

Taxes can be an important variable in determining the acquisition method used to acquire the target corporation's stock or assets. All parties also need to consider the nontax variables associated with the transaction. For example, a stock-for-stock acquisition may minimize taxes but leave the target corporation's shareholders controlling the acquiring corporation. Facing loss of control, the acquiring corporation's owners may prefer to have the transaction financed with borrowed funds (and make the acquisition taxable to the seller) while retaining control over the acquiring corporation.

COMPARISON OF TAXABLE AND NONTAXABLE STOCK ACQUISITIONS

For this discussion, we assume that the acquiring corporation acquires all the target corporation stock instead of its assets and that the target corporation becomes a controlled subsidiary of the acquiring corporation. If the acquiring corporation uses cash and/or other property alone or along with its own stock to acquire the target stock, the acquisition is taxable. If the acquiring corporation uses solely its voting stock or voting stock of its parent corporation to acquire the target stock, the acquisition may qualify as a nontaxable reorganization.

TAX CONSEQUENCES TO THE TARGET CORPORATION. The target corporation's basis in its assets does not change as a result of either a taxable or nontaxable stock acquisition (unless the acquiring corporation makes a Sec. 338 election after a taxable stock purchase). Any depreciation recapture potential on the transaction date stays with target corporation assets and, therefore, is inherited by the purchaser. Also, the target

Topic Review C:7-2

Comparison of Taxable and Nontaxable Asset Acquisitions

Tax Feature	Taxable Acquisition	Nontaxable Reorganization
1. Consideration used in acquisition	Primarily cash and debt instruments; may involve some stock of the acquiring corporation or its parent corporation.	Primarily stock and limited amount of cash or debt of the acquiring corporation or its parent corporation.
2. Target corporation		
a. Amount of gain or loss	All gains and losses are recognized. Installment method available if payments are deferred.	Generally, no gain or loss recognized. Gain recognized on an asset transfer when the target corporation receives boot property and does not distribute the boot property to its shareholders. Gain also recognized on the distribution of appreciated boot or retained property.
b. Character of gain or loss	Depends on nature of each asset transferred or distributed.	Depends on nature of each asset transferred or distributed.
c. Depreciation recapture	Sec. 1245 or 1250 depreciation is recaptured.	Sec. 1245 or 1250 depreciation is not recaptured unless boot triggers the recognition of gain.
3. Acquiring corporation		
a. Gain or loss when stock is exchanged for property	None recognized.	None recognized.
b. Gain or loss when boot is exchanged for property	Gain or loss recognized if noncash boot property is transferred to the target corporation.	Gain or loss recognized if noncash boot property is transferred to the target corporation.
c. Basis of acquired assets	Cost.	Same as the target corporation's basis, increased by gain recognized.
d. Holding period of acquired assets	Begins the day after the transaction date.	Includes holding period of the target corporation.
e. Acquisition of target tax attributes	No.	Yes.
4. Target corporation shareholders		
a. Amount of gain or loss	Realized gain or loss is recognized. Installment method available if payments are deferred.	Gain is recognized to the extent of boot received; losses are not recognized.
b. Character of gain or loss	Capital gain or loss; may be Sec. 1244 loss.	Capital gain and/or dividend income in some circumstances.
c. Basis of stock and securities received	Cost; generally FMV of stock, securities, or other property received.	Substituted basis referenced to the stock and securities surrendered; FMV for boot property.
d. Holding period of stock and securities received	Begins the day after the transaction date.	Includes holding period for the stock and securities surrendered; day after the transaction date for boot property.

corporation retains any loss or credit carryovers, which may be subject to special limitations in the post-acquisition tax years.

If the acquiring corporation is a member of an affiliated group that files a consolidated tax return, the target corporation must join in the consolidated return election if the acquiring corporation owns at least 80% of the target stock, and the target corporation is an includible corporation. Otherwise, the acquiring corporation and the target corportion can make an initial consolidated tax return election (see Chapter C:8).

TAX CONSEQUENCES TO THE ACQUIRING CORPORATION. In either a taxable or nontaxable stock acquisition, the acquiring corporation recognizes no gain or loss when it exchanges its own stock for target stock. In a taxable acquisition, the acquiring corporation's basis in the target stock is its acquisition cost. A taxable acquisition may qualify for the Sec. 338 deemed sale election. In a reorganization, the acquiring corporation's basis in the target stock is the same as that in the hands of target shareholders, and a Sec. 338 election is not available. The acquiring corporation recognizes gain or loss when it exchanges noncash boot property for target stock.

TAX CONSEQUENCES TO TARGET CORPORATION SHAREHOLDERS. The gain recognized on a taxable stock sale is capital in character if the target stock is a capital asset in the seller's hands. The seller can account for the gain under the installment method if payment of part or all of the consideration is deferred to a later tax year and if the stock is not traded on an established securities market. Consideration received by the seller that represents compensation for an agreement not to compete with the purchaser for a specified time period is taxable as ordinary income.

Because only voting stock may be used in a nontaxable stock acquisition, the target corporation's shareholders recognize no gain or loss. The shareholders take a substituted basis in the acquiring corporation stock, which is the same as their basis in the target stock.

Topic Review C:7-3 compares taxable and nontaxable stock acquisitions.

Topic Review C:7-3

Comparison of Taxable and Nontaxable Stock Acquisitions

Tax Feature	Taxable Acquisition	Nontaxable Reorganization
1. Consideration used in acquisition	Primarily cash and debt instruments; may include some stock of the acquiring corporation or its parent corporation.	Solely voting stock of the acquiring corporation or its parent corporation.
2. Target corporation		
a. Parent-subsidiary relationship established	Yes.	Yes.
b. Consolidated tax return election available	Yes.	Yes.
c. Basis in assets	Unchanged by stock acquisition unless a Sec. 338 election is made.	Unchanged by stock acquisition. No Sec. 338 election available.
d. Tax attributes	Retained by the target corporation.	Retained by the target corporation.
3. Acquiring corporation		
a. Basis in stock acquired	Cost basis.	Carryover basis from the target corporation shareholders.
4. Target corporation shareholders		
a. Amount of gain or loss recognized	Realized gain or loss is recognized.	No boot is received; therefore, no gain is recognized.
b. Character of gain or loss	Capital gain or loss; may be Sec. 1244 loss.	Not applicable.
c. Basis of stock, securities, or other property received	Cost; generally FMV of stock, securities, or other property received.	Substituted basis from stock surrendered.
d. Holding period of stock, securities, or other property received	Begins the day after the transaction date.	Includes holding period for the stock surrendered.

TYPES OF REORGANIZATIONS

OBJECTIVE 3

Explain the types of nontaxable reorganizations and their requirements

Section 368(a)(1) authorizes seven types of nontaxable reorganizations corresponding to the principal forms of business acquisitions, divestitures, and restructurings. Generally, tax practitioners refer to the reorganization type by the subparagraph of Sec. 368(a)(1) that defines it. For example, a merger is referred to as a *Type A* reorganization because it is defined in Sec. 368(a)(1)(A). The seven types of reorganizations also can be classified according to the transactional form, with the most common forms being acquisitive and divisive. In an **acquisitive reorganization**, the acquiring corporation obtains part or all of a target (or transferor) corporation's assets or stock. Types A, B, and C reorganizations generally are acquisitive. In a **divisive reorganization**, some of a transferor corporation's assets are transferred to a second corporation that is controlled by either the transferor or its shareholders. As part of the reorganization, the controlled (or transferee) corporation's stock or securities exchanged for the transferor's assets are distributed to the transferor's shareholders. Subsequent to the transfer, the transferor corporation can either remain in existence or be liquidated. If the transferor corporation remains in existence, its assets usually are divided between at least two corporations. Types D and G reorganizations may be either acquisitive or divisive.

TYPICAL MISCONCEPTION

For an acquisition to be treated as nontaxable, the transaction must qualify as a reorganization. The term *reorganization* includes only transactions specifically enumerated in Sec. 368. Other transactions that may constitute reorganizations in a more general context are not considered nontaxable reorganizations.

KEY POINT

A summary of the acquisitive reorganizations is presented below:

Type	*Description*
A	Merger or consolidation
B	Stock-for-stock
C	Asset-for-stock
D	Asset-for-stock
G	Bankruptcy

Two types of reorganizations are neither acquisitive or divisive. A Type E reorganization—a recapitalization—involves a change in a corporation's capital structure. A Type F reorganization—a change in identity, legal form, or state of incorporation—involves the transfer of an existing corporation's assets to a new corporation, but the shareholders of the transferor corporation generally retain the same equity interest in the transferee corporation.

Not all reorganizations fit neatly into one of the seven categories. Some reorganizations satisfy the requirements of two or more reorganization provisions. When this situation occurs, the IRC or the IRS generally determines which reorganization rules prevail. In other situations, a reorganization may satisfy the requirements of a reorganization provision, but for various reasons the IRS and courts prescribe an entirely different tax treatment (e.g., if the transaction lacks a business purpose, it may be treated as taxable). These issues are discussed further in the next section.

TAX CONSEQUENCES OF REORGANIZATIONS

OBJECTIVE 4

Determine the tax consequences of a nontaxable reorganization to the target corporation

This section examines the tax consequences of a reorganization to the target (or transferor) corporation, the acquiring (or transferee) corporation, and the shareholders and other security holders.[23]

TARGET OR TRANSFEROR CORPORATION

RECOGNITION OF GAIN OR LOSS ON ASSET TRANSFER. Under Sec. 361(a), the target corporation recognizes no gain or loss on the exchange of property exclusively for stock in another corporation that is a party to the reorganization.[24] In addition, under Sec. 361(b), the target corporation recognizes no gain if it also receives money or noncash boot property as part of the reorganization and distributes such property to its shareholders or

[23] The corporation that transfers its assets as part of a reorganization is referred to as either a **target or transferor corporation.** The term *target corporation* generally is used with respect to an acquisitive reorganization where substantially all of a corporation's assets are acquired by the acquiring corporation. The term *transferor corporation* is used with respect to divisive and other reorganizations where only part of a corporation's assets are transferred to a transferee corporation and the transferor corporation may remain in existence. Tax law provisions generally are applied the same to target or transferor corporations and acquiring or transferee corporations, so only a single reference to the target or acquiring corporation is provided in connection with an explanation.

[24] Section 361(a) permits securities (e.g., long-term debt obligations) to be received tax-free when the target corporation surrenders the same face amount of securities, or a larger amount. Generally, a securities exchange does not occur in an acquisitive reorganization, so all debt obligations received by the target corporation are boot property.

TYPICAL MISCONCEPTION

One perplexing aspect of the reorganization provisions is the overlap between the different statutory reorganizations. One transaction often can qualify as more than one type of reorganization.

creditors. On the other hand, the target corporation recognizes gain equal to the lesser of the realized gain or the amount of money plus the FMV of any noncash boot property received unless it distributes the property to its shareholders. However, because most acquisitive and divisive reorganization provisions require the target corporation to be liquidated or distribute all its assets, the target corporation generally retains no boot and thus recognizes no gain on the exchange. (Note: the target corporation might recognize gain on the distribution of appreciated property to its shareholders, as discussed below.)

EXAMPLE C:7-11 ▶ In a reorganization, Target Corporation transfers assets having a $175,000 adjusted basis to Acquiring Corporation in exchange for $400,000 of Acquiring common stock. In the exchange, Target realizes a $225,000 gain ($400,000 amount realized − $175,000 adjusted basis). Because Target received no boot, however, it recognizes none of the gain. If Target instead had received $350,000 of Acquiring common stock plus $50,000 of cash, Target would have recognized no gain if it had distributed the $50,000 of boot to its shareholders. ◀

TYPICAL MISCONCEPTION

Often, taxpayers do not realize that Sec. 361 applies to two exchanges. Section 361(a) applies to the exchange between the acquiring and target corporations (which already has been discussed). Section 361(c) deals with the exchange between the target corporation and its shareholders. Therefore, the target corporation is the only party to the reorganization that may recognize two separate gains.

DEPRECIATION RECAPTURE. The depreciation recapture rules of Secs. 1245 and 1250 do not override the gain or loss nonrecognition rules of Sec. 361.[25] The recapture potential that accumulates before the reorganization remains with the assets transferred to the acquiring corporation and is recognized when the acquiring corporation sells or exchanges the assets in a taxable transaction.

ASSUMPTION OF LIABILITIES. Neither the acquiring corporation's assuming the target corporation's liabilities nor its acquiring the target corporation's property subject to a liability triggers gain recognition on the asset transfer. Section 357(c), however, requires the target corporation to recognize gain if the sum of the liabilities assumed or acquired exceeds the total adjusted bases of the property transferred *and* the transaction is a divisive Type D reorganization.

SELF-STUDY QUESTION

How can the target corporation distribute appreciated boot property to its shareholders if it receives a FMV basis in all such property received from the acquiring corporation?

ANSWER

If the property appreciates in the hands of the target corporation before it is distributed, gain will result under Sec. 361(c). In addition, the target corporation may retain some of its own assets and distribute these assets to its shareholders, again causing the target corporation to recognize gain.

RECOGNITION OF GAIN OR LOSS ON DISTRIBUTION OF STOCK AND SECURITIES. The target corporation recognizes no gain or loss when it distributes to its shareholders or creditors pursuant to a plan of reorganization either (1) its stock, stock rights, or obligations or (2) any stock, stock rights, or obligations of a party to a reorganization that it received in the reorganization (see page C:7-47 for an explanation of a plan of reorganization).[26] Distributions of noncash boot property (including property retained by the target corporation) pursuant to the reorganization plan result in the recognition of gain (but not loss) in the same manner as if the target corporation had sold such property at its FMV.[27] Normally the gain recognized upon the distribution of boot property is inconsequential because of the brief period of time between the receipt of the boot from the acquiring corporation (with a basis equal to its FMV) and its distribution to the shareholders.

EXAMPLE C:7-12 ▶ In a statutory merger (Type A reorganization), Target Corporation transfers all its assets and liabilities to Acquiring Corporation, which exchanges $300,000 of its common stock and $100,000 of cash to Target for Target assets. Target's basis in the assets is $250,000. In the exchange, Target realizes a $150,000 [($300,000 + $100,000) − $250,000] gain. Target recognizes none of this gain, even though it receives boot, because Target must liquidate as a reorganization requirement. Upon distributing the Acquiring stock to its shareholders Target recognizes no gain. On the other hand, Target shareholders who receive cash may have to recognize gain. ◀

OBJECTIVE 5

Determine the tax consequences of a nontaxable reorganization to the acquiring corporation

ACQUIRING OR TRANSFEREE CORPORATION

AMOUNT OF GAIN OR LOSS RECOGNIZED. Under Sec. 1032, the acquiring corporation recognizes no gain or loss when it receives money or other property in exchange for its stock. Similarly, a target corporation recognizes no gain or loss when in a reorganiza-

[25] Secs. 1245(b)(3) and 1250(d)(3). Similar provisions are found in the other recapture rules.

[26] Secs. 361(c)(1)–(c)(3).

[27] Sec. 361(c).

SELF-STUDY QUESTION

Because the acquiring corporation is merely purchasing assets, can it ever recognize gain or loss on the transaction?

ANSWER

Yes. If the acquiring corporation uses noncash boot property, it recognizes gain or loss to the extent of the built-in gain or loss in the noncash boot property (Sec. 1001(a)).

tion it receives money or other property in exchange for its securities. Under Sec. 1001, however, the acquiring corporation recognizes gain or loss when it transfers noncash boot property to the target corporation or its shareholders.[28]

BASIS OF ACQUIRED PROPERTY. Under Sec. 362(b), property acquired from the target corporation in a reorganization takes a carryover basis, increased by the amount of gain recognized by the target corporation on the exchange. As a practical matter, however, because the target corporation generally recognizes no gain on the asset transfer, the carryover basis is not stepped up.

EXAMPLE C:7-13 ▶ Assume the same facts as in Example C:7-12. Acquiring's basis in the acquired property is the same as Target's basis, or $250,000. ◀

HOLDING PERIOD OF ACQUIRED PROPERTY. The acquiring corporation's holding period for acquired property includes the target corporation's holding period.[29]

SHAREHOLDERS AND SECURITY HOLDERS

OBJECTIVE 6

Determine the tax consequences of a nontaxable reorganization to target corporation shareholders and security holders

AMOUNT OF GAIN OR LOSS RECOGNIZED. Under Sec. 354(a), shareholders recognize no gain or loss if, pursuant to a plan of reorganization, stock or securities in a corporate party to a reorganization are exchanged solely for stock or securities in the same corporation or another corporate party to the reorganization. The receipt of property other than stock or securities (nonqualifying property) does not necessarily disqualify the entire transaction from tax-free treatment. Section 356(a) requires that a shareholder or security holder recognize gain to the extent of the lesser of the realized gain or the amount of money received plus the FMV of any other property received. Thus, a shareholder recognizes gain to the extent he or she receives nonqualifying property that does not represent a continuation of the equity interest.

EXAMPLE C:7-14 ▶ Upon the liquidation of Target Corporation in a reorganization, Brian surrenders 1,000 Target shares having a $13,000 basis for Acquiring Corporation stock having a $28,000 FMV. Brian's realized gain is $15,000 ($28,000 − $13,000), none of which is recognized. If instead Brian had received $25,000 of Acquiring stock and $3,000 of cash, he would have recognized $3,000 of the $15,000 realized gain. ◀

ADDITIONAL COMMENT

The acquiring corporation may increase its basis in assets received only by the gain recognized by the target corporation on its exchange with the acquiring corporation. Any gain recognized by the target corporation on distributing stock or other property to its shareholders does not increase the basis of any assets.

With some limitations, the general rule of Sec. 354(a) permits a nontaxable exchange of stock with securities. The receipt of securities is completely nontaxable only if the principal amount of the securities surrendered equals or exceeds the principal amount of the securities received. If the principal amount of securities received exceeds the principal amount of securities surrendered, the FMV of the "excess" constitutes boot.[30] If no securities are surrendered, the FMV of the entire principal amount received constitutes boot. Certain types of preferred stock (e.g., preferred stock that the issuer must redeem) also may constitute boot.

EXAMPLE C:7-15 ▶ Assume the same facts as in Example C:7-14 except Brian instead receives $25,000 of Acquiring stock and Acquiring debt securities having a $3,000 principal amount and a $2,850 FMV. Brian's realized gain is $14,850 [($25,000 + $2,850) − $13,000], of which $2,850 is recognized. If Brian had received $3,000 in Acquiring securities and surrendered $2,000 of Target securities, the FMV of the $1,000 "excess" principal amount, or $950 [$1,000 × ($2,850 FMV/$3,000 principal)], would have been treated as boot. ◀

SELF-STUDY QUESTION

In addition to receiving stock in Acquiring Corporation, shareholder Sue receives debt securities with a FMV of $120,000 and a principal amount of $100,000. In the exchange, Sue surrenders securities of Target Corporation with a FMV and principal amount of $80,000. Is Sue treated as having received any boot?

CHARACTER OF THE RECOGNIZED GAIN. Section 356(a)(2) requires that the recognized gain be taxed as a dividend if the receipt of the boot property has the same effect as the payment of a dividend. The amount of this dividend equals the lesser of the shareholder's recognized gain or the shareholder's ratable share of the transferor or target cor-

[28] Rev. Rul. 72-327, 1972-2 C.B. 197.
[29] Sec. 1223(1).
[30] Secs. 354(a)(2) and 356(d)(2)(B). The FMV of the debt obligations surrendered is irrelevant when determining the amount of recognized gain.

ANSWER

Yes. $100,000 − $80,000 = $20,000 of excess principal amount received. The boot received is $24,000. This amount represents the FMV of the excess principal amount [($20,000/$100,000) × $120,000].

poration's current and accumulated earnings and p
nized gain generally is capital in character.

The Sec. 302(b) stock redemption rules determine
of a dividend.[31] (See Chapter C:4 for a review of the
generally do not involve the actual redemption of the
poses of Sec. 356, however, they involve the hypotheti
acquiring corporation's stock. When the distribution
redemption for sale treatment under Sec. 302(b), the sh

The following example applies the dividend equivale
reorganization.

EXAMPLE C:7-16 ▶ Betty owns all 60 shares of Fisher Corporation's outstandi ... sher merges with Gulf Corporation in a reorganization, with Betty receiving $250,000 in cash and 35 shares of Gulf stock worth $350,000. Four other individuals own the remaining 100 shares of Gulf stock. Betty's Fisher stock has a $200,000 basis. Fisher and Gulf have E&P balances of $300,000 and $500,000, respectively. Betty's realized gain is $400,000 [($350,000 stock + $250,000 cash) − $200,000 adjusted basis], of which $250,000 must be recognized because the cash is treated as boot property.

The Fisher stock initially is treated as having been exchanged for only Gulf stock. Because the Fisher stock is worth $600,000 and the Gulf stock is worth $10,000 per share ($350,000 ÷ 35), Betty is initially treated as owning 60 of the 160 (100 + 60) shares of Gulf stock immediately after the merger. The $250,000 in cash Betty receives is treated as having been exchanged for 25 ($250,000 ÷ $10,000 per share) of the 60 shares of Gulf stock that would have been received in an all-stock transaction. Because Betty owns 37.5% (60 shares ÷ 160 shares) of Gulf stock before the hypothetical redemption and 25.93% (35 shares ÷ 135 shares) after the hypothetical redemption, the $250,000 gain is capital in character under the Sec. 302(b)(2) substantially disproportionate redemption rules (i.e., 25.93% is less than 80% × 37.5% = 30%). ◀

TYPICAL MISCONCEPTION

Before the *Clark* decision, the IRS looked to a target corporation's E&P to measure the amount of dividend income. The IRS thus far has declined to rule whether it has changed this position with respect to the E&P "pool" used to determine the amount of dividend income now that *Clark* treats the receipt of boot as a redemption between the target corporation shareholder and the acquiring corporation.

The Sec. 302(b) test would apply in the same manner if securities were received in the reorganization. In such a case, the boot portion of the transaction would equal the FMV of the "excess" principal amount received by the shareholder or security holder.

Whether capital gain treatment is available for boot received in a reorganization depends on the relative sizes of the target and acquiring corporations. If the acquiring corporation is larger than the target corporation, the Sec. 302(b)(2) (substantially disproportionate redemption) or Sec. 302(b)(1) (not essentially equivalent to a dividend) rules generally will allow capital gain treatment. (See Chapter C:4 for an explanation of these rules.) If the acquiring corporation is smaller than the target corporation, the target corporation's shareholder could be considered as having received dividend income or a combination of dividend income and capital gain (e.g., if the boot received exceeds the shareholder's ratable share of E&P).

Prior to the 2003 Act, many noncorporate shareholders preferred capital gain treatment for their recognized gains because a 20% or lower capital gains tax rate was substantially less than the maximum tax rate applicable to ordinary dividend income. The 2003 Act reduced the maximum capital gains tax rate to 15% and extended the 15% rate to qualified dividends received by noncorporate shareholders. Thus, shareholders are taxed at 15% whether the gain is characterized as capital or a dividend, thereby diminishing the difference between the two types of treatments. Nevertheless, capital gains treatment can provide a benefit not available to dividend treatment in that the capital gains can be offset by (1) capital losses recognized in the current year or (2) capital loss carryovers from prior tax years. Dividend income, even though taxed at a 15% rate, cannot be offset by capital losses.

Corporate shareholders may prefer dividend treatment because they can claim a 70%, 80%, or 100% dividends-received deduction to reduce their tax liability. On the other hand, capital gains recognized in the reorganization can be offset by capital losses

[31] *CIR v. Donald E. Clark*, 63 AFTR 2d 89-1437, 89-1 USTC ¶9230 (USSC, 1989). The IRS has agreed to follow the *Clark* decision in Rev. Rul. 93-61, 1993-2 C.B. 118.

recognized by corporate and noncorporate shareholders in other transactions. Finally, Sec. 453(f)(6)(C) permits a corporate or noncorporate shareholder who is a party to a reorganization to use the installment method to defer recognizing part of the gain realized, provided such gain is not characterized as a dividend.[32]

STOP & THINK

Question: The character of the shareholder's recognized gain is determined under the Sec. 302(b) stock redemption rules. Why are the relative sizes of the acquiring and target corporations important in determining the character of the gain recognized in a reorganization?

Solution: If the target corporation is smaller than the acquiring corporation, the receipt of boot almost always will qualify for capital gains treatment under the redemption rules because generally no shareholder(s) will own more than 50% of the acquiring corporation's stock before and after the hypothetical redemption. If the boot is distributed proportionately to stock ownership, the pre-and post-redemption interests of the target corporation shareholder(s) are likely to be reduced. If the target corporation is larger than the acquiring corporation, a shareholder could own more than 50% of the acquiring corporation stock, resulting in the characterization of boot as a dividend.

KEY POINT

In a nontaxable reorganization, shareholders defer recognition of their realized gain or loss. Consequently, they take a substituted basis in the new nonrecognition property received (i.e., any deferred gain or loss is reflected in the basis of the nonrecognition property received).

BASIS OF STOCK AND SECURITIES RECEIVED. The basis of stock and securities (nonrecognition property) received by target corporation shareholders and security holders is determined according to the Sec. 358 rules, as discussed in Chapter C:2. Accordingly, the basis of nonrecognition property is calculated as follows:

Adjusted basis of stock and securities exchanged
Plus: Any gain recognized in the exchange
Minus: Money received in the exchange
FMV of any noncash property received in the exchange
Basis of nonrecognition property received

basis of stock & sec =
- basis of old
+ gain rec'd
- boot rec'd

If a shareholder or security holder receives no boot, the stock and securities take a substituted basis from the stock and securities exchanged. If the shareholder recognizes gain, the basis of stock and securities exchanged is increased by the amount of such gain and then reduced by the amount of money plus the FMV of any other boot property received in the reorganization. The basis of any other boot property is its FMV.

EXAMPLE C:7-17 ▶ Keith owns Target Corporation stock having a $10,000 adjusted basis. In a reorganization, Keith exchanges his Target stock for $12,000 of Acquiring stock and $4,000 of Acquiring securities. Keith realizes a $6,000 gain [($12,000 + $4,000) − $10,000], of which he must recognize $4,000 because he received securities worth $4,000 but surrendered no securities. The basis of the Acquiring securities that Keith received is $4,000. Keith's basis in the Acquiring stock is $10,000 ($10,000 basis of Target stock + $4,000 gain recognized − $4,000 FMV of Acquiring securities). ◀

When the target corporation shareholders initially own a single class of stock (or a single class of securities) and exchange that stock for two or more classes of stock or securities in a reorganization, the total basis in the nonrecognition property as calculated under the above formula must be allocated among the stock and/or securities in proportion to the relative FMVs of each class.[33]

HOLDING PERIOD. The holding period for the stock and securities that are nonrecognition property includes the holding period for the stock and securities surrendered. The holding period for boot property begins the day after the exchange date.[34]

[32] *King Enterprises, Inc. v. U.S.*, 24 AFTR 2d 69-5866, 69-2 USTC ¶9720 (Ct. Cls., 1969).

[33] Reg. Sec. 1.358-2(a)(2)-(4).

[34] Sec. 1223(1).

Topic Review C:7-4 summarizes the tax consequences of a reorganization to the target corporation, acquiring corporation, and target corporation shareholders and security holders.

Topic Review C:7-4

Tax Consequences of a Nontaxable Reorganization

TARGET CORPORATION

1. The target corporation recognizes no gain or loss on the asset transfer except to the extent that it receives and retains money or other boot property (Secs. 361(a)–(b)). Generally, boot is not retained because the reorganization provisions require the target corporation to liquidate or distribute all its assets.
2. The character of any recognized gain or loss depends on the nature of the assets transferred.
3. The acquiring corporation's assumption or acquisition of target corporation liabilities does not trigger recognition of gain on the asset transfer except in "excess" liability situations involving divisive Type D reorganizations (Sec. 357(a)).
4. The target corporation recognizes no gain or loss when it distributes qualified property (i.e., stock and securities) to its shareholders and security holders. The target corporation recognizes gain (but not loss) when it distributes to shareholders or security holders noncash boot property or retained assets (Sec. 361(c)).

ACQUIRING CORPORATION

1. The acquiring corporation recognizes no gain or loss when it receives money or other boot property in exchange for its stock or debt obligations (Sec. 1032).
2. On the other hand, the acquiring corporation recognizes gain or loss when it transfers noncash boot property to the target corporation or its shareholders (Sec. 1001).
3. The basis of noncash property received by the acquiring corporation equals its basis in the transferor's hands increased by any gain recognized by the transferor (Sec. 362(b)).
4. The acquiring corporation's holding period for this property includes the transferor's holding period (Sec. 1223(1)).

SHAREHOLDERS AND SECURITY HOLDERS

1. Shareholders and security holders recognize no gain or loss if they receive only stock (Sec. 354(a)). They recognize gain (but not loss) when they receive money, excess securities, or other boot property. The amount of recognized gain equals the lesser of the realized gain or the amount of money plus the FMV of any other boot property received (Sec. 356(b)).
2. The character of recognized gain is based on Sec. 302(b) as applied to receipt of acquiring corporation stock. Dividend income cannot exceed the shareholder's ratable share of the transferor or target corporation's E&P (Sec. 356(a)(2)).
3. The total basis of stock and securities received equals the adjusted basis of stock and securities exchanged plus any gain recognized by the shareholders and security holders on the exchange minus the sum of money and FMV of other boot property received. This basis is allocated among the stock and securities received according to their relative FMVs. The basis of boot property is its FMV (Sec. 358(a)).
4. The holding period for stock and securities received includes the holding period for stock and securities surrendered. The holding period for boot property received begins the day after the exchange date (Sec. 1223(1)).

ACQUISITIVE REORGANIZATIONS

This section is devoted to Types A, B, C, D, and G acquisitive reorganizations. Each of these types is explained below. Topic Review C:7-5 summarizes the requirements for acquisitive reorganizations.

TYPE A REORGANIZATION

Type A reorganizations encompass four transactional structures: mergers, consolidations, triangular mergers, and reverse triangular mergers. Each of these structures is discussed on the next page.

Topic Review C:7-5

Summary of Major Acquisitive Reorganizations

Type of Reorganization	Target (T) Corporation Property Acquired	Consideration That Can Be Used	What Happens to the Target (T) Corporation?	Shareholders' Recognized Gain	Other Requirements
A—Merger or consolidation	Assets and liabilities of T Corporation.[a]	Voting and nonvoting stock, securities, and other property of A Corporation.[b]	T Corporation liquidates as part of the merger.	Lesser of realized gain or boot received.	For advance ruling purposes, at least 50% of the consideration must be A stock (continuity of interest requirement)
B—Stock for stock	At least 80% of the voting and 80% of the nonvoting T stock.	Voting stock of A Corporation.	Becomes a subsidiary of A Corporation.	None	Noncash boot paid by the transferor may result in gain recognition
C—Assets for stock	Substantially all T Corporation assets (and possibly some or all of its liabilities).	A Corporation stock, securities, and other property, provided at least 80% of the assets are acquired for voting stock.	Stock, securities, and boot received in the reorganization and all of T's remaining properties must be distributed to its shareholders and creditors; as a practical matter, T liquidates.	Lesser of realized gain or FMV of boot.	For advance ruling purposes, "substantially all" is 70% of the gross assets and 90% of the net assets of T Corporation.
D—Acquisitive	Substantially all T Corporation assets (and possibly some or all of its liabilities) are acquired by a "controlled" transferee corporation (A Corporation[b]).	A Corporation stock, securities, and other property.	Stocks, securities, and boot received in the reorganization and all of T's remaining property must be distributed to its shareholders and creditors; as a practical matter, T liquidates.	Lesser of realized gain or FMV of boot.	"Substantially all" definition is same as in a Type C reorganization; continuity of interest requirement applies for advance ruling purposes; control is defined as 50% of the voting power or 50% of the value of A's stock.

[a]T Corporation is the target or transferor corporation.
[b]A Corporation is the acquiring or controlled transferee corporation. In a Type D reorganization, A Corporation is 50% or more controlled by T Corporation shareholders.

KEY POINT

The Type A reorganization is unique in comparison to the other statutory reorganizations because corporation law is an important factor in determining whether a transaction qualifies as a nontaxable merger.

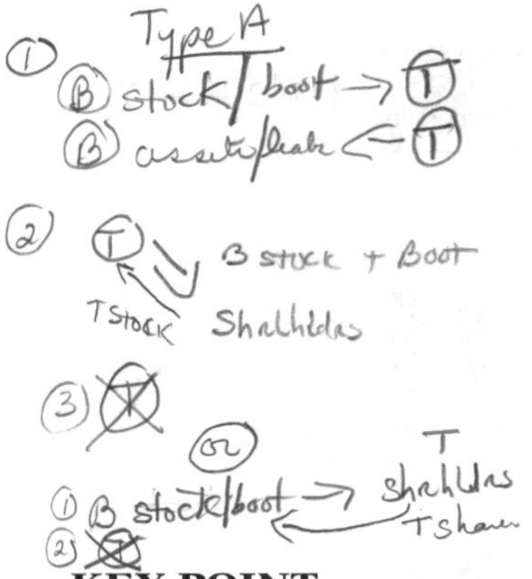

KEY POINT

The Type A reorganization is the most flexible reorganization with respect to the type of consideration that must be used. The only requirement that must be satisfied is the continuity of interest test, which is discussed later in the chapter.

MERGER OR CONSOLIDATION. In its broadest sense, a Type A reorganization is a **merger** or a **consolidation** that satisfies the corporation laws of the United States, a state, the District of Columbia, or a foreign country.[35] State law authorizes several different merger forms. Two common forms are discussed below. Other permitted forms, such as triangular mergers and reverse triangular mergers, are discussed later in this chapter. The first form involves the acquiring corporation's transferring its stock, securities, and other consideration (boot) to the target corporation in exchange for its assets and liabilities. The acquiring corporation stock, securities, and other consideration received by the target corporation are distributed to its shareholders and security holders in exchange for their target corporation stock and securities. The target corporation then goes out of existence. Figure C:7-1 illustrates this type of merger. The second form involves the acquiring corporation's exchanging its stock, securities, and other consideration directly for target corporation stock and securities held by target shareholders and security holders. The acquiring corporation then liquidates the target corporation and acquires its assets and liabilities.

In a consolidation, a new corporation uses stock, securities, and other consideration to acquire the assets of two or more existing target corporations. Each target corporation distributes the stock, securities, and other consideration to its shareholders and security holders in exchange for its own stock and securities. It then liquidates. Figure C:7-2 illustrates this type of consolidation. In another type, the new acquiring corporation transfers its stock, securities, and other consideration directly to target corporation shareholders and security holders in exchange for their stock and securities. Each target corporation transfers its assets and liabilities to the acquiring corporation and then liquidates.

Requirements for Mergers and Consolidations. The Type A reorganization provides the acquiring corporation with the greatest flexibility of consideration. Section 368 places no restrictions on the kind of consideration that can be used. Under the continuity

ADDITIONAL COMMENT

The actual exchange of acquiring corporation stock for target corporation stock may be different from the illustrations provided in this chapter. These illustrations represent how the IRC construes the steps in each reorganization. As a practical matter, the exchange of stock between the parties usually is performed by an independent stock transfer agent rather than flowing from the acquiring corporation to the target corporation and finally to the target corporation shareholders.

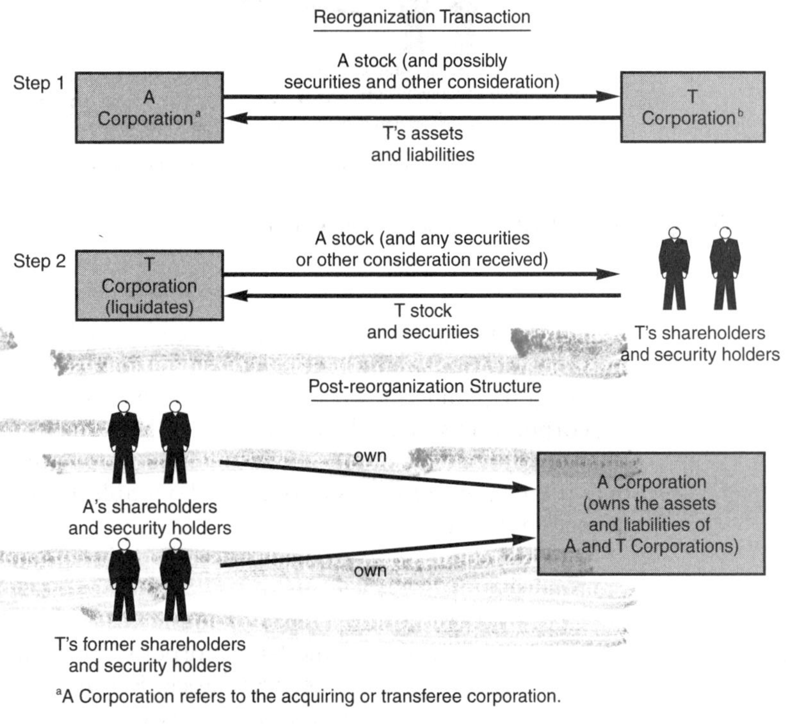

[a] A Corporation refers to the acquiring or transferee corporation.

[b] T Corporation refers to the target or transferor corporation.

FIGURE C:7-1 ▶ TYPE A REORGANIZATION—MERGER

[35] Sec. 368(a)(1)(A) and Reg. Sec. 1.368-2(b)(1).

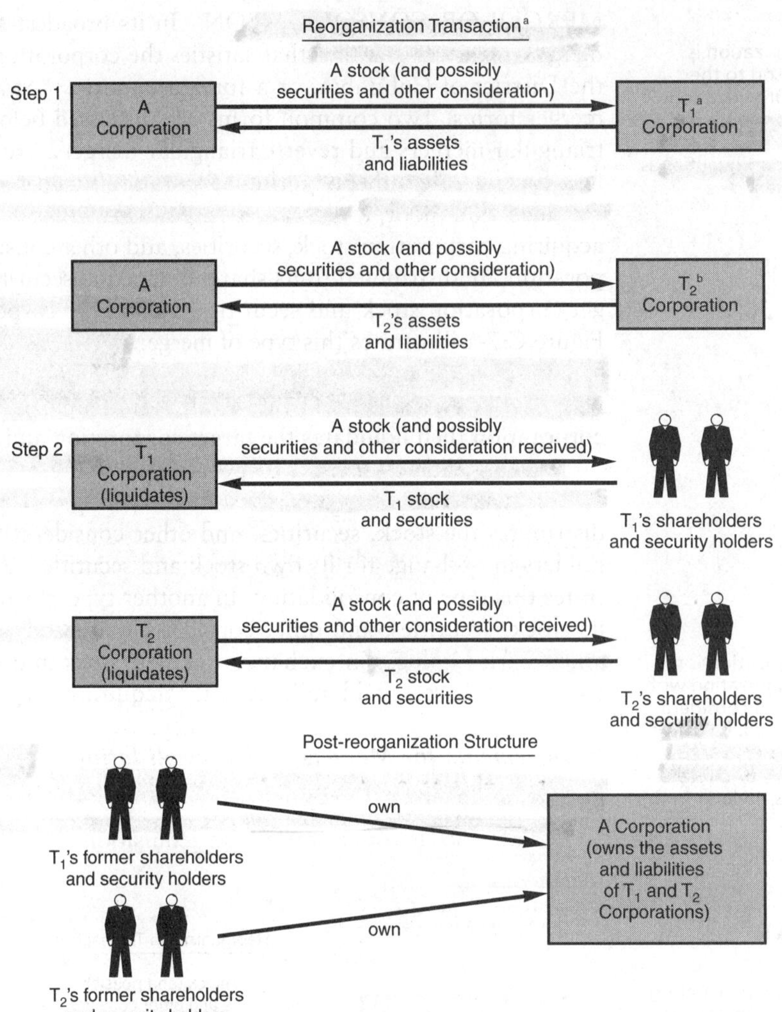

[a] T_1 Corporation is the first of two target corporations that are parties to the reorganization.

[b] T_2 Corporation is the second of two target corporations that are parties to the reorganization.

FIGURE C:7-2 ▶ TYPE A REORGANIZATION: CONSOLIDATION

of interest judicial doctrine, as interpreted by the IRS, stock of the acquiring corporation must be at least 50% of the total consideration used. The IRS will not issue a private letter ruling regarding the tax-free nature of the transaction if the percentage of the acquiring corporation stock is less than 50%.[36] The stock can be voting, nonvoting, or a combination of the two, and it can be common or preferred. The 50% minimum must be met only if the taxpayer wants to obtain a favorable advance ruling regarding the tax consequences of the transaction.

The IRS requires that, to qualify as a Type A reorganization, the merger must meet the requirements of the applicable federal, state, or foreign corporate merger law. In addition, the target corporation must go out of existence.[37] An acquisition does not qualify as a Type A reorganization if the target corporation retains some assets and target corporation shareholders retain some target stock. Revenue Ruling 2000-5 holds that, if a target corporation merges under state law into two or more acquiring corporations and the target corporation does not go out existence, the transaction does not qualify as a Type A reorganization.

[36] Rev. Proc. 77-37, 1977-2 C.B. 568, Sec. 3.02. In recent years, tax opinions from tax counsel have largely replaced private letter rulings for most acquisitive reorganizations.

[37] Rev. Rul. 2000-5, 2000-1 C.B. 436.

ADDITIONAL COMMENT

Shareholder approval is time consuming, expensive, and not always possible to obtain.

Because a merger or consolidation must comply with state, federal, or foreign corporation laws, transactions that qualify as mergers or consolidations, and the procedures that must be followed to effect them, vary according to the laws of the jurisdictions in which the acquiring and target corporations are incorporated. Generally, these laws require approval by a majority of shareholders of the corporate parties to the merger. Where the stock in one or both of the companies is publicly traded, holding a shareholder's meeting, soliciting proxies, and obtaining the necessary corporate approvals may be costly and time consuming.

The rights of any dissenting shareholders are defined in the merger law. Among these rights are the right to dissent and have shares independently valued and purchased for cash. Liquidating the interests of a substantial number of dissenting shareholders may require a large cash outlay and may violate the continuity-of-interest doctrine.

A transaction that does not satisfy the requirements of the applicable corporation law does not qualify as a Type A reorganization.[38] Generally, this failure renders the entire transaction taxable.

Advantages and Disadvantages of a Type A Reorganization. A Type A reorganization offers a number of advantages and disadvantages.

Advantages:

- ▶ A Type A reorganization is more flexible than other types of reorganizations because the consideration need not be solely voting stock, as in the case of some other reorganization types. Money, securities, other property, and the assumption of the target corporation's liabilities can be 50% or more of the total consideration used.[39]
- ▶ Substantially all the assets of the target corporation need not be acquired, as in the case of a Type C reorganization. Thus, dispositions of unwanted assets by the target corporation prior to, or as part of, the acquisition generally do not render the merger taxable.

Disadvantages:

- ▶ The parties to the merger must comply with applicable corporation laws. In most states, the shareholders of both the acquiring and target corporations must approve a plan of merger. Such approvals can take time and be costly if stock in one or both of the corporations is publicly traded.
- ▶ Dissenting shareholders of both corporations generally have the right to have their shares independently appraised and purchased for cash, which may require a substantial cash outlay.
- ▶ All liabilities of the target corporation, including unknown and contingent liabilities, must be assumed.
- ▶ A merger requires the transfer of real estate titles, leases, and contracts. The target corporation may have licenses, rights, or other privileges that are nontransferable. This impediment may necessitate use of a reverse triangular merger or other transactional structures discussed below.

Tax Consequences of a Merger. The following example illustrates the tax consequences of a merger.

EXAMPLE C:7-18 ▶ In a merger that qualifies as a Type A reorganization, Target Corporation transfers to Acquiring Corporation all its assets having a FMV and an adjusted basis of $2 million and $1.3 million, respectively, and $400,000 in liabilities in exchange for $1 million of Acquiring common stock and $600,000 of cash. At the time of the transfer, Acquiring's E&P balance is $1 million, and Target's is $750,000. Target distributes the Acquiring stock and cash to its sole shareholder, Millie, in exchange for all her Target stock, which has a $175,000 basis. If Millie had received only Acquiring stock, she would have held 6.25% of Acquiring stock (100,000 out of 1.6 million shares) immediately after the exchange.

---

[38] *Edward H. Russell v. CIR*, 15 AFTR 2d 1107, 65-2 USTC ¶9448 (5th Cir., 1965).

[39] Advance ruling requirements generally limit nonstock consideration to 50% of the total consideration. In certain circumstances, the courts have permitted the 50% ceiling to be exceeded.

In the asset transfer, Target realizes a $700,000 gain [($1,000,000 stock + $600,000 cash + $400,000 liabilities) − $1,300,000 adjusted basis] but recognizes none of this gain. Acquiring takes a $1.3 million carryover basis in the assets it receives. Target recognizes no gain when it distributes the stock and cash to Millie. Upon Target's liquidation, Millie realizes a $1,425,000 gain [($1,000,000 stock + $600,000 cash) − $175,000 adjusted basis], of which $600,000 must be recognized because of the cash received. Each share of Acquiring stock is worth $16 ($1,600,000 total consideration ÷ 100,000 shares that would have been held if all stock had been received). The hypothetical redemption of Millie's Acquiring stock required under the *Clark* case and Rev. Rul. 93-61 (see pages C:7-16 and C:7-17) qualifies for Sec. 302(b)(2) sale treatment because the deemed redemption of 37,500 ($600,000 cash ÷ $16) shares of Acquiring stock reduces Millie's interest from 6.25% (100,000 shares ÷ 1,600,000 shares) to 4.00% (62,500 shares ÷ 1,562,500 shares). Millie's basis in her Acquiring stock is $175,000 ($175,000 basis of Target stock + $600,000 gain recognized − $600,000 cash received). Millie's holding period for the Acquiring stock includes her holding period for the Target stock. ◀

ADDITIONAL COMMENT

If the IRS applies Sec. 351 to the drop down transaction, and if the total adjusted basis for all property transferred exceeds the total FMV of that property, the subsidiary's total basis will be limited to the total FMV (see Chapter C:2 for details).

DROP-DOWN TYPE A REORGANIZATION. The reorganization rules permit the acquiring corporation to transfer (drop down) to a controlled subsidiary part or all the assets and liabilities acquired in the merger or consolidation.[40] The drop down does not affect the nontaxable nature of the transaction. Thus, neither the parent nor subsidiary recognize gain or loss. The subsidiary takes from its parent a carryover basis in the assets.

TRIANGULAR MERGERS. **Triangular mergers** are authorized by Sec. 368(a)(2)(D). They are similar to straight mergers (previously discussed) except the parent corporation uses a controlled subsidiary to acquire target stock or assets. The target corporation then merges into the subsidiary under one of the two merger structures described earlier (see Figure C:7-3).

Triangular mergers must satisfy the same legal requirements as straight mergers. In addition, the stock used as consideration in the transaction is restricted to that of the parent corporation. On the other hand, a limited amount of subsidiary cash and securities can be used, and the subsidiary can assume the target corporation's liabilities.

The "Substantially All" Requirement. To qualify for nontaxable treatment, the subsidiary must acquire substantially all of target corporation's assets pursuant to a plan of reorganization. For advance ruling purposes, the IRS has defined *substantially all* to be at least 70% of the FMV of the target corporation's gross assets and 90% of the FMV of its net assets.[41]

EXAMPLE C:7-19 ▶ In a triangular merger, Acquiring Corporation's subsidiary, Acquiring-Sub Corporation, plans to acquire $2.5 million (FMV) in Target Corporation assets and $1 million in liabilities. Under the IRS's advance ruling policy, Acquiring must acquire at least 70% of Target's gross assets ($1,750,000 = $2,500,000 FMV of assets × 0.70) and 90% of its net assets [$1,350,000 = ($2,500,000 FMV of assets − $1,000,000 liabilities) × 0.90], or $1.75 million in assets. Target can sell or otherwise dispose of the remaining assets. ◀

PRACTICAL APPLICATION

The triangular merger is a very popular type of acquisition because the consideration that must be used is still very flexible and yet the parent corporation does not have to assume the known or unknown liabilities of the target corporation. Rather, the controlled subsidiary assumes these liabilities.

Advantages of a Triangular Merger. The tax treatment of a triangular merger is the same as for a straight merger. A triangular merger, however, offers three advantages over a straight merger:

- ▶ In a triangular merger, the target corporation's assets and liabilities become the responsibility of the subsidiary. Thus, the parent corporation generally cannot be held liable for any unknown or contingent liabilities. Potential claims against the parent corporation from the target's creditors are thus minimized.
- ▶ Because the parent corporation is the principal shareholder in the acquiring subsidiary, shareholder approval for the transaction is readily available. If the parent corporation's stock is widely held, the cost of obtaining shareholder approval may be reduced.

[40] Sec. 368(a)(2)(C). As defined in Sec. 368(c), *control* requires the parent corporation to own at least 80% of the voting power and 80% of each class of nonvoting stock. The ability to "drop down" the assets acquired to a subsidiary corporation without recognizing any gain also applies to Type B, C, and G reorganizations.

[41] Rev. Proc. 77-37, 1977-2 C.B. 568, Sec. 3.01. Also see Rev. Rul. 2001-46, 2001-2 C.B. 321.

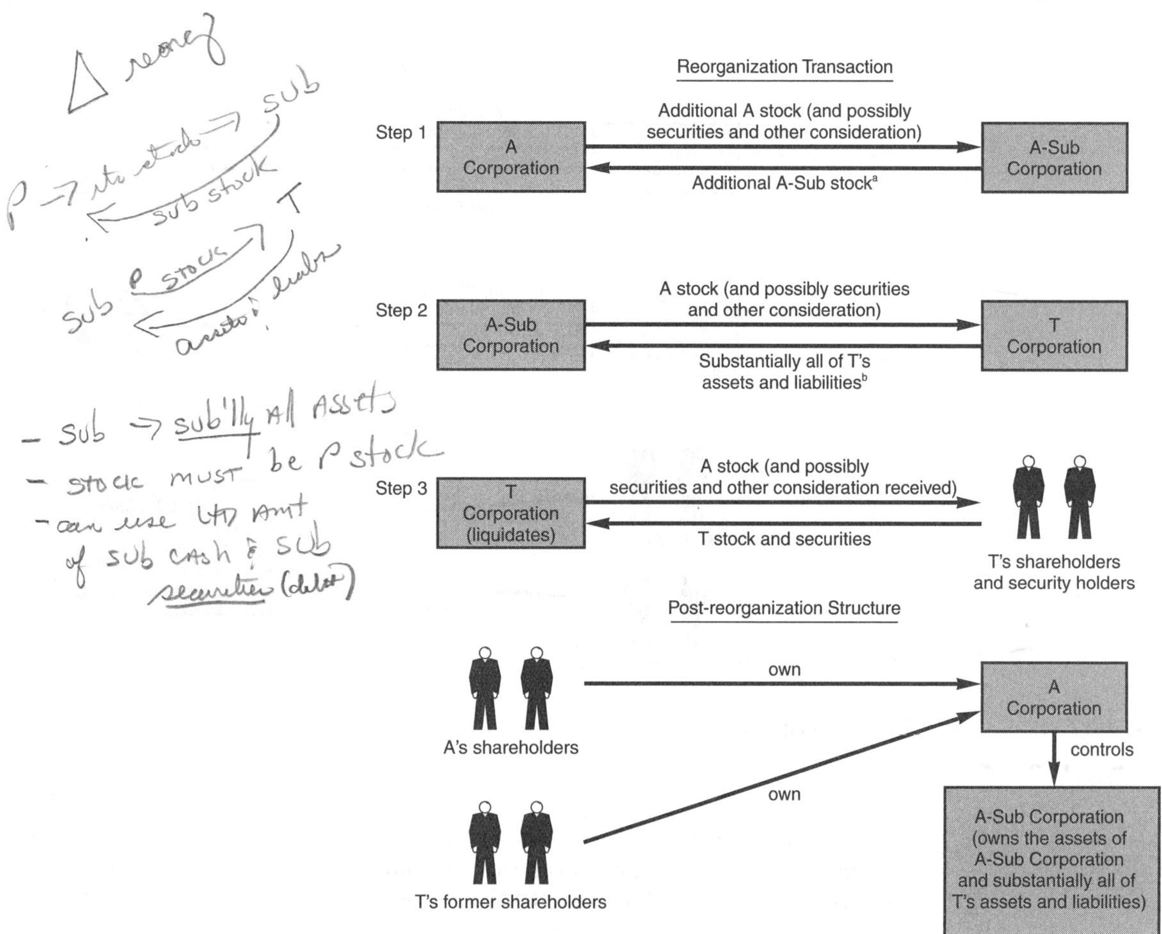

[a]A Corporation must control A-Sub Corporation. If A already owns 100% of A-Sub, the A stock may be treated as additional paid-in capital for the shares that are already owned.

[b]T's shareholders may receive any remaining T Corporation assets that A Corporation did not acquire and that T Corporation did not sell to third parties.

FIGURE C:7-3 ▶ TRIANGULAR TYPE A REORGANIZATION

- Target corporation shareholders may prefer to receive parent corporation stock because of its increased marketability. By selling shares of this stock over an extended period of time, target shareholders can recognize the gain as if they were using the installment method of accounting.

ADDITIONAL COMMENT

In addition to the Type B reorganization, which will be discussed later, the reverse triangular merger is an acquisitive reorganization that keeps the target corporation in existence. It is a popular reorganization form because, unlike the Type B reorganization, the acquiring corporation can use a limited amount of boot.

REVERSE TRIANGULAR MERGERS. A **reverse triangular merger** is similar to the triangular merger illustrated in Figure C:7-3 except the subsidiary (A-Sub Corporation) merges into the target corporation (T Corporation), the target corporation remains in existence as a subsidiary of the parent corporation (A Corporation), and A-Sub Corporation goes out of existence. Continuing the target corporation as a going concern may be desirable from a business standpoint because of nontransferable rights, licenses, and contracts that it owns. Technical details of this type of acquisition are beyond the scope of this text.

TYPE C REORGANIZATION

A **Type C reorganization** is an asset-for-stock acquisition. This type of transaction, illustrated in Figure C:7-4, requires the acquiring corporation to obtain substantially all the target corporation's assets in exchange for acquiring corporation voting stock and possibly a limited amount of other consideration.[42]

[42] Sec. 368(a)(1)(C).

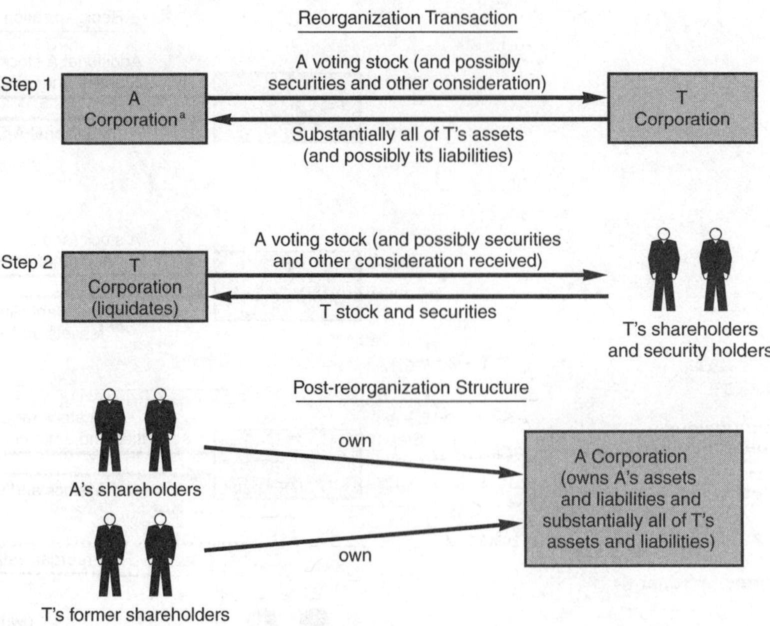

FIGURE C:7-4 ► TYPE C (ASSET-FOR-STOCK) REORGANIZATION

The term "substantially all" is not defined in the IRC or Treasury Regulations. For advance ruling purposes, however, the same minimum standard that applies to triangular Type A mergers (i.e., 70% of the FMV of gross assets and 90% of the FMV of net assets) applies to Type C reorganizations.[43]

In a Type C reorganization the target corporation must distribute the stock, securities, and other property it receives, plus any other property it retains, to its shareholders as part of the reorganization. Although the corporation need not formally dissolve, as a practical matter it usually liquidates.[44] Because the economic effect of a Type C reorganization is the same as that of a merger (i.e., the acquisition of target corporation assets) without dissolving the target corporation, many tax practitioners call it a practical merger.

In a Type C reorganization, the target corporation can retain its corporate charter to prevent others from using its corporate name or sell its corporate name to a third party. Assets other than the corporate charter can be retained to satisfy the minimum capital requirements of state law.[45]

ADDITIONAL COMMENT

Because of the solely-for-voting-stock requirement, a Type C reorganization is much less flexible than a Type A reorganization in terms of the consideration that can be used.

CONSIDERATION USED TO EFFECT THE REORGANIZATION. Section 368(a)(1)(C) requires that the consideration used to effect the reorganization be solely voting stock of the acquiring corporation (or its parent corporation). Both the acquiring corporation's assumption of part or all of target corporation liabilities and its acquiring property subject to a liability are disregarded for purposes of the solely-for-voting-stock requirement.

Section 368(a)(2)(B) permits the acquiring corporation to use other consideration in the reorganization, provided it obtains at least 80% of target property solely for its voting stock. Efffectively, this provision allows the acquiring corporation to use money, securities, nonvoting stock, or other property to acquire up to 20% of target assets. Liabilities assumed or acquired reduce on a dollar-for-dollar basis the amount of money the acquiring corporation can use in the reorganization. If the liabilities assumed or acquired exceed 20% of the FMV of target assets, the transaction will qualify as a Type C reorganization only if the acquiring corporation uses no money, securities, nonvoting stock, or other property as consideration.

---

[43] Rev. Proc. 77-37, 1977-2 C.B. 568, Sec. 3.01.
[44] Sec. 368(a)(2)(G).
[45] Rev. Proc. 89-50, 1989-1 C.B. 631.

EXAMPLE C:7-20 ▶ Acquiring Corporation wants to acquire all of Target Corporation's assets and liabilities in a Type C reorganization. The following table illustrates how the solely-for-voting-stock test applies in four different situations:

	Situation 1	*Situation 2*	*Situation 3*	*Situation 4*
FMV of Target assets	$200,000	$200,000	$200,000	$200,000
Target liabilities assumed by Acquiring	–0–	30,000	100,000	100,000
Consideration given by Acquiring:				
FMV of Acquiring voting stock	160,000	160,000	100,000	99,900
Cash	40,000	10,000	–0–	100

In Situation 1, because the FMV of the Acquiring stock equals 80% of total assets, the transaction qualifies as a Type C reorganization. In Situation 2, although the liabilities assumed reduce the amount of cash Acquiring can pay, the transaction is still a Type C reorganization because the amount of cash and liabilities, in total, do not exceed 20% of the FMV of Target assets. In Situation 3, the high percentage of liabilities does not disqualify the transaction from Type C reorganization treatment because Acquiring paid no cash.[46] In Situation 4, the transaction fails as a Type C reorganization because Acquiring uses cash and stock, and the total amount of cash given plus liabilities assumed by Acquiring exceed 20% of the total FMV of Target assets. ◀

ADDITIONAL COMMENT

Target corporation liabilities assumed by the acquiring corporation are not a problem unless the target corporation receives boot as part of the consideration. In this case, when applying the 20% boot relaxation rule, liabilities are treated as money. Situation 4 in Example C:7-20 illustrates that, if the target corporation has liabilities exceeding 20% of the FMV of its assets, the boot relaxation rule is of no benefit.

SELF-STUDY QUESTION

Must the acquiring corporation assume all liabilities of the target corporation in a Type C reorganization?

ANSWER

No. The acquiring corporation may leave liabilities in the target corporation. These liabilities would then have to be satisfied with assets retained by the target corporation or with assets acquired by the target corporation in the reorganization.

ADVANTAGES AND DISADVANTAGES OF A TYPE C REORGANIZATION. Relative to a merger, a Type C reorganization offers the following advantages and disadvantages.

- In a Type C reorganization, the acquiring corporation obtains only assets specified in the acquisition agreement. However, to qualify for nontaxable treatment, it needs to acquire substantially all the target corporation's assets. The target corporation might sell, dispose of, or retain assets the acquiring corporation does not want. These unwanted assets are not counted toward the "substantially all" test. Thus, disposition of a significant number of assets shortly before an asset-for-stock acquisition may prevent the transaction from qualifying as a Type C reorganization. By contrast, the "substantially all" test does not apply to a merger, and dispositions of unwanted assets generally will not prevent a merger from qualifying as a Type A reorganization.
- In a Type C reorganization, the acquiring corporation assumes only target liabilities specified in the acquisition agreement. Unknown and contingent liabilities are not assumed, as they are in a merger.
- In a Type C reorganization, shareholders of the acquiring corporation generally need not approve the acquisition, thereby reducing the total transaction cost. In a merger, however, acquiring and target corporation shareholders must approve the transaction.
- In many cases, target liabilities assumed by the acquiring corporation are so substantial (i.e., exceeding 20% of total consideration) as to preclude the use of consideration other than voting stock. In a Type A reorganization, up to 50% of the consideration may be nonstock.
- In both a Type A and Type C reorganization, dissenting shareholders of the target corporation may have the right under state law to have their shares independently appraised and purchased for cash.

TAX CONSEQUENCES OF A TYPE C REORGANIZATION. The following example illustrates the tax consequences of a Type C reorganization.

EXAMPLE C:7-21 ▶ Acquiring Corporation acquires all Target Corporation's assets and liabilities in exchange for $1.2 million of Acquiring voting stock. Target distributes the Acquiring stock to its sole shareholder, Andrew, in exchange for all his Target stock. Target's assets have a $1.4 million FMV and a $600,000 adjusted basis. Acquiring assumes liabilities of $200,000. Target has a $500,000 E&P

[46] The IRS, however, may attempt to treat a transaction as a purchase under the continuity of proprietary interest doctrine (see page C:7-41) when the amount of liabilities assumed or acquired is high relative to the total FMV of the assets acquired.

balance. Andrew's basis in his Target stock is $400,000. Target realizes an $800,000 gain [($1,200,000 + $200,000) − $600,000], none of which is recognized. Acquiring recognizes no gain when it exchanges its stock for the assets, in which it takes a $600,000 basis. Upon surrendering his Target shares, Andrew realizes an $800,000 ($1,200,000 − $400,000) gain, none of which is recognized. Andrew's basis in the Acquiring stock is $400,000. Andrew's holding period for the Acquiring stock includes his holding period for the Target stock. Acquiring inherits all of Target's tax attributes, including the $500,000 E&P balance. ◀

TYPICAL MISCONCEPTION

As with a Type A reorganization, a Type C reorganization can be structured as a triangular (but not reverse triangular) acquisition. Although this ability provides greater flexibility in tax planning, it makes the area more confusing because of the substantial overlap between the different types of reorganizations.

DROP-DOWN AND TRIANGULAR TYPE C REORGANIZATIONS. Section 368(a)(2)(C) permits the acquiring corporation to transfer tax-free part or all of the assets and liabilities acquired in a Type C reorganization to a controlled subsidiary. Section 368(a)(1)(C) permits an acquiring subsidiary to use parent corporation voting stock to acquire substantially all the target corporation's assets. The triangular Type C reorganization requirements are the same as those for a basic Type C reorganization except the voting stock used by the acquiring subsidiary to acquire target assets must consist solely of the parent's stock. The acquiring subsidiary, however, can provide additional consideration in the form of securities, money, or other property.

TYPE D REORGANIZATION

KEY POINT

When a Type D reorganization is used as an acquisitive reorganization, it generally involves commonly controlled corporations. However, its most common usage is as part of a divisive reorganization under Sec. 355 (discussed later in this chapter).

Type D reorganizations can be either acquisitive or divisive. (Divisive Type D reorganizations are discussed on pages C:7-33 through C:7-38.) In an acquisitive Type D reorganization, a target (transferor) corporation transfers substantially all its asssets to an acquiring (transferee) corporation in exchange for the transferee's stock and securities (and possibly other consideration) pursuant to a plan of reorganization. The exchange must be followed by a distribution of the stock, securities, and other consideration received in the reorganization, plus any other property retained by the transferor corporation, to the transferor's shareholders and security holders pursuant to a complete liquidation.[47] (See Figure C:7-5 for an illustration of an acquisitive Type D reorganization.)

What constitutes "substantially all" is based on the facts and circumstances. For advance ruling purposes, however, the 70% of the FMV of gross assets and 90% of the FMV of net assets test used in the triangular Type A and Type C reorganizations also applies here.[48]

ADDITIONAL COMMENT

The 50% control requirement makes the Type D reorganization a useful tool for the IRS to recast certain tax avoidance transactions.

CONTROL REQUIREMENTS. The transferor (target) corporation or one or more of its shareholders must control the transferee (acquiring) corporation immediately after the asset transfer. Section 368(a)(2)(H) defines control as either 50% or more of the total combined voting power of all classes of voting stock, or 50% or more of the total value of all classes of stock.

In one version of an acquisitive Type D reorganization, an acquiring corporation acquires all the assets of a larger corporation (target corporation), and target corporation shareholders control the acquiring corporation after the reorganization. Type C reorganizations (in which the target corporation does not control the acquiring corporation) and Type A reorganizations (which must comply with state, federal, or foreign merger law) are more common than acquisitive Type D reorganizations.

Section 368(a)(1)(D) does not limit the type of consideration that may be used in the transaction. The IRS and the courts, however, require that the transferor corporation's shareholders maintain a continuing equity interest in the transferee corporation. For advance ruling purposes, the IRS requires that transferor corporation shareholders receive transferee corporation stock equal to at least 50% of the value of the transferor corporation's outstanding stock.[49]

TAX CONSEQUENCES OF A TYPE D REORGANIZATION. Acquisitive Type D reorganization requirements are similar to those for a Type C reorganization. If the reorganization satisfies both the Type C and Type D reorganization requirements, Sec.

---

47 Secs. 368(a)(1)(D) and 354(b)(1).

48 Rev. Proc. 77-37, 1977-2 C.B. 568, Sec. 3.01.

49 Rev. Proc. 77-37, 1977-2 C.B. 568, Sec. 3.02.

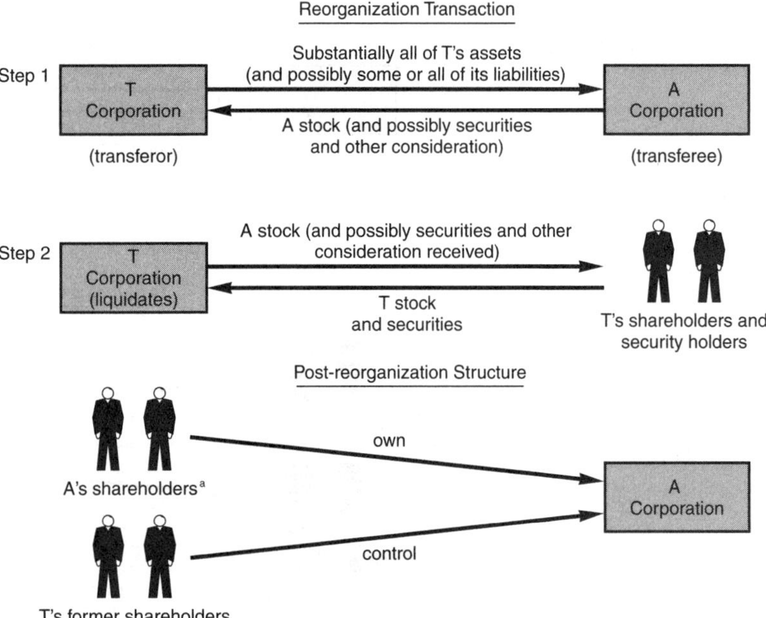

FIGURE C:7-5 ▶ ACQUISITIVE TYPE D REORGANIZATION

368(a)(2)(A) mandates that the reorganization be treated as Type D. The basic tax consequences of a Type D reorganization to the target corporation, the acquiring corporation, and target corporation shareholders are the same as those for a Type C reorganization.

ADDITIONAL COMMENT

If the acquiring corporation wants the target corporation to remain in existence, the two choices in Sec. 368 that can accomplish this objective are a Type B reorganization or a reverse triangular merger.

TYPE B REORGANIZATION

A **Type B reorganization** is the simplest of acquisitive reorganizations. In this type of reorganization, target corporation shareholders exchange their stock for acquiring corporation voting stock, and the target corporation remains in existence as the acquiring corporation's subsidiary (see Figure C:7-6).

A Type B reorganization generally preserves the target corporation as a going concern. The basis of the target's assets (inside basis) and its tax attributes generally remain the same. After the reorganization, the target corporation and its parent may elect to file a consolidated tax return (see Chapter C:8). If the target corporation liquidates into its parent shortly after the stock-for-stock exchange, the IRS may attempt to collapse the two-step transaction into a single transaction and treat it as a Type C asset-for-stock reorganization.[50]

KEY POINT

The IRC allows no relaxation of the solely-for-voting-stock requirement for the Type B reorganization. Thus, the Type B reorganization has the least flexible consideration requirement of any of the reorganizations.

SOLELY-FOR-VOTING-STOCK REQUIREMENT. Under Sec. 368(a)(1)(B), the acquiring corporation must acquire target corporation stock in exchange solely for acquiring corporation voting stock. The acquiring corporation must own sufficient stock to be in control of the target corporation immediately after the exchange.

The solely-for-voting-stock requirement generally precludes the use of other property as consideration in the transaction. However, the voting stock used can be either common or preferred. If the acquiring corporation uses consideration other than voting stock (e.g., nonvoting preferred stock), the transaction will not qualify as a Type B reorganization and will be taxable to target corporation shareholders.

In a Type B reorganization, acquiring corporation debt obligations can be exchanged for target corporation debt obligations held by target shareholders, who will not recognize gain or loss if the face amounts of the two obligations are the same.[51]

---

[50] Rev. Rul. 67-274, 1967-2 C.B. 141. If the transaction is "collapsed" into a Type C reorganization, the Type C reorganization requirements (and not the Type B) must be satisfied.

[51] Rev. Rul. 98-10, 1998-1 C.B. 643.

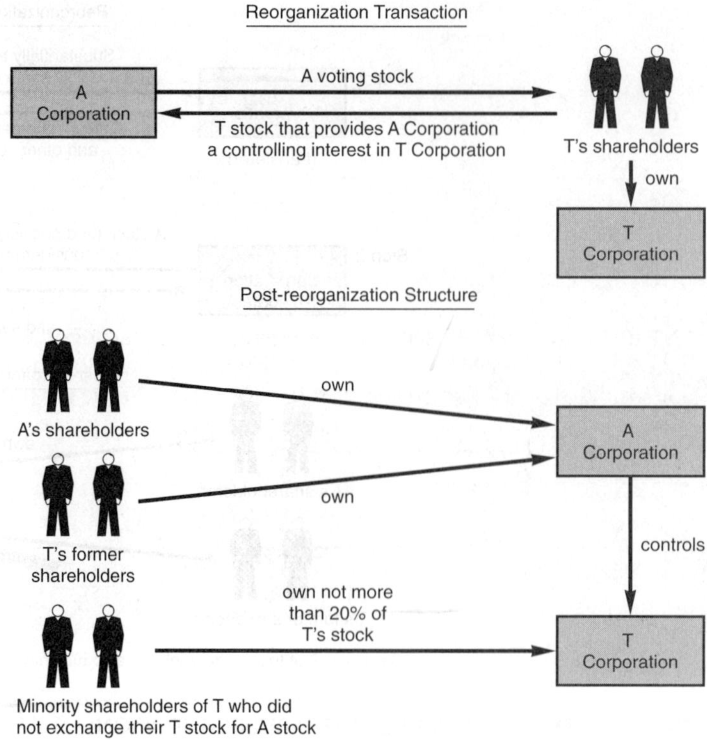

FIGURE C:7-6 ▶ TYPE B (STOCK-FOR-STOCK) REORGANIZATION

SELF-STUDY QUESTION

How can dissenters in a Type B reorganization be handled given the no-boot restriction?

ANSWER

The target corporation can redeem out the dissenters before the reorganization. Also, the nondissenting shareholders could buy out the dissenters' stock.

ADDITIONAL COMMENT

"Creeping acquisitions" are allowed in a Type B reorganization because the requirement is merely that the acquiring corporation own 80% after the transaction. Transactions within 12 months generally are considered related transactions. This aggregation rule can be either an advantage or a disadvantage depending on what consideration the acquiring corporation used in the various acquisition steps.

Exceptions. The acquiring corporation can use cash in limited circumstances without violating the solely-for-voting-stock requirement. For example:

- Target corporation shareholders can receive cash in exchange for their right to receive a fractional share of acquiring corporation stock.[52]
- The acquiring corporation can pay reorganization expenses (such as legal expenses, accounting fees, and administrative costs) of the target corporation without violating the solely-for-voting-stock requirement.[53]

Control. For Type B reorganizations, Section 368(c) defines control as 80% of the total combined voting power of all classes of voting stock and 80% of each class of nonvoting stock. Because the acquiring corporation need not acquire all the target corporation stock, a minority interest of up to 20% may remain. Under state law, minority shareholders can have their shares independently valued and acquired for cash without impairing the tax-free nature of the transaction. The target corporation can use its cash to redeem the minority shareholders' stock before or after the reorganization. The acquiring corporation, however, cannot use cash to purchase the dissenting minority shareholders' stock either before or as part of the reorganization. Doing so will render the entire transaction taxable.[54]

Timing of the Transaction. Some Type B reorganizations are conducted by exchanging stock of the acquiring corporation for 100% of target corporation shares in a single transaction. In other instances, the reorganization is accomplished through a series of transactions occurring over an extended period of time. Regulation Sec. 1.368-2(c) provides that a cash purchase of stock may be disregarded for purposes of the solely-for-voting-stock requirement if it was independent of the stock-for-stock exchange. According to this regulation, stock acquisitions over a relatively short period of time—12 months or less—are to be aggregated for purposes of the solely-for-voting-stock requirement.

[52] Rev. Rul. 66-365, 1966-2 C.B. 116.
[53] Rev. Rul. 73-54, 1973-1 C.B. 187.
[54] Rev. Rul. 68-285, 1968-1 C.B. 147.

EXAMPLE C:7-22 ▶ In July 2007, Acquiring Corporation purchased for cash 12% of Target Corporation's single class of stock. In January 2008, Acquiring acquires the remaining 88% in a stock-for-stock exchange. The IRS probably will aggregate the cash and stock-for-stock acquisitions because they occurred within a 12-month period. Even though Acquiring achieves 80% control in a single stock-for-stock transaction, this transaction does not qualify as a Type B reorganization because, if the two stock acquisitions are aggregated, the solely-for-voting-stock requirement is not met. The transaction could qualify as a Type B reorganization if Acquiring unconditionally sold its 12% interest in Target and then acquired the requisite 80% interest in a single stock-for-stock exchange, or if Acquiring postponed the stock-for-stock exchange until after July 2008, when the exchange might be considered independent of the cash purchase.[55] ◀

EXAMPLE C:7-23 ▶ In April 2000, Acquiring Corporation acquired 85% of Target Corporation's single class of stock in a transaction that qualified as a Type B reorganization. In December 2007, Acquiring acquires the remaining 15% of Target stock in a stock-for-stock exchange. Even though Acquiring already controls Target, the second transaction qualifies for Type B reorganization treatment because Acquiring owns at least 80% of Target after the exchange. ◀

TAX CONSEQUENCES OF A TYPE B REORGANIZATION. The tax consequences of a Type B reorganization are as follows:

- Target corporation shareholders recognize no gain or loss on the exchange unless their fractional shares are acquired for cash or the target corporation redeems some of their stock.
- Target corporation shareholders take a substituted basis in their acquiring corporation stock referenced to the basis of their target corporation stock surrendered. The holding period for the acquiring corporation stock includes the holding period for the target corporation stock.
- The acquiring corporation recognizes no gain or loss when it issues its voting stock for target corporation stock.
- The acquiring corporation's basis in the target corporation stock is the same as in the hands of target corporation shareholders.

EXAMPLE C:7-24 ▶ Mark owns all of Target Corporation's single class of stock, which has a $400,000 basis. Mark exchanges his Target stock for $700,000 of Acquiring Corporation voting stock. Mark realizes a $300,000 gain ($700,000 − $400,000), none of which is recognized. Mark's basis in the Acquiring stock is $400,000. Acquiring recognizes no gain or loss when it issues its stock to Mark, and it takes a $400,000 basis in the acquired Target stock. ◀

STOP & THINK

Question: Assume that stock in both Acquiring and Target Corporations is publicly traded and each corporation has several thousand shareholders. Acquiring Corporation acquires Target Corporation stock in a Type B reorganization. What problems might arise in determining Acquiring's basis in the Target stock?

Solution: Under Sec. 358(a), Acquiring's basis in the Target stock is the same as that in the hands of Target's shareholders. Many shareholders may not know their basis in stock purchased several years ago. The basis for these shares may have changed as a result of stock dividends, stock splits, or nonliquidating distributions. This lack of information may make it difficult to accurately determine Acquiring's basis in the Target stock acquired. The IRS allows sampling to extrapolate from the stock holdings of a small number of Target shareholders' total stock basis.

ADDITIONAL COMMENT

The IRS has concluded that compliance with the sampling standards in Rev. Proc. 81-70, 1981-2 C.B. 729, may be "unduly burdensome or impossible." Thus, the IRS is seeking comments from those who perform basis studies and other interested parties in an effort to revise the revenue procedure (see Notice 2004-44, 2004-28 I.R.B. 32). So far, the IRS has not issued new guidance.

ADVANTAGES OF A TYPE B REORGANIZATION. A Type B reorganization has a number of advantages. First, as explained earlier, the acquisition of target stock usually can be accomplished in a single transaction without formal shareholder approval. Even if the target corporation's management does not approve the transaction, the acquiring

[55] See, for example, *Eldon S. Chapman et al. v. CIR*, 45 AFTR 2d 80-1290, 80-1 USTC ¶9330 (1st Cir., 1980).

WHAT WOULD YOU DO IN THIS SITUATION?

Tobin Rote, a wealthy investor, owns the single class of stock of Detroit Corporation, a calendar year taxpayer. Mr. Rote has wanted to acquire Cleveland Corporation, which produces metal and plastic parts for the automobile industry. On August 1 of the current year, Detroit Corporation purchases for cash 4.9% of Cleveland voting stock, which trades on the New York Stock Exchange. The acquisition gives Tobin Rote, as a Cleveland shareholder, access to its books and records. The 4.9% ownership, however, is below the 5% threshold at which Detroit must file with the SEC a Tender Offer Statement (Schedule 14-D) regarding its stock position. Based on an analysis of Cleveland's books and records made shortly after becoming a shareholder, Tobin Rote wants to make a tender offer sometime in the next two months. In the tender offer, part or all of the remaining Cleveland voting and nonvoting stock would be acquired in exchange for Detroit stock. Mr. Rote comes to you for advice concerning the tender offer, which he wants to complete by December 31 of the current year. No shares would be acquired unless Cleveland shareholders tendered to Detroit Corporation 80% of the voting stock and 80% of all other classes of stock. Mr. Rote wants to use the pooling method to account for the transaction for book purposes. As Mr. Rote's CPA, you know that he used this method to account for his acquisitions several years ago. Mr. Rote explains to you that he hopes to avoid reporting on Cleveland's financial statements the goodwill that results from a cash purchase of target corporation stock because the impairment of goodwill reduces corporate earnings per share. As Mr. Rote's CPA, you have advised him about numerous acquisitions accounted for under the pooling method. You know that the FASB has issued pronouncements that apply to Mr. Rote's situation. What information do you need to advise Mr. Rote about these changes? What advantages do these pronouncements offer for his post-acquisition business?

corporation can acquire the necessary number of shares through a tender offer directly to target corporation shareholders. Second, the target corporation remains in existence, and its assets, liabilities, and tax attributes need not be transferred to the acquiring corporation. However, the use of its NOLs may be limited under Sec. 382 (see pages C:7-43 through C:7-46).[56] Third, the corporate name, goodwill, licenses, and rights of the target corporation may be preserved after the acquisition. Fourth, the acquiring corporation does not directly assume the target corporation's liabilities, as is the case of some other reorganizations. Finally, the acquiring and target corporations can report their post-acquisition results on a consolidated basis (see Chapter C:8).

DISADVANTAGES OF A TYPE B REORGANIZATION. Offsetting those advantages are a number of disadvantages. First, the acquiring corporation can use only voting stock as consideration in the transaction. Issuing this additional stock can dilute the voting power and control of acquiring corporation shareholders. Second, the acquiring corporation must end up with at least 80% of target corporation stock even though effective control can be achieved through ownership of less than 80%. Third, the acquisition of less than 100% of target corporation stock may give rise to dissenting minority shareholders. These shareholders have the right under state law to have their shares appraised and purchased for cash. Fourth, the bases of target corporation stock (outside basis) and assets (inside basis) are not stepped-up (or stepped-down) to their FMVs upon the change in ownership, as would be the case in a taxable asset acquisition.

DROP-DOWN AND TRIANGULAR TYPE B REORGANIZATIONS. As with Type A and C reorganizations, a triangular Type B reorganization, or a drop down of target corporation stock into a subsidiary before the stock-for-stock exchange, can be accomplished tax-free. In a triangular Type B reorganization, the acquiring subsidiary exchanges its parent stock for a controlling interest in the target corporation. As in a basic Type B reor-

[56] A Type B reorganization can result in an ownership change that restricts the ability of the target corporation's NOL carryovers to be used under Sec. 382 but does not, in total, diminish the amount of its carryovers.

ganization, the target corporation remains in existence as a subsidiary of the acquiring subsidiary. Thus, it becomes a second-tier subsidiary of the parent corporation.

TYPE G REORGANIZATION

Section 368(a)(1)(G) defines a **Type G reorganization** as "a transfer by a corporation of part or all of its assets to another corporation in a Title 11 [bankruptcy] or similar case, but only if, in pursuance of the plan, stock or securities of the corporation to which the assets are transferred are distributed in a transaction that qualifies under sections 354, 355, or 356." Type G reorganizations are infrequent because the reorganization must occur pursuant to a court-approved plan in a bankruptcy, receivership, or similar situation.

In an acquisitive Type G reorganization, an insolvent corporation might transfer substantially all its assets to an acquiring corporation under a court-approved plan (e.g., a bankruptcy reorganization plan). It then might distribute all the stock, securities, and other property received in the exchange, plus any property retained, to its shareholders and creditors in exchange for their stock and debt obligations.

DIVISIVE REORGANIZATIONS

A divisive reorganization involves the transfer of some of a transferor corporation's assets to a controlled corporation in exchange for its stock and securities (and possibly boot property).[57] The transferor then distributes the stock and securities (and possibly boot property) to its shareholders. A divisive reorganization generally is governed by the Type D reorganization rules, although a divisive reorganization involving a financially troubled corporation could be governed by the Type G reorganization rules. Topic Review C:7-6 summarizes the requirements for divisive and other reorganizations.

DIVISIVE TYPE D REORGANIZATION

A divisive Type D reorganization must satisfy the requirements of Secs. 368(a)(1)(D) and 355, which are explained below.[58] Divisive Type D reorganizations can assume three forms: spin-offs, split-offs, and split-ups (see Figure C:7-7).

In the reorganization, a distribution of a controlled corporation's stock may be nontaxable under Sec. 355 even if the distributing corporation transfers no assets to the controlled corporation, in which case the division is not classified as a reorganization. To be a nontaxable Type D reorganization, however, both the asset transfer and the Sec. 355 distribution must be part of a single transaction governed by a plan of reorganization.

TYPICAL MISCONCEPTION

The existence of a corporate business purpose is necessary before the stock of a controlled subsidiary can be distributed to the shareholders of the distributing corporation. This requirement is much more difficult to satisfy in a Sec. 355 distribution than it is in an acquisitive reorganization.

A divisive Type D reorganization can accomplish various business objectives, including

- Dividing an enterprise into two or more corporations to separate high-risk business from low-risk business
- Splitting up a single business among two or more disputing shareholders
- Dividing an enterprise according to functions, profit centers, or geographical areas
- Divesting operations because of antitrust laws

FORMS OF DIVISIVE TYPE D REORGANIZATIONS. Three types of divisive transactions are nontaxable under Sec. 368(a)(1)(D):

- **Split-off**—the distributing corporation transfers some of its assets to a controlled corporation in exchange for stock and possibly securities, money, or other boot property. The distributing corporation then distributes stock in the controlled corporation to some or all of its shareholders in exchange for some of its stock. The context for such a

[57] In a divisive Type D reorganization, control is defined by Sec. 368(c) because Sec. 355 (not Sec. 354) governs the distribution. Section 368(c) requires ownership of at least 80% of the voting and nonvoting stock to constitute control. An acquisitive Type D reorganization, on the other hand, requires ownership of only 50% of the voting and nonvoting stock for control.

[58] The requirements of a divisive Type D reorganization are contrasted with the acquisitive Type D reorganization (previously discussed), where substantially all the transferor's assets must be transferred to a controlled corporation.

Topic Review C:7-6

Summary of Divisive and Other Reorganizations

Type of Reorganization	Distributing (D) or Transferor (T) Corporation Property Acquired	Consideration That Can Be Used	What Happens to the Distributing (D) or Transferor (T) Corporation?	Shareholders' Recognized Gain	Other Requirements
D—Divisive	D Corporation transfers part or all of its assets (and possibly some or all of its liabilities) to C Corporation.	Stock, securities, and other property of C Corporation.	D or T Corporation must distribute stock, securities, and boot received in the reorganization to its shareholders. D Corporation may liquidate or remain in existence.	Lesser of realized gain or FMV of boot received.	Transactions can assume three forms—spin-off, split-off, or split-up. Control is defined as 80% under Sec. 368(c).
E—Recapitalization	No increase or decrease in assets. A change in the capital structure of T Corporation occurs.	Stock, securities, and other property of T Corporation.	T Corporation remains in existence.	Lesser of realized gain or FMV of boot received.	May involve stock-for-stock, bond-for-bond, or bond-for-stock exchanges.
F—Change in form, identity, or place of organization	Old T Corporation transfers assets or stock to new T Corporation.	Stock, securities, and other property of new T Corporation.	Old T Corporation liquidates.	Lesser of realized gain or FMV of boot received.	Must involve only a single operating company.
G—Acquisitive or divisive	T Corporation transfers part or all of its assets (and possibly some or all of its liabilities) to A Corporation in bankruptcy.	Stock, securities, and other property of A Corporation.	T Corporation may liquidate, divide, or remain in existence.	Lesser of realized gain or FMV of boot received.	Stock and securities of A Corporation received by T Corporation must be distributed to its shareholders, security holders, or creditors.

Key:
D Corporation refers to the distributing corporation.
C Corporation refers to the controlled corporation.
T Corporation refers to the transferor corporation.
A Corporation refers to the transferee or acquiring corporation.

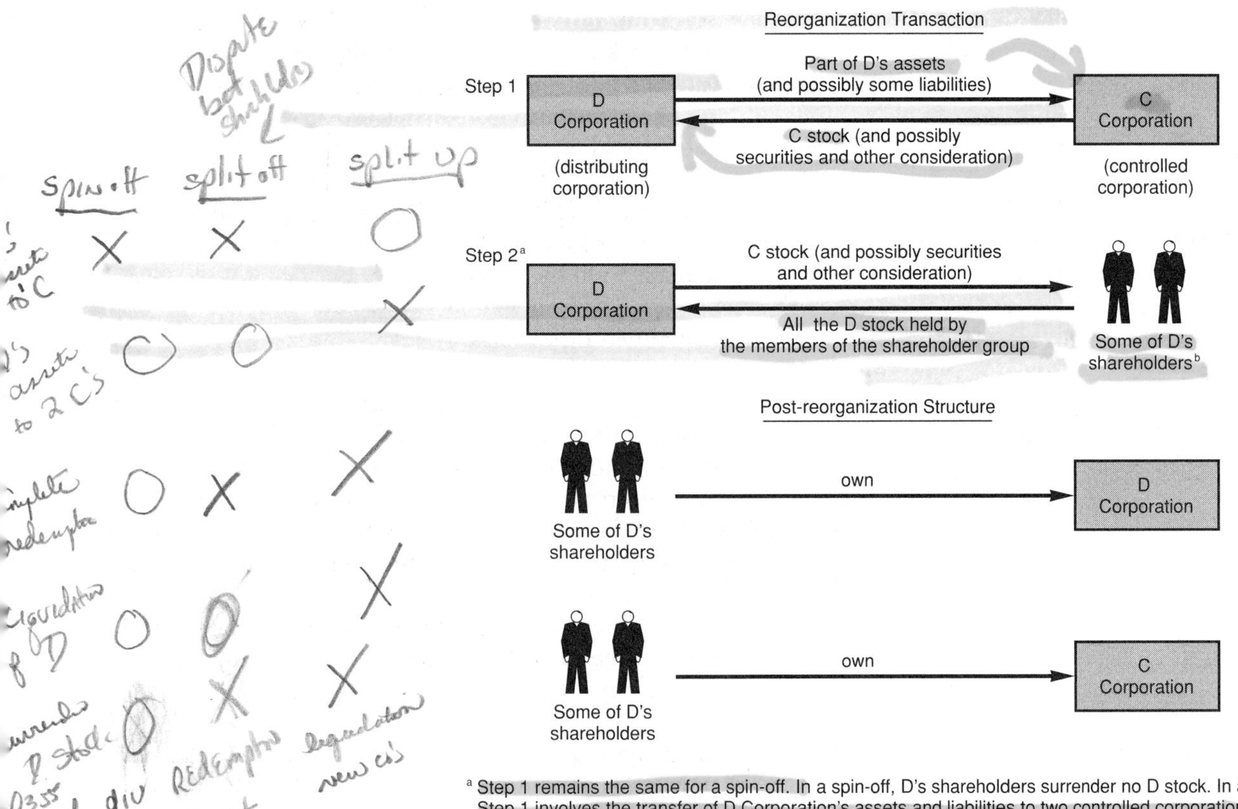

[a] Step 1 remains the same for a spin-off. In a spin-off, D's shareholders surrender no D stock. In a split-up, Step 1 involves the transfer of D Corporation's assets and liabilities to two controlled corporations. Step 2 involves the distribution of the stock of the two controlled corporations pursuant to the liquidation of D Corporation.

[b] This distribution also could occur on a pro rata basis to all of D's shareholders, in which case the shareholders surrender only a portion of their D shares.

FIGURE C:7-7 ▶ DIVISIVE TYPE D REORGANIZATION (SPLIT-OFF FORM)

transaction might be a management dispute between two dissenting shareholder groups. To resolve the dispute, the parent corporation might redeem all the stock of one of the groups (see Figure C:7-7).

- **Spin-off**—the distributing corporation transfers some of its assets to a controlled corporation in exchange for stock and possibly securities, money, or other boot property. The distributing corporation then distributes stock in the controlled corporation ratably to all its shareholders who do not surrender their distributing corporation stock. The context for such a transaction might be a desire to reduce risk inherent in distinct operations (e.g., steel and glass manufacturing) within a single corporation.
- **Split-up**—the distributing corporation transfers all its assets to two controlled corporations in exchange for stock and possibly securities, money, or other boot property. The distributing corporation then distributes stock in the two controlled corporations to all its shareholders, in exchange for all its own outstanding stock. Such a transaction might be motivated by a desire to separate and continue distinct operations of an old corporation that has lost goodwill.

ADDITIONAL COMMENT

If the IRS applies Sec. 351 to the asset transfer, and if the total adjusted basis for all property transferred exceeds the total FMV of that property, the subsidiary's total basis will be limited to the total FMV (see Chapter C:2 for details).

If the Sec. 355 requirements discussed below are *not* met, a spin-off is taxed as a dividend to the shareholders, a split-off is taxed as a stock redemption to the shareholders, and a split-up is taxed to its shareholders as a liquidation of the distributing corporation.

ASSET TRANSFER. The distributing corporation recognizes no gain or loss on the asset transfer except where it receives and retains boot property or where the controlled corporation acquires or assumes distributing corporation liabilities and total liabilities exceed the total adjusted bases of the assets transferred.[59] The controlled corporation recognizes no gain or loss when it exchanges its stock for the distributing corporation's property. The controlled corporation takes a carryover basis in the acquired assets, increased by any gain recognized by the distributing corporation on the asset transfer. Its holding period includes the distributing corporation's holding period for the assets.

TYPICAL MISCONCEPTION

Section 355 can apply to a distribution of stock of an existing subsidiary as well as the distribution of stock of a new subsidiary that is created as part of the transaction.

DISTRIBUTION OF STOCK AND SECURITIES. In a Type D reorganization, the distributing corporation recognizes no gain or loss when it distributes controlled corporation stock (or securities) to its shareholders.[60] On the other hand, the distributing corporation recognizes gain (but not loss) when it distributes nonmoney boot property to its shareholders and when it makes a disqualified distribution of stock or securities in the controlled corporation.

The shareholders recognize no gain or loss on the receipt of the stock (and securities) except to the extent they receive boot property.[61] A shareholder's basis in the stock (or securities) equals his or her basis in the stock (or securities) held before the distribution, increased by any gain recognized and decreased by the sum of any money and the FMV of any other boot property received. If the shareholder holds more than one class of stock or securities before or after the distribution, the total basis in the nonrecognition property is allocated to each class based on their relative FMVs. The basis in any boot property (other than money) is its FMV. The holding period for the stock and nonboot securities received includes the holding period for the stock and securities surrendered. The holding period for boot property begins on the day after the distribution date.

EXAMPLE C:7-25 ▶

Distributing Corporation transfers assets having a $600,000 FMV and a $350,000 adjusted basis to Controlled Corporation in exchange for all of Controlled's single class of stock. Distributing is owned equally by Ruth and Pat who are unable to agree on how Distributing should be managed. Ruth and Pat agree to divide the business by exchanging Pat's Distributing shares for Controlled shares while leaving Ruth's equity interest intact (i.e., a split-up). Pat's basis in her Distributing shares is $400,000. In the asset transfer, Distributing realizes a $250,000 gain ($600,000 – $350,000), none of which is recognized. Distributing recognizes no gain on the distribution of the Controlled shares to Pat. Upon surrendering her Distributing shares, Pat realizes a $200,000 ($600,000 – $400,000) gain, none of which is recognized. Her basis in the Controlled stock is $400,000. The holding period for the Controlled shares includes Pat's holding period for the Distributing shares. Upon issuing its stock for Distributing assets, Controlled recognizes no gain and takes a $350,000 basis in the acquired assets. ◀

SELF-STUDY QUESTION

Does the receipt of boot make the entire Sec. 355 transaction taxable to the shareholders?

ANSWER

No. The shareholders may have a partial recognition of gain. The amount and type of gain recognized depends on whether the shareholders surrender stock of the distributing corporation in the transaction.

Under Sec. 355, boot consists of money, short-term debt, property other than stock or securities of a controlled corporation, stock in the controlled corporation purchased within the previous five years in a taxable transaction, securities of the controlled corporation to the extent the principal amount of securities received exceeds the principal amount of securities surrendered, and stock or securities attributable to accrued interest.[62] When the shareholder receives boot, the amount and character of the recognized income or gain depend on whether he or she surrendered stock and securities in the distributing corporation (i.e., a split-off or split-up) or retained stock or securities (i.e., a spin-off).

When the shareholder receives boot in a spin-off, the FMV of the boot is treated as a dividend to the extent of the shareholder's ratable share of the distributing corporation's E&P. Any securities the shareholders receive in a spin-off are treated as boot because the

[59] Secs. 361(a) and 357(c)(1)(B).

[60] Sec. 361(c)(1). Two special rules may require the distributing corporation to recognize gain when it distributes stock and securities. A disqualifying distribution occurs if, immediately after the distribution, any person holds a 50% disqualified stock interest in either the distributing corporation or the controlled corporation. Disqualified stock generally is defined as any stock in the distributing or a controlled corporation purchased within the five-year period ending on the distribution date. The disqualifying distribution rules prevent a divisive transaction from following a stock purchase to accomplish the disposition of a significant part of the historic shareholders' interests in one or more of the divided corporations. A second set of rules, the anti-Morris Trust rules, also requires the distributing corporation to recognize gain when a distribution of stock or securities is made and is preceded or followed by a disposition of the stock or securities.

[61] Sec. 355(a). As with an acquisitive reorganization, Sec. 361(a) permits securities (e.g., long-term debt obligations) to be received tax-free in a divisive transaction when the shareholders surrender the same face amount of securities, or a larger amount. Excess securities received are boot property.

[62] Secs. 355(a)(3) and 356(b).

shareholders do not surrender any securities in this type of transaction. Thus, the FMV of the securities is a dividend to the extent of the shareholder's ratable share of the distributing corporation's E&P.

TYPICAL MISCONCEPTION

In a spin-off, the FMV of the boot received is treated as a Sec. 301 distribution to the shareholder. In a split-off or split-up, the shareholders recognize gain to the extent of the lesser of boot received or the gain realized. This gain may be a dividend or capital gain under Sec. 302.

In a split-off or split-up, in addition to the exchange of stock, a shareholder may receive boot property. If the shareholder realizes a loss on the exchange, the loss is not recognized, whether boot is received or not.[63] If the shareholder realizes a gain on the exchange, he or she recognizes the gain to the extent of the FMV of any boot received.

If the exchange is essentially equivalent to a dividend under the Sec. 302 stock redemption rules, the recognized gain is treated as a dividend to the extent of the shareholder's ratable share of the distributing corporation's E&P.[64] Otherwise it is treated as a capital gain. In either case, the income is taxed at a 15% rate. Under the Sec. 302 rules, the shareholder is treated as though he or she continued to own stock in the distributing corporation and surrendered only the portion of his or her shares equal in value to the amount of boot received. This hypothetical redemption is then tested under the Sec. 302(b) rules to determine whether the shareholder is entitled to sale or dividend treatment.[65]

EXAMPLE C:7-26 ▶ Distributing Corporation owns assets with a $60,000 FMV plus all the outstanding shares of Controlled Corporation stock valued at $40,000. Distributing formed Controlled by transferring some of its assets to Controlled as part of the reorganization. Distributing's E&P balance is $35,000. Carl and Diane each own 100 shares of Distributing stock. In a split-off, Distributing distributes all the Controlled stock to Carl in exchange for his 100 shares. Carl also receives $10,000 in cash. Carl's basis in the surrendered Distributing shares is $22,000. Carl has a $28,000 realized gain, calculated as follows:

FMV of Controlled stock	$40,000
Plus: Cash received	10,000
Amount realized	$50,000
Minus: Basis of Distributing stock	(22,000)
Realized gain	$28,000

Carl recognizes $10,000 of this gain (i.e., the lesser of the $28,000 realized gain or the $10,000 FMV of boot received). If Carl surrenders Distributing stock solely for the $10,000 cash, he would effectively be exchanging 20 Distributing shares ($10,000 boot ÷ $500 FMV for each share of Distributing stock) worth $10,000. Before this hypothetical redemption, he owns 50% of the outstanding Distributing shares (100 ÷ 200). Afterward, he owns 44% (80 ÷ 180). Thus, the hypothetical redemption is not substantially disproportionate under Sec. 302(b)(2) because the 44% post-redemption stock ownership exceeds 80% of the pre-redemption stock ownership (50% × 0.80 = 40%). If the exchange can meet one of the other tests for sale treatment (e.g., not essentially equivalent to a dividend), the $10,000 will be treated as a capital gain. Otherwise it will be treated as a dividend. ◀

TYPICAL MISCONCEPTION

Unlike Sec. 351, securities (long-term debt) can be exchanged in a Sec. 355 transaction without the recognition of gain as long as the principal amount surrendered is equal to or greater than the principal amount received.

In a split-off or split-up, a shareholder will receive securities of the controlled corporation tax-free only if the shareholder surrenders securities in the distributing corporation with an equal or larger principal amount. To the extent the principal amount of securities received exceeds the principal amount of securities surrendered, the excess will be taxable.

THE SEC. 355 REQUIREMENTS. Under Sec. 355, a distributing corporation's distribution of a controlled corporation's stock is nontaxable to the shareholders if the following six conditions are met:[66]

- ▶ The property distributed consists solely of stock or securities of a corporation controlled by the distributing corporation immediately before the distribution. The distributing corporation owns and distributes stock possessing at least 80% of the total

[63] Sec. 356(c).
[64] Sec. 356(a)(2).
[65] Rev. Rul. 93-62, 1993-2 C.B. 118.
[66] Sec. 355(a) and Reg. Secs. 1.355-2(b) and (c). Also, Rev. Proc. 2003-48, 2003-2 C.B. 86, is a checklist questionnaire of the information that must be included in a ruling request coming under Sec. 355. Appendix A of this revenue procedure contains guidelines regarding the business purpose requirement for Sec. 355 transactions including information submission requirements for nine specific situations where rulings may or may not be granted.

ADDITIONAL COMMENT

The control requirement for Sec. 355 is the same control requirement relating to the formation of a corporation under Sec. 351 (see Chapter C:2).

combined voting power of all classes of stock entitled to vote and at least 80% of the total number of shares of all other classes of stock.[67]

- The distribution has not been used principally as a device to distribute the E&P of the distributing corporation, the controlled corporation, or both. Whether the distribution has been used as such a device will be based on the facts and circumstances of each case. A sale or exchange of distributing or controlled corporation stock after the distribution is evidence that the distribution was used as such a device, especially if the sale was prearranged.[68]

TYPICAL MISCONCEPTION

The active trade or business requirement has two parts: a pre-distribution five-year history must exist, and both the distributing and controlled corporations must be actively engaged in a trade or business immediately after the distribution.

- Immediately after the distribution, the distributing and controlled corporations each engage in the active conduct of a trade or business that was actively conducted for at least five years before the distribution. This requirement prevents a corporation from spinning off a newly formed subsidiary whose only assets are unneeded cash and other liquid assets. The shareholders then could sell or liquidate the subsidiary and obtain the liquid assets in a transaction characterized as a sale rather than a dividend.[69]
- The distributing corporation distributes either all controlled corporation stock and securities held by it immediately before the distribution or an amount of controlled corporation stock constituting control. The distributing corporation may retain some stock if it can establish to the IRS's satisfaction that the stock was not retained as part of a tax avoidance plan.

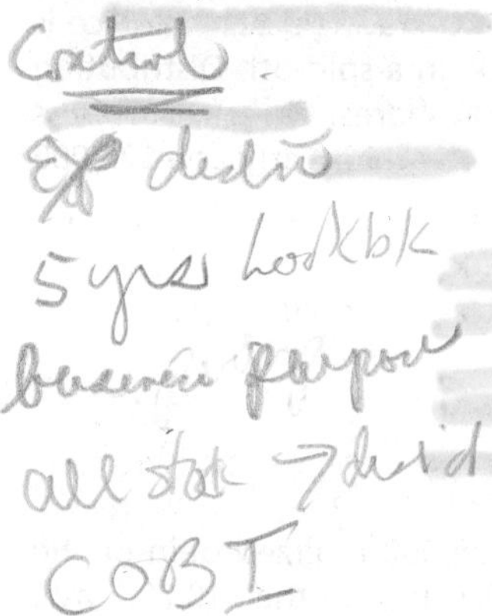

- The distribution has a substantial corporate business purpose. Qualifying distributions include those made to comply with antitrust laws and those made to separate businesses where the shareholders have major disagreements.[70]
- Shareholders who directly or indirectly owned the controlled corporation(s) and a substantial number of shareholders who owned the distributing corporation's stock before the distribution maintain a continuing equity interest in one or more of the corporations following the division.[71] The distribution of stock and securities need not be pro rata. Disproportionate distributions may be used to eliminate the stock ownership of dissenting shareholders. In a split-off, some shareholders may exchange all their distributing corporation stock for all the controlled corporation stock.

DIVISIVE TYPE G REORGANIZATION

A divisive Type G reorganization involves the transfer of some of a corporation's assets to a second corporation under a court-approved plan. The transferor corporation then distributes the transferee corporation's stock and securities to its shareholders, security holders, and creditors. The transferor corporation may continue as a separate going concern after restructuring its operations. Alternatively, the transferor corporation may liquidate under a court approved bankruptcy plan.

OTHER REORGANIZATIONS

Two types of transactions do not fit into the acquisitive or divisive reorganization categories: Type E reorganizations, which are recapitalizations, and Type F reorganizations, which are changes in identity, form, or state of incorporation. Topic Review C:7-6 presented earlier summarizes the requirements for Type E and Type F reorganizations.

TYPE E REORGANIZATION

Section 368(a)(1)(E) refers to a **Type E reorganization** simply as a "recapitalization." A 1942 Supreme Court opinion defined **recapitalization** as "the reshuffling of the corporate

[67] Sec. 368(c).

[68] Reg. Sec. 1.355-2(d).

[69] Sec. 355(b)(2). A corporation is engaged in the active conduct of a trade or business if it actively conducts all activities needed for generating a profit and these activities encompass all steps in the process of earning income. Specifically excluded are passive investment activities such as simply holding stock, securities, and land.

[70] Reg. Sec. 1.355-2(b)(5), Exs. (1) and (2).

[71] Reg. Sec. 1.355-2(c).

KEY POINT

A Type E reorganization is neither acquisitive nor divisive in nature. Instead, it simply allows a single corporation to restructure its capital without creating a taxable exchange between the corporation and its shareholders or creditors.

structure within the framework of an existing corporation."[72] To qualify as a nontaxable reorganization, a recapitalization must have a bona fide business purpose. One reason for a recapitalization is to reduce a corporation's interest payments and debt-to-equity ratio by exchanging additional common or preferred stock for outstanding bonds. Alternatively, a family corporation might exchange newly issued preferred stock for part or all of the common stock held by a retiring, controlling shareholder so that shareholder can transfer management control to his or her children. This type of recapitalization also facilitates estate planning (see discussion after Example C:7-28).

Three types of corporate capital structure adjustments can qualify as a Type E reorganization: a stock-for-stock exchange, a bond-for-stock exchange, and a bond-for-bond exchange.[73] Normally, these exchanges do not result in an increase or decrease in the corporation's assets except to the extent shareholders or creditors receive a distribution of money or other property.

STOCK-FOR-STOCK EXCHANGE. An exchange of common stock for common stock, or preferred stock for preferred stock, in the same corporation can qualify as a recapitalization if it is pursuant to a plan of reorganization. Section 1036 permits similar types of exchanges in a non-reorganization context. In either context, shareholders recognize no gain or loss on the exchange and take a substituted basis in the shares received that references the basis in the shares surrendered.

EXAMPLE C:7-27 ▶ The shareholders of Pilot Corporation exchange all their nonvoting Class B common stock for additional shares of Pilot's voting Class A common stock. The exchange is nontaxable under Sec. 1036 even if not pursuant to a plan of reorganization. An exchange of some of Pilot's Class A preferred stock for Class B preferred stock also would be nontaxable under Sec. 1036. ◀

Section 1036 does not apply to an exchange of common stock for preferred stock, or preferred stock for common stock, in the same corporation, or an exchange of stock of two corporations. On the other hand, the reorganization rules apply to an exchange of two different classes of stock (e.g., common for preferred) in the same corporation if the exchange is pursuant to a plan of reorganization. Under the Sec. 354(a) nonrecognition rules, the exchange is nontaxable to the shareholders except to the extent they receive boot property. If the FMV of stock received differs from that of stock surrendered, the difference may be recharacterized as a gift, a contribution to capital, compensation for services, dividend, or payment to satisfy a debt obligation, depending on the facts and circumstances.[74] The tax consequences of that portion of the exchange will not be governed by the reorganization rules.

EXAMPLE C:7-28 ▶ John owns 60% of Boise Corporation's common stock and all its preferred stock. The remainder of Boise's common stock is held by 80 unrelated individuals. John's basis in his preferred stock is $300,000. The preferred stock is valued at $500,000. John exchanges his preferred stock for $400,000 of additional common stock and $100,000 in cash. In the exchange, John realizes a $200,000 [($400,000 + $100,000) − $300,000] gain, of which he recognizes $100,000 as dividend income (assuming Boise has sufficient E&P). None of the Sec. 302(b) exceptions that permit capital gain treatment applies. John's basis in the additional common stock is $300,000 ($300,000 + $100,000 gain recognized − $100,000 money received). ◀

A recapitalization often is used as an estate planning device whereby a parent's controlling common stock interest is exchanged for both common and preferred stock. The common stock often is gifted to a child who, following the recapitalization, owns a controlling common stock interest in the corporation and manages its business. The parent will derive annual income from preferred stock dividends. The preferred stock's value is

---

72 *Helvering v. Southwest Consolidated Corp.*, 28 AFTR 573, 42-1 USTC ¶9248 (USSC, 1942).

73 An exchange of stock for bonds has been held in *J. Robert Bazely v. CIR* (35 AFTR 1190, 47-2 USTC ¶9288 [USSC, 1947]) not to be a recapitalization. Even if it were a recapitalization, it generally would be taxable because receipt of the entire principal amount of the bonds represents boot under Sec. 356. The IRS has held that, if no stock is held after the exchange, the Sec. 302 stock redemption rules apply to the transaction, thereby resulting in sale or exchange treatment (Rev. Rul. 77-415, 1977-2 C.B. 311).

74 Rev. Ruls. 74-269, 1974-2 C.B. 87 and 83-120, 1983-2 C.B. 170.

unlikely to increase significantly over time, thereby freezing the value of that portion of the parent's estate and limiting the estate tax liability. Relatively more capital appreciation will accrue to the child who owns the common stock.

Substantial income, estate, and gift tax planning opportunities previously existed in the recapitalization of a closely held corporation. To prevent abuses, Congress added Secs. 2701–2704, which, for transfer tax purposes, set forth procedures for more accurately valuing interests transferred to, and retained in, corporations and partnerships. Additional coverage of this topic is presented in Chapter C:12.

BOND-FOR-STOCK EXCHANGE. A bond-for-stock exchange is nontaxable to the shareholder except to the extent the shareholder receives a portion of the stock in satisfaction of the corporation's liability to him or her for accrued interest.[75] The latter portion is taxed as ordinary income.

BOND-FOR-BOND EXCHANGE. These exchanges are nontaxable only where the principal amount of the bonds received does not exceed the principal amount of the bonds surrendered. If the principal amount of the bonds received exceeds the principal amount of the bonds surrendered, the FMV of the "excess" is taxed to the bondholder as boot.

TYPE F REORGANIZATION

Section 368(a)(1)(F) defines a **Type F reorganization** as a "mere change in identity, form, or place of organization of one corporation, however effected." Typically, Type F reorganizations are used to change either the state in which the business is incorporated or the name of a corporation, without requiring the old corporation or its shareholders to recognize gain or loss. In a Type F reorganization, the assets and liabilities of the old corporation are transferred to a new corporation in exchange for stock and possibly debt obligations. The shareholders and creditors of the old corporation then exchange their stock and debt interests for similar interests in the new corporation.

EXAMPLE C:7-29 ▶ Rider Corporation is incorporated in Illinois. Its management decides to change its state of incorporation to Delaware because of that state's favorable securities and corporation laws. To effect the change, old Rider exchanges its assets for all the stock in new Rider, incorporated in Delaware. The shareholders of old Rider then exchange their stock for new Rider stock. Old Rider goes out of existence. Neither the shareholders nor the "two" corporations recognize gain or loss. Each shareholder takes a substituted basis in the new Rider stock that references their basis in the old Rider stock. Their holding period for the new Rider stock includes their holding period for the old Rider stock. New Rider's asset bases are the same as old Rider's asset bases, and new Rider acquires old Rider's tax attributes. Although the two corporations are legally distinct, they represent the same enterprise that merely has changed its state of incorporation. ◀

The reorganization illustrated in Example C:7-29 also could be accomplished if old Rider's shareholders exchanged their old Rider stock for new Rider stock. Old Rider then would liquidate into new Rider. The tax consequences would be the same for both transactions.

JUDICIAL RESTRICTIONS ON THE USE OF CORPORATE REORGANIZATIONS

The U.S. Supreme Court has held that compliance with the letter of the law of reorganization provisions does not necessarily make a transaction nontaxable.[76] Through various judicial doctrines, the courts have placed four restrictions on reorganizations:

[75] Sec. 354(a)(2)(B).

[76] *Evelyn F. Gregory v. Helvering*, 14 AFTR 1191, 35-1 USTC ¶9043 (USSC, 1935).

OBJECTIVE 7

Understand judicial doctrines that govern the tax treatment of corporate reorganizations

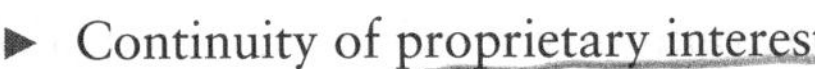

- Continuity of proprietary interest
- Continuity of business enterprise
- A bona fide business purpose
- The step transaction doctrine

All four requirements elevate economic substance over legal form.

CONTINUITY OF PROPRIETARY INTEREST

TYPICAL MISCONCEPTION

The continuity of interest requirement has nothing to do with the relative sizes of the acquiring and target corporations. The target shareholders may end up with a minimal amount of the total outstanding stock of the acquiring corporation, and yet the merger will be a valid reorganization as long as 50% of the consideration received by the target shareholders is an equity interest in the acquiring corporation.

The continuity of proprietary interest doctrine is based on the principle that the tax deferral associated with a reorganization is available because the shareholder merely has changed his or her investment from one form to another rather than liquidate it. According to Reg. Sec. 1.368-1(b), the requirements of this doctrine are met by a continuity of the business enterprise under a modified corporate form and a continuity of interest on the part of the shareholders who, directly or indirectly, own the enterprise before its reorganization. In a series of decisions, the courts have held that a continuing proprietary interest is ensured through ownership of common or preferred stock.[77] Thus, a transaction that involves the receipt of only cash or short-term debt obligations by the target corporation or its shareholders does not qualify as a nontaxable reorganization.

The IRC does not specify how much stock is necessary for continuity of proprietary interest. For advance ruling purposes, however, the IRS requires that at least 50% of the total consideration received by target corporation shareholders consist of acquiring corporation stock. The 50% rule applies only for advance ruling purposes, and the courts have accepted lower percentages.[78] Nevertheless, the 50% rule indicates the threshold below which the IRS may challenge the transaction.

SELF-STUDY QUESTION

For which reorganizations is the continuity-of-interest requirement most important?

ANSWER

The only limitation on consideration used for both regular and triangular mergers is the continuity-of-interest requirement. The other reorganizations, including reverse triangular mergers, have statutory requirements more restrictive than the continuity-of-interest doctrine.

EXAMPLE C:7-30 ▶ In a Type C reorganization, Target Corporation transfers all its assets to Acquiring Corporation in exchange for $200,000 of Acquiring stock and the assumption of $800,000 of Target liabilities. Target distributes the Acquiring stock to its sole shareholder, Nancy, in exchange for all her Target stock. Even though the transaction meets the statutory requirements for a Type C reorganization, the IRS probably will claim that the transaction does not qualify for tax-free treatment because it lacks continuity of proprietary interest. Only 20% of the total consideration paid consists of an equity interest in Acquiring. ◀

Recently, the IRS amended Reg. Sec. 1.368-1(b) to clarify that neither the continuity of interest nor the continuity of business enterprise doctrine applies to Type E and Type F reorganizations.

CONTINUITY OF BUSINESS ENTERPRISE

SELF-STUDY QUESTION

Does the acquiring corporation have to continue its own historic business?

ANSWER

No. The IRS has specifically ruled that continuity of business enterprise requires only that the historic business of the target corporation be continued (Rev. Rul. 81-25, 1981-1 C.B. 132).

Continuity of business enterprise implies that the acquiring corporation either continue the target corporation's business or use a significant portion of the target corporation's operating assets in a new business.[79] This doctrine limits nontaxable reorganizations to transactions involving *continuing interests* in the target's business or target property under a modified corporate form. The **continuity of business enterprise doctrine**, however, does not require that the target corporation's historic business be continued.

Whether the continuity of business enterprise requirement is met depends on the facts and circumstances of each case. The historic business requirement can be satisfied if the acquiring corporation continues one or more of the target corporation's significant lines of business.

EXAMPLE C:7-31 ▶ Historically, Target Corporation has manufactured resins and chemicals and has distributed chemicals for the production of plastics. All three lines of business generate the same level of revenues. Target merges into Acquiring Corporation. Two months after the merger, Acquiring sells the resin manufacturing and chemicals distribution lines to an unrelated party for cash. The transaction satisfies the continuity of business enterprise requirement because Acquiring continues at least one of Target's three significant lines of business.[80] ◀

---

[77] See, for example, *V. L. LeTulle v. Scofield,* 23 AFTR 789, 40-1 USTC ¶9150 (USSC, 1940).

[78] Rev. Proc. 77-37, 1977-2 C.B. 568, Sec. 3.02. See also *John A. Nelson Co. v. Helvering,* 16 AFTR 1262, 36-1 USTC ¶9019 (USSC, 1935), in which the Supreme Court permitted a nontaxable reorganization where the stock exchanged constituted only 38% of the total consideration.

[79] Reg. Sec. 1.368-1(d)(1).

[80] Reg. Secs. 1.368-1(d)(3) and -1(d)(5), Ex. (1).

The business (asset) continuity requirement is satisfied if the acquiring corporation uses in its business a significant portion of the assets used in the target corporation's business. Significance is based on the relative importance of the assets to target's historic business operations.

EXAMPLE C:7-32 ▶ Both Acquiring and Target Corporations manufacture computers. Target merges into Acquiring. Acquiring terminates Target's manufacturing activities and retains Target's equipment as a source of supply for its components. Acquiring satisfies the continuity of business enterprise requirement by continuing to use Target's business assets. Thus, Acquiring need not continue Target's historic business to satisfy the continuity of business enterprise requirement.[81] If instead Acquiring had sold Target's assets for cash and placed the proceeds in an investment portfolio, the continuity of business enterprise requirement would not have been met. ◀

ADDITIONAL COMMENT

Because the target corporation and its shareholders have the most to lose, they should protect themselves by stipulating that the acquiring corporation retain the historic assets. If not, the acquiring corporation can unilaterally dispose of the historic assets and destroy the nontaxable reorganization.

Moreover, the acquiring corporation need not hold the target corporation's business assets for a prolonged period of time. The assets (business activities) may be held (conducted) by an 80%-or-more-owned subsidiary corporation included in a chain of corporations that includes the acquiring corporation. In some cases, the acquired assets can be held by (or business conducted by) a partnership or LLC owned in full or in part by the acquiring corporation or one of its subsidiaries.

BUSINESS PURPOSE REQUIREMENT

A transaction must serve a **bona fide business purpose** to qualify for reorganization treatment.[82] Regulation Sec. 1.368-1(c) states that a transactional scheme that uses "the form of a corporate reorganization as a disguise for concealing its real character, and the object and accomplishment of which is the consummation of a preconceived plan having no business or corporate purpose, is not a plan of reorganization."

EXAMPLE C:7-33 ▶ Distributing Corporation transfers appreciated stock from its investment portfolio to newly created Controlled Corporation in exchange for all its stock. It then distributes the Controlled stock to its sole shareholder, Kathy, in exchange for some of her Distributing stock. Shortly after the stock transfer, Controlled liquidates, and Kathy receives the appreciated stock held by Controlled. If the liquidation were treated as a separate event, Kathy would recognize a capital gain, which she could use to offset capital loss carryovers from other tax years. In addition, she could step up the basis in the appreciated stock to its FMV without incurring a tax liability. Even though the stock transfer to Controlled complies with the letter of Sec. 368(a)(1)(D) for a divisive Type D reorganization, the IRS probably will claim that the Sec. 355 trade or business requirement has not been met. It also will rely on the Supreme Court's decision in *Gregory v. Helvering* to rule that the series of transactions serves no business purpose. As a result, Kathy's receipt of the appreciated stock from Controlled most likely will be treated as a dividend. ◀

KEY POINT

Business purpose is much more difficult to establish in divisive (Sec. 355) transactions than it is in acquisitive (Sec. 354) transactions.

STEP TRANSACTION DOCTRINE

The IRS can invoke the **step transaction doctrine** to collapse a multistep reorganization into a single taxable transaction. Alternatively, the IRS can invoke the doctrine to collapse a series of steps, which the taxpayer claims as independent taxable events, into a single nontaxable reorganization. Both IRS actions prevent the taxpayer from elevating legal form over economic substance.

EXAMPLE C:7-34 ▶ Jody transfers business property from his sole proprietorship to wholly owned Target Corporation. Three days after this transaction, purportedly in a Type C reorganization, Target transfers all its assets to Acquiring Corporation in exchange for Acquiring stock. Subsequently, Target liquidates and distributes the Acquiring stock to Jody. After the liquidation, Jody owns 15% of the Acquiring stock. The IRS might collapse the two steps (the Sec. 351 asset transfer to Target and the Type C asset-for-stock reorganization) into a single transaction: an asset transfer by Jody to Acquiring. It might claim that the Sec. 351 requirements have not been met because Jody does not own at least 80% of the Acquiring stock immediately after the transfer. Furthermore, it might rule that, because Jody owns only 15% of Acquiring stock, Jody must recognize gain or loss on the asset transfer.[83] ◀

---

81 Reg. Secs. 1.368-1(d)(4) and -1(d)(5), Ex. (2).

82 *Evelyn F. Gregory v. Helvering*, 14 AFTR 1191, 35-1 USTC ¶9043 (USSC, 1935). Other Sec. 355 requirements, such as not constituting a device for distributing of E&P, probably were not met in this case.

83 Rev. Rul. 70-140, 1970-1 C.B. 73.

TAX ATTRIBUTES

Under Sec. 381(a), the target or transferor corporation's tax attributes (e.g., loss or tax credit carryovers) are inherited by the acquiring or transferee corporation in certain types of reorganizations. Sections 269, 382, 383, and 384, however, restrict the taxpayer's ability to use certain corporate tax attributes (e.g., NOL carryovers) following the acquisition of a loss corporation's stock or assets.

OBJECTIVE 8

Explain what happens to tax attributes in a reorganization

ASSUMPTION OF TAX ATTRIBUTES

In Type A, C, acquisitive D, F, and acquisitive G reorganizations, the acquiring corporation obtains both the target corporation's tax attributes and assets. The tax attributes do not change hands in either the Type B or Type E reorganization because assets are not transferred from one corporation to another. Even though assets are transferred in divisive Type D and G reorganizations, the only tax attribute allocated to the transferee corporation is a pro rata portion of the transferor corporation's E&P.[84]

KEY POINT

An often-cited advantage to a nontaxable asset reorganization over a taxable acquisition is that the tax attributes (e.g., NOLs and net capital losses) carry over to the acquiring corporation.

In acquisitive reorganizations, tax attributes carried over under Sec. 381(c) include

- Net operating losses
- Capital losses
- Earnings and profits (E&P)
- General business credits
- Inventory methods

KEY POINT

The thrust of Sec. 381, as it relates to NOLs, is to allow Target's NOL carryovers to offset only the post-acquisition income of the acquiring corporation.

The target corporation's NOL carryover is determined as of the acquisition date and carries over to tax years ending after such date. Generally, the acquisition date for a reorganization is that on which the transferor or target corporation transfers the assets. When losses carryover from more than one tax year, the loss from the earliest tax year is used first. NOLs from the period following the acquisition date cannot be carried back by the acquiring corporation to offset target corporation profits earned in tax years preceding the acquisition date.[85]

EXAMPLE C:7-35 ▶ Target Corporation merges into Acquiring Corporation at the close of business on June 30, 2007. Both corporations use the calendar year as their tax year. At the beginning of 2007, Target reports a $200,000 NOL carryover from 2006. Target must file a final tax return for the period January 1, 2007, through June 30, 2007. Target reports $60,000 of taxable income (before any NOL deductions) on its tax return for the short period. Target's taxable income for the January 1 through June 30, 2007 period reduces its NOL carryover to $140,000 ($200,000 − $60,000). Acquiring assumes this carryover. ◀

Section 381(c) restricts the acquiring corporation's use of the NOL carryover in its first tax year ending after the acquisition date. The NOL deduction is limited to the portion of the acquiring corporation's taxable income allocable on a daily basis to the post-acquisition period.

EXAMPLE C:7-36 ▶ Assume the same facts as in Example C:7-35 except Acquiring's accountants determine that its taxable income is $146,000, earned evenly throughout 2007. Acquiring can use Target's NOL carryover to offset $73,600 [(184 ÷ 365) × $146,000] of its taxable income attributable to the 184 days in the July 1 through December 31, 2007 post-acquisition period. The remaining NOL of $66,400 ($140,000 − $73,600) carries forward to offset Acquiring's taxable income in 2008. Both the pre- and post-acquisition portions of 2007 are treated as full tax years for loss carryover purposes. ◀

OBJECTIVE 9

Explain restrictions on the use of NOL carryovers following an acquisition

LIMITATION ON USE OF TAX ATTRIBUTES

Sections 382 and 269 discourage taxpayers from purchasing the assets or stock of a corporation having loss carryovers (known as the **loss corporation**) primarily to acquire the corporation's tax attributes. Similarly, Secs. 382 and 269 discourage a loss corporation

[84] Reg. Sec. 1.312-10.

[85] Special rules apply to Type F reorganizations. Because only a change in form or identity involving a single corporation occurs in such a transaction, NOLs incurred following the acquisition date can be carried back in a Type F reorganization to offset profits earned in pre-acquisition tax years.

from acquiring assets or stock of a profitable corporation primarily to use its carryovers. Section 383 imposes similar restrictions on acquisitions intended to facilitate the use of capital loss and tax credit carryovers. Additionally, Sec. 384 restricts use of pre-acquisition losses to offset built-in gains.

SECTION 382. The Sec. 382 NOL restrictions are triggered when a substantial change in the stock ownership of the loss corporation occurs.

TYPICAL MISCONCEPTION

To create an ownership change, the 5% shareholders must increase their stock ownership by more than 50 *percentage points*. For example, if shareholder A increases her stock ownership from 10% to 20%, this increase is not an ownership change even though it doubles A's ownership.

Stock Ownership Change. A substantial change in stock ownership occurs where

- ▶ Stock ownership of any person(s) owning 5% or more of a corporation's stock has changed or a reorganization (other than a divisive Type D or G reorganization or a Type F reorganization) has occurred *and*
- ▶ The percentage of stock in the new loss corporation owned by one or more 5% shareholders has increased by more than 50 percentage points over the lowest percentage of stock in the old loss corporation owned by such shareholder(s) at any time during the preceding three-year (or shorter) "testing" period.[86]

The 5% shareholder test is based on the value of the loss corporation's stock. Nonvoting preferred stock is excluded from this ownership calculation.

An **old loss corporation** is any corporation entitled to use an NOL carryover or that has an NOL for the tax year in which the ownership change occurs, and that undergoes the requisite stock ownership change. A **new loss corporation** is any corporation entitled to use an NOL carryover after the stock ownership change.[87] The old and new loss corporations are the same in most taxable acquisitions (e.g., the purchase of a loss corporation's stock by a new shareholder group). The old and new loss corporations differ, however, in many acquisitive reorganizations (e.g., a merger transaction where an unprofitable target [old loss] corporation merges into the acquiring [new loss] corporation).

KEY POINT

One of the burdensome aspects of Sec. 382 is that each time the stock ownership of a 5% shareholder changes, all 5% shareholders must be tested at that date to see whether an ownership change has occurred.

Ownership changes are tested any time a transaction affects a person owning 5% or more of the stock either before or after the change. Such change may occur because a stock transaction involving a 5% shareholder or a person who does not own a 5% interest in the loss corporation affects the size of the stock interest owned by another 5% shareholder (i.e., a stock redemption). When applying the 5% rule, all shareholders owning less than 5% of the loss corporation's stock are considered to be a single shareholder.

EXAMPLE C:7-37 ▶ Stock in Spencer Corporation is publicly traded with no single individual owning more than 5% of its outstanding shares. In recent years, Spencer has incurred a series of NOLs. On July 3, Barry acquires 80% of Spencer's single class of stock for cash. Barry owned none of the Spencer stock before the acquisition. A substantial stock ownership change has occurred because, as a result of a stock purchase, a 5% shareholder (Barry) now owns 80 percentage points more stock than the 0% he owned at any time during the three-year testing period. Because Spencer incurred the losses prior to the ownership change and can use the NOLs after the change, it is considered to be both the old and new loss corporation. Consequently, Spencer's NOLs are subject to the Sec. 382 limitations. ◀

In many acquisitive reorganizations, the Sec. 382 stock ownership test applies first with respect to the old loss (or target) corporation and then with respect to the new loss (or acquiring) corporation.

EXAMPLE C:7-38 ▶ Target Corporation has a single class of stock. None of its 300 shareholders owns more than 5% of the outstanding shares. Target has incurred substantial NOLs in recent years. Pursuant to a merger agreement, Target merges into Jackson Corporation. Jackson also has a single class of stock, and none of its 500 shareholders owns more than 5% of its outstanding shares, or any of the Jackson shares before the merger. After the merger, Target shareholders own 40% of the

[86] Sec. 382(g). Special rules permit a testing period of less than three years for applying the 50-percentage-point ownership change rule. One such situation is where a recent change in stock ownership involving a 5% shareholder has occurred. In such case, the testing period begins on the date of the earlier ownership change.

[87] Secs. 382(k)(1)–(3).

Jackson stock. For purposes of applying the Sec. 382 stock ownership test, the stockholdings of all Jackson shareholders are aggregated. The Sec. 382 rules limit the use of Target NOL carryovers because Jackson shareholders owned none of the old loss corporation (Target) stock before the reorganization and own 60% of the new loss corporation (Jackson) stock immediately after the reorganization. ◀

Divisive Type D and G reorganizations or Type F reorganizations may be subject to the Sec. 382 limitations if the underlying transactions result in a more than 50 percentage point increase in the transferor corporation's stock ownership.

TYPICAL MISCONCEPTION

Section 382 does not necessarily disallow NOLs. It merely limits the amount of NOL carryovers the new loss corporation can use on an annual basis.

Loss Limitation. The Sec. 382 loss limitation for any tax year ending after the stock ownership change equals the value of the old loss corporation's stock (including nonvoting preferred) immediately before the ownership change multiplied by the long-term tax-exempt federal rate.[88] The IRS publishes the long-term tax-exempt federal rate, which is the highest of the adjusted federal long-term tax-exempt rates applicable in any month during the three-calendar-month period ending with the month in which the stock ownership change occurs.[89]

ADDITIONAL COMMENT

The new loss corporation's use of the old loss corporation's NOLs is limited annually to the FMV of the old loss corporation multiplied by the long-term tax-exempt federal rate because this limitation approximates the rate at which the old loss corporation could have used the NOLs.

A new loss corporation first claims its current year deductions. It then deducts any NOLs from the old loss corporation (pre-change tax years) not limited by Sec. 382. If the NOL carryovers from the old loss corporation exceed the Sec. 382 loss limitation, the unused portion is deferred until the following year, provided the 20-year NOL carryforward period has not expired. If the Sec. 382 loss limitation exceeds the new loss corporation's taxable income for the current year, the unused loss portion carries forward and increases the Sec. 382 loss limitation in the following year.[90] Finally, any of its NOL and other carryovers from post-change taxable years are deducted. A new loss corporation that discontinues the business of the old loss corporation throughout the two-year period beginning on the stock ownership change date must use a zero Sec. 382 limitation for any post-change year. This zero limitation, in effect, disallows the use of the NOL carryovers.[91]

EXAMPLE C:7-39 ▶

Peter purchased all the stock in Taylor Corporation (the old and new loss corporation) from Karl at the close of business on December 31, 2006. Taylor manufactures brooms and has a $1 million NOL carryover from 2006. Taylor continues to manufacture brooms after Peter's acquisition and in 2007 earns $300,000 of taxable income. The value of the Taylor stock immediately before the acquisition is $3.5 million. Assume the applicable long-term tax-exempt federal rate is 5%. The requisite stock ownership change has occurred because Peter has increased his stock ownership from zero during the three-year testing period to 100% immediately after the acquisition. The Sec. 382 loss limitation for 2007 is $175,000 ($3,500,000 × 0.05). Thus, Taylor can claim a $175,000 NOL deduction in 2007, thereby reducing its taxable income to $125,000. The remaining $825,000 ($1,000,000 − $175,000) NOL carries over to 2008 and later years, subject to the Sec. 382 limitation in those years. ◀

KEY POINT

If the old loss corporation is a very large corporation relative to its NOL carryovers, Sec. 382 will not be a real obstacle in the use of the NOLs by the new loss corporation. Only when the old loss corporation has a small FMV relative to its NOL carryovers does Sec. 382 present a major obstacle.

ADDITIONAL COMMENT

Although the legislative intent of Sec. 382 has not been seriously opposed, the complexity of the statute with its accompanying Treasury Regulations is of concern to many tax practitioners.

Special rules apply to the loss corporation for the year in which the stock ownership change occurs. Taxable income earned before the change is not subject to the Sec. 382 limitation. Taxable income earned after the change, however, is subject to the limitation. Allocation of income earned during the tax year to the time periods before and after the stock ownership change is based on the number of days in each of the two time periods according to procedures similar to those for allocating tax attributes under Sec. 381.

Old loss corporation NOLs incurred before the date of the stock ownership change are limited by Sec. 382. These include NOLs incurred in tax years ending before the date of change plus the pre-change portion of the NOL for the tax year that includes the date of change. Allocation of an NOL for the tax year that includes the date of change is based on the number of days before and after the change.[92]

---

[88] Sec. 382(b)(1).
[89] Sec. 382(f).
[90] Sec. 382(b)(2).
[91] Sec. 382(c). Failure to continue the old loss corporation's business enterprise also may cause a corporate reorganization to lose its nontaxable status.
[92] Sec. 382(b)(3).

SECTION 383. Section 383 restricts the use of tax credit and capital loss carryovers when stock ownership changes under Sec. 382 occur. The same restrictions that apply to NOLs apply to the general business credit, the minimum tax credit, and the foreign tax credit.

SECTION 384. Section 384 restricts the use of pre-acquisition losses of either the acquiring or target corporation (the loss corporation) to offset built-in gains recognized by another corporation (the gain corporation) during the five-year post-acquisition recognition period. Such gains may be offset only by pre-acquisition losses of the gain corporation. This limitation applies if a corporation acquires either a controlling stock interest or the assets of another corporation and either corporation is a gain corporation.

ADDITIONAL COMMENT

Section 269 represents the IRS's oldest and broadest weapon in dealing with trafficking in NOLs. However, because of the subjectivity of the statute, Secs. 382, 383, and 384 have turned out to be the IRS's main statutory weapons in this area.

SECTION 269. Section 269 applies where control of a corporation is obtained and the principal purpose of the transaction is "the evasion or avoidance of federal income tax by securing the benefit of a deduction" or credit that otherwise would not be available. The IRC defines control as 50% of the voting power or 50% of the value of the outstanding stock. The IRS can use this provision to disallow a loss or credit carryover in situations where Sec. 382 does not apply.

TAX PLANNING CONSIDERATIONS

WHY USE A REORGANIZATION INSTEAD OF A TAXABLE TRANSACTION?

Choosing between a taxable and nontaxable transaction can be difficult. The advantages and disadvantages of a nontaxable reorganization are important to both the buyer and the seller. Depending on their relative importance, they may serve as points of negotiation and compromise in the effort to structure the transaction.

ETHICAL POINT

The choice between making an acquisition a taxable or nontaxable transaction involves a large number of considerations for both the buyer and the seller. All parties must examine the tax, financial, and legal considerations with the assistance of their own experts. Because what may be good for the buyer may not be good for the seller in an acquisition, it probably is not a good idea for both parties to save money by using the same experts.

From the target shareholders' perspective, several factors are relevant. First, a nontaxable reorganization affords shareholders a tax deferral except to the extent they receive boot. This tax deferral may permit a shareholder to preserve a higher percentage of his or her capital investment than would be possible in a taxable acquisition. Second, a taxable transaction permits the target corporation shareholders to convert their former equity interests into liquid assets (e.g., when they receive cash or property other than stock or securities of the acquiring corporation). These liquid assets can be invested however the shareholder chooses.

In a reorganization, the shareholder must obtain a proprietary interest in the acquiring corporation. The future success of the acquiring corporation is likely to enhance the value of this interest. Conversely, if the acquiring corporation encounters financial difficulties, the value of the shareholder's investment may diminish. Third, losses realized in a reorganization cannot be recognized. A taxable transaction permits the immediate recognition of realized losses. Fourth, gains recognized in a reorganization are taxed as dividends if the distribution of boot is equivalent to a dividend. Taxable transactions generally result in the shareholder's recognizing capital gains. This difference is not as important now as in the past because both capital gains and dividend income are taxed at a maximum 15% rate. Finally, a taxable transaction permits the shareholder to step-up the basis of stock and securities received to their FMV. A nontaxable transaction, however, results in a substituted basis.

SELF-STUDY QUESTION

Is a nontaxable reorganization always preferable to a taxable acquisition?

ANSWER

No. The determination of what form an acquisition should take involves resolving a myriad of issues relating to the parties involved in the transaction. A number of these issues are discussed in this section.

From the transferor corporation's point of view, a reorganization permits the exchange of assets without gain recognition. In addition, depreciation is not recaptured in a reorganization. Instead, the recapture potential shifts to the acquiring corporation.

From the acquiring corporation's point of view, a reorganization permits an acquisition without the expenditure of substantial amounts of cash or securities. Because the target corporation shareholders do not recognize gain unless they receive boot, they may be

TYPICAL MISCONCEPTION

When a plan for an acquisition is developed, the tax consequences are only one of many considerations the parties must address. Often, the form of the final acquisition plan will not be optimal from a tax perspective because other factors were deemed more important.

willing to accept a lower sales price than would otherwise be the case in a taxable acquisition. In a reorganization, the transferee takes the same property basis as the transferor's. The inability to step-up basis to cost or FMV reduces the attractiveness of a reorganization and could lower the price the acquiror is willing to pay.

In a reorganization, the acquiror obtains the benefits of NOL, tax credit, and other carryovers from the target corporation (subject to limitations). In a taxable transaction, such tax attributes are not inherited by the buyer although they can be used to reduce the seller's tax cost in the sale.

AVOIDING THE REORGANIZATION PROVISIONS

TYPICAL MISCONCEPTION

The reorganization provisions are not elective. If a transaction qualifies as a Sec. 368 reorganization, it must be treated as such. It usually is not difficult to bust a nontaxable reorganization if the desire is for a taxable acquisition.

An acquisition can be converted from a nontaxable reorganization into a taxable transaction if the restrictions on the use of consideration incidental to a particular type of reorganization are violated. For example, the Type B reorganization rules can be skirted if the acquiring corporation obtains target corporation stock using a combination of acquiring corporation stock and cash. Because this structure does not meet the solely-for-voting-stock requirement, the transaction is taxable to the selling shareholders. It also is treated as a stock purchase, thereby permitting the acquiring corporation to make a Sec. 338 election and step-up the basis in target corporation assets.

EXAMPLE C:7-40 ▶ Acquiring Corporation offers to exchange one share of its common stock (valued at $40) plus $20 cash for each share of Target Corporation's single class of common stock. All of Target's shareholders accept the offer and exchange a total of 2,000 Target shares for 2,000 Acquiring shares and $40,000 cash. At the time of the exchange, Target's assets have a $35,000 adjusted basis and a $110,000 FMV. Target recognizes no gain or loss in the exchange. The basis of its assets remains $35,000 unless Acquiring makes a Sec. 338 election. Target's shareholders recognize gain or loss in the exchange whether or not Acquiring makes a Sec. 338 election. ◀

COMPLIANCE AND PROCEDURAL CONSIDERATIONS

SECTION 338 ELECTION

The acquiring corporation makes a Sec. 338 election by filing Form 8023 (Corporate Qualified Stock Purchase Election) with the IRS. This election must be made by the fifteenth day of the ninth month beginning after the month of the acquisition date. The required information about the acquiring corporation, the target corporation, and the election is set forth in Reg. Sec. 1.338-1(d).

PLAN OF REORGANIZATION

Nonrecognition of gain by a transferor corporation in an asset acquisition (Sec. 361) or a shareholder in a stock acquisition (Sec. 354) requires that the acquisition be pursuant to a plan of reorganization. A **plan of reorganization** is a consummated transaction specifically defined as a reorganization. Nonrecognition of gain or loss is limited to exchanges or distributions that are a direct part of a reorganization undertaken to continue the business of a corporation that is a party to a reorganization.[93] Although a written plan is not required, it would be prudent for all parties to the reorganization to reduce the plan to writing either as a communication to the shareholders, a document in the corporate records, or a written agreement between the parties. The transaction generally is taxable if a plan of reorganization does not exist or if a transfer or distribution is not pursuant to a plan.[94]

[93] Reg. Sec. 1.368-2(g).

[94] *A. T. Evans*, 30 B.T.A. 746 (1934), *acq.* XIII-2 C.B. 7; and *William Hewitt*, 19 B.T.A. 771 (1930).

PARTY TO A REORGANIZATION

Under Secs. 354 and 361, a shareholder or a transferor must be a party to a reorganization for the asset or stock transfer to be nontaxable. Section 368(b) includes as a party to a reorganization "any corporation resulting from a reorganization, and both corporations involved in a reorganization where one corporation acquires the stock or assets of a second corporation." In a triangular reorganization, the corporation controlling the acquiring corporation and whose stock is used to effect the reorganization also is a party to the reorganization.

RULING REQUESTS

Before proceeding with an acquisition or disposition, some taxpayers request an advance ruling from the IRS on the tax consequences of the transaction. They generally do so because of the complexity of tax reorganization law and the substantial dollar amounts involved in the transaction. An after-the-fact determination by the IRS or the courts that a completed transaction is taxable could be costly to all parties. The IRS will issue an advance ruling only for reorganizations that conform to the guidelines of Rev. Proc. 77-37 and other IRS pronouncements. It will not issue an advance ruling for a reorganization if the consequences are adequately addressed in the IRC, Treasury Regulations, Supreme Court decisions, tax treaties, revenue rulings, revenue procedures, notices, or other IRS pronouncements.[95] Because of IRS policy not to issue these so-called "comfort rulings," many taxpayers instead seek opinion letters from tax counsel.

FINANCIAL STATEMENT IMPLICATIONS

OBJECTIVE 10

Understand the financial statement implications of corporate acquisitions

Under SFAS No. 141, an acquiring corporation must use the purchase method for financial statement purposes whether the business combination is a taxable purchase or a nontaxable reorganization. Under SFAS No. 109, however, differences occur in the recording of deferred tax accounts and the treatment of goodwill. Also, a stock acquisition has its own particularities because recording the transaction occurs in the process of consolidating the financial statements of the acquiring parent and the acquired subsidiary.

For subsequent illustrations, assume Theta Corporation (the target corporation) has the following balance sheet of identified assets and liabilities, where the tax basis and book basis are the same. Thus, prior to the acquisition, Theta has no temporary differences or deferred tax accounts.

	FMV	*Basis*	*Difference*
Accounts receivable	$ 12,000	$ 12,000	$ -0-
Inventory	30,000	25,000	5,000
Plant and equipment	100,000	75,000	25,000
Land	50,000	40,000	10,000
Total assets	$192,000	$152,000	$40,000
Liabilities	$ 20,000	$ 20,000	
Equity	172,000	132,000	
Total liabilities and equity	$192,000	$152,000	

TAXABLE ASSET ACQUISTION

In a taxable purchase, the acquiring corporation's tax basis in the purchased assets likely will be the same as the recorded book basis. If so, deferred tax liabilities and assets will not arise as a result of the business combination. Also, if tax goodwill and book goodwill

[95] 1977-2 C.B. 568. In Rev. Proc. 2007-1, 2007-1, I.R.B. 1, and Rev. Proc. 2007-3, 2007-1 I.R.B. 108.

are equal, future amortization of tax goodwill under Sec. 197 will create temporary differences because book goodwill can be expensed under SFAS No. 142 only if impaired. (If tax and book goodwill differ in a taxable business combination, the financial statement treatment gets complicated beyond the scope of this textbook.)

For example: At the beginning of the current year, Alpha Corporation purchases all of Theta Corporation's assets for $207,000 cash and does not assume Theta's liabilities. For both book and tax purposes, each asset gets a FMV allocation of this purchase price with the remainder allocated to goodwill. Because the book and tax bases are equal, Alpha records no deferred tax accounts. Accordingly, Alpha makes the following book journal entry to record the purchase:

Accounts receivable	12,000	
Inventory	30,000	
Plant and equipment	100,000	
Land	50,000	
Goodwill	15,000	
Cash		207,000

In the acquisition year, Alpha deducts $1,000 of goodwill amortization for tax purposes but takes no impairment loss for book purposes. Assuming no other book-tax differences, $150,000 of pretax book income, and a 35% tax rate, Alpha realizes the following results for this year.

Net income before FIT expense	$150,000
Goodwill amortization (temporary difference)	(1,000)
Taxable income	$149,000

Thus, Alpha's federal income tax expense is $52,500 ($150,000 × 0.35), and its federal tax liability is $52,150 ($149,000 × 0.35). Also, Alpha records a deferred tax liability of $350 ($1,000 × 0.35). Accordingly, Alpha makes the following book journal entry:

Federal income tax expense	52,500	
Deferred tax liability		350
Federal income taxes payable		51,150

The deferred tax liability will increase by the same amount each year of the 15-year tax amortization period and will reverse if and when Alpha takes an impairment loss on the book goodwill.

NONTAXABLE ASSET ACQUISTION

In a nontaxable business combination, such as a Type A or Type C reorganization, the bases recorded for financial statement purposes differ from the carryover tax bases of acquired assets. For business combinations, SFAS No. 109 prescribes that the acquiring corporation recognize a deferred tax asset or liability for differences between the assigned financial statement values and the tax bases of the transferred assets and liabilities. Goodwill for which the corporation is not allowed an amortization deduction for tax purposes, the usual situation in a nontaxable acquisition, does not give rise to a temporary difference.

For example: At the beginning of the current year, Alpha Corporation acquires all of Theta's assets and assumes Theta's liabilities in a Type A merger. In addition to assuming the liabilities, Alpha issues $187,000 worth of its preferred stock as consideration, for a total consideration of $207,000. For tax purposes, Alpha takes a carryover basis in each asset, but for financial statement purposes, Alpha records each asset at its FMV. Assuming a 35% corporate tax rate, the $40,000 difference between the total book value and total tax basis creates a $14,000 ($40,000 × 0.35) deferred tax liability. Thus, aside from $15,000 of goodwill from the excess of consideration paid ($207,000) over the FMV of identified assets ($192,000), Alpha records $14,000 of additional goodwill. Accordingly, Alpha makes the following book journal entry to record the acquisition:

Accounts receivable	12,000	
Inventory	30,000	
Plant and equipment	100,000	
Land	50,000	
Goodwill	29,000	
Deferred tax liability		14,000
Liabilities		20,000
Preferred stock		187,000

In the acquisition year, Alpha's book net income before federal income tax (FIT) expense is $150,000, which includes $12,000 of book depreciation on the acquired plant and equipment and $2,800 of book goodwill impairment. For tax purposes, Alpha recognizes a $5,000 gain on the sale of the acquired inventory and takes $9,000 of depreciation on the acquired plant and equipment, but it amortizes no goodwill. The difference between the $2,800 book goodwill impairment and the zero tax goodwill amortization produces a permanent difference. The other book-tax differences are temporary, resulting in the following net income to taxable income reconciliation:

Net income before FIT expense	$150,000
Goodwill (permanent difference)	2,800
Net income after permanent differences	$152,800
Inventory sale (temporary difference)	5,000
Depreciation (temporary difference)	3,000
Taxable income	$160,800

Thus, assuming a 35% tax rate, Alpha's federal income tax expense is $53,480 ($152,800 × 0.35), and its federal tax liability is $56,280 ($160,800 × 0.35). Also, Alpha reduces its deferred tax liability by $2,800 ($8,000 × 0.35). Accordingly, Alpha makes the following book journal entry:

Federal income tax expense	53,480	
Deferred tax liability	2,800	
Federal income taxes payable		56,280

STOCK ACQUISTION

In a stock acquisition, the target corporation remains intact as a subsidiary of the acquiring corporation. The adjustments necessary to implement SFAS No. 141 purchase accounting rules and SFAS No. 109 income tax accounting rules occur when the corporations prepare their consolidated financial statements.

For example: At the beginning of the current year, Alpha Corporation acquires 100% of Theta's stock for $187,000 cash. As a result, Theta's shareholders recognize gain or loss on their sale of the stock. Alpha makes the following book journal entry to record the purchase:

Investment in Theta Corporation	187,000	
Cash		187,000

If Alpha instead acquired the Theta stock in a Type B reorganization using $187,000 of common voting stock, Alpha would have made a similar journal entry with the credit being to common stock rather than cash. In the consolidating journal entry for either type acquisition, Alpha eliminates the investment account, adjusts Theta's tax bases to book value, and records the necessary deferred accounts as follows:

Inventory	5,000	
Plant and equipment	25,000	
Land	10,000	
Goodwill	29,000	
Theta's equity	132,000	
Deferred tax liability		14,000
Investment in Theta Corporation		187,000

PRICING THE ACQUISITION

In the above examples, the numerical amount of consideration is the same for the taxable and nontaxable asset acquisitions ($207,000). Economically, however, they are not comparable because, in the taxable purchase, the seller bears the tax burden. In the nontaxable asset acquisition, however, the acquiring corporation assumes the tax burden because it pays the same amount of consideration for assets having a low tax basis and a built-in gain. Consequently, it incurs the tax liability when it sells or depreciates the low basis assets. To shift the tax burden back to the seller in a nontaxable acquisition, the acquiring corporation might want to negotiate a reduced price for the assets. Similarly in either a taxable or nontaxable stock acquisition, the acquiring corporation obtains a subsidiary with low basis assets. Hence, it might want to negotiate a stock price that reflects that built-in tax liability.

NET OPERATING LOSSES

If the target corporation has net operation loss carryovers (NOLs), the acquiring corporation must establish a deferred tax asset along with a valuation allowance if necessary. See Chapter C:3 for a discussion of the valuation allowance as well as a general discussion of the financial implications of federal income taxes.

PROBLEM MATERIALS

DISCUSSION QUESTIONS

C:7-1 From the standpoint of Target Corporation's shareholders, what is the advantage of a taxable stock acquisition by Purchaser Corporation compared to Purchaser acquiring all of Target's assets in a taxable transaction followed by a liquidating distribution from Target to its shareholders?

C:7-2 What tax advantages exist for the buyer when he or she acquires the assets of a corporation in a taxable transaction? For the seller when he or she exchanges stock in a taxable transaction? In a nontaxable transaction?

C:7-3 What tax and nontax advantages and disadvantages accrue when an acquiring corporation purchases all of a target corporation's stock for cash and subsequently liquidates the target corporation?

C:7-4 Why might a parent corporation make a Sec. 338 election after acquiring a target corporation's stock? When would such an election not be advisable?

C:7-5 Explain the following items related to a Sec. 338 election:

a. The rule used to determine the time period within which the Sec. 338 stock purchase(s) can be made.
b. The types of stock acquisitions that are counted and not counted when determining whether a qualified stock purchase has occurred.
c. The method for determining the sale price for target corporation assets.
d. The method for determining the total basis for target corporation assets.
e. The effect of the deemed sale on the target corporation's tax attributes.
f. The date by which the Sec. 338 election must be made.
g. Assuming goodwill results from a Sec. 338 election, can the goodwill be amortized? If so, over what period does amortization occur?

C:7-6 a. Holt Corporation acquires all the stock of Star Corporation and makes a timely Sec. 338 election. The adjusted grossed-up basis of the Star stock is $2.5 million. The FMV of tangible assets on Star's balance sheet is $1.8 million. Explain to Holt's president how the new bases in Star's individual assets are determined.
b. How would your answer change if instead the adjusted grossed-up basis were $1.4 million?

C:7-7 Compare the tax consequences of a taxable asset acquisition and an asset-for-stock reorganization, based on the following factors:

a. Consideration used to effect the transaction.
b. Recognition of gain or loss by the target corporation on the asset transfer.
c. Basis of property to the acquiring corporation.
d. Recognition of gain or loss when the target corporation liquidates.
e. Use and/or carryover of the target corporation's tax attributes.

C:7-8 Which of the following events that occur as part of an acquisitive reorganization require the target corporation to recognize gain? Assume in all cases that the target corporation liquidates as part of the reorganization.

a. Transfer of appreciated target corporation assets in exchange for acquiring corporation stock and short-term notes.
b. Transfer of appreciated target corporation assets in exchange for acquiring corporation stock and the assumption of the target corporation's liabilities.
c. Assume the same facts as in Part b except the amount of liabilities assumed by the acquiring corporation exceeds the adjusted basis of the target corporation's assets transferred.
d. Transfer of appreciated target corporation assets in exchange for stock and money. Target distributes the money to its shareholders.
e. Transfer of appreciated target corporation assets in exchange for stock and money. Target uses the money to pay off its liabilities.

C:7-9 A shareholder receives stock and cash in a reorganization. The shareholder recognizes a gain because of the boot (cash) received. What rules determine whether the character of the shareholder's recognized gain is dividend income or capital gain?

C:7-10 Evaluate the following statement: Individual shareholders who recognize gain as the result of receiving boot in a corporate reorganization generally prefer to report capital gain, whereas corporate shareholders generally prefer to report dividend income.

C:7-11 How is basis for nonboot stock and securities received by a shareholder determined? How is basis in boot property determined?

C:7-12 Which reorganization(s) are acquisitive transactions? Divisive transactions? Which reorganization(s) are neither acquisitive nor divisive? Which reorganization(s) can be either acquisitive or divisive?

C:7-13 Compare the type of consideration that can be used in Type A, B, and C reorganizations.

C:7-14 How does the IRS interpret the continuity of interest doctrine for a Type A reorganization?

C:7-15 How does the IRS interpret the continuity of business enterprise requirement for a Type A reorganization?

C:7-16 What are the advantages of using a Type C asset-for-stock reorganization instead of a Type A merger reorganization? The disadvantages?

C:7-17 How does the IRS interpret the "substantially all" asset requirement for a Type C reorganization?

C:7-18 Explain why an acquiring corporation might be prohibited from using cash as part of the consideration given in a Type C reorganization.

C:7-19 Some acquisitive transactions may be characterized as either a Type C or a Type D reorganization. Which reorganization provision controls in the case of an overlap?

C:7-20 What is the difference between an acquisitive Type C reorganization and an acquisitive Type D reorganization?

C:7-21 Explain the circumstances in which money and other property can be used in a Type B reorganization.

C:7-22 Acquiring Corporation purchased for cash a 5% interest in Target Corporation's stock. After buying the stock and examining Target's books, Acquiring's management wants to make a tender offer to acquire the remaining Target stock in exchange for Acquiring voting stock. Can this tender offer be accomplished as a Type B reorganization? What problems may be encountered in structuring the acquisition as a nontaxable reorganization?

C:7-23 Acquiring Corporation wants to exchange its voting common stock for all of Target Corporation's single class of stock in a tender offer. Only 85% of Target's shareholders agree to tender their shares. After the tender, what options exist for Acquiring to acquire the remaining shares as part of the reorganization? At a later date? How will a subsequent cash acquisition of the remaining outstanding shares effect the tax treatment for the tender offer?

C:7-24 Explain the structure of a triangular reorganization? What advantages would a triangular reorganization provide the acquiring corporation?

C:7-25 Compare and contrast the requirements for, and the tax treatment of, the spinoff, split-off, and split-up forms of divisive Type D reorganizations.

C:7-26 Stock in a controlled subsidiary corporation can be distributed tax-free to the distributing corporation's shareholders under Sec. 355. Explain the difference between such a distribution and a divisive Type D reorganization.

C:7-27 When is the distribution of a controlled corporation's stock or securities nontaxable to the distributing corporation's shareholders? What events trigger the recognition of gain or loss by the shareholders?

C:7-28 When does the distributing corporation recognize gain or loss on the distribution of stock or securities of a controlled corporation to its shareholders?

C:7-29 What is a recapitalization? What types of recapitalizations can take place tax-free?

C:7-30 How can a recapitalization reorganization be used to transfer voting control within a family corporation from a senior generation that is in the process of retiring to a junior generation without incurring income taxes?

C:7-31 Explain why a transaction might satisfy the letter of Sec. 368 for a reorganization yet fail to be treated as a reorganization.

C:7-32 Which types of reorganizations (acquisitive, divisive, and other) permit the carryover of tax attributes from a target or transferor corporation to an acquiring or transferee corporation?

C:7-33 What restrictions are placed on the acquisition and use of a loss corporation's tax attributes?

C:7-34 Explain why Sec. 382 will not be an obstacle to the use of NOL carryovers following a purchase transaction if the value of the old loss corporation is large relative to its NOL carryovers.

C:7-35 What is a plan of reorganization? Does such a plan need to be reduced to writing?

C:7-36 Why do some taxpayers secure an advance ruling regarding a reorganization transaction?

C:7-37 Does the receipt of a favorable advance ruling provide the taxpayer with a guarantee that the IRS will follow the ruling when auditing the completed transaction?

ISSUE IDENTIFICATION QUESTIONS

C:7-38 Rodger Powell owns all the stock in Fireside Bar and Grill Corporation in Pittsburgh. Rodger would like to sell his business and retire to sunny Florida now that he has turned 65. Karin Godfrey, a long-time bartender at Fireside, offers to purchase all the corporation's noncash assets in exchange for a 25% down payment, with the remaining 75% being paid in five equal annual installments. Interest will be charged at a market rate on the unpaid installments. Rodger plans to liquidate the corporation that has operated the Bar and Grill and have Fireside Bar and Grill distribute the installment notes and any remaining assets. What tax issues should Fireside Bar and Grill, Rodger, and Karin consider with respect to the proposed purchase?

C:7-39 Adolph Coors Co. transferred part of its assets to ACX Technologies Corporation in exchange for all of ACX's stock. The assets transfered included its aluminum unit, which makes aluminum sheet; its paper packaging unit, which makes consumer-products packaging; and its ceramic unit, which makes high-technology ceramics used in computer boards and automotive parts. The ACX Technologies stock received for the assets was distributed to the Coors shareholders. What tax issues should the parties to the divisive reorganization consider?

C:7-40 Johnson & Johnson announced that it had entered into a merger agreement with Alza Corporation, a research-based pharmaceutical company and a leader in drug delivery technologies. Alza shareholders were offered a fixed exchange ratio of 0.49 shares of Johnson & Johnson common stock for each share of Alza stock in a nontaxable reorganization. Alza had approximately 295 million shares outstanding at the time of the announcement. The boards of directors of both companies approved the merger. What tax issues were important to the two companies and to the two shareholder groups?

PROBLEMS

C:7-41 ***Qualified Stock Purchase.*** Acquiring Corporation purchased 20% of Target Corporation's stock on each of the following dates: January 2, 2007; April 1, 2007; June 1, 2007; October 1, 2007; and December 31, 2007.

a. Has a qualified stock purchase occurred? When must Acquiring make an election to have the stock purchase treated as an asset acquisition under Sec. 338?

b. How would your answer to Part a change if instead the purchase dates were January 1, 2007; April 1, 2007; September 2, 2007; January 3, 2008; and April 15, 2008?

c. If either Part a or b fails to be a qualified stock purchase, what is the latest date on which Acquiring can make the final stock purchase needed to qualify for a Sec. 338 election?

C:7-42 ***Sec. 338 Election.*** Acquiring Corporation purchases 20% of Target Corporation stock from Milt on August 10, 2007. Acquiring purchases an additional 30% of the stock from Nick on November 15, 2007. Acquiring purchases the remaining 50% of the Target stock from Phil on April 10, 2008. The total price paid for the stock is $1.9 million. Target's balance sheet on April 10, 2008, shows assets with a $2.5 million FMV, a $1.6 million adjusted basis, and $500,000 in liabilities.

a. What is the acquisition date for the Target stock for Sec. 338 purposes? By what date must Acquiring make the Sec. 338 election?

b. If Acquiring makes a Sec. 338 election, what is the aggregate deemed sale price for the assets?
c. What is the total basis of the assets following the deemed sale, assuming a 34% corporate tax rate?
d. How does the tax liability attributable to the deemed sale affect the price Acquiring should be willing to pay for the Target stock?
e. What happens to Target's tax attributes following the deemed sale?

C:7-43 *Sec. 338 Election.* Gator Corporation is considering the acquisition of Bulldog Corporation's stock in exchange for cash. Two options are being considered: (1) Gator purchases the assets from Bulldog for $1.4 million or (2) Gator purchases the Bulldog stock for $1 million and makes a Sec. 338 election shortly after the stock purchase. Bulldog has no NOL or capital loss carryovers. Bulldog's balance sheet is presented below.

Assets	*Adjusted Basis*	*FMV*	*Liabilities and Equity*	*Amount*
Cash	$100,000	$ 100,000	Short-term debt	$ 200,000
Marketable securities	140,000	200,000	Long-term debt	200,000
Accounts receivable	100,000	100,000	Paid-in capital	300,000
Inventory (FIFO)	$100,000	$ 150,000	Retained earnings	$ 700,000
Plant and equipment	200,000	500,000		
Intangibles	–0–	350,000		
Total	$640,000	$1,400,000	Total	$1,400,000

a. What advantages would accrue to Gator if it purchases the assets directly? What disadvantages would accrue to Bulldog if it sells the assets and then liquidates?
b. What advantages would accrue to Gator if it purchases the Bulldog stock for cash and subsequently makes a Sec. 338 election? What advantage would accrue to Bulldog if its shareholders sell the Bulldog stock?
c. How would your answers change if Bulldog had incurred $250,000 of NOLs in the current year that it cannot carry back in full due to low taxable income in the preceding two years?

C:7-44 *Sec. 338 Basis Allocation.* Apache Corporation purchases all of Target Corporation's stock for $300,000 cash. Apache makes a timely Sec. 338 election. Target's balance sheet at the close of business on the acquisition date is as follows:

Assets	*Adjusted Basis*	*FMV*	*Liabilities and Equity*	*Amount*
Cash	$ 50,000	$ 50,000	Accounts payable	$ 40,000
Marketable securities	18,000	38,000	Note to bank	60,000
Accounts receivable	66,000	65,000	Owner's equity	300,000
Inventory (FIFO)	21,000	43,000		
Equipment[a]	95,000	144,000		
Land	6,000	12,000		
Building[b]	24,000	48,000		
Total	$280,000	$400,000	Total	$400,000

[a]The equipment cost $200,000.
[b]The building is a MACRS property on which Target has claimed $10,000 of depreciation.

a. What is the aggregate deemed sale price for the Target assets (assume a 34% corporate tax rate)?
b. What amount and character of gain or loss must Target recognize on the deemed sale?
c. What is the adjusted grossed-up basis for the Target stock? What basis is allocated to each of the individual properties?
d. What happens to "old" Target's tax attributes? Do they carry over to "new" Target?
e. What amount (if any) of goodwill can Target amortize following the acquisition? Over what period and under what method does Target amortize the goodwill?

C:7-45 *Amount of Corporate Gain or Loss.* Thomas Corporation transfers all of its assets and $100,000 of its liabilities in exchange for Andrews Corporation voting common stock, having a $600,000 FMV, in a merger in which Thomas liquidates. Thomas's basis for its assets is $475,000.

a. What is the amount of Thomas's realized and recognized gain or loss on the asset transfer?
b. What is Andrews's basis in the assets received?
c. What is the amount of Thomas's realized and recognized gain or loss when it distributes the stock to its shareholders?
d. How would your answers to Parts a–c change if Thomas's basis in the assets instead had been $750,000?
e. How would your answers to Parts a–c change if Andrews instead had exchanged $600,000 cash for Thomas assets and Thomas subsequently liquidated. Assume a 34% corporate tax rate.

C:7-46 ***Amount of Shareholder Gain or Loss.*** Silvia exchanges all her Talbot Corporation stock (acquired August 1, 2004) for $300,000 of Alpha Corporation voting common stock pursuant to Talbot's merger into Alpha. Immediately after the stock-for-stock exchange Silvia owns 25% of Alpha's 2,000 outstanding shares of stock. Silvia's adjusted basis in the Talbot stock is $200,000 before the merger.
a. What are the amount and character of Silvia's recognized gain or loss?
b. What is Silvia's basis in the Alpha stock? When does her holding period begin?
c. How would your answers to Parts a and b change if instead Silvia received Alpha common stock worth $240,000 and $60,000 cash?

C:7-47 ***Amount and Character of Shareholder Gain or Loss.*** Yong owns 100% of Target Corporation's stock having a $600,000 adjusted basis. As part of the merger of Target into Allied Corporation, Yong exchanges his Target stock for Allied common stock having a $3 million FMV and $750,000 in cash. Yong retains a 60% interest in Allied's 100,000 shares of outstanding stock immediately after the merger.
a. What are the amount and character of Yong's recognized gain?
b. What is Yong's basis in the Allied stock?
c. How would your answer to Parts a and b change if instead Yong's 60,000 Allied shares were one-third of Allied's outstanding shares?

C:7-48 ***Amount and Character of Gain Recognized.*** Springs Corporation has developed a nature park at the site of Blue Springs and has been extremely profitable. Newberry Corporation wants to merge with Springs under Florida law because Newberry wants to further develop these natural springs along with several other springs in the area. Newberry offers $650,000 of nonvoting preferred shares plus 1,000 shares of voting common (FMV of $50,000) to Springs in exchange for all of Springs' assets. As part of the merger of Springs into Newberry, Springs' sole shareholder, Mr. High, exchanges all his shares in Springs for the shares in Newberry. Immediately before this transaction, Mr. High had a $240,000 basis in his Springs shares. Before this transaction, Mr. High had no shares in Newberry, and after the transaction he owns 20% of the value of Newberry's stock.
a. Does this transaction qualify as a Type A reorganization?
b. Does Springs recognize any gain or loss on the asset sale or the exchange of shares with Mr. High?
c. Does Mr. High recognize any gain or loss? What is his basis and holding period in his Newberry shares?

C:7-49 ***Characterization of the Shareholder's Gain or Loss.*** Turbo Corporation has one million shares of common stock and 200,000 shares of nonvoting preferred stock outstanding. Pursuant to a merger agreement, Ace Corporation exchanges its common stock worth $15 million for the Turbo common stock and pays $10 million in cash for the Turbo preferred stock. Some shareholders of Turbo received only Ace common stock for their common stock, some shareholders received only cash for their preferred stock, and some shareholders received both cash and Ace common stock for their Turbo preferred and common stock, respectively. Shareholders owning approximately 10% of the Turbo common stock also owned Turbo preferred stock. The total cash received by these shareholders amounted to $1.5 million. The Turbo common stockholders end up owning 15% of the Ace stock. What is the tax treatment of the common stock and/or cash received by each of the three groups of Turbo shareholders? Assume that some Turbo shareholders realize a gain on the transaction while other shareholders realize a loss.

C:7-50 ***Requirements for a Type A Reorganization.*** Anchor Corporation plans to acquire all the assets of Tower Corporation in a merger. Tower's assets have a $5 million FMV and a $2.2 million adjusted basis. Which of the following transactions qualify as a Type A reorganization assuming Tower liquidates?

a. The assets are exchanged for $5 million of Anchor common stock.
b. The assets are exchanged for $5 million of Anchor nonvoting preferred stock.
c. The assets are exchanged for $5 million of Anchor securities.
d. The assets are exchanged for $3.5 million of Anchor nonvoting preferred stock and $1.5 million in cash.
e. The assets are exchanged for $3 million of Anchor common stock and Anchor's assumption of $2 million of Tower liabilities.
f. The assets are exchanged for $5 million in cash provided by Anchor. An "all cash" merger transaction is permitted under state law.

C:7-51 *Tax Consequences of a Merger.* Armor Corporation exchanges $1 million of its common stock and $300,000 of Armor bonds for all of Trail Corporation's outstanding stock. As part of the same transaction, Trail then merges into Armor, with Armor receiving assets having a $1.3 million FMV and an $875,000 adjusted basis. As part of the merger, Antonello exchanges his 20% interest (4,000 shares) in Trail's single class of stock, having an adjusted basis of $100,000, for $200,000 in Armor stock and $60,000 in Armor bonds. Following the reorganization, Antonello owns 5% (1,000 shares) of Armor's stock. Armor's E&P balance is $375,000.
a. What is the amount of Trail's recognized gain or loss on the asset transfer?
b. What is Armor's basis in the assets received in the exchange?
c. What are the amount and character of Antonello's recognized gain or loss?
d. What is Antonello's basis in the Armor stock? In the Armor bonds?

C:7-52 ***Requirements for a Type C Reorganization.*** Arnold Corporation plans to acquire all the assets of Turner Corporation in an asset-for-stock (Type C) reorganization. Turner's assets have a $600,000 adjusted basis and a $1 million FMV. Which of the following transactions qualify as a Type C reorganization (assuming Turner liquidates as part of the reorganization)?
a. The assets are exchanged for $800,000 of Arnold voting common stock and $200,000 of cash.
b. The assets are exchanged for $800,000 of Arnold voting common stock and $200,000 of Arnold bonds.
c. The assets are exchanged for $1 million of Arnold nonvoting preferred stock.
d. The assets are exchanged for $700,000 of Arnold voting common stock and Arnold's assumption of $300,000 of Turner's liabilities.
e. The assets are exchanged for $700,000 of Arnold voting common stock, Arnold's assumption of $200,000 of Turner's liabilities, and $100,000 in cash.

C:7-53 *Tax Consequences of a Type C Reorganization.* Ash Corporation exchanges $250,000 of its voting common stock and $50,000 of its bonds for all of Texas Corporation's assets as part of a Type C reorganization. Texas liquidates, with each of its two shareholders receiving equal amounts of the Ash stock and bonds. Barbara has a $50,000 basis in her stock, and George has a $200,000 basis in his stock. George and Barbara, who are unrelated, each own 8% of Ash's stock (5,000 shares) immediately after the reorganization. At the time of the reorganization, Texas's E&P balance is $75,000, and its assets have an adjusted basis of $225,000.
a. What is the amount of Texas's recognized gain or loss on the asset transfer? On the distribution of the stock and bonds?
b. What is Ash's basis in the assets it acquired?
c. What are the amount and character of each shareholder's recognized gain or loss?
d. What is the basis of each shareholder's Ash stock? Ash bonds?

C:7-54 *Tax Consequences of a Type C Reorganization.* Tulsa Corporation exchanges assets having a $300,000 FMV and a $175,000 adjusted basis for $250,000 of Akron Corporation voting common stock and Akron's assumption of $50,000 of Tulsa's liabilities as part of a Type C reorganization. Tulsa liquidates, with its sole shareholder, Michelle, receiving the Akron stock in exchange for her Tulsa stock having an adjusted basis of $100,000. Michelle owns 12% (2,500 shares) of Akron's stock immediately after the reorganization.
a. What is the amount of Tulsa's recognized gain or loss on the asset transfer? On the distribution of the stock?
b. What is Akron's basis in the assets it receives?
c. What effect would the transfer of Tulsa's assets to Subsidiary Corporation (a subsidiary controlled by Akron) have on the reorganization?

d. What are the amount and character of Michelle's recognized gain or loss?
e. What is Michelle's basis and holding period for her Akron stock?
f. What are the tax consequences of the transaction if Akron first transfers its stock to Akron-Sub Corporation who then acquires Tulsa's assets?

C:7-55 *Requirements for a Type B Reorganization.* Allen Corporation plans to acquire all the stock in Taylor Corporation in a stock-for-stock (Type B) reorganization. Which of the following transactions will qualify as a Type B reorganization?
a. All of Taylor's common stock is exchanged for $1 million of Allen voting preferred stock.
b. All of Taylor's common stock is exchanged for $1 million of Allen voting common stock, and $500,000 face amount of Taylor bonds are exchanged for $500,000 face amount of Allen bonds. Both bonds are trading at their par values.
c. All of Taylor's stock is exchanged for $750,000 of Allen voting common stock and $250,000 of Allen bonds.
d. All of Taylor's stock is exchanged for $1 million of Allen voting common stock, and the shareholders of Taylor end up owning less than 1% of Allen's stock.
e. Ninety percent of Taylor's stock is exchanged for $900,000 of Allen voting common stock. One shareholder who owns 10% of the Taylor stock exercises his right under state law to have his shares independently appraised and redeemed for cash by Taylor. He receives $100,000.
f. Assume the same facts as in Part d except the Allen stock is contributed to Allen-Sub Corporation. The Allen stock is exchanged by Allen-Sub for all the Taylor stock.

C:7-56 *Tax Consequences of a Type B Reorganization.* Trent Corporation's single class of stock is owned equally by Juan and Miguel, who are unrelated. Juan has a $125,000 basis in his 1,000 shares of Trent stock, and Miguel has a $300,000 basis in his Trent stock. Adams Corporation exchanges 2,500 shares of its voting common stock having a $100 per share FMV for each shareholder's Trent stock in a single transaction. Immediately after the reorganization, each shareholder owns 15% of the Adams stock.
a. What are the amount and character of each shareholder's recognized gain or loss?
b. What is each shareholder's basis in his Adams stock?
c. What is Adams's basis in the Trent stock?
d. How would your answers to Parts a–c change if Adams instead exchanged 2,000 shares of Adams common stock and $50,000 in cash for each shareholder's Trent stock?

C:7-57 *Tax Consequences of a Type B Reorganization.* Austin Corporation exchanges $1.5 million of its voting common stock for all of Travis Corporation's single class of stock. Ingrid, who owns all the Travis stock, has a $375,000 basis in her stock. Ingrid owns 25% of the 15,000 outstanding shares of Austin stock immediately after the reorganization.
a. What are the amount and character of Ingrid's recognized gain or loss?
b. What is Ingrid's basis in her Austin stock?
c. What is Austin's basis in the Travis stock?
d. What are the tax consequences for all parties to the acquisition if Austin subsequently liquidates Travis as part of the plan of reorganization?
e. As part of the reorganization, Austin exchanges $1 million of its 7% bonds for $1 million Travis 7% bonds held equally by ten private investors.

C:7-58 *Tax Consequences of a Type B Reorganization.* Ashton Corporation purchased 10% of Todd Corporation stock from Cathy for $250,000 in cash on January 30, 2006. Andrea and Bill each exchange one-half of the remaining 90% of the Todd stock for $1.2 million of Ashton voting common stock on May 30, 2007. Andrea and Bill each have a $150,000 basis in their Todd stock. Andrea and Bill each own 15% of the Ashton stock (12,000 shares) immediately after the reorganization.
a. What are the amount and character of each shareholder's recognized gain or loss?
b. What is each shareholder's basis in his or her Ashton stock?
c. What is Ashton's basis in the Todd stock?
d. How would your answer to Parts a–c change if instead Ashton had acquired the remaining Todd stock on May 30, 2006?
e. What effect would the stock acquisition have on the adjusted bases of individual assets and the tax attributes of Todd?

f. Can the Ashton-Todd corporate group file a consolidated tax return?
g. Can a Sec. 338 election be made with respect to Todd's assets?

C:7-59 *Tax Consequences of a Divisive Type D Reorganization.* Road Corporation is owned equally by four shareholders. It conducts activities in two operating divisions: the road construction division and meat packing division. To separate the two activities into corporations, Road transferred the assets and liabilities of the meat packing division (60% of Road's total net assets) to Food Corporation in exchange for all of Food's single class of stock. The assets of the meat packing division have a $2.75 million FMV and a $1.1 million adjusted basis. A total of $500,000 of liabilities are transferred to Food. The $2.25 million of Food stock (90,000 shares) is distributed ratably to each of the four shareholders.

a. What is the amount of Road's recognized gain or loss on the asset transfer? On the distribution of the Food stock?
b. What are the amount and character of each shareholder's recognized gain or loss on the distribution? (Assume each shareholder's basis in Road stock is $200,000.)
c. What is the basis of each shareholder's Road and Food stock after the reorganization? (Assume the Road stock is worth $1.5 million immediately after the distribution.)

C:7-60 *Tax Consequences of a Divisive Type D Reorganization.* Light Corporation is owned equally by two individual shareholders, Bev and Tarek. The shareholders no longer agree on how to manage Light's operations. Tarek agrees to a plan whereby $500,000 of Light's assets (having an adjusted basis of $350,000) and $100,000 of Light's liabilities are transferred to Dark Corporation in exchange for all its single class of stock (5,000 shares). Tarek will exchange all his Light common stock, having a $150,000 adjusted basis, for the $400,000 of Dark stock. Bev will continue to operate Light.

a. What is the amount of Light's recognized gain or loss on the asset transfer? On the distribution of the Dark stock?
b. What are the amount and character of Tarek's recognized gain or loss?
c. What is Tarek's basis in his Dark stock?
d. What tax attributes of Light will be allocated to Dark?

C:7-61 *Distribution of Stock: Spin-Off.* Parent Corporation has been in the business of manufacturing and selling trucks for the past eight years. Its subsidiary, Diesel Corporation, has been in the business of manufacturing and selling diesel engines for the past seven years. Parent acquired control of Diesel six years ago when it purchased 100% of its single class of stock from Large Corporation. A federal court has ordered Parent to divest itself of Diesel as the result of an antitrust judgment. Consequently, Parent distributes all its Diesel stock to its shareholders. Alan owns less than 1% of Parent's outstanding stock having a $40,000 basis. He receives 25 shares of Diesel stock having a $25,000 FMV as a result of Parent's distribution. Parent distributes no cash or other assets. Parent's E&P at the end of the year in which the spinoff occurs is $2.5 million. The Parent stock held by Alan has a $75,000 FMV immediately after the distribution.

a. What are the amount and character of the gain, loss, or income Alan must recognize as a result of Parent's distributing the Diesel stock?
b. What basis does Alan take in the Diesel stock he receives?
c. When does Alan's holding period for the Diesel stock begin?
d. What amount and character of gain or loss does Parent recognize on the distribution?
e. How would your answer to Part a change if Parent had been in the truck business for only three years before the distribution and that it had acquired the Diesel stock in a taxable transaction only two years ago?

C:7-62 *Distribution of Stock: Split-Off.* Parent Corporation has owned all 100 shares of Subsidiary Corporation common stock since 2000. Parent has been in the business of manufacturing and selling light fixtures, and Subsidiary has been in the business of manufacturing and selling light bulbs. Amy and Bill are the two equal shareholders of the Parent stock and have owned their stock since 2000. Amy's basis in her 50 shares of Parent stock is $80,000, and Bill's basis in his 50 shares of Parent stock is $60,000. On April 10, 2007, Parent distributes all 100 shares of Subsidiary stock to Bill in exchange for all his Parent stock (which is cancelled). The distribution has a bona fide business purpose. The Subsidiary stock had a $30,000 basis to Parent on the distribution date. At the end of 2007, Parent has $150,000 of E&P. Immediately after the distribution, the FMVs of the Parent and Subsidiary stocks are $3,000 and $1,000 per share, respectively.

a. What are the amount and character of the gain, loss, or income Bill must recognize as a result of Parent's distributing the Subsidiary stock?
b. What basis does Bill take in the Subsidiary stock?
c. When does Bill's holding period for the Subsidiary stock begin?
d. Assume instead that Andrew formed Subsidiary in 2003 to manufacture and sell light-bulbs. Andrew sold the Subsidiary stock to Parent for cash in 2005. How would your answer to Parts a-c change?

C:7-63 ***Distribution of Stock and Securities: Split-Off.*** Ruby Corporation has 100 shares of common stock outstanding. Fred, a shareholder of Ruby, exchanges his 25% interest in the Ruby stock for Garnet Corporation stock and securities. Ruby purchased 80% of the Garnet stock ten years ago for $25,000. At the time of the exchange, Fred has a $50,000 basis in his Ruby stock, and the stock has an $80,000 FMV. Fred receives Garnet stock that has a $60,000 FMV and Garnet securities that have a $20,000 FMV. Ruby has $50,000 of E&P. Assume that all the requirements of Sec. 355 are met except for the receipt of boot.
a. What are the amount and character of Fred's recognized gain or loss on the exchange?
b. What is Fred's basis in the Garnet stock and the Garnet securities?
c. What are the amount and character of Ruby's recognized gain or loss on the distribution?
d. When does Fred's holding period begin for the Garnet stock and the Garnet securities?
e. How would your answer to Part a change if the exchange did not meet the requirements of Sec. 355 or Sec. 356?

C:7-64 ***Distribution of Stock and Securities: Split-Up.*** Jean Corporation has two divisions—home cookware and electric home appliances. Bill and Bob Jean own all of Jean Corporation's single class of stock. Bill, the older brother, owns 70% of the Jean stock with Bob owning the remaining 30%. Bill and Bob's adjusted bases in their Jean stock investments are $700,000 and $300,000, respectively. They have owned the stock for eight years. The divisions have the following assets:

Division	*FMV Assets*	*Adjusted Basis*
Cookware	$980,000	$600,000
Home appliances	420,000	300,000

To divide the business, Jean transfers the cookware assets to Cookware Corporation in exchange for all of Cookware's stock. Jean transfers the home appliance assets to Home Appliance Corporation in exchange for all of Home Appliance's stock. Jean transfers the Cookware stock to Bill in exchange for all of his Jean stock. Jean transfers the Home Appliance stock to Bob in exchange for all of his Jean stock. Finally, Jean liquidates with its remaining cash being used to pay its liabilities.
a. What gain or loss is recognized on the transfer of the Jean assets to Cookware and Home Appliance? What basis do the two corporations take in the assets transfered?
b. What gain or loss do Bill and Bob recognize when they transfer their Jean stock for the Cookware and Home Appliance stock? What basis does each shareholder take in his or her new stock?

C:7-65 ***Requirements for a Type E Reorganization.*** Master Corporation plans a recapitalization. Explain the tax consequences of each of the following independent transactions:
a. Holders of Class A nonvoting preferred stock exchange their stock for newly issued common stock. Master paid $300,000 of cash dividends in the current year and each prior year on the preferred stock.
b. Holders of Master bonds in the amount of $3 million exchange their bonds for a similar dollar amount of preferred stock. In addition, $180,000 of unpaid interest will be paid by issuing additional Master preferred stock to the former bondholders.
c. Master 9% bonds in the amount of $3 million are called and exchanged by their holders before their maturity date for a similar dollar amount of Master 6% bonds because of a decline in the prevailing market rate of interest. In addition, Master will pay $180,000 of unpaid interest in cash.

C:7-66 ***Tax Consequences of a Type E Reorganization.*** Milan Corporation is owned by four shareholders. Andy and Bob each own 40% of the outstanding common and preferred stock. Chris and Doug each own 10% of the outstanding common and preferred stock. The shareholders want to retire the preferred stock that was issued five years ago when the corporation was in the midst of a major expansion. Retirement of the preferred stock will eliminate the need to pay annual preferred dividends. Explain the tax consequences of the following two alternatives to the shareholders:

- Milan redeems the $100 par preferred stock for its $120 call price. Each shareholder purchased his preferred stock at its par value five years ago.
- The shareholders exchange each share of the $100 par value preferred stock for $120 of additional common stock.

What nontax advantages might exist for selecting one alternative over the other?

C:7-67 ***Types of Reorganizations.*** Identify the type of each of the following reorganizations.

a. Briggs Corporation originally incorporated in Georgia but now conducts most of its business activities in Florida. The firm transfers substantially all its Georgia assets to a new Florida corporation. The Georgia entity liquidates shortly after the transfer. All "Georgia" shareholders swap their "old" Briggs stock for "new" Briggs stock giving them an ownership interest in the Florida entity.

b. Jones Corporation exchanges all $1 million of its $1,000 face amount, 6% bonds for a similar amount of new convertible bonds paying a lower interest rate.

c. Bill Smith owns 100% of Smith Corporation and James Jones owns 100% of Jones Corporation. The two corporations are combined into a single entity called Smith & Jones Corporation. Each shareholder in the two original corporations receives stock in the new combined entity in proportion to the value of his original stock holdings.

d. Dupree Corporation is in bankruptcy. The corporation works out an agreement whereby bondholders and other creditors receive Dupree notes and stock in exchange for forgiving their original claims.

C:7-68 ***Reorganization Requirements.*** Discuss the tax consequences of the following corporate reorganizations to the parties to the reorganization:

a. Adobe Corporation and Tyler Corporation merge under Florida law. Tyler shareholders receive $300,000 of Adobe common stock and $700,000 of Adobe securities for their Tyler stock.

b. Alabama Corporation exchanges $1 million of its voting common stock for all the noncash assets of Texas Corporation. The transaction meets all requirements for a Type C reorganization. Alabama then splits the acquired business into two operating divisions: meat packing and meat distribution. Alabama retains the meat packing division's assets and continues to conduct its activities but sells for cash the assets of the meat distribution division. The meat distribution division's assets constitute 40% of Texas's noncash assets.

c. Parent Corporation transfers $500,000 of investment securities to Subsidiary Corporation in exchange for all its single class of stock. The Subsidiary stock is exchanged for one-third of the stock held by each of Parent's shareholders. Six months after the reorganization, Subsidiary distributes the investment securities to its shareholders pursuant to the liquidation of Subsidiary.

C:7-69 ***Determining the Type of Reorganization Transaction.*** For each of the following transactions, indicate its reorganization type (e.g., Type A, Type B, etc.). Assume all common stock is voting stock.

a. Anderson and Brown Corporations exchange their assets for all the single class of stock of newly created Computer Corporation. Following the exchange, Anderson and Brown liquidate. The transaction satisfies Michigan corporation law requirements.

b. Price Corporation (incorporated in Texas) exchanges all its assets for all the single class of stock of Price Corporation (incorporated in Delaware). Following the exchange, Price (Texas) liquidates.

c. All of Gates Corporation's noncumulative, 10% preferred stock is exchanged for Gates common stock.

d. Hobbs Corporation exchanges its common stock for 90% of the outstanding common stock and 80% of the outstanding nonvoting preferred stock of Calvin Corporation. The remaining Calvin stock is held by about 30 individual investors.

e. Scale Corporation transfers the assets of its two operating divisions to Major and Minor Corporations in exchange for all of each corporation's single class of stock. Scale then distributes the Major and Minor stock pursuant to the liquidation of Scale.

f. Tobias Corporation has $3 million of assets and $1 million of liabilities. Andrew

Corporation exchanges $2 million of its voting common stock for all of Tobias' assets and liabilities. Tobias liquidates, and its shareholders end up owning 11% of the Andrew stock following the transaction.

g. How would your answer to Part f change (if at all) should Tobias' balance sheet indicate that liabilities constituted 90% of the corporation's capital structure and common stock the remaining 10%?

C:7-70 ***Tax Attribute Carryovers.*** Alaska Corporation exchanges $2 million of its voting common stock for all the noncash assets of Tennessee Corporation at the close of business on May 31, 2007. Tennessee uses its cash to pay off its liabilities and then liquidates. Tennessee and Alaska report the following taxable income:

Tax Year Ending	*Alaska Corp.*	*Tennessee Corp.*
December 31, 2004	($100,000)	($95,000)
December 31, 2005	60,000	20,000
December 31, 2006	70,000	(90,000)
May 31, 2007	XXX	(40,000)
December 31, 2007	73,000	XXX

a. What tax returns must Alaska and Tennessee file for 2007?

b. What amount of the NOL carryover does Alaska acquire?

c. Ignoring any implications of Sec. 382, what amount of Tennessee's NOL can Alaska use in 2007?

C:7-71 ***Sec. 382 Limitation: Purchase Transaction.*** Murray Corporation's stock is owned by about 1,000 shareholders, none of whom own more than 1% of the outstanding shares. Pursuant to a tender offer, Said purchases all the Murray stock for $7.5 million cash at the close of business on December 31, 2006. Before the acquisition, Said owned no Murray stock. Murray had incurred substantial NOLs, which at the end of 2006 totaled $1 million. Murray's taxable income is expected to be $200,000 and $600,000, respectively, for 2007 and 2008. Assuming the long-term tax-exempt federal rate is 5% and Murray continues in the same trade or business, what amount of NOLs can Murray use in 2007 and/or 2008? What amount of NOLs and Sec. 382 limitation carryover to 2009?

C:7-72 ***Sec. 382 Limitation: Nontaxable Reorganization.*** Albert Corporation is a profitable publicly traded corporation. None of its shareholders owns more than 1% of its outstanding shares. On December 31, 2006, Albert exchanges $8 million of its stock for all the stock of Turner Corporation as part of a merger. Turner is owned by Tara, who receives 15% of the Albert stock as part of the reorganization. Tara owned none of the Albert stock before the merger. Turner accumulated $2.5 million in NOL carryovers before merging into Albert. Albert expects to earn $1 million and $1.5 million in taxable income during 2007 and 2008, respectively. Assuming the long-term tax-exempt federal rate is 4.5%, what amount of NOLs can Albert use in 2007 and 2008?

COMPREHENSIVE PROBLEM

C:7-73 Sid Kess, a long-time tax client of yours, has decided to acquire the snow blower manufacturing firm owned by Richard Smith, one of his closest friends. Richard has a $200,000 adjusted basis in his Richard Smith Snow Blowers (RSSB) stock. Sid Kess Enterprises (SKE), a C corporation 100%-owned by Sid Kess, will make the acquisition. RSSB operates as a C corporation and reports the following assets and liabilities as of November 1 of the current year.

Assets	*Adj. Basis*	*FMV*
Cash	$ 200,000	$ 200,000
Inventory (LIFO)	470,000	600,000
Equipment	100,000	275,000
Building	200,000	295,000
Land	80,000	120,000
Goodwill	–0–	250,000
Total	$1,050,000	$1,740,000

Equities	Amount
Accounts payable	$ 60,000
Mortgage payable	120,000
Paid-in capital	220,000
Retained earnings	650,000
Total	$1,050,000

RSSB has claimed depreciation of $200,000 and $80,000 on the equipment and building, respectively, and has claimed no amortization on the goodwill. Retained earnings approximate RSSB's E&P. No NOL, capital loss, or credit carryovers exist at the time of the acquisition. What are the tax consequences of each alternative acquisition methods to SKE and RSSB? Assume a 34% corporate tax rate.

a. SKE acquires all the single class of RSSB stock for $1.56 million in cash. RSSB is not liquidated.
b. SKE acquires all the noncash assets of RSSB for $1.54 million in cash. RSSB is liquidated.
c. SKE acquires all the RSSB stock for $1.56 million in cash. RSSB is liquidated into SKE shortly after the acquisition.
d. SKE acquires all the RSSB stock for $1.56 million in cash. SKE makes a timely Sec. 338 election. RSSB's tax rate is 34%.
e. SKE exchanges $1.54 million of its common stock for all of RSSB's noncash assets ($1,540,000 = $1,740,000 total assets − $200,000 cash). SKE has 10,000 shares of stock outstanding with a $3 million FMV before the acquisition. RSSB liquidates as part of the transaction. RSSB uses part of the retained cash to pay off the corporation's liabilities. The remaining cash is distributed with the SKE stock in the liquidation of RSSB.

f. SKE exchanges $1.56 million of its common stock for all of Richard Smith's RSSB stock. Assume that RSSB does not liquidate. Each share of SKE stock has a $300 FMV.
g. Assume the same facts as in Part d except SKE transfers $1.56 million of its common stock to SKE-Sub. SKE-Sub serves as the acquiring corporation for the transaction and uses $1.56 million of the SKE stock to acquire RSSB's stock.
h. Assume the same facts as in Part e except SKE transfers $1.54 million of its common stock to SKE-Sub. SKE-Sub serves as the acquiring corporation for the transaction and uses $1.54 million of the SKE stock to acquire RSSB's noncash assets.

TAX STRATEGY PROBLEMS

C:7-74 Angel Macias is considering selling his business. The business (Target Corporation) has the following assets and liabilities:

Assets	Adjusted Basis	FMV
Cash	$ 400,000	$ 400,000
Securities	400,000	300,000
Inventory (LIFO)	100,000	200,000
Equipment	200,000	400,000
Building	50,000	300,000
Goodwill	–0–	200,000
Total	$1,150,000	$1,800,000

Target owes $200,000 of accounts payable and $400,000 in bank loans. No NOL carryovers or carrybacks are available. Bill Jones and Sam Smith, each of whom have a net worth exceeding $1 million, are interested in purchasing the business using their S&J Corporation as the vehicle for making the purchase. Target's management and its owners are interested in selling the business. Assume that both entities are C corporations and that they are taxed at a flat 34% rate. The individual owners are taxed at a 35% tax rate on their ordinary income and a 15% rate on their capital gains. What advice would you give Bill and Sam about acquiring the assets directly from Target, or indirectly by purchasing Target's stock from its shareholders and then liquidating Target into S&J? Bill and Sam also have expressed a concern about possible differences in the financial reporting of a nontaxable versus a taxable acquisition.

C:7-75 Tom Smith owns 100% of Alpha Corporation's single class of stock, and Alpha owns 100% of Beta Corporation's single class of stock. Alpha and Beta have filed separate tax returns for a number of years. Neither corporation has any NOL carryovers. Although Alpha and Beta have been profitable in recent years, Beta needs an infusion of additional capital from outside investors. The corporations have received a proposal from an investor, Karla Boroff, to invest $2 million in Beta to enable Beta to expand its operations and to eliminate a current working capital shortage that cannot be remedied without additional funds. Karla has imposed one constraint on her capital contribution—that Alpha and Beta become two independent entities. Alpha would continue to be completely owned by Tom, but Beta would be owned by the two individuals, Tom and Karla, with each owning 50% of Beta's stock. What strategies can you offer for separating the two companies?

CASE STUDY PROBLEMS

TAX & FINANCIAL ACCOUNTING

C:7-76 *Comparative Acquisition Forms.* Bailey Corporation owns a number of automotive parts shops. Bill Smith owns an automotive parts shop that has been in existence for 40 years and has competed with one of Bailey's locations. Bill is thinking about retirement and would like to sell his business. He has his CPA prepare a balance sheet, which he takes to John Bailey, president, who has been a long-time friend.

Assets	*Adjusted Basis*	*FMV*
Cash	$ 250,000	$ 250,000
Accounts receivable	75,000	70,000
Inventories (LIFO)	600,000	1,750,000
Equipment	200,000	250,000
Building	30,000	285,000
Land	30,000	115,000
Total	$1,185,000	$2,720,000

If Bailey makes the acquisition, it intends to operate the automotive parts shop under its own tradename in the location Bill has used for 40 years. The president has asked you to prepare a summary of the tax consequences of the following three transactions: (1) a purchase of the noncash assets using cash, (2) a purchase of the stock of Bill's corporation using cash and Bailey notes, and (3) an asset-for-stock reorganization for solely Bailey stock. Upon interviewing Bill, you obtain the following additional information: Bill's business is operated as a C corporation, with a $160,000 adjusted basis for his stock. Accounts payable of $200,000 are outstanding. The corporation has depreciated the building under the straight-line method and has claimed $100,000 in depreciation. The equipment is Sec. 1245 property for which the corporation has claimed $150,000 in depreciation. The after-tax profits for each of the last three years have exceeded $300,000, and Bill suspects that some goodwill value exists that is not shown on the balance sheet. No NOL carryovers are available from prior years.

Required: Prepare a memorandum that outlines the tax consequences of each of the three alternative acquisition transactions assuming that the anticipated cash purchase price is $2.55 million for the noncash assets and $2.6 million for the stock and that the transaction takes place in 2007. How would the acquiring corporation report each of the three alternatives for financial reporting purposes under GAAP?

C:7-77 The following advertisement appeared in *The Wall Street Journal*:

$17 MILLION CASH WITH
ADDITIONAL CASH AVAILABLE
$105 MM TAX LOSS GOOD THROUGH 2021
TIGERA GROUP, INC.
NASDAQ listed w/300 shareholders
WANTS TO ACQUIRE COMPANY
with Net Before Tax Audited Earnings of $7MM to $10MM
Exceptional Opportunity and Participation for Sellers and
Existing Management. Contact: Albert M. Zlotnick or Ross P.
Lederer, Tel: (000)-000-0000 and Fax: (000)-000-0000.

Required: Prepare a memorandum explaining the tax advantages that would accrue to the Tigera Group if it acquired the stock or assets of a profitable corporation in a nontaxable reorganization or a taxable transaction. Would the advantages be the same if a profitable corporation acquired Tigera? In addition, explain any tax law provisions that might restrict the use of these loss carryovers.

TAX RESEARCH PROBLEMS

C:7-78 Austin Corporation acquires 8% of Travis Corporation's single class of stock for cash on January 10 of the current year. On August 25 of the current year, Austin makes a tender offer to exchange Austin common stock for the remaining Travis stock. Travis shareholders tender an additional 75% of the outstanding Travis stock. The exchange is completed on September 25 of the current year. Austin ends up owning slightly more than 83% of the Travis stock. The remaining 17% of the Travis stock is owned by about 100 former shareholders of Travis who own small blocks of stock. Your tax manager has asked you to draft a memorandum explaining whether one or both of the two acquisition transactions qualify as a nontaxable reorganization? If part or all of either transaction is taxable to Travis' shareholders, offer any suggestions for restructuring the acquisitions to improve the tax consequences of the transaction assuming that Austin does not desire to make a Sec. 338 election.

Matt Bonner, CEO of Travis, asked a question that might be relevant to reporting the transaction: To simplify the corporate structure, can Austin liquidate Travis into Austin without recognizing any gain or loss?

At a minimum you should consider:

- IRC Sec. 368(a)(1)(B)
- Reg. Sec. 1.368-2(c)
- *Eldon S. Chapman, et al. v. CIR*, 45 AFTR 2d 80-1290, 80-1 USTC ¶9330 (1st Cir., 1980)
- *Arden S. Heverly, et al. v. CIR*, 45 AFTR 2d 80-1122, 80-1 USTC ¶9322 (3rd Cir., 1980)

C:7-79 ABC Corporation is the subject of a hostile takeover bid by XYZ Corporation. ABC incurs a total of $400,000 in attorneys' fees, accounting fees, and printing costs for information mailed to ABC shareholders in an effort to defeat the XYZ takeover bid. XYZ finally gives up, and ABC remains a separate corporation. What is the appropriate tax treatment of the $400,000 in fees? Is that treatment different if XYZ succeeds in acquiring ABC? Tax sources you should consider include the following:

- IRC Sec. 162
- IRC Sec. 165
- *INDOPCO, Inc. v. Comm.*, 69 AFTR 2d 92-694, 92-1 USTC ¶50,113 (USSC, 1992)
- *U.S. v. Federated Department Stores, Inc.*, 74 AFTR 2d 94-5519, 94-2 USTC ¶50,418 (S.D. Ohio, 1994)
- *A.E. Staley Manufacturing Co. v. Comm.*, 80 AFTR 2d 97-5060, 97-2 USTC ¶50,521 (7th Cir., 1997)
- Reg. Sec. 1.263(a)-5

C:7-80 Diversified Corporation is a successful bank with ten branches. Al, Bob, and Cathy created Diversified six years ago and own equally all the Diversified stock. Diversified has constructed a new building in downtown Metropolis that houses a banking facility on the first floor, offices for its employees on the second and third floors, and office space to be leased out to third party lessees on the fourth through twelfth floors. Since the building was completed six months ago, approximately 75% of the floor space on the upper floors has been occupied. Pursuant to a plan of reorganization, Diversified proposes to transfer the building to Metropolis Real Estate (MRE) Corporation in exchange for all the MRE common stock. A team of commercial real estate experts has been hired to manage MRE. The building will be the only property owned by MRE following the reorganization. Diversified owns no other real estate because it currently leases from third parties the locations for its ten retail banking branches. Diversified will distribute the MRE common stock ratably to Al, Bob, and Cathy, who will end up holding all the Diversified and MRE common stock. Your tax manager has asked you to draft a memorandum explaining whether or not the proposed transaction will satisfy the requirements for a nontaxable divisive reorganization? At a minimum you should consider:

- IRC Sec. 368(a)(1)(D)
- Reg. Sec. 1.355-3(b), (c)
- *Appleby v. Comm.*, 9 AFTR 2d 372, 62-1 USTC ¶9178 (3rd Cir., 1962)

CHAPTER 8

CONSOLIDATED TAX RETURNS

LEARNING OBJECTIVES

After studying this chapter, you should be able to

1. Determine whether a group of corporations is an affiliated group
2. Explain the advantages and disadvantages of filing a consolidated tax return
3. Calculate consolidated taxable income for an affiliated group
4. Calculate the consolidated regular tax liability for an affiliated group
5. Calculate the consolidated AMT liability for an affiliated group
6. Determine whether a transaction is an intercompany transaction
7. Explain the reporting of an intercompany transaction
8. Calculate an affiliated group's consolidated NOL
9. Calculate the carryback or carryover of a consolidated NOL
10. Determine how the special loss limitations restrict the use of separate and consolidated NOL carrybacks and carryovers
11. Explain the procedures for making an initial consolidated return election
12. Understand the financial statement implications of various consolidated transactions

CHAPTER OUTLINE

Affiliated corporations (i.e., a parent corporation and at least one subsidiary corporation) have two options for filing their federal income tax returns:

- Each member of the group can file separate tax returns that report its own income and expenses. No special treatment is generally provided for transactions between group members.[1] However, the group can elect to claim a 100% dividends-received deduction for intragroup dividends.
- The affiliated group can file a single tax return, called a consolidated tax return, that reports the results for all its group members. A number of special treatments are applied to transactions between group members (e.g., deferring gains and losses on intercompany transactions and eliminating intragroup dividends).

Some consolidated tax returns include as few as two corporations. Other consolidated tax returns include hundreds of corporations. Moreover, most of the nation's largest corporate groups file consolidated tax returns. In recent years, affiliated groups filing on a consolidated basis reported 90% of total taxable income for all C corporations and paid more than 80% of the income taxes paid by all C corporations even though they made up less than 3% of all C corporation tax returns that were filed.[2]

This chapter considers the advantages and disadvantages of filing a consolidated tax return. It also examines the basic requirements for computing the consolidated tax liability.

SOURCE OF THE CONSOLIDATED TAX RETURN RULES

ADDITIONAL COMMENT

Filing a consolidated tax return does not affect the reporting of other taxes such as payroll, sales, or property taxes. Also, some states do not allow the filing of consolidated tax returns for state income tax purposes.

REAL-WORLD EXAMPLE

Several years ago, Mobil Oil filed a federal consolidated income tax return that was 6,300 pages long and weighed 76 pounds. Work papers for the return constituted 146,000 documents. The return took 57 person years to prepare at a cost of $10 million. In addition, more than $5 million of expenses were incurred annually in connection with the IRS's audit of the Mobil return.

Sections 1501–1504 are the primary statutory provisions governing the filing of a consolidated tax return. These four sections are very general and primarily define the composition of the affiliated groups eligible to elect to file a consolidated tax return. This topic is quite complex. The Treasury Department was given the responsibility of drafting the Treasury Regulations needed to determine (1) the consolidated tax liability and (2) the filing requirements for a consolidated tax return. Because it is unusual for the Treasury Department to have the authority to draft both statutory and interpretive regulations for a particular topical area, Sec. 1501 requires that all affiliated groups filing a consolidated tax return must consent to all the consolidated tax return regulations in effect when the return is filed. The purpose of Sec. 1501 is to reduce or avoid conflicts in applying the statutory and interpretive regulations. The consolidated return regulations have nearly the same authority as the Internal Revenue Code because of the consent requirement and the fact that they are legislative in nature.

These regulations are seldom challenged in court and even more rarely found invalid. In 2001, the Federal Circuit Court of Appeals ruled in *Rite Aid Corporation v. United States*[3] that one of the consolidated return regulations was invalid. This ruling was the first time in 22 years that a court overturned a consolidated return regulation. In overturning the regulation, the court reasoned that the invalid regulation "addresses a situation that arises . . . regardless of whether corporations file separate or consolidated returns" and that the difference in treatment between consolidated corporations and corporations filing separately was not justified. As a result of the *Rite Aid* decision, Congress was concerned that the IRS would be inundated with cases based on the assertion by taxpayers that their results would be different under the consolidated return regulations than they would be if the corporations filed separately. Accordingly, in the 2004 Jobs Act, Congress added a sentence to Sec. 1502 to specifically provide that the rules for consolidated entities may be different from the rules that would apply if the corporations filed separate returns.

---

[1] Some special treatments apply to related corporations filing separate returns under the controlled group rules. These include but are not limited to matching of income and deductions, Sec. 267(a)(1); deferral of loss on intragroup sales, Sec. 267(f)(2); and ordinary income recognition on intragroup sales of depreciable property, Sec. 1239.

[2] IRS Web site: *www.irs.gov*. For fiscal year 2002, affiliated groups filed 52,733 consolidated returns.

[3] 88 AFTR 2d 2001-5058, 2001-2 USTC ¶50,516 (Fed. Cir., 2001).

DEFINITION OF AN AFFILIATED GROUP

OBJECTIVE 1

Determine whether a group of corporations is an affiliated group

REQUIREMENTS

STOCK OWNERSHIP REQUIREMENT. Only an affiliated group of corporations can elect to file a consolidated return. Section 1504(a) outlines the stock ownership requirements that must be satisfied, as follows:

- A parent corporation must directly own stock[4] having at least 80% of the total voting power of all classes of stock entitled to vote and at least 80% of the total value of all outstanding stock in at least one includible corporation.
- For *each* other corporation eligible to be included in the affiliated group, stock having at least 80% of the total voting power of all classes of stock entitled to vote and at least 80% of the total value of all outstanding stock must be owned directly by the parent corporation and the other group members.

EXAMPLE C:8-1 ▶ P Corporation owns 90% of S_1 Corporation's single class of stock and 30% of S_2 Corporation's single class of stock.[5] S_1 Corporation owns 50% of S_2's stock. The remainder of S_1 and S_2's stock is owned by 100 individual shareholders. P, S_1, and S_2 Corporations form the P-S_1-S_2 affiliated group because P owns at least 80% of the S_1 stock needed to satisfy the direct ownership requirement and P and S_1 together own 80% (50% + 30%) of S_2's stock. The P-S_1-S_2 group can elect to file a consolidated tax return with P as the common parent corporation. ◀

EXAMPLE C:8-2 ▶ Ted owns all the stock of Alpha and Beta Corporations. Alpha and Beta Corporations do not constitute an affiliated group, even though each corporation is directly owned by the same individual shareholder. Because a parent-subsidiary relationship is not present, they are ineligible to make a consolidated return election (see below). The Tax Strategy Tip on page C:8-4 suggests ways to reform the corporations into an affiliated group. ◀

SELF-STUDY QUESTION

What issues determine whether an affiliated group exists?

ANSWER

In determining whether an affiliated group exists, three questions must be addressed. Does a corporation (common parent) own directly 80% or more of at least one includible corporation? What are the includible corporations? What chains of includible corporations are connected by at least 80% ownership?

INCLUDIBLE CORPORATION REQUIREMENT. As few as two corporations may satisfy the affiliated group definition. In many of the nation's largest affiliated groups, however, the number of related corporations runs into the hundreds. Some of these corporate groups may have a number of subsidiary corporations that are not able to participate in the consolidated tax return election because they are not includible corporations under Sec. 1504(b). Because they are not includible corporations, their stock ownership cannot be counted toward satisfying the 80% stock ownership minimums, nor can their operating results be reported as part of the consolidated tax return. In general, each excluded corporation must file its own separate corporate tax return.

The following special tax status corporations are not includible corporations:

- Corporations exempt from tax under Sec. 501
- Insurance companies subject to tax under Sec. 801[6]
- Foreign corporations
- Corporations claiming the Puerto Rico and U.S. possessions tax credit
- Regulated investment companies
- Real estate investment trusts
- Domestic international sales corporations
- S corporations

If both the stock ownership and includible corporation requirements are satisfied, the subsidiary corporation must be included in the consolidated return election made by a parent corporation.

BOOK-TO-TAX ACCOUNTING COMPARISON

Because of the different stock ownership rules, the corporations included in a consolidated group for financial reporting purposes may be quite different from the includible corporations when producing a consolidated tax return for federal income tax purposes. Page 1 of Schedule M-3 reconciles these differences (see Chapter C:3).

[4] The term *stock* does not include nonvoting preferred stock that is limited and preferred as to its dividends (and does not participate in corporate growth to any significant extent), has redemption or liquidation rights limited to its issue price (plus a reasonable redemption or liquidation premium), and is not convertible into another class of stock (Sec. 1504(a)(4)).

[5] All corporations referred to in the examples are includible domestic corporations unless otherwise indicated. See definition of *includible corporation* later in this chapter.

[6] Two or more Sec. 801 domestic life insurance companies may join together to form an affiliated group. If an affiliated group contains one or more Sec. 801 domestic life insurance companies, Sec. 1504(c)(2)(A) permits the parent corporation to elect to treat all such companies that have met the affiliated group stock ownership test for the five immediately preceding tax years as includible corporations. As recently as 2005, a bill was introduced into Congress to remove the limitation on life insurance companies being included in consolidated returns. This topic continues to be a political issue.

EXAMPLE C:8-3 ▶ P Corporation owns all the single class of stock of S_1 and S_2 Corporations. S_1 Corporation owns all of S_3 Corporation's stock. S_2 Corporation owns all of S_4 Corporation's stock. P, S_1, and S_3 are domestic corporations. S_2 and S_4 are foreign corporations. P, S_1 and S_3 Corporations constitute the P-S_1-S_3 affiliated group with P as the common parent corporation. S_2 and S_4 are not members of the affiliated group because as foreign corporations they are not includible corporations. ◀

ADDITIONAL COMMENT

Even if S_4 were an includible corporation, S_4 would not be part of the P-S_1-S_3 affiliated group. The chain is broken because S_2 is not an includible corporation.

REAL-WORLD EXAMPLE

The check-the-box regulations permit partnerships and LLCs to elect C corporation tax treatment. If the election is made, an LLC or partnership can be a member of an affiliated group filing a consolidated tax return.

Under the check-the-box regulations, noncorporate entities can elect to be taxed as a C corporation. Partnerships and LLCs that elect to be taxed as a C corporation under the check-the-box regulations and that meet all the requirements for inclusion in an affiliated group come under the consolidated return rules of Secs. 1501–1504. Partnerships and LLCs that are wholly- or partially-owned by a member of an affiliated group are not considered members of the affiliated group unless the election is made to have the entity taxed as a C corporation. Partnerships and LLCs for which such an election is made are taxed like a corporate group member. Each group member investing in a partnership or LLC for which no C corporation election is made reports its ratable share of the income/loss earned by the conduit entity in its separate tax return. Such income/loss becomes part of the consolidated tax return of the affiliated group. Partnerships and LLCs for which no C corporation election is made are not subject to the various special consolidated tax return rules, such as those applying to intercompany sales.

TYPICAL MISCONCEPTION

The terms *affiliated group, consolidated group,* and *controlled group* are sometimes used interchangeably. However, these terms have different definitions and applications.

TAX STRATEGY TIP

A brother-sister controlled group cannot file a consolidated tax return. To convert a brother-sister group into a parent-subsidiary affiliated group at a minimal cost, the owner(s) of one corporation could make a capital contribution of 80% or more of the corporation's stock to the other brother-sister group member in a tax-free transaction meeting the Sec. 351 requirements. The two corporations, being in a parent-subsidiary relationship, then can make the initial consolidated return election and begin filing on a consolidated basis. Alternatively, the owner(s) could contribute the stock of all the corporations to a new corporation, e.g., a holding company that would be the common parent.

COMPARISON WITH CONTROLLED GROUP DEFINITIONS

Three types of controlled groups—brother-sister groups, parent-subsidiary groups, and combined groups—were defined in Chapter C:3. As illustrated in Example C:8-2, the brother-sister category of controlled groups cannot elect to file a consolidated tax return because they do not satisfy the direct stock ownership requirement. However, most parent-subsidiary controlled groups and the parent-subsidiary portion of a combined controlled group can elect to file a consolidated tax return.

Only affiliated groups can elect to file consolidated tax returns. Four differences between the definitions of Sec. 1504 (affiliated group) and Sec. 1563 (parent-subsidiary controlled group) exist. These differences include:

- A parent corporation must own at least 80% of total voting power *and* total value (instead of voting power or value) of a subsidiary's stock to include the subsidiary in the affiliated group.
- The stock attribution rules are not used in determining the inclusion of a subsidiary in an affiliated group but are used in determining the existence of a controlled group.
- The types of corporations excluded from an affiliated group are different from those that are excluded from a controlled group.
- The affiliated group definition is tested on each day of the tax year (instead of only on December 31 for a controlled group).

These differences can cause some members of a controlled group to be excluded from the affiliated group.

SHOULD A CONSOLIDATED RETURN BE FILED?

OBJECTIVE 2

Explain the advantages and disadvantages of filing a consolidated tax return

ADVANTAGES OF FILING A CONSOLIDATED TAX RETURN

Filing a consolidated tax return offers a number of advantages and disadvantages, some of the more important of which are discussed below. Some of the advantages that may be gained by filing a consolidated tax return include the following:

- The separate return losses of one affiliated group member may be offset against the taxable income of other group members in the current tax year. Such losses provide an immediate tax benefit by reducing the tax due on the other group member's income or eliminating the need to carry a loss back to a prior tax year or forward to a subsequent tax year.

- Capital losses of one group member may be offset against the capital gains of other group members in the current tax year. Again, this offset avoids carrying these losses back to a prior tax year or over to a subsequent tax year.
- Dividends paid from one group member to a second group member are "eliminated" in the consolidated tax return.
- The various credit and deduction limitations are computed on a consolidated basis (e.g., charitable contributions). If the group members filed separate tax returns, some members' credits or deductions might be only partially used due to the limitations, while other members' credits or deductions fall short of the limitations. By filing a consolidated tax return, group members with "excess" credits or deductions can take advantage of other members' "excess" limitation.
- Gains on intercompany transactions are deferred until a subsequent event occurs that causes the profit or gain to be included in the consolidated return.
- Calculation of the alternative minimum tax (AMT) takes place on a consolidated basis (rather than for each group member) and may reduce the negative effects of tax preference items and adjustments. This treatment may eliminate the need for the affiliated group as a whole to pay an AMT liability. On the other hand, the affiliated group is limited to a single $40,000 AMT exemption.

KEY POINT

The elimination of intercompany dividends is an advantage of filing consolidated tax returns. However, even if a consolidated tax return is not filed, the owning member should be eligible for a 100% dividends-received deduction.

DISADVANTAGES OF FILING A CONSOLIDATED TAX RETURN

Some disadvantages of filing a consolidated tax return include the following:

- A consolidated return election is binding on all subsequent tax years unless the IRS grants the group permission to discontinue filing a consolidated return or the affiliated group is terminated.
- All group members must use the same taxable year.
- Losses and deductions on intercompany transactions are deferred until a subsequent event occurs that causes the losses or deductions to be included in the consolidated tax return.[7]
- Operating losses and capital losses of group members may reduce or eliminate the ability of profitable group members to take advantage of credits or deductions by lowering the applicable credit or deduction limitation for the affiliated group.
- Additional administrative costs may be incurred in maintaining the necessary records to account for deferred intercompany transactions and the special loss limitations, although some savings may occur by filing a single return and filing all tax returns at the same time.

No general rule can be applied to determine whether an affiliated group should elect to file a consolidated tax return. Each group should examine the long- and short-term advantages and disadvantages of filing a consolidated tax return before making a decision.

ADDITIONAL COMMENT

One disadvantage of filing a consolidated tax return that should be apparent after going through this chapter is the added recordkeeping costs necessary to file a consolidated tax return.

CONSOLIDATED TAXABLE INCOME

OBJECTIVE 3

Calculate consolidated taxable income for an affiliated group

The heart of the computation of the consolidated federal income tax liability is the calculation of **consolidated taxable income**. The calculation of consolidated taxable income is divided into the following five steps. An overview of the five-step consolidated taxable income calculation is presented in Table C:8-1.

[7] The deferral of losses and deductions in a consolidated tax return is less of a disadvantage now that related-party loss and deduction rules also apply to controlled groups in Sec. 267.

TYPICAL MISCONCEPTION
This table illustrates that the filing of a consolidated tax return instead of separate tax returns is clearly not easier from a compliance point of view.

▼ **TABLE C:8-1**
Consolidated Taxable Income Calculation

Step 1: Compute each group member's taxable income (or loss) based on the member's own accounting methods as if the corporation were filing its own separate tax return.

Step 2: Adjust each group member's taxable income as follows:
1. Gains and losses on certain intercompany transactions are deferred. If a restoration event occurs during the year, previously deferred gains and losses are included in the calculation.
2. An inventory adjustment may be required.
3. Dividends received by a group member from another group member are excluded from the recipient's gross income.
4. An adjustment for an excess loss (negative investment basis) account of an affiliate may be required.
5. Built-in deductions may be deferred.

Step 3: The following gains, losses, and deductions are removed from each member's taxable income because they must be computed on a consolidated basis:
1. Net operating loss (NOL) deductions
2. Capital gains and losses
3. Section 1231 gains and losses (including net casualty gain)
4. Charitable contribution deductions
5. Dividends-received deductions
6. Percentage depletion deductions
7. The U.S. production activities deduction

The result of making the adjustments to a member's taxable income in Steps 2 and 3 is the member's separate taxable income.

Step 4: Combine the members' separate taxable income amounts. This amount is called the group's combined taxable income.

Step 5: Adjust the group's combined taxable income for the following items that are reported on a consolidated basis:
1. Deduct the consolidated Sec. 1231 net loss.
2. Deduct the consolidated net casualty loss.
3. Add the consolidated capital gain net income (taking into account capital loss carrybacks and carryovers and Sec. 1231 gains).
4. Deduct the consolidated charitable contribution deduction.
5. Deduct the consolidated percentage depletion deduction.
6. Deduct the consolidated NOL deduction (taking into account any allowable NOL carryovers and carrybacks).
7. Deduct the consolidated dividends-received deductions.
8. Deduct the consolidated U.S. production activities deduction.

Consolidated taxable income (or consolidated NOL)

STEP 1. The starting point is the determination of each member's taxable income. The amount of a group member's taxable income is determined as if the group member were filing a separate tax return.

STEP 2. Once each group member's taxable income has been determined, a series of adjustments (e.g., deferral of gain on certain intercompany transactions) must be made to take into account the special treatment that certain transactions receive in consolidated returns.

STEP 3. Any income, loss, or deduction items that must be reported on a consolidated basis are removed from the taxable income calculation. The resulting amounts are each group member's **separate taxable income.**

STEP 4. The separate taxable income amounts of the individual group members are aggregated into a **combined taxable income** amount.

STEP 5. Each of the tax items stated on a consolidated basis (which were removed in Step 3) are added to or subtracted from the combined taxable income amount. The resulting amount is the affiliated group's consolidated taxable income.[8]

Consolidated taxable income is subject to the corporate tax rates of Sec. 11 to determine the consolidated regular tax liability. This amount is increased if the affiliated group owes an additional tax under the corporate AMT, one of the other special tax levies, or as the result of recapturing previously claimed tax credits. The group subtracts any tax credits and estimated tax payments from the total tax liability to determine the tax due or refund upon filing the consolidated tax return. A sample consolidated tax return worksheet is included in Appendix B, which illustrates the consolidated taxable income calculation.

INCOME INCLUDED IN THE CONSOLIDATED TAX RETURN

KEY POINT

Two basic rules exist for determining what income must be included in a consolidated tax return: common parent's income for the entire tax year and a subsidiary's income only for the time period the subsidiary is a member of the consolidated group.

A consolidated tax return includes the parent corporation's income for its entire tax year, except for any portion of the year that it was a member of another affiliated group that filed a consolidated tax return. A subsidiary corporation's income is included in the consolidated tax return only for the portion of the affiliated group's tax year for which it was a group member. When a corporation is a member of an affiliated group for only a portion of its tax year, the member's income for the remainder of its tax year is included in a separate tax return or the consolidated tax return of another affiliated group.[9]

A corporation that becomes or ceases to be a group member during a consolidated return year[10] changes its status at the end of the day on which such change occurs (i.e., the change date). Its tax year ends for federal income tax purposes at the end of the change date. Transactions that occur on the change date that are allocable to the portion of the day after the event resulting in the change (e.g., a stock sale or merger) are accounted for by the group member (and all related parties) as having occurred on the next day.[11]

WHAT WOULD YOU DO IN THIS SITUATION?

The P-S-T affiliated group has filed consolidated tax returns using the calendar year as its tax year for many years. On October 1, P Corporation created a new subsidiary, X Corporation, with a $10,000 initial capital contribution, and X Corporation issued its stock to P Corporation. A bank account was opened when X Corporation was created. A federal tax identification number was also applied for and obtained. X did not conduct any business activities before year-end. Its only income was $125 in interest earned on the initial capital contribution. Due to a lack of communication or an oversight, P's tax department did not include X Corporation in the affiliated group's current year consolidated tax return.

Your CPA firm has provided federal tax advice to P Corporation for a number of years, but your client's tax department has handled the federal tax return filings. Most of your work for P Corporation has been in the state and local taxation area and on special federal tax assignments. You were aware of the affiliated group's future business plans for creating X Corporation. Will the oversight with respect to X Corporation disqualify the affiliated group from filing a consolidated tax return for the current year and all future years? Can you avoid having to file a federal tax return for X Corporation because of the small amount of interest income the corporation earned? Does the failure to include X Corporation in this year's consolidated tax return prevent it from being included in future years? What advice can you give your client about needing to include X Corporation in the consolidated tax return?

---

[8] Reg. Sec. 1.1502-12.

[9] Reg. Sec. 1.1502-76(b)(1)(i). See Rev. Proc. 2006-45, 2006-45 I.R.B. 851, for the procedures governing automatic approval for a company to change its annual accounting period under Sec. 442 and related Treasury Regulations.

[10] **A consolidated return year** is defined by Reg. Sec. 1.1502-1(d) as a tax year for which a consolidated return is filed or is required to be filed by the affiliated group. A **separate return year** is defined by Reg. Sec. 1.1502-1(e) as a tax year for which a corporation files a separate return or joins in the filing of a consolidated tax return with a different affiliated group.

[11] Reg. Sec. 1.1502-76(b)(1)(ii).

EXAMPLE C:8-4 ▶ P and S Corporations file separate tax returns for calendar year 2007. At the close of business on April 30, 2008, P Corporation acquires all of S Corporation's stock. If the P-S affiliated group files a consolidated tax return for 2008, P's income is included in the consolidated tax return for all of 2008, and S's income is included only for the period May 1 through December 31, 2008. S Corporation must file a separate tax return to report its income for the pre-affiliation period January 1 through April 30, 2008. ◀

EXAMPLE C:8-5 ▶ P and S Corporations have filed consolidated tax returns for a number of years. At the close of business on April 30, 2008, P sells all of its S stock to Peter Gabriel. P and S file a consolidated tax return including P's income for all 12 months of 2008, and S's income for January 1 through April 30, 2008. S files a separate tax return for May 1 through December 31, 2008. ◀

Tax returns for the years that end and begin with a corporation becoming or ceasing to be a member of an affiliated group are separate return years. The separate returns, in general, are short period returns (i.e., for applying the MACRS rules) but do not require annualization of the tax liability or estimated tax calculations when a corporation joins an affiliated group. The short period return is a full tax year for purposes of NOL and other attribute carryovers. Allocation of income between the consolidated tax return and a member's separate return year takes place according to the accounting methods used by each individual corporation. If this allocation cannot be readily determined, allocation of items included in each tax return (other than ones considered below to be extraordinary) can be based on the relative number of days of the original tax year included in each tax year. A ratable allocation of income, expense, gain, loss, and credit items between periods is permitted if the new or departing group member is not required to change its annual accounting period or accounting method as a result of its change in status, and an irrevocable election is made by the group member and the parent corporation of the affected group. Extraordinary items are allocated to the day they are reported using the group member's accounting methods. Extraordinary items include but are not limited to gains or losses arising from the disposition or abandonment of capital assets, Sec. 1231 property, or inventory; NOL carrybacks or carryovers; settlements of a tort or third-party liability; and compensation-related deductions arising from the group member's change in status (e.g., bonuses, severance pay, and option cancellation payments).[12]

AFFILIATED GROUP ELECTIONS

TAX YEARS. An affiliated group's consolidated tax return must be filed using the parent corporation's tax year. Beginning with the initial consolidated return year for which it is includible in the consolidated tax return, each subsidiary corporation must adopt the parent corporation's tax year. The requirement for a common tax year applies to affiliated group members both when an initial consolidated tax return is being filed and when the stock of a new member is acquired.[13]

EXAMPLE C:8-6 ▶ P and S Corporations filed separate tax returns for 2006. P Corporation uses a calendar year as its tax year. S Corporation uses a fiscal year ending June 30 as its tax year. At the close of business on April 30, 2007, P Corporation acquires all of S Corporation's stock. If the P-S affiliated group files a consolidated tax return for 2007, S must change its tax year so that it ends on December 31. S must file a short-period tax return for the period July 1, 2006, through April 30, 2007. P's income for all of 2007 and S's income for the period May 1, 2007, through December 31, 2007, are included in the initial consolidated tax return. ◀

SELF-STUDY QUESTION

When a subsidiary leaves an affiliated group that has filed consolidated tax returns, may it select any year-end it wishes?

ANSWER

Without permission from the IRS to do otherwise, a subsidiary must retain the group's year-end (if filing a separate tax return) or adopt the year-end of the acquiring consolidated group, if applicable.

METHODS OF ACCOUNTING. Unless the IRS grants permission for a change in accounting method, the accounting methods used by each group member are determined by using the same rules as if the member were filing a separate tax return.[14] This requirement applies when a consolidated tax return election is made or a new corporation joins an existing affiliated group. Thus, one group member may use the cash method of accounting and another group member may use the accrual method of accounting during a consolidated return year. The possibility of finding a mixture of cash and accrual

[12] Reg. Sec. 1.1502-76(b)(2).
[13] Reg. Sec. 1.1502-76(a).
[14] Reg. Sec. 1.1502-17(a).

method corporations in an affiliated group is limited because of the Sec. 448 restrictions on the use of the cash method of accounting by C corporations described in Chapter C:3.

KEY POINT

Even though members of a consolidated group must use the same year-end, members are not required to use the same accounting methods. It is common to find different inventory methods (e.g., LIFO and FIFO) within the same affiliated group.

TERMINATION OF THE AFFILIATED GROUP

An affiliated group that elects to file a consolidated tax return must continue to file on a consolidated basis as long as the affiliated group exists unless the IRS grants permission for it to do otherwise. Under Reg. Sec. 1.1502-75(d)(1), an affiliated group "remains in existence for a tax year if the common parent remains as the common parent and at least one subsidiary that was affiliated with it at the end of the prior year remains affiliated with it at the beginning of the year." The parent corporation need not own the *same* subsidiary throughout the entire tax year nor own any subsidiary throughout the entire tax year as long as the parent owns a prior year subsidiary at the beginning of the current tax year.

EXAMPLE C:8-7 ▶ P and S_1 Corporations have filed a consolidated tax return for several calendar years. At the close of business on August 31 of the current year, P purchases all of S_2 Corporation's stock. S_2 uses the calendar year as its tax year. At the close of business on September 30, P sells its entire holding of S_1 stock. The affiliated group, with P as the parent corporation, must file a consolidated tax return for the current year because P remained the common parent and at least one subsidiary that was affiliated with it at the end of the prior year remained affiliated with it at the beginning of the current year (i.e., S_1).

Alternatively, assume the order of the purchase and sale transactions are reversed, i.e., P sells the S_1 stock on August 31 and purchases the S_2 stock on September 30. In this case, the affiliated group still must file a consolidated tax return for the current year. Even though P did not have a subsidiary from September 1 through September 30, it nevertheless remained as the common parent, and S_1 was affiliated with it at the end of the prior year and at the beginning of the current year. ◀

EXAMPLE C:8-8 ▶ P and S Corporations have filed a consolidated tax return for several calendar years. At the close of business on December 31 of the current year, P Corporation sells its entire holding of S stock to Arthur. On January 1 of next year, P purchases all of T Corporation's stock. P's and S's income is included in the current year consolidated tax return for the entire year. However, the affiliated group terminates at the end of the current year, and a new one is created when P purchases T. P and T may elect to file a consolidated tax return for next year but are not required to do so. ◀

ADDITIONAL COMMENT

Permission to discontinue the filing of consolidated tax returns is seldom granted by the IRS when the request relates to a change in the tax situation of the affiliated group that is not related to a law change.

SELF-STUDY QUESTION

In the second half of Example C:8-7, the order of the transactions is reversed. In this case, what tax returns are required, and what income is included in these returns?

ANSWER

(1) Consolidated return that includes P's income for the entire year, S_1's income from 1/1 through 8/31, and S_2's income from 10/1 through 12/31. (2) Short period separate return for S_1 from 9/1 through 12/31. (3) Short period separate return for S_2 from 1/1 through 9/30.

GOOD CAUSE REQUEST TO DISCONTINUE STATUS. Permission to discontinue filing a consolidated tax return sometimes is granted by the IRS in response to a "good cause" request initiated by the taxpayer. A good cause reason for discontinuing the consolidated tax return election includes a substantial adverse effect on the consolidated tax liability for the tax year (relative to what the aggregate tax liability would be if the group members filed separate tax returns) originating from amendments to the IRC or Treasury Regulations having effective dates in the tax year in question.[15]

EFFECTS ON FORMER MEMBERS. The termination of an affiliated group affects its former members in several ways, two of which are examined in subsequent sections of this chapter.

- ▶ Any gains and losses that have been deferred on intercompany transactions (e.g., intercompany profits on sales of inventory between group members) may have to be recognized.
- ▶ Consolidated tax attributes (such as NOL, capital loss, tax credit, and charitable contribution carryovers) must be allocated among the former group members.

In addition, disaffiliation of a corporation from an affiliated group prevents the corporation from being included in a consolidated return with the same affiliated group until five years after the beginning of its first tax year in which it ceased to be a group member. The IRS can waive the five-year requirement and permit the departing group member to join in a consolidated return at an earlier date.

[15] Reg. Sec. 1.1502-75(c).

Special rules apply when a corporation is included in, or is required to be included in, a consolidated tax return filed by an affiliated group for a tax year and the corporation ceases to be a member of the affiliated group in the tax year. Under Sec. 1504(a)(3), the corporation cannot be included in a consolidated tax return filed by the affiliated group, or an affiliated group having the same common parent corporation, for a 60-month period beginning after the first tax year in which the corporation ceased to be a member. The IRS has issued procedures for granting certain taxpayers an automatic waiver of the 60-month period before reconsolidation of returns is otherwise possible.[16]

COMPUTATION OF THE AFFILIATED GROUP'S TAX LIABILITY

OBJECTIVE 4

Calculate the consolidated regular tax liability for an affiliated group

REGULAR TAX LIABILITY

The affiliated group determines its consolidated regular income tax liability by applying the corporate tax rates found in Sec. 11 to the group's consolidated taxable income. Thus, the aggregate group obtains the benefit of the 15% tax rate for the first $50,000 of consolidated taxable income and the 25% tax rate for the next $25,000 of consolidated taxable income. If consolidated taxable income exceeds $100,000, however, a 5% surtax applies until consolidated taxable income reaches $335,000, at which point the benefits of the 15% and 25% tax brackets are completely recaptured.[17]

The result for consolidated tax returns has some similarities to the total tax liability for a controlled group (see Chapter C:3). Section 1561 limits a controlled group of corporations to an aggregate of $50,000 for which the 15% tax rate applies and an aggregate of $25,000 for which the 25% tax rate applies. In the controlled group situation, however, each corporation computes its separate tax liability with the benefits of the reduced rates allocated among the members of the group.

OBJECTIVE 5

Calculate the consolidated AMT liability for an affiliated group

KEY POINT

Determining the alternative minimum tax for corporations is discussed in Chapter C:5. Determining the alternative minimum tax for a consolidated group merely adds to the complexity of this already difficult computation.

CORPORATE ALTERNATIVE MINIMUM TAX LIABILITY

The corporate alternative minimum tax (AMT) liability is determined on a consolidated basis for all group members. The consolidated AMT is determined under an approach that generally parallels the determination of the group's consolidated taxable income. The starting point for the calculation is consolidated taxable income. The AMT procedures and definitions of Secs. 55-59 apply in determining consolidated AMT. Consolidated alternative minimum taxable income (AMTI) is computed using the rules of Reg. Sec. 1.1502-55(b). These Treasury Regulations require the deferral and restoration of AMT items. Consolidated AMTI equals consolidated preadjustment AMTI plus or minus 75% of the difference between consolidated adjusted current earnings (ACE) and consolidated preadjustment AMTI and decreased by the consolidated alternative tax NOL.[18] The negative ACE adjustment limitation is determined on a consolidated basis and requires the tracking of separate return and consolidated return positive and negative ACE adjustments. AMTI also must be adjusted for the difference (if any) between the U.S. production activities deduction for AMT purposes and the deduction for consolidated taxable income purposes. (See Chapter C:5 for a discussion of this adjustment.)

The consolidated AMT is the excess of the consolidated tentative minimum tax (TMT) over the consolidated regular tax liability for the tax year. The consolidated TMT amount is determined by first computing 20% of the excess of consolidated AMTI over a consolidated statutory exemption amount. This amount is reduced by the consolidated AMT foreign tax credit amount to arrive at the consolidated TMT. Any excess of the consoli-

[16] Rev. Proc. 2002-32, 2002-1 C.B. 959.

[17] A similar recapture of the tax savings produced by the 34% corporate tax rate applies when taxable income is between $15 million and $18,333,333 (see Chapter C:3).

[18] Reg. Secs. 1.1502-55(h)(4) and (i).

dated TMT over the consolidated regular tax must be paid by the affiliated group and is available in future years as a minimum tax credit.

A group's consolidated minimum tax credit (MTC) equals the sum of the consolidated return year MTCs and any prior separate return year MTCs. Use of the consolidated minimum tax credit is limited to the excess (if any) of the modified consolidated regular tax over the consolidated TMT for the year. Modified consolidated regular tax equals the consolidated regular tax amount reduced by any credits allowable for the AMT (other than the MTC).[19]

Affiliated groups of corporations filing a consolidated tax return, like corporations filing separate tax returns, are eligible for the small corporation exemption from the corporate alternative minimum tax. The $5 million and $7.5 million gross receipts ceilings on the small corporation AMT exemption apply to the entire affiliated group.

CONSOLIDATED TAX CREDITS

The affiliated group can claim all tax credits available to corporate taxpayers. The discussion that follows examines the two major credits claimed by most affiliated groups—the general business credit and the foreign tax credit.

GENERAL BUSINESS CREDIT. The affiliated group's general business credit is determined on a consolidated basis, with all of the group members' separate component credit amounts being combined into a single amount for the affiliated group. For these credits, an affiliated group is limited to the excess of the affiliated group's net income tax over the greater of (1) the affiliated group's tentative minimum tax for the year or (2) 25% of the affiliated group's net regular tax liability for the year exceeding $25,000.[20] Any unused general business tax credits may be carried back one year and forward 20 years under Sec. 39(a). (See Chapter C:3 for more detailed coverage of the tax credit limitation.)

A profitable group member may find that use of the consolidated tax liability as the basis for the general business credit limitation may result in a reduced credit amount because the losses of other group members are used to offset its separate taxable income. An unprofitable member, however, may find its general business credit limitation increased by the separate taxable income of another member, so that credits that otherwise would have been carried back or forward if separate returns were filed may be used currently by the group.

EXAMPLE C:8-9 ▶ The P-S affiliated group files a consolidated tax return for the current year. P and S Corporations contribute separate taxable income (or loss) amounts of $300,000 and ($100,000), respectively, to the group's $200,000 consolidated taxable income. P and S can tentatively claim a $40,000 research credit and a $10,000 targeted jobs credit, or a tentative $50,000 consolidated general business credit. The P-S group's regular tax liability is $61,250. The P-S group's tentative minimum tax liability (assuming no differences between AMTI and taxable income other than the statutory exemption) is $34,500.[21] The group's general business credit limitation is calculated as follows:

Regular tax		$61,250
Plus: Alternative minimum tax		–0–
Minus: Credits allowed under Secs. 21-30A		–0–
Net income tax		$61,250
Minus: Greater of:		
(1) 25% of group's net regular tax liability exceeding $25,000 [0.25 × ($61,250 − $25,000)]	$ 9,062	
(2) Group's tentative minimum tax for the year	34,500	(34,500)
General business credit limitation		$26,750

The $23,250 ($50,000 tentative credit − $26,750 credit limitation) of unused general business credits can be carried back one year and forward 20 years. ◀

[19] Reg. Sec. 1.1502-55(h)(4)(iii)(B)(1).
[20] Sec. 38(c).

[21] $200,000 AMTI − {$40,000 statutory exemption − [0.25 × ($200,000 AMTI − $150,000 threshold)]} × 0.20 = $34,500.

FOREIGN TAX CREDIT. An affiliated group's foreign tax credit for a consolidated return year is determined on a consolidated basis. The parent corporation makes the election to claim either a deduction or a credit for the group's foreign taxes. If the credit is chosen, the affiliated group's foreign tax credit limitation is computed by taking into account the group's income from U.S. and foreign sources, the consolidated taxable income, and the consolidated regular and alternative minimum tax amounts in the manner described in Chapter C:16.

INTERCOMPANY TRANSACTIONS

OBJECTIVE 6

Determine whether a transaction is an intercompany transaction

ADDITIONAL COMMENT

The rules that apply to intercompany transactions are an excellent example of the additional record-keeping necessary to file consolidated tax returns.

An **intercompany transaction** is defined as a transaction between corporations that are members of the same affiliated group immediately after the transaction.[22] Intercompany transactions include:

- Sales, exchanges, contributions, or other transfers of property from one group member to a second group member whether or not the gain or loss is recognized.
- The performance of services by one group member for a second group member, and the second member's payment or accrual of its expense.
- The licensing of technology, renting of property, or lending of money by one group member to a second group member, and the second member's payment or accrual of its expense.
- Payment of a dividend distribution by a subsidiary corporation to its parent corporation in connection with the parent's investment in the subsidiary's stock.

For purposes of our discussion, we will divide our coverage into two categories (1) property acquired in intercompany transactions, and (2) **other intercompany transactions.**

OBJECTIVE 7

Explain the reporting of an intercompany transaction

TAX STRATEGY TIP

A member of an affiliated group should consider a loss recognition transaction to a party outside the group in lieu of a deferred recognition intercompany transaction. For example, P Corporation has a machine that it intends to sell to its wholly owned subsidiary, S Corporation. The machine has a $15,000 adjusted basis and a $9,000 FMV. An intercompany sale of the machine from P to S results in a $6,000 ($9,000 – $15,000) Sec. 1231 loss that is deferred until a restoration event occurs, for example depreciation of the machine by S. A sale of the same property to an entity that is not part of the affiliated group permits P Corporation to deduct the $6,000 loss immediately. Thus, P should consider recognizing the loss to accelerate its income tax savings.

PROPERTY TRANSACTIONS

GENERAL RULE. Gains and losses on intercompany transactions receive special treatment under the consolidated return Treasury Regulations. In general, gains and losses on intercompany transactions involving the sale or exchange of property between two group members (also known as an intercompany item) are recognized in calculating the group member's separate taxable income. Exceptions to this general rule include intercompany transactions that qualify for nonrecognition treatment under Secs. 351 (corporate formation transaction) and 1031 (like-kind exchange). The recognized gain/loss is deferred under the consolidated tax return regulations and therefore not included in determining consolidated taxable income until a subsequent event occurs that requires the recognition of income, gain, deduction or loss (also known as a corresponding item) by the buyer (see Step 2 in Table C:8-1). Events that can trigger the recognition of an intercompany item include:

- The claiming of a depletion, depreciation, or amortization deduction with respect to a property acquired in an intercompany transaction.
- Amortization of services, or any other nonproperty asset, acquired by a group member in an intercompany transaction that has previously been capitalized.
- The disposition outside the affiliated group of a property acquired in an intercompany transaction.
- The departure from an affiliated group of the group member that either sells or owns a property that is acquired in an intercompany transaction.
- The first day of a separate return year for the parent corporation.

In general, buyers and sellers engaging in an intercompany transaction are treated as separate entities.[23] A sale of property by one group member to a second group member is reported on the selling and buying corporations' books using the same basic rules that

[22] Reg. Sec. 1.1502-13(b)(1)(i).

[23] Reg. Sec. 1.1502-13(a)(2).

would apply if the sale involved two unrelated parties. Of course, different rules would be used if the property were acquired in a like-kind exchange, or corporate formation transaction where part or all of the realized gain or loss is not recognized. The basic rules for reporting an intercompany property transaction are presented below.

AMOUNT AND CHARACTER OF THE INTERCOMPANY GAIN OR LOSS. At the time of the transaction, the amount and character of the intercompany gain or loss are determined as if the transaction had occurred in a separate return year.

BASIS AND HOLDING PERIOD. The basis and holding period for a property acquired in an intercompany transaction are determined as if the acquisition occurred in a separate return year. Thus, the adjusted basis for an asset is the property's acquisition cost if the property is purchased by the buying member for cash, or cash and a debt obligation, from the selling member. The holding period for such property begins on the day after the acquisition date.

EXAMPLE C:8-10 ▶ S (Seller) and B (Buyer) Corporations have filed consolidated tax returns for several years, with S being the common parent of the affiliated group.[24] S and B Corporations both use the accrual method of accounting. S acquired a block of marketable securities several years ago, which have been held as a capital asset since that date. The adjusted basis for the securities is $120,000. S sells the marketable securities to B for $200,000 cash on August 8, 2007. This gain is determined on a separate entity basis and is reported in S's separate tax return calculation. S's deferred intercompany capital gain is $80,000 ($200,000 − $120,000). The $80,000 deferred gain is not reported in the 2007 consolidated tax return. An adjustment is made to remove the deferred gain from consolidated taxable income (as illustrated in Step 2 of Table C:8-1). B's basis for the securities is their $200,000 cost. Its holding period for determining the character of the gain or loss on a subsequent sale of the securities begins with August 9, 2007. S recognizes no gain until one of the events described above that produces a corresponding item for B occurs. At that time, part or all of the deferred gain will be included in the consolidated return (but not S's separate tax return calculation). ◀

A sample completed consolidated tax return (Form 1120) and worksheet appears in Appendix B. The worksheet shows the reporting of an intercompany sale of inventory (see worksheet footnote 1) followed by the sale of the inventory outside the affiliated group. The use of the worksheet to report intercompany transactions will be further developed within the examples that follow.

The intercompany transaction rules are based on two concepts—intercompany items and corresponding items. An **intercompany item** is the Seller's income, gain, deduction, or loss from an intercompany transaction.[25] A **corresponding item** is the Buyer's income, gain, deduction, or loss from an intercompany transaction, or from property acquired in an intercompany transaction.[26]

MATCHING AND ACCELERATION RULES. Two principles are used to implement the single entity approach to reporting intercompany transactions. They are the matching rule and the acceleration rule. The matching rule generally treats the Seller and Buyer as divisions of a single corporation for purposes of taking into account the intercompany items. In general, a transfer of an asset between two divisions of a single corporation is not considered a taxable event. A taxable event can occur when, for example, a division sells an asset to a third party. The acceleration rule provides a series of exceptions to the matching rule for taking items into account if the treatment of the Seller and Buyer as divisions within a single entity cannot be achieved (e.g., if either S or B leaves the group and becomes a nonmember).

---

[24] S and B Corporations are used to designate the two members of the consolidated group, instead of our usual P and S Corporations, to make it easier to remember which group member is the seller (S) and which group member is the buyer (B).

[25] Reg. Sec. 1.1502-13(b)(2)(i).

[26] Reg. Sec. 1.1502-13(b)(3)(i).

The intercompany transaction rules override the basic accounting method elections used by the seller. Assume that S's sale to B in Example C:8-10 was instead made for a series of notes payable in equal amounts over a five-year period. Normally, the Sec. 453 installment sale rules would require the $80,000 gain to be reported as the collections were made over the five-year period. Instead, the $80,000 gain is an intercompany item which, in general, is not reported until a corresponding item is reported by the Buyer.[27]

INTERCOMPANY ITEM AMOUNT. When determining the intercompany item amount, all the Seller's direct and indirect costs related to the sale or the providing of services are included. As a result, the Uniform Capitalization rules of Sec. 263A apply in determining (1) the basis of inventory sold, (2) an employee's wages and other related costs included in determining the intercompany item when services are performed, and (3) depreciation and other direct expenses included in determining the intercompany item when property is rented.[28]

CORRESPONDING ITEM AMOUNT. Corresponding items are the Buyer's income, gain, deduction, and loss from an intercompany transaction, or from property acquired in an intercompany transaction.[29] Three corresponding items are illustrated in the text that follows, where the term "third party" refers to an entity that is not a member of the affiliated group:

- When a Buyer acquires property from a Seller and later sells it to a third party, the Buyer's gain or loss from the sale to the third party is a corresponding item.
- When a Buyer acquires property from a Seller and later makes an installment sale of the property to a third party, the Buyer's gain from the installment sale is a corresponding item.
- When a Buyer acquires depreciable property from a Seller, the Buyer's depreciation deductions are corresponding items.

Buyer's corresponding items also include disallowed losses and expenses or excluded income. Examples of such items include tax-exempt income, expenses related to the production of tax-exempt income and disallowed under Sec. 265, and losses disallowed on the distribution of appreciated property as a dividend under Sec. 311(a).[30]

In Example C:8-10 above, if B later sells the marketable securities to a third party for $250,000, the corresponding item would be B's $50,000 ($250,000 − $200,000) gain on the sale. The Buyer (B) reports its corresponding item using its regular accounting method. The Seller (S) reports its intercompany item (i.e., the deferred gain) at the same time. In our example, Treasury Regulations have matched the intercompany item and the corresponding item to affect consolidated taxable income simultaneously as if the two corporations were divisions of one corporation. Although the regulations contain an acceleration rule, which requires the intercompany item and the corresponding item to be taken into account when matching can no longer produce a single entity effect, this exception to the matching rule is not needed since the Seller and Buyer remained members of the affiliated group at the time of the Buyer's sale to the unrelated party.

The Seller and Buyer report their individual parts of an intercompany transaction as if they were separate entities when calculating their separate return taxable income. For this purpose, the Seller and Buyer are treated as engaging in their actual transaction and owning any actual property involved in the transaction. The intercompany transaction rules require a recomputation of the affiliated group's gain or loss at the time a corresponding item is reported. When making the recomputation of the affiliated group's gain or loss, the Buyer takes the Seller's basis for the securities instead of the step-up in basis that normally occurs with cash sales between two related or unrelated corporations.[31]

REPORTING SELECTED INTERCOMPANY TRANSACTIONS. The reporting of the intercompany securities transaction originally illustrated in Example C:8-10 is presented

[27] Reg. Sec. 1.1502-13(a)(3)(i).
[28] Reg. Sec. 1.1502-13(b)(2)(ii).
[29] Reg. Sec. 1.1502-13(b)(3)(i).
[30] Reg. Sec. 1.1502-13(b)(3)(ii).
[31] Reg. Sec. 1.1502-13(c)(3).

below in four different situations. The four examples demonstrate that the overall gain or loss on an intercompany sale followed by a sale to a third party emulates the results of a sale between divisions of a single firm. To illustrate, if Division S sells property to Division B (e.g., for $200,000), Division S recognizes no gain or loss, and Division B takes Division S's basis in the property (e.g., $120,000). When Division B sells the property to a third party (e.g., for $250,000), the firm recognizes gain or loss on the difference between the selling price to the third party and the original basis (e.g., $250,000 − $120,000 = $130,000 gain). Hence, gain or loss on the sale between S and B is deferred (e.g., $80,000). In the consolidated return context, the buying affiliated corporation (B) takes a cost basis in the property (e.g., $200,000), but the affiliated group must determine a recomputed gain or loss to arrive at the group's total gain. This total gain will be the same as in the sales between divisions followed by a sale to a third party.

EXAMPLE C:8-11 ▶ **Buyer sells securities to a third party at a profit.** Assume the same facts as in Example C:8-10 except B sells the securities to a third party for $250,000 in 2009. The affiliated group will report a $130,000 ($250,000 proceeds − $120,000 basis) recomputed capital gain in 2009. Of this gain, B reports $50,000 in its separate taxable income calculation. Since the affiliated group reported none of the $80,000 deferred gain in prior years, all the $80,000 ($130,000 − $50,000) difference between the affiliated group's total gain and B's separate taxable income gain is reported as an adjustment on the consolidated return worksheet (as illustrated in Step 2 of Table C:8-1). ◀

The reporting of the two sales made by S and B in Examples C:8-10 and C:8-11 can be presented in the worksheet format used in the completed consolidated tax return contained in Appendix B (see worksheet below). Each transaction is initially reported in the selling (S) corporation's separate tax return column. The adjustment for the deferred gain on S's sale of the securities to B in Example C:8-10 appears as a negative entry in the adjustments and eliminations column of the worksheet. The adjustment removes the $80,000 profit earned on the intercompany sale from the consolidated tax return. The adjustment for the restoration of the deferred gain when B sells the securities outside the affiliated group in Example C:8-11 is reported as a positive entry in the adjustments and eliminations column of the worksheet. The adjustment increases the profit resulting from B's sale of the securities to a third party included in the consolidated tax return from $50,000 to $130,000.

Transaction	*Consolidated Taxable Income*	*Adjustments & Eliminations*	*S Corporation's Tax Return*	*B Corporation's Tax Return*
S's sale to B in 2007	$ –0–	($80,000)	$80,000	
B's sale to a third party in 2009	130,000	80,000		$50,000
Total	$130,000	$ –0–	$80,000	$50,000

EXAMPLE C:8-12 ▶ **Buyer sells securities to a third party at a loss.**[32] Assume the same facts as in Example C:8-11 except the securities were instead sold by B to a third party for $190,000. The recomputed gain is $70,000 ($190,000 − $120,000). In 2009, B reports a $10,000 ($190,000 − $200,000 adjusted basis) capital loss in its separate taxable income calculation. Since the affiliated group reported none of the $80,000 deferred gain in prior years, all of the $80,000 ($70,000 + $10,000) difference between the affiliated group's total gain and B's separate taxable income loss is reported as an adjustment on the consolidated return worksheet. ◀

The separate return reporting of the transaction by S is the same as in Examples C:8-10 and C:8-11. The $50,000 capital gain that B reported when it sold the securities to a third party in Example C:8-11 becomes a $10,000 capital loss because the stock was sold for $190,000 rather than $250,000. Restoration of S's $80,000 deferred gain causes the

[32] Section 267(f)(2) requires a realized loss to be deferred when a sale of property occurs between members of a controlled group. Regulation Sec. 1.267(f)-1 provides special rules for property sales involving members of a controlled group that parallel the intercompany transaction rules for consolidated groups. These rules apply to the members of an affiliated group who sell property to a member of its controlled group that is unable to join in the consolidated return election. A discussion of these rules is beyond the scope of this introductory text.

$10,000 separate return capital loss reported by B to become a $70,000 consolidated capital gain in 2009. The worksheet is as follows:

Transaction	*Consolidated Taxable Income*	*Adjustments & Eliminations*	*S Corporation's Tax Return*	*B Corporation's Tax Return*
S's sale to B in 2007	$ –0–	($80,000)	$80,000	
B's sale to a third party in 2009	70,000	80,000		($10,000)
Total	$70,000	$ –0–	$80,000	($10,000)

EXAMPLE C:8-13 ▶ **Buyer sells inventory to a third party at a profit.** Assume the same facts as in Example C:8-11 except the securities were instead inventory in B's hands prior to their sale for $250,000. Although S held the securities as a capital asset, the character of the reported gain is based on the character of the asset at the time B sold it. Thus, both S's $80,000 gain and B's $50,000 gain are ordinary income. The consolidated return worksheet is the same as for Example C:8-11 except the income character changes. ◀

EXAMPLE C:8-14 ▶ **Buyer sells noninventory property to a third party using installment sale.** Assume the same facts as in Example C:8-11 except B's $250,000 sale proceeds are from the sale of a noninventory item and are to be collected in two equal, annual installments starting in 2009. B charges the third party an interest rate acceptable to the IRS on the unpaid balance. The recomputed gain and the individual group member's gains are the same as in Example C:8-11. After selling the securities, B reports the transaction in its separate taxable income using the installment sale provisions of Sec. 453 applicable to nondealers. Likewise, the affiliated group does not report the entire amount of the deferred gain in 2009. Instead, the affiliated group reports the deferred gain as B collects the amounts due under the installment contract.

TYPICAL MISCONCEPTION

Even though the restoration event illustrated in Example C:8-14 is based on the receipt of installment obligations, remember that intercompany sales cannot be reported by the selling group member on the installment method.

The following formula is used to determine the affiliated group's reported gain:

$$\frac{\text{Amount of the installment payment received}}{\text{Total contract price}} \times \text{Deferred intercompany gain} = \text{Affiliated group's restored gain or loss}$$

The affiliated group reports $40,000 of the deferred gain [($125,000 ÷ $250,000) × $80,000] in each 2009 and 2010 as an adjustment to determine consolidated taxable income. B reports its $50,000 gain in two installments of $25,000 each ($50,000 ÷ 2) in 2009 and 2010 plus reporting annually any interest earned on the unpaid balance. ◀

S's separate return reporting of the transaction in 2007 is the same as in Examples C:8-10 through C:8-12. S reports its $80,000 gain in its 2007 separate tax return. A negative $80,000 adjustment is made when preparing the 2007 consolidated tax return thereby resulting in no gain being included in consolidated taxable income. The $50,000 capital gain that B reported when it sold the securities to a third party in Example C:8-11 is reported in its separate tax returns when the obligations are collected in 2009 and 2010. In summary, $25,000 of gain is recognized each year, $40,000 of the deferred gain is restored as a positive adjustment in preparing the 2009 and 2010 consolidated tax returns, and therefore $65,000 of gain is included in consolidated taxable income in each 2009 and 2010.

Transaction	*Consolidated Taxable Income*	*Adjustments & Eliminations*	*S Corporation's Tax Return*	*B Corporation's Tax Return*
S's sale to B in 2007	$ –0–	($80,000)	$80,000	
B's sale to third party in 2009	–0–			$ –0–
B's collection of installment receivable in 2009	65,000	40,000		25,000

B's collection of installment receivable in 2010	65,000	40,000		25,000
Total	$130,000	$ –0–	$80,000	$50,000

DEPRECIATION OF RECOVERY PROPERTY BY THE BUYER. Recovery property sold between two group members in an intercompany transaction results in a continuation of the selling group member's recovery period and recovery method under the Sec. 168(i)(7) anti-churning rules to the extent the purchasing group member's basis equals or is less than the selling group member's adjusted basis. To the extent that the purchasing group member's basis exceeds the selling group member's basis, the excess is treated under Reg. Sec. 1.1502-13(c)(7) as a separate property acquired from an unrelated party. The purchasing party depreciates the step-up in basis as a new property and uses the appropriate MACRS depreciation method and recovery period. The purchaser's depreciation for the carryover portion of the basis is the same each year as the seller's depreciation would have been had the seller not sold the property. The amount of the intercompany gain attributable to the sale that the seller must report in any year (that is, the amount of the increased depreciation deduction to the group) is the amount of the depreciation deduction attributable to the purchaser's step-up in basis. This scenario is illustrated in the following example.

EXAMPLE C:8-15 ▶ S and B Corporations form the S-B affiliated group. On July 1, 2007, S pays $10,000 to a third party for machinery that under the MACRS rules is five-year property. Assuming no Sec. 179 election, S claims the following depreciation deductions:

Year and Type	*Deduction*
2007 regular depreciation	$2,000 ($10,000 × 0.20)
2008 regular depreciation	$3,200 ($10,000 × 0.32)

On January 3, 2009, S sells the machinery to B for $9,000. All the depreciation for 2009 is allocated to B. Under the MACRS rules, the purchaser is allocated the depreciation for the month of transfer when depreciable property is transferred between related parties.[33] S's $4,200 ($9,000 proceeds − $4,800 adjusted basis) Sec. 1245 gain is recognized ratably while B depreciates the asset.

KEY POINT

Depending on when an asset is placed in service and then sold in a deferred intercompany transaction, an asset can be divided into two pieces for depreciation purposes. These situations are covered by special anti-churning rules.

B is treated as continuing the MACRS depreciation on the $4,800 portion of the acquisition price that equals the carryover portion of S's adjusted basis for the machinery. The MACRS provisions also would apply to the $4,200 portion of the acquisition price that represents a step-up in basis (or gain portion of the basis) on B's books. This portion of B's basis is treated as new five-year MACRS property. The amount of the capital recovery deductions claimed by B in its separate taxable income calculation and the intercompany gain or loss reported by the affiliated group as an adjustment to determine consolidated taxable income during B's holding period for the asset are as follows:[34]

ADDITIONAL COMMENT

The result of the depreciation restoration event is to synchronize the depreciation deductions on the stepped-up basis with the restoration of the intercompany gain. Notice that the net depreciation reported in the 2011 consolidated return of $1,152 ($1,958 − $806 restored gain) is the same amount that would have been reported had S never transferred the property.

		Depreciation on			
Year		*Carryover Basis*	*Step-Up in Basis*	*Total Depreciation*	*Restoration of Deferred Gain*
2009	$10,000 × 0.1920	$1,920		$1,920	
	$4,200 × 0.2000		$ 840	840	$ 840
				$2,760	
2010	$10,000 × 0.1152	1,152		$1,152	
	$4,200 × 0.3200		1,344	1,344	1,344
				$2,496	
2011	$10,000 × 0.1152	1,152		$1,152	
	$4,200 × 0.1920		806	806	806
				$1,958	

[33] Reg. Sec. 1.168-5(b).

[34] Intercompany sales of property that will be depreciated in the purchasing group member's hands generally result in the recognition of ordinary income under Sec. 1239 because the selling and purchasing group members are usually also members of a controlled group and, therefore, are related parties under Sec. 1239(b).

2012	$10,000 × 0.0576	576		$ 576	
	$4,200 × 0.1152		484	484	484
				$1,060	
2013	$4,200 × 0.1152		484	484	484
2014	$4,200 × 0.0576		242	242	242
Total depreciation and restoration		$4,800	$4,200	$9,000	$4,200

S's reporting of the sale of the machine to B and B's depreciation of the machine in 2009 is illustrated in the following worksheet. No net gain is reported on the sale of the machine in 2009. The affiliated group reports net depreciation of $1,920 ($2,760 depreciation − $840 restored gain) on the machine in 2009.

Transaction Title	*Consolidated Taxable Income*	*Adjustments & Eliminations*	*S Corporation's Tax Return*	*B Corporation's Tax Return*
Gain on sale of the machine by S to B in 2009	$ -0-	($4,200)	$4,200	
Depreciation of the machine by B in 2009	(1,920)	840		($2,760)
Total	($1,920)	($3,360)	$4,200	($2,760)

S recognizes the $4,200 intercompany gain as ordinary income under Sec. 1245. A sample consolidated tax return is included in Appendix B, which includes the restoration of an intercompany gain via depreciation. ◀

PRACTICE NOTE

Some firms that make infrequent intercompany sales will follow the practice of making the sale at the asset's tax book value to avoid having to defer and restore a gain or loss.

DEPARTING GROUP MEMBER. The Seller's intercompany items and Buyer's corresponding items are taken into account under the acceleration rule when they no longer can be taken into account to produce the effect of treating the two entities as divisions of a single corporation.

If the Seller leaves the affiliated group and the intercompany item originated from a sale, exchange, or distribution, the acceleration rule treats the item as having been sold by the Buyer for a cash payment equal to the Buyer's adjusted basis in the property.

EXAMPLE C:8-16 ▶ Assume the same facts as in Example C:8-15 except that S's stock is sold by its parent corporation on the last day of 2010, and S immediately leaves the affiliated group. B continues to be owned by its parent corporation (and S's former parent corporation). Of S's $4,200 deferred gain, $2,184 has been recognized in the group's consolidated taxable income ($840 in 2009 and $1,344 in 2010). The affiliated group must report the remaining $2,016 ($4,200 − $2,184) of deferred gain immediately before S becomes a nonmember. B continues to depreciate the property's carryover basis using its regular accounting methods. ◀

If the S and B stock had been sold together by their parent company, the two corporations would continue to be treated as divisions of a single corporation for as long as S and B continued to file a consolidated tax return. Therefore, a deemed sale of the securities would not occur, and none of S's intercompany profit would be reported.

SELF-STUDY QUESTION

Why are the other intercompany transactions not given any special treatment?

ANSWER

Because both sides of the transaction are reported in the same consolidated return, they simply net each other out. If, due to accounting method differences, the items would be reported in different tax periods, both the income and deduction must be reported in the later of the two tax years.

OTHER INTERCOMPANY TRANSACTIONS

Any income, gain, deduction, or loss realized or incurred on other intercompany transactions is included in the income and expense classifications for the tax year in which the transaction is ordinarily reported. Both parties report their sides of the transaction in determining separate taxable income.[35] When both parties use the same accounting method, these amounts net to zero because the income and expense are included in consolidated taxable income.

Section 267(a)(2) imposes a special rule on related party transactions requiring the matching of the recognition of the payer's deduction item and the payee's income item.

[35] Reg. Sec. 1.1502-13(b)(1) and (2). This procedure may be contrasted with financial accounting, in which both sides of the transaction are eliminated in preparing the consolidated financial statements.

Thus, when two group members would ordinarily report the income and deduction items in different consolidated return years under their regular accounting methods, the payer must defer the reporting of the deduction until the tax year in which the payee member reports the income.

Section 267(b)(3) includes two corporations that are members of the same controlled group as related parties. This definition includes most members of affiliated groups, whether separate returns or a consolidated return are filed. It also may include certain corporations that are not included in the affiliated group because they are not includible corporations (for example, brother-sister corporations included in a combined controlled group).

Regulation Sec. 1.1502-13(a)(2) requires the two group members to match the income and expense items as if they were incurred by two divisions of a single corporation. As two divisions, S and B would report a recomputed expense amount of zero (i.e., the income of one division would exactly offset the expense of the other division, so that neither income nor loss would be reported to external parties). Because S's intercompany items are recognized when B's corresponding items are incurred, amounts earned by S from an intercompany transaction can be included in the consolidated tax return before they are taken into account under its separate entity method of accounting.

EXAMPLE C:8-17 ▶ S and B Corporations have filed calendar year consolidated tax returns for several years. S and B Corporations use the accrual method of accounting. S lends B $100,000 on March 1, 2007; this debt and the related interest are unpaid at the end of 2007. Interest is charged by S at an annual rate of 12%. The $10,000 interest charge owed at year-end is paid by B on March 1, 2008. S accrues $10,000 of interest income in 2007, and B accrues $10,000 of interest expense in 2007. S and B Corporations report the interest income and expense in a worksheet format similar to that used for the earlier intercompany sales. No net income or loss is reported in the consolidated tax return as a result of the loan being made by S in 2007.

Transaction	*Consolidated Taxable Income*	*Adjustments & Eliminations*	*S Corporation's Tax Return*	*B Corporation's Tax Return*
Accrual of interest income by S in 2007	$10,000		$10,000	
Accrual of expense interest by B in 2007	(10,000)			($10,000)
Total	$ –0–		$10,000	($10,000) ◀

EXAMPLE C:8-18 ▶ Assume the same facts as in Example C:8-17 except that S Corporation is a cash method of accounting taxpayer. Ordinarily, S, a cash method corporation, would report no interest income and B, an accrual method corporation, would report $10,000 of interest expense in the computation of their separate taxable incomes for 2007's consolidated tax return. Because B has reported $10,000 of interest expense in its separate return and the recomputed expense amount is zero, an adjustment must be made to nullify the interest expense in the 2007 consolidated tax return. After the adjustment, no "net" interest income or expense is reported.

In 2007, B normally would report its $10,000 of interest expense related to the loan using its overall accrual method of accounting. The consolidated tax return Treasury Regulations require B to defer the $10,000 of interest expense from 2007 to 2008. At this time, S will report $10,000 of interest income from the loan and B likewise will report its $10,000 interest expense. The consolidated return regulations require B to defer the reporting of its tax deduction until the point in time when B reports its interest income. The consolidated return worksheet is as follows:

Transaction	*Consolidated Taxable Income*	*Adjustments & Eliminations*	*S Corporation's Tax Return*	*B Corporation's Tax Return*
Interest income reported by S in 2007	$ –0–		$ –0–	
Interest expense reported by B in 2007	–0–	$10,000		($10,000)

Transaction	Consolidated Taxable Income	Adjustments & Eliminations	S Corporation's Tax Return	B Corporation's Tax Return
Interest income reported by S in 2008	10,000		10,000	
Interest expense reported by B in 2008	(10,000)	(10,000)		–0–
Total	$ –0–	$ –0–	$ 10,000	($10,000)

At the end of the two years, S reports $10,000 of income in its separate tax return, and B reports $10,000 of expense in its separate tax return. These two amounts net to the same zero amount reported in Example C:8-17 when both taxpayers were accrual method corporations. ◀

A Seller's profit or loss from the sale of the capitalized services to another group member is an intercompany item. When a Buyer capitalizes the acquisition cost of the services, the Buyer's amortization deduction becomes the corresponding item. Thus, Buyer's capitalization of the purchase under its separate method of accounting permits the Seller to spread the recognition of its profit, which otherwise would be recognized under its separate method of accounting, over the amortization time period.

EXAMPLE C:8-19 ▶ S and B Corporations have filed consolidated tax returns for a number of years. S Corporation, an accrual method of accounting taxpayer, drills wells. B Corporation, operates a farm, and uses the cash method of accounting. S drills a well in the current year for B for $10,000, which creates a $2,000 profit. B pays S the cost of the well, capitalizes the well cost, and begins to amortize it over a five-year period. Under the accrual method of accounting, S would report its income and expenses when the drilling occurred. Because it is an intercompany transaction, S reports its profit over the five-year amortization period used by B.

Transaction	*Consolidated Taxable Income*	*Adjustments & Eliminations*	*S Corporation's Tax Return*	*B Corporation's Tax Return*
Amortization of well-drilling cost by B in the current year	($2,000)			($2,000)
Accrual of well-drilling income by S in the current year	2,000	($8,000)	$10,000	
Total	$ –0–	($8,000)	$10,000	($2,000)

◀

Topic Review C:8-1 summarizes the intercompany transaction rules.

DIVIDENDS RECEIVED BY GROUP MEMBERS

SELF-STUDY QUESTION

Are dividends received from members of the same affiliated group entitled to a dividends-received deduction?

ANSWER

Not if the affiliated group files a consolidated tax return because intercompany dividends are excluded; hence, no dividends-received deduction is necessary.

Dividends received by group members are treated differently depending on whether they come from corporations within the affiliated group or from firms outside it. In determining consolidated taxable income, the dividends received from other group members are excluded, while those received from nonmembers of the group are eligible for a 70%, 80%, or 100% dividends-received deduction.

EXCLUSION PROCEDURE

A dividend distribution from one group member (the distributing member) to a second group member (the distributee member) during a consolidated return year is an intercompany transaction. An intercompany distribution is not included in the gross income of the distributee member. The exclusion applies only to distributions that otherwise would be

Topic Review C:8-1

Reporting Intercompany Transactions

INTERCOMPANY TRANSACTIONS

1. Intercompany transaction definition: a transaction taking place during a consolidated return year between corporations that are members of the same affiliated group immediately after the transaction.
2. Two types of intercompany transactions:
   a. Property transactions—the intercompany item (gain or loss) is deferred until a corresponding event occurs.
   b. Other transactions—the intercompany item (income or expense item) is reported in the year in which the corresponding event occurs.
3. The selling and buying members of the affiliated group generally are treated as separate entities when reporting the intercompany transaction.
   a. **Exception:** the selling and buying members are treated as two divisions of the same entity when determining the recomputed corresponding gain, income, loss, or deduction item.
4. The reporting of intercompany transactions are based on two concepts.
   a. **Intercompany items** are the Seller's income, gain, deduction, or loss from an intercompany transaction.
   b. **Corresponding items** are the Buyer's income, gain, deduction or loss from an intercompany transaction, or from property acquired in an intercompany transaction.
5. The following are some of the corresponding items that can trigger the recognition of an intercompany item (e.g., gain, loss, income, or deduction amount).
   a. The Buyer sells property to a nonmember of the group.
   b. Property acquired by the Buyer is depreciated, depleted, or amortized.
   c. The corporation that sold a property or acquired a property leaves the affiliated group.
   d. The affiliated group discontinues filing a consolidated tax return and begins filing separate tax returns.

TYPICAL MISCONCEPTION

One difference between consolidated tax returns and separate tax returns is that, in a consolidated setting, intercompany distributions exceeding both E&P and basis in the shareholder member's stock investment do not create a capital gain but rather create an excess loss account (i.e., a negative basis account for the distributee's investment in the distributing corporation).

REAL-WORLD EXAMPLE

When each corporation within an affiliated group prepares its own separate tax return, dividends received from related corporations may be included in gross income. In such a situation, a worksheet adjustment is then needed during the consolidation process to remove the dividend amount from consolidated taxable income.

taxable if paid to a nonaffiliated corporation and that produce a corresponding negative adjustment to the basis of the distributing member's stock.[36]

Within an affiliated group, nondividend distributions (e.g., distributions exceeding the earnings and profits balance) reduce the distributee member's basis in the distributing member's stock.[37] If the amount of the distribution exceeds the distributee's adjusted basis in the stock, the excess either creates a new, or increases an existing, excess loss account (i.e., a negative investment account). However, the distributee does not recognize any gain from the portion of the distribution that exceeds its basis in the distributing member's stock (as it would with nonaffiliated corporations).[38] The creation of an excess loss account is discussed in the basis adjustment section of this chapter.

The amount of any distribution received by one group member from another equals the money distributed plus the sum of the adjusted basis of any property distributed and the gain recognized by the distributing member. Because under Sec. 311(b) gain is recognized on most distributions of appreciated property, the gain recognized plus the adjusted basis of the distributed property generally will equal its FMV where a distribution of appreciated property takes place between group members. Gain recognized by the distributing member under Sec. 311(b) due to the distribution of property to another group member is treated as an intercompany item. The deferred gain is included in consolidated taxable income by the distributing member when a corresponding item is reported by the distributee (e.g., the distributee member depreciates the property).[39]

CONSOLIDATED DIVIDENDS-RECEIVED DEDUCTION

The basic dividends-received deduction rules, as set forth in Chapter C:3, apply to the calculation of the consolidated dividends-received deduction. The dividends-received

[36] Reg. Sec. 1.1502-13(f)(2).
[37] Reg. Sec. 1.1502-13(f)(7).
[38] Reg. Sec. 1.1502-14(a)(2). The amount of the excess loss account's negative balance is reported as either ordinary income or capital gain when a disposition of the subsidiary corporation's stock occurs.
[39] Reg. Sec. 1.1502-13(f).

deduction for dividends received from nonmembers is computed on a consolidated basis. It is not applied to the separate taxable income of each group member. The consolidated dividends-received deduction equals the sum of 70% of dividends received from unaffiliated domestic corporations in which a less than 20% interest is held, 80% of dividends received from unaffiliated domestic corporations in which a 20% or more interest is held, and 100% of dividends received from an 80% or more owned domestic corporation that is not included in the consolidated return election (e.g., a 100%-owned life insurance company prohibited from being part of a consolidated tax return). The 70% and 80% dividends-received deductions are separately limited by consolidated taxable income. The 80% dividends-received deduction limitation is calculated first, and the deduction cannot exceed 80% of consolidated taxable income excluding the consolidated dividends-received deduction, any consolidated NOL, or capital loss carryback. The 70% dividends-received deduction limitation is then calculated and the deduction cannot exceed 70% of consolidated taxable income reduced by the amount of the dividends eligible for the 80% dividends-received deduction and excluding the consolidated dividends-received deduction, any consolidated NOL, or capital loss carryback. The limitations do not apply if the full amount of the deduction creates or increases a consolidated NOL.[40]

EXAMPLE C:8-20 ▶ P, S_1, and S_2 Corporations create the P-S_1-S_2 affiliated group. Consolidated taxable income (without considering any dividends-received exclusions or deductions, NOLs, and capital losses) is $200,000. The following dividend income is received by the group members from unaffiliated corporations that are less than 20%-owned: P, $6,000; S_1, $10,000; and S_2, $34,000. In addition, P receives a $40,000 dividend from S_1, and S_1 receives a $60,000 dividend from a 100%-owned life insurance company that cannot join in the consolidated return election at the present time. S_1's distribution reduces P's basis for its investment in S_1.

- ▶ The $40,000 dividend that P receives from S_1 is excluded from P's gross income since it results in a basis reduction for P's investment in S_1.
- ▶ S_1's $60,000 dividend from the 100%-owned life insurance company is eligible for a 100% dividends-received deduction. This $60,000 deduction is not subject to any limitation and reduces consolidated taxable income before applying the 70% limitation.
- ▶ The 70% dividends-received deductions included in the separate taxable income calculations are P, $4,200 (0.70 × $6,000); S_1, $7,000 (0.70 × $10,000); and S_2, $23,800 (0.70 × $34,000), or a total $35,000 reduction in consolidated taxable income. The 70% dividends-received deduction ($35,000) is not restricted by the dividends-received deduction limitation [($200,000 consolidated taxable income given in the facts − $60,000 dividends-received deduction) × 0.70 = $98,000].

The consolidated dividends-received deduction is $95,000 ($35,000 + $60,000). ◀

SELF-STUDY QUESTION

What is the dividends-received deduction in Example C:8-20 if the group has consolidated taxable income before special deductions of (a) $95,000? (b) $94,999?

ANSWER

(a) $84,500 [$60,000 + (0.70 × $35,000)] due to the consolidated taxable income limitation.
(b) All $95,000 ($60,000 + $35,000) is allowed because the full dividends-received deduction creates an NOL. Should a $1 difference in consolidated taxable income make a $10,500 difference in the dividends-received deduction?

STOP & THINK *Question:* Alpha Corporation has owned the stock of a 100%-owned subsidiary for a number of years. Peter Gray, the CPA, who has prepared both corporations' tax returns since their creation has been trying to sell Alpha's Director of Federal Taxes on beginning to file a consolidated tax return based on the tax exemption for intragroup dividends. Is he right or wrong in his approach?

Solution: He is wrong. If the two companies file separate tax returns, a 100% dividends-received deduction is available for intragroup dividends. If a consolidated return were filed, the dividend can be excluded from Alpha's gross income. Typically, these two alternatives provide the same outcome. A difference between these two alternatives may be found when preparing state tax returns (see page C:8-36). Peter should be concentrating on advantages, such as offsetting profits and losses between the two companies should one company incur a loss, deferring intercompany profits, etc.

A discussion of the financial statement implications of intercompany transactions appears at the end of this chapter.

[40] Reg. Sec. 1.1502-26(a)(1).

CONSOLIDATED CHARITABLE CONTRIBUTIONS DEDUCTION

KEY POINT

Taking the charitable contribution deduction on a consolidated basis rather than for each corporation separately may or may not be beneficial. The outcome depends on the actual numbers in each individual situation.

The basic charitable contributions deduction rules, as set forth in Chapter C:3, apply to the calculation of the consolidated charitable contribution deduction. The affiliated group's charitable contributions deduction is computed on a consolidated basis. The consolidated charitable contributions deduction equals the sum of the charitable contributions deductions of the individual group members for the consolidated return year (computed without regard to any individual group member's limitation) plus any charitable contribution carryovers from earlier consolidated or separate return years. The charitable contributions deduction is limited to 10% of adjusted consolidated taxable income. Adjusted consolidated taxable income is computed without regard to the consolidated dividends-received deduction, any consolidated NOL or capital loss carrybacks, and the consolidated charitable contributions deduction. Any charitable contributions made by the group that exceeds the 10% limitation carry over to the five succeeding tax years.[41] Any unused contributions remaining at the end of the carryover period are lost.

EXAMPLE C:8-21 ▶ P, S_1, and S_2 Corporations form the P-S_1-S_2 affiliated group. The group members report the following charitable contributions and adjusted consolidated taxable income for the current year:

ADDITIONAL COMMENT

In Example C:8-21, if a consolidated tax return had not been filed, the charitable contribution deduction would have been $12,500 for P, $0 for S_1, and $1,000 for S_2. The total of these three deductions is $6,000 less than the $12,000 consolidated charitable contribution deduction.

Group Member	*Charitable Contributions*	*Adjusted Consolidated Taxable Income*
P	$12,500	$150,000
S_1	5,000	(40,000)
S_2	2,000	10,000
Total	$19,500	$120,000

The P-S_1-S_2 affiliated group's charitable contributions deduction is the lesser of its actual charitable contributions ($19,500) or 10% of its adjusted consolidated taxable income ($12,000). The $7,500 ($19,500 − $12,000) of excess charitable contributions carry over to the next five tax years. ◀

A member leaving the affiliated group takes with it any excess contributions arising in a prior separate return year plus its allocable share of any excess consolidated charitable contributions for a consolidated return year. The excess consolidated charitable contributions are allocated to each group member based on the relative amount of their contributions (when compared to the total contributions of all group members) for the consolidated return year.

CONSOLIDATED U.S. PRODUCTION ACTIVITIES DEDUCTION

For tax years beginning after 2004, the U.S. production activities deduction also can be taken on a consolidated basis. (See Chapter C:3 for a detailed discussion of this deduction.) The deduction for an affiliated group must be calculated as for a single corporation and is based on the lesser of (1) consolidated qualified production activities income or (2) consolidated taxable income before this deduction. For purposes of calculating the U.S. production activities deduction only, Congress expanded the definition of an affiliated group by reducing the stock ownership threshold from 80% to 50% and by including, as eligible, insurance companies and corporations that use the possessions tax credit. Accordingly, the calculation of this deduction may involve entities that are not part of the group filing the consolidated return. The members of this extended affiliated group must calculate a single consolidated U.S. production activities deduction and then allocate the deduction among the members of the group based on the relative

41 Reg. Sec. 1.1502-24(a).

amount of qualified production activities income that each member of the affiliated group earns. Because of the potential for an extremely complex calculation being necessary when the extended affiliated group and the consolidated group differ, Treasury Regulations under Sec. 199 provide some guidance.

NET OPERATING LOSSES (NOLs)

OBJECTIVE 8

Calculate an affiliated group's consolidated NOL

One advantage of filing a consolidated tax return is the ability of an affiliated group to offset one member's current NOLs against the taxable income of other group members. If these losses cause the affiliated group to report a consolidated NOL, the NOL may be carried back or carried forward to other consolidated return years of the affiliated group. In some cases, part or all of the consolidated NOL can be carried back or carried over to separate return years of the individual group members. NOLs of group members arising in separate return years also may be carried back or carried over to consolidated return years, subject to the separate return limitation year (SRLY) limit. In addition, NOLs, capital losses, and excess credits of a loss corporation that is a member of an affiliated group can be subject to the consolidated Secs. 382–384 limitations. The rules that apply to carrybacks and carryovers are examined below.

KEY POINT

Generally, the most significant benefit to filing consolidated tax returns is the ability to offset losses of one member against the income of other members.

CURRENT YEAR NOLs

Each member's separate taxable income is combined to determine combined taxable income before any adjustment is made for NOL carryovers (see Table C:8-1).[42] The combining process allows the losses of one group member to offset the taxable income of other group members. A group member cannot elect separately to carry back its own losses from a consolidated return year to one of its earlier profitable separate return years. Only the consolidated group's NOL (if any) may be carried back or over.

EXAMPLE C:8-22 ▶ P and S Corporations form the P-S affiliated group. During 2006, the initial year of operation, P and S file calendar year separate tax returns. Beginning in 2007, the P-S group elects to file a consolidated tax return. P and S report the following results for 2006 and 2007:

Group Member	Taxable Income 2006	Taxable Income 2007
P	($15,000)	$40,000
S	250,000	(27,000)
Consolidated taxable income	N/A	$13,000

N/A = Not applicable

P's 2006 NOL may not be used to offset S's 2006 profits because separate returns were filed. This NOL carryover may be used only to reduce the $13,000 of 2007 consolidated taxable income reported after S's 2007 loss is offset against P's 2007 separate taxable income. Because S's 2007 loss must be offset against P's 2007 taxable income, S cannot carry its 2007 NOL back against its 2006 taxable income to increase the value of the tax savings obtained from the loss. The remaining NOL of $2,000 ($15,000 loss from 2006 − $13,000 2007 consolidated taxable income) carries over to 2008. ◀

OBJECTIVE 9

Calculate the carryback or carryover of a consolidated NOL

CARRYBACKS AND CARRYFORWARDS OF CONSOLIDATED NOLs

The consolidated NOL rules are similar to the NOL rules applying to a corporation filing a separate tax return. A consolidated NOL is determined after the following computation:[43]

---

[42] Reg. Sec. 1.1502-12(h).

[43] Reg. Sec. 1.1502-21(e).

Separate taxable income of each group member (from Table C:8-1)
Plus: Consolidated capital gain net income
Minus: Consolidated Sec. 1231 net loss
Consolidated charitable contributions deduction
Consolidated dividends-received deduction

Consolidated NOL

A consolidated NOL may be carried back to the two preceding consolidated return years or carried over to the 20 succeeding consolidated return years. The parent corporation also may elect for the affiliated group to relinquish the entire carryback period for a consolidated NOL and use it only as a carryforward to succeeding years.[44] (See Chapter C:3 for a discussion of the reasons for making this election and how this election is made.)

TYPICAL MISCONCEPTION

As a general rule, a consolidated NOL may be carried back two years and carried forward 20 years. This procedure is not complicated unless the members of the group change before the loss is fully used.

A carryback or carryforward of the consolidated NOL to a tax year in which the members of the affiliated group have not changed poses no real problem. The amount of the consolidated NOL absorbed in a given tax year is determined according to the basic Sec. 172 rules for NOLs outlined in Chapter C:3.

Determining the amount of the consolidated NOL that may be absorbed in a tax year is more difficult when the group members are not the same in the carryback or carryforward year. In such a case, the consolidated NOL is apportioned to each corporation that was both a member of the affiliated group and incurred a separate NOL during the loss year. When a loss corporation is not also a group member in the carryback or carryforward year, the rules relating to carrybacks and carryforwards to separate return years (discussed below) must be applied.

CARRYBACK OF CONSOLIDATED NOL TO SEPARATE RETURN YEAR

GENERAL RULE. A consolidated NOL may be carried back and absorbed against a member's taxable income from the preceding two separate return years. To effect a carryback, part or all of the consolidated NOL must be apportioned to the member. To the extent a member uses its allocable share of the consolidated NOL, such an amount is not available to the remaining members as a carryback or carryforward to a consolidated return year. The consolidated NOL is apportioned to a loss member in the following manner:[45]

$$\frac{\text{Separate NOL of the individual member}}{\text{Sum of the separate NOLs incurred by all members having such losses}} \times \text{Consolidated NOL} = \text{Portion of consolidated NOL attributable to member}$$

EXAMPLE C:8-23 ▶ P and S Corporations form the P-S affiliated group. The P-S group filed separate tax returns in 2005 and 2006. S reported taxable income of $275,000 in 2005. The group elects to file a consolidated tax return for 2007. The P-S group reports a $150,000 consolidated NOL for 2007, all of which is attributable to S. S carries the $150,000 NOL back to 2005 and uses the loss to partially offset the taxable income it reported in 2005. The loss is used up in 2005 and therefore cannot be used by S in 2006 or by the P-S group in any subsequent consolidated return year. Alternatively, an election by P to forgo the carryback permits the 2007 loss to be used sequentially in 2008 and the next 19 consolidated return years. ◀

KEY POINT

In Example C:8-23, because P-S did not file a consolidated tax return in 2005, P must either forgo the two-year carryback or allow all the consolidated NOL to be carried back to S's 2005 separate tax return year.

SPECIAL CARRYBACK RULE FOR NEW MEMBERS. When the consolidated NOL is apportioned to a member, it normally is carried back to the two immediately preceding consolidated return years or the loss corporation's separate return years. A special rule permits

[44] Reg. Sec. 1.1502-21(b)(3)(i).

[45] Reg. Sec. 1.1502-21(b)(2)(iv). The member's separate NOL is determined in a manner similar to the calculation of separate taxable income except for a series of adjustments to account for the member's share of the consolidated charitable contributions and dividends-received deductions, the member's capital gain net income, and the member's net capital loss or Sec. 1231 net loss minus any portion of the consolidated amounts attributable to the member that were absorbed currently.

an affiliated group member to carry an NOL back two years to a separate return year of its common parent corporation or a consolidated return year of the affiliated group if

- The member corporation with the loss carryback did not exist in the carryback year, and
- The loss corporation has been a member of the affiliated group continually since its organization.

If these two requirements are met, the portion of the consolidated NOL attributable to the loss member is carried back to the two preceding consolidated return years of the affiliated group (or separate return year of the common parent corporation) only if the common parent was not a member of a different consolidated group or affiliated group filing separate returns for the year to which the loss is carried or a subsequent year in the carryback period.[46]

EXAMPLE C:8-24 ▶ P and S_1 Corporations were affiliated for 2005 and 2006 and filed consolidated tax returns. P acquires all of S_2 Corporation's stock on January 1, 2007, the date on which S_2 is created by P, and S_2 becomes a member of the affiliated group. P, S_1, and S_2 report the following results (excluding NOL deductions) for 2005 through 2007:

Group Member	Taxable Income 2005	2006	2007
P	$12,000	$10,000	$16,000
S_1	8,000	7,000	4,000
S_2	XXX	XXX	(30,000)
Consolidated taxable income	$20,000	$17,000	($10,000)

All the 2007 consolidated NOL is attributable to S_2. As illustrated, S_2's separate NOL of $30,000 is first used to offset P and S_1's taxable income in 2007, leaving only a $10,000 consolidated NOL. Two options are available with respect to the consolidated NOL: the NOL may be carried over to subsequent tax years, or the NOL may be carried back to 2005 and 2006. If the first alternative is selected, the NOL offsets consolidated taxable income reported in 2008 and up to 19 subsequent tax years. If the second alternative is selected, the $10,000 NOL is carried back to offset part of the 2005 consolidated taxable income. This result is possible because S_2 did not exist at the end of 2006 and because it joined the affiliated group immediately after it was created on January 1, 2007, and has been a group member continually since its organization. ◀

SELF-STUDY QUESTION

What is the reason for allowing S_2's portion of the consolidated NOL to be carried back to 2005 and 2006?

ANSWER

Because the assets that make up S_2 in 2007 were really P's assets in 2005 and 2006, it makes sense to allow the NOLs to be carried back against whatever tax return P filed in 2005 and 2006.

If the loss corporation is not a member of the affiliated group immediately after its organization, that member's portion of the consolidated NOL is carried back only to its prior separate return years.

EXAMPLE C:8-25 ▶ Assume the same facts as in Example C:8-24 except S_2 Corporation existed separately and filed a separate tax return for 2006 prior to its stock being acquired by P on January 1, 2007. P, S_1, and S_2 report the following results (excluding NOL deductions) for 2005 through 2007:

Group Member	Taxable Income 2005	2006	2007
P	$12,000	$10,000	$16,000
S_1	8,000	7,000	4,000
S_2	XXX	8,000	(30,000)
Consolidated taxable income	$20,000	$17,000[a]	($10,000)

[a] Including only the results of P and S_1.

The $10,000 2007 consolidated NOL can be carried back by S_2 to 2006. The NOL offsets all $8,000 of S_2's 2006 separate return taxable income. The remaining loss carryback of $2,000 can-

SELF-STUDY QUESTION

Is there any reason for P to elect not to carry back the NOL to S_2's separate tax return years?

ANSWER

Probably not. But if S_2 has minority shareholders, because the refund is issued to S_2, the minority stock interest will share in the increase in FMV of S_2's stock. Don't overlook minority shareholders!

[46] Reg. Sec. 1.1502-21(b)(2)(ii)(B). A consolidated group is an affiliated group that has elected to file a consolidated tax return.

not be used to reduce the taxable income reported in 2005 or 2006 by P and S_1. It can be carried over, however, to offset the affiliated group's 2008 and later taxable income. Alternatively, the P-S_1-S_2 affiliated group could elect to carry the entire loss over to offset 2008 and later years taxable income (see Chapter C:3's discussion regarding why such an election might be advisable). ◀

CARRYFORWARD OF CONSOLIDATED NOL TO SEPARATE RETURN YEAR

If a corporation ceases to be a member of the affiliated group during the current year, the portion of the consolidated NOL allocable to the departing member becomes the member's separate carryforward. However, the allocation of the NOL to the departing group member cannot be made until the available carryover is absorbed in the current consolidated return year. This requirement exists even when all of the carryover is attributable to the departing member. The departing member's share of the NOL carryforward then may be used in its first separate return year.[47]

EXAMPLE C:8-26 ▶ P, S_1, and S_2 Corporations form the P-S_1-S_2 affiliated group, with P owning all the S_1 and S_2 stock. The group files consolidated tax returns for several years. At the close of business on September 30, 2007, P sells its investment in S_1. S_1 must file a separate tax return covering the period October 1, 2007, through December 31, 2007. During pre-2007 tax years, P, S_1, and S_2 incurred substantial NOLs. At the beginning of 2007, a consolidated NOL carryover of $100,000 is still available. Two-thirds of this loss is allocable to S_1; the remainder is allocable to S_2. The affiliated group reports the following results (excluding NOL deductions) for 2007:

TYPICAL MISCONCEPTION

In Example C:8-26, it is important to understand that the group is entitled to use the consolidated NOL before S_1 determines its NOL carryover. This can have an impact on negotiating an equitable purchase price for S_1.

	Group Member	*Taxable Income*
P		$20,000
S_1:	January 1 through September 30	30,000
	October 1 through December 31	15,000
S_2		10,000
Total		$75,000

The consolidated NOL carryover of $100,000 offsets the $60,000 ($20,000 + $30,000 + $10,000) of taxable income reported by P, S_1, and S_2 in their 2007 consolidated tax return. This leaves $40,000 of carryover to be allocated between S_1 and S_2. Assume an agreement is reached where S_1 receives $26,667 (0.667 × $40,000), and S_2 receives $13,333 (0.333 × $40,000) of the carryover. Of S_1's carryover, $15,000 can be used in its separate tax return for October 1 through December 31, 2007. The remaining $11,667 is carried over to S_1's 2008 separate tax return. The affiliated group can carry over S_2's $13,333 allocable share of the NOL to 2008 and subsequent years. ◀

OBJECTIVE 10

Determine how the special loss limitations restrict the use of separate and consolidated NOL carrybacks and carryovers

SPECIAL LOSS LIMITATIONS

Two special loss limitations, the **separate return limitation year (SRLY) rules** and the **Sec. 382 loss limitation rules**, are imposed on affiliated groups. The SRLY rules limit the separate return NOL amount that can be deducted as a NOL carryback or carryover by an affiliated group to a member's contribution to consolidated taxable income.[48] This treatment prevents the affiliated group from offsetting its current taxable income by purchasing loss corporations solely to use their NOLs. The Sec. 382 loss limitation rules, which were explained in Chapter C:7 on a separate return basis, also apply to affiliated groups filing consolidated returns. The special Sec. 382 consolidated return rules restrict an affiliated group from using NOLs following an ownership change that results from a purchase transaction or a tax-free reorganization. Each set of rules is explained below.

KEY POINT

The SRLY rules limit a group from acquiring already existing losses and offsetting those losses against the group's income.

SEPARATE RETURN LIMITATION YEAR RULES. A member incurring an NOL in a separate return year (that is available as a carryback or a carryforward to a consolidated return year) is subject to a limit on the use of the NOL when the loss year is designated a

[47] Reg. Sec. 1.1502-21(b)(2)(ii)(A).

[48] The SRLY rules do not apply to the foreign tax credit, general business credit, minimum tax credit, and overall foreign losses for corporations joining the affiliated group.

ADDITIONAL COMMENT

These two exceptions to the SRLY rules exist because in both cases the group has not acquired already existing NOLs.

separate return limitation year. A **separate return limitation year** is defined as any separate return year, except

- A separate return year of the group member designated as the parent corporation for the consolidated return year to which the tax attribute (e.g., NOL) is carried, or
- A separate return year of any corporation that was a group member for every day of the loss year (i.e., a consolidated return was not elected or the corporation was not eligible to participate in the filing of a consolidated return in the loss year).

NOL Carryovers. An NOL incurred in a SRLY may be used as a carryover in a consolidated return year equal to the lesser of (1) the aggregate of the consolidated taxable income amounts for all consolidated return years of the group determined by taking into account only the loss member's items of income, gain, deduction, and loss minus any NOL carryovers previously absorbed, (2) consolidated taxable income, or (3) the amount of the NOL carryover.[49] A SRLY carryover cannot be used when a member's cumulative contribution is less than zero. Any NOL carryovers or carrybacks that cannot be used currently because of the member's contribution to consolidated taxable income or the group's current year consolidated taxable income must be carried over to subsequent tax years.

EXAMPLE C:8-27 ▶ P and S Corporations form the P-S affiliated group. P acquires the S stock at the close of business on December 31, 2007.[50] P and S file separate tax returns for 2007 and begin filing a consolidated tax return in 2008. Assume the U.S. production activities deduction does not apply. The group reports the following results (excluding NOL deductions) for 2007 through 2011:

SELF-STUDY QUESTION

What is the consequence of having losses subject to the SRLY limitations?

ANSWER

The effect of having a loss tainted as a SRLY loss is that it can be used only to offset taxable income of the subsidiary member (or possibly a loss subgroup) that created the NOL.

	Taxable Income				
Group Member	*2007*	*2008*	*2009*	*2010*	*2011*
P Corporation	($ 9,000)	$17,000	$ 6,000	($6,000)	$ 2,000
S Corporation	(20,000)	(2,000)	5,000	5,000	16,000
Consolidated taxable income	$ XXX	$15,000	$11,000	($1,000)	$18,000

Under the SRLY rules, the separate NOLs are used as follows:

- P's 2007 loss is offset against the group's $15,000 of 2008 consolidated taxable income (CTI). None of S's 2007 loss can be used because it incurred a separate NOL in 2008, which already has been offset against P's $17,000 profit. The group's 2008 CTI is reduced to $6,000 ($15,000 – $9,000).
- $3,000 of S's 2007 loss is offset against 2009 CTI: the smaller of S's $3,000 cumulative contribution to CTI [($2,000) + $5,000], its $20,000 NOL carryover, or the $11,000 of CTI. The $3,000 of NOL used reduces S's NOL carryover to $17,000.
- None of S's 2007 loss can be used in 2010 because the group reported a consolidated NOL. Assuming the 2010 NOL is carried back, 2008's CTI is reduced from $6,000 to $5,000 ($15,000 – $9,000 carryover from 2007 – $1,000 carryback from 2010).
- $17,000 of S's 2007 loss is offset against 2011 CTI, which is the smaller of S's $21,000 cumulative contributions to CTI in 2008 through 2011 ($24,000 net contributions to CTI in 2008–2011 – $3,000 NOL used in 2009), its $17,000 remaining loss carryover, or the $18,000 of CTI. Consolidated taxable income is reduced to $1,000 ($18,000 – $17,000), and no carryovers remain to 2012. ◀

The SRLY rules generally apply to each individual corporation that has a loss carryover from a separate return limitation year. The SRLY limitation must be determined for a subgroup of two or more corporations within an affiliated group that are continuously

[49] Reg. Sec. 1.1502-21(b)(1). Any unused NOLs that are carried to the consolidated return year from tax years ending before the separate return limitation year reduce the SRLY limitation on a first-in, first-out (FIFO) basis. Tax years ending on the same date reduce the SRLY limitations on a pro rata basis. A loss member's contribution to CTI is determined on a "with" and "without" basis. The difference between CTI "with" the loss member and "without" the loss member is the loss member's contribution to CTI.

[50] P's acquisition of the S stock can trigger both the SRLY rules and the Sec. 382 rules. The overlap rules have not yet been discussed. To simplify the example, assume that the Sec. 382 limitation does not apply.

affiliated after ceasing to be members of a former affiliated group, that joined the affiliated group at the same time, and where at least one of the corporations carries over losses from the former group to the current group. If the subgroup has remained continuously affiliated up to the beginning of the year to which the loss is carried, the subgroup's loss carryovers can be used to the extent the subgroup contributes to consolidated taxable income.[51]

EXAMPLE C:8-28 ▶ P Corporation owns 100% of S Corporation's stock, and the two corporations have filed consolidated tax returns together for a number of years. At the close of business on December 31, 2007, A Corporation purchases all of P's stock. The taxable income for P, S, and A Corporations for 2007 and 2008 are as follows:

	Taxable Income	
Group Member	*2007*	*2008*
A	xxx	$120
P	$100	40
S	(250)	30
CTI	($150)	$190

P and S are a subgroup when calculating the use of the SRLY losses in 2008. Their $150 NOL can be used to the extent of the smaller of their contribution to CTI ($70 = $40 + $30), the NOL carryover ($150), or CTI ($190), or $70. The remaining $80 NOL ($150 − $70) carries over to 2009, and the subgroup rules are applied again. ◀

KEY POINT

The SRLY rules apply to both carryovers and carrybacks. Remember that SRLYs stem from either a year in which a member files a separate return or a year in which a member joins in the filing of a consolidated return with a different affiliated group.

NOL Carrybacks. The SRLY rules also apply to NOL carrybacks from a separate return limitation year to a consolidated return year. For example, assume that S Corporation in Example C:8-27 leaves the P-S group at the end of 2009. Any NOL that S incurs in a subsequent separate return year (2010) that is carried back to the 2008 consolidated return year is subject to the SRLY rules. Its use is restricted under the SRLY rules to S's contribution to consolidated taxable income for all consolidated return years. However, S has not provided a contribution to consolidated taxable income in those years and would be prevented from using the carryback in those earlier years.

The use of built-in deductions also is limited by the SRLY rules. A **built-in deduction** is a deduction that accrues in a separate return year but is recognized for tax purposes in a consolidated return year. One example of such a deduction is the depreciation connected with a subsidiary corporation's asset that declines in value between the time it was acquired in a separate return year and the beginning of the initial consolidated return year. Built-in deductions also can result from the sale of a capital or noncapital asset at a loss in a consolidated return year when the decline in value takes place in a prior separate return year. For example, S purchases inventory in a separate return year for $60,000. The inventory declines to a $45,000 FMV before the time P purchases the S stock and the two corporations start filing on a consolidated basis. The $15,000 ($60,000 − $45,000) built-in deduction can be deducted by S when it sells the inventory only if its SRLY limitation equals or exceeds the built-in deduction amount.[52]

ADDITIONAL COMMENT

The built-in deduction rules eliminate the ability to circumvent the SRLY rules by acquiring a corporation with losses that have economically accrued and having these losses recognized after the subsidiary is a member of the group.

A discussion of the financial statement implications of SRLY losses appears at the end of this chapter.

SECTION 382 LOSS LIMITATION. Section 382 prevents the purchase of assets or stock of a corporation having loss carryovers (known as the loss corporation) where a substantial portion of the purchase price is related to the acquisition of the corporation's tax attributes.[53] Trafficking in NOLs and other tax attributes is prevented by applying the Sec. 382 loss limitation to any tax year ending after the ownership change. The 50 percentage point minimum stock ownership change needed to trigger the Sec. 382 rules

[51] Reg. Sec. 1.1502-21(c)(2)(i). This rule holds only if the losses were non-SRLY losses to the former affiliated group.

[52] Reg. Sec. 1.1502-15(a).

[53] The Sec. 382 limitation rules apply to the tax attributes limited by Secs. 382–384 (e.g., NOLs, capital losses, foreign tax credits, general business credits, minimum tax credit, built-in gains, and built-in losses).

can occur in acquisitive transactions involving a single corporation or a group of corporations that file separate or consolidated returns. (See Chapter C:7 for a discussion of Sec. 382.)

The consolidated Sec. 382 rules generally provide that the ownership change and Sec. 382 limitation are determined with respect to the entire affiliated group (or a subgroup of affiliated corporations) and not for individual entities.[54] Following an ownership change for a loss group, the consolidated taxable income for a post-change tax year that may be offset by a pre-change NOL cannot exceed the consolidated Sec. 382 limitation. If the post-change tax year includes the ownership change date, the Sec. 382 limitation applies to the consolidated taxable income that is earned in the portion of the tax year following the ownership change date.

ADDITIONAL COMMENT

Section 382 adopts a single-entity approach in determining ownership changes and Sec. 382 limitations. This means that the members of a consolidated group are treated like divisions of a single taxpayer.

A loss group is an affiliated group entitled to use an NOL carryover (other than a SRLY carryover) to the tax year in which the ownership change occurs, or has a consolidated NOL for the tax year in which the ownership change occurs.[55] An affiliated group can have two forms of ownership changes: a parent ownership change and a subgroup ownership change. A parent ownership change occurs when (1) the loss group's common parent corporation (a) has a shift in stock ownership involving a 5% or more shareholder or (b) is involved in a tax-free reorganization, and (2) the percentage of stock of the new loss corporation owned by one or more 5% shareholders has increased by more than 50 percentage points over the lowest percentage of stock owned in the old loss corporation by such shareholders during the preceding three-year (or shorter) testing period.[56] A parent ownership change is illustrated in the following example.

EXAMPLE C:8-29 ▶ Dwayne owns all of P Corporation's stock. P owns 80% of the S Corporation stock. The remaining 20% of the S stock is owned by Mitzi. For the current year, the P-S group has a consolidated NOL that can be carried over to next year. The P-S affiliated group is a loss group. On December 31 of the current year, Dwayne sells 51% of the P stock to Carter, who has owned no P stock previously. The Sec. 382 stock ownership requirements are applied to P to determine whether an ownership change has occurred. The 51 percentage point increase in Carter's stock ownership is an ownership change that causes the Sec. 382 loss limitation to apply to the carryover of the current year NOL to next year. If Carter had instead acquired only 49% of the P stock, the requisite ownership change would not have occurred, and the Sec. 382 limit would not apply. ◀

The preceding example applied the ownership change rules to a parent corporation. An ownership change also can occur with respect to a loss subgroup. A loss subgroup generally consists of two or more corporations that are continuously affiliated after leaving one affiliated group when at least one of the corporations brings with it NOLs from the old group to the new group.[57] The loss subgroup can have an ownership change if, for example, the common parent of the loss subgroup has an ownership change (e.g., when an acquisition of subsidiaries from another affiliated group occurs). The 50 percentage point ownership change test is applied to the common parent of the loss subgroup. Further discussion of this type of ownership change is beyond the scope of an introductory text.

The consolidated Sec. 382 limitation (or subgroup limitation) for any post-change tax year equals the value of the loss group (or subgroup) times the highest adjusted federal long-term tax-exempt rate that applies with respect to the three-month period ending in the month of the ownership change. The value of the loss group is the value of the common and preferred stock of each member, other than stock owned by other group members, immediately before the ownership change.

EXAMPLE C:8-30 ▶ Assume the same basic facts as in Example C:8-29. In addition, the value of the P stock is $1 million, and the value of the S stock is $750,000. The value of the P-S affiliated group when applying the Sec. 382 limitation is $1.15 million [$1,000,000 value of P stock + (0.20 minority interest

---

[54] Reg. Sec. 1.1502-91(a)(1).

[55] Reg. Sec. 1.1502-91(c).

[56] Reg. Sec. 1.1502-92(b)(1)(i).

[57] Reg. Sec. 1.1502-92(b)(1)(ii).

ADDITIONAL COMMENT

In Example C:8-30, the value of P's 80% ownership interest in S is not taken into account because it is part of the $1 million value of P's stock.

× $750,000 value of S stock owned by Mitzi)]. The $1.15 million value is multiplied by the appropriate federal long-term tax-exempt rate to determine the maximum amount of the current year consolidated NOL that can be used next year.[58] ◀

Two special Sec. 382 rules that apply to affiliated groups deserve brief recognition here.

- ▶ If the Sec. 382 limitation for a post-change tax year exceeds the consolidated taxable income that may be offset by a pre-change NOL, the excess limitation amount carries forward to the next tax year to increase that year's Sec. 382 limitation.[59]
- ▶ A loss group (or loss subgroup) is treated as a single entity for purposes of determining whether it satisfies the Sec. 382 continuity of enterprise requirement. The group's Sec. 382 limitation is zero should the loss group not meet the continuity of enterprise requirement at any time in its first two years.[60]
- ▶ When an affiliated group terminates or a member leaves the affiliated group, the Sec. 382 limitation is apportioned to the individual group members.[61] Failure to allocate any of the Sec. 382 limitation to a departing group member prevents the member from using any of its NOLs in post-departure tax years.

EXAMPLE C:8-31 ▶ In the P-S-T affiliated group, P owns 100% of the S stock, and S owns 100% of the T stock. The group has an annual Sec. 382 limit of $100, and 30% of the group's losses are allocable to T. When S sells the T stock to individual A, T receives its allocable share of the consolidated NOL. If T is allocated none of the affiliated group's Sec. 382 loss limitation, T's separate Sec. 382 limitation is set to zero. Consequently, T can use none of its allocable loss carryover. ◀

SRLY-SEC. 382 OVERLAP. An overlap problem exists because transactions that qualify under the SRLY rules (for example, the purchase by an acquiring corporation of 100% of the stock of a target corporation having a NOL) also may qualify under the Sec. 382 loss limitation rules. Under previous law, both the SRLY rules and Sec. 382 rules could apply to a single transaction involving members of an affiliated group. This overlap caused difficulty in complying with the consolidated tax return rules.

To alleviate this problem, Treasury Regulations eliminate the application of the SRLY rules in many SRLY-Sec. 382 overlap situations. To qualify for the overlap rule, a corporation must become a member of an affiliated group filing a consolidated tax return within six months of the date of an ownership change that creates a Sec. 382 limitation. If the Sec. 382 event precedes the SRLY event by six months or less, the overlap rule applies beginning with the tax year that includes the SRLY event. If the SRLY event precedes the Sec. 382 event by six months or less, the overlap rule applies for the first tax year beginning after the Sec. 382 event (and the SRLY rules apply for the interim period).

EXAMPLE C:8-32 ▶ The P-S affiliated group has filed consolidated tax returns for a number of years. The P-S group has a $200 consolidated NOL, of which $100 is allocable to each corporation. The A-B affiliated group also has filed consolidated returns for a number of years. The A-B group acquires the P-S affiliated group in a taxable transaction. The P-S affiliated group is a SRLY subgroup and a Sec. 382 subgroup. The overlap rule eliminates the application of the SRLY rules in the surviving A-B-P-S affiliated group for the $200 consolidated NOL it acquired from the P-S group. The Sec. 382 rules, however, still apply. ◀

The overlap rule does not apply if all the corporations included in a Sec. 382 loss subgroup are not included in a SRLY subgroup. A similar set of overlap rules applies to built-in losses.

Topic Review C:8-2 summarizes the rules applying to carrybacks and carryovers of consolidated return and separate return NOLs.

---

[58] A daily allocation of the loss is not needed because the acquisition occurred on the last day of the loss corporation's tax year.
[59] Reg. Sec. 1.1502-93(a).
[60] Reg. Sec. 1.1502-93(d).
[61] Reg. Sec. 1.1502-95(b).

Topic Review C:8-2

Rules Governing Affiliated Group NOL Carrybacks and Carryovers

Loss Year	Carryover/ Carryback Year	Rule and Special Limitations
CRY[a]	CRY	1. Consolidated NOLs carry back two years and over 20 years. The parent corporation can elect to forgo the carryback period. No special problems arise if the group members are the same in the loss year and the year to which the loss is carried back or carried over. 2. Section 382 limitation can apply to the loss carryover if an ownership change has occurred.
CRY	SRY[b]	1. Carryback to a member's prior separate return year is possible only if part or all of the NOL is apportioned to the member. Offspring rule permits carryback of an offspring member's allocable share of the consolidated NOL to a separate return year of the parent corporation or a consolidated return year of the affiliated group. 2. The departing member is allocated part of the consolidated NOL carryover. The consolidated NOL is used first in the consolidated return year in which the departing member leaves the group before an allocation is made. The allocated share of the loss is then used in the departing member's first separate return year. The departing member may be allocated a portion of the Sec. 382 loss limitation by the parent corporation.
SRY	CRY	1. A separate return year NOL can be carried over and used in a consolidated return year. SRLY rules will apply to NOLs other than those of a corporation that is the parent corporation in the carryover year or that is a group member on each day of the loss year. 2. Carryback of a loss of a departed group member to a consolidated return year is a SRLY loss.

[a]Consolidated return year.
[b]Separate return year.

Consolidated Capital Gains and Losses

In the previous discussion of separate taxable income (see page C:8-5), all capital gains and losses, Sec. 1231 gains and losses, and casualty and theft gains and losses were excluded. These three types of gains and losses are reported by the affiliated group on a consolidated basis. For a consolidated return year, the affiliated group's consolidated net capital gain or loss is composed of

- The aggregate amount of the capital gains and losses of the group members (without regard to any Sec. 1231 transactions or net capital loss carryovers or carrybacks)
- The net Sec. 1231 gain
- The net capital loss carryovers or carrybacks to the year[62]

Any capital gain net income that is part of consolidated taxable income is taxed at the regular corporate tax rates. Any consolidated net capital loss carries back three years or forward five years as a short-term capital loss.

ADDITIONAL COMMENT

Netting Sec. 1231 gains/losses on a consolidated basis rather than on a separate corporation basis can dramatically alter the amount of ordinary versus capital gain income.

Section 1231 Gains and Losses

A group member's Sec. 1231 gains and losses exclude any such amounts deferred when an intercompany transaction occurs. These intercompany gains and losses are reported when a corresponding item triggers the recognition of the intercompany item. The consolidated

[62] Reg. Sec. 1.1502-22(a)(1).

Sec. 1231 net gain or loss for the tax year is determined by taking into account the aggregate gains and losses of the group members' Sec. 1231 results. If the group's total Sec. 1231 gains (including net gain from casualty and theft occurrences involving Sec. 1231 property and certain capital assets) exceed similar losses, the net gain from these transactions is the consolidated net Sec. 1231 gain and is eligible for long-term capital gain treatment unless recaptured as ordinary income because of prior net Sec. 1231 losses. If the group reports a net loss either from Sec. 1231 transactions or from its casualty and theft occurrences, the net Sec. 1231 loss is treated as an ordinary loss and is deductible in determining consolidated taxable income.

CAPITAL GAINS AND LOSSES

SELF-STUDY QUESTION

How do intercompany transactions affect the calculation of capital gains/losses?

ANSWER

Deferred intercompany gains/losses are included in the netting of capital gains/losses only when a corresponding item triggers the recognition of the intercompany item.

DETERMINING THE AMOUNT OF GAIN OR LOSS. The amount of any group member's capital gains and losses excludes any such gains deferred when an intercompany transaction occurs. These intercompany gains and losses are reported when a corresponding item triggers the recognition of the intercompany item. Once the recognized gains and losses of each group member are determined, each member's short- and long-term transactions (including any consolidated Sec. 1231 net gain not treated as ordinary income) are combined into separate net gain or net loss positions. The sum of these separate positions then determines the amount of the affiliated group's aggregate short- or long-term capital gain or loss. These aggregate amounts are combined to determine the group's consolidated capital gain net income.

CARRYBACKS AND CARRYOVERS. The treatment of consolidated capital loss carrybacks and carryovers is similar to NOLs. The losses that carry back or over to other consolidated return years are treated as short-term capital losses and serve as a component of the consolidated capital gain or loss position.

The capital loss carrybacks or carryovers that can be used in a consolidated return year equal the sum of the affiliated group's unused consolidated capital loss carrybacks or carryovers and any unused capital loss carrybacks or carryovers of individual group members arising in separate return years. These capital loss carrybacks and carryovers are absorbed according to the same rules described earlier for NOLs (see pages C:8-24 through C:8-32).[63]

EXAMPLE C:8-33 ▶ P, S_1, and S_2 Corporations form the P-S_1-S_2 affiliated group. This group has filed consolidated tax returns for several years. During the current year, the affiliated group reports $100,000 of ordinary income, and the following property transaction results:

	Capital Gains and Losses		
Group Member	*Short-Term*	*Long-Term*	*Sec. 1231 Gains and Losses*
P	$2,000	($1,000)	($2,500)
S_1	(1,000)	7,000	2,000
S_2	(2,000)	3,000	2,000
Total	($1,000)	$9,000	$1,500

In addition, the group carries over a consolidated capital loss of $3,000 from the preceding year. No net Sec. 1231 losses have been recognized in prior years. The P-S_1-S_2 affiliated group's $1,500 consolidated net Sec. 1231 gain is combined with the $8,000 aggregate amount of capital gains and losses ($9,000 – $1,000) and the $3,000 consolidated net capital loss carryover to obtain the current year consolidated capital gain net income of $6,500 ($1,500 + $8,000 – $3,000). This entire amount is taxed at the regular corporate tax rates. ◀

Carryback of a Consolidated Net Capital Loss. A carryback of a member's apportionment of a consolidated capital loss to one of its preceding separate return years is required

[63] Reg. Sec. 1.1502-22(b).

when capital gains are available in the carryback year against which the loss may be offset. Apportionment of the consolidated capital loss to the loss members occurs in a manner similar to that described for NOLs.

TYPICAL MISCONCEPTION

The allocation of net capital losses to the individual group members is based in part on each member's Sec. 1231 losses. Thus, it is possible for a member with only a Sec. 1231 loss to share in the net capital loss carryforward or carryback.

SRLY Limitation. Carryovers or carrybacks of capital losses from a separate return limitation year invoke the SRLY rules. The amount of the loss carryback or carryover from a separate return limitation year that may be used in a consolidated return year equals the lesser of the loss member's contribution to the consolidated capital gain net income or consolidated capital gain net income.[64]

Sec. 382 Limitation. The Sec. 382 loss limitation rules apply to consolidated and separate return capital loss carryovers as well as consolidated and separate return NOLs. Under Sec. 383(b), capital losses are subject to the general Sec. 382 limitation described earlier.

ADDITIONAL COMMENT

The IRC provides that no election is available to forgo the three-year carryback for a net capital loss. This restriction can complicate matters when the three prior years include separate tax return years of the members of the group.

Taxable Income Limitation. In addition to the special capital loss limitations outlined above, Sec. 1212(a)(1)(A)(ii) contains a general limitation that prevents a capital loss from being carried back or over and creating or increasing the NOL for the tax year to which it is carried. Therefore, use of a capital loss also is limited to the group's consolidated taxable income.

Departing Group Members' Losses. A member leaving the affiliated group may take with it an apportionment of any consolidated capital loss carryover and any of its unused capital loss carryovers that originated in a separate return year. These losses are used in subsequent years until they expire. Apportionment of the consolidated capital loss to the departing group member occurs in a manner similar to that described above for NOLs.

STOCK BASIS ADJUSTMENTS

KEY POINT

Positive stock basis adjustments will reduce the amount of gain reported when a sale of the stock of an affiliated group member occurs.

The basis for an investment in a subsidiary corporation is adjusted annually for its profits and losses as well as for distributions made to higher-tier subsidiaries or to its parent corporation. These rules parallel those used by S corporations and partnerships. If the stock of a profitable subsidiary is sold, a "net" positive basis adjustment produces a smaller capital gain than the gain that would otherwise have been recognized if separate tax returns were filed.[65] The basis adjustment prevents the income earned by the subsidiary during the affiliation from being taxed a second time when the parent corporation disposes of the subsidiary's stock.

The starting point for the calculation is the original basis of the parent corporation's investment in the subsidiary, which depends on the acquisition method used to acquire the stock (e.g., purchase, tax-free corporate formation, or tax-free reorganization). The following basis adjustments must be made to the original basis:

- Basis is increased for the subsidiary's income and gain items and decreased for the subsidiary's deduction and loss items taken into account in determining consolidated taxable income. The adjustment includes net operating losses but excludes deferred gains and losses, and unused capital losses.
- Basis is increased for income permanently excluded from taxation (e.g., tax-exempt bond interest and federal income tax refunds).
- The distributee's (or higher-tier corporation's) basis is increased for distributions received from lower-tier group members.
- Basis is increased for a deduction that does not represent a recovery of basis or an expenditure of money (for example, a dividends-received deduction).

[64] As with a NOL, the SRLY rules can apply a single-year or multiple-year contribution comparison.

[65] Losses realized on the sale of a consolidated subsidiary present extremely complex calculations beyond the scope of this text. On March 3, 2005, the Treasury Department issued a new set of regulations disallowing certain duplicate losses from the sale of subsidiary stock by members of a consolidated group. The Treasury Department also announced that it will issue another regulation in the future detailing an alternative method of calculating the loss and tax results.

- Basis is decreased for NOLs used in the current year against other group members' taxable income or carried back and used in an earlier year. NOL carryovers and other suspended losses reduce basis in the year they are used. Expiring NOLs and capital losses reduce basis in the year they expire.
- Basis is decreased for noncapital expenses that are not deductible (e.g., federal income taxes, the 50% of meals and entertainment expenses that are nondeductible, expenses related to tax-exempt income, and losses disallowed under Sec. 267).
- The stock basis for an investment in a lower-tier corporation incurring a pre-acquisition separate return NOL or capital loss is reduced when the loss is used in the current year to offset income or gains reported by other group members. If the pre-acquisition loss expires unused, the unused loss reduces the basis of the stock investment unless the use of part or all of such losses is waived.
- Basis is decreased for all distributions without regard to the E&P balance, or whether such amounts were accumulated in pre- or post-affiliation years.
- If the negative basis adjustments for losses and distributions, etc. are sufficiently large, the basis of the subsidiary's stock is reduced to zero. Additional basis reductions that occur create an excess loss account. No recognition of income or gain is triggered by the creation of this "negative basis account." Subsequent profits or additional capital contributions may reduce or eliminate the excess loss account and, if large enough, can produce a positive basis for the subsidiary.

EXAMPLE C:8-34 ▶ On January 1 of the current year, Parent Corporation purchased all of Subsidiary Corporation's stock for $1 million. Parent and Subsidiary elected to begin filing a consolidated tax return in the current year. Subsidiary reported taxable income of $300,000, tax-exempt bond interest of $25,000, and a $5,000 nondeductible capital loss in the current year. On January 1 of next year, Parent sells the Subsidiary stock for $1.4 million. The portion of the consolidated tax liability allocable to Subsidiary is $102,000 ($300,000 × 0.34). Parent recognizes a $177,000 [$1,400,000 − ($1,000,000 + $300,000 + $25,000 − $102,000)] capital gain on the sale. This gain is $223,000 ($400,000 gain if no consolidated return election is made − $177,000 gain with a consolidated return election) smaller than the gain that would have been reported had Parent and Subsidiary not elected to file a consolidated return.[66] ◀

EXAMPLE C:8-35 ▶ On January 1 of the current year, Parent Corporation purchased all of Subsidiary Corporation's stock for $1 million. During the current year, Subsidiary reported a $750,000 NOL and made a $300,000 distribution to Parent. The $750,000 NOL offsets part of Parent's $2.5 million of taxable income. The basis of the Subsidiary stock is first reduced to zero ($1,000,000 − $750,000 loss − $250,000 distribution). The remaining $50,000 of distribution creates an excess loss account. No gain is recognized by the creation of this "negative basis" account. The excess loss account will be reduced or eliminated in subsequent years by profits in those years or capital contributions, or increased by additional losses and distributions. ◀

TAX PLANNING CONSIDERATIONS

100% DIVIDENDS-RECEIVED DEDUCTION ELECTION

Intercompany dividends are excluded when a consolidated tax return is filed. The 100% dividends-received deduction election (as discussed in Chapter C:4) may be used by the affiliated group to exempt from taxation any dividends received from corporations not eligible to be included in the consolidated return (e.g., a 100%-owned life insurance company).

[66] Separate basis calculations are required for regular tax and AMT purposes. The AMT basis calculations parallel those made for regular tax purposes but use the appropriate numbers from the AMT calculation. Because of the possible differences in these two amounts, the sale of a stock investment may result in different gain or loss amounts for regular tax and AMT purposes.

If a state does not permit the filing of a consolidated tax return for state income tax purposes,[67] it may be necessary for an affiliated group to elect the 100% dividends-received deduction for both state and federal tax purposes. In such a case, the state requires the filing of separate tax returns by each member of the affiliated group. Generally, the state also permits the claiming of any dividends-received deduction elected for federal income tax purposes. When a consolidated tax return is not filed for state income tax purposes, no exclusion of the dividends is possible, and the 100% dividends-received deduction (which was elected but not used on the federal tax return) is substituted on the state income tax return.

ESTIMATED TAX PAYMENTS

Once consolidated tax returns have been filed for two consecutive years, the affiliated group must pay estimated taxes on a consolidated basis.[68] The affiliated group is treated as a single corporation for this purpose. Thus, the estimated tax payments and any underpayment exceptions or penalties are based on the affiliated group's income for the current year and the immediately preceding tax year without regard to the number of corporations that comprise the affiliated group. This treatment can be advantageous if new, profitable corporations are added to the affiliated group.

EXAMPLE C:8-36 ▶ The P-S_1 affiliated group files consolidated tax returns for several years. In the preceding year, the P-S_1 group reported a $100,000 consolidated tax liability. The P-S_1 affiliated group acquires all of S_2 Corporation's stock during the current year. S_2 is very profitable and causes the P-S_1-S_2 group to report a $300,000 consolidated tax liability in the current year. Assuming the P-S_1-S_2 group does not fall under the large corporation rules outlined below, its current year estimated tax payments can be based on the P-S_1 group's $100,000 consolidated tax liability for the prior tax year. No underpayment penalties are imposed provided the P-S_1-S_2 group makes $25,000 ($100,000 ÷ 4) estimated tax payments by the fifteenth day of the fourth, sixth, ninth, and twelfth months of the tax year, because the prior year's tax liability exception to the underpayment rules is satisfied. The balance of the consolidated tax liability must be paid by the due date for the consolidated tax return (without regard to any extensions) to avoid penalty. ◀

UNDERPAYMENT RULES. Affiliated groups also are subject to the special underpayment rules of Sec. 6655(d)(2) for large corporations (that is, corporations having taxable income of at least $1 million in any one of the three immediately preceding tax years). An affiliated group is considered one corporation when applying the large corporation rules. Only the actual members of the affiliated group for the three preceding tax years are used in applying the $1 million threshold. New members entering the group are ignored for the three-preceding-years test.[69]

CONSOLIDATED OR SEPARATE BASIS. For the first two years for which a group files consolidated tax returns, the affiliated group may elect to make estimated tax payments on either a consolidated or separate basis. Starting in the third year, however, the affiliated group must make consolidated estimated tax payments. It must continue to do so until separate tax returns are again filed. During the first two tax years for which the election is in effect, the affiliated group sometimes can reduce its quarterly payments by making separate estimated tax payments in the first year and consolidated estimated tax payments in the second year or vice versa. Application of the exceptions to the penalty for underpayment of estimated taxes depends on whether estimated taxes are paid on a separate or consolidated basis. Different exceptions (e.g., prior year's liability or annualization of current year's income) to the underpayment rules should be used by the individual group members if it will reduce the amount of the required estimated tax payments. Determination of the actual separate or consolidated limitations, however, is beyond the scope of this book.

---

[67] Rev. Rul. 73-484, 1973-2 C.B. 78.
[68] Reg. Sec. 1.1502-5(a).

[69] Proposed Reg. Sec. 1.6655-4(d)(3) requires the $1 million threshold to be apportioned among all members of the controlled group.

ADDITIONAL COMMENT

The final estimated tax payment for a member joining a consolidated group is due the fifteenth day of the last month of the short taxable year. If a member is acquired after the fifteenth, the final estimated tax payment is already overdue.

SHORT-PERIOD RETURN. If a corporation joins an affiliated group after the beginning of its tax year, a short-period return covering the pre-affiliation time period generally must be filed. The payment rules covering the short-period return are found in Reg. Sec. 1.6655-3. If a corporation leaves an affiliated group, it must make the necessary estimated tax payments required of a corporation filing a separate tax return for the post-affiliation, short-period tax year, unless it joins in the filing of a consolidated tax return with another affiliated group. No estimated tax payment is required for a short tax year that is less than four months.

COMPLIANCE AND PROCEDURAL CONSIDERATIONS

OBJECTIVE 11

Explain the procedures for making an initial consolidated return election

THE BASIC ELECTION AND RETURN

An affiliated group makes an election to use the consolidated method for filing its tax return by filing a consolidated tax return (Form 1120) that includes the income, expenses, etc. of all its members. The election must be made no later than the due date for the common parent corporation's tax return including any permitted extensions.[70] An affiliated group can change from a consolidated tax return to separate tax returns,[71] or from separate tax returns to a consolidated tax return, at any time on or before the last day for filing the consolidated tax return. Once that day has passed, no change can be made.

Appendix B presents a sample Form 1120 for reporting the current year's results for the Alpha affiliated group described in Example C:8-37. The Form 1120 involves the five intercompany transactions mentioned in the example, and a worksheet that summarizes the income and expense items for the five companies illustrates the reporting of the intercompany transactions and presents the details of the consolidated taxable income calculation.

EXAMPLE C:8-37 ▶

Alpha Manufacturing Corporation owns 100% of the stock of Beta, Charlie, Delta, and Echo corporations. The affiliated group has filed consolidated returns for a number of years using the calendar year as their tax year. The components of the separate taxable income amounts of the five corporations are reported on the supporting schedule of the group's consolidated tax return contained in Appendix B. This return illustrates five common transactions involving members of an affiliated group. These are as follows:

- The sale of inventory from Alpha to Beta, which increases Alpha's deferred intercompany profit amount. Beta sells additional inventory to outsiders.
- Intragroup dividends paid from Beta and Echo to Alpha
- Payment of interest from Delta to Alpha
- The sale of a truck from Alpha to Beta
- Beta's depreciation of the truck acquired in the intercompany transaction ◀

ADDITIONAL COMMENT

If a group is considering making a consolidated return election, a properly executed Form 1122 should be obtained before any corporation is sold during the election year. After the sale, the consent form may be difficult to obtain.

Students should review this sample return to see how the transactions are reported and how the numbers from the consolidated taxable income schedule are reported in the affiliated group's Form 1120. Although not displayed in Appendix B, the consolidated return should include a Schedule M-3 if applicable (see Chapter C:3).

In addition to filing the necessary Form 1120 reflecting the consolidated results of operations, each corporation that is a member of the affiliated group during the initial consolidated return year must consent to the election. The parent corporation's consent is evidenced by its filing the consolidated tax return (Form 1120). Subsidiary corporations consent to the election by filing a Form 1122 (Authorization and Consent of Subsidiary Corporation To Be Included in a Consolidated Income Tax Return) and

[70] Reg. Sec. 1.1502-75(a)(1).

[71] Such a change can take place only for the initial consolidated return year or for a tax year for which the IRS has granted permission to discontinue the consolidated return election.

submitting it as a part of the initial consolidated tax return. Only newly acquired subsidiary corporations file Form 1122 with subsequent consolidated tax returns.

Each consolidated tax return also must include an Affiliations Schedule (Form 851). This form includes the name, address, and identification number of the corporations included in the affiliated group, the corporation's tax prepayments, the stock holdings at the beginning of the tax year, and all stock ownership changes occurring during the tax year.

Affiliated groups commonly use two types of consolidated tax return formats. One type is a schedular format where the affiliated group files a single tax return with separate spreadsheets showing the calculation of consolidated taxable income and any supporting data. (This format is used in the sample consolidated tax return included in Appendix B.) A second type is a "pancake" format where individual Form 1120s report the activity of each group member. In addition, a separate Form 1120 for an "eliminations" company reports all the adjustments and eliminations needed to go from the various separate tax returns to a single consolidated return, and a final Form 1120 reports the affiliated group's combined results. The pancake format tends to be used by affiliated groups comprised of large firms.

ADDITIONAL COMMENT

All states other than Louisiana, New Hampshire, and Ohio that require combined reporting of affiliated corporations allow taxpayers to elect to file a consolidated tax return for parent-subsidiary groups. The percent of required direct or indirect ownership is 80% for federal consolidated tax return purposes as opposed to the 50% minimum typically used for combined reporting under the state income tax rules.

The due date for the consolidated tax return is 2½ months after the end of the affiliated group's tax year. A six-month extension for filing the consolidated tax return is permitted if the parent corporation files Form 7004 and pays the estimated balance of the consolidated tax liability. The due date for the tax return of a subsidiary corporation that is not included in the consolidated return depends on whether the affiliated group's consolidated tax return has been filed by the due date for the subsidiary corporation's tax return. These rules are beyond the scope of this introductory text but can be reviewed in Reg. Sec. 1.1502-76(c).

PARENT CORPORATION AS AGENT FOR THE AFFILIATED GROUP

The parent corporation acts as agent for each subsidiary corporation and for the affiliated group. As agent for each subsidiary, the parent corporation is authorized to act in its own name in all matters relating to the affiliated group's tax liability for the consolidated return year.[72]

No subsidiary corporation can act in its own behalf with respect to a consolidated return year except to the extent that the parent corporation is prohibited from acting in its behalf. Thus, a subsidiary corporation is prevented from making or changing any election used in computing separate taxable income, carrying on correspondence with the IRS regarding the determination of a tax liability, filing any requests for extensions of time in which to file a tax return, filing a claim for a refund or credit relating to a consolidated return year, or electing to deduct or credit foreign tax payments.

ADDITIONAL COMMENT

Each member corporation is severally liable for the entire tax liability of the affiliated group. Anyone purchasing a corporation out of an affiliated group should consider this factor when negotiating the purchase price of the target corporation.

LIABILITY FOR TAXES DUE

The parent corporation and every other corporation that was a group member for any part of the consolidated return year are severally liable for that year's consolidated taxes.[73] Thus, the entire consolidated tax liability may be collected from one group member if, for example, the other group members are unable to pay their allocable portion. The IRS can ignore attempts made by the group members to limit their share of the liability by entering into agreements with one another or with third parties. Thus, the potential consolidated tax liability and any deficiencies could accrue to a corporation that is a member of an affiliated group for even a few days during a tax year.

An exception to this several liability principle occurs when a subsidiary corporation ceases to be a group member as a result of its stock being sold or exchanged before a deficiency is assessed against the affiliated group. Thus, the IRS can opt to assess a former subsidiary corporation for only its allocable portion of the total deficiency if it believes that the assessment and collection of the balance of the deficiency from the other group members will not be jeopardized.

[72] Reg. Sec. 1.1502-77(a).

[73] Reg. Sec. 1.1502-6(a).

FINANCIAL STATEMENT IMPLICATIONS

OBJECTIVE 12

Understand the financial statement implications of various consolidated transactions

INTERCOMPANY TRANSACTIONS

Intercompany transactions can raise deferred tax issues depending on the type of transaction and whether the affiliated group files consolidated tax returns or separate tax returns. The following discussion assumes a 100%-owned subsidiary to avoid the complications of accounting for noncontrolling interests. It also addresses just two types of intercompany transactions: (1) distributed and undistributed subsidiary profits and (2) intercompany sales of property.

For a parent with a 100%-owned subsidiary, intercompany dividends and undistributed subsidiary earnings cause no temporary differences. If the group files a consolidated tax return, the intercompany dividend is eliminated for both tax and consolidated financial statement purposes. If the group files separate tax returns, the parent takes a 100% dividends-received deduction because it owns at least 80% of the subsidiary's stock. Therefore, in either case, no book-tax difference occurs that would create a temporary difference. Undistributed subsidiary earnings are included in consolidated financial statements, but a parent filing separate tax return would not include these earnings in its income until the subsidiary distributed them as dividends. However, when ultimately distributed, the parent can take the 100% dividends-received deduction, thereby negating any tax on the dividend. Consequently, undistributed subsidiary earnings also present no deferred tax issues (within the assumed parameters of this discussion).

Intercompany sales, however, do raise deferred tax issues in certain cases. If the group files a consolidated tax return, the group defers income on intercompany sales for both tax and consolidated financial statement purposes. Thus, temporary differences and deferred tax issues do not arise. On the other hand, if the group members each file a separate tax return, the selling member recognizes income for tax purposes but not for consolidated financial statement purposes, thereby creating a temporary difference. SFAS No. 109 does not amend ARB No. 51, *Consolidated Financial Statements*, "for income taxes paid on intercompany profits on assets remaining within the group, and prohibits recognition of a deferred tax asset for the difference between the tax basis of the assets in the buyer's jurisdiction and their cost as reported in the consolidated financial statements." Thus, even though the buyer's tax basis (the intercompany purchase price) may exceed the financial statement basis (e.g., the original cost), the buyer does not recognize a deferred tax asset. Instead, the group recognizes a deferred tax asset on the difference between the seller's profit deferred in the consolidated financial statements and the taxes paid on the seller's separate tax return.

For example: Parent forms Subsidiary on January 2 of the current year as a 100%-owned subsidiary. The corporations have no temporary or permanent differences aside from those that might arise on intercompany transactions. For the current year, Parent and Subsidiary report the following transactions:

	Parent	*Subsidiary*
Net income before intercompany transactions	$300,000	$120,000
Profit on sale of inventory from Parent to Subsidiary	50,000	
Profit on partial sale of same inventory from Subsidiary to third parties		6,000
Dividend from Subsidiary to Parent	40,000	

The $50,000 profit to Parent is the difference between the inventory's $60,000 cost to Parent and its $110,000 selling price to Subsidiary. Subsidiary, in turn, sold 30% of this inventory to third parties for $39,000. This portion of the inventory had a $33,000 ($110,000 × 0.30) tax basis to Subsidiary, thereby generating the $6,000 profit.

If Parent and Subsidiary file a consolidated tax return for the current year, the $40,000 intercompany dividend and the $35,000 ($50,000 × 0.70) profit in the remaining inventory will be eliminated in both the consolidated financial statements and the consolidated tax return, leaving no temporary differences. Thus, consolidated taxable income (as well as net income before federal income taxes will equal $441,000 ($300,000 + $120,000 + $50,000 + $40,000 + $6,000 − $40,000 − $35,000), and the federal income tax liability will be $149,940 ($441,000 × 0.34). Accordingly, the group makes the following book journal entry:

Federal income tax expense	149,940	
Federal income taxes payable		149,940

If instead Parent and Subsidiary file separate tax returns, Parent will claim a $40,000 dividends-received deduction. Parent, however, will not eliminate the $35,000 inventory profit deferred for consolidated financial statement purposes but not for tax purposes. Thus, Parent's separate taxable income will be $350,000 ($300,000 + $50,000 + $40,000 − $40,000), and Subsidiary's taxable income will be $126,000 ($120,000 + $6,000). Even though Parent and Subsidiary do not file a consolidated tax return, they still comprise a parent-subsidiary controlled group. Consequently, Sec. 1563 limits the use of the 15% and 25% tax brackets. However, because the group's total taxable income ($350,000 + $126,000) exceeds $335,000, the benefit of the low brackets is completely phased out. Consequently, all taxable income for the group is taxed a flat 34% tax rate, giving Parent a $119,000 ($350,000 × 0.34) tax liability and Subsidiary a 42,840 ($126,000 × 0.34) tax liability, for a total of $161,840. At the same time, the group's consolidated net income before federal income taxes remains at $441,000, its federal income tax expense is $149,940 ($441,000 × 0.34), and its deferred tax asset is $11,900 ($35,000 × 0.34). Accordingly, the group makes the following book journal entry:

Federal income tax expense	149,940	
Deferred tax asset	11,900	
Federal income taxes payable		161,840

Next year, Parent and Subsidiary earn the same income before intercompany transactions ($300,000 and $120,000, respectively) and file separate tax returns. However, they have no intercompany transactions next year, and Subsidiary sells the remaining inventory to third parties for a $14,000 profit. Thus, Parent's taxable income is $300,000, and Subsidiary's taxable income is $134,000 ($120,000 + $14,000). In addition, Parent's tax liability is $102,000 ($300,000 × 0.34), and Subsidiary's tax liability is $45,560 ($134,000 × 0.34), for a total of $147,560. At the same time, the group's consolidated net income after recognizing the $35,000 deferred profit but before federal income taxes is $469,000 ($300,000 + $134,000 + $35,000), and its federal income tax expense is $159,460 ($469,000 × 0.34). Accordingly, the group makes the following book journal entry:

Federal income tax expense	159,460	
Deferred tax asset		11,900
Federal income taxes payable		147,560

SRLY LOSSES

A net operating loss (NOL) from a separate return limitation year (SRLY) will create a deferred tax asset, possibly subject to a valuation allowance.

For example: Parent and Subsidiary (100% owned) have filed separate tax returns for many years, but the group now wishes to file a consolidated tax return. At the beginning of the first consolidated tax return year, Subsidiary has a $200,000 NOL. Because of the SRLY restrictions, management estimates that the group will be able to use only $150,000 of the NOL. The group's tax rate is 34%. The deferred tax asset is $68,000 ($200,000 × 0.34), and the valuation allowance is $17,000 ($50,000 × 0.34), for a net of $51,000. Accordingly, the group makes the following book journal entry:

Deferred tax asset	68,000	
Valuation allowance		17,000
Federal income tax expense		51,000

See Chapter C:3 for a general discussion of financial implications of federal income taxes.

PROBLEM MATERIALS

DISCUSSION QUESTIONS

C:8-1 What minimum level of stock ownership is required for a corporation to be included in an affiliated group?

C:8-2 In what way are the consolidated return regulations different from most of the other tax regulations?

C:8-3 Which of the following entities are includible in an affiliated group (if the 80% stock ownership requirement is met)?
a. C corporation
b. Foreign corporation
c. Life insurance company taxed under Sec. 801
d. Limited liability company.

C:8-4 Explain the difference between the stock ownership requirements for having a group of companies that can consolidate their financial reporting activities and an affiliated group and a parent-subsidiary controlled group as used within the tax law.

C:8-5 P Corporation is 100% owned by Peter McKay. P Corporation owns 100% of S Corporation and 49% of T Corporation. S Corporation owns the remaining 51% of T Corporation. S Corporation also owns 100% of PeterM, a limited liability company (LLC). The LLC has elected to be taxed as a C corporation. Peter McKay also owns 100% of Z Corporation's stock. All are U.S. entities. Which entities are included in an affiliated group? In a controlled group? Would your answer change if the LLC had not elected to be taxed as a C corporation? If so, describe the change.

C:8-6 P, S_1, S_2, and S_3 Corporations form a controlled group of corporations. Because S_3 Corporation is a nonincludible insurance corporation, only P, S_1, and S_2 Corporations are permitted to file their income tax returns on a consolidated basis. Explain to P Corporation's president the alternatives available for allocating the tax savings from the 15%, 25%, and 34% tax rates to the members of the controlled group.

C:8-7 P Corporation has two subsidiaries, S_1 and S_2, both of which are 100%-owned. All three corporations are currently filing separate tax returns. P and S_1 have been profitable. S_2 is a start-up company that has reported losses for its first two years of existence. S_2 eventually will be selling cosmetics to S_1 for distribution to retailers. Explain to P Corporation's president the advantages (and disadvantages) of the three corporations filing a consolidated tax return.

C:8-8 Briefly explain how consolidated taxable income is calculated starting with the financial accounting (book) income information for each individual group member. Explain how the consolidated taxable income calculation is different from the taxable income calculation for a C corporation filing a separate tax return.

C:8-9 Determine whether each of the following statements is true or false:
a. One member of an affiliated group may elect to use the accrual method of accounting even though another group member uses the cash receipts and disbursements method of accounting.
b. A corporation that uses the calendar year as its tax year acquires all the stock of another corporation that has for years used a fiscal year as its tax year. Both corporations may continue to use their previous separate return tax years when filing their initial consolidated tax return.
c. T Corporation, a calendar year taxpayer, becomes a member of the P-S affiliated group at the close of business on February 28 of a non-leap year. The P-S group has filed consolidated tax returns using the calendar year for a number of years. The P-S-T affiliated group's consolidated tax return includes all of T's separate taxable income for the year.

C:8-10 What events permit an affiliated group to terminate its consolidated tax return election? If a corporation leaves an affiliated group, how long must the corporation be disaffiliated before it can again be included in its former group's consolidated tax return? In a new affilated group filing a consolidated tax return?

C:8-11 The P-S_1-S_2 affiliated group has filed consolidated tax returns using a calendar year for a number of years. At the close of business on September 15, P Corporation sells all its S_1 Corporation stock to Mickey. P Corporation retains its investment in S_2 Corporation.
a. Explain what tax returns are required of the three corporations for the current year.
b. What effect does the sale have on the P-S_1-S_2 group's prior year intercompany items and its charitable contributions carryover that is unused in the current year consolidated tax return?

C:8-12 Assume the same facts as in Question C:8-11 except that the original affiliated group was just P and S_1 Corporations and that the S_1 stock was sold to Mickey at the close of business on July 15. What affect does the sale have on the P-S_1 group's prior year intercompany items and its charitable contribution carryover that is unused in the final consolidated tax return?

C:8-13 Briefly explain how the consolidated alternative minimum tax is calculated.

C:8-14 Define the following terms:
a. Intercompany transaction

b. Intercompany item
c. Corresponding item
d. Matching rule
e. Acceleration rule

C:8-15 Explain how the rules governing depreciation recapture, basis, and depreciation operate when a seven-year recovery class property under the MACRS rules is sold at a profit by one group member to a second group member after the property has been held for three years. The purchasing group member will depreciate the property using the MACRS rules over a seven-year recovery period.

C:8-16 Compare and contrast the reporting of interest income and interest expense by P and S Corporations for financial accounting and consolidated tax return purposes when P Corporation lends money to S Corporation on August 1 for a three-year period. Both corporations use the calendar year as their tax year, and interest is paid on July 31 each year. Assume both corporations use the accrual method of accounting.

C:8-17 P and S_1 Corporations constitute the P-S_1 affiliated group on January 1. S_1 Corporation acquires all the stock of S_2 Corporation at the close of business on April 1. Which of the following transactions are intercompany transactions?
a. P Corporation sells inventory to S_1 Corporation throughout the current year.
b. S_2 Corporation performs services for S_1 Corporation between May 1 and December 31 of the current year.
c. S_1 Corporation sells machinery (Sec. 1245 property) to S_2 Corporation on September 1.
d. P Corporation sells inventory to the PS_1 Partnership, which is owned equally by P and S_1 Corporations, on July 23.

C:8-18 P, S_1, and S_2 Corporations constitute the P-S_1-S_2 affiliated group. The group members use the accrual method of accounting and the calendar year as their tax year. Determine whether each of the following transactions that take place during the current year are intercompany transactions. For each item, indicate the intercompany item and corresponding item.
a. P Corporation lends S_1 Corporation money, and P charges interest at a 10% annual rate. The money and interest remains unpaid at the end of the tax year.
b. S_1 Corporation sells inventory to P Corporation. At year end, P Corporation holds the entire inventory purchased from S_1 Corporation.
c. P Corporation sells land (Sec. 1231 property) to S_2 Corporation. S_2 Corporation holds the land (Sec. 1231 property) at year-end.
d. S_2 Corporation pays a cash dividend to P Corporation.
e. S_1 Corporation provides engineering services that are capitalized as part of the cost of S_2's new factory building.

C:8-19 Indicate for each of the following dividend payments the tax treatment available in computing consolidated taxable income:
a. Dividend received from a C corporation that is 10%-owned by the parent corporation.
b. Dividend received from a C corporation that is 100%-owned by the parent corporation and included in the consolidated tax return election.
c. Dividend received from a foreign corporation that is 80%-owned by the parent corporation. The foreign corporation earns no U.S. source income.
d. Dividend received from an unconsolidated life insurance corporation that is 100%-owned by the parent corporation.

C:8-20 Explain the circumstances in which a consolidated NOL arising in the current year can be carried back to a preceding separate return year.

C:8-21 What advantages can accrue to an affiliated group or an individual group member by electing to forgo the carryback of an NOL incurred in a consolidated return year? A separate return year? Who makes the election to forgo each carryback?

C:8-22 Define the term SRLY and explain its significance and application to an affiliated group filing a consolidated tax return.

C:8-23 What is a Sec. 382 ownership change? What is the Sec. 382 loss limitation? Explain their significance and application to an affiliated group filing a consolidated tax return.

C:8-24 P Corporation purchases 100% of the stock of S Corporation on January 1. S Corporation is P Corporation's only subsidiary. Explain to the president of P Corporation what basis adjustment must be made at year-end for its $2 million investment in S Corporation when S earns $350,000 of taxable income and $30,000 of tax-exempt interest income, while it distributes a $100,000 dividend to its parent corporation. Each company paid its own tax liability. Assume a 34% corporate tax rate.

C:8-25 Explain why an affiliated group filing a consolidated tax return might make a federal tax election to claim a 100% dividends-received deduction for a tax year even though all dividends received during that year are received from corporations that are 100%-owned by the parent company.

C:8-26 During what time period can an affiliated group elect to file a consolidated tax return? How is the election made? During what time period is the election to disaffiliate made?

C:8-27 Indicate for which of the following tax-related matters the parent corporation can act as the affiliated group's agent:
a. Making an initial consent for a subsidiary corporation to participate in a consolidated return election
b. Changing an accounting method election for a subsidiary corporation

c. Carrying on correspondence with the IRS during an audit regarding a transaction entered into by a subsidiary corporation that affects the group's determination of consolidated taxable income

d. Requesting an extension of time within which to file a consolidated tax return

C:8-28 You are the managing partner of a local CPA firm. The president of your largest client, a medium-size manufacturing firm, advises you that the firm is about to acquire its largest supplier. Both firms have been profitable for the past ten years and have filed separate tax returns. The president wants to know what tax return filing options are available for the two companies. What additional information do you need to make an informed decision? What factors do you think are most important in the firm's decision?

ISSUE IDENTIFICATION QUESTIONS

C:8-29 Mark owns all the stock of Red and Green Corporations. Red Corporation has been reporting $125,000 in taxable income for each of the past five years. Green Corporation annually has been reporting $30,000 NOLs, which have accumulated to $150,000. Approximately one-third of Red's profits come from sales to Green. Intercompany sales between Red and Green have increased during each of the last five years. What tax issues should Mark consider with respect to his investments in Red and Green Corporations?

C:8-30 Alpha and Baker Corporations, two accrual method of accounting corporations that use the calendar year as their tax year, have filed consolidated tax returns for a number of years. Baker Corporation, a 100%-owned subsidiary of Alpha, is transferring a patent, equipment, and working capital to newly created Charter Corporation in exchange for 100% of its stock. In the current year, Charter will begin to produce parts for the automotive industry. Charter expects to incur organizational expenditures of $10,000 and start-up expenditures of $60,000. What tax issues should Charter consider with respect to the selection of its overall accounting method, inventory method, and tax year, the proper reporting of its organizational and start-up expenditures, and the type of income tax return to file?

C:8-31 Wildcat Corporation is the parent company of a three-member affiliated group. Wildcat and Badger Corporations have been affiliated for a number of years. Both corporations have filed consolidated tax returns for ten years. Early in the current year, Wildcat Corporation purchased Hawkeye Corporation, a start-up business, which incurred net operating losses in each of its first three years. Hawkeye's losses total $260,000. Can the management of the Wildcat-Badger-Hawkeye group use all the losses in the first year after affiliation? The group expects profits in the first year after affiliation to be $300,000 with Hawkeye's contribution to the total being $50,000. What tax issues should the three corporations consider when deciding how to use the NOL?

PROBLEMS

C:8-32 ***Affiliated Group Definition.*** Which of the following independent situations result in an affiliated group being created? In each case, indicate the corporations that are eligible to be included in the consolidated tax return election. All corporations are domestic corporations unless otherwise indicated.

a. Zeke, an individual, owns all the stock of A and B Corporations.

b. Kelly, an individual, owns all the stock of P and W Corporations. P Corporation owns all of the stock of both S_1 and S_2 Corporations.

c. P Corporation owns all the stock of S_1 and S_2 Corporations. S_1 Corporation owns 40% of the stock of S_3 Corporation. P Corporation owns the remaining S_3 stock. S_2 Corporation is a French corporation.

C:8-33 ***Affiliated Group Definition.*** P Corporation owns 100% of L Corporation, a domestic manufacturing firm. They have filed a consolidated return for many years. In each of the independent situations below, determine whether any other entities also could join the consolidated return.

a. L owns 100% of F, a French manufacturing firm.

b. P owns 70% and L owns 15% of D, a domestic corporation that owns restaurants. Unrelated individuals own the remaining 15%.

c. P owns 90% of K Corporation, a domestic manufacturing firm, and K owns 70% of R, a domestic corporation. Unrelated investors own the remaining 10% of K and 30% of R.

d. P purchases 100% of I Corporation, a domestic insurance company, during the current year.

e. P owns 100% of S, a domestic corporation that has elected to be taxed as an S corporation.

C:8-34 ***Stock Ownership Requirement.*** P Corporation is the parent corporation of the P-S_1-S_2 affiliated group. P Corporation is conducting negotiations to purchase the stock of T Corporation. The management of P would like to include T in the affiliated group's consolidated tax return. T Corporation's outstanding shares are as listed.

Type of Stock	*Shares Outstanding*	*Par Value*	*Market Value*
Common stock (1 vote per share)	50,000	$ 1	$30
Voting preferred stock (4 votes per share)	5,000	100	95
Nonvoting preferred stock	20,000	100	90

The nonvoting preferred stock also is nonparticipating and nonconvertible. Determine a plan that permits P to acquire enough stock to include T in the affiliated group. Are other plans available for including T in the affiliated group?

C:8-35 ***Consolidated Return Election.*** P and S Corporations have been in existence for a number of years. P uses the calendar year as its tax year. S Corporation uses a fiscal year ending June 30 as its tax year. Both corporations are involved in manufacturing electronic circuitry and use the FIFO method of accounting for their inventories. At the close of business on July 31, 2007, P acquires all the S stock and elects to file a consolidated tax return for 2007.

a. What tax year must be used in filing the consolidated tax return?

b. What overall accounting method(s) can P and S Corporations elect?

c. What is the last date on which the election to file a consolidated tax return can be made?

d. What income of P and S is included in the consolidated tax return? In a separate return?

C:8-36 ***Consolidated Return Election.*** The P-S_1 affiliated group has filed consolidated tax returns for several years. All P-S_1 returns have been filed using the calendar year as the tax year. At the close of business on August 8, 2007, P Corporation purchases all the stock of S_2 Corporation. S_2 has been filing its separate tax returns using a fiscal year ending September 30. At the close of business on November 9, 2007, P Corporation sells all its S_1 stock.

a. What tax year must S_2 Corporation use after joining the affiliated group?

b. What tax returns are required of S_2 Corporation to report its results from October 1, 2006, through December 31, 2007?

c. What tax year must S_1 Corporation use after leaving the affiliated group?

d. What action is needed (if any) should S_1 desire to change to a fiscal year filing basis?

C:8-37 ***Income Included in Consolidated Return.*** Park and Sub1 Corporations form the Park-Sub1 affiliated group, which has filed consolidated tax returns on a calendar year basis for a number of years. At the close of business on February 25 of the current year, Park sells all the stock of Sub1. Park acquires all the stock of Sub2 Corporation at the close of business for both firms on September 25. Sub2 has always used the calendar year as its tax year. What tax returns are required of Park, Sub1, and Sub2 with respect to reporting the current year's income?

C:8-38 ***Alternative Minimum Tax.*** Peoria and Salem Corporations are members of the Peoria-Salem affiliated group, which has filed consolidated tax returns for a number of years. Consolidated adjusted current earnings are $750,000. Consolidated preadjustment alternative minimum taxable income is $400,000. Consolidated taxable income is $300,000. The consolidated general business credit amount (computed without regard to the overall limitation) is $15,000. Assume Peoria and Salem are not eligible for the small corporation AMT exemption that is based on gross receipts. Also assume no adjustment pertains to the U.S. production activities deduction. What is the Peoria-Salem group's federal tax liability? Are any carryovers created to subsequent tax years? How are the credit carryovers used?

C:8-39 ***Intercompany Transactions.*** P, S_1, and S_2 Corporations form the P-S_1-S_2 affiliated group, with P Corporation owning all the stock of S_1 and S_2 Corporations. The P-S_1-S_2 group has filed consolidated tax returns for several years. In 2007, S_1 sells land it has held for a possible expansion to S_2 for $275,000. The land originally cost S_1 $120,000 several years ago. S_2 constructs a new plant facility on the land. The land and the plant facility are sold for cash to a third party in 2009 with $400,000 of the sales price attributable to the land.

a. What are the amount and character of S_1's recognized gain or loss? In what year(s) is the gain or loss included in S_1's separate taxable income? In what year(s) is the gain or loss included in consolidated taxable income?
b. What are the amount and character of S_2's recognized gain or loss? In what year(s) is the gain or loss included in S_2's separate taxable income? In what year(s) is the gain or loss included in consolidated taxable income?

C:8-40 *Intercompany Transactions.* P and S Corporations form the P-S affiliated group. The P-S group has filed consolidated tax returns for several years. S acquired some land from P Corporation in 2006 for $60,000. P acquired the land several years ago as an investment at a cost of $20,000. S used the land for four years as additional parking space for its employees and made no improvements to the land. S sells the land to an unrelated party in 2010 for $180,000. Terms of the sale require a 20% down payment in the year of sale and four equal installments to be paid annually in years 2011 through 2014. Interest is charged at a rate acceptable to the IRS. Assume all payments are made in a timely fashion.
a. What are the amount and character of P's recognized gain or loss? In what year(s) is the gain or loss included in P's separate taxable income? In what year(s) is it included in consolidated taxable income?
b. What are the amount and character of S's recognized gain or loss? In what year(s) is the gain or loss included in S's separate taxable income? In what year(s) is it included in consolidated taxable income?
c. How is the interest income reported?

C:8-41 *Intercompany Transactions.* P and S Corporations form the P-S affiliated group, which has filed consolidated tax returns for several years. On June 10, 2005, P purchased a new machine (five-year MACRS property) for $20,000 cash. P made no expensing election under Sec. 179. On April 4, 2007, P sells the machine to S for $18,000 cash. S uses the property for two years before selling it to an unrelated party on March 10, 2009, for $15,000.
a. What are the amount and character of P's recognized gain or loss? In what year(s) is the gain or loss included in P's separate taxable income? In what year(s) is the gain or loss included in consolidated taxable income?
b. What is S's basis for the equipment?
c. What depreciation method should S use for the equipment?
d. What are the amount and character of S's recognized gain or loss? In what year(s) is the gain or loss included in S's separate taxable income? In what year(s) is the gain or loss included in consolidated taxable income?

C:8-42 P Corporation owns all the stock of S Corporation. Both corporations use the accrual method of accounting. P Corporation engages in two transactions with its 100%-owned subsidiary, S Corporation. In the first transaction, P sold an automobile having an $18,000 adjusted basis and a $30,000 FMV to S. In the second transaction, S provided cleaning services to P in the amount of $6,000. What are the similarities and differences in how P and S report the two transactions?

C:8-43 *Intercompany Transactions.* P and S Corporations form the P-S affiliated group, which has filed consolidated tax returns for a number of years. On January 1, 2005, P Corporation purchased a new machine (seven-year MACRS property) for $50,000. P does not make a Sec. 179 election for this acquistion. At the close of business on June 6, 2008, P sells the machine to S for $37,500. The machine is still classified as seven-year MACRS property in S's hands. S holds the asset until March 15, 2011, at which time S sells it to an unrelated party for $20,000.
a. What are the amount and character of P's recognized gain or loss? In what year(s) is the gain or loss included in P's separate taxable income? In what year(s) is it included in consolidated taxable income?
b. What are the amount and character of S's recognized gain or loss? In what year(s) is the gain or loss included in S's separate taxable income? In what year(s) is it included in consolidated taxable income?

C:8-44 *Intercompany Transactions.* P and S Corporations form the P-S affiliated group, which has filed consolidated tax returns for a number of years. During 2007, P Corporation began selling inventory items to S Corporation. P and S use the first-in, first-out inventory method. The intercompany profit on P's sales to S was $75,000 in 2007. Goods remaining in S's inventory at the end of 2007 accounted for $35,000 of the intercompany profit. During 2008, all of S's beginning inventory of goods acquired from P in 2007 was sold to unrelated parties and the intercompany profit on P's current sales of inventory to S amounted to $240,000. Goods remaining in S's inventory at the end of 2008 accounted for $70,000 of the intercompany profit. Taxable income for the P-S affiliated group (excluding the deferral and restoration of profits on intercompany inventory sales) is $100,000 in each year. What is consolidated taxable income for 2007 and 2008 for the P-S group?

C:8-45 ***Intercompany Transactions.*** P and S Corporations form the P-S affiliated group. The affiliated group has filed consolidated tax returns for several years. No intragroup inventory sales occurred before 2006. During 2006, P sells S 100,000 widgets, earning $5 per unit profit on the sale. S uses the FIFO method to account for its inventories. On January 1, 2007, 25,000 widgets remain in S's inventory. During 2007, S sells the beginning widget inventory and purchases 175,000 additional widgets from P. P earns a $6 per unit profit on the sale. S retains 40,000 of these units in its 2007 ending inventory. No additional widgets are purchased in 2008. All widgets in beginning inventory are sold by S during 2008. In all years, S sells the widgets for the same price it paid P for them.

a. What intercompany profit amounts are deferred in 2006? In 2007? In 2008?
b. How would your answer to Part a change if the LIFO inventory method were instead used? (Assume the 2007 year-end LIFO inventory includes 25,000 units acquired in 2006 and 15,000 units acquired in 2007.)

C:8-46 ***Intercompany Transactions.*** P Corporation has owned all of the stock of S Corporation for several years. The P-S affiliated group began filing a consolidated tax return in 2005 using the calendar year as its tax year. Both corporations use the accrual method of accounting. On July 1, 2006, P loaned S $250,000 on a one-year note. Interest is charged at a 12% simple rate. P repays the loan plus interest on June 30, 2007.

a. When does P report its interest income in its separate tax return? When does S report its interest expense in its separate tax return?
b. How would your answer to Part a change if P instead used the cash method of accounting?

C:8-47 ***Intercompany Transactions.*** P and S Corporations form the P-S affiliated group. S Corporation owns 80% of an LLC that is engaged in a manufacturing business. Peter Hart owns the remaining 20% of the LLC. The LLC has not elected under the check-the-box regulations to be taxed as a corporation. S Corporation sells inventory costing $125,000 to the LLC for $250,000. How does S Corporation report the profit on the sale?

C:8-48 ***Dividends-Received Deduction.*** P, S, and T Corporations form the P-S-T affiliated group. The P-S-T group has filed consolidated tax returns for several years. P, S, and T report separate taxable income amounts (excluding any dividend payments, eliminations, and dividends-received deductions) of $200,000, ($70,000), and $175,000, respectively, for the current year. Cash dividend payments received by P and S this year are as follows:

Shareholder Corporation	*Distributing Corporation*	*Amount*
P	T	$125,000
P	100%-owned nonconsolidated U.S.-based life insurance company	15,000
S	20%-owned domestic corporation	40,000
P	51%-owned nonconsolidated foreign corporation	10,000

a. What is the amount of the gross income reported in the P and S separate tax returns as a result of the four distributions?
b. What is the amount of the consolidated dividends-received deduction?
c. Why might P elect to claim a 100% dividends-received deduction for the dividend received from T for federal income tax purposes, even though a consolidated tax return is being filed?

C:8-49 ***Charitable Contribution Deduction.*** P and S Corporations form the P-S affiliated group. This group has filed consolidated tax returns for several years. The group reports consolidated taxable income (excluding charitable contributions) for the current year of $90,000. Included in this amount are a consolidated dividends-received deduction of $8,000 and an NOL deduction of $25,000 that represents a carryover of last year's consolidated NOL. P and S Corporations make cash contributions to public charities of $18,000 and $12,000, respectively, during this year. In addition, S Corporation accrues an unpaid contribution in the amount of $10,000. It paid the contribution in the first 30 days of the new tax year.

a. What is the P-S group's consolidated taxable income?
b. What is the amount of the charitable contribution carryover? How long can it be carried forward?

C:8-50 *NOL Carrybacks and Carryovers.* P and S Corporations form the P-S affiliated group, which files consolidated tax returns for the period 2006 through 2009. The affiliated group reports the following results for this period:

	Taxable Income			
Group Member	*2006*	*2007*	*2008*	*2009*
P	$10,000	($6,000)	$20,000	$15,000
S	2,000	2,000	(30,000)	10,000
Consolidated taxable income (excluding NOL deduction)	$12,000	($4,000)	($10,000)	$25,000

No elections were made to forgo the NOL carrybacks. Assume the U.S. production activities deduction does not apply.

a. What portion of the 2007 and 2008 consolidated NOLs can be carried back to 2006? Over to 2009?
b. Who files for the tax refund when the 2007 and 2008 NOLs are carried back?

C:8-51 *NOL Carryover.* P, S_1, and S_2 Corporations form the P-S_1-S_2 affiliated group, which has filed consolidated tax returns since the creation of all three corporations in 2006. At the close of business on July 10, 2008, P Corporation sells its entire interest in S_2 Corporation. The affiliated group remains in existence after the sale because P Corporation still owns all the S_1 stock. Assume the U.S. production activities deduction does not apply. The P-S_1-S_2 group reports the following results for 2006 through 2008:

	Taxable Income		
Group Member	*2006*	*2007*	*2008*
P	$ 8,000	($12,000)	$16,000
S_1	9,000	(24,000)	(4,000)
S_2	10,000	(36,000)	6,000[a]
S_2 (7/11–12/31)			8,000[b]
Consolidated taxable income (excluding NOL deduction)	$27,000	($72,000)	$18,000[c]

[a]Taxable income earned from January 1, 2008, through July 10, 2008.
[b]Taxable income from July 11, 2008, through December 31, 2008, is included in S_2's separate tax return.
[c]$16,000 − $4,000 + $6,000.

What amount of 2007's consolidated NOL can the P-S_1 affiliated group carry over to 2008 and 2009? What amount can S_2 carry over to 2008 and 2009? When does the carryover expire?

C:8-52 *NOL Carryovers and Carrybacks.* P Corporation acquires S Corporation on January 1, 2008. Each company filed separate calendar year tax returns for 2007. P and S report the following results for 2007 and 2008:

Group Member	*2007*	*2008*
P	$40,000	($30,000)
S	(30,000)	20,000
Taxable income	N/A	($10,000)

N/A = Not applicable

a. What are the 2008 tax consequences assuming a consolidated tax return is filed? What are the tax consequences if separate tax returns had instead been filed? (Ignore the Sec. 382 loss limitation that might apply to the acquisition of S, and ignore the U.S. production activities deduction.)
b. Assume P and S report the following taxable income in 2009 before any NOL carryover: P, $21,000; S, $6,000. What is the consolidated taxable income assuming a consolidated return was filed in 2008?

C:8-53 *Special NOL Limitation.* P, S_1, and S_2 Corporations form the P-S_1-S_2 affiliated group. P Corporation was created by Bart on January 1, 2007. P purchased all the S_1 and S_2 Corporation stock on September 1, 2007, after both corporations were in operation for about six months. All three corporations filed separate tax returns in 2007. The P-S_1-S_2 affiliated group elected to file a consolidated tax return starting in 2008. Assume the U.S. production activities deduction does not apply. The P-S_1-S_2 group, which is still owned by Bart, reports the following results for 2007 through 2009:

	Taxable Income		
Group Member	*2007*	*2008*	*2009*
P	($8,000)	$50,000	$10,000
S_1	(24,000)	20,000	(18,000)
S_2	(16,000)	(10,000)	15,000
Consolidated taxable income (excluding NOL deduction)	XXX	$60,000	$7,000

a. What loss carryovers are available to be used in 2008, 2009, and 2010? (Ignore the Sec. 382 loss limitation that might apply to the acquisitions of S_1 and S_2.)
b. How would your answer to Part a change if Bart instead created P, S_1, and S_2 Corporations as an affiliated group on January 1, 2007?

C:8-54 *Sec. 382 Loss Limitation.* Mack owns all of the stock of P Corporation. P Corporation owns all the stock of S_1 and S_2 Corporations. At the close of business on December 31, 2006, Mack sold his P Corporation stock to Jack for $9 million. The P-$S_1$-$S_2$ affiliated group has a consolidated NOL carryover to 2007 of $1.5 million at the end of 2006. Assume the U.S. production activities deduction does not apply.
a. Has a Sec. 382 ownership change occurred? Explain.
b. What is the P-S_1-S_2 affiliated group's consolidated Sec. 382 limitation for 2007 if the federal long-term tax-exempt rate is 3.5%? (Ignore the SRLY loss limitation that might apply to Jack's acquisition of the P Corporation stock.)
c. How much of the consolidated NOL carryover can be used in 2007 if the affiliated group's taxable income is $750,000? In 2008 if the affiliated group's consolidated taxable income is $200,000?

C:8-55 *Consolidated Taxable Income.* P and S Corporations have filed consolidated tax returns for a number of years. P is an accrual method of accounting taxpayer, and S is a cash method of accounting taxpayer. P and S report separate return taxable income (before adjustments, the NOL deduction, and special deductions) for the current year of $100,000 and $150,000, respectively. These numbers include the following current year transactions or events accounted for appropriately on a separate return basis.

- P sold land held for investment purposes to S at a $25,000 profit three years ago. S sold the land (a Sec. 1231 asset) to an unrelated corporation this year for a $16,000 gain. The current year's gain is included in S's separate taxable income.
- P's separate taxable income includes a $12,000 dividend received from S Corporation.
- P sold inventory to S last year for which the deferred intercompany profit at the beginning of this year was $50,000. All this inventory was sold outside the affiliated group this year. Additional inventory was sold by P to S this year. Some of this inventory remained unsold at year-end. The intercompany profit on the unsold inventory included in P's separate taxable income is $80,000.
- The P-S group has a $20,000 NOL carryover available from last year.
- S received a $10,000 dividend from an unrelated corporation.
- P and S made charitable contributions of $16,000 and $12,000, respectively, this year that are included in the separate taxable income calculations.
- P lent S $150,000 early in the current year. S repaid the loan before year-end. In addition, S paid P $6,000 of interest at the time of the repayment for the use of the borrowed money.
- P and S had qualified production activities income of $75,000 and $140,000, respectively. The applicable percentage for 2007 is 6%.

a. What is consolidated taxable income for the P-S affiliated group for 2007?
b. What is the consolidated tax liability for 2007?

COMPREHENSIVE PROBLEM

C:8-56 Using the facts from Problem C:8-58 below calculate the separate return tax liabilities of P and S Corporations for 2006. How much larger (or smaller) will the total of the two separate return tax liabilities be than the affiliated group's consolidated return tax liability? What taxes are due (or refund available) if Flying Gator made $125,000 of estimated tax payments and T Corporation made $25,000 of estimated tax payments?

TAX STRATEGY PROBLEM

C:8-57 Sandra and John, who are unrelated, own all of Alpha and Beta Corporations. John owns 60% of Alpha's stock and 40% of Beta's stock. Sandra owns 40% of Alpha's stock and 60% of Beta's stock. For five years, Alpha has conducted manufacturing activities and sold machine parts primarily in the eastern United States. Alpha has reported $75,000 of operating profits in each of the last two years. Alpha's operating profits are expected to grow to $150,000 during the next five years. Alpha still has $100,000 of NOLs that need to be used before it starts paying federal income taxes. Alpha sells 25% of its product to Beta. Beta has been working to establish a market niche for reselling Alpha products in the southwestern United States. In the start-up phase of establishing the market, Beta incurred $200,000 of NOLs. Under the sales arrangement with Alpha, probably the best that Beta can hope to achieve in the short-run is reach a break-even point.

Required: What suggestions can you offer Sandra and John about the short-term possibility of using Alpha and Beta's NOLs against the profits that Alpha expects to earn and about minimizing their overall tax liabilities if both businesses become profitable? Sandra has specifically asked about merging the two companies into a single entity so the losses of one entity can offset the profits of the other and delay the need to pay income taxes to the federal government. Sandra indicates that the two companies were created for business reasons and not tax avoidance reasons. The operating situation has changed and, according to Sandra, now may be the time to combine the entities into one. However, John is not sure that bringing the two businesses together is a good idea.

TAX FORM/RETURN PREPARATION PROBLEM

C:8-58 The Flying Gator Corporation and its 100%-owned subsidiary, T Corporation, have filed consolidated tax returns for a number of years. Both corporations use the hybrid method of accounting and the calendar year as their tax year. During 2006, they report the operating results as listed in Table C:8-2. Note the following additional information:

- Flying Gator and T Corporations are the only members of their controlled group.
- Flying Gator's address is 2101 W. University Ave., Gainesburg, FL 32611. Its employer identification number is 38-2345678. Flying Gator was incorporated on June 11, 1994. Its total assets are $430,000. Flying Gator made estimated tax payments of $150,000 for the affiliated group in the current year. Stephen Marks is Flying Gator's president.
- A $50,000 NOL carryover from the immediately preceding year is available. P Corporation incurred the NOL last year.
- Flying Gator uses the last-in, first-out (LIFO) inventory method. T began selling inventory to Flying Gator in the preceding year, which resulted in a $40,000 year-end deferred intercompany profit. An additional LIFO inventory layer was created by T's sales to Flying Gator during the current year that remained unsold at year-end. The intercompany profit on the additional inventory is $45,000. None of the original LIFO layer was sold during the current year.
- All of Flying Gator's dividends are received from T. T's dividends are received from a 60%-owned domestic corporation. All distributions received by T are from E&P.
- Flying Gator received its interest income from T. The interest is paid on March 31 of the current year on a loan that was outstanding from October 1 of the preceding year through March 31 of the current year. No interest income was accrued at the end of the preceding tax year. T paid $5,000 of its interest expense to a third party.
- Officer's salaries are $80,000 for Flying Gator and $65,000 for T Corporation. These amounts are included in salaries and wages in Table C:8-2.

▼ **TABLE C:8-2**
Flying Gator Corporation's Current Year Operating Results (Problem C:8-58)

Income or Deductions	Flying Gator	T	Total
Gross receipts	$2,500,000	$1,250,000	$3,750,000
Cost of goods sold	(1,500,000)	(700,000)	(2,200,000)
Gross profit	$1,000,000	$ 550,000	$1,550,000
Dividends	100,000	50,000	150,000
Interest	15,000		15,000
Sec. 1231 gain		20,000	20,000
Sec. 1245 gain		25,000	25,000
Long-term capital gain (loss)	(5,000)	6,000	1,000
Short-term capital gain (loss)		(3,000)	(3,000)
Total income	$1,110,000	$ 648,000	$1,758,000
Salaries and wages	175,000	200,000	375,000
Repairs	25,000	40,000	65,000
Bad debts	10,000	5,000	15,000
Taxes	18,000	24,000	42,000
Interest	30,000	20,000	50,000
Charitable contributions	22,000	48,000	70,000
Depreciation (other than that included in cost of goods sold)	85,000	40,000	125,000
Other expenses	160,000	260,000	420,000
Total deductions	$ 525,000	$ 637,000	$1,162,000
Separate return taxable income (before the USPAD, NOL ded, and DRD)	$ 585,000	$ 11,000	$ 596,000

- Flying Gator's capital losses include a $10,000 long-term loss on a sale of land to T in the current year. T held the land at year-end.
- These corporations have no non-recaptured net Sec. 1231 losses from prior tax years.
- T's Sec. 1245 gains include $20,000 recognized on the sale of equipment to Flying Gator at the close of business on September 30 in the current year. The asset cost $100,000 and had been depreciated for two years by T as five-year property under the MACRS rules. T claimed nine months of depreciation in the current (second) year. Flying Gator began depreciating the property in the current year by using the MACRS rules and a five-year recovery period. Flying Gator claimed the appropriate first-year MACRS depreciation on the property in the current year.
- Qualified production activities income for Flying Gator is $490,000 and for T is $(35,000). The applicable percentage for 2006 is 3%.

Determine the affiliated group's 2006 consolidated tax liability. Prepare the front page of the affiliated group's current year corporate income tax return (Form 1120). Hint: Prepare a spreadsheet similar to the one included in Appendix B to arrive at consolidated taxable income.

CASE STUDY PROBLEMS

C:8-59 P Corporation operates six automotive service franchises in a metropolitan area. The service franchises have been a huge success in their first three years of operation and P's annual taxable income exceeds $600,000. The real estate associated with the six service franchises is owned by J Corporation. P Corporation leases its automotive service franchise locations from J Corporation. J Corporation is reporting large interest and MACRS depreciation deductions because of a highly leveraged, capital intensive operation. As a result, J Corporation has reported NOLs in its first three years of operation. Both P and J Corporations file separate tax returns.

Both corporations are owned by Carol, who is in her late 20s. Carol sees the idea for the automotive service franchise chain starting to really develop and expects to add six more locations in each of the next two years. You and Carol have been friends for a number of years. Because of the rapid expansion that is planned, she feels that she has outgrown her father's accountant and needs to have new ideas to help her save tax dollars so that she can reinvest more money in the business.

Required: The tax partner that you are assigned to requests that you prepare a memorandum outlining your thoughts about Carol's tax problems and suggested solutions to those problems in preparation for his meeting next week with Carol.

TAX RESEARCH PROBLEMS

C:8-60 Angela owns all the stock of A, B, and P Corporations. P Corporation has owned all the stock of S_1 Corporation for six years. The P-S_1 affiliated group has filed a consolidated tax return in each of these six years using the calendar year as its tax year. On July 10 of the current year (a nonleap year), Angela sells her entire stock investment in A Corporation, which uses the calendar year as its tax year. No change takes place in Angela's ownership of B stock during the tax year. At the close of business on November 25 of this year, S_1 Corporation purchases 90% of the common stock and 80% of the nonconvertible, nonvoting preferred stock (measured by value) of S_2 Corporation. A, P, S_1, and S_2 Corporations are domestic corporations that do not retain any special filing status. Which corporations are included in the affiliated group? In the controlled group? What income is included in the various tax returns? How is the allocation of the income between tax years made if the books are not closed on the sale or acquisition dates? If no special allocations are made, what portion of the reduced tax rate benefits of Sec. 11(b) can be claimed in the current year by the affiliated group? In future years?

A partial list of resources includes:

- IRC Sec. 1504
- IRC Sec. 1563
- Reg. Sec. 1.1502-75
- Reg. Sec. 1.1561-2

C:8-61 P, S, and T Corporations have filed a consolidated tax return for a number of years using the calendar year as its tax year. Current plans call for P Corporation to purchase all of X Corporation's stock at the close of business on June 30 of the current year from three individuals. X Corporation was created seven years ago and always has been an S corporation using the calendar year as its tax year. The chief financial officer of P Corporation comes to your office and makes a number of inquiries about the tax consequences of the acquisition including: Can X Corporation retain its S election? If so, does it file a federal income tax return separate from the affiliated group? Does X Corporation have to be included in the P-S-T group's consolidated tax return? Assuming the acquisition takes place as planned, what tax returns are required of the affiliated group and X Corporation? What income is included in the pre-affiliation tax return of X Corporation (if required) and the affiliated group's post-acquisition consolidated tax return? Prepare a brief memo for the chief financial officer outlining the answers to these questions and any other questions you feel are relevant.

A partial list of resources includes:

- IRC Sec. 1361(b)
- Reg. Sec. 1.1502-76

C:8-62 Mary owns all the shares of Able Corporation. Able owns all the shares of Baker Corporation and Cross Corporations. The three corporations have filed a consolidated calendar year tax return for several years. After consulting with her tax accountant, Mary decides that it will be more beneficial if the corporations are restructured as S corporations so their income is subject to a single layer of tax. The restructuring process is complex because Baker holds some valuable franchises that cannot be transferred. The restructuring occurred on October 23 of the current year. On October 23, Able transfers all of its assets and liabilities to Baker, and the two corporations merge with Baker as the survivor. As part of the restructuring, Mary receives all the stock of Baker. Six hours after the first transaction, Baker sells Mary all the stock in Cross for $2 million. Thus, the consolidated group survived for only six hours during the restructuring. Immediately after the restructuring, Baker incurs substantial losses. Can Baker file a consolidated return for the restructuring year and deduct the post-restructuring losses against prior year consolidated income? A partial list of resources includes:

- Reg. Sec. 1.1502-75(a)(2)
- Reg. Sec. 1.1502-75(d)(2)
- Reg. Sec. 1.1502-76(b)(1)
- *The Falconwood Corporation v. U.S.* (96 AFTR 2d 2005-5977), 2005-2 USTC ¶50,597 (Fed. Cir., 2005)

9

C H A P T E R

PARTNERSHIP FORMATION AND OPERATION

LEARNING OBJECTIVES

After studying this chapter, you should be able to

1. Differentiate between general and limited partnerships
2. Explain the tax results of a contribution of property or services in exchange for a partnership interest
3. Determine the permitted tax years for a partnership
4. Differentiate between items that must be separately stated and those that are included in ordinary income or loss for partnerships that are not electing large partnerships
5. Calculate a partner's distributive share of partnership income, gain, loss, deduction, or credit items
6. Explain the requirements for a special partnership allocation
7. Calculate a partner's basis in a partnership interest
8. Determine the limitations on a partner's deduction of partnership losses
9. Determine the tax consequences of a guaranteed payment
10. Explain the requirements for recognizing the holder of a partnership interest as a partner in a family partnership
11. Determine the allocation of partnership income between a donor and a donee of a partnership interest
12. Determine the requirements for filing a partnership tax return

CHAPTER OUTLINE

Partnerships have long been one of the major entities for conducting business activities. Partnerships vary in complexity from the corner gas station owned and operated by two brothers to syndicated tax partnerships with their partnership interests traded on major security markets. Two different sets of rules apply to partnerships depending on their size. The rules discussed in Chapter C:9 and most of Chapter C:10 apply to the majority of partnerships. The rules discussed at the end of Chapter C:10 apply to very large partnerships (known as electing large partnerships), which make a specific election to be taxed under a different system. The partnership rules are found in Subchapter K of the IRC, which includes the provisions from Secs. 701–777.

Chapters C:9 and C:10 discuss the income tax rules applying to partnership business operations. The first part of this chapter defines a partnership, describes the types of partnerships, and discusses the formation of a partnership. The remainder of this chapter deals with the ongoing operations of a partnership, such as the annual taxation of partnership earnings, transactions between partners and the partnership, and a partner's basis in a partnership interest. This chapter also considers procedural matters, such as reporting the annual partnership income and IRS audit procedures for partnerships and their partners. Chapter C:10 continues by discussing distributions to the partners and the tax implications of the numerous transactions that can be used to terminate a partner's interest in a partnership. Chapter C:10 also discusses the unique problems of limited partnerships and the taxation of publicly traded partnerships and electing large partnerships.

DEFINITION OF A PARTNERSHIP

ADDITIONAL COMMENT

Even though the formation of a partnership requires no legal documentation, the partners should draft a formal written partnership agreement to prevent subsequent disagreements and arguments.

For tax purposes, the definition of a partnership includes "a syndicate, group, pool, joint venture, or other unincorporated organization" that carries on a business or financial operation or venture. However, a trust, estate, or corporation cannot be treated as a partnership. Unlike a corporation, which can exist only after incorporation documents are finalized, formation of a partnership requires no legal documentation. If two people (or business entities) work together to carry on any business or financial operation with the intention of making a profit and sharing that profit as co-owners, a partnership exists for federal income tax purposes.[1]

The IRC and Treasury Regulations define a **partner** simply as a member of a partnership. Years of case law and common business practice, however, have made clear that a partner can be an individual, trust, estate, or corporation. The only restriction on the number of partners is that a partnership must have at least two partners, but a large syndicated partnership may have hundreds or even thousands of partners.

GENERAL AND LIMITED PARTNERSHIPS

OBJECTIVE 1

Differentiate between general and limited partnerships

Each state has laws governing the rights and restrictions of partnerships. Almost all state statutes are modeled on the Uniform Partnership Act (UPA) or the Uniform Limited Partnership Act (ULPA) and thus have strong similarities to each other. A partnership can take two legal forms: a general partnership or a limited partnership. The differences between the two forms are substantial and extend to the partners' legal rights and liabilities as well as the tax consequences of operations to the partners. Because these differences are so important, we examine the two partnership forms before proceeding with further discussion of the partnership tax rules.

GENERAL PARTNERSHIPS. A **general partnership** exists any time two or more partners join together and do not specifically provide that one or more of the partners is a limited partner (as defined below). In a general partnership, each partner has the right to par-

[1] Section 761(a) allows an election to avoid the Subchapter K rules for a very limited group of business owners.

ticipate in the management of the partnership. However, the general partnership form is flexible enough to allow the business affairs of the general partnership to be managed by a single partner chosen by the general partners.

REAL-WORLD EXAMPLE

For 2003, 2.38 million domestic partnerships filed returns. Of these, 757,000 were general partnerships, 379,000 were limited partnerships, 88,000 were limited liability partnerships, and 1,092,000 were limited liability companies. The average general partnership had 3.8 partners, the average limited partnership had 16.5 partners, the average limit liability partnership had 3.9 partners, and the average limited liability company had 4.4 members.

Although only one (or a few) of the general partners may exercise management duties, each **general partner** has the ability to make commitments for the partnership.[2] In a general partnership, each partner has unlimited liability for all partnership debts. If the partnership fails to pay its debts, each partner may have to pay far more than the amount he or she has invested in the venture. Thus, each partner faces the risk of losing personal assets if the partnership incurs business losses. This exposure is the single biggest drawback to the general partnership form of doing business.

LIMITED PARTNERSHIPS. A **limited partnership** has two classes of partners. It must have at least one general partner, who essentially has the same rights and liabilities as any general partner in a general partnership,[3] and at least one **limited partner.** Even if a partnership becomes bankrupt, a limited partner can lose no more than his or her original investment plus any additional amount he or she has committed to contribute. However, a limited partner has no right to be active in the partnership's management.

The broad rights and obligations of general partners could make a general partnership an unwieldy form for operating a business with a large number of owners. On the other hand, a limited partnership having one (or a small number of) general partners can be useful for a business operation that needs to attract a large amount of capital. In fact, one common form for a tax shelter investment is a limited partnership having a corporation with a small amount of capital as its sole general partner. Such an arrangement allows the tax advantages of the partnership form (detailed in the remainder of this chapter and in the next chapter) while retaining the limited liability feature for virtually every investor.

Many of these limited partnerships are so large and widely held that in many ways they appear more like corporations than partnerships. As discussed in Chapter C:10, the tax laws provide that publicly traded partnerships may be reclassified for tax purposes as corporations.

LIMITED LIABILITY LIMITED PARTNERSHIP. A recent variation on the limited partnership is the limited liability limited partnership (LLLP). As discussed above, a limited partnership, in addition to having limited partners, has one or more general partners whose personal liability exposure is unlimited. The LLLP is a partnership formed under a state's limited partnership laws but that can elect under the state's laws to provide the general partners with limited liability. Thus, the LLLP is similar to an LLC. Only about 20 states, however, provide for this type partnership. It becomes potentially useful in states that do not extend LLC status to personal service firms but allow such firms to operate as an LLLP.[4]

REAL-WORLD EXAMPLE

The number of limited liability companies has increased from 48,000 in 1994 to 1,092,000 in 2003. Moreover, from 1994 to 2003, the number of general partnership returns has decreased each year while the number of limited liabilities company returns has increased.

LIMITED LIABILITY COMPANIES (LLCs). With the advent of LLCs, businesses have the opportunity to be treated as a partnership for tax purposes while having limited liability protection for every owner. State law provides this limited liability. Unique tax rules for LLCs have not been developed. Instead, the check-the-box regulations (discussed in Chapter C:2) permit each LLC to choose whether to be treated as a partnership or taxed as a corporation. If an LLC is considered a partnership for tax purposes, the same tax rules apply to the LLC that apply to a traditional partnership. Chapter C:10 further discusses the tax treatment of LLCs.

TAX STRATEGY TIP

A business that expects losses in its early years may wish to form an LLC initially so that losses pass through to the owners. Later, if the business expects to grow, it can consider incorporating as a C corporation and retaining its earnings to fund this expansion.

LIMITED LIABILITY PARTNERSHIPS (LLPs). Initially, professional organizations in certain fields (e.g., public accounting and law) were not permitted to operate as LLCs and therefore remained general partnerships. Subsequently, many states have added LLPs to the list of permissible business forms. The primary difference between a general partnership and an LLP is that, in an LLP, a partner is not liable for damages resulting from failures in

[2] Uniform Partnership Act.

[3] Uniform Limited Partnership Act.

[4] For a detailed discussion, see Shop Talk, "Service Firms Practicing as LLLPs: What Are the Tax Consequences?" *Journal of Taxation,* August 2005.

the work of other partners or of people supervised by other partners. Under the check-the-box regulations, an LLP can be treated as a partnership or as a corporation. Like an LLC, the default tax classification of an LLP is a partnership. The same tax rules apply to an LLP that apply to a traditional partnership. Chapter C:10 further discusses the taxation of LLPs.

REAL-WORLD EXAMPLE

For 2003, only 102 partnerships filed as electing large partnerships.

ELECTING LARGE PARTNERSHIPS. Partnerships that qualify as "large partnerships" may elect to have a simplified set of reporting rules apply. To qualify as a large partnership, the partnership must not be a service partnership and must not be engaged in commodity trading. Further, to qualify to make this election, the partnership must have at least 100 partners (excluding partners who provide substantial services in connection with the partnership's business activities) throughout the tax year. Once the partnership makes the election, it reports its income under a simplified reporting scheme, is subject to different rules about when the partnership terminates, and is subject to a different system of audits. The election is irrevocable without IRS permission. Chapter C:10 presents details about the tax treatment of electing large partnerships.

OVERVIEW OF TAXATION OF PARTNERSHIP INCOME

REAL-WORLD EXAMPLE

In 2003, 56.4% of all partnerships and LLCs were in finance, insurance, and real estate industries, and 19.6% were in service industries.

The following overview gives a broad perspective of the taxation of partnership income other than income earned by electing large partnerships. (Appendix F compares the tax characteristics of a partnership, a C corporation, and an S corporation.) More detailed descriptions follow this overview.

PARTNERSHIP PROFITS AND LOSSES

A partnership is not a taxpaying entity, and income earned by a partnership is not subject to two layers of federal income taxes. Instead, each partner reports a share of the partnership's income, gain, loss, deduction, and credit items as a part of his or her income tax return. The partnership, however, must file Form 1065 (U.S. Partnership Return of Income), an information return that provides the IRS with information about partnership earnings as well as how the earnings are allocated among the partners. The partnership must elect a tax year and accounting methods to calculate its earnings. (Appendix B includes a completed partnership tax return that shows a Form 1065 and Schedule K-1 for a partner along with a set of supporting facts.)

ADDITIONAL COMMENT

Because most partnerships use the calendar year as their tax year, the K-1s are not due until April 15. Because a calendar year corporate partner's return is due on March 15 and an individual partner's return is due on April 15, partners often must request extensions for filing their returns. An electing large partnership must provide K-1s by March 15 following the close of the partnership tax year.

Each partner receives a Schedule K-1 from the partnership, which informs the partner of the amount and character of his or her share of partnership income. The partner then combines his or her partnership earnings and losses with all other items of income or loss to be reported for the tax year, computes the amount of taxable income, and calculates the tax bill. Partnership income is taxed at the applicable tax rate for its partners, which can range from 10% to 35% (in 2007) for partners who are individuals, trusts, or estates. Corporate partners pay tax on partnership income at rates ranging from 15% to 39%.

One of the major advantages of the partnership form of doing business is that partnership losses are allocated among the partners. If the loss limitation rules (explained later in this chapter) do not apply, these losses combine with the partners' other income and result in an immediate tax savings for the partners. The immediate tax saving available to the partner contrasts sharply with the net operating loss (NOL) carrybacks or carryforwards that result from a C corporation's tax loss.

SELF-STUDY QUESTION

Why does a partner need to know his or her basis in his or her partnership interest?

ANSWER

Three important reasons are (1) to determine the gain or loss on a sale of the partnership interest, (2) to determine the amount of partnership losses a partner can deduct, and (3) to determine the amount of distributions that are tax-free to the partner.

THE PARTNER'S BASIS

A partner's basis in his or her partnership interest is a crucial element in partnership taxation. When a partner makes a contribution to a partnership or purchases a partnership interest, he or she establishes a beginning basis. Because partners can be personally liable for partnership debts, a partner's basis in his or her partnership interest is increased by his or her share of any partnership liabilities. Accordingly, the partner's basis fluctuates as the partnership borrows and repays loans or increases and decreases its accounts payable. In addition, a partner's basis in his or her partnership interest is increased by the partner's share of partnership income and decreased by his or her share of partnership losses. Because a partner's basis in his or her partnership interest can never be negative, the basis serves as one limit on the amount of deductible partnership losses. (See the discussion on pages C:9-26 and C:9-27 about the various loss limitations.)

EXAMPLE C:9-1 ▶ Tom purchases a 20% interest in the XY Partnership for $8,000 on January 1, 2007, and begins to materially participate in the partnership's business. The XY Partnership uses the calendar year as its tax year. At the time of the purchase, the XY Partnership has $2,000 in liabilities, of which Tom's share is 20%. Tom's basis in his partnership interest on January 1 is $8,400 [$8,000 + (0.20 × $2,000)]. ◀

EXAMPLE C:9-2 ▶ Assume the same facts as in Example C:9-1 except, during 2007, the XY Partnership incurs $10,000 in losses, and its liabilities increase by $4,000. What is Tom's basis on December 31, 2007?

January 1, 2007, basis	$8,400
Plus: Share of liability increase ($4,000 × 0.20)	800
Minus: Share of partnership losses ($10,000 × 0.20)	(2,000)
December 31, 2007, basis	$7,200 ◀

EXAMPLE C:9-3 ▶ Assume the same facts as in Example C:9-2, and further assume that, during 2008, the XY Partnership incurs $60,000 in losses and its liabilities increase by $10,000. Tom's share of the losses is $12,000 ($60,000 × 0.20). What is the maximum amount he can deduct in 2008?

January 1, 2008, basis	$7,200
Plus: Share of liability increase	2,000
December 31, 2008, basis before losses	$9,200
Minus: Maximum loss deduction allowed	(9,200)
December 31, 2008, basis	$ -0-

Tom's remaining $2,800 in losses carry over to subsequent years, and he can deduct them when he regains sufficient basis in his partnership interest. ◀

ADDITIONAL COMMENT

The increase in a partner's basis for earnings prevents double taxation of those earnings upon a subsequent distribution, sale of the partnership interest, or liquidation of the partnership.

PARTNERSHIP DISTRIBUTIONS

When a partnership makes a current distribution, the distribution generally is tax-free to the partners because it represents the receipt of earnings that already have been taxed to the partners and that have increased the partners' bases in their partnership interests. Subsequent distributions reduce a partner's basis in his or her partnership interest. If a cash distribution is so large, however, that it exceeds a partner's basis in his or her partnership interest, the partner recognizes gain equal to the amount of the excess. When the partnership goes out of business or when a partner withdraws from the partnership, the partnership makes liquidating distributions to the partner. Like current distributions, these distributions cause the partner to recognize gain only if the cash received exceeds the partner's basis in his or her partnership interest. A partner may recognize a loss if he or she receives only cash, inventory, and unrealized receivables in complete liquidation of his or her partnership interest. (Chapter C:10 presents detailed coverage of current and liquidating distributions.)

TAX IMPLICATIONS OF FORMATION OF A PARTNERSHIP

When two or more individuals or entities decide to operate an unincorporated business together, they form a partnership. The following sections examine the tax implications of property contributions, service contributions, and organization and syndication expenditures.

OBJECTIVE 2

Explain the tax results of a contribution of property or services in exchange for a partnership interest

CONTRIBUTION OF PROPERTY

NONRECOGNITION OF GAIN OR LOSS. Section 721 governs the formation of a partnership. In most cases, a partner who contributes property in exchange for a partnership interest recognizes no gain or loss on the transaction. Likewise, the partnership recognizes no gain or loss on the contribution of property. The partner's basis for his or her partnership interest and the partnership's basis for the property are both the same as basis of the property transferred.[5]

Nonrecognition treatment is limited to transactions in which a partner receives a partnership interest in exchange for a contribution of property. As in the corporate formation area, the term *property* includes cash, tangible property (e.g., buildings and land), and intangible property (e.g., franchise rights, trademarks, and leases).[6] Services are specifically excluded from the definition of property, so a contribution of services for a partnership interest is not a tax-free transaction.

ADDITIONAL COMMENT

For contributions to a corporation to be nontaxable, the contributing shareholders must control (own at least 80%) the corporation immediately after the transaction. No such control requirement exists for contributions to a partnership to be nontaxable.

RECOGNITION OF GAIN OR LOSS. The general rule of Sec. 721(a) provides that neither the partnership nor any partner recognizes gain or loss when partners contribute property in exchange for a partnership interest. Three exceptions to this general rule may require a partner to recognize a gain upon the contribution of property to a partnership in exchange for a partnership interest:

- Contribution of property to a partnership that would be treated as an investment company if it were incorporated
- Contribution of property followed by a distribution in an arrangement that may be considered a sale rather than a contribution
- Contribution of property to a partnership along with the partnership's assumption of liabilities previously owed by the partner

The investment company exception of Sec. 721(b) requires recognition of gain only if the exchange results in diversification of the transferor's property interest.[7] If the contribution of property is to an investment partnership, the contributing partner must recognize any gain (but not loss) realized on the property transfer as if he or she sold the stock or securities.

Sections 707(a)(2)(A) and (B) set out the second exception, which holds that a property contribution followed by a distribution (or an allocation of income or gain) may be treated as a sale of property by the partner to the partnership rather than as a contribution made by the partner to the partnership. For example, Treasury Regulations may require sale treatment (and the recognition of gain or loss) if the distribution would not have occurred except for the contribution.

EXAMPLE C:9-4 ▶ In return for a 40% interest in the CD Partnership, Cara contributed land with a $100,000 fair market value (FMV). The partners agreed that the partnership would distribute $100,000 in cash to Cara immediately after the contribution. Because the cash distribution would not have occurred had Cara not first contributed the land and become a partner, the transaction is likely to be treated as a sale of the land by Cara to the partnership. ◀

If the distribution does not occur simultaneously with the contribution, the transaction is treated as a sale if the later distribution is not dependent on the normal business risk of the enterprise.

EXAMPLE C:9-5 ▶ Elena received a 30% interest in the DEF Partnership in return for her contribution of land having a $60,000 FMV. The partnership waits six months and then distributes $60,000 in cash to Elena. If the $60,000 distribution is not contingent on the partnership's earnings or ability to borrow funds or other normal risks of doing business, the distribution and contribution will be treated as a sale of land by Elena to the partnership. ◀

---

[5] Secs. 722 and 723.

[6] For an excellent discussion of the definition of the term *property*, see footnote 6 of *D.N. Stafford v. U.S.*, 45 AFTR 2d 80-785, 80-1 USTC ¶9218 (5th Cir., 1980).

[7] Reg. Sec. 1.351-1(c)(1). This investment is taxed only when immediately after the exchange more than 80% of the value of the partnership's assets (excluding cash and nonconvertible debt obligations) is held for investment or is readily marketable stocks, securities, or interests in regulated investment companies or real estate investment trusts.

KEY POINT

A partner's relief of debt is treated as if the partner receives a cash distribution. A partner's assumption of debt is treated as if the partner makes a cash contribution. These two simple rules are critical to understanding transactions such as formations of partnerships, distributions from partnerships, and sales or liquidations of partnership interests.

EFFECTS OF LIABILITIES. The third condition that may cause a partner to recognize gain (but not loss) on the formation of a partnership is the contribution of property to a partnership along with the partnership's assumption of liabilities previously owed by the partner. Because each partner is liable for his or her share of partnership liabilities, increases and decreases in the partnership liabilities are reflected in each partner's basis. Specifically, Sec. 752 provides that two effects result from a partner's contribution of property to a partnership if the partnership also assumes the partner's liabilities.

- Each partner's basis is increased by his or her share of the partnership's liabilities as if he or she had contributed cash to the partnership in the amount of his or her share of partnership liabilities.
- The partner whose personal liabilities are assumed by the partnership has a reduction in the basis of his or her partnership interest as if the partnership distributed cash to him or her in the amount of the assumed liability. A cash distribution first reduces the partner's basis in the partnership interest. If the cash distribution exceeds the partner's predistribution basis in the partnership interest, the partner recognizes gain.

The net effect of these two basis adjustments, however, is seldom large enough to cause a transferor partner to recognize gain when he or she contributes property to the partnership. The transferor partner is deemed first to have made a contribution of property plus a contribution of cash equal to the partner's share of any partnership liabilities existing prior to his or her entrance into the partnership (or contributed by other partners concurrently with this transaction). The partner then is deemed to have received a cash distribution equal to the total amount of his or her own liability assumed by the *other* partners. (No basis adjustment is required for the portion of the liability transferred to the partnership by the transferor that he or she will retain as a partner.)

EXAMPLE C:9-6 ▶ In return for a 20% partnership interest, Mary contributes land having a $60,000 FMV and a $30,000 basis to the XY Partnership. The partnership assumes Mary's $15,000 liability arising from her purchase of the land, and Mary's share of partnership liabilities is 20%. The XY Partnership has $4,000 in liabilities immediately before her contribution. What is Mary's basis in her partnership interest?

Basis of contributed property	$30,000
Plus: Mary's share of existing partnership liabilities ($4,000 × 0.20)	800
Minus: Mary's liabilities assumed by the other partners ($15,000 × 0.80)	(12,000)
Mary's basis in her partnership interest	$18,800

Mary recognizes no gain on the partnership's assumption of her liability because the deemed cash distribution from the assumption of her $12,000 in liabilities by the partnership does not exceed her $30,800 basis in the partnership interest immediately preceding the fictional distribution. ◀

ADDITIONAL COMMENT

In Example C:9-6, the $12,000 reduction in basis also can be viewed as the net of $3,000, which is Mary's 20% share of the $15,000 increase in partnership liabilities, and $15,000, which is Mary's liability assumed by the partnership.

EXAMPLE C:9-7 ▶ Assume the same facts as in Example C:9-6 except the amount of the liability assumed by the XY Partnership is $50,000. Mary's basis in her partnership interest is calculated as follows:

Basis of contributed property	$30,000
Plus: Mary's share of existing partnership liabilities ($4,000 × 0.20)	800
Predistribution basis	$30,800
Minus: Mary's liabilities assumed by the other partners ($50,000 × 0.80)	(40,000)
Basis in partnership interest (cannot be negative)	$ –0–

The cash deemed distributed in excess of Mary's predistribution basis causes her to recognize a $9,200 ($40,000 − $30,800) gain. Mary reduces her basis to zero by the distribution because a partner's basis in the partnership interest can never be less than zero. ◀

ADDITIONAL COMMENT

In contrast to partnership formations, had Example C:9-7 involved a formation of the XY Corporation, Mary would have recognized a $20,000 Sec. 357(c) gain.

STOP & THINK

Question: Assume the land Mary contributed in Example C:9-6 has a $60,000 FMV and an $85,000 adjusted basis. Should Mary contribute it to the partnership?

Solution: If Mary contributes the land, she cannot recognize her $25,000 ($60,000 FMV − $85,000 adjusted basis) loss until the partnership disposes of the property. Accordingly, Mary might prefer to sell the property and recognize her loss now. If the partnership can afford the $60,000 price and needs this property, Mary could sell the land to the partnership, recognize her loss on the sale, and then contribute the cash she receives from the partnership in exchange for her partnership interest. If the partnership does not need the property, Mary could sell the land to a third party, recognize her loss, and contribute the sales proceeds to the partnership in exchange for her partnership interest. However, a problem arises if the partnership needs this property and cannot afford to buy it from Mary. In that case, contributing the property to the partnership may be the only alternative despite the less-than-optimal tax results.

TYPICAL MISCONCEPTION

Example C:9-7 illustrates another difference between partnership and corporate formations. In the example, XY Partnership does not increase its basis in the property for the gain recognized by Mary, but if XY were a corporation, XY would increase its basis in the property by Mary's recognized gain.

Because the partnership's assumption of a partner's liabilities is treated as a cash distribution, the character of any gain recognized by the partner is controlled by the partnership distribution rules. Cash distributions exceeding predistribution basis always result in gain recognition, and that gain is deemed to be gain from the sale of the partnership interest.[8] Because a partnership interest is usually a capital asset, any gain arising from assumption of a partner's liabilities normally is a capital gain.

PARTNER'S BASIS IN THE PARTNERSHIP INTEREST (COMMONLY CALLED THE OUTSIDE BASIS). In general, the transferor partner's beginning basis in the partnership interest equals the sum of money contributed plus his or her basis in contributed property. If the partner recognizes any gain on the contribution because the partnership is an investment company, the amount of recognized gain increases his or her basis in the partnership interest.[9] Beginning basis is adjusted to reflect liability share. Any gain recognized because of the effects of liabilities on the partner's basis does not increase the basis for the partnership interest because in this situation the basis is zero.

In some instances, a partner may contribute valuable property having little or no basis. For example, accounts receivable or notes receivable of a partner using the cash method of accounting can be a valued contribution to a partnership, but if the receivables' bases are zero, the beginning basis of the partnership interest also is zero.

TYPICAL MISCONCEPTION

If a partner contributes both ordinary income property and capital gain property to a partnership, the partner apparently has two different holding periods for his or her partnership interest.

HOLDING PERIOD FOR PARTNERSHIP INTEREST. The holding period for the partnership interest includes the transferor's holding period for the contributed property if that property is a capital asset or a Sec. 1231 asset in the transferor's hands.[10] If the contributed property is an ordinary income asset (e.g., inventory) to the partner, the holding period for the partnership interest begins the day after the contribution date.[11]

EXAMPLE C:9-8 ▶ On April 1, Sue contributes a building (a Sec. 1231 asset) to the ST Partnership in exchange for a 20% interest. Sue purchased the building three years ago. Her holding period for her partnership interest includes the three years she held the contributed building. ◀

EXAMPLE C:9-9 ▶ On April 1, Ted contributes inventory to the ST Partnership in exchange for a 20% interest. No matter when Ted acquired the inventory, his holding period for his partnership interest begins on April 2, the day after the date of his contribution. ◀

PARTNERSHIP'S BASIS IN PROPERTY. Under Sec. 723, the partnership's basis for contributed property is the same as the property's basis in the hands of the contributing partner. If, however, the contributing partner recognizes gain because the partnership is an investment company, such gain increases the partnership's basis in the contributed property. Gain recognized by the contributing partner because of the assumption of a partner's liability does not increase the partnership's basis in the property.[12]

Not only does the property's basis carry over to the partnership from the contributing partner, but for some property the character of gain or loss on a subsequent disposition of the property by the partnership also references the character of the property in the contributing partner's hands. Section 724 prevents the transformation of ordinary income

[8] Sec. 731(a).
[9] Sec. 722.
[10] Sec. 1223(1).
[11] Reg. Sec. 1.1223-1(a).
[12] Rev. Rul. 84-15, 1984-1 C.B. 158.

into capital gains (or capital losses into ordinary losses) when a partner contributes property to a partnership. Properties that were (1) unrealized receivables, inventory, or capital loss property in the hands of the contributing partner and (2) contributed to a partnership retain their character for some subsequent partnership dispositions.[13]

Unrealized Receivables. The concept of unrealized receivables plays a key role for tax purposes in many different partnership transactions. An **unrealized receivable** is any right to payment for goods or services the holder has not included in income because of the accounting method used.[14] The most common examples of unrealized receivables are the accounts receivable of a cash method taxpayer.

If property is an unrealized receivable in the hands of the contributing partner, any gain or loss recognized on the partnership's later disposition of the property is treated as ordinary income or loss. This rule mandates ordinary income or loss treatment regardless of how long the partnership holds the property before disposition or the character of the property in the partnership's hands.

Inventory. If property was inventory in the hands of the contributing partner, its character remains ordinary for five years. Consequently, any gain or loss recognized by the partnership on the disposition of such property during the five-year period beginning on the date of contribution is ordinary gain or loss. Ordinary gain or loss treatment occurs even if the property is a capital asset or Sec. 1231 asset in the partnership's hands.

EXAMPLE C:9-10 ▶ On June 1, Jose, a real estate developer, contributes ten acres of land in an industrial park he developed to the Hi-Tech Partnership in exchange for a 30% interest in the partnership. Although Jose held the acreage in inventory, the land serves as the site for Hi-Tech's new research facility. Four years later Hi-Tech sells its research facility and the land. Although gain on the sale of the land usually would be taxed as Sec. 1231 gain, Hi-Tech must report it as ordinary income under Sec. 724. ◀

ADDITIONAL COMMENT

Congress enacted Sec. 724 to eliminate the ability to transform the character of gain or loss on property by contributing the property to a partnership and having the partnership subsequently sell it.

Capital Loss Property. The final type of property whose character is fixed at the time of the contribution is property that would generate a capital loss if sold by the contributing partner rather than contributed to the partnership. A loss recognized by the partnership on the disposition of the property within five years of the date it is contributed to the partnership is a capital loss. However, the amount of loss characterized as capital may not exceed the capital loss the contributing partner would have recognized had the partner sold the property on the contribution date. The character of any loss exceeding the difference between the property's FMV and its adjusted basis on the contribution date is determined by the property's character in the hands of the partnership.

EXAMPLE C:9-11 ▶ Pam holds investment land that she purchased six years ago for $50,000. The FMV of the land was only $40,000 two years ago when she contributed it to the PK Partnership, which is in the business of developing and selling lots. PK develops the contributed land and sells it in the current year for $28,000, or at a $22,000 loss. The $10,000 loss that accrued while Pam held the land as a capital asset retains its character as a capital loss. The remaining $12,000 of loss that accrues while the land is part of the partnership's inventory is an ordinary loss. ◀

PARTNERSHIP'S HOLDING PERIOD. Under Sec. 1223(2), the partnership's holding period for its contributed assets includes the holding period of the contributing partner. This rule applies without regard to the character the property has in the contributing partner's hands or the partnership's hands.

SECTION 1245 AND 1250 PROPERTY RULES. Although the Sec. 1245 and Sec. 1250 depreciation recapture rules override many gain nonrecognition provisions in the IRC, the partner incurs no depreciation recapture unless he or she recognizes gain upon contributing

---

[13] Sec. 724. The determination of whether property is an unrealized receivable, inventory, or a capital loss property in the contributing partner's hands occurs immediately before the contribution.

[14] Section 724(d)(1) references the unrealized receivables definition found in Sec. 751(c). For distributions and sale transactions, the unrealized receivables definition is broadened to include certain recapture items. This difference is discussed more fully in Chapter C:10.

property in exchange for a partnership interest.[15] Instead, both the adjusted basis and depreciation recapture potential carry over to the partnership. If the partnership later sells the property at a gain, the Sec. 1245 and 1250 provisions affect the character of the gain. In addition, any Sec. 1250 gain potential carries over to the partnership to affect gain characterization upon a future sale. Section 1250 gain is taxed to individuals at a 25% capital gains tax rate under Sec. 1(h)(1)(D).

CONTRIBUTION OF PROPERTY AFTER FORMATION. Any time a partner contributes property in exchange for a partnership interest, the rules outlined above apply whether the contribution occurs during the formation of the partnership or at a later date. This treatment contrasts sharply with corporate contributions, where a tax-free contribution after formation is rare because of the 80% control requirement. Most contributions of property in exchange for a partnership interest are tax-free even if they occur years after the partnership was formed.

CONTRIBUTION OF SERVICES

A partner who receives a partnership interest in exchange for services has been compensated as if he or she receives cash and thus must recognize ordinary income. The amount and timing of the income to be recognized are determined under Sec. 83. Consequently, receipt of an unrestricted interest in a partnership requires the service partner to immediately recognize income equal to the FMV of the partnership interest less any cash or property contributed by the partner. Generally, the service partner recognizes no income upon receiving a restricted interest in a partnership until the restriction lapses or the interest can be freely transferred.

ADDITIONAL COMMENT

The Treasury Department has issued proposed regulations, and the IRS will issue a new revenue procedure that will alter the landscape of taxing partnership interests transferred for services. The new rules also will make Rev. Proc. 93-27, discussed on the next page, obsolete. However, taxpayers may not rely on the proposed rules until they are finalized and may continue to rely on existing rules and procedures. See Notice 2005-43, 2005-24 I.R.B. 1221.

Although a partnership interest seems to be a unified interest, it really is made up of two components: a capital interest and a profits interest. A partner may receive both components or only a profits interest in exchange for his or her services. (A capital interest without a profits interest rarely occurs.) Treasury Regulations indicate that a **capital interest** can be valued by determining the amount the partner would receive if the partnership liquidated on the day the partner receives the partnership interest.[16] If the partner would receive proceeds from the sale of the partnership's assets or receive the assets themselves, he or she is considered to own a capital interest. Alternatively, if the partner's only interest is in the future earnings of the partnership (with no interest in the current partnership assets), the partner owns a **profits interest** (but not a capital interest).

Tax law has long been settled that receipt of a capital interest in a partnership in exchange for services is taxable under the rules outlined above. A profits interest, however, is no more than a right to future income taxable to the partners as the partnership earns it. To the extent the profits interest itself has a value, one might expect that value to be taxed when the partner receives the profits interest, as any other property received for services would be taxed.

EXAMPLE C:9-12 ▶ Carl arranges favorable financing for the purchase of an office building and receives a 30% profits interest in a partnership formed to own and operate the building. Less than three weeks later, Carl sells his profits interest to his partner for $40,000. Carl must recognize $40,000 as ordinary income from the receipt of a partnership profits interest in exchange for services. ◀

The facts in Example C:9-12 approximate those of *Sol Diamond,* a landmark partnership taxation case, which was the first case to tax the partner upon receipt of a profits interest.[17] The Tax Court pointed out that Sec. 61 included all compensation for services, and no other provision contained in the IRC or Treasury Regulations removed this transaction from taxation. The Seventh Circuit Court of Appeals seemed to limit the inclusion

---

[15] Secs. 1245(b)(3) and 1250(d)(3). Property acquired as a capital contribution where gain is not recognized under Sec. 721 is subject to the MACRS anti-churning rules of Sec. 168(i)(7)(A). In general, the anti-churning rules require the partnership to use the same depreciation method as the partner who contributed the property. See Chapter C:2 for a discussion of these rules in connection with a corporate formation transaction.

[16] Reg. Sec. 1.704-1(e)(1)(v). The capital interest definition in this regulation relates to family partnerships, but such definition should apply generally in the partnership area.

[17] 33 AFTR 2d 74-852, 74-1 USTC ¶9306 (7th Cir., 1974), *aff'g.* 56 T.C. 530 (1971).

of a profits interest to situations in which the market value of the profits interest could be determined. The IRS resolved much of the uncertainty in this area of tax law when it issued Rev. Proc. 93-27, which provides that the IRS generally will tax a profits interest received for services only in three specified instances in which a FMV is readily ascertainable.[18] In the general case, therefore, an income tax is not levied on the profits interest separately, but all partnership profits that pass through to the partner are taxed under the normal rules of partnership taxation.

CONSEQUENCES TO THE PARTNERSHIP. Payments by the partnership for services are either deductible as an expense or capitalized, including those paid for services with an interest in the partnership. If the payment constitutes a deductible expense, the partnership takes the deduction in the same year the partner includes the value of his or her partnership interest in income.[19] This rule matches the timing of the partnership's deduction to the partner's income recognition.

Allocating the Expense Deduction. The partnership allocates the expense deduction or the amortization of the capital expenditure among the partners other than the service partner. This allocation occurs because these partners make the outlay by relinquishing part of their interest in the partnership.

EXAMPLE C:9-13 ▶ In June of the current year Jay, a lawyer, receives a 1% capital and profits interest (valued at $4,000) in the JLK Partnership in return for providing legal services to JLK's employees during the first five months of the current year. The legal services were a fringe benefit for JLK's employees and were deductible by JLK. Jay must include $4,000 in his current year gross income, and JLK can deduct the expense in the current year. JLK allocates the $4,000 expense to all partners other than Jay. ◀

If the service performed is of a nature that should be capitalized, the partnership capitalizes the amount and amortizes it as appropriate. The related asset's basis is increased at the same time and in the same amount as the partner's gross income inclusion.[20]

EXAMPLE C:9-14 ▶ In June of the current year, Rob, an architect, receives a 10% capital and profits interest in the KLB Partnership for his services in designing a new building to house the partnership's operations. The June value of the partnership interest is $24,000. Rob must recognize $24,000 of ordinary income in the current year as a result of receiving the partnership interest. The KLB Partnership must capitalize the $24,000 as part of the building's cost and depreciate that amount (along with the building's other costs) over its recovery period. ◀

The timing of the partner's recognition of income is the same in the preceding two examples even though the partnership could deduct one payment but had to capitalize the other.

Partnership Gain or Loss. By exchanging an interest in the partnership for services, the partnership, in effect, pays for services by transferring an interest in the underlying partnership property. Generally, when a debtor uses property to pay a debt, the debtor must recognize gain or loss equal to the difference between the property's FMV and adjusted basis. Likewise, the partnership must recognize the gain or loss existing in the proportionate share of its assets deemed to be transferred to the service partner.[21] Furthermore, because the partnership recognizes gain or loss, it must adjust the bases of the assets.

EXAMPLE C:9-15 ▶ On January 1 of the current year, Maria is admitted as a 25% partner in the XYZ Partnership in exchange for services valued at $16,500. The partnership has no liabilities at the time but has assets with a basis of $50,000 and FMV of $66,000. The transaction is treated as if Maria received an undivided one-fourth interest in each asset. She is taxed on the $16,500 FMV of the

---

[18] 1993-2 C.B. 343. The three exceptions involve receipt of a profits interest having a substantially certain and predictable income stream, the partner disposes of the profits interest within two years of receipt, or the profits interest is a limited interest in a publicly traded partnership.

[19] Reg. Sec. 1.83-6(a)(1).

[20] Reg. Sec. 1.83-6(a)(4).

[21] Reg. Sec. 1.83-6(b).

assets and takes a $16,500 basis in her partnership interest. The partnership recognizes $4,000 of gain [0.25 × ($66,000 FMV − $50,000 adjusted basis)] on the assets deemed paid to Maria. The partnership calculates gain or loss for each asset XYZ holds, and the character of each asset determines the character of the gain or loss recognized. The recognized gain is allocated to the partners other than Maria. Also, the partnership's original basis in its assets ($50,000) is increased by the $4,000 recognized gain. ◀

SELF-STUDY QUESTION

What is the importance of the distinction between organizational expenditures and syndication expenditures?

ANSWER

Organizational expenditures can be deducted up to $5,000 and then amortized over a period of 180 months, but syndication expenditures are *not* deductible or amortizable.

ORGANIZATIONAL AND SYNDICATION EXPENDITURES

The costs of organizing a partnership are capital expenditures. However, the partnership can elect to deduct the first $5,000 of these expenditures in the tax year it begins business. As a limit, the partnership must reduce the $5,000 by the amount by which cumulative organizational expenditures exceed $50,000, although the $5,000 cannot be reduced below zero. The partnership can amortize the remaining organizational expenditures over an 180-month period beginning in the month it begins business.[22] This rule applies to organization expenditures incurred after October 22, 2004. Prior to October 23, 2004, a partnership was not allowed an initial deduction but could elect to amortize its organizational expenditures over a period of at least 60 months beginning in the month it began business.

Organizational expenditures that can be capitalized and amortized must meet the same requirements as the costs incurred by a corporation making the Sec. 248 election to amortize organizational expenditures (see Chapter C:3). The organizational expenditures must be incident to the creation of the partnership, chargeable to a capital account, and of a character that would be amortizable over the life of the partnership if the partnership had a limited life. Eligible expenditures include legal fees for negotiating and preparing partnership agreements, accounting fees for establishing the initial accounting system, and filing fees. Syndication expenditures for the issuing and marketing of interests in the partnership are not organizational expenditures and cannot be included in this election.[23] The partnership deducts unamortized organizational expenditures when it is terminated or liquidated.

Topic Review C:9-1 summarizes the tax consequences of forming a partnership.

PARTNERSHIP ELECTIONS

OBJECTIVE 3

Determine the permitted tax years for a partnership

Once formed, the partnership must make a number of elections. For example, a partnership must select a tax year and elect accounting methods for all but a few items affecting the computation of partnership taxable income or loss.

PARTNERSHIP TAX YEAR

The partnership's selection of a tax year is critical because it determines when each partner reports his or her share of partnership income or loss. Under Sec. 706(a), each partner's tax return includes his or her share of partnership income, gain, loss, deduction, or credit items for any taxable year of the partnership ending within or with the partner's tax year.

EXAMPLE C:9-16 ▶ Vicki is a member of a partnership having a November 30 year-end. In her tax return for calendar year 2007, she must include her share of partnership items from the partnership tax year that ends November 30, 2007. Results of partnership operations in December 2007 are reported in Vicki's 2008 tax return along with her share of other partnership items from the partnership year that ends on November 30, 2008. She receives, in essence, a one-year deferral of the taxes due on December's partnership income. ◀

SECTION 706 RESTRICTIONS. Because of a substantial opportunity for tax deferral, Congress enacted Sec. 706 to restrict the available choices for a partnership's tax year. The partnership must use the same tax year as the one or more **majority partners** who have an

[22] Sec. 709(b).

[23] Reg. Sec. 1.709-2(b).

Topic Review C:9-1

Formation of a Partnership

	Contribution to a Partnership	
	Property	**Services**
Recognition of gain, loss, or income by partner	Tax-free unless (1) liabilities assumed by the partnership exceed partner's predistribution basis in partnership interest (gain recognized is amount by which liabilities assumed by partnership exceed predistribution basis), (2) the partnership formed is an investment partnership (gain recognized is excess of FMV of partnership interest over basis of assets contributed), or (3) a contribution is followed by a distribution that is treated as a sale (gain or loss recognized on sale transaction).	Taxable to partner equal to FMV of partnership interest received in exchange for the services.
Basis of partnership interest	Substituted basis from property contributed plus share of partnership liabilities assumed minus the partner's liabilities assumed by the partnership. Gain recognized because of the investment company rules increases the basis of the partnership interest.	Amount of income recognized plus share of partnership liabilities assumed by the partner minus partner's liabilities assumed by the partnership.
Gain or loss recognized by the partnership	No gain or loss recognized by the partnership.	1. Deduction or capitalized expense is created depending on the type of service rendered. 2. Gain or loss recognized equals difference between FMV of portion of assets used to pay service partner and the basis of such portion of the assets.
Basis of assets to the partnership	Carryover basis is increased by a partner's gain recognized only if gain results from the formation of an investment partnership. No basis adjustment occurs when assumption of partner's liabilities results in a partner's gain recognition. In a sale transaction, assets take a cost basis.	Increased or decreased to reflect the FMV of the assets paid to the service partner.

aggregate interest in partnership profits and capital exceeding 50%. This rule must be used only if these majority partners have a common tax year and have had this tax year for the shorter of the three preceding years or the partnership's period of existence. If the tax year of the partner(s) owning a majority interest cannot be used, the partnership must use the tax year of all its principal partners (or the tax year to which all of its principal partners are concurrently changing). A **principal partner** is defined as one who owns a 5% or more interest in capital or profits.[24] If the principal partners do not have a common tax year, the partnership must use the tax year that allows the least aggregate deferral. The least aggregate deferral test provided in Treasury Regulations[25] requires that, for each possible tax year-end, each partner's ownership percentage be multiplied by the number of months the partner would defer income (number of months from partnership year-end to partner year-end). The number arrived at for each partner is totaled across all partners. The same procedure is followed for each alternative tax year, and the partnership must use the tax year that produces the smallest total.

EXAMPLE C:9-17 ▶ Jane, Kerry Corporation, and Lanier Corporation form the JKL Partnership. The three partners use tax years ending on December 31, June 30, and September 30, respectively. Jane, Kerry Corporation, and Lanier Corporation own 40%, 40%, and 20%, respectively, of the partnership. Neither the majority partner rule nor the principal partner rule can be applied to determine

[24] Sec. 706(b)(3).

[25] Reg. Sec. 1.706-1.

WHAT WOULD YOU DO IN THIS SITUATION?

Bob Krause and his large family corporation have been longtime clients of your accounting firm. During the current year, Bob and his adult son, Tom, formed the BT Partnership to develop and sell vacation homes on the Suwanee River. Bob contributed a 1,000-acre tract of land in exchange for a 50% interest in BT Partnership's profits and losses. The land had a $300,000 FMV and a $30,000 adjusted basis. Tom contributed $150,000 in cash for the remaining 50% interest in the partnership. Two months after being formed, BT Partnership used the land as security for a $200,000 loan from a local bank. Of the $200,000 loan proceeds, the partnership used $50,000 to subdivide and plot the land. The partnership then distributed the other $150,000 of the loan proceeds to Bob. Bob plans not to report these transactions because property contributions in exchange for a partnership interest and distributions of money by a partnership that do not exceed the partner's basis are tax-free transactions. What would you advise your client to do in this situation?

JKL's tax year because each partner has a different year-end. To determine the least aggregate deferral, all three possible year-ends must be analyzed as follows:

			Possible Tax Year-Ends					
			6/30		*9/30*		*12/31*	
Partner	*Partnership Interest*	*Partner Tax Year*	*Months Deferred*[a]	*Total*[b]	*Months Deferred*	*Total*	*Months Deferred*	*Total*
Jane	40%	12/31	6	2.4	3	1.2	0	0
Kerry	40%	6/30	0	0	9	3.6	6	2.4
Lanier	20%	9/30	3	0.6	0	0	9	1.8
				3.0		4.8		4.2

[a] Months from possible partnership tax year-end to partner tax year-end.
[b] Partnership interest × months deferred = Total.

The partnership must use a June 30 year-end because, with a total score of 3.0, that tax year-end produces the least aggregate deferral. ◀

If the partnership has a business purpose for using some tax year other than the year prescribed by these rules, the IRS may approve use of another tax year. Revenue Procedure 2002-39[26] states that an acceptable business purpose for using a different tax year is to end the partnership's tax year at the end of the partnership's natural business year. This revenue procedure explains that a business having a peak period and a nonpeak period completes its natural business year at the end of its peak season (or shortly thereafter). For example, a ski lodge has a natural business year that ends in early spring. Partnerships that do not have a peak period cannot use the natural business year exception.

EXAMPLE C:9-18 ▶ Amy, Brad, and Chris are equal partners in the ABC Partnership. Each partner uses a December 31 tax year-end. ABC earns 30% of its gross receipts in July and August each year and has experienced this pattern of earnings for more than three years. This two-month period is the peak season for their business each year. The IRS probably would grant approval for the partnership to use an August 31 tax year-end. ◀

KEY POINT
Because of the Sec. 706 requirements, most partnerships are required to adopt a calendar year. As a compromise, a Sec. 444 election permits a fiscal tax year as long as no more than a three-month deferral exists and as long as the deferral is not increased from any deferral already approved.

Section 444 provides an election that permits a partnership to use a year-end that results in a deferral of the lesser of the current deferral period or three months. The deferral period is the time from the beginning of the partnership's fiscal year to the close of the first required tax year ending within such year (i.e., usually December 31). The Sec. 444

[26] 2002-1 C.B. 1046. The IRS in Rev. Rul. 87-57, 1987-2 C.B. 117, has provided a series of situations illustrating the business purpose requirement. In addition, Rev. Proc. 2006-46, 2006-45 I.R.B. 859, provides expeditious IRS approval if the natural business year satisfies a 25% test. This test requires that 25% of the partnership's gross receipts be earned in the last two months of the requested year and in the last two months of the two preceding similar 12-month periods.

election is available to both new partnerships making an initial tax year election or existing partnerships that are changing tax years. A partnership that satisfies the Sec. 706 requirements described above or has established a business purpose for its choice of a year-end (i.e., natural business year) does not need a Sec. 444 election.

STOP & THINK

Question: Suppose the ABC Partnership has had a December 31 year-end for many years. All its partners are individuals with calendar tax year-ends. Using Sec. 444, what tax year-ends are available for ABC?

Solution: Only December 31 can be used for a tax year-end for ABC even with Sec. 444. Section 444 allows a minimum deferral of the shorter of three months or the existing deferral. Because the existing deferral is zero months (the required tax year-end and the existing tax year-end are both December 31), no deferral is allowed under Sec. 444. The section allows a deferral only for new partnerships or for partnerships that already have a deferral.

HISTORICAL NOTE

Congress enacted Sec. 444, in part, as a concession to tax return preparers who already have the majority of their clients with calendar year-ends.

A partnership that makes a Sec. 444 election must make a required payment under Sec. 7519. (See the Compliance and Procedural Considerations section of this chapter for a discussion of the Sec. 444 election and Sec. 7519 required payment.) The required payment has the effect of assessing a tax on the partnership's deferred income at the highest individual marginal tax rate plus one percentage point.

Topic Review C:9-2 summarizes the allowable partnership tax year elections.

OTHER PARTNERSHIP ELECTIONS

With the exception of three specific elections reserved to the partners, Sec. 703(b) requires that the partnership make all elections that can affect the computation of taxable income derived from the partnership.[27] The three elections reserved to the individual partners relate to income from the discharge of indebtedness, deduction and recapture of certain mining exploration expenditures, and the choice between deducting or crediting foreign income taxes. Other than these elections, the partnership makes all elections at the entity level. Accordingly, the partnership elects its overall accounting method, which can differ from the methods used by its partners. The partnership also elects its inventory and depreciation methods.

Topic Review C:9-2

Allowable Tax Year for a Partnership

Section 706 requires that a partnership select the highest ranked tax year-end from the ranking that follows:

1. The tax year-end used by the partners who own a majority interest in the partnership capital and profits.
2. The tax year-end used by all principal partners (i.e., partners who each owns an interest in at least 5% of the partnership capital or profits).
3. The tax year-end determined by the least aggregate deferral test.

The IRS may grant permission for the partnership to use a fiscal year-end if the partnership has a natural business year. If the partnership does not have a natural business year, it must either

- Use the tax year-end required by Sec. 706 or
- Elect a fiscal year-end under Sec. 444 and make a required payment that approximates the tax due on the deferred income.

[27] The partnership does not include depletion from oil or gas wells in its computation of income (Sec. 703(a)(2)(F)). Instead each partner elects cost or percentage depletion (Sec. 613A(c)(7)(D)).

PARTNERSHIP REPORTING OF INCOME

PARTNERSHIP TAXABLE INCOME

OBJECTIVE 4

Differentiate between items that must be separately stated and those that are included in ordinary income or loss for partnerships that are not electing large partnerships

Although the partnership is not a taxable entity, the IRC requires that the partnership calculate **partnership taxable income** for various computational reasons, such as adjusting the partners' basis in their partnership interests. Partnership taxable income for partnerships that are not electing large partnerships is calculated in much the same way as the taxable income of individuals, with a few differences mandated by the IRC. First, taxable income is divided into separately stated items and ordinary income or loss. Section 703(a) specifies a list of deductions available to individuals but that cannot be claimed by a partnership. The forbidden deductions include income taxes paid or accrued to a foreign country or U.S. possession, charitable contributions, oil and gas depletion, and net operating loss (NOL) carrybacks or carryovers. The first three items must be separately stated and may or may not be deductible by the partner. Because all losses are allocated to the partners for deduction on their tax returns, the partnership itself never has an NOL carryover or carryback. Instead, a partner may have an NOL if his or her deductible share of partnership losses exceeds his or her other business income. These NOLs are used at the partner level without any further regard for the partnership entity.

SEPARATELY STATED ITEMS

Each partner must report his or her distributive share of partnership income. However, Sec. 702 establishes a list of items that must be separately stated at the partnership level so that their character can remain intact at the partner reporting level. Section 702(a) lists the following items that must be separately stated:

- Net short-term capital gains and losses
- Net long-term capital gains and losses
- Sec. 1231 gains and losses
- Charitable contributions
- Dividends eligible for the dividends-received deduction or the 15% maximum tax rate
- Taxes paid or accrued to a foreign country or to a U.S. possession
- Any other item provided by Treasury Regulations

Regulation Sec. 1.702-1(a)(8) adds several other items to this list, including:

- Tax-exempt or partially tax-exempt interest
- Any items subject to special allocations (discussed below)

As a general rule, an item must be separately stated if the income tax liability of any partner that would result from treating the item separately is different from the liability that would result if that item were included in partnership ordinary income.[28]

EXAMPLE C:9-19 ▶ Amy and Big Corporation are equal partners in the AB Partnership, which purchases new equipment during 2007 at a total cost of $300,000. In 2007, AB elects to expense $112,000 under Sec. 179 and allocates $56,000 to each partner. Big already has expensed $35,000 under Sec. 179 this year. The Sec. 179 expense must be separately stated because Big is subject to a separate $112,000 limit of its own (in 2007). After the partnership allocation, Big has a remaining Sec. 179 expense limitation of $21,000 ($112,000 − $35,000 − $56,000). ◀

Once the partnership separately states each item and allocates a distributive share to each partner, the partners report the separately stated items on their tax returns as if the partnership entity did not exist. A partner's share of partnership net long-term capital

[28] Reg. Sec. 1.702-1(a)(8)(ii).

ADDITIONAL COMMENT

The pass-through aspect of partnerships reflects the aggregate theory of partnerships, which holds that the partnership is merely an aggregate of its partners. In other ways, however, partnerships conform to the entity theory, for example, they report income and make elections at the entity level.

TYPICAL MISCONCEPTION

Partnership ordinary income or loss is the sum of all taxable income or loss items not separately stated. The partnership reports this amount as a residual number on line 22 of Form 1065. Partnership taxable income includes both the taxable separately stated items and the partnership ordinary income or loss. These two terms are not interchangeable.

gains or losses is combined with the partner's personal long-term capital gains and losses to calculate the partner's net long-term capital gain or loss. Likewise, a partner's share of partnership charitable contributions is combined with the partner's own charitable contributions with the total subject to the partner's charitable contribution limitations. In summary, Sec. 702(b) requires that the character of each separately stated item be determined at the partnership level. The amount then passes through to the partners and is reported in each partner's return as if the partner directly realized the amount.

PARTNERSHIP ORDINARY INCOME

All taxable items of income, gain, loss, or deduction that do not have to be separately stated are combined into a total called **partnership ordinary income** or **loss.** This ordinary income amount sometimes is incorrectly referred to as partnership taxable income. Partnership taxable income is the sum of all taxable items among the separately stated items plus the partnership ordinary income or loss. Therefore, partnership taxable income often is substantially greater than partnership ordinary income.

Included in the partnership's ordinary income are items such as gross profit on sales, administrative expenses, and employee salaries. Such items are always ordinary income or expenses not subject to special limitations. Partnership ordinary income also includes Sec. 1245 depreciation recapture because such ordinary income is not eligible for preferential treatment.

The partnership allocates a share of partnership ordinary income or loss to each partner. Such an allocation is reported on Schedules K and K-1 of the partnership's Form 1065 (see the completed partnership tax return in Appendix B). An individual partner reports his or her distributive share of ordinary income, or the deductible portion of his or her distributive share of ordinary loss, on Schedule E of Form 1040. Schedule E includes rental and royalty income and income or losses from estates, trusts, S corporations, and partnerships. A corporate partner reports partnership ordinary income or loss in the Other Income category of Form 1120.

U.S. PRODUCTION ACTIVITIES DEDUCTION

The 2004 Jobs Act added a new deduction for businesses engaged in U.S. production activities for tax years beginning after 2004. Chapter C:3 describes the corporate version of this deduction, whereby the U.S. production activities deduction equals a percentage (6% in 2007) times the lesser of (1) qualified production activities income for the year or (2) taxable income before the U.S. production activities deduction. Individuals use a modified form of AGI instead of taxable income for this computation. The deduction, however, cannot exceed 50% of the employer's W-2 wages for the year. In the case of a partnership, the deduction applies at the partner level, so the partnership must report each partner's share of qualified production activities income on the partner's Schedule K-1. For the 50% salary limitation, each partner is allocated a share of the partnership's W-2 wages.

PARTNER REPORTING OF INCOME

OBJECTIVE 5

Calculate a partner's distributive share of partnership income, gain, loss, deduction, or credit items

PARTNER'S DISTRIBUTIVE SHARE

Once the partnership determines separately stated income, gain, loss, deduction, or credit items, and partnership ordinary income or loss, the partnership must allocate the totals among the partners. Each partner must report and pay taxes on his or her distributive share. Under Sec. 704(b), the partner's distributive share normally is determined by the terms of the partnership agreement or, if the partnership agreement is silent, by the partner's overall interest in the partnership as determined by taking into account all facts and circumstances.

Note that the term **distributive share** is misleading because it has nothing to do with the amount actually distributed to a partner. A partner's distributive share is the portion of partnership taxable and nontaxable income that the partner has agreed to report for tax purposes. Actual distributions in a given year may be more or less than the partner's distributive share.

PARTNERSHIP AGREEMENT. The **partnership agreement** may describe a partner's distributive share by indicating the partner's profits and loss interest, or it may indicate separate profits and loss interests. For example, the partnership agreement may state that a partner has a 10% interest in both partnership profits and losses or a partner has only a 10% interest in partnership profits (i.e., profits interest) but has a 30% interest in partnership losses (i.e., loss interest).

If the partnership agreement states only one interest percentage, it is used to allocate both partnership profit and loss. If the partnership agreement states profit and loss percentages separately, the partnership's taxable income for the year is first totaled to determine whether a net profit or net loss has occurred. Then the appropriate percentage (either profit or loss) applies to each class of income for the year.[29]

EXAMPLE C:9-20 ▶ The ABC Partnership reports the following income and loss items for the current year:

Net long-term capital loss	$100,000
Net Sec. 1231 gain	90,000
Ordinary income	220,000

Carmelia has a 20% profits interest and a 30% loss interest in the ABC Partnership. Because the partnership earns a $210,000 ($90,000 + $220,000 − $100,000) net profit, Carmelia's distributive share is calculated using her 20% profits interest and is reported as follows:

Net long-term capital loss	$ 20,000
Net Sec. 1231 gain	18,000
Ordinary income	44,000

Her loss percentage is used only in years in which the partnership has a net loss. ◀

VARYING INTEREST RULE. If a partner's ownership interest changes during the partnership tax year, the income or loss allocation takes into account the partner's varying interest.[30] This varying interest rule applies for changes occurring to a partner's interest as a result of buying an additional interest in the partnership, selling part (but not all) of a partnership interest, giving or being given a partnership interest, or admitting a new partner. The partner's ownership interest generally applies to the income earned on a pro rata basis.

EXAMPLE C:9-21 ▶ Maria owns 20% of the XYZ Partnership from January 1 through June 30 of the current year (not a leap year). On July 1 she buys an additional 10% interest in the partnership. During this year, XYZ Partnership has ordinary income of $120,000, which it earned evenly throughout the year. Maria's $30,049 ($11,901 + $18,148) distributive share of income is calculated as follows:

Pre-July 1: $$\$120{,}000 \times \frac{181 \text{ days}}{365 \text{ days}} \times 0.20 = \$11{,}901$$

Post-June 30: $$\$120{,}000 \times \frac{184 \text{ days}}{365 \text{ days}} \times 0.30 = \$18{,}148$$

Similar calculations would be made if the XYZ Partnership reported separately stated items such as capital gains and losses. ◀

OBJECTIVE 6

Explain the requirements for a special partnership allocation

SPECIAL ALLOCATIONS

Special allocations are unique to partnerships and allow tremendous flexibility in sharing specific items of income and loss among the partners. Special allocations can provide a specified partner with more or less of an item of income, gain, loss, or deduction than

[29] This rule is derived from the House and Senate reports on the original Sec. 704(b) provisions. The two reports are identical and read, "The income ratio shall be applicable if the partnership has taxable income . . . and the loss ratio shall be applicable [if] the partnership has a loss." H. Rept. No. 1337, 83d Cong., 2d Sess., p. A223 (1954); S. Rept. No. 1622, 83d Cong., 2d Sess., p. 379 (1954).

[30] Sec. 706(d)(1).

would be available using the partner's regular distributive share. Special allocations fall into two categories. First, Sec. 704 requires certain special allocations with respect to contributed property. Second, other special allocations are allowed as long as they meet the tests set forth in Treasury Regulations for having substantial economic effect. If the special allocation fails the substantial economic effect test, it is disregarded, and the income, gain, loss, or deduction is allocated according to the partner's interest in the partnership as expressed in the actual operations and activities.

BOOK-TO-TAX ACCOUNTING COMPARISON

For tax purposes, the partnership takes a carryover basis in contributed property. For book purposes, however, the partnership records the contributed property at its FMV.

ALLOCATIONS RELATED TO CONTRIBUTED PROPERTY. As previously discussed, when a partner contributes property to a partnership, the property takes a carryover basis that references the contributing partner's basis. With no special allocations, this carryover basis rule would require the partnership (and each partner) to accept the tax burden of any gain or loss that accrued to the property before its contribution.

EXAMPLE C:9-22 ▶ In the current year, Elizabeth contributes land having a $4,000 basis and a $10,000 FMV to the DEF Partnership. Assuming the property continues to increase in value, or at least does not decline in value, DEF's gain on the ultimate sale of this property is $6,000 greater than the gain that accrues while the partnership owns the property. Without a special allocation, this $6,000 precontribution gain would be allocated among all partners. ◀

Section 704(c), however, requires precontribution gains or losses to be allocated to the contributing partner. Thus, the precontribution gain of $6,000 in Example C:9-22 would be allocated to Elizabeth. In addition, income and deductions reported with respect to contributed property must be allocated to take into account the difference between the property's basis and FMV at the time of contribution.

EXAMPLE C:9-23 ▶ Kay and Sam form an equal partnership when Sam contributes cash of $10,000 and Kay contributes land having a $6,000 basis and a $10,000 FMV. If the partnership sells the land two years later for $12,000, the $4,000 precontribution gain ($10,000 FMV − $6,000 basis) is allocated only to Kay. The $2,000 gain that accrued while the partnership held the land ($12,000 sales price − $10,000 FMV at contribution) is allocated to Kay and Sam equally. Kay reports a total gain of $5,000 ($4,000 + $1,000), and Sam reports a $1,000 gain on the sale of the land. ◀

The allocation of depreciation is another common example of the special deduction allocation related to contributed property that is necessary under these rules. Tax Research Problem C:9-60 addresses the depreciation allocation issue.

SUBSTANTIAL ECONOMIC EFFECT. Special allocations not related to contributed property must meet several specific criteria established by Treasury Regulations. These criteria ensure that the allocations affect the partner's economic consequences and not just their tax consequences.

BOOK-TO-TAX ACCOUNTING COMPARISON

The capital accounts for meeting the substantial economic effect requirements are maintained using book value accounting rather than tax accounting.

To distinguish transactions affecting only taxes from those affecting the partner's economic position, Treasury Regulations look at whether the allocation has an economic effect and whether the economic effect is substantial. Under the Sec. 704 regulations, the allocation has economic effect if it meets all three of the following conditions:

- The allocation results in the appropriate increase or decrease in the partner's capital account.
- The proceeds of any liquidation occurring at any time in the partnership's life cycle are distributed in accordance with positive capital account balances.
- Partners must make up negative balances in their capital accounts upon the liquidation of the partnership, and these contributions are used to pay partnership debts or are allocated to partners having positive capital account balances.[31]

EXAMPLE C:9-24 ▶ Arnie and Bonnie each contribute $100,000 to form the AB Partnership on January 1, 2006. The partnership uses these contributions plus a $1.8 million mortgage to purchase a $2 million

[31] Reg. Sec. 1.704-1(b)(2)(ii). Treasury Regulations provide other alternatives for meeting this portion of the requirements.

office building. To simplify the calculations, assume the partnership depreciates the building using the straight-line method over a 40-year life and that in each year income and expenses are equal before considering depreciation. AB makes a special allocation of depreciation to Arnie. The allocation reduces Arnie's capital account, and the partnership makes any liquidating distributions in accordance with the capital account balances. Allocations through 2008 are as follows:

	Capital Account Balance	
	Arnie	*Bonnie*
January 1, 2007, balance	$100,000	$100,000
2007 loss	(50,000)	–0–
2008 loss	(50,000)	–0–
2009 loss	(50,000)	–0–
December 31, 2009, balance	($ 50,000)	$100,000

If we assume that the property has declined in value in an amount equal to the depreciation claimed and that the partnership now liquidates, the need for the requirement to restore negative capital account balances becomes apparent.

Sales price of property on December 31, 2009	$1,850,000
Minus: Mortgage principal	(1,800,000)
Partnership cash to be distributed to partners	$ 50,000

If Arnie does not have to restore his negative capital account balance, Bonnie can receive only $50,000 in cash even though her capital account balance is $100,000. In effect, Bonnie has borne the economic burden of the 2009 depreciation. Without a requirement to restore the negative capital account balance, the special allocation to Arnie would be ignored for 2009, and Bonnie would receive the depreciation deduction. However, if Arnie must restore any negative capital account balance, he will contribute $50,000 when the partnership liquidates at the end of 2009, and Bonnie will receive her full $100,000 capital account balance. The 2009 special allocation to Arnie will then have economic effect. Note that Arnie's allocation for 2007 and 2008 is acceptable even without an agreement to restore negative capital account balances. This result occurs in each of these two years because Arnie has sufficient capital to absorb the economic loss if the property declines in value in an amount equal to the depreciation allocated to him.[32] ◀

ADDITIONAL COMMENT

The substantial economic effect rules ensure that cash flows ultimately conform to allocations and that allocations do not allow for abusive shifting of tax benefits among partners.

The second requirement for a special allocation to be accepted under Treasury Regulations is that the economic effect must be substantial, which requires that a reasonable possibility exists that the allocation will substantially affect the dollar amounts to be received by the partners independent of tax consequences.[33] Moreover, allocations that involve shifting will not pass the substantiality test. Shifting occurs when the following two conditions are present:

- ▶ The net change in the partner's capital accounts will be the same for a normal allocation and the special allocation.
- ▶ The total tax liability of the partners will be less with the special allocation than with a normal allocation.[34]

EXAMPLE C:9-25 ▶ The AB Partnership earns $10,000 in tax-exempt interest income and $10,000 in taxable interest income each year. Andy and Becky each have 50% capital and profit interests in the partnership. An allocation of the tax-exempt interest income to Andy, a 35% tax bracket partner, and the taxable interest income to Becky, a 15% tax bracket partner, does not have substantial economic effect. In particular, the allocation lacks substantiality because of shifting. The allocation increases each partner's capital account by $10,000 as would an equal allocation, and it reduces the partner's overall tax liability (see Problem C:9-36 at the end of this chapter). ◀

---

[32] Such allocations do not literally meet the three requirements outlined above for special allocations. However, allocations that meet the alternate standard—having sufficient capital to absorb the economic loss—are considered to have economic effect and will be allowed. See Reg. Sec. 1.704-1(b)(2)(ii)(d).

[33] Reg. Sec. 1.704-1(b)(2)(iii)(a). It should be noted that the substantial economic effect regulations go far beyond the rules covered in this text.

[34] Reg. Sec. 1.704-1(b)(2)(iii)(b). An allocation also can fail the substantiality test by being transitory, which is something like shifting except an allocation in one year is offset by another allocation in a future year (Reg. Sec. 1.704-1(b)(2)(iii)(c)).

STOP & THINK *Question:* The special allocation rules require that a partner who receives a special allocation of loss or expense receive less cash or property when the partnership liquidates. As we will see later in this chapter, losses reduce the partner's basis in the partnership interest, so a sale or liquidation of the partnership interest will cause the partner to recognize a larger gain (or a smaller loss) than would have resulted without this loss allocation. Because the basis is reduced, the partner also is more likely to recognize taxable gain on a distribution from the partnership. With these negative consequences, why would anyone want to be given a special allocation of partnership loss or expense?

Solution: The answer is a matter of timing. The specially allocated loss reduces taxable income now and saves more taxes now for the partner than would a "normal" loss allocation. The negative consequences occur when the partner incurs a larger gain (or smaller loss) upon a future sale or liquidation of his or her partnership interest. The special allocation scenario may have a greater after-tax present value to the partner than would the after-tax present value of receiving a normal share of losses and an increased liquidating distribution.

BASIS FOR PARTNERSHIP INTEREST

OBJECTIVE 7

Calculate a partner's basis in a partnership interest

The calculation of a partner's beginning basis in a partnership interest depends on the method used to acquire the interest, with different valuation techniques for a purchased interest, a gifted interest, and an inherited interest. The results of the partnership's operations and liabilities both cause adjustments to the beginning amount. Additional contributions to the partnership and distributions from the partnership further alter the partner's basis.

ADDITIONAL COMMENT

A partner's basis in a partnership interest commonly is referred to as "outside basis" as opposed to "inside basis," which is the partnership's basis in its assets.

BEGINNING BASIS

A partner's beginning basis for a partnership interest received for a contribution of property or services has been discussed. However, a partner also can acquire a partnership interest by methods other than contributing property or services to the partnership. If a person purchases the partnership interest from an existing partner, the new partner's basis is the price paid for the partnership interest, including assumption of partnership liabilities. If a person inherits the partnership interest, the heir's basis is the FMV of the partnership interest on the decedent's date of death or, if elected by the executor, the alternate valuation date but not less than liabilities assumed. If a person receives the partnership interest as a gift, the donee's basis generally equals the donor's basis (including the donor's ratable share of partnership liabilities) plus the portion of any gift tax paid by the donor that relates to appreciation attaching to the gift property. In summary, the usual rules for the method of acquisition dictate the beginning basis for a partnership interest.

SELF-STUDY QUESTION

What are some of the common methods of acquiring a partnership interest, and what is the beginning basis?

ANSWER

1. Contribution—substituted basis from contributed property
2. Purchase—cost basis
3. Inheritance—FMV
4. Gift—usually donor's basis with a possible gift tax adjustment

EFFECTS OF LIABILITIES

The early part of this chapter briefly discussed the effect of partnership liabilities on the basis of a partnership interest in connection with the contribution of property subject to a liability. However, further explanation is necessary to fully convey the pervasive impact of liabilities on partnership taxation.

INCREASES AND DECREASES IN LIABILITIES. Two changes in a partner's liabilities are considered contributions of cash by the partner to the partnership.[35] The first is an increase in the partner's share of partnership liabilities. This increase can arise from either an increase in the partner's profit or loss interests or from an increase in total partnership liabilities. Accordingly, if a partnership incurs a large debt, the partners' bases in their partnership interests increase. The second way to increase a partner's basis is to have the partner assume partnership liabilities in his or her individual capacity.

[35] Sec. 752.

Conversely, two liability changes are treated as distributions of cash from the partnership to the partner. These changes are a decrease in a partner's share of partnership liabilities and a decrease in the partner's individual liabilities resulting from the partnership's assumption of the partner's liability. Often, both an increase and a decrease in a partner's basis for his or her interest can result from a single transaction. The framework below illustrates the steps used to calculate the partner's basis in his or her partnership interest.

	Partner's basis before changes in liabilities
Plus:	Increases in share of partnership liabilities
Minus:	Decreases in share of partnership liabilities
Plus:	Partnership liabilities assumed by this partner
Minus:	This partner's liabilities assumed by the partnership
	Partner's basis in the partnership interest

EXAMPLE C:9-26 ▶ Juan, a 40% partner in the ABC Partnership, has a $30,000 basis in his partnership interest before receiving a partnership distribution of land. As part of the transaction, Juan agrees to assume a $10,000 mortgage on the land. First, Juan's basis in his partnership interest will decrease by $4,000 for the decline in Juan's share of partnership liabilities resulting from the partnership no longer owing the $10,000 mortgage. Second, his basis in the partnership interest will increase by $10,000, which is the partnership liability he assumes in his individual capacity. The net change in basis in his partnership resulting from the liabilities is $6,000 (−$4,000 + $10,000). His basis in his partnership interest also must be decreased for the land distribution he receives. Distributions will be discussed further in Chapter C:10. ◀

A PARTNER'S SHARE OF LIABILITIES. Having explained the general impact of liabilities on a partner's basis for his or her partnership interest, we now turn to how the specific amount of the partner's share of a partnership's liabilities is determined. All examples so far have considered only general partners who have the same interest in profits and losses. Partnerships, however, commonly have one or more limited partners, and thus partners can have differing profit and loss ratios. Moreover, the type of liability affects how it is allocated. Treasury Regulations provide guidelines for allocating partnership liabilities to the individual partners.

ADDITIONAL COMMENT

That a partner gets basis for his or her share of recourse debt is not controversial. That a partner gets basis for debt on which the partner is not personally liable seems questionable, yet other rules limit the benefit of the basis created by the nonrecourse debt.

TYPICAL MISCONCEPTION

Nonrecourse debt is allocated among all partners primarily according to their profit ratios. Recourse debt, on the other hand, is allocated to the limited partners to the extent they bear an economic risk of loss, but generally a limited partner's economic risk of loss is not greater than any additional amounts that partner has pledged to contribute. The remaining recourse debt is allocated among the general partners according to their economic risk of loss.

Recourse and Nonrecourse Loans. A **recourse loan** is the usual kind of loan for which the borrower remains liable until the loan is paid. If the recourse loan is secured and the borrower fails to make payments as scheduled, the lender can sell the property used as security. If the sales proceeds are insufficient to repay a recourse loan, the borrower must make up the difference. Under Treasury Regulations, a recourse loan is one for which any partner or a related party will stand an economic loss if the partnership cannot pay the debt.[36] In contrast, a **nonrecourse loan** is one in which the lender may sell property used as security if the loan is not paid, but no partner is liable for any deficiency. In short, the lender has no recourse against the borrower for additional amounts. Nonrecourse debts most commonly occur in connection with the financing of real property that is expected to substantially increase in value over the life of the loan.

General and Limited Partners. A limited partner normally is not liable to pay partnership debts beyond the original contribution (which already is reflected in his or her basis in the partnership interest) and any additional amount the partner has pledged to contribute.[37] Therefore, recourse debt increases a limited partner's basis only to the extent the partner has a risk of economic loss. Nonrecourse debts increase a limited partner's basis based primarily on the profit ratio.[38]

---

[36] Reg. Sec. 1.752-1(a).

[37] This rule may be modified by the limited partner agreeing to assume some of the risk of economic loss despite his or her limited partner status. For example, a limited partner may guarantee the debt or may agree to reimburse the general partner some amount if the general partner has to pay the debt. These arrangements mean that the limited partner shares the risk of loss.

[38] Some nonrecourse debt allocations involve two steps before an allocation according to profits interests. These two steps of the allocation process are beyond the scope of this explanation.

A general partner's share of nonrecourse liabilities also is determined primarily by his or her profit ratio. On the other hand, because limited partners seldom receive an allocated share of the recourse liabilities, the general partners share all recourse liabilities beyond any amounts the limited partners can claim according to their economic loss potential.

The Sec. 752 Treasury Regulations require that recourse liabilities be allocated to the partner who will bear the economic loss if the partnership cannot pay the debt. The regulations provide a complex procedure using a hypothetical liquidation to determine who would bear the loss. In this text, we assume that the hypothetical liquidation analysis has been completed and that the appropriate shares of economic loss as determined by the hypothetical liquidation procedure are stated as part of the problem or example information.

EXAMPLE C:9-27 ▶ The ABC Partnership has one general partner (Anna) and a limited partner (Clay) with the following partnership interests:

	Anna (General)	*Clay (Limited)*
Loss interest	75%	25%
Profits interest	60%	40%
Basis before liabilities	$100,000	$100,000

Clay has an obligation to make an additional $5,000 contribution. He has made no other agreements or guarantees. The partnership has two liabilities at year-end: a $300,000 nonrecourse liability and a $400,000 liability with recourse to the partnership. Clay has a risk of economic loss only to the extent that he has agreed to make additional contributions. The partners' year-end bases are calculated as follows:

	Anna (General)	*Clay (Limited)*
Year-end basis (excluding liabilities)	$100,000	$100,000
Share of:		
Recourse liability	395,000	5,000
Nonrecourse liability	180,000[a]	120,000[b]
Year-end basis	$675,000	$225,000

[a] 60% × $300,000 = $180,000
[b] 40% × $300,000 = $120,000 ◀

If the partnership has more than one general partner, the economic risk of loss computation entails computing a hypothetical loss and allocating that loss to the general partners. The hypothetical loss computation assumes the partnership sells all its assets (including cash) for the amount of nonrecourse liabilities. If the partnership does not have nonrecourse liabilities, the assets are deemed sold for zero dollars. The hypothetical loss then is subtracted from the partners' capital accounts to determine the economic risk of loss.

EXAMPLE C:9-28 ▶ Assume the same facts as in Example C:9-27 except that Clay is a general partner. In addition, the partnership has $900,000 of assets, and each partner's capital account is $100,000. If the partnership sold its assets for the amount of the nonrecourse liability, it would realize a $600,000 loss ($300,000 − $900,000). The economic risk of loss is calculated as follows:

	Anna (General)	*Clay (General)*
Capital accounts	$100,000	$100,000
Minus: Hypothetical loss (allocated according to loss percentages)	(450,000)	(150,000)
Economic risk of loss	($350,000)	($ 50,000)

The partners' year-end bases are calculated as follows:

	Anna (General)	*Clay (General)*
Year-end basis (excluding liabilities)	$100,000	$100,000
Share of:		
Recourse liability	350,000	50,000
Nonrecourse liability	180,000	120,000
Year-end basis	$630,000	$270,000 ◀

Determination of the partners' share of recourse liabilities can be simplified if the partners have the same interest in losses as they do for profits and if their capital accounts are in accordance with those percentages. In this situation, the recourse liability allocation also will be in accordance with the profit/loss percentages.

EFFECTS OF OPERATIONS

A partner's basis is a summary of his or her contributions and the partnership's liabilities, earnings, losses, and distributions. Basis prevents a second tax levy on a distribution of income that was taxed previously as a partner's distributive share. Section 705 mandates a basis increase for additional contributions made by the partner to the partnership plus the partner's distributive share for the current and prior tax years of the following items:

- Partnership taxable income (both separately stated items and partnership ordinary income)
- Tax-exempt income of the partnership

BOOK-TO-TAX ACCOUNTING COMPARISON

Although a partner's basis in the partnership cannot go below zero, a partner's book capital account (equity) may be negative.

Basis is decreased (but not below zero) by distributions from the partnership to the partner plus the partner's distributive share for the current and prior tax years of the following items:

- Partnership losses (both separately stated items and partnership ordinary loss)
- Expenditures that are not deductible for tax purposes and that are not capital expenditures

The positive basis adjustment for tax-exempt income and the negative basis adjustment for nondeductible expenses preserve that tax treatment for the partner. If these adjustments were not made, tax-exempt income would be taxable to the partner upon a subsequent distribution or upon the sale or other disposition of the partnership interest.

EXAMPLE C:9-29 ▶ LMN Partnership has only one asset—a $100,000 municipal bond. Marta has a $20,000 basis in her 20% partnership interest. In the current year, the partnership collects $4,000 tax-exempt interest from the bond. Marta's basis at year-end is calculated as follows:

Beginning basis	$20,000
Share of tax-exempt income	800
Basis at year end	$20,800

On the first day of the next year, the partnership sells the bond for $100,000 cash. At this point, the partnership has $104,000 in cash and no other assets. The partnership liquidates and distributes her 20% share of the cash ($20,800) to Marta. Marta has no gain or loss because her $20,800 basis exactly equals her distribution. If the tax-exempt income had not increased her basis, she would have recognized an $800 gain on the distribution ($20,800 cash distribution − $20,000 basis if no increase were made for the tax-exempt income). Thus, her basis must be increased by tax-exempt income to prevent a taxable gain upon its distribution. ◀

OBJECTIVE 8

Determine the limitations on a partner's deduction of partnership losses

LOSS LIMITATIONS. Each partner is allocated his or her distributive share of ordinary income or loss and separately stated income, gain, loss, or deduction items each year. The partner always reports income and gain items in his or her current tax year, and these items increase the partner's basis in the partnership interest. However, the partner may not be able to use his or her full distributive share of losses because Sec. 704(d) limits a partner's loss deduction to the amount of his or her basis in the partnership interest before the loss. All positive basis adjustments for the year and all reductions for actual or deemed distributions must be made before determining the amount of the deductible loss.[39]

EXAMPLE C:9-30 ▶ On January 1 of the current year, Miguel has a $32,000 basis for his general interest in the MT Partnership. He materially participates in the partnership's business activities. On December 1, Miguel receives a $1,000 cash distribution. His distributive share of MT's current items are a $4,000 net long-term capital gain and a $43,000 ordinary loss. Miguel's deductible loss is calculated as follows:

[39] Reg. Sec. 1.704-1(d)(2).

January 1 basis	$32,000
Plus: Long-term capital gain	4,000
Minus: Distribution	(1,000)
Limit for loss deduction	$35,000

SELF-STUDY QUESTION

What happens to losses that are disallowed due to lack of basis in a partnership interest?

ANSWER

The losses are suspended until that partner obtains additional basis.

Miguel can deduct $35,000 of the ordinary loss in the current year, which reduces his basis to zero. He cannot deduct the remaining $8,000 of ordinary loss currently but can deduct it in the following year if he regains sufficient basis in his partnership interest. ◀

Any distributive share of loss that a partner cannot deduct because of the basis limit is simply noted in the partner's financial records. It is not reported on the partner's tax return, nor does it reduce the partner's basis. However, the losses carry forward until the partner again has positive basis from capital contributions, additional partnership borrowings, or partnership earnings.[40]

EXAMPLE C:9-31 ▶ Assume the same facts as in Example C:9-30. Miguel makes no additional contributions in the following year, and the MT Partnership's liabilities remain unchanged. Miguel's distributive share of MT's partnership items in the following year is $2,500 of net short-term capital gain and $14,000 of ordinary income. These items restore his basis to $16,500 ($0 + $2,500 + $14,000), and he can deduct the $8,000 loss carryover. After taking these transactions into account, Miguel's basis is $8,500 ($16,500 − $8,000). ◀

Topic Review C:9-3 summarizes the rules for determining the initial basis for a partnership interest and the annual basis adjustments required to determine the adjusted basis of a partnership interest.

Topic Review C:9-3

Basis of a Partnership Interest

METHOD OF ACQUISITION	BEGINNING BASIS IS
Property contributed	Substituted basis from property contributed plus gain recognized for contributions to an investment partnership
Services contributed	Amount of income recognized for services rendered (plus any additional amount contributed)
Purchase	Cost
Gift	Donor's basis plus gift tax on appreciation
Inheritance	Fair market value at date of death or alternative valuation date
LIABILITY IMPACT ON BASIS	
Increase basis for	Increases in the partner's share of partnership liabilities Liabilities of the partnership assumed by the partner in his or her individual capacity
Decrease basis for	Decreases in the partner's share of partnership liabilities Liabilities of the partner assumed by the partnership
OPERATIONS IMPACT ON BASIS	
Increase basis for	Partner's share of ordinary income and separately stated income and gain items (including tax-exempt items) Additional contributions to the partnership Precontribution gain recognized
Decrease basis for	Distributions from the partnership to the partner Partner's share of ordinary loss and separately stated loss and deduction items (including items that are not deductible for tax purposes and are not capital expenditures) Precontribution loss recognized

[40] Reg. Sec. 1.704-1(d)(1).

SPECIAL LOSS LIMITATIONS

Three sets of rules limit the loss from a partnership interest that a partner may deduct. The Sec. 704(d) rules explained above limit losses to the partner's basis in the partnership interest. Two other rules establish more stringent limits. The at-risk rules limit losses to an amount called *at-risk basis.* The passive activity loss or credit limitation rules disallow most net passive activity losses.

AT-RISK LOSS LIMITATION

The Sec. 704(d) loss limitation rules were the only loss limits for many years. However, Congress became increasingly uncomfortable with allowing partners to increase their basis by a portion of the partnership's nonrecourse liabilities and then offset this basis with partnership losses. Accordingly, Congress established the **at-risk rules**, which limit loss deductions to the partner's at-risk basis. The **at-risk basis** is essentially the same amount as the regular partnership basis with the exception that liabilities increase the at-risk basis only if the partner is at risk for such an amount. The at-risk rules apply to individuals and closely held C corporations. Partners that are widely held C corporations are not subject to these rules.

Although much of the complexity of the *at-risk* term is beyond the scope of this text, a simplified working definition is possible. A partner is at risk for an amount if he or she would lose that amount should the partnership suddenly become worthless. Because a partner would not have to pay a partnership's nonrecourse liabilities even if the partnership became worthless, the usual nonrecourse liabilities cannot be included in any partner's at-risk basis. Under the at-risk rules, a partner's loss deduction may be substantially less than the amount deductible under the Sec. 704(d) rules.[41]

EXAMPLE C:9-32 ▶ Keesha is a limited partner in the KM Manufacturing Partnership. At the end of the partnership's tax year, her basis in the partnership interest is $30,000 ($10,000 investment plus a $20,000 share of nonrecourse financing). Keesha's distributive share of partnership losses for the tax year is $18,000. Although she has sufficient basis in the partnership interest, the at-risk rules limit her deduction to $10,000 because she is not at risk for the nonrecourse financing. ◀

TYPICAL MISCONCEPTION

The at-risk rules severely limit the use of nonrecourse debt to obtain loss deductions except for certain qualified real estate financing, yet this real estate exception is more apparent than real because of the final set of rules that must be satisfied: the passive activity limitations.

The IRC allows one significant exception to the application of the at-risk rules. At-risk rules do not apply to nonrecourse debt if it is qualified real estate financing. The partner is considered at risk for his or her share of nonrecourse real estate financing if all of the following requirements are met:

- ▶ The financing is secured by real estate used in the partnership's real estate activity.
- ▶ The debt is not convertible to any kind of equity interest in the partnership.
- ▶ The financing is from a qualified person or from any federal, state, or local government, or is guaranteed by any federal, state, or local government.[42] A qualified person is an unrelated party who is in the trade or business of lending money (e.g., bank, financial institution, or mortgage broker).

PASSIVE ACTIVITY LIMITATIONS

Subsequent to enacting the at-risk rules, Congress added still a third set of limitations to losses a partner may deduct: the passive activity loss and credit limitations of Sec. 469. Under these rules, income falls into one of three categories: (1) amounts derived from passive activities; (2) active income such as salary, bonuses, and income from businesses in which the taxpayer materially participates; and (3) portfolio income such as dividends, interest, and capital gains from investments other than passive activities. Generally, losses of an individual partner from a passive activity cannot be used to offset either active income or portfolio income. However, passive losses carry over to future years where they can offset passive income in those years. Moreover, passive losses are allowed in full when a taxpayer disposes of the entire interest in the passive activity. Passive losses generated by

[41] Sec. 465(a).

[42] Sec. 465(b)(6).

a passive rental activity in which an individual partner is an active participant can be deducted up to a maximum of $25,000 per year. This deduction phases out by 50% of the amount of the partner's adjusted gross income (AGI) that exceeds $100,000, so that no deduction is allowed if the partner has AGI of $150,000 or more. (The phase-out begins at $200,000 for low-income housing or rehabilitation credits.) Losses disallowed under the phase-out are deductible to the extent of passive income.

TAX STRATEGY TIP

If a partner is unable to use all of his or her share of partnership losses due to a lack of basis, contributions to capital or increasing partnership liabilities may provide the additional needed tax basis. If the passive activity limitation rules are the reason the partnership losses cannot be used, the possibility of investing in passive activities that generate passive income may be the best planning alternative. See Tax Planning Considerations for further discussion.

A passive activity is any trade or business in which the taxpayer does not materially participate. A taxpayer who owns a limited partnership interest in any activity generally fails the material participation test. Accordingly, losses from most limited partnership interests can be used only to offset income from passive activities even if the limited partner has sufficient Sec. 704(d) and at-risk basis.[43]

Although passive activity limitations may greatly affect the taxable income or loss reported by a partner, they have no unusual effect on basis. Basis is reduced (but not below zero) by the partner's distributive share of losses whether or not the losses are limited under the passive loss rules.[44] When the suspended passive losses later become deductible, the partner's basis in the partnership interest is not affected.

EXAMPLE C:9-33 ▶ Chris purchases a 20% capital and profits interest in the CJ Partnership in the current year, but he does not participate in CJ's business. Chris owns no other passive investments. His Sec. 704(d) basis in CJ is $80,000, and his at-risk basis is $70,000. Chris's distributive share of the CJ Partnership's loss for the current year is $60,000. Chris's Sec. 704(d) basis is $20,000 ($80,000 −$60,000), and his at-risk basis is $10,000 ($70,000 − $60,000) after the results of this year's operations are taken into account. However, Chris cannot deduct any of the CJ loss in the current year because it is a passive activity loss. The $60,000 loss, however, can be used in a subsequent year if the partner generates passive income. Because the $60,000 loss already has reduced basis for purposes of both Sec. 704(d) and the at-risk rules, the disallowed loss need not be tested against those rules a second time. ◀

TRANSACTIONS BETWEEN A PARTNER AND THE PARTNERSHIP

The partner and the partnership are treated as separate entities for many transactions. Section 707(b) restricts sales of property between the partner and partnership by disallowing certain losses and converting certain capital gains into ordinary income. Section 707(c) permits a partnership to make guaranteed payments for capital and services to a partner that are separate from the partner's distributive share. Each of these rules is explored below.

SALES OF PROPERTY

LOSS SALES. Without restrictions, a controlling partner could sell property to the partnership to recognize a loss for tax purposes while retaining a substantial interest in the property through ownership of a partnership interest. Congress closed the door to such loss recognition with the Sec. 707(b) rules.

KEY POINT

The IRC disallows losses on sales between persons and certain related partnerships, similar to the related party rules of Sec. 267. The concern is that tax losses can be artificially recognized without the property being disposed of outside the economic group.

The rules for partnership loss transactions are quite similar to the Sec. 267 related party rules discussed in Chapter C:3. Under Sec. 707(b)(1), no loss can be deducted on the sale or exchange of property between a partnership and a person who directly or indirectly owns more than 50% of the partnership's capital or profits interests. (Indirect ownership includes ownership by related parties such as members of the partner's family.[45]) Similarly, losses are disallowed on sales or exchanges of property between two partnerships in which the same persons own, directly or indirectly, more than 50% of the capital

[43] Sec. 469(h)(2).

[44] S. Rept. No. 99-313, 99th Cong., 2d Sess., p. 723, footnote 4 (1986).

[45] For purposes of Sec. 707, related parties include an individual and members of his or her family (spouse, brothers, sisters, lineal descendants, and ancestors), an individual and a more-than-50%-owned corporation, and two corporations that are members of the same controlled group.

or profits interests. If the seller is disallowed a loss under Sec. 707(b)(1), the purchaser can reduce any subsequent gain realized on a sale of the property by the previously disallowed loss.

EXAMPLE C:9-34 ▶ James, Karen, and Thelma own equal interests in the JKT Partnership. Karen and Thelma are siblings, but James is unrelated to the others. For purposes of Sec. 707, Karen owns 66.66% of the partnership (33.33% directly and 33.33% indirectly from Thelma). Likewise, Thelma also owns 66.66%, but James has only a direct ownership interest of 33.33%. ◀

EXAMPLE C:9-35 ▶ Pat sold land having a $45,000 basis to the PTA Partnership for $35,000, its FMV. If Pat has a 60% capital and profits interest in the partnership, Pat realizes but cannot recognize a $10,000 loss on the sale. If Pat owns only a 49% interest, directly and indirectly, he can recognize the loss. ◀

EXAMPLE C:9-36 ▶ Assume the same facts as in Example C:9-35 except the partnership later sells the land for $47,000. The partnership's realized gain is $12,000 ($47,000 − $35,000 basis). If Pat has a 60% capital and profits interest, his previously disallowed loss of $10,000 reduces the partnership's recognized gain to $2,000. This $2,000 gain is then allocated to the partners according to the partnership agreement. ◀

GAIN SALES. When gain is recognized on the sale of a capital asset between a partnership and a related partner, Sec. 707(b)(2) requires that the gain be ordinary (and not capital gain) if the property will not be a capital asset to its new owner. Sales or exchanges resulting in the application of Sec. 707(b)(2) include transfers between (1) a partnership and a person who owns, directly or indirectly, more than 50% of the partnership's capital or profits interests, or (2) two partnerships in which the same persons own, directly or indirectly, more than 50% of the capital or profits interests.[46] This provision prevents related parties from increasing the depreciable basis of assets (and thereby reducing future ordinary income) at the cost of recognizing only a current capital gain.

EXAMPLE C:9-37 ▶ Sharon and Tony have the following capital and profits interests in two partnerships:

Partner	*ST Partnership (%)*	*QRS Partnership (%)*
Sharon	42	58
Tony	42	30
Other unrelated partners	16	12
Total	100	100

The ST Partnership sells land having a $150,000 basis to the QRS Partnership for $180,000. The land was a capital asset for the ST Partnership, but QRS intends to subdivide and sell the land. Because the land is ordinary income property to the QRS Partnership and because Sharon and Tony control both partnerships, the ST Partnership must recognize $30,000 of ordinary income on the land sale. ◀

GUARANTEED PAYMENTS

A corporate shareholder can be an employee of the corporation. However, a partner generally is not an employee of the partnership, and most fringe benefits are disallowed for a partner who is "employed" by his or her partnership.[47]

OBJECTIVE 9

Determine the tax consequences of a guaranteed payment

A partner who provides services to the partnership in an ongoing relationship might be compensated like any other employee. Section 707(c) provides for this kind of payment and labels it a **guaranteed payment.** The term *guaranteed payment* also includes certain payments made to a partner for the use of invested capital. These payments are similar to interest. Both types of guaranteed payments must be determined without regard to the partnership's income.[48] Conceptually, this requirement separates guaranteed payments from distributive shares. As indicated below, however, such a distinction may not be so clear in practice.

46 Sec. 707(b)(2).

47 Rev. Rul. 91-26, 1991-1 C.B. 184, holds that accident and health insurance premiums paid for a partner by the partnership are guaranteed payments.

48 Sec. 707(c).

TYPICAL MISCONCEPTION

If a partner, acting in his or her capacity as a partner, receives payments from the partnership determined without regard to the partnership's income, the partner has received a guaranteed payment. If the partner is acting as a nonpartner, the partner is treated as any other outside contractor.

DETERMINING THE GUARANTEED PAYMENT. Sometimes the determination of the guaranteed payment is quite simple. For example, some guaranteed payments are expressed as specific amounts (e.g., $20,000 per year), with the partner also receiving his or her normal distributive share. Other times, the guaranteed payment is expressed as a **guaranteed minimum.** However, these guaranteed minimum arrangements make it difficult to distinguish the partner's distributive share and guaranteed payments because no guaranteed payment occurs under this arrangement unless the partner's distributive share is less than his or her guaranteed minimum. If the distributive share is less than the guaranteed minimum, the guaranteed payment is the difference between the distributive share and the guaranteed minimum.

EXAMPLE C:9-38 ▶ Tina manages the real estate owned by the TAV Partnership, in which she also is a partner. She receives 30% of all partnership income before guaranteed payments, but no less than $60,000 per year. In the current year, the TAV Partnership reports $300,000 in ordinary income. Tina's 30% distributive share is $90,000 (0.30 × $300,000), which exceeds her $60,000 guaranteed minimum. Therefore, she has no guaranteed payment. ◀

EXAMPLE C:9-39 ▶ Assume the same facts as in Example C:9-38 except the TAV Partnership reports $150,000 of ordinary income. Tina has a guaranteed payment of $15,000, which represents the difference between her $45,000 distributive share (0.30 × $150,000) and her $60,000 guaranteed minimum.[49] ◀

TAX IMPACT OF GUARANTEED PAYMENTS. Like salary or interest income, guaranteed payments are ordinary income to the recipient. The guaranteed payment must be included in income for the recipient partner's tax year during which the partnership year ends and the partnership deducts or capitalizes the payments.[50]

EXAMPLE C:9-40 ▶ In January 2008, a calendar year taxpayer, Will, receives a $10,000 guaranteed payment from the WRS Partnership, which uses the accrual method of accounting. WRS accrues and deducts the payment during its tax year ending November 30, 2007. Will must report his guaranteed payment in his 2007 tax return because that return includes the 2007 partnership income that reflects the impact of the guaranteed payment. ◀

The partnership treats the guaranteed payment as if it is made to an outsider. If the payment is for a service that is a capital expenditure (e.g., architectural services for designing a building for the partnership), the guaranteed payment must be capitalized and, if allowable, amortized. If the payment is for services deductible under Sec. 162, the partnership deducts the payment from ordinary income. Thus, deductible guaranteed payments offset the partnership's ordinary income but never its capital gains. If the guaranteed payment exceeds the partnership's ordinary income, the payment creates an ordinary loss that is allocated among the partners.[51]

EXAMPLE C:9-41 ▶ Theresa is a partner in the STU Partnership. She is to receive a guaranteed payment for deductible services of $60,000 and 30% of partnership income computed after the partnership deducts the guaranteed payment. The partnership reports $40,000 of ordinary income and a $120,000 long-term capital gain before deducting the guaranteed payment. Theresa's income from the partnership is determined as follows:

		Theresa's Share	
	STU Partnership	*Ratable Share*	*Amount*
Ordinary income (before guaranteed payment)	$ 40,000		
Minus: Guaranteed payment	(60,000)	100%	$60,000
Ordinary loss	($ 20,000)	30%	(6,000)
Long-term capital gain	$120,000	30%	36,000 ◀

[49] Reg. Sec. 1.707-1(c), Exs. (1) and (2).
[50] Reg. Secs. 1.707-1(c) and 1.706-1(a).
[51] Reg. Sec. 1.707-1(c), Ex. (4).

FAMILY PARTNERSHIPS

OBJECTIVE 10

Explain the requirements for recognizing the holder of a partnership interest as a partner in a family partnership

CAPITAL OWNERSHIP

Because each partner reports and pays taxes on a distributive share of partnership income, a family partnership is an excellent way to spread income among family members and minimize the family's tax bill. However, to accomplish this tax minimization goal, the IRS must accept the family members as real partners. The question of whether someone is a partner in a family partnership is often litigated, but safe-harbor rules under Sec. 704(e) provide a clear answer if three tests are met: the partnership interest must be a capital interest, capital must be a material income-producing factor in the partnership's business activity, and the family member must be the true owner of the interest.

A capital interest gives the partner the right to receive assets if the partnership liquidates immediately upon the partner's acquisition of the interest. Capital is a material income-producing factor if the partnership derives substantial portions of gross income from the use of capital. For example, capital is a material income-producing factor if the business has substantial inventory or significant investment in plant or equipment. Capital is seldom considered a material income-producing factor in a service business.[52]

TAX STRATEGY TIP

In certain situations, family partnerships provide an excellent tax-planning tool, but the family members must be real partners. The rules that determine who is a real partner in a family partnership are guided by the assignment-of-income principle.

The remaining question is whether the family member is the true owner of the interest. Ownership is seldom questioned if one family member purchases the interest at a market price from another family member. However, when one family member gifts the interest to another, the major question is whether the donor retains so much control over the partnership interest that the donor is still the owner of the interest. If the donor still controls the interest, the donor is taxed on the distributive share.

DONOR RETAINED CONTROL. No mechanical test exists to determine whether the donor has retained too much control, but several factors may indicate a problem:[53]

- Retention of control over distributions of income can be a problem unless the retention occurs with the agreement of all partners or the retention is for the reasonable needs of the business.
- Retention of control over assets that are essential to the partnership's business can indicate too much control by the donor.
- Limitation of the donee partner's right to sell or liquidate his or her interest may indicate that the donor has not relinquished full control over the interest.
- Retention of management control that is inconsistent with normal partnership arrangements can be another sign that the donor retains control. This situation is not considered a fatal problem unless it occurs in conjunction with a significant limit on the donee's ability to sell or liquidate his or her interest.

If the donor has not directly or indirectly retained too much control, the donee is a full partner. As a partner, the donee must report his or her distributive share of income.

KEY POINT

A valid family partnership is a useful method for allocating income among family members. However, the distributive share of income from a partnership interest to a partner under age 14 is subject to the "kiddie tax."

MINOR DONEES. When income splitting is the goal of a family, the appropriate donee for the partnership interest is often a minor. With the problem of donor-retained controls in mind, gifts to minors should be made with great attention to detail. Further, net unearned income of a child under age 14 is taxed to the child at the parents' marginal tax rate. This provision removes much of the incentive to transfer family partnership interests to young children, but gifting partnership interests to minors age 14 or older still can reap significant tax advantages.

OBJECTIVE 11

Determine the allocation of partnership income between a donor and a donee of a partnership interest

DONOR-DONEE ALLOCATIONS OF INCOME

Partnership income must be properly allocated between a donor and a donee to be accepted by the IRS. Note that only the allocation between the donor and donee is questioned, with no impact on the distributive shares of any other partners.

[52] Reg. Sec. 1.704-1(e)(1)(iv).

[53] Reg. Sec. 1.704-1(e)(2)(ii).

Two requirements apply to donor-donee allocations. First, the donor must be allocated reasonable compensation for services rendered to the partnership. Then, after reasonable compensation is allocated to the donor, any remaining partnership income must be allocated based on relative capital interests.[54] This allocation scheme apparently overrides the partnership's ability to make special allocations of income.

EXAMPLE C:9-42 ▶ Andrew, a 40% partner in the ABC Partnership, gives one-half of his interest to his brother, John. During the current year, Andrew performs services for the partnership for which reasonable compensation is $65,000 but for which he accepts no pay. Andrew and John are each credited with a $100,000 distributive share, all of which is ordinary income. Reallocation between Andrew and John is necessary to reflect the value of Andrew's services.

Total distributive shares for the brothers	$200,000
Minus: Reasonable compensation for Andrew	(65,000)
Income to allocate	$135,000

John's distributive share: $\frac{20\%}{40\%} \times \$135{,}000 = \$67{,}500$

Andrew's distributive share: $\left(\frac{20\%}{40\%} \times \$135{,}000\right) + \$65{,}000 = \$132{,}500$ ◀

ETHICAL POINT

CPAs have a responsibility to review an entity's conduct of its activities to be sure it is operating as a partnership. If a donee receives a partnership interest as a gift and the donee is not the true owner of the interest (e.g., the donor retains too much control over the donee's interest), the partnership return must be filed without a distributive share of income or loss being allocated to the donee.

TAX PLANNING CONSIDERATIONS

TIMING OF LOSS RECOGNITION

The loss limitation rules provide a unique opportunity for tax planning. For example, if a partner knows that his or her distributive share of active losses from a partnership for a tax year will exceed the Sec. 704 basis limitation for deducting losses, he or she should carefully examine the tax situation for the current and upcoming tax years. Substantial current personal income may make immediate use of the loss desirable. Current income may be taxed at a higher marginal tax rate than will future income because of, for example, an extraordinarily good current year, an expected retirement, or a decrease in future years' tax rates. If the partner chooses to use the loss in the current year, he or she can make additional contributions just before year-end (perhaps even from funds the partner borrows, as long as the additional benefit exceeds the cost of the funds). Alternatively, one partner may convince the other partners to have the partnership incur additional liabilities so that each partner's basis increases. This last strategy should be exercised with caution unless a business reason (rather than solely a tax reason) exists for the borrowing.

EXAMPLE C:9-43 ▶ Ted, a 60% general partner in the ST Partnership, expects to be allocated partnership losses of $120,000 for the current year from a partnership in which he materially participates but where his partnership basis is only $90,000. Because he has a marginal tax rate of 35% for the current year (and anticipates only a 25% marginal tax rate for next year), Ted wants to use the ST Partnership losses to offset his current year income. He could make a capital contribution to raise his basis by $30,000. Alternatively, he could get the partnership to incur $50,000 in additional liabilities, which would increase his basis by his $30,000 ($50,000 × 0.60) share of the liability. The partnership's $50,000 borrowing must serve a business purpose for the ST Partnership. ◀

Alternatively, if a partner has little current year income and expects substantial income in the following year, the partner may prefer to delay the deduction of partnership losses that exceed the current year's loss limitation. Similarly, if a partner has loss, deduction, or

[54] Sec. 704(e)(2).

credit carryovers that expire in the current year, deferral of the distributive share of partnership losses to the following year again may be desirable. Should the partner opt to deduct the loss in a later year, he or she needs only to leave things alone so that the distributive share of losses exceeds the loss limitation for the current year.

Compliance and Procedural Considerations

OBJECTIVE 12

Determine the requirements for filing a partnership tax return

REPORTING TO THE IRS AND THE PARTNERS

FORMS. If the partnership is not an electing large partnership, the partnership must file a Form 1065 with the IRS by the fifteenth day of the fourth month after the end of the partnership tax year. (See Appendix B for a completed Form 1065.) The IRS, however, allows an automatic six-month extension of time to file Form 1065. To obtain the extension, the partnership must file Form 7004 on or before the partnership's normal filing date.[55] Penalties are imposed for failure to file a timely or complete partnership return. Because the partnership is only a conduit, Form 1065 is an information return and is not accompanied by any tax payment.[56] Included on the front page of Form 1065 are all the ordinary items of income, gain, loss and deduction that are not separately stated. Schedule K of Form 1065 reports both a summary of the ordinary income items and the partnership total of the separately stated items. Schedule K-1, which the partnership must prepare for each partner, reflects that partner's distributive share of partnership income including his or her special allocations. The partner's Schedule K-1 is notification of his or her share of partnership items for use in calculating income taxes and self-employment taxes.

HISTORICAL NOTE

Turn to the partnership Schedule K in Appendix B of this text. The large number of items that now have to be separately stated illustrates how certain tax laws, such as the passive activity limitation rules and the investment interest limitation rules, have complicated the preparation of Form 1065.

SCHEDULE M-3. For tax years ending on or after December 31, 2006, a partnership must file Schedule M-3 in lieu of Schedule M-1 if any one of the following conditions holds:

- The amount of total assets reported in Schedule L of Form 1065 (Balance Sheet per Books) equals or exceeds $10 million.
- The amount of adjusted total assets equals or exceeds $10 million, where adjusted total assets equal the Schedule L amount plus the following items that appear in Schedule M-2 of Form 1065: (1) capital distributions made during the year, (2) net book loss for the year, and (3) other adjustments.
- Total receipts equal or exceed $35 million.
- A reportable entity partner owns at least a 50% interest in the partnership on any day of the tax year, where a reportable entity partner is one that had to file its own Schedule M-3.

SECTION 444 ELECTION AND REQUIRED PAYMENTS. A partnership can elect to use a tax year other than a required year by filing an election under Sec. 444. This election is made by filing Form 8716 (Election to Have a Tax Year Other Than a Required Tax Year) by the earlier of the fifteenth day of the fifth month following the month that includes the first day of the tax year for which the election is effective or the due date (without regard to extension) of the income tax return resulting from the Sec. 444 election. In addition, a copy of Form 8716 must be attached to the partnership's Form 1065 for the first tax year for which the Sec. 444 election is made.

A partnership making a Sec. 444 election must make a required payment annually under Sec. 7519. The required payment has the effect of remitting a deposit equal to the

[55] Temp. Reg. 1.6081-2T. This temporary regulation applies to applications for extension filed after December 31, 2005, and before November 4, 2008.

[56] Reg. Sec. 301.6031-1(e)(2). Although the partnership pays no income tax, it still must pay the employer's share of social security taxes and any unemployment taxes as well as withhold income taxes from its employees' salaries. In addition, some publicly traded partnerships may pay a tax as explained in Chapter C:10.

tax (at the highest individual tax rate plus one percentage point) on the partnership's deferred income.

A partnership can obtain a refund if past payments exceed the tentative payment due on the deferred income for the current year. Similar refunds are available if the partnership terminates a Sec. 444 election or liquidates. The required payments are not deductible by the partnership and are not passed through to a partner. The required payments are in the nature of a refundable deposit.

The Sec. 7519 required payment is due on or before May 15 of the calendar year following the calendar year in which the election year begins. The partnership remits the required payment with Form 8752 (Required Payment or Refund Under Section 7519) along with a computational worksheet, which is illustrated in the instructions to Form 1065. Refunds of excess required payments also are obtained by filing Form 8752.

ESTIMATED TAXES. If the partnership is not an electing large partnership, it pays no income taxes and makes no estimated tax payments. However, the partners must make estimated tax payments based on their separate tax positions including their distributive shares of partnership income or loss for the current year. Thus, the partners are not making separate estimated tax payments for their partnership income but rather are including the effects of the partnership's results in the calculation of their normal estimated tax payments.

SELF-EMPLOYMENT INCOME. Every partnership must report the net earnings (or loss) for the partnership that constitute self-employment income to the partners. The instructions to Form 1065 contain a worksheet to make such a calculation. The partnership's self-employment income includes both guaranteed payments, partnership ordinary income and loss, and some separately stated items, but generally excludes capital gains and losses, Sec. 1231 gains and losses, interest, dividends, and rentals. The distributive share of self-employment income for each partner is shown on a Schedule K-1 and is included with the partner's other self-employment income in determining his or her self-employment tax liability (Schedule SE, Form 1040). The distributive share of partnership income allocable to a limited partner is not self-employment income.

EXAMPLE C:9-44 ▶ Adam is a general partner in the AB Partnership. His distributive share of partnership income and his guaranteed payment for the year are as follows:

Ordinary income	$15,000
Short-term capital gain	9,000
Guaranteed payment	18,000

Adam's self-employment income is $33,000 ($15,000 + $18,000). ◀

EXAMPLE C:9-45 ▶ Assume the same facts as in Example C:9-44 except that Adam is a limited partner. His self-employment income includes only the $18,000 guaranteed payment. ◀

IRS AUDIT PROCEDURES

Any questions arising during an IRS audit about a partnership item must be determined at the partnership level (instead of at the partner level).[57] Section 6231(a)(3) defines **partnership items** as virtually all items reported by the partnership for the tax year including tax preference items, credit recapture items, guaranteed payments, and the at-risk amount. In fact, almost every item that can appear on the partnership return is treated as a partnership item. Each partner must either report partnership items in a manner consistent with the Schedule K-1 received from the partnership or notify the IRS of the inconsistent treatment.[58]

The IRS can bring a single proceeding at the partnership level to determine the characterization or tax impact of any partnership item. All partners have the right to participate in the administrative proceedings, and the IRS must offer a consistent settlement to all partners.

[57] Sec. 6221.

[58] Sec. 6222.

KEY POINT

To alleviate the administrative nightmare of having to audit each partner of a partnership, Congress has authorized the IRS to conduct audits of partnerships in a unified proceeding at the partnership level. This process is more efficient and should provide greater consistency in the treatment of the individual partners than did the previous system.

The partnership generally assigns a **tax matters partner** to facilitate communication between the IRS and the partners of a large partnership and to serve as the primary representative of the partnership.[59] If the partnership fails to assign the tax matters partner, the designation goes to the general partner having the largest profits interest at the close of the partnership's tax year.

These audit procedures, however, do not apply to small partnerships. For this purpose, a small partnership is defined as one having no more than ten partners who must be natural persons (but excluding nonresident aliens), C corporations, or estates. In counting partners, a husband and wife (or their estates) count as a single partner. Further, the IRS has announced that a partnership can be excluded from the audit procedures only if it can be established that all partners fully reported their shares of partnership items on timely filed tax returns.[60]

PROBLEM MATERIALS

DISCUSSION QUESTIONS

C:9-1 Yvonne and Larry plan to begin a business that will grow plants for sale to retail nurseries. They expect to have substantial losses for the first three years of operations while they develop their plants and their sales operations. Both Yvonne and Larry have substantial interest income, and both expect to work full-time in this new business. List three advantages for operating this business as a partnership instead of a C corporation.

C:9-2 Bob and Carol want to open a bed and breakfast inn as soon as they buy and renovate a turn-of-the-century home. What would be the major disadvantage of using a general partnership rather than a corporation for this business? Should they consider any other form for structuring their business?

C:9-3 Sam wants to help his brother, Lou, start a new business. Lou is a capable auto mechanic but has little business sense, so he needs Sam to help him make business decisions. Should this partnership be arranged as a general partnership or a limited partnership? Why? Should they consider any other form for structuring their business?

C:9-4 Doug contributes services but no property to the CD Partnership upon its formation. What are the tax implications of his receiving only a profits interest versus his receiving a capital and profits interest?

C:9-5 An existing partner wants to contribute property having a basis less than its FMV for an additional interest in a partnership.

a. Should he contribute the property to the partnership?
b. What are his other options?
c. Explain the tax implications for the partner of these other options.

C:9-6 Jane contributes valuable property to a partnership in exchange for a general partnership interest. The partnership also assumes the recourse mortgage Jane incurred when she purchased the property two years ago.

a. How will the liability affect the amount of gain that Jane must recognize?
b. How will it affect her basis in the partnership interest?

C:9-7 Which of the following items can be deducted (up to $5,000) and amortized as part of a partnership's organizational expenditures?

a. Legal fees for drawing up the partnership agreement
b. Accounting fees for establishing an accounting system
c. Fees for securing an initial working capital loan
d. Filing fees required under state law in initial year to conduct business in the state
e. Accounting fees for preparation of initial short-period tax return
f. Transportation costs for acquiring machinery essential to the partnership's business
g. Syndication expenses

C:9-8 The BW Partnership reported the following current year earnings: $30,000 interest from tax-exempt bonds, $50,000 long-term capital gain, and $100,000 net income from operations. Bob saw these numbers and told his partner, Wendy, that the partnership had $100,000 of taxable income. Is he correct? Explain your answer.

C:9-9 How will a partner's distributive share be determined if the partner sells one-half of his or her beginning-of-the-year partnership interest at the beginning of the tenth month of the partnership's tax year?

---

[59] Sec. 6231(a)(7).

[60] Rev. Proc. 84-35, 1984-1 C.B. 509.

C:9-10 Can a recourse debt of a partnership increase the basis of a limited partner's partnership interest? Explain.

C:9-11 The ABC Partnership has a nonrecourse liability that it incurred by borrowing from an unrelated bank. It is secured by an apartment building owned and managed by the partnership. The liability is not convertible into an equity interest. How does this liability affect the at-risk basis of general partner Anna and limited partner Bob?

C:9-12 Is the Sec. 704(d) loss limitation rule more or less restrictive than the at-risk rules? Explain.

C:9-13 Jeff, a 10% limited partner in the recently formed JRS Partnership, expects to have losses from the partnership for several more years. He is considering purchasing an interest in a profitable general partnership in which he will materially participate. Will the purchase allow him to use his losses from the JRS Partnership?

C:9-14 Helen, a 55% partner in the ABC Partnership, owns land (a capital asset) having a $20,000 basis and a $25,000 FMV. She plans to transfer the land to the ABC Partnership, which will subdivide the land and sell the lots. Discuss whether Helen should sell or contribute the land to the partnership.

C:9-15 What is the difference between a guaranteed payment that is a guaranteed amount and one that is a guaranteed minimum?

C:9-16 The TUV Partnership is considering two compensation schemes for Tracy, the partner who runs the business on a daily basis. Tracy can be given a $10,000 guaranteed payment, or she can be given a comparably larger distributive share (and distribution) so that she receives about $10,000 more each year. From the standpoint of when the income must be reported in Tracy's tax return, are these two compensation alternatives the same?

C:9-17 Roy's father gives him a capital interest in the Family Partnership. Discuss whether the Sec. 704(e) family partnership rules apply to this interest.

C:9-18 Andrew gives his brother Steve a 20% interest in the AS Partnership, and he retains a 30% interest. Andrew works for the partnership but is not paid. How will this arrangement affect the income from the AS Partnership that Andrew and Steve report?

ISSUE IDENTIFICATION QUESTIONS

C:9-19 Bob and Kate form the BK Partnership, a general partnership, as equal partners. Bob contributes an office building with a $130,000 FMV and a $95,000 adjusted basis to the partnership along with a $60,000 mortgage, which the partnership assumes. Kate contributes the land on which the building sits with a $50,000 FMV and a $75,000 adjusted basis. Kate will manage the partnership for the first five years of operations but will not receive a guaranteed payment for her work in the first year of partnership operations. Starting with the second year of partnership operations, Kate will receive a $10,000 guaranteed payment for each year she manages the partnership. What tax issues should Bob, Kate, and the BK Partnership consider with respect to the formation and operation of the partnership?

C:9-20 Suzanne and Laura form a partnership to market local crafts. In April, the two women spent $1,600 searching for a retail outlet, $1,200 to have a partnership agreement drawn up, and $2,000 to have an accounting system established. During April, they signed contracts with a number of local crafters to feature their products in the retail outlet. The outlet was fitted and merchandise organized during May. In June, the store opened and sold its first crafts. The partnership paid $500 to an accountant to prepare an income statement for the month of June. What tax issues should the partnership consider with regard to beginning this business?

C:9-21 Cara, a CPA, established an accounting system for the ABC Partnership and, in return for her services, received a 10% profits interest (but no capital interest) in the partnership. Her usual fee for the services would be approximately $20,000. No sales of profits interests in the ABC Partnership occurred during the current year. What tax issues should Cara and the ABC Partnership consider with respect to the payment made for the services?

C:9-22 George, a limited partner in the EFG Partnership, has a 20% interest in partnership capital, profits, and losses. His basis in the partnership interest is $15,000 before accounting for events of the current year. In December of the current year, the EFG Partnership repaid a $100,000 nonrecourse liability. The partnership earned $20,000 of ordinary income this year. What tax issues should George consider with respect to reporting the results of this year's activities for the EFG Partnership on his personal return?

C:9-23 Katie works 40 hours a week as a clerk in the mall and earns $20,000. In addition, she works five hours each week in the JKL Partnership's office. Katie, a 10% limited partner in the JKL Partnership, has been allocated a $2,100 loss from the partnership for the current year. The basis for her interest in JKL before accounting for current operations is $5,000. What tax issues should Katie consider with respect to her interest in, and employment by, the JKL Partnership?

C:9-24 Daniel has no family to inherit his 80% capital and profits interest in the CD Partnership. To ensure the continuation of the business, he gives a 20% capital and profits interest in the partnership to David, his best friend's son, on the condition that David work in the partnership for at least five years. David receives guaranteed payments for his work. Daniel takes no salary from the partnership, but he devotes all his time to the business operations of the partnership. What tax issues should Daniel and David consider with respect to the gift of the partnership interest and Daniel's employment arrangement with the partnership?

PROBLEMS

C:9-25 ***Formation of a Partnership.*** Suzanne and Bob form the SB General Partnership as equal partners. They make the following contributions:

Individual	*Asset*	*Basis to Partner*	*FMV*
Suzanne	Cash	$45,000	$ 45,000
	Inventory (securities)	14,000	15,000
Bob	Land	45,000	40,000
	Building	50,000	100,000

The SB Partnership assumes the $80,000 recourse mortgage on the building that Bob contributes, and the partners share the economic risk of loss on the mortgage equally. Bob has claimed $40,000 in straight-line depreciation under the MACRS rules on the building. Suzanne is a stockbroker and contributed securities from her inventory. The partnership will hold them as an investment.

a. What amount and character of gain or loss must each partner recognize on the formation of the partnership?
b. What is each partner's basis in his or her partnership interest?
c. What is the partnership's basis in each asset?
d. What is the partnership's initial book value of each asset?
e. The partnership holds the securities for two years and then sells them for $20,000. What amount and character of gain must the partnership and each partner report?

C:9-26 ***Formation of a Partnership.*** On May 31, six brothers decided to form the Grimm Brothers Partnership to publish and print children's stories. The contributions of the brothers and their partnership interests are listed below. They share the economic risk of loss from liabilities according to their partnership interests.

Individual	*Asset*	*Basis to Partner*	*FMV*	*Partnership Interest*
Al	Cash	$15,000	$ 15,000	15%
Bob	Accounts receivable	–0–	20,000	20%
Clay	Office equipment	13,000	15,000	15%
Dave	Land	50,000	15,000	15%
Ed	Building	15,000	150,000	20%
Fred	Services	?	15,000	15%

The following other information about the contributions may be of interest:

- Bob contributes accounts receivable from his proprietorship, which uses the cash method of accounting.
- Clay uses the office equipment in a small business he owns. When he joins the partnership, he sells the remaining business assets to an outsider. He has claimed $8,000 of MACRS depreciation on the office equipment.
- The partnership assumes a $130,000 mortgage on the building Ed contributes. Ed claimed $100,000 of straight-line MACRS depreciation on the commercial property.

- Fred, an attorney, drew up all the partnership agreements and filed the necessary paperwork. He receives a full 15% capital and profits interest for his services.

a. How much gain, loss, or income must each partner recognize as a result of the formation?
b. How much gain, loss, or income must the partnership recognize as a result of the formation?
c. What is each partner's basis in his partnership interest?
d. What is the partnership's basis in its assets?
e. What is the partnership's initial book value of each asset?
f. What effects do the depreciation recapture provisions have on the property contributions?
g. How would your answer to Part a change if Fred received only a profits interest?
h. What are the tax consequences to the partners and the partnership when the partnership sells for $9,000 the land contributed by Dave? Prior to the sale, the partnership held the land as an investment for two years.

C:9-27 ***Formation of a Partnership.*** On January 1, Julie, Kay, and Susan form a partnership. The contributions of the three individuals are listed below. Julie received a 30% partnership interest, Kay received a 60% partnership interest, and Susan received a 10% partnership interest. They share the economic risk of loss from recourse liabilities according to their partnership interests.

Individual	*Asset*	*Basis to Partner*	*FMV*
Julie	Accounts receivable	$ –0–	$ 60,000
Kay	Land	30,000	58,000
	Building	45,000	116,000
Susan	Services	?	20,000

Kay has claimed $15,000 of straight-line MACRS depreciation on the building. The land and building are subject to a $54,000 mortgage, of which $18,000 is allocable to the land and $36,000 is allocable to the building. The partnership assumes the mortgage. Susan is an attorney, and the services she contributes are the drawing-up of all partnership agreements.

a. What amount and character of gain, loss, or income must each partner recognize on the formation of the partnership?
b. What is each partner's basis in her partnership interest?
c. What is the partnership's basis in each of its assets?
d. What is the partnership's initial book value of each asset?
e. To raise some immediate cash after the formation, the partnership decides to sell the land and building to a third party and lease it back. The buyer pays $40,000 cash for the land and $80,000 cash for the building in addition to assuming the $54,000 mortgage. Assume the partnership claim no additional depreciation on the building before the sale. What is each partner's distributive share of the gains, and what is the character of the gains?

C:9-28 ***Contribution of Services.*** Sean is admitted to the XYZ Partnership in December of the current year in return for his services managing the partnership's business during the year. The partnership reports ordinary income of $100,000 for the current year without considering this transaction.

a. What are the tax consequences to Sean and the XYZ Partnership if Sean receives a 20% capital and profits interest in the partnership with a $75,000 FMV?
b. What are the tax consequences to Sean and the XYZ Partnership if Sean receives only a 20% profits interest with no determinable FMV?

C:9-29 ***Contribution of Services and Property.*** Marjorie works for a large firm whose business is to find suitable real estate, establish a limited partnership to purchase the property, and then sell the limited partnership interests. In the current year, Marjorie received a 5% limited partnership interest in the Eldorado Limited Partnership. Marjorie received this interest partially in payment for her services in selling partnership interests to others, but she also was required to contribute $5,000 in cash to the partnership. Similar limited partnership interests sold for $20,000 at approximately the same time that Marjorie received her interest. What are the tax consequences for Marjorie and the Eldorado Limited Partnership of Marjorie's receipt of the partnership interest?

C:9-30 *Partnership Tax Year.* The BCD Partnership is being formed by three equal partners, Beta Corporation, Chi Corporation, and Delta Corporation. The partners' tax year-ends are June 30 for Beta, September 30 for Chi, and October 31 for Delta. The BCD Partnership's natural business year ends on January 31.

a. What tax year(s) can the partnership elect without IRS permission?
b. What tax year(s) can the partnership elect with IRS permission?
c. How would your answers to Parts a and b change if Beta, Chi, and Delta own 4%, 4%, and 92%, respectively, of the partnership?

C:9-31 *Partnership Tax Year.* The BCD Partnership is formed in April of the current year. The three equal partners, Boris, Carlton Corporation, and Damien have had tax years ending on December 31, August 30, and December 31, respectively, for the last three years. The BCD Partnership has no natural business year.

a. What tax year is required for the BCD Partnership under Sec. 706?
b. Can the BCD Partnership make a Sec. 444 election? If so, what are the alternative tax years BCD could select?

C:9-32 *Partnership Income and Basis Adjustments.* Mark and Pamela are equal partners in MP Partnership. The partnership, Mark, and Pamela are calendar year taxpayers. The partnership incurred the following items in the current year:

Sales	$450,000
Cost of goods sold	210,000
Dividends on corporate investments	15,000
Tax-exempt interest income	4,000
Section 1245 gain (recapture) on equipment sale	33,000
Section 1231 gain on equipment sale	18,000
Long-term capital gain on stock sale	12,000
Long-term capital loss on stock sale	10,000
Short-term capital loss on stock sale	9,000
Depreciation (no Sec. 179 component)	27,000
Guaranteed payment to Pamela	30,000
Meals and entertainment expenses	11,600
Interest expense on loans allocable to:	
Business debt	42,000
Stock investments	9,200
Tax-exempt bonds	2,800
Principal payment on business loan	14,000
Charitable contributions	5,000
Distributions to partners ($30,000 each)	60,000

a. Compute the partnership's ordinary income and separately stated items.
b. Show Mark's and Pamela's shares of the items in Part a.
c. Compute Mark's and Pamela's ending basis in their partnership interests assuming their beginning balances are $150,000 each.

C:9-33 *Financial Accounting and Partnership Income.* Jim, Liz, and Ken are equal partners in the JLK Partnership, which uses the accrual method of accounting. All three materially participate in the business. JLK reports financial accounting income of $186,000 for the current year. The partnership used the following information to determine financial accounting income.

Operating profit (excluding the items listed below)	$ 94,000
Rental income	30,000
Interest income:	
Municipal bonds (tax-exempt)	15,000
Corporate bonds	3,000
Dividend income (all from less-than-20%-owned domestic corporations)	20,000
Gains and losses on property sales:	
Gain on sale of land held as an investment (contributed by Jim six years ago when its basis was $9,000 and its FMV was $15,000)	60,000
Long-term capital gains	10,000
Short-term capital losses	7,000
Sec. 1231 gain	9,000
Sec. 1250 gain	44,000

Depreciation:	
Rental real estate	12,000
Machinery and equipment	27,000
Interest expense related to:	
Mortgages on rental property	18,000
Loans to acquire municipal bonds	5,000
Guaranteed payments to Jim	30,000
Low-income housing expenditures qualifying for credit	21,000

The following additional information is available about the current year's activities.

- The partnership received a $1,000 prepayment of rent for next year but has not recorded it as income for financial accounting purposes.
- The partnership recorded the land for financial accounting purposes at $15,000.
- MACRS depreciation on the rental real estate and machinery and equipment were $12,000 and $29,000, respectively, in the current year.
- MACRS depreciation for the rental real estate includes depreciation on the low-income housing expenditures.

a. What is JLK's financial accounting income?
b. What is JLK's partnership taxable income? (See Appendix B for an example of a financial accounting-to-tax reconciliation.)
c. What is JLK's ordinary income (loss)?
d. What are JLK's separately stated items?

C:9-34 ***Partner's Distributive Shares.*** On January of the current year, Becky (20%), Chuck (30%), and Dawn (50%) are partners in the BCD Partnership. During the current year, BCD reports the following results. All items occur evenly throughout the year unless otherwise indicated. Assume the current year is not a leap year.

Ordinary income	$120,000
Long-term capital gain (recognized September 1)	18,000
Short-term capital loss (recognized March 2)	6,000
Charitable contribution (made October 1)	20,000

a. What are the distributive shares for each partner, assuming they all continue to hold their interests at the end of the year?
b. Assume that Becky purchases a 5% partnership interest from Chuck on July 1 so that Becky and Chuck each own 25% from that date through the end of the year. What are Becky and Chuck's distributive shares for the current year?

C:9-35 ***Allocation of Precontribution Gain.*** Last year, Patty contributed land with a $4,000 basis and a $10,000 FMV in exchange for a 40% profits, loss, and capital interest in the PD Partnership. Dave contributed land with an $8,000 basis and a $15,000 FMV for the remaining 60% interest in the partnership. During the current year, PD Partnership reported $8,000 of ordinary income and $10,000 of long-term capital gain from the sale of the land Patty contributed. What income or gain must Patty and Dave report from the PD Partnership in the current year?

C:9-36 ***Special Allocations.*** Refer to Example C:9-25 in the text. Provide computations showing that the partners' total tax liability under the special allocation is less than their total liability under an equal allocation of the two types of interest income.

C:9-37 ***Special Allocations.*** Clark sold securities for a $50,000 short-term capital loss during the current year, but he has no personal capital gains to recognize. The C&L General Partnership, in which Clark has a 50% capital, profits, and loss interest, reported a $60,000 short-term capital gain this year. In addition, the partnership earned $140,000 of ordinary income. Clark's only partner, Lois, agrees to divide the year's income as follows:

Type of Income	*Total*	*Clark*	*Lois*
Short-term capital gain	$ 60,000	$50,000	$10,000
Ordinary income	140,000	50,000	90,000

Both partners and the partnership use a calendar year-end, and both partners have a 33% marginal tax rate.

a. Have the partners made a special allocation of income that has substantial economic effect?

b. What amount and character of income must each partner report on his or her tax return?

C:9-38 *Special Allocations.* Diane and Ed have equal capital and profits interests in the DE Partnership, and they share the economic risk of loss from recourse liabilities according to their partnership interests. In addition, Diane has a special allocation of all depreciation on buildings owned by the partnership. The buildings are financed with recourse liabilities. The depreciation reduces Diane's capital account, and liquidation is in accordance with the capital account balances. Depreciation for the DE Partnership is $50,000 annually. Diane and Ed each have $50,000 capital account balances on January 1, 2007. Will the special allocation be acceptable for 2007, 2008, and 2009 in the following independent situations?

a. The partners have no obligation to repay negative capital account balances, and the partnership's operations (other than depreciation) each year have no net effect on the capital accounts.
b. The partners have an obligation to repay negative capital account balances.
c. The partners have no obligation to repay negative capital account balances. The partnership operates at its break-even point (excluding any depreciation claimed) and borrows $200,000 on a full recourse basis on December 31, 2008.

C:9-39 *Basis in Partnership Interest.* What is Kelly's basis for her partnership interest in each of the following independent situations? The partners share the economic risk of loss from recourse liabilities according to their partnership interests.

a. Kelly receives her 20% partnership interest for a contribution of property having a $14,000 basis and a $17,000 FMV. The partnership assumes her $10,000 recourse liability but has no other debts.
b. Kelly receives her 20% partnership interest as a gift from a friend. The friend's basis (without considering partnership liabilities) is $34,000. The FMV of the interest at the time of the gift is $36,000. The partnership has liabilities of $100,000 when Kelly receives her interest. No gift tax was paid with respect to the transfer.
c. Kelly inherits her 20% interest from her mother. Her mother's basis was $140,000. The FMV of the interest is $120,000 on the date of death and $160,000 on the alternate valuation date. The executor chooses the date of death for valuing the estate. The partnership has no liabilities.

C:9-40 *Basis in Partnership Interest.* Yong received a 40% general partnership interest in the XYZ Partnership in each of the independent situations below. In each situation, assume the general partners share the economic risk of loss related to recourse liabilities according to their partnership interests. What is Yong's basis in his partnership interest?

a. Yong designs the building the partnership will use for its offices. Yong normally would charge a $20,000 fee for a similar building design. Based on the other partner's contributions, the 40% interest has a FMV of $25,000. The partnership has no liabilities.
b. Yong contributes land with a $6,000 basis and an $18,000 FMV, a car (which he has used in his business since he purchased it) with a $15,000 adjusted basis and a $6,000 FMV, and $2,000 cash. The partnership has recourse liabilities of $100,000.

C:9-41 *Basis in Partnership Interest.* Tina purchases an interest in the TP Partnership on January 1 of the current year for $50,000. The partnership uses the calendar year as its tax year and has $200,000 in recourse liabilities when Tina acquires her interest. The partners share economic risk of loss associated with recourse debt according to their loss percentage. Her distributive share of partnership items for the year is as follows:

Ordinary income (excluding items listed below)	$30,000
Long-term capital gains	10,000
Municipal bond interest income	8,000
Charitable contributions	1,000
Interest expense related to municipal bond investment	2,000

TP reports the following liabilities on December 31:

Recourse debt	$100,000
Nonrecourse debt (not qualified real estate financing)	80,000

a. What is Tina's basis on December 31 if she has a 40% interest in profits and losses? TP is a general partnership. Tina has not guaranteed partnership debt, nor has she made any other special agreements about partnership debt.

b. How would your answer to Part a change if Tina instead had a 40% interest in profits and a 30% interest in losses? Assume TP is a general partnership, and all other agreements continue in place. Also assume the partners share recourse liabilities in accordance with their loss interest percentages.

c. How would your answer to Part a change if Tina were instead a limited partner having a 40% interest in profits and 30% interest in losses? The partnership agreement contains no guarantees or other special arrangements.

C:9-42 ***At-Risk Loss Limitation.*** The KC Partnership is a general partnership that manufactures widgets. The partnership uses a calendar year as its tax year and has two equal partners, Kerry and City Corporation, a widely held corporation. On January 1 of the current year, Kerry and City Corporation each has a $200,000 basis in the partnership interest. Operations during the year produce the following results:

Ordinary loss	$900,000
Long-term capital loss	100,000
Short-term capital gain	300,000

The only change in KC's liabilities during the year is KC's borrowing $100,000 as a nonrecourse loan (not qualified real estate financing) that remains outstanding at year-end.

a. What is each partner's deductible loss from the partnership's activities before any passive loss limitation?

b. What is each partner's basis in the partnership interest after the year's operations?

c. How would your answers to Parts a and b change if the KC Partnership's business were totally in real estate but not a rental activity? Assume the loan is qualified real estate financing.

C:9-43 ***At-Risk Loss Limitation.*** Mary and Gary are partners in the MG Partnership. Mary owns a 40% capital, profits, and loss interest. Gary owns the remaining interest. Both materially participate in partnership activities. At the beginning of the current year, MG's only liabilities are $30,000 in accounts payable, which remain outstanding at year-end. In November, MG borrows $100,000 on a nonrecourse basis from First Bank. The loan is secured by property with a $200,000 FMV. These are MG's only liabilities at year-end. Basis for the partnership interests at the beginning of the year is $40,000 for Mary and $60,000 for Gary before considering the impact of liabilities and operations. MG has a $200,000 ordinary loss during the current year. How much loss can Mary and Gary recognize?

C:9-44 ***Passive Loss Limitation.*** Eve and Tom own 40% and 60%, respectively, of the ET Partnership, which manufactures clocks. The partnership is a limited partnership, and Eve is the only general partner. She works full-time in the business. Tom essentially is an investor in the firm and works full-time at another job. Tom has no other income except his salary from his full-time employer. During the current year, the partnership reports the following gain and loss:

Ordinary loss	$140,000
Long-term capital gain	20,000

Before including the current year's gain and loss, Eve and Tom had $46,000 and $75,000 bases for their partnership interests, respectively. The partnership has no nonrecourse liabilities. Tom has no further obligation to make any additional investment in the partnership.

a. What gain or loss should each partner report on his or her individual tax return?

b. If the partnership borrowed an additional $100,000 of recourse liabilities, how would your answer to Part a change?

C:9-45 ***Passive Loss Limitation.*** Kate, Chad, and Stan are partners in the KCS Partnership, which operates a manufacturing business. The partners formed the partnership ten years ago with Kate and Chad each as general partners having a 40% capital and profits interest. Kate materially participates; Chad does not. Stan has a 20% interest as a limited partner. At the end of the current year, the following information was available:

	Kate	*Chad*	*Stan*
Basis in partnership (before gains and losses)	$100,000	$100,000	$50,000
Distributive share of:			
Nonrecourse liability (already included in basis and not qualified real estate financing)	50,000	50,000	25,000
Operating loss	(80,000)	(80,000)	(40,000)
Capital gain	20,000	20,000	10,000

a. How much operating loss can each partner deduct in the current year?
b. How much loss could each partner deduct if the KCS Partnership were engaged in rental activities? Assume Kate and Chad both actively participate, but Stan does not.

C:9-46 ***At-Risk and Passive Loss Limitations.*** At the beginning of year 1, Ed and Fran each contributed $1,000 cash to EF Partnership as equal partners. The partnership immediately borrowed $98,000 on a nonrecourse basis and used the contributed cash and loan proceeds to purchase equipment costing $100,000. The partnership leases out the equipment on a five-year lease for $10,000 per year. Over the five-year period, the partnership makes the following principal and interest payments on the loan:

Year	*Principal*	*Interest*
1	$3,000	$7,000
2	3,500	6,500
3	3,500	6,500
4	4,000	6,000
5	4,000	6,000

Assume the partnership depreciates the equipment according to the following hypothetical schedule:

Year	*Depreciation*
1	$40,000
2	25,000
3	15,000
4	8,000
5	8,000
6	4,000

At the beginning of year 6, the partnership sells the equipment for $82,000. The partnership claims the last $4,000 of depreciation at the beginning of year 6 as an expense, so the equipment has a zero basis when sold. At the beginning of year 6, the partnership also pays off the $80,000 loan balance and distributes any remaining cash to Ed and Fran. Assume that each partner has a 35% ordinary tax rate and a 15% capital gains tax rate.

a. Determine the partnership's gain (loss) for each of the five years and the beginning of the sixth year.
b. Assume that depreciation recapture applies but that the at-risk and passive activity loss rules do not apply. Using the results from Part a and a 7% discount rate, determine the present value of tax savings for both partners combined over the five-year period including the beginning of the sixth year. Why do these tax savings occur?
c. Now assume the at-risk and passive activity loss rules do apply. Determine what the partners recognize over the five-year period including the beginning of the sixth year. Do the partners have any tax savings in this situation? Why or why not?
d. Provide a schedule analyzing each partner's outside basis over the five-year period including the sixth year.

C:9-47 ***Related Party Transactions.*** Susan, Steve, and Sandy own 15%, 35%, and 50%, respectively, in the SSS Partnership. Susan sells securities for their $40,000 FMV to the partnership. What are the tax implications of the following independent situations?

a. Susan's basis in the securities is $60,000. The three partners are siblings.
b. Susan's basis in the securities is $50,000. Susan is unrelated to the other partners.
c. Susan's basis in the securities is $30,000. Susan and Sandy are sisters. The partnership will hold the securities as an investment.
d. What are the tax consequences in Part a if the partnership subsequently sells the securities to an unrelated third party for $70,000? For $55,000? For $35,000?

C:9-48 ***Related Party Transactions.*** Kara owns 35% of the KLM Partnership and 45% of the KTV Partnership. Lynn owns 20% of KLM and 3% of KTV. Maura, Kara's daughter, owns 15% of KTV. No other partners own an interest in both partnerships or are related to other partners. The KTV Partnership sells to the KLM Partnership 1,000 shares of stock, which KTV has held for investment purposes, for its $50,000 FMV. What are the tax consequences of the sale in each of the following independent situations?

a. KTV's basis for the stock is $80,000.

b. KTV's basis for the stock is $23,000 and KLM holds the stock as an investment.
c. KTV's basis for the stock is $35,000 and KLM holds the stock as inventory.
d. What are the tax consequences in Part a if the KLM Partnership subsequently sells the stock to an unrelated third party for $130,000? For $70,000? For $40,000?

C:9-49 ***Guaranteed Payments.*** Scott and Dave each invested $100,000 cash when they formed the SD Partnership and became equal partners. They agreed that the partnership would pay each partner a 5% guaranteed payment on his $100,000 capital account. Before the two guaranteed payments, current year results were $23,000 of ordinary income and $14,000 of long-term capital gain. What amount and character of income will Scott and Dave report for the current year from their partnership?

C:9-50 ***Guaranteed Payments.*** Allen and Bob are equal partners in the AB Partnership. Bob manages the business and receives a guaranteed payment. What amount and character of income will Allen and Bob report in each of the following independent situations?
a. The AB Partnership earns $160,000 of ordinary income before considering Bob's guaranteed payment. Bob is guaranteed a $90,000 payment plus 50% of all income remaining after the guaranteed payment.
b. Assume the same facts as Part a except Bob's distributive share is 50% with a guaranteed minimum of $90,000.
c. The AB Partnership earns a $140,000 long-term capital gain and no ordinary income. Bob is guaranteed $80,000 plus 50% of all amounts remaining after the guaranteed payment.

C:9-51 ***Guaranteed Payments.*** Pam and Susan own the PS Partnership. Pam takes care of daily operations and receives a guaranteed payment for her efforts. What amount and character of income will each partner report in each of the following independent situations?
a. The PS Partnership reports a $10,000 long-term capital gain and no ordinary income. Pam receives a $40,000 guaranteed payment plus a 30% distributive share of all partnership income after deducting the guaranteed payment.
b. The PS Partnership reports $80,000 of ordinary income, before considering any guaranteed payment, and a $60,000 Sec. 1231 gain. Pam receives a $35,000 guaranteed payment plus a 20% distributive share of all partnership income after deducting the guaranteed payment.
c. The PS Partnership reports $120,000 of ordinary income before considering any guaranteed payment. Pam receives 40% of partnership income but no less than $60,000.

C:9-52 ***Family Partnership.*** Dad gives Son a 20% capital and profits interest in the Family Partnership. Dad holds a 70% interest, and Fred, an unrelated individual, holds a 10% interest. Dad and Fred work in the partnership, but Son does not. Dad and Fred receive reasonable compensation for their work. The partnership earns $100,000 ordinary income, and the partners agree to divide this amount based on their relative ownership interests. What income must Father, Son, and Fred report if Family Partnership is a manufacturing firm with substantial inventories?

C:9-53 ***Family Partnership.*** Steve wishes to pass his business on to his children, Tracy and Vicki, and gives each daughter a 20% partnership interest to begin getting them involved. Steve retains the remaining 60% interest. Neither daughter is employed by the partnership, which buys and manages real estate. Steve draws only a $40,000 guaranteed payment for his work for the partnership. Reasonable compensation for his services would be $70,000. The partnership reports ordinary income of $120,000 after deducting the guaranteed payment. Distributive shares for the three partners are tentatively reported as: Steve, $72,000; Tracy, $24,000; and Vicki, $24,000. What is the proper distributive share of income for each partner?

COMPREHENSIVE PROBLEMS

C:9-54 Rick has a $50,000 basis in the RKS General Partnership on January 1 of the current year, and he owns no other investments. He has a 20% capital interest, a 30% profits interest, and a 40% loss interest in the partnership. Rick does not work in the partnership. The partnership's only liability is a $100,000 nonrecourse debt borrowed several years ago, which remains outstanding at year-end. Rick's share of the liability is based on his profits interest and is included in his $50,000 partnership basis. Rick and the partnership each report on a calendar year basis. Income for the entire partnership during the current year is:

Ordinary loss	$440,000
Long-term capital gain	100,000
Sec. 1231 gain	150,000

a. What is Rick's distributive share of income, gain, and loss for the current year?
b. What partnership income, gain, and loss should Rick report on his tax return for the current year?
c. What is Rick's basis in his partnership interest on the first day of next year?

C:9-55 Charles and Mary formed CM Partnership on January 1 of the current year. Charles contributed Inventory A with a $100,000 FMV and a $70,000 adjusted basis for a 40% interest, and Mary contributed $150,000 cash for a 60% interest. The partnership operates on a calendar year. The partnership used the cash to purchase equipment for $50,000, Inventory B for $80,000, and stock in ST Corporation for $5,000. The partnership used the remaining $15,000 for operating expenses and borrowed another $5,000 for operating expenses. During the year, the partnership sold one-half of Inventory A for $60,000 (tax basis, $35,000), one-half of Inventory B for $58,000 (tax basis, $40,000), and the ST stock for $6,000. The partnership claimed $7,000 of depreciation on the equipment for both tax and book purposes. Thus, for the year, the partnership incurred the following items:

Sales—Inventory A	$60,000
Sales—Inventory B	58,000
COGS—Inventory A	35,000
COGS—Inventory B	40,000
Operating expenses	20,000
Depreciation	7,000
Short-term capital gain	1,000
Interest on business loan	500

On December 31 of the current year, the partnership made a $1,000 principal payment on the loan and distributed $2,000 cash to Charles and $3,000 cash to Mary.
a. Determine partnership ordinary income for the year and each partner's distributive share.
b. Determine the separately stated items and each partner's distributive share.
c. Determine each partner's basis in the partnership at the end of the current year.
d. Determine each partner's book capital account at the end of the current year.
e. Provide an analysis of the ending cash balance.
f. Provide beginning and ending balance sheets using tax numbers.
g. Provide beginning and ending balance sheets using book values.

TAX STRATEGY PROBLEM

C:9-56 Sarah and Rex formed SR Entity on December 28 of last year. The entity operates on a calendar tax year. Each individual contributed $800,000 cash in exchange for a 50% ownership interest in the entity (common stock if a corporation; partnership interest if a partnership). In addition, the entity borrowed $400,000 from the bank. The entity operates on a calendar year. On December 28 of last year, the entity used the $2 million cash (contributions and loan) to purchase assets as indicated in the following balance sheet as of December 28 of last year:

Cash	$ 100,000
Inventory	1,770,000
Investment in tax-exempt bonds	50,000
Investment in corporate stock (less than 20%-owned)	80,000
Total	$2,000,000
Liability	$ 400,000
Equity*	1,600,000
Total	$2,000,000

*If a partnership, each partner's beginning capital account is $800,000.

The balance sheet did not change between December 28 of last year and the beginning of the current year. Thus, the above balance sheet also represents the balance sheet at January 1 of the current year.

The following data apply to the entity for the current year:

Sales	$3,000,000
Purchase of additional inventory	2,100,000
Ending inventory at December 31 of the current year	1,650,000
Gain on sale of corporate stock on December 31 of the current year	20,000
Dividends received on stock prior to its sale	4,000
Tax-exempt interest received	2,200
Operating expenses	500,000
Interest paid on loan (no principal paid)*	30,000
Distribution on December 31 of the current year:	
Sarah	50,000
Rex	50,000

*For simplicity, assume all the $30,000 interest expense pertains to business (and not to investments).

Sarah and Rex actively manage the entity's business, and the business does not qualify for the U.S. production activities deduction. At the individual level, Sarah and Rex are each single with no dependents. Each individual claims a standard deduction and one personal exemption (if applicable). Neither individual has income from sources other than listed above.

a. First, assume the entity is a regular C corporation and the distributions are dividends to Sarah and Rex. For the current year, determine the following:
  (1) The corporation's taxable income and tax liability.
  (2) Sarah's and Rex's individual AGI, taxable income, and tax liability.
  (3) The total tax liability for the corporation and its owners.

b. Next, assume the entity is a partnership. For the current year, determine the following:
  (1) Partnership ordinary income and each partner's share of partnership ordinary income.
  (2) Partnership separately stated items and each partner's share of each item.
  (3) Sarah's and Rex's AGI, taxable income, and total tax liability. Assume each partner will incur a $15,000 self-employment tax.
  (4) Each partner's basis in the partnership (outside basis) at the end of the current year.

c. Based on your analysis for the current year, which entity is better from an overall tax perspective? What are the shortcomings of examining only one year?

d. Given the corporate form, explain how the corporation can restructure the $50,000 distribution to each individual to reduce the overall tax liability.

TAX FORM/RETURN PREPARATION PROBLEM

C:9-57 The Dapper-Dons Partnership (employer identification no. 89-3456798) was formed ten years ago as a general partnership to custom tailor men's clothing. Dapper-Dons is located at 123 Flamingo Drive in Miami, Florida 33131. Bob Dapper (Social Security No. 654-32-1098) manages the business and has a 40% capital and profits interest. His address is 709 Brumby Way, Miami, Florida 33131. Jeremy Dons (Social Security No. 354-12-6531) owns the remaining 60% interest but is not active in the business. His address is 807 9th Avenue, North Miami, Florida 33134. The partnership values its inventory using the cost method and did not change the method used during the current year. The partnership uses the accrual method of accounting. Because of its simplicity, the partnership is not subject to the partnership audit procedures. The partnership has no foreign partners, no foreign transactions, no interests in foreign trusts, and no foreign financial accounts. This partnership is neither a tax shelter nor a publicly traded partnership. No changes in ownership of partnership interests occurred during the current year. The partnership made cash distributions of $155,050 and $232,576 to Dapper and Dons, respectively, on December 30 of the current year. It made no other property distributions. Financial statements for the current year are presented in Tables C:9-1 and C:9-2. Assume that Dapper-Dons' business qualifies as a U.S. production activity and that its qualified production activities income is $600,000. The partnership uses the small business simplified overall method for reporting these activities (see discussion for Line 13d of Schedules K and K-1 in the Form 1065 instructions).

Prepare a current year partnership tax return for Dapper-Dons Partnership.

▼ **TABLE C:9-1**
Dapper-Dons Partnership Income Statement for the 12 Months Ending December 31 of the Current Year (Problem C:9-57)

Sales		$2,350,000
Returns and allowances		(20,000)
		$2,330,000
Beginning inventory (FIFO method)	$ 200,050	
Purchases	624,000	
Labor	600,000	
Supplies	42,000	
Other costs[a]	12,000	
Goods available for sale	$1,478,050	
Ending inventory[b]	(146,000)	(1,332,050)
Gross profit		$ 997,950
Salaries for employees other than partners (W-2 wages)	$51,000	
Guaranteed payment for Dapper	85,000	
Utilities expense	46,428	
Depreciation (MACRS depreciation is $74,311)[c]	49,782	
Automobile expense	12,085	
Office supplies expense	4,420	
Advertising expense	85,000	
Bad debt expense	2,100	
Interest expense (all trade- or business-related)	45,000	
Rent expense	7,400	
Travel expense (meals cost $4,050 of this amount)	11,020	
Repairs and maintenance expense	68,300	
Accounting and legal expense	3,600	
Charitable contributions[d]	16,400	
Payroll taxes	5,180	
Other taxes (all trade- or business-related)	1,400	
Total expenses		494,115
Operating profit		$ 503,835
Other income and losses:		
Gain on sale of AB stock[e]	$ 18,000	
Loss on sale of CD stock[f]	(26,075)	
Sec. 1231 gain on sale of land[g]	5,050	
Interest on U.S. treasury bills for entire year ($80,000 face amount)	9,000	
Dividends from 15%-owned domestic corporation	11,000	16,975
Net income		$ 520,810

[a] Additional Sec. 263A costs of $7,000 for the current year are included in other costs.
[b] Ending inventory includes the appropriate Sec. 263A costs, and no further adjustment is needed to properly state cost of sales and inventories for tax purposes.
[c] The partnership reports a $10,000 positive AMT adjustment for property placed in service after 1986. Dapper-Dons acquired and placed in service $40,000 of rehabilitation expenditures for a certified historical property this year. The appropriate MACRS depreciation on the rehabilitation expenditures already is included in the MACRS depreciation total.
[d] The partnership made all contributions in cash to qualifying charities.
[e] The partnership purchased the AB stock as an investment two years ago on December 1 for $40,000 and sold it on June 14 of the current year for $58,000.
[f] The partnership purchased the CD stock as an investment on February 15 of the current year for $100,000 and sold it on August 1 for $73,925.
[g] The partnership use the land as a parking lot for the business. The partnership purchased the land four years ago for $30,000 and sold it on August 15 of the current year for $35,050.

▼ TABLE C:9-2

Dapper-Dons Partnership Balance Sheet for January 1 and December 31 of the Current Year (Problem C:9-57)

	Balance January 1	Balance December 31
Assets:		
Cash	$ 10,000	$ 40,000
Accounts receivable	72,600	150,100
Inventories	200,050	146,000
Marketable securities[a]	220,000	260,000
Building and equipment	374,600	465,000
Minus: Accumulated depreciation	(160,484)	(173,100)
Land	185,000	240,000
Total assets	$901,766	$1,128,000
Liabilities and equities:		
Accounts payable	$ 35,000	$ 46,000
Accrued salaries payable	14,000	18,000
Payroll taxes payable	3,416	7,106
Sales taxes payable	5,200	6,560
Mortgage and notes payable (current maturities)	44,000	52,000
Long-term debt	210,000	275,000
Capital:		
Dapper	236,060	289,334
Dons	354,090	434,000
Total liabilities and equities	$901,766	$1,128,000

[a] Short-term investment.

CASE STUDY PROBLEMS

C:9-58 Abe and Brenda formed the AB Partnership ten years ago as a general partnership and have been very successful with the business. However, in the current year, economic conditions caused them to lose significant amounts, but they expect the economy and their business to return to profitable operations by next year or the year after. Abe manages the partnership business and works in it full-time. Brenda has a full-time job as an accountant for a $39,000 annual salary, but she also works in the partnership occasionally. She estimates that she spent about 120 hours working in the partnership this year. Abe has a 40% profits interest, a 50% loss interest, and a basis in his partnership interest on December 31 (before considering this year's operations) of $81,000. Brenda has a 60% profits interest, a 50% loss interest, and a basis of $104,000 on December 31 (before considering this year's operations). The partnership has no liabilities at December 31. Neither Abe nor Brenda currently has other investments. The AB Partnership incurs the following amounts during the year.

Ordinary loss	$100,000
Sec. 1231 gain	10,000
Tax-exempt municipal bond income	14,000
Long-term capital loss	14,000
Short-term capital loss	136,000

Early next year, the AB Partnership is considering borrowing $100,000 from a local bank to be secured by a mortgage on a building owned by the partnership with $150,000 FMV.

Required: Prepare a presentation to be made to Abe and Brenda discussing this matter. Points that should be discussed include: What amounts should Abe and Brenda report on their income tax return for the current year from the AB Partnership? What are their bases in their partnership interests after taking all transactions into effect? What happens to any losses they cannot deduct in the current year? What planning opportunities are presented by the need to borrow money early next year? What planning ideas would you suggest for Brenda?

C:9-59 On the advice of his attorney, Dr. Andres, a local pediatrician, contributed several office buildings, which he had previously owned as sole proprietor, to a new Andres Partnership in which he became a one-third general partner. He gave the remaining limited partnership interests to his two sons, Miguel and Esteban. Last year, when the partnership was formed, the boys were 14 and 16. The real estate is well managed and extremely profitable. Dr. Andres regularly consults with a full-time hired manager about the business, but neither of his sons has any dealings with the partnership. Under the terms of the partnership agreement, the boys can sell their partnership interest to no one but their father. Distributions from the partnership have been large, and Dr. Andres has insisted that the boys put all their distributions into savings accounts to pay for their college education.

Last year's return (the partnership's first) was filed by Mr. Jones, a partner in the local CPA firm of Wise and Johnson. Mr. Jones, who was Dr. Andres's accountant for a decade, retired last summer. Dr. Andres's business is extremely profitable and is an important part of the client base of this small-town CPA firm. Ms. Watson, the young partner who has taken over Dr. Andres's account, asked John, a second-year staff accountant, to prepare the current year's partnership return.

John has done considerable research and is positive that the Andres Partnership does not qualify as a partnership at all because the father has retained too much control over the sons' interests. John has briefly talked to Mr. Jones about his concerns. Mr. Jones said he was really rushed in the prior year when he filed the partnership return and admitted he never looked into the question of whether the arrangement met the requirements for being taxed as a partnership. After hearing more of the details, Mr. Jones stated that John was probably correct in his conclusion. Dr. Andres's tax bill will be significantly larger if he has to pay tax on all the partnership's income. When John approached Ms. Watson with his conclusions, her response was, "Oh, no! Dr. Andres already is unhappy because Mr. Jones is no longer preparing his returns. He'll really be unhappy if we give him a big tax increase, too." She paused thoughtfully, and then went on. "My first thought is just to leave well enough alone and file the partnership return. Are you positive, John, that this won't qualify as a partnership? Think about it and let me know tomorrow."

Required: Prepare a list of points you want to go over with the tax partner that would support finding that the business activity is a partnership. Prepare a second list of points that would support finding that the business activity is not a partnership.

TAX RESEARCH PROBLEMS

C:9-60 Caitlin and Wally formed the C & W Partnership on September 20, 2007. Caitlin contributed cash of $195,000, and Wally contributed office furniture with a FMV of $66,000. He bought the furniture for $60,000 on January 5, 2007, and placed it in service on that date. Wally will not claim a Sec. 179 expense deduction on the furniture. He also contributed an office building and land with a combined FMV of $129,000. The land's FMV is $9,000. Wally bought the land in 2000 for $8,000 and had the building constructed for $100,000. The building was placed in service in June 2003.

Required: Your tax manager has asked you to prepare a schedule for the file indicating the basis of property at the time of contribution that Wally contributed, the depreciation for each piece of property that the partnership can claim, and the allocation of the depreciation to the two partners. Also indicate the amount and type of any recapture to which the contributed property may be subject at the time of the contribution and at a later time when the partnership sells the property. Your tax manager knows that, under Reg. Sec. 1.704-3, several alternatives exist for allocating depreciation relating to contributed property. He remembers that the Treasury Regulations describe a traditional method and a couple of others, but he's not sure what method applies in this situation. He wants you to check the alternatives and indicate which method should be used. Be certain to clearly label your schedule so that anyone who looks at the file later can determine where your numbers came from and the authority for your calculations. The manager has suggested that, at a minimum, you consult the following authorities:

- IRC Secs. 1(h), 168, 704, 1231, 1245
- Prop. Reg. Sec. 1.168-5(b)

- Reg. Sec. 1.704-1(b)(2)(iv)(g)(3)
- Reg. Sec. 1.704-3

C:9-61 Your clients, Lisa and Matthew, plan to form Lima General Partnership. Lisa will contribute $50,000 cash to Lima for a 50% interest in capital and profits. Matthew will contribute land having a $35,000 adjusted basis and a $50,000 FMV to Lima for the remaining 50% interest in capital and profits. Lima will borrow additional funds of $100,000 from a bank on a recourse basis and then will subdivide and sell the land. Prepare a draft memorandum for your tax manager's signature outlining the tax treatment for the partnership formation transaction. As part of your memorandum, compare the reporting of this transaction on the tax and financial accounting books. References:

- IRC Sec. 721
- APB, *Opinions of the Accounting Principles Board No. 29* [Accounting for Nonmonetary Transactions]

C:9-62 Almost two years ago, the DEF Partnership was formed when Demetrius, Ebony, and Farouk each contributed $100,000 in cash. They are equal general partners in the real estate partnership, which has a December 31 year-end. The partnership uses the accrual method of accounting for financial accounting purposes but uses the cash method of accounting for tax purposes. The first year of operations resulted in a $50,000 loss. Because the real estate market plummeted, the second year of operations will result in an even larger ordinary loss. On November 30, calculations reveal that the year's loss is likely to be $100,000 for financial accounting purposes. Financial accounting results for the year are as follows:

	Quarter			
	First	*Second*	*Third*	*Fourth**
Revenue	$40,000	$60,000	$80,000	$100,000
Maintenance expense	(30,000)	(58,000)	(70,000)	(85,000)
Interest expense	(10,000)	(30,000)	(35,000)	(50,000)
Utilities expense	(3,000)	(3,000)	(3,000)	(3,000)
Projected loss	($ 3,000)	($31,000)	($28,000)	($38,000)

* Fourth quarter results are the sum of actual October and November results along with estimates for December results. December estimates are revenue, $33,000; maintenance, $60,000; interest, $20,000; and utilities, $1,000.

Cash has been short throughout the second year of operations, so more than $65,000 of expenses for second year operations have resulted in bills that are currently due or overdue. The unpaid bills are for July 1 through November 30 interest on a loan from the bank. In addition, all but essential maintenance has been postponed during the fourth quarter so that most of the fourth quarter maintenance is scheduled to be completed during December.

The DEF partners wants to attract a new partner to obtain additional capital. Raj is interested in investing $100,000 as a limited partner in the DEF Partnership if a good deal can be arranged. Raj would have a 25% profits and loss interest in the partnership but would expect something extra for the current year. In the current tax year, Raj has passive income of more than $200,000 from other sources, so he would like to have large passive losses allocated to him from DEF.

Required: Your tax partner has asked you to prepare a memorandum suggesting a plan to maximize the amount of current year loss that can be allocated to Raj. Assume none of the partners performs more than one-half of his or her personal service time in connection with real estate trades or businesses in which he or she materially participates. She reminded you to consider the varying interest rules for allocating losses to new partners found in Sec. 706 and to look into the possibilities of somehow capitalizing on the cash method of accounting or of using a special allocation. She wants you to be sure to check all the relevant case law for the plan you suggest.

C:9-63 Alice, Beth, and Carl formed the ABC partnership early in 2006. Alice and Beth each contributed $100,000 for their partnership interests, and Carl contributed land having a $100,000 FMV and $160,000 adjusted basis. The land remained a capital asset to the partnership. Late in 2007, Carl sold his interest in the partnership to Dan for $100,000.

Shortly after that transaction, the partnership sold the land to an outside party for $100,000. The partnership has no Sec. 754 election in effect (discussed in Chapter C:10). The partners have asked that you explain the consequences these transactions have to the partnership and the partners, especially Carl and Dan. At a minimum, you should consult the following resources:

- IRC Sec. 704
- Reg. Sec. 1.704-3(a)

10

CHAPTER

SPECIAL PARTNERSHIP ISSUES

LEARNING OBJECTIVES

After studying this chapter, you should be able to

1. Determine the amount and character of gain or loss a partner recognizes in a nonliquidating partnership distribution
2. Determine the partner's basis of assets received in a nonliquidating partnership distribution
3. Identify the partnership's Sec. 751 assets
4. Determine the tax implications of a cash distribution when the partnership has Sec. 751 assets
5. Determine the amount and character of gain or loss a partner recognizes in a liquidating partnership distribution
6. Determine the partner's basis of assets received in a liquidating distribution
7. Determine the amount and character of the gain or loss recognized when a partner retires from the partnership or dies
8. Determine whether a partnership has terminated for tax purposes
9. Understand the effect of optional and mandatory basis adjustments
10. Determine the appropriate reporting for the income of an electing large partnership

CHAPTER OUTLINE

Chapter C:10 continues the discussion of partnership taxation. The chapter first explains simple nonliquidating distributions and then discusses more complex nonliquidating and liquidating distributions. The chapter also explains methods of disposing of a partnership interest, including sales of the partnership interest and the retirement or death of a partner as well as transactions that terminate the entire partnership.

Finally, the chapter examines special partnership forms. These forms include publicly traded partnerships, limited liability companies, limited liability partnerships, and electing large partnerships.

NONLIQUIDATING DISTRIBUTIONS

Distributions from a partnership fall into two categories: liquidating distributions and nonliquidating (or current) distributions. A **liquidating distribution** is a single distribution, or one of a planned series of distributions, that terminates a partner's entire interest in the partnership. All other distributions, including those that substantially reduce a partner's interest in the partnership, are governed by the **nonliquidating (current) distribution** rules.

Although the tax consequences of the two types of distributions are similar in many respects, they are sufficiently different to require separate study. The chapter first discusses simple current distributions. It then covers complex current distributions involving Sec. 751 property and liquidating distributions.

OBJECTIVE 1

Determine the amount and character of gain or loss a partner recognizes in a nonliquidating partnership distribution

RECOGNITION OF GAIN

A current distribution that does not bring Sec. 751 into play cannot result in the recognition of a loss by either the partnership or the partner who receives the distribution. Moreover, the partnership usually recognizes no gain on a current distribution (except for Sec. 751 property, defined later in this chapter). Under Sec. 731, partners who receive distributions recognize a gain if they receive money distributions that exceed their basis in the partnership. For distribution purposes, money includes cash, deemed cash from reductions in a partner's share of liabilities, and the fair market value (FMV) of marketable securities.

EXAMPLE C:10-1 ▶

Melissa is a 30% partner in the ABC Real Estate Partnership until Josh is admitted as a partner in exchange for a cash contribution. After Josh's admission, Melissa holds a 20% interest. Because of large loss deductions, Melissa's basis (before Josh's admission) is $20,000 including her 30% interest in the partnership liabilities of $250,000. She is deemed to receive a cash distribution equal to the $25,000 [(0.30 − 0.20) × $250,000] reduction in her share of partnership liabilities. Because the cash distribution exceeds her basis, Melissa recognizes a $5,000 ($25,000 distribution − $20,000 basis) gain. ◀

KEY POINT

Reductions in a partner's share of liabilities are treated as cash distributions.

SELF-STUDY QUESTION

Can gain or loss be recognized in a current distribution?

ANSWER

Current distributions with no Sec. 751 implications do not create losses to either the partner or partnership. Ignoring Sec. 751, the partnership recognizes no gains. However, a partner recognizes a gain if the partner receives a money distribution exceeding his or her basis in his or her partnership interest. A distribution also may trigger recognition of precontribution gain or loss for a partner.

Precontribution Gain Recognition. Although a current distribution usually causes gain recognition only if money distributions exceed a partner's basis, a distribution also may trigger recognition of previously unrecognized precontribution gain or loss. A precontribution gain or loss is the difference between the FMV and adjusted basis of property when contributed to the partnership. Two different distribution events may trigger recognition of precontribution gain or loss.

First, if a partner contributes property with a deferred precontribution gain or loss, the contributing partner must recognize the precontribution gain or loss when the partnership distributes the property to any other partner within seven years of the contribution. The amount of precontribution gain or loss recognized by the contributing partner equals the amount of precontribution gain or loss remaining that would have been allocated to the contributing partner had the property instead been sold for its FMV on the distribution date. The partnership's basis in the property immediately before the distribution and the contributing partner's basis in his or her partnership interest are both increased for any gain recognized or decreased for any loss recognized.[1]

EXAMPLE C:10-2 ▶ Several years ago, Michael contributed land with a $3,000 basis and a $7,000 FMV to the AB Partnership. In the current year, the partnership distributed the land to Stephen, another partner in the partnership. At the time of the distribution, the land had a $9,000 FMV. Stephen recognizes no gain on the distribution. Michael must recognize his $4,000 precontribution gain when the partnership distributes the property to Stephen. Michael increases the basis in his partnership interest by $4,000, and the partnership's basis in the land immediately before the distribution increases by $4,000. This increase in the partnership's basis for the land also increases the land's basis to the distributee partner (Stephen). ◀

KEY POINT

Note the differences in the two distributions that cause a contributing partner to recognize remaining precontribution gains. In the first distribution, the *contributed property* is distributed to *another partner.* In the second distribution, *property other than the contributed property* is distributed to the *contributing partner.*

Second, under Sec. 737, property distributions to a partner may cause the partner to recognize his or her remaining precontribution gain if the FMV of the distributed property exceeds the partner's basis in his or her partnership interest before the distribution. The gain recognized under Sec. 737 is the lesser of the remaining precontribution net gain or the excess of the FMV of the distributed property over the adjusted basis of the partnership interest immediately before the property distribution (but after reduction for any money distributed at the same time).[2] The remaining precontribution gain is the net of all precontribution gains and losses for property contributed to the partnership in the seven years immediately preceding the distribution to the extent that such precontribution gains and losses have not already been recognized. The character of the recognized gain is determined by referencing the type of property that had precontribution gains or losses. The gain recognized under Sec. 737 is in addition to any gain recognized on the same distribution because of distributed cash exceeding the partner's basis in his or her partnership interest.

EXAMPLE C:10-3 ▶ Several years ago, Sergio contributed land, a capital asset, with a $20,000 FMV and a $15,000 basis to the STU Partnership in exchange for a 30% general interest in the partnership. The partnership still holds the land on January 31 of the current year, and none of the $5,000 precontribution gain has been recognized. On January 31 of the current year, Sergio has a $40,000 basis in his partnership interest when he receives an $8,000 cash distribution plus property purchased by the partnership with a $45,000 FMV and a $30,000 basis. Under the Sec. 731 distribution rules Sergio recognizes no gain because the cash distribution ($8,000) does not exceed Sergio's predistribution basis in his partnership interest ($40,000). However, under Sec. 737 he recognizes gain equal to the lesser of the $5,000 remaining precontribution gain or the $13,000 difference between the FMV of the property distributed ($45,000) and the basis of the partnership interest after the cash distribution but before any property distributions ($32,000 = $40,000 adjusted basis − $8,000 cash distributed). Thus, Sergio recognizes a $5,000 capital gain. ◀

EXAMPLE C:10-4 ▶ Assume the same facts as in Example C:10-3 except the distribution was $20,000 in cash and $23,000 (FMV) in marketable securities, which are treated like money, plus the property. Sergio recognizes a $3,000 gain under Sec. 731 because he received a money distribution exceeding his basis in the partnership interest ($43,000 money distribution − $40,000 adjusted basis before distributions). Under Sec. 737 he also recognizes gain equal to the lesser of the remaining precontribution gain ($5,000) or the excess of the FMV of the property distributed ($45,000) over the zero basis of the partnership interest after money distributions but before property distributions ($0 = $40,000 adjusted basis − $43,000 money distributed). Sergio, therefore, recognizes both a $5,000 capital gain under Sec. 737 and a $3,000 capital gain under Sec. 731. ◀

If a partner recognizes gain under Sec. 737, that gain increases the partner's basis in his or her partnership interest (illustrated in the next section). Further, the recognized gain also increases the partnership's basis in the property that was the source of the precontribution gain.

---

[1] Sec. 704(c). See Chapter C:9 for a discussion of precontribution gains and losses.

[2] Section 737 does not apply if the property distributed was contributed by this same partner. Only the provisions of Sec. 731 would be considered in such a situation.

EXAMPLE C:10-5 ▶ Assume the same facts as in Example C:10-3. At the time Sergio contributed the land, the partnership assumed Sergio's $15,000 basis in the land. Now, Sergio's $5,000 Sec. 737 gain increases the partnership's basis in the land to $20,000. ◀

OBJECTIVE 2

Determine the partner's basis of assets received in a nonliquidating partnership distribution

BASIS EFFECTS OF DISTRIBUTIONS

In general, the partner's basis for property distributed by the partnership carries over from the partnership. The partner's basis in the partnership interest is reduced by the amount of money received and by the partner's basis in the distributed property.

EXAMPLE C:10-6 ▶ Jack has a $35,000 basis for his interest in the MLV Partnership before receiving a current distribution consisting of $7,000 in money, accounts receivable having a zero basis to the partnership, and land having an $18,000 basis to the partnership. Jack takes a carryover basis in the land and receivables. Following the distribution, his basis in the partnership interest is calculated as follows:

Predistribution basis in partnership interest		$35,000
Minus:	Money received	(7,000)
	Carryover basis in receivables	(–0–)
	Carryover basis in land	(18,000)
Postdistribution basis in partnership interest		$10,000

◀

The total bases of all distributed property in the partner's hands is limited to the partner's predistribution basis in his or her partnership interest plus any gain recognized on the distribution under Sec. 737.[3] If the partner's predistribution basis plus Sec. 737 gain is less than the sum of the money received plus the carryover basis of any nonmoney property received, the order in which the basis is allocated becomes crucial. First, cash and deemed cash distributions reduce the partner's basis in his or her partnership interest. Next, the remaining basis is allocated to provide a carryover of the partnership's basis for receivables and inventory. If the partner's predistribution basis is not large enough to allow a carryover of the partnership's basis for these two property categories, the partner's remaining basis is allocated among the receivables and inventory items based on both the partnership's basis in the assets and their FMV.[4] First, each asset is given its basis to the partnership. Then, the difference between the carryover basis from the partnership and the partner's basis in the partnership interest is cal-

WHAT WOULD YOU DO IN THIS SITUATION?

You have done the personal and business tax work for Betty and Thelma for a number of years. Betty and Thelma are partners in a retail shop. In addition, the two have decided they want to exchange some property that is not associated with their partnership. Betty wants to exchange undeveloped land she personally holds as an investment, having a $40,000 FMV and a $10,000 adjusted basis, for machinery and office equipment that Thelma owns but no longer uses. Thelma's machinery and office equipment in total have a $40,000 FMV and a $28,000 adjusted basis. Recently, a friend told Betty that several years ago he and an associate did a similar swap tax-free by contributing both pieces of property to be exchanged to a partnership, having the partnership hold the property for a few months, and then having the partnership distribute the property to the partner who wanted to receive it. The friend said the arrangement was tax-free because the initial transfer qualified as a tax-free contribution of property to the partnership in exchange for a partnership interest, and the distribution was tax-free because it was simply a pro rata property distribution made by the partnership. Thelma and Betty have come to you asking that you structure their exchange using their retail shop partnership so that the transfer will be tax-free also. How should you respond to their request?

---

[3] Secs. 732(a)(2) and 737(c). Marketable securities have a basis equal to their Sec. 732 basis plus any gain recognized under Sec. 731(c).

[4] Sec. 732(c).

culated. A decrease must be allocated if the partner's basis in the partnership interest (after any money distribution) is less than the carryover basis from the partnership. The decrease is first allocated to any asset that has declined in value in an amount equal to the smaller of the decline in value for the asset or the asset's share of the decrease. If the decrease is not fully used at this point in the calculation, the remaining decrease is allocated to the assets based on their relative adjusted bases at this point in the calculation.

EXAMPLE C:10-7 ▶

KEY POINT

If different types of property are distributed, the partnership distribution rules assume that the property is distributed in the following order: (1) cash, (2) receivables and inventory, and (3) other property. This ordering can affect both the recognition of gain to the partner and the basis the partner takes in the distributed property.

Tracy has a $15,000 basis in her interest in the TP Partnership and no remaining precontribution gain immediately before receiving a current distribution that consists of $6,000 in money, power tools held as inventory with a $4,000 basis to the partnership and FMV of $3,500, and steel rod held as inventory with an $8,000 basis to the partnership and FMV of $9,200. The basis of the distributed property in Tracy's hands is determined as follows:

Predistribution basis in partnership interest	$15,000
Minus: Money received	(6,000)
Plus: Sec. 737 gain	–0–
Basis to be allocated	$ 9,000

The calculation of bases for the steel rod and power tools is as follows:

	Steel Rods	*Power Tools*	*Total*
FMV of asset	$9,200	$3,500	$12,700
Minus: Partnership's basis for asset	(8,000)	(4,000)	(12,000)
Difference	$1,200	($ 500)	$ 700
Step 1: Give each asset the partnership's basis for the asset	$8,000	$4,000	$12,000
Minus: Tracy's basis to be allocated			(9,000)
Decrease to allocate			$ 3,000
Step 2: Asset basis after Step 1	$8,000	$4,000	$12,000
Allocate the decrease first to assets that have declined in value	–0–	(500)	(500)
Adjusted bases at this point in the calculation	$8,000	$3,500	$11,500
Step 3: Allocate $2,500 remaining decrease based on relative adjusted bases at this point in the calculation	(1,739)[a]	(761)[b]	(2,500)
Tracy's bases in the assets	$6,261	$2,739	$ 9,000

[a][$8,000 ÷ ($8,000 + $3,500)] × $2,500 = $1,739
[b][$3,500 ÷ ($8,000 + $3,500)] × $2,500 = $ 761

This process results in Tracy's total basis in the two assets she receives being exactly equal to the $9,000 amount to be allocated. Moreover, Tracy's basis in her partnership interest is zero after the property distributions. ◀

EXAMPLE C:10-8 ▶

Assume the same facts as in Example C:10-7 except Tracy recognizes $1,000 of remaining precontribution gain under Sec. 737 as a result of the distribution. The basis of the distributed property in Tracy's hands is determined as follows:

Predistribution basis in partnership interest	$15,000
Minus: Money received	(6,000)
Plus: Sec. 737 gain	1,000
Amount to be allocated	$10,000

The calculation of the basis for the steel rods and power tools are as follows:

	Steel Rods	*Power Tools*	*Total*
FMV of asset	$9,200	$3,500	$12,700
Minus: Partnership's basis for asset	(8,000)	(4,000)	(12,000)
Difference	$1,200	($ 500)	$ 700

Step 1: Give each asset the partnership's basis for the asset	$8,000	$4,000	$12,000
Minus: Tracy's basis to be allocated			(10,000)
Decrease to allocate			$ 2,000
Step 2: Adjusted basis after Step 1	$8,000	$4,000	$12,000
Allocate the decrease first to assets that have declined in value	-0-	(500)	(500)
Adjusted basis at this point in the calculation	$8,000	$3,500	$11,500
Step 3: Allocate $1,500 remaining decrease based on relative adjusted bases at this point in the calculation	(1,043)[a]	(457)[b]	(1,500)
Tracy's bases in the assets	$6,957	$3,043	$10,000

[a][$8,000 ÷ ($8,000 + $3,500)] × $1,500 = $1,043
[b][$3,500 ÷ ($8,000 + $3,500)] × $1,500 = $ 457

Again, Tracy's basis in her partnership interest is zero after the distributions. ◀

If a partner's predistribution basis plus Sec. 737 gain recognized exceeds the sum of his or her money distribution plus the carryover basis for any receivables and inventory, a carryover basis is allocated to the other property received. If the partner has an insufficient basis in the partnership interest to provide a carryover basis for all the distributed property, the remaining basis for the partnership interest is allocated to the other property first to any decrease in FMV below basis and then based on the relative bases of such property in the partnership's hands just as was calculated above.

SELF-STUDY QUESTION

Assume the same facts as in Example C:10-9 except the basis in the two parcels of land is only $4,000 in total. What are the tax consequences of the distribution?

ANSWER

If the basis in the two parcels of land were only $4,000 in total, the partner would take a $4,000 carryover basis in the land and retain a $2,000 basis in his partnership interest.

EXAMPLE C:10-9 ▶ John has a $15,000 basis in his partnership interest and no remaining precontribution gain before receiving the following property as a current distribution:

Property	*Basis to the Partnership*	*FMV*
Money	$ 5,000	$5,000
Inventory	4,000	4,500
Land parcel 1	4,500	6,000
Land parcel 2	3,000	4,000

John's basis in his distributed property is calculated as follows:

Predistribution basis	$15,000
Minus: Money received	(5,000)
Plus: Sec. 737 gain	-0-
Basis for nonmoney property	$10,000
Minus: Carryover basis for inventory	(4,000)
Remaining basis to be allocated	$ 6,000

The calculation of the basis for the two parcels of land is as follows:

	Parcel One	*Parcel Two*	*Total*
FMV of asset	$6,000	$4,000	$10,000
Minus: Partnership's basis for asset	(4,500)	(3,000)	(7,500)
Difference	$1,500	$1,000	$ 2,500
Step 1: Give each asset the partnership's basis for the asset	$4,500	$3,000	$ 7,500
Minus: John's basis to be allocated			(6,000)
Decrease to allocate			$ 1,500
Step 2: Adjusted basis after Step 1	$4,500	$3,000	$ 7,500
Allocate the decrease first to assets that have declined in value	-0-	-0-	-0-
Adjusted basis at this point in the calculation	$4,500	$3,000	$ 7,500

Step 3: Allocate $1,500 remaining decrease based on relative adjusted bases at this point in the calculation	(900)[a]	(600)[b]	(1,500)
John's bases in the assets	$3,600	$2,400	$ 6,000

[a][$4,500 ÷ ($4,500 + $3,000)] × $1,500 = $900
[b][$3,000 ÷ ($4,500 + $3,000)] × $1,500 = $600

John's basis in his partnership interest is zero after the distribution because all its basis is allocated to the money and other property received. ◀

TYPICAL MISCONCEPTION

The partner's basis in his or her partnership interest cannot be less than zero. However, a partner's capital account can be less than zero. One must distinguish between references to a partner's basis in his or her partnership interest (his outside basis) and the balance in a partner's capital account.

Two other points should be noted. First, even when a partner's basis in the partnership interest is reduced to zero by a current distribution, he or she retains an interest in the partnership. If the partner has no remaining interest in the partnership (as opposed to a zero basis), the distribution would have been a liquidating distribution. Second, the distributee's basis in property distributed as a current distribution is always equal to or less than the carryover basis. Basis for distributed property cannot be increased above the carryover basis amount when received as a nonliquidating distribution.

HOLDING PERIOD AND CHARACTER OF DISTRIBUTED PROPERTY

The partner's holding period for property distributed as a current distribution includes the partnership's holding period for such property.[5] The length of time the partner owns the partnership interest is irrelevant when determining the holding period for the distributed property. Thus, if a new partner receives a distribution of property the partnership held for two years before he or she became a partner, the new partner's holding period for the distributed property is deemed to begin when the partnership purchased the property (i.e., two years ago) rather than on the more recent date when the partner purchases the partnership interest.

KEY POINT

Consistent with the discussion in Chapter C:9, certain rules ensure that neither contributions to nor distributions from a partnership can be used to alter the character of certain gains and losses on property held by the partnership or by the individual partners.

A series of rules regulate the character of the gain or loss recognized when a partner subsequently sells or exchanges certain property distributed to the partner. These rules are similar to provisions regulating the character of gain or loss on contributed property.

If the partnership distributes property that is an unrealized receivable in its hands, the distributee partner recognizes ordinary income or loss on a subsequent sale of that property. This ordinary income or loss treatment occurs without regard to the character of the property in the distributee partner's hands or the length of time the partner holds the property before its disposition.[6]

If the partnership distributes property that is inventory in its hands, the distributee partner recognizes ordinary income or loss on a subsequent sale that occurrs within five years of the distribution date.[7] The inventory rule mandates the ordinary income or loss result only for the five-year period beginning on the distribution date. After five years, the character of the gain or loss recognized on the sale of such property is determined by its character in the hands of the distributee partner.

NONLIQUIDATING DISTRIBUTIONS WITH SEC. 751

OBJECTIVE 3

Identify the partnership's Sec. 751 assets

So far, the discussion of current distributions has ignored the existence of the Sec. 751 property rules. Now, we must expand our discussion to include them.

SECTION 751 ASSETS DEFINED

Section 751 assets include unrealized receivables and inventory. These two categories encompass all property likely to produce ordinary income when sold or collected. Each of these categories must be carefully defined before further discussion of Sec. 751.

---

[5] Sec. 735(b).
[6] Sec. 735(a)(1).
[7] Sec. 735(a)(2).

KEY POINT

Section 751 property represents property in a partnership that is likely to produce ordinary income or loss. The application of Sec. 751 in conjunction with partnership distributions or sales of a partnership interest is of concern to individual partners because the rules may trigger ordinary income recognition rather than capital gains.

UNREALIZED RECEIVABLES. **Unrealized receivables** includes a much broader spectrum of property than the name implies. Unrealized receivables are certain rights to payments to be received by a partnership to the extent they are not already included in income under the partnership's accounting methods. They include rights to payments for services performed or to be performed as well as rights to payment for goods delivered or to be delivered (other than capital assets). A common example of unrealized receivables is the accounts receivable of a cash method partnership.

In addition to rights to receive payments for goods and services, the term unrealized receivables includes most potential ordinary income recapture items. A primary example of this type of unrealized receivable is the potential Sec. 1245 or 1250 recapture on the partnership's depreciable property, which is the amount of depreciation that would be recaptured as ordinary income under Sec. 1245 or 1250 if the partnership sold property at its FMV.[8]

EXAMPLE C:10-10 ▶ The LK Partnership has two assets: $10,000 cash and a machine having a $14,000 basis and a $20,000 FMV. The partnership has claimed $8,000 of depreciation on the machine since its purchase. If the partnership sells the machine for its FMV, all $6,000 of the gain would be recaptured as ordinary income under Sec. 1245. Therefore, the LK Partnership has a $6,000 unrealized receivable item. ◀

SELF-STUDY QUESTION

What is included in the definition of unrealized receivables?

ANSWER

Unrealized receivables include not only the obvious cash method accounts receivable that have yet to be recognized but also most of the potential ordinary income recapture provisions. Therefore, the term unrealized receivables is broader than it may appear.

The definition of unrealized receivables is not limited to Sec. 1245 and 1250 depreciation recapture. Among the other recapture provisions creating unrealized receivables are Sec. 617(d) (mining property), Sec. 1252 (farmland), and Sec. 1254 (oil, gas, and geothermal property). Assets covered by Sec. 1278 (market discount bonds) and Sec. 1283 (short-term obligations) generate unrealized receivables to the extent the partnership would recognize ordinary income if it sold the asset. This type of unrealized receivable is deemed to have a zero basis.

INVENTORY. Inventory is equally surprising in its breadth. Inventory for purposes of Sec. 751 includes three major types of property:

- Items held for sale in the normal course of partnership business
- Any other property that, if sold by the partnership, would not be considered a capital asset or Sec. 1231 property
- Any other property held by the partnership that, if held by the selling or distributee partner, would be property of the two types listed above[9]

TYPICAL MISCONCEPTION

The definition of inventory is broadly construed by Sec. 751. In fact, for purposes of determining whether inventory is substantially appreciated, even unrealized receivables are treated as inventory items.

In short, cash, capital assets, and Sec. 1231 assets are the only properties that are not inventory.

For purposes of calculating the impact of Sec. 751 on distributions, inventory is considered a Sec. 751 asset only if the inventory is **substantially appreciated.** (This substantially appreciated rule does not apply to sales of partnership interests, discussed later in this chapter.) The test to determine whether inventory is substantially appreciated (and therefore falling under Sec. 751) is purely mechanical. Inventory is substantially appreciated if its FMV exceeds 120% of its adjusted basis to the partnership. For purposes of testing whether the inventory is substantially appreciated (but *only* for that purpose), inventory also includes unrealized receivables. The inclusion of unrealized receivables in the definition of inventory increases the likelihood that the inventory will be substantially appreciated.

EXAMPLE C:10-11 ▶ The ABC Partnership owns the following assets on December 31:

Assets	*Basis*	*FMV*
Cash	$10,000	$ 10,000
Unrealized receivables	–0–	40,000
Inventory	30,000	34,000
Land (Sec. 1231 property)	40,000	70,000
Total	$80,000	$154,000

---

[8] Sec. 751(c). Unrealized receivables may have basis if costs or expenses have been incurred but not taken into account under the partnership's method of accounting (e.g., the basis of property sold in a nondealer installment sale).

[9] Sec. 751(d)(2).

OBJECTIVE 4

Determine the tax implications of a cash distribution when the partnership has Sec. 751 assets

For purposes of the substantially appreciated inventory test, both ABC's unrealized receivables and inventory are included. The inventory's $74,000 FMV exceeds 120% of its adjusted basis [($30,000 + 0) × 1.20 = $36,000]. Therefore, the ABC Partnership has substantially appreciated inventory. ◀

EXCHANGE OF SEC. 751 ASSETS AND OTHER PROPERTY

A current distribution receives treatment under Sec. 751 only if the partnership has Sec. 751 assets and an exchange of Sec. 751 property for non-Sec. 751 property occurs. Accordingly, if a partnership does not have *both* Sec. 751 property and other property, the rules discussed above for simple current distributions control the taxation of the distribution. Similarly, a distribution that is proportionate to all partners or (1) consists of only the partner's share of either Sec. 751 property or non-Sec. 751 property and (2) does not reduce the partner's interest in other property is not affected by the Sec. 751 rules.

However, any portion of the distribution that represents an exchange of Sec. 751 property for non-Sec. 751 property must be isolated and is not treated as a distribution at all. Instead, it is treated as a sale between the partnership and the partner, and any gain or loss realized on the sale transaction is fully recognized.[10] The character of the recognized gain or loss depends on the character of the property deemed sold. For the party deemed the seller of the Sec. 751 assets, the gain or loss is ordinary income or loss.

TYPICAL MISCONCEPTION

Even if a partnership has Sec. 751 property, Sec. 751 is not applicable as long as a partner's interest in the ordinary income type assets is not altered. However, if a distribution of the partnership assets is disproportionate, Sec. 751 treats that portion of the distribution as a deemed sale between the partnership and the distributee partner, with the corresponding income or loss being recognized.

Analyzing the transaction to determine what property was involved in the Sec. 751 transaction is best accomplished by using an orderly, step-by-step approach.

STEP 1: DIVIDE THE ASSETS INTO SEC. 751 ASSETS AND NON-SEC. 751 ASSETS. Inventory must be tested at this time to see whether it is substantially appreciated to know whether it is a Sec. 751 asset for distribution purposes.

STEP 2: DEVELOP A SCHEDULE, SUCH AS THE ONE IN TABLE C:10-1, TO DETERMINE WHETHER THE PARTNER EXCHANGED SEC. 751 ASSETS FOR NON-SEC. 751 ASSETS OR VICE VERSA. This schedule must be based on the FMV of all the partnership's assets. To make the determination, compare the partner's interest in the partnership's assets before the distribution with his or her interest in the assets after the distribution. This part of the analysis assumes a hypothetical nontaxable pro rata distribution equal to the partner's decreased interest in the assets. We can see whether the partner exchanged Sec. 751 assets for non-Sec. 751 assets by comparing the hypothetical distribution with the actual distribution. Thus, in Table C:10-1,

KEY POINT

Steps 2 and 3 try to identify whether a disproportionate distribution of Sec. 751 assets has taken place. In Table C:10-1, if the column 5 total for Sec. 751 assets is zero, Sec. 751 is not applicable. But as the table illustrates, Anne received $10,000 more than her share of the partnership cash without receiving any of her $10,000 share of Sec. 751 assets.

- Column 1 represents the partner's interest (valued at FMV) in each asset before the distribution.
- Column 2 represents the partner's interest (valued at FMV) in each asset after the distribution.
- Column 3 shows a hypothetical proportionate distribution that would have occurred had the partner's ownership interest been reduced by the partner taking a pro rata share of each asset. (As such, the proportionate distribution would be nontaxable.)
- Column 4 shows the amounts actually distributed.
- Column 5 shows the difference between the hypothetical and actual distributions. This column indicates whether a Sec. 751 exchange has occurred (see Step 3).

STEP 3: ANALYZE COLUMN 5 TO DETERMINE WHETHER SEC. 751 ASSETS WERE EXCHANGED FOR NON-SEC. 751 ASSETS. If the column 5 total for the Sec. 751 assets section of Table C:10-1 is zero, no Sec. 751 exchange has occurred. The partner simply received an additional amount of one type of Sec. 751 asset in exchange for relinquishing an interest in some other type of Sec. 751 asset. For example, no Sec. 751 exchange occurs if a partner exchanges an interest in substantially appreciated inventory for an interest in unrealized receivables. However, if the column 5 total for the Sec. 751

[10] Sec. 751(b).

▼ **TABLE C:10-1**
Analysis of Sec. 751 Nonliquidating Distribution (Example C:10-12)

	Beginning Partnership Amount[a]	(1) Anne's Interest Before Distribution[a] (1/3)	(2) Anne's Interest After Distribution[a] (1/5)	(3) Hypothetical Proportionate Distribution (3) = (1) − (2)[a]	(4) Actual Distribution[a]	(5) Difference[b] (5) = (4) − (3)
Sec. 751 assets:						
Unrealized receivables	$15,000	$ 5,000	$ 3,000	$ 2,000	$ –0–	$ (2,000)
Inventory	60,000	20,000	12,000	8,000	–0–	(8,000)
Total Sec. 751 assets	$75,000	$25,000	$15,000	$10,000	$ –0–	($ 10,000)
Non-Sec. 751 assets:						
Cash	$75,000	$25,000	$10,000[c]	$15,000	$25,000	$ 10,000
Total non-Sec. 751 assets	$75,000	$25,000	$10,000	$15,000	$25,000	$ 10,000

[a]Valued at fair market value.
[b]A negative amount means that Anne gave up her interest in a particular property. A positive amount means that she received more than her proportionate interest.
[c]One-fifth interest in remaining cash of $50,000.

assets is an amount other than zero, a Sec. 751 exchange has occurred. One (or more) Sec. 751 properties has been exchanged for one (or more) non-Sec. 751 properties.

EXAMPLE C:10-12 ▶ On January 1, the ABC Partnership holds the assets listed below before making a $25,000 cash distribution to Anne that reduces her interest in the partnership from one-third to one-fifth.

Assets	*Basis*	*FMV*
Cash	$ 75,000	$ 75,000
Unrealized receivables	–0–	15,000
Inventory	30,000	60,000
Total	$105,000	$150,000

ABC owes no liabilities on January 1. Before the distribution, Anne has a $35,000 basis in her partnership interest. The following three steps indicate that a Sec. 751 exchange has occurred:

STEP 1. Determine ABC's Sec. 751 and non-Sec. 751 assets. ABC's Sec. 751 assets include the unrealized receivables and the substantially appreciated inventory. The cash is ABC's only non-Sec. 751 property.

STEP 2. Complete the table used to analyze the Sec. 751 distribution (see Table C:10-1).

STEP 3. Analyze column 5 of Table C:10-1 to see whether a Sec. 751 exchange has occurred. Because Anne's Sec. 751 asset total declined by $10,000, we know she gave up $10,000 of her proportionate interest in ABC's Sec. 751 assets in exchange for cash. ◀

ADDITIONAL COMMENT

Step 4 is crucial if a student is to understand the deemed sale that Sec. 751 creates. In Example C:10-13, Anne is treated as if she had exchanged her $10,000 interest in the unrealized receivables and inventory for $10,000 of cash. Thus, Anne has a taxable gain or loss on the deemed sale. To determine Anne's gain or loss on the deemed sale, the adjusted basis of the unrealized receivables and inventory equals whatever her basis would have been had the partnership actually distributed those assets to her.

STEP 4: DETERMINE THE GAIN OR LOSS ON THE SEC. 751 DEEMED SALE. We must assume that the exchange occurring in Step 3 above was a sale of the exchanged property between the partnership and the partner. This step follows logically from the premise that the partner "bargained" to receive the amounts actually distributed rather than a proportionate distribution. She sold her interest in some assets to receive more than her proportionate interest in other assets. As with any sale, the gain (or loss) equals the difference between the FMV of the property received and the adjusted basis of the property given up. Note that, up to this point, we have been dealing only in terms of the FMV, so the adjusted basis of property given up must be determined as if the hypothetical distribution actually had occurred.

EXAMPLE C:10-13 ▶ Assume the same facts as in Example C:10-12. The Sec. 751 sale portion of the distribution is analyzed as Anne receiving $10,000 more cash than her proportionate share and giving up a $2,000 (FMV) interest in the unrealized receivables and an $8,000 (FMV) interest in the inventory. By examining the balance sheet, we can see that the partnership's bases for the unrealized receivables and inventory are $0 and $4,000 [$8,000 × ($30,000 ÷ $60,000)]. If Anne received these properties in a current distribution, her basis would be the same as the property's basis in the partnership's hands, or $0 and $4,000, respectively. Therefore, Anne's deemed sale of the Sec. 751 assets is analyzed as follows:

Amount realized (cash)	$10,000
Minus: Adjusted basis of property deemed sold	(4,000)
Realized and recognized gain	$ 6,000

The character of the recognized gain depends on the character of the property deemed sold (in this case, the unrealized receivables and inventory). Therefore, Anne's $6,000 gain is ordinary income. ◀

STEP 5: DETERMINE THE IMPACT OF THE CURRENT DISTRIBUTION. The last step in analyzing the distribution's effect on the partner is to determine the impact of the portion of the distribution that is not a Sec. 751 exchange. This distribution is treated exactly like any other nonliquidating distribution.

EXAMPLE C:10-14 ▶ Assume the same facts as in Examples C:10-12 and C:10-13. Examining the distribution, we see in column 4 of Table C:10-1 that, as part of the Sec. 751 exchange, Anne received only $10,000 of the $25,000 cash actually distributed. The remaining $15,000 represents a current distribution. As described earlier in this chapter, a partner recognizes gain on a current distribution only if the money distributed exceeds his or her basis in the partnership interest. Thus, Anne recognizes no gain because she has a $16,000 basis in the partnership interest immediately after the current distribution. This basis is calculated as follows:

Predistribution basis for partnership interest	$35,000
Minus: Basis of property deemed distributed in Sec. 751 exchange ($0 unrealized receivables + $4,000 inventory)	(4,000)
Basis before current distribution	$31,000
Minus: Money distributed	(15,000)
Postdistribution basis of partnership interest	$16,000

After the entire distribution is complete, Anne owns a one-fifth partnership interest with a basis of $16,000 and has $25,000 in cash. In addition, she has recognized $6,000 of ordinary income. ◀

STOP & THINK

Question: Do most current distributions made by a partnership require a Sec. 751 calculation?

Solution: No. A partnership makes many current distributions pro rata to all partners, so Sec. 751 is not involved. Even if the distribution is not pro rata, the distribution often does not create an exchange of an interest in Sec. 751 assets for an interest in other assets. This exchange happens only when (1) the partner is reducing his or her overall interest in the partnership, (e.g., from a 15% to a 5% general partner) or (2) an explicit agreement provides that the distribution results in a partner giving up all or part of his or her interest in some asset(s) maintained by the partnership. Most current distributions do not involve Sec. 751.

TERMINATING AN INTEREST IN A PARTNERSHIP

A partner can terminate or dispose of an interest in a partnership in a number of ways. The two most common are receiving a liquidating distribution and selling the interest. Other possibilities include giving the interest away, exchanging the interest for corporate stock, and transferring the interest at death. This part of the chapter considers each of these methods.

OBJECTIVE 5

Determine the amount and character of gain or loss a partner recognizes in a liquidating partnership distribution

LIQUIDATING DISTRIBUTIONS

The IRC defines a liquidating distribution as a distribution, or one of a series of distributions, that terminates a partner's interest in the partnership.[11] If the partner's interest is drastically reduced but not terminated, the distribution is treated as a current distribution. A liquidating distribution can occur when only one member of a partnership terminates his or her interest, several partners terminate their interests but the partnership continues, or the entire partnership terminates and each partner receives a liquidating distribution. Rules for taxation of a liquidating distribution are the same whether one partner terminates his or her interest or the entire partnership liquidates.

GAIN OR LOSS RECOGNITION BY THE PARTNER. The rule for recognizing gain on a liquidating distribution is exactly the same rule used for a current distribution. A partner recognizes gain only if any money distributed exceeds the partner's predistribution basis in his or her partnership interest.[12] Distributed money includes money deemed distributed to the partner from a liability reduction or the FMV of marketable securities treated as money.

Although a partner can never recognize a loss from a current distribution, he or she can recognize a loss from a liquidating distribution. A partner recognizes a loss only if (1) the liquidating distribution consists of money (including money deemed distributed), unrealized receivables, and inventory, but no other property and (2) the partner's basis in the partnership interest exceeds the total basis of these distributed properties (including cash).[13] The amount of the loss is the difference between the partner's basis in the partnership interest before the distribution and the sum of money plus the bases of the receivables and inventory (to the partnership immediately before the distribution) that the partner receives.

EXAMPLE C:10-15 ▶ Maria terminates her interest in the ABC Partnership when her basis in the partnership is $35,000. She receives a liquidating distribution of $10,000 cash and inventory with a $12,000 basis to the partnership. Her recognized loss is $13,000 [$35,000 − ($10,000 + $12,000)]. The inventory has a $12,000 basis to Maria. ◀

OBJECTIVE 6

Determine the partner's basis of assets received in a liquidating distribution

BASIS IN ASSETS RECEIVED. A partner's basis of an asset received in a liquidating distribution is determined using rules similar to those used to determine the basis of an asset received in a current distribution. For both kinds of distributions, the basis in unrealized receivables and inventory is generally the same as the property's basis in the partnership's hands. Under no condition is the basis of these two types of assets increased. Occasionally, however, the partner's basis in his or her partnership interest is so small that after making the necessary reduction for money (and deemed money) distributions, the basis in the partnership interest is smaller than the partnership's bases for the unrealized receivables and inventory distributed. In such cases, the remaining basis in the partnership interest must be allocated among the unrealized receivables and inventory items based first on their decline in value and then on their relative bases as adjusted to reflect the decline in value.[14] As a result, the bases for the unrealized receivables and inventory are reduced, and the amount of ordinary income a partner recognizes on their ultimate sale, exchange, or collection increases.

TYPICAL MISCONCEPTION

The basis to a partner of distributed unrealized receivables or inventory can never be greater than the partnership's basis in those assets. Also, if the partner's basis in his or her partnership interest is not sufficient, the partner's basis in the distributed unrealized receivables and inventory is less than the partnership's basis in those assets.

Remember that a liquidating distribution of money, unrealized receivables, and inventory having a total basis to the partnership less than the partner's basis in his or her partnership interest results in the recognition of a loss. However, the partner recognizes no loss if the distribution includes any property other than money, unrealized receivables, and inventory. Instead, all the remaining basis in the partnership interest must be allo-

[11] Sec. 761(d).
[12] Sec. 731(a)(1).
[13] Sec. 731(a)(2).
[14] Sec. 732(c).

cated to the other property received regardless of that property's basis to the partnership or its FMV. Application of this rule can create strange results.

EXAMPLE C:10-16 ▶ Assume the same facts as in Example C:10-15 except Maria's distribution also includes an office typewriter having a $50 basis to the partnership and a $100 FMV. The allocation of basis proceeds as follows:

Predistribution basis for partnership interest	$35,000
Minus: Money received	(10,000)
Basis after money distribution	$25,000
Minus: Basis of inventory to partnership	(12,000)
Remaining basis of partnership interest	$13,000

The entire $13,000 remaining basis of the partnership interest is allocated to the typewriter. ◀

TAX STRATEGY TIP

The partnership in Example C:10-16 should avoid distributing low basis property along with cash, unrealized receivables, and inventory so that the partner can obtain an immediate loss deduction.

The basis allocation procedure illustrated in Example C:10-16 delays loss recognition until Maria either depreciates or sells the typewriter. The allocation procedure also may change the character of the loss because Maria would recognize a capital loss when she receives the liquidating distribution in Example C:10-15. In Example C:10-16, however, the character of Maria's loss is determined by the character of the typewriter in her hands (or in some cases by a series of specific rules that are discussed below). Worst of all, if she converts the typewriter into personal-use property, the loss on its sale or exchange is nondeductible.

If the partnership distributes two or more assets other than unrealized receivables or inventory in the same distribution, the remaining basis in the partnership interest is allocated among them based on both their relative FMVs and bases in the partnership's hands. Such an allocation process can lead to either a decrease or increase in the total basis of these assets. This potential for increasing the assets' bases is unique to liquidating distributions.

The allocation that results in a decrease in the basis of a distributed asset is identical to the allocation process described for current distributions. However, if the amount to be allocated is greater than the carryover bases of the distributed assets, the basis is first allocated among the distributed assets in an amount equal to their carryover basis from the partnership. Then, allocations are made based on relative appreciation of the assets up to the amount of appreciation, and further allocations are made to the assets based on their relative FMVs.

EXAMPLE C:10-17 ▶ Before receiving a liquidating distribution, Craig's basis in his interest in the BCD Partnership is $62,000. The distribution consists of $10,000 in cash, inventory having a $2,000 basis to the partnership and a $4,000 FMV, and two parcels of undeveloped land (not held as inventory) having bases of $6,000 and $18,000 to the partnership and having FMVs of $10,000 and $24,000, respectively. Assume that Sec. 751 does not apply. His bases in the assets received are calculated as follows:

Predistribution basis for partnership interest	$62,000
Minus: Money received	(10,000)
Basis of inventory to the partnership	(2,000)
Basis allocated to two parcels of land	$50,000

The calculation of the basis for the two parcels of land are as follows:

	Parcel One	*Parcel Two*	*Total*
FMV of asset	$10,000	$24,000	$34,000
Minus: Partnership's basis for asset	(6,000)	(18,000)	(24,000)
Difference	$ 4,000	$ 6,000	$10,000
Step 1: Give each asset the partnership's basis for the asset	$ 6,000	$18,000	$24,000
Minus: Craig's basis to be allocated			(50,000)
Increase to allocate			$26,000

Step 2: Adjusted basis after Step 1	$ 6,000	$18,000	$24,000
Allocate the increase first to assets that have increased in value	4,000	6,000	10,000
Adjusted basis at this point in the calculation	$10,000	$24,000	$34,000
Step 3: Allocate $16,000 remaining increase based on relative FMVs	4,706[a]	11,294[b]	16,000
Craig's bases in the assets	$14,706	$35,294	$50,000

[a]$10,000 ÷ ($10,000 + $24,000) × $16,000 = $ 4,706
[b]$24,000 ÷ ($10,000 + $24,000) × $16,000 = $11,294 ◀

KEY POINT
If the partner recognizes neither gain nor loss in a liquidating distribution, the partner's total basis in the distributed assets always equals the partner's predistribution basis in his or her partnership interest.

In a liquidating distribution, the amount of money received plus the distributee partner's total basis of the nonmoney property received normally equals the partner's predistribution basis in the partnership interest. The only two exceptions to this rule apply when the money received exceeds the partner's basis in his or her partnership interest, causing the partner to recognize a gain, or when money, unrealized receivables, and inventory are the only assets distributed and the partner recognizes a loss. In all other liquidating distributions, the distributee partner recognizes no gain or loss. Instead, that partner's predistribution basis in his or her partnership interest is transferred to the cash and other property received.

Holding Period in Distributed Assets. The distributee partner's holding period for any assets received in a liquidating distribution includes the partnership's holding period for such property.[15] If the partnership received the property as a contribution from a partner, the partnership's holding period also may include the period of time the contributing partner held the property prior to making the contribution (see Chapter C:9). The distributee partner's holding period for his or her partnership interest is irrelevant in determining the holding period of the assets received.

EXAMPLE C:10-18 ▶ George purchases an interest in the DEF Partnership on June 1, 2007, but he cannot get along with the other partners. Therefore, on July 1, 2007, he receives a liquidating distribution that terminates his interest in the partnership. George's distribution includes land that the partnership has owned since August 1, 2001. George's holding period for the land begins on August 1, 2001, even though his holding period for the partnership interest begins much later. ◀

The character of the gain or loss recognized on a subsequent sale of distributed property is determined using the same rules as for a current distribution.

KEY POINT
The main difference in how the Sec. 751 rules apply to current versus liquidating distributions is that, after a liquidating distribution, the partner always has a zero interest in the partnership assets because he or she is no longer a partner in the partnership.

EFFECTS OF SEC. 751. Section 751 has essentially the same impact on both liquidating and current distributions. To the extent the partner exchanges an interest in Sec. 751 assets for an interest in other assets (or vice versa), that portion of the transaction bypasses the distribution rules. Instead, this portion of the transaction is treated as a sale occurring between the partnership and the partner. One notable difference occurs between liquidating distributions and current distributions having Sec. 751 implications: the postdistribution interest in partnership assets is zero for the liquidating distribution because it terminates the partner's interest in the partnership.

EXAMPLE C:10-19 ▶ The ABC Partnership holds the assets listed below on December 31 before making a $50,000 cash distribution that reduces Al's one-third interest in the partnership to zero.

Assets	*Basis*	*FMV*
Cash	$75,000	$ 75,000
Unrealized receivables	–0–	15,000
Inventory	15,000	60,000
Total	$90,000	$150,000

[15] Sec. 735(b).

The partnership has no liabilities, and Al's predistribution basis in his partnership interest is $30,000. The following steps lead to the tax effects of the liquidating distribution:

STEP 1. Determine ABC's Sec. 751 and non-Sec. 751 assets. The Sec. 751 assets include the unrealized receivables and the substantially appreciated inventory. The cash is ABC's only non-Sec. 751 asset.

STEP 2. Complete the table used to analyze the Sec. 751 distributions (see Table C:10-2).

STEP 3. Analyze column 5 of Table C:10-2 to see whether a Sec. 751 exchange has occurred. Table C:10-2 shows that Al exchanges $5,000 of unrealized receivables and $20,000 of inventory for $25,000 cash.

SELF-STUDY QUESTION

What is the deemed Sec. 751 exchange shown in Table C:10-2?

ANSWER

Column 5 shows that Al received $25,000 of excess cash in lieu of $25,000 of Sec. 751 assets. Thus, the Sec. 751 exchange is a deemed sale by Al of $25,000 of unrealized receivables and inventory to the partnership in exchange for $25,000 of cash. With a table similar to Table C:10-2, the Sec. 751 computations are much easier to understand.

STEP 4. Determine the gain or loss on the Sec. 751 deemed sale. Al is deemed to have sold unrealized receivables and inventory for cash. Assume Al first got the receivables and inventory in a current distribution. He obtains the partnership's bases for the assets of $0 and $5,000, respectively. The subsequent deemed sale results in Al recognizing a $20,000 gain.

Amount realized (cash)	$25,000
Minus: Adjusted basis of property deemed sold	(5,000)
Realized and recognized gain	$20,000

Al's gain is ordinary income because it results from his deemed sale of receivables and inventory to the partnership.

STEP 5. Determine the impact of the non-Sec. 751 portion of the distribution. The liquidating distribution is only the $25,000 cash he receives that was *not* a part of the Sec. 751 transaction. To determine its impact, we first must find Al's basis in his partnership interest after the Sec. 751 transaction but before the $25,000 liquidating distribution.

Predistribution basis in the partnership interest	$30,000
Minus: Basis of receivables and inventory deemed distributed in Sec. 751 exchange	(5,000)
Basis before money distribution	$25,000
Minus: Money distribution	(25,000)
Gain recognized on liquidating distribution	$ –0–

Al recognizes no further gain or loss from the liquidating distribution portion of the transaction. ◀

▼ TABLE C:10-2

Analysis of Sec. 751 Liquidating Distribution (Example C:10-19)

	Beginning Partnership Amount[a]	(1) Al's Interest Before Distribution[a] (1/3)	(2) Al's Interest After Distribution[a] (–0–)	(3) Hypothetical Proportionate Distribution[a] (3) = (1) − (2)	(4) Actual Distribution[a]	(5) Difference[b] (5) = (4) − (3)
Sec. 751 assets:						
Unrealized receivables	$15,000	$ 5,000	$ –0–	$ 5,000	$ –0–	$ (5,000)
Inventory	60,000	20,000	–0–	20,000	–0–	(20,000)
Total Sec. 751 assets	$75,000	$25,000	$ –0–	$25,000	$ –0–	($ 25,000)
Non-Sec. 751 assets:						
Cash	$75,000	$25,000	$ –0–	$25,000	$50,000	$ 25,000
Total non-Sec. 751 assets	$75,000	$25,000	$ –0–	$25,000	$50,000	$ 25,000

[a]Valued at fair market value.
[b]A negative amount means that Al gave up his interest in a particular property. A positive amount means that Al received more than his proportionate interest.

SELF-STUDY QUESTION

What is the character of gain or loss on the sale of a partnership interest?

ANSWER

Because a partnership interest is generally a capital asset, the sale of a partnership interest results in the partner recognizing a capital gain or loss. However, if a partnership has Sec. 751 assets, the partner is deemed to sell his or her share of the underlying Sec. 751 assets, thereby causing a corresponding ordinary gain or loss to be recognized.

EFFECTS OF DISTRIBUTION ON THE PARTNERSHIP. A partnership generally recognizes no gain or loss on liquidating distributions made to its partners.[16] If a Sec. 751 deemed sale occurs, however, the partnership may recognize gain or loss on assets deemed sold to its partner. Although a liquidating distribution normally does not itself terminate the partnership, the partnership terminates if none of the remaining partners continue to operate the business of the partnership in a partnership form. In this case, all partners will receive liquidating distributions. Finally, the partnership's assets may be subject to optional or mandatory basis adjustments (see pages C:10-28 and C:10-29).

Topic Review C:10-1 summarizes the tax consequences of current and liquidating distributions.

SALE OF A PARTNERSHIP INTEREST

Absence any contrary rules, a partner's sale or exchange of a partnership interest would generate a capital gain or loss under Sec. 741 because a partnership interest is usually a capital asset. Section 751, however, modifies this result by requiring the partner to recognize ordi-

Topic Review C:10-1

Current and Liquidating Distributions

Tax Consequences	Current Distributions	Liquidating Distributions
Impact on Partner:		
Money (or deemed money from liability changes or marketable securities) distributed	Gain recognized only if money distributed exceeds basis in partnership interest before distribution.	Gain recognized only if money distributed exceeds basis in partnership interest before distribution.
Unrealized receivables and/or inventory distributed	Carryover basis (limited to basis in partnership interest before distribution reduced by money distributed).	Carryover basis (limited to basis in partnership interest before distribution reduced by money distributed).
	No gain or loss recognized.[a]	Loss recognized if partnership distributes money, inventory, and receivables with basis less than partner's basis in partnership interest before distribution and partnership distributes no other property.[a]
Other property distributed	Carryover basis (limited to basis in partnership interest before distribution reduced by money and carryover basis in inventory and receivables).	Basis equal to basis in partnership interest before distribution reduced by money and carryover basis in inventory and receivables.
	No gain or loss recognized.[a]	No gain or loss recognized.[a]
Impact on Partnership:		
General rule	No gain or loss recognized.	No gain or loss recognized.
Partnership assets	May be subject to optional basis adjustments (see pages C:10-28 and C:10-29).	May be subject to optional or mandatory basis adjustments (see pages C:10-28 and C:10-29).
Other Tax Consequences:	If a Sec. 751 deemed sale or exchange occurs, the partner and/or the partnership may recognize gain or loss on the deemed sale.	If a Sec. 751 deemed sale or exchange occurs, the partner and/or the partnership may recognize gain or loss on the deemed sale.

[a] A partner may recognize precontribution gain (but not loss) under Sec. 737 if a precontribution net gain remains and the FMV of the property distributed exceeds the adjusted basis of the partnership interest immediately before the property distribution (but after any money distribution). The contributing partner also may recognize precontribution gain or loss if the partnership distributes the contributed property to another partner within seven years of the contribution (Sec. 704(c)).

[16] Sec. 731(b).

nary income or loss (and possibly Sec. 1250 gain) on the sale or exchange of a partnership interest to the extent the consideration received is attributable to the partner's share of unrealized receivables and inventory items. The sale of a partnership interest also may have two other effects: the purchaser acquires the partner's share of the partnership's liabilities, and the partnership may be terminated. Each of these situations related to the sale of a partnership interest is examined below.

SECTION 751 PROPERTY. The definition of Sec. 751 property is slightly different for sales or exchanges than for distributions because inventory does not have to be substantially appreciated to be included as Sec. 751 property. Thus, all inventory and all unrealized receivables are Sec. 751 assets in a sale or exchange situation.[17]

Treasury Regulations under Sec. 751 take a hypothetical asset sale approach to determine the amount of ordinary income or loss the partner recognizes on the sale or exchange of a partnership interest.[18] Under the regulations, the partnership is deemed to sell all its assets for their FMV immediately before the partner sells his or her interest in the partnership. The partner then is allocated his or her share of ordinary gain or loss (and possibly Sec. 1250 gain) attributable to the Sec. 751 assets. With this approach, the results of the sale or exchange can be determined using the following three steps:

STEP 1. Determine the total gain or loss on the sale or exchange of the partnership interest.

STEP 2. Determine the ordinary gain or loss component and the Sec. 1250 gain component, if applicable, using the hypothetical asset sale approach.[19]

STEP 3. Determine the capital gain component by calculating the residual gain or loss after assigning the ordinary gain or loss and the Sec. 1250 gain components.

EXAMPLE C:10-20 ▶ Troy sells his one-fourth interest in the TV Partnership to Steve for $50,000 cash when the partnership's assets are as follows:

Assets	*Basis*	*FMV*
Cash	$ 20,000	$ 20,000
Unrealized receivables	–0–	24,000
Inventory	20,000	68,000
Building	40,000	56,000
Land	40,000	32,000
Total	$120,000	$200,000

The partnership has no liabilities on the sale date and has claimed $19,000 of straight-line depreciation on the building. Troy's basis in his partnership interest is $30,000 on such date. Both the receivables and inventory are Sec. 751 assets, and the building is Sec. 1250 property. Application of Step 1 yields the following gain on Troy's sale of his partnership interest:

Amount realized on sale	$50,000
Minus: Adjusted basis of partnership interest	(30,000)
Total gain realized	$20,000

Application of Step 2 yields the following allocation to Sec. 751 and Sec. 1250 property:

Deemed Sale of Assets	*Partnership Gain (Loss)*	*Troy's Share (25%)*
Unrealized receivables	$24,000	$ 6,000
Inventory	48,000	12,000
Building	16,000	4,000
Land	(8,000)	(2,000)

[17] Regulation Sec. 1.751-1(a)(1) is outdated to some extent and still speaks in terms of substantially appreciated inventory. However, Sec. 751(a) in the IRC, which deals with the sale or exchange of a partnership interest, includes all inventory items, not just those that are substantially appreciated.

[18] Reg. Sec. 1.751-1(a)(2). This hypothetical sale approach allows for easy incorporation of special allocations under Sec. 704 into the Sec. 751 calculation.

[19] The Sec. 1250 gain is the lesser of the hypothetical gain on Sec. 1250 property (e.g., buildings) or the amount of depreciation claimed on the Sec. 1250 property (assuming straight-line depreciation). This gain applies to noncorporate taxpayers and is subject to the 25% capital gains tax rate. A similar rule applies to a collectibles gain subject to the 28% capital gains tax rate. See Reg. Sec. 1.1(h)-1.

Thus, on the sale of his partnership interest, Troy recognizes ordinary income of $18,000 ($6,000 + $12,000). Because the $19,000 of depreciation exceeds the hypothetical gain on the building, the entire $16,000 gain is Sec. 1250 gain, $4,000 of which is Troy's share.

Application of Step 3 yields the following residual allocation to capital gain or loss:

Total gain realized	$20,000
Minus: Allocation to ordinary income and Sec. 1250 gain	(22,000)
Capital loss recognized	($ 2,000)

In summary, on the sale of his partnership interest, Troy recognizes $18,000 of ordinary income, $4,000 of Sec. 1250 gain, and a $2,000 capital loss. Without Sec. 751, these three components would have been netted together as a $20,000 capital gain. ◀

STOP & THINK *Question:* Bill owns 20% of Kraco and plans to sell his ownership interest for a $40,000 gain. Kraco has both unrealized receivables and inventory. If Kraco is a corporation, Bill will report a $40,000 capital gain. If Kraco is a partnership, part of the $40,000 gain (the gain on his 20% share of the Sec. 751 assets) will be ordinary income, and the remainder will be capital gain. Why did Congress decide to tax the gain on the sale of corporate stock differently from the gain on the sale of a partnership interest?

Solution: The corporation itself will pay tax on the ordinary income realized when it collects unrealized receivables or sells inventory, and the corporation's tax is unaffected by the identity of the shareholder. Under no conditions will the shareholder have to report any of the corporation's ordinary income. Accordingly, the sale of the corporate stock does not provide an opportunity to avoid ordinary income for the owner, nor can the owner convert ordinary income into capital gain by selling the corporate stock.[20]

Because the partners report and pay taxes on the ordinary income earned by the partnership, a sale of a partnership interest that produces only capital gains would represent an opportunity for a partner to avoid recognizing ordinary income and recognize capital gains instead. Imagine, for example, that Kraco is a cash basis service business whose only asset is a large account receivable where all work has been completed. If Bill stays in the partnership, he will recognize ordinary income when the partnership collects the receivable. If he were allowed to sell his partnership interest in this setting for a capital gain, he could convert his ordinary income into capital gain. However, Sec. 751 prevents this conversion from happening by requiring him to recognize ordinary income on the sale of the partnership interest to the extent the sales proceeds are attributable to Sec. 751 assets.

ADDITIONAL COMMENT

Section 751 treatment is another application of the aggregate theory of partnership taxation as opposed to the entity theory.

LIABILITIES. When a partnership has liabilities, each partner's distributive share of any liabilities is always part of the basis for the partnership interest. When a partner sells his or her partnership interest, the partner is relieved of the liabilities. Accordingly, the amount realized on the sale of a partnership interest is made up of money plus the FMV of nonmoney property received plus the seller's share of partnership liabilities assumed or acquired by the purchaser.

EXAMPLE C:10-21 ▶ Andrew is a 30% partner in the ABC Partnership when he sells his entire interest to Miguel for $40,000 cash. At the time of the sale, Andrew's basis is $27,000 (which includes his $7,000 share of partnership liabilities). The partnership has no Sec. 751 assets. Andrew's $20,000 gain on the sale is calculated as follows:

Amount realized:		
Cash	$40,000	
Liabilities assumed by purchaser	7,000	$47,000
Minus: Adjusted basis		(27,000)
Gain recognized on sale		$20,000

◀

[20] An exception used to exist for a so-called collapsible corporation. However, the 2003 Act repealed these provisions for tax years beginning after 2003 and before 2011. A discussion of collapsible corporations is beyond the scope of this text.

IMPACT ON THE PARTNERSHIP. When one partner sells his or her partnership interest, the sale usually has no more impact on the partnership than the sale of corporate stock by one shareholder has on the corporation. Only the partner and the purchaser of the interest are affected. However, the partnership itself is affected if the partnership interest sold is sufficiently large that, under Sec. 708, its sale terminates the partnership for tax purposes. This effect is discussed later in this chapter. Also, the partnership may have to make optional or mandatory basis adjustments to its assets (see pages C:10-26 through C:10-28).

OBJECTIVE 7

Determine the amount and character of the gain or loss recognized when a partner retires from a partnership or dies

RETIREMENT OR DEATH OF A PARTNER

If a partner dies or retires from a partnership, that partner's interest can be sold either to an outsider or to one or more existing partners.[21] The results of such a sale are outlined above. Often, however, a partner or a deceased partner's successor-in-interest departs from the partnership in return for payments made by the partnership itself. When the partnership buys out the partner's interest, the analysis of the tax results focuses on two types of payments: payments made in exchange for the partner's interest in partnership property and other payments.

PAYMENTS FOR PARTNERSHIP PROPERTY. Generally, the IRS accepts the valuation placed on the retiring partner's interest in the partnership property by the partners in an arm's-length transaction. Payments made for the property interest are taxed under the liquidating distribution rules. Like any liquidating distribution made to a partner, payments made to a retiring partner or a deceased partner's successor-in-interest[22] in exchange for his or her property interest are not deductible by the partnership.[23]

If the retiring or deceased partner was a general partner and the partnership is a service partnership (i.e., capital is not a material income producing factor), payments made to a general partner for unrealized receivables and goodwill (when the partnership agreement does not provide for a goodwill payment on retirement or death) are not considered payments for property. Instead, any such payments are treated as other payments. The other payment treatment permits the partnership to deduct the amounts paid to the retiring or deceased partner or to reduce the distributive share allocable to the other partners.

TYPICAL MISCONCEPTION

The significance of the two different kinds of payments is not readily apparent to some taxpayers. The payments for partnership property are not deductible by the partnership and often are not income to the retiring partner. However, payments considered in the second category are deductible by the partnership (or they reduce the distributive shares that other partners must recognize) and usually are income to the retiring partner.

OTHER PAYMENTS. Payments made to a retiring partner or to a deceased partner's successor-in-interest that exceed the value of that partner's share of partnership property have a different tax result for both the retiring partner and for the partnership. A few payments that do represent payments for property (e.g., payments to a general partner retiring from a service partnership for his or her interest in unrealized receivables and for his or her interest in partnership goodwill) also are taxed under these rules.

Under these rules, a payment is treated as either a distributive share or a guaranteed payment. If the excess payment is a function of partnership income (e.g., 10% of the partnership's net income), the income is considered a distributive share of partnership income.[24] Accordingly, the character of the income flows through to the partner, and each of the remaining partners is taxed on a smaller amount of partnership income. The income must be reported in the partner's tax year that includes the partnership year-end from which the distributive share arises, regardless of when the partner actually receives the distribution.

TYPICAL MISCONCEPTION

The main difference between a payment being taxed as a distributive share or as a guaranteed payment is the character of the income recognized by the recipient partner. If the payment is taxed as a distributive share, the character of the income is determined by the type of income earned by the partnership. In contrast, the payment is always ordinary income if it is treated as a guaranteed payment.

If the amount of the excess payment is determined without regard to the partnership income, the payment is treated as a guaranteed payment.[25] If the payment is a guaranteed payment, the retiring partner recognizes ordinary income, and the partnership generally has an ordinary deduction. Like all guaranteed payments, the income is includible in the

[21] Retirement from the partnership in this context has nothing to do with reaching a specific age and leaving the employ of the partnership but instead refers to the partner's withdrawal at any age from a continuing partnership.

[22] A deceased partner's successor-in-interest is the party that succeeds to the rights of the deceased partner's partnership interest (e.g., the decedent's estate or an heir or legatee of the deceased partner). A deceased partner's successor-in-interest is treated as a partner by the tax laws until his or her interest in the partnership has been completely liquidated.

[23] Sec. 736(b).

[24] Sec. 736(a)(1).

[25] Sec. 736(a)(2).

recipient's income for his or her tax year within which ends the partnership tax year in which the partnership claims its deduction (see Chapter C:9).

EXAMPLE C:10-22 ▶ When Sam retires from the STU Partnership, he receives a cash payment of $30,000. At the time of his retirement, his basis for his one-fourth limited partnership interest is $25,000. The partnership has no liabilities and the following assets:

Assets	*Basis*	*FMV*	*Sam's 1/4 FMV*
Cash	$ 40,000	$ 40,000	$10,000
Marketable securities	25,000	32,000	8,000
Land	35,000	48,000	12,000
Total	$100,000	$120,000	$30,000

In the absence of a valuation agreement, the partnership presumably pays Sam a ratable share of the FMV of each asset (and he receives no payment for any partnership goodwill). The $30,000 amount paid to Sam equals the FMV of his one-fourth interest in the partnership assets. The $30,000 Sam receives in exchange for his interest in partnership property is analyzed as a liquidating distribution in the following manner:

Cash distribution received	$30,000
Minus: Basis in partnership interest	(25,000)
Gain recognized on liquidating distribution	$ 5,000

Because the partnership holds no Sec. 751 assets, the entire gain is a capital gain. The partnership gets no deduction for the distribution. ◀

EXAMPLE C:10-23 ▶ Assume the same facts as in Example C:10-22 except Sam receives $34,000 instead of $30,000. This amount represents payment for Sam's one-fourth interest in partnership assets plus an excess payment of $4,000. Accordingly, this excess payment must be either a distributive share or a guaranteed payment. Because the $4,000 payment is not contingent on partnership earnings, it is taxed as a guaranteed payment. The partnership deducts the $4,000 payment, and Sam recognizes $4,000 of ordinary income.

In summary, Sam receives $34,000 as a payment on his retirement from the STU Partnership, $4,000 of which is considered a guaranteed payment taxed as ordinary income to Sam and deductible by the partnership. The remaining $30,000 Sam receives is in exchange for his interest in partnership property. Because the $30,000 cash payment exceeds his $25,000 basis in his partnership interest, he recognizes a $5,000 gain on the liquidating distribution. The partnership gets no deduction for the $30,000, which is considered a distribution. ◀

If the partnership has Sec. 751 assets, the calculations for a retiring partner are slightly more difficult. First, payments for substantially appreciated inventory and unrealized receivables are payments for property and must be analyzed using the liquidating distribution rules along with Sec. 751. The remainder of the transaction is analyzed as indicated above. (For partnership retirements only, unrealized receivables do not include recapture items.)

A retiring partner who receives payments from the partnership is considered to be a partner in that partnership for tax purposes until he or she receives the last payment. Likewise, a deceased partner's successor-in-interest is a member of the partnership until receiving the last payment.[26]

EXCHANGE OF A PARTNERSHIP INTEREST

EXCHANGE FOR ANOTHER PARTNERSHIP INTEREST. A partner also may terminate a partnership interest by exchanging it for either an interest in another partnership or a different interest in the same partnership. Exchanges involving interests in different partnerships do not qualify for like-kind exchange treatment.[27] Nevertheless, the IRS allows exchanges of interests within a single partnership.[28]

---

[26] Reg. Sec. 1.736-1(a)(1)(ii).

[27] Sec. 1031(a)(2)(D).

[28] Rev. Rul. 84-52, 1984-1 C.B. 157.

EXAMPLE C:10-24 ▶ Pam and Dean are equal partners in the PD General Partnership, which owns and operates a farm. The two partners agree to convert PD into a limited partnership, with Pam becoming a limited partner and Dean having both a general and a limited partnership interest in PD. Even though the partners exchange a general partnership interest for a limited partnership interest (plus an exchange of a general partnership interest for a general partnership interest for Dean), they recognize no gain or loss on the exchange. If, however, a partner's interest in the partnership's liabilities is changed, that partner's basis must be adjusted. If liabilities are reduced and a deemed distribution exceeding the basis for the partnership interest occurs, the partner must recognize gain on the excess. ◀

EXCHANGE FOR CORPORATE STOCK. A partnership interest may be exchanged for corporate stock in a transaction that qualifies under the Sec. 351 nonrecognition rules (see Chapter C:2). For Sec. 351 purposes, a partnership interest is property. If the other Sec. 351 requirements are met, a single partner's partnership interest can be transferred for stock in a new or an existing corporation in a nontaxable exchange. The partner treats this as if he or she had transferred any other property under the Sec. 351 rules. The basis in the corporate stock is determined by the partner's basis in the partnership interest. The holding period for the stock received in the exchange includes the holding period for the partnership interest. As a result of the exchange, one of the corporation's assets is an interest in a partnership, and the corporation (not the transferor) is now the partner of record. Thus, the corporation must report its distributive share of partnership income along with its other earnings.

INCORPORATION. When limited liability is important, the entire partnership may choose to incorporate. Normally such an incorporation can be structured to fall within the Sec. 351 provisions and can be partially or totally tax exempt. When a partnership chooses to incorporate, three possible alternatives are available:

- ▶ The partnership contributes its assets and liabilities to the corporation in exchange for the corporation's stock. The partnership then distributes the stock to the partners in a liquidating distribution of the partnership.
- ▶ The partnership liquidates by distributing its assets to the partners. The partners then contribute the property to the new corporation in exchange for its stock.
- ▶ The partners contribute their partnership interests directly to the new corporation in exchange for its stock. The partnership liquidates, with the corporation receiving all the partnership's assets and liabilities.

The tax implications of the incorporation and the impact of partnership liabilities, gain to be recognized, basis in the corporate assets, and the new shareholders' bases in their stock and securities may differ depending on the form chosen for the transaction.[29]

FORMATION OF AN LLC, LLP, OR LLLP. A second option for obtaining limited liability protection for all owners is for the partnership to become an LLC. Under Rev. Rul. 95-37,[30] the conversion is viewed as a partnership-to-partnership transfer. The property transfer does not cause the partners to recognize gain or loss nor does the transfer terminate the tax year for the partnership or any partner. The basis for the partners' interest in the partnership will be changed only if the liability shares for the partners change. Under the check-the-box regulations, an LLC with more than one member is treated as a partnership unless it elects to be taxed as a corporation (see Chapter C:2). If the LLC elects to be taxed as a C or an S corporation, the transfer of the property to the LLC falls under the incorporation rules discussed above.

If a partnership chooses LLP status to reduce some of the liability risks facing the partners, the change from partnership to LLP status also falls under the partnership-to-partnership transfer rules described above. The transfer does not cause the partners to recognize

[29] Rev. Rul. 84-111, 1984-2 C.B. 88. In addition, Reg. Secs. 301.7701-1, 2, and 3 describe the tax consequences of a partnership electing to be taxed as a corporation under the check-the-box regulations.

[30] 1995-1 C.B. 130.

gain or loss nor does the property transfer terminate the tax year for the partnership or any partner. Basis for the partners' interest in the partnership will be changed only if the liability shares for the partners change.[31] Finally, in some states, partners can achieve limited liability through a limited liability limited partnership (LLLP) (see page C:10-31).

Topic Review C:10-2 summarizes the tax consequences of a number of alternative methods for terminating an investment in a partnership.

INCOME RECOGNITION AND TRANSFERS OF A PARTNERSHIP INTEREST

The partnership tax year closes with respect to any partner who sells or exchanges his or her entire interest in a partnership or any partner whose interest in the partnership is liquidated. The partnership tax year closes on the sale or exchange date or the date of final payment on a liquidation. As a result, that partner's share of all items earned by the partnership must be reported in the partner's tax year that includes the transaction date.[32]

A partner's tax year also closes on the date of death. The partner's final return will include all partnership income up to the date of death.

OBJECTIVE 8

Determine whether a partnership has terminated for tax purposes

TERMINATION OF A PARTNERSHIP

EVENTS CAUSING A TERMINATION TO OCCUR. Because of the complex relationships among partners and their liability for partnership debts, state partnership laws provide for the termination of a partnership under a wide variety of conditions. Section 708(b), however, avoids the tax complexity created by the wide variety of state laws and the numerous termination conditions. This IRC section provides that a partnership terminates for tax purposes only if

Topic Review C:10-2

Terminating an Investment in a Partnership

Method	Tax Consequences to Partner
Death or retirement:	
Amounts paid for property[a]	Liquidating distribution tax consequences apply to the amount paid.
Amounts paid in excess of property values:	
Amounts not determined by reference to partnership income	Ordinary income.
Amounts determined by reference to partnership income	Distributive share of partnership income.
Sale of partnership interest to outsider	Capital gain (loss) except for ordinary income (loss) reported on Sec. 751 assets and Sec. 1250 gain on depreciable real property.
Exchange for partnership interest:	
In same partnership	No tax consequences
In different partnership	Capital gain (loss) except for ordinary income (loss) on Sec. 751 assets and Sec. 1250 gain on depreciable real property.
Exchange for corporate stock	No gain or loss generally recognized if it qualifies for Sec. 351 tax-free treatment. If the exchange does not qualify for Sec. 351 treatment, capital gain (loss) except for ordinary income (loss) on Sec. 751 assets and Sec. 1250 gain on depreciable real property.
Incorporation of partnership	Tax consequences depend on form of transaction used for incorporation.
Formation of LLC or LLP	No tax consequences except for distributions or contributions deemed to occur if liability shares change.

[a]Only for a general partner departing from a service partnership, property excludes unrealized receivables and goodwill if it is not mentioned in the partnership agreement.

[31] Ibid.

[32] Sec. 706(c)(2).

- No part of any business, financial operation, or venture of the partnership continues to be carried on by any of its partners in a partnership or
- Within a 12-month period a sale or exchange of at least 50% of the total interest in partnership capital and profits occurs.

TYPICAL MISCONCEPTION

Taxpayers often do not understand the difference between a partnership tax year closing for a specific partner versus a partnership tax year closing for all partners due to a termination of the partnership itself. The tax consequences of these two events are drastically different.

NO BUSINESS OPERATED AS A PARTNERSHIP. If no partner continues to operate any business of the partnership through the same or another partnership, the original partnership terminates. To avoid termination, the partnership must maintain partners and business activity. For example, if one partner retires from a two-person partnership and the second partner continues the business alone, the partnership terminates. However, if one partner in a two-member partnership dies, the partnership does not terminate as long as the deceased's estate or successor-in-interest continues to share in the profits and losses of the partnership business.[33]

Likewise, a partnership terminates if it ceases to carry on any business or financial venture. The courts, however, have allowed a partnership to continue under this rule even though the partnership sold all its assets and retained only a few installment notes.[34] Despite the courts' flexibility in these circumstances, a partnership should maintain more than a nominal level of assets if continuation of the partnership is desired.

KEY POINT

For the 50% rule to terminate a partnership, a *sale* or *exchange* of 50% or more of the capital *and* profits interests must occur. Sales or exchanges occurring within a 12-month period are aggregated. However, if the same interest is sold twice within 12 months, it is only counted once.

SALE OR EXCHANGE OF AT LEAST A 50% INTEREST. The second condition that terminates a partnership is the sale or exchange of at least a 50% interest in both partnership capital and profits within a 12-month period.[35] The relevant 12-month period is determined without reference to the tax year of either the partnership or any partner but rather is any 12 consecutive months. To cause termination, the partner must transfer the partnership interest by sale or exchange. Transactions or occurrences that do not constitute a sale or exchange (e.g., the gifting of a partnership interest or the transferring of a partnership interest at death) do not cause a partnership to terminate as long as partners continue the partnership business. Likewise, as long as at least two partners remain, the removal of a partner who owns more than 50% of the total partnership capital and profits interests can be accomplished without terminating the partnership by making a liquidating distribution.[36]

Measuring the portion of the total partnership capital and profits interest transferred often presents difficulties. Multiple exchanges of the same partnership interest are counted only once for purposes of determining whether the 50% maximum is exceeded. When several different small interests are transferred within a 12-month period, the partnership's termination occurs on the date of the transfer that first crosses the 50% threshold.[37]

EXAMPLE C:10-25 ▶

On August 1, 2007, Miguel sells his 30% capital and profits interest in the LMN Partnership to Steve. On June 1, 2008, Steve sells the 30% interest acquired from Miguel to Andrew. For purposes of Sec. 708, the two sales are considered to be the transfer of a single partnership interest. Thus, the LMN Partnership does not terminate unless other sales of partnership interests occur totaling at least 20% of LMN's capital and profits interests during any 12-month period that includes either August 1, 2007, or June 1, 2008. ◀

EXAMPLE C:10-26 ▶

On July 15, 2007, Kelly sells Carlos a 37% capital and profits interest in the KRS Partnership. On November 14, 2007, Rick sells Diana a 10% capital and profits interest in the KRS Partnership. On January 18, 2008, Sherrie sells Evan a 5% capital and profits interest in the KRS Partnership. The KRS Partnership terminates on January 18, 2008, because the cumulative interest sold within the 12-month period that includes January 18, 2008, first exceeds 50% on that date. ◀

EFFECTS OF TERMINATION.

Importance of Timing. When a partnership terminates, its tax year closes, requiring the partners to include their share of partnership earnings for the short-period partnership tax

---

[33] Reg. Sec. 1.708-1(b)(1)(i)(A).

[34] For example, see *Max R. Ginsburg v. U.S.*, 21 AFTR 2d 1489, 68-1 USTC ¶9429 (Ct. Cls., 1968).

[35] Under Sec. 774(c), an electing large partnership does *not* terminate solely because 50% or more of its interests are sold within a 12-month period.

[36] Reg. Sec. 1.708-1(b)(1)(ii).

[37] Ibid.

year in their tax returns. If the termination is not properly timed, partnership income for a regular 12-month tax year already may be included in the same return that must include the short tax year, resulting in more than 12 months of partnership income or loss being reported in some partners' tax returns. As partners and partnerships are increasingly forced to adopt the same tax year, this problem will lessen.

EXAMPLE C:10-27 ▶ Joy is a calendar year taxpayer who owns a 40% capital and profits interest in the ATV Partnership. ATV has a natural business year-end of March 31 and with IRS permission uses that date as its tax year-end. For the partnership tax year ending March 31, 2007, Joy has an $80,000 distributive share of ordinary income. Pat, who owns the remaining 60% capital and profits interests, sells his interest to Collin on November 30, 2007. Because more than 50% of the capital and profits interests have changed hands, the ATV Partnership terminates on November 30, 2007, and the partnership's tax year ends on that date.

Joy's tax return for the tax year ending December 31, 2007, must include the $80,000 distributive share from the partnership tax year for the period April 1, 2006, through March 31, 2007, and the distributive share of partnership income for the short tax year including the period April 1, 2007, through November 30, 2007. ◀

Liquidating Distributions and Contributions. When a termination occurs for tax purposes, the partnership is deemed to have made a pro rata liquidating distribution to all partners. Accordingly, the partners must recognize gain or loss under the liquidating distribution rules. An actual liquidating distribution may occur if the termination occurs because of the cessation of business. However, if the termination occurs because of a 50% or greater change in ownership of the capital and profits interests, an actual distribution usually does not occur. In this case, the new group of partners continue the business, and Treasury Regulations provide for the termination of the old partnership and the formation of a new partnership. Specifically, the old partnership is deemed to contribute all its property and liabilities to a new partnership in exchange for the interests in the new partnership. The old partnership then is deemed to liquidate by distributing its only remaining asset (the interests in the new partnership) to its partners.[38]

EXAMPLE C:10-28 ▶ The AB Partnership terminates for tax purposes on July 15 when Anna sells her 60% capital and profits interest to Diane for $123,000. The partnership has no liabilities, and its assets at the time of termination are as follows:

Assets	*Basis*	*FMV*
Cash	$ 20,000	$ 20,000
Receivables	30,000	32,000
Inventory	22,000	28,000
Building	90,000	95,000
Land	40,000	30,000
Total	$202,000	$205,000

Beth, a 40% partner in the AB Partnership, has an $80,800 basis in her partnership interest at the time of the termination. She has held her AB Partnership interest for three years at the time of the termination.

The old AB Partnership is deemed to transfer all its assets to a new partnership (NewAB) on July 15 in exchange for all the interests in NewAB. The old partnership then is deemed to transfer all the NewAB interests to the partners of the old partnership (Diane and Beth). At this point, the old AB Partnership ceases to exist because it no longer has partners, nor does it carry on any business.

The basis and holding period of the assets held by NewAB are identical to the basis and holding period of the old AB Partnership assets.[39] The basis of Beth's interest in NewAB is identical to her basis in her interest in the AB Partnership ($80,800).[40] Her holding period for the NewAB partnership interest begins when she acquired the old AB Partnership interest. Diane's basis in her partnership interest is its $123,000 cost, and her holding period begins when she purchases the interest. ◀

---

[38] Reg. Sec. 1.708-1(b)(1)(iv).

[39] Secs. 723 and 1223(2).

[40] Sec. 722.

Changes in Accounting Methods. The termination ends all partnership elections. Thus, the new partnership must make all elections concerning its tax year and accounting methods in its first new tax year.

KEY POINT

The principal concern when two or more partnerships combine is which partnership's tax year, accounting methods, and elections will survive the merger. This determination is made by examining the capital and profits interests of the partners of the old partnerships.

MERGERS AND CONSOLIDATIONS

When two or more partnerships join together to form a new partnership, the parties to the transaction must determine which, if any, of the old partnerships are continued and which are terminated. An old partnership whose partner(s) own more than 50% of the profits and capital interests of the new partnership is considered to be continued as the new partnership.[41] Accordingly, the new partnership must continue with the tax year and accounting methods and elections of the old partnership that is considered to continue. All the other old partnerships are considered to have been terminated.

EXAMPLE C:10-29 ▶ The AB and CD Partnerships merge to form the ABCD Partnership. April and Ben each own 30% of ABCD, and Carole and David each own 20% of ABCD. The ABCD Partnership is considered a continuation of the AB Partnership because April and Ben, the former partners of AB, own 60% of ABCD. ABCD is bound by the tax year, accounting method, and other elections made by AB. CD, formerly owned by Carole and David, is considered to terminate on the merger date. ◀

In some combinations, the partners of two or more of the old partnerships might hold the requisite profits and capital interest in the new partnership. When two or more old partnerships satisfy this requirement, the old partnership credited with contributing the greatest dollar value of assets to the new partnership is considered the continuing partnership, and all other partnerships terminate. Sometimes, none of the old partnerships account for more than 50% of the capital and profits of the new partnership. In that case, all the old partnerships terminate, and the merged partnership is a new entity that can make its own tax year and accounting method elections.

EXAMPLE C:10-30 ▶ Three partnerships merge to form the ABCD Partnership. The AB Partnership (owned by Andy and Bill) contributes assets valued at $140,000 to ABCD. BC Partnership (owned by Bill and Cathy) and CD Partnership (owned by Cathy and Drew) contribute assets valued at $180,000 and $120,000, respectively. The capital and profits interests of the partners in the new partnership are Andy, 20%; Bill, 35%; Cathy, 19%; and Drew, 26%. Both the AB and BC Partnerships had partners who now own more than 50% of the new partnership (Andy and Bill own 55%, and Bill and Cathy own 54%). The BC Partnership contributed more assets ($180,000) to the new partnership than did the AB Partnership ($140,000). Therefore, the ABCD Partnership is a continuation of the BC Partnership. Both the AB and CD Partnerships terminate on the merger date. ◀

KEY POINT

The principal concern of a partnership division is to determine which of the new partnerships is the continuation of the prior partnership.

DIVISION OF A PARTNERSHIP

When a partnership divides into two or more new partnerships, all the new partnerships whose partners own collectively more than 50% of the profits and capital interests in the old partnerships are considered a continuation of the old partnership.[42] All partnerships that are continuations of the old partnership are bound by the old partnership's tax year and accounting method elections. Any other partnership created by the division is considered a new partnership eligible to make its own tax year and accounting method elections. If no new partnership meets the criteria for continuation of the divided partnership, the divided partnership terminates on the division date. The interest of any partner of the divided partnership who does not own an interest in a continuing partnership is considered to be liquidated on the division date.

EXAMPLE C:10-31 ▶ The RSTV Partnership is in the real estate and insurance business. Randy owns a 40% interest and Sam, Thomas, and Vicki each own 20% of RSTV. The partners agree to split the partnership, with the RS Partnership receiving the real estate operations and the TV Partnership receiving the insurance business. Because Randy and Sam own more than 50% of the RSTV Partnership (40% + 20% = 60%), the RS Partnership is a continuation of the RSTV Partnership and must report its results using the same tax year and accounting method elections that RSTV used.

---

[41] Sec. 708(b)(2)(A).

[42] Sec. 708(b)(2)(B).

Thomas and Vicki are considered to have terminated their interests in RSTV and to have received a liquidating distribution of the insurance business property. The TV Partnership makes its tax year and accounting method elections following the rules for a new partnership. ◀

OPTIONAL AND MANDATORY BASIS ADJUSTMENTS

OBJECTIVE 9

Understand the effect of optional and mandatory basis adjustments

In general, a partnership makes no adjustment to the basis of its property when a partner sells or exchanges his or her interest in the partnership, when a partner's interest transfers upon the partner's death, or when the partnership makes a property distribution to a partner. A partnership, however, may adjust basis of its assets if the partnership makes an **optional basis adjustment** election under Sec. 754. The following paragraphs compare the consequences of having no election to having such an election. The discussion focuses primarily on sale transactions but also briefly mentions distributions. Once made, the Sec. 754 election applies to all subsequent transfers of partnership interests (e.g., sales, exchanges, and transfers upon death) and all subsequent distributions. In addition, the partnership may have to make a **mandatory basis adjustment** in certain circumstances even if a Sec. 754 election is not in effect.

ADJUSTMENTS ON TRANSFERS

OPTIONAL ADJUSTMENT. If a new incoming partner purchases his or her partnership interest from an existing partner, the new partner's basis in the partnership interest equals the purchase price plus the new partner's share of partnership liabilities. The new partner's basis in the partnership is likely to be different from his or her share of basis of the underlying assets in the partnership. This difference could lead to inequitable results as demonstrated by the following example.

EXAMPLE C:10-32 ▶ Amy, Bill, and Corey each own a one-third interest in ABC partnership, which has the following simple balance sheet:

	Basis	*FMV*
Assets:		
Cash	$30,000	$ 30,000
Inventory	60,000	90,000
Total	$90,000	$120,000
Liabilities and capital:		
Liabilities	$15,000	$ 15,000
Capital—Amy	25,000	35,000
—Bill	25,000	35,000
—Corey	25,000	35,000
Total	$90,000	$120,000

Eric purchases Amy's one-third interest for $35,000 cash and assumes her $5,000 share of partnerships liabilities. Eric pays this amount because one-third the FMV of the underlying partnership assets is $40,000 (1/3 × $120,000). In addition, the cash paid plus Eric's share of partnership liabilities gives him a $40,000 basis in his new partnership interest. Amy's basis at the time of sale is $30,000. Therefore, Amy recognizes a $10,000 gain ($40,000 amount realized − $30,000 basis). Amy's $10,000 gain also reflects her share of the difference between the inventory's FMV and basis at the partnership level. Thus, her gain will be ordinary income under Sec. 751.

Now suppose the partnership later sells the inventory for $90,000. The partnership recognizes $30,000 of ordinary income. Therefore, each partner, Bill, Corey, and Eric, recognizes a $10,000 distributive share of ordinary income from that sale, and each partner increases the basis of his partnership interest by the same amount. Accordingly, Eric increases his basis in the partnership from $40,000 to $50,000. In this situation, Eric appears to be taxed on the same gain as was Amy even though he paid a FMV price for his partnership interest (and the underlying partnership assets).

However, this result primarily is an issue of timing and possibly character of income and loss. For example, suppose further that, sometime after selling the inventory, the partnership distributes the $120,000 cash to the partners in liquidation. Eric would receive $40,000 and recognize a $10,000 ($40,000 distribution − $50,000 basis) capital loss.

In short, with no optional basis adjustment election in effect, Eric recognizes $10,000 of ordinary income when the partnership sells the inventory and a $10,000 capital loss when the partnership liquidates. This timing difference could be substantial if the partnership remains in existence for a long time. Also, the capital loss may offset only capital gains and up to $3,000 of ordinary income in the partner's personal tax return. ◀

ADDITIONAL COMMENT

The situation of a new partner purchasing an interest in a partnership is a good example of where a partner's outside basis can differ significantly from his or her share of the partnership's inside basis. The Sec. 754 election mitigates this difference.

AMOUNT OF THE ADJUSTMENT. An incoming partner might view the situation in Example C:10-32 as unacceptable and wish the partnership to make a Sec. 754 election. If the partnership makes such an election or has a Sec. 754 election already in effect, Sec. 743 mandates a special basis adjustment equal to the difference between the transferee (purchasing) partner's basis in the partnership interest and the transferee partner's share of basis of partnership assets. This basis adjustment, arising from a transfer, belongs only to the transferee partner (and not to the other partners), and it eliminates the inequities noted in Example C:10-32.

EXAMPLE C:10-33 ▶ Assume the same facts as in Example C:10-32 except the partnership makes a Sec. 754 election. Eric's optional basis adjustment is calculated as follows:

Cash purchase price	$35,000
Share of partnership liabilities	5,000
Initial basis in partnership	$40,000
Minus: Eric's share of partnership's basis in assets (1/3 × $90,000)[43]	(30,000)
Optional basis adjustment	$10,000

Now when the partnership sells the inventory, Eric has an additional $10,000 basis in his share of the inventory that offsets the $10,000 income he otherwise would recognize. The other partners, however, still recognize their $10,000 distributive shares of income. Because Eric recognizes no income, he does not increase his partnership basis. Suppose the partnership liquidates sometime after selling the inventory. Again, Eric receives a $40,000 distribution, but he recognizes no capital gain or loss ($40,000 distribution − $40,000 basis). Thus, the optional basis adjustment eliminated both the timing and character differences that occurred in Example C:10-32. ◀

MANDATORY ADJUSTMENT. For sales or exchanges of partnership interests occurring after October 22, 2004, the IRC imposes a mandatory basis adjustment if the partnership has a substantial built-in loss and has no Sec. 754 optional basis adjustment election in effect. A substantial built-in loss exists if the partnership's adjusted basis in its property exceeds the FMV of the property by more than $250,000. Congress enacted this provision to prevent the doubling of losses. Exceptions to the new rule apply to certain specialized partnerships, discussion of which is beyond the scope of this textbook.

EXAMPLE C:10-34 ▶ David, Ellen, and Frank each own a one-third interest in DEF partnership, which has the following simple balance sheet:

	Basis	*FMV*
Assets:		
Cash	$ 100,000	$100,000
Land	1,100,000	800,000
Total	$1,200,000	$900,000

[43] In some cases, the calculation of the transferee's share of the partnership's basis in assets can be more complicated than shown in this example. See Reg. Sec. 1.743-1(d).

Capital:		
David	$ 400,000	$300,000
Ellen	400,000	300,000
Frank	400,000	300,000
Total	$1,200,000	$900,000

Gwen purchases David's one-third interest for $300,000 cash, which gives Gwen a $300,000 initial basis in her new partnership interest. David's partnership interest basis at the time of sale is $400,000. Therefore, he recognizes a $100,000 loss. David's $100,000 loss also reflects his share of the difference between the land's FMV and basis at the partnership level.

Now suppose the partnership has no optional basis adjustment election in effect and later sells the land for $800,000. The partnership recognizes a $300,000 loss. As a result, each partner, Ellen, Frank, and Gwen, recognizes a $100,000 distributive share of that loss, and each partner decreases the basis of his or her partnership interest by the same amount. As a result, both David and Gwen recognize a $100,000 loss. To prevent this doubling of losses, the partnership must make a $100,000 mandatory downward basis adjustment with respect to Gwen's share of the land, thereby nullifying her distributive share of loss on the land sale. The adjustment is mandatory because the partnership has a substantial built-in loss (i.e., its $300,000 built-in loss exceeds $250,000). Note that, without this mandatory adjustment, Gwen's $100,000 loss would be temporary because her partnership basis would be reduced to $200,000, causing her to recognize a $100,000 gain should the partnership liquidate and distribute $300,000 to her. Nevertheless, Congress chose to eliminate the initial doubling of losses by requiring the mandatory basis adjustment. ◀

OTHER ISSUES. Examples C:10-32 through C:10-34 assume inventory or land is the only asset other than cash. If the assets instead had been depreciable property, the basis adjustments would give the transferee partner additional depreciation deductions in Examples C:10-32 and C:10-33 or reduced depreciation deductions in example C:10-34. Also, if a partnership has more than one asset other than cash, the optional or mandatory basis adjustment must be allocated to the assets under special rules found in Sec. 755 and related Treasury Regulations. These allocation rules are beyond the scope of this text.

ADJUSTMENTS ON DISTRIBUTIONS

OPTIONAL ADJUSTMENT. As mentioned earlier, if a partnership distributes property to a partner, the partnership makes no adjustment to the basis of its remaining property unless an optional basis adjustment election is in place or unless the mandatory basis adjustment rule discussed later applies. If the partnership has made a Sec. 754 election, the partnership makes the following adjustments upon the distribution to a partner:

- Increases the basis of *partnership* property by:
  1. Any gain recognized by the distributee partner on the distribution (e.g., cash distribution exceeding the partner's basis in his or her partnership interest)
  2. The amount by which the distributee partner decreases the basis of property received in a property distribution from the basis of the property in the partnership's hands
- Decreases the basis of *partnership* property by:
  1. Any loss recognized by the distributee partner on a liquidating distribution
  2. The amount by which the distributee partner increases the basis of property received in a property distribution from the basis of the property in the partnership's hands

Unlike the optional basis adjustments arising from a transfer of partnership interest, the basis adjustments arising from a distribution belong to the partnership as a whole. These adjustments eliminate many (but not all) basis and timing disparities resulting from distributions.

A partnership should take care in making a Sec. 754 election because, once made, the election affects many transactions in complicated ways. Moreover, the election can cause downward as well as upward adjustments. Finally, the election has long-range implications because it can be revoked only with IRS approval. The IRS will not grant such approval if the primary purpose of the revocation is to avoid reducing the basis of partnership assets.

MANDATORY ADJUSTMENT. The discussion of the optional basis adjustment for distributions included increases and decreases to partnership property. For distributions occuring after October 22, 2004, the IRC makes the decreasing basis adjustment mandatory if it exceeds $250,000. As with exchange transactions, Congress enacted this provision to prevent the doubling of losses. In effect, the mandatory adjustment rule applies only to liquidating distributions because such decreasing adjustments cannot occur in nonliquidating distribution situations.

SPECIAL FORMS OF PARTNERSHIPS

Here, we examine a series of special partnership forms, including tax shelters organized as limited partnerships, publicly traded partnerships, limited liability companies, limited liability partnerships, and electing large partnerships.

TAX SHELTERS AND LIMITED PARTNERSHIPS

ADDITIONAL COMMENT

The passive activity loss limitations eliminate the deferral benefit of tax shelters.

Tax shelters at their best are good investments that reduce and/or defer the amount of an investor's tax bill. Traditionally, shelter benefits arise from leverage, income deferral, deduction acceleration, and tax credits.

Before the Tax Reform Act of 1986, limited partnerships were the primary vehicle for tax shelter investments. However, the Tax Reform Act of 1986 greatly reduced the benefits of limited partnerships as tax shelters by invoking the passive activity loss limitations for activity conducted in a limited partnership form. The limited partnership, however, still allows an investor to limit liability while receiving the benefits of the shelter's tax attributes to save taxes on other passive income. Since the Tax Reform Act of 1986, limited partnerships that generate passive income rather than losses have become popular investments for investors who already hold loss-generating limited partnership interests. (See Problem C:9-46 in the previous chapter for an example of tax deferred benefits and their elimination by the at-risk and passive activity loss limitations.)

PUBLICLY TRADED PARTNERSHIPS

The IRC restricts still further the benefits of tax shelter ownership by imposing special rules on **publicly traded partnerships** (PTPs). A PTP is a partnership whose interests are traded either on an established securities exchange or in a secondary market or the equivalent thereof. A partnership that meets the requirements is taxed as a C corporation under Sec. 7704.

Two exceptions apply to partnerships that otherwise would be classified as PTPs:

- ▶ Partnerships that have 90% or more of their gross income being "qualifying income" continue to be taxed under the partnership rules.
- ▶ Partnerships that were in existence on December 17, 1987 and have not added a substantial new line of business since that date are grandfathered. In general, application of the PTP rules for these partnerships was delayed until tax years beginning after December 31, 1997.

REAL-WORLD EXAMPLE

The Chicago Board of Partnerships acts as a secondary market for limited partnership interests. Trades can range from a few thousand dollars to millions of dollars. This market increases the liquidity of limited partnership investments. Some partnerships are publicly traded on the major stock exchanges.

The Taxpayer Relief Act of 1997 added an election that allows the grandfathered partnerships to continue to be treated as partnerships after the original ten-year window and until the election is revoked. To elect to continue to be treated as a partnership, the publicly traded partnership (which must have been taxed as a partnership under the grandfather provision) must agree to pay a 3.5% annual tax on gross income from the active conduct of any trade or business.[44] The election may be revoked by the partnership, but once revoked, it cannot be reinstated.

[44] Sec. 7704(g)(3).

For the 90% of gross income test, Sec. 7704(d) defines qualifying income to include certain interest, dividends, real property rents (but not personal property rents), income and gains from the sale or disposition of a capital asset or Sec. 1231(b) trade or business property held for the production of passive income, and gain from the sale or disposition of real property. It also includes gains from certain commodity trading and natural resource activities. Any PTP not taxed as a corporation because of this 90% exception is subject to separate and more restrictive Sec. 469 passive loss rules than are partnerships that are not publicly traded.

If a partnership is first classified as a PTP taxed as a corporation during a tax year, the PTP incurs a deemed contribution of all partnership assets and all partnership liabilities to a corporation in exchange for all the corporation's stock. The stock is then deemed distributed to the partners in complete liquidation of the partnership. This transaction is taxed exactly as if it had physically occurred.

LIMITED LIABILITY COMPANIES

In recent years, the limited liability company (LLC) has emerged as a popular form of business entity in the United States. The LLC combines the legal and tax benefits of partnerships and S corporations. Currently, all 50 states have adopted LLC laws. The LLC business form combines the advantage of limited liability for all its owners with the ability of achieving the conduit treatment and the flexibility of being taxed as a partnership.

In the past, whether an LLC was characterized as a corporation or a partnership for federal tax purposes depended on the number of corporate characteristics the entity possessed, such as limited liability, free transferability of interests, centralized management, and continuity of life. The process of determining tax treatment was complex and time consuming. However, in December 1996, the Treasury Department issued regulations that allow entities (other than corporations and trusts) to choose whether to be taxed as a partnership or as an association. (An association is an unincorporated entity taxed as a corporation.) According to these check-the-box regulations, an LLC with two or more members can choose either partnership or association tax treatment. With a written and properly filed election, any LLC can choose to be taxed as an association. If the LLC makes no such election, an LLC with two or more members is treated as a partnership for tax purposes, while a single member LLC is treated as a sole proprietorship.

TAX STRATEGY TIP

The list of advantages of an LLC over an S corporation is substantial and suggests that an LLC should always be seriously considered as an option for a pass-through entity. However, one current, important advantage of an S corporation is that the shareholders are not subject to self-employment taxes on their share of the entity's earnings.

As already mentioned, an LLC with two or more members that does not elect association status is a partnership for tax purposes and is subject to all the rules applicable to other partnerships. Thus, the formation of the LLC; income, gain, loss, and deductions that flow through to the LLC members; current and liquidating distributions; and sale, gift, or exchange of an interest in the LLC all fall under the partnership rules. An LLC treated as a partnership is subject to the Sec. 704 rules for special allocations and allocations of precontribution gain or loss, to the Sec. 736 rules for retirement distributions, and to the Sec. 751 rules pertaining to unrealized receivables and inventory.

Using the LLC form for a business with publicly traded ownership interests is likely to result in taxation as a corporation. Even if the LLC does not elect association status, the public trading of the ownership interest brings the LLC under the publicly traded partnership rules. As discussed above, these rules result in the business being taxed as a corporation unless 90% or more of the income is qualifying income or unless the LLC is covered under the grandfather rules. However, given the recency of LLCs as a form for conducting business, the grandfather provisions are unlikely to apply.

REAL-WORLD EXAMPLE

All the Big 4 accounting firms and a number of other national accounting firms operate as LLPs. Many local and regional professional accounting and law firms also have changed to LLPs.

If an LLC is treated as a partnership, it offers greater flexibility than does an S corporation because it is not subject to the restrictions that apply to S corporations as to the number of shareholders, the number of classes of stock, or the types of investments in related entities that the entity can make. Moreover, unlike S corporations, LLCs can use the special allocation rules of Sec. 704 to allocate income, gain, loss or deductions to their members. Finally, each member's basis in the LLC interest includes that member's share of the organization's debts (and not just shareholder debt as with an S corporation).

LIMITED LIABILITY PARTNERSHIPS

REAL-WORLD EXAMPLE

Even though the non-responsible partners in an LLP are not liable for the responsible partner's negligence, all partners and employees can suffer if the partnership itself is deemed guilty, as demonstrated by the demise of a former Big 5 accounting firm several years ago.

Many states have added limited liability partnerships (LLPs) to the list of business forms that can be formed. Under the current state laws, the primary difference between a general partnership and an LLP is that in a limited liability partnership, a partner is not liable for damages resulting from failures in the work of other partners or of people supervised by other partners. For example, assume that a limited liability accounting partnership is assessed damages in a lawsuit that resulted from an audit partner in New York being negligent in an audit. The tax partner for the same firm, who is based in San Diego and who had no involvement with the audit or the auditor, should not be liable to pay damages resulting from the suit.

Like a general or limited partnership, this business form is a partnership for tax purposes. All the partnership tax rules and regulations apply to this business form just as they do to any other partnership.

STOP & THINK

Question: What issues do you expect the check-the-box regulations to raise for new businesses making their initial choice of entity decision? What effect do you expect these regulations to have on existing corporations?

Solution: Consider the options facing a new business. The business can be formed as a C corporation, which provides limited liability protection to owners but subjects the corporate income to double taxation. A business formed as a C corporation can make an S election for tax purposes, which keeps the limited liability protection for the owners and eliminates the double taxation by taxing all income directly to the owners. However, as you will see in Chapter C:11, a number of restrictions prevent many corporations from electing S status. In addition, all income and loss of an S corporation must be allocated among the shareholders on a pro rata basis. A partnership offers the most flexible tax treatment with no double taxation of income, but the traditional partnership must have at least one general partner whose liability for partnership debts is not limited. An LLC, which is treated as a partnership, provides limited liability protection to its owners while avoiding both the double taxation of income found in a regular C corporation as well as the restrictions placed on S corporations. Because an LLC is treated as a partnership, the income and loss shares reported by each partner is flexible, and the partner's basis for his partnership interest includes his or her share of the LLC's liabilities. Thus, in some ways, the LLC has the best attributes of both the corporation and the partnership.

These are strong reasons why a new entity would choose to form as an LLC and be treated as a partnership. However, because the LLC is a relatively new business form, statutes, case law, and regulations are still being developed, and thus many areas of uncertainty remain to be resolved over time.

The check-the-box regulations are not helpful to existing C corporations and S corporations because an existing corporation cannot elect to be treated as a partnership. Instead, it must liquidate (with all the tax consequences of a liquidation, as described in Chapter C:6) before it can form as a partnership or an LLC. Potentially, the change in entity form has a high tax cost for an existing corporation.

LIMITED LIABILITY LIMITED PARTNERSHIP

Another recent innovation is the limited liability limited partnership (LLLP). Remember that a limited partnership, in addition to having limited partners, has one or more general partners whose personal liability exposure is unlimited. The LLLP is a partnership formed under a state's limited partnership laws but that can elect under the state's laws to provide the general partners with limited liability. Thus, the LLLP is similar to an LLC. Only about 20 states, however, provide for this type of partnership. It becomes potentially useful in states that do not extend LLC status to personal service firms but allow such firms to operate as an LLLP.[45]

[45] For a detailed discussion, see Shop Talk, "Service Firms Practicing as LLLPs: What Are the Tax Consequences?" *Journal of Taxation*, August 2005.

OBJECTIVE 10

Determine the appropriate reporting for the income of an electing large partnership

ELECTING LARGE PARTNERSHIPS

Partnerships that qualify as "large partnerships" may elect to be taxed under a simplified reporting arrangement.[46] The partnership must meet the following four qualifications to be treated as an electing large partnership:

- ▶ It must not be a service partnership.
- ▶ It must not be engaged in commodity trading.
- ▶ It must have at least 100 partners.
- ▶ It must file an election to be taxed as an electing large partnership.

Section 775 defines a service partnership as one in which substantially all the partners perform substantial services in connection with the partnership's activities or the partners are retired but in the past performed substantial services in connection with the partnership's activities. One example of a partnership that could not make this election is a partnership that provides accounting services. An electing large partnership also cannot be engaged in commodity trading. Further, to qualify to make this election, the partnership must have at least 100 partners (excluding those partners who do provide substantial services in connection with the partnership's business activities) throughout the tax year.

Once it makes the election, the partnership reports its income under a simplified reporting scheme, is subject to different rules about when the partnership terminates, and is subject to a different system of audits. The election is irrevocable without IRS permission.

ELECTING LARGE PARTNERSHIP TAXABLE INCOME. Much like other partnerships, the calculation of electing large partnership taxable income includes separately stated income and other income. However, the items that must be separately stated are very different for the electing large partnership. Likewise, the items included in other income differ significantly. The main reason that Congress added electing large partnerships to the IRC was to provide a form of flow-through entity that does not require so much separate reporting to each partner of many different income, loss, and deduction items. Simpler reporting from the partnership to the partners was the goal, so fewer items are separately stated and many more items are combined at the partnership level.

Like a regular partnership, calculation of an electing large partnership's taxable income is similar to the calculation for an individual. For an electing large partnership (just like for other partnerships), the deductions for personal exemptions and net operating losses are disallowed as well as most additional itemized deductions, such as medical expenses and alimony. However, calculation of the items that would qualify as miscellaneous itemized deductions for an individual differs from the calculation for either individuals or other partnerships. For an electing large partnership, miscellaneous itemized deductions are combined at the partnership level and subject to a 70% deduction at the partnership level. After the 70% deduction, the remaining miscellaneous itemized deductions are combined with other income and passed through to the partners. Because they are combined with other income at the partnership level, they are not subject to the 2% nondeductible floor at the individual partner level.[47]

Instead of flowing through as a separately stated item as they do with a regular partnership, charitable contributions made by an electing large partnership are subject to the 10% of taxable income limit similar to the limit that normally applies to corporations. Once the limit is applied, the partnership deducts allowable charitable contribution from its ordinary income, and the partners do not report the charitable contributions as a separate item.[48]

For a regular partnership, the first-year expensing deduction allowed under Sec. 179 is both limited at the partnership level and is separately stated and limited at the partner level. For an electing large partnership, the only limit is at the partnership level. The allowable deduction is calculated at the partnership level, and the deduction amount offsets the partnership's ordinary income. For an electing large partnership, the Sec. 179

[46] Sec. 775.
[47] Sec. 773(b).
[48] Sec. 773(b)(2).

deduction is not separately stated and the impact of the Sec. 179 deduction is buried in the ordinary income amount reported by the partnership to the partners.

SEPARATELY STATED LARGE PARTNERSHIP ITEMS. An electing large partnership nevertheless is a pass-through entity, so some items still must be separately stated at the partnership level, and these items maintain their character when reported in the partners' tax returns. Section 772 lists the following items the electing large partnership must report separately:

- Taxable income or loss from passive loss limitation activities
- Taxable income or loss from other partnership activities
- Net capital gain or loss from passive loss limitation activities
- Net capital gain or loss from other partnership activities
- Tax-exempt interest
- Applicable net alternative minimum tax adjustment separately computed for passive loss limitation activities and other activities
- General credits
- Low income housing credit
- Rehabilitation credit
- Foreign income taxes
- Credit for producing fuel from a nonconventional source
- Any other item the IRS determines should be separately stated

The differences between the treatment of other partnerships versus electing large partnerships is significant. The most interesting aspect of this list is what items are combined for reporting by an electing large partnership. For example, Sec. 1231 gains and losses are netted at the partnership level, net 1231 losses are included in ordinary income or loss, and net 1231 gains are reported with capital gains and losses. The capital gains and losses also are combined at the partnership level with only a single, net number reported to the partners. The capital gain or loss is treated as long-term at the partner level. However, if the net is a short-term capital gain, that gain is treated as ordinary income and combined at the partnership level with other ordinary income items. All the partnership's credits are combined at the partnership level with the exceptions of the low income housing credit and the rehabilitation credit.

Both ordinary income and capital gains attributed to passive loss activities are reported separately from the results of other partnership activities. In addition, the taxable income or loss from activities other than passive activities generally are treated as items of income or expense with respect to property held for investment rather than as active trade or business income. Dividend income, for example, would fall into this category.

For the electing large partnership, all limits, such as the charitable contributions limit and the Sec. 179 expensing deduction limit, are applied at the partnership level rather than at the individual partner level with three exceptions. The three limits applied at the partner level are the Sec. 68 limit on itemized deductions, the limit on at risk losses, and the limit on passive activity losses.[49] For the limitation to be applied at the partner level, these items must be separately stated.

For separately stated items, the character of amounts flowing through the partnership retain their character when reported on the partners' tax returns. However, because many more items are combined at the partnership level and not separately stated, the character of many fewer kinds of income is retained to flow through with the electing large partnership form.

EXAMPLE C:10-35 ▶ The ABC Partnership is an electing large partnership that reports the following transactions for the current year. ABC has no passive activities.

[49] Sec. 773(a)

Net long-term capital loss	$100,000
Sec. 1231 gain	120,000
Ordinary income	40,000
Dividend income	10,000
Charitable contributions	30,000
Tax-exempt income	4,000

ABC will report these earnings to its partners as follows:

Long-term capital gain	$20,000
Ordinary income	33,000
Dividend income	10,000
Tax-exempt income	4,000

Because the partnership has a net Sec. 1231 gain, it is treated as a long-term capital gain ($120,000) and combined at the partnership level with the long-term capital loss ($100,000) to result in a net long-term capital gain of $20,000. At the partnership level, the charitable contribution deduction is limited to 10% of taxable income, or $7,000 [0.10 × ($20,000 capital gain + $10,000 dividend income + $40,000 ordinary income)] and is subtracted from ordinary income of $40,000 before ordinary income is reported to the partners. The character of the long-term capital gain, dividend income, tax-exempt income, and ordinary income pass through to the partner. ◀

REPORTING REQUIREMENT. An electing large partnership must provide a Schedule K-1 to each of its partners on or before March 15 following the close of the partnership tax year without regard to when the partnership tax return is due.[50] Partnerships that are not electing large partnerships are only required to provide the information return by the due date of the partnership tax return—which, for a calendar year partnership, is April 15. The IRS expects that the March 15 provision will reduce the number of partners who must file an extension of their individual tax returns because they do not receive the Schedule K-1 from a regular partnership early enough to file a timely individual return.

TERMINATION OF THE PARTNERSHIP. Because electing large partnerships are quite large and often may be widely traded, Congress decided to change the conditions under which these partnership will be considered to terminate. An electing large partnership terminates only if its partners cease to conduct any business, financial operation, or venture in a partnership form. Unlike other partnerships, an electing large partnership will not terminate because of the sale or exchange of partnership interests involving at least a 50% interest in partnership capital or profits during a 12-month period.[51]

ELECTING LARGE PARTNERSHIP AUDITS. An electing large partnership is not subject to the partnership audit rules but is subject to a much more restrictive set of partnership audit procedures.[52] First, all electing large partnership partners must report all items of partnership income, gain, loss, or deduction in the way the partnership reports the item. Deviations from that partnership reporting will be "corrected" by the IRS just as a math mistake is corrected.[53]

Because all partners are required to use identical reporting for partnership items, it becomes somewhat easier to audit partnership results only at the partnership level. Notice of audit proceedings, determination of errors, settlement offers, appeals proceedings, and court cases are all handled at the partnership level, and no individual partner can request separate treatment or refuse to participate in the partnership level result. In general, any adjustments determined at the partnership level by an audit agreement or court decision will be considered to be income or deduction that occurs in the year of the agreement or decision.[54] Accordingly, the effect of adjustments is borne by the partners who own interests in the year of the agreement or decision and not by the partners who originally reported the contested transaction results.

[50] Sec. 6031.
[51] Sec. 774(c).
[52] Sec. 6240.
[53] Sec. 6241.
[54] Sec. 6242.

TAX PLANNING CONSIDERATIONS

LIQUIDATING DISTRIBUTION OR SALE TO PARTNERS

An unusual tax planning opportunity exists when one partner withdraws from a partnership and the remaining partners proportionately increase their ownership of the partnership. The partners can structure the ownership change as either a liquidating distribution made by the partnership or as a sale of the partnership interest to the remaining partners. In fact, the substance of the two transactions is the same, only the form is different. However, this difference in form can make a substantial difference in the tax consequences in a number of areas.

- If the transferor partner receives payment for his or her interest in the partnership's Sec. 751 assets, he or she must recognize ordinary income no matter how the transaction is structured. The partnership's basis in Sec. 751 assets is increased in the case of a liquidating distribution. When a sale transaction takes place, the partnership's basis in Sec. 751 assets is increased only if the partnership has an optional basis adjustment election in effect.
- If the partnership has an optional basis adjustment election in effect, the allocation of the adjustment to the individual partnership assets can be different depending on whether the transaction is structured as a sale or as a liquidating distribution.
- If the interest being transferred equals or exceeds 50% of the profits and capital interests, a sale to the remaining partners terminates the partnership. A liquidating distribution does not cause a termination to occur.

Because the tax implications of the sale transaction and liquidating distribution alternatives are both numerous and complex, the partners should make their choice only after careful consideration. (See the Tax Strategy Problem below.)

PROBLEM MATERIALS

DISCUSSION QUESTIONS

C:10-1 Javier is retiring from the JKL Partnership. In January of the current year, he has a $100,000 basis in his partnership interest when he receives a $10,000 cash distribution. The partnership plans to distribute $10,000 each month this year, and Javier will cease to be a partner after the December payment. Is the January payment to Javier a current distribution or a liquidating distribution?

C:10-2 Lia has a $40,000 basis in her partnership interest just before receiving a parcel of land as a nonliquidating (current) distribution. The partnership purchased the land, and Lia has no precontribution gain. Under what conditions will Lia's basis in the land be $40,000? Under what conditions will Lia's basis in the land be a carryover basis from the partnership's basis in the land?

C:10-3 Mariel has a $60,000 basis in her partnership interest just before receiving a parcel of land as a liquidating distribution. She has no remaining precontribution gain and will receive no other distributions. Under what conditions will Mariel's basis in the land be $60,000?

C:10-4 Cindy has a $4,000 basis in her partnership interest before receiving a nonliquidating (current) distribution of property having a $4,500 basis and a $6,000 FMV from the CDE Partnership. Cindy has a choice of receiving either inventory or a capital asset. She will hold the distributed property as an investment for no more than two years before she sells it. What tax difference (if any) will occur as a result of Cindy's selection of one property or the other to be distributed by the partnership?

C:10-5 The AB Partnership purchases plastic components and assembles children's toys. The assembly operation requires a number of special machines that are housed in a building the partnership owns. The partnership has depreciated all its property under MACRS. The partnership sells the toys on account to a number of retail establishments and uses the accrual method of accounting. Identify any items you think might be classified as unrealized receivables.

C:10-6 Which of the following items are considered to be inventory for purposes of Sec. 751?

a. Supplies
b. Inventory
c. Notes receivable
d. Land held for investment purposes
e. Lots held for resale

C:10-7 Explain the conditions under which Sec. 751 has an impact on nonliquidating (current) distributions.

C:10-8 What conditions are required for a partner to recognize a loss upon receipt of a distribution from a partnership?

C:10-9 Can the basis of unrealized receivables and inventory received in a liquidating distribution be greater to the partner than to the partnership? Can the basis of unrealized receivables and inventory received in a distribution be smaller to the partner than to the partnership? Explain.

C:10-10 Can a partner recognize both a gain and a loss on the sale of a partnership interest? If so, under what conditions?

C:10-11 Tyra has a zero basis in her partnership interest and a share in partnership liabilities, which are quite large. Explain how these facts will affect the taxation of her departure from the partnership using the following methods of terminating her interest in the partnership.
a. A liquidating distribution of property
b. A sale of the partnership interest to a current partner for cash

C:10-12 Tom is a 55% general partner in the RST Partnership. Tom wants to retire, and the other two partners, Stacy and Rich, want to continue the partnership business. They agree that the partnership will liquidate Tom's interest in the partnership by paying him 20% of partnership profits for each of the next ten years. Explain why Sec. 736 does (or does not) apply to the partnership's payments to Tom.

C:10-13 Lucia has a $20,000 basis in her limited partnership interest before her retirement from the partnership. Her share of partnership assets have a $23,000 FMV, and the partnership has no Sec. 751 assets. In addition to being paid cash for her full share of partnership assets, Lucia will receive a share of partnership income for the next three years. Explain Lucia's tax treatment for the payments she receives.

C:10-14 What are the advantages and disadvantages to the partnership and its partners when a partnership termination is caused by a sale of at least a 50% capital and profits interest?

C:10-15 What is a publicly traded partnership? Are all publicly traded partnerships taxed as corporations?

C:10-16 What are the advantages of a firm being formed as a limited liability company (LLC) instead of as a limited partnership?

C:10-17 What is an electing large partnership? What are the advantages to the partnership of electing to be taxed under the electing large partnership rules?

ISSUE IDENTIFICATION QUESTIONS

C:10-18 When Kayla's basis in her interest in the JKL Partnership is $30,000, she receives a current distribution of office equipment. The equipment has an FMV of $40,000 and basis of $35,000. Kayla will not use the office equipment in a business activity. What tax issues should Kayla consider with respect to the distribution?

C:10-19 Joel receives a $40,000 cash distribution from the JM Partnership, which reduces his partnership interest from one-third to one-fourth. The JM Partnership is a general partnership that uses the cash method of accounting and has substantial liabilities. JM's inventory has appreciated substantially since it was purchased. What issues should Joel consider with regard to the distribution?

C:10-20 Scott sells his one-third partnership interest to Sally for $43,000 when his basis in the partnership interest is $33,000. On the date of sale, the partnership has no liabilities and the following assets:

Assets	*Basis*	*FMV*
Cash	$30,000	$30,000
Inventory	12,000	21,000
Building	45,000	60,000
Land	12,000	18,000

The partnership has claimed $5,400 of straight-line depreciation on the building. What tax issues should Scott and Sally consider with respect to the sale transaction?

C:10-21 David owns a 60% interest in the DDD Partnership, a general partnership, which he sells to the two remaining partners—Drew and Dana. The three partners have agreed that David will receive $150,000 in cash from the sale. David's basis in the partnership interest before the sale is $120,000, which includes his $30,000 share of partnership recourse liabilities. The partnership has assets with a $300,000 FMV and a $200,000 adjusted basis. What issues should David, Drew, and Dana consider before this sale takes place?

C:10-22 Andrew and Beth are equal partners in the AB Partnership. On December 30 of the current year, the AB Partnership agrees to liquidate Andrew's partnership interest for a cash payment on December 30 of each of the next five years. What tax issues should Andrew and Beth consider with respect to the liquidation of Andrew's partnership interest?

C:10-23 Alex owns 60% of the Hot Wheels LLC, which is treated as a partnership. He plans to give 15% of the LLC (one-fourth of his interest) to his daughter Haley for her high school graduation. He plans to put her interest in a trust, and he will serve as the trustee until Haley is 21. The trust will receive any distributions from the LLC, but Haley is unlikely to be given any of the cash until she is age 21. Alex's 60% interest has a $120,000 FMV and an $80,000 adjusted basis including his $48,000 share of the LLC's liabilities. Alex works full time for the LLC for a small salary and his share of LLC income. Alex also has a special allocation of income from rental property he manages for the LLC. What issues should Alex consider before he completes the gift?

C:10-24 Three individuals recently formed Krypton Company as a limited liability company (LLC). The three individuals—Jeff, Susan, and Richard—own equal interests in the company, and they all have substantial income from other sources. Krypton is a manufacturing firm and expects to earn approximately $130,000 of ordinary income and $30,000 of long term capital gain each year for the next several years. Jeff will be a full time manager and will receive a salary of $60,000 each year. What tax issues should the owners consider regarding the LLC's initial year of operations?

C:10-25 XYZ Limited Partnership has more than 300 partners and is publicly traded. XYZ was grandfathered under the 1987 Tax Act and has consistently been treated as a partnership. In the current year, XYZ will continue to be very profitable and will continue to pay out about 30% of its income to its owners each year. The managing partners of XYZ want to consider the firm's options for taxation in the current and later years.

PROBLEMS

C:10-26 *Current Distributions.* Lisa has a $25,000 basis in her partnership interest before receiving a current distribution of $4,000 cash and land with a $30,000 FMV and a $14,000 basis to the partnership. Assume that any distribution involving Sec. 751 property is pro rata and that any precontribution gains have been recognized before the distribution.

a. Determine Lisa's recognized gain or loss, Lisa's basis in distributed property, and Lisa's ending basis in her partnership interest.
b. How does your answer to Part a change if the partnership's basis in the land is $24,000 instead of $14,000?
c. How does your answer to Part a change if Lisa receives $28,000 cash instead of $4,000 (along with the land)?
d. How does your answer to Part a change if, in addition to the cash and land, Lisa receives inventory with a $25,000 FMV and a $10,000 basis and receivables with a $3,000 FMV and a zero basis?
e. Suppose instead that Lisa receives the distribution in Part a from a C corporation instead of a partnership. The corporation has $100,000 of E&P before the distribution, and Lisa's stock basis before the distribution is $25,000. What are the tax consequences to Lisa and the C corporation?
f. Note: This part can be answered only after the student studies Chapter C:11 but is placed here to allow comparison with Parts a and e. Suppose instead that Lisa receives the distribution in Part a from an S corporation instead of a partnership. Lisa is a 50% owner in the corporation, and her stock basis before the distribution is $25,000. What are the tax consequences to Lisa and the S corporation?

C:10-27 *Current Distributions.* Complete the chart for each of the following independent distributions. Assume all distributions are nonliquidating and pro rata to the partners, and no contributed property was distributed. All precontribution gain has been recognized before these distributions.

	Partner's Basis and Gain/Loss	Property Distributed	Property's Basis to Partnership	Property's FMV	Property's Basis to Partner
a. Basis:					
Predistribution	$20,000	Cash	$ 6,000	$ 6,000	
Postdistribution	$_____	Land	4,000	15,000	$_____
Gain or loss	$_____	Machinery	3,000	2,000	$_____
b. Basis:					
Predistribution	$20,000	Cash	$ 3,000	$ 3,000	
Postdistribution	$_____	Land	6,000	4,000	$_____
Gain or loss	$_____	Inventory	7,000	7,500	$_____
c. Basis					
Predistribution	$26,000	Cash	$35,000	$35,000	
Postdistribution	$_____	Land—Parcel 1	6,000	10,000	$_____
Gain or loss	$_____	Land—Parcel 2	18,000	18,000	$_____
d. Basis:					
Predistribution	$28,000	Land—Parcel 1	$ 4,000	$ 6,000	$_____
Postdistribution	$_____	Land—Parcel 2	6,000	10,000	$_____
Gain or loss	$_____	Land—Parcel 3	4,000	10,000	$_____

C:10-28 ***Current Distribution with Precontribution Gain.*** Three years ago, Mario joined the MN Partnership by contributing land with a $10,000 basis and an $18,000 FMV. On January 15 of the current year, Mario has a basis in his partnership interest of $20,000, and none of his precontribution gain has been recognized. On January 15, Mario receives a current distribution of a property other than the contributed land with a $15,000 basis and a $23,000 FMV.

a. Does Mario recognize any gain or loss on the distribution?
b. What is Mario's basis in his partnership interest after the distribution?
c. What is the partnership's basis in the land Mario contributed after Mario receives this distribution?

C:10-29 ***Current Distribution of Contributed Property.*** Andrew contributed investment land having an $18,000 basis and a $22,000 FMV along with $4,000 in money to the ABC Partnership when it was formed. Two years later, the partnership distributed the investment land Andrew had contributed to Bob, another partner. At the time of the distribution, the land had a $21,000 FMV, and Andrew and Bob's bases in their partnership interests were $21,000 and $30,000, respectively.

a. What gain or loss must be recognized on the distribution, and who must recognize it?
b. What are the bases for Andrew and Bob's interests in the partnership after the distribution?
c. What is Bob's basis in the distributed land?

C:10-30 ***Current Distribution of Contributed Property.*** The ABC Partnership made the following current distributions in the current year. The dollar amounts listed are the amounts before considering any implications of the distribution.

	Property Received			
Partner	Type of Property	Basis	FMV	Partner's Basis in Partnership Interest
Alonzo	Land	$ 4,000	$10,000	$19,000
Beth	Inventory	1,000	10,000	15,000
Cathy	Cash	10,000	10,000	18,000

The land Alonzo received had been contributed by Beth two years ago when its basis was $4,000 and its FMV was $8,000. The inventory Beth received had been contributed by Cathy two years ago when its basis was $1,000 and its FMV was $4,000. For each independent situation, what gain or loss must be recognized? What is the basis of the distributed property after the distribution? What are the bases of the partnership interests after the distribution? Assume the distribution has no Sec. 751 implications.

C:10-31 ***Current Distribution with Sec. 751.*** The KLM Partnership owns the following assets on March 1 of the current year:

Assets	Partnership's Basis	FMV
Cash	$ 30,000	$ 30,000
Receivables	–0–	16,000
Inventory	50,000	52,000
Supplies	6,000	6,500
Equipment[a]	9,000	10,500
Land (investment)	40,000	65,000
Total	$135,000	$180,000

[a]The partnership has claimed depreciation of $4,000 on the equipment.

a. Which partnership items are unrealized receivables?
b. Is the partnership's inventory substantially appreciated?
c. Assume the KLM Partnership has no liabilities and that Kay's basis for her partnership interest is $33,750. On March 1 of the current year, Kay receives a $20,000 current distribution in cash, which reduces her partnership interest from one-third to one-fourth. What are the tax results of the distribution (i.e., the amount and character of any gain, loss, or income recognized and Kay's basis in her partnership interest)?

C:10-32 ***Current Distribution with Sec. 751.*** The JKLM Partnership owns the following assets on October 1 of the current year:

Assets	Partnership's Basis	FMV
Cash	$ 48,000	$ 48,000
Receivables	12,000	12,000
Inventory	21,000	24,000
Machinery[a]	190,000	240,000
Land	36,500	76,000
Total	$307,500	$400,000

[a]Sale of the machinery for its FMV would result in $50,000 of Sec. 1245 depreciation recapture. Thus, the machinery's FMV and original cost are the same numerical value, $240,000.

a. Which partnership items are unrealized receivables?
b. Is the partnership's inventory substantially appreciated?
c. Assume the JKLM Partnership has no liabilities and Jack's basis in his partnership interest is $76,875. On October 1 of the current year, Jack receives a $25,000 current distribution in cash, which reduces his partnership interest from one-fourth to one-fifth. What are the tax results of the distribution (i.e., the amount and character of any gain, loss, or income recognized and Jack's basis in his partnership interest)?

C:10-33 ***Current Distribution with Sec. 751.*** The PQRS Partnership owns the following assets on December 30 of the current year:

Assets	Partnership's Basis	FMV
Cash	$ 20,000	$ 20,000
Receivables	–0–	40,000
Inventory	80,000	100,000
Total	$100,000	$160,000

The partnership has no liabilities, and each partner's basis in his or her partnership interest is $25,000. On December 30 of the current year, Paula receives a current distribution of inventory having a $10,000 FMV, which reduces her partnership interest from one-fourth to one-fifth. What are the tax consequences of the distribution to the partnership, Paula, and the other partners?

C:10-34 ***Liquidating Distributions.*** Assume the same four independent distributions as in Problem C:10-27. Fill in the blanks in that problem assuming the only change in the facts is that the distributions are now liquidating distributions instead of nonliquidating distributions.

C:10-35 ***Liquidating Distribution.*** Marinda is a one-third partner in the MWH Partnership before she receives $100,000 cash as a liquidating distribution. Immediately before Marinda receives the distribution, the partnership has the following assets:

Assets	*Partnership's Basis*	*FMV*
Cash	$100,000	$100,000
Marketable securities	50,000	90,000
Investment land	90,000	140,000
Total	$240,000	$330,000

At the time of the distribution, the partnership has $30,000 of outstanding liabilities, which the three partners share equally. Marinda's basis in her partnership interest before the distribution was $80,000, which includes her share of liabilities. What are the amount and character of the gain or loss recognized by Marinda and the MWH Partnership on the liquidating distribution?

C:10-36 ***Liquidating Distributions.*** The AB Partnership pays its only liability (a $100,000 mortgage) on April 1 of the current year and terminates that same day. Alison and Bob were equal partners in the partnership but have partnership bases immediately preceding these transactions of $110,000 and $180,000, respectively, including his or her share of liabilities. The two partners receive identical distributions with each receiving the following assets:

Assets	*Partnership's Basis*	*FMV*
Cash	$ 20,000	$ 20,000
Inventory	33,000	35,000
Receivables	10,000	8,000
Building	40,000	60,000
Land	15,000	10,000
Total	$118,000	$133,000

The building has no depreciation recapture potential. What are the tax implications to Alison, Bob, and the AB Partnership of the April 1 transactions (i.e., basis of assets to Alison and Bob, amount and character of gain or loss recognized, etc.)?

C:10-37 ***Liquidating Distribution.*** The LQD Partnership distributes the following property to Larry in a distribution that liquidates Larry's interest in the partnership. Larry's basis in his partnership interest before the distribution is $40,000. The adjusted bases and FMVs of the distributed property to the partnership before the distribution are as follows:

	Partnership's Basis	*FMV*
Cash	$ 2,500	$ 2,500
Inventory	8,000	9,000
Capital asset 1	10,000	15,000
Capital asset 2	15,000	17,500
Total	$35,500	$44,000

a. Determine Larry's basis in each distributed asset.
b. Same as Part a except Larry's partnership basis before the distribution is $46,500.
c. Same as Part b except the basis of capital asset 2 is $20,000 instead of $15,000.
d. Same as Part c except Larry's partnership basis before the distribution is $34,500.

C:10-38 ***Sale of a Partnership Interest.*** Pat, Kelly, and Yvette are equal partners in the PKY Partnership before Kelly sells her partnership interest. On January 1 of the current year, Kelly's basis in her partnership interest, including her share of liabilities, was $35,000. During January, the calendar year partnership earned $15,000 ordinary income and $6,000 of tax-exempt income. The partnership has a $60,000 recourse liability on January 1, and this amount remains constant throughout the tax year. Kelly's share of that liability is $20,000. The partnership has no other liabilities. Kelly sells her interest on February 1 to Margaret for a cash payment of $45,000. On the sale date the partnership had the following assets:

Assets	*Partnership's Basis*	*FMV*
Cash	$ 20,000	$ 20,000
Inventory	60,000	120,000
Building	36,000	40,000
Land	10,000	15,000
Total	$126,000	$195,000

The partnership has claimed $5,000 of depreciation on the building using the straight-line method.

a. What is Kelly's basis in her partnership interest on February 1 just before the sale?
b. What are the amount and character of Kelly's gain or loss on the sale?
c. What is Margaret's basis in her partnership interest?
d. What is the partnership's basis in its assets after the sale?

C:10-39 ***Sale of Partnership Interest and Termination.*** Clay owned 60% of the CAP Partnership and sold one-half of his interest (30%) to Steve for $75,000 cash. Before the sale, Clay's basis in his entire partnership interest was $168,000 including his $30,000 share of partnership liabilities and his share of income up to the sale date. Partnership assets on the sale date were

Assets	*Partnership's Basis*	*FMV*
Cash	$ 50,000	$ 50,000
Inventory	30,000	60,000
Land	200,000	190,000
Total	$280,000	$300,000

a. What are the amount and character of Clay's recognized gain or loss on the sale? What is his remaining basis in his partnership interest?
b. What is Steve's basis in his partnership interest?
c. How will the partnership's basis in its assets be affected?
d. How would your answers to Parts a and c change if Clay sold his entire interest to Steve for $150,000 cash?

C:10-40 ***Sale of a Partnership Interest.*** Alice, Bob, and Charles are one-third partners in the ABC Partnership. The partners originally formed the partnership with cash contributions, so no partner has precontribution gains or losses. Prior to Alice's sale of her partnership interest, the partnership has the following balance sheet:

Assets	*Partnership's Basis*	*FMV*
Cash	$ 12,000	$ 12,000
Receivable	–0–	21,000
Inventory	57,000	72,000
Machinery[a]	90,000	132,000
Building[b]	120,000	165,000
Land	36,000	30,000
Investments[c]	15,000	48,000
Total	$330,000	$480,000
Liabilities and capital		
Liabilities	$105,000	$105,000
Partners' capital:		
Alice	75,000	125,000
Bob	75,000	125,000
Charles	75,000	125,000
Total	$330,000	$480,000

[a]The machinery cost $126,000, and the partnership has claimed $36,000 of depreciation.
[b]The building cost $150,000, and the partnership has claimed $30,000 of straight-line depreciation.
[c]The partnership has held the investments for more than one year.

Alice has a $110,000 basis in her partnership interest including her share of partnership liabilities, and she sells her partnership interest to Darla for $125,000 cash.

a. What are the amount and character of Alice's recognized gain or loss on the sale?
b. What is Darla's basis in her partnership interest?

C:10-41 ***Retirement of a Partner.*** Suzanne retires from the BRS Partnership when the basis of her one-third interest is $105,000, which includes her share of liabilities. At the time of her retirement, the partnership had the following assets:

Assets	*Partnership's Basis*	*FMV*
Cash	$145,000	$145,000
Receivables	40,000	40,000
Land	130,000	220,000
Total	$315,000	$405,000

The partnership has $60,000 of liabilities when Suzanne retires. The partnership will pay Suzanne cash of $130,000 to retire her partnership interest.

a. What are the amount and character of the gain or loss Suzanne must recognize?

b. What is the impact of the retirement on the partnership and the remaining partners?

C:10-42 ***Retirement of a Partner.*** Brian owns 40% of the ABC Partnership before his retirement on April 15 of the current year. On that date, his basis in the partnership interest is $40,000 including his share of liabilities. The partnership's balance sheet on that date is as follows:

	Partnership's Basis	*FMV*
Assets:		
Cash	$ 60,000	$ 60,000
Receivables	24,000	24,000
Land	16,000	40,000
Total	$100,000	$124,000
Liabilities and capital:		
Liabilities	$ 20,000	$ 20,000
Capital—Abner	16,000	20,800
—Brian	32,000	41,600
—Charles	32,000	41,600
Total	$100,000	$124,000

What are the amount and character of gain or loss that Brian and the ABC Partnership recognize for the following independent retirement payments?

a. Brian receives $41,600 cash on April 15.

b. Brian receives $50,000 cash on April 15.

C:10-43 ***Retirement of a Partner.*** Kim retires from the KLM Partnership on January 1 of the current year. At that time, her basis in the partnership is $75,000, which includes her share of liabilities. The partnership reports the following balance sheet:

	Partnership's Basis	*FMV*
Assets:		
Cash	$100,000	$100,000
Receivables	30,000	30,000
Inventory	40,000	40,000
Land	55,000	100,000
Total	$225,000	$270,000
Liabilities and capital:		
Liabilities	$ 75,000	$ 75,000
Capital—Kim	50,000	65,000
—Larry	50,000	65,000
—Michael	50,000	65,000
Total	$225,000	$270,000

Explain the tax consequences (i.e., amount and character of gain or loss recognized and Kim's basis for any assets received) of the partnership making the retirement payments described in the following independent situations. Kim's share of liabilities is $25,000.

a. Kim receives $65,000 cash on January 1.

b. Kim receives $75,000 cash on January 1.

C:10-44 ***Death of a Partner.*** When Jerry died on April 16 of the current year, he owned a 40% interest in the JM Partnership, and Michael owns the remaining 60% interest. All his assets are held in his estate for a two-year period while the estate is being settled. Jerry's estate is his successor-in-interest for the partnership interest. Under a formula contained in the partnership agreement, the partnership must pay Jerry's successor-in-interest $40,000 cash shortly after his death plus $90,000 for each of the two years immediately following a partner's death. The partnership agreement provides that all payments to a retiring partner will first be payments for the partner's share of assets, and then any additional payments will be Sec. 736(a) payments. When Jerry died, the partnership had the following assets:

Assets	*Partnership's Basis*	*FMV*
Cash	$100,000	$100,000
Land	200,000	300,000
Total	$300,000	$400,000

Jerry's basis for the partnership interest on the date of his death was $120,000 including his $30,000 share of partnership liabilities.

a. How will the payments be taxed to Jerry's successor-in-interest?

b. What are the tax implications of the payments for the partnership?

C:10-45 ***Death of a Partner.*** Bruce died on June 1 of the current year. On the date of his death, he held a one-third interest in the ABC Partnership, which had a $100,000 basis including his share of liabilities. Under the partnership agreement, Bruce's successor-in-interest, his wife, is to receive the following amounts from the partnership: $130,000 cash, the partnership's assumption of Bruce's $20,000 share of partnership liabilities, plus 10% of partnership net income for the next three years. The partnership's assets immediately before Bruce's death are as follows:

Assets	*Partnership's Basis*	*FMV*
Cash	$100,000	$100,000
Receivables	90,000	90,000
Inventory	40,000	40,000
Land	70,000	220,000
Total	$300,000	$450,000

a. What are the amount and character of the gain or loss that Bruce's wife must recognize when she receives the first year's payment?

b. What is the character of the gain recognized from the partnership interest when she receives the payments in each of the following three years?

c. When does Bruce's successor-in-interest cease to be a member of the partnership?

C:10-46 ***Liquidation or Sale of a Partnership Interest.*** John has a 60% capital and profits interest in the JAS Partnership with a basis of $333,600, which includes his share of liabilities, when he decides to retire. Andrew and Stephen want to continue the partnership's business. On the date John retires, the partnership's balance sheet is as follows:

	Partnership's Basis	*FMV*
Assets:		
Cash	$160,000	$160,000
Receivables	100,000	100,000
Building[a]	200,000	300,000
Land	96,000	180,000
Total	$556,000	$740,000
Liabilities and capital:		
Liabilities	$120,000	$120,000
Capital—John	261,600	372,000
—Andrew	87,200	124,000
—Stephen	87,200	124,000
Total	$556,000	$740,000

[a]The partnership has claimed $60,000 of straight-line depreciation on the building.

a. What are the tax implications for John, Andrew, Stephen, and the JAS Partnership if Andrew and Stephen each purchase one-half of John's partnership interest for a cash price of $186,000 each? Include in your answer the amount and character of the recognized gain or loss, basis of the partnership assets, and any other relevant tax implications.

b. What are the tax implications for John, Andrew, Stephen, and the JAS Partnership if the partnership pays John a liquidating distribution equal to 60% of each partnership asset other than cash plus $24,000 of cash? Assume the assets are easily divisible.

C:10-47 ***Liquidation or Sale of a Partnership Interest.*** Amy, a one-third partner, retires from the AJS Partnership on January 1 of the current year. Her basis in her partnership interest is $120,000 including her share of liabilities. Amy receives $160,000 in cash from the partnership for her interest. On that date, the partnership balance sheet is as follows:

	Partnership's Basis	*FMV*
Assets:		
Cash	$180,000	$180,000
Receivables	60,000	60,000
Land	120,000	300,000
Total	$360,000	$540,000
Liabilities and capital:		
Liabilities	$ 60,000	$ 60,000
Capital—Amy	100,000	160,000
—Joan	100,000	160,000
—Stephanie	100,000	160,000
Total	$360,000	$540,000

a. What are the amount and character of Amy's recognized gain or loss?

b. How would your answers to Part a change if Joan and Stephanie each purchased one-half of Amy's partnership interest for $80,000 cash instead of having the partnership distribute the $160,000 in cash to Amy?

C:10-48 ***Exchange of Partnership Interests.*** Josh holds a general partnership interest in the JLK Partnership having a $40,000 basis and a $60,000 FMV. The JLK Partnership is a limited partnership that engages in real estate activities. Diana has an interest in the CDE Partnership having a $20,000 basis and a $60,000 FMV. The CDE Partnership is a general partnership that also engages in real estate activities. Neither partnership has any Sec. 751 assets or any liabilities.

a. What are the tax implications if Josh and Diana simply exchange their partnership interests?

b. What are the tax implications if instead Diana exchanges her general partnership interest in the CDE Partnership for a limited partnership interest in the same partnership (and Josh retains his general partnership interest in the JLK Partnership)?

C:10-49 ***Termination of a Partnership.*** Wendy, Xenia, and Yancy own 40%, 8%, and 52%, respectively, of the WXY Partnership. For each of the following independent situations occurring in the current year, determine whether the WXY Partnership terminates and, if so, the date on which the termination occurs.

a. Wendy sells her entire interest to Alan on June 1. Alan sells one-half of the interest to Beth on November 15.

b. Yancy receives a series of liquidating distributions totaling $100,000. He receives four equal annual payments on January 1 of the current year and the three subsequent years.

c. Wendy and Xenia each receive a liquidating distribution on September 14.

d. Yancy sells his interest to Karen on June 1 for $10,000 cash and a $90,000 installment note. The note will be paid in monthly installments of $10,000 principal plus interest (at a rate acceptable to the IRS) beginning on July 1.

e. The WXY and ABC Partnerships combine their businesses on December 30. Ownership of the new, combined partnership is as follows: Wendy, 20%; Xenia, 4%; Yancy, 26.5%; Albert, 20%; Beth, 19.5%; and Carl, 10%.

f. On January 1, the WXY Partnership divides its business into two new businesses. The WX Partnership is owned equally by Wendy and Xenia. Yancy continues his share of the business as a sole proprietorship.

C:10-50 ***Termination of a Partnership.*** For each of the following independent situations, determine which partnership(s) (if any) terminate and which partnership(s) (if any) continue.

a. The KLMN Partnership is created when the KL Partnership merges with the MN Partnership. The ownership of the new partnership is held 25% by Katie, 30% by Laura, 25% by Michael, and 20% by Neal.
b. The ABC Partnership, with $150,000 in assets, is owned equally by Amy, Beth, and Chuck. The CD Partnership, with $100,000 in assets, is owned equally by Chuck and Drew. The two partnerships merge, and the resulting ABCD Partnership is owned as follows: Amy, 20%; Beth, 20%; Chuck, 40%; and Drew, 20%.
c. The WXYZ Partnership results when the WX and YZ Partnerships merge. Ownership of WXYZ is held equally by the four partners. WX contributes $140,000 in assets, and YZ contributes $160,000 in assets to the new partnership.
d. The DEFG Partnership is owned 20% by Dawn, 40% by Eve, 30% by Frank, and 10% by Greg. Two new partnerships are formed by the division of DEFG. The two new partnerships, the DE and FG Partnerships, are owned in proportion to their relative interests in the DEFG Partnership by the individuals for whom they are named.
e. The HIJK Partnership is owned equally by its four partners, Hal, Isaac, Juan, and Katherine, before its division. Two new partnerships, the HI and JK Partnerships, are formed out of the division with the new partnerships owned equally by the partners for whom they are named.

C:10-51 *Disposal of a Tax Shelter.* Maria purchased an interest in a real estate tax shelter many years ago and deducted losses from its operation for several years. The real property owned by the tax shelter when Maria made her investment has been fully depreciated on a straight-line basis. Her basis in her limited partnership interest is zero, but her share of partnership liabilities is $100,000. Explain the tax results if Maria sells her partnership interest for $5 cash.

C:10-52 *Optional Basis Adjustment.* Patty pays $100,000 cash for Stan's one-third interest in the STU Partnership. The partnership has a Sec. 754 election in effect. Just before the sale of Stan's interest, STU's balance sheet appears as follows:

	Partnership's Basis	*FMV*
Assets:		
Cash	$ 80,000	$ 80,000
Land	160,000	220,000
Total	$240,000	$300,000
Partners' capital		
Stan	$ 80,000	$100,000
Traffic Corporation	80,000	100,000
Union Corporation	80,000	100,000
Total	$240,000	$300,000

a. What is Patty's total optional basis adjustment?
b. If STU Partnership sells the land for its $220,000 FMV immediately after Patty purchases her interest, how much gain or loss will the partnership recognize?
c. How much gain will Patty report as a result of the sale?

C:10-53 *Taxation of LLC Income.* ABC Company, a limited liability company (LLC) organized in the state of Florida, reports using a calendar tax year-end. The LLC chooses to be taxed as a partnership. Alex, Bob, and Carrie (all calendar year taxpayers) own ABC equally, and each has a basis of $40,000 in his or her ABC interest on the first day of the current tax year. ABC has the following results for the current year's operation:

Operating income	$30,000
Short-term capital gain	12,000
Long-term capital loss	6,000

Each owner received a $12,000 cash distribution during the current year.
a. What are the amount and character of the income, gain, and loss Alex must report on his tax return as a result of ABC's operations?
b. What is Alex's basis in his ownership interest in ABC after the current year's operations?

C:10-54 *Electing Large Partnership.* Austin & Becker is an electing large partnership. During the current year, the partnership has the following income, loss, and deduction items:

Ordinary income	$5,200,000
Rental loss	(2,000,000)
Long-term capital loss from investments	(437,100)
Short-term capital gain from investments	827,400
Charitable contributions	164,000

a. What ordinary income will Austin & Becker report?
b. What are the separately stated items for Austin & Becker?

C:10-55 ***Electing Large Partnership.*** Happy Times Film Distributions is an electing large partnership. During the current year, the partnership has the following income, loss, and deduction items:

Ordinary income	$ 700,000
Passive income	3,000,000
Sec. 1231 gains	27,000
Sec. 1231 losses	(134,800)
Long-term capital gains from investments	437,600
General business tax credits	43,000

a. What ordinary income will Happy Times report?
b. What are the separately stated items reported by Happy Times?

COMPREHENSIVE PROBLEMS

C:10-56 Refer to the facts in Comprehensive Problem C:6-54. Now assume the entity is a partnership named Lifecycle Partnership. Additional facts are as follows:

- Except for precontribution gains and losses, the partners agree to share profits and losses in a 60% (Able)—40% (Baker) ratio.
- The partners actively and materially participate in the partnership's business. Thus, the partnership is not a passive activity.
- Partnership debt is recourse debt.
- The salary to Able is a guaranteed payment.
- The refund for the NOL is not relevant to the partnership, nor are the E&P numbers.
- In addition to the numbers provided for the assets on January 2, 2010, the following partnership book values apply:

Equipment	$ 215,000
Building	926,000
Land A	30,000
Land B	20,000
Total	$1,191,000

- On January 2, 2010, the partnership sells its assets and pays off the $1.87 million debt. The partnership then makes liquidating distributions of the remaining cash to Able and Baker in accordance with their book capital account balances.

Required:

a. Determine the tax consequences of the partnership formation to Able, Baker, and Lifecycle Partnership.
b. For 2007–2009, prepare a schedule showing:
 (1) Partnership ordinary income and other separately stated items
 (2) Able's and Baker's book capital accounts at the end of 2007, 2008, and 2009
 (3) Able's and Baker's bases in their partnership interests at the end of 2007, 2008, and 2009
c. For 2010, determine:
 (1) The results of the asset sales
 (2) Able's and Baker's book capital accounts after the asset sales but before the final liquidating distribution
 (3) Able's and Baker's bases in their partnership interests after the asset sales but before the final liquidating distribution
 (4) The results of the liquidating distributions

C:10-57 Anne decides to leave the ABC Partnership after owning the interest for many years. She owns a 52% capital, profits, and loss interest in the general partnership (which is not a service partnership). Anne's basis in her partnership interest is $120,000 just before she leaves the partnership. The partnership agreement does not mention payments to partners who leave the partnership. The partnership has not made an optional basis adjustment election (Sec. 754). All partnership liabilities are recourse liabilities, and Anne's share is equal to her loss interest. When Anne leaves the partnership, the assets and liabilities for the partnership are as follows:

	Partnership's Basis	*FMV*
Assets:		
Cash	$240,000	$240,000
Receivables	–0–	64,000
Inventory	24,000	24,000
Land	60,000	100,000
Total	$324,000	$428,000
Liabilities	$ 60,000	$ 60,000

Analyze the following two alternatives, and answer the associated questions for each alternative.

a. Anne could receive a cash payment of $220,000 from the partnership to terminate her interest in the partnership. Does Anne or the partnership have any income, deduction, gain, or loss? Determine both the amount and character of any items.

b. Carrie already owns a 30% general interest in the ABC partnership prior to Anne's departure. Carrie is willing to buy Anne's partnership interest for a cash payment of $220,000. What income, gain, loss, or deduction will Anne recognize on the sale? What are the tax implications for the partnership if Carrie buys Anne's interest?

TAX STRATEGY PROBLEM

C:10-58 Consider the following balance sheet for DEF Partnership:

	Partnership's Basis	*FMV*
Assets:		
Cash	$60,000	$ 60,000
Receivables	–0–	60,000
Land A	10,000	20,000
Land B	10,000	20,000
Land C	10,000	20,000
Total	$90,000	$180,000
Partners' capital:		
Daniel	$30,000	$ 60,000
Edward	30,000	60,000
Frances	30,000	60,000
Total	$90,000	$180,000

Note: Land A, B, and C are Sec. 1231 property, and each partner's outside basis is $30,000.

Suppose Daniel wishes to exit the partnership completely. After discussions with Edward and Frances, the partners agree to let Daniel choose one of three options:

1. Daniel takes a liquidating distribution of $60,000 cash.
2. Daniel takes a pro rata liquidating distribution of $20,000 cash, $20,000 receivables, and Land A (FMV $20,000).
3. Daniel sells his entire partnership interest to Doris for $60,000 cash.

Required:

a. Determine the tax consequences to Daniel of each option including gains (losses) realized, recognized, and deferred; character of gains (losses); and bases of assets.

b. Discuss the relative merits of each option to Daniel, that is, what are the advantages and disadvantages of each option? What factors could sway your recommendation one way or the other?

Note: See Case Study Problem C:10-59 for another situation involving various exit strategies.

CASE STUDY PROBLEM

C:10-59 Mark Green and his brother Michael purchased land in Orlando, Florida many years ago. At that time, they began their investing as Green Brothers Partnership with capital they obtained from placing second mortgages on their homes. Their investments have flourished both because of the prosperity and growth of the area and because they have shown an ability to select prime real estate for others to develop. Over the years, they have acquired a great amount of land and have sold some to developers.

Their current tax year has just closed, and the partnership has the following balance sheet:

	Partnership's Basis	*FMV*
Assets:		
Cash	$200,000	$ 200,000
Accounts receivable	90,000	90,000
Land held for investment	310,000	1,010,000
Total	$600,000	$1,300,000
Liabilities and capital:		
Mortgages	$400,000	$ 400,000
Capital—Mark	100,000	450,000
—Michael	100,000	450,000
Total	$600,000	$1,300,000

Mark and Michael each have a basis in their partnership interest of $300,000 including their share of liabilities. They share the economic risk of loss from the liabilities equally. Last spring, Mark had a serious heart attack. On his doctor's advice, Mark wants to retire from all business activity and terminate his interest in the partnership. He is interested in receiving some cash now but is not averse to receiving part of his payment over time.

You have been asked to provide the brothers with information on how to terminate Mark's interest in the partnership. Several possibilities have occurred to Mark and Michael, and they want your advice as to which is best for Mark from a tax standpoint. Michael understands that the resulting choice may not be the best option for him. The possibilities they have considered include the following:

- Michael has substantial amounts of personal cash and could purchase Mark's interest directly. However, the brothers think that option probably would take almost all the cash Michael could raise, and they are concerned about any future cash needs Michael might have. They would prefer to have Mark receive $120,000 now plus $110,000 per year for each of the next three years. Mark also would receive interest at a market rate on the outstanding debt. This alternative would qualify for installment reporting. However, the installment sale rules for related parties would apply.
- The partnership could retire Mark's interest. They have considered the option of paying Mark $150,000 now plus 50% of partnership profits for the next three years. Alternatively, they could arrange for Mark to have a $150,000 payment now and a guaranteed payment of $100,000 per year for the next three years. They expect that the dollar amounts to be received by Mark would be approximately the same for the next three years under these two options. Mark also would receive interest at a market rate on any deferred payments.
- John Watson, a long-time friend of the family, has expressed an interest in buying Mark's interest for $450,000 cash immediately. Michael and John are comfortable that they could work well together.

Mark has substantial amounts of money in savings accounts and in stocks and bonds that have a ready market. He has invested in no other business directly. Assume that Mark's ordinary tax rate is 35% in each year and that his capital gains tax rate is 15%.

Required: Prepare a memorandum summarizing the advice you would give the two brothers on the options that they have considered.

TAX RESEARCH PROBLEMS

C:10-60 Arnie, Becky, and Clay are equal partners in the ABC General Partnership. The three individuals have tax bases in their partnership interests of $80,000, $120,000, and $160,000, respectively, and their financial accounting capital accounts are equal. For business reasons, the partnership needs to be changed into the ABC Corporation, and all three owners agree to the change. The partnership is expected to have the following assets on the date that the change is to occur:

Assets	*Partnership's Tax Basis*	*FMV*	*Partnership's Fin. Acctg. Book Value*
Cash	$ 50,000	$ 50,000	$ 50,000
Accounts receivable	60,000	55,000	55,000
Inventory	150,000	200,000	150,000
Land	200,000	295,000	235,000
Total	$460,000	$600,000	$490,000

Liabilities of $100,000 are currently outstanding and will be owed on the exchange date. Liabilities are shared equally and, as always, are already included in the bases of the partnership interest. The structure being considered for making the change is as follows:

- ABC Partnership transfers all its assets and liabilities to the new ABC Corporation in exchange for all the corporation's stock.
- ABC Partnership then liquidates by distributing the ABC stock to Arnie, Becky, and Clay.

Required: The tax manager you work for has asked you to determine the tax and financial accounting consequences. Describe the financial and tax treatments in a short memorandum to the partnership. Be sure to mention any relevant IRC sections, Treasury Regulations, revenue rulings, and APB or FASB opinions.

C:10-61 Della retires from the BCD General Partnership when her basis in her partnership interest is $70,000 including her $10,000 share of liabilities. The partnership is in the business of providing house cleaning services for local residences. At the date of Della's retirement, the partnership's balance sheet is as follows:

	Partnership's Basis	*FMV*
Assets:		
Cash	$ 50,000	$ 50,000
Receivables	–0–	30,000
Equipment[a]	40,000	50,000
Building[b]	90,000	100,000
Land	30,000	40,000
Total	$210,000	$270,000
Liabilities and capital:		
Liabilities	$ 30,000	$ 30,000
Capital—Bruce	60,000	80,000
—Celia	60,000	80,000
—Della	60,000	80,000
Total	$210,000	$270,000

[a]If the equipment were sold for $50,000, the entire gain would be recaptured as Sec. 1245 ordinary income.
[b]The building has been depreciated using the straight-line method.

Della will receive payments of $20,000 cash plus 5% of partnership ordinary income for each of the next five years. The partnership agreement specifies that goodwill will be paid for when a partner retires. Bruce, Celia, and Della agree that the partnership has $21,000 in goodwill when Della retires and that she will be paid for her one-third share.

Required: A tax manager in your firm has asked you to determine the amount and character of the income Della must report for each of the next five years. In addition, he wants you to research the tax consequences of the retirement on the partnership for the next five years. (Assume the partnership earns $100,000 of ordinary income each year for the next five years.) Prepare an oral presentation to be made to Della explaining the tax consequences of the payments she will receive.

C:10-62 Pedro owns a 60% interest in the PD General Partnership having a $40,000 basis and $200,000 FMV. His share of partnership liabilities is $100,000. Because he is nearing retirement age, he has decided to give away his partnership interest on June 15 of the current year. The partnership's tax year ends on December 31. Pedro's tax year ends on June

30. He intends to give a 30% interest to his son, Juan, and the remaining 30% interest to the American Red Cross.

Required: A tax manager in your firm has asked you to prepare a letter to Pedro explaining fully the tax consequences of this gift to him, the partnership, and the donees. She reminds you to be sure to include information about the allocation of the current year's partnership income.

C:10-63 Frank, Greta, and Helen each have a one-third interest in the FGH Partnership. On December 31, 2006, the partnership reported the following balance sheet:

Assets	*Partnership's Basis*	*FMV*
Cash	$120,000	$120,000
Asset 1	262,380	360,000
Asset 2	115,200	90,000
Total	$497,580	$570,000
Partners' Capital		
Frank	$165,860	$190,000
Greta	165,860	190,000
Helen	165,860	190,000
Total	$497,580	$570,000

The partnership placed Asset 1 (seven-year property) in service in 2004 and Asset 2 (five-year property) in service in 2005. The partnership did not elect Sec. 179 expensing and did not claim bonus depreciation. Accordingly, it computed the assets' adjusted bases at December 31, 2006 as follows:

		Asset 1		*Asset 2*
Cost		$600,000		$240,000
Depreciation:				
2004	$85,740			
2005	146,940		$48,000	
2006	104,940	(337,620)	76,800	(124,800)
Adjusted basis		$262,380		$115,200

On January 2, 2007, Helen sold her partnership interest to Hank for $190,000. At the time of sale, the partnership had a Sec. 754 optional basis election in effect but has not elected to use the remedial method for allocating partnership items.

Required: The partners have asked you to determine (1) the amount and character of Helen's gain or loss; (2) Hank's optional basis adjustment and its allocation to Asset 1 and Asset 2; and (3) the amount of depreciation allocated to Hank in 2007, including the effects of the optional basis adjustment. At a minimum, you should consult the following resources:

- IRC Secs. 743 and 751
- Reg. Sec. 1.743-1(j)
- Reg. Sec. 1.755-1

11

CHAPTER

S CORPORATIONS

LEARNING OBJECTIVES

After studying this chapter, you should be able to

1. Explain the requirements for being taxed under Subchapter S
2. Apply the procedures for electing to be taxed under Subchapter S
3. Identify the events that will terminate an S election
4. Determine the permitted tax years for an S corporation
5. Calculate ordinary income or loss
6. Calculate the amount of any special S corporation taxes
7. Calculate a shareholder's allocable share of ordinary income or loss and separately stated items
8. Determine the limitations on a shareholder's deduction of S corporation losses
9. Calculate a shareholder's basis in his or her S corporation's stock and debt
10. Determine the taxability of an S corporation's distributions to its shareholders
11. Apply the procedures for filing an S corporation tax return
12. Determine the estimated tax payments required of an S corporation and its shareholders

CHAPTER OUTLINE

This chapter discusses a special type of corporate entity known as an S corporation. The S corporation rules, located in Subchapter S of the Internal Revenue Code, permit small corporations to enjoy the nontax advantages of the corporate form of organization without being subject to the possible tax disadvantages of the corporate form (e.g., double taxation when the corporation pays a dividend to its shareholders). When enacting these rules, Congress stated three purposes:

- To permit businesses to select a particular form of business organization without being influenced by tax considerations
- To provide aid for small businesses by allowing the income of the business to be taxed to shareholders rather than being taxed at the corporate level
- To permit corporations realizing losses for a period of years to obtain a tax benefit of offsetting the losses against income at the shareholder level[1]

As discussed in Chapter C:2, S corporations are treated as corporations for legal and business purposes. For federal income tax purposes, however, they are treated much like partnerships.[2] As in a partnership, the profits and losses of the S corporation pass through to the owners, and the S corporation can make tax-free distributions of earnings previously taxed to its shareholders. Although generally taxed like a partnership, the S corporation still follows many of the basic Subchapter C tax provisions (e.g., S corporations use the corporate tax rules regarding formations, liquidations, and tax-free reorganizations instead of the partnership rules). A tabular comparison of the S corporation, partnership, and C corporation rules appears in Appendix F.

ADDITIONAL COMMENT

An LLC (or partnership) that wishes to be treated as an S corporation can file the S election (Form 2553) and automatically be classified as an association (corporation) under the check-the-box regulations without having to file the entity classification election (Form 8832).

Changes over the past several years have caused many businesses to reexamine the implications of an S election. First, the restrictive nature of the S corporation requirements has caused many new businesses that were potential S corporations to look at alternative business forms. All 50 states have adopted limited liability company (LLC) legislation. LLCs offer many of the same tax advantages of S corporations because they are treated as partnerships. LLCs, however, are not subject to the same requirements that an S corporation and its shareholders must satisfy to make and retain an S election. Partially because of the S corporation restrictions, some new businesses have organized as LLCs to take advantage of the greater operational flexibility the LLC form provides the entity and its owners, as well as its liability protection. A number of small businesses, however, elected to be S corporations because of the greater certainty available within the legal system for corporate entities.

Recent tax legislation has relaxed restrictions and increased the S corporation's popularity. For example, the shareholder limit was increased to 100, and the prohibitions against certain entities and trusts becoming S corporation shareholders were lessened. Moreover, current law now treats family members as one shareholder for the 100-shareholder limit. In effect, these changes have reduced some of the differences between S corporations and LLCs and have renewed interest in the S corporation form of doing business.

For many existing C corporations, the tax cost of liquidating the corporate entity and creating an LLC may be a prohibitively expensive way to avoid the corporate level income tax (see Chapter C:6). However, many of these C corporations have taken the next best alternative, that is, making an S election.

This chapter examines the requirements for making an S election and the tax rules that apply to S corporations and their shareholders.

---

[1] S. Rept. No. 1983, 85th Cong., 2d Sess., p. 87 (1958).

[2] Some states do not recognize an S corporation as a conduit for state income tax purposes. Instead, they are taxed under the state income tax laws in the same manner as a C corporation.

SHOULD AN S ELECTION BE MADE?

ADVANTAGES OF S CORPORATION TREATMENT

A number of advantages are available to a corporation that makes an S election.

REAL-WORLD EXAMPLE

The number of S corporations has grown from 725,000 in 1985 to 3.15 million in 2002. As a result of this rapid increase, the IRS has announced a major study of S corporation compliance to be conducted by the National Research Program (NRP). Under this program, the IRS will examine 5,000 randomly selected S corporation returns from 2003 and 2004 filings. See News Release IR 2005-76.

- The corporation's income is exempt from the corporate income tax. An S corporation's income is taxed only to its shareholders, whose tax bracket may be lower than a C corporation's tax bracket.
- The corporation's losses pass through to its shareholders and can be used to reduce the taxes owed on other types of income. This feature can be especially important for new businesses. The corporation can make an S election, pass through the start-up losses to the owners, and terminate the election once a C corporation becomes advantageous.
- Undistributed income taxed to the shareholder is not taxed again when subsequently distributed unless the distribution exceeds the shareholder's basis for his or her stock.
- Capital gains, dividends, and tax-exempt income are separately stated and retain their character when passed through to the shareholders. Such amounts become commingled with other corporate earnings and are taxed as dividends when distributed by a C corporation. Through 2010, however, the 15% maximum tax rate on qualified dividends alleviates the detrimental tax effect of C corporation dividends.
- Deductions, losses, and tax credits are separately stated and retain their character when passed through to the shareholders. These amounts may be subject to the various limitations at the shareholder level. This treatment can permit the shareholder to claim a tax benefit when it otherwise would be denied to the corporation (e.g., a shareholder can claim the general business credit benefit even though the S corporation reports a substantial loss for the year).
- Splitting the S corporation's income among family members is possible. However, income splitting is restricted by the requirement that reasonable compensation be provided to family members who provide capital and services to the S corporation.
- An S corporation's earnings that pass through to the individual shareholders are not subject to the self-employment tax. In contrast, a partnership must determine what portion of each general partner's net earnings constitutes self-employment income.
- An S corporation is not subject to the personal holding company tax or the accumulated earnings tax (although, as discussed later, passive income can trigger a corporate-level tax in special circumstances).

DISADVANTAGES OF S CORPORATION TREATMENT

A number of tax disadvantages also exist for a corporation that makes an S election.

KEY POINT

The structure of an S corporation can create a real hardship for a shareholder if large amounts of income flow through without any compensation payments or distributions of cash to help pay the tax on the income.

- A C corporation is treated as a separate tax entity from its shareholders, thereby permitting its first $50,000 of income to be taxed at a 15% marginal rate instead of the shareholder's marginal rate.
- The S corporation's earnings are taxed to the shareholders even though they are not distributed. This treatment may require the corporation to make distributions or salary payments so the shareholder can pay taxes owed on the S corporation's earnings.
- S corporations are subject to an excess net passive income tax and a built-in gains tax. Partnerships are not subject to either of these taxes.
- Dividends received by the S corporation are not eligible for the dividends-received deduction, as is the case for a C corporation.
- Allocation of ordinary income or loss and the separately stated items is based on the stock owned on each day of the tax year. Special allocations of particular items are not permitted, as they are in a partnership.

- The loss limitation for an S corporation shareholder is smaller than for a partner in a partnership because of the treatment of liabilities. Shareholders can increase their loss limitations by the basis of any debt they loan to the S corporation. Partners, on the other hand, can increase their loss limitation by their ratable share of all partnership liabilities.
- S corporations and their shareholders are subject to the at-risk, passive activity limitation, and hobby loss rules. C corporations generally are not subject to these rules.
- An S corporation is somewhat restricted in the type and number of shareholders it can have and the capital structure it can use. Partnerships and C corporations are not so restricted.
- S corporations must use a calendar year as their tax year unless they can establish a business purpose for a fiscal year or unless they make a special election to use an otherwise nonpermitted tax year. Similar restrictions also apply to partnerships.

Once the owners decide to incorporate, no general rule determines whether the corporation should make an S election. Before making a decision, management and the shareholders should examine the long- and short-run tax and nontax advantages and disadvantages of filing as a C corporation versus filing as an S corporation. Unlike a consolidated return election, the S election can be revoked or terminated at any time with minimal effort.

S CORPORATION REQUIREMENTS

OBJECTIVE 1

Explain the requirements for being taxed under Subchapter S

The S corporation requirements are divided into two categories: shareholder-related and corporation-related requirements. A corporation that satisfies all the requirements is known as a small business corporation. Only small business corporations can make an S election. Each set of requirements is outlined below.

SHAREHOLDER-RELATED REQUIREMENTS

Three shareholder-related requirements must be satisfied on each day of the tax year.[3]

- The corporation must not have more than 100 shareholders.
- All shareholders must be individuals, estates, certain tax-exempt organizations, or certain kinds of trusts.
- None of the individual shareholders can be classified as a nonresident **alien**.

ADDITIONAL COMMENT

The Sec. 1244 stock rules (Chapter C:2) and the S corporation rules both use the term *small business corporations.* The definitions have different requirements, although most S corporation stock can qualify as Sec. 1244 stock.

100-SHAREHOLDER RULE. For purposes of applying the 100-shareholder limit, members of a family (and their estates) count as one shareholder. Members of a family include the common ancestor, lineal descendants of the common ancestor, spouses (or former spouses) of the common ancestor or lineal descendents, and estates of family members. An individual will not be considered a common ancestor if he or she is more than six generations removed from the youngest generation of family member shareholders. When two unmarried or nonfamily individuals own stock jointly (e.g., as tenants in common or as joint tenants), each owner is considered a separate shareholder.

REAL-WORLD EXAMPLE

In 2003, 59.1% of all S corporations had one owner. Only 0.09% of the 3.3 million S corporations that filed in 2003 had more than 30 owners.

ELIGIBLE SHAREHOLDERS. C corporations and partnerships cannot own S corporation stock. This restriction prevents a corporation or a partnership having a large number of owners from avoiding the 100-shareholder limitation by purchasing S corporation stock and being treated as a single shareholder. Organizations exempt from the federal

[3] Sec. 1361.

income tax under Sec. 501(a) (e.g., a tax-exempt public charity or private foundation) can hold S corporation stock, and each such organization counts as one shareholder when calculating the 100-shareholder limit.

Seven types of trusts can own S corporation stock: grantor trusts, voting trusts,[4] testamentary trusts, **qualified Subchapter S trusts** (QSSTs),[5] qualified retirement plan trusts, small business trusts, and beneficiary-controlled trusts (i.e., trusts that distribute all their income to a single income beneficiary who is treated as the owner of the trust). Grantor trusts, QSSTs, and beneficiary-controlled trusts can own S corporation stock only if the grantor or the beneficiary is a qualified shareholder. Each beneficiary of a voting trust also must be an eligible shareholder. A qualified retirement plan trust is one formed as part of a qualified stock bonus, pension, or profit sharing plan or employee stock ownership plan (ESOP) that is exempt from the federal income tax under Sec. 501(a).

Small business trusts can own S corporation stock. These trusts can be complex trusts and primarily are used as estate planning devices. No interest in a small business trust can be acquired in a purchase transaction, that is, a transaction where the holder's interest takes a cost basis under Sec. 1012. Interests in small business trusts generally are acquired as a result of a gift or bequest. All current beneficiaries of a small business trust must be individuals, estates, or charitable organizations. Current beneficiaries are parties that can receive an income distribution for the period in question. Each beneficiary counts separately for purposes of the 100-shareholder limit. QSSTs and tax-exempt trusts are ineligible to elect to be a small business trust. The trustee must make an election to obtain small business trust status.

ETHICAL POINT

Tax professionals must assist their clients in monitoring that the S corporation requirements are met on each day of the tax year. Failing to meet one of the requirements for even one day terminates the election. Ignoring a terminating event until the IRS discovers it upon an audit probably will cause the corporation to be taxed as a C corporation and prevent it from having the termination treated as being inadvertent.

A testamentary trust (i.e., a trust created under the terms of a will) that receives S corporation stock can hold the stock and continue to be an eligible shareholder for a two-year period, beginning on the date the stock transfers to the trust. A grantor trust that held S corporation stock immediately before the death of the deemed owner, and which continues in existence after the death of the deemed owner, can continue to hold the stock and be an eligible shareholder for the two-year period beginning on the date of the deemed owner's death. Charitable remainder unitrusts and charitable remainder annuity trusts do not qualify as small business trusts.

EXAMPLE C:11-1 ▶ Joan, a U.S. citizen, owns 25% of Walden Corporation's stock. Walden is an S corporation. At the time of Joan's death in the current year, the Walden stock passes to her estate. The estate is a qualifying shareholder, and the transfer does not affect the S election. If the stock subsequently transfers to a trust provided for in Joan's will, the testamentary trust can hold the Walden stock for a two-year period before the S election terminates. ◀

ADDITIONAL COMMENT

The 2004 Jobs Act added one other narrowly defined trust situation. A bank that otherwise would qualify for making an S election can now do so even if an IRA trust holds some of its stock. This provision applies only with respect to bank stock held in IRA trusts on October 22, 2004. In this situation, the beneficiary of the IRA trust is treated as the shareholder.

The trust in Example C:11-1 can hold the S corporation stock for an indefinite period only if the trust's income beneficiary makes an election to have it treated as a QSST or small business trust. Otherwise, the S election terminates at the end of the two-year period.

ALIEN INDIVIDUALS. Individuals who are not U.S. citizens (i.e., alien individuals) can own S corporation stock only if they are U.S. residents or are married to a U.S. citizen or resident alien and make an election to be taxed as a resident alien. The S election terminates if an alien individual purchases S corporation stock and does not reside in the United States or has not made the appropriate election.

CORPORATION-RELATED REQUIREMENTS

The corporation must satisfy the following three requirements on each day of the tax year:

[4] A **voting trust** is an arrangement whereby the stock owned by a number of shareholders is placed under the control of a trustee, who exercises the voting rights possessed by the stock. One reason for creating a voting trust is to increase the voting power of a group of minority shareholders in the selection of corporate directors or the establishment of corporate policies.

[5] A QSST is a domestic trust that owns stock in one or more S corporations and distributes (or is required to distribute) all its income to its sole income beneficiary. The income beneficiary must make an irrevocable election to have the QSST rules of Sec. 1361(d) apply. The beneficiary is treated as the owner (and, therefore, the shareholder) of the portion of the trust consisting of the S corporation stock. A separate election is made for each S corporation's stock owned by the trust.

ADDITIONAL COMMENT

An unincorporated eligible entity that makes a valid S election is automatically treated as making an election to be treated as a corporation under the check-the-box regulations. Thus, the entity does not have to make two separate elections.

- The corporation must be a domestic corporation or an unincorporated entity that elects to be treated as a corporation under the check-the-box regulations.
- The corporation must not be an "ineligible" corporation.
- The corporation must have only one class of stock.[6]

The first requirement precludes a foreign corporation from making an S election.

A corporation may be an ineligible corporation and thereby violate the second requirement in one of two ways:

- Corporations that maintain a special federal income tax status are not eligible to make an S election. For example, financial institutions (e.g., banks) that use the reserve method to account for bad debts and insurance companies are not eligible.
- Corporations that have elected the special Puerto Rico and U.S. possessions tax credit (Sec. 936) or that had elected the special Domestic International Sales Corporation tax exemption are ineligible to make the S election.

ADDITIONAL COMMENT

Current S corporation stock ownership rules and the approval of the check-the-box regulations permit great flexibility in creating groups of entities that fit the business needs of their owners.

S corporations can own the stock of a C corporation or an S corporation without any limitation on the percentage of voting power or value held. However, as mentioned earlier, a C corporation cannot own the stock of an S corporation. An S corporation that owns the stock of a C corporation cannot participate in the filing of a consolidated tax return. An S corporation also can own the stock of a **Qualified Subchapter S Subsidiary (QSub)**. A QSub is a domestic corporation that qualifies as an S corporation, is 100% owned by an S corporation, and for which the parent S corporation elects to treat the subsidiary as a QSub. The assets, liabilities, income, deductions, losses, etc. of the QSub are treated as those of its S corporation parent and reported on the parent's tax return.[7]

A corporation that has two classes of stock issued and outstanding has violated the third requirement and cannot be an S corporation. The single class of stock determination is more difficult than it appears at first glance because of the many different financial arrangements that are possible between an S corporation and its shareholders. A corporation is treated as having only one class of stock if all of its outstanding shares of stock possess identical rights to distribution and liquidation proceeds and the corporation has not issued any instrument or obligation, or entered into any arrangement, that is treated as a second class of stock.[8] A second class of stock is not created if the only difference between the two classes of stock pertains to voting rights.[9]

EXAMPLE C:11-2 ► Kelly Corporation has two classes of common stock outstanding. The Class A and Class B common stock give the shareholders identical rights and interests in the profits and assets of the corporation. Class A stock has one vote per share. Class B stock is nonvoting. Kelly Corporation is treated as having only one class of stock outstanding and can make an S election. ◄

GENERAL RULES. The determination of whether all outstanding shares of stock confer identical rights to distribution and liquidation proceeds is based on the corporate charter, articles of incorporation, bylaws, applicable state law, and binding agreements relating to distribution and liquidation proceeds (i.e., the governing agreements).[10] Treasury Regulations permit certain types of state laws, agreements, distributions, etc., to be disregarded in determining whether all of a corporation's outstanding shares confer identical rights to distribution and liquidation proceeds. These include

- Agreements to purchase stock at the time of death, divorce, disability, or termination of employment
- Distributions made on the basis of the shareholder's varying stock interests during the year
- Distributions that differ in timing (e.g., one shareholder receives a distribution in the current year and a second shareholder receives a similar dollar amount distribution shortly after the beginning of the next tax year)

---

[6] Sec. 1361(b)(1).
[7] Sec. 1361(b)(3).
[8] Reg. Sec. 1.1361-1(l).
[9] Sec. 1361(c)(4).
[10] Reg. Sec. 1.1361-1(l)(2).

Agreements to increase cash or property distributions to shareholders who bear heavier state income tax burdens so as to provide equal after-tax distributions provide unequal distribution and liquidation rights. The unequal distributions probably will cause a second class of stock to be created. However, state laws that require a corporation to pay or withhold state income taxes on behalf of some or all of a corporation's shareholders are disregarded.

DEBT INSTRUMENTS. Debt instruments, corporate obligations, and deferred compensation arrangements, in general, are not treated as a second class of stock.[11] A number of safe harbors exist for characterizing corporate obligations as debt (and not as a second class of stock):

- Unwritten advances from a shareholder that do not exceed $10,000 during the tax year, are treated as debt by the two parties, and are expected to be repaid within a reasonable time
- Obligations that are considered equity under the general tax laws but are owned solely by the shareholders in the same proportion as the corporations's outstanding stock

KEY POINT

If debt instruments satisfy the safe harbor rules, such instruments cannot be construed as equity. However, such debt must have been issued in an S corporation tax year.

In addition, Sec. 1361(c)(5) provides a safe harbor for straight debt instruments so that the debt is not treated as a second class of stock. For debt to qualify under the safe harbor, it must meet the following requirements if issued while an S election is in effect:

- The debt must represent an unconditional promise to pay a certain sum of money on a specified date or on demand.
- The interest rate and interest payment dates must not be contingent on profits, the borrower's discretion, or similar factors.[12]
- The debt must not be convertible directly or indirectly into stock.
- The creditor must be an individual, estate, or trust eligible to be an S corporation shareholder, or a nonindividual creditor actively and regularly engaged in the business of lending money.[13]

The safe harbor rules can apply to debt even if the debt otherwise would be considered a second class of stock under case law or other IRC provisions. An obligation that originally qualifies as straight debt may no longer qualify if it is materially modified so that it no longer satisfies the safe harbor or is transferred to a third party who is not an eligible shareholder.[14]

ELECTION OF S CORPORATION STATUS

OBJECTIVE 2

Apply the procedures for electing to be taxed under Subchapter S

The S election exempts a corporation from all taxes imposed by Chapter 1 of the Internal Revenue Code (Secs. 1-1399) except for the following:

- Sec. 1374 built-in gains tax
- Sec. 1375 excess net passive income tax
- Sec. 1363(d) LIFO recapture tax

This rule exempts the S corporation from the regular income tax, accumulated earnings tax, the personal holding company tax, and the corporate alternative minimum tax for all tax years the election remains in effect.

---

[11] Reg. Sec. 1.1361-1(l)(4)(i). An exception applies to debt instruments, corporate obligations, and deferred compensation arrangements that are treated as stock under the general principles of the federal tax law where the principal purpose for the debt instrument, etc., is to circumvent the distribution or liquidation proceeds rights provided for by the outstanding stock or to circumvent the 100-shareholder limit.

[12] That the interest rate depends on the prime rate or a similar factor not related to the debtor corporation will not disqualify the instrument from coming under the safe harbor rules. If the interest being paid is unreasonably high, an appropriate portion may be treated as a payment of something other than interest.

[13] Sec. 1361(c)(5).

[14] Reg. Sec. 1.1361-1(l)(5)(ii) and (iii).

The S election affects the shareholders in three ways:

- Shareholders report their pro rata share of the S corporation's ordinary income or loss as well as any separately stated items.
- Shareholders treat most distributions as a nontaxable recovery of their stock investments.
- Shareholders' stock bases are adjusted for the shareholders' ratable share of ordinary income or loss and any separately stated items.

MAKING THE ELECTION

Only small business corporations can make the S election.[15] For a small business corporation to make a valid S election, the corporation must file a timely election (Form 2553), and all the corporation's shareholders must consent to the election. Existing corporations can make a timely S election at any time during the tax year preceding the year for which the election is to be effective or on or before the fifteenth day of the third month of the year for which the election is to be effective.

For a new corporation, the S election can be made at any time on or before the fifteenth day of the third month of its initial tax year. A new corporation's initial tax year begins with the first day the corporation has shareholders, acquires assets, or begins business.

If the corporation makes the S election during the first 2½ months of the tax year for which the election is first to be effective, the corporation also must meet all the small business corporation requirements on each day of the tax year preceding and including the election date. If the corporation fails to satisfy this requirement, the election becomes effective in the corporation's next tax year.

The tax law, however, provides some relief for improper elections. First, if the corporation misses the deadline for making the S corporation election, the IRS can treat the election as timely made if the IRS determines that the corporation had reasonable cause for making the late election. Second, if the election was ineffective because the corporation inadvertently failed to qualify as a small business corporation or because it inadvertently failed to obtain shareholder consents (see below), the IRS nevertheless can honor the election if the corporation and shareholders take steps to correct the deficiency within a reasonable period of time.[16]

EXAMPLE C:11-3 ▶ Wilco Corporation, a calendar year taxpayer, has been in existence for several years. Wilco wants to be treated as an S corporation for 2008 and subsequent years. The corporation can make the election any time during 2007 or from January 1 through March 17, 2008 (March 15 falls on a Saturday). If the corporation makes the election after March 17, 2008, it becomes effective in 2009. However, if Wilco can show reasonable cause for making the late election, the IRS may allow the election to be effective for 2008. ◀

SELF-STUDY QUESTION

Would the answer to Example C:11-3 change if Wilco is a member of an affiliated group through January 15, 2008?

ANSWER

Yes. Because Wilco is an ineligible corporation for a portion of the 2½-month period of 2008, an S election would not be effective until January 1, 2009.

CONSENT OF SHAREHOLDERS. Each person who is a shareholder on the election date must consent to the election. The consent is binding on the current tax year and all future tax years. No additional consents are required of shareholders who acquire the stock between the election date and its effective date or at any subsequent date.

Section 1362(b)(2) imposes a special rule on the shareholders when the corporation makes an election after the beginning of the tax year for which it is to be effective. Each shareholder who owned stock during any portion of the year preceding the election date, and who is not a shareholder on the election date, also must consent to the election.

EXAMPLE C:11-4 ▶ Sara and Harry own all of Kraft Corporation's stock. Sara sells all her Kraft stock to Lisa on February 10. The next day Kraft makes an S election. For the election to apply in the current year, Sara, Harry, and Lisa must consent to the election. If Sara refuses to consent, the election will not be effective until next year. ◀

---

[15] Election rules are in Sec. 1362.

[16] For situations other than those added by the 2004 Job Act, the IRS spells out detailed procedures for relief in Rev. Proc. 2003-43, 2003-23 C.B. 998, and Rev. Proc. 2004-48, 2004-32 I.R.B. 172. The IRS probably will update these procedures for the new provisions.

Each tenant (whether or not husband and wife) must consent to the S election if the shareholders own the stock as tenants in common, joint tenants, or tenants in the entirety. If the shareholders own the S corporation stock as community property, each person having a community property interest must consent to the election. If the shareholder is a minor, either the minor or the minor's legal representative (e.g., a natural parent or legal guardian) can make the consent.

Topic Review C:11-1 summarizes the S corporation requirements and procedures for making the S election.

OBJECTIVE 3

Identify the events that will terminate an S election

TERMINATION OF THE ELECTION

Once made, the S election remains in effect until the corporation either revokes the election or terminates the election because it ceases to meet the small business corporation requirements. The following discussion examines each action and outlines the requirements for making a new S election following a termination.[17]

REVOCATION OF THE ELECTION. A corporation can revoke its S election in any tax year as long as it meets the requirements regarding shareholder consent and timeliness. Shareholders owning more than one-half the corporation's stock (including nonvoting stock) on the day the corporation makes the revocation must consent to the revocation. A revocation made on or before the fifteenth day of the third month of the tax year is effective on the first day of that tax year. A revocation made after the first 2½ months of the tax year takes effect on the first day of the next tax year. An exception permits the S corporation to select a prospective date for the revocation to be effective. The prospective date can be the date the corporation makes the revocation or any subsequent date.

Topic Review C:11-1

S Corporation Requirements and Election Procedures

Requirements

Shareholder-related:

1. The corporation may have no more than 100 shareholders. Family members and their estates count as one shareholder.
2. All shareholders must be individuals, estates, certain kinds of trusts, or certain kinds of tax-exempt organizations. Eligible trusts include grantor trusts, voting trusts, testamentary trusts, beneficiary-controlled trusts, qualified Subchapter S trusts, qualified retirement plan trusts, and small business trusts.
3. All the individual shareholders must be U.S. citizens or resident aliens.

Corporation-related:

1. The corporation must be a domestic corporation or an unincorporated entity. An unicorporated entity that makes an S election is automatically treated as having elected to be taxed as a domestic corporation under the check-the-box regulations.
2. The corporation must not be an ineligible corporation (e.g., an ineligible bank or other financial institution, an insurance company, or a foreign corporation).
3. The corporation must have only one class of stock issued and outstanding. Differences in voting rights are ignored.

Making the Election

1. The corporation can make the S election any time during the tax year preceding the year for which the election is effective or on or before the fifteenth day of the third month of the tax year for which the election is effective. Late elections are effective with the next tax year unless the corporation obtains IRS relief for reasonable cause.
2. Each shareholder who owns stock on the date the corporation makes the election must consent to the election. If the corporation makes the election after the beginning of the tax year, each person who was a shareholder during the portion of the tax year preceding the election also must consent to the election.

---

[17] Termination and revocation rules are in Sec. 1362.

EXAMPLE C:11-5 ▶ Adobe Corporation, a calendar year taxpayer, has been an S corporation for several years. However, the corporation has become quite profitable, and management feels that it would be advantageous to make a public stock offering to obtain additional capital during 2008. Adobe can revoke its S election any time before March 18, 2008 (March 15 falls on a Saturday), making the revocation effective on January 1, 2008. If the corporation revokes the election after March 17, 2008, it takes effect January 1, 2009. In either case, the corporation may specify a prospective 2008 effective date as long as the date occurs on or after the date it makes the revocation. ◀

TAX STRATEGY TIP

When it is difficult to obtain the majority shareholder vote necessary for revocation, consideration should be given to purposely triggering a termination event.

TERMINATION OF THE ELECTION. The S election terminates if the corporation fails one or more of the small business corporation requirements any time after the election's effective date. The termination generally occurs on the day of the terminating event. Events that can terminate the election include

- Exceeding the 100-shareholder limit
- Having an ineligible shareholder own some of the stock
- Creating a second class of stock
- Attaining a prohibited tax status
- Selecting an improper tax year
- Failing the passive investment income test for three consecutive years

The passive investment income test applies annually. It terminates the S election if more than 25% of the corporation's gross receipts are passive investment income for each of three consecutive tax years *and* the corporation has Subchapter C earnings and profits (E&P) at the end of each of the three consecutive tax years. If the corporation meets these conditions for three consecutive tax years, the election terminates on the first day of the next (fourth) tax year.

Passive investment income includes royalties, rents,[18] dividends, interest, annuities, and gains from the sale or exchange of stocks and securities. Treasury Regulations hold that passive investment income excludes income derived from the active conduct of a trade or business. Subchapter C E&P includes only earnings that accrued in tax years in which an S election was not in effect (i.e., the corporation was taxed under the C corporation rules).

EXAMPLE C:11-6 ▶ Shareholders formed Silver Corporation in the current year, and the corporation promptly made an S election. Silver can earn an unlimited amount of passive income during a tax year without any fear of losing its S corporation status or being subject to the Sec. 1375 tax on excess net passive income because it has never been a C corporation and thus has no Subchapter C E&P. However, if a C corporation containing E&P merged into Silver, Silver would then have potential exposure to the passive income rules. (See page C:11-16 for a discussion of the Sec. 1375 tax.) ◀

HISTORICAL NOTE

Previously, a termination was deemed effective on the first day of the tax year in which the terminating event occurred. To stop potential abuse, Congress changed the rule so that an S election terminates on the day of the terminating event.

ALLOCATION OF INCOME. A terminating event occurring at some time other than the first day of the tax year creates an S termination year. The **S termination year** is divided into an S short year and C short year. The **S short year** begins on the first day of the tax year and ends on the day preceding the termination date. The **C short year** begins on the termination date and continues through the last day of the corporation's tax year.

EXAMPLE C:11-7 ▶ Dixon Corporation has been an S corporation for several years. Paula and Frank each own one-half of Dixon's stock. Paula sells one-half of her Dixon stock to Eagle Corporation on July 1. The sale terminates the S election on July 1 because Eagle is an ineligible shareholder. Assuming Dixon is a calendar year taxpayer, the S short year runs from January 1 through June 30. The C short year runs from July 1 through December 31. ◀

---

[18] Regulation Sec. 1.1362-2(c)(5)(ii)(B)(2) excludes from rents payments received for the use or occupancy of property if the corporation provides significant services or incurs substantial costs in the rental business. See page C:11-37 for additional explanations of the significant services and substantial costs definitions.

TAX STRATEGY TIP

Income or loss can be allocated in the termination year under either of two methods. Careful consideration should be given to the possible tax advantages of a daily allocation versus an actual closing of the books. See Tax Planning Considerations for further details.

ADDITIONAL COMMENT

To use an actual closing of the books to allocate Dixon's income or loss in Example C:11-7, Eagle must consent. Due to the consequences of such an election, the method of allocation should be considered in negotiating the Dixon stock sale.

The S corporation's shareholders report the S short year income according to the normal reporting rules described below. The C corporation reports the income earned during the C short year and calculates its C short year income tax liability on an annualized basis (see Chapter C:3). The S short year and C short year returns are due on the due date for the corporation's tax return for the tax year had the termination not occurred (including any extensions).

An S corporation can use either of two rules to allocate the termination year's income between the S short year and the C short year. The general rule of Sec. 1362(e)(2) allocates the ordinary income or loss and the separately stated items between the S short year and C short year based on the number of days in each year. A special election under Sec. 1362(e)(3) permits an allocation that accords with the corporation's normal tax accounting rules if all persons who were shareholders at any time during the S short year and all persons who are shareholders on the first day of the C short year consent to the election. The corporation cannot use a daily allocation when an S termination year occurs and, during such year, sales or exchanges of 50% or more of the corporation's outstanding stock occur. In such a case, the corporation must use its normal accounting rules to make the allocation.

INADVERTENT TERMINATION. Special rules permit the corporation to continue its S election if an inadvertent termination occurs by its ceasing to be a small business corporation or by its failing the passive investment income test for three consecutive years. If such a termination occurs, the S corporation or its shareholders must take the necessary steps, within a reasonable time period after discovering the event creating the termination, to restore the corporation's small business status. If the IRS determines that the termination was inadvertent, the corporation and all persons owning stock during the termination period must agree to make the adjustments necessary to report the income for this period as if the S election had been in effect continuously.[19]

EXAMPLE C:11-8 ▶

Shareholders formed Frye Corporation in 2004 and operated it as a C corporation during that year. Frye made an S election in 2005. During 2004, the corporation incorrectly computed its E&P and believed that no Subchapter C E&P existed for its only pre–S corporation tax year. From 2005 through 2007, Frye earned large amounts of passive income but did not pay the Sec. 1375 excess net passive income tax or worry about terminating its election because it thought it had no accumulated E&P from 2004. Upon auditing Frye's tax returns, the IRS finds that Subchapter C E&P, in fact, did exist from 2004 and terminates the S election effective on January 1, 2008. If the corporation distributes the E&P and the shareholders report the dividend income, the IRS probably will treat the occurrence as an inadvertent termination and not revoke the election. ◀

The IRS also can grant relief for inadvertent terminations of the election to treat a subsidiary as a Qualified Subchapter S Subsidiary (QSub). For example, a parent S corporation might inadvertently transfer shares of a QSub to another person, thereby violating the 100% ownership requirement. If the S corporation takes the necessary steps to correct the inadvertent transfer, the IRS can grant relief, thereby allowing the election to remain in effect.

OTHER IRS WAIVERS. The IRS not only can waive a termination it deems to be inadvertent, it also can validate certain invalid elections. Validation of an invalid election can occur when the election failed to meet the basic S corporation requirements of Sec. 1361 or failed to provide the necessary shareholder consents. The IRS also can exercise this authority in situations where a corporation never filed an election. In addition, the IRS can treat a late S election as being timely filed if the IRS determines that reasonable cause

[19] Regulation Sec. 1.1362-4(b) holds that a termination will be inadvertent if the terminating event was not reasonably within the control of the corporation and was not part of a plan to terminate the election or if it took place without the corporation's knowledge and reasonable safeguards were in place to prevent the event from occurring.

existed for failing to make a timely election and the corporation meets certain other requirements.[20]

NEW ELECTION FOLLOWING A TERMINATION. A corporation that revokes or terminates its S election must wait five tax years before making a new election.[21] This delay applies unless the IRS consents to an earlier reelection. Regulation Sec. 1.1362-5(a) indicates that permission for an early reelection can occur (1) when more than 50% of the corporation's stock is owned by persons who did not own stock on the termination date or (2) when the event causing the termination was not reasonably within the control of the corporation or the shareholders having a substantial interest in the corporation *and* was not part of a plan to terminate the election involving the corporation or such shareholders.

EXAMPLE C:11-9 ▶ Terri owned Vector Corporation, a calendar year taxpayer that has been an S corporation for ten years. In January 2006, Terri sold all the Vector stock to Michelle with payments to be made over a five-year period. In March 2008, Michelle fails to make the necessary payments, and Terri repossesses the stock. During the time Michelle held the stock, Vector revoked its S election. Vector should immediately apply for reelection of S status because a more than 50% ownership change occurred since the revocation date. ◀

AVOIDING TERMINATION OF AN S ELECTION. Termination of an S election potentially can increase corporate or shareholder taxes. The S corporation's owners, management, and tax advisor need to understand the various events that can cause the termination of the S election. Some steps shareholders can take to prevent an untimely termination include the following:

- Monitor all transfers of S corporation stock. Make certain the purchaser or transferee of the stock is not an ineligible shareholder (e.g., corporation, partnership, or nonresident alien) or that the total number of shareholders does not exceed 100 (e.g., an excess shareholder resulting from creation of a joint interest).
- Establish procedures for the S corporation to purchase the stock of deceased shareholders to avoid the stock being acquired by a trust that is ineligible to be a shareholder.
- Establish restrictions on the transferability of the S corporation stock by having shareholders enter into a stock purchase agreement. Such an agreement could provide that the stock cannot be transferred without the prior consent of all other shareholders

WHAT WOULD YOU DO IN THIS SITUATION?

Harry Baker formed Xeno Corporation on January 4, 2005. The corporation filed a valid S corporation election on January 17, 2005, to be effect for 2005. Harry, the corporation's sole shareholder, consented to the election. The corporation had business ties to Mexico, and to strengthen these ties, Harry sold 25% of his Xeno shares to Pedro Gonzales on February 12, 2006. Pedro is one of Harry's business associates and is a citizen and resident of Mexico. Harry continued to operate Xeno as an S corporation throughout 2006. Early in March 2007, Harry became aware that, by selling stock to an ineligible shareholder, he may have jeopardized the corporation's S election. Thus, Harry immediately contacted Pedro and persuaded Pedro to sell his Xeno shares back to him (Harry). Harry hires you as his tax advisor on December 16, 2007, at which time you learn about the sale and repurchase of the Xeno shares. However, Harry tells you not to worry because, by buying back the shares, he already has rectified the situation, and thus the IRS need not be told about the transfers. How do you advise Harry on this matter?

[20] See Rev. Procs. 97-48, 1997-2 C.B. 521, and 2003-43, 2003-23 C.B. 998, for additional guidance on this issue and a special transition rule.

[21] *Termination* includes both revocation of the S election and loss of the election because one or more of the small business corporation requirements were not met.

and, if the necessary consent cannot be obtained, the corporation will repurchase the stock at a specified price (e.g., at book value).

- Monitor the passive income earned by an S corporation that previously had been a C corporation for one or more years. Make certain the passive income requirement is not failed for three consecutive years by reducing the level of passive income or by distributing the Subchapter C E&P.

S CORPORATION OPERATIONS

S corporations make the same accounting period and accounting method elections that a C corporation makes. Each year, the S corporation must compute and report to the IRS and to its shareholders its ordinary income or loss and its separately stated items. The special S corporation rules are explained below.

OBJECTIVE 4

Determine the permitted tax years for an S corporation

TAXABLE YEAR

Section 1378(a) requires that the S corporation's taxable year be a permitted year, defined as

- A tax year ending on December 31 (including a 52–53 week year)
- Any fiscal year for which the corporation establishes a business purpose[22]

Section 1378(b) specifically notes that income deferral for the shareholders is not a necessary business purpose. An S corporation that adopts a fiscal year coinciding with its natural business year has satisfied the business purpose requirement. The natural business year for an S corporation depends on the type of business conducted. When a trade or business has nonpeak and peak periods of business, the natural business year is considered to end at, or soon after, the close of the peak business period. A business whose income is steady throughout the year, does not have a natural business year.[23]

EXAMPLE C:11-10 ▶ Sable Corporation, an S corporation, operates a ski resort and reports $1 million of gross receipts for each of its last three tax years. If at least $250,000 (25% of gross receipts) of the receipts occurred in February and March for each of the three consecutive years, Sable can adopt, or change to, or continue to use a natural business year ending March 31.[24] ◀

An S corporation's adoption of, or a change to, a fiscal year that is an ownership tax year also is permitted. An ownership tax year is the same tax year used by shareholders owning more than 50% of the corporation's outstanding stock. The 50% requirement must be met on the first day of the tax year to which the change relates. Failure to meet the 50% ownership requirement on the first day of any later tax year requires a change to a calendar year or other approved fiscal year. S corporations also can adopt or change to a fiscal year for which it obtains IRS approval, based on the facts and circumstances of the situation.[25]

ADDITIONAL COMMENT

The requirement that all S corporations adopt calendar years (with March 15 return due dates) caused a hardship for tax return preparers. Section 444 is a compromise provision that allows a fiscal year for filing purposes, but it mandates a special payment of the deferred taxes.

Section 444 permits an S corporation to elect a fiscal year other than a permitted year. The fiscal year elected under Sec. 444 must have a deferral period of three months or less (e.g., a September 30 or later fiscal year-end for an S corporation otherwise required to use a calendar year). An S corporation that changes its tax year can elect to use a new fiscal year under Sec. 444 only if the deferral period is no longer than the shorter of three months or the deferral period of the tax year being changed.[26] A Sec. 444 election is not required of an S corporation that satisfies the business purpose exception.

[22] Some S corporations use a "grandfathered" fiscal year, which is a fiscal year for which IRS approval was obtained after June 30, 1974. Excluded are fiscal years that result in an income deferral of three months or less.

[23] Rev. Procs. 2002-39, 2002-1 C.B. 1046, and 2006-46, 2006-45 I.R.B. 859.

[24] See Rev. Proc. 2006-46, 2006-45 I.R.B. 859, for an explanation of the 25% test.

[25] Regulation Sec. 1.1378-1 and Rev. Proc. 2006-46, 2006-45 I.R.B. 859, explain the procedures for an S corporation adopting a fiscal year or changing the tax year of a new or existing S corporation. Rev. Rul. 87-57, 1987-2 C.B. 117, examines eight situations concerning whether the tax year is a permitted year.

[26] Special Sec. 444 transitional rules for 1986 permitted many S corporations to retain a previously adopted fiscal year (e.g., January 31) even though the deferral period is longer than three months.

S corporations that elect a fiscal year under Sec. 444 must make required payments under Sec. 7519, which approximate the deferral benefit of the fiscal year. Revocation or termination of the S election also terminates the Sec. 444 election unless the corporation becomes a personal service corporation. Termination of the Sec. 444 election permits the S corporation to obtain a refund of prior Sec. 7519 payments.

Topic Review C:11-2 summarizes the alternative tax years available to an S corporation.

ACCOUNTING METHOD ELECTIONS

As with a partnership, an S corporation makes accounting method elections independent of accounting method elections made by its shareholders. Three elections generally reserved for the S corporation's shareholders are as follows:

- Sections 108(b)(5) or (c)(3) relating to income from the discharge of indebtedness
- Section 617 election relating to deduction and recapture of mining exploration expenditures
- Section 901 election to take a credit for foreign income taxes[27]

OBJECTIVE 5

Calculate ordinary income or loss

ORDINARY INCOME OR LOSS AND SEPARATELY STATED ITEMS

S corporations are treated much like partnerships and thus report both an ordinary income or loss amount and a series of separately stated items. Ordinary income or loss is the net of income and deductions other than the separately stated items described in the next paragraph.

KEY POINT

S corporations are much like partnerships in their method of reporting income and losses. Both are pass-through entities that provide K-1s to their owners with their respective shares of income and loss items.

The S corporation's separately stated items are the same ones that apply in partnership taxation under Sec. 702(a).[28] The items required to be separately stated by Sec. 702(a) include

- Net short-term capital gains and losses
- Net long-term capital gains and losses
- Sec. 1231 gains and losses
- Charitable contributions

Topic Review C:11-2

Alternative S Corporation Tax Years

Tax Year	Requirements
Calendar year (including certain 52–53 week years)	The permitted tax year unless an exception applies.
Permitted fiscal year:	IRS will grant approval if:
a. Ownership year	The tax year requested is the same as that used by shareholders owing more than 50% of the corporation's outstanding stock. This test must be met on the first day of the year for which approval is requested as well as for each succeeding year.
b. Natural business year	25% or more of the gross receipts for each of the three most recent 12-month periods are in the last two months of the requested tax year.
c. Facts and circumstances year	The corporation establishes a business purpose (other than an ownership year or natural business year) using the facts and circumstances of the situation.
Nonpermitted fiscal year	A Sec. 444 election permits the S corporation to use an otherwise nonpermitted tax year if the deferral period is three months or less and the corporation makes the necessary required payments.

---

27 Secs. 1363(c).

28 Sec. 1366(a).

- Dividends eligible for the 15% maximum tax rate or treated as investment income[29]
- Taxes paid to a foreign country or to a U.S. possession
- Any other item provided by Treasury Regulations

Regulation Sec. 1.702-1(a)(8) adds for partnerships several other items to the list. The same additions from the Treasury Regulations apply to S corporations and include the following:

- Tax-exempt or partially tax-exempt interest
- Soil and water conservation expenditures
- Intangible drilling and development costs
- Certain mining exploration expenditures

Additional separately stated items not mentioned in Sec. 702 or its regulations include

- Passive income and loss
- Portfolio income (e.g., dividends and interest)

For a more complete list of the separately stated items see Form 1120S, Schedule K included in Appendix B.

Section 1366(b) requires that the character of any separately stated item be determined as if the item were (1) realized directly by the shareholder from the same source from which it was realized by the corporation or (2) incurred by the shareholder in the same manner as it was incurred by the corporation. Thus, the character of an income, gain, deduction, loss, or credit item does not change merely because the item passes through to the shareholders.

DEDUCTIONS THAT CANNOT BE CLAIMED. S corporations also have several deductions that it cannot claim, including

- The 70%, 80%, or 100% dividends-received deduction (because dividends pass through to the S corporation's shareholders)
- The U.S. production activities deduction (because that deduction passes through to the S corporation's shareholders)
- The same deductions disallowed to a partnership under Sec. 703(a)(2) (e.g., personal and dependency exemptions, additional itemized deductions for individuals, taxes paid or accrued to a foreign country or to a U.S. possession, charitable contributions, oil and gas depletion, and NOL carrybacks and carryforwards).[30]

SIMILARITY TO C CORPORATION TREATMENT. S corporations are treated as corporations for certain tax matters. For example, an S corporation can elect to amortize its organizational expenditures under Sec. 248 (after deducting up to $5,000). Also, the 20% reduction in certain tax preference benefits under Sec. 291 applies to an S corporation if the corporation was a C corporation in any of its three preceding tax years.[31]

ADDITIONAL COMMENT

The 20-year carryover period continues to run on C corporation NOLS even during subsequent S corporation years.

CARRYOVERS AND CARRYBACKS WHEN STATUS CHANGES. Some S corporations may operate as C corporations during a period of years that either precede the making of an S election or follow the termination of an S election. No carryovers or carrybacks that originate in a C corporation tax year can carry to an S corporation tax year other than carryovers that can be used to offset the built-in gains tax (see pages C:11-16 through C:11-18). Similarly, no carryovers or carrybacks created in an S corporation tax year can carry to a C corporation tax year.[32] Losses from an S corporation tax year pass through to the shareholder and, if greater than the shareholder's income for the year, can create an NOL carryover or carryback for the shareholder.

---

[29] Partnerships are permitted to have C corporations as owners of partnership interests. Thus, dividends eligible for the dividends-received deduction also are separately stated. Such is not the case with an S corporation, which cannot have a corporate shareholder.

[30] Sec. 1363(b)(2).

[31] Secs. 1363(b)(3) and (4).

[32] Sec. 1371(b).

U.S. PRODUCTION ACTIVITIES DEDUCTION

The 2004 Jobs Act added a new deduction for businesses engaged in U.S. production activities for tax years beginning after 2004. Chapter C:3 describes the C corporation version of this deduction, whereby the U.S. production activities deduction equals a percentage (6% in 2007) times the lesser of (1) qualified production activities income for the year or (2) taxable income before the U.S. production activities deduction. Individuals use a modified form of AGI instead of taxable income for this computation. The deduction, however, cannot exceed 50% of the employer's W-2 wages for the year. In the case of an S corporation, the deduction applies at the shareholder level, so the S corporation must report each shareholder's share of qualified production activities income on the shareholder's Schedule K-1. For the 50% salary limitation, each shareholder is allocated his or her share of the S corporation's W-2 wages.

OBJECTIVE 6

Calculate the amount of any special S corporation taxes

SPECIAL S CORPORATION TAXES

The S corporation is subject to three special taxes: the excess net passive income tax, the built-in gains tax, and the LIFO recapture tax. Each of these taxes is explained below.

EXCESS NET PASSIVE INCOME TAX. The **excess net passive income (or Sec. 1375) tax** applies when an S corporation has passive investment income for the tax year that exceeds 25% of its gross receipts and, at the close of the tax year, the S corporation has Subchapter C E&P. The excess net passive income tax equals the S corporation's excess net passive income times the highest corporate tax rate (35% in 2007).[33]

The **excess net passive income** is determined as follows:

$$\text{Excess net passive income} = \text{Net passive income} \times \frac{\text{Passive investment income} - 25\% \text{ of gross receipts}}{\text{Passive investment income}}$$

KEY POINT

The excess net passive income tax is of concern to a former C corporation that has accumulated E&P. A corporation that always has been an S corporation will not have a passive income problem.

The excess net passive income is limited to the corporation's taxable income, which is defined as a C corporation's taxable income except with no reduction for the NOL deduction or the dividends-received deduction. Net passive income equals passive investment income minus any deductions directly related to its production. Passive investment income excludes income derived from the active conduct of a trade or business.[34]

EXAMPLE C:11-11 ▶ Paoli Corporation, an S corporation, reports the following results for the current year:

Service (nonpassive) income	$35,000
Dividend income	37,000
Interest income	28,000
Passive income-related expenses	10,000
Other expenses	25,000

At the end of this year, Paoli's E&P from its prior C corporation tax years amounts to $60,000. Paoli's excess net passive income is determined as follows:

$$\$33,846 = (\$65,000 - \$10,000) \times \frac{\$65,000 - (0.25 \times \$100,000)}{\$65,000}$$

The excess net passive income tax is $11,846 ($33,846 × 0.35). The special tax reduces (on a pro rata basis) the dividend income and interest income items that pass through to the shareholders. The S election is not terminated at the end of the current year unless Paoli also was subject to the tax in the prior two tax years. ◀

TAX STRATEGY TIP

A former C corporation can avoid the Sec. 1375 tax (and the possibility of having its S election terminated) by electing to distribute its Subchapter C E&P. See Tax Planning Considerations for further details.

BUILT-IN GAINS TAX. A second corporate level tax may apply to gains recognized by an S corporation that formerly was a C corporation. This tax, called the **built-in gains (or Sec. 1374) tax**, applies to any income or gain the corporation would have included in

[33] *Passive investment income* and *Subchapter C E&P* for this purpose have the same definition here as given on pages C:11-9 and C:11-10.

[34] Reg. Sec. 1.1362-2(c)(5). Also, Reg. Sec. 1.1375-1(f), Ex. (2) indicates that passive income subject to the Sec. 1375 tax includes municipal bond interest that otherwise is exempt from the federal income tax.

gross income while a C corporation had the corporation used the accrual method of accounting (known as a **built-in gain**) and that the corporation reports during the ten-year period beginning on the date the S election took effect (known as the recognition period). **Built-in losses** are any deductions or losses the corporation would have deducted while a C corporation had the corporation used the accrual method of accounting and that the corporation reports during the ten-year period beginning on the date the S election took effect. Built-in gains and losses also include the differences between the FMVs and adjusted bases of assets held at the time the S election takes effect. Built-in losses reduce the amount of recognized built-in gains in determining the built-in gains tax liability.

REAL-WORLD EXAMPLE

The special S corporation taxes account for only a small amount of federal revenues. In 2003, collections on the built-in gains and excess net passive income taxes were $336.4 and $4.4 million, respectively. In contrast, total C corporation tax revenues collected in 2003 were $177.5 billion.

Congress enacted this tax to prevent taxpayers from avoiding the corporate level tax by making an S election before distributing or selling its assets. The built-in gains tax applies to S corporation tax years beginning after December 31, 1986, where the S corporation was formerly a C corporation and made the current S election after December 31, 1986.

EXAMPLE C:11-12 ▶ Theta Corporation, a calendar year taxpayer, incorporated in 1986 and operated as a C corporation through the end of 2006. On February 4, 2007, Theta filed an S election that was effective for 2007 and later tax years. Because Theta filed its S election after December 31, 1986, it is subject to the built-in gains tax for ten years starting with January 1, 2007. ◀

The Sec. 1374 tax is determined by using the following four-step calculation:

STEP 1: Determine the corporation's net recognized built-in gain for the tax year.

STEP 2: Reduce the net recognized built-in gain from Step 1 (but not below zero) by any NOL or capital loss carryovers from prior C corporation tax years.

STEP 3: Compute a tentative tax by multiplying the amount determined in Step 2 by the highest corporate tax rate (35% in 2007).

STEP 4: Reduce the tax determined in Step 3 (but not below zero) by the general business credit and minimum tax credit carryovers from any prior C corporation tax years and by the nonhighway use of gasoline and other fuels credit.

TAX STRATEGY TIP

An S corporation with NOL, capital loss, general business credit, and minimum tax credit carryovers from C corporation years can use these carryovers to reduce the effect of the built-in gains tax. Both NOL and capital loss carryforwards reduce the amount of recognized built-in gain taxed under Sec. 1374. The general business and minimum tax credit carryforwards reduce the actual built-in gains tax.

A recognized built-in gain or loss is any gain or loss recognized on an asset disposition during the ten-year recognition period unless the S corporation can establish that it did not hold the asset on the first day of the first tax year to which the S election applies. A recognized built-in gain cannot exceed the excess of a property's FMV over its adjusted basis on the first day of the ten-year recognition period. Dispositions include sales or exchanges and other events, including the collection of accounts receivable by a cash basis taxpayer, collection of an installment sale obligation, and the completion of a long-term contract by a taxpayer using the completed contract method.[35]

Built-in losses include not only losses originating from a disposition of property, but also any deductions claimed during the ten-year recognition period that are attributable to periods before the first S corporation tax year. A recognized built-in loss cannot exceed the excess of a property's adjusted basis over its FMV on the first day of the ten-year recognition period. Built-in losses, however, do not include any loss, deduction, or carryover originating from the disposition of an asset acquired before or during the recognition period where the principal purpose of such acquisition was avoiding the Sec. 1374 tax.

PRACTICAL APPLICATION

The application of the Sec. 1374 tax requires detailed records, which enable the taxpayer to track the built-in gain assets and determine when the corporation recognizes these gains.

The net recognized built-in gain for a tax year is limited to the smaller of:

- The excess of (1) the net unrealized built-in gain (i.e., excess of the FMV of the S corporation's assets at the beginning of its first tax year for which the S election is in effect over their total adjusted basis on such date) over (2) the total net recognized built-in gain for prior tax years beginning in the ten-year recognition period.[36]

---

[35] Income and gains potentially can be taxed under both the excess net passive income (Sec. 1375) and built-in gains (Sec. 1374) taxes. Any such income or gain is fully taxed under the Sec. 1374 rules. The portion of the income or gain taxed under the Sec. 1374 tax is exempt from the Sec. 1375 tax.

[36] The recognition period can be extended beyond ten years if property having a carryover basis is acquired in a tax-free transaction (e.g., a tax-free reorganization) from a C corporation. For such property, the ten-year recognition period begins on the date the S corporation acquired the property.

- The S corporation's taxable income as if it were a C corporation but with no dividends-received deduction or NOL deduction allowed.

If the net of the recognized built-in gains and losses exceeds the corporation's taxable income and the corporation made the S election after March 30, 1988, the excess built-in gain carries over to the next tax year, where it may be subject to the Sec. 1374 built-in gains tax in the carryover year. The built-in gain carryover consists of a ratable share of each of the income categories (e.g., ordinary income or capital gains) making up the net recognized built-in gain for the tax year.

The built-in gains tax passes through to the shareholders as if it were a loss. The loss must be allocated proportionately among the net recognized built-in gains that resulted in the tax being imposed.

EXAMPLE C:11-13 Assume the same facts as in Example C:11-12 and that Theta Corporation uses the accrual method of accounting. Theta owns the following assets on January 1, 2007:

Assets	*Adjusted Basis*	*FMV*
Cash	$ 10,000	$ 10,000
Marketable securities	39,000	45,000
Accounts receivable	60,000	60,000
Inventory (FIFO)	60,000	75,000
Building	27,000	44,000
Land	10,000	26,000
Machinery and equipment[a]	74,000	140,000
Total	$280,000	$400,000

[a] $50,000 of the gain is subject to recapture under Sec. 1245.

ETHICAL POINT

A C corporation that has substantially appreciated assets and wants to make an S election should obtain an appraisal of its assets on or about the first day of the S election period. The S corporation's tax accountant must make sure the appraiser does not assign an artificially low value to these assets to minimize the potential built-in gains tax burden.

During 2007, Theta collects $58,000 of accounts receivable and declares $2,000 uncollectible. It sells the FIFO inventory at a $25,000 profit in the first quarter of 2007, replacing the sold inventory with new inventory. It also sells two machines during 2007. One machine, having an $18,000 FMV and an $11,000 adjusted basis on January 1, produced a $7,000 gain (Sec. 1245 recapture income) on September 2. A second machine, having a $15,000 FMV and a $19,000 adjusted basis on January 1, produced a $4,000 loss on March 17.

- Theta recognizes no built-in gain or loss on collecting the receivables because it is an accrual method taxpayer. The $2,000 uncollectible debt is not a built-in loss because the loss arose after January 1. It is deductible as part of the ordinary income or loss calculation.
- Of the $25,000 inventory profit, $15,000 ($75,000 – $60,000) is a built-in gain taxed under Sec. 1374. Theta includes the entire $25,000 profit in ordinary income or loss.
- Theta recognizes a $7,000 built-in gain ($18,000 – $11,000) and a $4,000 ($15,000 – $19,000) built-in loss on the sale of the two machines. The $7,000 gain is ordinary income due to Sec. 1245 recapture and becomes part of Theta's S corporation ordinary income or loss. The $4,000 Sec. 1231 loss passes through separately to the shareholders.

In total, an $18,000 ($15,000 + $7,000 – $4,000) net recognized built-in gain is taxed under Sec. 1374, subject to the taxable income ceiling. Assuming C corporation taxable income (with no NOL deduction or dividends-received deduction) is at least $18,000, the built-in gains tax is $6,300 ($18,000 × 0.35). The entire tax amount reduces the shareholder's ordinary income from the inventory and machinery sales. ◀

LIFO RECAPTURE TAX. If a C corporation using the LIFO inventory method makes an S election, Sec. 1363(d)(3) requires the corporation to include its LIFO recapture amount in gross income for its last C corporation tax year. The LIFO recapture amount is the excess of the inventory's basis for tax purposes under the FIFO method over its basis under the LIFO method at the close of the final C corporation tax year. Any tax increase incurred in the final C corporation tax year is payable in four annual installments, on or before the due date for the final C corporation tax return and on or before the due date for the first three S corporation tax returns. The S corporation's inventory basis is increased by the LIFO recapture amount included in gross income.

EXAMPLE C:11-14 ▶ Taylor Corporation, a calendar year C corporation since its inception in 1990, makes an S election on December 23, 2006, effective for its 2007 tax year. Taylor has used the LIFO inventory method for a number of years. Its LIFO inventory has a $400,000 adjusted basis, a $650,000 FIFO inventory value, and an $800,000 FMV. Taylor's LIFO recapture amount is $250,000 ($650,000 – $400,000). Taylor includes this amount in gross income reported on its 2006 corporate tax return. Assuming a 34% corporate tax, Taylor's increased tax liability is $85,000 (0.34 × $250,000), of which $21,250 (0.25 × $85,000) is due with Taylor's 2006 C corporation tax return. An additional $21,250 is due with the 2007 through 2009 S corporation tax returns. Taylor increases the basis of its inventory by the $250,000 LIFO recapture amount. ◀

STOP & THINK

Question: Former C corporations that are now treated as S corporations are subject to three corporate level taxes—the **LIFO recapture tax**, the built-in gains tax, and the excess net passive income tax. Why did Congress enact these three taxes?

Solution: In 1986, Congress debated making the conversion of a C corporation into an S corporation a taxable event subject to the corporate liquidation rules. The corporation would have recognized all gains and losses at the time of conversion. As a compromise, only LIFO users are subject to an "automatic" tax when conversion occurs, and this tax applies only to the LIFO recapture amount and not all inventory appreciation. The built-in gains tax applies only when the corporation sells or exchanges assets during its first ten years after the S election. Assets not sold or exchanged during this time period escape the tax. The excess net passive income tax encourages S corporations to distribute their accumulated E&P. No tax is imposed, however, if the corporation keeps its passive income below the 25% of gross receipts threshold. Thus, former C corporations and their shareholders generally are better off under the current system than had Congress mandated corporate liquidation treatment.

TAXATION OF THE SHAREHOLDER

OBJECTIVE 7

Calculate a shareholder's allocable share of ordinary income or loss and separately stated items

INCOME ALLOCATION PROCEDURES

An S corporation's shareholders must report their pro rata share of the ordinary income or loss and separately stated items for the S corporation's tax year that ends with or within the shareholder's tax year.[37] Each shareholder's pro rata share of these items is determined by

1. Allocating an equal portion to each day in the tax year (by dividing the amount of the item by the number of days in the S corporation's tax year)
2. Allocating an equal portion of the daily amount to each share of stock outstanding on each day (by dividing the daily amount for the item by the number of shares of stock outstanding on a particular day)
3. Totaling the daily allocations for each share of stock
4. Totaling the amounts allocated for each share of stock held by the shareholder

TYPICAL MISCONCEPTION

An S corporation's income or loss is allocated basically the same as a partnership's except that a partnership may have the added flexibility of making certain special allocations under Sec. 704(b).

These allocation rules are known as the "per day/per share" method. Special allocations (such as those possible under the partnership tax rules) of the ordinary income or loss and separately stated items are not permitted.

If a sale of the S corporation stock occurs during the year, the transferor reports the earnings allocated to the transferred shares through the day of the transfer.[38] The transferee reports his or her share of the earnings from the day after the transfer date through the end of the tax year.

[37] Sec. 1366(a). If the shareholder dies during the S corporation's tax year, the income earned during the portion of the tax year preceding death is reported on the shareholder's tax return. Income for the period the estate holds the S corporation stock is reported on the estate's fiduciary tax return.

[38] Reg. Sec. 1.1377-1(a)(2)(ii). Also see examples under Reg. Sec. 1.1377-1(c).

EXAMPLE C:11-15 ▶ Fox Corporation is an S corporation owned equally by Arnie and Bonnie during all of the current year (not a leap year). During this year, Fox reports ordinary income of $146,000 and a long-term capital gain of $36,500. Arnie and Bonnie each report $73,000 (0.50 × $146,000) of ordinary income and $18,250 (0.50 × $36,500) of long-term capital gain. ◀

EXAMPLE C:11-16 ▶ Assume the same facts as in Example C:11-15, except Bonnie sells one-half of her shares to Clay on March 31 of the current year (the 90th day of Fox's tax year). Arnie reports the same ordinary income and long-term capital gain from his investment. Bonnie and Clay report ordinary income and long-term capital gain as follows:

Ordinary Income

$$\text{Bonnie: } \left(\$146{,}000 \times \frac{1}{2} \times \frac{90}{365}\right) + \left(\$146{,}000 \times \frac{1}{4} \times \frac{275}{365}\right) = \$45{,}500$$

$$\text{Clay: } \$146{,}000 \times \frac{1}{4} \times \frac{275}{365} = 27{,}500$$

Total $73,000

Long-Term Capital Gain

$$\text{Bonnie: } \left(\$36{,}500 \times \frac{1}{2} \times \frac{90}{365}\right) + \left(\$36{,}500 \times \frac{1}{4} \times \frac{275}{365}\right) = \$11{,}375$$

$$\text{Clay: } \$36{,}500 \times \frac{1}{4} \times \frac{275}{365} = 6{,}875$$

Total $18,250 ◀

KEY POINT

Shareholders of an S corporation need to be aware that when they dispose of their stock, they have the option of having income or loss determined by an actual closing of the books rather than an allocation on a daily basis.

A special election is available for allocating the ordinary income or loss and separately stated items when the shareholder's interest in the S corporation terminates or is substantially reduced during the tax year. Under this election, the income is allocated according to the accounting methods used by the S corporation (instead of on a daily basis). The election divides the S corporation's tax year into two parts ending on

- The day the shareholder's interest in the corporation terminates
- The last day of the S corporation's tax year

The corporation can make this election only if all affected shareholders agree to the election.[39] Affected shareholders include the shareholder whose interest terminated and all shareholders who received S corporation shares during the year. The Tax Planning Considerations section of this chapter explores this election in greater detail.

OBJECTIVE 8

Determine the limitations on a shareholder's deduction of S corporation losses

LOSS AND DEDUCTION PASS-THROUGH TO SHAREHOLDERS

The S corporation's ordinary loss and separately stated loss and deduction items pass through to the shareholders at the end of the corporation's tax year. The shareholders report these items in their tax year in which the S corporation's tax year ends.

ALLOCATION OF THE LOSS. Under the rules outlined above, allocation of the loss also occurs on a daily basis. Thus, shareholders receive an allocation of ordinary loss and separately stated items even if they own the stock for only a portion of the year. If ordinary loss and other separately stated loss and deduction pass-through items exceed the shareholder's income, the excess may create an NOL for the shareholder and result in a carryback or carryover at the shareholder level.

EXAMPLE C:11-17 ▶ Kauai Corporation, an S corporation, reports a $73,000 ordinary loss during the current year (not a leap year). At the beginning of the currrent year, Edward and Frank own equally all of Kauai's stock. On June 30 of the current year (the 181st day of Kauai's tax year), Frank gives

[39] Sec. 1377(a)(2).

one-fourth of his stock to his son George. Edward is allocated $36,500 ($73,000 × 0.50) of ordinary loss. Frank and George are allocated ordinary losses as follows:

$$\text{Frank:} \quad \left(\$73{,}000 \times \frac{1}{2} \times \frac{181}{365} \right) + \left(\$73{,}000 \times \frac{3}{8} \times \frac{184}{365} \right) = \$31{,}900$$

$$\text{George:} \quad \$73{,}000 \times \frac{1}{8} \times \frac{184}{365} = \underline{\quad 4{,}600}$$

$$\text{Total} \quad \underline{\underline{\$36{,}500}}$$

All three shareholders can deduct these losses on their individual tax returns subject to the loss limitations described below. ◀

REAL-WORLD EXAMPLE

A U.S. Supreme Court case held that discharge of indebtedness income excluded from gross income under Sec. 108 nevertheless is a pass-through item that increases the shareholders' stock bases, thereby allowing loss pass-through items to be deducted by the shareholders. *Gitlitz et al. v. Comm.* 87 AFTR 2d 2001-417, 2001-1 USTC ¶50,147 (USSC, 2001). A subsequent tax act (2002), however, disallowed the pass-through and stock basis increase for debt cancellations after October 11, 2001. This situation is a good example of Congress "overruling" the Supreme Court with its legislative power.

SHAREHOLDER LOSS LIMITATIONS. Each shareholder's deduction for his or her share of the ordinary loss and the separately stated loss and deduction items is limited to the sum of the adjusted basis for his or her S corporation stock plus the adjusted basis of any indebtedness owed *directly* by the S corporation to the shareholder. Thus, a shareholder must account for stock basis and debt basis. Unlike the partnership taxation rules, however, a shareholder cannot increase his or her stock basis by a ratable share of the general S corporation liabilities.[40]

In determining the stock basis limitation for losses, the shareholder makes the following positive and negative adjustments:[41]

- Increase stock basis for any capital contributions during the year
- Increase stock basis for ordinary income and separately stated income or gain items
- Decrease stock basis for distributions not included in the shareholder's income
- Decrease stock basis for nondeductible, noncapital expenditures (unless the shareholder elects to determine the loss limitation without this decrease)

Sequencing the basis reduction for distributions ahead of losses means that distributions reduce the deductibility of S corporation loss and deduction pass-throughs, but losses do not affect the treatment of S corporation distributions.

TAX STRATEGY TIP

Rather than having the corporation borrow money, an S corporation shareholder might consider borrowing money directly from the bank and then lending the loan proceeds to the corporation with the corporation guaranteeing the bank loan. In this way, the shareholder obtains debt basis.

Many S corporations are nothing more than incorporated forms of sole proprietorships or partnerships. As a result, banks and other lending institutions often require one or more shareholders to personally guarantee loans the institutions make to the S corporation. The IRS and courts, however, have held that these guaranteed loans do not create corporate indebtedness to the shareholder. As a result, the shareholder's loss limitation does not increase until the shareholder pays part or all of the corporation's liability or the shareholder executes a note at the bank in full satisfaction of the corporation's liability. Such action by the shareholder converts the guarantee into an indebtedness of the corporation to the shareholder, which increases the shareholder's debt basis and loss limitation.[42]

The adjusted basis of S corporation stock and debt generally is determined as of the last day of the S corporation's tax year. If the shareholder disposes of the S corporation stock before that date, the stock and debt bases are instead determined immediately prior to the disposition.

Loss and deduction pass-through items are allocated to each share of stock and reduce each share's basis. Once the losses and deductions have reduced stock basis to zero, they then reduce the basis of any debt owed by the S corporation to the shareholder.

EXAMPLE C:11-18 ▶ Pat and Bill equally own Tillis Corporation, an S corporation. During the current year, Tillis reports an ordinary loss of $104,000. Tillis's liabilities at the end of the current year include $110,000 of accounts payable, $150,000 of mortgage payable, and a $20,000 note owed to Bill.

---

[40] Sec. 1366(d)(1). Amounts owed by an S corporation to a conduit entity that has the shareholder as an owner or beneficiary will not increase the shareholder's loss limitation.

[41] Sec. 1366(d) and Reg. Sec. 1.1366-2(a)(3). Special basis adjustment rules apply to oil and gas depletion.

[42] Rev. Ruls. 70-50, 1970-1 C.B. 178; 71-288, 1971-2 C.B. 319; and 75-144, 1975-1 C.B. 277. See also *Estate of Daniel Leavitt v. CIR*, 63 AFTR 2d 89-1437, 89-1 USTC ¶9332 (4th Cir., 1989) among a series of decisions that uphold the IRS's position. However, see *Edward M. Selfe v. U.S.*, 57 AFTR 2d 86-464, 86-1 USTC ¶9115 (11th Cir., 1986) for a transaction where a guarantee was held to increase the shareholder's loss limitation because the transaction was structured so the bank looked primarily to the shareholder instead of the corporation for repayment.

Thus, Bill has a $20,000 debt basis for the amount he loaned to the corporation. Pat and Bill each had a $40,000 adjusted basis in their Tillis stock on January 1. The ordinary loss is allocated equally to Pat and Bill. Pat's $52,000 loss allocation is only partially deductible this year (i.e., up to $40,000) because the loss exceeds his $40,000 stock basis. Bill's $52,000 loss allocation is fully deductible this year because his loss limitation is $60,000 ($40,000 stock basis + $20,000 debt basis). After the loss pass-through, Pat and Bill each have a zero stock basis and Bill has an $8,000 debt basis.[43] ◀

Any loss or deduction pass-through not currently deductible is suspended until the shareholder regains basis in his stock or debt. The carryover period for the loss or deduction item is unlimited.[44] The additional adjusted basis amount can originate from a number of sources, including subsequent profits earned by the S corporation, additional capital contributions or loans made by the shareholder to the corporation, or purchases of additional stock from other shareholders.

EXAMPLE C:11-19 ▶ Assume the same facts as in Example C:11-18 and that Tillis Corporation reports ordinary income of $24,000 next year. Pat and Bill each are allocated $12,000 of ordinary income. This income provides Pat with the necessary $12,000 stock basis to deduct the $12,000 loss carryover. The $12,000 income allocated to Bill restores his debt basis to $20,000 (see pages C:11-25 through C:11-27). ◀

If a shareholder sells his or her S corporation stock still having unused losses due to lack of stock or debt basis, these losses do not transfer to the new shareholder. Instead, the unused losses lapse when the shareholder sells the stock. If the shareholder transfers the S corporation stock to a spouse or former spouse incident to a divorce, however, the suspended losses transfer to the spouse or former spouse. Thus, the spouse or former spouse can deduct the losses when he or she obtains sufficient basis.

SPECIAL SHAREHOLDER LOSS AND DEDUCTION LIMITATIONS. S corporation shareholders are subject to three special loss and deduction limitations. These limitations may prevent an S corporation's shareholder from using losses or deductions even though the general loss limitation described above does not otherwise apply. Application of the special loss limitations occurs as follows:

KEY POINT

An oft-quoted advantage of an S election is that losses pass through to the shareholders. This advantage is significantly limited by the at-risk and passive activity rules.

- *At-Risk Rules:* The Sec. 465 at-risk rules apply at the shareholder level. Thus, a shareholder can deduct a loss from a particular S corporation activity only to the extent the shareholder is at risk in the S corporation's activity at year-end.
- *Passive Activity Limitation Rules:* Losses and credits from a passive activity offset income earned from that passive activity or other passive activities in the same or subsequent tax year. An S corporation shareholder personally must meet the material participation standard for an activity to avoid the passive activity limitation. The S corporation's material participation in an activity does not allow a passive investor to deduct S corporation losses against his or her salary and other "active" income.
- *Hobby Loss Rules:* S corporation losses are subject to the Sec. 183 hobby loss rules, which limit deductions to the activity's gross income unless the S corporation can establish that it is engaged in the activity for profit.

In addition, various separately stated loss and deduction items are subject to shareholder limitations (e.g., charitable contributions, capital losses, and investment interest expenses), but they are not subject to corporate limitations. Conversely, some separately stated items are subject to corporate limitations but not shareholder limitations (e.g., the 50% nondeductible portion of meal and entertainment expenses).

POST-TERMINATION LOSS CARRYOVERS. Loss and deduction carryovers incurred in S corporation tax years can carry over at the shareholder level even though the S elec-

[43] See pages C:11-24 through C:11-27 for a detailed discussion of basis adjustments.

[44] Sec. 1366(d)(2). If more than one type of loss or deduction item passes through to the shareholder, the carryover amount is allocated to each of the pass-through items based on their relative amounts.

SELF-STUDY QUESTION

If losses are suspended due to the lack of basis in S corporation stock, do the losses expire when the S election terminates?

ANSWER

No. These loss carryovers may be deducted in the post-termination transition period (usually one year) if the shareholder creates additional stock basis in that period of time.

tion has terminated. Shareholders can deduct these carryovers only in the **post-termination transition period.**[45] The length of the post-termination transition period depends on the event causing the termination. In general, the period begins on the day after the last day of the corporation's final S corporation tax year and ends on the later of one year after the last day or the due date for the final S corporation tax return (including any extensions).

If the S election terminates for a prior tax year as a result of a determination, the period runs for 120 days beginning on the determination date. Section 1377(b)(2) defines a determination as a court decision that becomes final, a closing agreement entered into, a final disposition of a refund claim by the IRS, or an agreement between the corporation and the IRS that the corporation failed to qualify as an S corporation.

The shareholder can deduct the loss carryovers only up to his or her adjusted basis of the stock at the end of the post-termination transition period.[46] Losses that cannot be deducted because of the basis limitation are lost forever. Deducted losses reduce the shareholder's stock basis.

EXAMPLE C:11-20 ▶ Pearson Corporation has been a calendar year S corporation for several years. Helen's stock basis is $45,000. On July 1, 2007, its S election terminates when an ineligible shareholder acquires part of its stock. For the period ended June 30, 2007, Helen is allocated $60,000 of Pearson's ordinary loss. Helen can deduct only $45,000 of this loss because of her Pearson stock basis, which the loss reduces to zero. The $15,000 unused loss carries over to the post-termination transition period, which ends on June 30, 2008 (assuming Pearson does not extend the March 17, 2008 due date for the S short year tax return; March 15 falls on Saturday). Helen must have an adjusted basis for the Pearson stock of at least $15,000 at the close of business on June 30, 2008, to use the loss. Helen should consider making additional capital contributions of at least $15,000 between July 1, 2007, and June 30, 2008, to use the loss. ◀

Topic Review C:11-3 summarizes the rules governing deductibility of S corporation losses and deductions that pass through to the shareholders.

Topic Review C:11-3

Deductibility of S Corporation Losses and Deductions

Allocation Process

1. Losses and deductions are allocated based on the number of shares of stock owned by each shareholder on each day of the tax year. Special allocations of losses and deductions are not permitted.
2. Termination of the S election requires the tax year to be divided into two parts. The corporation can elect (with the shareholders' consent) to allocate the loss or deduction according to the corporation's accounting methods. This election also is available when a shareholder's interest in the S corporation terminates.

Loss Limitations

1. Losses and deductions pass through on a per-share basis and are limited to the shareholder's basis in stock and debt. Once the basis for all the shareholder's stock is reduced to zero, the losses reduce the basis of any S corporation indebtedness to the shareholder.
2. Losses and deductions that are not deducted carry over to a tax year in which the shareholder regains stock or debt basis. The time period for the carryover is unlimited. The unused losses lapse if the shareholder transfers the stock to anyone other than a spouse or former spouse incident to a divorce.
3. S corporation shareholders are subject to three special loss limitations:
   - ▶ At-risk rules
   - ▶ Passive activity limitations
   - ▶ Hobby loss rules

   Some separately stated loss and deduction items also are subject to shareholder limitations (e.g., investment interest expense). Other separately stated items are subject to corporate limitations but not shareholder limitations (e.g., the 50% nondeductible portion of meal and entertainment expenses).

---

[45] Sec. 1366(d)(3). The loss carryovers that carry over include those disallowed by the at-risk rules.

[46] Sec. 1366(d)(3)(B).

FAMILY S CORPORATIONS

Family S corporations have been an important tax planning device. This type of tax planning often involves a high-tax-bracket taxpayer gifting stock to a minor child who generally has little other income. The transfer results in income splitting among family members. The IRS has enjoyed success in litigating cases dealing with intrafamily transfers of S corporation stock when the transferor (usually a parent) retains the economic benefits and control over the stock transferred to the transferee (usually a child).[47] The IRS has attained less success when one family member purchases the stock from another family member at its market value.

ADDITIONAL COMMENT

The advantages of family S corporations have been somewhat curtailed. For example, income from stock of an S corporation gifted to a child under age 18 is subject to the "kiddie tax," where unearned income exceeding $1,700 (in 2007) is taxed at the parents' marginal tax rate.

The IRS also has the statutory authority to adjust the income, loss, deduction, or credit items allocated to a family member to reflect the value of services rendered or capital provided to the corporation. Section 1366(e) defines family as including spouse, ancestors, lineal descendants, and trusts created for such individuals. This provision permits the reallocation of income to provide for full compensation of a shareholder or nonshareholder for services and capital provided to the corporation. It also reduces the residual income reported by the S corporation and allocated to the shareholders according to their stock ownership. Such a reallocation prevents not only the shifting of income from the family member providing the services or capital to other family members, but also the avoidance of employment taxes. Alternatively, the IRS can determine that the corporation paid too much compensation to a shareholder and reduce that shareholder's salary and increase the residual income allocated based on stock ownership.

EXAMPLE C:11-21 ▶ Harvest Corporation, an S corporation, reports ordinary income of $200,000 after it claims a $20,000 deduction for Sid's salary. Sid and his three children own the Harvest stock equally. Harvest employs none of Sid's three children. The IRS subsequently determines that reasonable compensation for Sid is $80,000. This adjustment increases Sid's salary income and Harvest's compensation deduction by $60,000 ($80,000 − $20,000) and reduces Harvest's ordinary income to $140,000 ($200,000 − $60,000). Each shareholder's ratable share of ordinary income is reduced from $50,000 ($200,000 ÷ 4) to $35,000 ($140,000 ÷ 4). These adjustments have a twofold effect. First, they increase the amount of income allocable to Sid ($80,000 + $35,000 vs. $20,000 + $50,000), where Sid may be in a higher tax bracket than his children. Second, the increased salary increases Sid's employment taxes. Alternatively, if the IRS can prove that the stock transfer to the three children is not a bona fide transfer, all $220,000 of Harvest's income is taxed to Sid—$80,000 as salary and $140,000 as an allocation of ordinary income. ◀

BASIS ADJUSTMENTS

OBJECTIVE 9

Calculate a shareholder's basis in his or her S corporation's stock and debt

Shareholder's must adjust their S corporation stock basis annually. In addition, if the S corporation is indebted to the shareholder, he or she may have to adjust the debt basis downward for loss or deduction pass-throughs and upward to reflect restoration of the debt basis when the corporation earns subsequent profits. Each of these adjustments is described below.

BASIS ADJUSTMENTS TO S CORPORATION STOCK

Basis adjustments to the shareholder's stock are made in the following order:[48]

Initial investment (or basis at beginning of tax year)
Plus: Additional capital contributions made during the year
Allocable share of ordinary income
Allocable share of separately stated income and gain items

[47] See, for example, *Gino A. Speca v. CIR*, 47 AFTR 2d 81-468, 80-2 USTC ¶9692 (7th Cir., 1980) and *Henry D. Duarte*, 44 T.C. 193 (1965), where the IRS's position prevailed. See also *Gavin S. Millar*, 1975 PH T.C. Memo ¶75,113, 34 TCM 554, and *Donald O. Kirkpatrick*, 1977 PH T.C. Memo ¶77,281, 36 TCM 1122, where the taxpayers prevailed.

[48] Sec. 1367(a) and Reg. Sec. 1.1367-1(f).

SELF-STUDY QUESTION

Why is the determination of stock basis in an S corporation important?

ANSWER

To determine gain or loss on the sale of the stock, to determine the amount of losses that can be deducted, and to determine the amount of distributions to shareholders that are tax-free.

Minus: Distributions excluded from the shareholder's gross income
Allocable share of any expense not deductible in determining ordinary income (loss) and not chargeable to the capital account (A shareholder, however, can elect to make this adjustment *after* the two following adjustments.)
Allocable share of ordinary loss
Allocable share of separately stated loss and deduction items

Adjusted basis for stock (but not less than zero)

A shareholder's initial basis for S corporation stock depends on how he or she acquires it. Stock purchased from the corporation or another shareholder takes a cost basis. Stock received as part of a corporate formation takes a substituted basis from the assets transferred. Stock acquired by gift takes the donor's basis (adjusted for gift taxes paid) or FMV (if lower). Stock acquired at death takes its FMV on the decedent's date of death or the alternate valuation date (if elected). The basis of S corporation stock inherited from a deceased shareholder is its FMV minus any corporate income that would have been income in respect of a decedent (see Chapter C:14) if the income had been acquired from the decedent. No basis adjustment occurs when the corporation makes the initial S election.

The basis adjustments to the S corporation stock parallel those made to a partnership interest. The ordinary income and separately stated income and gain items increase the shareholder's basis whether they are taxable, tax-exempt, or receive preferential tax treatment.

EXAMPLE C:11-22 ▶ Cathy owns Marlo Corporation, an S corporation. At the beginning of the current year, Cathy's adjusted basis in her Marlo stock is $105,000. Marlo reports the following operating results this year:

Ordinary income	$70,000
Municipal bond interest income	15,000
Dividends from domestic corporations	6,000
Long-term capital gain	8,000
Short-term capital loss	17,000

Cathy's adjusted basis in her Marlo stock at year-end is $187,000 ($105,000 + $70,000 + $15,000 + $6,000 + $8,000 − $17,000). ◀

Cathy makes the basis adjustment at the end of the S corporation's tax year, when the results for the entire period are known. Because profits and losses are allocated ratably on a daily basis to all shares held on each day of the tax year, a shareholder's gain or loss realized on the sale of S corporation stock during the tax year is not determinable until the ordinary income or loss and separately stated items allocable to the shares sold are known. Similarly, when S corporation stock becomes worthless during a tax year, the shareholder must make the necessary positive and negative basis adjustments before determining the amount of the worthless security loss.

EXAMPLE C:11-23 ▶ Mike, Carlos, and Juan equally own Diaz Corporation, an S corporation. Mike's 100 shares of Diaz stock have a $25,000 adjusted basis at the beginning of the current year (not a leap year). Diaz reports ordinary income of $36,500 and municipal bond interest income of $14,600 in the current year. On February 14 of the current year (the 45th day of Diaz's tax year), Mike sells all his Diaz stock for $30,000. Assuming the corporation uses the daily method to allocate the income items, Mike's basis for the Diaz stock is $27,100, determined as follows:

$$\$27,100 = \$25,000 + \left(\$36,500 \times \frac{45}{365} \times \frac{1}{3}\right) + \left(\$14,600 \times \frac{45}{365} \times \frac{1}{3}\right)$$

Mike reports a $2,900 ($30,000 − $27,100) gain on the sale. ◀

KEY POINT

Losses first reduce basis in stock and then any amount of debt owed to the shareholder by the S corporation. Subsequent *net* increases in basis are added first to debt and then to stock.

BASIS ADJUSTMENTS TO SHAREHOLDER DEBT

After the shareholder's basis in S corporation stock is reduced to zero, basis in any S corporation indebtedness to the shareholder is reduced (but not below zero) by the remainder of the available loss and deduction items.[49] If a shareholder has more than one loan outstanding at year-end, the basis reduction applies to all the indebtednesses based on the relative adjusted basis of each loan. Ordinary income and separately stated gain or income items allocated to the shareholder in subsequent tax years (net of distributions and losses to the shareholders) first restore debt basis. Once all previous decreases to debt basis are restored, any additional positive basis adjustments increase the shareholder's stock basis.[50]

Repayment of a shareholder indebtedness results in gain recognition to the shareholder if the payment amount exceeds the debt's adjusted basis. If the indebtedness is secured by a note, the difference is a capital gain. If the indebtedness is not secured by a note or other evidence of the indebtedness, the repayment is ordinary income.[51]

EXAMPLE C:11-24 ▶ At the beginning of 2006, Betty owns one-half the stock of Trailer Corporation, an S corporation. Betty's basis in the Trailer stock is $40,000. Trailer owes Betty $20,000 on January 1, 2006, evidenced by a note. Thus, Betty has a $20,000 debt basis. During 2006, Trailer reports an ordinary loss of $100,000 and during 2007 reports ordinary income of $10,000. Betty's $50,000 loss pass-through from 2006 first reduces her stock basis from $40,000 to zero. Next, the $10,000 remainder of the loss pass-through reduces Betty's debt basis from $20,000 to $10,000. Betty's $5,000 allocation of 2007's ordinary income increases her debt basis from $10,000 to $15,000. If the corporation repays the note before the end of 2007, Betty reports a $5,000 ($20,000 – $15,000) long-term capital gain resulting from the repayment plus $5,000 of ordinary income from Trailer's 2007 operations. If the debt instead were unsecured (i.e., an advance from the shareholder not secured by a note), the gain would be ordinary income. ◀

STOP & THINK *Question:* The text preceding Example C:11-24 says that ordinary income and separately stated gain or income items (net of losses and distributions) restore debt basis before increasing stock basis; that is, debt is restored first by any net increase. The following rule also applies: total basis for the loss limitation equals (1) stock basis *after* all current year adjustments other than for losses plus (2) debt basis *before* any current year adjustments.

Consider the following situation: Omega Corporation is an S corporation with one shareholder. At the beginning of last year, the shareholder's stock basis was $15,000, and her debt basis was $20,000. Last year, Omega incurred a $45,000 ordinary loss, $35,000 of which the shareholder could deduct and $10,000 of which carries over. The loss affected basis as follows:

	Stock Basis	*Debt Basis*
Basis at beginning of last year	$15,000	$20,000
Ordinary loss last year ($45,000)	(15,000)	(20,000)
Basis at beginning of current year	$ –0–	$ –0–

In the current year, Omega earns $18,000 of ordinary income. What does the shareholder recognize in the current year, and what is the effect on her stock and debt bases? Why is the net increase rule for debt basis restoration beneficial to the shareholder?

Solution: The shareholder recognizes $18,000 of ordinary income and deducts the entire $10,000 loss carryover. Current year basis adjustments are as follows:

	Stock Basis	*Debt Basis*
Balance at beginning of current year	$ –0–	$ –0–
Ordinary income	10,000	8,000
Loss carryover allowed	(10,000)	–0–
Basis at end of current year	$ –0–	$8,000

The net increase approach benefits the shareholder because it allows her to deduct the $10,000 loss carryover in the current year rather than next year. The net increase for debt

[49] The shareholder makes no basis reductions to debt repaid before the end of the tax year. Regulation Sec. 1.1367-2(d)(1) holds that restoration occurs immediately before a shareholder repays or disposes of indebtedness during the tax year.

[50] Sec. 1367(b)(2)(B).

[51] Rev. Ruls. 64-162, 1964-1 (Part I) C.B. 304 and 68-537, 1968-2 C.B. 372.

restoration is $8,000 ($18,000 − $10,000), which leaves $10,000 of the $18,000 ordinary income to increase stock basis. This net increase approach to debt restoration allows a stock basis increase sufficient to use the loss carryover. Alternatively, if debt were restored by ordinary income without netting, the debt basis would increase by the entire $18,000, leaving no positive adjustment to the stock basis. This increase to debt basis would not help the shareholder in the current year because debt basis for the loss limitation is the balance before any current year adjustments. Under this hypothetical alternative approach, the shareholder could deduct the loss next year because next year's beginning debt basis would be $18,000. However, the net increase approach is better than the alternative because it allows the shareholder to deduct the loss in the current year.

S CORPORATION DISTRIBUTIONS

OBJECTIVE 10

Determine the taxability of an S corporation's distributions to its shareholders

Two sets of rules apply to S corporation distributions. One applies to S corporations having accumulated E&P. Accumulated E&P may exist if an S corporation was a C corporation in a pre–S election tax year. Another set of distribution rules applies to S corporations that do not have E&P (e.g., a corporation formed after 1982 that makes a timely S election in its initial tax year). These rules are explained below.

CORPORATIONS HAVING NO EARNINGS AND PROFITS

For S corporations with no accumulated E&P, a two-tier rule applies. Distributions are initially nontaxable and reduce the shareholder's stock basis (but not below zero). If the distribution exceeds the shareholder's stock basis, the shareholder treats the excess as a gain from the sale or exchange of the stock. Stock basis for determining excess distributions is that after positive adjustments for ordinary income and separately stated income and gain items but before negative adjustments.[52]

EXAMPLE C:11-25 ▶ Sandy owns 100% of Liberty Corporation, an S corporation. At the beginning of the current year, Sandy's adjusted basis in her Liberty stock (a capital asset) is $20,000. In the current year, Liberty reports ordinary income of $30,000 and a long-term capital loss of $7,000. Liberty makes a $35,000 cash distribution to Sandy on June 15. Sandy's basis for the stock must be adjusted for the ordinary income before determining the taxability of the distribution. Because Sandy's $50,000 ($20,000 + $30,000) adjusted stock basis exceeds the $35,000 distribution, she excludes the entire distribution from her gross income. The distribution reduces her stock basis to $15,000 ($50,000 − $35,000). Because Sandy still has sufficient stock basis, she can deduct the $7,000 capital loss, which further reduces her stock basis to $8,000.

If Liberty instead reports only $5,000 of ordinary income and a $7,000 capital loss, $10,000 of the distribution is taxable. The ordinary income increases the stock's basis to $25,000 ($20,000 + $5,000). Because the distribution exceeds the stock's adjusted basis by $10,000 ($35,000 − $25,000), Sandy recognizes a capital gain on the excess distribution. The distribution not included in Sandy's income ($25,000) reduces her stock basis to zero at year-end. Because the stock basis after the distribution is zero, Sandy cannot deduct the $7,000 capital loss in the current year. She must wait until she regains a positive stock basis (or obtains debt basis). ◀

SELF-STUDY QUESTION

Can distributions that exceed stock basis be tax-free to the extent of shareholder loans?

ANSWER

No. Although the amount of deductible losses can be increased by the amount of shareholder loans, tax-free distributions are strictly limited to stock basis. Also, distributions never reduce debt basis.

If an S corporation distributes appreciated property to its shareholders, the S corporation recognizes gain as if it sold the property.[53] The corporation recognizes no loss, however, when it distributes property that has declined in value. The gain recognized on the distribution may be taxed at the corporate level as part of the S corporation's built-in gains or excess net passive income. The gain also becomes part of the S corporation's ordinary income or loss, or is passed through as a separately stated item, depending on the type of property distributed and the character of the gain recognized. After this recognition

[52] Secs. 1368(b)and (d).

[53] Sec. 311(b).

occurs, the distributed property causes no further taxation provided the sum of the money plus the FMV of the nonmoney property distributed does not exceed the shareholder's stock basis. The shareholder's stock basis is reduced by the FMV of the distribution, and the shareholder takes a FMV basis in the distributed property.

EXAMPLE C:11-26 ▶ Tad owns 100% of Echo Corporation, which always has been an S corporation. Tad's stock basis at the beginning of the current year is $50,000. Echo reports $30,000 of ordinary income for this year (exclusive of the effects of a property distribution to Tad). On December 1, Echo distributes some Cable Corporation stock to Tad. The stock cost $40,000 and has a $100,000 FMV, and Echo has held it as an investment for three years. Echo reports $60,000 ($100,000 − $40,000) of capital gain from distributing the stock. Tad reports $30,000 of ordinary income and $60,000 of long-term capital gain from Echo's current year activities. Tad's stock basis increases to $140,000 ($50,000 + $30,000 + $60,000). The distribution is free of further taxation because the $140,000 stock basis exceeds the $100,000 distribution. The stock basis is $40,000 ($140,000 − $100,000) at year-end. Tad takes a $100,000 FMV basis in the Cable stock. ◀

ADDITIONAL COMMENT

The distribution of appreciated stock in Example C:11-26 produced income to Echo, which passed through to Tad. A similar distribution by a C corporation would result in a double tax by causing income recognition to both Echo and Tad.

CORPORATIONS HAVING ACCUMULATED EARNINGS AND PROFITS

PRIOR RULES. Under pre-1983 rules, a corporation's undistributed taxable income was taxed to its shareholders as a deemed distribution at year-end. This income accumulated in a **previously taxed income (PTI)** account, which can be a source of S corporation distributions. For simplicity in this text, however, the following discussion assumes that S corporation status occurs after 1982 and thus ignores the implications of PTI.

KEY POINT

The AAA represents the cumulative income and loss recognized in post-1982 S corporation years. To the extent the AAA is positive and sufficient basis exists in the stock, distributions from an S corporation are tax-free and reduce stock basis.

CURRENT RULES. Under current (post-1982) rules, some S corporations have a post-1982 accumulated E&P balance earned while a C corporation. Part or all of a distribution may be treated as made from this balance. The current rules, however, also require S corporations that have accumulated E&P balances to maintain an **accumulated adjustments account (AAA)** from which they make most of their distributions. The existence of accumulated E&P and AAA balances makes the tax treatment of cash and property distributions somewhat more complicated than do the rules explained in the preceding section.

MONEY DISTRIBUTIONS. For corporations making a post-1982 S election and having an accumulated E&P balance, money distributions come from the two tiers of earnings illustrated in Table C:11-1. The corporation makes distributions from the first tier until it is exhausted. The corporation then makes distributions from the second tier until that tier is used up. Amounts distributed after the two tiers of earnings are exhausted reduce the shareholder's remaining basis in his or her S corporation stock. Any additional amounts distributed once stock basis has been reduced to zero are taxed to the shareholder as a capital gain. The corporation usually maintains these tiers as working paper accounts and not as general ledger accounts.

The AAA is the cumulative total of the ordinary income or loss and separately stated items accumulated for the S period but excluding tax-exempt income and expenses related to its production. The S period is the most recent continuous period during which the corporation has been an S corporation. No tax years beginning before 1983 are included in this period.[54]

The year-end AAA balance is determined as follows:

AAA balance at the beginning of the year
Plus: Ordinary income
Separately stated income and gain items (except for tax-exempt income)

[54] Sec. 1368(e). An S corporation without accumulated E&P need not maintain the AAA to determine the tax effect of its distributions. If an S corporation having no E&P subsequently acquires E&P in a transaction where it assumes tax attributes under Sec. 381(a) (e.g., a merger), the corporation must calculate its AAA at the merger date to determine the tax effects of post-merger distributions. To accomplish this calculation, a firm may need to make calculations back to the original S election date. To reduce this hardship, the IRS, in the Form 1120S instructions, recommends that all S corporations maintain AAA information.

▼ **TABLE C:11-1**
Source of Distributions Made by S Corporations Having Accumulated Earnings and Profits

		Types of Distributions Coming from Tier		
Tier	**Classification**	**Money Distributions?**	**Property (Nonmoney) Distributions?**	**Taxable or Tax-Free Distributions?**
1	Accumulated adjustments account	Yes	Yes	Tax-free[a]
2	Accumulated E&P	Yes	Yes	Taxable
3	Basis of S corporation stock	Yes	Yes	Tax-free[a]
4	Excess over stock basis	Yes	Yes	Taxable

[a] These distributions reduce the basis of the S corporation stock. Although generally tax-free, gain can be recognized if the amount of money plus the FMV of the nonmoney property distributed exceeds the shareholder's adjusted basis in the S corporation stock as indicated in Tier 4.

Minus: Distributions made from AAA (see first bullet item below)
Ordinary loss
Separately stated loss and deduction items (except for expenses or losses related to the production of tax-exempt income)
Expenses not deductible in determining ordinary income (loss) and not chargeable to the capital account

AAA balance at the end of the year

Four differences exist between the positive and negative adjustments required for the AAA and the basis calculation for S corporation stock:

- Distributions not included in gross income reduce *stock* basis *before* other negative adjustments. Distributions reduce the AAA *after* other negative adjustments unless the other negative adjustments, when netted against positive adjustments, produce a "net negative adjustment." In this case, positive adjustments increase the AAA and negative adjustments other than distributions reduce the AAA to the extent of the positive adjustments. Then, distributions reduce the AAA before the net negative adjustment, and the net negative adjustment reduces the AAA after the distribution.[55]
- Tax-exempt income does not increase the AAA but increases the basis of S corporation stock.
- Nondeductible expenses that reduce stock basis also reduce the AAA except for expenses related to the production of tax-exempt income and federal income taxes related to a C corporation tax year.
- The AAA balance can be negative (e.g., when the cumulative losses exceed the cumulative profits), but a shareholder's stock basis cannot be less than zero.

TYPICAL MISCONCEPTION

Even though stock basis cannot be less than zero, the AAA can be negative if cumulative losses exceed cumulative profits.

Allocation of the AAA balance to individual distributions occurs at year-end after taking into account current year income and loss items. In general, the AAA balance is allocated ratably to individual distributions within a tax year (other than distributions coming from E&P) based on the amount of money or FMV of nonmoney property distributed.

[55] Reg. Secs. 1.1367-1(f) and 1.1368-2(a)(5). This ordering for AAA preserves tax-free treatment for S corporation earnings from prior years distributed in the loss year.

Corporations also maintain an Other Adjustments Account (OAA) if they have accumulated E&P at year-end. The corporation increases this account for tax-exempt income earned and decreases it by expenses incurred in earning the tax-exempt income, distributions out of the OAA, and federal taxes paid by the S corporation that are attributable to C corporation tax years. The effect of creating a separate account for tax-exempt income earned by companies having accumulated E&P is that the AAA is determined by taking into account only the taxable portion of the S corporation's income and any expenses and losses other than those related to the production of the tax-exempt income. Although the corporation reports the OAA balance on page 4 of the Form 1120S, it is not an accumulated earnings account. Municipal bond interest and other forms of tax-exempt income (net of related deductions) become part of the stock basis and thus appear after accumulated E&P in the distribution order. A corporation having an accumulated E&P balance might consider having the tax-exempt income-producing property owned at the shareholder level rather than at the corporate level.

EXAMPLE C:11-27 ▶ Omega Corporation is an S corporation with one shareholder, George. George's stock basis at the beginning of the current year is $22,000. Omega reports the following results for the current year:

Ordinary loss	$10,000
Dividend income	2,000

In addition, at the beginning of the current year, the corporation has a $12,000 AAA balance and a $4,000 accumulated E&P balance. In December of the current year, Omega distributes $7,500 cash to George. Because the ordinary loss and dividend income produce an $8,000 ($2,000 – $10,000) net negative adjustment, the predistribution AAA remains at $12,000 while the $2,000 dividend increases predistribution stock basis. Accordingly, the predistribution balances are as follows:

	Stock Basis	*AAA*	*E&P*
Beginning balances	$22,000	$12,000	$4,000
Dividend income	2,000	2,000	
Partial ordinary loss		(2,000)	
Predistribution balance	$24,000	$12,000	$4,000

Given these predistribution balances, the distribution has the following effects:

	Stock Basis	*AAA*	*E&P*
Predistribution balance	$24,000	$12,000	$4,000
AAA distribution	(7,500)	(7,500)	
Ordinary loss	(10,000)		
Net negative adjustment		(8,000)	
Ending balance	$ 6,500	($3,500)	$4,000

Because the net negative adjustment to the AAA occurs after the distribution, the entire distribution comes out of the AAA, and none comes out of accumulated E&P. Also, the distribution does not exceed the predistribution stock basis. Thus, the entire distribution is nontaxable. ◀

EXAMPLE C:11-28 ▶ Sigma Corporation, an S corporation, reports the following results during the current year:

Ordinary income	$30,000
Long-term capital gain	15,000
Municipal bond interest income	5,000
Dividend from domestic corporation	3,000
Charitable contribution	8,000

Sigma's sole shareholder, Silvia, has a $60,000 stock basis on January 1. On January 1, Sigma has a $40,000 AAA balance, a $27,000 accumulated E&P balance, and a zero OAA balance. Sigma makes $50,000 cash distributions to Silvia, its sole shareholder, on June 1 and December 1. The stock basis, AAA, OAA, and accumulated E&P activity for the year (before any distributions) is summarized as follows:

TYPICAL MISCONCEPTION

If shareholders sell their S corporation stock, the AAA account remains with the S corporation. But if an S election terminates, other than for the post-termination transition period, the AAA disappears.

	Stock Basis	*AAA*	*E&P*	*OAA*
Beginning balance	$ 60,000	$40,000	$27,000	$ -0-
Ordinary income	30,000	30,000		
Long-term capital gain	15,000	15,000		
Municipal bond interest	5,000			5,000
Dividend income	3,000	3,000		
Charitable contribution		(8,000)		
Predistribution balance	$113,000	$80,000	$27,000	$5,000

The $80,000 AAA balance is allocated ratably to each of the distributions as follows:

$$\$40{,}000 = \$50{,}000 \times \frac{\$80{,}000}{\$50{,}000 + \$50{,}000}$$

The charitable contribution does not reduce the predistribution stock basis but does reduce the predistribution AAA because the reduction does not produce a net negative adjustment. Accordingly, $40,000 of each distribution comes out of AAA. This portion of the distribution is tax-free because the AAA distributions in total are less than the stock's $113,000 predistribution basis. The remaining $10,000 ($50,000 – $40,000) of each distribution comes out of accumulated E&P and is taxable as dividend income. Accumulated E&P is reduced to $7,000 ($27,000 – $20,000) at year-end. The OAA balance reported on Form 1120S is not affected by the distribution because the accumulated E&P has not been exhausted. The stock's basis is $25,000 ($113,000 – $80,000 – $8,000) at year-end because a dividend distribution from accumulated E&P does not reduce its basis, but the charitable contribution does. After adjustment for the distribution, the AAA is zero. The effects of the distribution are summarized below:

	Stock Basis	*AAA*	*E&P*	*OAA*
Predistribution balance	$113,000	$80,000	$27,000	$5,000
AAA distribution	(80,000)	(80,000)		
E&P distribution			(20,000)	
Charitable contribution	(8,000)			
Ending balance	$ 25,000	$ -0-	$ 7,000	$5,000

◀

PROPERTY DISTRIBUTIONS. Property distributions (other than money) made by an S corporation having accumulated E&P trigger gain recognition according to the general rules described on page C:11-28. The FMV of the nonmoney property distributed reduces AAA.

TAX STRATEGY TIP

If a shareholder has NOL carryforwards that are about to expire, the election to treat distributions as dividend income to the extent of E&P (as opposed to AAA distributions) may make sense. Also, after 2010, the 15% maximum tax rate on dividends expires. Thus, shareholders may want to recognize dividend income before ordinary tax rates again apply to dividends.

DISTRIBUTION ORDERING ELECTIONS. An S corporation can elect to change the distribution order of E&P and the AAA. Specifically, the S corporation can elect to skip over the AAA in determining the source of a cash or property distribution, in which case distributions will come from accumulated E&P and then AAA. This election permits the S corporation to distribute Subchapter C E&P so as to avoid the excess net passive income tax and termination of the S election. The Tax Planning Considerations section of this chapter contains further discussion of this election.

POST-TERMINATION TRANSITION PERIOD. Distributions of money made during the S corporation's post-termination transition period can be made tax-free to those shareholders who owned S corporation stock on the termination date. These distributions come first from the former S corporation's AAA balance and then from current and accumulated E&P. The amounts from the AAA are tax-free and reduce the shareholder's stock basis.[56] The AAA balance disappears when the post-termination period ends. Even though the profits earned during the S election period no longer can be distributed tax-free from the AAA after the post-termination period ends, they still can be distributed tax-free to the extent of the shareholder's stock basis once the corporation distributes its

[56] Sec. 1371(e).

Topic Review C:11-4

Taxation of S Corporation Income and Distributions

Taxation of Income to the Corporation

1. Unlike with a partnership, special entity level taxes apply to an S corporation.
   a. Built-in gains tax: applicable to the net recognized built-in gain of an S corporation that formerly was a C corporation and that made its S election after December 31, 1986.
   b. Excess net passive income tax: applicable to S corporations that have Subchapter C E&P at year-end and that earn passive investment income exceeding 25% of gross receipts during the tax year.
   c. LIFO recapture tax: imposed when a C corporation that uses the LIFO inventory method in its final C corporation tax year makes an S election.

Allocation of Income to the Shareholders

1. Income and gains are allocated based on the number of shares of stock owned by each shareholder on each day of the tax year.
2. Termination of the S election or termination of the shareholder's interest in the S corporation during the tax year requires the tax year to be divided into two parts. The S corporation can elect to allocate the income or gain according to the general rule in (1) or the accounting methods used by the corporation.

Shareholder Distributions

1. Income and gain allocated to the shareholder increase the basis of the S corporation stock. For any S corporation that does not have an E&P balance, the amount of money plus the FMV of any nonmoney property distributed is tax-free provided it does not exceed the shareholder's stock basis, determined before negative adjustments. The corporation recognizes gain (but not loss) when it distributes nonmoney property. The gain passes through to the shareholders.
2. If the S corporation made the S election after 1982 and has accumulated E&P, two earnings tiers must be maintained: the AAA and accumulated E&P. Distributions come from each tier in succeeding order until the tier is exhausted. Distributions out of accumulated E&P are taxable to the shareholder as dividends. Other distributions are tax-free unless stock basis is reduced to zero, in which case the shareholder recognizes capital gain on the excess distribution.

current and accumulated E&P. Any distributions made from current or accumulated E&P and nonmoney distributions made during the post-termination transition period are taxable.

Topic Review C:11-4 summarizes the taxation of S corporation income and gains that pass through to the shareholders and the treatment of S corporation distributions.

STOP & THINK

Question: Special earnings tracking rules apply to S corporations that formerly were C corporations. Why do we need to have these special rules, which add complexity to the distribution topic?

Solution: Former C corporations that were profitable usually have an accumulated E&P balance when they become an S corporation. These earnings have never been taxed as a dividend to the corporation's shareholders. If separate tracking of the S corporation earnings (AAA) and C corporation earnings (accumulated E&P) did not occur, it would be impossible to determine which cash and property distributions came from S corporation earnings and which ones came from C corporation earnings, thereby frustrating the government's ability to collect taxes on distributed E&P.

OTHER RULES

In addition to the differences discussed above, S corporations differ from C corporations in a number of other ways. As discussed below, these differences include tax preference items and other alternative minimum tax (AMT) adjustments, expenses owed by the S corporation to a shareholder, related party sales and exchanges, and fringe benefits paid by the S corporation to a shareholder-employee.

TAX PREFERENCE ITEMS AND OTHER AMT ADJUSTMENTS

The S corporation is not subject to the corporate AMT. Instead, the S corporation computes and passes through tax preference items contained in Sec. 57(a) to its shareholders. The shareholders then include these tax preference items in their individual AMT calculations. Allocation of the tax preference items occurs on a daily basis unless the corporation makes one of the two special elections to allocate the items based on the corporation's tax accounting methods.

Section 56(a) prescribes a number of adjustments to the tax reporting of certain transactions and occurrences for AMT purposes from that used for income tax purposes. As with tax preference items, these special AMT adjustments pass through to the S corporation's shareholders to be included in their individual AMT calculations.

S corporations do not have to make an adjustment for the difference between adjusted current earnings and preadjustment alternative minimum taxable income that a C corporation makes in calculating its AMT liability. For certain corporations, this difference may make an S election attractive.[57]

TRANSACTIONS INVOLVING SHAREHOLDERS AND OTHER RELATED PARTIES

The Sec. 267(a)(2) related party transaction rules deny a payor a deduction for an expense paid to a related payee when a mismatching of the expense and income items occurs because of differences in accounting methods. A number of related party situations directly involve S corporations. Some of these transactions involve two S corporations or an S corporation and a C corporation where the same shareholders directly or indirectly own more than 50% of the value of each corporation's stock. Section 267(a)(2), for example, prevents an S corporation using the accrual method from currently deducting a year-end expense accrued for an item owed to a second S corporation that uses the cash method when the same shareholders own both corporations. The first S corporation can deduct the expense on the day the second S corporation includes the income in its gross income.

The S corporation, being a pass-through entity, is subject to Sec. 267(e), which extends the Sec. 267(a)(2) related party transaction rules described above to any payment made by the S corporation to *any* person who directly or indirectly owns S corporation stock. This rule prevents the S corporation from deducting a payment to be made to one of its shareholders or to someone who indirectly owns such stock until the payee reports the income. Payments made to the S corporation by a person who directly or indirectly owns S corporation stock are similarly restricted.

EXAMPLE C:11-29 ▶ Vassar Corporation, an S corporation, uses the accrual method of accounting and a calendar tax year. On September 1, 2007, Vassar borrows $50,000 from Joan, a cash basis taxpayer who owns 10% of the Vassar stock. Joan charges interest at an 8% annual rate. At year-end, Vassar accrues $1,000 of interest expense on the loan. The corporation pays six months of interest (including the $1,000 of accrued interest) to Joan on April 1, 2008. Vassar cannot deduct the 2007 accrued interest until it pays the interest in 2008. ◀

Section 267(a)(1) denies a deduction for losses incurred on the sale or exchange of property directly or indirectly between related parties. The same definition of a related party applies for this purpose as in applying Sec. 267(a)(2) to expense transactions involving an S corporation. Any loss disallowed to the seller on the related party sale or exchange can offset gains realized by the purchaser on a subsequent sale or exchange.

FRINGE BENEFITS PAID TO A SHAREHOLDER-EMPLOYEE

The S corporation is not treated as a corporate taxpayer with respect to many fringe benefits paid to 2% shareholders.[58] Instead, the S corporation is treated the same as a partnership,

---

[57] Sec. 56(g)(6).

[58] Section 1372(b) defines a 2% shareholder as any person who directly or indirectly owns on any day of the S corporation's tax year more than 2% of its outstanding stock or stock possessing more than 2% of its voting power. The Sec. 318 stock attribution rules apply to determine whether the 2% threshold has been exceeded.

TYPICAL MISCONCEPTION

Most fringe benefits provided by a C corporation are deductible to the corporation and nontaxable to the employee. However, fringe benefits paid to a more-than-2% shareholder-employee of an S corporation are in many cases nondeductible unless taxable to the shareholder-employee as compensation.

and a 2% shareholder is treated as a partner of such partnership.[59] Because of this restriction, many fringe benefits paid to a 2% shareholder-employee of an S corporation are taxable as compensation to the shareholder and deductible by the corporation if the benefit is not excludible from the shareholder's the gross income. Shareholders owning 2% or less of the S corporation stock are treated as ordinary employees.

The special fringe benefit rules apply only to statutory fringe benefits. They do not apply to stock options, qualified retirement plans, and nonqualified deferred compensation. The fringe benefits limited by the more-than-2%-shareholder rule include group term life insurance premiums (Sec. 79), accident and health benefit plan insurance premiums and payments (Secs. 105 and 106), meals and lodging furnished by the employer (Sec. 119), cafeteria plan benefits (Sec. 125), and employer-provided parking (Sec. 132). Fringe benefits that may be excluded by more-than-2%-shareholders include compensation for injuries and sickness (Sec. 104); educational assistance program benefits (Sec. 127); dependent care assistance program benefits (Sec. 129); and no-additional-cost benefits, qualified employee discounts, working condition fringe benefits, de minimis fringe benefits, and on-premises athletic facilities (Sec. 132). For purposes of the Sec. 162(l) above-the-line deduction for self-employed taxpayer's health insurance premiums, a more-than-2%-shareholder is deemed to be self-employed.

EXAMPLE C:11-30 ▶ Bill and his wife Cathy equally own Edison Corporation, an S corporation. Edison employs Bill and ten other individuals. All employees receive group term life insurance benefits based on their annual salaries. All employees except Bill can qualify for the Sec. 79 group term life insurance premium exclusion. Bill is treated as a partner and, therefore, does not qualify as an employee. Bill's premiums are treated as compensation and taxable to Bill. Edison can deduct the premiums paid to all its employees, including Bill. Because Bill is treated as self-employed under the 2% shareholder rules, he can deduct a portion of the premiums paid on the health insurance as a "for" AGI deduction under the Sec.162(l) rules applicable to health insurance payments made by all self-employed individuals. ◀

TAX PLANNING CONSIDERATIONS

ELECTION TO ALLOCATE INCOME BASED ON THE S CORPORATION'S ACCOUNTING METHODS

As a general rule, the S corporation's ordinary income or loss and separately stated items are allocated based on the amount of stock owned by each shareholder on each day of the S corporation's tax year. A special "closing of books" election allows the income to be allocated based on the S corporation's accounting methods when the S election terminates or when a shareholder terminates or substantially reduces his or her entire interest in the S corporation.[60] The use of the S corporation's tax accounting method to allocate the year's profit or loss can permit income shifting among shareholders.

EXAMPLE C:11-31 ▶ At the beginning of the current year (not a leap year), Rod and Dana equally own Apex Corporation, an S corporation. During the current year, Apex reports ordinary income of \$146,000. On March 31 of the current year (the 90th day of Apex's tax year), Dana sells all his Apex stock to Randy. Apex earns \$125,000 of its ordinary income after March 31 of the current year. Rod is allocated \$73,000 (\$146,000 × 0.50) of ordinary income. His income allocation is the same whether the corporation uses the daily allocation method or the special allocation election. In total, Dana and Randy are allocated \$73,000 of ordinary income. Dana and Randy can allocate the ordinary income amount in the following ways:

[59] Sec. 1372(a).

[60] The shareholder, however, still can be a creditor, director, or employee of the corporation. Sections 1362(e) and 1377(a) prevent the daily allocation method from applying to any items resulting from a sale or exchange of 50% or more of the S corporation's stock during an S termination year.

	Daily Allocation	*Closing of Books Election*
Dana:	$\$146{,}000 \times \frac{1}{2} \times \frac{90}{365} = \$18{,}000$	$(\$146{,}000 - \$125{,}000) \times \frac{1}{2} = \$10{,}500$
Randy:	$\$146{,}000 \times \frac{1}{2} \times \frac{275}{365} = \$55{,}000$	$\$125{,}000 \times \frac{1}{2} = \$62{,}500$

The shifting of the $7,500 in income from Dana ($18,000 – $10,500) to Randy ($62,500 – $55,000) under the special election also reduces Dana's adjusted basis for his Apex stock when determining his gain or loss on the sale. The $7,500 difference between the income allocations under the two methods may be a point for negotiation between Dana and Randy, particularly if their marginal tax rates differ. ◀

By electing to use the S corporation's tax accounting method to allocate profits or losses between the C short year and S short year in the termination year, the corporation can shift losses into an S short year where the shareholders obtain an immediate benefit at a marginal tax rate of up to 35% (in 2007), or it can shift profits into a C short year to take advantage of the 15% and 25% marginal corporate tax rates. The C corporation, however, must annualize its short-year income in determining its tax liability.

EXAMPLE C:11-32 ▶ Delta Corporation has been an S corporation for several years using a calendar year as its tax year. The corporation has one shareholder whose marginal tax rate is 35%. Delta's S election terminates on July 1. The S short year includes January 1 through June 30, and the C short year includes July 1 through December 31. Total ordinary income this year is $10,000. If the corporation closes its books on June 30, $40,000 of ordinary loss is allocable to the S short year, and $50,000 of ordinary income is allocable to the C short year. Assuming each month has 30 days, the following income allocations are possible:

Period	*Daily Allocation*	*Closing of Books Election*
S short year	$ 5,000	($40,000)
C short year	5,000	50,000
Total	$10,000	$10,000

With the daily allocation, one-half the income is taxed to the shareholder, and the other half is taxed to the C corporation.[61] The daily allocation method causes the shareholder's tax to be $1,750 ($5,000 × 0.35) on the pass-through income and the C corporation's tax to be $750 ($5,000 × 2 × 0.15 × 0.5) on its annualized income, for a total tax of $2,500. By closing the books, the corporation passes the $40,000 S short year loss through to its shareholder and is taxed on the $50,000 C short year income as a C corporation. This method provides the shareholder with a $14,000 ($40,000 pass-through loss × 0.35) tax savings and causes the C corporation's tax to be $11,125 ($22,250 tax on $100,000 of annualized income × 0.5), for a net tax savings of $2,875 ($14,000 – $11,125). Thus, in this situation, the closing of books method provides the greater overall tax advantage ($2,875 vs. $2,500). ◀

INCREASING THE BENEFITS FROM S CORPORATION LOSSES

At the shareholder level, the deduction for S corporation pass-through losses is limited to the S corporation stock basis plus the basis of debt owed by the S corporation to the shareholder. Pass-through losses exceeding this limitation carry over to a subsequent tax year when the shareholder regains stock or debt basis. If the shareholder expects his or her marginal tax rate to be the same or lower in a carryover tax year, the shareholder should consider either increasing his or her stock basis or loaning additional funds to the corporation before the end of the current tax year. Conversely, if the shareholder never expects the loans to be repaid, he or she should not lend the S corporation additional amounts just to secure an additional tax deduction, which is worth at most 35 cents (at 2007 rates) for

[61] Section 1362(e)(5)(A) requires calculation of the tax liability for the C short year to be based on the annualized income of the former S corporation (see Chapter C:3 for a discussion of annualization).

each dollar loaned. If the shareholder expects his or her marginal tax rate to be higher in future tax years, the shareholder should consider deferring additional capital contributions or loans until after the end of the current tax year.

EXAMPLE C:11-33 ▶ Nancy owns 100% of Bailey Corporation, an S corporation. Bailey expects a $100,000 ordinary loss in 2007. Nancy's stock basis (before adjustment for the current loss) is $35,000. Bailey also owes Nancy $25,000. Nancy's 2007 marginal tax rate is 35%, but she expects her marginal tax rate to decline to 15% in 2008. Nancy should consider making $40,000 [$100,000 loss – ($35,000 stock basis + $25,000 debt basis)] of additional capital contributions or loans before the end of 2007 to obtain an additional $8,000 [(0.35 – 0.15) × $40,000] of tax benefits from deducting the loss in 2007 rather than in 2008. If Nancy instead expects her 2007 and 2008 marginal tax rates to be 15% and 35%, respectively, she can defer $8,000 [(0.35 – 0.15) × $40,000] of tax benefits (less the time value of money for one year) by postponing her capital contributions or loans until 2008. Alternatively, Nancy could use the loss carryover to offset profits reported in 2008. These profits would restore part or all of her debt basis (and possibly increase her stock basis). The stock basis then would be partially or fully offset by the $40,000 loss carryover. ◀

KEY POINT

If an S corporation shareholder has losses that have been suspended due to lack of basis, either contributions to capital or bona fide loans to the corporation will create the necessary basis to use the losses.

The S corporation loss carryover is available only to the shareholder who held the stock when the loss occurred. A shareholder should consider increasing the stock basis to take advantage of the carryover before selling the stock. The purchasing shareholder does not acquire the carryover.

PASSIVE INCOME REQUIREMENTS

The S corporation can earn an unlimited amount of passive income each year without incurring any penalty provided it has no E&P accumulated in a C corporation tax year (known as Subchapter C E&P) at the end of its tax year. Thus, a corporation can make an S election to avoid the personal holding company tax that otherwise might apply to a C corporation's passive income.

S corporations that have operated as C corporations and have accumulated Subchapter C E&P are potentially liable for the excess net passive income tax. In addition, their S election may terminate if the passive investment income exceeds 25% of gross receipts for three consecutive tax years. The S corporation can avoid both of these possible problems by making a special election under Sec. 1368(e)(3) to distribute its entire Subchapter C E&P balance to its shareholders. A corporation that elects to distribute Subchapter C E&P before distributing from its accumulated adjustments account (AAA) can make a second special election to treat part or all of this "distribution" as a deemed dividend, which is deemed distributed to the shareholders and immediately contributed by the shareholders to the corporation on the last day of the corporation's tax year.[62] Such an election requires no cash outlay. The distribution, however, results in a tax cost for the shareholders who pay tax on the resulting deemed dividend income. To the shareholders, the cost of the election can be small if the accumulated E&P balance is insignificant or if the shareholder has a current year NOL (excluding the distribution) or an NOL carryover. The tax cost also is low given the current 15% maximum tax rate on dividends. The ultimate long-run benefit, however, may be great because it permits the S corporation to earn an unlimited amount of passive investment income free from corporate taxes in subsequent tax years.

EXAMPLE C:11-34 ▶ Hawaii Corporation incorporated 12 years ago and operated for a number of years as a C corporation, during which time it accumulated $30,000 of E&P. Most of Hawaii's gross income now comes from rentals and interest, constituting passive investment income. Hawaii makes an S election starting in the current year. The excess net passive income tax will apply in the current year if Hawaii's rentals and interest exceed 25% of its gross receipts for the year unless the corporation elects to distribute the accumulated E&P and then distributes the earnings by the end of the currrent year. ◀

[62] Reg. Sec. 1.1368-1(f)(3).

S corporations that earn rental income also can avoid the passive income tax and the possibility of having its election terminated if the corporation renders significant services to the occupant of the space or if the corporation incurs significant costs in the rental business.[63] Whether the corporation performs significant services or incurs substantial costs in the rental business depends on the facts and circumstances including, but not limited to, the number of persons employed to provide the services and the types and amounts of costs and expenses incurred (other than depreciation).

EXAMPLE C:11-35 ▶ Assume the same facts as in Example C:11-34 except Hawaii Corporation provides significant services to its tenants in connection with its rental activities. Because the services are significant, Hawaii has a passive income problem only if its interest income exceeds 25% of its gross receipts. If the 25% threshold is not exceeded, Hawaii can avoid having to distribute its Subchapter C E&P in the current year. ◀

S corporations that experience a passive income problem in two consecutive tax years should carefully monitor their passive income in the next year. If they see that their passive income for the third year will exceed the 25% threshold, they should elect to distribute their accumulated Subchapter C E&P before year-end. This strategy not only will prevent loss of the S election but also will avoid having to pay the Sec. 1375 tax.

COMPLIANCE AND PROCEDURAL CONSIDERATIONS

MAKING THE ELECTION

A corporation makes the S election by filing Form 2553 (Election by Small Business Corporation). Any person authorized to sign the S corporation's tax return under Sec. 6037 can sign the election form. The corporation files Form 2553 with the IRS Service Center designated in the instructions. The IRS can treat a late election as timely made if the corporation can show reasonable cause.[64]

A shareholder can consent to the S election either on Form 2553 or on a separate consent statement signed by the shareholder and attached to the corporation's election form. Regulation Sec. 1.1362-6(b) outlines other information that must be provided with a separate consent. The IRS can grant extensions of time for filing shareholder consents to the S election.[65]

A corporation makes a Sec. 444 election to use a fiscal year on Form 8716, which the corporation must file by the earlier of (1) the fifteenth day of the fifth month following the month that includes the first day of the tax year for which the election will first be effective or (2) the due date for the income tax return resulting from the election.[66] The corporation must attach a copy of Form 8716 to Form 1120S for the first tax year for which the Sec. 444 election is effective. A corporation desiring to make a Sec. 444 election also must state its intention in a statement attached to its S election form (Form 2553).[67]

OBJECTIVE 11

Apply the procedures for filing an S corporation tax return

FILING THE CORPORATE TAX RETURN

All S corporations, whether or not they owe taxes under Secs. 1374 or 1375, must file a tax return if they exist for part or all of the tax year. An S corporation must file its corporate tax return not later than the fifteenth day of the third month following the end of the tax year.[68] The S corporation reports its results on Form 1120S (U.S. Income Tax Return for an S Corporation). A completed S corporation tax return and the facts supporting the return appear in Appendix B. An S corporation is allowed an automatic six-month extension of

---

[63] According to Reg. Sec. 1.1362-2(c)(5)(ii)(B)(3), however, significant services are not rendered and substantial costs are not incurred in connection with net leases.

[64] Sec. 1362(b)(5), Rev. Proc. 2003-43, 2003-23 C.B. 998, and Rev. Proc. 2004-48, 2004-32 I.R.B. 172.

[65] Reg. Sec. 1.1362-6(b)(3)(iii).

[66] Temp. Reg. Sec. 1.444-3T(b)(1).

[67] Temp. Reg. Sec. 1.444-3T(b)(3).

[68] Sec. 6072(b).

time for filing its tax return by filing Form 7004 (Application for Automatic 6-month Extension of Time to File Certain Business Income Tax, Information, and Other Returns), also illustrated in Appendix B.[69]

EXAMPLE C:11-36 ▶ Simpson Corporation, an S corporation, uses the calendar year as its tax year. Its tax return generally is due on March 15. Simpson can file Form 7004 and obtain an automatic six-month extension for the return, thereby extending its due date until September 15. ◀

REAL-WORLD EXAMPLE

The IRS recently resumed its program of matching Schedule K-1 information to the shareholders' individual tax returns.

All S corporations that file a tax return must furnish each person who is a shareholder at any time during the tax year with pertinent information from the tax return, usually via Form 1120S, Schedule K-1. The corporation must make the Schedule K-1 available to the shareholder not later than the day on which it files its tax return.[70] An individual shareholder reports the S corporation's pass-through ordinary income or loss and certain passive income or loss items on his or her Form 1040, Schedule E. The shareholder reports most separately stated items on other supporting schedules to Form 1040, as illustrated on the Form 1120S, Schedule K-1 presented in Appendix B.

An S corporation is subject to the same basic three-year statute of limitations that applies to other taxpayers. This three-year limitations period applies for purposes of determining the time period during which

- The corporation remains liable for assessments of the excess net passive income and built-in gains taxes
- The IRS can question the correctness of an S election made for a particular tax year[71]

The limitation period for assessing the income tax liability of an S corporation shareholder (e.g., for an erroneous S corporation loss deduction claimed), however, runs from the date on which the shareholder files his or her return and not from the date the S corporation files its tax return.[72]

If the corporation elects a fiscal year under Sec. 444, it determines the Sec. 7519 required payment on a computation worksheet provided in the instructions for the Form 1120S. The corporation need not make a required payment if the total of such payments for the current year and all preceding years is $500 or less. Amounts equal to or less than the $500 threshold carry over to succeeding years. The required payment is due on or before May 15 regardless of the fiscal year used. The required payment and the computation worksheet must accompany a Form 8752, which also is used to secure a refund of prior Sec. 7519 payments.[73]

OBJECTIVE 12

Determine the estimated tax payments required of an S corporation and its shareholders

ESTIMATED TAX PAYMENTS

S corporations must make estimated tax payments if their estimated tax liability is reasonably expected to be $500 or more.[74] Estimated tax payments are required for the corporate liability attributable to the built-in gains tax (Sec. 1374) and the excess net passive income tax (Sec. 1375). In addition, the S corporation's shareholders must include their income, gain, loss, deduction, and credit pass-through items in their own estimated tax calculations.

The corporate estimated tax payment requirements described for a C corporation in Chapter C:3 also apply to an S corporation's tax liabilities. The required quarterly installment is 25% of the lesser of (1) 100% of the tax shown on the return for the tax year or (2) the sum of 100% of the built-in gains tax shown on the return for the tax year plus 100% of the excess net passive income tax shown on the return for the preceding tax year.

An S corporation cannot use the prior year tax liability exception when determining the required payment to be made with respect to the built-in gains tax. This exception, however, is available with respect to the excess net passive income tax portion of the

---

69 Reg. Sec. 1.6081-3.

70 Sec. 6037(b).

71 Sec. 6233.

72 *Sheldon B. Bufferd v. CIR*, 71 AFTR 2d 93-573, 93-1 USTC ¶50,038 (USSC, 1993).

73 Temp. Reg. Sec. 1.7519-2T.

74 Estimate tax rules appear in Sec. 6655.

SELF-STUDY QUESTION

Is an S corporation required to make estimated tax payments?

ANSWER

Yes. An S corporation is required to pay estimated taxes if the corporation is subject to built-in gains or excess net passive income taxes. Also, shareholders are required to include their S corporation income, loss, and credit pass-through items in determining their estimated tax payments.

required payment without regard to whether the corporation owed any tax in the prior year. All corporations can use the prior year tax liability exception for the excess net passive income tax whether or not they are "large" corporations under Sec. 6655(d)(2). The annualization election of Sec. 6655(e) also is available when determining the quarterly estimated tax payment amounts. An S corporation's failure to make timely estimated tax payments, or a timely final payment when it files the tax return, will trigger interest and penalties.

The S corporation's shareholders must include their ratable share of ordinary income or loss and separately stated items in determining their estimated tax liability. Such amounts are treated as having been received concurrently by the shareholders throughout the S corporation's tax year. Thus, ordinary income or loss and separately stated items for an S corporation tax year that ends with or within the shareholder's tax year are included in the estimated tax calculation to the extent they are attributable to months in the S corporation tax year that precede the month in which the installment is due.[75]

CONSISTENCY RULES

ADDITIONAL COMMENT

When examining an S corporation, the IRS conducts the audit in a unified proceeding at the corporate level rather than in separate audits of each S corporation shareholder.

Section 6037(c) requires an S corporation shareholder to report on his or her return a Subchapter S item in a manner consistent with the treatment accorded the item on the S corporation's return. A Subchapter S item is any item (e.g., income, gain, deduction, loss, credit, accounting method, or tax year) of an S corporation where the reporting of the item is more appropriately determined at the corporation level than at the shareholder level. A shareholder must notify the IRS of any inconsistency when the corporation has filed a return but the shareholder's treatment on his return is (or may be) inconsistent with the treatment of the item on the corporation return. Failure to do so may result in the imposition of a negligence penalty under Sec. 6662. Any adjustment required to produce consistency with the corporate return is treated as a mathematical or clerical error for penalty calculation purposes. A similar notification also is required when the corporation has not filed a return. If a shareholder receives incorrect information from the S corporation regarding a Subchapter S item, the shareholder's consistent reporting of the item consistently with the information provided by the corporation generally will eliminate the imposition of any penalty.

SAMPLE S CORPORATION TAX RETURN

REAL-WORLD EXAMPLE

In 2003, of the 5.4 million corporate tax returns filed, 61.9% were S corporations.

A sample S corporation Form 1120S and supporting Schedule K-1 appear in Appendix B, along with the facts supporting the return. Two differences should be noted between the S corporation tax return and a partnership tax return. First, the S corporation tax return provides for the determination of a corporate tax liability and the payment of the special taxes that can be levied on the S corporation. No such items appear in the partnership return. Second, the S corporation return does not require a reconciliation of the shareholders' basis adjustments as occurs on a partnership tax return. Schedule M-1, M-2, and M-3 reconciliations similar to those required of a C corporation are required of an S corporation. Schedule M-1 requires a reconciliation of book income with the income or loss reported on line 23 of Schedule K, which includes not only the ordinary income (loss) amount but also separately stated income and deduction items. For tax years ending on or after December 31, 2006, an S corporation must file Schedule M-3 in lieu of Schedule M-1 if the amount of total assets reported in Schedule L of Form 1120S (Balance Sheet per Books) equals or exceeds $10 million. The S corporation also may file Schedule M-3 voluntarily even if not required to do so. If the corporation files Schedule M-3, in either case, it checks the appropriate box on page 1 of Form 1120S and does not file Schedule M-1. (The sample tax return in Appendix B does not include Schedule M-3.) Schedule M-2 requires a reconciliation of the AAA, OAA, and PTI accounts. (The PTI account pertains to pre-1983 S corporations.) Only S corporations that have an accumulated E&P balance must provide the AAA reconciliation and OAA balance although the IRS recommends that all S corporations maintain AAA and OAA balances.

[75] For example, see Ltr. Rul. 8639008 (June 23, 1986).

PROBLEM MATERIALS

DISCUSSION QUESTIONS

C:11-1 List five advantages and five disadvantages of making an S election. Briefly explain each item.

C:11-2 Julio, age 50, is a U.S. citizen who has a 28% marginal tax rate. He has operated the A&B Automotive Parts Company for a number of years as a C corporation. Last year, A&B reported $200,000 of pre-tax profits, from which it paid $50,000 in salary and $25,000 in dividends to Julio. The corporation expects this year's pre-tax profits to be $300,000. To date, the corporation has created no fringe benefits or pension plans for Julio. Julio asks you to explain whether an S corporation election would reduce his taxes. How do you respond to Julio's inquiry?

C:11-3 Celia, age 30, is leaving a major systems development firm to establish her own firm. She will design computer-based systems for small- and medium-sized businesses. Celia will invest $100,000 in the business. She hopes to operate near her breakeven point during her first year, although a small loss is possible. Profits will build up slowly over the next four years until she is earning $150,000 a year in her fifth year. Celia has heard about S corporations and asks you whether the S corporation form would be advisable for her new business. How do you respond to Celia's inquiry?

C:11-4 Lance and Rodney are contemplating starting a new business to manufacture computer software games. They expect to encounter losses in the initial years. Lance's CPA has talked to them about using an S corporation. Rodney, while reading a business publication, encounters a discussion on limited liability companies (LLCs). The article talks about the advantages of using an LLC instead of an S corporation. How would you respond to their inquiry?

C:11-5 Which of the following classifications make a shareholder ineligible to own stock in an S corporation?

a. U.S. citizen
b. Domestic corporation
c. Partnership where all the partners are U.S. citizens
d. Estate of a deceased U.S. citizen
e. Grantor trust created by a U.S. citizen
f. Nonresident alien individual

C:11-6 Which of the following taxes do not apply to an S corporation?

a. Regular (income) tax
b. Accumulated earnings tax
c. Corporate alternative minimum tax
d. Built-in gains tax
e. Personal holding company tax
f. Excess net passive income tax
g. LIFO recapture tax

C:11-7 Will the following events cause an S election to terminate?

a. The S corporation earning 100% of its gross receipts in its first tax year from passive sources
b. The S corporation issuing nonvoting stock that has a dividend preference
c. The S corporation purchasing 100% of the single class of stock of a second domestic corporation that has conducted business activities for four years
d. An individual shareholder donating 100 shares of S corporation stock to a charity that is exempt from tax under Sec. 501(c)(3)
e. The S corporation earning tax-exempt interest income

C:11-8 What is an inadvertent termination? What actions must the S corporation and its shareholders take to correct an inadvertent termination?

C:11-9 After an S corporation revokes or terminates its S election, how long must the corporation wait to make a new election? What circumstances permit an early reelection?

C:11-10 What tax years can a newly created corporation that makes an S election adopt for its first tax year? If a fiscal year is permitted, does it require IRS approval?

C:11-11 At the time Cable Corporation makes its S election, it elects to use a fiscal year based on a Sec. 444 election. What other requirements must Cable satisfy to continue to use its fiscal year election for future tax years?

C:11-12 What are Subchapter C earnings and profits (E&P)? How does the existence of such E&P affect the S corporation's ability to earn passive income?

C:11-13 Explain the procedures for allocating an S corporation's ordinary income or loss to each of the shareholders. What special allocation elections are available?

C:11-14 What limitations apply to the amount of loss pass-through an S corporation shareholder can deduct? What happens to any losses exceeding this limitation? What happens to losses if the shareholder transfers his or her stock?

C:11-15 What actions can an S corporation shareholder take before year-end to increase the amount of the S corporation's losses he or she can deduct in the year they are incurred?

C:11-16 What is a post-termination transition period? What loss carryovers can an S corporation shareholder deduct during this period?

C:11-17 Explain the positive and negative adjustments to the basis of an S corporation shareholder's stock investment and the basis of an S corporation debt owed to the shareholder.

C:11-18 Explain the differences between the tax treatment accorded nonliquidating property distributions made by S corporations and partnerships.

C:11-19 What nonliquidating distributions made by an S corporation are taxable to its shareholders? Tax-free to its shareholders?

C:11-20 What is an accumulated adjustments account (AAA)? What income, gain, loss, and deduction items *do not* affect this account assuming the S corporation has an accumulated E&P balance?

C:11-21 Explain the differences between the way the following items are reported by a C corporation and an S corporation:

a. Ordinary income or loss
b. Dividend income
c. Capital gains and losses
d. Tax-exempt interest income
e. Charitable contributions
f. Nonliquidating property distributions
g. Fringe benefits paid to a shareholder-employee

C:11-22 When is the S corporation's tax return due? What extensions are available for filing the return?

C:11-23 What taxes must an S corporation prepay by making quarterly estimated tax payments? Can a shareholder owning S corporation stock use the corporation's estimated tax payments to reduce the amount of his or her individual estimated tax payments? Explain.

C:11-24 Review the completed C corporation, partnership, and S corporation tax returns presented in Appendix B. List three major tax reporting similarities and three major tax reporting differences in either content or format among the three tax returns.

ISSUE IDENTIFICATION QUESTIONS

C:11-25 Jennelle and Paula are equal partners in the J&P Manufacturing Partnership. The partnership will form J&P Corporation by exchanging the assets and liabilities of the J&P Manufacturing Partnership for all the corporation's stock on September 1 of the current year. The partnership then will liquidate by distributing the J&P Corporation stock equally to Jennelle and Paula. Both shareholders use the calendar year as their tax year and desire that the corporation make an S election. What tax issues should Jennelle and Paula consider with respect to the incorporation?

C:11-26 Williams Corporation has operated as a C corporation for the last seven years. The corporation has assets with a $450,000 adjusted basis and an $800,000 FMV. Liabilities amount to $100,000. Dan Williams, who uses a calendar year as his tax year, owns all the Williams Corporation stock. The corporation uses the accrual method of accounting and a June 30 year-end. Dan's CPA has suggested that he convert the corporation to S corporation status to reduce his total corporate/personal federal income tax liability. Dan would like to complete the conversion on the last day of the corporation's tax year. What tax issues should Dan and his CPA consider with respect to the S election?

C:11-27 Peter owns 50% of Air South Corporation, an air charter service. His S corporation stock basis at beginning of the year is $100,000. Air South has not done well this year and will report an ordinary loss of $375,000. Peter's marginal tax rate for the current year is 35%. What tax issues should Peter consider with respect to the loss?

C:11-28 Glacier Smokeries has been an S corporation since its inception six years ago. On January 1 of the current year, the corporation's two equal shareholders, Adam and Rodney, had adjusted bases of $175,000 and $225,000, respectively, for their S corporation's stock. The shareholders plan to have the corporation distribute land with a $75,000 adjusted basis and a $300,000 FMV in the current year. The shareholders also expect ordinary income to be $125,000 in the current year. What tax issues should Adam and Rodney consider with respect to the distribution?

PROBLEMS

C:11-29 *Comparison of Entity Forms.* Ken Munro, a single taxpayer, owns 100% of King Corporation. During 2007, King reports $100,000 of taxable income. Ken Munro reports no income other than that earned from King, and Ken claims the standard deduction.

a. What is King Corporation's income tax liability assuming Ken withdraws none of the earnings from the C corporation? What is Ken's income tax liability? What is the total tax liability for the corporation and its shareholder?

b. Assume that King instead distributes 100% of its after-tax earnings to Ken as a dividend in the current year. What is the total income tax liability for the C corporation and its shareholder?
c. How would your answer to Part a change if Ken withdrew $50,000 from the business in salary? Must any taxes other than corporate and individual income taxes be considered now that the corporation pays a salary?
d. How would your answers to Parts a–c change if King were instead an S corporation?

C:11-30 *Making the Election.* Voyles Corporation, a calendar year taxpayer formed five years ago, desires to make an S election beginning in 2007. Sue and Andrea each own one-half of the Voyles stock.
a. How does Voyles make the S election?
b. When can Voyles file its election form?
c. If in Part b the corporation does not file the election in a timely manner, when will the election take effect?

C:11-31 *Termination of the Election.* Orlando Corporation, a calendar year taxpayer, has been an S corporation for several years. On July 10, 2007, Orlando authorizes a second class of nonvoting preferred stock that pays a 10% annual dividend. The corporation issues the stock to Sid on September 12, 2007, to raise additional equity capital. Sid owns no other Orlando stock.
a. Does Orlando's S election terminate? If so, when is the termination effective?
b. What tax returns must Orlando file for 2007? When are they due?
c. How would your answer to Parts a and b change if instead the second class of stock were nonvoting Class B common stock?

C:11-32 *Revocation of the Election.* Tango Corporation, a calendar year taxpayer, has been an S corporation for several years. Tango's business activities have become very profitable in recent years. On June 15, 2007, its sole shareholder, who is in the 35% marginal tax bracket, desires to revoke the S election.
a. How does Tango revoke its S election? When does the revocation take effect?
b. Assume the revocation is effective July 1, 2007. What tax returns are required of Tango for 2007? For 2008? When are these returns due?
c. If the corporation makes a new S election after the revocation, when does it take effect?

C:11-33 *Sale of S Corporation Interest.* Peter and his wife, Alice, own all the stock of Galleon Corporation. Galleon made its S election 12 years ago. Peter and Alice sold one-half their Galleon stock to a partnership owned by Rob and Susan (not husband and wife) at the close of business on December 31, 2007, for a $75,000 profit. What are the tax consequences of the sale transaction for Peter and Alice? For the corporation? As Peter and Alice's CPA, do you have any advice for them if all parties would like the S election to continue?

C:11-34 *Selecting a Tax Year.* Indicate in each of the following situations whether the taxpayer can accomplish what is proposed. Provide adequate authority for your answer including any special elections that are needed or requirements that must be satisfied. Assume all individuals use the calendar year as their tax year unless otherwise indicated.
a. Will and Carol form Classic Corporation. They want the corporation to adopt a fiscal year ending January 31 as its tax year to provide a maximum deferral for their income. The corporation makes an S election for its initial tax year ending January 31, 2008.
b. Mark and Dennis have owned and operated the Plastic Corporation for several years. Plastic has used a fiscal year ending June 30 since its organization as a C corporation because it conforms to the corporation's natural business year. The corporation makes an S election for its tax year beginning July 1, 2007.

C:11-35 *Passive Income Tax.* Oliver organized North Corporation 15 years ago. The corporation made an S election last year after it accumulated $60,000 of E&P as a C corporation. As of December 31 of the current year, the corporation has distributed none of its accumulated E&P. In the current year, North reports the following results:

Dividends from domestic corporations	$ 60,000
Rental income	100,000
Services income	50,000
Expenses related to rental income	30,000
Expenses related to services income	15,000
Other expenses	5,000

The corporation has not provided significant services nor incurred substantial costs in connection with earning the rental income. The services income is derived from the active conduct of a trade or business.

a. Is North subject to the excess net passive income tax? If so, what is its tax liability?
b. What is the effect of the excess net passive income tax liability on North's pass-throughs of ordinary income and separately stated items?
c. What advice would you give North regarding its activities?

C:11-36 ***Built-in Gains Tax.*** Theta Corporation formed 15 years ago. In its first year, it elected to use the cash method of accounting and adopted a calendar year as its tax year. It made an S election on August 15 of last year, effective for Theta's current tax year. At the beginning of the current year, Theta had assets with a $600,000 FMV and a $180,000 adjusted basis. During the current year, Theta reports taxable income of $400,000.

- In the current year, Theta collects all $200,000 of accounts receivables outstanding on January 1 of the current year. The receivables had a zero adjusted basis.
- On February 1, Theta sells an automobile for $3,500. The automobile had a $2,000 adjusted basis and a $3,000 FMV on January 1 of the current year. Theta claimed $800 of MACRS depreciation on the automobile in the current year.
- On March 1, Theta sells land (a Sec. 1231 asset) that it held three years in anticipation of building its own office building for a $35,000 gain. The land had a $45,000 FMV and a $25,000 adjusted basis on January 1 of the current year.
- In the current year, Theta paid $125,000 of accounts payable outstanding on January 1 of the current year. All the payables are deductible expenses.

What is the amount of Theta's built-in gains tax liability?

C:11-37 ***Determination of Pass-Throughs and Stock Basis Adjustments.*** Mike and Nancy are equal shareholders in MN Corporation, an S corporation. The corporation, Mike, and Nancy are calendar year taxpayers. The corporation has been an S corporation during its entire existence and thus has no accumulated E&P. The shareholders have no loans to the corporation. The corporation incurred the following items in the current year:

Sales	$300,000
Cost of goods sold	140,000
Dividends on corporate investments	10,000
Tax-exempt interest income	3,000
Section 1245 gain (recapture) on equipment sale	22,000
Section 1231 gain on equipment sale	12,000
Long-term capital gain on stock sale	8,000
Long-term capital loss on stock sale	7,000
Short-term capital loss on stock sale	6,000
Depreciation	18,000
Salary to Nancy	20,000
Meals and entertainment expenses	7,800
Interest expense on loans allocable to:	
Business debt	32,000
Stock investments	6,400
Tax-exempt bonds	1,800
Principal payment on business loan	9,000
Charitable contributions	2,000
Distributions to shareholders ($15,000 each)	30,000

a. Compute the S corporation's ordinary income and separately stated items.
b. Show Mike's and Nancy's shares of the items in Part a.
c. Compute Mike's and Nancy's ending stock bases assuming their beginning balances are $100,000 each. When making basis adjustments, apply the adjustments in the order outlined on pages C:11-24 and C:11-25 of the text.

C:11-38 ***Allocation of Income to Shareholders.*** John owns all the stock of Lucas Corporation, an S corporation. John's basis for the 1,000 shares is $130,000. On June 11 of the current year (assume a non-leap year), John gifts 100 shares of stock to his younger brother Michael, who has been working in the business for one year. Lucas Corporation reports $125,000 of ordinary income for the current year. What amount of income is allocated to John? To Michael?

C:11-39 *Sale of S Corporation Interest.* Al and Ruth each own one-half the stock of Chemical Corporation, an S corporation. During the current year (assume a non-leap year), Chemical earns $15,000 per month of ordinary income. On April 5, Ruth sells her entire stock interest to Patty. The corporation sells a business asset on August 18 and realizes a $75,000 Sec. 1231 gain. What alternatives (if any) exist for allocating Chemical's current year income?

C:11-40 *Allocation of Income to Shareholders.* Toyland Corporation, an S corporation, uses the calendar year as its tax year. Bob, Alice, and Carter own 60, 30, and 10 shares, respectively, of the Toyland stock. Carter's basis for his stock is $26,000 on January 1 of the current year (assume a non-leap year). On June 30, Alice gifted one-half of her stock to Mike. On November 30, Carter sold his stock to Mike for $45,000. Toyland reports the following results for the current year:

Ordinary income	$120,000
Long-term capital loss	10,000
Charitable contributions	6,000

a. What amount of income, loss, or deduction do the four shareholders report (assuming the corporation makes no special allocation election)?
b. What gain or loss does Carter recognize when he sells the Toyland stock?

C:11-41 *Allocation of Income to Shareholders.* Redfern Corporation, a calendar year taxpayer, has been an S corporation for several years. Rod and Kurt each own 50% of Redfern's stock. On July 1 of the current year (assume a non-leap year), Redfern issues additional common stock to Blackfoot Corporation for cash. Rod, Kurt, and Blackfoot each end up owning one-third of Redfern's stock. Redfern reports ordinary income of $125,000 and a short-term capital loss of $15,000 in the current year. Eighty percent of the ordinary income and all the capital loss accrue after Blackfoot purchases its stock. Redfern makes no distributions to its shareholders in the current year. What income and losses do Redfern, Blackfoot, Rod, and Kurt report as a result of the current year's activities?

C:11-42 *Allocation of Income Between Family Members.* Bright Corporation, an S corporation, has been 100% owned by Betty since its creation 12 years ago. The corporation has been profitable in recent years and, in the current year (assume a non-leap year), reports ordinary income of $240,000 after paying Betty a $60,000 salary. On January 1, Betty gifts 15% of her Bright stock to each of her three sons, John, Andrew, and Stephen, hoping they will work in the family business. Betty pays gift taxes on the transfers. The sons are ages 19, 12, and 10 at present and are not currently active in the business. Bright distributes $7,500 in cash to each son and $27,500 in cash to Betty in the current year.
a. What income does Betty, John, Andrew, and Stephen report for the current year as a result of Bright's activities assuming the sons are considered bona fide owners of the stock? How will the income be taxed to the children?
b. Assuming the IRS determines a reasonable salary for Betty to be $120,000, how would your answer to Part a change?
c. How would your answer to Part a change if the sons were not considered bona fide owners of the stock?

C:11-43 *Use of Losses by Shareholders.* Monte and Allie each own 50% of Raider Corporation, an S corporation. Both individuals actively participate in Raider's business. On January 1, Monte and Allie have adjusted bases for their Raider stock of $80,000 and $90,000, respectively. During the current year, Raider reports the following results:

Ordinary loss	$175,000
Tax-exempt interest income	20,000
Long-term capital loss	32,000

Raider's balance sheet at year-end shows the following liabilities: accounts payable, $90,000; mortgage payable, $30,000; and note payable to Allie, $10,000.
a. What income and deductions will Monte and Allie report from Raider's current year activities?
b. What is Monte's stock basis on December 31?
c. What are Allie's stock basis and debt basis on December 31?
d. What loss carryovers are available for Monte and Allie?
e. Explain how the use of the losses in Part a would change if instead Raider were a partnership and Monte and Allie were partners who shared profits, losses, and liabilities equally.

C:11-44 *Use of Loss Carryovers.* Assume the same facts as in Problem C:11-43. Assume further that Raider Corporation reports $75,000 of ordinary income, $20,000 of tax-exempt income, and a $25,000 long-term capital gain in the next year.

a. What income and deductions will Monte and Allie report from next year's activities?
b. What is Monte's stock basis on December 31 of next year?
c. What are Allie's stock basis and note basis on December 31 of next year?
d. What loss carryovers (if any) are available to Monte and Allie?

C:11-45 *Use of Losses by Shareholders.* Tom owns 100% of Hammer Corporation, an S corporation. Tom has a $100,000 stock basis on January 1. Tom actively participates in Hammer's business. Hammer operating results were not good in the current year, with the corporation reporting an ordinary loss of $175,000. The size of the loss required Tom to lend Hammer $50,000 on August 10 of the current year to provide funds needed for operations. The loan is secured by a Hammer Corporation note. Hammer rebounds during the next year and reports ordinary income of $60,000. Hammer repays the $50,000 note on December 15.

a. What amount of Hammer's current year loss can Tom deduct on his income tax return?
b. What is Tom's basis for the Hammer stock and note at the end of the loss year?
c. What income and deductions will Tom report next year from Hammer's activities and the loan repayment?

C:11-46 *Allocation of Losses to Shareholders.* Harry and Rita formed Alpha Corporation as an S corporation, with each shareholder contributing $10,000 in exchange for stock. In addition, Rita loaned the corporation $7,000, and the corporation borrowed another $8,000 from the bank. In the current year, the corporation incurred a $26,000 operating loss. In the next year, the corporation will earn $16,000 of operating income.

a. For the current year and next year, determine the pass-through items for each shareholder and each shareholder's stock basis at the end of each year. Also, determine Rita's debt basis at the end of each year.
b. Same as Part a except the corporation also distributes $6,000 cash to each shareholder at the end of next year.
c. Assume the same facts as in Part b and that Alpha is a partnership instead of an S corporation. For the current year and next year, determine the pass-through items for each partner and each partner's basis in his or her partnership interest at the end of each year.

C:11-47 *Post-Termination Loss Use.* Stein Corporation, an S corporation, has 400 shares of stock outstanding. Chuck and Linda own an equal number of these shares, and both actively participate in Stein's business. Chuck and Linda each contributed $60,000 when they organized Stein on September 10, 2006. Start-up losses during 2006 resulted in Stein reporting a $210,000 ordinary loss. Stein's activities have since become profitable, and the corporation voluntarily revokes the S election on March 1, 2007, with no prospective revocation date being specified. In 2007, Stein reports $360,000 of taxable income ($30,000 per month). Stein makes no distributions to its shareholders in either year.

a. What amount of loss can Chuck and Linda deduct in 2006?
b. What amount of loss do Chuck and Linda carry over to 2007?
c. If Chuck reported only $5,000 of other business income in 2006, what happens to the "excess" deductible S corporation losses?
d. What portion of the loss carryover from Part b can Chuck and Linda deduct in 2007? What happens to any unused portion of the loss?
e. What advice can you offer to Chuck and Linda to enhance their use of the Stein loss?

C:11-48 *Use of Losses by Shareholders.* Tina, a single taxpayer, owns 100% of Rocket Corporation, an S corporation. She has an $80,000 stock basis for her investment on January 1. During the first 11 months of 2007, Rocket reports an ordinary loss of $100,000. The corporation expects an additional $20,000 loss for December. Tina earns $285,000 of ordinary income from her other activities in 2007. She expects her other income to decline to $155,000 in 2008 and continue at that level in future years. The corporation expects 2008 losses to be only $20,000. Rocket projects a $50,000 profit for 2009 and each of the next four years. What advice can you offer Tina about using her Rocket losses and retaining S corporation status in future years? How would your answer change if Tina expected her income from other activities to be $75,000 in 2007 and $285,000 in 2008.

C:11-49 *Stock Basis Adjustment.* For each of the following items, indicate whether the item will increase, decrease, or cause no change in the S corporation's ordinary income (loss), AAA, and in the shareholder's stock basis. The corporation was formed four years ago and made its S election two years ago. During the time it was a C corporation, it accumulated $30,000 of E&P. The corporation has not distributed any of this accumulated E&P.

a. Operating profit
b. Dividend income received from domestic corporation
c. Interest income earned on corporate bond held as an investment
d. Life insurance proceeds paid on death of corporate officer
e. Long-term capital gain
f. Section 1231 loss
g. Section 1245 gain (recapture)
h. Charitable contributions
i. Fines paid for having overweight trucks
j. Depreciation
k. Pension plan contributions for employees
l. Salary paid to owner
m. Premiums paid on life insurance policy in Part d
n. Distribution of money (but not exceeding current year's earnings)

C:11-50 ***Taxability of Distributions.*** Tammy organized Sweets Corporation in January of the current year, and the corporation immediately elected to be an S corporation. Tammy, who contributed $40,000 in cash to start the business, owns 100% of the corporation's stock. Sweets' current year results are reported below:

Ordinary income	$36,000
Short-term capital loss	5,000

On July 10, Sweets makes a $10,000 cash distribution to Tammy.

a. What income (if any) do Sweets and Tammy recognize as a result of the distribution?
b. What is Tammy's basis for the Sweets stock on December 31?
c. How would your answers to Parts a and b change if Sweets' distribution were instead $80,000?

C:11-51 ***Property Distributions.*** George and Martha formed Washington Corporation as an S corporation several years ago. George and Martha each have a 50% interest in the corporation. At the beginning of the current year, their stock bases are $45,000 each. In the current year, the corporation earns $40,000 of ordinary income. In addition, the corporation distributes property to George having a $26,000 FMV and a $40,000 adjusted basis and distributes property to Martha having a $26,000 FMV and a $16,000 adjusted basis.

a. Determine what George and Martha recognize in the current year, and determine their ending stock bases. What bases do George and Martha have in the distributed property?
b. What tax planning disadvantages do you see with these property distributions?

C:11-52 ***Taxability of Distributions.*** Curt incorporates Vogel Corporation on January 15 of the current year. Curt makes a $70,000 capital contribution including land having a $12,000 FMV, and Vogel makes a timely S election for this year. Vogel reports $60,000 of ordinary income, $40,000 of Sec. 1231 gain, $5,000 of tax-exempt interest income, and $3,000 of charitable contributions this year. On December 1, Vogel distributes $5,000 cash plus the land contributed by Curt because the corporation no longer needs it in the business. The land, which had a $10,000 basis and a $12,000 FMV when contributed to the corporation in January, has an $18,000 FMV when distributed.

a. What income do Vogel Corporation and Curt report as a result of the distribution?
b. What is Curt's basis in the Vogel stock on December 31?
c. What is Vogel's accumulated adjustments account (AAA) balance on December 31?

C:11-53 ***Taxability of Distributions.*** Hal organized Stable Corporation five years ago and has continued to own all its stock. The corporation made an S election one year after its incorporation. At the beginning of the current year, Stable reports the following earnings accumulations:

Accumulated adjustments account (AAA)	$85,000
Accumulated E&P	22,000

Hal's basis in his Stable stock on January 1 of the current year is $120,000. During the current year, Stable reports the following results from its operations:

Ordinary income	$30,000
Tax-exempt interest income	15,000
Long-term capital loss	20,000

Stable makes a $65,000 cash distribution to Hal on August 8.

a. What income, gain, or loss (if any) do Stable and Hal recognize as a result of the distribution?

b. What is Hal's basis in the Stable stock on December 31?

c. What are Stable's AAA, E&P, and OAA balances on December 31?

d. How would your answers to Parts a-c change if Stable instead distributed $117,000?

C:11-54 ***Taxability of Distributions.*** Sigma Corporation, an S corporation with one shareholder, incurred the following items 2006 and 2007:

2006	
Tax-exempt income	$ 5,000
Ordinary income	30,000
2007	
Ordinary loss	$(40,000)
Cash distribution	15,000

At the beginning of 2006, the corporation had a AAA balance of zero and accumulated E&P of $6,000. At the beginning of 2006, the shareholder had a $10,000 basis in stock and a $12,000 basis in debt he loaned to the corporation.

a. Determine items reported by the shareholder in 2006 and 2007.

b. Determine the balances in each corporate account and the shareholder's stock and debt bases at the end of each year.

c. Determine the results if the distribution in 2007 is $35,000 instead of $15,000.

d. How does the answer to Part c change if, in 2007, the corporation has an $18,000 long-term capital gain in addition to the $40,000 ordinary loss?

C:11-55 ***Taxability of Distributions.*** Beta Corporation, an S corporation with one shareholder, incurred the following items:

2006	
Ordinary loss	$(40,000)
2007	
Ordinary income	$27,000
Cash distribution	10,000
2008	
Ordinary income	$22,000
Cash distribution	17,000

At the beginning of 2006, the shareholder's stock basis was $20,000, and her debt basis was $16,000.

a. Assuming the corporation has no accumulated E&P, show items reported by the shareholder in each year, show all basis adjustments to stock and debt, and show the stock and debt bases at the end of each year.

b. Redo Part a for 2007 and 2008 assuming ordinary income in 2007 is $8,000 instead of $27,000.

c. Go back to the original facts and again redo Part a for all years assuming that, at the beginning of 2006, the corporation had a AAA balance of zero and accumulated E&P of $12,000.

COMPREHENSIVE PROBLEMS

C:11-56 ***Comparison of Entity Formations.*** Cara, Bob, and Steve want to begin a business on January 1, 2007. The individuals are considering three business forms—C corporation, partnership, and S corporation.

- Cara has investment land with a $36,000 adjusted basis and a $50,000 FMV that she is willing to contribute. The land has a rundown building on it having a $27,000 basis and a $15,000 FMV. Cara has never used the building nor rented it. She would like to get rid of the building. Because she needs cash, Cara will take out a $25,000 mortgage on the property before the formation of the new business and have the new business assume the debt. Cara obtains a 40% interest in the entity.

- Bob will contribute machinery and equipment, which he purchased for his sole proprietorship in January 2002. He paid $100,000 for the equipment and has used the MACRS rules with a half-year convention on this seven-year recovery period property. He did not make a Sec. 179 expensing election for this property, and he elected not to take bonus depreciation. The FMV of the machinery and equipment is $39,000. Bob obtains a 39% interest in the entity.
- Steve will contribute cash of $600 and services worth $20,400 for his interest in the business. The services he will contribute include drawing up the necessary legal documentation for the new business and setting up the initial books. Steve obtains a 21% interest in the entity.

To begin operations, the new business plans to borrow $50,000 on a recourse basis from a local bank. Each owner will guarantee his or her ownership share of the debt.

What are the tax and nontax consequences for the new business and its owners under each alternative? Assume that any corporation will have 200 shares of common stock authorized and issued. For the partnership alternative, each partner receives a capital, profits, and loss interest. How would your answer to the basic facts change if instead Steve contributes $2,600 in cash and $18,400 in services?

C:11-57 ***Comparison of Operating Activities.*** RST business entity reported the following items during 2007:

Dividends from 25%-owned domestic corporation	$19,000
State of Florida bond interest	18,000
General Electric Corporation bond interest	29,000
Gain on land contributed by Karen[a]	40,000
Operating profit (excluding depreciation)[b]	120,000
MACRS depreciation	36,000
Section 1245 gain (recapture)	5,000
Section 1231 loss	28,000
Long-term capital losses	4,000
Short-term capital losses	5,000
Charitable contributions	23,000
Investment interest expense (related to General Electric bonds)	16,000
Salary (guaranteed payment)	37,000

[a] Karen held the land as an investment prior to contributing it to RST business entity three years ago in exchange for her ownership interest. When Karen contributed the land, it had a basis of $15,000 and a FMV of $40,000. RST sold the land in the current year for $55,000. RST business entity held the land as an investment. Assume that Sec. 351 applied to any corporate formation transaction.

[b] Assume that qualified production activities income is $47,000 and that operating profit includes sufficient W-2 wages so as not to be a limiting factor.

a. What is the corporate taxable income and income tax liability for the current year if RST is taxed as a C corporation?
b. What is the ordinary income and separately stated items for the current year if RST elects to be an S corporation? Assume that RST has never operated as a C corporation.
c. What are the ordinary income and separately stated items if RST is treated as a general partnership?

C:11-58 ***Comparison of Nonliquidating Distributions.*** Jeff and John organized Tampa Corporation 18 years ago and have each owned 50% of the corporation since its inception. In the current year, Tampa reports ordinary income/taxable income of $40,000. Assume the business does not qualify for the U.S. production activities deduction. On April 5, Tampa distributes $100,000 cash to Jeff and distributes land with a $100,000 FMV and a $70,000 adjusted basis to John. Tampa had purchased the land as an investment two years ago. What are the tax implications to Tampa, Jeff, and John of the land distribution in each of the four situations that follow?

a. Tampa has been a C corporation since its formation. On January 1 of the current year, Jeff's basis in his stock is $50,000, and John's stock basis is $45,000. Tampa has accumulated E&P of $155,000 on January 1 of the current year.

b. Tampa was formed as a C corporation but made an S election three years after its formation. On January 1 of the current year, Jeff's basis in his stock is $100,000, and John's stock basis is $80,000. Tampa had the following earnings balances on January 1 of the current year:

Accumulated Adjustments Account	$125,000
Accumulated E&P	30,000

c. Tampa was formed as a partnership and continues to operate in that form. On January 1 of the current year, Jeff's basis in his partnership interest is $100,000, and John's partnership basis is $80,000. The partnership has no liabilities and no unrecognized precontribution gains.

d. How would your answers to Parts a–c change if the land held as an investment and then distributed to John had been contributed to Tampa by Jeff two years ago? At the time of Jeff's contribution, the land had a FMV of $95,000 and a $70,000 basis.

TAX STRATEGY PROBLEMS

C:11-59 Alice, a single taxpayer, will form Morning Corporation in the current year. Alice plans to acquire all of Morning's common stock for a $100,000 contribution to the corporation. Morning will obtain additional capital by borrowing $75,000 from a local bank. Morning will conduct a variety of service activities with little need to retain its capital in the business. Alice expects start-up losses of $90,000 during Morning's first year of operation. She expects the corporation to earn pre-tax operating profits of $250,000 (before reduction for Alice's salary) starting next year. Alice plans to withdraw $100,000 of Morning's profits as salary. Her other income consists primarily of ordinary income (no dividends) from other sources, and she expects these amounts to total $120,000 annually. What advice can you provide Alice about the advisability of making an S election in the initial tax year? In the next tax year? In answering these questions, compare the following alternatives: (1) S corporation in both the current year and the next year, (2) S corporation in the current year and C corporation in the next year (i.e., by revoking the S election next year), (3) C corporation in both the current year and the next year, and (4) C corporation in the current year and S corporation in the next year. When analyzing these alternatives, consider the total taxes associated with each alternative, specifically, at the corporate and shareholder levels and across both years. Ignore payroll taxes, however. Also, assume the following facts: (1) For both years, Alice's combined standard deduction and exemption is $8,800 (ignore phase-outs regardless of AGI levels); (2) 2007 tax rate schedules remain the same for both years; and (3) a 7% discount rate applies for present value calculations. Although this problem asks for only a two-year analysis, discuss some shortcomings of such a short time frame. Ignore the U.S. production activities deduction for this problem.

C:11-60 One way to compare the accumulation of income by alterative business entity forms is to use mathematical models. The following models express the investment after-tax accumulation calculation for a particular entity form:

Flow-through entities (S corporations, partnerships, and LLCs): $ATA = [1 + R(1 - t_p)]^n$

C corporation: $ATA = [1 + R(1 - t_c)]^n(1 - t_g) + t_g$

where: ATA = after-tax accumulation in n years
- R = before-tax rate of return;
- t_p = owner's marginal tax rate on ordinary income
- t_c = corporation's marginal tax rate
- t_g = owner's tax rate on capital gains
- n = number of periods

For each alternative business form, the owner makes an initial investment of $1. The following operating assumptions apply:

Before-tax rate of return (R) = 0.18
Marginal tax rate for owner (t_p) = 0.35
Corporate tax rate (t_c) = 0.34
Capital gains rate (t_g) = 0.15 for regular capital gains (assume the Sec. 1202 50% exclusion for small business corporations does not apply)
Investment horizon (n) = 2, 4, 20, 50, or 101 years

A flow-through entity distributes only enough cash each year for the owners to pay their taxes. The corporation pays no dividends. The shareholders sell their stock at the end of the investment horizon, and their gains are taxed at capital gains rates. (See Chapter I:18 of the *Individuals* volume for a detailed explanation of these models.)

Required: What is the after-tax accumulation if each business form is operated for the investment horizon and then sold for the amount of the accumulation? Which entity form is best for each investment horizon? How would your calculations and conclusions change if the C corporation's tax rate is 25%?

C:11-61 Problem C:6-56 considered two alternative forms for doing business. Now consider a third alternative. The C corporation could make an S election effective at the beginning of the current year, operate as an S corporation for the next 20 years, and liquidate the S corporation at that time (32 years in total). Compare this alternative to the other two alternatives in Problem C:6-56.

C:11-62 Assume the corporation in Problem C:11-61 (and C:6-56) had been an S corporation for its first 12 years, during which it distributed just enough cash for the shareholder to pay taxes on the pass-through income. Thus, the S corporation reinvested after-tax income. Now the corporation is considering revoking its S election and operating as a C corporation for the remaining 20 years with no dividend distributions. Show the results of remaining an S corporation versus revoking the election. Also show supporting models and calculations. Which alternative should the corporation adopt? Ignore the accumulated earnings tax for C corporations. How does your answer change if the C corporation's tax rate is 15% instead of 35%?

TAX FORM/RETURN PREPARATION PROBLEM

C:11-63 Bottle-Up, Inc., was organized on January 8, 1997, and made its S election on January 24, 1997. The necessary consents to the election were filed in a timely manner. Its federal tax identification number is 38-1507869. Its address is 1234 Hill Street, Gainesville, FL 32607. Bottle-Up, uses the calendar year as its tax year, the accrual method of accounting, and the first-in, first-out (FIFO) inventory method. Bottle-Up manufactures ornamental glass bottles. It made no changes to its inventory costing methods this year. It uses the specific identification method for bad debts for book and tax purposes. Herman Hiebert (S.S. No. 123-45-6789) and Melvin Jones (S.S. No. 100-67-2000) own 500 shares each. Both individuals materially participate in Bottle-Up's single activity. Herman Hiebert is the tax matters person. Financial statements for Bottle-Up for the current year are shown in Tables C:11-2 through C:11-4. Assume that Bottle-Up's business qualifies as a U.S. production activity and that its qualified production activities income is $90,000. The S corporation uses the small business simplified overall method for reporting these activities (see discussion for Line 12d of Schedules K and K-1 in the Form 1120S instructions). Prepare a current year S corporation tax return for Bottle-Up, showing yourself as the paid preparer.

CASE STUDY PROBLEM

C:11-64 Debra has operated a family counseling practice for a number of years as a sole proprietor. She owns the condominium office space that she occupies in addition to her professional library and office furniture. She has a limited amount of working capital and little need to accumulate additional business assets. Her total business assets are about $150,000, with an $80,000 mortgage on the office space being her only liability. Typically, she has withdrawn any unneeded assets at the end of the year. Debra has used her personal car for business travel and charged the business for the mileage at the appropriate mileage rate provided by the IRS. Over the last three years, Debra's practice has grown so that she now forecasts $80,000 of income being earned this year. Debra has contributed small amounts to an Individual Retirement Account (IRA) each year, but her contributions have never reached the annual limits. Although she has never been sued, Debra recently has become concerned about legal liability. An attorney friend of hers has suggested that she incorporate her business to protect herself against being sued and to save taxes.

Required: You are a good friend of Debra's and a CPA; she asks your opinion on incorporating her business. You are to meet with Debra tomorrow for lunch. Prepare a draft of the points you feel should be discussed over lunch about incorporating the family counseling practice.

▼ **TABLE C:11-2**

Bottle-Up, Inc. Income Statement for the Year Ended December 31 of the Current Year (Problem C:11-63)

Sales		$2,500,000
Returns and allowances		(15,000)
Net sales		$2,485,000
Beginning inventory	$ 102,000	
Purchases	900,000	
Labor	200,000	
Supplies	80,000	
Utilities	100,000	
Other manufacturing costs	188,000[a]	
Goods available for sale	$1,570,000	
Ending inventory	(96,000)	1,474,000[b]
Gross profit		$1,011,000
Salaries[c]	$ 451,020	
Utilities expense	54,000	
Depreciation (MACRS depreciation is $36,311)	11,782	
Automobile and truck expense	26,000	
Office supplies expense	9,602	
Advertising expense	105,000	
Bad debts expense	620	
Rent expense	30,000	
Interest expense[d]	1,500	
Meals and entertainment expense	21,000	
Selling expenses	100,000	
Repairs and maintenance expense	38,000	
Accounting and legal expense	4,500	
Charitable contributions[e]	9,000	
Insurance expense[f]	24,500	
Hourly employees' fringe benefits	11,000	
Payroll taxes	36,980	
Other taxes	2,500	
Penalties (fines for overweight trucks)	1,000	(938,004)
Operating profit		$ 72,996
Other income and losses:		
Long-term gain on sale of capital assets	$ 48,666[g]	
Sec. 1231 loss	(1,100)[h]	
Interest on U.S. Treasury bills	1,200	
Interest on State of Florida bonds	600	
Dividends from domestic corporations	11,600	
Investment expenses	(600)	60,366
Net income		$ 133,362

[a] Total MACRS depreciation is $74,311. Assume that $38,000 of depreciation has been allocated to cost of sales for both book and tax purposes so that the book and tax inventory and cost of sales amounts are the same. The AMT depreciation adjustment on personal property is $9,000.

[b] The cost of goods sold amount reflects the Uniform Capitalization Rules of Sec. 263A. The appropriate restatements have been made in prior years.

[c] Officer salaries of $120,000 are included in the total. All are employer's W-2 wages.

[d] Investment interest expense is $500. All other interest expense is trade- or business-related. None of the interest expense relates to the production of tax-exempt income.

[e] The corporation made all contributions in cash to qualifying charities.

[f] Includes $3,000 of premiums paid for policies on lives of corporate officers. Bottle-Up is the beneficiary for both policies.

[g] The corporation acquired the capital assets on March 3, 2004 for $100,000 and sold them on September 15, 2006 for $148,000.

[h] The corporation acquired the Sec. 1231 property on June 5, 2005 for $10,000 and sold it on December 21, 2006 for $8,900.

▼ **TABLE C:11-3**

Bottle-Up, Inc. Balance Sheet for January 1 and December 31 of the Current Year (Problem C:11-63)

	January 1	December 31
Assets:		
Cash	$ 15,000	$116,948
Accounts receivable	41,500	45,180
Inventories	102,000	96,000
Stocks	103,000	74,000
Treasury bills	15,000	16,000
State of Florida bonds	10,000	10,000
Building and equipment	374,600	375,000
Minus: Accumulated depreciation	(160,484)	(173,100)
Land	160,000	190,000
Total	$660,616	$750,028
Liabilities and equities:		
Accounts payable	$ 36,000	$ 10,000
Accrued salaries payable	12,000	6,000
Payroll taxes payable	3,416	7,106
Sales taxes payable	5,200	6,560
Due to Mr. Hiebert	10,000	5,000
Mortgage and notes payable (current maturities)	44,000	52,000
Long-term debt	210,000	260,000
Capital stock	10,000	10,000
Retained earnings	330,000	393,362
Total	$660,616	$750,028

▼ **TABLE C:11-4**

Bottle-Up, Inc. Statement of Change in Retained Earnings, for the Current Year Ended December 31 (Problem C:11-63)

Balance, January 1		$330,000[a]
Plus: Net income	$133,362	
Minus: Dividends	(70,000)	63,362
Balance, December 31		$393,362

[a] The January 1 accumulated adjustments account balance is $274,300.

TAX RESEARCH PROBLEMS

C:11-65 Cato Corporation incorporated on July 1, 2002, in California, with Tim and Elesa, husband and wife, owning all the Cato stock. On August 15, 2002, Cato made an S election effective for 2002. Tim and Elesa filed the necessary consents to the election. On March 10, 2006, Tim and Elesa transferred 15% of the Cato stock to the Reid and Susan Trust, an irrevocable trust created three years earlier for the benefit of their two minor children. In early 2007, Tim and Elesa's tax accountant learns about the transfer and advises the couple that the transfer of the stock to the trust may have terminated Cato's S election. Prepare a memorandum for your tax manager indicating any action Tim and Elesa can take that will permit Cato to retain its S election? Research sources suggested by the tax manager include Secs. 1361(c)(2), 1362(d)(2), and 1362(f).

C:11-66 One of your wealthy clients, Cecile, invests $100,000 for sole ownership of an electing S corporation's stock. The corporation is in the process of developing a new food product.

Cecile anticipates that the new business will need approximately $200,000 in capital (other than trade payables) during the first two years of its operations before it starts to earn sufficient profits to pay a return on the shareholder's investment. The first $100,000 of this total is to come from Cecile's contributed capital. The remaining $100,000 of funds will come from one of the following three sources:

- Have the corporation borrow the $100,000 from a local bank. Cecile is required to act as a guarantor for the loan.
- Have the corporation borrow $100,000 from the estate of Cecile's late husband. Cecile is the sole beneficiary of the estate.
- Have Cecile lend $100,000 to the corporation from her personal funds.

The S corporation will pay interest at a rate acceptable to the IRS. During the first two years of operations, the corporation anticipates losing $125,000 before it begins to earn a profit. Your tax manager has asked you to evaluate the tax ramifications of each of the three financing alternatives. Prepare a memorandum to the tax manager outlining the information you found in your research.

C:11-67 Frank Wilson formed Gamma Corporation on January 5, 2006, and the corporation immediately elected to be treated as an S corporation beginning in 2006. Upon formation, Frank contributed $300,000 in exchange for the corporation's common stock. As 2006 progressed, Frank realized the corporation was going to incur heavy losses, so on July 31, 2006, he advanced the corporation $400,000 on open account. For 2006, the corporation ended the year with a $550,000 ordinary loss from operations, and Frank claimed this loss in his personal tax return. Early in 2007, the corporation's operations were doing well, and the corporation repaid the $400,000 advance to Frank. However, later in 2007, things took a turn for the worse, and the corporation seemed headed for a net loss for the year. Therefore, Frank advanced an additional $500,000 to the corporation on July 31, 2007 in a similar fashion to the prior year's advance. For 2007, the corporation ended the year with a $200,000 ordinary loss. Frank suspects this pattern of advances and repayments may continue next year as well, although he hopes for profitable years after that. Frank asks your help in determining the tax consequences of these transactions. At a minimum, you should consider the following resources:

- IRC Sec. 1367
- Reg. Sec. 1.1367-2
- *Fleming G. Brooks, et ux. v. Commissioner, et al.*, TC Memo 2005-204, 90 TCM 172 (2005)

12

CHAPTER

THE GIFT TAX

LEARNING OBJECTIVES

After studying this chapter, you should be able to

1. Understand the concept of the unified transfer tax system
2. Describe the gift tax formula
3. Identify a number of transactions subject to the gift tax
4. Determine whether an annual gift tax exclusion is available
5. Identify deductions available for gift tax purposes
6. Apply the gift-splitting rules
7. Calculate the gift tax liability
8. Understand how basis affects the overall tax consequences
9. Recognize the filing requirements for gift tax returns

CHAPTER OUTLINE

The **gift tax** is a **wealth transfer tax** that applies if a person transfers property while alive. It is similar to the estate tax, which applies to transfers associated with death. Both the gift tax and the estate tax are part of the unified transfer tax system that subjects gratuitous transfers of property between persons to taxation. The vast majority of all property transfers are exempt from these transfer taxes because of the annual exclusion and the various deductions and credits. However, planning for reducing these transfer taxes is a significant matter for wealthy or moderately wealthy individuals. In recent years, there has been considerable discussion about permanently abolishing the estate tax or increasing the amount exempt from the tax.[1] The Economic Growth and Tax Relief Reconciliation Act of 2001 (the 2001 Act) provided for phased in increases to the unified credit and phased in reductions in the unified tax rate schedule beginning in 2002. In addition, it repealed the estate and generation skipping transfer taxes, *but not the gift tax,* effective January 1, 2010. However, if no further legislation passes, the 2001 Act provides that the rules for gift, estate, and generation skipping taxes will revert on January 1, 2011, to what they were before the 2001 Act. Congress adopted this "sunsetting" provision to comply with the Congressional Budget Act of 1974.

This chapter discusses both the structure of the gift tax (including the exclusion, deduction, and credit provisions) and exactly which property transfers fall within its purview. It reviews the income tax basis rules in the context of their implications for selecting properties to transfer by gift instead of at death. Consider, however, that an individual who believes Congress will eventually repeal the estate tax prior to such person's anticipated date of death will likely decide against making sizable gifts.

CONCEPT OF TRANSFER TAXES

OBJECTIVE 1

Understand the concept of the unified transfer tax system

The recipient of a gift incurs no income tax liability because Sec. 102 explicitly excludes gifts and inheritances from the recipient's gross income.[2] The gift tax, a type of excise tax, is levied on the donor, the person who transferred the property. The gift tax applies to the act of transferring property to a recipient who pays either no consideration or consideration smaller than the value of the property received.

HISTORY AND PURPOSE OF TRANSFER TAXES

The United States has had an estate tax since 1916 and a gift tax continuously since 1932. The structure of the gift and estate taxes has remained fairly constant, but details such as the amount of the exclusion and the rate schedules have changed numerous times. The Tax Reform Act of 1976 (the 1976 Act) made a very significant change by enacting a unified rate schedule for gift and estate tax purposes.

The gift tax has had several purposes, one of the most important of which was to raise revenue. However, because of the fairly generous annual exclusion and unified credit legislated by Congress, the gift tax yields only a small fraction of the federal government's total revenues. Only donors making relatively large gifts owe any gift taxes. Another purpose of the gift tax is to serve as a backstop to the estate tax and to prevent individuals from avoiding a significant amount of—or all—estate taxes by disposing of property before death. For example, without the gift tax, persons who know they are terminally ill could dispose of property "on their deathbed" and escape the transfer tax. In addition, the gift tax provides revenue to offset some of the income tax revenue lost because of income from the gifted property sometimes being shifted to a person in a lower income tax bracket. Another purpose for levying gift and estate taxes is to redistribute wealth.

ADDITIONAL COMMENT

In 2006, the House of Representatives passed a bill that would increase the amount exempt from the estate, gift, and generation-skipping transfer taxes to $5 million. The bill also would apply the capital gains tax rate to taxable amounts between $5 and $25 million and double the capital gains tax rate to amounts above $25 million.

ADDITIONAL COMMENT

The new lower tax rate on dividend income will reduce or eliminate the income tax savings from having dividends taxed to donees in low tax brackets.

[1] Proposals to abolish the estate tax received criticism, in part, because in 1998, for example, only 47,500 estates owed any tax, and most of the tax was paid by estates above $5 million. See "House Republicans Shift Their Strategy in Effort to Push Two Popular Tax Cuts," *The Wall Street Journal* (August 22, 2000), p. A20.

[2] The income earned from property received as a gift or an inheritance, however, is not exempt from the income tax.

No one knows what the distribution of wealth would have been had Congress not enacted transfer taxes. However, one study estimated that the top 1% of the population held 22.5% of this nation's personal wealth in 1995, about the same percentage as in 1992.[3]

THE UNIFIED TRANSFER TAX SYSTEM

In 1976, Congress greatly revamped the transfer tax system by combining the separate estate and gift tax systems into one unified transfer tax system. Although Chapters C:12 and C:13 use the terms *gift tax* and *estate tax,* these taxes actually are components of the same unified transfer tax system. The system also includes the generation-skipping transfer tax, a topic discussed in Chapter C:13. The unification of the transfer tax system removed the previous law's bias favoring the tax treatment of lifetime gifts in comparison with transfers at death. The three most significant elements of the unified system—the unified rate schedule, the inclusion of taxable gifts in the death tax base, and the unified credit—are discussed below.

UNIFIED RATE SCHEDULE

SELF-STUDY QUESTION

Use the rate schedule inside the back cover of this text to determine the amount of gift tax (before credits) on 2007 taxable gifts of $4 million.

ANSWER

The tax is: On the first $1.5 million, $555,800; plus 45% of the excess over $1.5 million, or $1,125,000. Thus, the gross tax equals $1,680,800.

Before the 1976 Act mandated a **unified rate schedule,** effective for gifts made after 1976 and deaths occurring after 1976 and applicable to both lifetime transfers and transfers at death, the gift tax rates were only 75% of the estate tax rates on a transfer of the same size. The rates are progressive and have varied over the years. The 2001 Act reduced the unified transfer tax rates beginning in 2002 by replacing the former top two brackets (on amounts exceeding $2.5 million) with a 50% maximum tax rate in 2002. The top rate declined to 49% in 2003, 48% in 2004, 47% in 2005, and 46% in 2006. In those years, the top rate applies to tax bases above $2 million. In 2007 through 2009, for both estate and gift tax purposes, the maximum tax rate of 45% will apply to tax bases exceeding $1.5 million.

As mentioned earlier, the 2001 Act repeals the estate and generation skipping taxes effective January 1, 2010. At that date, the maximum gift tax rate will decline to 35% and will apply to tax bases exceeding $500,000. Congress retained the gift tax to make up for the loss in income tax revenue that could occur should wealthy individuals shift assets free of gift tax to donees in lower income tax brackets. (See the inside back cover for the unified transfer tax rates.)

IMPACT OF TAXABLE GIFTS ON DEATH TAX BASE

Before 1977, a separate system applied to lifetime gifts compared with dispositions at death. By making gifts, an individual could shift the taxation of property from the top of the estate tax rate schedule to the bottom of the gift tax rate schedule. Few taxpayers could take advantage of this shifting, however, because only people with a relatively large amount of property could afford to part with sizable amounts of their assets while alive.

ADDITIONAL COMMENT

At the taxpayer's death, the unified tax is computed on the sum of the taxable estate plus the adjusted taxable gifts. The tax on this sum is reduced by the tax that would have been payable (at current rates) on the taxable gifts made after December 31, 1976.

Under today's unified system, taxable gifts affect the size of the tax base at death. Any post-1976 taxable gifts (other than gifts included in the gross estate) are called **adjusted taxable gifts**, and such gifts are included in the donor's death tax base. Although they are valued at their fair market value (FMV) on the date of the gift, the addition of such taxable gifts to the tax base at death can cause the donor-decedent's estate to be taxed at a higher marginal tax rate. However, such gifts are not taxed for a second time upon the donor's death because gift taxes (computed at current rates) on these gifts are subtracted in determining the estate tax liability.

[3] "Tax Report," *The Wall Street Journal* (April 19, 2000), p. A1.

EXAMPLE C:12-1 ▶ In 1994, Dan made taxable gifts totaling $500,000. When Dan dies in the current year, the value of the gifted property has tripled. Dan's death tax base includes the $500,000 of post-1976 taxable gifts. They are valued for estate tax purposes at their FMV on the date of the gift; the post-gift appreciation escapes the transfer tax system. Thus, the transfer tax value is fixed or frozen at the date-of-gift value. ◀

Note that unification (including taxable gifts that become part of the tax base at death) extends only to gifts made after 1976. Congress exempted gifts made before 1977 from unification because it did not want to retroactively change the two separate transfer tax systems of the prior tax regime.

UNIFIED CREDIT

The **unified credit** reduces dollar for dollar a certain amount of the tax computed on the taxable gifts or the taxable estate. The amount of the credit has varied depending on the year of the transfer. However, for years 2002 through 2009 the credit for gift tax purposes is $345,800. In the gift and estate tax formulas, the full credit is available for lifetime transfers and again in determining the tax payable at death. In concept, however, an individual's estate does not receive the benefit of this unified credit amount at death to the extent the decedent had used the credit against lifetime transfers (as explained in Chapter C:13). The gift tax formula, including the unified credit, is discussed below.

GIFT TAX FORMULA

OBJECTIVE 2

Describe the gift tax formula

The formula described in this section is used to calculate a donor's gift tax liability for the year of the transfer. Gift tax reporting is done on an annual basis, always on a calendar year. Figure C:12-1 illustrates the formula for determining the donor's annual gift tax liability. This formula is discussed in detail later in the chapter.

ADDITIONAL COMMENT

The gift tax applies to cumulative lifetime gifts made since the enactment of the gift tax in 1932. The unified gift and estate tax, enacted in 1976, applies only to cumulative lifetime taxable gifts made after 1976. Thus, a taxable gift of $75,000 made in 1970 would not be included in a decedent's unified tax base for calculating the estate tax but would affect the gift tax payable by that person.

DETERMINATION OF GIFTS

The starting point in the process is to determine which, if any, of the taxpayer's transfers constitute gifts. The next section discusses the various types of transfers that the statute views as gifts. All gifts are valued at their FMVs on the date of the gift. Next, the aggregate amount of gifts for the period is determined. The aggregate gifts are then reduced by any exclusions and deductions. Finally, the tax is computed according to the formula illustrated in Figure C:12-1.

EXCLUSIONS AND DEDUCTIONS

For many years the maximum amount excludible annually was a fixed amount of $10,000 per donee, but Congress amended the IRC to allow indexation beginning with gifts made after 1998. Inflation adjustments are rounded to the next *lowest* multiple of $1,000.[4] Accordingly, the annual exclusion rose to $11,000 in 2002 and to $12,000 beginning in 2006. If the gifts made to a donee are less than the annual exclusion amount, the amount excludible is limited to the amount of the gift made to that donee. A donor may claim exclusions for transfers to an unlimited number of donees.

Two types of deductions (marital and charitable) reduce the amount of the taxable gifts. Most transfers to one's spouse generate a marital deduction; there is no ceiling on the amount of this deduction. Similarly, most transfers to charitable organizations are cancelled out by the charitable contribution deduction, which also is unlimited.

KEY POINT

The annual exclusion applies to each *donee* per year; therefore, the total amount of tax-free gifts in a given year can be much greater than the annual exclusion amount. Also, gift-splitting can double the tax-free amount per donee.

GIFT-SPLITTING ELECTION

Congress authorized gift-splitting provisions to achieve more comparable tax consequences between taxpayers of community property and noncommunity property (common law) states.[5] Under **community property law**, assets acquired after marriage are com-

---

[4] Sec. 2503(b).

[5] The eight traditional community property states are Louisiana, Texas, New Mexico, Arizona, California, Washington, Idaho, and Nevada. Wisconsin's marital property law, though not providing for community property, is basically the same as community property.

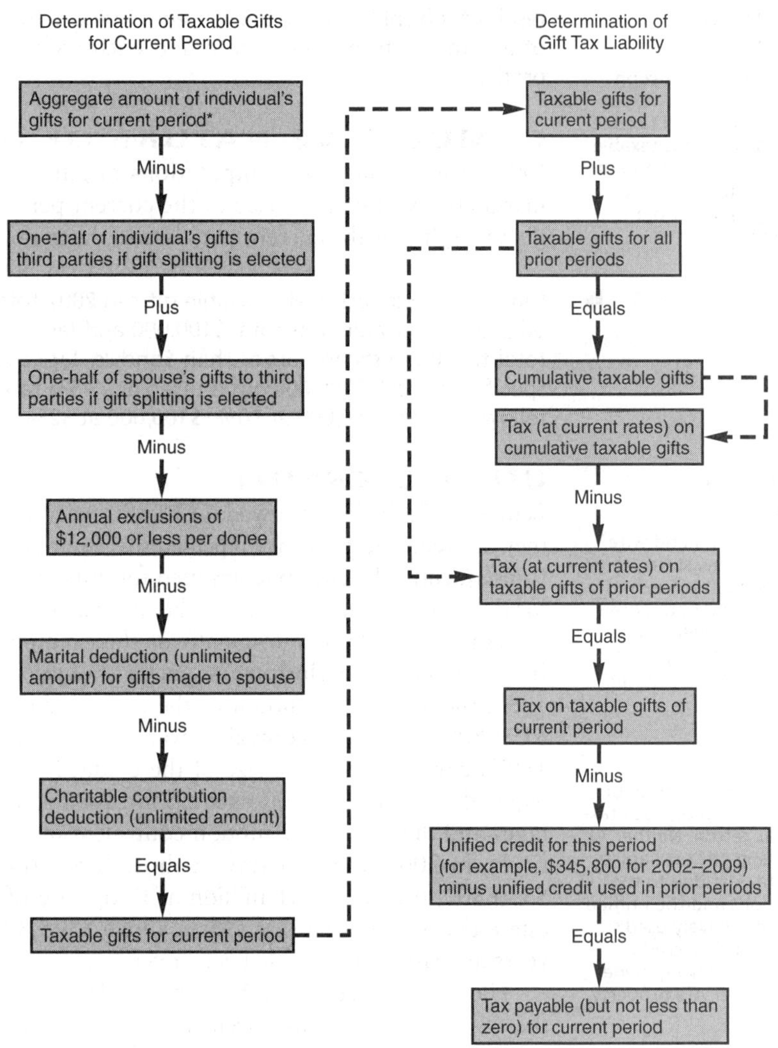

FIGURE C:12-1 ▶ THE GIFT TAX FORMULA

munity property unless they are acquired by gift or inheritance. Typically, in a **community property state**, a large portion of the spouses' assets is community property, property in which each spouse has a one-half interest. One-half of a community property gift is automatically considered to be given by each spouse. By contrast, in a **common law state**, all assets acquired during the marriage are the property of the acquiring spouse. The other spouse does not automatically acquire an interest in the property. Thus, often only one spouse owns enough assets to consider making large gifts.

Section 2513 authorizes spouses to elect gift splitting, which treats gifts made by each spouse to third parties as if each spouse made one-half of the gift. As a result, spouses in common law states can achieve the same benefits that apply automatically for gifts of community property. Thus, both spouses can claim a $12,000 per donee exclusion although only one spouse actually makes the gift, and the spouses can give each donee a total of $24,000 before either spouse's gift becomes taxable.

EXAMPLE C:12-2 ▶ Andy and Bonnie, residents of a common law state, are married throughout 2007. In that year, Andy gives his brother $100,000 cash. Andy and Bonnie may elect gift splitting and thereby treat the $100,000 gift as if each spouse gave $50,000. As a result, the excludible portion of the gift totals $24,000 ($12,000 per donee for each of the two deemed donors). If they elect gift splitting, each donor's $38,000 taxable gift may be taxed at a lower marginal tax rate. In addition, Bonnie can use a unified credit amount that she might not otherwise be able to use. As a

ADDITIONAL COMMENT

Because the gift tax is a tax on *cumulative* lifetime gifts, taxpayers must keep track of all taxable gifts because all previous taxable gifts are part of the calculation for current gift tax due, and post-1976 taxable gifts affect the estate tax liability.

result of gift splitting, the tax consequences are the same as if Andy and Bonnie were residents of a community property state and each gave $50,000 of community property to Andy's brother. ◀

CUMULATIVE NATURE OF GIFT TAX

Unlike the income tax, computations of gift tax liabilities are cumulative in nature. The marginal tax rate applicable to the current period's taxable gifts is a function of both the taxable gifts for the current period and the aggregate taxable gifts for all earlier periods.

EXAMPLE C:12-3 ▶ Sandy and Jack each make taxable gifts in 2007 totaling $200,000. However, for previous periods, Sandy's taxable gifts total $100,000 and Jack's total $1.5 million. Because Jack's cumulative total taxable gifts are larger than Sandy's, Jack's current marginal tax rate exceeds Sandy's. Specifically Jack's $200,000 gift is taxed at a 45% rate, while Sandy's $200,000 gift is taxed at the following rates: $50,000 at 30%, $100,000 at 32%, and $50,000 at 34%. ◀

SELF-STUDY QUESTION

Al and Beth, husband and wife, live in a common law state. Al gives a $620,000 gift to each of two children. Al and Beth agree to split the gift. Neither Al nor Beth has made taxable gifts in any prior year. Explain their gift tax liability.

ANSWER

One-half of each gift, a total of $620,000, is reported on each taxpayer's gift tax return. Neither Al nor Beth has any gift tax liability for the current year due to the annual exclusions and the unified credit. Al has effectively used some of Beth's unified credit without Beth ever having ownership or control over Al's property.

UNIFIED CREDIT

Before 1977, the IRC allowed a $30,000 specific exemption deductible by donors whenever they desired. The 1976 Act repealed this exemption and replaced it with the unified credit.[6] Consequently, the gift tax computed for gifts made in 1977 and later years is reduced dollar for dollar by the unified credit. The unified credit allows donors to make a certain amount of taxable gifts (known originally as the **exemption equivalent** and now referred to in the IRC as **applicable exclusion amount**) without needing to pay the gift tax. For 1977 through 1987, the maximum amount of the credit increased progressively until in 1987 it reached $192,800, which was equivalent to a $600,000 exemption from the gift tax. Legislation in 1997 again increased the size of the credit. For 2000 and 2001, the credit was $220,550 (equivalent to a $675,000 exemption). As a result of the 2001 Act, the credit against gift taxes and the gift tax exemption equivalent increased to $345,800 and $1 million, respectively, in 2002 and will stay at those levels through 2009. In 2010, the credit will be $330,800, the tax on $1 million at a top rate of 35%. On the other hand, the credit for estate tax purposes later increases above $345,800. The unified credit amount for various years appears on the inside back cover.

The amount creditable for a particular year is the credit amount for that year minus the credit that could have been claimed for the taxable gifts made by the individual in earlier years. Recall that no credit was allowed for gifts made before 1977.

EXAMPLE C:12-4 ▶ Zheng made her first taxable gift,[7] $500,000 in amount, in 1986. Zheng used the $155,800 unified credit available for 1986 (as shown on the inside back cover) to reduce her $155,800 gift tax liability to zero. Zheng made her next taxable gift in 1994. The taxable amount was $250,000. Zheng's 1994 gift tax of $92,500 ($248,300 − $155,800) was reduced by a unified credit of $37,000 ($192,800 − $155,800). The $92,500 represents the tax on the $750,000 of cumulative taxable gifts, which is $248,300, minus the tax on the $500,000 of prior taxable gifts, which was $155,800. If she makes taxable gifts in 2007, the maximum credit she can claim against her current tax is $153,000 ($345,800 − $192,800 already used). ◀

ADDITIONAL COMMENT

Taxpayers must keep a record of how much of the specific exemption they used between September 9 and December 31, 1976, to determine how much of the unified credit is available to them.

After passage of the 1976 Act, prospective donors quickly realized they could make gifts before the end of 1976 and avoid the unification provisions, but Congress adopted a special rule that affects donors who used any portion of their specific exemption between September 9, 1976, and December 31, 1976.[8] The rule reduced the amount of unified credit otherwise available to such donors by 20% of the amount of the specific exemption they claimed against gifts made between September 9 and December 31, 1976. The maximum reduction in the unified credit as a result of this provision is $6,000 (0.20 × $30,000 maximum specific exemption).

EXAMPLE C:12-5 ▶ In November 1976, Maria made a large taxable gift, her first gift, and used her $30,000 specific exemption. As a result, the unified credit that Maria could otherwise claim after 1976 is reduced by $6,000 (0.20 × $30,000). Her 1976 taxable gifts are not includible in her death tax base. ◀

---

[6] Sec. 2505.

[7] No credit is used for a gift that is completely nontaxable.

[8] Sec. 2505(b). Congress repealed this exemption for post-1976 years.

TRANSFERS SUBJECT TO THE GIFT TAX

OBJECTIVE 3

Identify a number of transactions subject to the gift tax

In general, property transferred for less than adequate consideration in money or money's worth is deemed to be a gift in the gift tax context. The gift occurs when the donor gives up control over the transferred property. Congress has legislated several provisions that exempt various property transfers that otherwise might be viewed as gifts from the scope of the gift tax. These exemptions include direct payments of medical expenses and tuition, transfers to political organizations, property settlements in conjunction with a divorce, and qualified disclaimers.

TRANSFERS FOR INADEQUATE CONSIDERATION

As mentioned earlier, the initial step in determining the donor's gift tax liability is deciding which transactions constitute gifts for gift tax purposes. Section 2501(a) states that a gift tax is imposed on "the transfer of property by gift." Thus, if *property* is transferred *by gift,* the transferor potentially incurs a gift tax liability. Perhaps surprisingly, the IRC does not define the term *gift.* Section 2511(a) expands on Sec. 2501(a) by indicating that the tax is applicable "whether the transfer is in trust or otherwise, whether the gift is direct or indirect, and whether the property is real or personal, tangible or intangible."

A transaction is subject to the gift tax even though not entirely gratuitous if "the value of the property transferred by the donor exceeds the value in money or money's worth of the consideration given therefor."[9] In such circumstances, the amount of the gift is the difference between the value of the property the donor gives up and the value of the consideration in money or money's worth received. The following discussion examines in more depth the scope of the rule regarding transfers for less than adequate consideration.

ADDITIONAL COMMENT

At times, a transferor can inadvertently make a gift by selling property to a family member for an amount determined in an IRS audit to be less than its fair market value.

BARGAIN SALES. Often, an individual wants to sell an asset to a family member, but the prospective buyer cannot afford to pay the full FMV of the property. If the buyer pays consideration of less than the FMV of the transferred property, the seller makes a gift to the buyer equal to the bargain element of the transaction, which is the excess of the property's FMV over its sales price.

EXAMPLE C:12-6 ▶ Martha sells her ranch, having a $1 million FMV, to her son Stan, who can afford to pay only $300,000 of consideration. In the year of the sale, Martha makes a gift to Stan of $700,000, the excess of the ranch's FMV over the consideration received. ◀

TRANSFERS IN NORMAL COURSE OF BUSINESS. Treasury Regulations provide an exception to the general rule that a transfer for inadequate consideration triggers a gift. Specifically, a transaction arising "in the ordinary course of business (a transaction which is bona fide, at arm's length, and free from any donative intent)" is considered to have been made for adequate consideration.[10] Thus, no gift arises when a buyer acquires property for less than its FMV *if* the acquisition is in the ordinary course of business.

EXAMPLE C:12-7 ▶ John, a merchant, has a clearance sale and sells a diamond bracelet valued at $30,000 to Bess who pays $12,000, the clearance sale price. Because the clearance sale arose in the ordinary course of John's business, the bargain element ($18,000) does not constitute a gift to Bess. ◀

STATUTORY EXEMPTIONS FROM THE GIFT TAX

For various reasons, including simplifying the administration of the gift tax, Congress enacted several provisions that exempt certain transactions from the purview of the gift tax. In the absence of these statutory rules, some of these transactions could constitute gifts.

---

[9] Reg. Sec. 25.2512-8.

[10] Ibid.

PAYMENT OF MEDICAL EXPENSES OR TUITION. Section 2503(e) states that a qualified transfer is not treated as a transfer of property by gift. The IRC defines *qualified transfer* as an amount paid on behalf of an individual to an educational organization for tuition or to any person who provides medical care as payment for such medical care. Such payments are exempt from gift treatment only if made *directly* to the educational organization or to the person or entity providing the medical care. *Educational organization* has the same definition as for charitable contribution purposes,[11] and *medical care* has the same definition as for medical expense deduction purposes.[12] Note that the rule addresses only tuition, not room, board, and books. Note also that the identity of the person whose expenses are paid is not important. The special exemption applies even if an individual makes payments on behalf of a non-relative.

SELF-STUDY QUESTION

Ben's adult son Clarence, who is not Ben's dependent, needs a liver transplant. Because Clarence cannot afford the surgical procedure, Ben pays the medical fee directly to the hospital. Is the payment for Clarence's benefit a taxable gift?

ANSWER

The payment is not a taxable gift because of Sec. 2503(e).

If one taxpayer pays amounts benefitting someone else and the expenditures constitute support that the payor must furnish under state law, such payments are support, not gifts. State law determines the definition of support. Generally, payments of medical expenses for one's minor child would be categorized as support and not a gift, even in the absence of Sec. 2503(e). On the other hand, state law generally does not require parents to pay medical expenses or tuition for an adult child. Thus, the enactment of Sec. 2503(e) removed such payments from the gift tax.

According to the Staff of the Joint Committee on Taxation, special rules concerning tuition and medical expense payments were enacted because

> Congress was concerned that certain payments of tuition made on behalf of children who have attained their majority, and of special medical expenses on behalf of elderly relatives, technically could be considered gifts under prior law. The Congress believed such payments should be exempt from gift taxes.[13]

EXAMPLE C:12-8 ▶ Sergio pays $20,000 for his adult grandson's tuition at medical school and $14,000 for the grandson's room and board in the medical school's dormitory. Sergio makes all payments directly to the educational organization. Section 2503(e) exempts the direct payment of the tuition to the medical school (but not the room and board) from being treated as a gift. Because Sergio is not required under state law to pay room and board for an adult grandson, such payments are not support. Sergio has made a $14,000 gift to the grandson. ◀

EXAMPLE C:12-9 ▶ Assume the same facts as in Example C:12-8 except that Sergio writes a $34,000 check to his grandson, who in turn pays the medical school. Sergio has made a $34,000 gift. Because Sergio does not pay the tuition directly to the school, Sergio does not meet all the conditions for exempting the tuition payments from gift tax treatment. Here, and in Example C:12-8, Sergio receives a $12,000 annual exclusion. ◀

TRANSFERS TO POLITICAL ORGANIZATIONS. Congress adopted a provision specifically exempting transfers to political organizations from being deemed to be a transfer of property by gift.[14] Without this special rule, these transfers generally would be subjected to gift tax treatment.

EXAMPLE C:12-10 ▶ Ann transfers $2,000 to a political organization founded to promote Thomas's campaign for governor. Ann's $2,000 transfer does not fall within the statutory definition of a gift. ◀

PROPERTY SETTLEMENTS IN CONJUNCTION WITH DIVORCE. To reduce litigation, Congress enacted special rules addressing property transfers in the context of a divorce. Section 2516 specifies the circumstances in which it automatically exempts property settlements in connection with a divorce from being treated as gifts.

For Sec. 2516 to be applicable, the spouses must adopt a written agreement concerning their marital and property rights and the divorce must occur during a three-year

---

[11] Section 170(b)(1)(A)(ii) defines *educational organization* in the context of the charitable contribution deduction.

[12] Section 213(d) defines *medical care* in the context of the medical expense deduction.

[13] U.S. Congress, Staff of the Joint Committee on Taxation, *General Explanation of the Economic Recovery Tax Act of 1981* (Washington, DC: U.S. Government Printing Office, 1981), p. 273.

[14] Sec. 2501(a)(5).

WHAT WOULD YOU DO IN THIS SITUATION?

You are a CPA with a very wealthy elderly client, Ms. Atsushi Trong. She is a model of the U.S. success story. Having struggled in her native country, she immigrated to the United States as a teenager and studied clothing trends among her peers in both high school and college. She started her own clothing company and over the years has led the way by promoting such trends as miniskirts, bell-bottom pants, the so-called "Mature Elvis" look, and the hip-hop-rap grunge fashion. She has a net worth of over $100 million and no immediate family.

She has decided to plow some of her good fortune back into the educational system, which provided the intellectual foundation for her success. She selected the current class of her old high school, P.S. 101, and in 2007 gave each of 100 graduating students $100,000 to be used to pay tuition costs for four years at her college alma mater. Each of the 100 student donees used the $100,000 to prepay the four-year tuition costs. All these transactions took place during the current tax year.

You have now been asked to determine the tax consequences of these transactions. What position would you take after considering the requirements of the IRC and *Treasury Department Circular 230*?

period beginning one year before they make the agreement. No gift arises from any transfer made in accordance with such agreement if a spouse transfers property to settle the other spouse's marital or property rights or to provide reasonable support for the children while they are minors.

EXAMPLE C:12-11 ▶ In June 2006, Hal and Wanda signed a property agreement whereby Hal is to transfer $750,000 to Wanda in settlement of her property rights. Hal makes the transfer in May 2007. Hal and Wanda receive a divorce decree in July 2007. Hal is not deemed to have made a gift to Wanda when he transferred property to her. ◀

QUALIFIED DISCLAIMERS. Sometimes a person named to receive property under a decedent's will prefers not to receive such property and would like to disclaim (not accept) it. Typically, the person is quite ill and/or elderly or very wealthy. State disclaimer statutes allow individuals to say "no thank you" to the property willed to them. State law or another provision in the will addresses how to determine who will receive the property after the original beneficiary (the disclaimant) declines to accept it.

ADDITIONAL COMMENT

Individuals who execute disclaimers, in a sense, participate in shifting wealth to another.

Section 2518(a) states that people making a qualified disclaimer are treated as if the disclaimed property were never transferred to them. Thus, the person making the disclaimer is not deemed to have made a gift to the person who receives the property because of the disclaimer.

A **qualified disclaimer** must meet the following four tests:

- It must be an irrevocable, unqualified, written refusal to accept property.
- The transferor or his or her legal representative must receive the refusal no later than nine months after the later of the day the transfer is made or the day the person named to receive the property becomes age 21.
- The disclaiming person must not have accepted the property interest or any of its benefits.
- As a result of the disclaimer, the property must pass to the decedent's spouse or a person other than the one disclaiming it. In addition, the person disclaiming the property cannot direct who is to receive the property.[15]

EXAMPLE C:12-12 ▶ Doug dies on February 1, 2007, and wills 500 acres of land to Joan. If Joan disclaims the property in a manner that meets all four of the tests for a qualified disclaimer, Joan will not be treated as making a gift to the person who receives the property as a result of her disclaimer. ◀

[15] Sec. 2518(b).

EXAMPLE C:12-13 ▶ Assume the same facts as in Example C:12-12 except Joan instead disclaims the property on January 2, 2008. Joan's action arose too late to meet the second qualified disclaimer test above. Thus, Joan makes a gift to the person who receives the property she disclaims. ◀

CESSATION OF DONOR'S DOMINION AND CONTROL

A gift occurs when a transfer becomes complete and is valued as of the date the transfer becomes complete. Thus, the concept of a completed transfer is important in two contexts: determination of whether a gift has arisen and, if so, the value of the gift. According to Treasury Regulations, a gift becomes complete—and is thus deemed made and valued—when the donor "has so parted with dominion and control as to leave in him no power to change its disposition, whether for his own benefit or for the benefit of another."[16] A gift is not necessarily complete just because the transferor cannot receive any further personal benefits from the property. If the transferor still can influence the benefits others may receive from the transferred property, the transfer is incomplete with respect to the portion of the property over which the transferor retained control.

REVOCABLE TRUSTS. A transferor who conveys property to a revocable trust has made an incomplete transfer because the creator of a revocable trust can change the trust provisions, including the identity of the beneficiaries. Moreover, the creator may demand the return of the trust property. Because the transferor does not give up any control over property conveyed to a revocable trust, the individual does not make a gift upon funding the trust. Once the trustee distributes trust income to a beneficiary, however, the creator of the trust loses control over the distributed funds and then makes a completed gift of the income the trustee pays out.

EXAMPLE C:12-14 ▶ On May 1, Ted transfers $500,000 to a revocable trust with First National Bank as trustee. The trustee must pay out all the income to Ed during Ed's lifetime and at Ed's death distribute the property to Ed, Jr. On December 31, the trustee distributes $35,000 of income to Ed. The May 1 transfer is incomplete because Ted may revoke the trust; thus, no gift arises upon the funding of the trust. A $35,000 gift to Ed occurs on December 31 because Ted no longer has control over the income distributed to Ed. The gift is eligible for the annual exclusion. ◀

EXAMPLE C:12-15 ▶ Assume the same facts as in Example C:12-14 and that Ted amends the trust instrument on July 7 of the next year to make the trust irrevocable. By this date, the trust property has appreciated to $612,000. Ted makes a completed gift of $612,000 on July 7 of the next year because he gives up his powers over the trust. The gift is eligible for the annual exclusion. ◀

KEY POINT
If the donor retains control over any portion of the property, no gift is considered to have been made with respect to the portion of the property the donor still controls.

OTHER RETAINED POWERS. Even transfers to an irrevocable trust can be deemed incomplete with respect to the portion of the trust over which the creator kept control. Treasury Regulations state that if "the donor reserves any power over its [the property's] disposition, the gift may be wholly incomplete, or may be partially complete and partially incomplete, depending upon all the facts in the particular case."[17] They add that one must examine the terms of the power to determine the scope of the donor's retention of control. The regulations elaborate by indicating that "[a] gift is . . . incomplete if and to the extent that a reserved power gives the donor the power to name new beneficiaries or to change the interests of the beneficiaries."[18]

EXAMPLE C:12-16 ▶ On May 3, Art transfers $300,000 of property in trust with a bank as trustee. Art names his friends Bob and/or Sue to receive the trust income for 15 years and Karl to receive the trust property at the end of 15 years. Art reserves the power to determine how that income is to be divided between Bob and Sue each year, but the trustee must distribute all of the income each year. Because Art reserves the power over payment of the income for the 15-year period, this portion of the transfer is incomplete on May 3. Actuarial tables discussed in the next section of the chapter address the valuation of the completed gift to Karl. ◀

---

[16] Reg. Sec. 25.2511-2(b).
[17] Ibid.
[18] Reg. Sec. 25.2511-2(c).

EXAMPLE C:12-17 ▶ Assume the same facts as in Example C:12-16 and that on December 31 Art instructs the trustee to distribute the trust's $34,000 of income as follows: $18,000 to Bob and $16,000 to Sue. Once the trustee pays out income, Art loses control over it. Thus, Art makes an $18,000 gift to Bob and a $16,000 gift to Sue on December 31. Each gift qualifies for the annual exclusion. ◀

EXAMPLE C:12-18 ▶ Assume the same facts as in Example C:12-16 and that on May 3 of the next year, when the trust assets are valued at $360,000, Art relinquishes his powers over payment of income and gives this power to the trustee. Art's transfer of the income interest (with a remaining term of 14 years) becomes complete on May 3 of the next year. The valuation of the gift of a 14-year income interest is determined from actuarial tables in Appendix H. ◀

Topic Review C:12-1 provides examples of various complete, incomplete, and partially complete transfers.

VALUATION OF GIFTS

ADDITIONAL COMMENT

Because the determination of value is such a subjective issue, a large number of gift tax controversies are nothing more than valuation disagreements.

GENERAL RULES. All gifts are valued at their FMV as of the date of the gift (i.e., the date the transfer becomes complete). Treasury Regulations state that a property's value is "the price at which such property would change hands between a willing buyer and a willing seller, neither being under any compulsion to buy or to sell, and both having reasonable knowledge of relevant facts."[19] According to the regulations, stocks and bonds traded on a stock exchange or over the counter are valued at the mean of the highest and lowest selling price on the date of the gift.[20] In general, the guidelines for valuing properties are the same, regardless of whether the property is conveyed during life or at death. An exception is life insurance policies, which are less valuable while the insured is alive. Valuation of life insurance policies is discussed in a later section of this chapter, as well as in Chapter C:13's coverage of the estate tax.

KEY POINT

The value of the life estate plus the value of the remainder interest equals the total FMV of the property.

LIFE ESTATES AND REMAINDER INTERESTS. Often a donor transfers less than his or her entire interest in an asset. For example, an individual may transfer property in trust and reserve the right to the trust's income for life and name another individual to receive the property upon the transferor's death. In such a situation, the transferor retains a **life estate** and gives a **remainder interest.** In general, only the remainder interest is subject to the gift tax. An exception applies if the gift is to a family member, as discussed in the estate freeze section below. If the transferor keeps an annuity (a fixed amount) for life and names another person to receive the remainder at the transferor's death, in all situations the gift is of just the remainder interest.

A grantor also may transfer property in trust with the promise that another person will receive the income for a certain number of years and at the end of that time period the

Topic Review C:12-1

Examples of Complete and Incomplete Transfers

1. Complete Transfers, Subject to Gift Tax:
   a. Property transferred outright to donee
   b. Property transferred to an irrevocable trust over which the donor retains no powers
2. Incomplete Transfers, Not Subject to Gift Tax:
   a. Property transferred to a revocable trust
   b. Property transferred to an irrevocable trust for which the donor retains discretionary powers over both income and the remainder interest
3. Partially Complete Transfers, Only a Portion Subject to Gift Tax:
   a. Property transferred to an irrevocable trust for which the donor retains discretionary powers over who receives the income but not the remainder interest[a]

[a]The gift of the remainder interest constitutes a completed transfer.

[19] Reg. Sec. 25.2512-1.

[20] Reg. Sec. 25.2512-2.

TAX STRATEGY TIP

When gifting a remainder interest, the donor should consider giving property with an anticipated appreciation rate greater than the Sec. 7520 interest rate.

property will revert to the grantor. In this case, the donor retains a reversionary interest, whereas the other party receives a **term certain interest**.[21] As explained later, unless the donee is a family member, only the term certain interest is subject to the gift tax. Trusts in which the grantor retains a reversionary interest have disadvantageous income tax consequences to the grantor if they were created after March 1, 1986. Chapter C:14 discusses the income tax treatment of such trusts.

Life estates, annuity interests, remainders, and term certain interests are valued from actuarial tables that incorporate the Sec. 7520 interest rate. In general, these tables must be used regardless of the actual earnings rate of the transferred assets. Excerpts from the tables appear in Appendix H. Table S is used for valuing life estates and remainders and Table B for term certain interests. The factor for a life estate or term certain interest is 1.0 minus the remainder factor. The remainder factor simply represents the present value of the right to receive a property at the end of someone's life (in the case of Table S) or at the end of a specified time (in the case of Table B). The value of the income interest plus the remainder interest is 1.0, the entire value of the property. The factor for an annuity is the life estate or the term factor divided by the Sec. 7520 interest rate. Section 7520 calls for the interest rate to be revised every month to the rate, rounded to the nearest 0.2%, that is 120% of the federal midterm rate applicable for the month of the transfer.[22] Congress mandated revisions to the tables to reflect mortality experience at least once every ten years, and the Treasury Department issued revised life tables effective for transfers on May 1, 1999, and later.

EXAMPLE C:12-19 ▶ Refer to Example C:12-16, in which on May 3 Art transfers $300,000 of property in trust with a bank as trustee. Art names his friends Bob and Sue to receive the trust income for 15 years but reserves the power to determine how the income is to be divided between them each year. However, the trustee must distribute all the income. Art specifies that Karl is to receive the trust property at the end of the fifteenth year. Only the gift of the remainder interest is a completed transfer on May 3. The gift is valued from Table B. If the interest rate is 10%, the amount of the gift is $71,818 (0.239392 × $300,000), the present value of the property to be received by Karl at the end of 15 years. ◀

EXAMPLE C:12-20 ▶ Assume the same facts as in Example C:12-19 and that three years later, when the trust assets are valued at $360,000, Art relinquishes to the trustee his power over the payment of trust income. The income interest has a remaining term of 12 years. The gift is the present value of the 12-year income interest, which is valued from Table B by subtracting the factor for a remainder interest (0.318631 if the interest rate is 10%) from 1.0. Thus, the amount of the gift is $245,293 [(1.0 − 0.318631) × $360,000]. ◀

EXAMPLE C:12-21 ▶ On July 5 of the current year, Don transfers $100,000 of property in trust and names his friends Larry (age 60) to receive all of the income for the rest of Larry's life and Ruth (age 25) to receive the trust assets upon Larry's death. Don names a bank as the trustee. The amount of each donee's gift is determined from Table S. If the interest rate is 10% and Larry is age 60, the value of the remainder interest gift to Ruth, as calculated from the single life remainder factors column of Table S, is $21,196 (0.21196 × $100,000). This amount represents the present value of the property Ruth will receive after the death of Larry, age 60. The remaining portion of the $100,000 of property, $78,804 ($100,000 − $21,196), is the value of the life estate transferred to Larry. The total value of the income plus remainder interests is 1.0. ◀

EXAMPLE C:12-22 ▶ In July of the current year, Amy (age 62) transferred $1 million of stock to a trust from which she retained the right to receive $120,000 per year for five years. She provided that the remainder will pass to her son, Arthur, at the end of the fifth year. Assume that 7% was the Sec. 7520 rate at the time of her transfer. She anticipated that the stock would continued to appreciate at its recent appreciation rate of 9% a year. The factor for a five-year annuity, assuming a 7%

---

21 *Term certain interest* means that a particular person has an interest in the property held in trust for a specified time period. The person having such interest does not own or hold title to the property but has a right to receive the income from such property for a specified time period. At the end of the time period, the property reverts to the grantor (or passes to another person, the remainderman).

22 The IRS regularly issues revenue rulings with applicable rate information.

rate, is 4.1002 [(1.0 − 0.712986, the factor for a remainder interest)/(0.07, the Sec. 7520 rate)]. Thus, Amy is deemed to have retained $492,024 (4.1002 × $120,000) and is deemed to have gifted the difference of $507,976 ($1,000,000 − $492,024). ◀

STOP & THINK *Question:* In which scenario would the amount of the gift be larger: (1) a gift of a remainder interest to a friend if a 68-year-old donor retained the income for life or (2) a gift of a remainder interest to a friend if an 86-year-old donor retained the income for life? Assume that each donor makes the gift on the same day so that the applicable interest rates are the same for each scenario.

Solution: The gift of the remainder interest would be larger if the donor is 86, instead of 68, because the actuarial value of the income interest the donor retains would be smaller if the donor is older. Under actuarial assumptions, older donors have shorter life expectancies.

ADDITIONAL COMMENT

In estate freeze transfers, Congress provided rules that generally increase the amount classified as a gift at the time of the actual transfer.

SPECIAL VALUATION RULES: ESTATE FREEZES. A number of years ago, Congress became concerned that individuals were able to shift wealth to other individuals, usually in a younger generation, without paying their "fair share" of the transfer taxes. An approach donors commonly used was to recapitalize a corporation (by exchanging common stock for both common and preferred shares) and then to give the common stock to individuals in the younger generation. This technique was one of a variety of transactions known as estate freezes.

In 1990, Congress decided to address the perceived problem of estate freezes by writing new valuation rules that apply when a gift occurs. The thrust of these rules—current IRC Chapter 14 (Secs. 2701 through 2704)—is to ensure that gifts are not undervalued. A couple of the more common situations governed by the new rules are described below, but the rules are too complicated to warrant a complete discussion. If a parent owns 100% of a corporation's stock and then gives the common stock to his or her children and retains the preferred stock, the value of the right to the preferred dividends is treated as zero unless the stock is cumulative preferred. Unless the donor retains *cumulative* preferred stock, the value assigned to the common stock given away is relatively high. If the donor creates a trust in which he or she retains an interest and in which he or she gives an interest to a family member, the value of the transferor's retained interest is treated as zero unless the interest is an annuity interest (fixed payments) or a unitrust interest (calling for distributions equal to a specified percentage of the current FMV of the trust). Thus, the donor who retains an income interest is treated as having kept nothing. The effect of these rules increases the gift amount, compared with the result under prior law, unless the transferor structures the transaction to avoid having a zero value assigned to his or her retained interest.[23]

GIFT TAX CONSEQUENCES OF CERTAIN TRANSFERS

Some transactions that cause the transferor to make a gift are straightforward. It is easy to see that the disposition is within the scope of the gift tax if, for example, an individual places the title to stock or real estate solely in another person's name and receives less than adequate consideration in return. Treasury Regulations include the following examples of transactions that may be subject to the gift tax: forgiving of a debt; assignment of the benefits of a life insurance policy; transfer of cash; and transfer of federal, state, or municipal bonds.[24] The gratuitous transfer of state and local bonds falls within the scope of the gift tax, even though interest on such bonds is exempt from federal income taxation. The following discussion concerns the gift tax rules for several transfers that are more complicated than, for example, transferring the title to real property or stock to another person.

---

[23] See Reg. Secs. 25.2701-1 through -6 and 25.2702-1 through -6 for guidance concerning the estate freeze provisions.

[24] Reg. Sec. 25.2511-1(a).

CREATION OF JOINT BANK ACCOUNTS. Parties depositing money to a jointly owned bank account potentially face gift tax consequences. Funding a joint bank account is an incomplete transfer because the depositor is free to withdraw the amount deposited into the account. A gift occurs when one party withdraws an amount exceeding the amount he or she deposited.[25] The transfer is complete at that time because only the person who made the withdrawal can control the withdrawn funds.

EXAMPLE C:12-23 ▶ On May 1, Connie deposits $100,000 into a joint bank account in the names of Connie and Ben. Her friend Ben makes no deposits. On December 1, Ben withdraws $30,000 from the joint account and purchases an automobile. No gift arises upon the creation of the bank account. However, on December 1, Connie makes a gift to Ben of $30,000, the excess of Ben's withdrawal over Ben's deposit. ◀

CREATION OF OTHER JOINT TENANCIES. **Joint tenancy** is a popular form of property ownership from a convenience standpoint because, when one joint owner dies, the property is automatically owned by the survivor(s). Each joint tenant is deemed to have an equal interest in the property. A completed gift arises when the transferor titles real estate or other property in the names of himself or herself and another (e.g., a spouse, a sibling, or a child) as joint tenants. The person furnishing the consideration to acquire the property is deemed to have made a gift to the other joint tenant in an amount equal to the value of the donee's pro rata interest in the property.[26]

EXAMPLE C:12-24 ▶ Kwame purchases land for $250,000 and immediately has it titled in the names of Kwame and Kesha, as joint tenants with right of survivorship. Kwame and Kesha are not husband and wife. Kwame makes a gift to Kesha of $125,000, or one-half the value of the property. ◀

TAX STRATEGY TIP

An owner of a life insurance policy who wishes to gift the ownership to someone else, such as the beneficiary, can use the following strategies to avoid the gift tax:

(1) Before making the gift, borrow enough against the policy to reduce its net value to the amount of the annual exclusion ($12,000 in 2007). The former owner (borrower) then can pay premiums and make loan repayments, not to exceed the annual exclusion in any given year.

(2) Have the insurance company rewrite the policy into separate policies, each having a value that does not exceed the annual exclusion. Then, gift one policy each year for several years.

TRANSFER OF LIFE INSURANCE POLICIES. The mere naming of another as the beneficiary of a life insurance policy is an incomplete transfer because the owner of the policy can change the beneficiary designation at any time. However, if an individual irrevocably assigns all ownership rights in an insurance policy to another party, this event constitutes a gift of the policy to the new owner.[27] Ownership rights include the ability to change the beneficiary, borrow against the policy, and cash the policy in for its cash surrender value.

The payment of a premium on an insurance policy owned by another person is considered a gift to the policy's owner. The amount of the gift is the amount of the premium paid. The tax result is the same as if the donor transferred cash to the policy owner and the owner used the cash to pay the premium.

According to Reg. Sec. 25.2512-6, the value of the gift of a life insurance policy is the amount it would cost to purchase a comparable policy on the date of the gift. The regulations point out, however, that if the policy is several years old, the cost of a comparable policy is not readily ascertainable. In such a situation, the policy is valued at its interpolated terminal reserve (i.e., an amount similar to the policy's cash surrender value) plus the amount of any unexpired premiums. The insurance company will furnish information concerning the interpolated terminal reserve.

EXAMPLE C:12-25 ▶ On September 1, Bill transfers his entire ownership rights in a $300,000 life insurance policy on his own life to his sister Susan. The policy's interpolated terminal reserve is $24,000 as of September 1. On July 1, Bill had paid the policy's $4,800 annual premium. Bill makes a gift to Susan on September 1 of $28,000 [$24,000 + (10/12 × $4,800)] because he transferred ownership to Susan. If, however, the policy had been a term insurance policy, which has no interpolated terminal reserve, the gift would have been $4,000 (10/12 × $4,800), the amount of the unexpired premium.

On July 1 of the next year, Bill pays the $4,800 annual premium on the policy now owned by Susan. As a result of the premium payment, Bill makes a $4,800 gift to Susan that year, the same result as if he had given her $4,800 of cash to pay the premium. ◀

[25] Reg. Sec. 25.2511-1(h)(4).

[26] Reg. Sec. 25.2511-1(h)(5). If the two joint tenants are husband and wife, no taxable gift will arise because of the unlimited marital deduction.

[27] Reg. Sec. 25.2511-1(h)(8).

EXAMPLE C:12-26 ▶ Assume the same facts as in Example C:12-25 except that Susan, who now owns the policy, changes the beneficiary of the policy from Frank to John. Susan does not make a gift because she has not given up control; she can change the beneficiary again in the future. ◀

EXERCISE OF A GENERAL POWER OF APPOINTMENT. Section 2514 provides the rules concerning powers of appointment. A **power of appointment** exists when a person transfers property (perhaps in trust) and grants someone else the power to specify who eventually will receive the property. Thus, possession of a power of appointment has some of the same benefits as ownership of the property. Powers can be general or special. *Potential* gift tax consequences are associated with the powerholder's exercise of a **general power of appointment.** A person possesses a general power of appointment if he or she has the power to appoint the property (have the property distributed) to him- or herself, his or her creditors or estate, or the creditors of his or her estate. The words *his or her estate* mean that there are no restrictions concerning to whom the individual may bequeath the property.

A gift occurs when a person exercises a general power of appointment and names some other person to receive the property.[28] The donee is the person the powerholder names to receive the property. A person who exercises a general power of appointment in favor of himself or herself does not make a gift (i.e., one cannot make a gift to him- or herself).

EXAMPLE C:12-27 ▶ In 2007, Tina funds an irrevocable trust with $600,000 and names Van to receive the income for life. In addition, Tina gives Van a general power of appointment exercisable during his life as well as at his death. Tina made a gift to Van of $600,000 at the time she transferred the property to the trust in 2007. In 2008, Van instructs the bank trustee to distribute $50,000 of trust property to Kay. Through the exercise of his general power of appointment in favor of Kay, Van makes a $50,000 gift to Kay in 2008 because he diverted property to her. ◀

NET GIFTS. A **net gift** occurs when an individual makes a gift to a donee who agrees to pay the gift tax as a condition of receiving the gift. The donee's payment of the gift tax is treated as consideration paid to the donor. The amount of the gift is the excess of the FMV of the transferred property over the amount of the gift tax paid by the donee. Because the amount of the gift depends on the amount of gift tax payable, which in turn depends on the amount of the gift, the calculations require the use of simultaneous equations.[29]

The net gift strategy is especially attractive for people who would like to remove a rapidly appreciating asset from their estate but are unable to pay the gift tax because of liquidity problems. However, a net gift has one potential disadvantage: the Supreme Court has ruled that the donor must recognize as a gain the excess of the gift tax payable over his or her adjusted basis in the property.[30] The Court's rationale is that the donee's payment of the donor's gift tax liability constitutes an "amount realized" for purposes of determining the gain or loss realized on a sale, exchange, or other disposition. From a practical standpoint, this decision affects only donors who transfer property so highly appreciated that the property's adjusted basis is less than the gift tax liability.

EXAMPLE C:12-28 ▶ Mary transfers land with a $3 million FMV to her son, Sam, who agrees to pay the gift tax liability. Mary's adjusted basis in the land is $15,000. Earlier in the year, she gave him $12,000. The amount of the taxable gift is $3 million, less the gift tax paid by Sam. Simultaneous equations are used to calculate the amount of the gift and the gift tax liability. Mary must recognize gain equal to the excess of the gift tax liability paid by Sam minus Mary's $15,000 basis in the property.

---

[28] In general, the exercise of a special power of appointment is free of gift tax consequences. In the case of special powers of appointment, the holder of the power does not have an unrestricted ability to name the persons to receive the property. For example, he or she may be able to appoint to only his or her descendants.

[29] In Rev. Rul. 75-72 (1975-1 C.B. 310), the IRS explained how to calculate the amount of the net gift and the gift tax. In Ltr. Rul. 7842068 (July 20, 1978), the IRS stated that the donor's available unified credit, not the donee's, is used to calculate the gift tax payable.

[30] *Victor P. Diedrich v. CIR*, 50 AFTR 2d 82-5054, 82-1 USTC ¶9419 (USSC, 1982).

TAX STRATEGY TIP

As a general rule, substantially appreciated property should not be transferred by gift. It should be transferred at death to take advantage of the step-up in basis to the estate tax value (usually FMV at date of death). If Mary in Example C:12-28 were elderly, it might be better to transfer an asset other than the land to preserve the step-up in basis for the land.

Assume that, because of sizable previous taxable gifts, any additional gifts Mary makes will be subject to the 45% maximum gift tax rate. Assume Mary has used all of her unified credit. If G represents the amount of the gift and T is the amount of the tax, then

$$G = \$3{,}000{,}000 - T$$
$$T = 0.45G$$

Substituting 0.45G for T in the first equation and solving for G yields G = $3,000,000 ÷ 1.45 = $2,068,966, the amount of the gift. The tax is 45% of this amount, or $931,035. The calculation increases in difficulty when, because of splitting brackets, more than one gift tax rate applies. Mary's gain equals the $931,035 gift tax paid by Sam minus her $15,000 basis in the property, or $916,035. ◀

EXCLUSIONS

OBJECTIVE 4

Determine whether an annual gift tax exclusion is available

In many instances, a portion or all of a transfer by gift is tax-free because of the annual exclusion authorized by Sec. 2503(b). In 1932, the Senate Finance Committee explained the purpose of the **annual exclusion** as follows:

> Such exemption . . . is to obviate the necessity of keeping an account of and reporting numerous small gifts, and . . . to fix the amount sufficiently large to cover in most cases wedding and Christmas gifts and occasional gifts of relatively small amount.[31]

In most gift transactions, the donor makes no taxable gift because of the annual exclusion. Consequently, administration of the gift tax provisions is a much simpler task than it otherwise would be.

AMOUNT OF THE EXCLUSION

The amount of this exclusion, which is analogous to an exclusion from gross income for income tax purposes, currently is $12,000.[32] It is available each year for an unlimited number of donees. For transfers made in trust, each beneficiary is deemed to be a separate donee. Any number of donors may make a gift to the same donee, and each is eligible to claim the exclusion. The only limitations on the annual exclusion are the donor's wealth, generosity, and imagination in identifying donees.

EXAMPLE C:12-29 ▶ In 2007, Ann and Bob each give $12,000 cash to each of Tad and Liz. Ann and Bob again make $12,000 cash gifts to Tad and Liz in 2008. For both 2007 and 2008, Ann receives $24,000 of exclusions ($12,000 for the gift to Tad and $12,000 for the gift to Liz). The same result applies to Bob. ◀

TAX STRATEGY TIP

Gifts up to the amount of the annual exclusion not only remove the gifted amounts from the donor's estate with no gift taxes but also remove the property's future income from the donor's estate. In addition, the property's income can be shifted to someone whose tax bracket might be lower than the donor's, thereby reducing income taxes.

The annual exclusion is a significant tax planning device that has no estate tax counterpart. So long as a donor's gifts to a particular donee do not exceed the excludable amount, the donor will never make any taxable gifts or incur any gift tax liability. Because taxable gifts will be zero, the donor's estate tax base will not include any adjusted taxable gifts. A donor, who each year for ten years prior to 2002 gave $10,000 per donee to each of ten donees, removed $1 million (10 × $10,000 × 10) from being taxed in his or her estate. The donor accomplished these transfers without making any taxable gifts or paying any gift tax. If retained, the $1 million would have been taxed in the donor's estate, at perhaps the top estate tax rate, unless the property was willed to the donor's surviving spouse.

PRESENT INTEREST REQUIREMENT

Although we generally speak of the annual exclusion as if it were available automatically for all gifts, in actuality it is not. A donor receives an exclusion only for gifts that constitute a present interest.

---

[31] S. Rept. No. 665, 72nd Cong., 1st Sess. (1932), reprinted in 1939-1 C.B. (Part 2), pp. 525–526.

[32] On January 1, 1982, Congress increased the annual exclusion from $3,000 to $10,000. Later, Congress provided that the exclusion would be indexed after 1998, with inflation adjustments rounded to the next lowest multiple of $1,000. In 2002, the exclusion rose to $11,000 and remained there through 2005. It rose to $12,000 in 2006 and remains there in 2007.

DEFINITION OF PRESENT INTEREST. A **present interest** is "an unrestricted right to the immediate use, possession, or enjoyment of property or the income from property (such as a life estate or term certain)."[33] Only present interests qualify for the annual exclusion. If only a portion of a transfer constitutes a present interest, the excluded portion of the gift may not exceed the value of the present interest.

DEFINITION OF FUTURE INTEREST. A future interest is the opposite of a present interest. A **future interest** "is a legal term, and includes reversions, remainders, and other interests . . . which are limited to commence in use, possession, or enjoyment at some future date or time."[34] Gifts of future interests are ineligible for the annual exclusion. The following examples help demonstrate the attributes of present and future interests.

EXAMPLE C:12-30 ▶ Nancy transfers $500,000 of property to an irrevocable trust with a bank serving as trustee. Nancy names Norm (age 55) to receive all the trust income quarterly for the rest of Norm's life. At Norm's death, the property is to pass to Ellen (age 25) or Ellen's estate. Norm receives an unrestricted right to immediate enjoyment of the income. Thus, Norm has a present interest. Ellen, however, has a future interest because Ellen cannot enjoy the property or any of the income until Norm dies. The taxable gift is $488,000 ($500,000 − $12,000). ◀

EXAMPLE C:12-31 ▶ Greg transfers $800,000 of property to an irrevocable trust with a bank serving as trustee and instructs the trustee to distribute all the trust income semiannually to Greg's three adult children, Jill, Katy, and/or Laura. The trustee is to use its discretion in deciding how much to distribute to each beneficiary. Moreover, it is authorized to distribute nothing to a particular beneficiary if it deems such action to be in the beneficiary's best interest. Although all the income must be paid out, the trustee has complete discretion to determine how much to pay to a particular beneficiary. None of the beneficiaries has the assurance that he or she will receive a trust distribution. Thus, Greg created no present interests, and the annual exclusion does not apply. The taxable gift, therefore, is $800,000. ◀

SPECIAL RULE FOR TRUSTS FOR MINORS. Congress realized that many donors would not want trusts for minor children to be required to distribute all their income to the young children. Accordingly, Congress enacted Sec. 2503(c), which authorizes special trusts for minors, to address donors' concerns about the distribution of trust income to minors. Section 2503(c) authorizes an annual exclusion for gifts to trusts for beneficiaries under age 21 even though the trusts need not distribute all their income annually. Such trusts, known as **Sec. 2503(c) trusts**, allow donors to claim the annual exclusion if the following two conditions are met:

- Until the beneficiary becomes age 21, the trustee may pay the income and/or the underlying assets to the beneficiary.
- Any income and underlying assets not paid to the beneficiary will pass to that beneficiary when he or she reaches age 21. If the beneficiary should die before becoming age 21, the income and underlying assets are payable to either the beneficiary's estate or to any person the minor may appoint if the minor possesses a general power of appointment over the property.

ADDITIONAL COMMENT

The donor may serve as trustee of a Sec. 2503(c) trust, but this approach generally is not advisable. If the donor's powers are not sufficiently limited, the trust property will be included in the donor's estate if the donor's death occurs before the trust terminates.

If the trust instrument contains both the provisions listed above, no part of the trust is considered to be a gift of a future interest. Therefore, the entire transfer is treated as a present interest and is eligible for the annual exclusion.

As a result of Sec. 2503(c), donors creating trusts for donees under age 21 receive an exclusion even though the trustee has discretion over paying out the trust income. However, the trustee must distribute the assets and accumulated income to the beneficiary at age 21.

ADDITIONAL COMMENT

The holder of a *Crummey* power must be given notice of a contribution to the trust to which the power relates and must be given a reasonable time period within which to exercise the power. The donor receives the annual exclusion regardless of whether the donee exercises the power.

CRUMMEY TRUST. The **Crummey trust** is yet another technique that allows the donor to obtain an annual exclusion upon funding a discretionary trust. The trust can terminate at whatever age the donor specifies and can be created for a beneficiary of any age. Thus, the *Crummey* trust is a much more flexible arrangement than the Sec. 2503(c) trust.

[33] Reg. Sec. 25.2503-3(b).

[34] Reg. Sec. 25.2503-3(a).

The *Crummey* trust is named for a Ninth Circuit Court of Appeals decision holding that the trust beneficiaries had a present interest as a result of certain language in the trust instrument.[35] That language, which is referred to interchangeably as a *Crummey* power, *Crummey* demand power, or *Crummey* withdrawal power, entitled each beneficiary to demand a distribution of the lesser of $4,000 (the amount in the actual case) or the amount transferred to the trust that year. If the beneficiary did not exercise the power by a specified date, it expired. The trust instrument included the "lesser of" language for the demand power because the largest present interest the donor needs to create is equal to the annual exclusion amount. In years in which the gift is smaller than the annual exclusion amount, the donor simply needs to be able to exclude the amount of that year's gift. In addition, the donor wants to restrict the amount to which the beneficiary can have access. The trust instrument often states that the maximum amount the beneficiary can withdraw is "an amount equal to the annual exclusion for federal gift tax purposes" or twice that amount if gift splitting is anticipated.

The court held that the demand power provided each beneficiary with a present interest equal to the maximum amount the beneficiary could require the trustee to pay over to him or her that year. Use of the *Crummey* trust technique entitles the donor to receive the annual exclusion while creating a discretionary trust that terminates at whatever age the donor deems appropriate. The donor thereby avoids the restrictive rules of Sec. 2503(c). Generally, the donor hopes the beneficiary will not exercise the demand right.

EXAMPLE C:12-32 ▶ Al funds two $100,000 irrevocable trusts and names First Bank the trustee. The first trust is for the benefit of Kay, his 15-year-old daughter. The trustee has discretion to distribute income and/or principal to Kay until she reaches age 21. If she dies before age 21, the trust assets are payable to whomever she appoints in her will or to her estate if she dies without a will. The second trust is for the benefit of Bob, Al's 25-year-old son. Income and/or principal are payable to Bob in the trustee's discretion until Bob reaches age 35, whereupon Bob will receive the trust assets. Bob may demand by December 31 of each year that the trustee pay him the lesser of the amount of the gift tax annual exclusion or the amount transferred to the trust that calendar year. The trust for Kay is a Sec. 2503(c) trust, and the one for Bob is a *Crummey* trust. An annual exclusion is available for each trust. ◀

STOP & THINK

Question: For which of the following gifts would the donor receive an annual exclusion:

- A gift of a remainder interest in land if the donor retains the income interest for life
- A gift outright of a life insurance policy that has a cash surrender value
- A gift to a discretionary trust that is classified as a Sec. 2503(c) trust
- A gift to a Crummey trust?

Solution: All the transfers except the gift of the remainder interest (a future interest) are eligible for the annual exclusion. Even though the gift to the Sec. 2503(c) trust does not literally involve a gift of a present interest (the right to current income or enjoyment), the IRC explicitly allows this kind of transfer to qualify for the annual exclusion.

GIFT TAX DEDUCTIONS

OBJECTIVE 5

Identify deductions available for gift tax purposes

The formula for determining taxable gifts allows both an unlimited marital deduction and an unlimited charitable contribution deduction. The **marital deduction** is for transfers to one's spouse. The **charitable contribution deduction** is for gifts to charitable organizations. Section 2524 states that the deductible amount in either case may not exceed the amount of the "includible gift"—that is, the amount of the gift exceeding the annual exclusion. Thus, the lowest possible taxable gift is zero, not a negative number, as could be the case if the deduction equaled the total amount of the gift.

---

[35] *D. Clifford Crummey v. CIR*, 22 AFTR 2d 6023, 68-2 USTC ¶12,541 (9th Cir., 1968).

MARITAL DEDUCTION

ADDITIONAL COMMENT

Congress allowed a marital deduction because a taxpayer who transfers property to his or her spouse has not made a transfer outside the economic (husband/wife) unit. For similar reasons, the interspousal gift has no *income* tax consequences. The donor spouse recognizes no gain or loss, and the donee spouse takes a carryover basis.

Generally, the marital deduction results in tax-free interspousal transfers, but an exception discussed below applies to gifts of certain terminable interests. Congress first enacted the marital deduction in 1948 to provide more uniform treatment of community property and noncommunity property donors. To recap, in community property states, most property acquired after marriage is owned equally by each spouse. In noncommunity property states, however, the spouses' wealth often is divided unequally, and such spouses can equalize each individual's share of the wealth only by engaging in a gift-giving program. As a result of the marital deduction, spouses can shift wealth between themselves completely free of any gift tax consequences.

UNLIMITED AMOUNT. Over the years, the maximum marital deduction has varied, but since 1981 one spouse has been able to deduct up to 100% of the amount of gifts made to the other spouse. The amount of the marital deduction, however, is limited to the portion of the gift that exceeds the annual exclusion.[36] Beginning after 1981, transfers of community property became eligible for the marital deduction.

EXAMPLE C:12-33 ▶ A wife gives her husband stock valued at $450,000. She excludes $12,000 because of the annual exclusion and claims a $438,000 marital deduction. Thus, no taxable gift arises. ◀

GIFTS OF TERMINABLE INTERESTS: GENERAL RULE.

Nondeductible Terminable Interests. A **terminable interest** is an interest that ends or is terminated when some event occurs (or fails to occur) or a specified amount of time passes. Some, but not all, terminable interests are ineligible for the marital deduction.[37] A marital deduction is denied only when the transfer is of a *nondeductible* terminable interest. A nondeductible terminable interest has one of the following characteristics:

- The donee-spouse's interest ceases at a set time (such as at death) and the property then either passes back to the donor or passes to a third party who does not pay adequate consideration.
- Immediately after making the gift, the donor has the power to name someone else to receive an interest in the property, and the person named may possess the property upon the termination of the donee-spouse's interest.[38]

The next three examples illustrate some of the subtleties of the definition of nondeductible terminable interests. In Example C:12-34, a marital deduction is available because neither characteristic exists for a nondeductible terminable interest.

EXAMPLE C:12-34 ▶ A donor gives a patent to a spouse. A patent is a terminable interest because the property interest terminates at the end of the patent's legal life. Nevertheless, the patent does not constitute a nondeductible terminable interest. When the patent's legal life expires, a third party will not possess an interest in the patent. Thus, a donor will receive a marital deduction. ◀

In Example C:12-35, a marital deduction is denied because the first of the two alternative characteristics of a nondeductible terminable interest exists.

EXAMPLE C:12-35 ▶ A donor transfers property in trust and (1) names his wife to receive trust income, at the trustee's discretion, annually for the next 15 years and (2) states that at the end of the 15-year period the trust's assets are to be distributed to their child. The donor has given his wife a nondeductible terminable interest. When the spouse's interest ceases, the property passes to their child, a recipient who did not pay adequate consideration. Thus, the donor receives no marital deduction. ◀

In Example C:12-36, a marital deduction is available. In addition to having a lifetime income interest, the donee-spouse has a general power of appointment over the trust's assets and can specify who eventually receives the property.

[36] Sec. 2524.
[37] Sec. 2523(b).
[38] Ibid.

EXAMPLE C:12-36 ▶ The donor gives his wife the right to all the income from a trust annually for life plus a general power of appointment over the trust's assets. He has transferred an interest eligible for the marital deduction. The general power of appointment may be exercisable during life, at death, or at both times. In addition, the donee-spouse is entitled to receive the income annually. ◀

TAX STRATEGY TIP

A general power of appointment can qualify a transfer for the marital deduction. For example, assume that last year Brad transferred property to a trust, income to be distributed annually to his wife Sonia until her death, with a general power of appointment in Sonia over the remainder. Sonia's general power of appointment allowed the transfer to be eligible for the gift tax marital deduction.

The rationale behind the nondeductible terminable interest rule is that a donor should obtain a marital deduction only if he or she conveys an interest that will have transfer tax significance to the donee-spouse. In other words, when a donee spouse later gives away property that he or she received as a result of an interspousal transfer, a transfer subject to the gift tax occurs. If the donee-spouse retains such property until death, the asset is included in the donee-spouse's gross estate.

QTIP PROVISIONS. Beginning in 1982, Congress made a major change to the nondeductible terminable interest rule and allowed transfers of qualified terminable interest property to be eligible for the marital deduction.[39] Such transfers are commonly referred to as *QTIP transfers*. **Qualified terminable interest property** is property

TAX STRATEGY TIP

By using a QTIP, a donor can achieve a marital deduction while exercising some control over the property. For example, assume the same facts as in the previous annotation except that Brad has been married twice. He had two children by his first wife and three children with Sonia. Brad could not be sure his first two children would ever receive anything from the trust because Sonia could exercise her general power of appointment in favor of just their three children (or someone else). If Brad funded a QTIP, the trust instrument could specify that the remainder, on Sonia's death, would go equally to all five children. Brad could thus control the ultimate disposition of the remainder and still receive a marital deduction.

- ▶ That is transferred by the donor-spouse,
- ▶ In which the donee has a "qualifying income interest for life," and
- ▶ For which a special election has been made.

A spouse has the necessary "qualifying income interest for life" if

- ▶ The spouse is entitled to all the income from the property annually or more often, and
- ▶ No person has a power to appoint any part of the property to any person other than the donee-spouse unless the power cannot be exercised while the spouse is alive.

The QTIP rule enhances the attractiveness of making transfers to one's spouse because a donor can receive a marital deduction—and thereby make a nontaxable transfer—without having to grant the spouse full control over the gifted property. The QTIP rule is especially attractive for a donor who wants to ensure that the children by a previous marriage will receive the property upon the donee-spouse's death.

The donor does not have to claim a marital deduction even though the transfer otherwise qualifies as a QTIP transfer. Claiming the deduction on such transfers is elective.[40] If the donor elects to claim a marital deduction, the donee-spouse must include the QTIP trust property in his or her estate at its value as of the donee-spouse's date of death. Thus, as with other transfers qualifying for the marital deduction, the interspousal transfer is tax-free, and the taxable event is postponed until the donee-spouse transfers the property.

EXAMPLE C:12-37 ▶ Jo transfers $1 million of property in trust with a bank acting as trustee. All the trust income is payable to Jo's husband, Ed (age 64), quarterly for the rest of his life. Upon Ed's death, the property will pass to Jo's nieces. This gift is eligible for a marital deduction. If Jo elects to claim the marital deduction, she will receive a $988,000 ($1,000,000 − $12,000) marital deduction. The deduction is limited to the amount of the includible gift, i.e., the gift exceeding the annual exclusion. Jo's taxable gift will be zero. ◀

Note that Jo's marital deduction in the preceding example is for $988,000 and not for the value of Ed's life estate. If Jo elects to claim the marital deduction, Ed's gross estate will include the value of the entire trust, valued as of the date of Ed's death. The QTIP provision permits Jo to receive a marital deduction while still being able to specify who will receive the property upon her husband's death.

Topic Review C:12-2 summarizes the eligibility of a transfer for the marital deduction and the amount of the marital deduction that can be claimed.

---

[39] Sec. 2523(f).

[40] The donor might decide not to claim the marital deduction if the donee-spouse has substantial assets already or a short life expectancy, especially if the gifted property's value is expected to appreciate at a high annual rate.

Topic Review C:12-2

Eligibility for and Amount of the Marital Deduction

Examples of Transfers Eligible for the Marital Deduction

Property transferred to spouse as sole owner

Property transferred in trust with all the income payable to the spouse for life and over which the donee-spouse has a general power of appointment

Property transferred in trust with all the income payable annually or more often to the spouse for life and for which the donor-spouse designated the remainderman—marital deduction available if elected under QTIP rule

Examples of Transfers Ineligible for the Marital Deduction

Property transferred in trust with the income payable in the trustee's discretion to the spouse for life, and for which the donor-spouse designated the remainderman

Property transferred in trust with all the income payable to the spouse for a specified number of years and for which the donor-spouse designated the remainderman

Amount of the Marital Deduction, if Available

The amount of the transfer minus the portion eligible for the annual exclusion

CHARITABLE CONTRIBUTION DEDUCTION

If a donor is not required to file a gift tax return to report noncharitable gifts, the donor does not have to report gifts to charitable organizations on a gift tax return, provided a charitable contribution deduction is available and the charitable organization receives the donor's entire interest in the property. Claiming an income tax deduction for a charitable contribution does not preclude the donor from also obtaining a gift tax deduction. In contrast with the income tax provisions, the gift tax charitable contribution deduction has no percentage limitation. The only ceiling on the deduction is imposed by Sec. 2524, which limits the deduction to the amount of the gift that exceeds the excluded portion.

EXAMPLE C:12-38 ▶ Julio gives stock valued at $76,000 to State University. Julio receives an $12,000 annual exclusion and a $64,000 charitable contribution deduction for *gift* tax purposes. However, he need not report the gift on a gift tax return if he does not have to file a return to report gifts to noncharitable donees. On his *income* tax return, he receives a $76,000 charitable contribution deduction, subject to AGI limitations. ◀

TAX STRATEGY TIP

A charitably minded taxpayer could avoid the gift (and the estate) tax entirely by giving all his or her property to a qualified charitable organization. Actually, in 2007 the taxpayer could give up to $1 million plus the amount shielded by the annual exclusion to noncharitable donees and still pay no gift tax.

TRANSFERS ELIGIBLE FOR THE DEDUCTION. To be deductible, the gift must be made to a charitable organization. The rules defining charitable organizations are quite similar for income, gift, and estate tax purposes.[41] According to Sec. 2522, a gift tax deduction is available for contributions to the following:

- The United States or any subordinate level of government within the United States as long as the transfer is solely for public purposes
- A corporation, trust fund, etc., organized exclusively for religious, charitable, scientific, literary, or educational purposes, or to foster amateur sports competition, including the encouragement of art and the prevention of cruelty to children or animals
- A fraternal society or similar organization operating under the lodge system if the gifts are to be used in the United States only for religious, charitable, scientific, literary, or educational purposes
- A war veterans' post or organization organized in the United States or one of its possessions if no part of its net earnings accrues to the benefit of private shareholders or individuals

[41] In contrast to the income tax rules, a charitable contribution deduction is available under the gift tax rules for transfers made to foreign charitable organizations. No deduction is available, however, for gifts made to foreign governments.

SPLIT-INTEREST TRANSFERS. Specialized rules apply when a donor makes a transfer for both private (i.e., an individual) and public (i.e., a charitable organization) purposes. Such arrangements are known as **split-interest transfers**. An example of a split-interest transfer is the gift of a residence to one's sister for life with the remainder interest to a university. If a donor gives a charitable organization a remainder interest, the donor forfeits the charitable contribution deduction unless the remainder interest is in either a personal residence (not necessarily the donor's principal residence), a farm, a charitable remainder annuity trust or unitrust, or a pooled income fund.[42] A split-interest gift of a present interest to a charity qualifies for a charitable contribution deduction only if the charity receives a guaranteed annuity interest or a unitrust interest. Actuarial tables are used to value split-interest transfers (see Appendix H).

EXAMPLE C:12-39 ▶ Al transfers $800,000 of property to a charitable remainder annuity trust. He reserves an annuity of $56,000 per year for his remaining life and specifies that upon his death the trust property will pass to the American Red Cross. Al must report this transaction on a gift tax return because the Red Cross did not receive his entire interest in the property. In the same year, Al gives a museum a remainder interest in his antique furniture collection and reserves a life estate for himself.

Each of these is a split-interest transfer. Unfortunately for the donor, only the remainder interest in the charitable remainder annuity trust is eligible for a charitable contribution deduction. Consequently, Al makes a taxable gift equal to the value of the remainder interest in the antique furniture. (If Al had given a remainder interest in a personal residence or farm, he would have received a charitable contribution deduction for this gift.) Even though the furniture is not an income-producing property, the value of the remainder interest is determined from the actuarial tables found in Appendix H.

Assume that Al was age 60 at the time of the gifts and that the Sec. 7520 interest rate was 10%. What is the amount of Al's charitable contribution deduction?

Answer: The portion of the annuity trust retained by Al is $441,302 {[(1.0 − 0.21196) ÷ 0.10] × $56,000}. The charitable deduction on the gift tax return is $358,698 ($800,000 − $441,302). The same amount also is allowable—subject to the ceiling rules—as a charitable contribution deduction on Al's income tax return for that year. ◀

SELF-STUDY QUESTION

In Example C:12-39, does Al receive an annual exclusion for the gift of the furniture?

ANSWER

No. The remainder interest is a future interest, as is the remainder in the trust.

THE GIFT-SPLITTING ELECTION

OBJECTIVE 6

Apply the gift-splitting rules

The gift-splitting provisions of Sec. 2513 allow spouses to treat a gift actually made by just one of them as if each spouse made one-half of the gift. This election offers several advantages, as follows:

- ▶ If only one spouse makes a gift to a particular donee, the election enables a spouse to give $24,000 (instead of $12,000) to the donee before a taxable gift arises.
- ▶ If per-donee annual transfers exceed $24,000 and taxable gifts occur, the election may reduce the applicable marginal gift tax rate.
- ▶ Each spouse may use a unified credit to reduce the gift tax payable.

To take advantage of the gift-splitting election, the spouses must meet the following requirements at the time of the transfer:

- ▶ They must be U.S. citizens or residents.
- ▶ At the time of the gift(s) for which the spouses make an election, the donor-spouse must be married to the person who consents to gift splitting. In addition, the donor-spouse must not remarry before the end of the year.

The gift-splitting election is effective for all transfers to third parties made during the portion of the year that the spouses were married to each other.

TAX STRATEGY TIP

Donors can magnify the benefits of the annual exclusion by using gift splitting techniques.

[42] In a **charitable remainder annuity trust**, an individual receives trust distributions for a certain time period or for life. The annual distributions are a uniform percentage (5% or higher) of the value of the trust property, valued on the date of the transfer. For a **charitable remainder unitrust**, the distributions are similar, except that they are a uniform percentage (5% or higher) of the value of the trust property, revalued at least annually. Thus, the annual distributions from a unitrust, but not an annuity trust, vary from one year to the next. Both unitrusts and annuity trusts must meet the requirements that the payout rate does not exceed 50% of the value of the property and the value of the remainder interest is at least 10% of the initial FMV. A **pooled income fund** is similar in concept to a mutual fund. The various individual beneficiaries receive annual distributions of their proportionate shares of the pooled income fund's total income.

ADDITIONAL COMMENT

A wife makes a gift of $40,000 to a child in March and a gift of $60,000 to another child in November of the same year. The gift-splitting election, if made, will apply to both gifts because the election to gift split applies to all gifts made during the year. With gift splitting, her husband will be treated as making one-half of each gift.

A spouse living in a community property state who makes a gift of separate property (e.g., an asset received by inheritance) may desire to use gift splitting. In this case, the election automatically extends to gifts of community property even though splitting each spouse's gifts of community property has no impact on the "bottom-line" amount of taxable gifts.

Note that gift splitting is an all-or-nothing proposition. Spouses wanting to elect it for one gift must elect it for all gifts to third parties for that year. Each year's election stands alone, however, and is not binding on future years.[43] The procedural aspects of the gift-splitting election are discussed in the Compliance and Procedural Considerations section of this chapter.

EXAMPLE C:12-40 ▶ Eli marries Joy on April 1 of the current year. They are still married to each other at the end of the year. In March, Eli gave Amy $60,000. In July, Eli gave Barb $52,000, and Joy gave Claire $28,000. If the couple elects gift splitting, the election is effective only for the July gifts. Each spouse is treated as giving $26,000 and $14,000 to Barb and Claire, respectively. Because they may not elect gift splitting for the gift Eli makes before their marriage, Eli is treated as giving $60,000—the amount he actually transfers—to Amy. Under gift splitting, both Eli and Joy exclude $12,000 of gifts to both Barb and Claire, or a total of $48,000. Eli also excludes $12,000 of his gift to Amy. ◀

ADDITIONAL COMMENT

The gift-splitting election is a year-by-year election. For example, a husband and wife could elect to gift split in 2002, 2004, and 2006, but not elect to gift split in 2003, 2005, and 2007.

Upon the death of the actual donor or the spouse who consented to gift splitting, such decedent's estate tax base includes that decedent's post-1976 taxable gifts, known as adjusted taxable gifts. By electing gift splitting, a couple can reduce the amount of the taxable gifts the donor-decedent is deemed to have made. Under gift splitting, the adjusted taxable gifts include only the portions of the gifts that are taxable on the gift tax returns filed by the donor-decedent. Of course, the nondonor-spouse's estate reports his or her post-1976 taxable gifts.

STOP & THINK

Question: Bob made taxable gifts of $4 million in 2001, and Betty, his spouse, has not made any taxable gifts. Betty inherited a large fortune last year and is contemplating gifting $500,000 in 2007 to each of her two children. Bob does not anticipate making any taxable gifts in 2007. Should they elect gift splitting for Betty's gifts?

Solution: They should not necessarily elect gift splitting because the main advantage of the election will be that the aggregate annual exclusions will be $48,000 instead of $24,000. An adverse effect will be that Bob, who has exhausted his unified credit (except for the increase from $220,550 in 2001 to $345,800) and is in a higher marginal tax bracket, will be the deemed donor of $476,000 [(0.50 × $1,000,000) − $24,000] of taxable gifts.

COMPUTATION OF THE GIFT TAX LIABILITY

OBJECTIVE 7

Calculate the gift tax liability

EFFECT OF PREVIOUS TAXABLE GIFTS

The gift tax computation involves a cumulative process. All the donor's previous taxable gifts (i.e., those made in 1932 or later years) plus the donor's taxable gifts for the current year affect the marginal tax rate for current taxable gifts. Thus, two donors making the same taxable gifts in the current period may incur different gift tax liabilities because one donor may have made substantially larger taxable gifts in earlier periods than did the other donor. The process outlined below must be used to compute the gross tax levied on the current period's taxable gifts.

---

[43] If the nondonor-spouse has made substantial taxable gifts relative to those made by the donor-spouse, the gift tax liability for the period in question may be lower if the spouses do not elect gift splitting because the nondonor-spouse may have little or no unified credit left and may have reached the highest marginal transfer tax rate.

1. Determine the gift tax liability (at current rates) on the donor's cumulative taxable gifts (taxable gifts of current period plus aggregate taxable gifts of previous periods).
2. Determine the gift tax liability (at current rates) on the donor's cumulative taxable gifts made through the end of the preceding period.
3. Subtract the gift tax determined in Step 2 from that in Step 1. The difference equals the gross gift tax on the current period's taxable gifts.

This calculation process results in taxing the gifts on a progressive basis over the donor's lifetime.

Note that, although the gift tax rates have varied over the years, the current rate schedules are used in the calculation even when the donor made some or all the gifts when different rates were in effect. This process ensures that current taxable gifts are taxed at the appropriate rate, given the donor's earlier gift history.

EXAMPLE C:12-41 ▶ In 1975, Tony made $2 million in taxable gifts. These gifts were the first Tony ever made. The tax imposed under the 1975 rate schedule was $564,900. Tony's next taxable gifts are made in 2007. The taxable amount of these gifts is $400,000. The tax on Tony's 2007 taxable gifts before applying the unified credit is calculated as follows:

Tax at current rates on $2.4 million of cumulative taxable gifts	$960,800
Minus: Tax at current rates on $2 million of prior period taxable gifts	(780,800)
Tax on $400,000 of taxable gifts made in the current period	$180,000 ◀

This cumulative process results in the $400,000 gift in Example C:12-41 being taxed at the maximum 45% gift tax rate, which is applicable to taxable transfers exceeding $1.5 million. If the gift tax computations were not cumulative, the tax on the $400,000 of gifts would be determined by using the lowest marginal rates and would have been only $121,800. Because the tax on taxable transfers made in previous periods is determined by reference to the current rate schedule, Tony's actual 1975 gift tax liability, incurred when the gift tax rates were lower, is not relevant to the determination of his current gift tax. As discussed below, the unified credit will reduce the tax liability.

UNIFIED CREDIT AVAILABLE

Congress enacted a unified credit for both gift and estate tax purposes beginning in 1977. The unified credit reduces the amount of the gross gift tax owed on current period gifts. The amount of the credit has increased over the years (see inside back cover). As a result of the 2001 Act, the credit for gift tax purposes rose to $345,800 in 2002 and will remain at that amount through 2009 even though the credit against estate taxes will increase further through 2009. Donors who have made taxable gifts in the post-1976 period have used some of their credit. The amount of the credit available to those donors for the current year is reduced by the aggregate amount allowable as a credit in all preceding years.

EXAMPLE C:12-42 ▶ Hu made her first taxable gift in 1985. The taxable amount of the 1985 gift was $100,000, which resulted in a gross gift tax of $23,800. Hu claimed $23,800 (of the $121,800 credit then available) on her 1985 return to reduce her net gift tax liability to zero. Hu made her next taxable gift in 1994. The taxable amount of the gift was $400,000. The tax on the $400,000 gift equaled (1) the tax on $500,000 of total gifts (at 1994 gift tax rates) of $155,800 minus (2) the tax on $100,000 of previous gifts (at 1994 gift tax rates) of $23,800, or $132,000. The credit amount for 1994 was $192,800. Hu's gift tax was reduced to zero by a credit of $132,000 because for 1994 she had a credit of $169,000 ($192,800 − $23,800) left. If in 2007 Hu makes additional taxable gifts, $190,000 [$345,800 − ($23,800 + $132,000)] of unified credit will be available to reduce Hu's gift tax liability in 2007. ◀

STOP & THINK

Question: You are reviewing a 2007 gift tax return that a co-worker prepared. The tax return reflects current taxable gifts of $1 million and $500,000 of taxable gifts made in 1992. You note that on the return your colleague (a new staff member) calculated tax of $345,800, claimed a unified credit of $345,800, and thus reported zero gift tax payable. What should you discuss with your colleague?

Solution: You should explain that the 2007 unified credit of $345,800 (which equals the tax on the first $1 million of taxable gifts) is not an annual credit maximum but rather is the credit available during a donor's lifetime. Because in 1992 the donor made $500,000 of taxable gifts, he exhausted $155,800 of his $192,800 unified credit then available. In addition, you should explain the cumulative nature of the gift tax calculations. The tax calculated on the first $1 million of taxable gifts is $345,800. If the colleague claimed a $345,800 unified credit and showed zero tax payable, he did not calculate the tax on the $1 million current taxable gift by performing the cumulative calculations that take into effect the $500,000 of earlier taxable gifts. The tax *before* the credit was calculated incorrectly. The credit available is $190,000 ($345,800 − $155,800), the 2007 credit less the credit already used. Therefore, the donor will owe some gift tax.

COMPREHENSIVE ILLUSTRATION

The following comprehensive illustration demonstrates the computation of one donor's gift tax liability for the situation where the spouses elect gift splitting. It demonstrates the computation of the wife's gift tax liability.

BACKGROUND DATA

Hugh and Wilma Brown are married to each other throughout 2006. Hugh made no taxable gifts in earlier periods. Wilma's previous taxable gifts were $300,000 in 1975 and $200,000 in 1988. In August 2006, Wilma makes the following gratuitous transfers:

- $80,000 in cash to son Billy
- $28,000 in jewelry to daughter Betsy
- $30,000 in medical expense payments to Downtown Infirmary for medical care of grandson Tim
- Remainder interest in vacation cabin to friend Ruth Cain. Wilma (age 60) retains a life estate. The vacation cabin is valued at $100,000.
- $600,000 of stocks to a bank in trust with all of the income payable semiannually to husband Hugh (age 72) for life and remainder payable at Hugh's death to Jeff Bass, Wilma's son by an earlier marriage, or Jeff's estate. Wilma wants to elect the marital deduction.

In 2006, Hugh's only gifts were

- $80,000 of stock to State University
- $600,000 of land to daughter Betsy

Assume the applicable interest rate for valuing life estates and remainders is 10%.

CALCULATION OF TAX LIABILITY

Section 2503(e) exempts the medical expense payments from the gift tax. The Browns need to report the gift made to State University even though the university received Hugh's entire interest in the property, and even though the transfer is nontaxable, because they must file a gift tax return to report gifts to noncharitable donees. The vacation cabin is valued at $100,000, and the remainder interest therein at $21,196 (0.21196 × $100,000) (see Table S, age 60 in Appendix H). The stock is transferred to a QTIP trust, and the marital deduction election treats the entire interest (not just the life estate) as having been given to Hugh Brown.

Table C:12-1 shows the computation of Wilma's gift tax liability for 2006. Recall that the annual exclusion for 2006 was $12,000. These same facts are used for the sample United States Gift Tax Return, Form 709, in Appendix B. The form's format for reporting the gift-splitting aspects differs slightly from the format in the table. On the form, Part 1 of Schedule A splits the gift earlier than Table C:12-1 does.

▼ TABLE C:12-1
Comprehensive Gift Tax Illustration

Wilma's actual 2006 gifts:		
Billy, cash		$ 80,000
Betsy, jewelry		28,000
Ruth, remainder interest in vacation cabin (future interest)		21,196
Husband Hugh and son Jeff, transfer to QTIP trust		600,000
Total gifts made by Wilma		$729,196
Minus: One-half of Wilma's gifts made to third parties that are deemed made by Hugh [0.50 × ($80,000 + $28,000 + $21,196)]		(64,598)
Plus: One-half of Hugh's gifts made to third parties (Betsy and State University) that are deemed made by Wilma [0.50 × ($80,000 + $600,000)]		340,000
Minus: Annual exclusions for gifts of present interests ($12,000 each for gifts made to Billy, Betsy, Hugh, and State University)		(48,000)
Minus: Marital deduction ($600,000 − $12,000 exclusion)		(588,000)
Minus: Charitable contribution deduction ($40,000 deemed gift by Wilma − $12,000 exclusion)		(28,000)
Taxable gifts for current period		$340,598
Tax on cumulative taxable gifts of $840,598[a]		$283,633
Minus: Tax on previous taxable gifts of $500,000 (current rate schedule)		(155,800)
Tax on taxable gifts of $340,598 for the current period		$127,833
Minus: Unified credit:		
Credit for 2006	$345,800	
Minus: Credit allowable for prior periods	(68,000)[b]	(277,800)[c]
Tax payable for 2006		$ –0–

[a]$300,000 (in 1975) + $200,000 (in 1988) + $340,598 (in 2006).
[b]$0 (for 1975) + $68,000 (for 1988). The $68,000, which is smaller than the maximum credit of $192,800 for1988, is the excess of the $155,800 tax on cumulative taxable gifts less the $87,800 tax on the $300,000 previous taxable gifts.
[c]Actually, for 2006 Wilma uses only $127,833 of her remaining credit. In 2007, she will have available a credit of $149,967 [$345,800 − ($127,833 + $68,000)].

BASIS CONSIDERATIONS FOR A LIFETIME GIVING PLAN

OBJECTIVE 8

Understand how basis affects the overall tax consequences

Prospective donors should consider the tax-saving features of making a series of lifetime gifts (discussed in the Tax Planning Considerations section of this chapter). Lifetime giving plans can remove income from the donor's income tax return and transfer it to the donee's income tax return, where it may be taxed at a lower marginal tax rate. A series of gifts may permit property to be transferred to a donee without incurring a gift tax liability and thus enable the donor to eliminate part or all of his or her estate tax liability. These two advantages must be weighed against the unattractive basis rules (discussed below) applicable for such transfers.

PROPERTY RECEIVED BY GIFT

The carryover basis rules apply to property received by gift. Provided the property's FMV on the date of the gift exceeds its adjusted basis, the donor's basis in the property carries over as the donee's basis. In addition, the donee's basis may be increased by some or all of the gift tax paid by the donor. For pre-1977 gifts, all the gift taxes paid by the donor may be added to the donor's adjusted basis. For post-1976 transfers, however, the donee may add only the portion of the gift taxes represented by the following fraction:

$$\frac{\text{Amount of property's appreciation from acquisition date through date of gift}}{\text{FMV of property on the date of the gift minus exclusions and deductions}}$$

In no event, however, can the gift tax adjustment increase the donee's basis above the property's FMV on the date of the gift.[44]

If the gifted property's FMV on the date of the gift is less than the donor's adjusted basis, the basis rules are more complicated. For purposes of determining gain, the donee's basis is the same as the donor's adjusted basis. For purposes of determining loss, the donee's basis is the property's FMV on the date of the gift. If the donee sells the property for an amount between its FMV as of the date of the gift and the donor's adjusted basis, the donee recognizes no gain or loss. The property's basis cannot be increased by any gift taxes paid if the donor's adjusted basis exceeds the property's FMV as of the date of the gift. In general, prospective donors should dispose of property that has declined in value by selling it instead of gifting it.

SELF-STUDY QUESTION

Barkley purchased land in 1955 for $90,000. In 1974, when the FMV of the land was $300,000, he gave the land to his son Tracy and paid gift taxes of $23,000. What is Tracy's basis in the land? What if the gift had been made in 2007? For simplicity, assume the 2007 tax was $23,000.

ANSWER

If the gift were made in 1974, Tracy's basis is $90,000 plus the $23,000 gift tax, or $113,000. Had Barkley made the gift in 2007, Tracy's basis would be $90,000 plus [($210,000/$288,000) × $23,000], or $106,771.

PROPERTY RECEIVED AT DEATH

In general, the basis rules that apply to property received as a result of another's death call for a step up or step down to the property's FMV as of the decedent's date of death. The recipient's basis is the same as the amount at which the property is valued on the estate tax return, which is its FMV on either the decedent's date of death or the alternate valuation date. Generally, the alternate valuation date is six months after the date of death. Although these rules are usually thought of as providing for a step-up in basis, if the property has declined in value as of the transferor's death, the basis is stepped-down to its FMV at the date of death or alternate valuation date.

ADDITIONAL COMMENT

Phil owns investment property worth $350,000 in which his adjusted basis is $500,000. Unless there are reasons why the property should be kept in the family, Phil should sell the property and recognize an income tax loss. If he gifts the property to his child, the loss basis in the child's hands is $350,000 (and the gain basis is $500,000). Thus, if the value does not increase, the income tax loss for the $150,000 decline in market value can never be taken. If Phil dies holding the loss property, his heirs will take the estate tax return value (FMV) as their basis, and the potential income tax loss will not be recognized.

In certain circumstances, no step up in basis occurs for appreciated property transferred at death.[45] This exception applies if both of the following conditions are present:

- The decedent receives the appreciated property as a gift during the one-year period preceding his or her death, and
- The property passes to the donor or to the donor's spouse as a result of the donee-decedent's death.

Before the enactment of this rule, a widely publicized planning technique was the transfer of appreciated property to an ill spouse who, in turn, could will the property back to the donor-spouse, who would receive the property at a stepped-up basis. Interspousal transfers by gift and at death are tax-free because of the unlimited marital deduction for both gift tax and estate tax purposes. Consequently, before the rule change, the property received a step-up in basis at no transfer tax cost.

EXAMPLE C:12-43 ▶ In June 2006, Sarah gave property valued at $700,000 to Tom, her husband. Sarah's adjusted basis in the property was $120,000. Tom dies in March 2007. At this time, the property is worth $740,000. If the property passes back to Sarah under Tom's will upon Tom's death, Sarah's basis will be $120,000. However, if the property passes to someone other than Sarah at Tom's death, its basis will be stepped-up to $740,000. If Tom lives for more than one year after receiving the gift, the basis is stepped-up to its FMV as of Tom's date of death regardless of whether the property passes at Tom's death to Sarah or someone else. If Tom (the donee) sold the property a few months before his death in March 2007, Tom's basis would be the same as Sarah's was, or $120,000. ◀

In conjunction with the repeal of the estate tax in 2010, the step-up in basis rule for property received from a decedent will be replaced with a modified carryover basis rule. Under this rule, a person receiving property from a decedent will have a basis equal to the lesser of (1) the decedent's adjusted basis in the property or (2) the property's fair market value at the date of the decedent's death. A special rule, however, will allow a $1.3 million

[44] See Reg. Sec. 1.1015-5(c) for examples of how to calculate the gift tax that can increase the property's basis.

[45] Sec. 1014(e).

basis increase (and an additional $3 million basis increase for property transferred to a surviving spouse) not to exceed the property's fair market value. For example, assume the decedent's entire estate consists of land the decedent purchased for $2 million. He dies in 2010, when the land is worth $12 million and leaves the land to his surviving spouse. Her basis will be $6.3 million ($2,000,000 + $1,300,000 + $3,000,000), compared with $12 million under current law. Some additional special rules will apply to the basis of property received from a decedent but are not detailed in this text.

BELOW-MARKET LOANS: GIFT AND INCOME TAX CONSEQUENCES

GENERAL RULES

Section 7872 provides rules concerning the gift and income tax consequences of below-market loans. In general, it treats the lender as both making a gift to the borrower and receiving interest income. The borrower is treated as receiving a gift and paying interest expense.

In the case of a demand loan, the lender is treated as having made a gift in each year in which the loan is outstanding. The amount of the gift equals the forgone interest income for the portion of the year the loan is outstanding. The forgone interest income is calculated by referring to the excess of the federal short-term rate of Sec. 1274(d), for the period in question, over the interest rate the lender charged.

For income tax purposes, the forgone interest is treated as being retransferred from the borrower to the lender on the last day of each calendar year in which the loan is outstanding. The amount of the forgone interest is the same as for gift tax purposes and is reported by the lender as income for the year in question. The borrower gets an interest expense deduction for the same amount unless one of the rules limiting the interest deduction applies (e.g., personal interest or investment interest limitations).

EXAMPLE C:12-44 ▶ On July 1, Frank lends $500,000 to Susan, who signs an interest-free demand note. The loan is still outstanding on December 31. Assume that 10% is the applicable annual interest rate. Frank is deemed to have made a gift to Susan on December 31 of $25,000 (0.10 × $500,000 × 6/12). Frank must report $25,000 of interest income. Susan deducts $25,000 of interest expense provided the interest expense deduction rules do not otherwise limit or disallow her deduction. ◀

DE MINIMIS RULES

Under one of the *de minimis* rules, neither the income nor the gift tax rules apply to any gift loan made directly between individuals for any day on which the aggregate loans outstanding between the borrower and the lender are $10,000 or less. The *de minimis* exception does not apply to any loan directly attributable to the purchase or carrying of income-producing assets.

A second *de minimis* exception potentially permits loans of $100,000 or less to receive more favorable income tax (but not gift tax) treatment by limiting the lender's imputed income to the borrower's net investment income (as defined in Sec. 163(d)(3)) for the year. Moreover, if the borrower's net investment income for the year is $1,000 or less, such amount is treated as being zero.

The *de minimis* provisions do not apply to transactions having tax avoidance as a principal purpose and do not apply to any day on which the total outstanding loans between the borrower and the lender exceed $100,000. For purposes of the $100,000 or $10,000 loan limitations, a husband and wife are treated as one person.

EXAMPLE C:12-45 ▶ On August 1, Mike lends $100,000 to Don. No other loans are outstanding between the parties. Avoidance of federal taxes is not a principal purpose of the loan. Don signs an interest-free demand note when 10% is the applicable interest rate. The loan is still outstanding on December 31. Mike is treated as having made a gift to Don on December 31 of $4,167 [$100,000 × 0.10 × 5/12]. Mike need not report this gift on a gift tax return unless his aggregate gifts to Don this year exceed the $12,000 gift tax annual exclusion.

The income tax consequences depend on Don's (the borrower's) net investment income. If Don's net investment income for the year exceeds $4,167, Mike reports $4,167 of imputed interest income under Sec. 7872. Subject to rules that may disallow some or all of the interest expense deduction, Don deducts the $4,167 interest expense imputed under Sec. 7872 . If Don's net investment income is between $1,001 and $4,167, each party reports imputed interest income or expense equal to Don's net investment income. Mike and Don report no interest income or expense under Sec. 7872 if Don's net investment income is $1,000 or less. ◀

TAX PLANNING CONSIDERATIONS

The 1976 Act, which introduced the unification concept, reduced the tax law's bias in favor of lifetime transfers. The 2001 Act, on the other hand, is more favorable toward transfers at death because the unified credit for gift tax purposes does not exceed $345,800 whereas the credit against the estate tax is higher. Nevertheless, lifetime gifts still provide more advantages than disadvantages unless the donor dies in 2010 or the estate tax is repealed permanently. Many factors, including the expected appreciation rate and the donor's expectations about whether permanant repeal of the estate tax will actually occur, affect the decision of whether to make gifts. Thus, the optimal result is not always clear. The pros and cons of lifetime gifts from an estate planning perspective are discussed below.

TAX-SAVING FEATURES OF INTER VIVOS GIFTS

USE OF ANNUAL EXCLUSION. The annual exclusion offers donors the opportunity to start making gifts to several donees per year relatively early in their lifetime and keep substantial amounts of property off the transfer tax rolls. The tax-free amount doubles if a husband and wife use the gift-splitting election.

The law provides no estate tax counterpart to the annual gift tax exclusion. Consequently, a terminally ill person whose will includes bequests of approximately $12,000 to each of several individuals would realize substantial transfer tax savings if gifts—instead of bequests—were made to these individuals.

REMOVAL OF POST-GIFT APPRECIATION FROM TAX BASE. Another important advantage of lifetime gifts is that their value is frozen at their date-of-gift value. That is, any post-gift appreciation escapes the transfer tax rolls. Consequently, transfer tax savings are maximized if the donor gives away the assets that appreciate the most.

REMOVAL OF GIFT TAX AMOUNT FROM TRANSFER TAX BASE. With one exception, gift taxes paid by the donor are removed from the transfer tax base. The lone exception applies to gift taxes paid on gifts the donor makes within three years of dying. Under the gross-up rule (discussed in Chapter C:13), the donor's gross estate includes only gift taxes paid on gifts made within three years of the donor's death.

ADDITIONAL COMMENT

If a terminally ill spouse, Sam, has no property, an election to gift split can effectively use up Sam's unified credit. Another method of using Sam's unified credit is to give Sam property in trust with the income payable to Sam for life, and the remainder subject to a general power of appointment in Sam. If the general power of appointment is not exercised during Sam's lifetime (or by will on Sam's death), the remainder must pass to specified beneficiaries other than the donor. If Sam exercises the general power while alive, he will be subject to gift tax. Otherwise, the trust will be in Sam's gross estate.

INCOME SHIFTING. Originally, one of the most favorable consequences of lifetime gifts was income shifting, but the compression of the income tax rate schedules beginning in 1987 has lessened these benefits. In addition, the 2003 Act, which lowered the tax rate on dividends, further reduced income shifting benefits from giving stock. The income produced by the gifted property is taxed to the donee, whose marginal income tax rate may be lower than the donor's. If income tax savings do arise, they accrue each year during the post-gift period. Thus, the income tax savings can be quite sizable over a span of several years. This tax saving aspect of gifts is a major reason Congress retained the gift tax in the 2001 Act.

GIFT IN CONTEMPLATION OF DONEE-SPOUSE'S DEATH. At times, a terminally ill spouse may have very few assets. If such a spouse died, a sizable portion of his or her unified credit would be wasted because the decedent's estate would be well below the amount of the exemption equivalent provided by the unified credit. If the healthier spouse is relatively wealthy, he or she could make a gift to the ill spouse to create an estate in an amount equal to the estate tax exemption equivalent. Because of the unlimited marital deduction, the gift would be tax-free. Upon the death of the donee-spouse, no estate tax would be payable because the estate tax liability would not exceed the unified credit. The donee-spouse should not transfer his or her property back to the donor-spouse at death. Otherwise, the donee-spouse's unified credit would be wasted, and the original tax planning would be negated. Moreover, the returned property would be included in the surviving spouse's estate.

A gift of appreciated property in contemplation of the donee-spouse's death provides an additional advantage. If the property does not pass back to the donor-spouse, its basis is increased to its value on the donee's date of death. In the event the property is willed to the donor-spouse, a step-up in basis still occurs if the date of the gift precedes the donee-spouse's date of death by more than one year.

LESSENING STATE TRANSFER TAX COSTS. Currently about 25 states levy an estate or inheritance tax, but only four states impose a gift tax.[46] State death taxes are deductible in calculating the taxable estate, but they still add to death-associated costs. Therefore, in some states, the tax cost of lifetime transfers is lower than that for transfers at death.

INCOME TAX SAVINGS FROM CHARITABLE GIFTS. Some individuals desire to donate a portion of their property to charitable organizations. Assuming the donation is eligible for a charitable contribution deduction, the transfer tax implications are the same—no taxable transfer—irrespective of whether the transfer occurs *inter vivos* or at death. From an income tax standpoint, however, a lifetime transfer is preferable because only lifetime transfers produce an income tax deduction for charitable contributions.

NEGATIVE ASPECTS OF GIFTS

LOSS OF STEP-UP IN BASIS. Taxpayers deliberating about whether to make gifts or which property to give should keep in mind that the donee receives no step-up in basis for property acquired by gift. From a practical standpoint, sacrifice of the step-up in basis is insignificant if the donee does not plan to sell the property or if the property is not subject to an allowance for depreciation. Also, keep in mind that gain on the sale is likely to be taxed at the preferential long-term capital gain rate (e.g., 15%), and property in the estate may be taxed at rate close to 50%.

PREPAYMENT OF ESTATE TAX. A donor who makes taxable gifts that exceed the exemption equivalent (applicable exclusion amount) must pay a gift tax. Upon the donor's death, the taxable gift is included in his or her estate tax base as an adjusted taxable gift. Because the gift tax paid during the donor's lifetime reduces the donor's estate tax liability, in a sense, the donor's payment of the gift tax results in prepayment of a portion of the estate tax.

COMPLIANCE AND PROCEDURAL CONSIDERATIONS

OBJECTIVE 9

Recognize the filing requirements for gift tax returns

FILING REQUIREMENTS

Section 6019 specifies the circumstances in which a donor should file a gift tax return. In general, the donor will file Form 709 (United States Gift Tax Return). A completed Form 709 appears in Appendix B. The facts used in the preparation of the completed Form 709 are the same as the facts in the comprehensive illustration, which uses a format for the gift-splitting aspects that differs slightly from that used in the form.

[46] The four states that impose a gift tax are Connecticut, Louisiana, North Carolina, and Tennessee. Connecticut adopted legislation phasing out its gift tax on gifts of $1 million or less during the period 2001–2006. In 2002, legislation delayed the phase out by two additional years.

As is the case for income tax returns, a return can be necessary even though the taxable amount and the tax payable are both zero. A donor must file a gift tax return for any calendar year in which the donor makes gifts other than

- Gifts to the spouse that qualify for the marital deduction
- Gifts that are fully shielded from taxation because they fall within the annual exclusion amount or are exempted from classification as a gift under the exception for educational or medical expenses
- Gifts to charitable organizations if the gift is deductible and the organization receives the donor's entire interest in the property

However, if the gift to the spouse is of qualified terminable interest property (QTIP), the donor must report the gift on the gift tax return. The marital deduction is not available for these transfers unless the donor makes the necessary election, which is done by claiming a marital deduction on the gift tax return.

United States persons who receive aggregate foreign gifts or bequests exceeding $13,258 (in 2007) must report such amounts as prescribed in Treasury Regulations.[47]

DUE DATE

All gift tax returns must be filed on a calendar-year basis. Under the general rule, gift tax returns are due no later than April 15 following the close of the year of the gift.[48] An extension of time granted for filing an individual income tax return is deemed to automatically extend the filing date for the individual's gift tax return for that year. The automatic extension period is until October 15.

If the donor dies early in the year in which a gift is made, the due date for the donor's final gift tax return may be earlier than April 15. Because information concerning the decedent's taxable gifts is necessary to complete the estate tax return, the gift tax return for the year of death is due no later than the due date (including extensions) for the donor's estate tax return.[49] Estate tax returns are due nine months after the date of death.

Receipt of an extension for filing a gift tax return does not postpone the due date for payment of the tax. Interest is imposed on any gift tax not paid by April 15. Donors should submit Form 8892 if they anticipate owing gift tax and/or if they need an extension for only their gift tax return. Unlike with the income tax, a donor does not have to make estimated payments of gift taxes.

GIFT-SPLITTING ELECTION

For taxable gifts to be computed under the gift-splitting technique, both spouses must indicate their consent to gift splitting in one of the following ways:[50]

- Each spouse signifies his or her consent on the other spouse's gift tax return.
- Each spouse signifies his or her consent on his or her own gift tax return.
- Both spouses signify their consent on one of the gift tax returns.

Treasury Regulations state that the first approach listed above is the preferred manner for designating consent.

KEY POINT

Similarly to a husband and wife filing a joint income tax return, if gift splitting is elected, the husband and wife have joint and several liability for the entire gift tax liability regardless of who actually made the gifts.

LIABILITY FOR TAX

The donor is responsible for paying the gift tax,[51] and if the spouses consent to gift splitting, the entire gift tax liability is a joint and several liability of the spouses.[52] Thus, if spouses do not pay the tax voluntarily, the IRS may attempt to collect whatever amount it deems appropriate from either spouse, irrespective of the size of the gift that spouse actually made.

In the rare event that the donor does not pay the gift tax, the donee becomes personally liable for the gift tax.[53] However, a donee's liability is limited to the value of the gift.

---

[47] Sec. 6039F.

[48] Sec. 6075(b).

[49] The decedent's post-1976 taxable gifts affect the size of his or her estate tax base, as discussed in the next chapter.

[50] Reg. Sec. 25.2513-2(a)(1).

[51] Sec. 2502(c).

[52] Sec. 2513(d).

[53] Reg. Sec. 301.6324-1.

DETERMINATION OF VALUE

One of the most difficult problems encountered by donors and their tax advisors is determining the gifted property's FMV. This task is especially difficult if the gifted property is stock in a closely held business, an oil and gas property, or land in an area where few sales occur.

If a transaction involves a sale, the IRS can argue that the asset's value exceeds its sales price and, thus, there is a gift to the extent of the bargain element. This problem is especially common with sales to family members. If the donor gives or sells to a family member property whose value is not readily determinable, the donor should obtain an appraisal of the property before filing the gift tax return.

ETHICAL POINT

A CPA who advises a client about the tax consequences of making a gift also has a responsibility to make sure the property is correctly valued. Otherwise, if the valuation claimed is too low, the IRS can levy a penalty on the donor. For example, a gift of noncash property (e.g., land) may require that an appraisal be obtained. Failure to obtain an appraisal, or failure to investigate an appraisal that seems too low, may result in an undervaluation of the gift property, which may lead to the IRS imposing additional gift taxes, interest, and penalties.

PENALTY FOR UNDERVALUATION. Section 6662 imposes a penalty, at one of two rates, on underpayments of gift or estate taxes resulting from too low a valuation of property. The amount on which the penalty is imposed is the underpayment of the transfer tax attributable to the valuation understatement.

No penalty applies if the valuation shown on the return exceeds 65% of the amount determined during an audit or court trial to be the correct value. For returns filed after August 17, 2006, if the value reported on the return is 65% or less of the correct value, the penalty rate is as shown below.

Ratio of Value per Return to Correct Value	*Penalty Rate*
More than 40% but 65% or less	20%
40% or less	40%

Section 6662(g)(2) exempts a taxpayer from the penalty if the underpayment is less than $5,000.

EXAMPLE C:12-46 ▶ Assume Donna already has used her available unified credit. She gives land to her son and reports its value at $400,000 on her gift tax return. The IRS audits Donna's return, and she agrees that $900,000 was the correct value of the property. Because the value stated on the return is 44.44% [($400,000 ÷ $900,000) × 100] of the correct value, the IRS levies a 20% penalty on the underpayment attributable to the valuation understatement. If Donna is in the 45% marginal gift tax bracket, the gift tax underpayment is $225,000 [0.45 × ($900,000 − $400,000)]. Thus, the penalty is $45,000 (0.20 × $225,000) unless Donna can demonstrate reasonable cause and good faith for the valuation. ◀

ADDITIONAL COMMENT

Even if a taxpayer questions whether a taxable gift has been made, it is a good idea to file a gift tax return and at least disclose the transaction. The filing of the return with adequate disclosure of the transaction causes the statute of limitations to begin and limits the time during which the IRS may question the valuation and the amount of the gift, if any.

STATUTE OF LIMITATIONS

In general, the statute of limitations for gift tax purposes is three years after the later of the date the return was filed or the return's due date.[54] The statute of limitations increases from three to six years if the donor omits from the gift tax return gifts whose total value exceeds 25% of the gifts reported on the return. If the donor files no return because, for example, he or she is unaware that he or she made any gifts, the IRS may assess the tax at any time.

The cumulative nature of the gift tax causes the taxable gifts of earlier years to affect the gift tax owed in subsequent periods. Once the statute of limitations expired for pre-1997 gifts, the IRS could not argue that taxable gifts of prior periods were undervalued (and thus that the current period's gifts should be taxed at a higher rate than that used by the donor) as long as the donor paid gift tax on the earlier gifts. However, for gifts reported after August 5, 1997, this rule applies even if the donor paid no gift tax.[55]

For gifts made in 1997 and later, it is important to adequately disclose potential gift transactions for which the gift status is unclear. The statute of limitations will not expire on a transaction unless the donor makes adequate disclosure.[56]

EXAMPLE C:12-47 ▶ Andy filed a gift tax return for 2006, reporting taxable gifts of $1.85 million made in October 2006. Andy paid gift tax. If Andy adequately disclosed all potential gifts, once the statute of limitations expires for 2006, the IRS cannot contend that, for purposes of calculating the tax on later taxable gifts, the 2006 taxable gifts exceeded $1.85 million. ◀

---

[54] Sec. 6501.
[55] Sec. 2504(c).
[56] Sec. 6501(c)(9).

PROBLEM MATERIALS

DISCUSSION QUESTIONS

C:12-1 Describe two ways in which the transfer tax (estate and gift tax) system is a unified system.

C:12-2 What was the Congressional purpose for enacting the gift-splitting provisions?

C:12-3 Determine whether the following statement is true or false: Every donor who makes a taxable gift incurs a gift tax liability. Explain your answer.

C:12-4 Under what circumstances must the amount of the unified credit usually available be reduced (by a maximum amount of $6,000) even though the donor has never claimed any unified credit?

C:12-5 Does the exemption from the gift tax for direct payment of tuition apply for payments of non-relatives' tuition? Explain.

C:12-6 Steve is considering the following actions. Explain to him which actions will constitute gifts for gift tax purposes.

a. Transferring all his ownership rights in a life insurance policy to another person
b. Depositing funds into a joint bank account in the names of Steve and another party (who deposits nothing)
c. Paying half the consideration for land and having it titled in the names of Steve and his son as joint tenants with right of survivorship if the son furnishes the other half of the consideration
d. Paying a hospital for the medical expenses of a neighbor
e. Making a $1 million demand loan to an adult child and charging no interest

C:12-7 Dick wants to transfer property with a $600,000 FMV to an irrevocable trust with a bank as the trustee. Dick will name his distant cousin Earl to receive all of the trust income annually for the next eight years. Then the property will revert to Dick. In the last few years, the income return (yield) on the property has been 9%. Assume this yield is not likely to decline and that the applicable rate from the actuarial tables is 7%.

a. What will be the amount of Dick's gift to Earl?
b. Would you recommend that Dick transfer the property yielding 9% to this type of a trust? Explain. If not, what type of property would you recommend that Dick transfer to the trust?

C:12-8 Antonio would like to make a gift of a life insurance policy. Explain to him what action he must take to make a completed gift.

C:12-9 In what circumstances might a potential donor be interested in making a net gift? Explain the potential income tax problem with making a net gift.

C:12-10 What is the purpose of the gift tax annual exclusion?

C:12-11 In what circumstances do gifts fail to qualify for the annual exclusion?

C:12-12 Compare and contrast a Sec. 2503(c) trust and a *Crummey* trust.

C:12-13 From a nontax standpoint, would a parent probably prefer to make a transfer to a minor child by using a Sec. 2503(c) trust or a *Crummey* trust?

C:12-14 Explain the requirements for classifying a transaction as a transfer of a qualified terminable interest property (QTIP).

C:12-15 Why do some donors consider the qualified terminable interest property (QTIP) transfer an especially attractive arrangement for making gifts to their spouses?

C:12-16 A client is under the impression that a donor cannot incur a gift tax liability if he or she makes gifts to only U.S. charitable organizations. What should you say to the client?

C:12-17 Describe to a married couple three advantages of making the gift-splitting election.

C:12-18 Both Damien and Latoya make taxable gifts of $250,000 in the current year. Will their current year gift tax liabilities necessarily be identical? Explain.

C:12-19 A donor made his first taxable gift in 1979 and his second taxable gift in the current year. In the intervening years, the highest gift tax rates declined. In calculating the tax on taxable gifts of previous periods, which rate schedule is used: the one for the year in which the donor made the earlier gift or the one for the current period?

C:12-20 A mother is trying to decide which of the two assets listed below to give to her adult daughter.

Asset	*FMV*	*Adjusted Basis*	*Annual Net Income from the Asset*
Apartment	$2,400,000	$1,500,000	$(10,000)
Bonds	2,400,000	2,300,000	80,000

The mother's marginal income tax rate exceeds her daughter's. Describe the pros and cons of giving each of the two properties.

C:12-21 Phil and Marcy have been married for a number of years. Marcy is very wealthy, but Phil is not. In fact, Phil has only $10,000 of property. Phil is very ill, and his doctor believes that he probably will die within the next few months. Make one (or more) tax planning suggestions for the couple.

C:12-22 Assume the same facts as in Problem C:12-21 and that Marcy has decided to give Phil property valued at $1.99 million. Phil probably will leave the gifted property to their children under his will.

a. What are the gift tax consequences to Marcy and the estate tax consequences to Phil of the transfer (assuming the property does not appreciate before his death)?

b. Assume Marcy is trying to decide whether to give Phil stock with an adjusted basis of $285,000 or land with an adjusted basis of $800,000. Each asset is valued at $1.99 million. Which asset would you recommend she give and why?

C:12-23 Carlos has heard about the unified transfer tax system and does not understand how making gifts can be beneficial. Explain to Carlos how a lifetime gift fixes (freezes) the gifted property's value for transfer tax purposes.

C:12-24 Describe for a client five advantages and two disadvantages of disposing of property by gift instead of at death.

C:12-25 In general, what is the due date for the gift tax return? What are two exceptions?

C:12-26 In 1999, Frank made an installment sale of real property to Stu, his son, for $1 million. Frank did not file a gift tax return. In 2008, the IRS audits Frank's 2006 income tax return and discovers the sale. The IRS then contends that the property Frank sold was worth $2.5 million in 1999 and that Frank made a $1.5 million gift to Stu in 1999.

a. Can the IRS collect the gift tax on the 1999 gift? If not, will the 1999 gift affect the tax due on later gifts that Frank makes?

b. Will Frank potentially incur any penalty? Explain.

ISSUE IDENTIFICATION QUESTIONS

C:12-27 Kwambe is thinking of making a substantial gift of stock to his fiancée, Maya. The wedding is scheduled for October 1 of the current year. Kwambe already has exhausted his unified credit. He also is considering giving $24,000 cash this year to each of his three children by a previous marriage. What tax issues should Kwambe consider with respect to the gifts he plans to make to Maya and his three children?

C:12-28 Janet is considering transferring assets valued at $4 million to an irrevocable trust (yet to be created) for the benefit of her son, Gordon, age 15, with Farmers Bank as trustee. Her attorney has drafted a trust agreement that provides that Gordon is to receive income in the trustee's discretion for the next 20 years and that at age 35 the trust assets will be distributed equally between Gordon and his sister Joanna. Janet anticipates that her husband will consent to gift splitting. What tax issues should Janet and her husband consider with respect to the trust?

C:12-29 Melvin funds an irrevocable trust with Holcomb Bank as trustee and reserves the right to receive the income for seven years. He provides that at the end of the seventh year the trust assets will pass outright to his adult daughter, Pamela, or to Pamela's estate should Pamela not be alive. Melvin transfers assets valued at $1 million to the trust; the assets at present are producing income of about 4.5% per year. Assume that the Sec. 7520 rate per the actuarial tables for the month of the transfer is 8%. What tax issues should Melvin consider regarding the trust?

PROBLEMS

C:12-30 *Calculation of Gift Tax.* In 2007, Sondra makes taxable gifts aggregating $2 million. Her only other taxable gifts amount to $700,000, all of which she made in 1997.

a. What is Sondra's 2007 gift tax liability?

b. What is her 2007 gift tax liability under the assumption that she made the $700,000 of taxable gifts in 1974 instead of 1997?

C:12-31 *Calculation of Gift Tax.* Amir made taxable gifts as follows: $800,000 in 1975, $1.2 million in 1999, and $600,000 in 2007. What is Amir's gift tax liability for 2007?

C:12-32 *Determination of Taxable Gifts.* In the current year, Beth, who is single, sells stock valued at $40,000 to Linda for $18,000. Later that year, Beth gives Linda $12,000 in cash.

a. What is the amount of Beth's taxable gifts?

b. How would your answer to Part a change if Beth instead gave the cash to Patrick?

C:12-33 *Determination of Taxable Gifts.* In the current year, Clay gives $32,000 cash to each of his eight grandchildren. His wife makes no gifts during the current year.

a. What are Clay's taxable gifts, assuming Clay and his wife do *not* elect gift splitting?

b. How would your answer to Part a change if the couple elects gift splitting?

C:12-34 *Determination of Taxable Gifts.* In the current year, David gives $180,000 of land to David, Jr. In the current year, David's wife gives $200,000 of land to George and $44,000 cash to David, Jr. Assume the couple elects gift splitting for the current year.

a. What are the couple's taxable gifts?
b. How would your answer to Part a change if David's wife gave the $44,000 of cash to Ollie (instead of to David, Jr.)?

C:12-35 *Recognition of Transactions Treated as Gifts.* In the current year, Emily, a widow, engages in the following transactions. Determine the amount of the completed gift, if any, arising from each of the following occurrences.

a. Emily names Lauren the beneficiary of a $100,000 life insurance policy on Emily's life. The beneficiary designation is not irrevocable.
b. Emily deposits $50,000 cash into a checking account in the joint names of herself and Matt, who deposits nothing to the account. Later that year, Matt withdraws $15,000 from the account.
c. Emily pays $22,000 of nephew Noah's medical expenses directly to County Hospital.
d. Emily transfers the title to land valued at $60,000 to Olive.

C:12-36 *Calculation of Gift Tax.* Refer to the facts of Problem C:12-35 and assume the current year is 2007. Emily's prior gifts are as follows:

Year	*Amount of Taxable Gifts*
1974	$ 500,000
1998	1,000,000

What is the gift tax liability with respect to Emily's 2007 gifts?

C:12-37 *Recognition of Transactions Treated as Gifts.* In the current year, Marge (age 67) engages in the following transactions. Determine the amount of the completed gift, if any, arising from each of the following events. Assume 10% is the applicable interest rate.

a. Marge transfers $100,000 of property in trust and irrevocably names herself to receive $8,000 per year for life and daughter Joy (age 37) to receive the remainder.
b. Marge pays her grandson's $15,000 tuition to State University.
c. Marge gives the same grandson stock valued at $72,000.
d. Marge deposits $150,000 into a revocable trust. Later in the year, the bank trustee distributes $18,000 of income to the named beneficiary, Gail.

C:12-38 *Recognition of Transactions Treated as Gifts.* Determine the amount of the completed gift, if any, arising from each of the following occurrences.

a. A parent sells real estate valued at $1.8 million to an adult child, who pays $1 million in consideration.
b. A furniture store holds a clearance sale and sells a customer a $5,000 living room suite for $1,500.
c. During the year, a father purchases food and clothing costing $8,500 for his minor child.
d. A citizen contributes $1,500 cash to a political organization.
e. Zeke lends $600,000 interest free to Henry, who signs a demand note on August 1. Assume 10% is the applicable interest rate and the note remains unpaid at year-end.

C:12-39 *Determination of Unified Credit.* In March 1976, Sue made a taxable gift of $200,000. In arriving at the amount of her taxable gift, Sue elected to deduct the $30,000 specific exemption formerly available. In 2007, Sue makes her next gift; the taxable amount is $1.5 million.

a. What unified credit can Sue claim on her 2007 return?
b. What unified credit can Sue claim on her 2007 return if she made the 1976 gift in December instead of March?

C:12-40 *Valuation of Gifts.* On September 1 of the current year, Mario irrevocably transfers a $100,000 whole life insurance policy on his life to Mario, Jr. as owner. On September 1, the policy's interpolated terminal reserve is $30,000. Mario paid the most recent annual premium ($1,800) on June 1. What is the amount of the gift Mario made in the current year?

C:12-41 *Determination of Gift Tax Deductions.* In June, Tina makes cash gifts of $700,000 to her husband and $100,000 to the City Art Museum. What are the amounts of the deductions available for these gifts when calculating Tina's income tax and gift tax liabilities if she does not elect gift splitting?

C:12-42 ***Determination of Annual Exclusion.*** For each of the following transactions that happen in the current year, indicate the amount of the annual exclusion available. Explain your answer.

a. Tracy creates a trust in the amount of $300,000 for the benefit of her eight-year-old daughter, May. She names a bank as trustee. Before May reaches age 21, the trustee in its discretion is to pay income or corpus (trust assets) to May or for her benefit. When May reaches age 21, she will receive the unexpended portion of the trust income and corpus. If May dies before reaching age 21, the unexpended income and corpus will be paid to her estate or a party (or parties) she appoints under a general power of appointment.

b. Assume the same facts as in Part a except May is age 28 when Tracy creates the trust and the trust agreement contains age 41 wherever age 21 appears in Part a.

c. Assume the same facts as in Part b except the trust instrument allows May to demand a distribution by December 31 of each year equal to the lesser of the amount of the annual exclusion for federal gift tax purposes or the amount transferred to the trust that year.

C:12-43 ***Determination of Annual Exclusion.*** During 2007, Will gives $40,000 cash to Will, Jr. and a remainder interest in a few acres of land to his friend Suzy. The remainder interest is valued at $32,000. Will and his wife, Helen, elect gift splitting, and during the current year Helen gives Joyce $8,000 of stock. What is the total amount of the annual gift tax exclusions available to Will and Helen?

C:12-44 ***Availability of Annual Exclusion.*** Bonnie, a widow, irrevocably transfers $1 million of property to a trust with a bank named as trustee. For as long as Bonnie's daughter Carol is alive, Carol is to receive all the trust income annually. Upon Carol's death, the property is to be distributed to Carol's children. Carol is age 32 and currently has three children. How many gift tax exclusions does Bonnie receive for the transfer?

C:12-45 ***Calculation of Gift Tax.*** Before last year, neither Hugo nor Wanda, his wife, made any taxable gifts. In 2006, Hugo gave $12,000 cash to each of his 30 nieces, nephews, and grandchildren. This year (2007), Wanda gives $32,000 of stock to each of the same people. What is the *minimum* legal gift tax liability (*before* reduction for the unified credit) for each spouse for each year?

C:12-46 ***Calculation of Marital Deduction.*** Hugh makes the gifts listed below to Winnie, his wife, age 37. What is the amount of the marital deduction, if any, attributable to each?

a. Hugh transfers $500,000 to a trust with a bank named as trustee. All the income must be paid to Winnie monthly for life. At Winnie's death, the property passes to Hugh's sisters or their estates.

b. Hugh transfers $300,000 to a trust with a bank named as trustee. Income is payable at the trustee's discretion to Winnie annually until the earlier of her death or her remarriage. When payments to Winnie cease, the trustee must distribute the property to Hugh's children by a previous marriage or to their estates.

C:12-47 ***Calculation of the Marital Deduction.*** In the current year, Louise makes the transfers described below to Lance, her husband, age 47. Assume 7% is the applicable interest rate. What is the amount of her marital deduction, if any, attributable to each transfer?

a. In June, she gives him land valued at $45,000.

b. In October, she gives him a 12-year income interest in a trust with a bank named as trustee. She names their daughter to receive the remainder interest. She funds the irrevocable trust with $400,000 in assets.

C:12-48 ***Charitable Contribution Deduction.*** Tien (age 67) transfers a remainder interest in a vacation cabin (with a total value of $100,000) to a charitable organization and retains a life estate in the cabin for herself.

a. What is the amount of the gift tax charitable contribution deduction, if any, attributable to this transfer? Assume that 10% is the applicable interest rate.

b. How will your answer to Part a change if Tien instead gives a remainder interest in a valuable oil painting (worth $100,000) to the organization?

C:12-49 ***Calculation of Gift Tax.*** In 2007, Homer and his wife, Wilma (residents of a non–community property state) make the gifts listed below. Homer's previous taxable gifts consist of $100,000 made in 1975 and $1.4 million made in 1996. Wilma has made no previous taxable gifts.

Wilma's current year gifts were	
to Art	$400,000
to Bart	6,000
Homer's current year gifts were	
to Linda	$600,000
to a charitable organization	100,000
to Norma (future interest)	200,000

a. What are the gift tax liabilities of Homer and Wilma for 2007 if they elect gift splitting and everyone except Norma receives a present interest?
b. How would the gift tax liabilities for each spouse in Part a change if they do not elect gift splitting?

C:12-50 *Calculation of Gift Tax.* In 2007, Henry and his wife, Wendy, made the gifts shown below. All gifts are of present interests. What is Wendy's gift tax payable for 2007 if the couple elects gift splitting and Wendy's previous taxable gifts (made in 1995) total $1 million?

Wendy's current gifts were	
to Janet	$80,000
to Cindy	70,000
to Henry	50,000
Henry's current gifts were	
to Janet	30,000

C:12-51 *Basis Rules.* In June 2006, Karen transfers property with a $75,000 FMV and a $20,000 adjusted basis to Hal, her husband. Hal dies in March 2007; the property has appreciated to $85,000 in value by then.
a. What is the amount of Karen's taxable gift in 2006?
b. What gain would Hal recognize if he sells the property for $95,000 in July 2006?
c. If Hal wills the property to Dot, his daughter, what basis would Dot have?
d. How would your answer to Part c change if Hal instead willed the property to Karen?
e. How would your answer to Part d change if Hal did not die until August 2007?

C:12-52 *Basis Rules.* Siu is considering giving away stock in Ace Corporation or Gold Corporation. Each has a current FMV of $500,000, and each has the same estimated future appreciation rate. Siu's basis in the Ace stock is $100,000, and her basis in the Gold stock is $450,000. Which stock would you suggest that she give away and why, or does it make any difference?

C:12-53 *Below-Market Loans.* On October 1, Sam lends Tom $10 million. Tom signs an interest-free demand note. The loan is still outstanding on December 31. Explain the income tax and gift tax consequences of the loan to both Sam and Tom. Assume that the federal short-term rate is 9%.

COMPREHENSIVE PROBLEM

C:12-54 In 2007, Ginger Graham, age 46 and wife of Greg Graham, engaged in the transactions described below. Determine Ginger's gift tax liability for 2007 if she and Greg elect gift splitting and Greg gave their son Stevie stock valued at $80,000 during 2007. Ginger's grandmother Mamie died November 12, 2006, and Mamie's will bequeathed $250,000 to Ginger. On March 4, 2007, Ginger irrevocably disclaimed the $250,000 in writing, and, as a result, the property passed instead to Ginger's sister Gertie. In 2007, Ginger gave $100,000 cash to her alma mater, State University. In 1996, Ginger had given ownership of a life insurance policy on her own life to her daughter, Denise, and in 2007 Ginger paid the $22,000 annual premium on the policy. In 2006, Ginger deposited $45,000 into a bank account in the name of herself and son Stevie, joint tenants with rights of survivorship. Stevie deposited nothing. Neither party made a withdrawal until 2007, when Stevie withdrew $30,000. In 2007, Ginger created a trust with County Bank as trustee and transferred $300,000 of stock to the irrevocable trust. She named her husband Greg (age 47) to receive all the trust income semi-annually for life and daughter Drucilla to receive the remainder. In 2007, she gave a remainder interest in her beach cottage to the American Red Cross and kept the right to use the cottage rent free for the rest of her life. The fair market value of the cottage was $70,000.

Other information: Ginger's earlier *taxable* gifts are $175,000, all made in 1996. Ginger will make whatever elections are necessary to minimize her current gift tax liability. Assume the Sec. 7520 interest rate is 8%.

TAX STRATEGY PROBLEM

C:12-55 Ilene Ishi is planning to fund an irrevocable charitable remainder annuity trust with $100,000 of cash. She will designate her sister, age 60, to receive an annuity of $8,000 per year for 15 years and State University to receive the remainder at the end of the fifteenth year. The valuation of the charitable portion of the transfer, according to Reg. Sec. 25.2522(c)-3(d)(2)(i), is to be determined under Reg. Sec. 1.664-2(c), an income tax regulation. Regulation Sec. 1.664-2(c) provides that, in valuing the remainder interest, the donor may elect to use the Sec. 7520 interest rate for either of the two months preceding the month of the transfer as an alternative to using the rate for the actual month of transfer. Otherwise, the value will be determined by using the Sec. 7520 rate for the month of the transfer. Assume that in the month of the transfer the interest rate was 7% but that in the two preceding months the rate was 7.2%. Should the donor elect to calculate the value of the remainder interest by using the interest rate for one of the two preceding months? Explain your answer. Note: The 7.2% rate does not appear in the excerpts from the actuarial tables, but the absence of such rate from the tables will not preclude you from answering this question.

TAX FORM/RETURN PREPARATION PROBLEMS

C:12-56 Dave and Sara Moore, of 10105 Lake View Lane, Chicago, Illinois 60108, engage in the transactions described below in August 2006. Use this information to prepare a gift tax return (Form 709) for Dave. He and Sara want to use gift splitting. Both are U.S. citizens. His Social Security number is 477-11-1333 and hers is 272-92-4403. For simplicity, assume the rate for the actuarial tables used is 10%. Dave's transactions are summarized below.

	Amount
1. Tuition paid to State University for son-in-law, Jim Smith.	$ 22,000
2. Room and board paid to State University for Jim Smith.	13,000
3. Sports car purchased for Jim Smith.	34,000
4. Premium paid on life insurance policy on Dave's life. Dave transferred the policy to his sister, Amy Lane, as owner in 1996.	14,000
5. Land given to daughter, Glenda Muñoz.	90,000
6. Remainder interest in personal residence given to State University. Dave (age 70) retains a life estate. The total value of the residence is $200,000.	
7. Stocks transferred to an irrevocable trust with First National Bank as trustee. The trust income is payable to Sara (age 60) semiannually for life. The remainder is payable at Sara's death to daughter, Amanda Webb, or her estate.	500,000

Sara gave $68,000 of cash to Dave's sister, Amy Lane. Dave's gift history includes a $600,000 taxable gift made in 1975 and a $400,000 taxable gift made in 1994.

C:12-57 Alice Arnold, Social Security number 572-13-4409, a widow, engages in the transactions listed below in 2006. Use this information to prepare a gift tax return (Form 709) for Alice.

	Amount
1. Stock given to daughter, Brenda Bell.	$700,000
2. Cash transferred to son, Al Arnold.	600,000
3. $500,000 interest-free demand loan made to Brenda Bell on July 1. The loan is still outstanding on December 31.	
4. Land given to niece, Lou Lane	100,000

Assume 8% is the applicable interest rate. Alice has made only one previous taxable gift: $300,000 (taxable amount) in 2000. Alice, a U.S. citizen, resides at 105 Peak Rd., Denver, Colorado 80309.

CASE STUDY PROBLEMS

C:12-58 Your client, Karen Kross, recently married Larry Kross. Karen is age 72, quite wealthy, and in reasonably good health. To date, she has not made any taxable gifts, but Larry made taxable gifts totaling $700,000 in 1998. Karen is considering giving each of her five college-age grandchildren approximately $24,000 of cash for them to use to pay their college expenses of tuition and room and board for the year. In addition, she is considering giving her three younger grandchildren $3,000 each to use for orthodontic bills. Karen wants to give her daughter property valued at $400,000. She is trying to choose between giving her daughter cash or stock with a basis of $125,000. She would like to give her son $400,000 of property also, but prefers to tie the property up in a discretionary trust with a bank as trustee for the son for at least 15 years. An agricultural museum approached Karen about making a contribution to it and, as a result, she is contemplating deeding her family farm to the museum but retaining a life estate in the farm.

Required: Prepare a memorandum to the tax partner of your firm that discusses the transfer tax and income tax consequences of the proposed transactions described above. Also, make any recommendations that you deem appropriate.

C:12-59 Morris Jory, a long-time tax client of the firm you work for, has made substantial gifts during his lifetime. Mr. Jory transferred Jory Corporation stock to 14 donees in December 2006. Each donee received shares valued at $12,000. Two of the donees were Mr. Jory's adult children, Amanda and Peter. The remaining 12 donees were employees of Jory Corporation who are not related to Mr. Jory. Mr. Jory, a widower, advised the employees that within two weeks of receiving the stock certificates they must endorse such certificates over to Amanda and Peter. Six of the donees were instructed to endorse their certificates to Amanda and six to Peter. During 2006, Mr. Jory also gave $35,000 cash to his favorite grandchild, Robin. Your firm has been engaged to prepare Mr. Jory's 2006 gift tax return. In January 2007, you meet with Mr. Jory, who insists that his 2006 taxable gifts will be only $23,000 ($35,000 to Robin − $12,000 annual exclusion). After your meeting with Mr. Jory, you are uncertain about his position regarding the amount of his 2006 gifts and have scheduled a meeting with your firm's senior tax partner, who has advised Mr. Jory for more than 20 years. In preparation for the meeting, prepare a summary of the tax and ethical considerations (with supporting authority where possible) regarding whether you should prepare a gift tax return that reports the taxable gifts in accordance with Mr. Jory's wishes.

TAX RESEARCH PROBLEMS

C:12-60 Karl Kremble funded an irrevocable trust in March 2007 with oil and gas property valued at $400,000. Assume the Sec. 7520 interest rate for the actuarial tables was 7% on the date of funding. Karl named a bank trustee and provided that his distant cousin, Louise Lane, will receive all the trust income annually for the next 34 years. Then the assets will revert (pass back) to Karl or his estate. The trust instrument specifically states that the trust is not to maintain a reserve for depletion (that is, no portion of the royalties received from the oil and gas properties is to be transferred to the trust's principal account to account for the wasting nature of the trust assets). Your manager has requested that you research whether the amount of Karl's gift to Louise may be determined by using the actuarial tables and that you write a memo summarizing your conclusions. Your manager indicated further that your memo should address the amount of the gift Karl is deemed to have made.

C:12-61 Sarah Studer, resident of Arkansas, is the daughter of Maude Mason, a widow, who died intestate March 12, 2007. Under Arkansas law, Sarah, Maude's only child, received all of her mother's probate estate, $780,000 in amount. Sarah owes the IRS $820,000 in "back taxes" and interest, and under Sec. 6321 there is a tax lien against all of Sarah's property and rights to property. Sarah has virtually no property and knows that if she accepts the property from her mother's estate she will have to use it to pay her debts to the IRS. It is now November 20, 2007, and Sarah has inquired whether a disclaimer would allow her mother's property to stay within the family unit, given that, if she disclaimed the property, it would pass under state law to her son, Steven Studer, Jr.

Your manager has requested that you write a memorandum in which you address the consequences to Sarah of a disclaimer. Your manager suggested that you consult *Rohn F. Drye, Jr.*, 84 AFTR 2d 99-7160, 99-2 USTC ¶51, 006 (USSC, 1999).

C:12-62 Janet Mason filed a 2005 gift tax return to report the gift on June 3, 2005 of closely held stock in Mason Meat Co., Inc. The tax return, which your firm prepared, reflected a value of $1,500 per share (determined by an appraiser) and a taxable gift of $1.1 million. This was Janet's first taxable gift, and she exhausted her full unified credit of $345,800. On October 22, 2006, Janet's father, Mason Meat's CEO and founder, died unexpectedly at age 59. In addition, two months prior to her father's death the firm had recalled much of its meat from distributors and supermarkets because of contamination in the meat plant. The meat plant closed for six weeks while the contamination problem was corrected. An appraiser valued the stock for her father's estate at $1,000 per share. Janet would like for your firm to prepare an amended gift tax return and value her gift at $1,000 per share because of the decline in value resulting from the two events described. She would like to receive a refund of the gift tax she paid and have some of her unified credit restored. Prepare a memo that addresses whether Janet should be entitled to a refund of the gift tax paid and restoration of some of her unified credit.

C:12-63 ***Internet Research Problem.*** In 2007, Calvin Carter, of Raleigh, North Carolina, made a $2.1 million taxable gift to his niece, Camille Carter Donovan. Use the Internet to determine what the marginal tax bracket will be for the North Carolina state gift tax he will owe on this gift if it is his first taxable gift.

C:12-64 ***Internet Research Problem.*** Your manager wants you to participate in delivering a staff training course on the basics of gift taxation. Your assignment is to discuss *Crummey* trusts. You want to improve your understanding of some of the advantages and disadvantages of such trusts. Do research on the Internet and summarize the advantages and disadvantages. Also indicate which site(s) is (are) the source(s) of your information.

C:12-65 ***Internet Research Problem.*** What is the Sec. 7520 rate for August, September, and October 2006?

13

CHAPTER

THE ESTATE TAX

LEARNING OBJECTIVES

After studying this chapter, you should be able to

1. Describe the formula for the estate tax
2. Describe the methods for valuing interests in the gross estate
3. Determine which interests are includible in the gross estate
4. Identify deductions available for estate tax purposes
5. Calculate the estate tax liability
6. Identify tax provisions that alleviate liquidity problems
7. Recognize the filing requirements for estate tax returns

CHAPTER OUTLINE

Gift taxes and estate taxes, wealth transfer taxes that are part of the unified transfer tax system, account for only a small portion of the federal government's collections from taxation. Chapter C:12 discussed their history and purposes.

As previously noted, the term *gift taxes* applies to lifetime transfers and the term *estate taxes* applies to dispositions of property resulting from the transferor's death. This chapter discusses the structure of the federal estate tax and examines the types of interests and transactions that cause inclusions in the decedent's gross estate. It also discusses the various deductions and credits affecting the federal estate tax liability and the rules concerning the taxable gifts that affect the estate tax base, an important issue because of the unified nature of the tax levied at death.

It is essential to keep in mind that the estate tax is a *wealth transfer tax,* not a property or an income tax. Understanding that the estate tax is levied on the transfer of property makes it easier to understand the rules for estate taxation, which are part of the unified transfer tax system.

ADDITIONAL COMMENT

Congress continues to deliberate whether to make the estate tax repeal permanent or to increase the amount exempt from taxation.

As described in Chapter C:12, the Economic Growth and Tax Relief Reconciliation Act of 2001 (the 2001 Act) provided phased-in increases to the unified credit and phased-in reductions to the unified tax rate schedule beginning with 2002. In addition, it repeals the estate and generation skipping transfer taxes, effective January 1, 2010. However, the 2001 Act further provides that, in the absence of additional legislation, the rules for gift, estate, and generation skipping taxes will revert on January 1, 2011 to what they were before the 2001 Act.

ESTATE TAX FORMULA

OBJECTIVE 1

Describe the formula for the estate tax

The tax base for the federal estate tax is the *total* of the decedent's taxable estate (i.e., the gross estate less the deductions discussed below) and adjusted taxable gifts (post-1976 taxable gifts). After the gross tax liability on the tax base is determined, various credits—including the unified credit—are subtracted to arrive at the net estate tax payable. The estate tax formula appears in Figure C:13-1.

GROSS ESTATE

REAL-WORLD EXAMPLE

In 2001, the top 7.36 million wealth holders held total assets worth $15.2 trillion in the following proportions:

Personal residences	11.8%
Other real property	9.8
Closely held stock	8.1
Other stock	23.0
Tax exempt bonds	5.8
Various other assets	41.5

As illustrated in Figure C:13-1, calculation of the decedent's estate tax liability begins with determining which items are included in the gross estate. Such items are valued at either the decedent's date of death or the alternate valuation date.[1] As a transfer tax, the estate tax is levied on dispositions that are essentially testamentary in nature. Transactions are viewed as being essentially **testamentary transfers** if the transferor's control or enjoyment of the property in question ceases at death, not before death.[2]

Inclusions in the gross estate extend to a much broader set of properties than merely assets the decedent holds title to at the time of death. Making a lifetime transfer that generates a taxable gift does not guarantee that the donor removes the transferred property from his or her gross estate. Although an individual usually removes property from his or her gross estate by giving it to another before death, the donor's gross estate must include the gifted property if the donor retains either the right to receive the income generated by the transferred property or control over the property for the donor's lifetime.

EXAMPLE C:13-1 ▶ In the current year, Ted transfers stocks to an irrevocable trust with a bank named as trustee. Under the terms of the trust agreement, Ted is to receive the trust income annually for the rest of his life and Ted's cousin Ed (or Ed's estate) is to receive the remainder. For gift tax purposes in the current year, Ted made a taxable gift of the remainder interest (but not the income inter-

[1] Under Sec. 2032, the alternate valuation date is the earlier of six months after the date of death or the date the property is disposed of.

[2] An example of a transaction that is essentially **testamentary** in nature is a situation where the donor transfers property in trust but reserves a lifetime right to receive the trust income and, thus, continues to enjoy the economic benefits.

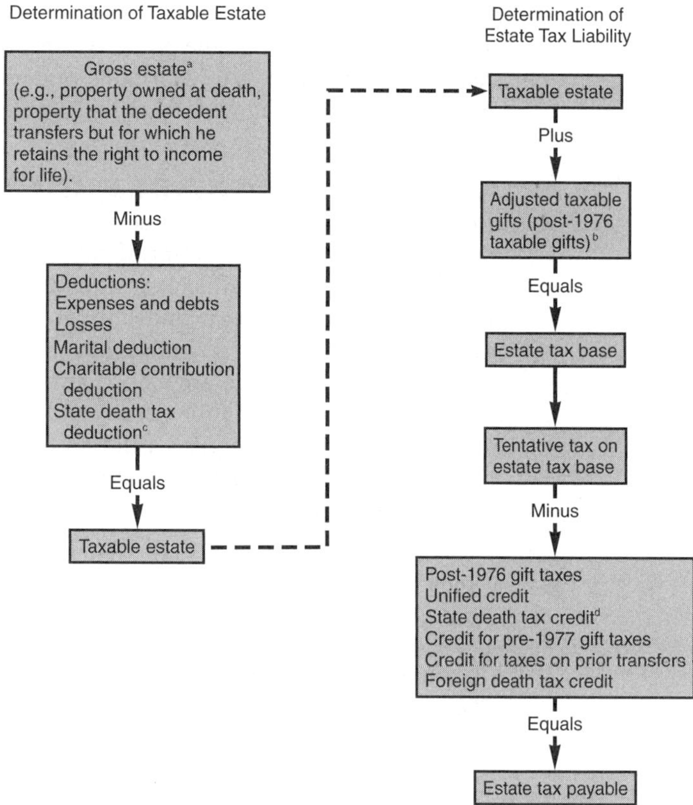

[a]Valued at decedent's date of death or alternate valuation date.
[b]Valued at date of gift.
[c]For decedents dying after 2004.
[d]For decedents dying before 2005.

FIGURE C:13-1 ▶ ESTATE TAX FORMULA

SELF-STUDY QUESTION

In 2002, Barb transferred $500,000 in trust, income for life to herself, remainder to her daughter. What part, if any, of the value of the trust's assets will be included in Barb's estate?

ANSWER

The value of the entire trust will be included in Barb's estate, because she retained the income from the trust until her death.

ADDITIONAL COMMENT

If a decedent leaves all his or her property to his or her spouse, the decedent wastes his or her unified credit. In addition, the estate of the surviving spouse is increased and may be pushed into higher tax brackets.

est) in the trust. If, for example, Ted already has used his entire unified credit, he incurs a gift tax liability. When Ted dies, the entire value of the trust is included in Ted's gross estate, even though Ted does not have legal title to the property. Because the shift in the right to the income does not occur until Ted's death, the transfer is testamentary in nature. ◀

The categories of items included in the gross estate and their valuation are examined in detail later in this chapter. Once the components of the gross estate have been determined and valued, the deductions from the gross estate are calculated.

DEDUCTIONS

The IRC authorizes five categories of items that may be deducted in arriving at the amount of the taxable estate:

- ▶ Expenses and debts
- ▶ Casualty and theft losses
- ▶ Transfers to the decedent's spouse
- ▶ Transfers to charitable organizations
- ▶ State death taxes

Deductible expenses include funeral expenses and expenses of administering the decedent's property. As is true for gift tax purposes, there is no ceiling on the marital deduction. Thus, the death of the first spouse is free of estate taxes if the decedent's spouse receives all the decedent's property, or all the property except for an amount equal to the exemption equivalent.[3] Property passing to charitable organizations qualifies, in general, for a charitable contribution deduction, with no ceiling on the amount of such deductions.

ADJUSTED TAXABLE GIFTS AND TAX BASE

Under the unified transfer tax concept, adjusted taxable gifts are added to the taxable estate to determine the amount of the estate tax base. Section 2001(b) defines adjusted taxable gifts as taxable gifts made after 1976 *other than* gifts included in the gross estate. Because very few gifts are included in the gross estate, almost every post-1976 taxable gift is classified as an adjusted taxable gift.

Adjusted taxable gifts are valued at their date-of-gift values. Therefore, any post-gift appreciation escapes both the gift tax and estate tax. Allowable deductions and exclusions are subtracted from the gift's value in determining the adjusted taxable gifts amount. Increasing the taxable estate by adjusted taxable gifts potentially forces the estate into a higher marginal tax rate.

EXAMPLE C:13-2 ▶ In 1992, Amy made $5 million of taxable gifts, none of which were included in her gross estate. In 2007, Amy dies with a taxable estate of $4 million. The property Amy gave away in 1992 appreciated to $7 million in value by her date of death. In 1998, Amy gave stock valued at $10,000 to one of her children. Amy made no taxable gifts and incurred no transfer tax on the 1998 transaction. The stock had appreciated to $70,000 when Amy died. Amy's estate tax base is calculated as follows:

Taxable estate	$4,000,000
Plus: Adjusted taxable gifts (valued at date-of-gift values)	5,000,000
Estate tax base	$9,000,000

The $2 million of post-gift appreciation on the property gifted in 1992 escapes transfer taxation. Amy's $9 million tax base includes the gifted property, whose value is "frozen" at its date-of-gift value. The 1998 gift does not affect Amy's estate tax base because the 1998 *taxable* gift was zero. ◀

ADDITIONAL COMMENT

Income earned on gifted property is the donee's and is not included in the donor's estate.

TENTATIVE TAX ON ESTATE TAX BASE

Once the amount of the tax base has been determined, the next step is to calculate the tax on this base. Section 2001(c) contains the unified tax rates, which are reproduced on the inside back cover. In 2006, a top marginal tax rate of 46% applied to tax bases exceeding $2 million. In 2007 through 2009, a maximum tax rate of 45% will apply to tax bases exceeding $1.5 million for both estate and gift tax purposes.

EXAMPLE C:13-3 ▶ Assume the same facts as in Example C:13-2. The gross tax on Amy's $9 million tax base is $3,930,800. The estate is taxed at a 45% marginal tax rate, the highest rate applicable in the year Amy dies. ◀

REDUCTION FOR POST-1976 GIFT TAXES

Adjusted taxable gifts, in effect, are not taxed twice because Sec. 2001(b)(2) allows a reduction to the estate tax for gift taxes imposed on post-1976 taxable gifts. If the rate schedule for the year of death differs from the schedule applicable for the year of the gift, the tax on post-1976 taxable gifts is determined by using the rate schedule in effect for the year of death. This rule works to the disadvantage of decedents who made taxable gifts and paid taxes at a higher rate than the rate in effect on the date of death. This rule

[3] The estate tax exemption equivalent ($2 million for 2007), as explained in Chapter C:12, is the size of the tax base for which the estate tax liability is exactly cancelled by the unified credit of $780,800.

ensures that the estate pays tax at the current marginal tax rate applicable for the decedent's amount of taxable estate and adjusted taxable gifts.

EXAMPLE C:13-4 ▶ Assume the same facts as in Examples C:13-2 and C:13-3. Recall that in 1992 Amy made $5 million of taxable gifts. The tax on $5 million of 1992 taxable gifts was $2,390,800. Amy was entitled to a $192,800 unified credit and paid $2,198,000 of gift taxes. Amy's 1992 gifts were taxed at a 55% marginal rate. For the year of Amy's death (2007), the marginal rate for $5 million of transfers is 45%. Consequently, the reduction for gift taxes on post-1976 taxable gifts is limited to the amount of gift taxes that would be payable if the 2007 rate schedule were in effect in the year of the gift. This amount is calculated as follows:

Tax on $5 million at 2007 rates	$2,130,800
Minus: Unified credit for 1992 (the year of the gift)	(192,800)
Tax that would have been payable on $5 million if 2007 rates were in effect	$1,938,000

Note that the only change to the gift tax computation is that the 2007 transfer tax rates are used. The actual credit applicable for the year of the gift (and not the credit for the year of death) is subtracted. ◀

EXAMPLE C:13-5 ▶ From Examples C:13-3 and C:13-4, Amy's estate tax, before reduction for any credits, is calculated as follows:

Tax on $9 million tax base (Example C:13-3)	$3,930,800
Minus: Tax that would have been payable on $5 million of post-1976 taxable gifts, at 2007 rates (Example C:13-4)	(1,938,000)
Estate tax, before reduction for credits (discussed below)	$1,992,800 ◀

SELF-STUDY QUESTION

Taxpayer made $3 million of taxable gifts in 1992 and paid gift taxes of $1,098,000 (gross tax of $1,290,800 minus the unified credit of $192,800). Taxpayer died in 2007 with a taxable estate of $100,000. At current rates, the gift taxes payable on $3 million would be $1,038,000 ($1,230,800 − $192,800). Determine the amount of her estate tax liability.

ANSWER

The unified transfer tax base is $3.1 million, the sum of the $3 million of 1992 taxable gifts and the $100,000 estate. The current tax on $3.1 million is $1,275,800. The unified credit of $780,800 and the subtraction for gift taxes of $1,038,000 reduce the tax liability to zero.

UNIFIED CREDIT

As shown in the inside back cover, the unified credit of Sec. 2010 has varied over the years since its inception in 1977. The credit enables a certain size tax base, referred to as the exemption equivalent or applicable exclusion amount, to be completely free of transfer taxes. The credit and exemption equivalent amounts for 2006 through 2009 are as follows:

Year of Death	*Amount of Credit*	*Exemption Equivalent*
2006	$ 780,800	$2,000,000
2007	780,800	2,000,000
2008	780,800	2,000,000
2009	1,455,800	3,500,000

The estate tax computation permits an estate to subtract the entire unified credit applicable for the year of death (reduced by any phaseout for certain pre-1977 gifts) regardless of how much unified credit the decedent claimed for gift tax purposes. As a conceptual matter, however, only one unified credit is available. Under the unification concept, the estate tax is computed on a tax base consisting of the taxable estate plus the adjusted taxable gifts. The tentative tax on the tax base is reduced not by the amount of the "gross" tax on the adjusted taxable gifts, but by the "gross" tax on such gifts reduced by the unified credit. Ignoring changes in the amount of the unified credit, this computation achieves the same result as allowing the unified credit amount to be subtracted only once against all of a person's transfers but allowing a reduction to the estate tax for the gift tax liability *before* reduction for the unified credit.

OTHER CREDITS

In addition to the unified credit—the only credit available for gift tax purposes—the IRC authorizes three credits for estate tax purposes. (Prior to 2005, estates also were allowed a credit for state death taxes.) These additional credits (shown in Figure C:13-1) are discussed in more detail on pages C:13-24 and C:13-25.

THE GROSS ESTATE: VALUATION

OBJECTIVE 2

Describe the methods for valuing interests in the gross estate

DATE-OF-DEATH VALUATION

All property included in the gross estate is valued at either its fair market value (FMV) on the date of death or the alternate valuation date. The valuation date election is an all-or-nothing proposition. Each item included in the gross estate must be valued as of the same date. In other words, the executor (called the personal representative in some states) may not value some items as of the date of death and others as of the alternate valuation date.

Fair market value is defined as "the price at which the property would change hands between a willing buyer and a willing seller, neither being under any compulsion to buy or to sell and both having reasonable knowledge of relevant facts."[4] In general, the FMV of a particular asset on a certain date is the same regardless of whether the property is being valued for gift or estate tax purposes. Life insurance on the life of the transferor is an exception to this rule. Upon the death of the insured, the policy is valued at its face value, whereas it is valued at a lesser amount while the insured is alive. Generally, this lesser amount is either the cost of a comparable contract or the policy's interpolated terminal reserve plus the unexpired portion of the premium.

For certain types of property, Treasury Regulations contain detailed descriptions of the valuation approach. However, the valuation of interests in closely held businesses is described in only very general terms. Judicial decisions and revenue rulings provide additional guidance for valuation of assets. Valuation rules for several interests are discussed below. For purposes of this discussion, it is assumed that date-of-death valuation is elected.

TYPICAL MISCONCEPTION

The basis of inherited property is the FMV of the property on the decedent's date of death, which could be higher or lower than the decedent's basis. This change is referred to as a step-up or a step-down in basis. Many taxpayers hear so much about step-up that they forget that a step-down also may occur.

ETHICAL POINT

Valuation of interests in closely held corporations and real estate is an area where a CPA or attorney may need to engage a qualified appraiser. Because appraisals are subjective, two appraisers may arrive at different values. Using the highest appraisal may mean additional estate taxes, but it will provide a greater step-up in basis. Using too low an appraisal may subject the estate to undervaluation penalties (see page C:13-36).

LISTED STOCKS. Stocks traded on a stock exchange are valued at the average of their highest and lowest selling prices on the date of death.[5] If no sales occur on the date of death, but sales do take place within a few days of such date, the estate tax value is a weighted average of the high and low sales prices on the nearest trade dates before and after the date of death. The average is weighted inversely in relation to the number of days separating the sales dates and the date of death.

EXAMPLE C:13-6 ▶ Juan, who dies on November 15, owns 100 shares of Jet Corporation stock. Jet stock, traded on the New York Stock Exchange, traded at a high of $120 and a low of $114 on November 15. On Juan's estate tax return, the stock is valued at $117 per share, the average of $120 and $114. The total value of the block of Jet stock is $11,700 (100 × $117). ◀

EXAMPLE C:13-7 ▶ Susan, who dies on May 7, owns 100 shares of Top Corporation stock, traded on the New York Stock Exchange. No sales of Top stock occur on May 7. The sales occurring closest to May 7 take place two business days before May 7 and three business days after May 7. On the earlier date, the stock trades at a high of $500 and a low of $490, with an average of $495. On the later date, the high is $492 and the low is $490, for an average of $491. The date-of-death per-share valuation of the stock is computed under the inverse weighted average approach, as follows:

$$\frac{[3 \times \$495] + [2 \times \$491]}{5} = \$493.40$$

The total value of the block of Top stock is $49,340 (100 × $493.40). ◀

In certain circumstances, the decedent may own such a large block of stock that the price at which the stock trades in the market may not represent the FMV per share for the decedent's number of shares. In such circumstances, Treasury Regulations allow a departure from the traditional valuation rule for stocks. These regulations, referred to as the blockage regulations, state that

[4] Reg. Sec. 20.2031-1(b).

[5] Reg. Sec. 20.2031-2(b).

> In certain exceptional cases, the size of the block of stock to be valued in relation to the number of shares changing hands in sales may be relevant in determining whether selling prices reflect the fair market value of the block of stock to be valued. If the executor can show that the block of stock to be valued is so large in relation to the actual sales on the existing market that it could not be liquidated in a reasonable time without depressing the market, the price at which the block could be sold as such outside the usual market, as through an underwriter, may be a more accurate indication of value than market quotations.[6]

INTERESTS IN FIRMS WHOSE STOCK IS NOT PUBLICLY TRADED. Often, the decedent owns stock in a firm whose shares are not publicly traded. Treasury Regulations do not specifically address the valuation rules for this type of an interest. However, detailed guidelines about relevant factors, including book value and earning capacity, are found in Rev. Rul. 59-60.[7] If the stock is a minority interest in a closely held firm, the courts often grant a discount for the minority interest.

REAL ESTATE. Perhaps surprisingly, Treasury Regulations do not specifically address the valuation approach for real estate. Thus, the general valuation principles concerning a price that would be acceptable to a willing buyer and a willing seller must be implemented without the benefit of more specific guidance. Appraisal literature discusses three techniques for valuing real property: comparable sales, reproduction cost, and capitalization of earnings.[8] Unfortunately, for some properties, it may be difficult to locate a comparable real estate sale. The reproduction cost, of course, is not applicable to valuing land. Capitalization of earnings often is used in valuing commercial real property. At times, an appraiser may use all three approaches.

ANNUITIES, INTERESTS FOR LIFE OR A TERM OF YEARS, REVERSIONS, REMAINDERS. Actuarial tables are used to value annuities, interests for life or a term of years, reversions, and remainders included in the gross estate.[9] The same tables apply for both estate and gift tax purposes. (See Chapter C:12 for a discussion of the use of these tables.) The following example illustrates a situation when the actuarial tables must be used to value an inclusion in the decedent's estate.

EXAMPLE C:13-8 ▶ Tony gives property to a trust with a bank named as trustee and his cousin named to receive all of the trust income for the next 15 years (i.e., a term certain interest). At the end of the fifteenth year, the property reverts to Tony or his estate. Tony dies exactly four years after creating the trust, and the trust property is valued at $100,000 at Tony's death. At Tony's death, the trust has 11 years to continue until the property reverts to Tony's estate. The inclusion in Tony's estate is the value of a reversionary interest following a term certain interest with 11 remaining years. If 10% is the applicable rate, the reversionary interest is valued at $35,049 (0.350494 × $100,000) from Table B of the actuarial tables included in Appendix H. ◀

ALTERNATE VALUATION DATE

Section 2032 authorizes the executor to elect to value all property included in the gross estate at its FMV on the alternate valuation date. Congress enacted this provision in response to the stock market crash of 1929 to make sure that an entire estate could not be confiscated for taxes because of a sudden, substantial drop in values.

In general, the **alternate valuation date** is six months after the date of death. However, if the property is distributed, sold, exchanged, or otherwise disposed of within six months of the date of death, the alternate valuation date is the date of sale or other disposition.

EXAMPLE C:13-9 ▶ Ron dies on March 3. Ron's estate includes two items: stock and land. The estate still owns the stock on September 3, but the executor sold the land on August 20. If Ron's executor elects the

---

[6] Reg. Sec. 20.2031-2(e). As examples of cases dealing with the blockage discount, see *Horace Havemeyer v. U.S.*, 33 AFTR 1069, 45-1 USTC ¶10,194 (Ct. Cls., 1945); *Estate of Charles M. Prell*, 48 T.C. 67 (1967); and *Estate of David Smith*, 57 T.C. 650 (1972). The *Smith* case extended the blockage concept to large holdings of works of art.

[7] 1959-1 C.B. 237.

[8] For a discussion of techniques for appraising real estate, see The Appraisal Institute, *The Appraisal of Real Estate*, 11th ed. (Arlington Heights, IL: The Appraisal Institute, 1996).

[9] Section 7520 provides that the interest rate potentially changes every month. Regulation Sec. 20.7520-1(a)(2) provides these tables. An excerpt from these tables is included in Appendix H.

alternate valuation date, the stock is valued as of September 3. The land, however, is valued as of August 20 because it is disposed of before the end of the six-month period. Of course, the value of land generally would change very little, if any, between August 20 and September 3. ◀

If the executor elects the alternate valuation date, generally any changes in value that occur *solely* because of a "mere lapse of time" must be ignored in determining the property's value.[10] In a limited number of situations, one must concentrate on the meaning of the phrase "the mere passage of time." For example, if the executor elects the alternate valuation date to value a patent, he or she must ignore any change in value attributable to the fact that the patent's remaining life is six months shorter on the alternate valuation date than it was on the date of death. Changes in value resulting from the marketing of a competing patented product are relevant.

The alternate valuation date election can be made only if it decreases the value of the gross estate *and* the estate tax liability (after reduction for credits).[11] As a result of this provision, electing the alternate valuation date cannot produce a higher step-up in basis. Congress enacted this strict rule because the alternate valuation date formerly offered a substantial tax planning advantage in situations where, because of the unlimited marital deduction, no estate tax was owed. If the property appreciated between the date of death and the alternate valuation date, the recipient could receive an increased basis if the executor elected the alternate valuation date.[12] Because of the unlimited marital deduction, the estate formerly could achieve an additional step-up in basis without increasing the estate tax liability.

STOP & THINK

Question: Joan died on April 1. Her estate consisted of three assets: an apartment building valued at $1.2 million on April 1, stock valued at $1.7 million on April 1, and $400,000 of cash. On October 1, the values were as follows: apartment building—$1.5 million, stock—$1.1 million, and cash of $400,000. Joan willed all her property to her son, who anticipates owning the property for a long time. The deductions for Joan's estate are negligible. Is there an estate tax benefit in electing the alternate valuation date? Is there an income tax benefit in electing the alternate valuation date?

Solution: An estate tax benefit results from using the alternate valuation date. The estate tax liability would be lower because the taxable estate would be $300,000 smaller if the alternate valuation date value ($3 million minus deductions) were used instead of the date of death value ($3.3 million minus deductions). Some income tax benefit also results from using the alternate valuation date. By using the alternate valuation date value, the tax basis for calculating cost recovery on the apartment building is $300,000 higher, ignoring any allocation of value to the land. However, a related detriment occurs because the basis of the stock is $600,000 less with the alternate valuation date. If it is anticipated that the stock will be sold in the near future, the $600,000 capital loss that would be available by using the date of death value might permit Joan's son to sell a number of highly-appreciated assets and offset a very large capital gain with the $600,000 capital loss.

THE GROSS ESTATE: INCLUSIONS

OBJECTIVE 3

Determine which interests are includible in the gross estate

As Figure C:13-1 illustrates, the process of calculating the decedent's estate tax liability begins with determining the components of the gross estate. The **gross estate** is analogous to gross income. Once the components of the gross estate have been identified, they must be valued. As previously mentioned, the gross estate encompasses a much wider array of items than merely those to which the decedent held title at death. For example, under cer-

10 Reg. Sec. 20.2032-1(f).

11 Sec. 2032(c).

12 Sec. 1014(a).

SELF-STUDY QUESTION

Which of the following properties will be included in (1) the probate estate, (2) the gross estate, (3) both the probate and gross estate, or (4) neither estate?
1. Real property held in joint tenancy with the decedent's spouse. (The answer is 2.)
2. Real property held as a tenant in common with the decedent's spouse. (The answer is 3.)
3. A life insurance policy owned by the decedent in which the decedent's spouse is named the beneficiary. (The answer is 2.)
4. A life insurance policy always owned by the decedent's spouse in which the decedent's children are named the beneficiaries. (The answer is 4.)

tain statutory provisions, referred to as the *transferor sections,* the gross estate includes items previously transferred by the decedent. For decedents other than nonresident aliens, the fact that property is located in a foreign country does not preclude it from being included in the gross estate. Table C:13-1 provides an overview of the inclusions in the gross estate.

COMPARISON OF GROSS ESTATE WITH PROBATE ESTATE

The gross estate is a federal tax law concept, and the probate estate is a state law concept. To oversimplify, the **probate estate** can be defined as encompassing property that passes subject to the will (or under an intestacy statute) and is subject to court administration. Often, a decedent's gross estate is substantially larger than his or her probate estate. For example, suppose that at the time of death, a decedent owns a life insurance policy on his own life with his daughter as the beneficiary. The policy is not a part of the decedent's probate estate because the policy proceeds are payable directly to the daughter, but it is included in the gross estate.

STOP & THINK

Question: Karl died recently, and Karl's executor has included the following properties in Karl's gross estate: life insurance payable to the beneficiary, Karl's wife; savings account solely in Karl's name; land titled in the names of Karl and his son as joint tenants with right of survivorship; and a trust created under the will of Karl's mother. Karl had an income interest in the trust for his lifetime and complete power to designate the owners of the property on his death. With the exception of the trust assets (willed to his children), Karl's will leaves all his property to his beloved cousin, Karla. Which assets pass under the terms of Karl's will? Which assets will Karla receive?

Solution: This scenario illustrates the difference between the property included in a decedent's gross estate and in the probate estate. Karl's gross estate is larger than his probate estate. Only two assets included in his gross estate—the savings account and the trust property—pass under the terms of Karl's will. Karla will receive only the savings account because Karl wills the trust property to his children. The life insurance passes to the named beneficiary, the spouse, and the land passes to the surviving joint tenant, the son.

▼ TABLE C:13-1
Inclusions in the Gross Estate

IRC Section	Type of Property or Transaction Included
2033	Property in which the decedent had an interest
2035	Gift taxes on property given away within three years of death *plus* certain property (primarily life insurance) given away within three years of death
2036	Property that the decedent transferred during life but in which the decedent retained economic benefits or the power to control enjoyment
2037	Property that the decedent transferred during life but for which the decedent has too large a reversionary interest
2038	Property that the decedent transferred during life but over which the decedent held the power to alter, amend, revoke, or terminate an interest
2039	Annuities
2040	Jointly owned property
2041	Property over which the decedent possessed a general power of appointment
2042	Life insurance on the decedent's life
2044	QTIP trust for which a marital deduction was claimed by the decedent's spouse

PROPERTY IN WHICH THE DECEDENT HAD AN INTEREST

Section 2033, sometimes called the *generic section,* provides that the gross estate includes the value of all property the decedent beneficially owned at the time of death. Its broad language taxes such items as a personal residence, an automobile, stocks, and any other asset titled in the decedent's name. Because the rule refers to beneficial ownership, however, its scope extends beyond assets to which the decedent held title. For example, such items as remainder interests also are included in the gross estate.

EXAMPLE C:13-10 ▶ At the time of his death, the following assets are in Raj's name: personal residence, mountain cabin, Zero Corporation stock, checking account, and savings account. Raj beneficially owns each of these items when he dies. Under Sec. 2033, each item is included in Raj's gross estate. ◀

EXAMPLE C:13-11 ▶ Ken's will named Ann to receive trust income for life and Raj or Raj's estate to receive the trust remainder upon Ann's death. Raj's gross estate, therefore, includes the value of the remainder interest if Raj predeceases Ann because Raj's will controls the passage of the remainder interest. The transfer is associated with Raj's death, and, hence, is subject to the estate tax. ◀

DOWER OR CURTESY RIGHTS

Certain state laws provide wealth protection to surviving spouses through **dower** or **curtesy** rights.

- Dower is a widow's interest in her deceased husband's property.
- Curtesy is a widower's interest in his deceased wife's property.

ADDITIONAL COMMENT

Any property that passes outright to the decedent's spouse, due to dower or curtesy rights under state law, is eligible for the marital deduction and will not increase the unified tax base.

Dower or curtesy rights entitle the surviving spouse to a certain portion of the decedent spouse's estate, even though the decedent may have willed a smaller portion to the spouse. Because the decedent spouse does not have complete control over the portion of his or her estate that is subject to dower or curtesy rights, some might argue that the portion of the estate that the surviving spouse is entitled to receive is excluded from the gross estate. Thus, Congress made it crystal clear that the decedent's gross estate is not reduced for the value of the property in which the surviving spouse has a dower or curtesy interest or some other statutory interest.[13]

EXAMPLE C:13-12 ▶ The laws of a certain state provide that widows are entitled to receive one-third of their deceased husband's property. The husband's gross estate does not exclude his widow's dower rights (one-third interest) in his property. ◀

SELF-STUDY QUESTION

When Dorothy died on April 10, she owned Z Corporation bonds, which paid interest on April 1 and October 1, and stock in X and Y Corporations. X Corporation had declared a dividend on March 15 payable to stockholders of record on April 1. Y Corporation had declared a dividend on March 31 payable to stockholders of record on April 15. Dorothy's estate received the interest and dividends on the payment dates. Should any of the interest or dividends be included in Dorothy's gross estate?

ANSWER

The X Corporation dividend must be included because the date of record preceded Dorothy's death. The Y Corporation dividend will not be included because the date of record was after her death. The Z Corporation bond interest that must be included is the interest that accrued between the April 1 payment date and the April 10 date of death.

TRANSFEROR PROVISIONS

Sections 2035 through 2038 are called the *transferor provisions.* They apply if the decedent made a transfer while alive of a type specified in the IRC section in question, *and* the decedent did not receive adequate consideration in money or money's worth for the transferred interest. If one of the transferor provisions applies, the gross estate includes the transferred property at its date-of-death or alternate valuation date value.

GIFTS MADE WITHIN THREE YEARS OF DEATH. Section 2035(a) specifies the circumstances in which a gift that a decedent makes within three years of death triggers an inclusion in the gross estate. The scope of this provision, which is relatively narrow, encompasses the following two types of transfers made by the donor-decedent within three years before death:

- A life insurance policy on the decedent's life that would have been taxed under Sec. 2042 (life insurance proceeds received by the executor or for the benefit of the estate) had the policy not been given away, or
- An interest in property that would have been taxed under Sec. 2036 (transfers with a retained life estate), Sec. 2037 (transfers taking effect at death), or Sec. 2038 (revocable transfers) had it not been transferred.

[13] Sec. 2034.

Of these situations, the most common involves the insured's gifting a life insurance policy on his or her own life and dying within three years of the transfer. With new insurance policies, the potential for an inclusion can be avoided if the decedent never owns the new policy. In other words, instead of the insured purchasing a new policy and then giving it to a transferee as owner, the other party should buy the new policy. A common planning technique involves a transfer of cash by an individual to a trust, and the trust (a life insurance trust) using the cash to purchase an insurance policy on the transferor's life.

EXAMPLE C:13-13 ▶ On April 1, 2004, Roy transferred to Sally ownership of a $400,000 life insurance policy on his own life purchased in 1996. Sally is the policy's beneficiary. Roy dies on February 3, 2007. Because Roy dies within three years of giving away the policy, the policy is included in Roy's gross estate. The estate tax value of the policy is its $400,000 face value. If Roy had lived until at least April 2, 2007, the policy transfer would have fallen outside the three-year rule, and the policy would not have been included in Roy's gross estate. ◀

EXAMPLE C:13-14 ▶ Roy made a gift of stock to Troy on May 1, 2006. Roy dies on February 3, 2007. The stock was worth $80,000 on the gift date and is worth $125,000 at the time of Roy's death. The gifted property is not included in Roy's gross estate because it is not life insurance on Roy's life, nor is it property that would have been taxed in Roy's estate under Secs. 2036 through 2038 had he kept such property. ◀

GROSS-UP RULE. The donor-decedent's gross estate is increased by any gift tax that he or she, or his or her estate pays on any gift the decedent or his or her spouse makes during the three-year period ending with the decedent's death.[14] This provision, known as the gross-up rule, applies to the gift tax triggered by a gift of any type of property during the three-year look-back period.

The purpose of the gross-up rule is to foreclose the opportunity that existed under pre-1977 law to reduce one's gross estate (and thereby one's taxable estate) by removing the gift tax on "deathbed" gifts from the gross estate. Because the donor's estate received a credit for some or all of the gift tax paid, under the pre-1977 rules, a person on his or her deathbed in effect could prepay a portion of his or her estate tax and at the same time reduce his or her gross estate by the amount of the gift tax.

The gross-up rule, as illustrated in the two examples below, reinstates the estate to the position it would have been in had no gift tax liability been incurred.

EXAMPLE C:13-15 ▶ In late 2004, Cheron made her first gift, a $2 million taxable gift of stock, and paid a gift tax of $435,000 ($780,800 gross tax − $345,800 unified credit). Cheron dies in early 2007. Cheron's gross estate does not include the stock, but it does include the $435,000 gift tax paid because she made the gift within three years of her death. ◀

EXAMPLE C:13-16 ▶ In late 2004, Hal gave Jody stock having a $4,022,000 FMV, and he and Wanda, his wife, elected gift splitting. Each is deemed to have made a $2 million [($4,022,000 ÷ 2) − $11,000 annual exclusion] taxable gift, and each paid $435,000 ($780,800 gross tax − $345,800 unified credit) of gift tax. Wanda dies in early 2007. Wanda's gross estate includes the $435,000 in gift tax she paid on the portion of her husband's gift that she is deemed to have made within three years of her death. Her cash balance declined because of paying the gift tax, and the gross-up for the tax reinstates her estate to the position it would have been in had she paid no gift tax. ◀

SELF-STUDY QUESTION

Refer to Example C:13-16. Assume that Hal, the spouse who actually made the gift, paid Wanda's $435,000 gift tax as well as his own $435,000 gift tax. Would Wanda's $435,000 gift tax be included in her gross estate?

ANSWER

No. It would not be included because payment of the tax from Hal's account did not reduce Wanda's cash balance.

TRANSFERS WITH RETAINED LIFE ESTATE. Section 2036, although titled "Transfers with Retained Life Estate," extends beyond taxing solely lifetime transfers made by the decedent in which he or she retained a life estate (the right to income or use for life). The two primary types of transfers taxed under Sec. 2036 are those for which the decedent

- ▶ Kept possession or enjoyment of the property or the right to its income
- ▶ Retained the power to designate the person who is to possess or enjoy the property or to receive its income

[14] Sec. 2035(b).

Thus, Sec. 2036 applies when the transferor kept the income or enjoyment *or* the right to control other individuals' income or enjoyment.

The direct or indirect retention of voting rights in stock of a controlled corporation that the decedent transferred also can cause the gifted stock to be included in the transferor's gross estate.[15] A controlled corporation is one in which the decedent owned (directly, indirectly, or constructively), or had the right to vote, stock that possessed at least 20% of the voting power.[16]

The retention of income, control, or voting rights for one of the three retention periods listed below causes the transferred property to be included in the transferor's gross estate. The three periods are

- The transferor's lifetime
- A period that cannot be determined without referring to the transferor's death (e.g., the transferor retained the right to quarterly payments of income, but payments ceased with the last quarterly payment before the transferor's death)
- A period that does not end, in fact, before the transferor's death

An implied agreement or understanding is sufficient to trigger inclusion. For example, if a mother gives a residence to her daughter and continues to occupy the residence alone and rent-free, the residence probably will be included in the mother's gross estate under the argument that the parties had an implied understanding allowing the mother to occupy the residence for life.

If Sec. 2036 applies to a transfer and if the decedent's retention of enjoyment or control extends to all the transferred property, 100% of the transferred property's value is included in the transferor's gross estate.[17] However, if the transferor keeps the right to only one-third of the income for life and retains no control over the remaining two-thirds, his estate includes just one-third of the property's date-of-death value. The following three examples illustrate some of the transactions that cause Sec. 2036 to apply.

EXAMPLE C:13-17 ▶ In 2002, David (age 30) transferred an office building to Ellen but retained the right to collect all the income from the building for life. David dies in 2007. Because David retained the income right for life, the Sec. 2036 inclusion applies. The amount included is 100% of the building's date-of-death value. ◀

EXAMPLE C:13-18 ▶ Assume the same facts as in Example C:13-17 except that David retains the right to income for only 15 years. David dies five years after the transfer; therefore, David has the right to receive the income for the remaining ten-year period. Because the retention period does not *in fact* end before David's death, his gross estate includes 100% of the property's date-of-death value. ◀

EXAMPLE C:13-19 ▶ Tracy creates a trust with a bank as trustee and names Alice, Brad, and Carol to receive the trust income for their joint lives and Dick to receive the remainder upon the death of the first among Alice, Brad, or Carol to die. Tracy reserves the right to designate the portion of the income to be paid to each income beneficiary each year. Only the transfer to Dick was a completed transfer and subject to gift taxes. Tracy predeceases the other parties. Because her control over the flow of income does not end before Tracy's death, the date-of-death value of the trust assets is included in Tracy's gross estate even though a portion of the transfer was subject to gift taxes. If Tracy had instead "cut the string" and not kept control over the income flow, she could have removed the trust property from her estate. ◀

SELF-STUDY QUESTION

Refer to Example C:13-19. Assume the same facts except that the trustee is directed to distribute its annual income equally to Alice, Brad, and Carol for their joint lives. Also assume that Tracy names Dick the remainderman. Will the value of the trust be included in Tracy's gross estate?

ANSWER

No, because Tracy retained no power to control the enjoyment of the property.

REVERSIONARY INTERESTS. If the chance exists that the property will pass back to the transferor under the terms of the transfer, the transferor has a **reversionary interest.** Under Sec. 2037, the transferor's gross estate includes earlier transferred property if the decedent stipulates that another person must survive him or her to own the property and the value of the decedent's reversionary interest exceeds 5% of the value of the transferred property. Actuarial techniques are used to value the reversionary interest.[18] Section 2037 does not apply if the value of the reversionary interest does not exceed the 5% *de minimis* amount.

---

[15] Sec. 2036(b)(1).

[16] Sec. 2036(b)(2).

[17] Reg. Sec. 20.2036-1(a).

[18] The **reversionary interest** is the interest that will return to the transferor. Often, it will return only if certain contingencies occur. The value of Beth's reversionary interest in Example C:13-20 is a function of the present value of the interest Beth would receive after the deaths of Tammy and Doug, valued as from actuarial tables (see Appendix H), and coupled with the probability that Tammy and Doug would die before Beth.

EXAMPLE C:13-20 ▶ Beth transfers an asset to Tammy for life and then to Doug for life. The asset is to revert to Beth, if Beth is still alive, upon the death of either Tammy or Doug, whoever dies second. If Beth is not alive upon the death of the survivor of Tammy and Doug, the asset is to pass to Don or to a charitable organization if Don is not alive. Thus, Don must live longer than Beth to receive the property. The property is included in Beth's estate if the value of Beth's reversionary interest exceeds 5% of the property's value. The amount included is not the value of Beth's reversionary interest, but rather the date-of-death value of the asset less the value of Tammy's and Doug's intervening life estates. ◀

ADDITIONAL COMMENT

Sections 2036 through 2038 draw back into the gross estate certain previously transferred property and include it at its FMV on the date of the decedent's death. For income tax purposes, if the property has appreciated in value, donees will obtain a stepped-up basis rather than a carryover gift tax basis.

REVOCABLE TRANSFERS. Section 2038 covers the rules for revocable transfers (i.e., revocable trusts). However, this provision also taxes all transfers over which the decedent has, at the time of his or her death, the power to change the enjoyment by altering, amending, revoking, or terminating an interest. Revocable trusts, sometimes called living trusts, are popular arrangements from a non-tax standpoint because assets held by a revocable trust pass outside of probate. Advantages of avoiding probate include lower probate costs and easier administration for real property located in a state that is not the decedent's state of domicile. In addition, unlike a will, a revocable trust is not a matter of public record.

Section 2038 can apply even though the decedent does not originally retain powers over the property. The crucial factor is that the transferor possesses the powers at the time of death regardless of whether the transferor retained such powers originally. The estate must include only the value of the interest that is subject to the decedent's power to change. Sections 2038 and 2036 overlap greatly, and if one amount is taxable under one section and a different amount is taxable under the other section, the gross estate includes the larger amount. Two types of transfers taxed by Sec. 2038 are illustrated in the following examples.

EXAMPLE C:13-21 ▶ Joe funds a revocable trust and names his son to receive the income for life and his grandson to receive the property upon the son's death. Because the trust is revocable, Joe may change the terms of the trust or take back the trust property during his lifetime. Joe's power to revoke the transfer extends to the entire trust. Thus, Joe's gross estate includes the date-of-death value of the entire trust. ◀

EXAMPLE C:13-22 ▶ Vicki creates a trust and names Gina to receive the income for life and Matt to receive the remainder. Vicki, however, retains the right to substitute Liz (for Matt) as remainderman. When Vicki dies, she has the authority to change the enjoyment of the remainder. Thus, the value of the trust's remainder interest is includible in Vicki's estate. ◀

SELF-STUDY QUESTION

Reggie purchased an annuity and elected to collect benefits for 15 years. If Reggie dies before the end of the 15-year term of the annuity, his estate will be entitled to the remaining payments. Assume Reggie died after receiving nine payments. Will the value of the remaining six payments be included in Reggie's estate?

ANSWER

Yes. Section 2039 requires that the cost of a comparable contract of six payments be included in his gross estate.

ANNUITIES AND OTHER RETIREMENT BENEFITS

Section 2039 explicitly addresses the estate tax treatment of annuities. Even if this section had not been enacted, some annuities probably would have been taxable under the general language of Sec. 2033 because the decedent would have been viewed as having an interest in the property. For an annuity to be included in the gross estate, it must involve payments made under a contract or an agreement. In addition, the decedent must be receiving such payments at the time of his or her death or must have the right to collect such payments alone or with another person. If the annuity simply ceases with the death of the decedent in question, nothing is to be received by another party and nothing is included in the gross estate. For the payments to be included in the decedent's estate, they must be paid for the decedent's life, a period that may not be determined without referring to the decedent's date of death or for a period that does not actually end before the decedent's death.

ANNUITIES NOT RELATED TO EMPLOYMENT. The purchase of an annuity designed to pay benefits to the purchaser and then to a named survivor upon the purchaser's death, or to both parties simultaneously and then to the survivor, is a form of wealth shifting. The other party receives wealth that originates with the purchaser. This type of transfer is different from most other wealth transfers because it involves a series of annuity payments instead of a transfer of a tangible property.

The amount included in the gross estate with respect to annuities or other retirement benefits is a fraction (described below) of the value of the annuity or lump-sum payment to be received by the surviving beneficiary. Annuities are valued at the cost of a comparable contract.[19] To determine the inclusion in the gross estate, this cost is multiplied by a fraction that represents the portion of the purchase price the decedent contributed.

EXAMPLE C:13-23 ▶ Twelve years ago, Jim purchased a joint and survivor annuity and selected benefits to be paid to himself and his son concurrently and then to the survivor for life. Jim and his son started collecting payments four years ago. Jim dies in the current year, survived by his son. At the time of Jim's death, the cost of a comparable contract providing the same benefits is $180,000. Because Jim provided all the consideration to purchase the annuity, his gross estate includes 100% of the $180,000 cost of a comparable contract. This annuity arrangement represents a shifting of wealth from Jim to his son upon Jim's death. ◀

SELF-STUDY QUESTION

On his retirement at age 65, Winslow elected to take a joint and survivor annuity from his qualified pension plan. The plan provided Winslow and his wife with a monthly pension of $2,500 until the death of the survivor. Winslow died seven years later. What amount (if any) must be included in Winslow's gross estate if his wife survives?

ANSWER

The gross estate includes the cost of a comparable contract providing $2,500 a month for the rest of the spouse's life. The spouse's age would affect the cost.

EMPLOYMENT-RELATED RETIREMENT BENEFITS. Recall that, to determine the amount of an annuity includible in the decedent's gross estate, the cost of a comparable contract is multiplied by a fraction representing the portion of the purchase price contributed by the decedent. Section 2039(b) states that contributions from the decedent's employer (or former employer) are treated as contributions made by the decedent, provided such payments are made as a result of the employment relationship. Thus, 100% of the benefits from an employment-related annuity are included in the gross estate.

EXAMPLE C:13-24 ▶ Pat was employed by Wheel Corporation at the time of his death. Wheel Corporation maintains a qualified retirement plan to which it makes 60% of the contributions and its employees contribute 40%. Pat's spouse is to receive an annuity valued at $350,000 from the retirement plan. Because the employer's contributions are considered to have been made by the employee, Pat is deemed to have provided all the consideration for the retirement benefits. Consequently, Pat's gross estate includes 100% of the annuity's $350,000 date-of-death value. ◀

JOINTLY OWNED PROPERTY

Section 2040 addresses the estate tax treatment of jointly owned property (i.e., property owned in a joint tenancy with right of survivorship or tenancy by the entirety arrangement).[20] An important characteristic of this form of ownership is that, upon the death of one joint owner, the decedent's interest passes automatically (by right of survivorship) to the surviving joint owner(s). Thus, the property is not part of the probate estate and does not pass under the will. Section 2040 contains two sets of rules, one for property jointly owned by spouses and one for all other jointly owned properties.

OWNERSHIP INVOLVING PERSONS OTHER THAN SPOUSES. When persons other than spouses or persons in addition to spouses own property as joint owners, the amount includible is determined by the consideration-furnished test.[21] Under this test, property is included in a joint owner's gross estate in accordance with the portion of the consideration he or she furnished to acquire the property. Obviously, this portion can range between 0% and 100%.

---

[19] Reg. Sec. 20.2031-8(a).

[20] Both joint tenancies with right of survivorship and tenancies by the entirety have the feature of survivorship. When one joint owner dies, his or her interest passes by right of survivorship to the remaining joint owner(s). Only spouses may use the tenancy by the entirety arrangement, whereas any persons may own as joint tenants with right of survivorship. A joint tenancy with right of survivorship may be severed by the action of any joint owner, whereas a tenancy by the entirety arrangement continues unless severed by the joint action of both joint owners.

The following definitions are from Henry Campbell Black, *Black's Law Dictionary,* Rev. 6th ed., Ed. by Joseph R. Nolan and Jacqueline M. Nolan-Haley (St. Paul, MN: West Publishing Co., 1990), p. 1465.

Joint tenancy with right of survivorship: The primary incident of joint tenancy is survivorship, by which the entire tenancy on the decease of any joint tenant remains to the survivors, and at length to the last survivor.

Tenancy by the entirety: A tenancy which is created between husband and wife and by which together they hold title to the whole with right of survivorship so that upon death of either, other takes whole to exclusion of deceased heirs. It is essentially a "joint tenancy" modified by the common-law theory that husband and wife are one person, and survivorship is the predominant and distinguishing feature of each. Neither party can alienate or encumber the property without the consent of the other.

[21] Sec. 2040(a).

EXAMPLE C:13-25 ▶

Seven years ago, Fred and Jack provided $10,000 and $30,000 of consideration, respectively, to purchase real property titled in the names of Fred and Jack as joint tenants with right of survivorship. Fred dies in the current year and is survived by Jack. The real property is valued at $60,000. Fred's gross estate includes $15,000 (0.25 × $60,000) because Fred furnished 25% of the consideration to acquire the property. If Jack instead predeceases Fred, his estate would include $45,000 (0.75 × $60,000). ◀

ADDITIONAL COMMENT

The tracing rule is easy to understand but difficult to implement. Suppose a joint tenancy between a parent and a child was created in a parcel of real estate 30 years ago when the parent paid for the property. The child died of a heart attack, and the parent is senile. Nothing should be included in the child's gross estate. Unfortunately the burden of proof to keep a portion of the property out of the estate is on the estate, not the IRS.

If part of the consideration furnished by one joint tenant is originally received gratuitously from another joint tenant, the consideration is attributable to the joint tenant who made the gift. If all joint owners acquire their interests by gift, devise, bequest, or inheritance, the decedent joint owner's estate includes his or her proportionate share of the date-of-death value of the jointly owned property.

EXAMPLE C:13-26 ▶

Ray gives stock valued at $50,000 to Sam. Three years later Sam transfers this stock (now valued at $60,000) as partial consideration to acquire real property costing $120,000. Ray furnishes the remaining $60,000 of consideration. The real property is titled in the names of Ray and Sam as joint tenants with right of survivorship. Because Sam received the asset that he used for consideration as a gift from Ray (the other joint tenant), Sam is treated as having furnished no consideration. If Sam dies before Ray, Sam's estate will include none of the real property's value. If Ray predeceases Sam, however, Ray's estate will include the entire date-of-death value. ◀

SELF-STUDY QUESTION

Fred and Myrtle, husband and wife, hold title to their home in joint tenancy with right of survivorship. Fred is killed in an airplane crash. What part of the value of the residence will be included in Fred's gross estate? Who will own the residence if Fred wills all his property to their children?

OWNERSHIP INVOLVING ONLY SPOUSES. If spouses are the only joint owners, the property is classified as a **qualified joint interest**. Section 2040(b)(1) provides that, in the case of qualified joint interests, the decedent's gross estate includes one-half the value of the qualified joint interest. The 50% inclusion rule applies automatically regardless of the relative amount of consideration provided by either spouse.

EXAMPLE C:13-27 ▶

Wilma provides all the consideration to purchase stock costing $80,000. She registers the stock in her name and her husband's name as joint tenants with right of survivorship. The estate of the first spouse to die, regardless of which spouse it is, will include 50% of the value of the jointly owned stock. Upon the second spouse's death, all the property will be included in that spouse's gross estate because it no longer will be jointly owned property. ◀

ANSWER

One-half the value of the residence will be included in Fred's gross estate. Myrtle will own the residence after Fred's death because it passes to her by right of survivorship.

GENERAL POWERS OF APPOINTMENT

Section 2041 requires inclusion in the gross estate of certain property interests that the decedent never owns in a legal sense. Inclusion occurs because the decedent had the power to designate who eventually would own the property. The authority to designate the owner—a significant power—is called a power of appointment. Powers of appointment can be general or special (i.e., more restricted).

Only a general power of appointment results in an addition to the gross estate. If a general power was created before October 22, 1942, however, no inclusion occurs unless the decedent exercised the power. For a post-1942 general power of appointment, inclusion occurs regardless of whether the power is exercised. A general power of appointment exists if the holder can exercise the power in favor of him- or herself, his or her estate or creditors, *or* the creditors of his or her estate. Being exercisable in favor of the decedent's estate means there is no restriction on the powerholder's ability to specify the person(s) to receive the property. The power may be exercisable during the decedent's life, by his or her will, or both.

Sometimes a powerholder can exercise a power for only specified purposes and/or in favor of only certain persons. Appointment powers that are governed by a so-called "ascertainable standard" are free of estate tax consequences because they may be exercised solely for purposes of the decedent's health, support, maintenance, or education.

EXAMPLE C:13-28 ▶

When Kathy died in 1991, her will created a trust from which Doris is to receive the income for life. In addition, Doris is granted the power to designate by will the person or persons to receive the trust's assets. Doris has a testamentary general power of appointment. The trust's assets are included in Doris's gross estate regardless of whether Doris exercises the power. If Kathy had instead died in 1940, Doris would have had a pre-1942 power of appointment. Such powers are taxed only if exercised. ◀

EXAMPLE C:13-29 ▶ Assume the same facts as in Example C:13-28 except that Kathy's will merely empowers Doris to name which of her descendants shall receive the trust assets. Doris now has only a special power of appointment because she does not have the power to leave the property to whomever she desires (e.g., the power to appoint the property to her estate). Because Doris's power of appointment is only a special power, the value of the trust is not included in Doris's gross estate. ◀

LIFE INSURANCE

TYPICAL MISCONCEPTION

Many taxpayers who own life insurance policies on their own lives mistakenly believe that their estates will not owe estate taxes on the life insurance proceeds if they name someone other than their estate as the beneficiary. Life insurance will be included in the gross estate of the decedent if, at the time of death, the decedent held *any* (one) of the incidents of ownership in the policy.

Section 2042 addresses the estate tax treatment of life insurance policies on the decedent's life. Life insurance policies owned by the decedent on the lives of others are taxed under the general language of Sec. 2033. According to Sec. 2042, a decedent's gross estate includes the value of policies on his or her own life if the proceeds are receivable by the executor or for the benefit of the estate, or if the decedent had any "incidents of ownership" in the policy at the time of death. Treasury Regulations list the following powers as a partial inventory of the incidents of ownership:

- To change the beneficiary
- To surrender or cancel the policy
- To borrow against the policy
- To pledge the policy for a loan
- To revoke an assignment of the policy[22]

Examples in the regulations pertaining to incidents of ownership involve economic rights over the insurance policies. Judicial decisions also have been important in defining what constitutes incidents of ownership. In some jurisdictions, the phrase has been interpreted to be broader than simply relating to economic powers.[23]

If the decedent could have exercised the incidents of ownership only in conjunction with another party, the policy nevertheless is included in the gross estate. Moreover, it is the legal power to exercise ownership rights, not the practical ability to do so, that leads to an inclusion. The Supreme Court in the *Estate of Marshal L. Noel* emphasized the importance of the decedent-insured's legal powers in a situation where the insured was killed in a plane crash and the policies he owned on his life were on the ground in the possession of his spouse. The Court held that the decedent possessed incidents of ownership and thus the policies were includible in his gross estate.[24]

EXAMPLE C:13-30 ▶ Tracy purchased an insurance policy on her life, and several years later she transferred all her incidents of ownership in the policy to her daughter. Seven years after the transfer, Tracy dies. Tracy's niece has always been the policy's beneficiary. The policy is not included in Tracy's gross estate because Tracy did not have any incidents of ownership in the policy at the time of her death, nor is her estate the beneficiary. (Also, she did not give the policy away within three years of death.) ◀

EXAMPLE C:13-31 ▶ Assume the same facts as in Example C:13-30 except that Tracy's estate instead is the policy's beneficiary. Because Tracy's estate is designated as the beneficiary, the policy is included in her gross estate and valued at its face value. ◀

It is not sufficient to consider only Sec. 2042 in determining whether a life insurance policy on the decedent's life is includible in the gross estate. Recall from the discussion earlier in this chapter that a life insurance policy is includible in a decedent's gross estate if the individual makes a gift of a life insurance policy on his or her own life within three years of dying.[25]

EXAMPLE C:13-32 ▶ Two years ago, Peng gave all his incidents of ownership in a life insurance policy on his own life to his son, Phong. The face value of the policy is $400,000. Phong has always been the

---

[22] Reg. Sec. 20.2042-1(c)(2).

[23] See, for example, *Estate of James H. Lumpkin, Jr. v. CIR,* 31 AFTR 2d 73-1381, 73-1 USTC ¶12,909 (5th Cir., 1973), wherein the court held that the right to choose how the proceeds were to be paid—in a lump sum or in installments—was an incident of ownership.

[24] *CIR v. Estate of Marshal L. Noel,* 15 AFTR 2d 1397, 65-1 USTC ¶12,311 (USSC, 1965).

[25] The gifted insurance policy is included under Sec. 2035(a)(2).

beneficiary. Peng dies in the current year. Because Peng died within three years of giving Phong the policy, Peng's gross estate includes the policy, valued at its $400,000 date-of-death value. The potential problem of making a transfer of a life insurance policy within three years of death could have been avoided had Phong been the original owner of the policy. In that case, Peng would not have made a transfer and need not have been concerned with the three-year rule. ◀

TAX STRATEGY TIP

An individual may be concerned that his or her estate will not have sufficient cash to pay its estate taxes. The individual could buy life insurance so his or her estate will have sufficient cash. However, if the individual owns the policy or names his or her estate the beneficiary of the policy, the proceeds of the policy will be taxed in the gross estate. In this case, the individual should have his or her children (or an irrevocable life insurance trust) buy the life insurance and name themselves the beneficiaries, even if the individual has to provide the funds for the premiums (by making gifts). If the children are the beneficiaries, they can use the policy proceeds to buy an asset from the estate so the estate can raise cash needed to pay the estate taxes.

CONSIDERATION OFFSET

Property is included in the gross estate at its FMV on the date of death or alternate valuation date. Section 2043 allows an offset against the amount included in the gross estate for consideration received in certain transactions.[26] This offset is allowed only if the decedent received some, but less than adequate, consideration in connection with an earlier transaction. The gross estate is reduced by an offset for the partial consideration received. The offset is for the actual dollars received, not for the pro rata portion of the cost paid by the decedent. This offset, called the consideration offset, serves the same function as a deduction in that it reduces the taxable estate. If the decedent receives consideration equal to the value of the property transferred, the property in question is not included in the gross estate. No offset is permitted if the property is excluded from the decedent's gross estate.

The consideration offset prevents a double counting of property in the decedent's estate. For example, if an individual makes a transfer that is includible in the gross estate and receives partial consideration in return, the consideration received is part of the gross estate unless it has been consumed. Sections 2035 through 2038 also require the transferred property to be included in the gross estate, even though the transferor does not own it at the date of death.

EXAMPLE C:13-33 ▶ Two years ago, Steve transferred a $300,000 life insurance policy on his life to Earl. The policy was worth $75,000 at the time of transfer, but Earl paid only $48,000 for the policy. Steve dies in the current year with the $48,000 still in his savings account. Steve's gross estate includes both the amount in the savings account and the $300,000 face value of the insurance policy. Under Sec. 2043, Steve's gross estate is reduced by the $48,000 consideration received on the transfer of the insurance policy. The insurance policy on Steve's life would be excluded from Steve's estate if Steve survived the transfer by more than three years, and no consideration offset would be permitted because the insurance is not included in the gross estate. ◀

RECIPIENT SPOUSE'S INTEREST IN QTIP TRUST

Recall from Chapter C:12 that a gift tax marital deduction is available for transferring qualified terminable interest property (QTIP) to one's spouse. A QTIP interest involves a transfer entitling the recipient spouse to all the income for life. The estate tax rules for QTIP interests are explained on page C:13-22. Claiming a marital deduction with respect to QTIP interests is voluntary. If the donor or the executor elects to claim a marital deduction for QTIP interests transferred to the spouse during life or at death, the transferred property generally is included in the recipient spouse's gross estate.[27] A QTIP interest included in the gross estate, like other property included in the gross estate, is valued at its date-of-death or alternate valuation date value.

The gross estate of the surviving spouse excludes the QTIP interest if the transferor spouse does not elect to claim a marital deduction. If the recipient spouse has a life estate, has no general power of appointment, and was not the transferor, no IRC sections other than Sec. 2044 (dealing with QTIPs) include the property in the gross estate.

No inclusion in the gross estate is required for QTIP interests for which a marital deduction is elected if the recipient spouse disposes of all or a portion of his or her income interest during his or her lifetime. However, dispositions of all or a portion of a spouse's income interest in a QTIP are treated under Sec. 2519 as a transfer of all interests in the QTIP other than the qualifying income interest. Thus, such dispositions are subject to the gift tax.

---

[26] Section 2043 provides a consideration offset for items included in the gross estate under Secs. 2035 through 2038 and Sec. 2041.

[27] Sec. 2044.

EXAMPLE C:13-34 ▶ Henry died five years ago. His will created a $2 million QTIP trust for his widow, Wendy, age 75. Henry's executor elected to claim a marital deduction for the QTIP trust. Wendy dies in the current year. By then, the assets in the QTIP trust have appreciated to $2.8 million. Wendy's gross estate includes the QTIP trust, which is valued at $2.8 million. If Henry's executor had not claimed a marital deduction for the QTIP trust, the value of the trust would be excluded from Wendy's estate. If Henry's executor had made a partial QTIP election for 70% of the trust, only 70% of the $2.8 million value would be in Wendy's gross estate. ◀

DEDUCTIONS

OBJECTIVE 4

Identify deductions available for estate tax purposes

As mentioned earlier in this chapter, deductions from the gross estate currently fall into five categories. Three of these categories (debts and funeral and administration expenses, casualty and theft losses, and state death taxes) allow the tax base to reflect the net wealth passed to the decedent's heirs, legatees, or devisees. Two other deduction categories reduce the estate tax base for transfers to the surviving spouse (the marital deduction) or to charitable organizations (the charitable contribution deduction). No deduction is available, however, for the amount of wealth diverted to the federal government in the form of estate taxes. The aggregate amount of the deductions is subtracted from the gross estate amount to determine the taxable estate. Each deduction category is examined below. Table C:13-2 provides an overview of the estate tax deductions.

TYPICAL MISCONCEPTION

Many taxpayers are so familiar with the fact that, for income tax purposes, expenses must be paid or accrued to be deductible, they do not recognize that the expenses of administering an estate can be estimated at the time the estate tax return is filed. Estimation is necessary because the administration of the estate can continue long after the estate tax return is filed.

DEBTS AND FUNERAL AND ADMINISTRATION EXPENSES

Section 2053 authorizes deductions for mortgages and other debts owed by the decedent, as well as for the decedent's funeral and administration expenses. Mortgages and all other debts of the decedent are deductible provided they represent bona fide contracts for an adequate and full consideration in money or money's worth. Even personal debts relating to an expenditure for which no income tax deduction would be allowable are deductible. Interest, state and local taxes, and trade or business expenses accrued at the date of death are deductible on both the estate tax return (as a debt of the decedent) and on the estate's income tax return (as an expense known as a deduction in respect of a decedent) when they are paid. (See Chapter C:14 for a discussion of the income tax implications.)

Examples of administration expenses include executor's commissions, attorneys' fees, court costs, accountants' fees, appraisers' fees, and expenses of preserving and distributing the estate. The executor must decide whether to deduct administration expenses on the estate tax return (Form 706) or the estate's income tax return (Form 1041). Such expenses cannot be deducted twice, although some may be deducted on the estate tax return and others on the estate's income tax return.

▼ TABLE C:13-2
Estate Tax Deductions

IRC Section	Type of Deduction
2053	Funeral and administration expenses[a] and debts
2054	Casualty and theft losses[a]
2055	Charitable contributions[b]
2056	Marital deduction[b]
2058	State death taxes[c]

[a]Deductible on the estate tax return or on the estate's income tax return.
[b]No limit on deductible amount.
[c]Available (instead of a credit) after 2004.

An estate that owes no estate tax (e.g., because of the unlimited marital deduction or the unified credit) should deduct administration expenses on its income tax return because no tax savings will result from a deduction on the estate tax return. If an estate owes estate taxes, its marginal estate tax rate will be at least 45% because the tax base will exceed the $2 million (in 2007) exemption equivalent. In 2006 and 2007 the highest income tax rate for an estate is 35%. Thus, for taxable estates exceeding $2 million, administration expenses should be deducted on the estate tax return.

Funeral expenses are deductible only on the estate tax return. The estate may deduct any funeral expenses allowable under local law including "[a] reasonable expenditure for a tombstone, monument, or mausoleum, or for a burial lot, either for the decedent or his family, including a reasonable expenditure for its future care."[28] The transportation costs of the person bringing the body to the burial place also are deductible as funeral expenses.

EXAMPLE C:13-35 ▶ At Ed's date of death, Ed owes a $75,000 mortgage on his residence, plus $280 of interest accrued thereon, and $320 of personal expenditures charged to a department store charge card. The estate's administration expenses are estimated to be $32,000. His funeral expenses total $12,000. Under Sec. 2053, Ed's estate can deduct $75,600 ($75,000 + $280 + $320) for debts and $12,000 for funeral expenses. The $32,000 of administration expenses are deductible on the estate tax return, on the estate's income tax return for the year in which they are paid, or some on each return. Ed's estate will receive an income tax deduction for the accrued mortgage interest whenever it is paid. ◀

TAX STRATEGY TIP

The executor should elect to deduct any casualty or theft loss, when such loss is allowable, from the estate tax return if the marginal estate tax rate exceeds the marginal income tax rate.

LOSSES

Section 2054 authorizes a deduction for losses incurred from theft or casualty while the estate is being settled. Just as in the context of the income tax, examples of casualties include fires, storms, and earthquakes. Any insurance compensation received affects the amount of the loss. If the alternate valuation date is elected, the loss may not be used to reduce the alternate value and then used again as a loss deduction. As with administration expenses, the executor must decide whether to deduct the loss on the estate tax return or the estate's income tax return. No double deduction is allowed for these losses, and the nondeductible floor applicable for income tax purposes does not exist for estate tax purposes.

EXAMPLE C:13-36 ▶ Sam dies on May 3. One of the items included in Sam's gross estate is a mountain cabin valued at $125,000. The uninsured cabin is totally destroyed in a landslide on August 18. If the date-of-death valuation is chosen, the cabin is included in the gross estate at $125,000. The executor must choose between claiming a Sec. 2054 loss deduction on the estate tax return or a Sec. 165 casualty loss deduction on the estate's income tax return. ◀

EXAMPLE C:13-37 ▶ Assume the same facts as in Example C:13-36 except that Sam's executor elects the alternate valuation date. The cabin is valued at zero when determining the value of the gross estate. No loss deduction is available for the casualty on the estate tax return. The estate cannot claim an income tax deduction for the casualty loss either because the property's adjusted basis in its hands is zero. ◀

CHARITABLE CONTRIBUTION DEDUCTION

Section 2055 authorizes a deduction for transfers to charitable organizations. The rules concerning eligible donee organizations are the same as for gift tax purposes.

Because the estate tax charitable contribution deduction is unlimited, a decedent could eliminate his or her estate tax liability by willing all his or her property (or all property except for an amount equal to the exemption equivalent) to a charitable organization. Similarly, a decedent could eliminate an estate tax liability by willing an amount equal to the exemption equivalent to the children and the rest of the estate to the surviving spouse and a charitable organization (e.g., in equal shares).[29] People who desire to leave some property to a charity at their death should be encouraged to consider giving the property before death, so they can obtain an income tax deduction for the gift and also reduce their gross estate by the amount of the gift.

---

[28] Reg. Sec. 20.2053-2.

[29] Another way the estate could owe no taxes is if all of the property, or all of the property except for the exemption equivalent, is shielded from taxation by the marital deduction.

COMPUTING THE DEDUCTION. In certain circumstances, computation of the estate tax charitable contribution deduction can be somewhat complicated. Suppose the decedent (a widow) has a $5 million gross estate and no Sec. 2053 or 2054 deductions. The decedent's will specifies that her son is to receive $3 million and a charitable organization is to receive the residue (the rest not explicitly disposed of). Assume that state law specifies that death taxes are payable from the residue. Because $3 million of property passes to the decedent's child, the estate will definitely owe some estate taxes. The charitable organization will receive $2 million, less the estate taxes payable therefrom. The estate tax liability depends on the amount of the charitable contribution deduction, which in turn depends on the amount of the estate tax liability. Simultaneous equations are required to calculate the amount of the charitable contribution deduction.[30]

EXAMPLE C:13-38 ▶ Ahmed, a widower, dies with a gross estate of $6 million. Ahmed wills State University $1 million and the residue of his estate to his children. Under state law, death taxes are payable from the residue. In this scenario, Ahmed's estate receives a charitable contribution deduction for $1 million because the estate taxes are charged against the children's share (the residue). ◀

SPLIT-INTEREST TRANSFERS. If the decedent's will provides for a split-interest transfer (i.e., a transfer of interests to both an individual and a charitable organization), the rules concerning whether a charitable contribution deduction is available are very technical. Basically, the rules are the same as for gift tax purposes (discussed in Chapter C:12).

EXAMPLE C:13-39 ▶ Jane dies in the current year with a gross estate of $3.5 million. Under Sec. 2036, Jane's gross estate includes her personal residence, valued at $350,000. She gave City Art Museum a remainder interest in the residence in 1995 but retained the right to live there rent-free for the rest of her life. Upon Jane's death, no other individuals have an interest in the residence. Jane received an income tax deduction in 1995 for the value of the remainder interest and incurred no gift tax liability. Her estate receives a $350,000 charitable contribution deduction.

Her lifetime transfer triggers no added estate tax cost. The residence is included in her gross estate, but the inclusion is a wash because of the estate tax charitable contribution deduction claimed for the value of the residence. ◀

MARITAL DEDUCTION

The fourth category of deductions is the marital deduction for certain property passing to the decedent's surviving spouse.[31] Because the marital deduction is unlimited, the decedent's estate does not owe any federal estate taxes if all the items includible in the gross estate (or all items except an amount equal to the exemption equivalent) pass to the surviving spouse.[32] If the surviving spouse is not a U.S. citizen, however, a marital deduction is not available unless the decedent's property passes to a special trust called a qualified domestic trust.

TAX STRATEGY TIP
The marital deduction defers the estate tax until the death of the surviving spouse and protects against liquidity problems when the first spouse dies. Moreover, the surviving spouse can reduce the overall estate tax through personal consumption and a lifetime gifting program.

The marital deduction provides equal treatment for decedents of common law and community property states. As mentioned in Chapter C:12, marital property is treated differently under each type of state law. In community property states, for example, a large portion of the assets acquired after a couple marries constitutes community property (i.e., property owned equally by each spouse). On the other hand, in common law states, one spouse may own the majority of the assets acquired after marriage. Thus, with no marital deduction, the progressive estate tax rates could cause the combined estate tax liability to be higher for a couple living in a noncommunity property state. Nevertheless, a marital deduction is available to decedents who own nothing but community property.

Only certain transfers to the surviving spouse are eligible for the marital deduction. The estate does not receive a marital deduction unless the interest conveyed to the surviving spouse will be subject to either the estate tax in the recipient spouse's estate or to the

[30] The simultaneous equation problem generally does not occur if a charity receives a bequest of a specific dollar amount. See Reg. Sec. 20.2055-3 for a discussion of death taxes payable from charitable transfers.

[31] Sec. 2056.

[32] Some states have not adopted an unlimited marital deduction; therefore, some estates may owe state death taxes even though no federal liability would otherwise exist. Payment of substantial sums to a state as taxes will reduce the amount passing to the spouse as a marital deduction and can cause federal taxes to be owed.

gift tax if transferred while the surviving spouse is alive. In other words, the surviving spouse generally can escape transfer taxation on the transferred property only by consuming it.

The following three tests must be met before an interest qualifies for the marital deduction:

- The property must be included in the decedent's gross estate.
- The property must pass to the recipient spouse in a qualifying manner.
- The interest conveyed must not be a nondeductible terminable interest.

TEST 1: INCLUSION IN THE GROSS ESTATE. No property passing to the surviving spouse is eligible for the marital deduction unless the property is included in the decedent's gross estate. The reason for this rule is obvious: Assets excluded from the gross estate cannot generate a deduction.

EXAMPLE C:13-40 ▶ Gail is insured under a life insurance policy for which her husband, Al, is the beneficiary. Gail's sister always had the incidents of ownership in the policy. Gail held the title to the personal residence in which she and Al lived. She willed the residence to Al, and the residence qualifies for the marital deduction. Even though the insurance proceeds are payable to Al, Gail's estate receives no marital deduction for the insurance. The policy is excluded from Gail's gross estate because she had no incidents of ownership, her estate was not the beneficiary, and the policy was not transferred within three years of her death. ◀

TEST 2: THE PASSING REQUIREMENT. Property is not eligible for the marital deduction unless it passes to the decedent's spouse in a qualifying manner. According to Sec. 2056(c), property is deemed to pass from one spouse to the other if the surviving spouse receives the property because of

- A bequest or devise under the decedent's will
- An inheritance resulting from the decedent dying intestate
- Dower or curtesy rights
- An earlier transfer from the decedent
- Right of survivorship
- An appointment by the decedent under a general power of appointment or in default of appointment
- A designation as the beneficiary of a life insurance policy on the decedent's life

In addition, a surviving spouse's interest in a retirement benefit plan is considered to have passed from the decedent to the survivor to the extent the retirement benefits are included in the gross estate.[33]

TEST 3: THE TERMINABLE INTEREST RULE. The last statutory test (also applicable for gift tax purposes) requires that the recipient-spouse's interest *not* be classified as a nondeductible terminable interest.[34] A terminable interest is one that ceases with the passage of time or the occurrence of some event. Some terminable interests qualify for the marital deduction, however, because only *nondeductible* terminable interests fail to generate a marital deduction. Nondeductible terminable interests have the following features:

- An interest in the property must pass or have passed from the decedent to a person other than the surviving spouse, and such person must have paid less than adequate consideration in money or money's worth.
- The other person may possess or enjoy any part of the property after the termination of the surviving spouse's interest.

Thus, if the decedent makes a transfer granting the surviving spouse the right to receive all the income annually for life and a general power of appointment over the

[33] Reg. Sec. 20.2056(e)-1(a)(6).

[34] Nondeductible terminable interests also are precluded from eligibility for the marital deduction for gift tax purposes.

property, the property is eligible for the marital deduction. As discussed below, as a result of the QTIP provisions a marital deduction is available for certain transfers that otherwise would be disqualified under the nondeductible terminable interest rule.

EXAMPLE C:13-41 ▶ At the time of Louis's death, he wills a copyright with a ten-year remaining life to his wife, Tina, age 42. His will also sets up a trust for the benefit of Tina, whom he entitles to receive all of the income semiannually until the earlier of her remarriage or her death. Upon Tina's remarriage or death, the trust property is to be distributed to the couple's children or their estates. Both the copyright and the trust are terminable interests. The copyright is eligible for the marital deduction because it is not a nondeductible terminable interest; the copyright simply ends at the expiration of its legal life. No person other than Tina receives an interest in the copyright. No marital deduction is available for the trust because it is a nondeductible terminable interest. Upon the termination of Tina's interest, the children will possess the property, and they receive their interests from Louis without paying adequate consideration. ◀

SELF-STUDY QUESTION

A decedent, by will, creates a trust with income to the surviving spouse for 25 years, the remainder to their children. The surviving spouse's life expectancy is 16 years. Does the property qualify for the marital deduction?

ANSWER

The property does not qualify because the surviving spouse's interest terminates at the end of a specified number of years. The spouse's shorter life expectancy is irrelevant.

QTIP TRANSFERS. Section 2056(b)(7) authorizes a marital deduction for transfers of qualified terminable interest property (called QTIP transfers). The QTIP provisions are somewhat revolutionary compared with earlier law because they allow a marital deduction in situations where the recipient spouse is not entitled to designate which parties eventually receive the property.

Qualified terminable interest property is defined as property that passes from the decedent, in which the surviving spouse has a qualifying income interest for life, and to which an election applies. A spouse has a qualifying income interest for life if the following are true:

- He or she is entitled to all the income from the property, payable at least annually.
- No person has a power to appoint any portion of the property to anyone other than the surviving spouse unless the power cannot be exercised during the spouse's lifetime (e.g., it is exercisable only at or after the death of the surviving spouse).

SELF-STUDY QUESTION

How does the donor spouse or decedent spouse who establishes a QTIP trust control the disposition of the trust corpus?

ANSWER

The donor or decedent spouse states in the trust instrument or in his or her will who will receive the remainder interest on the death of the recipient spouse.

Claiming the marital deduction with respect to QTIP transfers is not mandatory, and partial elections also are allowed. In the event the executor elects to claim a marital deduction for 100% of the QTIP transfer, the marital deduction is for the entire amount of the QTIP transfer. In other words, the deduction is not limited to the value of the surviving spouse's life estate.

If the marital deduction is elected in the first spouse's estate, the property is taxed in the surviving spouse's estate under Sec. 2044 or is subject to the gift tax in such spouse's hands if disposed of during the spouse's lifetime.[35] Thus, as with other interspousal transfers, the QTIP provisions allow a postponement of the taxable event until the second spouse dies or disposes of the interest by gift. If the taxable event is postponed, the property is valued at its FMV as of the date the second spouse transfers the property by gift or at death. See the Tax Planning Considerations section of this chapter for a discussion of planning opportunities (including partial QTIP elections) with the marital deduction.

EXAMPLE C:13-42 ▶ Tom died in 1995, survived by his wife, Mary, who lives until the current year. Tom's will called for setting up a $1 million trust from which Mary would receive all the income quarterly for the rest of her life. Upon Mary's death, the property is to be distributed to Tom's children by a previous marriage. If Tom's executor elects to claim a marital deduction, Tom's estate receives a $1 million marital deduction. At Mary's death, the trust assets are valued at $2.2 million. Section 2044 includes $2.2 million in Mary's gross estate. If Tom's executor forgoes electing the marital deduction, Mary's gross estate excludes the value of the trust. In either event, the trust assets will be taxed in the estate of one of the spouses, but not both. ◀

ADDITIONAL COMMENT

Refer to Example C:13-42. The executor may elect QTIP status for less than the entire property in the trust. For example, the executor might elect QTIP treatment for only 60% of the $1 million placed in the trust. On Mary's death, 60% of $1.7 million, or $1.02 million, is included in Mary's gross estate.

STATE DEATH TAXES. For estates of decedents dying after 2004, Sec. 2058 allows a deduction for state death taxes. Eligible taxes include estate, inheritance, legacy, and succession taxes paid to a state or the District of Columbia. The taxes must be paid no later than four years after the filing of the estate tax return. The amount of the deduction is the amount paid and, unlike the state death tax credit formerly available, is not restricted to a maximum amount.

---

[35] Section 2519 states that, if a recipient spouse disposes of a qualifying income interest for life for which the donor or the executor elected a marital deduction under the QTIP rules, the recipient spouse is treated as having made a gift of everything except the qualifying income interest. Under the generic gift rules of Sec. 2511, the gift of the income interest is treated as a gift.

COMPUTATION OF TAX LIABILITY

OBJECTIVE 5

Calculate the estate tax liability

As mentioned earlier, the estate tax base is the aggregate of the decedent's taxable estate and his or her adjusted taxable gifts. Figure C:13-1 earlier in this chapter illustrates how the estate tax formula combines these two concepts.

TAXABLE ESTATE AND TAX BASE

The gross estate's value is reduced by the deductions to arrive at the amount of the taxable estate. Under the unification provisions effective after 1976, the estate tax base consists of the taxable estate plus the adjusted taxable gifts, defined as *all* taxable gifts made *after 1976 other than* gifts included in the gross estate. The addition of the adjusted taxable gifts to the estate tax base may cause an estate to be taxed at a higher marginal tax rate. If the decedent elects gift splitting (discussed in Chapter 12), the decedent's adjusted taxable gifts equal the amount of the taxable gifts the individual is deemed to have made after applying the gift-splitting provisions. Adjusted taxable gifts can arise from consenting to gift splitting, even though the decedent never actually gives away any property.

Adjusted taxable gifts are valued at date-of-gift values; therefore, any post-gift appreciation is exempt from the transfer taxes. The estate tax computations for decedents who never made gifts exceeding the excludable amount reflect no adjusted taxable gifts.

SELF-STUDY QUESTION

Verda died penniless in 2007. Because of consenting to gift splitting, her taxable gifts made in 1999 were $1.75 million. She paid $457,000 of gift taxes on these gifts. What is her unified tax base?

ANSWER

Her unified tax base is $1.75 million, the amount of her lifetime taxable gifts. Note that the gifts are valued at what they were worth on the date of the gift.

SELF-STUDY QUESTION

Refer to the previous self-study question. What is the amount of the unified tax before credits? After credits?

ANSWER

The unified tax before credits is $668,300. This tax is reduced by the unified credit of $780,800 and by post-1976 gift taxes of $457,000, which leaves zero tax due. Verda's unified tax base of $1.75 million is below the $2 million exemption equivalent.

TENTATIVE TAX AND REDUCTION FOR POST-1976 GIFT TAXES

The tentative tax is computed on the estate tax base, which is the sum of the taxable estate and the adjusted taxable gifts, if any.[36] The unified transfer tax rates are found in Sec. 2001(c) and are reproduced on the inside back cover. The tentative tax is reduced by the decedent's post-1976 gift taxes. In determining the tax on post-1976 taxable gifts, the effect of gift splitting is taken into consideration. That is, the amount of the post-1976 gift taxes is usually the levy imposed on the taxable gifts the decedent is deemed to have made after applying any gift-splitting election.

If the tax rates change between the time of the gift and the time of death, the subtraction for gift taxes equals the amount of gift taxes that would have been payable on post-1976 gifts had the rate schedule applicable in the year of death been in effect in the year of the gift. The only "as if" computation is for the gross tax amount; the unified credit actually used on the gift tax return is subtracted to determine the amount of gift tax that would have been payable at current rates.

UNIFIED CREDIT

The excess of the tentative tax over the post-1976 gift taxes is reduced by the unified credit of Sec. 2010. The amount of this credit has changed over the years and will increase through 2009; in 2007 it is $780,800 (see inside back cover). With a credit of $780,800, the tax on a $2 million tax base is completely eliminated. The unified credit never generates a refund; the most relief it can provide is to eliminate an estate's federal estate tax liability.

Section 2010(c) provides that the unified credit otherwise available for estate tax purposes must be reduced because of certain pre-1977 gifts. Before 1977, a $30,000 lifetime exemption was available for the gift tax. Donors could claim some or all of this exemption whenever they so desired. For post-1976 years, Congress repealed the exemption and replaced it with the unified credit. If the decedent claimed any portion of the $30,000 exemption against gifts made after September 8, 1976, and before January 1, 1977, the unified credit was reduced by 20% of the exemption claimed.

[36] Sec. 2001(b).

EXAMPLE C:13-43 ▶ Carl dies in 2007 with a tax base of $2 million. In October 1976, Carl made his first taxable gift. Carl claimed the $30,000 exemption to reduce the amount of his taxable gifts. Thus, Carl's $780,800 unified credit is reduced by $6,000 (0.20 × $30,000). If Carl claimed the exemption by making a gift on or before September 8, 1976, his estate would be entitled to the full $780,800 credit. ◀

OTHER CREDITS

The IRC authorizes three additional credits: a gift tax credit on pre-1977 gifts, a credit for another decedent's estate taxes paid on prior transfers, and a credit for foreign death taxes. (Prior to 2005, the IRC also allowed a state death tax credit.) These credits apply less often than the unified credit. Like the unified credit, these credits cannot exceed the amount of the estate tax actually owed.

PRE-2005 STATE DEATH TAX CREDIT. For years all states levied some form of death tax: an inheritance tax, an estate tax, or both. Many states enacted a simple system whereby the state death tax liability equaled the credit for state death taxes allowed on the federal estate tax return.

Prior to 2005, Sec. 2011 allowed a credit calculated in accordance with the table contained in Sec. 2011(b). As mentioned earlier, beginning in 2005, a deduction replaced the credit. With the demise of the credit, if a jurisdiction had imposed a state death tax equal to the credit allowed on the federal return for state death taxes, no state death tax will be owed after 2004 *unless* that jurisdiction changes its tax rules.

EXAMPLE C:13-44 ▶ John died in 2007 with a taxable estate of $3.6 million. If he resided in a state whose statute imposes an estate tax equal to the credit available on the federal return for state death taxes, his estate will owe nothing to the state. In effect, his state no longer has an estate tax. On the other hand, if he resided in a state that levies an inheritance tax based on the value of the property the various heirs receive, his estate will receive a deduction (not a credit) for the inheritance tax paid. ◀

CREDIT FOR PRE-1977 GIFT TAXES. Section 2012(a) authorizes a credit for gift taxes paid by the decedent on pre-1977 gifts that must be included in the gross estate. Remember that Sec. 2001(b)(2) allows a reduction for gift taxes paid on post-1976 gifts, but the IRC does not refer to this item as a credit. The following transaction involves a situation in which the credit for pre-1977 gift taxes applies.

EXAMPLE C:13-45 ▶ In 1975, Yuji created a trust from which he is to receive the income for life and his son, Yuji, Jr., is to receive the remainder. Yuji paid a gift tax on the 1975 gift of the remainder. Upon Yuji's death in the current year, the date-of-death value of the trust's assets is included in his estate under Sec. 2036. Yuji's estate receives a credit for some or all of his 1975 gift taxes. ◀

In general, the credit for pre-1977 gift taxes equals the amount of gift taxes paid with respect to transfers included in the gross estate. Because of a ceiling rule, however, the amount of the credit sometimes is lower than the amount of gift taxes paid. A discussion of the credit ceiling computation is beyond the scope of this text.

CREDIT FOR TAX ON PRIOR TRANSFERS. The credit available under Sec. 2013 for the estate taxes paid on prior transfers reduces the cost of having property taxed in more than one estate in quick succession. Without this credit, the overall tax cost could be quite severe if the legatee dies soon after the original decedent. The credit applies if the person who transfers the property (i.e., the transferor-decedent) to the decedent in question (i.e., the transferee-decedent) dies no more than ten years before, or within two years after, the date of the transferee-decedent's death. The potential credit is the smaller of the federal estate tax of the transferor-decedent attributable to the transferred interest or the federal estate tax of the transferee-decedent attributable to the transferred interest.

To determine the final credit, the potential credit is multiplied by a percentage that varies inversely with the period of time separating the two dates of death. If the transferor dies no more than two years before or after the transferee, the credit percentage is 100%. As specified in Sec. 2013(a), the other percentages are as follows:

Number of Years by Which Transferor's Death Precedes the Transferee's Death	*Credit Percentage*
More than 2, but not more than 4	80
More than 4, but not more than 6	60
More than 6, but not more than 8	40
More than 8, but not more than 10	20

The following two examples illustrate situations in which the credit for the taxes paid on prior transfers applies.

EXAMPLE C:13-46 ▶ Mary died on March 1, 2002. All of Mary's property passed to Debra, her daughter. Debra dies on June 1, 2007. All of Debra's property passes to her son. Both Mary's and Debra's estates pay federal estate taxes. Debra's estate is entitled to a credit for a percentage of some, or all, of the taxes paid by Mary's estate. Because Mary's death preceded Debra's death by five years and three months, the credit for the tax paid on prior transfers is 60% of the potential credit. ◀

EXAMPLE C:13-47 ▶ Ed died on May 7, 2006. One of the items included in Ed's estate is a life insurance policy on Sam's life. Sam had given Ed all his incidents of ownership in this policy on December 13, 2005. Sam dies on June 15, 2007, which is within three years of making a gift of the insurance policy on his own life. The policy is included in Sam's gross estate under Sec. 2035. Because Sam dies within two years of Ed's death, Ed's estate is entitled to a credit for 100% of the potential credit and an amended return must be filed to claim this credit. ◀

SELF-STUDY QUESTION

What is the effect of the maximum credit provision for the foreign death tax credit?

ANSWER

The effect is to tax the property located in the foreign country at the higher of the U.S. estate tax rate or the foreign death tax rate.

FOREIGN DEATH TAX CREDIT. Under Sec. 2014, the estate is entitled to a credit for some or all of the death taxes paid to a foreign country for property located in that foreign country and included in the gross estate. The maximum credit is the smaller of the foreign death tax attributable to the property located in the foreign country that imposed the tax or the federal estate tax attributable to the property located in the foreign country and taxed by such country.

COMPREHENSIVE ILLUSTRATION

The following comprehensive illustration demonstrates the computation of the estate tax liability.

BACKGROUND DATA

Herman Estes dies on October 13, 2006. Herman, an Ohio resident, is survived by his widow, Ann, and three adult children. During his lifetime, Herman made three gifts, as follows:

- In 1974, he gave his son Billy $103,000 cash. Herman claimed the $30,000 exemption (then available) and a $3,000 annual exclusion available then. The taxable gift was $70,000.
- In 1978, he gave his daughter, Dotty, $203,000 cash. He claimed a $3,000 annual exclusion available then and thus made a $200,000 taxable gift on which he paid a $28,000 gift tax, after claiming the $34,000 unified credit.
- In December 2004, he gave his son, Johnny, stock then worth $1,511,000. Herman claimed an $11,000 annual exclusion and thus made a $1.5 million taxable gift. He claimed the available unified credit of $311,800 ($345,800 − $34,000) and paid a $287,900 gift tax. On October 13, 2006, the stock is worth $1.75 million.

Property discovered after Herman's death appears below. All amounts represent date-of-death values.

- Checking account containing $19,250.
- Savings account containing $75,000.
- Land worth $400,000 held in the names of Herman and Ann, joint tenants with right of survivorship (JTWROS). Herman provided all the consideration to buy the land in January 1993.
- Life insurance policy 123-A with a face value of $200,000. Herman had incidents of ownership; Johnny is the beneficiary.
- A personal residence titled in Herman's name worth $325,000.
- Stock in Ajax Corporation worth $1.6 million.
- Qualified pension plan to which Herman's employer made 60% of the contributions and Herman made 40%. Ann is to receive a lump-sum distribution of $240,000.
- A trust created under the will of Herman's mother, Amelia, who died in 1992. Herman was entitled to receive all the income quarterly for life. In his will, Herman could appoint the trust assets to such of his descendants as he desired. The trust assets are valued at $375,000.

At his death, Herman owes a $25,200 bank loan, including $200 accrued interest. Balances due on his various charge cards total $6,500. Herman's funeral expenses are $15,000, and his administration expenses are estimated to be $70,000. Assume that the maximum tax savings will occur by deducting the administration expenses on the estate tax return.

Herman's will contains the following provisions:

- "To my wife, Ann, I leave my residence, my savings account, and $10,000 from my checking account."
- "I leave $200,000 of property in trust with First Bank as trustee. My wife, Ann, is to receive all the income from this trust fund quarterly for the rest of her life. Upon Ann's death, the trust property is to be divided equally among our three children."
- "To the American Cancer Society I leave $10,000."
- "I appoint the property in the trust created by my mother, Amelia Estes, to my daughter, Dotty."
- "The residue of my estate is to be divided equally between my sons, Johnny and Billy."

CALCULATION OF TAX LIABILITY

Table C:13-3 illustrates the computation of Herman's estate tax liability. These same facts are used for the sample Estate Tax Return (Form 706) included in Appendix B. For illustration purposes, it is assumed that the executor elects to claim the marital deduction on the QTIP trust and that Herman's state levies death taxes equal to the maximum federal credit for state death taxes. As mentioned earlier, after 2004 an estate receives a deduction instead of a credit for state death taxes. Thus, because the federal government allows no credit for state death taxes, Herman's estate owes nothing to the state.

Note that several factors affect the computation set out in Table C:13-3:

- Herman had only a special power of appointment over the assets in the trust created by his mother because he could will the property only to his descendants. Therefore, the trust property is not included in his estate.
- Assets that pass to the surviving spouse outside the will, such as by survivorship and by beneficiary designation, can qualify for the marital deduction.
- Adjusted taxable gifts (added to the taxable estate) include only post-1976 taxable gifts.
- The estate tax payable is not reduced by pre-1977 gift taxes unless the gifted property is included in the gross estate.
- Because the highest marginal income tax rate for the estate is less than its 46% marginal estate tax rate and because the estate owes a tax liability (even with the available credits), administration expenses should be deducted on the estate tax return.

▼ **TABLE C:13-3**
Comprehensive Estate Tax Illustration

Gross estate:	
Checking account (Sec. 2033)	$ 19,250
Savings account (Sec. 2033)	75,000
Land held in joint tenancy with wife (0.50 × $400,000) (Sec. 2040)	200,000
Life insurance (Sec. 2042)	200,000
Personal residence (Sec. 2033)	325,000
Ajax stock (Sec. 2033)	1,600,000
Qualified pension plan (Sec. 2039)	240,000
Gross-up for gift tax paid on 2004 gift (Sec. 2035)	287,900
Total gross estate	$2,947,150
Minus:	
Debts (Sec. 2053):	
Bank loan, including $200 accrued interest	(25,200)
Charge cards	(6,500)
Funeral expenses (Sec. 2053)	(15,000)
Administration expenses (Sec. 2053)	(70,000)
Marital deduction (Sec. 2056):	
Residence (under will)	(325,000)
Checking account (under will)	(10,000)
Savings account (under will)	(75,000)
QTIP trust (under will)	(200,000)
Land (JTWROS)	(200,000)
Qualified pension plan (beneficiary)	(240,000)
Charitable contribution deduction (Sec. 2055)	(10,000)
Total reductions to gross estate	($1,176,700)
Taxable estate	$1,770,450
Plus adjusted taxable gifts (Sec. 2001(b)):	
1978 taxable gifts	200,000[a]
2004 taxable gifts	1,500,000[a]
Estate tax base	$3,470,450
Tentative tax on tax base (Sec. 2001)	$1,457,207
Minus:	
Reduction for post-1976 gift taxes (Sec. 2001(b))	(315,900)[b]
Unified credit (Sec. 2010)	(780,800)
Estate tax payable	$ 360,507

[a]Valued at date-of-gift fair market values.
[b]$28,000 (for 1978) + $287,900 (for 2004) = $315,900.

LIQUIDITY CONCERNS

OBJECTIVE 6

Identify tax provisions that alleviate liquidity problems

Liquidity is one of the major problems facing individuals planning their estates and executors eventually managing the estates. Individuals often use life insurance to help address this problem. In general, the entire amount of the estate tax liability is due nine months after the decedent's death. Certain provisions, however, allow the executor to pay some or all of the estate tax liability at a later date. Deferral of part or all of the estate tax payments and two other provisions aimed at alleviating a liquidity problem are discussed below.

DEFERRAL OF PAYMENT OF ESTATE TAXES

REASONABLE CAUSE. Section 6161(a)(1) authorizes the Secretary of the Treasury to extend the payment date for the estate taxes for a *reasonable period*, defined as a period of not longer than 12 months. Moreover, the Secretary of the Treasury may extend the payment date for a maximum period of ten years if the executor shows reasonable cause for not being able to pay some, or all, of the estate tax liability on the regular date.[37]

Whenever the executor pays a portion of the estate tax after the regular due date, the estate owes interest on the portion of the tax for which it postpones payment. In general, the interest rate, which is governed by Sec. 6621, is the same as that applicable to underpayments. The interest rate on underpayments potentially fluctuates quarterly with changes in the rate paid on short-term U.S. Treasury obligations.[38]

REMAINDER OR REVERSIONARY INTERESTS. If the gross estate includes a relatively large remainder or reversionary interest, liquidity problems could result if the estate has to pay the entire estate tax liability soon after the decedent's death. For example, the estate might include a remainder interest in an asset in which a healthy, 30-year-old person has a life estate. The estate might not gain possession of the assets until many years after the decedent's death. Section 6163 permits the executor to elect to postpone payment of the tax attributable to a remainder or reversionary interest until six months after the other interests terminate, which in the example would be after the person currently age 30 died. In addition, upon being convinced of reasonable cause, the Secretary of the Treasury may grant an additional extension of not more than three years.

TAX STRATEGY TIP

A person who owns a substantial interest in a small business might choose to gift property other than the business interest. He or she may want to retain the business interest so that his or her estate will qualify for the five-year deferral, ten-installment option of Sec. 6166. See Tax Planning Considerations for further details.

INTERESTS IN CLOSELY HELD BUSINESSES. Section 6166 authorizes the executor to pay a portion of the estate tax in as many as ten annual installments in certain situations. Executors may elect to apply Sec. 6166 if

- The gross estate includes an interest in a closely held business, and
- The value of the closely held business exceeds 35% of the value of the adjusted gross estate.

Closely held businesses are defined as proprietorships and partnerships or corporations having no more than 45 owners.[39] If a corporation or partnership has more than 45 owners, it can be classified as closely held if the decedent's gross estate includes 20% or more of the capital interest (in the partnership) or 20% or more of the value of the voting stock (in the corporation).[40]

The adjusted gross estate is defined as the gross estate less *allowable* Sec. 2053 and 2054 deductions. Consequently, in determining whether the estate meets the 35% requirement, all administration expenses and casualty and theft losses are subtracted, regardless of whether the executor elects to deduct them on the estate tax return or the estate's income tax return.

Once the election is chosen, the following provisions apply:

- The portion of the estate tax that can be paid in installments is the ratio of the value of the closely held business interest to the value of the adjusted gross estate.
- The first of the ten allowable installments generally is not due until five years after the due date for the return. (This provision defers the last payment for as many as 15 years.)
- Interest on the tax due is payable annually, even during the first five years.

Some or all of the installment payments may accrue interest at a rate of only 2%. The maximum amount of deferred tax to which the 2% rate applies is (1) the tax on the total of $1 million of value (as indexed) and the exemption equivalent amount less (2) the unified credit. In no event, however, may the amount exceed the tax postponed under Sec. 6166.[41] The $1 million amount is indexed for inflation with inflation adjustments rounded to the next lowest $10,000; for 2007, this amount is $1.25 million. The interest rate on any additional deferred tax is 45% of the rate applicable to underpayments. The

[37] Sec. 6161(a)(2).
[38] Sec. 6621. The interest rate is discussed in Chapter C:15.
[39] Sec. 6166(b)(1).
[40] Ibid.
[41] Sec. 6601(j).

downside is the interest paid is not deductible as interest expense on the estate's income tax return or as an administrative expense on the estate tax return.

EXAMPLE C:13-48 ▶ Frank dies on March 1, 2007. Frank's gross estate, which includes a proprietorship interest valued at $1 million, is $2.6 million. The executor deducts all $100,000 of the potential Sec. 2053 and 2054 deductions on the estate tax return. Frank has no marital or charitable contribution deductions and makes no taxable gifts. Frank's adjusted gross estate, taxable estate, and tax base are $2.5 million. His estate tax payable is $225,000 ($1,005,800 − $780,800). Frank's closely held business interest makes up 40% ($1,000,000 ÷ $2,500,000) of his adjusted gross estate.

Thus, $90,000 (0.40 × $225,000) may be paid in ten equal annual installments. The first installment payment is due on December 1, 2012. The 2% interest rate potentially applies to $562,500 [$1,343,300, the tax on $3.25 million ($1,250,000 + $2,000,000), minus the unified credit of $780,800] of deferred tax liability. However, because this estate's postponed tax is only $90,000, all the interest accrues at the 2% rate. ◀

STOCK REDEMPTIONS TO PAY DEATH TAXES

Sometimes an estate's major asset is stock in a closely held corporation. In this situation, the corporation may have to redeem some of the corporate stock to provide the estate sufficient liquidity to pay death taxes. As discussed in Chapter C:4, stock redemptions generally receive sale or exchange treatment only if they meet certain requirements under Sec. 302, such as being substantially disproportionate or involving a complete termination of the shareholder's interest. Without exchange treatment and assuming sufficient earnings and profits, the redeemed shareholder (e.g., the estate) recognizes a dividend equal to the redemption proceeds rather than a capital gain equal to the difference between the redemption proceeds and the stock's adjusted basis. Because of the 15% maximum tax rate on dividends, the primary benefit of sale or exchange treatment is being able to apply basis against proceeds. To reduce the income tax cost upon a shareholder's death, Sec. 303 allows the estate to treat a redemption as an exchange even if it does not satisfy the stringent Sec. 302 requirements. This treatment minimizes any gain recognized because the stock's adjusted basis, which is subtracted from the redemption proceeds, is stepped up to its FMV upon the decedent's death.

To qualify for Sec. 303 treatment, the stock in the corporation redeeming the shares must make up more than 35% of the value of the decedent's gross estate, less any *allowable* Sec. 2053 and 2054 deductions. The maximum amount of redemption proceeds eligible for exchange treatment is the total of the estate's death taxes and funeral and administration expenses, regardless of whether they are deducted on the estate tax return or the estate's income tax return.

SELF-STUDY QUESTION

Why might an heir to farmland want an estate to forego the special valuation method of Sec. 2032A?

ANSWER

The heir may contemplate selling the land and prefer the higher basis he or she would get if FMV is used rather than the special farmland value, especially if the estate taxes are payable out of the residual estate and the heir does not share in that residual.

SPECIAL USE VALUATION OF FARM REAL PROPERTY

In 1976, Congress became concerned that farms sometimes had to be sold to generate funds to pay estate taxes. This situation was attributable, in part, to the FMV of farm land in many areas being relatively high, perhaps because of suburban housing being built nearby. Congress enacted Sec. 2032A, which allows real property used for farming or in a trade or business other than farming to be valued using a formula approach that attempts to value the property at what it is worth for farming purposes. The lowest valuation permitted is $750,000 less than the property's FMV, but the $750,000 is indexed after 1998 with adjustments rounded to the next lowest $10,000. In 2007, the indexed amount is $940,000.

The estate must meet a number of requirements before the executor can elect the special valuation rules.[42] Moreover, if during the ten-year period after the decedent's death the new owner of the property disposes of it or no longer uses it as a farm, in general, an additional tax equal to the estate tax savings that arose from the lower Sec. 2032A valuation is levied.

---

[42] For example, the farm real and personal property must make up at least 50% of the adjusted value of the gross estate, and the farm real property must make up 25% or more of the adjusted value of the gross estate.

GENERATION-SKIPPING TRANSFER TAX

The Tax Reform Act of 1976 enacted a third transfer tax—the generation-skipping transfer tax (GSTT)—to fill a void in the gift and estate tax structure. In 1986, Congress repealed the original GSTT retroactive to its original effective date and replaced it with a revised GSTT. The revised GSTT generally applies to *inter vivos* transfers made after September 25, 1985 and transfers at death made after October 22, 1986.

For years, a popular estate planning technique, especially among the very wealthy, involved giving individuals in several generations an interest in the same property. For example, a decedent might set up a testamentary trust creating successive life estates for a child and a grandchild and a remainder interest for a great grandchild. Under this arrangement, an estate tax would be imposed at the death of the person establishing the trust but not again until the great grandchild's death. The GSTT's purpose is to ensure that some form of transfer taxation is imposed one time a generation. It accomplishes its purpose by subjecting transfers that escape gift or estate taxation for one or more generations to the GSTT.

The GSTT is levied at a flat rate, the highest estate tax rate.[43] The tax applies to direct skip gifts and bequests and to taxable terminations of and taxable distributions from generation-skipping transfers. A **generation-skipping transfer** involves a disposition that

- ▶ Provides interests for more than one generation of beneficiaries who are in a younger generation than the transferor, or
- ▶ Provides an interest solely for a person two or more generations younger than the transferor.[44]

The recipient must be a skip person, a person two or more generations younger than the decedent (or the donor). For family members, generation assignments are made according to the family tree. Transfers to skip persons outside of a trust are known as direct skips because they skip one or more generations.

EXAMPLE C:13-49 ▶ Tom transfers an asset directly to Tom, III, his grandson. This is a direct skip type of generation-skipping transfer because the transferee (Tom, III) is two generations younger than the transferor (Tom). ◀

The termination of an interest in a generation-skipping arrangement is known as a taxable termination.[45] This event triggers imposition of the GSTT. The tax is levied on the before-tax amount transferred, and the trustee pays the tax.

EXAMPLE C:13-50 ▶ Tom creates a trust with income payable to his son, Tom, Jr., for life and a remainder interest distributable to Tom, III, upon the death of Tom, Jr. (his father). This is a generation-skipping transfer because Tom, Jr., and Tom, III, are one and two generations younger, respectively, than the transferor (Tom). A taxable termination occurs when Tom, Jr. dies. ◀

EXAMPLE C:13-51 ▶ The trust in Example C:13-50 is worth $2 million when Tom, Jr. dies in 2007. Tom, Jr. used his GSTT exemption against other transfers. The amount of the taxable termination is $2 million. The tax is $900,000 (0.45 × $2,000,000). The trustee pays the tax and distributes the $1.1 million of remaining assets to the beneficiary. ◀

In the case of a direct skip, the amount subject to the GSTT is the value of the property received by the transferee.[46] The transferor is liable for the tax. If the direct skip occurs *inter vivos*, the GSTT paid by the transferor is treated as an additional transfer subject to the gift tax.[47] As a result, the total transfer tax liability (GSTT plus gift tax) can exceed the value of the property the donee received.

---

[43] Sec. 2641.
[44] Sec. 2611.
[45] Sec. 2612(a).
[46] Sec. 2623.
[47] Sec. 2515.

What Would You Do in This Situation?

You are a CPA specializing in wealth transfer taxation. You have established your practice in Aspen, Colorado, because there is a lot of wealth situated in that ski resort. You client is a long-time resident of Aspen, and his health has recently taken a downhill turn. His doctor told him to consider putting his affairs in order because he will probably not ski any moguls for more than six months.

Your client is a merchant who owns a number of assets with FMVs totaling $2.4 million under some estimates. His largest single asset is his Victorian era store building situated in the desirable and exclusive West End of Aspen. Based on comparable fair market sales in the area, your client's building appears to be worth approximately $760,000 in the current real estate market. Because your client is in poor health, he does not use all of the store space and occasionally rents out some space in his building to vendors for selling crafts and gifts. During the ski season, the full price fair market rental value of the space would be over $1,000 per week. Your client's only son has indicated that he is not interested in moving to Aspen. The son is independently wealthy, does not really need to liquidate the building, and plans to continue the rental practices initiated by his father.

The estate probably will have no deductions. You are interested in saving your client some estate taxes. Would you propose to him that this asset be listed in the estate as Special Use Value property pursuant to Sec. 2032A? Would it be ethical to propose a valuation method based on the historical income generated by this property for the client's estate tax return? Using the historical income stream, the capitalized value would be $350,000. With this value, his estate would be lower by $410,000 and no tax would be owed because of an overall valuation of slightly under $2 million (in 2007) for the entire estate.

EXAMPLE C:13-52 ▶ Susan gives $1 million to her granddaughter. Susan has used her entire unified credit and is in the 45% marginal gift tax bracket; ignore the annual exclusion and the exemption. The GSTT is $450,000 (0.45 × $1,000,000). The amount subject to the gift tax is the value of the property transferred ($1 million) plus the GSTT paid ($450,000). Thus, the gift tax is $652,500 (0.45 × $1,450,000). It costs $1,102,500 ($450,000 + $652,500) to shift $1 million of property to the granddaughter. ◀

Originally, every grantor was entitled to a $1 million exemption from the GSTT, but the exemption became indexed for inflation (with adjustments rounded to the next lowest $10,000) for estates of decedents dying after 1998.[48] Beginning in 2004, Congress changed the exemption to the same amount as the "applicable exclusion amount" for estate tax purposes, which is $2 million in 2007. The grantor elects when, and against which transfers, to apply this exemption. Appreciation on the property for which the exemption is elected is also exempt from the GSTT.

Tax Planning Considerations

The effectiveness of many of the pre-1977 transfer tax-saving strategies was diluted by the unification of the transfer tax system in general and by the adoption of a unified rate schedule and the concept of adjusted taxable gifts in particular. To some extent, provisions that allow a larger tax base to be free of estate taxes and permit most interspousal transfers to be devoid of transfer tax consequences counterbalance unification. This section discusses various tax planning considerations that tax advisors should explore to reduce the transfer taxes applicable to a family unit.

[48] Sec. 2631(a).

USE OF *INTER VIVOS* GIFTS

SELF-STUDY QUESTION

What types of property should one consider gifting?

ANSWER

Give property that is expected to appreciate substantially in future years, produces substantial amounts of income, or is a family heirloom that probably will be passed from the donee to the donee's heirs and not be sold.

One of the most significant strategies for reducing transfer taxes is a well-designed, long-term gift program. As long as the gifts to each donee do not exceed the per donee annual exclusion, there will be no additions to the gross estate and no adjusted taxable gifts. A donor may pass thousands of dollars of property to others free of any transfer tax consequences if he or she selects enough donees and makes gifts over a substantial number of years. If taxable gifts do occur, the donor removes the post-gift appreciation from the estate tax base. Moreover, if the donor lives more than three years after the date of the gift, the gift tax paid is removed from the gross estate.

Prospective donors should weigh the opportunities for reducing transfer taxes through the use of lifetime gifts against the income tax disadvantage of foregoing the step up in basis that occurs if the donor retains the property until death. However, unless the donee is the donor's spouse, income taxes on the income produced by the gifted property can be reduced if shifted to a donee in a lower tax bracket.

USE OF EXEMPTION EQUIVALENT

As a result of the exemption equivalent (or applicable exclusion amount), a certain amount of property—$2 million in 2007—may pass to people other than the decedent's spouse without any estate taxes being extracted therefrom. A donor can transfer property to the spouse tax-free without limit. Thus, because the spouse presumably will die before any children or grandchildren (i.e., individuals to whom people often will property), a wealthy person should contemplate leaving at least an amount equal to the exemption equivalent to people other than his or her spouse. (If one leaves this amount of property in trust, the trust is often called a credit shelter or bypass trust.) Otherwise, he or she will waste some or all of the exemption equivalent, and the property will be taxed when the surviving spouse dies.

Making full use of the exemption equivalent enables a husband and wife to transfer to third parties an aggregate of $4 million (using 2007 amounts) without incurring any estate taxes. The strategy of making gifts to an ill spouse, who is not wealthy, to keep the donee-spouse's exemption equivalent from being wasted was discussed earlier (see Chapter C:12). Under this technique, the wealthier spouse makes gifts to the other spouse free of gift taxes because of the marital deduction. The recipient spouse then has an estate that can be passed tax-free to children, grandchildren, or other individuals because of the exemption equivalent.

STOP & THINK

Question: Sol made $600,000 in taxable gifts six years before his death but did not have to pay any gift tax. Sol died in 2007, when the gifted property was worth $825,000. Sol's taxable estate (gross estate minus estate tax deductions) was $2 million. Because of the exemption equivalent, does Sol's estate owe zero tax?

Solution: No. In concept, the unified credit of $780,800, which cancels out the tax on the 2007 $2 million exemption equivalent, is available only once. Sol's total tranfers—by gift and at death—exceed $2 million. Calculation of Sol's estate tax payable would be as follows:

Taxable estate	$2,000,000
Plus: Adjusted taxable gifts	600,000
Estate tax base	$2,600,000
Tentative tax on estate tax base	$1,050,800
Minus:	
Post-1976 gift tax (on $600,000 gift)	-0-
Unified credit	(780,800)
Estate tax payable	$ 270,000

The $270,000 represents the tax on the incremental $600,000, the amount over and above the $2 million *aggregate* taxable amount that can be passed free of transfer taxes (both gift and estate).

WHAT SIZE MARITAL DEDUCTION IS BEST?

To reiterate, the tax law imposes no ceiling on the amount of property eligible for the marital deduction. Even so, the availability of an unlimited marital deduction does not necessarily mean that a person should use it. From a tax perspective, wealthier people should leave an amount equal to the exemption equivalent to someone other than the spouse. Alternatively, they could leave the spouse an income interest in property equal to the exemption equivalent along with the power to invade such property for reasons of health, support, maintenance, or education. These powers do not cause an inclusion in the gross estate.

In certain circumstances, it may be preferable for an amount exceeding the exemption equivalent to pass directly to third parties. It might be beneficial for the first spouse's estate to pay some estate taxes if the surviving spouse already has substantial property and has a relatively short life expectancy, especially if the decedent spouse's assets are expected to rapidly increase in value.

EXAMPLE C:13-53 ▶ Paul dies in 2007 with a $3.5 million gross estate and no deductions other than the marital deduction. At the time of Paul's death, his wife's life expectancy is two years. The assets she owns in the current year are estimated to be worth $6 million in two years. Paul's property is expected to increase in value by 25% during the two-year period following his death. Paul wills his wife, Jill, $1 million and his children the rest. The estate tax payable for each spouse's estate is as follows:

	Paul (in 2007)		*Jill (in 2009)*
Gross estate	$3,500,000		$7,250,000[a]
Minus: Marital deduction	(1,000,000)		–0–
Taxable estate and tax base	$2,500,000		$7,250,000
Estate tax, after unified credit[b]	$ 225,000		$1,687,500
Combined estate tax	→	$1,912,500	←

[a]$6,000,000 + (1.25 × $1,000,000) = $7,250,000.
[b]$780,800 in 2007 and $1,455,800 in 2009. The top rate in 2009 is 45%. ◀

EXAMPLE C:13-54 ▶ Assume the same facts as in Example C:13-53 except that Paul wills everything except $2 million to Jill. The estate tax payable for each spouse's estate is as follows:

	Paul (in 2007)		*Jill (in 2009)*
Gross estate	$3,500,000		$7,875,000[a]
Minus: Marital deduction	(1,500,000)		–0–
Taxable estate and tax base	$2,000,000		$7,875,000
Estate tax, after unified credit	$ –0–		$1,968,750
Combined estate tax	→	$1,968,750	←

[a]$6,000,000 + (1.25 × $1,500,000) = $7,875,000. ◀

The combined estate tax liability is $56,250 higher in Example C:13-54 than in Example C:13-53. However, in Example C:13-54, no tax is owed upon the first spouse's death. Because the estate taxes for the second spouse's estate are not payable until a later date, their discounted present value also should be considered. Also note that, if Paul's will had created a trust eligible for QTIP treatment instead of leaving the property to Jill outright, the arrangement would have been more flexible because of the availability of partial QTIP elections.

STOP & THINK

Question: Tarik died recently at age 78. He was survived by his wife, Saliah, and several children and grandchildren. Saliah is 54 and in excellent health. Tarik's adjusted gross estate is $6.2 million, and his will leaves $2 million outright to his children and the rest to a trust for Saliah. The trust is eligible for the QTIP election. An investment advisor believes that the trust assets will likely appreciate annually at the rate of at least 10%. Name two advantages and one disadvantage of electing the marital deduction on the entire trust.

Solution: One advantage is that the tax on the trust will be deferred, perhaps for a long time, given the wife's age and health. Another advantage is that, because no tax is owed at Tarik's death, the trust assets remain intact to appreciate and produce more income for Saliah. That is, there is no current capital drain to pay transfer taxes. If Congress does not permanently repeal the estate tax, a disadvantage is that, because of the anticipated appreciation and the long time before Saliah's estimated death, the amount taxed in Saliah's estate will likely be much greater than the residue (here, $4.2 million) Tarik willed to Saliah.

USE OF DISCLAIMERS

Because the IRC does not treat a **qualified disclaimer** as a gift, disclaimers can be valuable estate planning tools (see Chapter C:12). For example, if a decedent wills all his or her property to the surviving spouse, such spouse could disclaim an amount at least equal in size to the exemption equivalent and thereby enable the decedent's estate to take full advantage of the unified credit. Alternatively, a decedent's children might disclaim some bequests if, as a result of their disclaimer, the property would pass instead to the surviving spouse. This approach might be desirable if the estate otherwise would receive a relatively small marital deduction. Another scenario where a disclaimer could be appropriate is where the disclaimant is elderly and in poor health and wishes to preclude the property from being taxed again relatively soon. (Of course, the credit for tax on prior transfers would provide some relief from double taxation.) Bear in mind, however, that the person making the qualified disclaimer has no input concerning which people receive the disclaimed property.

ROLE OF LIFE INSURANCE

Life insurance is an important asset with respect to estate planning for the following reasons:

- It can help provide the liquidity for paying estate taxes and other costs associated with death.
- It has the potential for large appreciation. If the insured gives away his or her incidents of ownership in the policy and survives the gift by more than three years, his or her estate benefits by keeping the policy's increased value out of the estate.

Assume an individual is contemplating purchasing a new insurance policy on his or her life and transferring it to another individual as a gift. The insured must live for more than three years after making the gift to exclude the face amount of the policy from his or her gross estate. Should the insured die within three years of gifting the policy, the donor's gross estate includes the policy's face amount. If the donee instead purchases the policy, the insured will not make a gift of the policy, and the three-year rule will not be of concern.

QUALIFYING THE ESTATE FOR INSTALLMENT PAYMENTS

TAX STRATEGY TIP

The payment of estate taxes can be deferred as much as 14 years if the estate's executor makes a timely Sec. 6166 election. The interest charged on the deferred taxes is at a favorable rate.

It can be quite beneficial for an estate owning an interest in a closely held business to qualify for installment payment of estate taxes under Sec. 6166. In a sense, the estate can borrow a certain amount of dollars from the government at 2% and the rest at a higher, but still favorable, rate. The closely held business interest must comprise more than 35% of the adjusted gross estate, defined as the gross estate less Sec. 2053 and Sec. 2054 deductions.

Retaining closely held business interests and gifting other assets will increase the likelihood of the estate's being able to elect the installment payments. However, closely held business interests often have a potential for great appreciation. Consequently, from the standpoint of reducing the size of the estate by freezing values, they are good candidates for gifts.

People cannot make gifts to restructure their estates and thereby qualify for Sec. 6166 if they postpone restructuring until soon before their death. If the decedent makes gifts within three years of dying, the closely held business interest must make up more than 35% of the adjusted gross estate in both of the following calculations:

1. Calculate the ratio of the closely held business to the actual adjusted gross estate.
2. Redo the calculations after revising the ratio to include (at date-of-death values) any property given away within three years of death.

EXAMPLE C:13-55 ▶ Joe dies in 2007. Joe's gross estate includes a closely held business interest valued at $2 million and other property valued at $3.6 million. Joe's allowable Sec. 2053 and 2054 deductions total $100,000. In 2005, partly in hopes of qualifying his estate for Sec. 6166 treatment, Joe made gifts of listed securities of $300,000 (at 2007 valuations) and paid no gift tax on the gifts. The two tests for determining whether Joe's estate is eligible for Sec. 6166 are as follows:

Excluding gifts:	$2,000,000 ÷ $5,500,000 = 36.36%
Including gifts:	$2,000,000 ÷ $5,800,000 = 34.48%

The estate may not elect Sec. 6166 treatment because it meets the greater than 35% test in only one of the two computations. ◀

WHERE TO DEDUCT ADMINISTRATION EXPENSES

Another tax planning opportunity concerns the choice of where to deduct administration expenses: on the estate tax return, on the estate's income tax return, or some in each place. The executor should claim the deduction where it will yield the greatest tax savings. Thus, if the estate owes the estate tax, which it will in 2007 if the estate tax base exceeds $2 million, the executor should deduct the expenses on the estate tax return because the marginal estate tax rate exceeds the top income tax rate. If no estate taxes are owed because of the exemption equivalent or the marital and/or charitable contribution deduction, administration expenses should be deducted on the estate's income tax return.

COMPLIANCE AND PROCEDURAL CONSIDERATIONS

OBJECTIVE 7

Recognize the filing requirements for estate tax returns

FILING REQUIREMENTS

Section 6018 indicates the circumstances in which estate tax returns are necessary. In general, no return is necessary unless the value of the gross estate plus adjusted taxable gifts exceeds the exemption equivalent (also known as the applicable exclusion amount). An exception applies, however, if the decedent made any post-1976 taxable gifts or claimed any portion of the $30,000 specific exemption after September 8, 1976, and before January 1, 1977. In such circumstances, a return must be filed if the value of the gross estate exceeds the amount of the exemption equivalent minus the total of the decedent's adjusted taxable gifts and the amount of the specific exemption claimed against gifts made after September 8, 1976, and before January 1, 1977.

A completed sample Estate Tax Return (Form 706) appears in Appendix B. The facts on which the preparation of the return is premised are the same as for the comprehensive illustration appearing on pages C:13-25 through C:13-27.

REAL-WORLD EXAMPLE

The IRS expects 30,400 estate tax returns to be filed for 2007, declining to 17,600 in 2010.

DUE DATE

Estate tax returns generally must be filed within nine months after the decedent's death.[49] The Secretary of the Treasury is authorized to grant a reasonable extension of time for filing.[50] The maximum extension period is six months. Obtaining an extension does not extend the time for paying the estate tax. Section 6601 imposes interest on any portion of the tax not paid by the due date of the return, determined without regard to the extension period. Thus, to avoid interest, the estate must pay the tax by the original due date.

[49] Sec. 6075(a).

[50] Sec. 6081(a).

VALUATION

One of the most difficult tasks of preparing estate tax returns is valuing the items included in the gross estate. Some items (e.g., one-of-a-kind art objects) may truly be unique. For many properties the executor should arrange for appraisals by experts.

If the value of any property reported on the return is 65% or less of the amount determined to be the proper value during an audit or court case, a 20% undervaluation penalty is imposed.[51] The penalty is higher if a gross valuation misstatement occurs; that is, the estate tax valuation is 40% or less than the amount determined to be the proper value.[52] Chapter C:12 discusses these penalties in more detail.

ELECTION OF ALTERNATE VALUATION DATE

The executor may value the gross estate on the alternate valuation date instead of on the date of death by making an irrevocable election on the estate tax return. The election does not necessarily have to be made on a timely return, but no election is possible if the return is filed more than a year after the due date (including extensions).

DOCUMENTS TO BE INCLUDED WITH RETURN

The instructions for the Estate Tax Return (Form 706) indicate that the executor must file numerous documents and other papers with the return. Some of the more important items that should accompany the form include

- ► The death certificate
- ► A certified copy of the will if the decedent died testate (i.e., died with a valid will)
- ► A listing of the qualified terminable interest property and its value if the executor wishes to make the QTIP election
- ► Copies of gift tax returns the decedent filed
- ► Copies of appraisals for real estate
- ► A Form 712 (obtained from the insurance companies) for each life insurance policy on the decedent's life
- ► Copies of written trust and other instruments for lifetime transfers the decedent made
- ► A certified copy of the order admitting the will to probate if the will makes bequests for which a marital deduction or charitable contribution deduction is claimed

In addition, when filing the return (or as soon thereafter as possible), the executor should submit a certificate from the proper state officer that denotes the amount of the state death taxes and the date paid.

PROBLEM MATERIALS

DISCUSSION QUESTIONS

C:13-1 In general, at what amount are items includible in the gross estate valued? (Answer in words.) Indicate one exception to the general valuation rules and the reason for this exception.

C:13-2 A client requests that you explain the valuation rules used for gift tax and estate tax purposes. Explain the similarities and differences of the two sets of rules.

[51] Sec. 6662(g).

[52] Sec. 6662(h).

C:13-3 Compare the valuation for gift and estate tax purposes of a $150,000 group term life insurance policy on the transferor's life.

C:13-4 Explain how shares of stock traded on a stock exchange are valued. What is the blockage rule?

C:13-5 Assume that the properties included in Alex's gross estate have appreciated during the six-month period immediately after his death. May Alex's executor elect the alternate valuation date and thereby achieve a larger step-up in basis? Explain.

C:13-6 Explain to an executor an advantage and a disadvantage of electing the alternate valuation date.

C:13-7 A decedent transferred land to an adult child by gift two years before death. Is the land included in the decedent's gross estate? In the estate tax base?

C:13-8 From a tax standpoint, which of the following alternatives is more favorable for a client's estate?

a. Buying a new insurance policy on his life and soon thereafter giving it to another person

b. Encouraging the other person to buy the policy with funds previously received from the client

Explain your answer.

C:13-9 Explain the difference between the estate tax treatment for gift taxes paid on gifts made two years before death and on gifts made ten years before death.

C:13-10 A client is considering making a very large gift. She wants to know whether the gross-up rule will apply to the entire amount of gift taxes paid by both her and her spouse if the spouses elect gift splitting and she dies within three years of the gift. Explain.

C:13-11 A widow owns a valuable eighteenth-century residence that she would like the state historical society to own someday. Explain to her the estate tax consequences of the following two alternatives:

a. Deeding the state historical society a remainder interest in the residence and reserving the right to live there rent free for the rest of her life.

b. Giving her entire interest in the house to the society and moving to another home for the rest of her life.

C:13-12 Which three retention periods can cause Sec. 2036 (transfers with retained life estate) to apply to a transferor's estate?

C:13-13 What characteristics do Secs. 2035 through 2038 have in common?

C:13-14 When does the consideration furnished test apply to property that the decedent held as a joint tenant with right of survivorship?

C:13-15 In which two circumstances is life insurance on the decedent's life includible in the gross estate under Sec. 2042? If insurance policies on the decedent's life escape being included under Sec. 2042, are they definitely excluded from the gross estate? Explain.

C:13-16 Indicate two situations in which property that has previously been subject, at least in part, to gift taxation is nevertheless included in the donor-decedent's gross estate.

C:13-17 Joe died in the current year. Under Joe's will, property is put in trust with a bank as trustee. Joe's will names his sister Tess to receive the trust income annually for life and empowers Tess to will the property to whomever she so desires. In addition, Tess may require that the trustee make distributions of principal to her for her health or support needs. Tess plans to leave the property by will to two of her three children in equal shares. Tess seeks your advice about whether the trust will be included in her gross estate. Respond to Tess.

C:13-18 Determine the accuracy of the following statement: The gross estate includes a general power of appointment possessed by the decedent only if the decedent exercised the power.

C:13-19 Carlos died six years ago. His will called for the creation of a trust to be funded with $1 million of property. The bank trustee must distribute all the trust income semiannually to Carlos's widow for the rest of her life. Upon her death, the trust assets are to be distributed to the couple's children. The widow dies in the current year, by which time the trust assets have appreciated to $1.7 million. Are the trust assets included in the widow's gross estate? Explain.

C:13-20 List the various categories of estate tax deductions currently allowed, and compare them with the categories of gift tax deductions. What differences exist?

C:13-21 Compare the tax treatment of administration expenses with that of the decedent's debts.

C:13-22 Judy dies and is survived by her husband, Jason, who receives the following interests as a result of his wife's death. Does Judy's estate receive a marital deduction for them? Explain.

a. $400,000 of life insurance proceeds; Jason is the beneficiary; Judy held the incidents of ownership.

b. Outright ownership of $700,000 of land held by Judy and Jason as joint tenants. Jason provided all the consideration to purchase the land.

C:13-23 Compare the credits available for estate tax purposes with the credits available for gift tax purposes. What differences exist?

C:13-24 Explain to a client the tax policy reason Congress allowed an estate to make installment payments of the portion of the estate taxes attributable to closely held business interests.

C:13-25 Assume that Larry is wealthier than Jane, his wife, and that he is likely to die before her. From an overall tax standpoint (considering transfer taxes and income taxes), is it preferable for Larry to transfer property to Jane *inter vivos* or at death, or does it matter? Explain.

C:13-26 Bala desires to freeze the value of his estate. Explain which of the following assets you would recommend that Bala transfer during his lifetime (more than one asset may be suggested):
a. Life insurance on his life
b. Cash
c. Corporate bonds (assume interest rates are expected to rise)
d. Stock in a firm with a bright future
e. Land in a boom town

C:13-27 Refer to Problem C:13-26. Explain the negative tax considerations (if any) with respect to Bala's making gifts of the assets that you recommended.

C:13-28 From a tax standpoint, why is it advisable for a wealthy married person to dispose of an amount equal to the exemption equivalent (applicable exclusion amount) to individuals other than his or her spouse?

C:13-29 In general, when is the estate tax due? What are some exceptions?

ISSUE IDENTIFICATION QUESTIONS

C:13-30 Henry Arkin (a widower) is quite elderly and is beginning to do some estate planning. His goal is to reduce his transfer taxes. He is considering purchasing land with a high potential for appreciation and having it titled in his name and the name of his grandson as joint tenants with rights of survivorship. Henry would provide all of the consideration, estimated to be about $5 million. What tax issues should Henry Arkin consider with respect to the purchase of the land?

C:13-31 Annie James dies early in 2007. All her property passes subject to her will, which provides that her surviving husband, Dave James, is to receive all the property outright. Her will further states that any property Dave disclaims will pass instead to their children in equal shares. Annie's gross estate is about $5 million, and her Sec. 2053 deductions are very small. Dave, who is in poor health, already owns about $3 million of property. What tax issues should Dave James consider with respect to the property bequested to him by his wife?

C:13-32 Assume the same facts as in Problem C:13-31 except that Annie's will leaves all her property to a QTIP trust for Dave for life with the remainder to their children. What tax issues should Dave James and the estate's executor consider with respect to the property that passes to the QTIP trust?

C:13-33 Jeung Hong, a widower, died in March 2007. His gross estate is $3 million and, at the time of his death, he owed debts of $60,000. His will made a bequest of $200,000 to his undergraduate alma mater and left the rest of his property to his children. His administrative expenses are estimated to be about $75,000. Jeung made no taxable gifts. What tax issues should the estate's CPA consider when preparing Jeung's estate tax return and his estate's income tax return?

PROBLEMS

C:13-34 *Valuation.* Beth dies on May 5 of the current year. Her executor elects date-of-death valuation. Beth's gross estate includes the items listed below. What is the estate tax value of each item?
a. 4,000 shares of Highline Corporation stock, traded on a stock exchange on May 5 at a high of 30, a low of 25, and a close of 26.
b. Life insurance policy on the life of Beth having a face value of $600,000. The cost of a comparable policy immediately before Beth's death is $187,430.
c. Life insurance policy on the life of Beth's son having a face value of $100,000. The interpolated terminal reserve immediately before Beth's death is $14,000. Unexpired premiums are $920.
d. Beach cottage appraised at a FMV of $175,000 and valued for property tax purposes at $152,000.

C:13-35 *Valuation.* Mary dies on April 3, 2007. As of this date, Mary's gross estate is valued at $2.8 million. On October 3, Mary's gross estate is valued at $2.5 million. The estate neither distributes nor sells any assets before October 3. Mary's estate has no deductions or adjusted taxable gifts. What is Mary's *lowest* possible estate tax liability?

C:13-36 *Estate Tax Formula.* Sue dies on May 3, 2007. On March 1, 2006, Sue gave Tom land valued at $2,012,000. Sue applied a unified credit of $345,800 against the gift tax due on this transfer. On Sue's date of death the land is valued at $2.4 million.
a. With respect to this transaction, what amount is included in Sue's gross estate?
b. What is the amount of Sue's adjusted taxable gifts attributable to the 2006 gift?

C:13-37 *Transferor Provisions.* Val dies on May 13, 2007. On July 3, 2006, she gave a $400,000 life insurance policy on her own life to son Ray. Because the value of the policy was relatively low, the transfer did not cause any gift tax to be payable.

a. What amount is included in Val's gross estate as a result of the 2006 gift?

b. What amount is included in Val's gross estate if the property given is land instead of a life insurance policy?

c. Refer to Part a. What amount would be included in Val's gross estate if she instead dies on October 13, 2009?

C:13-38 *Transferor Provisions.* In December 2004, Jody transferred stock having a $1,111,000 FMV to her daughter Joan. Jody paid $41,000 of gift taxes on this transfer. When Jody died in January 2007, the stock was valued at $920,000. Jody made no other gifts during her lifetime. With respect to this gift transaction, what amount is included in Jody's gross estate and what amount is reported as adjusted taxable gifts?

C:13-39 *Transferor Provisions.* In December 2004, Curt and Kate elected gift splitting to report $2,222,000 million of gifts of stocks Curt made. Each paid gift taxes of $41,000 by spending his or her own funds. Kate died in January 2007 and was survived by Curt. Her only taxable gift was the one reported for 2004. When Kate died in 2007, the stock had appreciated to $2.8 million. With respect to the 2004 gift, what amount is included in Kate's gross estate and what amount is reported as adjusted taxable gifts?

C:13-40 *Transferor Provisions.* John died in 2007. What amount, if any, is included in his gross estate in each of the following situations:

a. In 1994, John created a revocable trust, funded it with $400,000 of assets, and named a bank as trustee. The trust instrument provides that the income is payable to John annually for life. Upon John's death, the assets are to be divided equally among John's descendants. When John dies at the age of 72, the trust is still revocable. The trust assets are then worth $480,000.

b. In 1995, John transferred title to his personal residence to a charitable organization but retained the right to live there rent free for 20 years. The residence was worth $150,000 on the transfer date. At John's death, the residence is worth $230,000.

c. In 1995, John created an irrevocable trust, funded it with $200,000 of assets, and named a bank as trustee. According to the trust agreement, all the trust income is to be paid out annually for 25 years. The trustee, however, is to decide how much income to pay each year to each of the three beneficiaries (John's children). Upon termination of the trust, the assets are to be distributed equally among John's three children (now adults) or their estates. The trust's assets are worth $500,000 when John dies.

d. In 1996, John created an irrevocable trust with a bank named as trustee. He designated his grandson Al as the beneficiary of all the income for life. Upon Al's death, the property is to be distributed equally among Al's descendants. The trust assets are worth $400,000 when John dies.

C:13-41 *Transferor Provisions.* Latoya transferred property to an irrevocable trust in 1996 with a bank trustee. Latoya named Al to receive the trust income annually for life and Pat or Pat's estate to receive the remainder upon Al's death. Latoya reserved the power to designate Mike or Mike's estate (instead of Pat or Pat's estate) to receive the remainder. Upon Latoya's death in August 2007, the trust assets are valued at $200,000; Al is age 50; Mike, age 27; and Pat, age 32. Assume a 10% rate for the actuarial tables.

a. How much, if any, is included in Latoya's gross estate?

b. How much would have been included in Latoya's gross estate if she had *not* retained any powers over the trust? (Assume that Latoya survives for more than three years after the transfer.)

C:13-42 *Annuities.* Maria dies in the current year, two years after her retirement. At the time of her death at age 67, she is covered by the two annuities listed below.

- An annuity purchased by Maria's father providing benefits to Maria upon her attaining age 65. Upon Maria's death, survivor benefits are payable to her sister. The sister's total benefits are valued at $45,000.
- An annuity purchased by Maria's former employer under a qualified plan to which only the employer contributed. Benefits became payable to Maria upon her retirement. Upon Maria's death a survivor annuity valued at $110,000 is payable to her son.

a. What is the amount of the inclusion in Maria's gross estate with respect to each annuity?

b. How would your answer for the first annuity change if Maria had instead purchased the annuity?

c. How would your answer for the second annuity change if the employer had instead made 70% of the contributions to the qualified plan and Maria had made the remaining 30%?

C:13-43 *Jointly Owned Property.* In 1994, Art purchased land for $60,000 and immediately titled it in the names of Art and Bart, joint tenants with right of survivorship. Bart paid no consideration. In 2007, Art dies and is survived by Bart, his brother. The land's value has appreciated to $300,000.

a. What is the amount of the inclusion in Art's gross estate?
b. Assume Bart died (instead of Art). What amount would be included in Bart's gross estate?
c. Assume that Art dies in 2007 and Bart dies in 2009, when the land is worth $320,000. What amount is included in Bart's gross estate?

C:13-44 *Jointly Owned Property.* Five years ago, Andy and Sandy, siblings, pooled their resources and purchased a warehouse. Andy provided $50,000 of consideration, and Sandy furnished $100,000. Andy dies and is survived by Sandy. The property, which they had titled in the names of Andy and Sandy, joint tenants with right of survivorship, is valued at $450,000 when Andy dies. What amount is included in Andy's gross estate?

C:13-45 *Jointly Owned Property.* Mrs. Cobb purchased land costing $80,000 in 1995. She had the land titled in the names of Mr. and Mrs. Cobb, joint tenants with right of survivorship. Mrs. Cobb dies and is survived by Mr. Cobb. At Mrs. Cobb's death, the land's value is $200,000.

a. What amount is included in Mrs. Cobb's gross estate?
b. What is the amount, if any, of the marital deduction that Mrs. Cobb's estate can claim for the land?
c. Assume Mr. Cobb dies after Mrs. Cobb and the land is worth $240,000 at his death. What amount is included in his gross estate?

C:13-46 *Powers of Appointment.* Tai, who dies in the current year, is the sole income beneficiary for life of each of the trusts described below. For each trust indicate whether and why it is includible in Tai's gross estate.

a. A trust created under the will of Tai's mother, who died in 1996. Upon Tai's death, the trust assets are to pass to those of Tai's descendants whom Tai directs by his will. Should Tai fail to appoint the trust property, the trust assets are to be distributed to the Smithsonian Institution. Tai wills the property to his twin daughters in equal shares.
b. An irrevocable *inter vivos* trust created in 2001 by Tai's father. The trust agreement authorizes Tai to appoint the property to whomever he so desires. The appointment could be made only by his will. In his will, Tai appoints the property to an elderly neighbor.
c. An irrevocable trust funded by Tai in 2002. The trust instrument specifies that, upon Tai's death, the property is to pass to his children.
d. A trust created under the will of Tai's great-grandmother, who died in 1941. Her will authorizes Tai to appoint the property by his will to whomever he so desires. In default of appointment, the property is to pass to Tai's descendants in equal shares. Tai's will does not mention this trust.
e. Assume the same facts as in Part b except that Tai's will does not mention the trust property.

C:13-47 *Life Insurance.* Joy dies on November 5, 2007. Soon after Joy's death, the executor discovers the following insurance policies on Joy's life. Indicate the amount includible in Joy's gross estate for each policy.

Policy Number	*Owner*	*Beneficiary*	*Face Value*
123	Joy	Joy's husband	$400,000
757	Joy's son	Joy's estate	225,000
848	Joy's son	Joy's son	300,000
414	Joy's daughter	Joy's husband	175,000

Joy transferred ownership of policies 757 and 848 to her son in 1997. She gave ownership of policy 414 to her daughter in 2006.

C:13-48 *Life Insurance.* Refer to Problem C:13-47. What is the net addition to Joy's *taxable estate* with respect to the insurance policies listed above if all the property passing under Joy's will goes to Joy's son?

C:13-49 *Deductions.* When Yuji dies in 2007, his gross estate is valued at $5 million. He owes debts totaling $300,000. Funeral and administration expenses are estimated at $12,000 and $120,000, respectively. The marginal estate tax rate will exceed his estate's marginal income tax rate. Yuji wills his church $300,000 and his spouse $1.1 million. What is Yuji's taxable estate?

C:13-50 *Marital Deduction.* Assume the same facts as in Problem C:13-49 except that Yuji's will also provides for setting up a trust to be funded with $400,000 of property with a bank named as trustee. His wife is to receive all the trust income semiannually for life, and upon her death the trust assets are to be distributed equally among Yuji's children and grandchildren.

a. What is the amount of Yuji's taxable estate? Provide two possible answers.
b. Assume Yuji's widow dies in 2009. With respect to Yuji's former assets, which items will be included in the widow's gross estate? Provide two possible answers, but you need not indicate amounts.

C:13-51 *Marital Deduction.* Assume the same facts as in Problem C:13-50 and that before Yuji's death his wife already owns property valued at $300,000. Assume that each asset owned by each spouse increases 20% in value by 2009 and that Yuji's executor elects to claim the maximum marital deduction possible. Assume there are no state death taxes. From a tax standpoint, was the executor's strategy of electing the marital deduction on the QTIP trust a wise decision? Support your answer with computations.

C:13-52 *Adjusted Taxable Gifts.* Will, a bachelor, dies in the current year. At the time he dies, his sole asset is cash of $2 million. Assume no debts or funeral and administration expenses. His gift history is as follows:

Date	*Amount of Taxable Gifts*	*FMV of Gift Property at Date of Death*
October 1987	$270,000	$290,000
October 1991	90,000	65,000

a. What is Will's estate tax base?
b. How would your answer to Part a change if Will made the first gift in 1974 (instead of 1987)?

C:13-53 *Estate Tax Base.* Bess dies in 2007. Her gross estate, which totals $3 million, includes a $100,000 life insurance policy on her life that she gave away in 2006. The taxable gift that arose from giving away the policy was $15,000. In 2005, Bess made a $740,000 taxable gift of stock whose value increased to $790,000 by the time Bess died. Assume her estate tax deductions total $80,000.

a. What is her estate tax base?
b. What unified credit may her estate claim?

C:13-54 *Installment Payments.* Elaine dies on May 1, 2007. Her gross estate consists of the following items:

Cash	$ 40,000
Stocks traded on a stock exchange	940,000
Personal residence	250,000
25% capital interest in a 60-person partnership	1,020,000

Elaine's Sec. 2053 deductions total $30,000. She has no other deductions.

a. What percentage of Elaine's federal estate taxes may be paid in installments under Sec. 6166? When is the first installment payment due?
b. May Elaine's estate elect Sec. 6166 treatment if the stocks are valued at $2.74 million instead of $940,000?

C:13-55 *State Death Taxes.* Giovanni dies in 2007 with a gross estate of $1.8 million and debts of $30,000. He made post-1976 taxable gifts of $100,000, valued at $80,000 when Giovanni dies. His estate pays state death taxes of $110,200. What is his estate tax base?

COMPREHENSIVE PROBLEMS

C:13-56 Bonnie dies on June 1, 2007, survived by her husband, Abner, and two sons, Carl and Doug. Bonnie's only lifetime taxable gift was made in October 2004 in the taxable amount of $1.25 million. She did not elect gift splitting. By the time of her death, the value of the gifted property (stock) had declined to $1.1 million.

Bonnie's executor discovers the items shown below. Amounts shown are the FMVs of the items as of June 1, 2007.

Cash in checking account in her name	$127,750
Cash in savings account in her name	430,000
Stock in names of Bonnie and Doug, joint tenants with right of survivorship. Bonnie provided all the consideration ($3,000) to purchase the stock.	25,000
Land in names of Bonnie and Abner, joint tenants with right of survivorship. Abner provided all the consideration to purchase the land.	360,000
Personal residence in only Bonnie's name	450,000
Life insurance on Bonnie's life. Bonnie is owner, and Bonnie's estate is beneficiary (face value)	500,000
Trust created under the will of Bonnie's mother (who died in 1990). Bonnie is entitled to all the trust income for life, and she could will the trust property to whomever she desired. She wills it to her sons in equal amounts.	700,000

Bonnie's debts, as of her date of death, are $60,000. Her funeral and administration expenses are $15,000 and $65,000, respectively. Her estate paid state death taxes of $65,000. The executor elects to deduct the administration expenses on the estate tax return.

Bonnie's will includes the following:

> I leave my residence to my husband Abner.
>
> $250,000 of property is to be transferred to a trust with First Bank named as trustee. All of the income is to be paid to my husband, Abner, semiannually for the rest of his life. Upon his death the property is to be divided equally between my two sons or their estates.
>
> I leave $47,000 to the American Cancer Society.

Assume the executor elects to claim the maximum marital deduction possible. Compute the following with respect to Bonnie's estate:

a. Gross estate
b. Taxable estate
c. Adjusted taxable gifts
d. Estate tax base
e. Tentative tax on estate tax base
f. Federal estate tax payable

C:13-57 Assume the same facts as in Problem C:13-56 except the joint tenancy land is held in the names of Bonnie and her son Doug, joint tenants with right of survivorship. Also assume that Bonnie provided 55% of the consideration to buy the land and that Bonnie's executor does not elect to claim the marital deduction on the QTIP trust. Assume further that no taxable gift arose on the purchase of the joint tenancy land.

TAX STRATEGY PROBLEM

C:13-58 Gaylord Gunnison (GG) died January 13, 2007, and his gross estate consisted of three properties—cash, land, and stock in a public company. The amount of cash on the date of his death was $1.9 million, which went into the estate. On January 13, 2007, the land had a fair market value of $1 million, and the stock had a fair market value of $2 million. On July 13, 2007, the fair market values of the land and stock were $1.1 million and $1.6 million, respectively, and the cash remained at $1.9 million. Assume, for simplicity, that the estate has no deductions and GG made no taxable gifts. GG willed all of his property to his daughter, Gilda, who anticipates that, beginning in July 2007, the stock will appreciate at the rate of 9% per year before taxes. She anticipates selling the stock on or about July 13, 2013. Assume that the land's fair market value will remain at $1.1 million through 2013 and that she anticipates retaining the land for the rest of her life.

Considering both income tax and estate tax effects, compare after-tax wealth using the alternate valuation date or the date of death to value the estate. Which date should the executor elect? For simplicity, assume that the cash is not invested. (Incidentally, the factor for the future value, six years hence, at 9% is 1.677.) Prepare a worksheet on which you calculate the amount of after-tax wealth using the two possible valuation dates. Assume that the gain will be taxed at a 20% rate in 2013.

TAX FORM/RETURN PREPARATION PROBLEMS

C:13-59 Prepare an Estate Tax Return (Form 706) for Judy Griffin (464-55-3434), who died on June 30, 2006. Judy is survived by her husband, Greg, and her daughter, Candy. Judy was a resident of 17 Fiddlers Way, Nashville, Tennessee 37205. She was employed as a corporate executive with Sounds of Country, Inc., a recording company, at the time of her death. The assets discovered at Judy's death are listed below at their date-of-death values.

Savings account in Judy's name	$190,000
Checking account in Judy's name	10,000
Personal residence (having a $200,000 mortgage)	500,000
Household furnishings	75,000
400 shares of stock in Omega Corporation (quotes on June 30, 2006 are high of 70, low of 60, close of 67)	?
Land in New York (inherited from her mother in 1991)	640,000
Porsche purchased by Greg in 2004 as an anniversary gift to Judy	45,000

Other items include the following:

1. Life insurance policy 1: Judy purchased a $200,000 life insurance policy on her life on November 1, 2003 and paid the first annual premium of $2,500. The next day, she transferred the policy to her brother, Todd Williams, who also is the beneficiary. Judy paid the premium on August 1, 2004, and August 1, 2005.
2. Life insurance policy 2: A $150,000 whole life policy on Greg's life. Judy purchased the policy in 1994 and has always paid the $1,200 semiannual premium due on March 30 and September 30. Interpolated terminal reserve is $25,000. The beneficiary is Judy or her estate. Judy is the owner of the policy.
3. Employer annuity: Judy's employer established a qualified pension plan in 1982. The employer contributes 60% and the employee pays 40% of the required annual contributions. Judy chose a settlement option that provides for annual payments to Greg until his death. The annuity receivable by Greg is valued at $600,000.

Other information includes the following:

1. In October 2003, Judy transferred to her brother, Todd, $1,522,000 of stock that she received as a gift. Judy and Greg elected gift splitting. This was the first taxable gift for each spouse, and they paid their own portion of the gift tax (if any) from their own funds. When Judy dies, the stocks have appreciated to $1.6 million.
2. Unpaid bills at death include $2,500 owed on a bank credit card.
3. The cost of Judy's funeral and tombstone totals $25,000.
4. Judy's administration expenses are estimated at $55,000. Her estate's marginal transfer tax rate will be higher than the estate's marginal income tax rate.
5. Judy's will includes the following dispositions of property:

> I leave $60,000 of property in trust with Fourth Bank named as trustee. All income is to be paid semiannually to my husband, Greg, for life or until he remarries, whichever occurs first. At the termination of Greg's interest, the property will pass to my daughter, Candy, or her estate.
>
> To my beloved husband, Greg, I leave my Omega stock. The rest of my property I leave to my daughter, Candy, except that I leave $10,000 to the University of Tennessee.

6. Assume that Judy's state imposes an estate tax equal to the maximum credit available on the federal return for state death taxes.
7. Make the QTIP election if possible.

C:13-60 Prepare an Estate Tax Return (Form 706) for Joe Blough (177-47-3217) of 1412 Robin Lane, Birmingham, Alabama 35208. Joe died on November 12, 2006; he was survived by his wife, Joan, and their daughter, Katy. Joe was a bank vice president. Date-of-death values of the assets discovered at Joe's death are listed below.

Checking and savings accounts in names of Joe and Joan, joint tenants with right of survivorship	$800,000

General power of appointment trust	150,000
Second home, in Joe's name	450,000
Life insurance policy on Joe's life; his estate is the beneficiary and Joan is the owner	250,000
Land in Joe's name	2,200,000

Other pertinent information is as follows:

1. In 1988, Joe gave his sister land then valued at $220,000. He and Joan elected gift splitting. This was Joe's first taxable gift. The land was worth $350,000 when Joe died.
2. Joan owns the house that had been the couple's principal residence. Its value is $750,000.
3. Joe appointed the trust assets to Joan.
4. Joe willed all his other property to their daughter, Katy.
5. For simplicity, assume no administration expenses and that funeral expenses are $11,000.
6. Assume that Joe's estate paid state death taxes of $25,000.

CASE STUDY PROBLEMS

C:13-61 Your long-time client, Harold (Hal) Holland will meet with your supervising partner next week for an estate planning appointment. Hal has been married to Winona Holland since 1990. Hal is age 68 and retired. Winona, age 60, retired early to spend more time with Hal. They are residents of Topeka, Kansas. Hal is a U.S. citizen, and Winona is a citizen of Australia. Winona has indicated she plans to return to Australia if Hal predeceases her. Your supervising partner has requested that you identify any potential pitfalls in Hal's current estate plan so she can bring them to his attention.

Hal has stated that, in addition to providing some wealth transfers to his wife Winona, he wants to treat his three children by his prior marriage (Gina, Halbert, and Julianna) approximately equally in terms of total wealth received from him while he is alive and as a result of his death.

Hal and Winona prepared and submitted via e-mail the list of assets shown below.

- Principal residence in Topeka titled in the names of Hal and Winona, joint tenants with right of survivorship; purchased with $280,000 of consideration furnished solely by Winona; fair market value of $400,000.
- Household furnishings in the Topeka house; fair market value of $34,000. Winona owned almost all of these furnishings before she married Hal.
- Portfolio of publicly traded stocks in Hal's name; fair market value of $5.12 million.
- Mountain cabin and land in Vail, Colorado. Hal purchased the property in 1988 for $60,000; fair market value is $460,000. Hal never visits the cabin, but Halbert spends every summer and several weeks during the winter at the cabin.
- Stock (12 shares) in Harold's Hammocks, Inc. (a closely held C corporation) transferred to the Oz State Bank Revocable Trust in 1992; fair market value of $226,000, and basis of $15,000. Hal acquired the 12 shares in 1988 in a Sec. 351 transaction. Julianna and Gina own the remaining stock, 44 shares each, which Hal gifted to them in 2005.
- Individual retirement account at ToKan State Bank. The account consists of the funds rolled directly into the IRA from the non-contributory qualified retirement plan of Hal's former employer when Hal retired. Fair market value of the IRA is $540,000. Hal has not yet received any distributions. He is the IRA beneficiary, and Winona is the contingent beneficiary if Hal predeceases her.
- Cash of $825,000 in checking and savings accounts in Hal's name.
- Mutual fund shares in the names of Hal and Julianna, joint tenants with right of survivorship. Hal provided all the consideration ($9,000); fair market value of $64,000. He intended to use the money to finance Julianna's education, but she received a full scholarship.
- Stock in Dolrah, Inc. (a firm that elected S corporation status in 1990 upon its formation). The stock is in Hal's name, and he is one of six stockholders; fair market value of $79,000.

Hal's current will reads as follows:

> To my wife, Winona, I leave outright any household furnishings that I own, $500,000 of stock from my portfolio of publicly traded stocks, and all of my stock in Dolrah, Inc.
>
> To my grandchild, Halbert, Jr., I leave $3,750,000 of stock from my portfolio.
>
> I leave the rest of my estate outright in equal shares to my children, Gina, Halbert, and Julianna.

Required:
Prepare a memo to your supervising partner to help her prepare for the appointment with Hal. In the memo, advise the partner of any pitfalls (problems) you have identified that she should discuss with Hal. You need not make any calculations of estate tax liabilities.

C:13-62 Your client is Jon Jake, the executor of the Estate of Beth Adams, a widow. Mrs. Adams died 11 years after the death of her husband, Sam. Mr. Jake seeks assistance in the preparation of the estate tax return for Mrs. Adams, whose estate consists primarily of real estate. Mrs. Adams's estate will be divided among her three adult children except for a small amount of property willed to charity. The real estate has been appraised at $2.2 million by her son-in-law (who is married to one of Mrs. Adams's three children), an experienced real estate appraiser. You have a number of real estate clients and have considerable familiarity with property values for real estate located in the same general area as the estate's property. Your "gut feeling" is that the appraised values may be somewhat understated. As a tax advisor, what responsibilities do you have to make additional inquiries? What information should you provide Mr. Jake concerning possible penalties?

TAX RESEARCH PROBLEMS

C:13-63 Arthur Zolnick died at age 84 on June 7, 2007. In March 2004, he transferred $4 million of stock to a charitable remainder annuity trust (CRAT) from which he named himself to receive $280,000 per year for life. He designated a charitable organization to receive the remainder interest after his death and appointed his nephew Luther as trustee. Luther never distributed cash to Arthur because Arthur indicated he had no need for additional funds that "would just add to my gross estate." At Arthur's date of death, the value of the assets in the CRAT had risen to $4.3 million. What charitable contribution deduction will Arthur's estate receive?

C:13-64 Val, a resident of Illinois, died on June 12 of the current year. On May 5, she wrote four checks for $12,000 each, payable to each of her four grandchildren. Val mailed the checks on May 6, and each donee received the check on or before May 9. None of the donees deposited his or her checks until after Val's death. As of Val's date of death, the balance in her checking account was $52,127. This balance includes the $48,000 of outstanding checks issued to her grandchildren. Assume the executor will elect date-of-death valuation.

Your senior requested that you prepare a memorandum concerning whether the checks can be subtracted from the $52,127 account balance in arriving at the cash includible in Val's gross estate. Your senior indicates that you should start with the following authorities:

- IRC Sec. 2031(a)
- Reg. Secs. 20.2031-5 and 25.2511-2(b)

C:13-65 Hal Harmon, a resident of California, died in 2007, survived by his spouse Winnie Harmon and their three sons. In 1997, he transferred property to an irrevocable trust with his spouse as trustee and provided in the trust instrument that during the rest of his life he was entitled to all the trust income, payable quarterly, and that he could withdraw from principal whatever amounts he desired. He made no principal withdrawals, and when he died, the value of the trust was $3.7 million. Another provision in the trust instrument provided that his sons, in equal shares, would receive the remainder interest in the trust after Winnie's death if he predeceased her or after his death if Winnie predeceased him. In addition, the trust instrument instructed the trustee to pay to Winnie quarterly for life, beginning immediately after his death, "all the trust income as the trustee in its reasonable discretion determines is proper for Winnie's health, education, support, maintenance, comfort, and welfare in accordance with Winnie's accustomed manner of living." Prepare a memo to your manager in which you discuss whether the trust qualifies for the marital deduction and whether Winnie possesses a general power of appointment over the trust.

C:13-66 *Internet Research Problem.* You have been asked to make a presentation to a group of laypersons and explain which types of property do not pass under the decedent's will (that is, they pass outside probate). Consult the Internet address *http://www.mtpalermo.com,* where you will find a number of estate tax related materials you can use to conduct the research for your presentation. Prepare a presentation explaining several types of property that do not pass under the terms of the will, that is, they pass outside probate.

C:13-67 *Internet Research Problem.* Soon you will be meeting with a client who is considering moving to one of several other states and who does not currently have a will. You want to do some research regarding how property typically passes if the decedent dies intestate (without a will). The client plans to execute a will soon but makes the inquiry because of his busy schedule and tendency to procrastinate. Consult the Internet address *http://www.suffolklaw.com.* On the left side, select "Legal News," then select "What Happens If You Die Without a Will?" Prepare a brief memo about what you learn.

14

CHAPTER

INCOME TAXATION OF TRUSTS AND ESTATES

LEARNING OBJECTIVES

After studying this chapter, you should be able to

1. Understand the basic concepts concerning trusts and estates
2. Distinguish between the accounting concepts of principal and income
3. Calculate the tax liability of a trust or an estate
4. Understand the significance of distributable net income
5. Determine the taxable income of a simple trust
6. Determine the taxable income of a complex trust and an estate
7. Recognize the significance of income in respect of a decedent
8. Explain the effect of the grantor trust provisions
9. Recognize the filing requirements for fiduciary returns

CHAPTER OUTLINE

Chapters C:12 and C:13 examined two components of the transfer tax system: the gift tax and the estate tax. This chapter returns to income taxation by exploring the basic rules for taxing trusts and estates, two special tax entities often called **fiduciaries.** Income generated by property owned by an estate or a **trust** is reported on an income tax return for that entity. In general, the tax rules governing estates and trusts are identical. Unless the text states that a rule applies to only one of these entities, the discussion concerns both estates and trusts. Subchapter J (Secs. 641-692) of the IRC contains the special tax rules applicable to estates and trusts. This chapter describes the basic provisions of Subchapter J.

This chapter also discusses principles of fiduciary accounting, a concept that influences the tax consequences. The chapter focuses on determining the fiduciary's taxable income and the amount taxable to the beneficiaries. It includes comprehensive examples concerning the computations of taxable income, and Appendix B displays completed tax returns (Form 1041) for both a simple and a complex trust. The chapter also explores the circumstances that cause the grantor (transferor) to be taxed on the trust's income.

BASIC CONCEPTS

OBJECTIVE 1

Understand the basic concepts concerning trusts and estates

INCEPTION OF TRUSTS

Often a relatively wealthy person (one concerned with gift and/or estate taxes) will create trusts for tax and/or other reasons (e.g., conserving assets). A person may create a trust at any point in time by transferring property to the trust. A **trustee** (named by the transferor) administers the trust property for the benefit of the beneficiary. The trustee may be either an individual or an institution, such as a bank, and there can be more than one trustee.

If the transfer occurs during the transferor's lifetime, the trust is called an **inter vivos trust,** meaning among the living. The transferor is known as the **grantor** or the **trustor.** A trust created under the direction of a decedent's will is called a **testamentary trust** and contains assets formerly held by the decedent's estate. A trust may continue to exist for whatever time the trust instrument or the will specifies subject to the constraints of the **Rule Against Perpetuities.**[1]

INCEPTION OF ESTATES

ADDITIONAL COMMENT

The IRS projects that 3.8 million fiduciary income tax returns will be filed in 2007.

Estates originate only upon the death of the person whose assets are being administered. The estate continues in existence until the executor[2] (i.e., the person(s) named in the will to manage the property and distribute the assets) or administrator (where the decedent died without a will) completes his or her duties. An executor's or administrator's duties include collecting the assets, paying the debts and taxes, and distributing the property. The time needed to perform the duties may vary from a year or two to over a decade, depending on many factors (e.g., whether anyone contests the will).

Because the estate is a separate tax entity, continuing the estate's existence creates an additional personal exemption and achieves having some income taxed to yet another taxpayer, but the estate's income tax rates are very compressed. Nevertheless, the decedent's survivors sometimes can reduce their personal income taxes by preserving the estate's existence as a separate taxpayer. Treasury Regulations provide, however, that if the IRS considers the administration of an estate to have been unreasonably prolonged, it will view the estate as having been terminated for federal tax purposes after the expiration of a reasonable period for performance of the administrative duties.[3] In such a situation, the income is taxed directly to the individuals entitled to receive the estate's assets, and sometimes these individuals have a higher marginal tax rate than does the estate.

---

[1] The Rule Against Perpetuities addresses how long property may be tied up in trust and is the "principle that no interest in property is good unless it must vest, if at all, not later than 21 years, plus period of gestation, after some life or lives in being at time of creation of interest." Henry Campbell Black, *Black's Law Dictionary,* Rev. 6th ed., Ed. by Joseph R. Nolan and Jacqueline M. Nolan-Haley (St. Paul, MN: West Publishing Co., 1990), p. 1331. Some states have abolished the Rule Against Perpetuities.

[2] In some states, this individual is called a personal representative.

[3] Reg. Sec. 1.641(b)-3(a).

REASONS FOR CREATING TRUSTS

A myriad of reasons—both tax and nontax—exist for creating trusts. A discussion of some of these reasons follows.

KEY POINT

A trust is a contract between two parties: the grantor and the trustee. The grantor gives the trustee legal title to property, which the trustee holds for the benefit of a third party(ies), the beneficiary(ies). The trustee, acting in a fiduciary capacity, manages the property for the duration of the trust. Beneficiaries of a trust may have an income interest, which means that they receive part or all of the trust's income, or they may have a remainder interest, which means that they will receive the property held by the trust on some specified future date. A beneficiary may hold both an income interest and a remainder interest. The grantor may be a beneficiary and/or the trustee.

TAX SAVING ASPECTS OF TRUSTS. If the trust is irrevocable, meaning the grantor cannot require the trustee to return the assets, one of the primary tax purposes for establishing the trust traditionally was to achieve income splitting. Historically, with income splitting, the income from the trust assets was taxed to at least one taxpayer (i.e., the trust or the beneficiary) at a lower marginal tax rate than that of the grantor. Today's compressed fiduciary tax rate schedules, under which the top rate of 35% (in 2007) occurs at an income level slightly above $10,000, often make achieving income tax reduction difficult. Sometimes the trust instrument authorizes the trustee to use his or her discretion in "sprinkling" the income among several beneficiaries or accumulating it within the trust. In such circumstances, the trustee may consider the tax effects of making a distribution of income to one beneficiary rather than to another or retaining income in the trust.

Individuals also have created trusts to minimize their estate taxes. As discussed in Chapter C:13, for the transferor to exclude the property conveyed to the trust from the gross estate, the transferor must not retain the right to receive the trust income or the power to control which other people receive the income or have, at the time of death, the power to alter the identity of anyone named earlier to receive such assets.[4]

NONTAX ASPECTS OF TRUSTS. Reduction of taxes is not always the foremost reason for establishing trusts. Individuals often use trusts, including Sec. 2503(c) trusts and *Crummey* trusts, when minors are the donees so that a trustee can manage the assets. (See Chapter C:12 for a discussion of such trusts.) Even when the donee is an adult, donors sometimes may prefer that the assets be managed by a trustee deemed to have better management skills than the donee. Other donors may want to avoid conveying property directly to a donee if they fear the donee would soon consume most of the assets. In addition, donors sometimes use trusts to protect assets from creditors.

The creation of a **revocable trust** (i.e., one in which the grantor may demand that the assets be returned) does not yield any income or estate tax savings for the grantor. Nevertheless, donors often establish revocable trusts, including ones in which the grantor is also the beneficiary, for nontax purposes such as having the property managed by an individual or an institution with superior management skills. Use of a revocable trust reduces probate costs because assets in a revocable trust avoid probate. Such a strategy is especially important in states where probate costs are high. In this text, a trust is deemed to be an **irrevocable trust** unless explicitly denoted as being revocable.

BASIC PRINCIPLES OF FIDUCIARY TAXATION

Throughout the rest of this chapter, you should keep several basic principles of **fiduciary taxation** in mind. These features (discussed below) apply to all trusts other than grantor trusts, a type of trust where generally the grantor instead of the trust or the beneficiary pays tax on the income. (See pages C:14-30 through C:14-33 for a description of the tax treatment of grantor trusts.)

TRUSTS AND ESTATES AS SEPARATE TAXPAYERS. An estate or a trust is a separate taxpaying entity that files a Form 1041, and if it has any taxable income, it pays an income tax. The 2007 tax rates applicable to estates and trusts appear on the inside back cover. These rates, which are indexed annually for inflation, are very compressed in comparison with the rates for individuals. As is true for individuals, an estate's or trust's long-term capital gains and qualified dividends are taxed at a top tax rate of 15% (through 2010).

---

[4] Sec. 2036, relating to retention of income or control, and Sec. 2038, relating to the power to alter the identity of beneficiaries.

EXAMPLE C:14-1 ▶ For calendar year 2007, a trust reports taxable income of $15,000, none from dividends or long-term capital gains. Its tax liability is $4,294. In contrast, an unmarried individual not qualifying as a head of household would owe taxes of $1,859 on $15,000 of taxable income. ◀

NO DOUBLE TAXATION. Unlike the situation for corporations, no double taxation of income earned by an estate or trust (a fiduciary taxpayer) occurs because an estate or trust receives a deduction for the income it distributes to its beneficiaries. The beneficiaries, in turn, report the taxable portion of their receipts as income on their individual returns. Thus, the current income is taxed once, to the fiduciary or to the beneficiary or some to each, depending on whether it is distributed. In total, all the estate or trust's current income is taxed, sometimes some to the fiduciary and the remaining amount to the beneficiary. One of the primary purposes of the Subchapter J rules is to address exactly where the estate or trust's current income is taxed.

EXAMPLE C:14-2 ▶ In the current year, the Lopez Trust receives corporate bond interest of $25,000, $15,000 of which the trustee in its discretion distributes to Lupe. Lupe is taxed on $15,000, the amount of the distribution. The trust is taxed on the income it retains or accumulates, $10,000 in this case, less a $100 personal exemption (discussed on pages C:14-9 and C:14-10). ◀

CONDUIT APPROACH. A conduit approach governs fiduciary income taxation. Under this approach, the distributed income has the same character in the hands of the beneficiary as it has to the trust. Thus, if the trust distributes tax-free interest income on state and local bonds, such income retains its tax-free character at the beneficiary level.

EXAMPLE C:14-3 ▶ In the current year, the Lopez Trust receives $15,000 of dividends and $10,000 of tax-free interest. It distributes all of its receipts to its beneficiary, who is deemed to receive $15,000 of dividend income and $10,000 of tax-free interest. The 15% tax rate applies to the dividends assuming the beneficiary's tax bracket equals or exceeds 15%. ◀

SELF-STUDY QUESTION

King Trust receives interest on a savings account and distributes it to Anne. Because the trust is treated as a conduit, the interest is reported by Anne as taxable interest. Why might this be important?

ANSWER

For purposes of the limitation on the investment interest deduction, the interest from the trust is part of Anne's investment income. For purposes of the passive loss limitations, it is classified as portfolio income.

SIMILARITY TO RULES FOR INDIVIDUALS. Section 641(b) states "[T]he taxable income of an estate or trust shall be computed in the same manner as in the case of an individual, except as otherwise provided in this part." Sections 641-683 appear in this part (Part I) of Subchapter J. Thus, the tax effect for fiduciaries is the same as for individuals if the provisions of Secs. 641-683 do not specify rules that differ from those applicable for individual taxpayers. Sections 641-683 do not provide any special treatment for interest income from state and local bonds or for state and local tax payments. Consequently, an estate or trust receives an exclusion for state and local bond interest and the same deductions as individuals for state and local taxes. On the other hand, Sec. 642(b) specifies the amount of the personal exemption for fiduciaries. Thus, this subsection preempts the Sec. 151 rule concerning the amount of the personal exemption for individuals.

PRINCIPLES OF FIDUCIARY ACCOUNTING

OBJECTIVE 2

Distinguish between the accounting concepts of principal and income

To better understand the special tax treatment of fiduciary income, especially the determination of to whom the estate or trust's current income is taxed, one needs a general knowledge of the principles of fiduciary accounting. In a sense, fiduciary accounting is similar to fund accounting for government entities. Instead of having separate funds, however, all receipts and disbursements are classified in either the income or principal (corpus) account.

THE IMPORTANCE OF IDENTIFYING INCOME AND PRINCIPAL

When computing taxable income, we generally are concerned with whether a particular item is included in or deducted from gross income. When answering fiduciary tax questions, however, we also need to consider whether an item is classified as principal (corpus) or income for fiduciary accounting purposes. For example, certain items (e.g., interest on state bonds) may constitute fiduciary accounting gross income but are not included in calculating gross income for tax purposes. Other items (e.g., capital gains) may be included in gross income but classified as principal for fiduciary accounting purposes. If the trust instrument stipulates that the trustee can distribute only income prior to the termination of the trust, the amount of fiduciary accounting income sets the ceiling on the current distribution that the trustee can make to a beneficiary.

One of the most difficult aspects of feeling comfortable with the fiduciary taxation rules is appreciating the difference between fiduciary accounting income and income in the general tax sense. To understand and apply the IRC, one has to know in which context the word *income* is used. Section 643(b) provides guidance for this matter by providing that the word *income* refers to income in the fiduciary accounting context unless other words, such as "distributable net," "undistributable net," "taxable," or "gross," modify the word *income*. In this text, the term **net accounting income** is used to refer to the excess of accounting gross income over expenses charged to accounting income.

Under state law, the definitions in the trust instrument that classify items as principal or income preempt any definitions contained in state statutes. In the absence of definitions in the trust instrument, the applicable state statute controls. For purposes of defining principal and income, many states have adopted the Revised Uniform Principal and Income Act (enacted in 1962 and hereafter referred to as the Uniform Act of 1962) in its entirety or with minor modifications.[5] However, in recent years a number of states have adopted the Uniform Principal and Income Act (1997).

SELF-STUDY QUESTION

A trust agreement provides that all trust income is to be distributed to Janet until her thirty-fifth birthday, at which time the trust is to terminate and distribute all of its corpus to Joe. Stock is the only property owned by the trust. If the trust sells the stock, is Janet entitled to a distribution equal to the gain?

ANSWER

This question stresses the importance of differentiating between income and principal. The trustee must follow the definitions of income and corpus stated in the trust agreement, or if not there, under state law. Janet receives no distribution if the proceeds are classified as corpus unless the trustee under the 1997 Act makes an adjustment and moves money from corpus to income.

The 1997 Act allows the trustee to make adjustments between the principal and income accounts to the extent the trustee deems them necessary (such as to increase the amount distributable), provided certain additional requirements are met. A trustee, however, will not always deem adjustments necessary. The rationale behind allowing adjustments is grounded in modern portfolio theory. By allowing trustees to transfer cash from principal to income, the 1997 Act enables a trustee to apply prudent investor standards when making investment decisions. If dividends are low because of investing in growth stocks, the trustee can transfer some cash to the income account, thereby increasing the amount distributable to a beneficiary entitled to receive only income.

The categorization of a receipt or disbursement as principal or income generally affects the amount that can be distributed and the amount taxed to the fiduciary or the beneficiary. For example, if a gain is classified as principal and the trustee can distribute only income, the trust is taxed on the gain. Even though a receipt constitutes gross income for tax purposes, the trustee cannot distribute it to a beneficiary if it constitutes principal under the fiduciary accounting rules unless the trust instrument authorizes the trustee to distribute principal or unless, under the 1997 Act, the trustee adjusts by transferring some cash from principal to income.

EXAMPLE C:14-4 ▶ In the current year, the Bell Trust collects $18,000 of dividends, classified as accounting income. In addition, it sells stock for a $40,000 capital gain. Under state law, which is based on the Uniform Act of 1962 (discussed below), the gain is allocated to principal. The trust instrument (which does not define principal or income) requires the trustee to distribute all the trust's income to Beth annually until she reaches age 45. The trust assets are to be held and paid to Beth on her forty-fifth birthday (five years from now). The trustee must distribute $18,000 to Beth in the current year. The capital gain cannot be distributed currently because it is allocated to principal, and the trustee is not empowered to make distributions of principal. The trust will pay tax on the gain. ◀

PRINCIPAL AND INCOME: THE UNIFORM ACT

INCOME RECEIPTS. The Uniform Act of 1962 defines *income* as "the return in money or property derived from the use of principal." It lists income as including the following: rent, interest, corporate distributions of dividends, distributions by a regulated investment company from ordinary income, and the net profits of a business. The rules are more

[5] The *Revised Uniform Principal and Income Act* (1962) is a model set of rules proposed by the National Conference of Commissioners on Uniform State Laws. States can voluntarily adopt such provisions verbatim or in amended form.

detailed for receipts from the disposition of natural resources. A portion (27.5%) of the receipts from royalties is added to principal as a depletion allowance. The remainder of the royalties constitutes income. The 1997 Act provides different rules for allocating of royalty receipts.

ADDITIONAL COMMENT

The Commissioners approved and recommended for enactment the *Uniform Principal and Income Act* (1997). A number of states have adopted the 1997 Act, which differs in many ways from the 1962 Act.

PRINCIPAL RECEIPTS. ***Principal*** is defined in the Uniform Act of 1962 as "the property which has been set aside by the owner or the person legally empowered so that it is held in trust eventually to be delivered to the **remainderman** while the return or use of the principal is in the meantime taken or received by or held for accumulation for an **income beneficiary**." Among the categories of receipts included in principal are the following: consideration received on the sale or other transfer of principal or on repayment of a loan, stock dividends, receipts from disposition of corporate securities, and 27.5% of royalties received from natural resources.

EXPENDITURES. The Uniform Act of 1962 provides guidance for expenditures also. Among the important charges that reduce income are the following:

- ▶ Ordinary expenses, including regularly recurring property taxes, insurance premiums, interest, and ordinary repairs
- ▶ A reasonable allowance for depreciation
- ▶ Tax payable by the trustee if it is levied on receipts classified as income

Some of the significant expenditures chargeable to principal are

- ▶ Principal payments on debts
- ▶ Extraordinary repairs or expenses incurred in making a capital improvement
- ▶ Any tax levied on gain or other receipts allocated to principal even if the tax is described as an income tax

Frequently, the agreement between the grantor and the trustee specifies the respective portions of the trustee's fee that are chargeable to income and corpus.

EXAMPLE C:14-5 ▶ The governing instrument for the Wang Trust does not define income and principal. The state in question has adopted the Uniform Act of 1962. In the current year, the trust reports the following receipts and disbursements:

Dividends	$12,000
Proceeds from sale of stock, including $20,000 of gain	70,000
Trustee's fee, all charged to income	1,000
CPA's fee for preparation of tax return	500

The trust's net accounting income is $10,500 ($12,000 − $1,000 − $500). The gain on the sale of stock and the remaining sales proceeds constitute corpus. Consequently, if the trustee can distribute nothing but income, the maximum distribution is $10,500. ◀

SELF-STUDY QUESTION

Wilson Trust, which owns a commercial building, is required to distribute all of its income each year. The building is leased to a tenant on a net lease, so the trust's only expense is depreciation. The rental income is $25,000, and the depreciation is $11,000. If depreciation is chargeable to income, the distribution to the income beneficiary will be $14,000, and the trustee will set aside $11,000 of the income for the remainderman. What is the impact if depreciation is chargeable to principal?

ANSWER

The income distribution will be $25,000. If the trust holds the building to the end of its useful life, the building will theoretically "turn to dust" overnight, and the remainderman would receive nothing (as far as the building is concerned) because the trust had no depreciation reserve.

CATEGORIZATION OF DEPRECIATION

As mentioned above, the Uniform Act of 1962 charges depreciation to income. Depreciation thereby reduces net accounting income and the maximum amount that can be distributed to a beneficiary if the trust instrument does not authorize the distribution of corpus. Many states have departed from the Uniform Act's treatment of depreciation by providing that depreciation is a charge against principal (instead of against income). If depreciation is charged against principal, the maximum amount that can be distributed to the income beneficiaries is not reduced by the depreciation deduction. This result is advantageous to the income beneficiary. (See page C:14-9 for a discussion of the tax treatment of depreciation.)

Some trust instruments require the trustee to set aside (and not distribute) a certain amount of income as a depreciation reserve. A statement in the trust instrument concerning the accounting treatment for depreciation overrides a provision of state law.

EXAMPLE C:14-6 ▶ Park Trust, whose trust instrument is silent with respect to depreciation, collects rental income of $17,000 and pays property taxes of $1,000. Its depreciation expense is $4,000. Under state law, all depreciation is charged to principal. Therefore, the trust's net accounting income is $16,000 ($17,000 − $1,000). If the trust instrument mandates current distribution of all the income, the beneficiary receives $16,000. If the trust instrument states that depreciation is charged against income, the income distribution is limited to $12,000. ◀

Topic Review C:14-1 summarizes the treatment under the Uniform Act of 1962 of the major receipts and expenditures of fiduciaries. The discussion in the rest of the chapter assumes the Uniform Act of 1962 governs the trust.

FORMULA FOR TAXABLE INCOME AND TAX LIABILITY

OBJECTIVE 3

Calculate the tax liability of a trust or an estate

With three major exceptions, the formula for determining a fiduciary's taxable income and income tax liability is very similar to the formula applicable to individuals. A fiduciary's deductions are not divided between deductions *for* and *from* adjusted gross income (AGI). Instead, a fiduciary's deductions are simply deductible in arriving at taxable income. A fiduciary receives no standard deduction. A type of deduction inapplicable to individuals—the distribution deduction—is available in computing a fiduciary's taxable income. Figure C:14-1 illustrates the formula for computing a fiduciary's taxable income and tax liability.

GROSS INCOME

The items included in a trust or estate's gross income are the same as those included in an individual's gross income. However, the categorization of a fiduciary's income is not identical for tax and accounting purposes. For example, a gain usually constitutes principal for accounting purposes, but it is part of gross income for tax purposes.

EXAMPLE C:14-7 ▶ In the current year, Duke Trust receives $8,000 interest on corporate bonds, $20,000 interest on state bonds, and a $50,000 capital gain. The trust reports gross income of $58,000 ($8,000 + $50,000). Its accounting income is $28,000 ($8,000 + $20,000) because tax-exempt interest is accounting income, and the gain is part of principal. ◀

DEDUCTIONS FOR EXPENSES

Fiduciaries incur numerous deductible expenses that parallel those of individuals and include interest, taxes (e.g., state and local income taxes and property taxes), fees for investment advice, fees for tax return preparation, expenses associated with producing income, and trade or business expenses. In addition, fiduciaries may deduct the trustee's fee. This fee, which is similar to a property management fee incurred by an individual, is deductible under Sec. 212 as an expense incurred for the management of property held for the production of income.

Topic Review C:14-1

Classification of Receipts and Expenditures as Principal or Income Under the Uniform Act of 1962

INCOME ACCOUNT	PRINCIPAL ACCOUNT
Income:	Receipts:
Rent	Consideration (including gains) received upon disposition of property
Interest	Stock dividends
Dividends	27.5% of royalties[a]
Net profits of a business	
72.5% of royalties[a]	
Expenses:	Expenditures:
Ordinary expenses (e.g., property taxes, insurance, interest, and ordinary repairs)	Principal payments on debt
Taxes levied on accounting income	Extraordinary repairs and capital improvements
Depreciation[b]	Taxes levied on gains and other items of principal

[a]The Uniform Principal and Income Act (1997) provides a different allocation.
[b]Many state laws depart from the Uniform Act and characterize depreciation as a charge to principal.

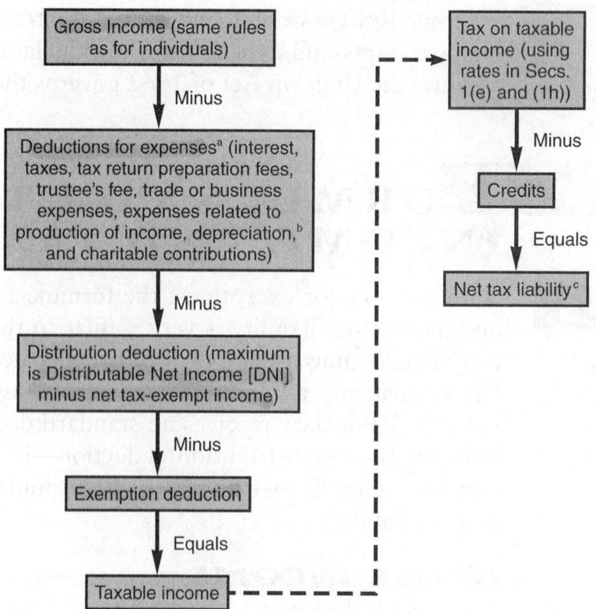

[a] No deduction is available for expenses allocable to tax-exempt income.

[b] When the trust instrument is silent, depreciation is allocated for tax purposes between the fiduciary and the beneficiary according to the portion of income attributable to each.

[c] Trusts and estates are subject to the alternative minimum tax (AMT). The AMT may be owed by a trust or estate in addition to the income tax levy described in this figure. The AMT is calculated in the same way as for individual taxpayers. Trusts and estates, however, are allowed only a $22,500 statutory exemption. This exemption is phased-out from $75,000 to $165,000 of alternative minimum taxable income.

FIGURE C:14-1 ▶ FORMULA FOR DETERMINING THE TAXABLE INCOME AND TAX LIABILITY OF A FIDUCIARY

For individuals, miscellaneous itemized deductions are deductible only to the extent the aggregate amount of such deductions exceeds 2% of the taxpayer's AGI. Estates and trusts do not literally have AGI, but Sec. 67(e) provides that a hypothetical AGI amount for an estate or trust is determined in the same fashion as for an individual *except* that (1) expenses paid or incurred in connection with the administration of the estate or trust *that would not have been incurred if the property were not held in such trust or estate,* (2) the personal exemption, and (3) the distribution deduction are treated as deductible for hypothetical AGI. Thus, these deductions are not subject to the 2% floor, and by being subtracted to arrive at hypothetical AGI, they reduce the amount of disallowed miscellaneous deductions. The trustees' or executors' fees and the cost of preparation of a fiduciary return would have been avoided if the trust or estate had not existed and therefore are excepted from the 2% floor. In *William J. O'Neill, Jr. Irrevocable Trust*[6] the Sixth Circuit reversed the Tax Court's decision and held that amounts paid for investment counsel fees were not subject to the floor because they were unique to the administration of estates and trusts. In *Mellon Bank, N.A.*,[7] the Federal Circuit upheld the decision of the U.S. Court of Federal Claims that fees for investment advice were subject to the 2% floor. The court reasoned that such fees failed the requirement that they would not have been incurred had there been no trust.

KEY POINT

Trustees' and executors' fees, as well as tax return preparation fees, are *not* subject to the 2% miscellaneous itemized deduction floor.

An executor can deduct administration expenses on the estate's income tax return if he or she does not deduct such items on the estate tax return. Unlike the situation for individuals, a fiduciary's charitable contribution deduction is not limited. The IRC does not allow a deduction, however, unless the trust instrument authorizes a charitable contribution.[8]

[6] 71 AFTR 2d 93-2052, 93-1 USTC ¶50,332 (6th Cir., 1993), reversing 98 T.C. 227 (1992), nonacq., I.R.B. 1994-38, 4.

[7] 88 AFTR 2d 2001-5800, 2001-2 USTC ¶50,621 (Fed. Cir., 2001). In *Scott*, 89 AFTR 2d 2002-1314, 2002-1 USTC ¶50,364 (DC, VA, 2002), a district court in Virginia concluded that fees were limited by the 2% floor rule. The Fourth Circuit, 91 AFTR 2d 2003-2100, 2003-1 USTC ¶50,428, affirmed *Scott*. In 2005, the Tax Court ruled in *Rudkin Testamentary Trust*, 124 T.C. No. 19 (2005), that investment management fees were subject to the 2% floor.

[8] Sec. 642(c)(1).

A depreciation or depletion deduction is available to an estate or trust only to the extent it is not allowable to beneficiaries under Secs. 167(d) or 611(b).[9] According to Sec. 167(d), the depreciation deduction for trusts is apportioned between the income beneficiaries and the trust pursuant to the terms of the trust instrument. If the instrument is silent, the depreciation is divided between the parties on the basis of the trust income allocable to each. For estates, however, the depreciation always must be apportioned according to the share of the income allocable to each party. The Sec. 611(b) rules for depletion parallel those described above for the allocation of depreciation.

EXAMPLE C:14-8 ▶ In the current year, Nunn Trust distributes 20% of its income to Bob and 50% to Clay. It accumulates the remaining 30%. The trust's current year depreciation is $10,000. The trust instrument is silent concerning the depreciation deduction. Under state law, depreciation is charged to principal. Even though net accounting income and the maximum distributable amount are not reduced by the depreciation deduction, Bob receives a $2,000 (0.20 × $10,000) depreciation deduction, and Clay receives a $5,000 (0.50 × $10,000) depreciation deduction. The remaining $3,000 (0.30 × $10,000) of depreciation is deducted in calculating the trust's taxable income. ◀

KEY POINT

If a trust *must* distribute all of its income currently, has no charitable beneficiary, *and* does *not* distribute corpus during the year, it is a simple trust for that year. *Income,* as used here, is accounting net income.

DISTRIBUTION DEDUCTION

SIMPLE TRUSTS. Some trusts must distribute all their income currently and are not empowered to make charitable contributions. Treasury Regulations refer to such trusts as **simple trusts.**[10] According to Sec. 651(a), these trusts receive a distribution deduction for the income required to be distributed currently, that is, 100% of the trust income. No words modify the word *income;* therefore, *income* means accounting income. If the accounting income that must be distributed exceeds the trust's distributable net income, the distribution deduction may not exceed the distributable net income (see discussion beginning on page C:14-10). As used in this context, distributable net income does not include any tax-free income (net of related deductions) that the trust earned.[11] Whatever amount is deductible at the trust level is taxed to the beneficiaries, and they are taxed on all the income, irrespective of the amount they receive.

COMPLEX TRUSTS. Trusts that are not required to distribute all their income currently are referred to as **complex trusts.**[12] The distribution deduction for complex trusts and all estates is the sum of the income required to be distributed currently and any other amounts (such as discretionary payments) properly paid, credited, or required to be distributed for the year. As is the case for simple trusts, the distribution deduction may not exceed the trust or estate's distributable net income (reduced by its tax-exempt income net of any related deductions).[13] The complex trust or estate's beneficiaries report, in the aggregate, gross income equal to the amount of the distribution deduction.[14]

EXAMPLE C:14-9 ▶ Green Trust must distribute 25% of its income annually to Amy. In addition, the trustee in its discretion may distribute additional income to Amy or Brad. In the current year, the trust has net accounting income and distributable net income of $100,000, none from tax-exempt sources. The trust makes a $25,000 mandatory distribution to Amy and discretionary distributions of $10,000 each to Amy and Brad. The trust's distribution deduction is $45,000 ($25,000 + $10,000 + $10,000). Amy and Brad report trust income of $35,000 and $10,000, respectively, on their individual returns. ◀

PERSONAL EXEMPTION

One of the differences between the rules for individuals and for fiduciaries is the amount of the personal exemption. Under Sec. 151, individuals are allowed personal exemptions. Section 642(b) authorizes an exemption for fiduciaries that applies in lieu of the amount for individuals. A trust or estate, however, receives no exemption in the year of its termination.

[9] Sec. 642(e).
[10] Reg. Sec. 1.651(a)-1.
[11] Sec. 651(b).
[12] Reg. Sec. 1.661(a)-1.
[13] Secs. 661(a) and (c).
[14] Sec. 662(a).

Estates are entitled to a $600 exemption. The exemption amount for trusts differs, depending on the terms of the trust. If the trust instrument requires that the trustee distribute all the income annually, the trust receives a $300 exemption. Otherwise, $100 is the exemption amount. Some trusts may be required to make current distributions of all their income in certain years, whereas in other years they may be directed to accumulate the income or to make distributions at the trustee's discretion. For such trusts the exemption amount is $300 in some years and $100 in other years.

EXAMPLE C:14-10 ▶ Gold Trust is established in 2007 with Jack as the beneficiary. The trust instrument instructs the trustee to make discretionary distributions of income to Jack during the years 2007 through 2011. Beginning in 2012, the trustee is to pay all the trust income to Jack currently. For 2007 through 2011, the trust's exemption is $100. Beginning in 2012, it rises to $300. ◀

Recall that a trust receives a distribution deduction for income currently distributed to its beneficiaries. At first blush, it appears that the distribution deduction balances out the income of trusts that must distribute all their income currently, and such trusts receive no tax benefits from their exemption deduction. True, the exemption produces no tax savings for such trusts if they have no gains credited to principal. Tax savings do result from the personal exemption, however, if the trust has undistributed gains. The exemption reduces the amount of gain otherwise taxed at the trust level.

EXAMPLE C:14-11 ▶ Rizzo Trust must distribute all of its income currently. Capital gains are characterized as principal. In the current year, Rizzo Trust has $25,000 of interest income from corporate bonds and a $10,000 capital gain. It has no expenses. It receives a distribution deduction of $25,000 and a $300 personal exemption. Its taxable income is $9,700 ($25,000 + $10,000 – $25,000 – $300). ◀

SELF-STUDY QUESTION

A trust, although not required to do so, distributes all of its income for the year. In the same year, it has a long-term capital gain. The trust agreement allocates the gain to principal. The trust does not distribute corpus, and none of its beneficiaries are charities. Is the trust a simple trust? What is its personal exemption?

ANSWER

It is a complex trust because it is not required to distribute all of its income. The exemption is $100 because distributions are discretionary.

The personal exemption amount for individuals is adjusted annually for changes in the consumer price index, but no comparable provision exists for the personal exemption for fiduciaries. On the other hand, the tax rate schedules for both fiduciaries and individuals are indexed for inflation.

CREDITS

In general, the rules for tax credits for fiduciaries are the same as those for individuals, but a fiduciary generally does not incur expenditures of the type that trigger some of the personal credits, such as the credit for household and dependent care expenses. Trusts and estates are allowed a foreign tax credit determined in the same manner as for individual taxpayers except that the credit is limited to the amount of foreign taxes not allocable to the beneficiaries.[15]

U.S. PRODUCTION ACTIVITIES DEDUCTION

The 2004 Jobs Act added a new deduction for businesses engaged in U.S. production activities for tax years beginning after 2004. Chapter C:3 describes the corporate version of this deduction, but the deduction also applies to individuals. If upon the death of a sole proprietor, his or her business passes to an estate or trust, the U.S. production activities deduction applies at the beneficiary level. Thus, the estate or trust will need to determine each beneficiary's share of the business's qualified production activities income and report these amounts to the beneficiaries. Further discussion of this topic with respect to estates and trusts is beyond the scope of this text.

DISTRIBUTABLE NET INCOME

OBJECTIVE 4

Understand the significance of distributable net income

As stated earlier in this chapter, the primary function of Subchapter J is to determine to whom—the fiduciary, the beneficiary, or some to each—the estate or the trust's current income is to be taxed. **Distributable net income (DNI)** plays a key role in determining the amount taxed to each party. In fact, DNI has been called the pie to be cut for tax purposes.[16]

---

[15] Sec. 642(a)(1).

[16] M. Carr Ferguson, James L. Freeland, and Richard B. Stephens, *Federal Income Taxation of Estates and Beneficiaries* (Boston, MA: Little, Brown, 1970), p. 1x.

SIGNIFICANCE OF DNI

DNI sets the ceiling on the amount of distributions taxed to the beneficiaries. As mentioned earlier, beneficiaries are taxed on the lesser of the amount of the distributions they receive or their share of DNI (reduced by net tax-exempt income).

Just as the total amount taxed to the beneficiaries equals the fiduciary's distribution deduction, DNI represents not only the maximum that can be taxed to the beneficiaries but also the maximum that can be deducted at the fiduciary level. Recall from the preceding section that the distribution deduction is the smaller of the amount distributed or the fiduciary's DNI. The distribution deduction, however, may not include any portion of tax-exempt income (net of any related deductions) deemed to have been distributed.

DNI also determines the character of the beneficiaries' income. Under the conduit approach, each beneficiary's distribution is deemed to consist of various categories of income (net of deductions) in the same proportion as the total of each class of income bears to the total DNI. For example, if 40% of the trust's income consists of dividends, 40% of each beneficiary's distribution is deemed to consist of dividends.

EXAMPLE C:14-12 ▶ Sun Trust has $30,000 of DNI for the current year. Its DNI includes $10,000 of rental income and $20,000 of corporate bond interest. The trust instrument requires that each year the trustee distribute 30% of the trust's income to Jose and 70% to Petra. Because the trust has no tax-exempt income and must distribute all of its income, it receives a $30,000 distribution deduction.

Jose reports $9,000 (0.30 × $30,000) of trust income, and Petra reports $21,000 (0.70 × $30,000) of trust income. Because rents make up one-third ($10,000 ÷ $30,000) of DNI, the composition of the income reported by Jose and Petra is one-third rental income and two-thirds corporate bond interest. ◀

SELF-STUDY QUESTION

What functions does distributable net income (DNI) serve?

ANSWER

1. It establishes the maximum amount on which the beneficiaries may be taxed.
2. It establishes the maximum amount the trust or estate may deduct as a distribution deduction.
3. It establishes the character of the income or expense in DNI that flows to the beneficiaries (income or expense flows to the beneficiaries in proportion to the part each different type of income or expense bears to DNI).

DEFINITION OF DNI

Section 643(a) defines *DNI* as the fiduciary's taxable income, adjusted as follows:

- No distribution deduction is subtracted.
- No personal exemption is subtracted.
- Capital gains are not included and capital losses are not subtracted unless such gains and losses are allocated to accounting income instead of to principal.
- Extraordinary dividends and taxable stock dividends are not included if they are allocable to principal.
- An addition is made for tax-exempt interest (minus the expenses allocable thereto).

Because one purpose of DNI is to set a ceiling on the distribution deduction, the distribution deduction is not subtracted from taxable income in determining DNI. If capital gains and extraordinary dividends are allocated to corpus, they are excluded from DNI because they cannot be distributed. Tax-exempt interest is part of accounting income and can be distributed even though it is excluded from gross income. Consequently, DNI includes tax-exempt income (net of the nondeductible expenses allocable to such income). Even though net tax-exempt income is included in DNI, no distribution deduction is available for the portion of the distribution deemed to consist of tax-exempt income.

KEY POINT

A significant difference between net accounting income and DNI is that DNI is reduced by certain expenses charged to principal. These expenses do not decrease net accounting income, nor do they decrease the amount of money that can be distributed.

Aside from complicated scenarios, net accounting income and DNI are the same, with one other exception. Any expenses (e.g., trustee's fees) charged to principal reduce DNI even though they do not lessen net accounting income. The trustee's fees (whether charged to income or to principal) are deductible in arriving at taxable income, and no adjustment is made to taxable income for such expenses when calculating DNI. Reducing DNI by the expenses charged to principal provides a tax advantage for the income beneficiary because these fees lessen the amount taxable to the beneficiary. However, such fees do not decrease the money that can be distributed to the beneficiary.

MANNER OF COMPUTING DNI

The amount of taxable income is in large measure a function of the distribution deduction, and the distribution deduction depends on the amount of DNI. The distribution deduction cannot exceed DNI. Thus, the Sec. 643(a) definition of DNI, which involves making adjustments to a fiduciary's taxable income, is not a workable definition from a practical standpoint because the computation is circular. The distribution deduction must be computed to arrive at the amount of income taxable to the fiduciary, and the distribution deduction depends, in part, on the amount of DNI.

However, there are two practical means of determining DNI. The first approach, as illustrated below, begins with taxable income exclusive of the distribution deduction and makes the adjustments (other than the distribution deduction) to taxable income that the IRC specifies.

EXAMPLE C:14-13 ▶ In the current year, Darby Trust reports the following results. The trust must distribute all of its income annually.

	Amounts Allocable to	
	Income	*Principal*
Corporate bond interest	$20,000	
Rental income	30,000	
Gain on sale of investment land		$40,000
Property taxes	5,000	
Trustee's fee charged to corpus		2,000
Distribution to beneficiary	45,000	

The trust's taxable income exclusive of the distribution deduction is computed as follows:

Corporate bond interest	$20,000
Rental income	30,000
Capital gain	40,000
Minus: Property taxes	(5,000)
Trustee's fee	(2,000)
Personal exemption	(300)
Taxable income exclusive of distribution deduction	$82,700

Now that taxable income exclusive of the distribution deduction has been determined, DNI can be computed in the following manner:

Taxable income exclusive of distribution deduction	$82,700
Plus: Personal exemption	300
Minus: Capital gain	(40,000)
DNI	$43,000 ◀

A second method that often can be used to determine DNI is to calculate net accounting income and reduce such amount by expenses charged to corpus (e.g., the trustee's fee). In some complicated situations, however, DNI would not be correctly arrived at under this approach, but the discussion of such situations is beyond the scope of this book.

EXAMPLE C:14-14 ▶ Assume the same facts as in Example C:14-13. The following steps illustrate the second approach to calculating the DNI amount.

Corporate bond interest	$20,000
Rental income	30,000
Minus: Property taxes	(5,000)
Net accounting income	$45,000
Minus: Trustee's fee charged to corpus	(2,000)
DNI	$43,000 ◀

Although the beneficiary receives a cash distribution of $45,000 (net accounting income), he or she reports only $43,000 (DNI) as income. The beneficiary receives $2,000 tax-free. Thus, an income beneficiary benefits from trustee's fees charged to principal by getting to report a smaller amount of gross income than the amount of cash he or she receives. The trust's distribution deduction cannot exceed $43,000 (DNI) even though the amount paid to the beneficiary exceeds this amount.

Topic Review C:14-2 summarizes the DNI concept.

STOP & THINK *Question:* Wei is the beneficiary of a two unrelated simple trusts. From which simple trust would Wei's after-tax cash flow be larger?

- Trust A collects corporate bond interest of $40,000 and pays a trustee's fee of $1,000. The trustee's fee is charged to corpus.
- Trust B collects corporate bond interest of $40,000 and pays a trustee's fee of $800. The trustee's fee is charged to income.

Solution: Wei would receive $40,000 in cash from Trust A but pay federal income taxes on only $39,000, which is the trust's DNI. The trust's distribution is based on net accounting income, which is not reduced by the trustee's fee charged to corpus. Wei's gross income is based on the trust's DNI, which is reduced by the trustee's fee. Wei would receive $39,200 in cash from Trust B. He would pay federal income taxes on the same $39,200 amount, which is the trust's DNI. The trustee's fee paid by Trust B reduces both net accounting income and DNI. Even though the trust's economic income is larger with Trust B, Wei would have a larger amount of after-tax cash flow from Trust A.

DETERMINING A SIMPLE TRUST'S TAXABLE INCOME

OBJECTIVE 5

Determine the taxable income of a simple trust

The term *simple trust* does not appear in the IRC. Treasury Regulations interpreting Secs. 651 and 652—the statutory rules for trusts that distribute current income only—introduce the term *simple trust.* The provisions of Secs. 651 and 652 govern only trusts whose trust agreements require that all income be distributed currently and do not authorize charitable contributions. Moreover, such provisions are inapplicable if the trust makes distributions of principal.

Some trust instuments may require trusts to pay out all their income currently in certain years but permit them to retain a portion of their income in other years. In some of the years in which the instument mandates distribution of all their income, it also permits distributions of principal. These trusts are simple trusts in some years and complex trusts in others. The amount of the personal exemption, however, turns not on whether the trust is simple or complex but on whether it must pay out all its income currently. Suppose, for

Topic Review C:14-2

The Distributable Net Income (DNI) Concept

Significance of DNI

DNI, exclusive of net tax-exempt interest included therein, sets the ceiling on:

1. The distribution deduction, and
2. The aggregate amount of gross income reportable by the beneficiaries.

Calculation of DNI

Taxable income, exclusive of distribution deduction[a]
Plus: Personal exemption
Minus: Capital gains (or plus deductible capital losses)
Plus: Tax-exempt interest (net of allocable expenses)
Distributable net income (DNI)[b]

[a]Gross income (dividends, taxable interest, rents, and capital gains) minus deductible expenses and the personal exemption.
[b]Frequently, DNI is the same amount as net accounting income minus trustee's fees charged to corpus.

▼ **TABLE C:14-1**
Trust Classification Rules and the Size of the Exemption

Situation	Classification	Exemption Amount
Required to pay out all of its income, makes no charitable contributions, distributes no principal	Simple	$300
Required to pay out all of its income, makes no charitable contributions, distributes principal	Complex	$300
Required to pay out all of its income, authorized to make charitable contributions, distributes no principal	Complex	$300
Authorized to make discretionary distributions of income, makes no charitable contributions, distributes no principal	Complex	$100
Authorized to make discretionary distributions of income and principal, makes no charitable contributions	Complex	$100

example, a trust must pay out all of its current income and one-fourth of its principal. Because the trust distributes principal, it is a complex trust. It claims a $300 personal exemption because of the mandate to distribute all of its income. Table C:14-1 highlights the trust classification rules and the $300 or $100 exemption dichotomy.

ALLOCATION OF EXPENSES TO TAX-EXEMPT INCOME

Recall that expenses related to producing tax-exempt income are not deductible.[17] Thus, if a trust with income from both taxable and tax-exempt sources incurs expenses that are not directly attributable to the production of taxable income, a portion of such expenses may not be deducted. Regulation Secs. 1.652(b)-3 and 1.652(c)-4(e) address the issue of the allocation of deductions. An expense directly attributable to one type of income, such as a repair expense for rental property, is allocated thereto. Expenses not directly related to a particular item of income, such as a trustee's fee for administering the trust's assets, may be allocated to any type of income included in computing DNI, provided a portion of the expense is allocated to nontaxable income. Regulation Sec. 1.652(b)-3 sets forth the following formula for determining the amount of indirect expenses allocable to nontaxable income:

$$\frac{\text{Tax-exempt income (net of expenses directly attributable thereto)}}{\text{Accounting income (net of all direct expenses)}^{18}} \times \text{Expenses not directly attributable to any item of income} = \text{Indirect expenses allocable to nontaxable income}$$

EXAMPLE C:14-15 ▶ In the current year, the Mason Trust reports the following results:

Dividends	$16,000
Interest from corporate bonds	6,000
Tax-exempt interest from state bonds	18,000
Capital gain (allocated to corpus)	20,000
Trustee's fee, all allocated to corpus	4,000

[17] Sec. 265(a)(1).

[18] A discrepancy exists in the Treasury Regulations with respect to how to allocate expenses to tax-exempt income. According to Reg. Sec. 1.652(b)-3(b), the denominator is accounting income net of direct expenses. Regulation Sec. 1.652(c)-4(e), however, shows computations where the denominator is accounting income unreduced by direct expenses. The text uses the latter approach.

SELF-STUDY QUESTION

A trust can allocate indirect expenses arbitrarily (after the appropriate allocation is made to tax-exempt income). Hill Trust has rental income, taxable interest income, and dividend income. Its sole beneficiary has unused rental losses of her own. To which income would you suggest allocating the trustee's fee?

ANSWER

If possible, the trust should take into consideration the tax status of its beneficiaries. The trust should not allocate the fee to its rental income so that rental income is maximized. Moreover, because of the low tax rate on dividends, the trust should allocate the fee against interest income.

Accounting gross income is $40,000 ($16,000 + $6,000 + $18,000). The trustee's fee is an indirect expense that must be allocated to the tax-exempt income as follows:

$$\frac{\$18,000}{\$40,000} \times \$4,000 = \$1,800$$

Thus, the Mason Trust cannot deduct $1,800 of its trustee's fee. The remaining $2,200 may be allocated to dividends or corporate bond interest in whatever amounts the return preparer desires. Because of the low tax rate on dividends, allocating the fee to the higher taxed interest income would reduce taxes. ◀

DETERMINATION OF DNI AND THE DISTRIBUTION DEDUCTION

As mentioned above, DNI is defined as taxable income with several adjustments, including a subtraction for capital gains credited to principal. As described earlier, a practical technique for determining DNI involves beginning with taxable income exclusive of the distribution deduction. Once DNI has been determined, both the distribution deduction and the trust's taxable income can be calculated.

A simple trust must distribute all of its net accounting income currently. Thus, a simple trust generally receives a distribution deduction equal to the amount of its net accounting income.[19] The following two exceptions modify this general rule:

- The distribution deduction may not exceed DNI. Therefore, if a trust has expenses that are charged to corpus (as in Example C:14-13), the distribution deduction is limited to the DNI amount because DNI is smaller than net accounting income.
- Because tax-exempt income is not included in the trust's gross income, no distribution deduction is available for tax-exempt income (net of the expenses allocable thereto) included in DNI.[20]

TAX TREATMENT FOR BENEFICIARY

The aggregate gross income reported by the beneficiaries equals the trust's net accounting income, subject to the constraint that the aggregate of their gross income amount does not exceed the trust's DNI. If DNI is lower than net accounting income and the trust has more than one beneficiary, each beneficiary's share of gross income is the following fraction of total DNI:[21]

$$\frac{\text{Income required to be distributed to such beneficiary}}{\text{Income required to be distributed to } \textit{all} \text{ beneficiaries}}$$

The income received by the beneficiaries retains the character it had at the trust level. Thus, if the trust receives tax-exempt interest, the beneficiaries are deemed to have received tax-exempt interest. Unless the trust instrument specifically allocates particular types of income to certain beneficiaries, each beneficiary is viewed as receiving income consisting of the same fraction of each category of income as the total of such category bears to total DNI.

EXAMPLE C:14-16 ▶ In the current year, Crane Trust has $22,000 of tax-exempt interest and $66,000 of dividends and pays $8,000 of trustee's fees from corpus. Its net accounting income is $88,000, and its DNI is $80,000: $20,000 of net tax-exempt interest and $60,000 of net dividends. The trust instrument requires distribution of one-eighth of the income annually to Matt and the remaining seven-eighths of the income to Pat. The distributions to Matt and Pat are $11,000 and $77,000, respectively. The distribution deduction and the aggregate gross income of the beneficiaries are limited to $60,000 ($80,000 DNI − $20,000 net tax-exempt interest). Matt and Pat will report gross income of $7,500 (0.125 × $60,000) and $52,500 (0.875 × $60,000), respectively. Dividends make up 75% ($60,000 ÷ $80,000) of DNI and 100% ($60,000 ÷ $60,000) of taxable DNI. Therefore, all of Matt's and Pat's *gross* income is deemed to consist of dividends. Matt and Pat also are deemed to receive $2,500 (0.125 × $20,000) and $17,500 (0.875 × $20,000), respectively, of tax-exempt interest. ◀

[19] Sec. 651(a).
[20] Sec. 651(b).
[21] Sec. 652(a).

Because a simple trust must distribute all of its income currently, trustees cannot defer the taxation of trust income to the beneficiaries by postponing distributions until the next year. Beneficiaries of simple trusts are taxed currently on their pro rata share of taxable DNI regardless of the amount distributed to them during the year.[22]

SHORTCUT APPROACH TO PROVING CORRECTNESS OF TAXABLE INCOME

A shortcut approach may be used to verify the correctness of the amount calculated as a simple trust's taxable income. Because a simple trust must distribute all of its income currently, the only item taxable at the trust level should be the amount of gains (net of losses) credited to principal, reduced by the personal exemption. The taxable income calculated under the shortcut approach should equal the taxable income determined under the formula illustrated in Figure C:14-1. The steps of the shortcut approach are as follows:

1. Start with the excess of gains over losses credited to principal.
2. Subtract the $300 personal exemption.

EXAMPLE C:14-17 ▶ In the current year, West Trust, which must distribute all of its income currently, reports $25,000 of corporate bond interest, a $44,000 long-term capital gain, and a $4,000 long-term capital loss. Under the shortcut approach, the test-check calculation of its taxable income is $39,700 [($44,000 − $4,000) − $300 personal exemption]. On its tax return, the trust reports $25,000 of gross income from interest, $40,000 from net long-term capital gains, a $25,000 distribution deduction, and a $300 exemption. ◀

EFFECT OF A NET OPERATING LOSS

If a trust incurs a net operating loss (NOL), the loss does not pass through currently to the beneficiaries unless the loss arises in the year the trust terminates, but the trust can carry the NOL back and forward. In determining the amount of the NOL, deductions are not allowed for charitable contributions or the distribution deduction.[23] In the year a trust terminates, any loss that would otherwise qualify for a loss carryover at the trust level passes through to the individual return of the beneficiary(ies) succeeding to the trust's property.[24]

EXAMPLE C:14-18 ▶ In 2007, the year it terminates, New Trust incurs a $10,000 NOL. It also has a $40,000 NOL carryover from 2005 and 2006. At termination, New Trust distributes 30% of its assets to Kay and 70% to Liz. Because 2007 is the termination year, Kay may report a $15,000 (0.30 × $50,000) NOL on her 2007 return, and Liz may report a $35,000 (0.70 × $50,000) NOL on her 2007 return. Before 2007, the beneficiaries cannot report any of the trust's NOLs on their returns. ◀

EFFECT OF A NET CAPITAL LOSS

The maximum capital loss that a trust can deduct is the lesser of $3,000 or the excess of its capital losses over capital gains.[25] Because simple trusts must distribute all of their accounting income currently and the distribution deduction reduces their taxable income to zero, they receive no current tax benefit from capital losses that exceed capital gains. Nevertheless, the trust's taxable income for the year of the loss is reduced by its net capital loss, up to $3,000. In determining the capital loss carryover, capital losses that produced no tax benefit are available as a carryover to offset capital gains realized by the trust in subsequent years. In addition, if all of the capital loss carryovers have not been absorbed by capital gains before the trust's termination date, the remaining capital loss is passed through in the termination year to the beneficiaries succeeding to the trust's property.[26]

---

22 Reg. Sec. 1.652(a)-1.

23 Reg. Sec. 1.642(d)-1(b).

24 Reg. Sec. 1.642(h)-1. A trust is never categorized as a simple trust in the year it terminates because in its final year it always makes distributions of principal.

25 Sec. 1211(b).

26 Reg. Sec. 1.642(h)-1.

EXAMPLE C:14-19 ▶ Old Trust, which must distribute all of its income currently, sells two capital assets before it terminates. In 2005, it sells an asset at a $20,000 loss. In 2006, it sells an asset for a $6,000 gain. In 2007, it terminates and distributes its assets equally between its two beneficiaries, Joy and Tim. The trust is not a simple trust in 2007 because it distributes principal that year. Because the $20,000 loss provided no benefit on the 2005 return, the carryover to 2006 is $20,000, and $6,000 of it offsets 2006's $6,000 capital gain. The remaining $14,000 carries over to 2007. Because 2007 is the termination year, a $7,000 (0.50 × $14,000) capital loss passes through to both Joy's and Tim's individual returns for 2007. Joy realizes a $12,000 capital gain by selling assets in 2007. Joy offsets the $7,000 trust loss against her own gain. Tim sells no assets in 2007. Therefore, Tim deducts $3,000 of the loss from the trust against his other income. His remaining $4,000 loss carries over to 2008. ◀

SELF-STUDY QUESTION

Why do Treasury Regulations (see footnotes 25 and 26) allow unused NOLs and capital losses to be used by the remainderman on the termination of a trust?

ANSWER

Losses have depleted the corpus of the trust. Because the remainderman's interest has been depleted by these losses, it is reasonable to allow the trust to pass these losses through to the remainderman at the end of its life.

Topic Review C:14-3 describes how to calculate a trust's taxable income.

COMPREHENSIVE ILLUSTRATION: DETERMINING A SIMPLE TRUST'S TAXABLE INCOME

The following comprehensive illustration reviews a number of the points discussed previously. The facts for this illustration are used to complete the Form 1041 for a simple trust that appears in Appendix B.

BACKGROUND DATA

Zeb Brown established the Bob Adams Trust by a gift in 1993. The trust instrument requires that the trustee (First Bank) distribute all of the trust income at least annually to Bob Adams for life. Capital gains are credited to principal. The 2006 results of the trust are as follows:

	Amounts Allocable to	
	Income	*Principal*
Dividends	$30,000	
Rental income from land	5,000	
Tax-exempt interest	15,000	
Rental expenses (realtor's commission on rental income)	1,000	
Trustee's fee		$ 1,200
Fee for preparation of tax return	500	
Capital gain on sale of stock[a]		12,000
Distribution of net accounting income to Bob	48,500	
Payments of estimated tax		2,600

[a]The trust sold the stock in October, having acquired it four years earlier.

Topic Review C:14-3

Calculation of Trust Taxable Income

Gross income[a]	
Minus:	Deductions for expenses[a]
	Distribution deduction[b]
	Personal exemption ($300 or $100)
Taxable income	

[a]Rules for calculating these amounts are generally the same as for individual taxpayers.
[b]Deduction cannot exceed the amount of DNI from taxable sources.

TRUSTEE'S FEE

As mentioned earlier, a portion of the trustee's fee is nondeductible because it must be allocated to tax-exempt income. The trust receives \$50,000 (\$30,000 + \$5,000 + \$15,000) of gross accounting income, of which \$15,000 is tax-exempt. Therefore, \$360 [(\$15,000 ÷ \$50,000) × \$1,200] of the trustee's fee is allocated to tax-exempt income and is nondeductible. The entire return preparation fee is deductible because no such fee would have been incurred had the trust's income been entirely from tax-exempt sources.

DISTRIBUTION DEDUCTION AND DNI

One of the key amounts affecting taxable income is the distribution deduction. Taxable income exclusive of the distribution deduction can be the starting point for determining the amount of DNI, a number crucial in quantifying the distribution deduction. The trust's taxable income, exclusive of the distribution deduction, is calculated as follows:

Dividends		\$30,000
Rental income		5,000
Capital gain on sale of stock		12,000
Minus:	Rental expenses	(1,000)
	Deductible portion of trustee's fee	(840)
	Fee for tax return preparation	(500)
	Personal exemption	(300)
Taxable income, exclusive of distribution deduction		\$44,360

DNI now can be calculated by making the adjustments shown below to taxable income, exclusive of the distribution deduction.[27]

Taxable income, exclusive of distribution deduction		\$44,360
Plus:	Personal exemption	300
Minus:	Capital gain on sale of stock	(12,000)
Plus:	Tax-exempt interest, net of \$360 of allocable expenses	14,640
DNI		\$47,300

Recall that the distribution deduction cannot exceed the DNI, as reduced by tax-exempt income (net of any allocable expenses). The distribution deduction may be computed as follows:

Smaller of:	Net accounting income (\$48,500) or DNI (\$47,300)		\$47,300
Minus:	Tax-exempt interest	\$15,000	
	Minus: Allocable expenses	(360)	(14,640)
Distribution deduction			\$32,660

TRUST'S TAXABLE INCOME

Once the amount of the distribution deduction is determined, the trust's taxable income can be calculated as illustrated in Table C:14-2.

CATEGORIZING A BENEFICIARY'S INCOME

Because income reported by the beneficiary retains the character it had at the trust level, the amount of each category of income received by the beneficiary must be determined. Bob is deemed to have received dividends, rents, and tax-exempt interest. Rental expenses are charged entirely against rental income. The deductible portion of the trustee's fee and the tax return preparation fee can be allocated in full to rents or dividends, or some to each. However, because of the low tax rate on dividends, the fees should be allocated against the higher taxed rents. Consequently, the character of Bob's income is determined as follows:

[27] Another way of determining the amount of DNI in this scenario is to reduce the net accounting income of \$48,500 by the \$1,200 of expenses charged to principal. The resulting amount is \$47,300.

	Dividends	Rents	Tax-Exempt Interest	Total
Accounting income	$30,000	$5,000	$15,000	$50,000
Minus: Expenses:				
Rental expenses		(1,000)		(1,000)
Trustee's fee		(840)	(360)	(1,200)
Tax return preparation fee		(500)		(500)
DNI	$30,000	$2,660	$14,640	$47,300

Bob reports $30,000 of dividend income and $2,660 of rental income on his individual return. His dividend income is taxed at the low rate applicable to dividends.

DETERMINING TAXABLE INCOME FOR COMPLEX TRUSTS AND ESTATES

OBJECTIVE 6

Determine the taxable income of a complex trust and an estate

The caption to Subpart C of Part I of Subchapter J (Secs. 661-664) reads "Distribution for Estates and Trusts Accumulating or Distributing Corpus." In general, the rules applicable to estates and these trusts (complex trusts) are the same. The IRC does not contain the term *complex trust,* but according to Treasury Regulations, "A trust to which subpart C is applicable is referred to as a 'complex' trust."[28] Recall from the discussion about simple trusts that a trust that must distribute all of its income currently can be classified as a complex trust for a particular year if it also pays out some principal during the year.

▼ TABLE C:14-2

Comprehensive Illustration: Determining a Simple Trust's Taxable Income and Tax Liability

Gross income:	
Dividends	$30,000
Rental income	5,000
Capital gain on sale of stock	12,000[a]
Minus: Expense deductions:	
Rental expenses	(1,000)
Deductible portion of trustee's fee	(840)
Tax return preparation fee	(500)
Minus: Distribution deduction	(32,660)
Minus: Personal exemption	(300)
Taxable income	$11,700[b]
Tax liability (2006 rates)	$ 1,550[c]
Minus: Estimated tax payments	(2,600)
Tax owed (refunded)	($ 1,050)

[a]The stock sale took place in October and involved stock purchased four years earlier.
[b]The short-cut approach to verifying taxable income is as follows:

Long-term capital gain	$12,000
Minus: Personal exemption	(300)
Taxable income	$11,700

[c]The taxable income consists of a long-term capital gain, which, in 2006, is taxed at a maximum rate of 5% on the first $2,050 and 15% on the rest.

ADDITIONAL COMMENT

The short-cut approach to computing taxable income used in Table C:14-2 consists of reducing the income allocated to corpus by the personal exemption.

[28] Reg. Sec. 1.661(a)-1.

Trusts that can accumulate income are categorized as complex trusts, even in years in which they make discretionary distributions of all their income. A trust also is a complex trust if the trust instrument provides for amounts to be paid to, or set aside for, charitable organizations (see Table C:14-1).

Many of the rules are the same for simple and complex trusts, but some differences exist. Different rules are used to determine the distribution deduction for the two types of trusts. The rules for determining an estate's distribution deduction are the same as those applicable to complex trusts. The personal exemption, however, is $600 for an estate and $300 or $100 for a complex trust. The $300 amount applies for years in which a trust must pay out all of its income; otherwise, the exemption is $100.

TAX STRATEGY TIP

Trust managers can reduce overall taxes by carefully planning the amount and timing of distributions. See Tax Planning Considerations later in text for details.

DETERMINATION OF DNI AND THE DISTRIBUTION DEDUCTION

Section 661(a) defines the distribution deduction for complex trusts and estates as the sum of the total current income *required* to be paid out currently plus any other amounts "properly paid or credited or required to be distributed" (i.e., discretionary distributions) to the beneficiary during the year. If the fiduciary can make mandatory distributions from either the income or the principal account, distributions are treated as "current income required to be paid" if paid out of the trust's income account; thus, some of the income is taxed to the beneficiary. Like simple trusts, the amount of the trust's DNI limits the amount of the distribution deduction.

EXAMPLE C:14-20 ▶ In the current year, Able Trust has net accounting income and DNI of $30,000, all from taxable sources. It makes a $15,000 mandatory distribution of income to Kwame and a $4,000 discretionary distribution to Kesha. Its distribution deduction is computed as follows:

Income required to be distributed currently	$15,000
Plus: Other amounts properly paid, etc.	4,000
Tentative distribution deduction	$19,000
DNI	$30,000
Distribution deduction (lesser of tentative distribution deduction or DNI)	$19,000 ◀

As is the case for simple trusts, an additional constraint applies to the amount of the distribution deduction. No distribution deduction is allowed with respect to tax-exempt income (net of allocable expenses).

EXAMPLE C:14-21 ▶ Assume the same facts as in Example C:14-20 except that net accounting income and DNI consist of $20,000 of corporate bond interest and $10,000 of tax-exempt interest. Because one-third ($10,000 ÷ $30,000) of the DNI is from tax-exempt sources, tax-exempt income is deemed to make up one-third of the distributions. Thus, the distribution deduction is only $12,667 (0.667 × $19,000). ◀

If a trust makes charitable contributions, DNI is not reduced by the charitable contribution deduction when determining the maximum distribution deduction for mandatory distributions. However, DNI is reduced by the charitable contribution deduction when calculating the deduction for discretionary distributions.

EXAMPLE C:14-22 ▶ Assume instead that the trust in Example C:14-20 has net accounting income and DNI (exclusive of the charitable contribution deduction) of $16,000. The trust makes a $15,000 mandatory distribution to Kwame and a $4,000 mandatory distribution to Kesha. In accordance with its trust instrument, the trust pays $3,000 to a charitable organization.

Tentative distribution deduction (required distributions)	$19,000
DNI (excluding charitable contribution deduction)	16,000
Distribution deduction (lesser of tentative distribution deduction or DNI)	16,000

If the distributions to both Kwame and Kesha were discretionary, the $3,000 charitable contribution would be deductible by the trust and would first reduce DNI to $13,000, thereby limiting the distribution deduction to $13,000. Thus, in total, the beneficiaries would report $3,000 less gross income. ◀

TAX TREATMENT FOR BENEFICIARY

KEY POINT

Distributions to beneficiaries retain the character that the income has at the fiduciary level; for example, the character of rents, interest, dividends, or tax-exempt income flows through to the beneficiary.

GENERAL RULES. In general, the amount of distributions from estates or complex trusts includible in a beneficiary's gross income equals the sum of income required to be distributed currently to the beneficiary plus any other amounts properly paid or credited, or required to be distributed (i.e., discretionary distributions) to the beneficiary during the year.[29] This general rule has three exceptions, all discussed later in this section.

Because income retains the character it has at the fiduciary level, beneficiaries do not include distributions of tax-exempt income in their gross income. Each beneficiary's distribution is deemed to consist of tax-exempt income in the proportion that total tax-exempt income bears to total DNI.[30] Thus, if 30% of DNI is from tax-exempt income, 30% of each beneficiary's distribution is deemed to consist of tax-free income.

Even in the absence of distributions of principal, mandatory payments to beneficiaries can exceed DNI because at times accounting income exceeds DNI. When the total income required to be distributed currently exceeds DNI (before reduction for the charitable contribution deduction), each beneficiary reports as gross income the following ratio of DNI attributable to taxable sources:

$$\frac{\text{Income required to be distributed currently to the beneficiary}}{\text{Aggregate income required to be distributed to all beneficiaries currently}^{31}}$$

In calculating the portion of DNI includible in the gross income of each beneficiary who receives mandatory distributions, DNI is not reduced for the charitable contribution deduction.

EXAMPLE C:14-23 ▶ In the current year, Yui Trust reports net accounting income of $125,000 but DNI of only $95,000 because of certain expenses charged to principal. The trust must distribute $100,000 of income to Tai and $10,000 to Tien. It makes no discretionary distributions or charitable contributions. Because the trust's mandatory distributions of $110,000 exceed its DNI of $95,000, the amount each beneficiary reports as gross income is as follows:

Beneficiary	*Gross Income*
Tai	$86,364 = ($100,000 ÷ $110,000) × $95,000
Tien	$8,636 = ($10,000 ÷ $110,000) × $95,000

◀

EXCEPTION—THE TIER SYSTEM. If both principal and income are distributed, distributions will exceed income even if net accounting income and DNI are equal. If the sum of current income required to be distributed currently and all other amounts distributed (e.g., discretionary payments of income or any payments of corpus) exceed DNI, the amount taxable to each beneficiary is calculated under a tier system. Beneficiaries to whom income distributions must be made are commonly called **tier-1 beneficiaries.**[32] All other beneficiaries are known as **tier-2 beneficiaries.** An individual who receives both mandatory and discretionary payments in the same year can be both a tier-1 and a tier-2 beneficiary.

Under the tier system, tier-1 beneficiaries are the first to absorb income. The total income taxed to this group is the lesser of the aggregate mandatory distributions or DNI, which is determined without reduction for charitable contributions. If required income distributions plus all other payments exceed DNI, each tier-2 beneficiary includes in income a fraction of the remaining DNI, the DNI minus the income required to be distributed currently. Section 662(a)(2) states that the fraction is as follows:

$$\frac{\text{Other amounts properly paid or required to be distributed to the beneficiary}}{\text{Aggregate of amounts properly paid or required to be distributed to } \textit{all} \text{ beneficiaries}}$$

[29] Sec. 662(a).
[30] Sec. 662(b).
[31] Sec. 662(a)(1).

[32] The terms *tier-1* and *tier-2* do not appear in the IRC or Treasury Regulations.

EXAMPLE C:14-24 ▶ In the current year, Eagle Trust reports net accounting income and DNI of $80,000, all from taxable sources. The trust instrument requires the trustee to distribute $30,000 of income to Holly currently. In addition, the trustee makes $60,000 of discretionary distributions, $15,000 to Holly and $45,000 to Irene. The trust pays $10,000 of the $60,000 discretionary distributions from corpus. The gross income reported by each beneficiary is determined as follows.

1. Gross income from mandatory distributions:	
Lesser of:	
a. Amount required to be distributed, or	$30,000
b. DNI	80,000
Amount reportable by Holly	30,000
2. Gross income from other amounts paid:	
Lesser of:	
a. All other amounts paid, or	60,000
b. DNI minus amount required to be distributed ($80,000 − $30,000)	50,000
Amount reportable by Holly and Irene	50,000
3. Total amount reportable (1) + (2) = (3)	80,000

The portions of the $50,000 from Step 2 to be reported by each beneficiary are calculated under a pro rata approach as follows:

Holly: $50,000 × ($15,000 ÷ $60,000) = $12,500
Irene: $50,000 × ($45,000 ÷ $60,000) = $37,500

A recapitulation of the beneficiaries' gross income is as follows:

	Amount Reported by	
Type of Distribution	*Holly*	*Irene*
Mandatory distributions	$30,000	$ –0–
Discretionary distributions	12,500	37,500
Total	$42,500	$37,500 ◀

Tier-1 beneficiaries generally have gross income equal to their total distributions if they receive no tax-exempt interest, whereas tier-2 beneficiaries are more likely to receive a portion of their distributions tax-free. Thus, tier-2 beneficiaries potentially receive more favorable tax treatment than tier-1 beneficiaries.

SELF-STUDY QUESTION

What is the ultimate effect of the separate share rule?

ANSWER

It has the effect of treating a trust or estate as two or more separate entities, each with its own DNI. This "separate" DNI is allocated to the specific beneficiary of each share of the trust or estate.

EXCEPTION—SEPARATE SHARE RULE. Some trusts and estates with more than one beneficiary can be treated as consisting of more than one entity in determining the amount of the distribution deduction and the beneficiaries' gross income.[33] In calculating the fiduciary's income tax liability, however, these trusts or estates are treated as one entity with the result that taxable income is taxed under one rate schedule. Entities eligible for this treatment, known as the **separate share rule**, have governing instruments requiring that distributions be made in substantially the same manner as if separate entities had been created.[34] If the separate share rule applies, the amount of the income taxable to a beneficiary can differ from the amount that otherwise would be taxable to such beneficiary. Because of this rule, beneficiaries often report gross income that is less than the distributions they receive.

EXAMPLE C:14-25 ▶ Bart Berry created the Berry Trust for the benefit of Dale and John. According to the trust instrument, no income is to be distributed until a beneficiary reaches age 21. Moreover, income is to be divided into two equal shares. Once a beneficiary reaches age 21, the trustee may make discretionary distributions of income and principal to such beneficiary, but distributions may not exceed a beneficiary's share of the trust. Each beneficiary is to receive his remaining share of the trust assets on his thirtieth birthday. Earlier distributions of income and principal must be taken into account in determining each beneficiary's final distribution.

On January 1 of the current year, Dale reaches age 21; John is age 16. In the current year, the trust has DNI and net accounting income of $50,000, all from taxable sources. During the current year, the trustee distributes $25,000 of income (Dale's 50% share) and $80,000 of principal

[33] Sec. 663(c).

[34] Reg. Sec. 1.663(c)-3(a).

to Dale. The trustee makes no distribution of income or corpus to John. Under the separate share rule, the trust's distribution deduction and Dale's gross income inclusion cannot exceed his share of DNI, or $25,000. Dale receives the remaining $80,000 distribution tax-free. Berry Trust pays tax on John's separate share of the income (all accumulated), or $25,000, less the personal exemption. In the absence of the separate share rule, Dale would be taxed on $50,000 (the lesser of DNI or his total distributions). ◀

EXCEPTION—SPECIFIC BEQUESTS. Recall that a beneficiary is taxed on other amounts properly paid, credited, or required to be distributed,[35] subject to the constraint that the maximum amount taxed to all beneficiaries is the fiduciary's DNI. Thus, a beneficiary can be required to report gross income even though he or she receives a distribution from the principal account.

EXAMPLE C:14-26 ▶ Doug died in 2006, leaving a will that bequeathed all his property to his sister Tina. During 2007, Doug's estate reports $50,000 of DNI, all from taxable sources. During 2007, the executor distributes Doug's coin collection, valued at $22,000, to Tina. The adjusted basis of the coin collection also is $22,000, its value at the date of death. The distribution of the coin collection is classified as an "other amount properly paid" and, even though the executor distributes nothing from the income account, Tina must report $22,000 of gross income. If the coin collection's adjusted basis and FMV exceed $50,000 (DNI), Tina's gross income would be only $50,000, the DNI amount. ◀

ADDITIONAL COMMENT

The executor of an estate should carefully consider the timing of property distributions where the property being distributed is not the subject of a specific bequest. If possible, property (other than specific bequests) should be distributed in a year when the trust has little or no DNI.

On the other hand, a distribution of property does not trigger a distribution deduction at the estate level or the recognition of gross income at the beneficiary level if such property constitutes a bequest of a specific sum of money or of specific property to be paid at one time or in not more than three installments.[36] If Doug's will in Example C:14-26 instead includes specific bequest language (e.g., "I bequeath my coin collection to Tina"), Tina would not report any gross income upon receiving the coin collection.

More income is generally taxed at the estate level (and less at the beneficiary level) if the decedent's will includes numerous specific bequests. If the estate has a lower marginal income tax rate than its beneficiaries' marginal tax rates, the optimal tax result is to have the income taxed to the estate because the tax liability is lower.

EXAMPLE C:14-27 ▶ Dick died in 2006 and bequeathed $100,000 cash to Fred and devised his residence, valued at $300,000, to Gary. The executor distributes the cash and the residence in 2007, when the estate has $80,000 of DNI, all from taxable sources. Because the cash and residence constitute specific bequests, the estate receives no distribution deduction and the beneficiaries report no gross income. ◀

STOP & THINK

Question: Sally is the sole beneficiary of her uncle Harry's estate. In the current year, the estate had DNI of $36,000, all from dividends and corporate interest. During the current year, the estate's executor distributed to Sally $12,200 of cash and her uncle Harry's rare book collection, valued at $5,400 on both date of death and date of distribution. Uncle Harry's will made one specific bequest, the rare book collection to Sally. How much gross income should Sally report from the estate during the current year? What is the amount of the estate's distribution deduction?

Solution: Sally does not have to report gross income as a result of receiving the specific bequest of the book collection. Because Sally's $12,200 cash distribution does not exceed the estate's $36,000 DNI, Sally should report gross income equal to the cash distributed to her ($12,200). The estate's distribution deduction equals the amount included in Sally's gross income ($12,200). If the book collection were not a specific bequest, its distribution by the estate would be taxable to Sally because the $17,600 ($12,200 + $5,400) distributed by the estate is less than the estate's DNI.

[35] Sec. 662(a)(2).

[36] Sec. 663(a)(1).

KEY POINT

Generally, the tax consequences of both NOLs and net capital losses are the same for estates, complex trusts, and simple trusts.

EFFECT OF A NET OPERATING LOSS

As with simple trusts, an NOL of an estate or complex trust can be carried back and carried forward. In the year the trust or estate terminates, any remaining NOL passes through to the beneficiaries who succeed to the assets. In addition, in its year of termination the estate passes through to its beneficiaries any excess of current nonoperating expenses (e.g., executor's fees) over current income. If the estate incurs NOLs over a series of years, a tax incentive exists for terminating the estate as early as possible so the loss can pass through to the beneficiaries.

EFFECT OF A NET CAPITAL LOSS

The tax effect of having capital losses that exceed capital gains generally is the same for estates and complex trusts as for simple trusts. As for an individual taxpayer, the maximum capital loss deduction is the lesser of $3,000 or the excess of its capital losses over capital gains.[37] Simple trusts, however, receive no immediate tax benefit when capital losses exceed capital gains. Estates and complex trusts often do not distribute all their income and, thus, have taxable income against which they can offset a capital loss.

EXAMPLE C:14-28 ▶ For 2006, Gold Trust reported $30,000 of net accounting income and DNI, all from taxable sources. It made discretionary distributions totaling $7,000 to Amy. It sold one capital asset at an $8,000 long-term capital loss. The trust deducted $3,000 of capital losses in arriving at its 2006 taxable income. The trust carries over the remaining $5,000 of capital loss to 2007. If in 2007, Gold Trust sells a capital asset for a $5,000 long-term capital gain, it will offset the $5,000 loss carryover against the $5,000 capital gain. ◀

COMPREHENSIVE ILLUSTRATION: DETERMINING A COMPLEX TRUST'S TAXABLE INCOME

The comprehensive illustration below reviews a number of points discussed earlier. A sample Form 1041 for a complex trust appears in Appendix B; it is prepared on the basis of the facts in this illustration.

BACKGROUND DATA

Ted Tims established the Cathy and Karen Stephens Trust on March 12, 1994. Its trust instrument empowers the trustee (Merchants Bank) to distribute income in its discretion to Cathy and Karen for the next 20 years. The trust will then be terminated, and the trust assets will be divided equally between Cathy and Karen, irrespective of the amount of distributions each has previously received. In other words, no separate shares are to be maintained. Under state law, capital gains are part of principal.

The 2006 income and expenses of the trust appear below. With the exception of the information concerning distributions and payments of estimated tax, the amounts are the same as in the comprehensive illustration for a simple trust discussed previously in the chapter. As before, the holding period for the stock sold in October was four years.

	Amounts Allocable to	
	Income	*Principal*
Dividends	$30,000	
Rental income from land	5,000	
Tax-exempt interest	15,000	
Rental expenses (realtor's commissions on rental income)	1,000	

[37] Sec. 1211(b).

Trustee's fee		$ 1,200
Fee for preparation of tax return	500	
Capital gain on sale of stock		12,000
Distribution of net accounting income to:		
Cathy	14,000	
Karen	7,000	
Payments of estimated tax	5,240	3,360

TRUSTEE'S FEE

Recall that some of the trustee's fee must be allocated to tax-exempt income, with the result that this portion is nondeductible. Of the trust's gross accounting income of $50,000 ($30,000 + $5,000 + $15,000), $15,000 is from tax-exempt sources. Consequently, the nondeductible trustee's fee is $360 [($15,000 ÷ $50,000) × $1,200]. The remaining $840 of the fee is deductible, as is the $500 tax return preparation fee.

DISTRIBUTION DEDUCTION AND DNI

Recall that the primary function of the Subchapter J rules is to provide guidance for calculating the amounts taxable to the beneficiaries and to the fiduciary. One of the crucial numbers in the process is the distribution deduction, which requires knowledge of the DNI amount. Taxable income, exclusive of the distribution deduction, is the starting point for calculating DNI and is computed as follows:

Dividends		$30,000
Rental income		5,000
Capital gain on sale of stock		12,000
Minus:	Rental expenses	(1,000)
	Deductible portion of trustee's fee	(840)
	Fee for tax return preparation	(500)
	Personal exemption	(100)
Taxable income, exclusive of distribution deduction		$44,560

DNI is calculated by adjusting taxable income, exclusive of the distribution deduction, as follows:

Taxable income, exclusive of distribution deduction		$44,560
Plus:	Personal exemption	100
Minus:	Capital gain on sale of stock	(12,000)
Plus:	Tax-exempt interest (net of $360 of allocable expenses)	14,640
DNI		$47,300

The distribution deduction is the lesser of (1) amounts required to be distributed, plus other amounts properly paid or credited, or required to be distributed, or (2) DNI. This lesser-of amount must be reduced by tax-exempt income (net of allocable expenses). DNI, exclusive of net tax-exempt income, is calculated as follows:

DNI		$47,300
Minus:	Tax-exempt income (net of $360 of allocable expenses)	(14,640)
DNI, exclusive of net tax-exempt income		$32,660

In no event may the distribution deduction exceed $32,660, the DNI, exclusive of net tax-exempt income. The DNI ceiling is of no practical significance in this example, however, because only $21,000 is distributed.

ADDITIONAL COMMENT

This example dealing with a complex trust clearly illustrates the computational complexity that exists in situations with multiple categories of income and multiple beneficiaries.

Because a portion of the payments to each beneficiary is deemed to consist of tax-exempt income, the distribution deduction is less than the $21,000 distributed. Each beneficiary's share of tax-exempt income is determined by dividing DNI into categories of income. In this categorization process, the rental expenses are direct expenses that must be charged against rental income, and $360 of the trustee's fees must be charged against tax-exempt income. In this example, the deductible trustee's fee and the tax return preparation fee are charged against rental income. Alternatively, they could be charged against dividend income or pro rata against each income category, but an allocation to dividend income would be disadvantageous because dividends are taxed at the preferential 15% rate. As with the simple trust illustrated earlier, total DNI of $47,300 consists of the following categories:

	Dividends	*Rents*	*Tax-Exempt Interest*	*Total*
Accounting income	$30,000	$5,000	$15,000	$50,000
Minus: Expenses:				
Trustee's fee		(840)	(360)	(1,200)
Rental expenses		(1,000)		(1,000)
Tax return preparation fee		(500)		(500)
DNI	$30,000	$2,660	$14,640	$47,300

Because the complex trust illustration involves two beneficiaries and three categories of income, we must calculate the amount of each beneficiary's distribution attributable to each income category. These steps were not needed in the simple trust illustration because it involved only one beneficiary.

Category of Income	*Proportion of DNI*
Dividends	63.4249% = $30,000 ÷ $47,300
Rental income	5.6237% = $ 2,660 ÷ $47,300
Tax-exempt income	30.9514% = $14,640 ÷ $47,300
Total	100.0000%

As shown above, 30.9514% of each beneficiary's distribution represents tax-exempt interest and is ineligible for a distribution deduction. The amount of the distribution deduction (which cannot exceed the $32,660 DNI, exclusive of net tax-exempt income) is determined as follows:

Total amount distributed	$21,000
Minus: Net tax-exempt income deemed distributed (0.309514 × $21,000)	(6,500)
Distribution deduction	$14,500

The distributions received by the beneficiaries are deemed to consist of three categories of income in the amounts shown below.

Components of Distributions	*Cathy*	*Karen*	*Total*
Dividends (63.4249%)	$ 8,879	$4,440	$13,319
Plus: Rental income (5.6237%)	788	393	1,181
Gross income (69.0486%)	$ 9,667	$4,833	$14,500
Plus: Tax-exempt interest (30.9514%)	4,333	2,167	6,500
Total income (100%)	$14,000	$7,000	$21,000

TRUST'S TAXABLE INCOME

Once the taxable and tax-exempt distributions have been quantified, the trust's taxable income can be calculated. Table C:14-3 illustrates this calculation. Unlike the simple trust situation, no short-cut approach exists for verifying taxable income for complex trusts and estates except in the years when they distribute all their income.

ADDITIONAL OBSERVATIONS

A few additional observations are in order concerning the Stephens Trust:

- If the entity is an estate instead of a trust, all amounts except the personal exemption are the same. The estate's personal exemption would be $600 instead of $100.

▼ **TABLE C:14-3**

Comprehensive Illustration: Determining a Complex Trust's Taxable Income and Tax Liability

Gross income:	
Dividends	$30,000
Rental income	5,000
Capital gain on sale of stock	12,000
Minus: Expense deductions:	
Rental expenses	(1,000)
Deductible portion of trustee's fee	(840)
Tax return preparation fee	(500)
Minus: Distribution deduction	(14,500)
Minus: Personal exemption	(100)
Taxable income	$30,060
Tax liability (2006 rates)[a]	$ 4,443
Minus: Estimated taxes	(8,600)
Tax owed (refunded)	($ 4,157)

[a]The $12,000 long-term capital gain and the $16,681 of dividends retained by the trust are taxed at the lower rates. The $16,681 amount is $30,000 minus the $13,319 dividends distributed, as calculated on p. C:14-26. The remaining taxable income of $1,379 ($30,060 − $12,000 − $16,681) is taxed at 15%. The tax liability is calculated as follows:

Tax on ordinary, non-dividend income (0.15 × $1,379)	$ 207
Plus: Tax on capital gains and dividends at 5% [0.05 × $671 (where $671 = $2,050 − $1,379)]	34
Tax on capital gains and dividends at 15% [0.15 × ($28,681 − $671)]	4,202
Total tax	$4,443

- Assume that (1) the trust owns a building instead of land and incurs $2,000 of depreciation expense, chargeable against principal under state law, and (2) the trust instrument does not require a reserve for depreciation. Because approximately 56% of the trust's income is accumulated (i.e., $26,300 of its $47,300 DNI), $1,120 (0.56 × $2,000) of the depreciation is deductible by the trust and its taxable income is $1,120 lower. The remaining $880 (0.44 × $2,000) is deductible on the beneficiaries' returns and is divided between them according to their pro rata share of the total distributions. Cathy deducts $587 [$880 × ($14,000 ÷ $21,000)], and Karen deducts $293 [$880 × ($7,000 ÷ $21,000)]. In summary, the depreciation is deductible as follows $1,120 to the trust, $587 to Cathy, and $293 to Karen.
- If the trust instrument had mandated a reserve for depreciation equal to the depreciation expense for tax purposes, accounting income would have been reduced by the depreciation. In addition, the entire $2,000 of depreciation would have been deducted by the trust, and DNI would have been $45,300 instead of $47,300.

INCOME IN RESPECT OF A DECEDENT

OBJECTIVE 7

Recognize the significance of income in respect of a decedent

DEFINITION AND COMMON EXAMPLES

Section 691 specifies the tax treatment for specific types of income known as income in respect of a decedent. **Income in respect of a decedent (IRD)** is gross income that the decedent earned before death but was not includible on the decedent's income tax return for the tax year ending with the date of death or for an earlier tax year because the decedent (a cash basis taxpayer) had not collected the income. Because most individuals use the cash method of accounting, IRD generally consists of income earned, but not actually or constructively received, prior to death. Common examples of IRD include the following:

- Interest earned, but not received, before death
- Salary, commission, or bonus earned, but not received, before death
- Dividends collected after the date of death, for which the record date precedes the date of death
- The gain portion of principal collected on a pre-death installment sale

SELF-STUDY QUESTION

Roger, a cash basis taxpayer, is a medical doctor. At the time of Roger's death, patients owe him $150,000. These accounts receivable are "property" in which Roger has an interest at the time of his death and are included in his gross estate. Why are the accounts receivable income in respect of a decedent?

ANSWER

Because they are income Roger earned while alive, but did not report as income under his accounting method, they constitute income to his estate (or his heirs) when they are collected. Thus, they are income in respect of a decedent (IRD).

SIGNIFICANCE OF IRD

DOUBLE TAXATION. Recall from Chapter C:13 that a decedent's gross estate includes property to the extent of his or her interest therein. The decedent has an interest in any income earned but not actually or constructively received before death. Thus, the decedent's gross estate includes income accrued as of the date of death. If the decedent used the cash method of accounting, the decedent did not include this accrued income in gross income because he or she had not yet collected it. The income is taxed to the party (i.e., the estate or a named individual) entitled to receive it. Thus, IRD is taxed under both the transfer tax system and the income tax system. The income also is taxed twice if the decedent collects a dividend check, deposits it into his or her bank account, and dies before consuming the cash. In the latter case, the dividend is included in the decedent's individual income tax return, and the cash (from the dividend check) is included in the decedent's gross estate. The income taxes owed on the dividend income are deductible as a debt on the estate tax return.

EXAMPLE C:14-29 ▶ Doug dies on July 1. Included in Doug's gross estate is an 8%, $1,000 corporate bond that pays interest each September 1 and March 1. Doug's gross estate also includes accrued interest for the period March 2 through July 1 of $27 ($\$1,000 \times 0.08 \times 4/12$). On September 1, Doug's estate collects $40 of interest, of which $27 constitutes IRD. The calendar year income tax return for Doug's estate includes $40 of interest income, consisting of $27 of IRD and $13 earned after death. ◀

SELF-STUDY QUESTION

Karl receives his regular monthly paycheck on May 1 and deposits the paycheck in his savings account. He dies on May 10. He made no withdrawals from the account before his death. On June 1, Karl's employer pays Karl's estate one-third of Karl's May salary (the amount Karl had earned prior to his death on May 10). What are the tax consequences?

ANSWER

Karl's gross estate will include his savings account. Karl's final income tax return will include his salary through April 30 (i.e., his May 1 check is subject to both the income and the estate tax). The income taxes owed on the April salary are deductible as a debt on his estate tax return.

Karl's gross estate will include the one-third of his May salary. The income tax return for his estate also will report this amount as income. The salary is income in respect of a decedent, so the estate will receive some relief under Sec. 691(c) from the double tax.

DEDUCTIONS IN RESPECT OF A DECEDENT. Section 691(b) authorizes **deductions in respect of a decedent** (**DRD**). Such deductions include trade or business expenses, expenses for the production of income, interest, taxes, depletion, etc. that are accrued before death but are not deductible on the decedent's final income tax return because the decedent used the cash method of accounting. Because these accrued expenses have not been paid before death, they also may be deductible as debts on the estate tax return. In addition, the accrued expenses are deductible on the estate's income tax return when paid by the estate (if they are for deductible expenses). Thus, a double benefit can be obtained for DRD.

EXAMPLE C:14-30 ▶ Dan dies on September 20. At the time of his death, Dan owes $18,000 of salaries to the employees of his proprietorship. The executor pays the total September payroll of $29,000 on September 30. The $18,000 of accrued salaries is deductible as a debt on the estate tax return. As a trade or business (Sec. 162) expense, the salaries also constitute DRD. The $18,000 of DRD, plus any other salaries paid, is deductible on the estate's income tax return for the period of payment. ◀

SECTION 691(c) DEDUCTION. The Sec. 691(c) deduction provides some relief for the double taxation of IRD. This deduction equals the federal estate taxes attributable to the net IRD included in the gross estate. The total Sec. 691(c) deduction is the excess of the decedent's actual federal estate tax over the federal estate tax that would be payable if the net IRD were excluded from the decedent's gross estate. Net IRD means IRD minus deductions in respect of a decedent (DRD). If the IRD is collected in more than one tax year, the Sec. 691(c) deduction for a particular tax year is determined by the following formula:[38]

$$\begin{matrix}\text{Sec. 691(c)}\\ \text{deduction}\\ \text{for the year}\end{matrix} = \begin{matrix}\text{Total}\\ \text{Sec. 691(c)}\\ \text{deduction}\end{matrix} \times \frac{\text{Net IRD included in gross income for the year}}{\text{Total Net IRD}}$$

[38] Sec. 691(c)(1).

EXAMPLE C:14-31 ▶ Latoya died in 2006 with a taxable estate and estate tax base of $2.5 million. Latoya's gross estate included $300,000 of IRD, none of which was received by her surviving spouse. Her estate had no DRD. The estate collects $250,000 of the IRD during its 2007 tax year. The Sec. 691(c) deduction for Latoya's estate for 2007 is calculated as shown below.

Actual 2006 federal estate tax on base of $2.5 million	$230,000
Minus: 2006 federal estate tax on base of $2.2 million determined by excluding net IRD from gross estate	(92,000)
Total Sec. 691(c) deduction	$138,000
Sec. 691(c) deduction available in 2007: ($250,000 ÷ $300,000) × $138,000 =	$115,000 ◀

NO STEP-UP IN BASIS. Most property received as the result of a decedent's death acquires a basis equal to its FMV on the date of death or the alternate valuation date. Property classified as IRD, however, retains the basis it had in the decedent's hands.[39]

This carryover basis rule for IRD items is especially unfavorable when the decedent sells a highly appreciated asset soon before death, collects a relatively small portion of the sales price before death, and reports the sale under the installment method of accounting. For example, if the gain is 80% of the sales price, 80% of each principal payment in the post-death period will continue to be characterized as gain. If the sale instead had been postponed until after the date of death, the gain would be restricted to the post-death appreciation (if any) because the step-up in basis rules apply to the asset.

EXAMPLE C:14-32 ▶ On June 3, 2007, Joel sells a parcel of investment land for $40,000. The land has a $10,000 adjusted basis in Joel's hands. The buyer pays $8,000 down and signs a $32,000 note at an interest rate acceptable to the IRS. The note is payable June 3, 2008. Joel, a cash basis taxpayer, uses the installment method for reporting the $30,000 ($40,000 – $10,000) gain. The gross profit ratio is 75% ($30,000 gain ÷ $40,000 contract price). Joel dies on June 13, 2007. Joel's final individual income tax return reports a gain of $6,000 (0.75 × $8,000). The estate reports a gain of $24,000 (0.75 × $32,000) on its 2008 tax return because it collects the $32,000 balance due on June 3, 2008. Had the sale contract been entered into immediately after Joel's death, the gain would have been zero because the land's basis would have been its $40,000 FMV at the date of death. ◀

SELF-STUDY QUESTION

Roger (a cash basis taxpayer) died leaving $150,000 of accounts receivable. What basis does his estate have in these accounts receivable?

ANSWER

Zero. The accounts receivable constitute IRD. If they were stepped-up in basis, they would never be subject to an income tax.

STOP & THINK

Question: Isaac, a cash basis, calendar year taxpayer, died on May 12 of the current year. On which income tax return—Isaac's or his estate's—should the following income and expenses be reported? Assume the estate's tax year is the calendar year.

- Dividends declared in January and paid in February
- Interest income on a corporate bond that pays interest each June 30 and December 31
- Rent collected in June for a vacation home rented to tenants for the month of March, but the tenants were allowed to pay after occupying the property
- Balance due on Isaac's state income taxes for the previous year, paid in July because the return was extended
- Federal estimated income tax for the previous year that Isaac paid in January

Solution: Income received before death and deductible expenses paid before death (in this case the dividends and nothing more) should be reported on his individual return. Income received after Isaac's death, even though earned before his death, is to be reported on the estate's income tax return. The same is true for deductible expenses paid by the estate. Items to be reported on the estate's income tax return include the interest income, the rental income, and the state income taxes. The federal income taxes paid are not deductible on the federal income tax return of either taxpayer. The tax payment, however, reduced the cash Isaac owned at his date of death.

[39] Sec. 1014(c).

GRANTOR TRUST PROVISIONS

OBJECTIVE 8

Explain the effect of the grantor trust provisions

This portion of the chapter examines the provisions affecting a special type of trust known as a **grantor trust**, which is governed by Secs. 671-679. As discussed previously, income of a regular (or nongrantor) trust or an estate is taxed to the beneficiary to the extent distributed or to the fiduciary to the extent accumulated. In the case of a grantor trust, however, the trust's grantor (creator) is taxed on some or all of the trust's income even if such income is distributed to the beneficiary. In certain circumstances, a person other than the grantor or the beneficiary (e.g., a person with powers over the trust) must pay taxes on the trust's income.

PURPOSE AND EFFECT

The grantor trust rules require grantors who do not give up enough control or economic benefits when they create a trust to pay a price by being taxed on part or all of the trust's income. A grantor must report some or all of a trust's income on his or her individual tax return if he or she does not part with enough control over the trust assets or give up the right to income produced by the assets for a sufficiently long time period. For transfers after March 1, 1986, the grantor generally is taxed on the trust's income if the trust property will eventually return to the grantor or the grantor's spouse.[40] According to the Tax Court, the grantor trust rules have the following purpose and result:

> This subpart [Secs. 671-679] enunciates the rules to be applied where, in described circumstances, a grantor has transferred property to a trust but has not parted with complete dominion and control over the property or the income which it produces. . . . [41]

Sections 671-679 use the term *treated as owner.* Section 671 specifies that when a grantor is treated as owner, the income, deductions, and credits attributable to the portion of the trust with respect to which the grantor is treated as owner are reported directly on the grantor's tax return and not on the trust's return. The fiduciary return contains only the items attributable to the portion of the trust for which the grantor is not treated as the owner.

ADDITIONAL COMMENT

Many trust provisions can cause the grantor trust rules to apply. A trust need *not* be a revocable trust to be a grantor trust.

Unfortunately, the rules governing when a transfer is complete for income tax purposes (meaning the grantor avoids being taxed on the trust's income) do not agree completely with the rules concerning whether the transfer is complete for gift tax purposes or the transferred property is removed from the donor's gross estate. In certain circumstances, a donor can make a taxable gift and still be taxed on the income from the transferred property. For example, if a donor transfers property to a trust with the income payable annually to the donor's cousin for six years and a reversion of the property to the donor at the end of the sixth year, the donor makes a gift, subject to the gift tax, of the value of a six-year income interest. Under the grantor trust rules, however, the donor is taxed on the trust's income because the property reverts to the donor within too short a time period.

Retention of certain powers over property conveyed in trust can cause the trust assets to be included in the donor's gross estate even though these powers do not result in the donor being taxed on the trust income. Assume a donor to a trust reserves the discretionary power to pay out or accumulate trust income until the beneficiary reaches age 21. The trust assets, including any accumulated income, are to be distributed to the beneficiary on his or her twenty-first birthday. The donor is not taxed on the trust income because he can exercise his powers only until the beneficiary reaches age 21. If the donor dies before the beneficiary attains age 21, however, the donor's gross estate will include the trust property because the donor retained control over the beneficiary's economic benefits (see discussion of Sec. 2036 in Chapter C:13).

---

[40] For trusts created before March 2, 1986, the grantor was treated as the owner with respect to the trust's capital gains but not its ordinary income if the property returned to the grantor after a period of more than ten years. In such a situation, the grantor is taxed on the capital gains and the trust and/or the beneficiary on the ordinary income. The trusts usually terminated slightly more than ten years after their funding. Thus, few of these trusts exist today.

[41] *William Scheft*, 59 T.C. 428, at 430-431 (1972).

REVOCABLE TRUSTS

The grantor of a revocable trust can control assets conveyed to the trust by altering the terms of the trust (including changing the identity of the beneficiaries) and/or withdrawing assets from the trust. Not surprisingly, Sec. 676 provides that the grantor is taxed on the income generated by a revocable trust. As Chapter C:12 points out, a transfer of assets to a revocable trust is an incomplete transfer and not subject to the gift tax.

EXAMPLE C:14-33 ▶ In the current year, Tom transfers property to a revocable trust and names Ann to receive the income for life and Beth to receive the remainder. The trust's income for the current year consists of $15,000 of dividends and an $8,000 long-term capital gain. The trustee distributes the dividends to Ann but retains the gain and credits it to principal. Because the trust is revocable, the dividend and capital gain income are taxed directly to Tom on his current year individual tax return. Nothing is taxed to the trust or its beneficiaries. ◀

ADDITIONAL COMMENT

A common use of the revocable trust is to avoid probate for the property held by the trust. On the death of the grantor, the trustee of the revocable trust distributes the trust property in accordance with the trust agreement. Because the trustee holds legal title to the property, he or she can distribute the property without going through the probate process.

POST-1986 REVERSIONARY INTEREST TRUSTS

The 1986 Tax Reform Act amended Sec. 673(a) for transfers made after March 1, 1986, to provide that, generally, the grantor is taxed on the accounting income of the trust if he or she has a reversionary interest in either income or principal. Under Sec. 672(e), a grantor is treated as holding any interest held by his or her spouse. These rules have two exceptions.

The first exception makes the grantor trust rules inapplicable if, as of the inception of the trust, the value of the reversionary interest does not exceed 5% of the value of the trust. The second exception applies if the reversion will occur only if the beneficiary dies before reaching age 21 and the beneficiary is a lineal descendant of the grantor.

EXAMPLE C:14-34 ▶ In the current year, Paul establishes a trust with income payable to his elderly parents for 15 years. The assets of the trust will then revert to Paul. The value of Paul's reversionary interest exceeds 5%. Because Paul has a reversionary interest valued at above 5% and the transfer arose after March 1, 1986, Paul is taxed currently on the trust's accounting income and capital gains. ◀

EXAMPLE C:14-35 ▶ In the current year, Paul transfers property to a trust with income payable to his daughter Ruth until Ruth reaches age 21. On Ruth's twenty-first birthday, she is to receive the trust property outright. In the event Ruth dies before reaching age 21, the trust assets will revert to Paul. Paul is not taxed on the accounting income because his reversion is contingent on the death of the beneficiary (a lineal descendant) before age 21. ◀

RETENTION OF ADMINISTRATIVE POWERS

Under Sec. 675, the grantor is taxed on the accounting income and gains if he or she or his or her spouse holds certain administrative powers. Such powers include, but are not limited to, the following:

- The power to purchase or exchange trust property for less than adequate consideration in money or money's worth
- The power to borrow from the trust without adequate interest or security except where the trustee (who is someone other than the grantor) has a general lending power to make loans irrespective of interest or security
- The power exercisable in a role other than as trustee to (1) vote stock of a corporation in which the holdings of the grantor and the trust are significant from the standpoint of voting control and (2) reacquire the trust property by substituting other property of equal value.

RETENTION OF ECONOMIC BENEFITS

Section 677 taxes the grantor on the portion of the trust with respect to which the income may be

- Distributed to the grantor or his or her spouse,
- Held or accumulated for future distribution to the grantor or his or her spouse, or
- Used to pay premiums on life insurance policies on the life of the grantor or his or her spouse

Use of trust income to provide support for a child whom the grantor is legally obligated to support yields obvious economic benefits to the grantor. A grantor is taxed on any trust income distributed by the trustee to support individuals whom the grantor is legally obligated to support (e.g., children). However, the mere existence of the discretionary power to use trust income for support purposes does not cause the grantor to be taxed on the trust income. Taxation turns on whether the trust income is actually used to meet the support obligation.

The next example concerns use of trust income to support the grantor's minor child.

EXAMPLE C:14-36 ▶ Hal creates a trust and empowers the bank trustee to distribute income to his minor son, Louis, until the son reaches age 21. When Louis reaches age 21, the trust assets including accumulated income are to be paid over to the child. In the current year, when Louis is age 15, the trustee distributes $5,000 that is used to support Louis and $8,000 that is deposited into Louis's savings account. The remaining $12,000 of income is accumulated. Hal (the grantor) is taxed on the $5,000 used to support his son. Louis includes $8,000 in his gross income, and the trust pays tax on $12,000 less its $100 exemption. ◀

The following example deals with the payment of premiums on an insurance policy on the grantor's life.

EXAMPLE C:14-37 ▶ Maria is the grantor of the Martinez Trust, one of whose assets is a life insurance policy on Maria's life. The trust instrument requires that $1,000 of trust income be used to pay the annual insurance premiums and that the rest be distributed to Maria's adult son Juan. Section 677 requires Maria (the grantor and insured) to be taxed on $1,000 of accounting income. The remaining income is taxed to Juan under the general trust rules. ◀

ADDITIONAL COMMENT

If the trust were created by a person other than the insured, say a parent, the income required to be used for paying life insurance premiums would not be taxed to the grantor because the insured is not the grantor or the grantor's spouse.

CONTROL OF OTHERS' ENJOYMENT

Section 674 taxes the grantor on trust income if he or she, his or her spouse, or someone without an interest in the trust (e.g., a trustee) has the power to control others' beneficial enjoyment such as by deciding how much income to distribute. Many exceptions, including one for independent trustees, exist for the general rule.

EXAMPLE C:14-38 ▶ Otto is grantor and trustee of a trust over which the trustee has complete discretion to pay out the income or corpus in any amount he deems appropriate to some or all of its three unrelated beneficiaries, Kay, Fay, and May. In the current year, the trustee distributes all the income to Kay. Otto, the grantor, is taxed on the income. If instead the trustee were independent, Kay would be taxed on the amount she received. ◀

Under Sec. 678, an individual other than the trust's grantor or beneficiary can be required to report the trust income. This individual is taxed on the trust income if he or she has the power under the trust instrument to vest the trust principal or the income in him- or herself, provided such power is exercisable solely by such individual.

Topic Review C:14-4 summarizes the grantor trust rules.

WHAT WOULD YOU DO IN THIS SITUATION?

You, a CPA, have prepared the income tax returns for the Candy Cain Trust, an irrevocable trust, since the inception of the trust five years ago. The grantor is Able Cain, another client and the father of Candy Cain, the income beneficiary. First Bank, the trustee, is authorized to distribute income at its descretion to Candy, who is now age 17. For the current year, the trust's DNI of $15,000, all from interest on corporate bonds, was distributed to Candy to pay her medical bills incurred in an accident. You advised Mr. Cain that he must include the $15,000 trust distribution on his individual tax return because the distribution was used to satisfy his obligation to support Candy. Mr. Cain reminds you of how many clients he has referred to you and demands that you instead show the distribution as taxable to Candy so the income will be taxed at his daughter's low rates instead of at his rate, the highest marginal rate. How will you react to Mr. Cain's request?

Topic Review C:14-4

Grantor Trust Rules

FACTUAL SITUATION	TAX TREATMENT
1. Trust is revocable.	Ordinary income (including dividends) and capital gains are taxed to grantor.
2. Irrevocable trust is funded on or after March 2, 1986, with income payable to third-party beneficiary for 20 years after which property reverts to grantor; the value of the reversionary interest exceeds 5% of the value of the trust.	Ordinary income (including dividends) and capital gains are taxed to grantor.
3. The grantor of an irrevocable trust retains administrative powers described in the IRC.	Ordinary income (including dividends) and capital gains are taxed to grantor.
4. The income of an irrevocable trust is disbursed to meet the grantor's obligation to support his or her children.	Ordinary income (including dividends) used for support are taxed to grantor.
5. The income of an irrevocable trust is disbursed to pay the premium on a life insurance policy on the life of the grantor or the grantor's spouse.	Ordinary income (including dividends) and capital gains are taxed to grantor to the extent they may be used to pay the premiums.

TAX PLANNING CONSIDERATIONS

ADDITIONAL COMMENT

In 2007, the first $2,150 of trust income is taxed at 15%. A complex trust pays no tax on $100 of income (because of its personal exemption) and only 15% on the next $2,150 of income. If the trust distributes income to a child under age 18 who is a dependent and has no other unearned income, the child pays no tax on the first $850 of that income and pays taxes at his or her own rate on the next $850. The rest is taxed at the parents' rates. If the parents are always in the top income tax bracket, non-trivial income tax savings still can be achieved by using a trust to spread non-dividend income over different taxpayers. For the situation described here, a Sec. 2503(c) trust (trust for minors) is commonly used.

Many tax planning opportunities exist with respect to estates and trusts, including the ability to shift income to the fiduciary and/or the beneficiaries and the opportunity for executors or trustees of discretionary trusts to consider the tax consequences of the timing of distributions. These and other tax planning considerations are discussed below.

ABILITY TO SHIFT INCOME

Before 1987, one of the primary tax advantages of using trusts was the ability to shift income from the grantor to the trust or the beneficiary. Three changes have reduced the tax advantages of shifting income. First, the tax rate schedules for all taxpayers—but especially for fiduciaries—are very compressed. In fact, an estate or trust has only $2,150 (in 2007) of income subject to the 15% tax rate. Second, unearned income exceeding $1,700 (in 2007) of children under age 18 is taxed at the higher of the parents' or the child's tax rate, even if distributed from a trust or estate. Third, dividend income is eligible for a maximum 15% tax rate regardless of whether it is taxed to the grantor, the beneficiary, or the trust. Depending on whether the income is distributed or retained, it is taxed to the trust or the beneficiary or a portion to each. Because the trust is a separate taxpayer, income taxed to the trust is taxed under the trust's rate schedule. If the beneficiary has income from other sources, the income shifted to the beneficiary is not necessarily taxed in the lowest tax bracket. An income tax savings nevertheless can occur whenever a portion of the shifted income is taxed at a rate lower than the rate the grantor would pay on such income.

KEY POINT

Given that one often cannot determine the exact amount of income a trust (or any other entity) has earned until after the end of the tax year, the importance of the 65-day rule for distribution planning becomes readily apparent.

TIMING OF DISTRIBUTIONS

Individuals managing estates and discretionary trusts can reduce taxes by carefully planning the timing of distributions. From a tax standpoint, the executor or trustee should consider the beneficiary's income from other sources and make distributions in amounts that equalize the marginal tax rates of the beneficiary and the fiduciary. If the trust is a **sprinkling trust** (a discretionary trust with several beneficiaries), the trustee can accomplish tax savings for the beneficiaries by making distributions to the beneficiaries who have the lowest marginal tax rate that year. Of course, nontax reasons might require a trustee to distribute income to other beneficiaries as well. A special 65-day rule allows trustees of complex trusts and estates to treat distributions made during the first 65 days of the new tax year as if they had been made on the last day of the preceding tax year. If the trustee or executor does not make the election, the distributed income is deducted by the fiduciary and taxed to the beneficiary in the year of the actual distribution.

PROPERTY DISTRIBUTIONS

Under the general rule affecting property distributions, the trust gets a distribution deduction equal to the lesser of the fiduciary's adjusted basis in the property or the property's FMV.[42] If the trust distributes appreciated property, however, the trustee can elect to recognize a gain on the distribution equal to the excess of the property's FMV over its adjusted basis on the distribution date. If the trustee does not make the election, the trust recognizes no gain when it distributes the property.

If the trustee elects to recognize the gain, the distribution deduction equals the property's FMV. The beneficiary, in turn, takes a basis equal to the property's adjusted basis to the trust plus the gain the trust recognized on the distribution. If the beneficiary likely will sell the property soon after distribution, the election provision allows the trustee to choose where the appreciation will be taxed, at the trust level or the beneficiary level. If the distribution involves appreciated capital gain property, the capital gain recognized by the trust can be offset by the trust's current capital loss and carryovers from prior tax years.

EXAMPLE C:14-39 ▶ Todd Trust owns a number of assets, including an asset with a FMV of $35,000 and an adjusted basis of $12,000. In the current year, the trust distributes the asset to its sole beneficiary, Susan. The trust does not make any other distributions to Susan. If the trustee elects to recognize gain of $23,000, the trust receives a distribution deduction of $35,000, the FMV of the asset. Susan includes $35,000 of income in her tax return and obtains a $35,000 basis in the asset. Thus, if she sells the asset for $35,000, she will report no gain. If the trustee had not elected to recognize gain on the in-kind distribution, the distribution deduction would have been $12,000, the asset's adjusted basis to the trust. Susan's basis in the asset also would have been $12,000. ◀

CHOICE OF YEAR-END FOR ESTATES

Distributions from an estate or trust are taxed to the beneficiaries in the beneficiaries' tax year in which the fiduciary's year ends.[43] Congress in 1986 required all trusts (even existing fiscal-year trusts) other than tax-exempt and wholly charitable trusts to use a calendar year as their tax year to eliminate their ability to defer the taxation of trust distributions to beneficiaries by choosing a noncalendar year.[44] Estates, however, are completely free to choose a year-end as long as the tax year does not exceed 12 months.

EXAMPLE C:14-40 ▶ Molly Madison died on February 7, 2006. Madison Estate adopted a fiscal year ending January 31. During the period February 7, 2006 through January 31, 2007, Madison Estate distributes $30,000 to Bob, a calendar year beneficiary. The estate's DNI exceeds $30,000. Bob reports $30,000 of estate income on his individual return for 2007, Bob's tax year during which the estate's tax year ended. By choosing the January 31 year-end (instead of a calendar year-end), the executor postpones the taxation of income to Bob from 2006 to 2007. ◀

DEDUCTION OF ADMINISTRATION EXPENSES

Chapter C:13 points out that the executor elects where to deduct administration expenses, i.e., on the estate tax return, the estate's income tax return, or some on each return. Unlike the situation for deductions in respect of a decedent, Sec. 642(g) denies a double deduction for administration expenses. Such expenses should be deducted where

---

[42] Sec. 643(d).
[43] Secs. 652(c) and 662(c).
[44] Sec. 645.

they will yield the greatest tax savings. Of course, if the surviving spouse receives all the decedent's property or all except for an amount equal to the exemption equivalent, deducting administration expenses on the estate tax return will produce no tax savings because the estate will owe no estate taxes.

COMPLIANCE AND PROCEDURAL CONSIDERATIONS

OBJECTIVE 9

Recognize the filing requirements for fiduciary returns

FILING REQUIREMENTS

GENERAL RULE. Every estate that has gross income of at least $600 for the tax year must file an income tax return (Form 1041-U.S. Fiduciary Income Tax Return). A trust income tax return (generally Form 1041) is required for every trust that has taxable income or has gross income of $600 or more.[45] In addition, every estate or trust that has a nonresident alien as a beneficiary must file a return.[46]

ETHICAL POINT

Individual beneficiaries report their share of income from trusts and estates on Schedule E of Form 1040. CPAs have a responsibility to monitor the beneficial interests that clients have in trusts and estates to prevent underreporting. Some clients may unintentionally forget to report income from a simple trust because they received no cash distributions from the fiduciary during the year.

DUE DATE FOR RETURN AND TAX

The due date for fiduciary returns (Form 1041) is the same as for individuals, the fifteenth day of the fourth month following the end of the tax year.[47] If an extension is desired, Form 7004 must be filed. The automatic extension period is six months.

Both trusts and estates generally must make estimated tax payments using the general rules applicable to individual taxpayers.[48] The IRC, however, exempts estates from making estimated tax payments for their first two tax years. If the fiduciary's tax liability exceeds the estimated tax payments, the balance of the tax is due on or before the due date for the return.[49] Estimated tax payments for a trust or an estate are made by using Form 1041-ES (Estimated Income Tax for Fiduciaries).

DOCUMENTS TO BE FURNISHED TO IRS

Although the executor or the trustee need not file a copy of the will or the trust instrument with the return, at times the IRS may request a copy of such documents. If the IRS makes such a request, the executor or the trustee also should transmit the following:

- A statement signed under penalty of perjury that the copy is true and complete
- A statement naming the provisions of the will or trust agreement that the executor or the trustee believes control how the income is to be divided among the fiduciary, the beneficiaries, and the grantor (if applicable)

SAMPLE SIMPLE AND COMPLEX TRUST RETURNS

Appendix B contains samples of simple and complex trust returns (Form 1041). The Appendix also illustrates completed Schedules K-1 for the reporting of distributed income, etc. to the beneficiaries. One copy of Schedule K-1 for each beneficiary is filed with Form 1041. In addition, each beneficiary receives a copy of his or her Schedule K-1, so that he or she knows the amount and type of gross income to report for the distributions received as well as other pertinent information.

In the two sets of facts illustrated in the sample returns, the trusts do not owe the alternative minimum tax (AMT). When trusts do owe the AMT, they report it on Schedule I of Form 1041.

---

[45] Secs. 6012(a)(3) and (4). A special grantor trust rule, however, permits a revocable trust's income to be reported on the grantor's tax return. See Reg. Sec. 1.671-4(b).

[46] Sec. 6012(a)(5).

[47] Sec. 6072(a).

[48] Sec. 6654(l).

[49] Sec. 6151(a).

PROBLEM MATERIALS

DISCUSSION QUESTIONS

C:14-1 Explain to a client in laymen's language what portion of the income of an estate or trust is subject to taxation at the fiduciary level.

C:14-2 Given the tax rate schedule for trusts, what reasons (tax and/or nontax) exist today for creating a trust?

C:14-3 List some major differences between the taxation of individuals and trusts.

C:14-4 Explain to a client the significance of the income and principal categorization scheme used for fiduciary accounting purposes.

C:14-5 List some common examples of principal and income items under the 1962 Act.

C:14-6 A client asks about the relevance of state law in classifying items as principal or income. Explain the relevance.

C:14-7 A trust whose instrument provides that Irene is entitled to receive for life only distributions of income and Beth is to receive the remainder interest sells property at a gain. Income and corpus are classified in accordance with the Uniform Act. Will Irene receive a distribution equal to the amount of the gain? Explain.

C:14-8 Refer to Question C:14-7. Which taxpayer (the trust, Irene, or Beth) pays the tax on the gain?

C:14-9 A trust owns an asset on which depreciation is claimed. The trust distributes all of its income to its sole income beneficiary. Whose taxable income is reduced by the depreciation?

C:14-10 What is the amount of the personal exemption for trusts and estates?

C:14-11 A client inquires about the significance of distributable net income (DNI). Explain.

C:14-12
a. Are net accounting income and DNI always the same amount?
b. If not, explain a common reason for a difference.
c. Are capital gains usually included in DNI?

C:14-13 Explain how to determine the deductible portion of a trustee's fee.

C:14-14 Assume that a trust collects rental income and interest income on tax-exempt bonds. Will a portion of the rental expenses have to be allocated to tax-exempt income and thereby become nondeductible? Explain.

C:14-15
a. Describe the shortcut approach for verifying that the amount calculated as a simple trust's taxable income is correct.
b. Can a shortcut verification process be applied for trusts and estates that accumulate some of their income? Explain.

C:14-16 When does the NOL of a trust or estate produce tax deductions for the beneficiaries?

C:14-17 The Mary Morgan Trust, a simple trust, sells one capital asset in the current year. The sale results in a loss.
a. When will the capital loss produce a tax benefit for the trust or its beneficiary? Explain.
b. Would the result necessarily be the same for a complex trust? Explain.

C:14-18 A peer states that simple trusts receive no tax benefit from a personal exemption. Is your peer correct?

C:14-19 Describe the tier system for taxing trust beneficiaries.

C:14-20 Determine the accuracy of the following statement: Under the tier system, beneficiaries who receive mandatory distributions of income are more likely to be taxed on the entire distributions they receive than are beneficiaries who receive discretionary distributions.

C:14-21
a. Describe to a client what income in respect of a decedent (IRD) is.
b. Describe to the client one tax disadvantage and one tax advantage that occur because of the classification of a receipt as IRD.

C:14-22 Describe three situations that cause trusts to be subject to the grantor trust rules.

C:14-23 Can a client escape the grantor trust rules by providing in a trust instrument that income is payable to a nephew for 20 years and that the trust assets pass at the end of 20 years to the client's spouse?

C:14-24 A client is under the impression that, if the grantor trust rules apply to a trust, the grantor is always taxed on the trust's ordinary income (including dividends) and capital gains. Is the client correct? Explain.

C:14-25 What is the benefit of the 65-day rule?

C:14-26
a. When are fiduciary income tax returns due?
b. Must estates and trusts pay estimated income taxes?

ISSUE IDENTIFICATION QUESTIONS

C:14-27 Art Rutter sold an apartment building in May 2006 for a small amount of cash and a note payable over five years. Principal and interest payments are due annually on the note in April of 2007 through 2011. Art died in August 2006. He willed all his assets to his daughter Amelia. Art's gross estate is about $3 million, and his estate tax deductions are very small. What tax issues should the executor of his estate consider with respect to reporting the sale of the building and the collection of the installments?

C:14-28 For the first five months of its existence (August through December 2007), the Estate of Amy Ennis had gross income (net of expenses) of $7,000 per month. For January through July 2008, the executor estimates that the estate will have gross income (net of expenses) totaling $5,000. The estate's sole beneficiary is Amy's son, Joe, who is a calendar year taxpayer. Joe incurred a large NOL from his sole proprietorship years ago, and $34,000 of the NOL carryover remains but expires at the end of 2007. During 2007, Joe received only $9,000 of income from part-time employment. What tax issues should the executor of Amy's estate consider with respect to distributions of the estate's income?

C:14-29 Raj Kothare funded an irrevocable simple trust in May of last year. The trust benefits Raj's son for life and grandson upon the son's death. One of the assets he transferred to the trust was Webbco stock, which had a $35,000 FMV on the transfer date. Raj's basis in the stock was $39,000, and he paid no gift tax on the transfer. The stock's value has dropped to $27,000, and the trustee thinks that now (October of the current year) might be the time to sell the stock and realize the loss. For the current year, the trust will have $20,000 of income exclusive of any gain or loss. Raj's taxable income is approximately $15,000. What tax and non-tax issues should the trustee consider concerning the possible sale of the stock?

PROBLEMS

C:14-30 *Calculation of the Tax Liability.* A trust has taxable income of $30,000 in 2007. The $30,000 includes $5,000 of long-term capital gains and $25,000 of interest. What is its income tax liability? Compare this tax to the amount of tax a married individual filing a joint return would pay on the same amount of taxable income.

C:14-31 *Determination of Taxable Income.* A simple trust has the following receipts and expenditures for the current year. The long-term capital gain and trustee's fees are part of principal.

Dividends	$20,000
Long-term capital gain	15,000
Trustee's fees	1,500
Distribution to beneficiary	20,000

a. What is the trust's taxable income under the formula approach of Figure C:14-1?
b. What is the trust's taxable income under the short-cut approach?

C:14-32 *Determination of Taxable Income.* Refer to Problem C:14-31. How would your answer to Part a change if the trust in addition received $8,000 interest from tax-exempt bonds, and it distributed $28,000 instead of $20,000?

C:14-33 *Determination of Taxable Income and Tax Liability.* A simple trust has the following receipts and expenditures for the current year. The trust instrument is silent with respect to capital gains, and state law concerning trust accounting income follows the Uniform Act. Assume the trustee's fee is charged to income.

Corporate bond interest	$40,000
Tax-exempt interest	9,000
Long-term capital gain	5,000
Trustee's fee	2,000
Distribution to beneficiary	47,000

a. What is the trust's taxable income under the formula approach of Figure C:14-1?
b. What is the trust's tax liability?

C:14-34 *Determination of Taxable Income.* During the current year, a simple trust has the following receipts and expenditures. Assume that trustee's fees are charged to income and that the Uniform Act governs for accounting.

Corporate bond interest	$60,000
Long-term capital gain	20,000
Trustee's fees	3,000

a. How much must be distributed to the beneficiary?
b. What is the trust's taxable income under the shortcut approach?

C:14-35 *Determination of Distribution Deduction.* A trust has net accounting income of $24,000 and incurs a trustee's fee of $1,000 in its principal account. What is its distribution deduction under the following situations:
a. It distributes $24,000, and all of its income is from taxable sources.
b. It distributes $24,000, and it has tax-exempt income (net of allocable expenses) of $2,000.
c. It distributes $10,000, and all of its income is from taxable sources.

C:14-36 *Determination of Beneficiary's Income.* A trust is authorized to make discretionary distributions of income and principal to its two beneficiaries, Roy and Sandy. Separate shares are not required. For the current year, it has DNI and net accounting income of $80,000, all from taxable sources. It distributes $60,000 to Roy and $40,000 to Sandy. How much gross income should each beneficiary report?

C:14-37 *Determination of Beneficiary's Income.* Refer to Problem C:14-36. How would your answer change if the trust instrument required that $10,000 per year be distributed to Sandy, and the trustee also made discretionary distributions of $60,000 to Roy and $30,000 to Sandy with separate shares not required?

C:14-38 *Determination of Accounting Income and Distribution.* The Trotter Trust has the receipts and expenditures listed below for the current year. Assume the Uniform Act (1962) governs an item's classification as principal or income. The trustee's fee is charged one-half to principal and one-half to income. What is the trust's net accounting income and the maximum amount it can distribute? Assume the trust cannot pay out principal.

Dividends	$15,000
Interest on tax-exempt bonds	7,000
Loss on sale of capital asset	(9,000)
Rental income from land	6,000
Property taxes on rental property	1,000
Trustee's fee	1,800

C:14-39 *Determination of Taxable Income.* Refer to Problem C:14-38. Assume the trustee must pay out all of its income currently to its beneficiary, Julio.
a. What is the deductible portion of the trustee's fee?
b. What is the trust's taxable income exclusive of the distribution deduction?
c. What is the trust's DNI?
d. What is the trust's taxable income using the formula approach of Figure C:14-1?

C:14-40 *Determination of Taxable Income.* Refer to Problem C:14-39. How would your answers change if the trust were a discretionary trust that distributes $12,000 to its beneficiary, Julio?

C:14-41 *Calculation of Deductible Expenses.* The George Grant Trust reports the receipts and expenditures listed below. What are the trust's *deductible* expenses?

U.S. Treasury interest	$25,000
Rental income	9,000
Interest from tax-exempt bonds	6,000
Property taxes on rental property	2,000
CPA's fee for tax return preparation	800
Trustee's fee	1,900

C:14-42 *Tax Treatment of Capital Losses.* A simple trust had a long-term capital loss of $10,000 for 2006 and a long-term capital gain of $15,000 for 2007. Its net accounting income and DNI are equal. Explain the tax treatment for the 2006 capital loss assuming the trust is in existence at the end of 2008.

C:14-43 *Tax Treatment of Capital Losses.* Refer to Problem C:14-42. How would your answer change if instead the trust were a complex trust that makes no distributions in 2006 and 2007? Assume the trust earns $8,000 of corporate bond interest income each year.

C:14-44 *Revocable Trusts.* A revocable trust created by Amir realizes $30,000 of rental income and a $5,000 capital loss. It distributes $25,000 to Ali, its beneficiary. How much income is taxed to the trust, the grantor, and the beneficiary?

C:14-45 *Reversionary Interest Trusts.* Holly funded the Holly Marx Trust in January 2007. The trust income is payable to her adult son, Jack for 20 years. At the end of the twentieth year, the trust assets are to pass to Holly's husband. In the current year, the trust realizes $30,000 of dividend income and a $15,000 long-term capital gain. How much income is taxed to the trust, the grantor, and the beneficiary in the current year?

C:14-46 *Reversionary Interest Trusts.* Refer to Problem C:14-45. Explain how your answers would change for each independent situation indicated below:

a. At the end of the trust term, the property passes instead to Holly's nephew.
b. Holly creates the trust in October 2007 for a term of 25 years, after which the property reverts to her.

C:14-47 *Income in Respect of Decedent.* The following items are reported on the first income tax return for the Ken Kimble Estate. Mr. Kimble, a cash method of accounting taxpayer, died on July 1, 2007.

Dividends	$10,000
Interest on corporate bonds	18,000
Collection on installment note from sale of investment land	24,000

The record date was June 14 for $6,000 of the dividends and October 31 for the remaining $4,000 of dividends. The bond interest is payable annually on October 1. Mr. Kimble's basis in the land was $8,000. He sold it in 2006 for a total sales and contract price of $48,000 and reported his gain under the installment method. Ignore interest on the installment note. What amount of IRD is reported on the estate's income tax return?

C:14-48 *Income in Respect of Decedent.* Julie Brown died on May 29 of the current year. She was employed before her death at a gross salary of $4,000 per month. Her pay day was the last day of each month, and her employer did not pro rate her last monthly salary payment. She owned preferred stock that paid quarterly dividends of $800 per quarter each March 31, June 30, September 30, and December 31. The record date for the June dividend was June 10. Assume her estate chooses a calendar year as its tax year. What amount of gross income should be reported on the estate's first income tax return? Identify the IRD included in gross income.

C:14-49 *Property Distributions.* In the current year, Maddox Trust, a complex trust, distributed an asset with a $42,000 adjusted basis and a $75,000 FMV to its sole beneficiary, Marilyn Maddox-Mason. The trustee elected to recognize gain on the distribution. Marilyn received no other distributions from the trust during the year. The distributable net income for the year was $87,000, and none of it was from tax-exempt sources.

a. What is the trust's distribution deduction?
b. On her individual income tax return, how much gross income should Marilyn report from the trust?
c. What is Marilyn's basis in the asset distributed in kind from the trust?

C:14-50 *Income Recognition by Beneficiary.* Joan died April 17, 2006. Joan's executor chose March 31 as the tax year end for the estate. The estate's only beneficiary, Kathy, reports on a calendar year. The executor of Joan's estate makes the following distributions to Kathy:

June 2006	$ 5,000
August 2006	10,000
March 2007	12,000
August 2007	14,000

The 2006 and 2007 distributions do not exceed DNI. How much income should Kathy report on her 2006 return as a result of the distributions from the estate? On her 2007 return?

COMPREHENSIVE PROBLEM

C:14-51 Dana Dodson died October 31, 2006, with a gross estate of $2.7 million, debts of $200,000, and a taxable estate of $2.5 million. Dana made no adjusted taxable gifts. All of her property passed under her will to her son, Daniel Dodson. The estate chose a June 30 year-end. Its receipts, disbursements, and gains for the period ended June 30, 2007, were as follows:

Dividend income	$27,000
Interest income from corporate bonds	18,000
Interest income from tax-exempt bonds	9,000
Gain on sale of land	10,000
Executor's fee (charged to principal)	4,000
Distribution to Daniel Dodson	–0–

Of the $27,000 dividends received, $7,000 were declared October 4, 2006, with a record date of October 25 and a payment date of November 4, 2006. The corporate bonds pay interest each August 31 and February 28. The estate collected $18,000 corporate bond interest in February 2007. The tax-exempt bonds pay interest each June 30 and December 31. The estate collected $4,500 in December 2006 and $4,500 in June 2007 from the tax-exempt bonds. Dana, a cash basis taxpayer, sold land in 2005 for a total gain of $60,000 and used installment reporting. She collected principal in 2005 and 2006 and reported gain of $30,000 on her 2005 return and $10,000 on her 2006 return. The estate collected additional principal in March 2007 and will collect the remaining principal payment in March 2008. The gain attributable to the March 2007 and March 2008 principal collections is $10,000 per year. Ignore interest on the sale.

Calculate the following:

a. Deductible executor's fee.

b. Total IRD and the IRD reported on the return for the period ended June 30, 2007.

c. Total Sec. 691(c) deduction if none of the debts are DRD.

d. Section 691(c) deduction deductible on the estate's income tax return for the period ended June 30, 2007.

e. Taxable income of the estate for its first tax year.

f. Marginal income tax rate for the estate for its first tax year.

TAX STRATEGY PROBLEM

C:14-52 Glorietta Trust is an irrevocable discretionary trust that Grant Glorietta funded in 1992. The discretionary income beneficiary for life is Grant's son, Gordon Glorietta (single). Gordon is a partner in a partnership in which he materially participates, and he has a large basis in his partnership interest. For 2007, the trust had $50,000 of corporate bond interest, net of expenses, and no other income. It made no distributions to Gordon in 2007. Assume that it is now February 22, 2008, and Gordon has just learned that his share of loss from the partnership will be $72,000. Gordon has other income for 2007 of approximately $52,000. The trustee anticipates distributing $40,000 cash to Gordon before the end of February. For the last few years, Gordon's marginal tax rate was 15%. He claims the standard deduction, has only one exemption, and files as a single individual. Discuss a tax-saving opportunity presented by this scenario. Also show a comparative analysis of the alternatives.

TAX FORM/RETURN PREPARATION PROBLEMS

C:14-53 Marion Mosley created the Jenny Justice Trust in 1995 with First Bank named as trustee. For 20 years, the trust is to pay out all its income semiannually to the beneficiary, Jenny Justice. At the end of the twentieth year, the trust assets are to be distributed to Jenny's descendants. Capital gains are credited to principal, and depreciation is charged to principal. For the current year, the irrevocable trust reports the following results:

	Amounts Allocable to	
	Income	*Principal*
Rental income	$15,000	
Corporate bond interest	27,000	
Interest on tax-exempt (non-private activity) bonds	8,000	

Long-term capital gain on sale of land		30,000[a]
Maintenance and repairs of rental property	1,500	
Property taxes on rental property	700	
Fee for tax return preparation	500	
Trustee's fee		2,000
Depreciation		2,400
Estimated federal income taxes paid		9,000

[a]The sales price and adjusted basis are $110,000 and $80,000, respectively. The trustee acquired the land in 2002 and the trustee sold it in November of the current year.

Prepare a Form 1041, including any needed Schedule K-1s, for the Jenny Justice Trust. Omit pages 3 through 5 of Form 1041. The trustee's address is P.O. Box 100, Dallas, TX 75202. The identification number of the trust is 74-6224343. Jenny, whose Social Security number is 252-37-1492, resides at 2 Mountain View, Birmingham, AL 35205.

C:14-54 In 2001, Belinda Barclay established the Barclay Trust, an irrevocable trust, and named as trustee Local Bank, 1234 Tide Freeway, Tuscaloosa, AL 35487. She funded the trust with corporate and municipal bonds. The trustee is directed to distribute income and/or principal at its discretion to Belinda's adult sons, Anthony Barclay (421-78-0443) and Patrick Barclay (421-78-0445), for 15 years and then to pay out the remaining trust assets, including any accumulated income, equally between the two sons. The tax ID number for the trust is 74-5434127. Half of the trustee's fee is charged to principal and half to income. During the current year, the trustee distributed $12,400 to Anthony, who resides at 37 Crimson Cove, Tuscaloosa, AL 35487, and nothing to Patrick. Other current year information for the trust is as follows:

Corporate bond interest	$17,000
Municipal bond interest	19,000
Long-term capital gain on sale of corporate bonds	2,200
CPA's fee for prior year's tax return	800
Trustee's fee	1,500
Estimated federal income taxes paid	3,700

The trust has a $700 short-term capital loss carryover from the prior year.

Prepare a Form 1041, and any needed Schedule K-1s, for the Barclay Trust. Omit pages 3 through 5 of Form 1041. The bonds are not private activity bonds.

C:14-55 Mark Meadows funded a trust in 1994 with Merchants Bank named as trustee. He paid no gift tax on the transfer. The trustee in its discretion is to pay out income to Mark's children, Angela and Barry, for 15 years. Then the trust will terminate, and its assets, including accumulated income, will be paid to Angela and Barry in equal amounts. (Separate shares are *not* to be maintained.) In the current year, the trustee distributes $3,000 to Angela and $9,000 to Barry. The trust paid estimated federal income taxes of $15,000 and reported the following additional results for the current year.

	Amounts Allocable to	
	Income	*Principal*
Dividends	$50,000	
Interest on corporate bonds	4,000	
Interest on City of Cleveland (non-private activity) bonds	9,000	
Long-term capital loss on sale of stock		$12,000[a]
Trustee's fee		2,400
CPA's fee for tax return preparation	400	

[a]Mr. Meadows purchased the stock for $30,000 in 1990. It was valued at $44,000 when he transferred it to the trust in 1994. The trust sold the stock for $18,000 in December of the current year.

Prepare a Form 1041, including any needed Schedule K-1s, for the trust established by Mr. Meadows. Omit pages 3 through 5 of Form 1041. The trustee's address is 201 Fifth Ave., New York, NY 10017. The trust's identification number is 74-5271322. Angela (127-14-1732) and Barry (127-14-1733) reside at 3 East 246th St., Huntington, NY 11743.

CASE STUDY PROBLEMS

C:14-56 Arthur Rich, a widower, is considering setting up a trust (or trusts) with a bank as trustee for his three minor children. He will fund the trust at $900,000 (or $300,000 each in the case of three trusts). A friend suggested that he might want to consider a January 31 year-end for the trusts. The friend also suggested that Arthur might want to make each trust a complex discretionary trust. Arthur is a little apprehensive about the idea of a trust that would be complex. The friend warned that trust income should not be spent on support of the children.

Required: Prepare a memorandum to the tax partner of your firm concerning the above client matter. As part of your analysis, consider the following:

a. What tax reasons, if any, can you think of for having three trusts instead of one?
b. Why do you think the friend suggested a January 31 year-end?
c. What is your reaction to the friend's suggestion about the year-end?
d. Which taxpayer, the beneficiary or the trust, is taxed on the income from a discretionary trust?
e. To what extent do trusts serve as income-shifting arrangements?
f. What can you advise Arthur concerning his apprehension about a complex trust?
g. Why did the friend warn against spending trust income for the children's support?

C:14-57 You are preparing a 2006 individual tax return for Robert Lucca, a real estate developer and long-time client. While preparing Robert's individual tax return you learn that he has income from a trust his 75-year-old father created in 2005. His 2006 income from the trust is properly reflected on a Schedule K-1 prepared by the accounting firm that prepared the trust's 2006 return. Robert prepared the trust's return for 2005, and decided that he should not be taxed on any of the trust's income because the trust distributed nothing to him. Upon reviewing Robert's copy of the trust instrument, you learn that the instrument calls for mandatory distributions of all the income to Robert every year. Assume that the trust reported only $3,300 of taxable income for 2005 and that Robert was in the highest marginal tax bracket for 2005.

a. What responsibility do you have in 2007 to correct the error made for the tax year 2005? Refer to the *Statements on Standards for Tax Services* in Appendix E.
b. Assume instead that an IRS agent has just begun to audit Robert's 2005 individual tax return. What is your responsibility if you have discovered the error on the 2005 trust return, and you are representing Robert in the audit?

TAX RESEARCH PROBLEMS

C:14-58 The Latimer Trust instrument directs that all income be paid annually to Laura Lee Latimer for life with remainder to Laura Lee's son Lance Latimer or his estate. The trust instrument does not authorize the trustee to make charitable contributions. The Latimer Trust owns a 15% interest in LLL Partnership, which operates a retail store. A Schedule K-1 the Latimer Trust received from the partnership reported, among other information, that the trust's share of charitable contributions made by the partnership for 2007 was $350. The trust had DNI of $25,000. What charitable contribution deduction, if any, may the trust deduct? Is the trust a simple or complex trust in 2007?

C:14-59 In 2006, Bill Ames died at age 48. One of the items included in his gross estate was the principal residence where he and his widow, Lynn (age 46), lived for 20 years. Its FMV in 2006 was $500,000. In accordance with Bill's will, the residence and numerous other assets passed to a trust. Lynn is entitled to all the trust income for the rest of her life.

In 2007, the trust sells the residence for $540,000 and later that year pays $370,000 for a new house that Lynn moves into as her principal residence. Your manager asks that you draft a letter to the trustee and in the letter explain whether the trust is eligible for the nonrecognition rules for sales of principal residences.

Your manager suggests that you consider at a minimum the following research sources:

- IRC Sec. 121
- Rev. Rul. 54-583, 1954-2 C.B. 158

You should attach to the letter a list of additional relevant authorities and their citations.

C:14-60 Joyce Ingalls is the daughter of the late Fred Ingalls, who died August 15, 2007. One of the items included in his gross estate was a traditional (regular/non-Roth) IRA valued at several million dollars. Mr. Ingalls's estate will owe taxes, but no estate taxes had been paid by March 1, 2008, the date Joyce filed her 2007 individual income tax return, which she prepared. Included in her gross income for 2007 was a $50,000 distribution from her father's IRA. After talking with a friend, she wonders whether a Sec. 691(c) deduction was available on her 2007 return, and she has contacted you to resolve this issue. Write a memo in which you address whether Joyce is entitled to claim a Sec. 691(c) deduction for income in respect of a decedent (IRD) she collected, given that no estate tax has yet been paid on the IRD or any other inclusion in her father's gross estate. Also address in a conceptual manner how the deduction, assuming it is available, is calculated. At a minimum you should consult the following sources:

- IRC Sec. 691(c)
- FSA 200011023

C:14-61 *Internet Research Problem.* Your client is considering funding a trust with some oil and gas properties. The trust will be governed by the laws of Virginia, which has adopted the 1997 version of the Uniform Principal and Income Act (the 1997 Act). Your client wants to know how royalty income will be allocated between the principal and income accounts under the 1997 Act, compared with the 1962 version of the Act. Start your research by going to *www.nccusl.org,* the Web site for the National Conference of Commissioners of Uniform State Laws. Go to "Final Acts & Legislation." Select "Principal and Income Act," and "Virginia." Consult Section 411 of the Act. Prepare a memo that addresses the client's question.

C:14-62 *Internet Research Problem.* You are preparing for a client meeting at which the client has indicated he wants to discuss revocable trusts. Use the search engine Google and locate a discussion about revocable trusts (also known as living trusts). Summarize the points from a site's discussion about revocable (living) trusts, and indicate which Web site you visited.

paid by March 1, 2008, the date she filed her 2007 individual income tax return, which she prepared, included in her gross income for 2007 was a $70,000 distribution from her father's IRA. After talking with a friend, she wonders whether a Sec. 691(c) deduction was available on her 2007 return, and she has contacted you to resolve the issue. Write a memo in which you address whether [illegible] is entitled to claim a Sec. 691(c) deduction for income in respect of a decedent (IRD). She believes that no estate tax has yet been paid on the IRD or any other inclusion in her father's gross estate. Also address in a conceptual manner how the deduction, assuming it is available, is calculated. At a minimum, you should consult the following sources:

- IRC Sec. 691(c)
- [illegible] 200011023

Internet Research Problem. Your client is considering funding a trust with some oil and gas properties. The trust will be governed by the laws of Virginia, which has adopted the 1997 version of the Uniform Principal and Income Act (the 1997 Act). Your client wants to know how royalty income will be allocated between the principal and income accounts under the 1997 Act, compared with the 1962 version of the Act. Start your research by going to www.nccusl.org, the Web site for the National Conference of Commissioners of Uniform State Laws. Go to "Final Acts & Legislation." Select "Principal and Income Act," and "Virginia." Consult section 411 of the Act. Prepare a memo that addresses the client's question.

Internet Research Problem. You are preparing for a client meeting at which the client has indicated he wants to discuss [illegible]

15

CHAPTER

ADMINISTRATIVE PROCEDURES

LEARNING OBJECTIVES

After studying this chapter, you should be able to

1. Understand the role of the IRS in our tax system
2. Discuss how returns are selected for audit and the alternatives available to taxpayers whose returns are audited
3. Describe the IRS's ruling process
4. Identify due dates for tax returns
5. Understand tax-related penalties generally
6. Calculate the penalty for not paying estimated taxes
7. Describe more severe penalties, including the fraud penalty
8. Understand the statute of limitations
9. Explain from whom the government may collect unpaid taxes
10. Understand government-imposed standards for tax practitioners

CHAPTER OUTLINE

This chapter provides an overview of the administrative and procedural aspects of tax practice, an area with which all tax advisors should be familiar. The specific matters discussed include the role of the Internal Revenue Service (IRS) in tax enforcement and collection, the manner in which the IRS chooses tax returns for audit, taxpayers' alternatives to immediately agreeing to pay a proposed deficiency, due dates for returns, taxpayer penalties, and the statute of limitations. Chapter C:1 discussed the AICPA's *Statements on Standards for Tax Services,* which guide CPAs engaged in tax practice. Chapter C:15 examines additional tax practice topics, including Internal Revenue Code (IRC) penalty provisions that affect tax advisors and tax return preparers.

ROLE OF THE INTERNAL REVENUE SERVICE

OBJECTIVE 1

Understand the role of the IRS in our tax system

The IRS is part of the Treasury Department. Its chief administrative officer is the IRS Commissioner. Overseeing the activities of the IRS is a nine-member board consisting of the Secretary of the Treasury, the IRS Commissioner, a public sector representative, and six private sector representatives. All board members are appointed by the President of the United States.

ENFORCEMENT AND COLLECTION

KEY POINT

The U.S. tax structure is based on a self-assessment system. The level of voluntary compliance actually is quite high, but one of the principal purposes of the IRS is to enforce the federal tax laws and identify taxpayers who willfully or inadvertently fail to pay their fair share of the tax burden.

One of the IRS's most significant functions is enforcing tax laws.[1] The IRS is responsible for ensuring that taxpayers file returns, correctly report their tax liabilities, and pay any tax due.

Voluntary compliance with U.S. tax laws is relatively high. However, because some persons do not voluntarily comply, the IRS must audit selected taxpayers' returns and investigate the activities of nonfilers. In addition, because numerous ambiguities (gray areas) in the tax law exist, taxpayers and the IRS do not always agree on the proper tax treatment of transactions and events. As part of its enforcement duties, the IRS attempts to discover whether the reporting of these transactions and events differs from the way the IRS thinks they should be reported. As we point out later, taxpayers who disagree with the IRS in an audit may litigate.

The IRS must ensure that taxpayers not only report the correct tax liability, but also pay their taxes on time. For various reasons, some taxpayers file returns without paying any or all of the tax owed. The IRS's collection agents are responsible for collecting as much of the tax as possible from such persons.

INTERPRETATION OF THE STATUTE

As noted in Chapter C:1, the statutory language of the Internal Revenue Code (IRC) often is so vague that the courts and IRS must interpret it so that it can be readily applied. The IRS publishes its interpretations in revenue rulings, revenue procedures, notices, and information releases, which are available to the general public. In addition, the IRS offers guidance to specific taxpayers in the form of letter rulings, which have no precedential value for third-party taxpayers. Each of these authorities is discussed in detail in Chapter C:1.

[1] The IRS, however, does not have enforcement duties with respect to the taxes on guns and alcohol.

ORGANIZATION OF THE IRS

The IRS performs its duties on a nationwide basis. It is organized *functionally* into four divisions: (1) Wage and Investment Income, (2) Small Business and Self-Employed, (3) Large and Mid-size Business, and (4) Tax Exempt (see Figure C:15-1). Each division is headed by a divisional director.

The Wage and Investment Income Division has authority over individual taxpayers who report only wage and investment income. Most of these taxpayers file Forms 1040, 1040A, or 1040EZ. The Small Business and Self-Employed Division has authority over sole proprietors, individuals with supplemental income, and small corporations and partnerships. Most of these taxpayers file Forms 1065 and 1120S or Schedules C, E, and F. The Large and Mid-size Business Division has authority over corporations with assets of $5 million or more. Most of these taxpayers file Form 1120. The Tax Exempt Division has authority over tax exempt organizations, employee plans, and state and local governments. Most of these entities file tax exempt status forms.

The shift to a functional mode of organization reflects Congress' desire to render the IRS more efficient and client oriented. Through this mode of organization, tax administrators can focus on their areas of technical expertise, and taxpayers can deal with the same technical experts wherever they reside.

AUDITS OF TAX RETURNS

OBJECTIVE 2

Discuss how returns are selected for audit and the alternatives available to taxpayers whose returns are audited

The IRS operates seven service centers, which receive and process tax returns.[2] One of the IRS's principal enforcement functions is auditing these returns. All returns are subject to some verification. One task the IRS service centers perform is checking whether amounts are properly calculated and faithfully carried from one line of a return to another. Another task is determining whether any items, such as signatures and Social Security numbers, are missing. Computers compare (or "match") by Social Security number the amounts reported on a taxpayer's return with employer- or payer-prepared documents (Forms W-2 and 1099) filed with the IRS service center.[3] To date, however, a 100% matching of these documents with tax return information has been difficult to achieve.

If the service center detects a calculation error in the tax reported on the return, it will send to the taxpayer a notice proposing an additional tax or granting a refund. If the information reported on a return is inconsistent with the information on Forms W-2 or 1099 reported by an employer or payer, the IRS asks the taxpayer to account for the discrepancy in writing or pay some additional tax.

PERCENTAGE OF RETURNS EXAMINED

Only a small fraction of all returns are examined. For example, for returns filed in 2004, the IRS examined only 0.93% of all individual returns, 1.24% of all C corporation returns, 0.33% of all partnership returns, 0.18% of all S corporation returns, and 0.12% of all fiduciary returns. For individuals with total positive income (i.e., gross income before losses and other deductions) of $100,000 or more, the audit rate was 1.41%, and corporations with assets of at least $250 million faced a 44.06% rate. As a result of its audit activities, the IRS recommended additional taxes and penalties totaling $48.6 billion in that year.[4]

The examination percentages described above may be misleading because over half the returns filed are subject to a computerized matching in which the IRS compares the tax return information with documents (Forms 1099 and W-2) submitted by payers and

[2] IRS Service Centers are located in Andover, Massachusetts; Atlanta, Georgia; Austin, Texas; Fresno, California; Kansas City, Missouri; Memphis, Tennessee; and Philadelphia, Pennsylvania.

[3] Form W-2 reports employees' salaries and withholding tax, and Form 1099 reports income such as interest and dividends.

[4] "Examination Coverage: Recommended and Average Recommended Additional Tax Examination, by Type and Size of Return, Fiscal Year 2004," *Internal Revenue Service 2004 Data Book*, available for download at *http://www.irs.gov*, Tax Statistics Link. Examinations are performed by revenue agents, tax auditors, and service center personnel.

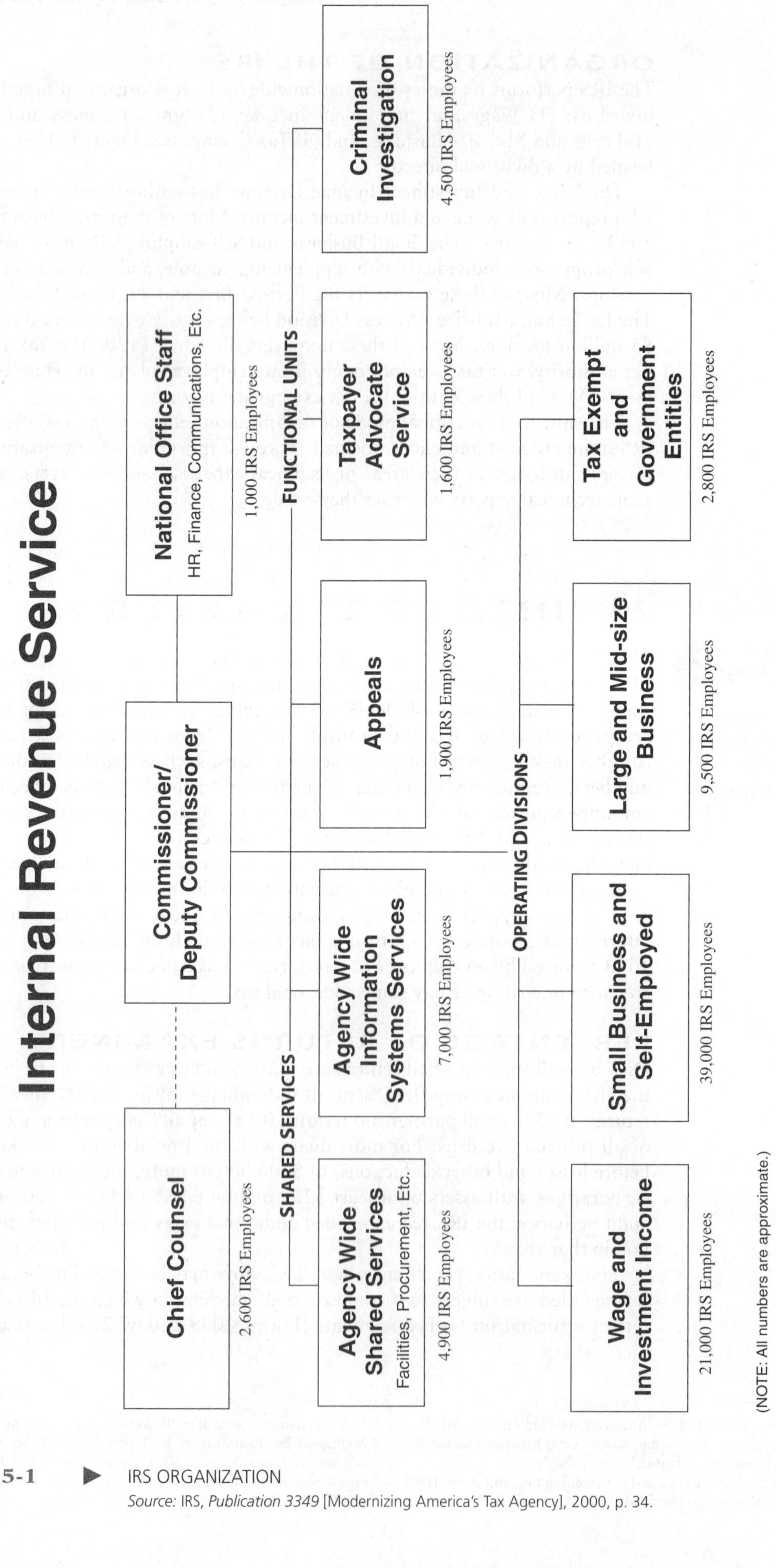

Internal Revenue Service

Chief Counsel
2,600 IRS Employees

Commissioner/ Deputy Commissioner

National Office Staff
HR, Finance, Communications, Etc.
1,000 IRS Employees

SHARED SERVICES

- **Agency Wide Shared Services** — Facilities, Procurement, Etc. — 4,900 IRS Employees
- **Agency Wide Information Systems Services** — 7,000 IRS Employees

FUNCTIONAL UNITS

- **Appeals** — 1,900 IRS Employees
- **Taxpayer Advocate Service** — 1,600 IRS Employees
- **Criminal Investigation** — 4,500 IRS Employees

OPERATING DIVISIONS

- **Wage and Investment Income** — 21,000 IRS Employees
- **Small Business and Self-Employed** — 39,000 IRS Employees
- **Large and Mid-size Business** — 9,500 IRS Employees
- **Tax Exempt and Government Entities** — 2,800 IRS Employees

(NOTE: All numbers are approximate.)

FIGURE C:15-1 ▶ IRS ORGANIZATION
Source: IRS, *Publication 3349* [Modernizing America's Tax Agency], 2000, p. 34.

employers. Because wages, interest, alimony, pensions, unemployment compensation, Social Security benefits, and other items of income are reported to the IRS by the payers, and because state income taxes, local real estate taxes, home mortgage interest, and other items of deduction are reported to the IRS by the payees, taxpayers who report only these items on their returns effectively face a 100% audit rate. According to a former IRS commissioner, "[M]ore than half of the individual returns filed are simple enough so that a matching with forms filed by employers and interest payors is sufficient to insure compliance."[5]

SELECTION OF RETURNS FOR AUDIT

Returns are chosen for audit in various ways, with many being selected under the *discriminant function (DIF)* process described below. The IRS's objective in using the DIF process is to make the audit process as productive as possible by maximizing the number of audits that result in the collection of additional taxes. The DIF process has improved the IRS's ability to select returns for audit. In recent years, the IRS failed to collect additional taxes on only 10% to 15% of the individual returns audited by its revenue agents and examiners. By comparison, in the late 1960s, before the advent of the DIF program, the IRS failed to collect additional taxes in 45% to 50% of its audits.[6] Recently, the IRS launched an audit initiative known as the Market Segment Specialization Program (MSSP). Examples of market segments include manufacturing, wholesale trade, retail trade (auto and boat dealers and service stations), and services (medical and health).[7] Under the MSSP, IRS personnel develop industry expertise, and the IRS prepares MSSP audit guidelines. As IRS personnel become more familiar with specific industries, their ability to spot industry-specific items that taxpayers incorrectly report likely will improve.

HISTORICAL NOTE

Taxpayers have made several attempts to make the DIF variables public information. However, so far the courts have refused to require the IRS to provide such information. The basic thrust of the DIF program is that a return will be flagged if enough items on the return are out of the norm for a taxpayer in that particular income bracket.

DISCRIMINANT FUNCTION (DIF) PROGRAM. Of the individual returns audited in 1982, the IRS selected two-thirds under the DIF program. In fiscal year 2005, the IRS selected only 29% under the DIF program, with the rest being selected under 12 different audit initiatives, some of which involve nonfilers, tax-shelter related write-offs, computer matching of third-party information, claims for refund, return preparers, and unallowable items.[8] The IRS laid the groundwork for the DIF program in the mid-1960s to

- Reduce the staff and computer time necessary to screen returns
- Identify returns most likely to contain errors
- Reduce the number of audited returns for which an examination results in little or no additional tax[9]

An assistant IRS commissioner described the DIF selection process in the following manner:

> DIF is a type of statistical analysis, using multiple variables or criteria to differentiate between two populations. For the IRS, those populations are tax returns needing examination versus those returns not needing examination. DIF essentially identifies items on tax returns having predictive power; that is, the selected items on returns in the "need to examine" group show up differently than those in the "no need to examine" group. DIF takes several items on a tax return and reduces them to a single score, which is then used as a major determinant as to whether a particular return will be examined.[10]

Returns with a relatively high DIF score have characteristics in common with returns for which the IRS earlier assessed a deficiency upon audit (e.g., the return may have reported a relatively high casualty loss or charitable contribution deduction). Because the

---

[5] Bureau of National Affairs, *BNA Daily Tax Reports,* June 20, 1984, p. G-1.

[6] Letter from Sheldon S. Cohen, former IRS Commissioner, to Representative Nancy L. Johnson, Chairman of House Ways and Means Subcommittee on Oversight Regarding the TCMP, dated July 20, 1995, reprinted in *Tax Notes Today,* August 10, 1995, Document 95 TNT 156-63.

[7] K. D. Bakhai and G. E. Bowers, "A New Era in IRS Auditing," *Florida CPA Today*, November 1994, pp. 26–30.

[8] J. L. Wedick, Jr., "Looking for a Needle in a Haystack—How the IRS Selects Returns for Audit," *The Tax Adviser,* November 1983, p. 673.

[9] Ibid., pp. 673–674.

[10] Ibid., p. 674.

WHAT WOULD YOU DO IN THIS SITUATION?

Cultural understanding and tolerance are hallmarks of modern American society. Yet in the tax sphere, are there limits to such understanding and tolerance?

Consider the case of Mr. Y and his difficulties with the IRS. Mr. Y was born, reared, and educated as a lawyer in his native country. His employment experience included working for his country's counterpart of the IRS. Mr. Y immigrated to the United States at age 46 and was self-employed as a tax preparer. He became a naturalized U.S. citizen, and his tax practice flourished.

The IRS audited Mr. Y's individual tax returns, which resulted in an assessment of $27,000 in additional taxes and penalties. Mr. Y proceeded to award the IRS audit agent $5,000 in return for a "no-change" letter. Unbeknownst to Mr. Y at the time, the transaction was secretly taped. Mr. Y was convicted of violating a U.S. law (18 USC 201(5)(1)(A)) that prohibits bribing a U.S. government official.

At his sentencing hearing, Mr. Y argued that his national origin should be taken into account in determining his punishment. Mr. Y explained that offering tax officials an "honorarium" to settle tax controversies was standard practice in his country. Not to do so would be insulting to these officials.

Do you believe that the $5,000 award to the IRS agent was appropriate in these circumstances? Assume you were representing Mr. Y. How should you have advised your client when he initially proposed offering an amount to the IRS agent?

IRS does not have the resources to audit all returns with a relatively high DIF score, IRS agents choose which of the higher scored returns should receive top priority for an audit.

The IRS has developed its DIF formulas based on data gathered in its **Taxpayer Compliance Measurement Program (TCMP)**. Under the TCMP, the IRS conducted special audits of taxpayers selected at random. In these audits, the IRS examined every line item of taxpayers' returns so as to develop a statistical norm for the taxpayers' industry or profession as a whole. If an item on the return of another taxpayer in the same industry or profession significantly departed from the norm, the return was flagged for examination. Before 1994, the IRS conducted TCMP audits of about 50,000 individuals every three years. It also regularly conducted TCMP audits of entities, such as corporations. Because of budget constraints, the IRS "indefinitely postponed" the TCMP in 1995.[11] Consequently, the data incorporated in the DIF formulas became outdated over time.

In 2002, the IRS launched the **National Research Program (NRP)** to select individual returns for audit. The NRP updates data compiled in TCMP audits and develops new statistical models for identifying returns most likely to contain errors. The NRP differs from the TCMP in two significant respects. First, it relies on pre-existing audit data as well as data complied in ordinary, as opposed to special, audits. Second, it focuses on specific portions of a tax return, not all line-by-line items. Like the TCMP, the NCR is based on data gathered primarily in audits of about 50,000 individual tax returns. It purports to be less intrusive and less burdensome than the TCMP.

The IRS also conducts what are called "financial status" or "lifestyle" audits. These audits seek to identify inconsistencies between the income that a taxpayer reports and income suggested by his or her lifestyle. In the course of the audit, IRS agents review the taxpayer's overall economic situation. They may ask questions concerning where the taxpayer vacations, where his or her children go to school, and the cost and model of his or her vehicles. Although the courts generally have sanctioned the use of financial status audits, Congress has limited their use to situations in which the IRS has a reasonable indication of unreported income.

OTHER METHODS. The IRS widely uses other methods for selecting returns for audit. Some returns are chosen because the taxpayer filed a claim for a refund of taxes paid previously, and the IRS decides to audit the tax return before refunding the requested

[11] "Rare Reprieve: IRS Postpones Its Superaudits," *The Wall Street Journal*, October 24, 1995, p. B1.

amount. A few returns are audited because the IRS receives a tip from one taxpayer (perhaps a disgruntled former employee or ex-spouse) that another taxpayer did not file a correct return. If the IRS does collect additional taxes as a result of the audit, it is authorized to pay a reward to the individual who provided the tip. The reward is completely discretionary, although it cannot exceed 10% of the additional tax and penalties due.[12] Sometimes, examining the return of an entity (e.g., a corporation) leads to an audit of a related party's return (e.g., a major stockholder).

Occasionally, the IRS investigates particular types of transactions or entities to ascertain taxpayer compliance with the tax law. As a result of these investigations, the IRS may select a number of returns for audit. For example, in 1989 the IRS examined 3,000 to 4,000 individual returns to determine whether taxpayers avoided classifying expenses as miscellaneous itemized deductions to escape the 2% floor. In 1997, the IRS investigated the returns of about 200,000 trusts (representing approximately 7% of total trust returns) to determine whether taxpayers had established them to avoid taxes.[13] In 2003, through a combination of audits, summons, and targeted litigation, the IRS launched an initiative to identify and deter promoters of abusive tax shelters.[14]

ALTERNATIVES FOR A TAXPAYER WHOSE RETURN IS AUDITED

When the IRS notifies a taxpayer of an impending audit, the notice indicates whether the audit is a correspondence, office, or field audit. In a correspondence audit, communication, such as documenting a deduction or explaining why the taxpayer did not report certain income, is handled through the mail. In an office audit, the taxpayer and/or his or her tax advisor meet with an IRS employee at a nearby IRS office. The audit notice indicates which items the IRS will examine and what information the taxpayer should bring to the audit. Field audits are common for business returns and complex individual returns. IRS officials conduct these audits either at the taxpayer's place of business or residence or at his or her tax advisor's office.

ADDITIONAL COMMENT

This special relief rule was designed to reduce the likelihood that the IRS could harass a taxpayer by repeatedly auditing a taxpayer on the same issue.

SPECIAL RELIEF RULE. A special relief rule exists for repetitive audit examinations of the same item. A taxpayer who receives an audit notice can request that the IRS suspend the examination and review whether the audit should proceed if (1) the IRS audited the taxpayer's return for the same item in at least one of the two previous years and (2) the earlier audit did not result in a change to his or her tax liability. To request the suspension, the taxpayer should call the IRS official whose name and telephone number appear on the audit notice.

EXAMPLE C:15-1 ▶ In October 2007, the IRS notifies Tony that it will audit his 2005 medical expense deduction. Two years ago, the IRS audited Tony's 2003 medical expense deduction but did not assess an additional tax. Consequently, Tony may request that the IRS suspend the audit of his 2005 return regarding this issue. ◀

EXAMPLE C:15-2 ▶ Assume the same facts as in Example C:15-1 except the IRS audited Tony's 2003 employee business expenses. Because that audit dealt with a different item, Tony may not request a suspension. ◀

ADDITIONAL COMMENT

Taxpayers should encourage the tax practitioner to handle an IRS audit. Because taxpayers usually have a limited understanding of the complexities of the tax law and its administration, having the taxpayer present at the audit generally is not a good idea.

MEETING WITH A REVENUE AGENT. Generally, the first step in the audit process is a meeting between the IRS agent and the taxpayer or the taxpayer's advisor. If the taxpayer is fortunate, the agent will agree that the return was correct as filed or, even better, that the taxpayer is entitled to a refund. In most instances, however, the agent will contend that the taxpayer owes additional taxes. Taxpayers who do not agree with the outcome of their meeting may ask to confer with the agent's supervisor. A meeting with the supervisor could lead to an agreement concerning the additional tax due.

---

[12] Reg. Sec. 301.7623-1(c).

[13] Jacob M. Schlesinger, "IRS Cracks Down on Trusts It Believes Were Set up as Tax-Avoidance Schemes," *The Wall Street Journal,* April 4, 1997, p. A2.

[14] I.R. 2003-51, April 15, 2003.

TYPICAL MISCONCEPTION

Taxpayers should be cautious in signing a Form 870. Once this form is executed, the taxpayer no longer is permitted to administratively pursue the items under audit.

Should the taxpayer agree and the agent's supervisor concur in the amount owed, the taxpayer must sign Form 870 (Waiver of Statutory Notice). This form indicates that the taxpayer waives any restrictions on the IRS's authority to assess the tax and consents to the IRS's collecting it. However, signing Form 870 does not preclude the taxpayer from filing a refund claim later.

If the taxpayer agrees that he or she owes additional tax and pays the tax upon signing the Form 870 waiver, interest accrues on the tax deficiency from the due date of the return through the payment date. Interest ceases to accrue 30 days after the Form 870 waiver is signed, and the IRS charges no additional interest if the taxpayer pays the tax due within ten days of the billing date.

TECHNICAL ADVICE MEMORANDA. Occasionally, a highly technical issue with which an IRS agent or appeals officer has had little or no experience arises in the course of the audit. Regardless of the type of audit, the official may request advice from the IRS's national office. Sometimes, the taxpayer urges the official to seek such advice. The advice is given in a Technical Advice Memorandum, which the IRS makes public in the form of a letter ruling. If the advice is favorable to the taxpayer, the agent or appeals officer must follow it. Even if the advice is pro-IRS, the official may consider the hazards of litigation in deciding whether to compromise.

APPEAL TO APPEALS DIVISION. If the taxpayer does not sign the Form 870 waiver, the IRS will send the taxpayer a **30-day letter**, detailing the proposed changes in the taxpayer's liability and advising the taxpayer of his or her right to pursue the matter with the IRS appeals office. The taxpayer has 30 days from the date of the letter to request a conference with an IRS appeals officer.

If the audit was a field audit and the amount of additional tax plus penalties and interest in question exceeds $10,000, the taxpayer must submit a **protest letter** within the 30-day period. Only a brief written statement is necessary if the amount is between $2,501 and $10,000. An oral request is acceptable in the case of office audits, regardless of the amount of the additional tax, penalties, and interest. If the taxpayer does not respond to the 30-day letter, the IRS will follow up with a 90-day letter, discussed below.

Protest letters are submitted to an official in the appropriate IRS functional division and should include the following information:

- The taxpayer's name, address, and telephone number
- A statement that the taxpayer wishes to appeal the IRS findings to the appeals office
- A copy of the letter showing the proposed adjustments
- The tax years involved
- A list of the proposed changes with which the taxpayer disagrees
- A statement of facts supporting the taxpayer's position on any issue with which he or she disagrees
- The law or other authority on which the taxpayer relied[15]

KEY POINT

The appeals officer currently has the authority to settle or compromise issues with the taxpayer. To alleviate some of the workload and to make the audit process more efficient, the IRS currently is considering giving more of this settlement authority to revenue agents.

The taxpayer must declare, under penalties of perjury, that the statement of facts is true. If the taxpayer's representative prepares the protest letter, the representative must indicate whether he or she knows personally that the statement of facts is true.

Unlike IRS agents, appeals officers generally have the authority to settle (compromise) cases after considering the hazards of litigation. For example, if the appeals officer believes that the IRS has approximately a 40% chance of winning in court, the appeals officer may agree to close the case if the taxpayer will pay an amount equal to 40% of the originally proposed deficiency. The settlement authority of appeals officers extends to questions of fact and law.

In some matters, however, an appeals officer has no settlement authority. For example, if the matter involves an appeals coordinated issue, the appeals officer must obtain con-

[15] IRS, *Publication No. 5* [Your Appeal Rights and How to Prepare a Protest If You Don't Agree], January 1999, p. 1. A sample protest letter is published in Robert E. Meldman and Richard J. Sideman, *Federal Taxation Practice and Procedure*, Seventh Edition (Chicago: CCH Incorporated, 2004).

currence or guidance from a director of appeals to reach a settlement. An **appeals coordinated issue** is an issue of wide impact or importance, frequently involving an entire industry or occupation group, for which the IRS desires consistent treatment. An example of an appeals coordinated issue is whether the taxpayer has in substance made a disposition of excess inventory and thus is entitled to claim a deduction for the loss on disposition.[16]

If, after the appeals conference, the taxpayer completely agrees with the IRS's position, he or she signs a Form 870 waiver. However, if the appeals officer makes some concessions and the parties agree that the additional tax is less than that originally proposed, the taxpayer signs Form 870-AD (Waiver of Restrictions on Assessment and Collection). Unlike the case of a Form 870 waiver, a Form 870-AD waiver generally does not permit the taxpayer later to file a refund claim for the tax year in question. A Form 870-AD waiver is effective only if accepted by the IRS.

90-DAY LETTER

If the taxpayer and appeals officer fail to reach an agreement, or if the taxpayer does not file a written protest within 30 days of the date of the initial letter, the IRS issues a **90-day letter** (officially, a "Statutory Notice of Deficiency").[17] The 90-day letter specifies the amount of the deficiency; explains how the amount was calculated; and states that the IRS will assess it unless, within 90 days of the date of mailing, the taxpayer files a petition with the Tax Court.[18] During the 90-day period (and whether or not the taxpayer files the petition), the IRS may not assess the deficiency or attempt to collect it. After the 90-day period (and only if the taxpayer timely files the petition), the IRS still may not assess or collect the deficiency until the Court's decision becomes final.

LITIGATION

As mentioned earlier, taxpayer litigation can begin in one of three courts of first instance: the Tax Court, a U.S. district court, and the U.S. Court of Federal Claims. After considering the time and expense of litigation, some taxpayers decide to pay the deficiency even though they believe their position is correct. Before deciding where to litigate, a taxpayer should consider the precedents, if any, of the various courts. Chapter C:1 discusses the issues of precedent and "forum shopping."

U.S. TAX COURT. Taxpayers seeking to litigate in the Tax Court must file their petition with the Tax Court within 90 days of the date on which the IRS mails the Statutory Notice of Deficiency. The Tax Court strictly enforces this time limit. Before the scheduled hearing date, taxpayers still may reach an agreement with the IRS. Going the Tax Court route has some advantages, including not having to pay the deficiency as a precondition to filing suit. If the amount in question does not exceed $50,000 for a given year, the taxpayer may use the informal small cases procedure, an alternative not available in other courts. A potential disadvantage of this procedure is that the taxpayer may not appeal the Court's decision.

Taxpayers must pay the additional tax, plus any interest and penalties, if they lose in Tax Court and choose not to appeal their case. In some situations, the Tax Court leaves the computation of the additional tax up to the litigating parties. When this happens, the phrase "Entered under Rule 155" appears at the end of the Tax Court's opinion.

U.S. DISTRICT COURT OR U.S. COURT OF FEDERAL CLAIMS. To litigate in either a U.S. district court or the U.S. Court of Federal Claims, the taxpayer must first pay the deficiency and then file a claim for a refund with the IRS. In all likelihood, the IRS will deny this claim on the ground that the IRS correctly calculated the deficiency amount and properly assessed it. Upon notice of denial or six months after filing the claim, whichever is earlier, the taxpayer may sue the IRS for a refund. In no event, however, may the taxpayer file this lawsuit two years after the IRS denies the claim.

---

[16] *Internal Revenue Manual,* Sec. 8776.(14).

[17] Upon request, the IRS may grant an extension of time for filing a protest letter.

[18] Sec. 6213(a). If the notice is addressed to a person outside the United States, the time period is 150 days instead of 90.

APPEAL OF A LOWER COURT'S DECISION. Whichever party loses—the taxpayer or the IRS—may appeal the lower court's decision to an appellate court. If the case began in the Tax Court or a federal district court, the case is appealable to the circuit court of appeals with jurisdiction over the taxpayer. For individuals, the taxpayer's place of residence generally determines which court of appeals has jurisdiction. In the case of corporations, the firm's principal place of business or state of incorporation generally controls. Cases originating in the U.S. Court of Federal Claims are appealable to the Circuit Court of Appeals for the Federal Circuit; that is, all the latter cases are heard by the same circuit, irrespective of the taxpayer's residence, principal place of business, or state of incorporation.

Either the taxpayer or the government can request that the Supreme Court review an appellate court's decision. If the Supreme Court decides to hear a case, it grants **certiorari**. If the Court decides not to hear a case, it denies certiorari. In any given year, the Supreme Court hears only a few cases dealing with tax matters.

STOP & THINK

Question: Two years ago, Pete deducted an expenditure in the year he paid it. Recently, the IRS began an audit of Pete's return for that year and contended that the expenditure is not deductible. Pete is a resident of California, which is in the Ninth Circuit. In a similar case a few years ago, the Tax Court held that the expenditure is deductible, and the IRS did not appeal the decision. In yet another similar case litigated in a U.S. district court in California, the government lost at the trial level but won on appeal to the Ninth Circuit. If Pete decides to litigate, in which forum (lower court) should he file suit, and why?

Solution: If he litigates in the Tax Court, he would not have to pay the proposed deficiency tax in advance. However, under the *Golsen* Rule (see Chapter C:1), the Tax Court would depart from its earlier pro-taxpayer decision and rule for the IRS. (Pete's case would be appealable to the Ninth Circuit, and the Ninth Circuit has adopted a pro-government position.) Because the court for his California district would be bound by Ninth Circuit precedent, he should not litigate in that court. This likely outcome would disappoint Pete if he believed that a jury would rule in his favor because only U.S. district courts allow for jury trials. The only forum in which he could win is the U.S. Court of Federal Claims. No precedent that this court must follow exists because neither the U.S. Supreme Court, the Court of Appeals for the Federal Circuit, nor the U.S. Court of Federal Claims has previously adjudicated the issue. (For a discussion of "forum-shopping," see Chapter C:1.)

BURDEN OF PROOF. In civil cases, the IRS has the burden of proving any factual issue relevant to a determination of the taxpayer's liability, provided the taxpayer meets four conditions.[19] First, the taxpayer introduces "credible evidence" regarding the issue. Credible evidence means evidence of a quality sufficient to serve as the basis of a court decision.[20] Second, the taxpayer complies with the recordkeeping and substantiation requirements of the IRC. These requirements include the proper documentation of meal and entertainment expenses (Sec. 274), charitable contributions (Sec. 170), and foreign controlled businesses (Sec. 6038). Third, the taxpayer "cooperates" with the reasonable requests of the IRS for witnesses, information, documents, meetings, and interviews. Cooperation includes providing access to, and inspection of, persons and items within the taxpayer's control. It also includes exhausting all administrative remedies available to the taxpayer.[21] Fourth, the taxpayer is either a legal person with net worth not exceeding $7 million, or a natural person.

---

[19] See Sec. 7491.
[20] See S. Rept. No. 105-174, 105th Cong., 1st Sess. (unpaginated).
[21] Ibid.

REQUESTS FOR RULINGS

OBJECTIVE 3

Describe the IRS's ruling process

As discussed in Chapter C:1, a taxpayer can seek to clarify the tax treatment of a transaction by requesting that the IRS rule on the transaction. The IRS will respond to certain requests by issuing a letter ruling (sometimes referred to as a private letter ruling) directly to the taxpayer. A letter ruling is a written determination that interprets and applies the tax laws to the taxpayer's specific set of facts.[22] The IRS releases letter rulings to the public but eliminates all confidential information before doing so. The IRS charges a user fee for issuing a ruling, with the 2007 fees ranging from $150 for identical accounting method changes to $50,000 for pre-filing agreements. The fee for ruling on a proposed transaction is $10,000.[23] The fee for a ruling on a proposed transaction is $7,000.

ADDITIONAL COMMENT

The information requirements for requesting a letter ruling are very precise (see Rev. Proc. 2007-1). In general, a tax professional experienced in dealing with the national office of the IRS should be consulted. Also, a good blueprint of what should be included in a ruling request often can be found by locating an already-published letter ruling and examining its format.

INFORMATION TO BE INCLUDED IN TAXPAYER'S REQUEST

Early each calendar year, the IRS issues a revenue procedure that details how to request a letter ruling and the information that the request must contain. Taxpayers or tax advisors should consult this procedure before requesting a ruling. Appendix B of the procedure contains a checklist the taxpayer may use to ensure that the request is in order. The IRS has issued additional guidelines concerning the data to be included in the ruling request. For example, the IRS has specified what information the taxpayer must provide in a request for a ruling on the tax effects of transfers to a controlled corporation under Sec. 351. Each ruling request must contain a statement of all the relevant facts, including the following:

- Names, addresses, telephone numbers, and taxpayer identification numbers of all interested parties
- The taxpayer's annual accounting period and method
- A description of the taxpayer's business operations
- A complete statement of the business reasons for the transaction
- A detailed description of the transaction[24]

The taxpayer also should submit copies of the contracts, agreements, deeds, wills, instruments, and other documents that pertain to the transaction. The taxpayer must provide an explicit statement of all the relevant facts and not merely incorporate by reference language from the documents. The taxpayer also should indicate what confidential data should be deleted from the ruling before its release to the public.

If the taxpayer takes a position, he or she must disclose the basis for this position and the authorities relied on. Even if the taxpayer does not argue for a particular position, he or she must furnish an opinion of the expected tax effects, along with a statement of authorities supporting this opinion. In addition, the taxpayer should disclose and discuss any authorities to the contrary. The IRS suggests that, if no authorities to the contrary exist, the taxpayer should state so.

The person on whose behalf a ruling is requested should sign the following declaration: "Under penalties of perjury, I declare that I have examined this request, including accompanying documents, and, to the best of my knowledge and belief, the request contains all the relevant facts relating to the request, and such facts are true, correct, and complete."[25]

WILL THE IRS RULE?

In income and gift tax matters, the IRS will rule only on proposed transactions and on completed transactions for which the taxpayer has not yet filed a return.[26] In estate tax matters, the IRS generally will not rule if the estate has filed a tax return. On the other hand, the IRS will rule on the estate tax consequences of a living person.[27] If no temporary

---

22 Rev. Proc. 2007-1, 2007-1 I.R.B. 1, Sec. 2.01.

23 Rev. Proc. 2007-1, 2007-1 I.R.B. 1, Sec. 15, Appendix A.

24 Rev. Proc. 2007-1, 2007-1 I.R.B. 1, Sec. 7.01. Certain revenue procedures provide a checklist of information to be included for frequently occurring transactions. See, for example, Rev. Proc. 83-59, 1983-2 C.B. 575, which includes guidelines for requesting rulings regarding a corporate formation under Sec. 351.

25 Rev. Proc. 2007-1, 2007-1 I.R.B. 1, Sec. 7.01.

26 Ibid., Sec. 5.01.

27 Ibid., Sec. 5.06.

TYPICAL MISCONCEPTION

It is easy to be confused about the difference between letter rulings, which pertain to either prospective transactions or completed transactions for which a return has not yet been filed, and Technical Advice Memoranda, which pertain to completed transactions for which the return has been filed and is under audit.

or final Treasury Regulations relating to a particular statutory provision have been issued, the following policies govern a ruling unless another IRS pronouncement holds otherwise:

- If the answer seems clear by applying the statute to the facts, the IRS will rule under the usual procedures.
- If the answer seems reasonably certain by applying the statute to the facts, but not entirely free from doubt, the IRS will likewise rule.
- If the answer does not seem reasonably certain, the IRS will rule if so doing is in the best interests of tax administration.[28]

The IRS will not rule on a set of alternative ways of structuring a proposed transaction or on the tax consequences of hypothetical transactions. Generally, the IRS will not rule on certain issues because of the factual nature of the problem involved or for other reasons.[29]

From time to time, the IRS discloses, by means of a revenue procedure, the topics with respect to which it will not rule. The list of topics, however, is not all-inclusive. The IRS may refuse to rule on other topics whenever, in its opinion, the facts and circumstances so warrant.

SELF-STUDY QUESTION

How are letter rulings different from other IRS administrative pronouncements (i.e., revenue rulings, revenue procedures, notices, and information releases)?

ANSWER

Letter rulings are written for specific taxpayers (not the general public) and have no precedential value.

According to Rev. Proc. 2007-3, the matters on which the IRS will not rule include the following:

- Whether property qualifies as the taxpayer's principal residence
- Whether compensation is reasonable in amount
- Whether a capital expenditure for an item ordinarily used for personal purposes (e.g., a swimming pool) has medical care as its primary purpose
- The determination of the amount of a corporation's earnings and profits.[30]

In addition, the IRS will not rule privately on issues that it proposes to address in revenue rulings, revenue procedures, or otherwise, or that the Treasury Department proposes to address in Treasury Regulations.

ADDITIONAL COMMENT

Requesting a letter ruling makes most sense for transactions that the taxpayer would not undertake without being assured of certain tax consequences. For example, certain divisive reorganizations are tax-free under Sec. 355. Taxpayers often request a ruling that a proposed transaction satisfies the intricate requirements of Sec. 355.

WHEN RULINGS ARE DESIRABLE

Private letter rulings serve to "insure" the taxpayer against adverse, after-the-fact tax consequences. They are desirable where (1) the transaction is proposed, (2) the potential tax liability is high, and (3) the law is unsettled or unclear. They also are desirable where the IRS has issued to another taxpayer a favorable ruling regarding similar facts and issues. Because only the other taxpayer may rely on the latter ruling, *this* taxpayer may seek a ruling on which he or she may confidently rely. On the other hand, private letter rulings are undesirable where the IRS has issued to another taxpayer an unfavorable ruling regarding similar facts and issues. They also are undesirable where the IRS might publicly rule on a related matter, and the taxpayer has an interest in this matter. Private letter rulings offer insight into the IRS's thinking on the tax treatment of proposed transactions. Although third parties may not cite them as authority for the tax consequences of their transactions, they may cite them as authority for avoiding a substantial understatement penalty (discussed later in this chapter).

DUE DATES

OBJECTIVE 4

Identify the due dates for tax returns

DUE DATES FOR RETURNS

Returns for individuals, fiduciaries, and partnerships are due on or before the fifteenth day of the fourth month following the year-end of the individual or entity.[31] C corporation and S corporation tax returns are due no later than the fifteenth day of the third month after the corporation's year-end. To be subject to reporting requirements, individu-

[28] Ibid., Sec. 5.14.

[29] Ibid., Sec. 6.

[30] Rev. Proc. 2007-3, 2007-1 I.R.B. 108, Sec. 3.

[31] Sec. 6072(a). Section 6072(c) extends the due date for returns of nonresident alien individuals to the fifteenth day of the sixth month after the end of their tax year.

als and fiduciaries, but not corporations and partnerships, must have earned a minimum level of gross income during the year.[32]

EXTENSIONS

Congress realized that, in some instances, gathering the requisite information and completing the return by the designated due date is difficult. Consequently, it authorized extensions of time for filing returns. Unless the taxpayer is abroad, the extension period cannot exceed six months.[33]

INDIVIDUALS. By filing Form 4868 (Application for Automatic Extension of Time to File U.S. Individual Income Tax Return), an individual taxpayer may request an automatic extension to file the tax return. The extension is automatic in the sense that the taxpayer need not convince the IRS that an extension is necessary. Prior to 2006, the automatic extension period was four months after the return's original due date. If taxpayers needed more time, they could request an additional two-month extension by filing Form 2688 (Application for Additional Extension of Time to File U.S. Individual Income Tax Return). On this form, taxpayers had to explain the reason for the request. For tax returns filed in 2006 through 2008, the IRS will grant an automatic six-month extension via Form 4868, making Form 2688 unnecessary.[34]

EXAMPLE C:15-3 ▶ Bob and Alice, his wife, are calendar year taxpayers. By filing Form 4868, they may get an automatic extension until October 15 of the following year for filing their current year's return. However, if the fifteenth falls on Saturday, Sunday, or a holiday, the due date is the next business day. ◀

CORPORATIONS. Corporations request an automatic extension by filing Form 7004 (Application for Automatic Extension of Time to File Corporation Income Tax Return) by the original due date for the return. Although the IRC specifies an automatic extension period of three months, Treasury Regulations and the Form 7004 instructions specify six months.[35] No additional extensions are available.

EXAMPLE C:15-4 ▶ Lopez Corporation reports on a fiscal year ending March 31. The regular due date for its return is June 15. It may file Form 7004 and request an automatic six-month extension that postpones the due date until December 15. ◀

DUE DATES FOR PAYMENT OF THE TAX

TYPICAL MISCONCEPTION

Obtaining an extension defers the date by which the return must be filed, but it does *not* defer the payment date of the tax liability. Therefore, an extension for filing must be accompanied by a payment of an estimate of the taxpayer's tax liability. Computing this estimated tax liability can be difficult because much of the information necessary to complete the return may be incomplete or not yet available.

The granting of an extension merely postpones the due date for filing the return. It does not extend the due date for paying the tax. In general, the due date for the tax payment is the same as the unextended due date for filing the return.[36] In addition, the first estimated tax installment for extinguishing an individual's annual income tax liability must be paid by the due date for the preceding year's return, and the remaining payments must be made, respectively, two, five, and nine months later. Taxpayers who elect to let the IRS compute their tax must pay it within 30 days of the date the IRS mails a notice of the amount payable.[37]

When individuals request an automatic extension, they should project the amount of their tax liability to the extent possible. Any tax owed, after reducing the projected amount by withholding and estimated tax payments, should be remitted with the extension request. In addition, if an extension for filing a gift tax return is requested (on the same form), the estimated amount of gift tax liability should be remitted. Similarly, corporations should remit with their automatic extension request the amount of tax they estimate to be due, reduced by any estimated tax already paid.

---

[32] Secs. 6012(a)(2) and 6031(a).

[33] Sec. 6081(a).

[34] Temp. Reg. Sec. 1.6081-4T.

[35] Sec. 6081(b) and Reg. Sec. 1.6081-3(a).

[36] Sec. 6151(a).

[37] Sec. 6151(b)(1). The estimated tax payment rules for C corporations, S corporations, and trusts and estates are described in Chapters C:3, C:11, and C:14, respectively, of this volume.

INTEREST ON TAX NOT TIMELY PAID

Interest accrues on any tax not paid by the original due date for the return even if the taxpayer extends the filing date.[38] Taxpayers incur interest charges in four situations.

- ▶ They file late, without having requested an extension, and pay late.
- ▶ They request an extension for filing but underestimate their tax liability and, thus, must pay additional tax when they file their return.
- ▶ They file in a timely manner but are not financially able to pay some, or all, of the tax.
- ▶ The IRS audits their return and determines that they owe additional taxes.

RATE DETERMINATION. The IRS fixes the interest rate that it charges taxpayers under rules provided in Sec. 6621. The rate varies with fluctuations in the quarterly federal short-term rate. Thus, the interest rate could change at the beginning of each calendar quarter. For noncorporate taxpayers, the interest rate on both underpayments and overpayments is three percentage points higher than the federal rate. For corporate tax overpayments exceeding $10,000, the interest rate is reduced to the federal short-term rate plus one-half percentage point. For corporate underpayments exceeding $100,000, the rate is five percentage points above the federal short-term rate if the deficiency is not paid before a certain date. Rates are rounded to the nearest full percent. Recent applicable interest rates are as follows:

Period	*General Rate for Underpayments and Overpayments*
July 1, 2006, through March 31, 2007	8%
October 1, 2005, through June 30, 2006	7%
April 1, 2005, through September 30, 2005	6%
October 1, 2004, through March 31, 2005	5%
July 1, 2004, through September 30, 2004	4%

EXAMPLE C:15-5 ▶ Ann filed her 2004 individual return in a timely manner, and the IRS audits it in March 2007. Ann is a calendar year taxpayer. The IRS contends that Ann owes $2,700 of additional taxes. Ann pays the additional taxes on March 31, 2007. Ann also must pay interest on the $2,700 deficiency for the period April 16, 2005, through March 31, 2007. The interest rate is 6% from April 16, 2005, through September 30, 2005, 7% from October 1, 2004, through September 30, 2004, 5% from October 1, 2004 through March 31, 2005, 6% from April 1, 2005 through September 30, 2005, 7% from October 1, 2005 through June 30, 2006, and 8% from July 1, 2006 through March 31, 2007. ◀

HISTORICAL NOTE

Probably two of the most significant changes in tax administration have been the daily compounding of interest and tying the interest rate charged to the federal short-term rate, which has resulted in a higher rate used to calculate the interest charge than in years past. Before these two changes, taxpayers who played the "audit lottery" and took aggressive positions incurred little risk.

DAILY COMPOUNDING. Daily compounding applies to both the interest taxpayers owe to the government and the interest the government owes to taxpayers who have overpaid their taxes. The IRS has issued Rev. Proc. 95-17 containing tables to be used for calculating interest.[39] The major tax services have published these tables. In addition, software packages are available for interest calculations.

ACCRUAL PERIOD. Interest usually accrues from the original due date for the return until the payment date. However, two important exceptions apply. First, if the IRS fails to send an individual taxpayer a notice within 18 months after the original due date or the date on which a return is timely filed, whichever is later, the accrual of interest (and penalties) is suspended.[40] The suspension period begins on the day after the 18-month period and ends 21 days after the IRS sends the requisite notice. Second, if the IRS does not issue a notice and demand for payment within 30 days after the taxpayer signs a Form 870 waiver, no interest is charged for the period between the end of the 30-day period and the date the IRS issues its notice and demand.[41] Taxpayers litigating in the Tax Court may

[38] Secs. 6601(a) and (b)(1).
[39] Rev. Proc. 95-17, 1995-1 C.B. 556.
[40] Sec. 6404(g).
[41] Sec. 6601(c).

make a deposit to reduce interest potentially owed. If the court decides that the taxpayer owes a deficiency, interest will not accrue on the deposit.

EXAMPLE C:15-6 ▶ Cindy receives an automatic extension for filing this year's return. On June 24 of the following year, she submits her return, along with the $700 balance she owes on this year's tax liability. She owes interest on $700 for the period April 16 of this year through June 24 of the following year. Interest is compounded daily based on the interest rate for underpayments determined under Sec. 6621. ◀

EXAMPLE C:15-7 ▶ After filing for an automatic extension, Hans files his 2007 return on August 15, 2008. On April 2, 2010, the IRS sends Hans a notice of deficiency in which it assesses interest. Because the IRS failed to send Hans the notice by February 15, 2010 (18 months after the date on which the return was timely filed), the accrual of interest is suspended. The suspension period begins on February 16, 2010 (the day after the 18-month period), and ends on April 23, 2010 (21 days after the IRS sends the requisite notice). ◀

EXAMPLE C:15-8 ▶ Raj filed his 2004 individual return on March 15, 2005. The IRS audits the return in 2007, and on January 24, 2007, Raj signs a Form 870 waiver, in which he agrees that he owes a $780 deficiency. The IRS does not issue a notice and demand for payment until March 20, 2007. Raj pays the deficiency two days later. Raj owes interest, compounded daily at the Sec. 6621 underpayment rate, for the period April 16, 2005, through February 24, 2007. No interest can be assessed for the period February 24 through March 20, 2007 because the IRS did not issue its notice and demand for payment until more than 30 days after Raj signed the Form 870 waiver. ◀

ABATEMENT. The IRS does not abate interest except for unreasonable errors or delays resulting from its managerial or ministerial acts.[42] A "managerial act" involves the temporary or permanent loss of records or the exercise of judgment or discretion relating to the management of personnel.[43] A "ministerial act" involves routine procedure without the exercise of judgment or discretion.[44] A decision concerning the proper application of federal law is neither a managerial nor a ministerial act.

EXAMPLE C:15-9 ▶ Omar provides documentation to an audit agent, who assures him that he will receive a copy of an audit report shortly. Before the agent has had an opportunity to act, however, the divisional manager transfers him to another office. An extended period of time elapses before the manager assigns another audit agent to Omar's case. The decision to reassign is a managerial act. The IRS may abate interest attributable to any unreasonable delay in payment resulting from this act. ◀

EXAMPLE C:15-10 ▶ Chanelle requests information from an IRS employee concerning the balance due on her current year tax liability. The employee fails to access the most current computerized database and provides Chanelle with incorrect information. Based on this information, Chanelle pays less than the full balance due. The employee's failing to access the most current database is a ministerial act. The IRS may abate interest attributable to any unreasonable delay in payment resulting from this act. ◀

FAILURE-TO-FILE AND FAILURE-TO-PAY PENALTIES

OBJECTIVE 5

Understand tax-related penalties generally

Penalties add teeth to the accounting and reporting provisions of the Internal Revenue Code. Without them, these provisions would be mere letters on the books of the legislature—words without effect. Tax-related penalties fall into two broad categories: taxpayer and preparer. As the name suggests, taxpayer penalties apply only to taxpayers, be they individuals, corporations, estates, or trusts. Preparer penalties apply only to tax return preparers, be they firms that employ tax professionals or the professionals themselves.

---

[42] Sec. 6404(e).
[43] Reg. Sec. 301.6404-2(b)(1).
[44] Reg. Sec. 301.6404-2(b)(2).

REAL-WORLD EXAMPLE

In 2005, as a result of the audit process, the IRS assessed a total of $7.97 billion in civil penalties and abated about $1.6 billion for reasonable cause.

Within these broad categories are two distinct subcategories: civil and criminal. Civil penalties are imposed on taxpayers for negligently, recklessly, or intentionally failing to fulfill their accounting or reporting obligations. Criminal penalties are imposed for maliciously or willfully failing to do so. Taxpayers may raise as a defense to some penalties "reasonable cause" and a good faith belief in the correctness of their position. Sometimes, for the defense to be valid, they also must disclose this position on their tax return. This section of the text discusses two commonly encountered penalties in income, estate, and gift taxation: failure to file and failure to pay. The IRS may assess these penalties, in addition to interest, on overdue tax liabilities. Subsequent sections of the text discuss other taxpayer and preparer penalties. Topic Review C:15-1 presents a summary of IRC penalty provisions. The Topic Review is provided here rather than later in the chapter to give readers a framework for following the discussion of the various penalties.

Topic Review C:15-1

Overview of Penalties

Penalty	IRC Section	Applicability	Rules/Calculation	Defenses/Waiver
A. TAXPAYER—CIVIL				
Failure to file	6651(a)	All persons	*General rule:* 5% per month or fraction thereof; 25% maximum *Minimum penalty if late more than 60 days:* lesser of $100 or 100% of tax due *Fraudulent reason for not filing: 15% per month or fraction thereof; 75% maximum*	Reasonable cause, not willful neglect
Failure to pay tax	6651(a)	All persons	*General rule:* 0.5% per month or fraction thereof; 25% maximum*	Reasonable cause, not willful neglect
Failure by individual to pay estimated tax	6654	Individuals, certain estates, trusts	*General rule:* penalty at same rate as interest rate for deficiency; imposed for period between due date for estimated tax payments and earlier of payment date or due date for return	Waiver in unusual circumstances
Failure by corporation to pay estimated tax	6655	Corporations	*General rule:* penalty at same rate as interest rate for deficiency; imposed for period between due date for estimated tax payments and earlier of payment date or due date for return	—
Negligence	6662(c)	All persons	*General rule:* 20% of underpayment attributable to negligence	Reasonable cause, good faith
Substantial understatement	6662(d)	All persons	*General rule:* 20% of underpayment attributable to substantial understatement (portion for which no substantial authority and no disclosure exists)	Reasonable cause, good faith; also, substantial authority, disclosure
Civil fraud	6663	All persons	*General rule:* 75% of portion of understatement attributable to fraud.	Reasonable cause, good faith
B. TAXPAYER—CRIMINAL				
Willful attempt to evade tax	7201	All persons	*General rule:* $100,000 ($500,000 for corporations) and/or up to five years in prison	—
Willful failure to collect or pay over tax	7202	All persons	*General rule:* $10,000 and/or up to five years in prison	—
Willful failure to pay or file	7203	All persons	*General rule:* $25,000 ($100,000 for corporations) and/or up to five years in prison	—
Willfully making false or fraudulent statements	7206	All persons	*General rule:* $25,000 ($100,000 for corporations) and/or up to one year in prison	—

Topic Review C:15-1 (cont.)

C. PREPARER—CIVIL				
Understatement of tax by preparer	6694(a)	Tax return preparers	*General rule:* $250	Reasonable cause, good faith; also, disclosure
Willful attempt to understate taxes	6694(b)	Tax return preparers	*General rule:* $1,000	—
Failure to furnish copy to taxpayer	6695(a)	Tax return preparers	*General rule:* $50; $25,000 maximum	Reasonable cause, not willful neglect
Failure to sign return	6695(b)	Tax return preparers	*General rule:* $50; $25,000 maximum	Reasonable cause, not willful neglect
Failure to furnish identifying number	6695(c)	Tax return preparers	*General rule:* $50; $25,000 maximum	Reasonable cause, not willful neglect
Failure to retain copy or list	6695(d)	Tax return preparers	*General rule:* $50; $25,000 maximum	Reasonable cause, not willful neglect
Failure to file correct information returns	6695(e)	Tax return preparers	*General rule:* $50 for each failure to file a return or each failure to set forth an item in a return; $25,000 maximum	Reasonable cause, not willful neglect
Improper negotiation of checks	6695(f)	Tax return preparers	*General rule:* $500 per check	—
Aiding and abetting in understatement	6701(b)	All persons	*General rule:* $1,000 ($10,000 for corporations)	—

* If the taxpayer owes both the failure-to-file and the failure-to-pay penalties for a given month, the total penalty for such month is limited to 5% of the net tax due.

FAILURE TO FILE

Taxpayers who do not file a return by the due date generally are liable for a penalty of 5% per month (or fraction thereof) of the net tax due.[45] A fraction of a month, even just a day, counts as a full month. The maximum penalty for failing to file is 25%. If the taxpayer receives an extension, the extended due date is treated as the original due date. In determining the net tax due (i.e., the amount subject to the penalty), the IRS reduces the taxpayer's gross tax by any taxes paid by the return's due date (e.g., withholding and estimated tax payments) and tax credits claimed on the return.[46] If any failure to file is fraudulent, the penalty rate is 15% per month up to a maximum penalty of 75%.[47] For purposes of this provision, "fraud" is actual, intentional wrongdoing or the commission of an act for the specific purpose of evading a tax known or believed to be due.[48]

ADDITIONAL COMMENT

The most common reason given by taxpayers to support reasonable cause for failing to file a timely tax return is reliance on one's tax advisor. Other reasons include severe illness or serious accident. Reliance on a tax advisor is not always sufficient cause to obtain a waiver of the penalties.

Penalties are not levied if a taxpayer can prove that he or she failed to file a timely return because of reasonable cause (as opposed to willful neglect). According to Treasury Regulations, reasonable cause exists if "the taxpayer exercised ordinary business care and prudence and was nevertheless unable to file the return within the prescribed time."[49] Not surprisingly, much litigation deals with the issue of reasonable cause.

Note that the penalty imposed for not filing on time generally is a function of the net tax due. However, a minimum penalty applies in some cases.[50] Congress enacted the minimum penalty provision because of the cost to the IRS of identifying nonfilers. If a taxpayer does not file an income tax return within 60 days of the due date (including any extensions), the penalty will be no less than the smaller of $100 or 100% of the tax due on the return. Taxpayers who owe no tax are not subject to the **failure-to-file penalty**. Also, the IRS may waive the penalty if the taxpayer shows reasonable cause for not filing.

---

[45] Sec. 6651(a).

[46] Sec. 6651(b)(1).

[47] Sec. 6651(f).

[48] *Robert W. Bradford v. CIR*, 58 AFTR 2d 86-5532, 86-2 USTC ¶9602 (9th Cir., 1996: *Chris D. Stoltzfus v. U.S.*, 22 AFTR 2d 5251, 68-2 USTC ¶9499 (3rd Cir., 1968): and *William E. Mitchell v. CIR*, 26 AFTR 684, 41-1 USTC ¶9317 (5th Cir., 1941).

[49] Reg. Sec. 301.6651-1(c)(1).

[50] Sec. 6651(a).

EXAMPLE C:15-11 ▶ Earl files his 2007 individual income tax return on July 5, 2008. Earl requested no extension and did not have reasonable cause for his late filing, but he committed no fraud. Earl's 2007 return shows a balance due of $400. Under the regular rules, the late filing penalty would be $60 (0.05 × 3 months × $400). Earl's penalty is $100 because of the minimum penalty provision applicable to his failure to file the return within 60 days of the due date. ◀

In general, interest does not accrue on any penalty paid within ten days of the date that the IRS notifies the taxpayer of the penalty. Under Sec. 6601(e)(2)(B), however, interest accrues on the failure-to-file penalty, from the due date of the return (including any extensions) until the payment date.

FAILURE TO PAY

The **failure-to-pay penalty** is imposed at 0.5% per month (or fraction thereof).[51] The maximum penalty is 25%. The penalty is based on the gross tax shown on the return less any tax payments made and credits earned before the beginning of the month for which the penalty is calculated.[52] As with the failure-to-file penalty, the IRS may waive the failure-to-pay penalty if the taxpayer shows reasonable cause.

Because the tax is due on the original due date for the return, taxpayers who request an extension without paying 100% of their tax liability potentially owe a failure-to-pay penalty. Treasury Regulations provide some relief by exempting a taxpayer from the penalty if the additional tax due with the filing of the extended return does not exceed 10% of the tax owed for the year.[53]

EXAMPLE C:15-12 ▶ Gary requests an extension for filing his 2007 individual income tax return. His 2007 tax payments include withholding of $4,500, estimated tax payments of $2,000, and $1,000 submitted with his request for an automatic extension. He files his return on June 6, 2008, showing a total tax of $8,000 and a balance due of $500. Gary is exempt from the failure-to-pay penalty because the $500 balance due does not exceed 10% of his 2007 liability (0.10 × $8,000 = $800). Had Gary's 2007 tax instead been $9,000, he would have owed an additional tax of $1,500 and a failure-to-pay penalty of $15 (0.005 × 2 months × $1,500). ◀

The 0.5% penalty increases to 1% a month, or fraction thereof, in certain circumstances. The rate is 1% for any month beginning after the earlier of

- Ten days after the date the IRS notifies the taxpayer that it plans to levy on his or her salary or property and
- The day the IRS notifies and demands immediate payment from the taxpayer because it believes that collection is in jeopardy

EXAMPLE C:15-13 ▶ Ginny filed her 2004 individual income tax return on April 12, 2005. However, Ginny did not pay her tax liability. On October 5, 2007, the IRS notifies Ginny of its plans to levy on her property. The failure-to-pay penalty is 0.5% per month for the period April 18, 2005 through October 17, 2006. Beginning on October 18, 2006, the penalty rises to 1% per month, or fraction thereof. ◀

SELF-STUDY QUESTION

If a taxpayer does not have sufficient funds to pay his or her tax liability by the due date, should the taxpayer wait until the funds are available before filing the tax return?

ANSWER

No. He or she should file the return on a timely basis. This filing avoids the 5% per month failure-to-file penalty. The taxpayer still will owe the failure-to-pay penalty, but at least this penalty is only 0.5% per month.

Some taxpayers file on time to avoid the failure-to-file penalty even though they cannot pay the balance of the tax due. Barring a showing of reasonable cause, these taxpayers still will incur the failure-to-pay penalty. Because taxpayers who do not timely file a return are likely to owe additional taxes, they often owe both the failure-to-file and the failure-to-pay penalties.

The IRC provides a special rule for calculating the 5% per month failure-to-file penalty for periods in which the taxpayer owes both penalties. The 5% per month failure-to-file penalty is reduced by the failure-to-pay penalty.[54] Thus, the total penalties for a given month will not exceed 5%. For months when the taxpayer incurs both penalties, the failure-to-file penalty is effectively 4.5% (5% − 0.5%). Note, however, that no reduction occurs if the minimum penalty for failure to file applies.

[51] Sec. 6651(a)(2).
[52] Sec. 6651(b)(2).
[53] Reg. Sec. 301.6651-1(c)(3) and (4).
[54] Sec. 6651(c)(1).

EXAMPLE C:15-14 ▶ Tien files her current year individual income tax return on August 5 of the following year, without having requested an extension. Her total tax is $20,000. Tien pays $15,000 in a timely manner and the $5,000 balance when she files the return. Although Tien committed no fraud, she can show no reasonable cause for the late filing and late payment. Tien's penalties are as follows:

Failure-to-pay penalty:		
$5,000 × 0.005 × 4 months		$ 100
Failure-to-file penalty:		
$5,000 × 0.05 × 4 months	$1,000	
Minus: Reduction for failure-to-pay penalty imposed for same period	(100)	900
Total penalties		$1,000 ◀

EXAMPLE C:15-15 ▶ Assume the same facts as in Example C:15-14 except that Tien instead pays the $5,000 balance on November 17 of the following year. The penalties are as follows:

Failure-to-pay penalty:		
$5,000 × 0.005 × 8 months (April 16 through November 17)		$ 200
Failure-to-file penalty:		
$5,000 × 0.05 × 4 months (April 16 through August 5)	$1,000	
Minus: Reduction for failure-to-pay penalty levied for April 16 through August 5 ($5,000 ×0.005 × 4 months)	(100)	900
Total penalties		$1,100 ◀

ESTIMATED TAXES

OBJECTIVE 6

Calculate the penalty for not paying estimated taxes

Individuals earning only salaries and wages generally pay their annual income tax liability through payroll withholding. The employer is responsible for remitting these withheld amounts, along with Social Security taxes, to a designated federal depository. By contrast, individuals earning other types of income, as well as C corporations, S corporations, and trusts, must estimate their annual income tax liability and prepay their taxes on a quarterly basis.[55] Estates must do the same with respect to income earned during any tax year ending two years after the decedent's death.[56] Although partnerships do not pay estimated income taxes, their separate partners do if they are individuals or taxable entities. Chapters C:3, C:11, and C:14 discuss the estimated income tax requirements for C corporations, S corporations, and fiduciaries, respectively.

PAYMENT REQUIREMENTS

Individuals should pay quarterly estimated income taxes if they have a significant amount of income from sources other than salaries and wages. The amount of each payment should be the same if this outside income accrues uniformly throughout the year. To avoid an estimated income tax penalty for the current year, individuals with AGI of $150,000 or less in the previous year should calculate each payment as follows:

Step 1: Determine the lesser of
- a. 90% of the taxpayer's regular tax, alternative minimum tax (if any), and self-employment tax for the current year, or
- b. 100% of the taxpayer's prior year regular tax, alternative minimum tax (if any), and self-employment tax if the taxpayer filed a return for the prior year and the year was not a short tax year.

Step 2: Calculate the total of
- a. Tax credits for the current year
- b. Taxes withheld on the current year's wages
- c. Overpayments of the prior year's tax liability the taxpayer requests be credited against the current year's tax

[55] S corporations must pay quarterly estimated taxes on their net recognized built-in gains, passive investment income, and credit recapture amounts.

[56] For example, if the decedent's death were June 15 of the current year, and the assets of the decedent's estate are not distributed by June 14 of the following year, the estate must pay estimated taxes on income earned on estate assets for the following tax year.

Step 3: Multiply the excess of the amount from Step 1 over the amount from Step 2 by 25%.[57]

Calendar year individual taxpayers should pay their quarterly installments on April 15, June 15, September 15, and January 15.

Individuals with AGI exceeding $150,000 ($75,000 for married filing separately) in the prior year can avoid the estimated tax penalty for the current year if they pay at least 90% of the current year's tax, or at least 110% of the prior year's tax.[58]

EXAMPLE C:15-16 ▶ Mike's regular tax on his current year taxable income is $35,000. Mike also owes $2,000 of self-employment tax but no alternative minimum tax. Mike's total tax liability last year for both income and self-employment taxes was $24,000. His AGI last year did not exceed $150,000. Taxes withheld from Mike's current year wages were $8,000. Mike did not overpay his tax last year or earn any credits this year. For the current year, Mike should have made quarterly estimated tax payments of $4,000, as calculated below.

Lesser of:	90% of current year's tax (0.90 × $37,000 = $33,300) or 100% of prior year's $24,000 tax liability	$24,000
Minus:	Taxes withheld from current year's wages	(8,000)
Minimum estimated tax payment to avoid penalty under general rule		$16,000
Quarterly estimated tax payments (0.25 × $16,000)		$ 4,000 ◀

ADDITIONAL COMMENT

Although it is simpler to use the amount of tax paid (or, if necessary, the applicable percentage of the amount of tax paid) in the preceding year as a safe harbor, the estimate of the current year's tax liability is preferable if the current year's tax liability is expected to be significantly less than the preceding year's tax liability.

The authority to make estimated tax payments based on the preceding year's income is especially significant for taxpayers with rising levels of income. To avoid an estimated income tax penalty, these taxpayers need to pay only an amount equal to the prior year's tax liability. Using this safe harbor eliminates the need for estimating the current year's tax liability with a high degree of accuracy.

EXAMPLE C:15-17 ▶ Peter, a single calendar year taxpayer, incurs a regular tax liability of $76,000 in the current year. Peter owes no alternative minimum tax liability nor can he claim any tax credits. No overpayments of last year's taxes are available to offset this year's tax liability. Taxes withheld evenly from Peter's wages throughout the current year are $68,000. Peter's AGI last year exceeded $150,000, and his regular tax liability was $60,000. Because Peter's $17,000 of withholding for each quarter exceeds the $15,000 minimum required quarterly payments, as calculated below, he incurs no underpayment penalty.

Lesser of:	90% of current year's (0.90 × $76,000 = $68,400) or 110% of prior year's $60,000 tax liability	$66,000
Minus:	Taxes withheld from current year's wages	(68,000)
Minimum estimated tax payment to avoid penalty under general rule		$ -0-

The $8,000 ($76,000 – $68,000) balance of the current's year taxes is due on or before April 15 of next year. ◀

ADDITIONAL COMMENT

If a taxpayer is having taxes withheld and making estimated tax payments, a certain amount of tax planning is possible. Withholdings are deemed to have occurred equally throughout the year. Thus, disproportionately large amounts could be withheld in the last quarter to allow the taxpayer to avoid the underpayment penalty.

PENALTY FOR UNDERPAYING ESTIMATED TAXES

With the exceptions discussed in the next section, taxpayers who do not remit the requisite amount of estimated tax by the appropriate date are subject to a penalty for underpayment of estimated taxes. The penalty is calculated at the same rate as the interest rate applicable under Sec. 6621 to late payments of tax.[59] The penalty for each quarter is calculated separately on Form 2210.

The amount subject to the penalty is the excess of the total tax that should have been paid during the quarter (e.g., $6,000 [$24,000 prior year's tax liability ÷ 4] in Example C:15-16) over the sum of the estimated tax actually paid during that quarter on or before

[57] Secs. 6654(d), (f), and (g).

[58] Sec. 6654(d)(1)(C). Included in the definition of *individuals* are estates and trusts. Section 67(e) defines AGI for estates and trusts. (See Chapter C:14.)

[59] Daily compounding is not applicable in calculating the penalty.

the installment date plus the withholding attributable to that quarter. Unless the taxpayer proves otherwise, the withholding is deemed to take place equally during each quarter. This rule creates a planning opportunity. Taxpayers who have not paid sufficient amounts of estimated tax in the first three quarters can avoid a penalty by having large amounts of tax withheld during the last quarter.

The penalty is assessed for the time period beginning on the due date for the quarterly installment and ending on the earlier of the date the underpayment actually is paid or the due date for the return (April 15 assuming a calendar year taxpayer). The next example illustrates the computation of the underpayment penalty.

EXAMPLE C:15-18 ▶ Assume the same facts as in Example C:15-16 except that Mike pays only $3,000 of estimated tax payments on April 15, June 15, and September 15 of the current year and January 15 of next year and, for simplicity, that 6% is the Sec. 6621 underpayment rate for the entire time period. Mike files his current year return on March 30 of next year and pays the $17,000 ($37,000 − $8,000 withholding − $12,000 estimated taxes) balance due at that time. Mike's underpayment penalty is determined as follows:

TYPICAL MISCONCEPTION

Many self-employed taxpayers assume they are not liable for estimated taxes if they have sufficient itemized deductions and exemptions to create zero taxable income or a taxable loss. However, a self-employment tax liability may exist even if the individual has no taxable income. Thus, taxpayers in this situation can end up with an overall tax liability and an accompanying estimated tax penalty.

	Quarter			
	First	*Second*	*Third*	*Fourth*
Amount that should have been paid ($24,000 ÷ 4)	$6,000	$6,000	$6,000	$6,000
Minus: Withholding	(2,000)	(2,000)	(2,000)	(2,000)
Estimated tax payment	(3,000)	(3,000)	(3,000)	(3,000)
Underpayment	$1,000	$1,000	$1,000	$1,000
Number of days of underpayment (ends March 30 of next year because earlier than April 15 of next year);	349	288	196	74
Penalty at 6% assumed annual rate for number of days of underpayment	$ 57	$ 47	$ 32	$ 12

The total penalty equals $148 ($57 + $47 + $32 + $12). The $148 penalty is not deductible. ◀

Interest does not accrue on underpayments of estimated tax.[60] However, if the entire tax is not paid by the due date for the return, interest and perhaps also a failure-to-pay penalty will be levied on the unpaid amount.

EXCEPTIONS TO THE PENALTY

In certain circumstances, individuals who have not remitted the required estimated tax payments nevertheless will be exempt from the underpayment penalty. The IRS imposes no penalty if the taxpayer's tax liability exceeds by less than $1,000 taxes actually withheld from wages during the year. Similarly, the taxpayer will not owe a penalty, regardless of the underpayment amount, if the taxpayer owed no taxes for the prior tax year, the prior tax year consisted of the full 12 months, and the taxpayer was a U.S. citizen or resident alien throughout that year. The Secretary of the Treasury can waive the penalty otherwise due in the case of "casualty, disaster, or other unusual circumstances" or for newly retired or disabled individuals.[61]

EXAMPLE C:15-19 ▶ Paul's current year tax liability is $2,200, the same as last year's. His wage withholding amounts to $1,730, and Paul does not pay any estimated taxes. Paul pays the $470 balance due on March 15 of next year. Under the general rules, Paul is subject to the underpayment penalty because he does not reach either the 90% of the current year tax threshold or 100% of the prior year

[60] Sec. 6601(h).

[61] Sec. 6654(e).

tax threshold. However, because Paul's tax exceeds wage withholding by less than $1,000, he owes no penalty for underpaying his estimated tax liability. ◀

Taxpayers are exempt from the underpayment penalty in certain other circumstances, a discussion of which is beyond the scope of this text. Chapter I:14 of *Prentice Hall's Federal Taxation: Principles* and *Comprehensive* texts, however, discusses one such circumstance where the taxpayer annualizes his or her income and bases the estimated tax payment on the annualized amount.[62]

OTHER MORE SEVERE PENALTIES

OBJECTIVE 7

Describe more severe penalties, including the fraud penalty

In addition to the penalties for failure to file, failure to pay, and underpayment of estimated tax, taxpayers may be subject to other more severe penalties. These include the accuracy-related penalty (applicable in several contexts) and the fraud penalty, each of which is discussed below.[63] A 20% accuracy-related penalty applies to any underpayment attributable to negligence, any substantial understatement of income tax, and various types of errors, a discussion of which is beyond the scope of this text. An accuracy-related penalty is not levied, however, if the government imposed the fraud penalty or if the taxpayer filed no return.

ADDITIONAL COMMENT

To shift the burden of proof to the IRS, the taxpayer must introduce credible evidence regarding a factual issue relating to his or her tax liability.

NEGLIGENCE

The accuracy-related **negligence penalty** applies whenever the IRS determines that a taxpayer has underpaid any part of his or her taxes as a result of negligence or disregard of the rules or regulations (but without intending to defraud).[64] The penalty is 20% of the underpayment attributable to negligence. Interest accrues on the negligence penalty at the rates applicable to underpayments.[65]

EXAMPLE C:15-20 ▶ The IRS audits Ted's individual return and assesses a $7,500 deficiency, of which $2,500 is attributable to negligence. Ted agrees to the assessment and pays the additional tax of $7,500 the following year. Ted incurs a negligence penalty of $500 (0.20 × $2,500). ◀

The IRC defines ***negligence*** as "any failure to make a reasonable attempt to comply with the provisions" of the IRC. It defines disregard of the rules or regulations as "any careless, reckless, or intentional disregard."[66] According to Treasury Regulations, a presumption of negligence exists if the taxpayer does not include in gross income an amount of income reported on an information return or does not reasonably attempt to ascertain the correctness of a deduction, credit, or exclusion that a reasonable and prudent person would think was "too good to be true."[67]

A taxpayer is careless if he or she does not diligently try to determine the correctness of his or her position. A taxpayer is reckless if he or she exerts little or no effort to determine whether a rule or regulation exists. A taxpayer's disregard is intentional if he or she knows about the rule or regulation he or she disregards.[68]

The penalty will not be imposed for any portion of an underpayment if the taxpayer had reasonable cause for his or her position and acted in good faith.[69] Failure to follow a regulation must be disclosed on Form 8275-R (Regulation Disclosure Statement).

EXAMPLE C:15-21 ▶ The IRS audits Mario's current year individual return, and Mario agrees to a $4,000 deficiency. Mario had reasonable cause for adopting his tax return positions (which were not contrary to

[62] Section 6654(d)(2) allows for computation of the underpayments, if any, by annualizing income. Relief from the underpayment penalty may result from applying the annualization rules. Corporations, but not individuals, are permitted a seasonal adjustment to the annualization rules.
[63] Secs. 6662(a) and (b).
[64] Secs. 6662(b) and (c).
[65] Sec. 6601(e)(2)(B).
[66] Sec. 6662(c).
[67] Reg. Sec. 1.6662-3(b)(1).
[68] Reg. Sec. 1.6662-3(b)(2).
[69] Sec. 6664(c).

the applicable rules or regulations) and acted in good faith. Mario will not be liable for a negligence penalty. ◀

SUBSTANTIAL UNDERSTATEMENT

ADDITIONAL COMMENT

Theoretically, penalties are designed to deter taxpayers from willfully disregarding federal tax laws. Some taxpayers have been concerned that the IRS has used the multitude of tax penalties primarily as a source of revenue. The IRS achieved this result by "stacking" penalties (i.e., applying several penalties to a single underpayment). Recent legislation has alleviated some of this concern.

Taxpayers who substantially understate their income tax are liable for an accuracy-related penalty for their substantial understatements. The IRC defines a substantial understatement as an understatement of tax exceeding the greater of 10% of the tax required to be shown on the return or $5,000 (or $10,000 in the case of a C corporation). For a C corporation, an additional rule applies. Specifically, if 10% of the required tax exceeds $10 million, a substantial understatement exists if the understatement exceeds $10 million.[70] The penalty equals 20% of the underpayment of tax attributable to the substantial understatement. It does not apply to understatements for which the taxpayer shows reasonable cause and good faith for his or her position.

SELF-STUDY QUESTION

How is an understatement different from an underpayment?

ANSWER

An underpayment can be larger than an understatement. Understatements do not include underpayments for which there was either substantial authority or adequate disclosure.

UNDERSTATEMENT VERSUS UNDERPAYMENT. The amount of tax attributable to the substantial understatement may be less than the amount of the underpayment. In general, the amount of the understatement is calculated as the amount by which the tax required to be shown (i.e., the correct tax) exceeds the tax shown on the return. Because the amount of tax attributable to certain items is not treated as an understatement, the additional tax attributed to such items is not subject to the penalty. An underpayment for an item other than a tax shelter is *not* an understatement if either of the following is true:

- The taxpayer has substantial authority for the tax treatment of the item.
- The taxpayer discloses, either on the return or in a statement attached to the return, the relevant facts affecting the tax treatment of the item, and the taxpayer has a reasonable basis for such treatment.

Although neither the IRC nor Treasury Regulations define "reasonable basis," Reg. Sec. 1.6662-3(b)(3) states that a "reasonable basis" standard is significantly higher than the "not frivolous" standard that usually applies to tax preparers. The latter standard involves a tax position that is not patently improper. The taxpayer meets the adequate disclosure requirement if he or she properly completes Form 8275 and attaches it to the return, or discloses information on the return in a manner prescribed by an annual revenue procedure.[71]

EXAMPLE C:15-22 ▶ The IRS examines Val's current year individual income tax return, and Val agrees to a $9,000 deficiency, which increases her tax liability from $25,000 to $34,000. Val neither made adequate disclosure concerning the items for which the IRS assessed the deficiency nor had substantial authority for her tax treatment. Thus, Val's understatement also is $9,000. This understatement is substantial because it exceeds both 10% of her correct tax liability ($3,400 = 0.10 × $34,000) and the $5,000 minimum. Val incurs a substantial understatement penalty of $1,800 (0.20 × $9,000). ◀

EXAMPLE C:15-23 ▶ Assume the same facts as in Example C:15-22 except Val has substantial authority for the tax treatment of an item that results in a $1,000 additional assessment. In addition, she makes adequate disclosure for a second item with respect to which the IRS assesses additional taxes of $1,500. Although Val's underpayment is $9,000, her understatement is only $6,500 [$9,000 − ($1,000 + $1,500)]. The $6,500 understatement is substantial because it is more than the greater of 10% of Val's tax or $5,000. Thus, the penalty in this case is $1,300 (0.20 × $6,500). ◀

Like the negligence penalty, the substantial understatement penalty bears interest at the rate applicable for underpayments. The interest accrues from the due date of the return.

---

[70] Sec. 6662(d)(1).

[71] Reg. Secs. 1.6662-4(f)(1) and (2). See Rev. Proc. 99-41, 1999-2 C.B. 566, Rev. Proc. 2001-11, 2001-1 C.B. 275, and Rev. Proc. 2001-52, 2001-2 C.B. 491, where the Treasury Department identifies circumstances where disclosure of a position on a taxpayer's return is adequate to reduce the understatement penalty of Sec. 6662(d) and tax preparer penalties of Sec. 6694(a).

ADDITIONAL COMMENT

Even though the substantial understatement penalty is a taxpayer penalty, tax preparers have a duty to make their clients aware of the potential risk of substantial understatement. In some situations, failure to do so has resulted in the client's attempting to collect the amount of the substantial understatement penalty from the preparer.

CONCEPT OF SUBSTANTIAL AUTHORITY. Treasury Regulations indicate that substantial authority

- Exists only if the weight of authorities supporting the tax treatment of an item is substantial relative to the weight of those supporting the contrary treatment, and
- Is based on an objective standard involving an analysis of law and its application to the relevant facts. This standard is more stringent than the "reasonable basis" standard that the taxpayer must meet to avoid the negligence penalty but less stringent than the "more likely than not" standard that applies to tax shelters.[72] (See discussion below.)

According to these regulations, the following are considered to be "authority": statutory provisions; proposed, temporary, and final regulations; court cases; revenue rulings; revenue procedures; tax treaties; Congressional intent as reflected in committee reports and joint statements of a bill's managers; private letter rulings; technical advice memoranda; information or press releases; notices; and any other similar documents published by the IRS in the *Internal Revenue Bulletin* and the *General Explanation of the Joint Committee on Taxation* (also known as the "Blue Book"). Conclusions reached in treatises, periodicals, and the opinions of tax professionals are not considered to be authority. The applicability of court cases in the taxpayer's district is not taken into account in determining the existence of substantial authority. On the other hand, the applicability of court cases in the taxpayer's circuit *is* taken into account in determining the existence of substantial authority.

EXAMPLE C:15-24 ▶ Authorities addressing a particular issue are as follows:

- For the government: Tax Court and Fourth Circuit Court of Appeals
- For taxpayers: U.S. District Court for Rhode Island and First Circuit Court of Appeals

The taxpayer (Tina) is a resident of Rhode Island, which is in the First Circuit. Tina would have substantial authority for a pro-taxpayer position because such a position is supported by the circuit court of appeals for Tina's geographical jurisdiction. ◀

Taxpayers should be aware that, while sparing them a substantial understatement penalty, disclosure (even with a reasonable basis for the tax treatment of the item) might raise a "red flag" that could prompt an IRS audit.

TAX SHELTERS. A different set of rules applies to a tax shelter, which is any arrangement for which a significant purpose is the avoidance or evasion of federal income tax.[73] See page C:15-33 for a discussion of this topic.[74]

CIVIL FRAUD

Fraud differs from simple, honest mistakes and negligence in that it involves a deliberate attempt to deceive. Because the IRS cannot establish intent per se, it attempts to prove intent indirectly by emphasizing the taxpayer's actions and the circumstances surrounding these actions. One leading authority refers to fraud cases in this manner:

> Fraud cases ordinarily involve systematic or substantial omissions from gross income or fictitious deductions or dependency claims, accompanied by the falsification or destruction of records or false or inconsistent statements to the investigating agents, especially where records are not kept by the taxpayer. The taxpayer's education and business experience are relevant.[75]

The fraud penalty equals 75% of the portion of the underpayment attributable to fraud. If the IRS establishes that any portion of an underpayment is due to fraud, the entire underpayment is treated as having resulted from fraud unless the taxpayer establishes otherwise by a preponderance of the evidence. Like the negligence penalty, the fraud penalty bears interest.[76]

---

[72] Reg. Sec. 1.6662-4(d).

[73] Sec. 6662(d)(2)(C).

[74] The discussion on that page covers the new rules ushered in by the 2004 Jobs Act.

[75] Boris I. Bittker and Lawrence Lokken, *Federal Taxation of Income, Estates, and Gifts* (Boston, MA: Warren, Gorham & Lamont, 1999), vol. 4, ¶ 114–6.

[76] Sec. 6601(e)(2)(B).

EXAMPLE C:15-25 ▶ The IRS audits Ned's individual return and claims that Ned's underpayment is due to fraud. Ned agrees to the $40,000 deficiency but establishes that only $32,000 of the deficiency is attributable to fraud. The remainder results from mistakes that the IRS did not believe were due to fraud. Ned's civil fraud penalty is $24,000 (0.75 × $32,000). ◀

The fraud penalty can be imposed on taxpayers filing income, gift, or estate tax returns. If it is imposed, the negligence and substantial understatement penalties are not assessed on the portion of the underpayment attributable to fraud.[77]

With respect to a joint return, no fraud penalty can be imposed on a spouse who has not committed fraud.[78] In other words, one spouse is not liable for the other spouse's fraudulent acts.

STOP & THINK

Question: A few years ago, Joyce filed her individual income tax return in which she reported $250,000 of taxable income. She paid all the tax shown on the return on the day she filed. She, however, fraudulently omitted an additional $100,000 of gross income and, of course, does not have substantial authority for this omission. Moreover, she did not make a disclosure of the omitted income. If the IRS proves that Joyce committed fraud, will she be liable for both the civil fraud penalty and the substantial understatement penalty? What are the rates for the two penalties?

Solution: Because the penalties cannot be stacked, Joyce will not owe both penalties. If the IRS successfully proves fraud, she will owe a penalty of 75% of the tax due on the omitted income. She will not owe the 20% penalty for substantial understatements.

CRIMINAL FRAUD

ADDITIONAL COMMENT

In fiscal 2005, the IRS initiated 4,269 criminal investigations (up from 3,917 in 2004), and it referred 2,859 for prosecution. During fiscal 2005, the IRS filed 2,406 indictments, and prison sentences were handed down in 2,095 of those cases.

Civil and criminal fraud are similar in that both involve a taxpayer's intent to misrepresent facts. They differ primarily in terms of the weight of evidence required for conviction. Civil fraud requires proof by a preponderance of the evidence. Criminal fraud requires proof beyond a reasonable doubt. Because the latter standard is more stringent than the former, the government charges relatively few taxpayers with criminal fraud. To do so, the IRS and Justice Department must agree on the charges.

CRIMINAL FRAUD INVESTIGATIONS. The Criminal Investigation Division of the IRS conducts criminal fraud investigations. The agents responsible for the investigation are called **special agents**. Under IRS policy, at the first meeting of the special agent and the taxpayer, the special agent must

- ▶ Identify himself or herself as such
- ▶ Advise the taxpayer that he or she is the subject of a criminal investigation
- ▶ Advise the taxpayer of his or her rights to remain silent and consult legal counsel

PENALTY PROVISIONS. Sections 7201-7216 provide for criminal penalties. Three of these penalties are discussed below.

ADDITIONAL COMMENT

Any time a tax professional learns a client has engaged in activities that may constitute criminal fraud, he or she immediately should refer the client to qualified legal counsel. Counsel should then hire the accountant as a consultant. Taxpayer's communications will be confidential under the attorney–client relationship. This relationship encompasses agents of the attorney.

Section 7201. Section 7201 provides for an assessment of a penalty against any person who "willfully attempts . . . to evade or defeat any tax." The maximum penalty is $100,000 ($500,000 for corporations), a prison sentence of up to five years, or both.

Section 7203. Section 7203 imposes a penalty on any person who willfully fails to pay any tax or file a return. The maximum penalty is $25,000 ($100,000 for corporations), a prison sentence of no more than one year, or both. If the government charges the taxpayer with willfully failing to prepare a return, it need not prove that the taxpayer owes additional tax.

---

[77] Sec. 6662(b).

[78] Sec. 6663(c).

Section 7206. Persons other than the taxpayer can be charged under Sec. 7206. This section applies to any person who

> [W]illfully aids or assists in, or procures, counsels, or advises the preparation or presentation under, or in connection with any matter arising under the internal revenue laws, of a return, affidavit, claim, or other document, which is fraudulent or is false as to any material matter, whether or not such falsity or fraud is with the knowledge or consent of the person authorized or required to present such return, affidavit, claim, or document.[79]

What constitutes a material matter has been litigated extensively.[80] The maximum penalty under Sec. 7206 is $100,000 ($500,000 for corporations), a prison sentence of up to three years, or both. The government need not prove that the taxpayer owes additional tax.

STATUTE OF LIMITATIONS

OBJECTIVE 8

Understand the statute of limitations

The **statute of limitations** has the same practical implications in a tax context as in other contexts. It specifies a timeframe (called the limitations period) during which the government must assess the tax or initiate a court proceeding to collect the tax. The statute of limitations also defines the limitations period during which a taxpayer may file a lawsuit against the government or a claim for a refund.

GENERAL THREE-YEAR RULE

Under the general rule of Sec. 6501(a), the limitations period is three years after the date on which the return is filed, regardless of whether the return is timely filed. A return filed before its due date is treated as if it were filed on the due date.[81]

EXAMPLE C:15-26 ▶ Ali files his 2007 individual return on March 5, 2008. The government may not assess additional taxes for 2007 after April 15, 2011. If instead, Ali files his 2007 individual return on October 6, 2008, the limitations period for his return expires on October 6, 2011. ◀

SIX-YEAR RULE FOR SUBSTANTIAL OMISSIONS

INCOME TAX RETURNS. In the case of substantial omissions, the limitations period is six years after the later of the date the return is filed or the return's due date. For income tax purposes, the six-year period is applicable if the taxpayer omits from gross income an amount exceeding 25% of the gross income shown on the return. If an item is disclosed either on the return or in a statement attached to the return, it is not treated as an omission if the disclosure is "adequate to apprise the [Treasury] Secretary of the nature and amount of such item."[82] In the case of taxpayers conducting a trade or business, gross income for purposes of the 25% omission test means the taxpayer's sales revenues (not the taxpayer's gross profit).[83] Taxpayers benefit from this special definition because it renders the 25% test applicable to a gross amount (implying a higher threshold).

EXAMPLE C:15-27 ▶ Peg files her 2007 return on March 31, 2008. Her return shows $6,000 of interest from corporate bonds and $30,000 of salary. Peg attaches a statement to her return that indicates why she thinks a $2,000 receipt is nontaxable. However, because of an oversight, she does not report an $8,000 capital gain. Peg is deemed to have omitted only $8,000 rather than $10,000 (the $8,000 capital gain plus the $2,000 receipt) because she disclosed the $2,000 receipt. The $8,000 amount is 22.22% ($8,000/$36,000) of her reported gross income. Because the omission does not exceed 25% of Peg's reported gross income, the limitations period expires on April 15, 2011. ◀

---

[79] Sec. 7206(2).

[80] See, for example, *U.S. v. Joseph DiVarco*, 32 AFTR 2d 73-5605, 73-2 USTC ¶9607 (7th Cir., 1973), wherein the court held that the source of the taxpayer's income as stated on the tax return is a material matter.

[81] Sec. 6501(b)(1).

[82] Sec. 6501(e).

[83] Regulation Sec. 1.61-3(a) defines *gross income* as sales less cost of goods sold.

WHAT WOULD YOU DO IN THIS SITUATION?

After working eight years for a large CPA firm, you begin your practice as a sole practitioner CPA. Your practice is not as profitable as you had expected, and you consider how you might attract more clients. One idea is to obtain for your clients larger refunds than they anticipate. Your reputation for knowing tax-saving tips might grow, and your profits might increase. You think further and decide that maybe you could claim itemized deductions for charitable contributions that actually were not made and for business expenses that actually were not paid. You are aware of Sec. 7206, regarding false and fraudulent statements but think that you can avoid the "as to any material matter" stipulation by keeping the deduction overstatements relatively insubstantial. Would you try this scheme for increasing your profits? If so, would you escape the scope of Sec. 7206? What ramifications might these deeds have on your standing as a CPA under the AICPA's *Statements on Standards for Tax Services* and *Code of Professional Conduct*?

EXAMPLE C:15-28 ▶ Assume the same facts as in Example C:15-27 except Peg does not make adequate disclosure of the $2,000 receipt. Thus, she is considered to have omitted $10,000 from gross income. The $10,000 amount is 27.77% ($10,000/$36,000) of her reported gross income. Therefore, the limitations period expires on April 15, 2014. ◀

EXAMPLE C:15-29 ▶ Rita conducts a business as a sole proprietorship. Rita's 2007 return, filed on March 17, 2008, indicates sales of $100,000 and cost of goods sold of $70,000. Rita inadvertently fails to report $9,000 of interest earned on a loan to a relative. For purposes of the 25% omission test, her gross income is $100,000, not $30,000. The omitted interest is 9% ($9,000/$100,000) of her reported gross income. Because the $9,000 does not exceed 25% of the gross amount, the limitations period expires on April 15, 2011. ◀

KEY POINT
A 25% omission of gross income extends the basic limitations period to six years, whereas a 25% overstatement of deductions is still subject to the basic three-year limitations period. However, if fraud can be shown, there is no limitations period.

Note that the six-year rule applies only to omitted income. Thus, claiming excessive deductions will not result in a six-year limitations period. Moreover, if the omission involves fraud, no limitations period applies.

GIFT AND ESTATE TAX RETURNS. A similar six-year limitations period applies for gift and estate tax purposes. If the taxpayer omits items that exceed 25% of the gross estate value or the total amount of gifts reported on the return, the limitations period expires six years after the later of the date the return is filed or the due date. Items disclosed on the return or in a statement attached to the return "in a manner adequate to apprise the [Treasury] Secretary of the nature and amount of such item" do not constitute omissions.[84] Understatements of the value of assets disclosed on the return also are not considered omissions.

EXAMPLE C:15-30 ▶ On April 3, 2008, John files a gift tax return for 2007. The return reports a cash gift of $600,000. In 2007, John sold land to his son for $700,000. At the time of the sale, John thought the land's FMV was $700,000 and did not disclose any additional amount on the gift tax return. Upon audit, the IRS determines that the FMV of the land on the sale date was $900,000. Thus, John effectively gave an additional $200,000 to his son. The $200,000 amount is 33⅓% ($200,000/$600,000) of all gifts reported. The limitations period expires on April 15, 2014. ◀

WHEN NO RETURN IS FILED

No limitations period exists if the taxpayer does not file a return.[85] Thus, the government may assess the tax or initiate a court proceeding for collection at any time.

EXAMPLE C:15-31 ▶ Jill does not file a tax return for 2007. No limitations period applies. Consequently, if the government discovers 20 years later that Jill did not file a return, it may assess the 2007 tax, along with penalties and interest. ◀

[84] Sec. 6501(e)(2).

[85] Sec. 6501(c)(3).

OTHER EXCEPTIONS TO THREE-YEAR RULE

SELF-STUDY QUESTION

Should a taxpayer ever agree to extend the limitations period?

ANSWER

Yes. When an audit is in progress, if a taxpayer refuses to extend the limitations period, the agent may assert a deficiency for each item in question. Had the taxpayer granted an extension, perhaps many of the items in question never would have been included in the examining agent's report.

EXTENSION OF THE THREE-YEAR LIMITATIONS PERIOD. The IRC provides other exceptions to the three-year statute of limitations rule, some of which are discussed here. The taxpayer and the IRS can mutually agree in writing to extend the limitations period for taxes other than the estate tax.[86] In such situations, the limitations period is extended until the date agreed on by the two parties. Such agreements usually are concluded when the IRS is auditing a return near the end of the statutory period. Taxpayers often agree to extending the limitations period because they think that, if they do not do so, the IRS will assess a higher deficiency than otherwise would have been the case. Before concluding such an agreement, the IRS must notify the taxpayer that he or she may refuse to extend the limitations period or may limit the extension to particular issues.

NOL CARRYBACKS. For a year to which a net operating loss (NOL) carries back, the applicable limitations period is for the year in which the NOL arose.[87]

WHEN FRAUD IS PROVEN.

Deficiency and Civil Fraud Penalty. If the government successfully proves that a taxpayer filed a false or fraudulent return "with the intent to evade tax" or engaged in a "willful attempt . . . to defeat or evade tax," there is no limitations period.[88] In other words, the government may at any time assess the tax or begin a court proceeding to collect the tax and the interest thereon. In addition, if the government proves fraud, it may impose a civil penalty. If it fails to prove fraud and the normal three-year limitations period and special six-year period for 25% omissions have expired, it may not assess additional taxes. The fraud issue is significant in tax litigation because the burden of proving fraud is unconditionally on the government.

EXAMPLE C:15-32 ▶ The IRS audits Trey's 2011 return late in 2014. It also examines Trey's prior years' returns and contends that Trey has willfully attempted to evade tax on his timely filed 2007 return. Trey litigates in the Tax Court, and the Court decides the fraud issue in his favor. Because the IRS did not prove fraud, it may not assess additional taxes for 2007. Had the IRS proven fraud, the limitations period for the 2007 return would have remained open, and the IRS could have assessed the additional taxes. ◀

ADDITIONAL COMMENT

Even though a taxpayer is home free from criminal prosecution after six years of an act or omission, he or she still is subject to civil fraud penalties if fraud is proven at any time after the six-year period.

Criminal Provisions. If taxpayers are not indicted for criminal violations of the tax law within a certain period of time, they are home free. For most criminal offenses, the maximum period is six years after the commission of the offense.[89] Taxpayers cannot be prosecuted, tried, or punished unless an indictment is made within that timeframe. The six-year period begins on the date the taxpayer committed the offense, not the date he or she files the return. Taxpayers who file fraudulent returns might commit offenses related to the returns at a subsequent date. An example of an offense that some taxpayers commit after filing a return is depositing money into a new bank account under a fictitious name.

EXAMPLE C:15-33 ▶ In March 2008, Tony files a fraudulent 2007 return through which he attempts to evade tax. Before filing, Tony keeps a double set of books. In 2007, Tony deposits some funds into a bank account under a fictitious name. In 2009, he moves to another state, and on May 4, 2009, he transfers these funds to a new bank account under a different fictitious name. Depositing money into the new account is an offense relating to the fraudulent return. Provided Tony commits no additional offenses, the limitations period for indictment expires on May 4, 2015. ◀

SELF-STUDY QUESTION

Suppose a taxpayer incorrectly includes a receipt in a tax return and then, after the limitations period has expired for that year, correctly includes the receipt in a subsequent return. Is it equitable for the taxpayer to have to pay tax on the same income twice?

REFUND CLAIMS

Taxpayers generally are not entitled to a refund for overpayments of tax unless they file a claim for refund by the later of three years from the date they file the return or two years from the date they pay the tax.[90] The limitations period for individuals is suspended when

[86] Sec. 6501(c)(4).

[87] Sec. 6501(h).

[88] Secs. 6501(c)(1) and (2).

[89] Sec. 6531.

[90] Sec. 6511(a).

ANSWER

No. A complicated set of provisions (Secs. 1311-1314) allows, in specific situations, otherwise closed years to be opened if a position taken in an open year is inconsistent with a position taken in a closed year.

the individual is financially disabled. A return filed before the due date is deemed to have been filed on the due date. The due date is determined without regard to extensions. In most cases, taxpayers pay the tax concurrently with filing the return. Typically, the taxpayer files a claim for a refund in the following circumstance: the IRS has audited the taxpayer's return, has proposed a deficiency, and has assessed additional taxes. The taxpayer may have paid the additional taxes two years after the due date for the return. In such a situation, the taxpayer may file a claim for a refund at any time within two years after making the additional payment (or a total of four years after the filing date). If the taxpayer does not file a claim until more than three years after the date of filing the return, the maximum refund is the amount of tax paid during the two-year period immediately preceding the date on which he or she files the claim.[91]

EXAMPLE C:15-34 ▶ Pat files his 2007 return on March 12, 2008. The return reports a tax liability of $5,000, and Pat pays this entire amount when he files his return. He pays no additional tax. Pat must file a claim for refund by April 15, 2011. The maximum refundable amount is $5,000. ◀

EXAMPLE C:15-35 ▶ Assume the same facts as in Example C:15-34 except the IRS audits Pat's 2007 return, and Pat pays a $1,200 deficiency on October 4, 2010. Pat may file a claim for refund as late as October 4, 2012. If Pat files the claim later than April 15, 2011, the refund may not exceed $1,200 (the amount of tax paid during the two-year period immediately preceding the filing of the claim). ◀

LIABILITY FOR TAX

Taxpayers are primarily liable for paying their tax. Spouses and transferees may be secondarily liable, as discussed below.

OBJECTIVE 9

Explain from whom the government may collect unpaid taxes

JOINT RETURNS

Ordinarily, if spouses file a joint return, their liability to pay the tax is joint and several.[92] **Joint and several liability** means that each spouse is potentially liable for the full amount due. If one spouse fails to pay any or all of the tax, the other spouse is responsible for paying the deficiency. Joint and several liability has facilitated IRS collection efforts where one spouse absconds from the country, and the other spouse remains behind.

VALIDITY OF JOINT RETURN. To be valid, a joint return generally must include the signatures of both spouses. However, if one spouse cannot sign because of a disability, the return still is valid if that spouse orally consents to the other spouse's signing for him or her.[93] A joint return is invalid if one spouse forces the other to file jointly.

INNOCENT SPOUSE PROVISION. Congress has provided for **innocent spouse relief** where holding one spouse liable for the taxes due from both spouses would be inequitable. Relief is available if all five of the following conditions are met:

- The spouses file a joint return.
- The return contains an understatement of tax attributable to the erroneous item(s) of an individual filing it.
- The other individual establishes that he or she neither knew nor had reason to know of any or all of the understatement.
- Based on all the facts and circumstances, holding the other individual liable for the deficiency would be inequitable.
- The other individual elects innocent spouse relief no later than two years after the IRS begins its collection efforts.

[91] Under Sec. 6512, special rules apply if the IRS has mailed a notice of deficiency and if the taxpayer files a petition with the Tax Court.

[92] Sec. 6015.

[93] Reg. Sec. 1.6012-1(a)(5).

The degree of relief available depends on the extent of the electing spouse's knowledge. If the spouse neither knew nor had reason to know of *an understatement,* full relief will be granted. Full relief encompasses liability for taxes, interest, and penalties attributable to the full amount of the understatement. On the other hand, if the spouse either knew or had reason to know of an understatement, but not *the extent of the understatement,* only partial relief will be granted. Partial relief encompasses liability for taxes, interest, and penalties attributable to that portion of the understatement of which the spouse was unaware.

EXAMPLE C:15-36 ▶ Jim and Joy jointly filed a tax return for 2006. Joy fraudulently reported on Schedule C two expenses: one amounting to $4,000 and the other amounting to $3,000. The IRS audits the return, assesses a $2,170 deficiency, and begins its collection efforts on June 2, 2008. If (1) Jim elects innocent spouse relief no later than June 2, 2010, (2) Jim establishes that he neither knew nor had reason to know of the understatement, and (3) if holding Jim liable for the deficiency would be inequitable under the circumstances, Jim will be relieved of liability for the full $2,170. ◀

EXAMPLE C:15-37 ▶ Same facts as in Example C:15-36 except Jim had reason to know the $3,000 expense was fraudulent. If (1) Jim elects innocent spouse relief no later than June 2, 2010, (2) Jim establishes that he neither knew nor had reason to know the *extent* of the understatement (i.e., $7,000 as opposed to $3,000), and (3) if holding Jim liable for the full amount of the deficiency would be inequitable under the circumstances, Jim will be relieved of liability for that portion of the deficiency attributable to the $4,000 expense. ◀

Proportional liability is liability for only that portion of a deficiency attributable to the taxpayer's separate taxable items. A joint filer incurs proportional liability if all the following conditions are met:

- The joint filer elects proportional liability within two years after the IRS begins its collection efforts.
- The electing filer is either divorced or separated at the time of the election.
- The electing filer did not reside in the same household as the other filer at any time during the 12-month period preceding the election.
- The electing filer does not have actual knowledge of any item giving rise to the deficiency.

The electing filer bears the burden of proving the amount of his or her proportional liability. The fraudulent transfer of property between joint filers immediately before the election will invalidate it.

EXAMPLE C:15-38 ▶ Sam and Sue jointly filed a 2005 tax return. Sam intentionally omitted to report $8,000 in gambling winnings. Sue fraudulently deducted $1,600 in business expenses. The IRS audits the return, assesses a $3,600 deficiency, and begins its collection efforts on August 15, 2008. Sam and Sue are subsequently divorced. If Sue (1) elects innocent spouse relief no later than August 16, 2010, (2) did not reside in the same household as Sam at any time during the 12-month period preceding the election, and (3) did not actually know of Sam's omission, she will be liable for only that portion of the deficiency attributable to her fraudulent deduction. ◀

The Effect of Community Property Laws. Community property laws are ignored in determining to whom income (other than income from property) is attributable. For example, if one spouse living in a community property state wins money by gambling, the gambling income is not treated as community property for purposes of the innocent spouse provisions. If the gambling winnings are omitted from a joint return, they are deemed to be solely the income of the spouse who gambled.

TYPICAL MISCONCEPTION

A taxpayer cannot escape paying taxes by transferring assets to a transferee (donee, heir, legatee, etc.) or a fiduciary (executor, trustee, etc.).

TRANSFEREE LIABILITY

Section 6901 authorizes the IRS to collect taxes from persons other than the taxpayer. The two categories of persons from whom the IRS may collect taxes are transferees and fiduciaries. Transferees include donees, heirs, legatees, devisees, shareholders of dissolved corporations, parties to a reorganization, and other distributees.[94] Fiduciaries include executors and administrators of estates. In general, the limitations period for transferees expires one year after the limitations period for transferors. The transferors may be income earners in the case of income taxes, executors in the case of estate taxes, and donors in the case of gift taxes.

EXAMPLE C:15-39 ▶ Lake Corporation is liquidated in the current year, and it distributes all its assets to its sole shareholder, Leo. If the IRS audits Lake's return and assesses a deficiency, Leo (the distributee) is responsible for paying the deficiency. ◀

TAX PRACTICE ISSUES

OBJECTIVE 10

Understand government-imposed standards for tax practitioners

A number of statutes and guidelines address what constitutes proper behavior of CPAs and others engaged in tax practice.[95]

STATUTORY PROVISIONS CONCERNING TAX RETURN PREPARERS

KEY POINT

As evidenced by the formidable list of possible penalties, an individual considering becoming a tax return preparer needs to be aware of certain procedures set forth in the IRC.

Sections 6694-6696 impose penalties on tax return preparers for misconduct. Section 7701(a)(36) defines an income tax return preparer as a "person who prepares for compensation, or who employs one or more persons to prepare for compensation, any return of tax imposed by subtitle A [income tax] or any claim for refund of tax imposed by subtitle A." Preparation of a substantial portion of a return or refund claim is treated as preparation of the full return or claim. These statutory provisions do not affect preparers of estate and gift tax returns and claims for refund of such taxes.

Section 6695 imposes penalties for

- Failure to furnish the taxpayer with a copy of the return or claim ($50 per failure)
- Failure to sign a return or claim ($50 per failure)
- Failure to furnish one's identification number ($50 per failure)
- Failure to keep a copy of a return or claim or, in lieu thereof, to maintain a list of taxpayers for whom returns or claims were prepared ($50 per failure, up to a maximum of $25,000 for a return period)
- Failure to file a return disclosing the names, identification numbers, and places of work of each income tax return preparer employed ($50 per return plus $50 for each failure to set forth an item in the return)
- Endorsement or other negotiation of an income tax refund check made payable to anyone other than the preparer ($500 per check)

The first five penalties are not assessable if the preparer shows that the failure is due to reasonable cause and not willful neglect.[96]

Under Sec. 6694, a preparer will owe a $250 penalty for understating a tax liability if any portion of the understatement is due to a position that does not have a realistic possibility of being sustained on its merits. The preparer will be liable for the penalty if he or she knew, or reasonably should have known, of the position and the position either was frivolous or was not disclosed. If any portion of the understatement results from the preparer's willful attempt to understate taxes or from reckless or intentional disregard of rules or regulations, the penalty will be $1,000.

REAL-WORLD EXAMPLE

In addition to these penalties, the IRS may suspend or bar a tax practitioner from practicing before the IRS. Each week the IRS publishes a list of suspended practitioners.

Regulation Sec. 1.6694-2(b)(2) states that the relevant authorities for the realistic-possibility-of-being-sustained test are the same as those that apply in the substantial authority context. The IRS "will treat a position as having a realistic possibility of being sustained

[94] Reg. Sec. 301.6901-1(b).

[95] Chapter C:1 discusses the AICPA's *Statements on Standards for Tax Services*, which provides guidelines for CPAs engaged in tax practice. See Appendix E for a reproduction of the statements.

[96] Regulation Sec. 1.6695-1(b)(5) states that, for the purpose of avoiding the failure-to-sign penalty, reasonable cause is "a cause which arises despite ordinary care and prudence exercised by the individual preparer."

on 'its merits' if a reasonable and well-informed analysis by a person knowledgeable in the tax law would lead such person to conclude that the position has approximately a one in three, or greater, likelihood of being sustained on its merits."[97]

Regulation Sec. 1.6694-3 states that preparers are considered to have willfully understated taxes if they have attempted to wrongfully reduce taxes by disregarding pertinent information. A preparer generally is deemed to have recklessly or intentionally disregarded a rule or regulation if he or she adopts a position contrary to a rule or regulation about which he or she knows, or is reckless in not knowing about such rule or regulation. A preparer may adopt a position contrary to a revenue ruling if a realistic possibility exists that the position can be sustained on its merits. In addition, a preparer may depart from following a Treasury Regulation without penalty if he or she has a good faith basis for challenging its validity and adequately discloses his or her position on Form 8275-R (Regulation Disclosure Statement).

STOP & THINK

Question: While preparing a client's tax return two days before the due date, Tevin reviews an item that arguably is deductible. He weighs the cost of researching whether the deduction has a realistic possibility of being sustained on its merits. He calculates that researching the issue will cost him $300 in forgone revenues and that not researching the issue will cost him $250 in preparer penalties. What should Tevin do?

Solution: Undoubtedly, Tevin should research the issue and determine whether the deduction either has a realistic possibility of being sustained on the merits or is not frivolous. If it is not frivolous, he should disclose his position on the tax return. At stake here is not merely $300 in foregone revenues but also Tevin's professional reputation. His taking a position that does not meet the realistic possibility standard or that is nonfrivolous but undisclosed subjects not only him as tax preparer, but also his client as taxpayer, to penalties. If the IRS imposes a penalty on the client, the client might terminate the professional relationship with Tevin or sue Tevin for negligence. Besides, Tevin may have miscalculated his own professional liability. If the IRS determines that Tevin recklessly or intentionally disregarded tax rules and regulations, it may impose a penalty of $1,000, not $250.

Tax preparers who offer advice relating to the preparation of a document, knowing that such advice will result in a tax understatement, will be liable for aiding and abetting in the understatement.[98] The penalty for aiding and abetting is $1,000 for advice given to noncorporate taxpayers and $10,000 for advice given to corporate taxpayers. If a preparer is assessed an aiding-and-abetting penalty, the preparer will not be assessed a Sec. 6694 preparer penalty for the same infraction.

TAX SHELTER DISCLOSURES

Section 6111 sets forth the obligations of tax shelter organizers and material advisors. It requires tax shelter organizers to register their tax schemes with the IRS. It also requires material advisors to maintain a list of tax shelter clients and file information returns with the IRS.

For purposes of Sec. 6111, a "tax shelter" is any investment with respect to which a person could reasonably infer that the tax benefits of investing in it exceed the investment amount by a ratio of two to one at the end of a prescribed five-year period. The investment must be required to be registered under state or federal securities law, sold pursuant to a securities law exemption, or offered to five or more investors in an amount exceeding $250,000. A tax shelter includes any entity, plan, arrangement, or transaction a significant purpose of which is to avoid or evade federal income tax law, offered for sale under conditions of confidentiality, and for which the tax shelter promoters may receive fees exceeding $100,000.

A "tax shelter organizer" is a person principally responsible for organizing a tax shelter and, potentially, any other person who participated in its organization, sale, or management. A "material advisor" is any individual who, in return for providing assistance or advice regarding a reportable transaction, derives at least $50,000 of gross income from the activity ($250,000, if derived from a legal entity). A "reportable transaction" is a

[97] Reg. Sec. 1.6694-2(b).

[98] Sec. 6701.

transaction with the potential for tax avoidance or evasion, information for which must be reported in a return or statement. A "listed transaction" is an abusive transaction that the IRS has identified in an official pronouncement.

Failure to disclose a tax shelter, register a tax shelter, keep a client list, or file an information return subjects a taxpayer, tax shelter organizer, or material advisor to severe penalties as follows:

- *Imposed on the taxpayer:* Failure to disclose a tax shelter (ranging from $10,000 to $200,000, depending on the nature of the transaction and the status of the taxpayer)[99]
- *Imposed on the taxpayer:* Accuracy-related penalty for listed and reportable transactions (20% of the understatement for disclosed transactions; 30% for undisclosed transactions)[100]
- *Imposed on the organizer or advisor:* Failure to furnish information on reportable transactions ($50,000; $200,000 or more for listed transactions)[101]
- *Imposed on the organizer or advisor:* Failure to maintain an investor list ($10,000 per day after the twentieth business day following notice)[102]
- *Imposed on the organizer or advisor:* Tax shelter fraud (50% of gross income derivable from the tax shelter)[103]

In addition, if a taxpayer fails to report information regarding a listed transaction on a required return or statement, the limitations period is extended to one year after the earlier of the date on which the information is furnished to the IRS or the date on which a material advisor meets the list maintenance requirements.[104]

RULES OF *CIRCULAR 230*

Treasury Department Circular 230 regulates the practice of attorneys, CPAs, enrolled agents, and enrolled actuaries before the IRS. Practice before the IRS includes representing taxpayers in meetings with IRS audit agents and appeals officers. Tax professionals who do not comply with the rules and regulations of *Circular 230* can be barred from practicing before the IRS and may be subject to censure and/or monetary penalties. Such professionals are entitled to an administrative hearing before being penalized.

Among the rules governing the conduct of practitioners before the IRS are the following:[105]

- If the practitioner knows that a client has not complied with federal tax laws or has made an error in or an omission from any return, the practitioner should promptly advise the client of the error or omission. The practitioner also must advise the client of possible corrective action and the consequences of not taking such action.
- Each person practicing before the IRS must exercise due diligence in preparing returns, determining the correctness of representations made to the Treasury Department, and determining the correctness of representations made to clients about tax matters.

ETHICAL POINT

In deciding whether to adopt a pro-taxpayer position on a tax return or in rendering tax advice, a tax advisor should keep in mind his or her responsibilities under the tax return preparer rules of the IRC, *Treasury Department Circular 230,* and the *Statements on Standards for Tax Services,* especially Statement No. 1. Statement No. 1 (discussed in Chapter C:1 and reproduced in Appendix E) requires that a CPA have a good faith belief that the position adopted on the tax return is supported by existing law or by a good faith argument for extending, modifying, or reversing existing law.

Like Sec. 6694, *Circular 230* provides that a tax practitioner should always give advice or prepare a return based on a position that has a realistic possibility of being sustained on its merits or that is not frivolous and is disclosed (or, a practitioner giving advice should inform the client of the opportunity to avoid a penalty by making a disclosure). The realistic possibility standard is met if a person knowledgeable in the tax law would conclude that the position has approximately a one in three, or greater, chance of being sustained on its merits.[106]

Circular 230 also lists best practices standards for tax advisors.[107] Such standards include the following:

- Communicate clearly with the client regarding the terms of the engagement.

[99] Sec. 6707A.
[100] Sec. 6662A.
[101] Sec. 6707.
[102] Sec. 6708.
[103] Sec. 6700(a).

[104] Sec. 6501(c)(10).
[105] *Treasury Department Circular 230* (2005), Secs. 10.21 and 10.22.
[106] Ibid., Sec. 10.34.
[107] Ibid., Sec. 10.33.

- Establish the relevant facts, evaluate the reasonableness of assumptions or representations, relate the applicable law to the relevant facts, and arrive at a conclusion supported by the law and relevant facts.
- Advise the client of the implications of conclusions reached, including the applicability of accuracy-related penalties.
- Act fairly and with integrity in practice before the IRS.

Finally, *Circular 230* provides detailed requirements for practitioners who provide covered opinions. A "covered opinion" is written advice concerning various tax shelter and other avoidance arrangements.[108]

TAX ACCOUNTING AND TAX LAW

Accountants and lawyers frequently deal with the same issues. These issues pertain to incorporation and merger, bankruptcy and liquidation, purchases and sales, gains and losses, compensation and benefits, and estate planning. Both types of professionals are competent to practice in many of the same areas. In some areas, however, accountants are more competent than lawyers, and in other areas, lawyers are more competent than accountants. What are these areas, and where does one draw the line?

In the realm of federal taxation, achieving a clear delineation always has been difficult. When an accountant prepares a tax return, he or she invariably delves into the intricacies of tax law. When a lawyer gives tax advice, he or she frequently applies principles of accounting. Toward clarifying the responsibilities of each, the AICPA and American Bar Association have issued the *Statement on Practice in the Field of Federal Income Taxation*.[109] This statement indicates five areas in which CPAs and attorneys are equally competent to practice and several areas in which each is exclusively competent to practice. The areas of mutual competence are as follows:

- Preparing federal income tax returns
- Determining the tax effects of proposed transactions
- Representing taxpayers before the Treasury Department
- Practicing before the U.S. Tax Court
- Preparing claims for refunds

Areas in which an accountant is exclusively competent to practice include:

- Resolving accounting issues
- Preparing financial statements included in financial reports or submitted with tax returns
- Advising clients as to accounting methods and procedures
- Classifying transactions and summarizing them in monetary terms
- Interpreting financial results

Areas in which an attorney is exclusively competent to practice include:

- Resolving issues of law
- Preparing legal documents such as agreements, conveyances, trust instruments, and wills
- Advising clients as to the sufficiency or effect of legal documents
- Taking the necessary steps to create, amend, or dissolve a partnership, corporation, or trust
- Representing clients in criminal investigations

State bar and CPA associations have issued similar guidelines for their constituencies, and the courts generally have followed these and the national guidelines.[110]

---

[108] Ibid., Secs. 10.35 and 10.36.

[109] National Conference of Lawyers and Certified Public Accountants, *Statement on Practice in the Field of Federal Income Taxation*, November 1981.

[110] See for example *Lathrop v. Donahue*, 367 U.S. 820, 81 S. Ct. 1826 (1961), *U.S. v. Gordon Buttorff*, 56 AFTR 2d 85-5247, 85-1 USTC ¶9435 (5th Cir., 1985), *Morton L. Simons v. Edgar T. Bellinger*, 643 F.2d 774, 207 U.S. App. D.C. 24 (1980), *Emilio L. Ippolito v. The State of Florida*, 824 F. Supp. 1562, 1993 U.S. Dist. LEXIS 13091 (M.D. Fla., 1993), *In re Application of New Jersey Society of Certified Public Accountants*, 102 N.J. 231, 507 A.2d 711 (1986).

What happens if an accountant oversteps his or her professional bounds? The transgression may constitute the **unauthorized practice of law.** The unauthorized practice of law involves the engagement, by nonlawyers, in professional activities traditionally reserved for the bar. In most states, it is actionable by injunction, damages, or both. Allegations of the unauthorized practice of law typically arise in the context of a billing dispute.[111] The CPA bills a client for professional services, and the client disputes the bill on the ground that the accountant engaged in the unauthorized practice of law. Occasionally, the court sustains the client's allegation and thus denies the accountant the amount in dispute. With this and the public interest in mind, accountants should always confine their practice to areas in which they are most competent.

ACCOUNTANT-CLIENT PRIVILEGE

According to judicial doctrine, certain communications between an attorney and a client are "privileged," i.e., nondiscoverable in the course of litigation. In 1998, Congress extended this privilege to similar communications between a federally authorized tax advisor and a client. A federally authorized tax advisor includes a certified public accountant.

The accountant-client privilege is similar to the attorney-client privilege in two respects. First, it encompasses communications for the purpose of obtaining or giving professional advice. Second, it excludes communications for the sole purpose of preparing a tax return. The accountant-client privilege is dissimilar in three respects. First, it is limited only to *tax* advice. Second, it may be asserted only in a noncriminal tax proceeding before a federal court or the IRS. Third, it excludes written communications between an accountant and a corporation regarding a tax shelter. A tax shelter is any plan or arrangement, a significant purpose of which is tax avoidance or evasion.

EXAMPLE C:15-40 ▶ Alec, Chief Financial Officer of MultiCorp, has solicited the advice of his tax accountant, Louise, concerning a civil dispute with the IRS. Louise has advised Alec in a series of letters spanning the course of five months. An IRS appeals officer asks Louise if he can review the letters. Louise may refuse the officer's request because her professional advice was offered in anticipation of civil litigation and therefore is "privileged." ◀

EXAMPLE C:15-41 ▶ Assume the same facts as in Example C:15-40 except Louise sends Alec a letter concerning a foreign sales scheme. Because Louise communicates tax advice to a corporation concerning a "tax shelter" and because this communication is written, it is *not* privileged. ◀

The creation of an accountant-client privilege reflects Congress' belief that the selection of a tax advisor should not hinge on the question of privilege. It ensures that all tax advice is accorded the same protection regardless of the tax advisor's professional status.

PROBLEM MATERIALS

DISCUSSION QUESTIONS

C:15-1 Describe how the IRS verifies tax returns at its service centers.

C:15-2 Name some of the IRS administrative pronouncements.

C:15-3 **a.** Through what programs has the IRS gathered data to develop its DIF statistical models?

b. How do these programs differ?

c. How has the IRS used these programs to select returns for audit?

C:15-4 On his individual return, Al reports salary and exemptions for himself and seven dependents. His itemized deductions consist of mortgage

[111] See for example, *In re Bercu,* 299 N.Y. 728, 87 N.E.2d 451 (1949), and *Agran v. Shapiro,* 46 AFTR 896, 127 Cal. App.2d 807 (App. Dept. Super. Ct., 1954).

interest, real estate taxes, and a large loss from breeding dogs. On his individual return, Ben reports self-employment income, a substantial loss from partnership operations, a casualty loss deduction equal to 25% of his AGI, charitable contribution deductions equal to 30% of his AGI, and an exemption for himself. Al's return reports higher taxable income than does Ben's. Which return is more likely to be selected for audit under the DIF program? Explain.

C:15-5 The IRS notifies Tom that it will audit his current year return for an interest deduction. The IRS audited Tom's return two years ago for a charitable contribution deduction. The IRS, however, did not assess a deficiency for the prior year return. Is any potential relief available to Tom with respect to the audit of his current year return?

C:15-6 The IRS informs Brad that it will audit his current year employee business expenses. Brad just met with a revenue agent who contends that Brad owes $775 of additional taxes. Discuss briefly the procedural alternatives available to Brad.

C:15-7 What course(s) of action is (are) available to a taxpayer upon receipt of the following notices:
a. The 30-day letter?
b. The 90-day letter?
c. IRS rejection of a claim for a refund?

C:15-8 List the courts in which a taxpayer can begin tax-related litigation.

C:15-9 Why do taxpayers frequently litigate in the Tax Court?

C:15-10 In what situations is a protest letter necessary?

C:15-11 What information should be included in a request for a ruling?

C:15-12 What conditions must the taxpayer meet to shift the burden of proof to the IRS?

C:15-13 In what circumstances will the IRS rule on estate tax issues?

C:15-14 On which of the following issues will the IRS likely issue a private letter ruling and why? In your answer, assume that no other IRS pronouncement addresses the issue and that pertinent Treasury Regulations are not forthcoming.
a. Whether the taxpayer correctly calculated a capital gain reported on last year's tax return.
b. The tax consequences of using stock derivatives in a corporate reorganization.
c. Whether a mathematical formula correctly calculates the fair market value of a stock derivative.
d. Whether the cost of an Internet course that purports to improve existing employment skills may be deducted this year as a business expense.

C:15-15 Tracy wants to take advantage of a "terrific business opportunity" by engaging in a transaction with Homer. Homer, domineering and impatient, wants Tracy to conclude the transaction within two weeks and under the terms proposed by Homer. Otherwise, Homer will offer the opportunity to another party. Tracy is unsure about the tax consequences of the proposed transaction. Would you advise Tracy to request a ruling? Explain.

C:15-16 Provide the following information relating to both individual and corporate taxpayers:
a. Due date for an income tax return assuming the taxpayer requests no extension.
b. Due date for the return assuming the taxpayer files an automatic extension request.
c. Latest possible due date for the return

C:15-17 Your client wants to know whether she must file any documents for an automatic extension to file her tax return. What do you tell her?

C:15-18 A client believes that obtaining an extension for filing an income tax return would give him additional time to pay the tax at no additional cost. Is the client correct?

C:15-19 Briefly explain the rules for determining the interest rate charged on tax underpayments. Is this rate the same as that for overpayments? In which months might the rate(s) change?

C:15-20 In April of the current year, Stan does not have sufficient assets to pay his tax liability for the previous year. However, he expects to pay the tax by August of the current year. He wonders if he should request an extension for filing his return instead of simply filing his return and paying the tax in August. What is your advice?

C:15-21 At what rate is the penalty for underpaying estimated taxes imposed? How is the penalty amount calculated?

C:15-22 The IRS audited Tony's return, and Tony agreed to pay additional taxes plus the negligence penalty. Is this penalty necessarily imposed on the total additional taxes that Tony owes? Explain.

C:15-23 Assume that a taxpayer owes additional taxes as a result of an audit. Give two reasons why the IRS might not impose a substantial understatement penalty on the additional amount owed.

C:15-24 Upon audit, the IRS determines Maria's tax liability to be $40,000. Maria agrees to pay a $7,000 deficiency. Will she necessarily have to pay a substantial understatement penalty? Explain.

C:15-25 Distinguish between the circumstances that give rise to the civil fraud penalty and those that give rise to the negligence penalty.

C:15-26 Distinguish between the burdens of proof the government must meet to prove civil and criminal fraud.

C:15-27 Explain why the government might bring criminal fraud charges against a taxpayer under Sec. 7206 instead of Sec. 7201. Compare the maximum penalties imposed under Secs. 7201, 7203, and 7206.

C:15-28 In general, when does the limitations period for tax returns expire? List four exceptions to the general rule.

C:15-29 What is the principal purpose of the innocent spouse provisions?

C:15-30 According to the IRC preparer provisions, under what circumstances should a CPA sign a tax return as a preparer?

C:15-31 List five IRC penalties that can be imposed on tax return preparers. Does the IRC require a CPA to verify the information a client furnishes?

C:15-32 According to *Treasury Department Circular 230,* what standard should a CPA meet to properly take a position on a tax return?

ISSUE IDENTIFICATION QUESTIONS

C:15-33 You are preparing the tax return of Bold Corporation, which had sales of $60 million. Bold made a $1 million expenditure for which the appropriate tax treatment—deductible or capitalizable—is a gray area. Bold's director of federal taxes and chief financial officer urgently wants to deduct the expenditure. What tax compliance issues should you consider in advising her?

C:15-34 Your client, Hank Goedert, earned $100,000 of salary and received $40,000 of dividends in the current year. His itemized deductions total $37,000. In addition, Hank received $47,000 from a relative who was his former employer. You have researched whether the $47,000 should be classified as a gift or compensation and are confident that substantial authority exists for classifying the receipt as a gift. What tax compliance issues should you consider in deciding whether to include or exclude the amount in Hank's gross income?

C:15-35 The IRS audited the tax returns of Darryl Strawberry, a former major league outfielder. It contended that, between 1986 and 1990, Strawberry earned $422,250 for autograph signings, appearances, and product endorsements, but he reported only $59,685 of income. Strawberry attributed the shortfall to his receipt of cash for autograph sessions and promotional events. He allegedly concealed the cash payments in separate bank accounts of which his CPA was unaware. What tax compliance issues regarding the alleged underreporting are pertinent?

PROBLEMS

C:15-36 *Calculation of Penalties.* Amy files her current year tax return on August 13 of the following year. She pays the amount due without requesting an extension. The tax shown on her return is $24,000. Her current year wage withholding amounts to $15,000. Amy pays no estimated taxes and claims no tax credits on her current year return.

a. What penalties will the IRS likely impose on Amy (ignoring the penalty for underpayment of estimated taxes)? Assume Amy committed no fraud.

b. On what dollar amount, and for how many days, will Amy owe interest?

C:15-37 *Calculation of Penalties.* In the preceding problem, how would your answers change if Amy instead files her return on June 18 and, on September 8 of the following year, pays the amount due? Assume her wage withholding tax amounts to

a. $19,000

b. $24,500

c. How would your answer to Part a change if Amy requests an automatic extension?

C:15-38 *Calculation of Penalties.* The taxes shown on Hu's tax returns for 2006 and 2007 are $5,000 and $8,000, respectively. Hu's wage withholding for 2007 was $5,200, and she paid no estimated taxes. Hu filed her 2007 return on March 17, 2008, but she did not have sufficient funds to pay any taxes on that date. She paid the $2,800 balance due on June 20, 2008. Hu's AGI for 2006 did not exceed $150,000. Calculate the penalties Hu owes with respect to her 2007 tax return.

C:15-39 *Calculation of Penalties.* Ted's 2007 return reported a tax liability of $1,800. Ted's wage withholding for 2007 was $2,200. Because of his poor memory, Ted did not file his 2007 return until May 28, 2008. What penalties (if any) does Ted owe?

C:15-40 *Calculation of Penalties.* Bob, a calendar year taxpayer, files his current year individual return on July 17 of the following year without having requested an extension. His return indicates an amount due of $5,100. Bob pays this amount on November 3 of the following year. What are Bob's penalties for failing to file and failing to pay his tax on time? Assume Bob committed no fraud.

C:15-41 *Calculation of Penalties.* Carl, a calendar year taxpayer, requests an automatic extension for filing his 2007 return. By April 15, 2008, he has paid $20,000 of taxes in the form of wage withholding and estimated taxes. He does not pay any additional tax with his extension request. Carl files his return and pays the balance of the taxes due on June 19, 2008. For 2006, his tax liability was $19,000, and his AGI did not exceed $150,000. What penalties will Carl owe if his 2007 tax is $23,000? $20,800?

C:15-42 *Determination of Interest.* Refer to the preceding problem.

a. Will Carl owe interest? If so, on what amount and for how many days?
b. Assume the applicable interest rate is 6%. Compute Carl's interest payable if his 2007 tax is $23,000. (See Rev. Proc. 95-17, 1995-1 C.B. 556, or a major tax service, for the compounding tables.)

C:15-43 *Penalty for Underpayment of Estimated Taxes.* Ed's tax liability for last year was $24,000. Ed projects that his tax for this year will be $34,000. Ed is self-employed and, thus, will have no withholding. His AGI for last year did not exceed $150,000. How much estimated tax should Ed pay for this year to avoid the penalty for underpaying estimated taxes?

C:15-44 *Penalty for Underpayment of Estimated Taxes.* Refer to the preceding problem. Assume that Ed expects his income for this year to decline and his tax liability for this year to be only $15,000. What minimum amount of estimated taxes should Ed pay this year? What problem will Ed encounter if he pays this minimum amount and his income exceeds last year's because of a large capital gain realized in December of this year?

C:15-45 *Penalty for Underpayment of Estimated Taxes.* Pam's 2006 income tax liability was $23,000. Her 2006 AGI did not exceed $150,000. On April 3, 2008, Pam, a calendar year taxpayer, files her 2007 individual return, which indicates a $30,000 income tax liability (before reduction for withholding). In addition, the return indicates self-employment taxes of $2,600. Taxes withheld from Pam's salary total $20,000; she has paid no estimated taxes.

a. Will Pam owe a penalty for not paying estimated taxes? Explain.
b. What amount (if any) per quarter is subject to the penalty? For what period will the penalty be imposed for each quarter's underpayment?
c. How would your answers to Parts a and b change if Pam's 2007 tax liability (including self-employment taxes) instead were $17,000?

C:15-46 *Penalty for Underpayment of Estimated Taxes.* Amir's projected tax liability for the current year is $23,000. Although Amir has substantial dividend and interest income, he does not pay any estimated taxes. Amir's withholding for January through November of the current year is $1,300 per month. He wants to increase his withholding for December to avoid the penalty for underpaying estimated taxes. Amir's previous year's liability (excluding withholding) is $21,000. His previous year's AGI did not exceed $150,000. What amount should Amir have withheld from his December paycheck? Explain.

C:15-47 *Negligence Penalty.* The IRS audits Tan's individual return for the current year and assesses a $9,000 deficiency, $2,800 of which results from Tan's negligence. What is the amount of Tan's negligence penalty? Does the penalty bear interest?

C:15-48 *Negligence Penalty.* The IRS audits Pearl's current year individual return and determines that, among other errors, she negligently failed to report dividend income of $8,000. The deficiency relating to the dividends is $2,240. The IRS proposes an additional $12,000 deficiency for the other errors that do not involve negligence. What is the amount of Pearl's negligence penalty for the $14,240 in deficiencies?

C:15-49 *Substantial Understatement Penalty.* Carmen's current year individual return reports a $6,000 deduction for a questionable item not relating to a tax-shelter. Carmen does not make a disclosure regarding this item. The IRS audits Carmen's return, and she consents to a deficiency. As a result, her tax liability increases from $20,000 to $21,860. Assume Carmen lacks substantial authority for the deduction.

a. What substantial understatement penalty (if any) will be imposed?
b. Will the penalty bear interest?
c. How would your answer to Parts a and b change if Carmen reported a $20,000 deduction instead of $6,000, and her tax liability increased by $6,200 to $26,200?

C:15-50 ***Substantial Understatement Penalty.*** Refer to Part c of the previous problem. Assume that Carmen discloses her position, which is not frivolous. How would your original answer change assuming the item does not involve a tax shelter?

C:15-51 ***Fraud Penalty.*** Luis, a bachelor, owes $56,000 of additional taxes, all due to fraud.

a. What is the amount of Luis' civil fraud penalty?

b. What criminal fraud penalty might the government impose on Luis under Sec. 7201?

C:15-52 ***Fraud Penalty.*** Hal and Wanda, his wife, are in the 35% marginal tax bracket in the current year. Wanda fraudulently omits from their joint return $50,000 of gross income. Hal does not participate in or know of her fraudulent act. Hal, however, overstates his deductions by $10,000 because of an oversight.

a. If the government successfully proves fraud in a civil suit against Wanda, what fines and/or penalties might she owe? If Hal and Wanda establish that the overstatement is not attributable to fraud, can the government impose a civil fraud penalty on Hal?

b. If the government successfully proves fraud in a criminal suit against Wanda, what fines or penalties might she owe? Could she or Hal be sentenced to prison?

C:15-53 ***Statute of Limitations.*** Frank, a calendar year taxpayer, reports $100,000 of gross income and $60,000 of taxable income on his 2007 return, which he files on March 12, 2008. He fails to report on the return a $52,000 long-term capital gain and a $10,000 short-term capital loss. When does the limitations period for the government's collecting the tax deficiency expire if

a. Frank's omission results from an oversight?

b. His omission results from a willful attempt to evade the tax?

C:15-54 ***Statute of Limitations.*** Refer to the previous problem. Assume Frank commits fraud with respect to his 2007 return as late as October 8, 2009. When does the limitations period for charging Frank with criminal tax fraud expire?

C:15-55 ***Claim for Refund.*** On March 12, 2008, Maria, a calendar year taxpayer, files her 2007 individual return and pays the amount of tax due. She later discovers that she overlooked some deductions that she should have reported on the return. By what date must she file a claim for refund?

C:15-56 ***Innocent Spouse Provisions.*** Wilma earns no income in 2007 but files a joint return with her husband, Hank. Their 2007 return reports $40,000 of gross income and AGI, and $24,000 of taxable income. Hank realizes $12,000 of gambling winnings (no losses) in 2007 but fails to report the winnings on the return. Wilma does not know about Hank's gambling activities, much less his winnings. The IRS audits the 2007 return and assesses additional taxes. Is Wilma entitled to innocent spouse relief? Explain.

C:15-57 ***Innocent Spouse Provisions.*** Joe and Joan file a joint return for the current year. They are in the 35% marginal tax bracket. Unbeknownst to Joe, Joan fails to report on the return the $8,000 value of a prize she won. She, however, used the prize to buy Joe a new boat. Is Joe entitled to innocent spouse relief? Explain.

C:15-58 ***Unauthorized Practice of Law.*** Your client, Meade Technical Solutions, proposes to merge with Dealy Cyberlabs. In advance of the merger, you (a) issue an opinion concerning the FMV of Dealy, (b) prepare pro forma financials for the merged entity to be, (c) draft Meade shareholder resolutions approving the proposed merger, (d) file a shareholder proxy statement with the U.S. Securities and Exchange Commission, and (e) advise Meade's board of directors concerning the advantages of a Type A versus a Type B reorganization. Which of these activities, if any, constitutes the unauthorized practice of law?

C:15-59 ***Unauthorized Practice of Law.*** Your client, Envirocosmetics, recently has filed for bankruptcy. In the course of bankruptcy proceedings, you (a) prepare a plan of reorganization that alters the rights of preferred stockholders, (b) notify the Envirocosmetics' creditors of an impending bulk transfer of the company's assets, (c) review IRS secured claims against these assets, (d) restructure the company's debt by reducing its principal amount and extending its maturity, (e) advise the bankruptcy court as to how this restructuring will impact the company's NOLs. Which of these activities, if any, constitutes the unauthorized practice of law?

C:15-60 ***Accountant-Client Privilege*** Which of the following communications between an accountant and client are privileged?

a. For tax preparation purposes only, client informs the accountant that she contributed $10,000 to a homeless shelter.

b. Client informs the accountant that he forgot to report on his tax return the $5,000 value of a prize and asks how he should correct the error.
c. Client informs the accountant that she no longer will pay alimony to her ex-husband.

C:15-61 *Accountant-Client Privilege.* Which of the following communications between an accountant and client are *not* privileged?
a. In a closed-door meeting, the accountant orally advises the client to set up a foreign subsidiary to shift taxable income to a low-tax jurisdiction.
b. In a closed-door meeting, the accountant submits to the client a plan for shifting taxable income to a low-tax jurisdiction.
c. In soliciting professional advice relating to criminal fraud, the client informs the accountant that he (the client) lied to the IRS.

COMPREHENSIVE PROBLEM

C:15-62 This year, Ark Corporation acquired substantially all the voting stock of BioTech Consultants, Inc. for cash. Subsequent to the acquisition, Ark's chief financial officer, Jonathan Cohen, approached Edith Murphy, Ark's tax advisor, with a question: Could Ark amortize the "general educational skills" of BioTech's employees? Edith researched the issue but found no primary authorities on point. She did, however, find a tax journal article, co-authored by two prominent academics, that endorsed amortizing "general educational skills" for tax purposes. The article referred to numerous primary authorities that support the amortization of "technical skills," but not "general educational skills." Edith consulted these authorities directly. Based on her research, Edith in good faith advised Jonathan that Ark could amortize the "general educational skills" over a 15-year period. In so doing, has Edith met the "realistic possibility standard" of
a. The IRC?
b. The AICPAs *Statements on Standards for Tax Services* (see Appendix E)?

TAX STRATEGY PROBLEM

C:15-63 The IRS is disputing a deduction reported on your 2006 tax return, which you filed on April 12, 2007. On April 2, 2010, the IRS audit agent asks you to waive the statute of limitations for the entire return so as to give her additional time to obtain a Technical Advice Memorandum. The agent proposes in return for the waiver a "carrot"—the prospect of an offer in compromise—and a "stick"—the possibility of a higher penalty. Although you have substantial authority for the deduction, you consider the following alternatives: (1) waive the statute of limitations for the entire return, (2) waive the statute of limitations for the deduction only, or (3) do not waive the statute of limitations in any way, shape, or form. Which alternative should you choose, and why?

CASE STUDY PROBLEM

C:15-64 A long-time client, Horace Haney, wishes to avoid currently recognizing revenue in a particular transaction. A recently finalized Treasury Regulation provides that, in such a transaction, revenue should be currently recognized. Horace insists that you report no revenue from the transaction and, furthermore, that you make no disclosure about contravening the regulation. The IRC is unclear about whether the income should be recognized currently. No relevant cases, revenue rulings, or letter rulings deal specifically with the transaction in question.

Required: Discuss whether you, a CPA, should prepare Horace's tax return and comply with his wishes. Assume that recognizing the income in question would increase Horace's tax liability by about 25%.

TAX RESEARCH PROBLEMS

C:15-65 Art is named executor of the Estate of Stu Stone, his father, who died on February 3 of the current year. Art hires Larry to be the estate's attorney. Larry advises Art that the estate must file an estate tax return but does not mention the due date. Art, a pharmacist, has no experience in tax matters other than preparing his own tax returns. Art provides

Larry with all the necessary information by June 15 of the current year. On six occasions, Art contacts Larry to check on the progress of the estate tax return. Each time, Larry assures Art that "everything is under control." On November 15, Art contacts Larry for the seventh time. He learns that because of a clerical oversight, the return—due on November 2 of the current year—has not been filed. Larry apologizes and says he will make sure that an associate promptly files the return. The return, which reports an estate tax liability of $75,200, is filed on December 7 of the current year. Your manager requests that you prepare a memorandum addressing whether the estate will owe a failure-to-file penalty. Your manager suggests that, at a minimum, you consult

- IRC Sec. 6151(a)
- *U.S. v. Robert W. Boyle,* 55 AFTR 2d 85-1535, 85-1 USTC ¶13,602 (USSC, 1985)

C:15-66 Harold and Betty, factory workers who until this year prepared their own individual tax returns, purchased an investment from a broker last year. Although they reviewed the prospectus for the investment, the broker explained the more complicated features of the investment. Early this year, they struggled to prepare their individual return for last year but, because of the investment, found it too complicated to complete. Consequently, they hired a CPA to prepare the return. The CPA deducted losses generated from the investment against income that Harold and Betty generated from other sources. The IRS audited the return for last year and contended that the loss is not deductible. After consulting their CPA, who further considered the tax consequences of the investment, Harold and Betty agreed that the loss is not deductible and consented to paying the deficiency. The IRS also contended that the couple owes the substantial understatement penalty because they did not disclose the value of the investment on their return and did not have substantial authority for their position. Assume you are representing the taxpayers before the IRS and intend to argue that they should be exempted from the substantial understatement penalty. Your tax manager reminds you to consult Secs. 6662 and 6664 when conducting your research.

C:15-67 Gene employed his attorney to draft identical trust instruments for each of his three minor children: Judy (age 5), Terry (age 7), and Grady (age 11). Each trust instrument names the Fourth City Bank as trustee and states that the trust is irrevocable. It provides that, until the beneficiary reaches age 21, the trustee at its discretion is to pay income and/or principal (corpus) to the beneficiary. Upon reaching age 21, the beneficiary will have 60 days in which to request that the trust assets be paid over to him or her. Otherwise, the assets will stay in the trust until the beneficiary reaches age 35. The beneficiary also is granted a general testamentary power of appointment over the trust assets. If the beneficiary dies before the trust terminates and does not exercise his or her power of appointment (because, for example, he or she dies without a will), trust assets will be distributed to family members in accordance with state intestacy laws. Each trust will be funded with property valued at $100,000. Before he signs the instruments, Gene wants to obtain a ruling from the IRS concerning whether the trusts qualify for the annual gift tax exclusion. Your task is to prepare a request for a letter ruling.

A partial list of research sources is

- IRC Secs. 2503(b) and (c)
- Reg. Sec. 25.2503-4
- Rev. Rul. 67-270, 1967-2 C.B. 349
- Rev. Rul. 74-43, 1974-1 C.B. 285
- Rev. Rul. 81-7, 1981-1 C.B. 474

C:15-68 On April 12, 2006, Adam and Renee Tyler jointly filed a 2005 return that reported AGI of $68,240 ($20,500 attributable to Renee) and a tax liability of $3,050. They paid this amount in a timely fashion. On their return, the Tylers claimed a $18,405 deduction for Adam's distributive share of a partnership loss. If not for the loss, the Tylers' tax liability would have been $8,358. In the previous year, Adam had withdrawn $20,000 cash from the partnership, which he used to buy Renee a new car. Although Renee, a marketing consultant, is not active in the partnership business, she has worked for the partnership as a part-time receptionist. Adam and his partner (who incidentally is Renee's brother) failed to file a partnership return for 2005. Upon audit, the IRS discovered that the 2005 partnership records were missing. In June 2007, Adam had a heart attack. He remains in serious condition. Unable to reach Adam, the IRS sends Renee a 30-day letter proposing a

$5,308 deficiency. She intends to protest. Your supervisor has asked you to write a memorandum discussing Renee's potential liabilities and defenses. In your memorandum, you should consult the following authorities:

- IRC Secs. 6013 and 6662
- *Rebecca Jo Reser v. CIR*, 79 AFTR 2d 97-2743, 97-1 USTC ¶50,416 (5th Cir., 1997)

C:15-69 A colleague comes to you with the following investment proposal that he would like to market for Client:

- Client obtains cash of $60,000 from Bank.
- Bank loan agreement specifies that $40,000 of this amount represents principal; the remaining $20,000 represents interest.
- Client contributes the $60,000 cash to Partnership, which agrees to assume Client's $40,000 debt.
- Under Sec. 752, Partnership's debt assumption is treated as a distribution of money that reduces Client's basis in partnership interest from $60,000 to $20,000.
- Partnership invests the $60,000 in a resort hotel project.
- Before the project comes onstream, Client sells partnership interest for $15,000.

Net result: Partnership, not Client, is responsible for repayment of Bank loan. Client realizes a $5,000 capital loss without having spent any of its own funds.

Prepare a memorandum that sets forth the tax and reporting implications of this investment proposal. At a minimum, consult the following authorities:

- IRC Secs. 6707A and 6111
- Reg. Secs. 1.6111-4 and 301.6112-1
- Notice 2000-44, 2000-2 C.B. 255

CHAPTER 16

U.S. TAXATION OF FOREIGN-RELATED TRANSACTIONS

LEARNING OBJECTIVES

After studying this chapter, you should be able to

1. Understand the principles underlying U.S. authority to tax foreign-related transactions
2. Determine the foreign tax credit available to U.S. taxpayers
3. Calculate the earned income exclusion available to U.S. individuals working abroad
4. Determine whether a foreign citizen is a U.S. resident or nonresident alien
5. Calculate the U.S. tax liability of a nonresident alien
6. Calculate the deemed paid credit available to a U.S. stockholder in a foreign corporation
7. Understand tax provisions applicable to controlled foreign corporations (CFCs)
8. Be aware of special international tax incentives formerly available to U.S. taxpayers
9. Explain the transactional structure and taxation of inversions
10. Understand the financial statement implications of various international transactions

CHAPTER OUTLINE

When making their business decisions, taxpayers must consider the potential U.S. tax consequences of international transactions. These consequences impact whether a foreign business should be conducted directly by a U.S. corporation or indirectly through a foreign subsidiary. They also impact the placement and compensation of U.S. employees abroad. In many cases, these employees can exempt part or all of their foreign salaries and housing allowances from U.S. taxation. Such an exemption reduces the cost of employing American citizens abroad.

This chapter presents a general overview of the U.S. taxation of cross-border and foreign-related transactions. Coverage also includes the U.S. taxation of income derived from domestic and foreign activities conducted by U.S. citizens, resident and nonresident aliens, and domestic and foreign entities.

JURISDICTION TO TAX

OBJECTIVE 1

Understand the principles underlying U.S. authority to tax foreign-related transactions

U.S. authority to tax foreign-related transactions is based on three factors:

- The taxpayer's country of citizenship
- The taxpayer's country of residence
- Where income is earned

The U.S. tax laws prescribe different tax treatments of income items according to the taxpayer's country of citizenship or country of organization. The United States taxes U.S. citizens and corporations[1] on their worldwide income and taxes foreign citizens and corporations primarily on income earned within U.S. territorial limits.

Individuals who are not U.S. citizens are called "aliens." The U.S. income tax laws divide aliens into two classes: resident and nonresident. A **resident alien** is an individual who resides in the United States *but* is not a U.S. citizen. A **nonresident alien** is an individual who resides outside the United States *and* is not a U.S. citizen.

TYPICAL MISCONCEPTION

Many people believe that income earned outside the United States is not subject to taxation by the United States. This belief is incorrect. U.S. citizens, resident aliens, and domestic corporations are taxed by the United States on their worldwide income.

Like U.S. citizens and domestic corporations, resident aliens are taxed on their worldwide income. In general, the same rules apply to the various classes of income they earn, whether the income is earned in the United States, a foreign country, or a U.S. possession. However, certain items of income earned in foreign countries or U.S. possessions are subject to special treatment.

- Compensation received by a U.S. citizen or resident alien who works in a foreign country for an extended period of time is eligible for a special inflation adjusted annual exclusion of up to $82,400 (in 2006).
- The income taxes paid by a U.S. taxpayer to a foreign country or a U.S. possession may be credited against the U.S. tax liability.

To some extent, the tax treatment accorded nonresident aliens and foreign corporations depends on whether they conducted a trade or business in the United States at some time during the year. If they conducted no such activities, the nonresident aliens and foreign corporations are taxed only on their U.S.-source investment income. If they conducted such activities, the nonresident aliens and foreign corporations are taxed on both their U.S.-source investment income and their U.S.-source (and certain foreign-source) income that is connected with the conduct of the U.S. trade or business. Trade or business and investment income earned outside the United States by nonresident aliens and foreign corporations generally escape U.S. taxation.

An overview of international tax issues relating to the various types of tax entities that operate in, or from within, the United States is presented in Table C:16-1. This table gives structure to the following discussion of the U.S. tax rules that apply to foreign-related transactions.

[1] Secs. 7701(a)(3) and (4). A domestic corporation is a corporation created or organized under federal law or the laws of one of the 50 states or the District of Columbia. All other corporations are **foreign corporations**. A domestic corporation includes a noncorporate entity that elects under the check-the-box regulations to be taxed as a corporation. See Chapter C:2.

▼ **TABLE C:16-1**
Overview of International Tax Issues

Entity Form	U.S. Tax Base	U.S. Tax Issues
Individuals:		
U.S. citizen	Worldwide income	1, 2
U.S. resident alien	Worldwide income	1, 2
U.S. nonresident alien	U.S. territorial	3, 4
Corporations:		
U.S. parent with foreign branch	Worldwide income	1, 3
U.S. parent with foreign subsidiary	Worldwide income	1, 5, 6
Foreign parent with U.S. branch	U.S. territorial	3, 4, 6, 7
Foreign parent with U.S. subsidiary	Worldwide	1, 3, 4, 6

U.S. Tax Issues Listing

1. Foreign tax credit
2. Foreign earned income exclusion
3. U.S. income tax liability
4. Withholding of U.S. taxes on payments by U.S. persons to non-U.S. persons
5. Deferral of U.S. taxation of foreign profits
6. Transfer pricing
7. Branch profits tax

TAXATION OF U.S. CITIZENS AND RESIDENT ALIENS

This section examines two foreign tax provisions applicable to U.S. citizens and resident aliens: the foreign tax credit and the foreign-earned income exclusion. Both provisions alleviate the double taxation of income earned by these individuals in a foreign country.

OBJECTIVE 2

Determine the foreign tax credit available to U.S. taxpayers

FOREIGN TAX CREDIT

The **foreign tax credit** alleviates double taxation by allowing U.S. taxpayers to credit income taxes paid or accrued to a foreign country (including its political subdivisions such as provinces and cities) or a U.S. possession[2] against the U.S. income tax liability. The foreign tax credit reduces a U.S. taxpayer's total effective tax rate on income earned in foreign countries or U.S. possessions to the higher of the U.S. or the foreign tax rate.

STOP & THINK

Question: The United States uses the foreign tax credit as its principal mechanism for alleviating double taxation. What are the advantages and disadvantages of the foreign tax credit?

Solution: The foreign tax credit is based on the premise that all taxable income should be subject to the same effective tax rate no matter where it is earned. The U.S. government taxes foreign source income but allows a credit for foreign income taxes paid or accrued up to the amount of U.S. taxes owed on all foreign-source income. The credit system requires that a taxpayer report the income, file a tax return, and apply the credit to reduce

[2] For Sec. 901 purposes, U.S. possessions include Puerto Rico, the Virgin Islands, Guam, the Northern Mariana Islands, and American Samoa.

his or her U.S. tax liability. This requirement ensures the reporting to the U.S. tax authorities of non-U.S. income taxed in a foreign jurisdiction and provides additional U.S. tax revenues to the extent that U.S. tax rates are higher than foreign tax rates. The reporting requirement, however, increases compliance costs for U.S. taxpayers. The credit provides an incentive for foreign governments to raise their tax rates to the level of U.S. tax rates (in the form of "soak up taxes"). Such increases will not alter a taxpayer's worldwide tax costs but will increase tax revenues accruing to a foreign treasury at the expense of the U.S. Treasury.

KEY POINT

This double taxation is caused by two different jurisdictions taxing the same income rather than one jurisdiction taxing the same income twice (such as dividends a shareholder receives from a C corporation).

CREDITABLE TAXES. Income taxes paid or accrued to a foreign country or a U.S. possession may be credited against the U.S. tax liability. Other foreign taxes are deductible under the rules of Sec. 164, which are explained in Chapter I:7 of the companion volume, *Prentice Hall's Federal Taxation: Individuals*. The IRS regularly issues pronouncements relating to the creditability of certain foreign taxes.[3] These pronouncements save taxpayers time and effort in determining whether a specific tax is creditable. Major tax services summarize these pronouncements, as well as judicial decisions concerning creditable taxes.

REAL-WORLD EXAMPLE

The foreign tax credit is the largest U.S. tax credit. In 2003, U.S. corporations claimed $50 billion in foreign tax credits, which is 5.2 times larger than their general business credits. These credits reduced their U.S. tax liability by 20.7%.

ELIGIBILITY FOR THE CREDIT. Section 901(a) permits U.S. citizens and resident aliens to elect to claim a foreign tax credit for income taxes paid or accrued to a foreign country or a U.S. possession. This type of tax credit is known as a *direct credit*. Most taxpayers annually elect to credit their foreign income taxes against their U.S. tax liability. As discussed in the Tax Planning Consideration section of this chapter, however, taxpayers sometimes prefer to deduct their foreign income taxes from gross income.

A taxpayer who uses the accrual method of accounting claims the foreign tax credit in the year in which the tax accrues. A taxpayer who uses the cash method of accounting claims the foreign tax credit in the year in which the tax is paid unless the taxpayer makes a special election to accrue the tax (the advantages of this election are discussed in the Tax Planning Considerations section of this chapter).

ADDITIONAL COMMENT

Foreign income taxes also are deductible under Sec. 164. However, taxpayers may not both deduct and credit the same foreign income taxes. Whether a taxpayer credits or deducts the foreign income taxes is an annual election.

TRANSLATION OF THE FOREIGN TAX PAYMENTS. Determining the credit amount necessitates translating the tax paid or accrued in a foreign currency into U.S. dollars. To do the translation, cash method taxpayers use the exchange rate as of the payment date. Accrual method taxpayers use the average exchange rate for the tax year over which the tax accrues. They may elect to translate the tax amount into U.S. dollars based on the exchange rate prevailing on the payment date, provided the tax is denominated in a currency other than that used in the taxpayer's regular course of business. (The latter currency is referred to as the taxpayer's "functional currency.") If accrual method taxpayers pay their taxes two years after the close of the tax year to which the taxes relate, they must use the exchange rate prevailing on the payment date to account for any potential currency fluctuation.[4]

EXAMPLE C:16-1 ▶ U.S. citizen Bill is a resident of Country A during the current year. Country A permits its residents to make a single tax payment on the first day of the third month following the close of the tax year. Bill's tax year for both U.S. and Country A tax reporting is the calendar year. Bill remits a 60,000 pirog payment for current year Country A taxes on March 1 of the following year. The average pirog-U.S. dollar exchange rate for the current calendar year is 1 pirog = $0.50 (U.S.). The exchange rate on the March 1 payment date is 1 pirog = $0.60 (U.S.). If Bill uses the cash method of accounting (and does not elect to accrue his foreign taxes), he can claim a $36,000 (60,000 pirogs × $0.60) foreign tax credit. If Bill uses the accrual method of accounting, he can claim a $30,000 (60,000 pirogs × $0.50) foreign tax credit based on the average dollar/pirog exchange rate for the accrual period. ◀

[3] Reg. Sec. 1.901-2. See, for example, Rev. Rul. 91-45, 1991-2 C.B. 336, relating to the creditability of the Mexican asset tax and the Mexican income tax.

[4] Temp. Reg. Sec. 1.905-3T. An amended U.S. tax return must be filed to report the increase or decrease in the credit amount if the taxpayer has filed his or her U.S. tax return by the date the foreign tax is paid. The average exchange rate translation method applies to 1998 and later tax years.

ADDITIONAL COMMENT

The numerator of the limiting fraction is U.S. taxable income from foreign sources. The foreign taxes actually paid or accrued are computed using the tax laws of the foreign jurisdiction. Because these tax laws may differ significantly from the U.S. tax laws, determining whether the fraction is a limiting factor cannot necessarily be determined by simply comparing the statutory tax rates of the two countries.

FOREIGN TAX CREDIT LIMITATION.

Calculating the General Limitation. Congress enacted the foreign tax credit limitation to prevent taxpayers from crediting foreign taxes owed on income earned outside the United States against U.S. taxes owed on income earned in the United States. This limit, which corresponds to the amount of U.S. tax payable on income earned outside the United States, is calculated as follows:

$$\text{Foreign tax credit limitation} = \text{Total U.S. tax liability} \times \frac{\text{Foreign source taxable income}}{\text{Total worldwide taxable income}}$$

The foreign tax credit equals the lesser of (1) creditable taxes paid or accrued to all foreign countries and U.S. possessions or (2) the foreign tax credit limitation. The limitation permits taxpayers to offset during the same tax year "excess" foreign taxes paid in one country against "excess" limitation amounts relative to taxes paid in other countries (known as cross-crediting). However, the total foreign taxes paid or accrued on foreign source taxable income may not exceed the total U.S. tax due on such income.[5] Also, only foreign taxes allocable to the same income baskets (discussed later) may be cross-credited. Before claiming the foreign tax credit, individuals must reduce taxable income by nonrefundable credits allowed under Secs. 21–26.[6]

EXAMPLE C:16-2 ▶ U.S. citizen Theresa earns $10,000 of taxable income (wages) from U.S. sources and $20,000 of taxable income (wages) from Country B in the current year. Theresa pays $6,000 of taxes to Country B in the current year. Assuming a 25% U.S. tax rate, Theresa's gross U.S. tax liability is calculated as follows:

Source of Income	*Taxable Income*	*U.S. Tax Liability before FTC*
United States	$10,000	$2,500
Country B	20,000	5,000
Total	$30,000	$7,500

Theresa's foreign tax credit limitation is determined as follows:

$$\$5{,}000 = \$7{,}500 \times \frac{\$20{,}000}{\$30{,}000}$$

Without a foreign tax credit limitation, Theresa could credit $1,000 of Country B taxes against the $2,500 of U.S. taxes assessed on her U.S. income. Accordingly, an unlimited credit would decrease her U.S. tax liability to $1,500 ($7,500 − $6,000). The foreign tax credit limitation, however, reduces the amount of foreign tax that Theresa can credit to the extent of U.S. taxes owed on the Country B income, or $5,000. This limitation ensures that Theresa pays the full $2,500 of U.S. taxes assessed on her U.S. income. The $1,000 ($6,000 − $5,000) excess credit carries back and over to other tax years as discussed below. ◀

SELF-STUDY QUESTION

Kathy Richards, a U.S. citizen, earns active business income of $100,000 in Country X, $200,000 in Country Z, and $200,000 in the United States. She pays $10,000 in taxes to X and $90,000 in taxes to Z. Assume a 35% U.S. tax rate. What is Richards's post-credit U.S. tax liability?

ANSWER

Pre-credit U.S. tax = $175,000 ($500,000 × 0.35). The credit is the lesser of the $100,000 ($10,000 + $90,000) of foreign taxes paid or the $105,000 ($175,000 × 300/500) foreign tax credit limitation. Although Richards pays taxes to Country Z at a much higher rate (45%) than the U.S. rate, all the foreign taxes are creditable because the limit is computed on an overall basis and because the Country X tax rate is so low (5%).

Section 904(j) exempts an individual with less than $300 of creditable foreign taxes ($600 for joint filers) from the foreign tax credit limitation, provided his or her foreign source income is exclusively passive.

Determining the Income Amounts. The taxable income amount in the numerator of the credit limitation formula is determined according to the source of income ("sourcing") rules found in Secs. 861–865. These rules are summarized as follows:

- ▶ *Personal service income:* Compensation for personal services is considered to be earned in the place where the taxpayer performs the services.

[5] Sec. 904(a). An "excess" foreign tax amount is the excess of the foreign taxes paid or accrued over the foreign tax credit limitation. An "excess" limitation amount is the excess of the foreign tax credit limitation over foreign taxes paid or accrued.

[6] Sec. 904(h).

- *Sales of personal property (other than inventory):* Income derived from a U.S. resident's sale of noninventory personal property (e.g., investment securities) is considered to be earned in the United States. Income derived from a nonresident's sale of such property is considered to be earned outside the United States.[7]
- *Sales of inventory:* Income derived from the sale of merchandise inventory (i.e., final goods purchased for resale) is considered to be earned in the country where the sale occurs. Income derived from the sale of manufactured inventory (i.e., goods manufactured and sold) is considered to be earned partly in the country of manufacture and partly in the country of sale.[8]
- *Sales of real property:* Income derived from the sale of real property is considered to be earned in the country where the property is located.
- *Rents and royalties:* Rents are considered to be earned in the place where the tangible property is located, and royalties in the place where the intangible property (e.g., patent, copyright, or trademark) is used. The latter rule applies to the sale of intangible property if the sale is contingent on the productivity, use, or disposition of the property.
- *Interest income:* Interest generally is considered to be earned in the debtor's country of residence. For purpose of this rule, a U.S. resident includes a foreign partnership or foreign corporation that has derived most of its income from a U.S. trade or business over the past three years.
- *Dividends:* Dividends generally are considered to be earned in the distributing corporation's country of incorporation.

In deriving foreign-source taxable income, a taxpayer allocates deductions and losses to foreign-source gross income according to the rules outlined in Reg. Sec. 1.861-8.

- For individual taxpayers, taxable income is computed without any reduction for personal exemptions.
- In general, deductions are matched with the income with which they are associated.
- Deductions not associated with a specific class of income (such as itemized deductions and the standard deduction) are allocated ratably among all classes of income.

Foreign Tax Credit Carrybacks and Carryovers. Excess foreign tax credits can be carried back one year and carried over ten years to a tax year in which the taxpayer has an excess foreign tax credit limitation (i.e., an unused limitation amount). The total of the foreign taxes paid or accrued in a tax year, plus any carryback or carryover to that year, cannot exceed the taxpayer's foreign tax credit limitation. When a taxpayer reports excess credits in more than one year, the excess credits are used on a first-in, first-out (FIFO) basis.[9]

EXAMPLE C:16-3 ▶ U.S. citizen Kathy accrues $95,000 of creditable foreign taxes in 2007. Kathy's 2007 foreign tax credit limitation is $80,000. The $15,000 of 2007 excess credits carry back to 2006, then over to 2008 through 2017, until used up. The credit carryback and carryover procedure is illustrated below:

	2006	*2007*	*2008*
Foreign tax accrual	$ 90,000	$95,000	$100,000
Foreign tax credit limitation	100,000	80,000	95,000
Excess credits		15,000	
Excess limitation	10,000		5,000

[7] Sec. 865(a). Income derived by a nonresident alien from the sale of personal property (including inventory) attributable to an office or place of business located in the United States is considered to be earned in the United States. Section 865(g) defines the terms *resident* and *nonresident* for the purpose of personal property sales. The definition generally is based on the individual's domicile.

[8] Sec. 865(b) and Reg. Secs. 1.863-3(b) and (c). For tax purposes, an inventory sale generally occurs at the location where title passes from the buyer to the seller. The IRS may depart from this general rule where the primary purpose of the sale is tax-avoidance .

[9] Sec. 904(c). For foreign tax credits arising before October 23, 2004, the carryback period is two years, and the carryover period is five years.

The excess credits first carry back to 2006, and Kathy must file an amended return for 2006 to claim the $10,000 carryback. The remaining $5,000 ($15,000 − $10,000) of excess credits carry over to 2008. If the carryover is not fully used before 2017, the remainer will expire. ◀

ADDITIONAL COMMENT

U.S. corporate tax rates tend to be lower than the tax rates of many foreign jurisdictions. This fact, coupled with the imposition of separate limitation baskets, has caused about 70% of all U.S. multinational corporations to remain in an excess foreign tax credit position.

Special Foreign Tax Credit Limitations. For some taxpayers, more than one foreign tax credit calculation is required. Before 2007, the Sec. 904 foreign tax credit limitation rules created nine baskets of income, for which separate foreign tax credit limitation calculations had to be made.[10] Common baskets included:

- Passive income: Income classified as foreign personal holding company income (see page C:16-26). This basket generally includes dividends, interest, annuities, rents, and royalties.
- High withholding tax interest: Interest income subject to tax withholding (or similar gross-basis tax) at a rate of at least 5% in a foreign country or U.S. possession.
- Financial services income: Income derived from (1) the active conduct of a banking, financing, or similar business, or the investment activities of an insurance company or (2) insurance activities under the Subpart F rules (see page C:16-26).
- Foreign oil and gas income.
- General limitation income, which is a residual basket that contains all other income.

Beginning in 2007, the number of foreign tax credit limitation baskets is reduced two, one for passive income and the other for general limitation income. The separate baskets prevent taxpayers from cross-crediting excess foreign taxes levied on one type of income against excess limitations associated with another type of income. Without the separate baskets, taxpayers could "load up" on income items traditionally taxed at low rates to inflate the numerator in the foreign tax credit limitation formula without increasing the total amount of taxes to be credited.

Dividends received by a U.S. shareholder from a foreign corporation in which the shareholder owns at least a 10% equity stake, as well as interest, rents, and royalties received by a U.S. shareholder from a controlled foreign corporation (i.e., a majority-U.S.-owned foreign corporation) are treated as income earned in the separate baskets on a look-through basis (i.e., as if the foreign corporation were a conduit entity).

Compensation and manufacturing income fall into the general limitation basket. Taxpayers who earn such income exclusively must make one foreign tax credit calculation. Other taxpayers must make two or three calculations. Many large multinational corporations must make all calculations.

Excess foreign taxes in one basket cannot offset excess limitation amounts in another basket. Because items in each basket must be accounted for separately, taxpayers generally cannot use excess credits arising from foreign taxes paid or accrued at a high rate (e.g., taxes on salary or business profits in one basket) to offset U.S. taxes owed on income taxed by a foreign country at a low rate or not taxed at all (e.g., taxes on interest or dividends).

EXAMPLE C:16-4 ▶ Assume the same facts as in Example C:16-2 except, in Country C, Theresa also earns $15,000 of interest income that is not subject to local taxation. The additional U.S. tax liability resulting from this interest income is $3,750 ($15,000 × 0.25). Theresa's total U.S. tax liability is $11,250 ($7,500 [from Example C:16-2] + $3,750). Two foreign tax credit limitations must be calculated for Theresa:

$$\text{Interest income } \$3{,}750 = \$11{,}250 \times \frac{\$15{,}000}{\$45{,}000}$$

$$\text{Wages } \$5{,}000 = \$11{,}250 \times \frac{\$20{,}000}{\$45{,}000}$$

[10] Sec. 904(d)(1). Other less common baskets include taxable income attributable to a foreign sales corporation (FSC) (see page C:16-31) and distributions from a FSC or former FSC.

SELF-STUDY QUESTION

Do any limitations restrict the carryback or carryforward of excess foreign taxes?

ANSWER

Yes. The carryback and carryover provision can occur only within the separate baskets. In Example C:16-4, the $1,000 of excess foreign taxes can be offset only against an excess limitation in the general limitation basket for a carryback or carryover year.

Theresa's foreign tax credit position is summarized in the following table:

Type of Income Earned	*U.S. Tax Liability before FTC*	*Foreign Taxes Paid or Accrued*	*Foreign Tax Credit Limitation*	*U.S. Tax Liability after FTC*	*Excess Foreign Tax Payments*
Interest	$ 3,750	$ -0-	$3,750	$3,750	$ -0-
Wages	7,500	6,000	5,000	2,500	1,000
Total	$11,250	$6,000	$8,750	$6,250	$1,000

Theresa can claim a $5,000 foreign tax credit—the lesser of the $5,000 foreign tax credit limitation or the $6,000 foreign tax paid—for the Country B wages. She can claim no foreign tax credit for the Country C interest income because she paid no foreign tax on this income. Even though the interest income is foreign-source and U.S. taxpayers calculate the foreign tax credit limitation based on worldwide income, the $1,000 of excess taxes paid on the Country B wages cannot be used to offset the U.S. taxes owed on the Country C interest income because the interest income is included in the passive income basket and the salary income is included in the general limitation basket. Theresa can carry the excess foreign taxes allocable to the general limitation basket back to the preceding tax year then forward up to ten years. ◀

Topic Review C:16-1 summarizes the foreign tax credit provisions. A discussion of the financial statement implications of the foreign tax credit appears at the end of this chapter.

FOREIGN-EARNED INCOME EXCLUSION

OBJECTIVE 3

Calculate the earned income exclusion available to U.S. individuals working abroad

Special income exclusions are available to individuals working in foreign countries, Puerto Rico, and certain U.S. possessions. One such exclusion—the foreign earned income exclusion under Sec. 911—is important to employers because it provides tax relief to their U.S. employees stationed in foreign countries. Many such employers reimburse their overseas employees for their incremental worldwide tax costs relative to the costs they would have incurred had they stayed in the United States. By reducing the U.S. tax liability of these employees, the Sec. 911 exclusion decreases the amount of this reimbursement and thus reduces employers' costs.

U.S. CITIZENS AND RESIDENT ALIENS WORKING ABROAD. The United States taxes U.S. citizens and resident aliens, including those working abroad, on their worldwide income. While working outside the country, these taxpayers may incur additional costs to

Topic Review C:16-1

Foreign Tax Credit

- Foreign income taxes paid or accrued to a foreign country or a U.S. possession are deductible or creditable by U.S. taxpayers.
- The election to deduct or credit foreign taxes is made annually. Generally, a taxpayer will elect to credit foreign taxes because of the dollar-for-dollar tax benefit derived from a credit as opposed to a deduction.
- Cash method taxpayers can elect to accrue their foreign taxes. This election can accelerate by one year the time for claiming the credit and may reduce the need to carry back or carry over excess credits.
- A direct credit is available for foreign taxes paid or accrued by the taxpayer, as well as for foreign taxes withheld by a foreign payer.
- Foreign taxes generally are translated into U.S. dollars at the exchange rate for the date on which they are paid or the period over which they accrue, depending on the taxpayer's accounting method.
- The foreign tax credit limitation prevents crediting foreign taxes against the U.S. tax liability on U.S. source income. The amount of credit that can be claimed is the lesser of (a) the creditable taxes paid or accrued to all foreign countries and U.S. possessions, or (b) the overall foreign tax credit limitation. Excess credits carry back one year and then forward ten years. Taxpayers must account for the credit by income type, or foreign tax credit basket. An excess credit in one basket cannot offset an excess credit limitation in another basket.

maintain the same standard of living they enjoyed in the United States. In addition, they may endure inconveniences, substandard living conditions, hardships, or political hazards that warrant additional compensation in the form of special allowances. The allowances may be taxed by both the United States and the country of residence. The U.S. employer generally reimburses U.S. employees for these incremental tax costs to relieve them of any increased tax burden. The total compensation package can make hiring a U.S. citizen or resident alien more expensive than hiring a foreign resident or citizen with the same set of skills.

ADDITIONAL COMMENT

The foreign income exclusion is elective and is made by filing Form 2555 with the income tax return (or amended return) for the first tax year for which the election is to be effective. A completed Form 2555 is reproduced in Appendix B.

To enable U.S. firms to compete abroad, the U.S. government established a policy of reducing the U.S. tax burden on U.S. citizens and resident aliens living abroad for an extended period of time. Taxpayers who are bona fide residents of a foreign country (or countries) for an entire tax year, or who are physically present in a foreign country (or countries) for 330 full days[11] out of a 12-month period, could exclude up to $82,400 of foreign-earned income from their gross income in 2006.[12] This benefit, which is known as the *foreign-earned income exclusion,* is indexed for inflation and is available to taxpayers who meet one of two tests: the bona fide residence test or the physical presence test.

KEY POINT

Whether a U.S. citizen has established foreign residency is based on all the pertinent facts and circumstances. This rule is different from the determination of whether a foreign citizen has established U.S. residency. The latter is based on either the green card test or the substantial physical presence test (discussed later in this chapter).

BONA FIDE RESIDENCE TEST. A U.S. citizen (but not a resident alien) satisfies the bona fide residence test of Sec. 911(d)(1)(A) if he or she has resided in a foreign country (or countries) for an uninterrupted period that includes an entire tax year and has maintained a tax home in a foreign country (or countries) during the period of residence.

For Sec. 911 purposes, an individual's tax home is defined in the same way it is for determining the deductibility of travel expenses incurred while away from home on business.[13] In other words, an individual's tax home is his or her regular or principal place of business. Temporary absences from the foreign country for trips back to the United States or to other foreign countries normally do not disqualify foreign residency.

An individual is not a bona fide resident of a foreign country if he or she submits to the taxing authorities of that country a statement claiming to be a nonresident and obtains from that country's taxing authorities an earned income exemption based on nonresident status.[14] An individual does not qualify for the foreign earned income exclusion until he or she has been a foreign resident for an *entire tax year.* At the end of that period, the individual can retroactively claim Sec. 911 benefits from the date he or she became a foreign resident.

EXAMPLE C:16-5 ▶

U.S. citizen Mark, who uses the calendar year as his tax year, is transferred by his employer to Country P. Mark becomes a Country P resident upon his arrival at noon on July 15, 2004. At that time, Mark establishes his tax home in P's capital. Mark's residency in P is maintained until his return to the United States at 2 p.m. on January 10, 2008. Mark first qualifies as a bona fide resident of a foreign country on December 31, 2005 after a full tax year. This qualification permits Mark to claim the foreign earned income exclusion as of July 15, 2004. Mark can continue to claim the exclusion through January 10, 2008. ◀

TYPICAL MISCONCEPTION

A day is not just any 24-hour period. To count a day, the taxpayer must be in a foreign country for a period of 24 hours beginning and ending at midnight.

SELF-STUDY QUESTION

During a 12-month period, U.S. citizen Robert's work requires him to be physically present in a foreign country for 317 days. If Robert delays his return to the U.S. by vacationing overseas for 13 more days, will he qualify for the foreign-earned income exclusion?

ANSWER

Yes. The foreign physical presence can be for any reason.

PHYSICAL PRESENCE TEST. A taxpayer who cannot satisfy the bona fide residence test still can qualify for Sec. 911 benefits by satisfying the physical presence test of Sec. 911(d)(1)(B). To do so, the taxpayer must meet two requirements:

- Be physically present in a foreign country (or countries) for at least 330 *full* days during a 12-month period.
- Maintain a tax home in a foreign country (or countries) during the period of physical presence.

The 330 days need not be consecutive, nor must the taxpayer be in the same country at all times. The 12-month period may begin on any day of the calendar year. The period ends on the day before the corresponding calendar day in the twelfth succeeding month.

---

[11] A full day is a continuous 24-hour period beginning with midnight and ending with the following midnight.

[12] The $80,000 foreign earned income exclusion applies for years 2002–2005. After 2005, the amount is adjusted for inflation.

[13] Sec. 911(d)(3).

[14] Sec. 911(d)(5). The Sec. 911 bona fide residence test is different from the Sec. 7701(b) test used to determine whether an alien individual is a resident or nonresident of the United States. The latter test is discussed on page C:16-14.

EXAMPLE C:16-6 ▶ Assume the same facts as in Example C:16-5. The 330 days of physical presence begin with the first full day Mark is present in Country P (July 16, 2004) and include a total of 169 days through the end of 2004. The 161 additional days needed to complete the 330 day period include January 1, 2005, through June 10, 2006. One possible 12-month period for Mark thus begins on July 16, 2004, and runs through July 15, 2005. An alternative 12-month period might be June 11, 2004, through June 10, 2005, where the 330 days of physical presence fall at the end of the period. ◀

ADDITIONAL COMMENT

Note that in Example C:16-6, Mark would prefer to use the 12-month period of June 11, 2004, through June 9, 2005, when computing the exclusion for 2005 to have more days of the year in the qualifying period and, hence, a larger exclusion. This 12-month period places the 330 days of qualifying time at the end of the 12-month period.

FOREIGN EARNED INCOME DEFINED. For purposes of the exclusion, earned income means wages, salaries, professional fees, and other compensation for personal services actually rendered.[15] Earned income is excludable only if it is foreign source. The sourcing rules previously discussed are used to determine whether income is earned in the United States or a foreign country. In general, income is sourced according to where the services are performed. If the taxpayer performs services in more than one location during the tax year, the income must be allocated between the two or more locations based on the number of days worked at each location.[16]

Fringe benefits excluded from gross income under an IRC provision other than Sec. 911 (e.g., meals and lodging furnished for the convenience of the employer, excludible under Sec. 119) do not diminish the excludible amount. Items that generally are taxable to the recipient, but which do not comprise earned income for Sec. 911 purposes, include pensions and annuities, compensation paid by the United States or one of its agencies to an employee,[17] and amounts received more than one tax year after the tax year in which services are performed.

AMOUNT OF THE EXCLUSION. The foreign earned income exclusion is available only for the number of days in the tax year during which the taxpayer meets either the bona fide residence test or the physical presence test. Section 911(b)(2)(A) limits the foreign earned income exclusion to the lesser of the following:

- ▶ The individual's foreign-earned income
- ▶ The amount of the daily exclusion times the number of days during the tax year that the individual qualifies for the exclusion

The 2006 annual and daily limits were $82,400 and $225.75 ($82,400 ÷ 365), respectively. For 2004 and 2005, the annual limit was $80,000, and the daily limits were $218.58 ($80,000 ÷ 366) and $219.18 ($80,000 ÷ 365), respectively.

EXAMPLE C:16-7 ▶ U.S. citizen Lee, who uses the calendar year as his tax year, establishes a tax home and residency in Country A on November 1, 2004 (the 306th day of the year). Lee maintains his tax home and residency until March 31, 2006 (the 90th day), when Lee returns to the United States. While employed abroad, Lee earns salary and allowances at $15,000 monthly. Lee's exclusion is calculated as follows:

Tax Year	*Foreign-Earned Income*	*Qualifying Days (1)*	*Daily Exclusion Amount (2)*	*Total Amount Excluded (3) = (1) × (2)*
2004	$ 30,000	61	218.58	$13,333
2005	180,000	365	219.18	80,000
2006	45,000	90	225.75	20,318 ◀

Individuals satisfying the bona fide residence test can claim the exclusion for each day they "reside" in a foreign country whether or not they are physically present in that country on each day. Individuals satisfying the physical presence test can claim the exclusion for each day of a 12-month period that falls within the tax year whether or not they are physically present in a foreign country on all 365 days. Because an individual need only be

[15] Sec. 911(d)(2).

[16] Sec. 911(b)(1)(A).

[17] Civilian officers and employees of the U.S. Government who are employed abroad can exclude from gross income certain foreign area and cost-of-living allowances under Sec. 912.

physically present in a foreign country for 330 days out of the 12-month period (365 days in a non-leap year, 366 days in a leap year) and because the exclusion applies to income earned during the full 12-month period, an individual might qualify for the exclusion for as many as 35 days before arrival in the foreign country or as many as 35 days after departure from the foreign country. Such an extension of the qualifying period in the year of arrival or departure may favor calculating the exclusion for these years based on the physical presence test.[18]

EXAMPLE C:16-8 ▶ Assume the same facts as in Example C:16-7 except Lee was physically present in Country A at all times from his arrival in 2004 to his departure in 2006. Lee's first 330 full days in Country A extend from November 2, 2004, through September 27, 2005. Lee's last 330 full days in Country A extend from May 5, 2005, through March 30, 2006. Lee's two corresponding 12-month periods extend from September 27, 2004 (the 270th day of 2004) through September 26, 2005, and from May 5, 2005, through May 4, 2006 (the 124th day of 2006). The amount of Lee's exclusion is calculated below:

Taxable Year	*Foreign-Earned Income*	*Qualifying Days (1)*[19]	*Daily Exclusion Amount (2)*	*Amount Excluded (3) = (1) × (2)*
2004	$ 30,000	96	$218.58*	$20,984
2005	180,000	365	219.18	80,000
2006	45,000	124	225.75	27,993

*Based on 366 days in a leap year.

Lee obtains a larger exclusion in 2004 and 2006 under the physical presence test because he effectively gets credit for the additional 35 days extending beyond the 330 day period, but included in the corresponding 12-month period. ◀

KEY POINT

A taxpayer may elect to use or not use the foreign-earned income exclusion and the housing cost exclusion. Once made, the exclusion election is effective for that year and all subsequent years. See pages C:16-34 and C:16-35 for a discussion of why a taxpayer might elect out of the Sec. 911 exclusion.

HOUSING COST EXCLUSION OR DEDUCTION. Section 911 permits a taxpayer who is eligible for the foreign earned income exclusion to exclude or deduct a **housing cost amount**, which is determined as follows:

$$\text{Housing cost amount} = \text{Housing expenses} - \text{Base housing amount}$$

$$\text{Base housing amount} = 0.16 \times \text{Maximum foreign earned income exclusion} \times \frac{\text{Number of qualifying days in the tax year}}{\text{Number of days in the tax year}}$$

For 2006, the maximum foreign earned income exclusion is $82,400.[20] Thus, for taxpayers qualifying for Sec. 911 benefits for the entire tax year, the base housing amount for 2006 is $13,184, and the daily base housing amount is $36.12.

Housing costs include any reasonable expense paid or incurred for foreign housing for the taxpayer, his or her spouse, and any dependents during the part of the year the taxpayer qualifies for Sec. 911 benefits. Housing costs also include expenses incurred for a second home outside the United States if, because of adverse living conditions, the taxpayer must maintain a home for his or her spouse and dependents at a location other than the tax home.[21]

ADDITIONAL COMMENT

Employer-provided amounts include all compensation provided by the employer (salary, bonus, allowances, etc.), not just the amount identified as the housing allowance.

The exclusion is limited to 30% of the maximum foreign earned income exclusion (computed on a daily basis). Employer-provided amounts encompass any income that is foreign earned and included in the employee's gross income (without regard to Sec. 911 benefits) for the tax year. Such amounts include, but are not limited to, salary or allowances paid by the

[18] Reg. Sec. 1.911-3(d).

[19] September 27, 2004, through December 31, 2004, encompasses 96 days, and January 1, 2006, through May 4, 2006, encompasses 124 days.

[20] As of this text's publication date, the government has not released the corresponding figure for 2007.

[21] Sec. 911(c)(2). The IRS provides a list of countries with adverse living conditions. Individuals residing in these countries were required to leave them because of war, civil unrest, or other similar conditions that precluded the normal conduct of business. The most recent list appeared in Rev. Proc. 2004-17, 2004-10 I.R.B. 562, that covered tax year 2003.

employer (including allowances other than for housing), reimbursements to the employee for housing expenses, in-kind housing (other than that excluded under Sec. 119), and reimbursements to third parties on behalf of the employee.

EXAMPLE C:16-9 ▶ U.S. citizen John is a bona fide resident of Country M for all of 2006. John, who uses the calendar year as his tax year, receives $120,000 in salary and allowances from his employer. Included in this total is a $15,000 housing allowance. In 2006, John incurred eligible housing expenses of $18,000. Thus, John's housing cost amount is $4,816 ($18,000 − $13,184). Because this amount is less than the foreign housing cost limit of $24,720 (0.30 × $82,400), John can exclude the full housing cost amount. In addition, he can exclude $82,400 of his foreign earned income because he qualified for all of 2006. Therefore, his total exclusion is $87,216 ($4,816 + $82,400), so only $32,784 ($120,000 − $87,216) of his total compensation is subject to U.S. taxation. ◀

ADDITIONAL COMMENT

If an individual has only W-2 income (no self-employment income), he or she is eligible for only the housing cost exclusion because the entire housing cost amount is attributable to employer-provided amounts. The housing cost exclusion and deduction can both be taken only in situations where an individual has both W-2 income and self-employment income. Proration of the housing cost amount between a deduction and an exclusion is based on the relative amounts of the taxpayer's W-2 income and self-employment income.

Any portion of the housing cost amount that is not provided by an employer is a *for*-AGI deduction.[22] Thus, if an individual has only self-employment income, the entire housing cost amount is deductible. Such would be the case in Example C:16-9 if John were self-employed and the $120,000 were commission income. His $4,816 housing cost amount could be claimed only as a *for*-AGI deduction.

The housing cost deduction is limited to the taxpayer's foreign earned income minus the sum of the foreign earned income and housing cost exclusions. If the deduction for housing costs exceeds its limitation, the excess amount carries forward as a deduction in the next year (subject to that year's limitation).

DISALLOWANCE OF DEDUCTIONS AND CREDITS. Section 911(d)(6) prohibits taxpayers from claiming deductions or credits relating to their excluded income. The rules used to determine the nondeductible portion of an individual's employment-related expenses and the noncreditable portion of an individual's foreign taxes are discussed below.

Employment-related Expenses. Any employment-related expense associated with a taxpayer's excluded foreign earned income is nondeductible. By contrast, expenses relating to the employee's taxable income are deductible in full.[23] However, although foreign housing expenses may be related to excludible foreign earned income, no restriction is placed on deducting the housing cost amount.

EXAMPLE C:16-10 ▶ In 2006, Don reports $150,000 of foreign-earned income and $15,000 of foreign employment-related expenses that are subject to the 2% of AGI floor. Don takes $12,000 of other itemized deductions not directly related to foreign earned income and not subject to the 2% of AGI floor. Don may exclude $80,000 (or 53.33%) of his foreign earned income. Based on the calculation below, the exclusion precludes Don from deducting 53.33% or $8,000 ($15,000 total expenses − $7,000 deductible expenses) of foreign employment-related expenses. Don can deduct the full $12,000 of the other itemized deductions.

$$\text{\$7,000 (Deductible expenses)}^{a} = \text{\$15,000 (Expenses directly attributable to foreign earned income)} \times \left[1 - \frac{\text{\$80,000 (Excluded foreign earned income)}}{\text{\$150,000 (Total foreign earned income)}}\right]$$

[a] Subject to the 2% AGI floor.

The employment-related expenses are deductible only to the extent they exceed 2% of Don's $70,000 AGI ($150,000 − $80,000). Don can deduct $5,600 [$7,000 − ($70,000 × 0.02)] of employment-related expenses plus the $12,000 of other itemized deductions not subject to the 2% floor. ◀

[22] Sec. 911(c)(3)(A).

[23] Sec. 911(d)(6) and Reg. Sec. 1.911-6(a). Miscellaneous itemized expenses are subject to the 2% AGI floor whether the taxpayer is eligible for the Sec. 911 exclusion or not.

Foreign Income Taxes. Foreign income taxes paid or accrued on excludible foreign earned income cannot be credited or deducted for U.S. income tax purposes. Creditable foreign taxes are determined under the following formula.[24]

REAL-WORLD EXAMPLE

A number of Web sites provide the costs of sending an employee on an overseas assignment or the cost of maintaining an employee who already is on an overseas assignment. Some sites also provide information on foreign, U.S., and state taxation. In addition, many of the sites provide cultural information and financial advice.

$$\text{Creditable taxes} = \text{Foreign income taxes paid or accrued} \times \left[1 - \frac{\text{Excludible foreign earned income (minus nondeductible foreign employment-related expenses)}}{\text{Total foreign earned income (minus expenses relating to foreign earned income) subject to foreign tax}}\right]$$

If foreign income taxes are paid or accrued on earned and other types of income, and the taxes cannot be allocated between the two amounts, the denominator of the fraction must include the total of all income subject to foreign tax (minus all related expenses).

EXAMPLE C:16-11 ▶ Assume the same facts as in Example C:16-10 except Don also incurs $33,750 of Country F income taxes on his foreign earned income. Don's $15,750 of creditable foreign taxes are 46.67% of the total foreign taxes. The creditable taxes are computed as follows:

$$\$15,750 = \$33,750 \times \left[1 - \frac{\$80,000 - \$8,000}{\$150,000 - \$15,000}\right]$$ ◀

Topic Review C:16-2 summarizes the foreign earned income and housing cost exclusions.

Topic Review C:16-2

Foreign Earned Income and Housing Cost Exclusions

1. Only U.S. citizens can qualify under the bona fide residence test. According to this test, they must have (a) resided in a foreign country(ies) for an uninterrupted period that includes an entire tax year and (b) maintained a tax home in a foreign country(ies) during the residence period.
2. U.S. citizens and resident aliens can qualify under the physical presence test. According to this test, they must have (a) been physically present in a foreign country(ies) for at least 330 full days during a 12-month period and (b) maintained a tax home in a foreign country(ies) during the period of physical presence.
3. The exclusion equals the lesser of the taxpayer's foreign earned income or the $225.75 daily exclusion (in 2006) times the number of days in the tax year that the taxpayer qualifies for the exclusion.
4. Under the bona fide residence test, qualifying days include the number of days in the tax year during which the taxpayer "resided" in a foreign country. Under the physical presence test, qualifying days encompass the full 12-month period within which at least 330 days of physical presence fall.
5. Subject to limitations, employees can exclude a housing cost amount in addition to foreign earned income. Self-employed individuals can deduct the housing cost amount. The housing cost amount equals housing expenses incurred minus the base housing amount (16% × maximum foreign earned income exclusion) for the part of the tax year during which the taxpayer qualifies for the foreign earned income exclusion.
6. Taxpayers who exclude foreign earned income may not claim deductions or credits associated with their excluded income.

[24] Reg. Sec. 1.911-6(c).

TAXATION OF NONRESIDENT ALIENS

Whether a foreign national is a U.S. resident or a nonresident determines the U.S. tax treatment of that person's income. Under Sec. 871, U.S. taxing authority over nonresident aliens is limited to their U.S.-source investment income and any U.S. (and certain foreign) income effectively connected with the conduct of a U.S. trade or business.

The taxation of nonresident aliens is important for both U.S. and foreign companies that employ foreign nationals in the United States. Just like companies that employ U.S. citizens or residents abroad, companies that employ foreign citizens in the United States often assist them in complying with the U.S. tax laws and reimburse them for additional tax costs. In addition, U.S. businesses that pay U.S.-source income to nonresident aliens, foreign corporations, or foreign conduit entities (e.g., foreign partnerships) must withhold U.S. taxes on this income to avoid certain penalties.

OBJECTIVE 4

Determine whether a foreign citizen is a U.S. resident or nonresident alien

DEFINITION OF NONRESIDENT ALIEN

With certain exceptions,[25] foreign nationals who do not satisfy the Sec. 7701(b) tests set forth below are nonresident aliens. Foreign nationals who satisfy the tests are resident aliens.

- *Lawful permanent residence test:* The foreign national must have been a lawful permanent resident of the United States at any time during the tax year. A foreign national with a "green card" is considered to be a lawful permanent resident.
- *Substantial presence test:* The foreign national must have been present in the United States for 31 or more days during the current calendar year *and* a total of 183 or more days during the current and the two preceding tax years. The 183-day prong of the test is based on a weighted average calculation, in which the more recent the period, the greater the weight. Specifically, each day in the current year is weighted one, each day in the first preceding year is weighted one-third, and each day in the second preceding year is weighted one-sixth.

EXAMPLE C:16-12 ▶ Marco, a citizen of Country X, is present in the United States for 122 days in each of 2005, 2006, and 2007. Marco satisfies the 31-day requirement because he is present in the United States for at least 31 days in 2007. The following table illustrates the weighting of days for purposes of the 183-day requirement:

Year	*Days Present In the United States*	*Portion of Day Counted*	*Total Days Counted*
2007	122	Full day	122.00
2006	122	1/3 of full day	40.67
2005	122	1/6 of full day	20.33
Total			183.00

Marco is a resident alien because he satisfies both the 31-day and 183-day requirements. ◀

Even though foreign nationals satisfy the physical presence test, they are nonresident aliens if they are nominally present in the United States (i.e., physically present in the United States for less than 30 days in the current year notwithstanding a three-year total of 183 or more days) or if they have a closer connection with a foreign country than with the United States. Under the "closer connection" rule, the individual is present in the United States for less than 183 days in the current year, maintains a tax home in a foreign

[25] A nonresident alien also can become a resident alien by marrying a U.S. citizen or resident alien and electing to be treated as a resident alien under Sec. 6013(g). (See the Tax Planning Considerations section of this chapter.)

country for the entire year, and has maintained more significant contacts with the foreign country than with the United States.

Foreign nationals typically have dual status in their first and last years of U.S. residency. Dual status implies that the foreign national resides in the United States for part of the year and in a foreign country for the other part. Therefore, his or her tax computation is based on nonresident alien status for part of the tax year and resident alien status for the other part. An individual who satisfies the lawful permanent residency test (but not the substantial presence test) begins his or her residency period on the first day of the first year in which he or she is physically present as a lawful permanent resident in the United States. An individual who satisfies the substantial presence test in his or her first year becomes a resident on the first day of the first year in which he or she is physically present in the United States.

Foreign nationals terminate their residency on the last day of the last year in which they are lawful permanent residents. Foreign nationals who satisfy the physical presence test for a particular year maintain residency through the last day of such year (ignoring periods of nominal U.S. presence).

The United States amended its tax laws to reduce the incentive for U.S. citizens and residents to forfeit their U.S. citizenship or residency. The U.S. government can impose an expatriation tax when an individual terminates his or her U.S. citizenship or long-term residency status. The IRC sets forth a tax avoidance presumption that references the individual's average taxes for the five-year period preceding the termination, as well as the individual's net worth. The expatriation tax is based on an expanded U.S. source of income definition that applies to nonresident aliens who are liable for the additional income tax.[26] Modified estate and gift tax rules subject certain property to U.S. taxation if transferred within ten years of the event triggering the loss of citizenship or residency.[27]

INVESTMENT INCOME

OBJECTIVE 5

Calculate the U.S. tax liability of a nonresident alien

Passive investment income is taxed to a nonresident alien only if it is U.S.-source. Section 871(a)(1)(A) places the following types of income in this category: interest, dividends, rents, salaries,[28] premiums; annuities; compensation; and other fixed or determinable annual or periodical gains and profits (sometimes referred to as "FDAP income"). Capital gains realized by a nonresident alien in the United States (other than in the conduct of a U.S. trade or business) are taxed to that individual only if he or she is physically present in the United States for at least 183 days during the tax year.[29] Two important exceptions to this general rule are as follows:

TYPICAL MISCONCEPTION

Alien individuals who are U.S. residents are taxed on their worldwide income, just as U.S. citizens are. They file Form 1040. Nonresident aliens who are subject to U.S. taxation file Form 1040NR.

- ▶ Interest income earned by a nonresident alien on deposits in a U.S. bank, the foreign office of a U.S. bank, or other financial institution is exempt from U.S. taxation, provided the interest is not effectively connected with the foreign national's conduct of a U.S. trade or business.
- ▶ Portfolio interest (i.e., interest on obligations issued by U.S. persons and held by a nonresident alien as a portfolio investment) is exempt from U.S. taxation.[30]

The sale of personal property in the United States is not considered to generate fixed or determinable annual or periodic income. As a result, casual sales of inventory that are not regular, continuous, and substantial are not subject to U.S. taxation. To the extent the sales proceeds are contingent on the productivity, use, or disposition of an intangible asset, gain from the sale of the asset (e.g., patent, copyright, trademark) is taxed as ordinary income. It is U.S.-source if the asset is used in the United States and foreign-source if the asset is used in a foreign country. To the extent the sales proceeds are noncontingent,

[26] Sec. 877.
[27] Secs. 2107 and 2501.
[28] Compensation for personal services ordinarily is trade or business income. Salaries are trade or business income even if the foreign national does not conduct a U.S. trade or business in the tax year in which the income is reported (e.g., no services are performed in the United States in the year in which a final paycheck is collected by a cash method taxpayer) if it is attributable to an earlier tax year and would have been treated as effectively connected with the conduct of a U.S. trade or business in that year.
[29] Sec. 871(a)(2). The capital gains are reduced by U.S. capital losses, and only the net gain is taxed.
[30] Portfolio obligations include, for example, bonds issued by a U.S. corporation in the Eurobond market.

the gain is capital in character. It is U.S.-source if a U.S. resident sells the asset and foreign-source if a nonresident sells the asset.

EXAMPLE C:16-13 ▶ Paula, a citizen and resident of Country A, sells a patent to a U.S. corporation in consideration for a $2 fee for each unit produced in the United States under the patent. In the current year, Paula receives $18,000 for 9,000 units produced. The $18,000 is a contingent payment. It is U.S.-source because the patent is used in the United States and thus is subject to U.S. taxing authority. If Paula instead received a single $18,000 payment in exchange for all rights to the patent, the $18,000 less Paula's adjusted basis in the patent would have been a capital gain. It would have been foreign-source, and thus would have escaped U.S. taxation, because Paula is a foreign resident. ◀

ADDITIONAL COMMENT
Many tax treaties reduce this flat 30% rate for specific types of income.

Investment income and capital gains earned by a nonresident alien are taxed at a flat 30% rate, applicable to the gross amount.[31] Often, this rate is reduced by tax treaty (see discussion under Tax Planning Considerations later in this chapter). The 30% rate applies to capital gains of a nonresident alien only if he or she is present in the United States for at least 183 days during a tax year. In many cases, an individual who is present in the United States for 183 or more days has already acquired resident alien status. In general, U.S. payers must withhold the tax from the gross amount and remit the tax to the IRS.[32] If the U.S. payer fails to do so, and the nonresident alien fails to pay the tax voluntarily, the U.S. payer may be liable for the tax, as well as penalties for failing to withhold.[33]

EXAMPLE C:16-14 ▶ First State Bank issues dividend checks for a domestic corporation. One of the corporation's shareholders is Kelly, a nonresident alien entitled to a $30,000 dividend. Because the dividend represents U.S.-source investment income paid to a nonresident alien, First State Bank must withhold $9,000 ($30,000 × 0.30) of U.S. tax from Kelly's payment and remit the tax to the IRS. Kelly need not report or voluntarily pay the tax to the IRS. ◀

TRADE OR BUSINESS INCOME

A nonresident alien is engaged in a U.S. trade or business if he or she, with the intent to make a profit, conducts an activity in the United States that is regular, continuous, and substantial. A partner in a partnership or a beneficiary of a trust or estate is considered to indirectly conduct a U.S. trade or business if the partnership, trust, or estate directly conducts the U.S. trade or business.

Nonresident aliens who (1) are in the United States for less than 90 days during the year; (2) are employed by a nonresident alien, foreign partnership, or foreign corporation that does not conduct a U.S. trade or business, or by a foreign office maintained by a U.S. person; and (3) do not earn more than $3,000 for their services are considered not to have conducted a U.S. trade or business. In addition, their wages are exempt from U.S. taxation because such wages are foreign source.

Nonresident aliens who invest in securities through a broker also are considered not to have conducted a U.S. trade or business. Their capital gains are exempt from U.S. taxation unless they are present in the United States for more than 183 days during the year.

SPECIAL ELECTION FOR REAL ESTATE INVESTORS. Nonresident aliens may elect to have their U.S. real estate activities be treated as a U.S. trade or business even though the activities are passive. This election permits the nonresident aliens to claim all deductions and losses associated with the activities and thus be taxed on a net basis. If the election is not made and the activity does not constitute a trade or business, the real estate income is subject to the flat 30% withholding tax levied on a gross basis (i.e., without any reduction for deductions and losses).[34] Gains from the sale of U.S. real property interests (whether capital or ordinary) are treated as effectively connected with the conduct of a U.S. trade or business. Ownership of a U.S. real estate interest may be direct or indirect

---

[31] Sec. 871(a).

[32] If a nonresident alien voluntarily files a tax return, he or she can deduct casualty and theft losses related to (1) personal use property that exceed the $100/10% of AGI floor and (2) transactions entered into for a profit even if not connected with a trade or business, and (3) charitable contributions otherwise deductible under Sec. 170.

[33] Secs. 1441(a) and 1461.

[34] Sec. 871(d).

(e.g., an investment in a corporation or a partnership that owns substantial U.S. real estate).[35]

PRACTICAL APPLICATION

Paula operates a U.S. business and qualifies as a nonresident alien. Paula invests the excess cash from the business in short-term securities. The investment income is effectively connected with the business under the asset-use test.

EFFECTIVELY CONNECTED TESTS. Income is effectively connected with the conduct of a U.S. trade or business if one of two tests is met: an "asset use" test or a "business activities" test. Under the asset use test, income is effectively connected with the conduct of a U.S. trade or business if the income is derived from assets used in the business. For example, interest earned on a certificate of deposit (CD) may be either investment or business related, depending on how the CD is used. If a nonresident alien holds the CD to support the operating cycle of his or her U.S. business, the interest is derived from an asset used in the business and thus is effectively connected with the conduct of the business. Under the business activities test, income is effectively connected with the conduct of a U.S. trade or business if the activities of the business are a material factor in generating the income. For example, short-term gains realized by the U.S. branch of a foreign securities firm are effectively connected with the conduct of a U.S. business because the activities of the business (i.e., securities trading) are a material factor in generating the income. Capital gain income that is effectively connected with the conduct of a U.S. trade or business under either test is taxable without regard to the number of days the individual is physically present in the United States.

Income from the sale of inventory or other personal property by a nonresident alien is U.S.-source and, therefore, taxable in the United States if the alien has a U.S. office and the sale is attributable to that office. On the other hand, the income is foreign-source and therefore exempt from U.S. taxation if the property is for foreign use or disposition and if a non-U.S. office materially participated in the sale. When a foreign national manufactures or creates personal property in the United States and then sells it abroad, a portion of the sales income is allocated to U.S. production and thus is subject to U.S. taxation. The remainder is allocated to the location where the sale occurred.

CALCULATING THE TAX. A foreign national who conducts a U.S. trade or business may have to make two separate tax calculations. Investment income that is unrelated to the conduct of a U.S. trade or business is taxed on a gross basis at a flat 30% rate (unless reduced by a tax treaty). This tax is collected through withholding. Trade or business income is taxed at graduated rates on a net basis (i.e., reduced by all associated expenses and losses). Nonresident aliens

- ► Cannot use the standard deduction otherwise available to individual taxpayers
- ► Must itemize their deductions
- ► Are generally limited to a single personal exemption[36]

Individual tax rates apply to taxable income derived from an unincorporated U.S. trade or business. The trade or business income of unmarried nonresident aliens is taxed at the marginal rates for single taxpayers. Married nonresident aliens use the tax rate schedule for married individuals filing separately unless they elect to file a joint return under Sec. 6013(g) (see the Tax Planning Considerations section of this chapter). The U.S. trade or business income of nonresident aliens may be subject to the alternative minimum tax for individuals. The taxes owed on trade or business income can be reduced by any available tax credits. The taxpayer then pays the net U.S. tax liability through estimated tax installments and, if a balance remains, through a final remittance when he or she files an annual return.

EXAMPLE C:16-15 ▶ Maria, a single taxpayer, is a citizen and resident of Country D. In the current year, Maria reports $40,000 of U.S. dividends that are unrelated to Maria's U.S. trade or business and $1,000 of itemized deductions. Maria's U.S. trade or business generates $300,000 of gross income from sales activities, $20,000 of interest income, $225,000 of expenses, and $500 of tax credits.

[35] Secs. 897(a) and (c).

[36] Section 873(b) permits certain personal deductions (for example, casualty losses, charitable contributions, and personal exemptions) not directly related to trade or business activities.

SELF-STUDY QUESTION

In Example C:16-15, assume Maria also earned $10,000 of capital gain income on the sale of investment property she had owned in the United States. How would this change Maria's total U.S. tax liability?

ANSWER

Maria's U.S. tax liability would not increase unless the capital gain was connected with a U.S. trade or business, or it was investment gain and Maria was present in the United States for 183 days or more, and the gain was U.S. source income.

Maria's tax liability on her dividend income is $12,000 ($40,000 × 0.30) unless a U.S. tax treaty with Country D reduces the 30% rate. The taxes owed on Maria's trade or business income are calculated as follows:

Gross income:	
Sales	$300,000
Interest	20,000
Total gross income	$320,000
Minus: Trade or business expenses	(225,000)
Adjusted gross income	$ 95,000
Minus: Personal exemption (2007)	(3,400)
Itemized deductions	(1,000)
Taxable income	$ 90,600
Gross tax liability (single rate schedule)	$ 19,479
Minus: Tax credits	(500)
Net tax liability	$ 18,979

Maria's total U.S. tax liability is $30,979 ($12,000 + $18,979). ◀

Topic Review C:16-3 summarizes the tax rules applicable to nonresident aliens.

TAXATION OF U.S. BUSINESSES OPERATING ABROAD

The IRC offers numerous tax breaks to U.S. enterprises that conduct business abroad. For example, it generally exempts from U.S. taxation income earned by foreign subsidiaries of U.S. corporations unless the income is derived from a U.S. trade or business or from a U.S. investment. This exemption extends to the foreign subsidiary's U.S. owners, who generally are not taxed on their share of the subsidiary's earnings until they receive the earnings in the form of a dividend (but see discussion of controlled foreign corporations below). The remainder of this chapter examines the conduct of overseas businesses and the special tax treatment of their owners.

DOMESTIC SUBSIDIARY CORPORATIONS

The use of domestic subsidiaries to sell goods or provide services to foreign consumers offers two nontax advantages to U.S. multinationals. First, the foreign activities of the multinationals can be conducted separately from their domestic activities. Second, a subsidiary's liabilities can be separated from those of its parent corporation, thereby shielding the parent's assets from the subsidiary's foreign creditors.

Profits from overseas business activities are taxed in the United States when earned. Losses are deductible when incurred. Because the foreign activities are conducted by a domestic corporation, they can be reported as part of a consolidated tax return that includes both the parent's and its domestic subsidiaries' operating results (see Chapter C:8 of this text). Thus, foreign losses can offset domestic profits and vice versa with respect to domestic losses.

ADDITIONAL COMMENT

The use of limited liability companies (LLCs) is popular with overseas activities. The profits and losses of an LLC pass through to its U.S. owners. In many cases, the U.S. owner of a foreign LLC is a U.S. corporation. Once the LLC becomes profitable, the U.S. owner can elect to be taxed as a C corporation under the check-the-box regulations and receive the benefits of the deferral privilege (see page C:16-19) or can continue to be treated as an LLC under its default classification.

FOREIGN BRANCHES

A domestic corporation may choose to conduct its overseas business through a foreign branch. A **foreign branch** is an unincorporated office or other fixed place of business (e.g., a manufacturing plant) maintained by a domestic entity in a foreign country. For tax purposes, a branch is treated as a legal extension of the domestic corporation. The domestic corporation reports profits attributable to the branch's foreign activities in the year in which the profits are earned. Whether or not the profits have been remitted to the United States is immaterial in determining the tax consequences. Foreign income taxes paid or accrued on these profits are creditable against the domestic corporation's U.S. tax liability.

Topic Review C:16-3

Taxation of Nonresident Aliens

1. Nonresident aliens are foreign nationals who do not reside in the United States. A foreign citizen can acquire U.S. resident alien status by satisfying either the lawful permanent residency test or the substantial presence test as set forth in the IRC.
2. Foreign nationals generally have dual status in their first and last years of U.S. residency. The foreign national may be taxed as a resident alien for part of the year and as a nonresident alien for the remainder of the year. Two different tax computations for the year may be required.
3. Passive investment income (e.g., dividends, interest, rents) is taxed to a nonresident alien only if such income is U.S. source. The income is taxed at a flat 30% rate, unless reduced by tax treaty, with no allowance for deductions or exemptions.
4. Capital gains earned in the United States (other than those related to the conduct of a U.S. trade or business) are taxed at the 30% rate only if the foreign national is physically present in the United States for 183 or more days during the tax year.
5. The U.S. tax on investment income or capital gains is collected through withholding by the U.S. person who pays the income or gains to the nonresident alien.
6. The United States taxes a nonresident alien's ordinary income and capital gains that are effectively connected with the conduct of a U.S. trade or business. Related business expenses and losses are deductible from effectively connected income. In computing their U.S. tax liability, nonresident aliens can claim a single personal exemption but not a standard deduction. Graduated individual tax rates apply to the nonresident alien's U.S. taxable income. The foreign national voluntarily pays the tax owed on the effectively connected income through estimated tax payments and an annual remittance.
7. A special election to file a joint return with their U.S.-citizen or resident-alien spouse is available to nonresident aliens. If the nonresident alien makes the election, he or she is subject to U.S. taxation on his or her worldwide income.

Similarly, the domestic corporation reports losses attributable to the branch's foreign activities in the year in which the losses are incurred. Because deducting the losses reduces taxes on domestic profits, such deductibility is a major advantage of conducting initial overseas activities through a branch. By using a branch, a domestic corporation can deduct start-up losses when incurred. Subject to branch loss recapture provisions, once the overseas activities become profitable, the domestic corporation can incorporate the branch in a foreign country and defer U.S. taxes on overseas profits until the profits are remitted to the United States.

FOREIGN CORPORATIONS

Conducting an overseas business through a foreign corporation offers the following four advantages:

- The foreign corporation's liabilities are separate from the assets of the parent corporation, thereby limiting the parent's losses to the extent of its capital investment in the foreign corporation.
- Unless the foreign corporation is "controlled" (see discussion of controlled foreign corporations below), the U.S. income tax on a U.S. stockholder's ratable share of the foreign corporation's earnings is deferred until the earnings are remitted to the United States.
- A domestic corporation that receives a dividend from a foreign corporation in which it has at least a 10% stock interest can claim a deemed paid tax credit for a ratable share of foreign income taxes paid or accrued by the foreign corporation.
- A domestic corporation that receives a dividend from a foreign corporation in which it has at least a 10% stock interest can claim a dividends-received deduction for the portion of any dividend paid out of the foreign corporation's undistributed profits that are effectively connected with the conduct of a U.S. trade or business. A dividends-received deduction is not available for dividends paid out of the foreign corporation's non-U.S. trade or business earnings.

The last three of these advantages, as well as the tax treatment of a foreign corporation's U.S. trade or business income, is discussed below.

ADDITIONAL COMMENT

Notwithstanding the fourth bullet item, in 2005, a domestic corporation receiving a dividend from a controlled foreign corporation (see discussion below) could, under certain conditions, have claimed a one-time 85% dividends-received deduction for the full amount of any dividend paid out of the controlled foreign corporation's undistributed profits whether or not such profits are effectively connected with a U.S. trade or business.

ADDITIONAL COMMENT

This deferral privilege is eliminated for certain types of income of controlled foreign corporations. This topic is discussed later in the chapter.

DEFERRAL PRIVILEGE. For U.S. tax purposes, foreign corporations are entities separate and distinct from their shareholders. The IRC effectively grants a **deferral privilege** to U.S. shareholders with respect to the foreign corporation's earnings. Under this privilege, the U.S. shareholders are not taxed on the foreign corporation's earnings until the earnings are remitted to them as dividends.

EXAMPLE C:16-16 ▶ Adobe, a U.S. corporation, owns all the stock in Delta, a foreign corporation. In 2003, Delta reported $300,000 in after-tax profits from foreign manufacturing activities. Delta reinvested these profits outside the United States and remitted them to Adobe as a dividend in 2007. No U.S. income taxes are due on Delta's profits until 2007. This result contrasts with that for a foreign branch, whose earnings would have been taxable in the United States to Adobe in 2003. The value of the tax deferral (known as the "deferral privilege") equals the amount of U.S. taxes deferred times the time value of money for four years. ◀

TAX STRATEGY TIP
To attain the deferral privilege consider using a corporation rather than a branch for foreign operations.

Losses incurred by a foreign corporation cannot be deducted by any of its U.S. shareholders. Instead, the losses reduce profits earned in other years.

EXAMPLE C:16-17 ▶ Boston, a U.S. corporation, owns all the stock in Gulf, a foreign corporation. In the current year, Gulf reports $125,000 in losses. None of Gulf's current losses can be used to reduce Boston's current profits. Instead, the losses can reduce Gulf's profits in other years that might be distributed to Boston as dividends. Had the $125,000 of losses instead been incurred by a foreign branch, Boston could have used the current losses to offset its current profits. ◀

ADDITIONAL COMMENT
The deemed paid foreign tax credit is not available to individual U.S. shareholders.

FOREIGN TAX CREDIT. If a U.S. corporation conducts a foreign business through a foreign branch, it is directly liable for foreign taxes owed on the branch's earnings and can claim a direct U.S. credit for all such taxes paid or accrued. On the other hand, if a U.S. corporation conducts a foreign business through a foreign subsidiary, the foreign subsidiary is directly liable for foreign taxes owed on the subsidiary's earnings, and the U.S. corporation can claim a direct U.S. credit only for foreign taxes withheld from the subsidiary's dividend payments. Because most foreign countries impose taxes on foreign profits that are higher than taxes withheld on dividends, the foreign tax credit rules could discourage the use of foreign subsidiaries to conduct foreign businesses. To remedy this situation, Congress enacted the Sec. 902 **deemed paid credit** provisions relating to foreign income taxes paid or accrued by a foreign corporation.

OBJECTIVE 6
Calculate the deemed paid credit available to a U.S. stockholder in a foreign corporation

For a U.S. corporation to claim a deemed paid credit, two conditions must be met:

- The foreign corporation must pay a dividend to the U.S. corporation out of the foreign corporation's earnings and profits (E&P).
- The U.S. corporation must own at least 10% of the foreign corporation's voting stock on the distribution date.[37]

TYPICAL MISCONCEPTION
The deemed paid credit is available from first- through sixth-tier foreign corporations (but not for seventh- and lower-tier corporations). The credit becomes available only as an *actual* dividend is paid from each subsidiary to its parent. The U.S. corporation claims the credit when the first-tier foreign corporation pays a dividend to the U.S. corporation.

Calculating the Deemed Paid Credit. The deemed paid credit for the post-1986 tax years of a domestic corporate shareholder is calculated as follows:[38]

$$\text{Deemed paid credit} = \frac{\text{Dividend paid to domestic corporation out of undistributed earnings}}{\text{Accumulated undistributed earnings}} \times \text{Creditable taxes paid or accrued by the foreign corporation}$$

ADDITIONAL COMMENT
The foreign corporation's earnings and profits must be calculated using U.S. tax concepts.

The undistributed earnings amount is not reduced by current dividends and is determined at the end of the current year. Dividends paid to all shareholders (U.S. and foreign) during the year reduce undistributed earnings at year-end. Creditable taxes also are determined at the end of the current year and include taxes paid, accrued, or deemed

[37] Secs. 902(a) and 902(b)(1)–(3). Foreign taxes paid by foreign subsidiaries of foreign corporations also qualify for the deemed paid credit.

[38] Sec. 902(a). Deemed paid foreign taxes are not deductible under Sec. 164. The calculation below pertains to post-1986 earnings and credits. Different rules apply to pre-1987 deemed paid credit calculations.

paid by the foreign corporation. Taxes attributable to all dividends paid during the current year reduce total taxes at year-end. The definition of "dividend" in the numerator of the fraction is the same as that for domestic corporate distributions out of E&P (see Chapter C:4).

Both the dividend received by the domestic corporation and the income equivalent of the pro rata share of foreign taxes associated with it are included in the domestic corporation's gross income.[39] This "gross up" for a pro rata share of foreign income taxes paid or accrued by the foreign corporation (equal to the amount of the deemed paid credit) precludes the domestic corporation's benefiting from both a deduction and a credit for such taxes (i.e., a deduction at the foreign corporate level and a credit at the domestic shareholder level).

EXAMPLE C:16-18 ▶ Coastal, a U.S. corporation, owns 40% of the stock in Bay, a foreign corporation. During the current year, Bay reports $200,000 of E&P, pays $50,000 in foreign income taxes, and remits $60,000 in dividends to Coastal. Bay withholds $6,000 in foreign taxes from the dividend payment. In prior tax years, Bay reported $100,000 of E&P, paid $40,000 in foreign income taxes, and paid no dividends. Based on a 34% corporate tax rate, Coastal's calculation of the deemed paid credit for the current year dividend is as follows:

$$\$18{,}000 = \frac{\$60{,}000}{\$200{,}000 + \$100{,}000} \times (\$50{,}000 + \$40{,}000)$$

The $18,000 credit amount is included in Coastal's income as a "gross up" and enters into the calculation of its U.S. tax liability:

Dividend	$60,000
Plus: Deemed paid credit gross up	18,000
Gross income	$78,000
Times: Corporate tax rate	× 0.34
Gross U.S. tax liability	$26,520
Minus: Deemed paid credit	(18,000)
Direct credit	(6,000)
Net U.S. tax liability	$ 2,520

◀

Translating the Dividend and Foreign Taxes into U.S. Dollars. Normally, a foreign corporation's books and records are maintained in the currency of the country in which the corporation operates. For U.S. tax reporting purposes, the dividend must be translated into U.S. dollars. If the distributee is a domestic corporation eligible for the deemed paid credit, the foreign corporation's E&P and foreign taxes also must be translated into U.S. dollars. The exchange rate for the date on which the dividend is included in gross income is used to translate the dividend paid by a noncontrolled foreign corporation, as well as the underlying E&P.[40] Translation of foreign taxes withheld from the dividend is based on the exchange rate in effect on the dividend payment date. For purposes of calculating the deemed paid credit, translation of foreign taxes is based on the exchange rate in effect on the date the foreign corporation pays the taxes.[41]

EXAMPLE C:16-19 ▶ Houston, a U.S. corporation, owns 40% of the stock in Far East, a foreign corporation that began operations in 2006. In 2007, Far East pays Houston a 70,000 pira dividend. In 2006 and 2007, Far East earns 400,000 pira in pretax profits. It pays 30,000 and 20,000 pira in home country taxes respectively in 2006 and 2007. On the dividend payment date, the pira-U.S. dollar exchange rate is 1 pira = $0.22 (U.S.). Far East paid the 2006 and 2007 foreign taxes when the exchange rates were 1 pira = $0.20 (U.S.) and 1 pira = $0.25 (U.S.), respectively. Far East's E&P is 350,000 (400,000 pretax profits − 50,000 taxes) pira. The translated dividend amount is 70,000 pira × $0.22 = $15,400. The translated foreign tax amount is $11,000 [(30,000 pira × $0.20) + (20,000 pira × $0.25)]. The translated foreign taxes attributable to the dividend are $2,200 [$11,000 × (70,000 pira ÷ 350,000 pira)]. ◀

[39] Sec. 78.

[40] Reg. Secs. 1.301-1(b) and 1.902-1(g) and *The Bon Ami Co.*, 39 B.T.A. 825 (1939).

[41] Sec. 986(b).

A discussion of the financial statement implications of deferred foreign earnings appears at the end of this chapter.

FOREIGN TAX CREDIT BASKETS. Before 2003, dividends received by a corporate shareholder owning at least 10% but no more than 50% of a foreign corporation's stock were accounted for in a separate limitation basket. These dividends are called Sec. 902 dividends because that IRC section governs their tax treatment. They also are called 10/50 dividends because of the range of required taxpayer ownership in the stock of the dividend paying corporation. Until 2003, separate foreign tax credit limitations were calculated for this basket. The existence of a separate 10/50 dividend basket permitted the cross-crediting of foreign taxes paid on dividends received from noncontrolled (10/50) foreign corporations. Cross-crediting was allowed only with respect to distributions made out of the foreign corporation's earnings and profits accumulated before January 1, 2003. As an illustration, in Example C:16-18 the dividends received by Coastal Corporation from Bay Corporation (as well as from all other 10/50 corporations) before 2003 would have been placed in Coastal's 10/50 dividend basket. Coastal then would have calculated separate limitations for the purpose of determining the amount of foreign taxes attributable to the dividends that were creditable.

Now, U.S. corporate taxpayers that receive dividends from a 10/50 corporation must "look through" the foreign corporation to ascertain the source and character of the foreign corporation's earnings and profits out of which the dividends were paid. They then must apportion the dividends according to this source and character and assign them to the baskets into which the underlying earnings and profits would have been placed. (See the previous discussion of Special Foreign Tax Credit Limitations on p. C:16-7.) To apply the Sec. 902 dividend "look through" rules, minority U.S. shareholders must rely on foreign corporations to supply them with information on the source and character of the corporation's earnings and profits.

ADDITIONAL COMMENT

Dividends paid by a foreign corporation out of its U.S. trade or business E&P are eligible for a dividends-received deduction.

TAXATION OF A FOREIGN CORPORATION'S U.S. TRADE OR BUSINESS INCOME

Regular and Alternative Minimum Taxes. A foreign corporation that invests in the United States or that conducts a U.S. trade or business is taxed by the U.S. government in the same way as a nonresident alien. Section 881(a) taxes the U.S.-source investment income of a foreign corporation on a gross basis at a flat 30% rate (or lower rate specified by tax treaty). Capital gains that are not effectively connected with the conduct of a U.S. trade or business are exempt from U.S. taxation. The U.S. taxes on the investment income are collected through withholding.[42] Section 882(a) taxes that portion of the foreign corporation's income that is effectively connected with the conduct of a U.S. trade or business on a net basis at graduated rates. These earnings are not taxed to the foreign corporation's U.S. shareholders until they are distributed.

ADDITIONAL COMMENT

In 2005, U.S. corporations were eligible for a one-time 85% deduction for cash dividends received from a controlled foreign corporation (CFC), whether or not paid out of the CFC's U.S. business profits. The deduction was intended to encourage the repatriation and reinvestment, in the United States, of CFC offshore earnings. It applied to distributions out of CFC earnings not previously taxed to the U.S. shareholder under Subpart F and was subject to certain conditions and limitations. After 2005, CFC cash dividends received by a domestic corporation are taxed according to the rules set forth in the text.

Section 245(a) allows a domestic corporation to deduct dividends (or a portion thereof) received from a foreign corporation in which it has at least a 10% stock interest. To be deductible, the dividends (or a portion thereof) must have been paid out of the foreign corporation's undistributed profits that are effectively connected with the conduct of a U.S. trade or business. The percentage (i.e., 70%, 80%, or 100%) of the effectively connected dividend amount that is deductible depends on the extent of the domestic corporation's stock ownership in the foreign corporation. The deductibility of the effectively connected dividend amount alleviates the double taxation of the foreign corporation's earnings that were previously taxed by the United States.

Branch Profits Tax. Income earned by a U.S. subsidiary of a foreign corporation is taxed twice: first, at the U.S. corporate level when earned; second, at the foreign shareholder level when distributed. The corporate level tax is assessed on a net basis at graduate rates. The U.S. subsidiary pays it voluntarily. The shareholder level tax is assessed on a gross dividend basis at a flat 30% rate, which may be reduced by treaty. The U.S. subsidiary withholds the tax and remits it to the IRS.

[42] Sec. 1442.

In a similar manner, income earned by an unincorporated U.S. branch of a foreign corporation also is taxed twice: first, at the branch level when earned; second, at the foreign corporate level when "remitted." The branch level tax is imposed on branch income effectively connected with the conduct of a U.S. trade or business. It is assessed on a net basis at graduated rates. The corporate level tax is imposed on a "dividend equivalent amount" deemed to have been paid by the U.S. branch to the foreign corporation. This tax is assessed on a gross basis at a flat 30% rate, which may be reduced by treaty. The foreign corporation pays both of these taxes voluntarily.

The latter tax on deemed-distributed branch earnings is called the **branch profits tax,**[43] It is analogous to the 30% withholding tax on U.S. corporate dividends paid to foreign shareholders. The branch profits tax effectively places foreign corporations that conduct their U.S. business through an unincorporated U.S. branch on par with foreign corporations that conduct their U.S. business through a U.S. subsidiary. It ensures that both sets of foreign corporations are treated in the same way.

The branch profits tax equals 30% (or a lower rate specified in a tax treaty) times the dividend equivalent amount. The dividend equivalent amount equals the foreign corporation's E&P that is effectively connected with the conduct of its U.S. trade or business increased by the decrease (or decreased by the increase) in the foreign corporation's net equity investment in its branch assets during the year. Thus, the branch profits tax base is (1) increased by earnings remitted to the foreign corporation during the year as reflected by a decrease in the branch's U.S. trade or business assets and (2) decreased by earnings reinvested in branch operations during the year as reflected by an increase in the branch's U.S. trade or business assets. Under allocable interest rules, certain interest paid by a U.S. branch is taxed as if it were paid by a U.S. corporation. The interest income accruing to foreign creditors is considered to be U.S. source and hence subject to a 30% U.S. withholding tax (or a lower rate specified in a tax treaty).

OBJECTIVE 7

Understand provisions applicable to controlled foreign corporations (CFCs)

CONTROLLED FOREIGN CORPORATIONS

UNDER PRE-SUBPART F RULES. Before the 1962 enactment of the **controlled foreign corporation** (CFC) provisions (known as the Subpart F rules, discussed later), U.S. corporations set up majority owned foreign subsidiaries in "tax-haven" countries to minimize their U.S. tax liability on income earned from overseas operations. The typical scenario was as follows:

- A U.S. manufacturer formed a sales subsidiary in a foreign country that imposed little or no corporate income tax.
- The U.S. manufacturer sold goods to foreign purchasers.
- The U.S. manufacturer shipped the goods directly to the foreign purchasers.
- The U.S. manufacturer billed the sales subsidiary for the goods at an artificially low price.
- The sales subsidiary, in turn, billed the foreign purchasers for the goods at an artificially high price.
- Through this scheme, the U.S. manufacturer effectively shifted its sale profits from the United States to the foreign country in which the sales subsidiary operated.

A U.S. firm that performed services for foreign clients could devise a similar scheme. The following example illustrates how, absent Subpart F rules, a U.S. corporation could defer recognition of U.S. taxable income by conducting its foreign business through a foreign subsidiary as opposed to a foreign branch.

EXAMPLE C:16-20 ▶ Under pre-CFC rules, Chicago, a U.S. corporation, forms a foreign branch to conduct its overseas widget sales. The foreign country in which the branch operates imposes no income taxes. Chicago's overseas widget sales generate $1 million of profits annually. Chicago pays $340,000 ($1,000,000 × 0.34) in U.S. taxes and no foreign taxes in the year the income is earned. Had the same profit been divided equally between Chicago and Island Corporation, a newly formed foreign sales subsidiary, the worldwide tax cost would have been reduced substantially. Figure C:16-1 illustrates this result.

[43] Sec. 884(a).

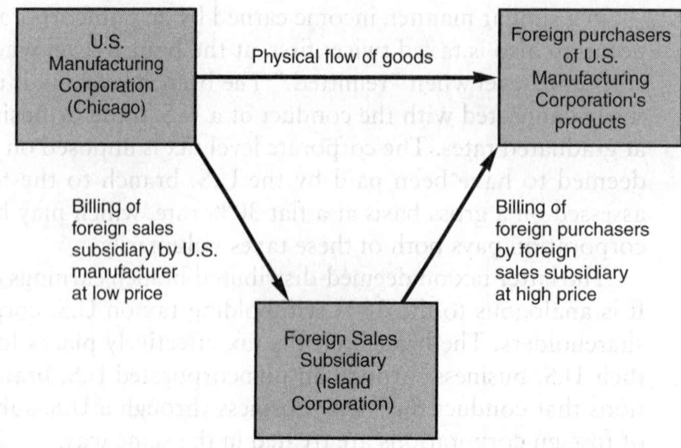

Sales made by Chicago's foreign branch:
$1,000,000 profit x 0.34 = $340,000 U.S. tax liability for Chicago. No foreign tax liability.

Sales made by Chicago. Profit divided equally between Chicago and Island Corporation in the absence of Subpart F rules:
Chicago: $500,000 profit x 0.34 = $170,000 U.S. tax liability.
Island: $500,000 profit x 0 = $0 Foreign Country tax liability (and no U.S. tax liability for Chicago until part or all of the profit is remitted to the United States.)

Sales made by Chicago. Profit divided equally between Chicago and Island Corporation in the absence of Subpart F rules:
Chicago: $500,000 profit on sales to Island x 0.34 = $170,000 U.S. tax liability.
$500,000 Subpart F income x 0.34 = $170,000 U.S. tax liability.
No U.S. tax liability when Island remits its profits to the United States.
Island: $500,000 profit x 0 = $0 Foreign Country tax liability and no U.S. tax liability.

FIGURE C:16-1 ▶ ILLUSTRATION OF USE OF FOREIGN SALES SUBSIDIARY (EXAMPLE C:16-20)

KEY POINT
The tainted income is taxable to Chicago (the CFC's U.S. parent) as a deemed paid dividend, rather than being taxed directly to the CFC.

Chicago's $500,000 share of the profit results in a $170,000 ($500,000 × 0.34) U.S. tax liability. Island owes no U.S. or foreign tax on its $500,000 share of the profit. Chicago owes no U.S. tax on Island's share of the profits because the earnings have not been remitted as a dividend to its parent corporation in the United States. An attempt by Chicago to maximize its tax deferral by selling its widgets to Island at an artificially low price probably would be challenged by the IRS under the Sec. 482 transfer pricing rules (see page C:16-30). Section 482 would limit Island's profit to the portion of the $1 million total profit that it had earned based on the value it had added to the goods. This amount may be less than the amount allocated under a 50–50 profit split method. ◀

UNDER SUBPART F RULES. In the foregoing scenario, the Subpart F rules eliminate tax deferral by accelerating U.S. recognition of certain types of "tainted" income (see Figure C:16-2 for a summary of the Subpart F income categories).

EXAMPLE C:16-21 ▶ Assume the same facts as in Example C:16-20 except that Island is a CFC. Under current U.S. tax law, Island's profit on widgets manufactured by a related party outside Island's country of incorporation and resold to third parties outside Island's country of incorporation is considered tainted or Subpart F income. This profit is deemed to be distributed to Chicago on the last day of Island's tax year. Only the portion, if any, of Island's profits attributable to widget sales in Island's country of incorporation is untainted and thus deferred. If Island sells all the widgets outside its country of incorporation, its $500,000 of profits would be taxed directly to Chicago under the Subpart F rules. This result is basically the same as if Chicago had conducted its foreign sales through a foreign branch. ◀

Because of the increased tax cost associated with the Subpart F rules, U.S. businesses often organize their overseas activities to avoid CFC status or structure their transactions to avoid generating Subpart F income.

CFC DEFINED. A CFC is a foreign corporation in which more than 50% of the voting stock or more than 50% of the value of all outstanding stock is owned by U.S. share-

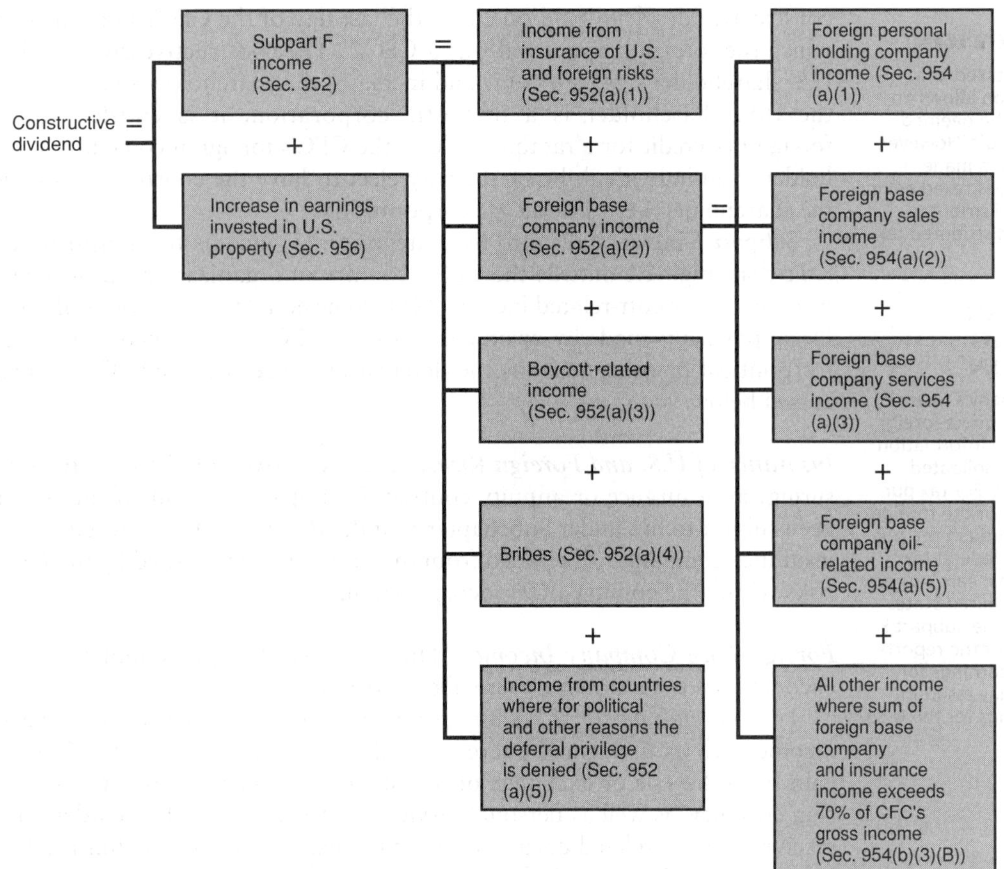

FIGURE C:16-2 ▶ TYPES OF INCOME EARNED BY A CONTROLLED FOREIGN CORPORATION (CFC) INCLUDIBLE IN THE GROSS INCOME OF ITS U.S. SHAREHOLDER(S)

holders on any day of the corporation's tax year.[44] A **U.S. shareholder** is a U.S. person who owns at least 10% of the foreign corporation's voting stock.[45] Ownership may be direct, indirect, or constructive. Constructive ownership is determined under the attribution rules of Sec. 318 (see Chapter C:4) with modifications specified in Sec. 958(b).

EXAMPLE C:16-22 ▶ Europa, a foreign corporation, is owned by five unrelated individuals. Al, Bill, and Connie are U.S. citizens who own 24%, 20%, and 9%, respectively, of Europa's voting and nonvoting stock. Duane and Elaine are nonresident aliens who own 40% and 7%, respectively, of Europa's voting and nonvoting stock. Only Al and Bill are considered U.S. shareholders because they are U.S. persons who own at least 10% of Europa's voting stock. Europa is not a CFC because Al and Bill together own only 44% of its voting and nonvoting stock. If Al instead were Connie's father, Connie would be a U.S. shareholder because, under the Sec. 318 family attribution rules, she would own 33% (9% directly + 24% constructively from Al) of Europa's voting stock. Europa then would be a CFC because its three U.S. shareholders together would own 53% (24% + 20% + 9%) of its voting and nonvoting stock. Double-counting Al's 24% interest to take into consideration both Al's and Connie's stockholdings is not permitted. ◀

CONSTRUCTIVE DISTRIBUTIONS OF SUBPART F INCOME. A U.S. shareholder is taxed on its ratable share of Subpart F income if the foreign corporation has been a CFC for at least 30 days during the tax year. Each U.S. shareholder reports its share as a

[44] Sec. 957(a). A CFC must adopt the same tax year as its majority U.S. shareholder if on the first day of the CFC's tax year (or other days as prescribed by the IRS) 50% or more of the voting power or value of all classes of the CFC's stock is directly, indirectly, or constructively owned by a single U.S. shareholder.

[45] Sec. 951(b). A U.S. person includes a U.S. citizen or resident alien, a domestic corporation, a domestic partnership, and a domestic trust or estate.

TYPICAL MISCONCEPTION

The election to be taxed as a domestic corporation allows an individual to take the deemed paid foreign tax credit. However, the election is seldom made because the income is taxed again when it is actually distributed rather than being distributed tax-free.

BOOK-TO-TAX ACCOUNTING COMPARISON

A U.S. parent company's financial statements may include a foreign subsidiary's financial information in its worldwide consolidated financial statements. For tax purposes, the earnings of the foreign subsidiary are included in the parent company's U.S. federal tax return only when the earnings are repatriated to the United States or are taxed under the Subpart F rules. This deferral of the reporting of the foreign earnings for U.S. tax purposes may result in significant tax savings for the U.S. parent company.

constructive dividend paid on either the last day of the CFC's tax year or the last day on which the foreign corporation was a CFC.[46] The constructive dividend is included in the U.S. shareholder's gross income and increases the shareholder's basis in the CFC stock. If the U.S. shareholder is a domestic corporation, it is entitled to a deemed paid foreign tax credit for a ratable share of the CFC's foreign income taxes. If the U.S. shareholder is an individual, he or she may elect to have the constructive dividend taxed as if the shareholder were a domestic corporation.

Subpart F income falls into five categories: (1) income from insuring U.S. and foreign risks that originate outside the CFC's country of organization, (2) foreign base company income, (3) boycott-related income, (4) income equal to the amount of any bribes or other illegal payments made by or on behalf of the CFC, and (5) income from countries where for political or other reasons the deferral privilege is denied. These categories are discussed below.

Insurance of U.S. and Foreign Risks. Income derived by the CFC from issuing (or reinsuring) an insurance or annuity contract is Subpart F income if the income would have been subject to tax under Subchapter L of the IRC had it been earned by a domestic (U.S.) insurance company.[47] Excluded from this rule is income earned by the CFC from insuring risks within the country of its incorporation.

Foreign Base Company Income. The broadest of all, this Subpart F income category encompasses the following four subcategories.

1. *Foreign personal holding company income* (FPHCI) includes passive investment income such as dividends, interest, royalties, annuities, and rents. FPHCI also includes gain from the sale or exchange of non-income-producing property, commodities, or foreign currency, as well as personal services contract income. It excludes rents and royalties received from a related corporation for the use of property within the CFC's country of incorporation. It also excludes income derived from the CFC's active conduct of a trade or business with an unrelated person. A special exception from the Subpart F rules applies to (1) active banking and finance income earned by a CFC predominantly or substantially engaged in a banking, financing, or similar business and (2) income from services related to the production of banking and finance income. An exception also applies to gains from property sales by security dealers. Dividends and interest are not FPHCI if received from a related corporation organized in the CFC's country of incorporation and whose principal assets are used in a trade or business in that country.[48]

EXAMPLE C:16-23 ▶ Time is a CFC incorporated in Country X. Time receives interest and dividends from its two foreign subsidiaries, East Corporation and West Corporation. East is incorporated in Country V and conducts all its business in that country. West is incorporated in Country X and conducts all its business in that country. Only the interest and dividends received from East are FPHCI because East is not incorporated in the same country as Time. West's interest and dividends are not FPHCI because West is incorporated in Country X. ◀

KEY POINT

For foreign base company sales income to exist, the goods must be both manufactured and sold for use outside the CFC's country of incorporation. If the goods are manufactured or sold in the CFC's country of incorporation, the assumption is that a good business reason exists for having set up the CFC in that country. Thus, the CFC has no foreign base company sales income.

2. *Foreign base company sales income* includes fees and profits earned from the sale, or purchase and sale, of personal property outside the CFC's country of incorporation to or from a related party. The related party transactions that result in foreign base company sales income are[49]

- The purchase of personal property from a related person and its sale to any person
- The sale of personal property to any person on behalf of a related person (e.g., commission income)
- The purchase of personal property from any person and its sale to a related person
- The purchase of personal property from any person on behalf of a related person

[46] Sec. 951(a).

[47] Sec. 953(a)(1).

[48] Sec. 954(c). Section 954(d)(3) defines "related person" for Subpart F purposes as (a) any individual, corporation, partnership, trust, or estate that controls, or is controlled by, the CFC, or (b) any corporation, partnership, trust, or estate controlled by the same persons who control the CFC. "Control" means direct, indirect, or constructive ownership of 50% or more of the total voting power or total value of the CFC's stock.

[49] Sec. 954(d)(1).

Foreign base company sales income excludes profits derived from the sale of products either manufactured in the CFC's country of incorporation, sold for use in the CFC's country of incorporation, or produced by the CFC.[50]

EXAMPLE C:16-24 ▶ Dublin Corporation is a CFC organized in Country F. Dublin purchases machine tools from its U.S. parent for sale to unrelated parties. Dublin sells 70% of the tools in Country E and 30% in Country F. Only the profit earned from the sale of tools in Country E constitutes foreign base company sales income. If Dublin manufactured the machine tools, none of its profit from the Country E or Country F sales would be foreign base company sales income. ◀

ADDITIONAL COMMENT

Goods are deemed to have been manufactured by the CFC if it substantially transforms the product (such as making screws and bolts from steel rods) or if its direct labor and factory overhead account for 20% or more of the total cost of goods sold.

3. *Foreign base company services income* includes compensation for services provided for or on behalf of a related person outside the CFC's country of incorporation. In general, compensation for personal services is considered to be earned at the location where the services are performed.[51]

EXAMPLE C:16-25 ▶ Andes Corporation, organized in Country A, is 100% owned by Hi-Tech, a U.S. corporation. Hi-Tech sells industrial machines to unrelated Amazon Corporation for use in Country B. Hi-Tech assigns the portion of the sales contract covering the installation and maintenance of the machines to Andes, and Hi-Tech pays Andes for these services. Earnings derived from the installation and maintenance is foreign base company services income because Andes performs these services for a related party (Hi-Tech) outside its country of incorporation (Country A). ◀

4. *Foreign base company oil-related income* includes earnings derived from oil and gas related activities (other than the extraction of oil and gas) conducted in a foreign country. Such activities include the transport, shipping, processing, and distribution of oil and gas and any related service. Foreign base company oil-related income is not taxed under Subpart F if it is earned in the foreign country in which the oil and gas was extracted.[52]

WHAT WOULD YOU DO IN THIS SITUATION?

You are a tax manager assigned to the U.S. Manufacturing and Export Corporation (USM&E) account. USM&E manufactures machine tools for distribution throughout North and South America. USM&E sells its products to six 100%-owned foreign subsidiaries that resell the products in various North and South American markets. In reviewing USM&Es operating results, you notice that sales to the U.S. and Canadian subsidiaries account for the largest profit margin. USM&E revenues from sales to the four Central and South American subsidiaries are barely above related manufacturing costs. Upon examining prior year information, you discover that Canadian income tax rates are nearly the same as U.S. rates while the rates in the other countries are substantially lower. The sales manager at USM&E tells you that this organizational structure has been in place for years and the operations of the six sales subsidiaries are substantially identical. He also informs you that none of the other tax professionals who have worked on the account has ever questioned USM&E's sales and pricing. In reviewing USM&E's data, you discover that additional costs were incurred to ship the goods from the United States to Central and South America, but these costs do not justify the price differences between the sales made in these regions and the sales made in the United States and Canada. You suspect that a transfer pricing problem exists. What benefit can USM&E derive from its current pricing arrangements? Can you advise your client about possible negative tax consequences of defective pricing? Under U.S. tax laws, are any alternatives available to USM&E that might permit it to use different pricing methods or non-arm's length transfer prices? Can USM&E obtain advice from the IRS concerning the soundness of its pricing methods?

[50] Sec. 954(d) and Reg. Sec. 1.954-3(a)(4)(i).
[51] Sec. 954(e).
[52] Sec. 954(h).

Subpart F income specifically excludes

- Income earned by the CFC in the conduct of a U.S. trade or business, which is taxed directly to the CFC.[53]
- Foreign base company income or insurance income that is subject to an effective foreign tax rate greater than 90% of the maximum U.S. corporate rate.[54]
- Foreign base company income and insurance income that in total are less than the smaller of 5% of the CFC's gross income or $1 million[55]
- Income earned by the CFC that cannot be repatriated to the United States because of currency or other restrictions[56]

When foreign base company income and insurance income exceed 70% of the CFC's total gross income, all the CFC's gross income is deemed to be foreign base company income or insurance income.[57]

REAL-WORLD EXAMPLE

Countries that participate in, or cooperate with, international boycotts include Bahrain, Kuwait, Lebanon, Libya, Oman, Qatar, Saudi Arabia, Syria, the United Arab Emirates, and the Republic of Yemen. In 2002, 3,421 boycott reports were filed. The tax effects were a $697,000 reduction in foreign tax credits, and a $5.5 million increase in Subpart F income.

Boycott-related Income. This category includes any income derived by the CFC from the participation in, or cooperation with, an international boycott against a particular nation (or group of nations). The portion of the CFC's profits that are boycott-related is determined under the rules of Sec. 999.

Bribes, Kickbacks, and Other Illegal Payments. The CFC loses its deferral privilege for the earnings equivalent of all bribes, kickbacks, and other illegal payments that it makes.

Earnings Derived in Certain Foreign Countries. U.S. shareholders of a CFC cannot defer income derived from activities in certain countries. These countries include those the U.S. government does not recognize, those with whom the U.S. Government has frozen or severed diplomatic relations, and those the U.S. Government believes support international terrorism.

Related Deductions. Subpart F income is reduced by any related deductions, the allocation of which are based on rules set forth in Reg. Sec. 1.861-8.[58]

ADDITIONAL COMMENT

Income derived from the following countries is not eligible for the deferral privilege: Cuba, Iran, Libya, North Korea, Sudan, and Syria.

INCREASE IN EARNINGS INVESTED IN U.S. PROPERTY. Dividends paid by a CFC to its U.S. shareholders may be both taxed to the shareholders in the United States and subject to tax withholding in the foreign country. In the absence of special rules, the CFC could avoid the U.S. tax by either investing its earnings in U.S. property or lending funds to its U.S. shareholders, thereby affording them the beneficial use of CFC earnings without an actual earnings distribution. To close this loophole, Congress enacted a special IRC provision that taxes the U.S. shareholders on their respective pro rata shares of any increase in CFC earnings invested in U.S. property. Under this provision, each U.S. shareholder is deemed to receive a constructive distribution equal to the lesser of the shareholder's ratable share of U.S. property held by the CFC over the CFC's E&P previously taxed as a constructive distribution, or the shareholder's ratable share of CFC earnings for the year.[59] CFC earnings previously taxed as Subpart F income may be invested in U.S. property without the shareholder's incurring additional tax liability. Such amounts, if distributed, would not constitute a dividend.

ADDITIONAL COMMENT

If the CFC guarantees an obligation of a U.S. person, it is deemed to hold that obligation. Thus, if a CFC guarantees a loan of its U.S. parent, the guarantee constitutes the acquisition of U.S. property. This result can be a tax trap for the unwary.

The U.S. property value is based on the average adjusted basis (minus any liability to which the property is subject) as of the last day of each quarter of the CFC's tax year. U.S. property includes tangible property located in the United States, stock in domestic corporations, obligations of U.S. persons, and intangibles developed by the CFC for use in the United States.[60] U.S. property excludes U.S. Government obligations, U.S. bank deposits, stock in domestic corporations that are not U.S. shareholders of the CFC or more than 25% owned by a U.S. shareholder, U.S. securities acquired by CFC security dealers, obligations issued by non-corporate U.S. persons unrelated to the CFC, and U.S. property acquired before the first and after the last day on which the foreign corporation was "controlled."

---

[53] Sec. 952(b).
[54] Sec. 954(b)(4).
[55] Sec. 954(b)(3)(A).
[56] Sec. 964(b).
[57] Sec. 954(b)(3)(B).
[58] Sec. 954(b)(5).
[59] Sec. 951(a)(2).
[60] Secs. 956(a)(3) and (b).

EXAMPLE C:16-26 ▶ Forco is a CFC in its initial year of operation. During the current year, Forco reports $1 million of earnings, none of which is taxed as Subpart F income. On December 31, Forco invests in U.S. property worth $400,000. Because of this additional investment, $400,000 of Forco's earnings are no longer deferred and are taxed ratably to Forco's U.S. shareholders. ◀

SELF-STUDY QUESTION

If $500,000 of the $1 million in Example C:16-26 had been Subpart F income (and thus currently taxed to the CFC's U.S. shareholders), would the acquisition of the U.S. property also be taxed currently?

ANSWER

The E&P invested in U.S. property comes first out of the E&P that has been previously taxed. Therefore, the U.S. shareholders would incur no additional tax levy as a result of the U.S. investment.

DISTRIBUTIONS FROM A CFC. Distributions by a CFC are deemed to be made first out of any increase in earnings invested in U.S. property and the CFC's most recently accumulated Subpart F income, then out of its U.S. tax-deferred earnings, if any. Distributions of previously taxed income (i.e., the increase in earnings invested in U.S. property and Subpart F income) are tax-free to the U.S. shareholder and reduce his or her basis in CFC stock.[61]

EXAMPLE C:16-27 ▶ Bulldog, a domestic corporation, owns all the stock in Marine, a CFC. Bulldog's cost basis in the Marine stock is $600,000. Since the time Bulldog acquired the stock, Marine generated $400,000 of E&P, of which $175,000 was taxed to Bulldog as Subpart F income. Marine distributes $200,000 cash to Bulldog. Of this amount, $175,000 is a tax-free distribution of previously taxed Subpart F income. The remaining $25,000 is a taxable distribution of earnings that were not previously taxed under Subpart F. After the distribution, Bulldog's basis in the Marine stock is $600,000 ($600,000 + $175,000 − $175,000). ◀

KEY POINT

Section 1248 is a backstop to the Subpart F rules in that it prevents the gain from the disposition of CFC stock from escaping taxation as ordinary income to the extent that it previously has not been taxed.

DISPOSITION OF CFC STOCK. Section 1248 applies to U.S. persons who own at least 10% of a foreign corporation's voting stock and who sell or exchange the stock within five years after any time the foreign corporation was a CFC. The gain recognized on the sale or exchange is taxed as a dividend to the extent of the U.S shareholder's pro rata share of the CFC's untaxed E&P. This amount is further prorated to reflect the time the U.S. person held the stock and the period during which the foreign corporation was a CFC.[62] The remaining portion of the gain is treated as capital in character. Foreign taxes associated with the dividend portion of the gain qualify for the deemed paid foreign tax credit.

EXAMPLE C:16-28 ▶ On October 30, 2005, Texas, a domestic corporation, purchased 200 of the 500 outstanding shares of Le Chien Corporation's stock. Texas holds the shares until March 31, 2007, when it sells the stock for a $60,000 gain. Le Chien is a CFC at all times while the stock is owned. Le Chien's E&P amounts not previously taxed to Texas under the Subpart F rules are as follows: 2005, $60,000; 2006, $30,000; and 2007, $70,000. The untaxed E&P attributable to the stock sold or exchanged is determined under the following formula:

$$\text{CFC's untaxed E\&P for tax year} \times \frac{\text{Number of shares sold or exchanged}}{\text{Number of shares outstanding}} \times \frac{\text{Number of days shares are owned while corporation is a CFC}}{\text{Number of days in CFC's tax year}} = \text{CFC's untaxed E\&P attributable to shares sold or exchanged}$$

$$2005\text{: } \$60{,}000 \times \frac{200}{500} \times \frac{61}{365} = \$\ 4{,}011$$

$$2006\text{: } \$30{,}000 \times \frac{200}{500} \times \frac{365}{365} = 12{,}000$$

$$2007\text{: } \$70{,}000 \times \frac{200}{500} \times \frac{90}{365} = 6{,}904$$

$$\text{Total} \quad \$22{,}915$$

Thus, $22,915 of the gain is treated as a dividend, and $37,085 ($60,000 − $22,915) is treated as capital in character. Texas can claim a deemed paid credit for a pro rata share of foreign taxes actually paid by Le Chien on the earnings out of which the CFC paid the dividend. ◀

ADDITIONAL COMMENT

For U.S. taxpayers operating in a foreign country with a high tax rate, Sec. 1248 is a tax benefit and not a tax detriment. The combination of Sec. 1248's dividend treatment and the availability of the Sec. 902 deemed paid credit reduces the U.S. tax liability to below the U.S. tax liability if the gain were instead taxed as a capital gain.

[61] Secs. 959(c) and 961(b).

[62] Sec. 1248(a).

TYPICAL MISCONCEPTION

Section 482 applies to transactions involving two U.S. entities as well as to transactions involving a U.S. entity and a foreign entity.

SECTION 482 RULES AND TAX AVOIDANCE. Transactions between a domestic corporation and its foreign subsidiary, or between a foreign corporation and its U.S. subsidiary, present an opportunity for tax avoidance. For example, the domestic corporation could sell goods to, or provide services for, the subsidiary at a price less than the price that would be obtained in an arm's-length dealing (see Figure C:16-1 and related text). Alternatively, the foreign subsidiary could pay a less-than-arm's-length price for the use of intangibles (such as patents or trademarks). Both transactions increase the foreign subsidiary's profits that may be deferred for U.S. tax purposes.

EXAMPLE C:16-29 ▶ Taylor, a U.S. corporation, sells widgets to its wholly owned foreign subsidiary, Wheeler Corporation. Wheeler is incorporated in, pays taxes to, and sells the widgets in Country Z. Taylor normally sells widgets at a price of $10 per unit to a U.S. wholesaler that provides services similar to those provided by Wheeler. Both the U.S. wholesaler and Wheeler incur similar costs. If Taylor sells the widgets to Wheeler at $8 per unit, Wheeler's profits increase by $2 per unit, and Taylor's profits decrease by $2 per unit. The additional profit is not Subpart F income because it is derived from sales by the CFC within its country of incorporation. Thus, the additional profit is isolated in Country Z. It is not taxed by the United States until Wheeler remits it to Taylor as a dividend. ◀

EXAMPLE C:16-30 ▶ Assume the same facts as in Example C:16-29 except Taylor instead issues a license to Wheeler to manufacture the widgets and charges a $1 per-unit royalty for each unit produced and sold. A licensing agreement between Taylor and an unrelated foreign widget producer specifies a $3 per-unit royalty payment. The reduced royalty rate increases Wheeler's profits by an additional $2 per unit. Because the profit is derived from manufacturing performed by a CFC, the additional profit is not taxed to Taylor as Subpart F income. Such profit is U.S. tax deferred until Wheeler remits it to Taylor as a dividend. ◀

REAL-WORLD EXAMPLE

An IRS study conducted in 1999 pegs the annual gross income tax gap related to Sec. 482 at $2.8 billion. Of this shortfall, $2 billion is from U.S. corporations that are subsidiaries of foreign parent corporations, and $800 million is from less-than-50%-foreign owned U.S. corporations. Eighty percent of this amount originates in the manufacturing and retailing sectors.

Section 482 authorizes the IRS to distribute, apportion, or allocate gross income, deductions, credits or allowances between or among controlled entities to prevent tax evasion and to clearly reflect income. The IRS may use this authority under the following circumstances:

- Two or more organizations, trades, or businesses exist.
- They are owned or controlled by the same persons.
- A transaction between or among the entities does not reflect the income that would have been earned in an arm's-length transaction.

The **Sec. 482 rules** can apply to transactions between two unincorporated entities, two incorporated entities, or one incorporated entity and one unincorporated entity. The related persons can be domestic or foreign and need not be members of an affiliated group that files a consolidated return. In the two preceding examples, Sec. 482 would authorize the IRS to adjust the prices and/or profits reported by Taylor and Wheeler to reflect an arm's-length transaction.

Treasury Regulations under Sec. 482 provide guidance for determining an arm's-length standard in various types of transactions, including

- Loans or advances
- Performance of services
- Sales, transfers, or use of intangible property
- Sales, transfers, or use of tangible property
- Cost sharing arrangements[63]

These rules create safe harbors for taxpayers engaged in related party transactions. If the transaction price meets the standard set forth in the Sec. 482 Treasury Regulations, the IRS generally will not challenge it.

Treasury Regulations finalized in 1994 offer additional guidance. For example, Reg. Sec. 1.482-3(b)(2) states that a transaction involving the transfer of tangible property (as in Example C:16-29) between controlled taxpayers meets the arm's-length standard if the

[63] Reg. Sec. 1.482-1 through -6 and -8.

REAL-WORLD EXAMPLE

The IRS entered into 610 advance pricing agreements (APAs) with taxpayers as of December 31, 2005. In addition to the completed APAs, the IRS has 240 more APAs under negotiation. APAs provide advance Sec. 482 approval for the transfer pricing procedures used by the taxpayer on transfers of tangible personal property or financial instruments. Most APAs cover a five-year period, at which time they must be renewed. Firms that have taken advantage of APAs include Apple Computer, Matsushita (makers of Panasonic and Qasar products), and Barclays Bank. Australia, Canada, Japan, and Belgium are among the countries that have APA rules in place.

ADDITIONAL COMMENT

Many federal government documents are available to the general public under the Freedom of Information Act (FOIA). Advance pricing arrangements (APAs), however, receive special treatment under the FOIA. APAs, both past and present, and their related background files are treated as confidential tax return information.

results are consistent with the outcome that would have been obtained had uncontrolled taxpayers engaged in a *comparable* transaction under *comparable* circumstances. The transaction and circumstances are comparable only if minor differences between the transactions have no effect on the amount charged, or if these differences can be reconciled through a reasonable number of adjustments to the uncontrolled transaction. If no uncontrolled transaction is comparable, the resale price, cost-plus, comparable profits, profit-split, or any other appropriate method approved by the IRS can be used.

For intangibles (as in Example C:16-30), the arm's-length price in a controlled transfer of an intangible is the same as that in a comparable uncontrolled transfer. An uncontrolled transfer is comparable to a controlled transfer if it involves comparable intangible property and occurs under comparable circumstances, as explained in Reg. Sec. 1.482-4(c)(2). If significant differences exist between the controlled and uncontrolled transfers that make them substantially dissimilar, the comparable profits method may not be used. The comparable profits method derives the arm's-length price paid in a controlled transfer of property from objective measures of profitability (e.g., profit level indicators such as rates of return) specific to uncontrolled persons engaged in similar business activities with other uncontrolled persons under similar circumstances. If the comparable profits method cannot be used, the taxpayer can petition the IRS to use another method.

Section 482 permits the IRS periodically to adjust the level of payments for the use of an intangible to reflect its current revenue yield. Thus, in setting the initial royalty rate, related parties should consider projected operating results, including changes in the income stream attributed to the intangible.

A net Sec. 482 transfer pricing adjustment for the provision of services, or the sale or use of property, could constitute a substantial valuation misstatement under Sec. 6662(e)(1)(B) if it exceeds the lesser of $5 million or 10% of the taxpayer's gross receipts. If so, an accuracy-related penalty equal to 20% of the tax underpayment attributable to the valuation misstatement may be imposed.

OBJECTIVE 8

Be aware of special international tax incentives formerly available to U.S. taxpayers

FOREIGN SALES CORPORATIONS REGIME AND EXTRATERRITORIAL INCOME EXCLUSION

Before 2005, two special tax incentives to encourage the export of U.S. goods abroad were available to U.S. taxpayers: the foreign sales corporation (FSC) regime and the extraterritorial income (ETI) exclusion. The FSC regime exempted from U.S. taxation a portion of foreign trade income earned by an FSC organized by a U.S. taxpayer in a treaty country. The ETI exclusion exempted from U.S. taxation foreign trading gross receipts accruing to a U.S. corporation as a result of activities conducted abroad. In response to World Trade Organization rulings that the FSC regime and the ETI exclusion constitute prohibited export subsidies, Congress repealed both measures. The ETI repeal, however, does not apply to transactions conducted in the ordinary course of business under a binding contract, between unrelated persons, in effect since September 2003. As a phase-out of the ETI exclusion, 80% of the otherwise available ETI benefits were available to U.S. taxpayers in 2005, and 60% of the benefits are available in 2006.

OBJECTIVE 9

Explain the transactional structure and taxation of inversions

INVERSIONS

In our federal system of taxation, the tax treatment of U.S. corporations differs significantly from the tax treatment of foreign corporations. Specifically, U.S. corporations are taxed on their worldwide income, both U.S.- and foreign-source. By contrast, foreign corporations are taxed almost exclusively on their U.S.-source business and investment income. Unless effectively connected with the conduct of a U.S. trade or business (or attributable to a U.S. "permanent establishment" under the terms of a treaty), the foreign-source income of foreign corporations largely escapes U.S. taxation.

This difference in tax treatment creates an incentive for U.S. corporations with substantial foreign-source income to reorganize as a foreign corporation in transactions known as **inversions**. Typically, in an inversion, a U.S. corporation (1) merges into a foreign entity or transfers substantially all of its assets to the foreign entity; (2) the owners of the U.S. business exchange stock in the U.S. corporation for equity in the foreign entity; and (3) the same owners continue to conduct their U.S. business, as well as their foreign operations, through the foreign entity. Following the merger or asset transfer, income from the U.S. business continues to be subject to U.S. taxation, but income from the foreign business largely escapes U.S. taxation.

Because inversions erode the U.S. corporate tax base, Congress added two anti-inversion provisions to Secs. 367 and 7874. Under the first provision, a foreign corporation will be deemed to be a U.S. corporation for U.S. tax purposes if (1) the foreign corporation acquired substantially all the assets of a U.S. corporation, (2) former shareholders of the U.S. corporation own 80% or more (by vote or value) of stock in the foreign corporation by reason of their U.S. stock ownership, and (3) the foreign corporation and its affiliates do not conduct substantial business in the foreign country of incorporation.

Under the second anti-inversion provision, income recognized in an inversion transaction, as well as related taxes, cannot be offset by the U.S. corporation's otherwise available tax attributes (e.g., net operating losses or foreign tax credits) for a ten-year period if conditions (1) through (3) in the previous paragraph are met, with the substitution of 60% ownership for 80% ownership. Thus, if in the inversion, (1) the foreign corporation acquires substantially all the assets of a U.S. corporation, (2) former shareholders of the U.S. corporation own between 60% and 80% of the foreign corporation's stock by reason of their U.S. stock ownership, and (3) the foreign corporation and its affiliates do not conduct substantial business in the foreign country of incorporation, income recognized on the asset transfer cannot be reduced by the U.S. corporation's otherwise available net operating losses, and taxes owed on this income cannot be offset with the U.S. corporation's otherwise available foreign tax credits. Excepted from the rule are sales of inventory and similar property to a foreign related person.

EXAMPLE C:16-31 ▶ Gomez, Nguyen, Jones, and Ahmed own equal shares of Wilmington-Domestic, a U.S. corporation. The corporation generates $20 million of income from its U.S. business and $60 million of income from a business conducted in Country X. In an attempt to remove its foreign business income from U.S. taxing jurisdiction, Wilmington-Domestic reorganizes as Wilmington-Foreign in Country Z. In the reorganization, Gomez, Nguyen, Jones, and Ahmed exchange their stock in Wilmington-Domestic for an equal number of shares in Wilmington-Foreign, and Wilmington-Domestic merges into Wilmington-Foreign. Following the reorganization, Wilmington-Foreign conducts the U.S. and Country X businesses but conducts no business in Country Z. Under the first anti-inversion rule, Wilmington-Foreign will be treated as a U.S. corporation, and thus taxed on its worldwide income, because (1) Wilmington-Foreign acquired substantially all the assets of Wilmington-Domestic; (2) Gomez, Nguyen, Jones, and Ahmed own more than 80% of Wilmington-Foreign stock by reason of their Wilmington-Domestic stock ownership; and (3) Wilmington-Foreign conducts no business in Country Z. ◀

EXAMPLE C:16-32 ▶ Assume the same facts as in the preceding example except that only Gomez, Nguyen, and Jones exchange their stock in Wilmington-Domestic for an equal number of shares in Wilmington-Foreign (75% of the total). Under the second anti-inversion rule, any income recognized on the merger of Wilmington-Domestic into Wilmington-Foreign cannot be reduced by Wilmington-Domestic's otherwise available net operating losses, if any. Moreover, taxes owed on this income cannot be offset by Wilmington-Domestic's otherwise available foreign tax credits, if any. ◀

TAX PLANNING CONSIDERATIONS

DEDUCTION VERSUS CREDIT FOR FOREIGN TAXES

Taxpayers may elect annually to deduct or credit any paid or accrued foreign income taxes.[64] Nearly all taxpayers elect to credit them. The advantage of doing so is illustrated in the following example.

---

[64] Sec. 901(a).

EXAMPLE C:16-33 ▶ Phil, a U.S. citizen, earns $100 of foreign income. Phil pays $25 in foreign income taxes and is subject to a 28% marginal tax rate. He makes the following calculations to compare the advantages of crediting the taxes versus deducting them.

	Deduction	*Credit*
Gross income	$100	$100
Minus: Foreign tax deduction	(25)	–0–
Taxable income	$ 75	$100
Times: Marginal tax rate	× 0.28	× 0.28
Gross U.S. tax liability	$ 21	$ 28
Minus: Foreign tax credit	–0–	(25)
Net U.S. tax liability	$ 21	$ 3

If Phil deducts the foreign income taxes, his total U.S. and foreign tax liability is $46 ($25 + $21). By claiming the credit, Phil reduces his total U.S. and foreign tax liability to $28 ($25 + $3). ◀

REAL-WORLD EXAMPLE

Seldom will it be advantageous for a taxpayer to deduct the foreign taxes paid when such taxes can be claimed as a foreign tax credit. Some taxpayers deduct their foreign taxes, when they are a small dollar amount, because of the complexity of complying with the foreign tax credit rules (e.g., figuring out the law and filing the necessary form(s)). The complexity of the foreign tax credit for individual taxpayers having less than $300 ($600 for joint filers) of foreign passive income is substantially reduced because they are not subject to foreign tax credit limitation.

Some taxpayers deduct their foreign income taxes when they incur foreign losses or when they cannot credit the taxes either in the current year or in any of the one carryback or ten carryover years. The deduction provides current tax benefits where U.S. profits exceed foreign losses. If no U.S. profits are earned, the foreign taxes increase the taxpayer's NOL.

ELECTION TO ACCRUE FOREIGN TAXES

Cash method taxpayers may elect to accrue foreign taxes for credit purposes. The election permits them to credit foreign income taxes that have accrued but have not yet been paid. It does not affect the application of the cash method of accounting to other taxable items. The election is not available for the purpose of deducting foreign taxes. It is binding on all tax years and can be revoked only with IRS consent.[65]

Topic Review C:16-4

Taxation of U.S. Persons Doing Business Abroad

TYPE OF ENTITY USED	TAX TREATMENT
Domestic subsidiary	Profits are taxed to the subsidiary (or the consolidated group) in the year earned. A direct foreign tax credit is available for foreign taxes paid or accrued. Losses are deducted in the year incurred.
Foreign branch	Foreign branches are unincorporated extensions of domestic entities. Branch profits are taxed to the entity in the year earned. A direct foreign tax credit is available for foreign taxes paid or accrued on branch profits. Branch losses are deducted in the year incurred.
Foreign corporation (less than 50% U.S.-owned)	A foreign corporation's earnings are tax deferred until repatriated to the United States. A domestic corporation can claim a deemed paid foreign tax credit with respect to dividends received from a foreign corporation in which it owns at least a 10% interest.
Controlled foreign corporation (CFC) (more than 50% U.S.-owned)	Same rules as for previous entry. Subpart F income of the CFC is taxed to its U.S. shareholders in the year in which earned. The increase in CFC earnings invested in U.S. property is subject to U.S. taxation. Previously taxed income is distributed tax-free. Special rules apply to the sale or exchange of CFC stock.

[65] Sec. 905(a).

Two advantages ensue from this election.

- It accelerates use of the foreign tax credit by one or more tax years.
- It eliminates the problem of matching foreign income with foreign taxes for credit limitation purposes. In many cases, it obviates the need for a carryback or carryover of excess credits.

EXAMPLE C:16-34 ▶ In 2004, Tulsa, a U.S. corporation and cash method taxpayer, began a business in Country Z. Z's tax laws require the use of a calendar year for tax reporting purposes. Taxes owed on income earned during the year must be paid by the first day of the third month following year-end. Tulsa conducts its foreign operations for three years before ceasing business on December 31, 2006. Its results are as follows:

	2004	*2005*	*2006*	*2007*
Foreign source taxable income	$1,000	$1,000	$1,000	$-0-
Foreign taxes accrued (30% rate)	300	300	300	-0-
Foreign taxes paid	-0-	300	300	300
Foreign tax credit limitation (34% U.S. corporate rate)	340	340	340	-0-
Foreign tax credit:				
Cash method	-0-	300	300	300
Accrual method	300	300	300	-0-

Under the cash method, Tulsa pays its 2004 U.S. taxes without the benefit of a foreign tax credit. In 2007, Tulsa generates $300 of excess credits because of the annual mismatching of income and tax payments. Of the 2007 foreign tax payment, $40 can be carried back to 2006, but $220 [$300 – ($40 + $40)] in foreign tax credits are lost because Tulsa discontinued its foreign activities in 2006. If such activities had not been discontinued, the excess foreign taxes could have been carried over and used in later years when the credit limitation exceeds foreign taxes paid. No mismatching occurs, however, where Tulsa uses the accrual method to report the foreign tax credit. ◀

SPECIAL EARNED INCOME ELECTIONS

Taxpayers may revoke a previous election to exclude foreign-earned income or not make the initial election if they find themselves in one of two situations:

- They are employed in a foreign country where the foreign tax rate exceeds the U.S. tax rate (e.g., Canada or Germany).
- They incur a substantial loss from overseas employment or in a trade or business.

In the first situation, the available foreign tax credits exceed the taxpayer's gross U.S. tax liability. The foreign-earned income exclusion diminishes the utility of the excess credits. By including foreign earned income in gross income, the taxpayer can use the entire amount of excess credits as a carryback or carryover (subject to separate basket limitations). These excess credits might be beneficial if, for example, the taxpayer earned self-employment income in another year in a foreign country where the tax rate is lower than the U.S. rate.

In the second situation, the foreign deductions of taxpayers who incur substantial losses may exceed their foreign gross income. If these taxpayers exclude part or all of their foreign-earned income from their total gross income, a pro rata portion of the related foreign expenses will be disallowed. This disallowance reduces the amount of any available NOL carryback or carryover. Including foreign earnings in the taxpayer's gross income allows the excess foreign expense portion to be deducted.

Taxpayers may not elect to exclude or deduct the housing cost amount. A qualifying taxpayer who receives only this amount (reported as W-2 income) from his or her employer must exclude it from gross income. If the taxpayer earns only self-employment income, he or she must deduct the housing cost amount. If the taxpayer earns both salary (or wages) and self-employment income, he or she must apportion the housing cost amount between an exclusion and a deduction based on the relative amounts of income earned.

A taxpayer can decline the foreign earned income benefits by so electing on his or her current return or on an amended return. If the taxpayer revokes the initial election, he or she may not make a new election for five years or until the IRS consents.[66] Thus, a taxpayer who revokes an election while residing in a country with a tax rate higher than the U.S. rate may not elect to exclude foreign earned income if shortly thereafter he or she moves to a country with a tax rate lower than that in the United States.

ADDITIONAL COMMENT

With certain exceptions, whenever a treaty and the IRC are in conflict, the treaty takes precedence.

TAX TREATIES

A treaty is an agreement between two or more sovereign nations. The United States has concluded tax treaties with over 60 countries. Income **tax treaties** have numerous objectives, including

- To reduce or eliminate double taxation
- To facilitate the exchange of information among taxing authorities
- To provide a mechanism for resolving disputes between residents or citizens of one country and residents or citizens of another country

In addition to income tax treaties, the United States has concluded estate and gift tax treaties, as well as Social Security tax totalization agreements.

A tax treaty to which the United States is a party cannot be used by U.S. citizens or U.S. corporations to reduce the scope of their income subject to U.S. taxation. Notwithstanding the provisions of any treaty, U.S. citizens and U.S. corporations are still taxed on their worldwide income at regular U.S. rates. On the other hand, a tax treaty can reduce the foreign taxes that U.S. citizens or U.S. corporations pay on their foreign-source investment income, and it allows them to credit against their U.S. tax liability foreign taxes paid on their foreign-source business income. Conversely, a tax treaty can reduce the U.S. taxes that foreign citizens or foreign corporations pay on their U.S.-source investment income, and it allows them to credit against their foreign tax liability U.S. taxes paid on their U.S.-source business income.

ADDITIONAL COMMENT

Tax treaties designate a competent authority to represent each country when an international tax dispute originates between the United States and a treaty partner. The U.S. competent authority is the Assistant Commissioner (International) of the IRS.

The second objective is intended to prevent or eliminate tax evasion. The third objective is achieved through a "competent authority" procedure under which taxpayers of one treaty partner can settle tax disputes with taxpayers of the other treaty partner through the latter country's tax authorities.

Section 6114 requires a taxpayer who takes a position based on a treaty provision that preempts an IRC provision to disclose such position on his or her tax return or on a statement attached to the return.

SPECIAL RESIDENT ALIEN ELECTIONS

Two special elections permit nonresident aliens to be treated as resident aliens for U.S. tax purposes. The first election is usually made when a foreign national moves to the United States too late in the year to qualify as a resident (see page C:16-14). This election is available if the foreign national

- Does not qualify as a resident under the lawful residence test or substantial presence test for the calendar year for which the election is made (i.e., election year)
- Does not qualify as a resident for the calendar year preceding the election year
- Qualifies as a resident under the substantial presence test in the calendar year immediately following the election year, and was present in the United States
    a. For at least 31 consecutive days in the election year and
    b. For at least 75% of the days during the period beginning with the first day of the 31-consecutive-day or longer period and ending with the last day of the election year.

The election is made on the nonresident alien's tax return for the election year and may not be revoked without the IRS's consent. The election cannot be made before the foreign national has met the substantial presence test for the calendar year following the election year.[67]

[66] Sec. 911(e)(2).

[67] Sec. 7701(b)(4).

ADDITIONAL COMMENT
The special resident alien election is made by attaching to a joint return a statement that the Sec. 6013(g) election is being made. This election must be made within the time period designated for filing a claim for credit or refund.

Section 6013(g) permits nonresident aliens who are married to U.S. citizens or resident aliens to elect to be taxed as resident aliens. Such an election requires both spouses to agree to be taxed on their worldwide income and to provide all books, records, and information necessary to determine either spouse's tax liability. The election permits nonresident aliens to file a joint tax return with their spouses. By filing a joint return, the spouses can take advantage of the lower tax rates available to married persons filing jointly.

Another election permits nonresident aliens to be treated as resident aliens for income tax and wage withholding purposes. To qualify for the election, the foreign national must be a nonresident alien at the beginning of the tax year and a resident alien at the end of the year and must be married to a U.S. citizen or resident alien at the end of the tax year. Both spouses must make the election, which provides the same tax benefits as a Sec. 6013(g) election and eliminates nonresident alien tax treatment for part of the year and resident alien tax treatment for the remainder of the year.

COMPLIANCE AND PROCEDURAL CONSIDERATIONS

FOREIGN OPERATIONS OF U.S. CORPORATIONS

U.S. corporations must provide a summary of their overseas business activities on Form 1120, Schedule N (Foreign Operations of U.S. Corporations). This form reports information relating to interests in foreign partnerships, stock in controlled foreign corporations, and foreign bank and securities accounts.

REPORTING THE FOREIGN TAX CREDIT

Individual taxpayers claim the foreign tax credit on Form 1116. Corporate taxpayers claim the credit on Form 1118. Separate forms must be filed for each of the foreign tax credit limitation baskets. A completed Form 1116 is illustrated in Appendix B. This form is based on the following situation:

EXAMPLE C:16-35 ▶ Andrew Roberts is a U.S. citizen and resident who files jointly with his wife. They have no children. His Social Security number is 123-45-6789. In 2006, he reports $30,000 (Canadian) of dividend income on which $4,500 (Canadian) in income taxes are withheld on December 31, 2006. On December 31, 2006, 1.5843 Canadian dollars equal $1 (U.S.). The Canadian dollars translate into $18,936 (U.S.) of dividend income and $2,840 (U.S.) of income taxes. Roberts owns 3% of the distributing foreign corporation's outstanding stock. The Canadian taxes are translated at the exchange rate for the date on which they were withheld (December 31, 2006). The $18,936 (U.S.) of gross income is reduced by an allocable portion of Andrew's deductions. Andrew can claim the entire $2,840 ($18,936 × 0.15) (U.S.) foreign tax withheld from the dividend, as a foreign tax credit subject to Andrew's credit limitation for the passive income basket. The Roberts' taxable income before exemptions (Form 1040, Line 41) is $86,000, and their tax before credits (Form 1040, Line 44) is $12,965. ◀

REPORTING THE EARNED INCOME EXCLUSION

The elections for the foreign earned income and housing cost exclusions are made separately on Form 2555 or Form 2555-EZ. The latter form can be used by a taxpayer who meets the bona fide residence or physical presence test and maintains a tax home in a foreign country during the requisite period. In addition, the taxpayer must (1) be a U.S. citizen or resident alien, (2) have earned wages/salaries in a foreign country, (3) report total foreign earned income of $82,400 (in 2006) or less, (4) file a tax return for a 12-month period, (5) have earned no self employment income, and (6) have incurred no business and/or moving expenses. Each election must be made on an income tax return that is timely filed (including any extensions), a later amended return filed within the appropriate limitations period, or an original income tax return filed within one year after the return's due date. Once made, the election remains in effect for that year and all subsequent years

KEY POINT

Taxpayers who regularly reside in a foreign country generally qualify under both the physical presence and bona fide residence tests. Tax practitioners must indicate on Form 2555 which one of the two tests has been met when claiming the foreign earned exclusion. Determining whether one is a foreign resident is more difficult than merely determining one's physical presence during the tax year. If a taxpayer fails the physical presence test, the client should retain documentation (e.g., rent receipts, employment contract, and visas) to support the bona fide residence claim should an IRS inquiry occur.

unless the IRS consents to revocation. Thus, a new election is not required when an individual either moves from one foreign country to another or moves to the United States and then returns to a foreign country years later.[68]

At the end of their first year in a foreign country, U.S. expatriates often face a dilemma. They would like to claim the foreign earned income and/or housing cost exclusion (deduction) for the current year but have not yet met either the bona fide residency or physical presence test. As a result, despite their intention to remain in the foreign country until such time as they have met one these tests, they might have to include their foreign earnings in gross income and pay U.S. taxes on an otherwise excludible amount. If in a subsequent year they eventually meet either test because of their extended stay in the foreign country, they might have to file an amended return or a refund claim to retroactively recover the foregone Sec. 911 benefits for the previous year. To avoid this result, Treasury Regulations grant these taxpayers an extension for filing their first year return until such time as they will have met either the residence or physical presence test.[69] Regulations also grant these taxpayers a general filing extension to the fifteenth day of the sixth month following the close of the tax year.[70]

Appendix B contains a completed Form 2555 based on the following situation:

EXAMPLE C:16-36 ▶ Lawrence Smith, a U.S. citizen, Social Security number 234-56-7890, is employed in 2006 by the Very Public Corporation in Paris, France. Smith is eligible for the Sec. 911 earned income exclusion for all of 2006 even though he spent five business days in the United States. For 2006, Smith can exclude up to $82,400 under the foreign earned income exclusion and an additional $8,116 ($21,300 qualifying expenses − $13,184 base housing amount) under the housing cost exclusion. This $90,516 ($82,400 + $8,116) is not reduced by any disallowed-for-AGI deductions because Smith deducts all his employment-related expenses as miscellaneous itemized deductions. ◀

FILING REQUIREMENTS FOR ALIENS AND FOREIGN CORPORATIONS

A nonresident alien reports income on Form 1040-NR on or before the fifteenth day of the sixth month following the close of the tax year. If the nonresident alien's wages are subject to tax withholding, Form 1040-NR must be filed on or before the fifteenth day of the fourth month following the close of the tax year.[71]

A foreign corporation reports income on Form 1120-F.[72] If the foreign corporation maintains no U.S. office or place of business, the due date for its income tax return is the fifteenth day of the sixth month following the close of its tax year. If the corporation maintains a U.S. office or place of business, the due date is the fifteenth day of the third month following the close of its tax year.

FINANCIAL STATEMENT IMPLICATIONS

OBJECTIVE 10

Understand the financial statement implications of various international transactions

FOREIGN TAX CREDIT

A corporation having excess foreign taxes because of the foreign tax credit (FTC) limitation will record a deferred tax asset, possibly subject to a valuation allowance. The valuation allowance, in turn, will increase the corporation's effective tax rate. On the other hand, full use of the foreign tax credit without limitation will not affect the corporation's effective tax rate.

For example: Upsilon Corporation operates in the United States and in Country Low using a foreign branch. Country Low's tax rate is 20%. In the current year, Upsilon earns $1 million from its U.S. operations and $400,000 from its Country Low operations. Thus,

[68] Reg. Sec. 1.911-7(a).
[69] Reg. Sec. 1.911-7(c).
[70] Reg. Sec. 1.6081-5(a).
[71] Reg. Sec. 1.6072-1(c).
[72] Reg. Secs. 1.6072-2(a) and (b) and 1.6081-5(a).

Upsilon pays $80,000 ($400,000 × 0.20) of foreign taxes to Country Low, producing the following tax results:

U.S.-source income	$1,000,000
Foreign-source income	400,000
Taxable income	$1,400,000
Times: U.S. tax rate	0.34
U.S. tax before FTC	$ 476,000
Minus: Foreign tax credit	(80,000)
U.S. taxes payable	$ 396,000

For book purposes, Upsilon's total income tax expense is $476,000 ($396,000 U.S. + $80,000 foreign). Accordingly, Upsilon makes the following book journal entry:

Total income tax expense	476,000	
Total income taxes payable		476,000

In this case, Upsilon reports the following book results:

Net income before income tax expense	$1,400,000
Minus: Total income tax expense	(476,000)
Net income	$ 924,000
U.S. taxes ($396,000/$1,400,000)	28.29%
Foreign taxes ($80,000/$1,400,000)	5.71%
Total effective tax rate	34.00%

Suppose instead that Upsilon's foreign branch is in Country High, which imposes a 45% tax rate. In this case, Upsilon's foreign taxes are $180,000 ($400,000 × 0.45), with the FTC limited to $136,000 ($476,000 × $400,000/$1,400,000). Assuming no carry-back opportunity, the $44,000 ($180,000 − $136,000) excess carries over for ten years. Upsilon's net U.S. tax is $340,000 ($476,000 − $136,000), and its total tax liability is $520,000 ($340,000 U.S. + $180,000 foreign).

For book purposes, Upsilon records a $44,000 deferred tax asset for the FTC carry-over. However, if Upsilon continues to operate only in Country High, it likely will not realize the deferred tax asset because of the FTC limitation. Therefore, Upsilon also must record a $44,000 valuation allowance. Accordingly, Upsilon makes the following book journal entry:

Total income tax expense	520,000	
Deferred tax asset	44,000	
Valuation allowance		44,000
Total income taxes payable		520,000

In this case, Upsilon reports the following book results:

Net income before income tax expense	$1,400,000
Minus: Total income tax expense	(520,000)
Net income	$ 880,000
U.S. taxes ($340,000/$1,400,000)	24.28%
Foreign taxes ($180,000/$1,400,000)	12.86%
Total effective tax rate	37.14%

This effective tax rate reconciles to the 34% statutory tax rate as follows:

Statutory tax rate	34.00%
Valuation allowance ($44,000/$1,400,000)	3.14%
Total effective tax rate	37.14%

Alternatively, Upsilon plans to open second branch in Country Low. Because all income falls into the general limitation basket, Upsilon can offset the excess foreign taxes from Country High against the excess FTC limitation from Country Low and thereby use the FTC carryover within the next ten years. With these alternative facts, Upsilon need not record the valuation allowance, so its U.S. income tax expense per books reflects the entire foreign tax credit. Thus, Upsilon's U.S. tax expense is $296,000 ($476,000 − $180,000), and its foreign tax expense is $180,000, for a total of $476,000. Accordingly, Upsilon makes the following book journal entry:

Total income tax expense	476,000	
Deferred tax asset	44,000	
Total income taxes payable		520,000

In this case, Upsilon reports the following book results:

Net income before income tax expense	$1,400,000
Minus: Total income tax expense	(476,000)
Net income	$ 924,000
U.S. taxes ($296,000/$1,400,000)	21.14%
Foreign taxes ($180,000/$1,400,000)	12.86%
Total effective tax rate	34.00%

DEFERRED FOREIGN EARNINGS

As discussed earlier in this chapter, a U.S. parent does not include a foreign subsidiary's earnings in its (the parent's) gross income until the subsidiary repatriates (remits) the earnings as a dividend. (An exception to this deferral privilege was discussed earlier in the text under Controlled Foreign Subsidiaries.) Under the normal principles of SFAS No. 109, this deferred income would create a deferred tax liability. However, in this situation, SFAS No. 109 adopts the so-called APB No. 23 exception for indefinite reinvestment. Specifically, SFAS No. 109 states that a reporting entity does not recognize a deferred tax asset for the excess of financial reporting basis over tax basis of an investment in a foreign subsidiary unless that temporary difference will reverse in the foreseeable future. Such a basis difference will occur if the consolidated financial statements recognize the foreign earnings but the U.S. parent's tax return does not. If the group does not invoke the APB No. 23 exception because it expects to repatriate the earnings in the future, the deferral and subsequent repatriation will not affect the effective tax rate. One the other hand, if the group does invoke the exception, the deferral is treated as a permanent difference that reduces the effective tax rate. However, if the subsidiary nevertheless remits the earnings in a future year, the repatriation will increase the effective tax rate. Thus, using the exception could cause wide swings in effective tax rates. These potential swings might induce management to forgo the exception or, if using the exception, inhibit management from repatriating the foreign earnings.

For example: Parent Corporation operates in the United States and in Country Low using Foreign Subsidiary in which Parent holds a 100% interest. Country Low's tax rate is 20%. In the current year, Parent earns $1 million from its U.S. operations, and Foreign earns $400,000 from its Country Low operations. Thus, Foreign pays $80,000 ($400,000 × 0.20) of foreign taxes to Country Low, and Parent incurs a $340,000 ($1,000,000 × 0.34) tax liability on its U.S.-source income. Thus, the total tax liability is $420,000 ($340,000 + $80,000), and Parent defers $56,000 of U.S. taxes on the foreign earnings, computed as follows:

Gross foreign earnings	$400,000
Times: U.S. tax rate	0.34
Tax liability before FTC	$136,000
Minus: Potential deemed paid FTC	(80,000)
Deferred tax liability	$ 56,000

For book purposes, the consolidated financial statements include the foreign earnings, so the group's U.S. income tax expense is $396,000, computed as follows:

U.S.-source income	$1,000,000
Foreign-source income	400,000
Net income before income tax expense	$1,400,000
Times: U.S. tax rate	0.34
U.S. income tax expense before FTC	$ 476,000
Minus: Deemed paid FTC	(80,000)
U.S. income tax expense	$ 396,000

Consequently, the group's total income tax expense is $476,000 ($396,000 U.S. + $80,000 foreign). Assuming the group does not invoke the APB No. 23 exception, the group recognizes a deferred tax liability and makes the following book journal entry:

Total income tax expense	476,000	
Deferred tax liability		56,000
Total income taxes payable		420,000

In this case, the group reports the following book results:

Net income before income tax expense	$1,400,000
Minus: Total income tax expense	(476,000)
Net income	$ 924,000
U.S. taxes ($396,000/$1,400,000)	28.29%
Foreign taxes ($80,000/$1,400,000)	5.71%
Total effective tax rate	34.00%

In a subsequent year, Parent again earns $1 million from its U.S. operations, but Foreign has no earnings that year. Nevertheless, Foreign remits a $320,000 dividend to Parent out of prior year earnings from which it paid the $80,000 of foreign taxes. For tax purposes, Parent grosses up the dividend by the deemed paid FTC to $400,000 ($320,000 + $80,000) and claims the deemed paid FTC. Consequently, Parent's U.S. tax on the foreign earnings is $56,000 ($136,000 − $80,000), and its total liability is $396,000 ($340,000 + $56,000).

For book purposes, the group recognizes only the $1 million of U.S.-source earnings, so its total income tax expense is $340,000. Accordingly, the group makes the following book journal entry:

Total income tax expense	340,000	
Deferred tax liability	56,000	
Total income taxes payable		396,000

In this case, the group reports the following book results:

Net income before income tax expense	$1,000,000
Minus: Total income tax expense	(340,000)
Net income	$ 660,000
U.S. taxes ($340,000/$1,000,000)	34.00%
Foreign taxes ($0/$1,000,000)	–0–%
Total effective tax rate	34.00%

Thus, the effective tax rate is the same in each year.

Now assume the group invokes the APB No. 23 exception in the first year thinking it will leave the foreign earnings invested in Foreign indefinitely. Nevertheless, subsequent events lead the group to repatriate the earnings in the later year. In the first year, the group treats the $56,000 deferral as permanent. For book purposes, the consolidated financial statements include the foreign earnings, but the income tax expense does not reflect the permanent difference, so the group's U.S. income tax expense is $340,000, computed as follows:

U.S.-source income	$1,000,000
Foreign-source income	400,000
Net income before income tax expense	$1,400,000
Minus: Foreign source income treated as a permanent difference	(400,000)
Net income after permanent differences	$1,000,000
Times: U.S. tax rate	0.34
U.S. income tax expense	$ 340,000

Consequently, the group's total tax income tax expense is $420,000 ($340,000 U.S. + $80,000 foreign), and the group makes the following book journal entry:

Total income tax expense	420,000	
Total income taxes payable		420,000

In this case, the group reports the following book results:

Net income before income tax expense	$1,400,000
Minus: Total income tax expense	(420,000)
Net income	$ 980,000
U.S. taxes ($396,000/$1,400,000)	24.29%
Foreign taxes ($80,000/$1,400,000)	5.71%
Total effective tax rate	30.00%

This effective tax rate reconciles to the 34% statutory tax rate as follows:

Statutory tax rate	34.00%
Foreign tax treated as a permanent difference ($56,000/$1,400,000)	(4.00%)
Total effective tax rate	30.00%

In the subsequent year when Foreign remits the dividend, the group reverses the "permanent" difference, so the group's U.S. income tax expense is $476,000, computed as follows:

U.S.-source income	$1,000,000
Foreign-source income	–0–
Net income before income tax expense	$1,000,000
Plus: Reversed permanent difference	400,000
Net income after permanent differences	$1,400,000
Times: U.S. tax rate	0.34
U.S. income tax expense before FTC	$ 476,000
Minus: Deemed paid FTC	(80,000)
U.S. income tax expense	$ 396,000

The group's total tax income tax expense also is $396,000 because it incurred no foreign taxes in this year. Accordingly, the group makes the following book journal entry:

Total income tax expense	396,000	
Total income taxes payable		396,000

In this case, the group reports the following book results:

Net income before income tax expense	$1,000,000
Minus: Total income tax expense	(396,000)
Net income	$ 604,000

U.S. taxes ($396,000/$1,000,000)	39.60%
Foreign taxes ($0/$1,000,000)	–0–%
Total effective tax rate	39.60%

This effective tax rate reconciles to the 34% statutory tax rate as follows:

Statutory tax rate	34.00%
Reversal of foreign tax treated as a permanent difference ($56,000/$1,000,000)	5.60%
Total effective tax rate	39.60%

Thus, the effective tax rate varied from 30% in the first year to 39.6% in the subsequent year.

One other point deserves mention. The foreign operations may occur in a high tax foreign country such that the deemed paid FTC completely eliminates the U.S. tax on the repatriated earnings. Consequently, the group would not reduce its effective tax rate by invoking the APB No. 23 exception for indefinite reinvestment. Therefore, corporations in this situation typically do not treat foreign earnings as indefinitely reinvested.

See Chapter C:3 for a general discussion of financial implications of federal income taxes.

PROBLEM MATERIALS

DISCUSSION QUESTIONS

C:16-1 What three elements have the drafters of U.S. tax laws considered in determining the scope of U.S. tax jurisdiction? Explain the importance of each element.

C:16-2 Why is it important for a foreign national to ascertain whether he or she is a resident of the United States?

C:16-3 Explain the alternatives available to individual taxpayers in accounting for foreign taxes paid or accrued on their taxable income.

C:16-4 What types of foreign taxes are eligible to be credited?

C:16-5 In what circumstances might a taxpayer prefer to deduct, rather than credit, foreign taxes?

C:16-6 Why did Congress enact the foreign tax credit limitation rules?

C:16-7 Explain how the separate basket approach to calculating the foreign tax credit has created excess foreign tax credit issues for some U.S. taxpayers.

C:16-8 What advantages does a cash method taxpayer gain by electing to accrue foreign taxes for foreign tax credit purposes?

C:16-9 What requirements must be satisfied for a U.S. citizen or resident living abroad to qualify for the foreign-earned income exclusion?

C:16-10 Tony, a U.S. citizen, uses the calendar year as his tax year. Tony is transferred to Foreign Country C on June 15, 2005, and he immediately becomes a resident of that country. His employer transfers him back to the United States on March 10, 2007. Does Tony qualify for the foreign-earned income exclusion as a bona fide resident? If not, can he qualify in any other way?

C:16-11 Explain why a taxpayer might prefer to claim his or her foreign-earned income exclusion under the physical presence test instead of the bona fide residency test.

C:16-12 Why might a taxpayer choose to forego the foreign-earned income exclusion? If the taxpayer does so in the current tax year, what negative tax consequences might this choice have in future tax years?

C:16-13 Compare the U.S. tax treatment of a nonresident alien and a resident alien, both of whom earn U.S. trade or business and U.S. investment income.

C:16-14 Explain how a nonresident alien is taxed in the year of arrival and departure if he or she arrives in the United States on July 1, 2005 and immediately establishes U.S. residency, and departs from the United States on October 1, 2007, thereby terminating his or her U.S. residency.

C:16-15 How is a nonresident alien's U.S. source investment income taxed? What planning tool(s) is (are) available to reduce the tax rate below 30%? What mechanism is used to collect the tax?

C:16-16 Why is the effectively connected income concept important in taxing a nonresident alien's trade or business?

C:16-17 During the current year, Manuel, a nonresident alien, conducts a U.S. business. He earns $100,000 in sales commissions and $25,000 of interest income. What factor(s) do U.S. taxing authorities consider to determine whether the interest is investment income not subject to U.S. taxation or business income subject to U.S. taxation?

C:16-18 What are the advantages of a U.S. corporation's conducting a foreign business through a foreign branch? Through a foreign subsidiary?

C:16-19 What is the deferral privilege? What tax provisions result in the current U.S. taxation of part or all of a foreign corporation's earnings?

C:16-20 Why did Congress enact the deemed paid foreign tax credit provisions?

C:16-21 What are the "look through" rules? To whom do they apply and for what purposes? What taxable items are subject to these rules?

C:16-22 Kilarney, a foreign corporation, is incorporated in Country J and is 100%-owned by Maine, a domestic corporation. During the current year, Kilarney earns $500,000 from its Country J operations and $100,000 from its U.S. trade or business activities. None of the Country J income is Subpart F. None of Kilarney's after-tax profits are distributed as a dividend to Maine.

a. Explain how Kilarney is taxed in the U.S. and whether any of Kilarney's income is taxed to Maine.

b. How would your answer change if Kilarney earned none of its income from U.S. operations and if Kilarney paid a $50,000 dividend to Maine?

C:16-23 What is the branch profits tax? Explain Congressional intent behind its enactment.

C:16-24 What is a controlled foreign corporation (CFC)? How does the tax treatment of a U.S. stockholder's share of distributed and undistributed CFC profits differ from that of U.S. stockholders in a noncontrolled foreign corporation?

C:16-25 Explain the concept of Subpart F income. What major income categories are taxed under the Subpart F rules?

C:16-26 A primary purpose of Subpart F is to prevent the use of related entities in tax-haven countries to shelter foreign profits from U.S. taxation. Explain how application of the following income concepts accomplish this purpose:

a. Foreign personal holding company income

b. Foreign base company sales income

c. Foreign base company services income

C:16-27 A U.S. manufacturer wants to conduct business through a foreign subsidiary organized in a low tax jurisdiction. How might it do so without being currently taxed on the subsidiary's foreign earnings?

C:16-28 What is the increase in CFC earnings invested in U.S. property? Explain why Congress decided to tax this amount to U.S. shareholders.

C:16-29 Explain the tax consequences to a U.S. shareholder of a CFC distribution of previously taxed Subpart F income.

C:16-30 How does the taxation of a gain recognized when a U.S. shareholder sells stock in a CFC differ from that of a gain recognized when a U.S. shareholder sells stock in a non-CFC?

C:16-31 Explain how the Sec. 482 transfer pricing and CFC rules work together to discourage a domestic corporation's use of a foreign sales subsidiary to avoid U.S. taxation.

C:16-32 What are the tax consequences of an inversion where former shareholders of the merged U.S. corporation own 85% of the voting stock in the new foreign corporation by reason of their U.S. stock ownership? Where they own 75% of this stock by reason of their U.S. stock ownership?

C:16-33 Adam, Britt, and Casey own equal shares of Yankee, Inc., a U.S. corporation. Yankee generates $10 million of taxable income from its U.S. business and $40 million of taxable income from a business conducted in the Republic of Boleckia. Yankee reincorporates as AlienCorp in Boleckia. In the reincorporation, Adam and Britt exchange their shares of Yankee voting stock for an equal number of shares of AlienCorp voting stock, and Yankee merges into AlienCorp. Subsequently, Adam and Britt conduct the U.S. and Boleckia businesses from an office in New York under the AlienCorp logo. Analyze the transaction under the anti-inversion rules, and indicate how it will be taxed.

C:16-34 King, a U.S. corporation, owns 25% of each of two foreign corporations. King's foreign business activities are taxed at foreign tax rates that are higher than those prevailing in the United States. Consequently, King finds itself in an excess foreign tax credit position. Corporation A is located in a country that has concluded a tax treaty with the United States. The treaty reduces from 15% to 5% the withholding on dividends paid to a U.S. corporation. Corporation B is located in a non-treaty country where the withholding rate is 15%. A and B both pay local income taxes at a 20% effective tax rate. If King wants to repatriate profits, which corporation(s) should pay the dividend to minimize the repatriation cost? Can King use such a payment to reduce its excess foreign tax credits associated with its other foreign income?

ISSUE IDENTIFICATION QUESTIONS

C:16-35 Plato Toys has created a new line of plastic toys that it wants to market in Canada. The corporation's headquarters are located in Detroit, Michigan. The company currently exports about $500,000 worth of toys to Canada each year. Most of the toys are sold in the province of Ontario through a Canadian distributor. Profits on current sales average 30% of the selling price to the Canadian distributor. Plato has never had a Canadian office or plant. Because of the corporation's desire to expand its operations, Plato is planning to open branch offices in other Canadian provinces that have large population centers. If a high volume of Canadian sales materializes, the company would like to open a manufacturing facility in Canada at a future date. Your accounting firm has performed audit and tax services for Plato for a number of years. One October morning, Plato's director of taxes, Kelly Hunt, comes to your office and asks that you prepare a presentation to corporate management about the U.S. tax consequences of the company's opening additional sales offices (or a Canadian sales subsidiary). If Canadian activities sufficiently expand, the firm might send U.S. personnel to work in Canada. Plato's CFO has had reservations about transferring employees to Canada and opening branch offices. She wants you to identify possible tax and business problems, in addition to explaining whether it is necessary to operate in Canada to obtain U.S. tax breaks. Prepare a list of tax and non-tax issues faced by Plato that you want to cover in your presentation.

C:16-36 In January of the current year, George Kratzer's U.S. firm assigned him to its Brussels office. During the year, George earned salary, a cost-of-living allowance, a housing allowance, a home leave allowance that permitted him to return home once each year, and an education allowance to pay for his daughter's U.S. schooling. George and his wife, Geneva, have rented an apartment in Brussels and paid Belgian income taxes. What U.S. tax issues should George consider when preparing his tax return?

C:16-37 During the current year, Bailey, a U.S. corporation, began operating overseas. It manufactures machine tools in the United States and sells them to Canadian customers through a branch office located in Toronto. Bailey purchased a 40% investment in a Brazilian corporation from which it later received a dividend. The company received royalties from an English firm that licences machine tool patents owned by Bailey. The English firm uses the patents to manufacture machine tools that the firm sells in England. What international tax issues regarding these activities should Bailey's director of taxes consider?

C:16-38 During the current year, Sanders, a U.S. corporation, organized a foreign subsidiary in Country Z. The subsidiary purchases components from Sanders, assembles them into finished products using Country Z labor, and sells the products to unrelated wholesalers in Countries X, Y, and Z through its own sales force. Assembly costs are 25% of the wholesale price. The foreign subsidiary has paid Sanders (its parent) no dividends this year. What tax issues regarding these activities should Sanders' director of taxes consider?

PROBLEMS

C:16-39 *Translation of Foreign Tax Payments.* Arnie, a U.S. citizen who uses the calendar year as his tax year and the cash method of accounting, operates a sole proprietorship in Country Z. In 2006, he reports 500,000 dubles of pretax profits. On June 1, 2007, he pays Country Z income taxes of 150,000 dubles for calendar year 2006. Duble-U.S. dollar exchange rates on various dates in 2006 and 2007 are as follows:

December 31, 2006	4.00 dubles = $1 (U.S.)
2006 average	3.75 dubles = $1 (U.S.)
June 1, 2007	4.25 dubles = $1 (U.S.)

a. What is the U.S. dollar amount of Arnie's foreign tax credit? In what year can Arnie claim the credit?

b. How would your answer to Part a change if Arnie elected to accrue his foreign income taxes on December 31, 2006, and filed his 2006 U.S. income tax return on April 15, 2007?

c. What adjustment to the credit claimed in Part b would Arnie have to make when he pays his Country Z taxes on June 1, 2007?

C:16-40 *Foreign Tax Credit Limitation.* During the current year, Jackson, a U.S. corporation and accrual method taxpayer, engages in both U.S. and foreign business activities. All its overseas activities are conducted by a branch in Country S. The results of Jackson's current year operations are as follows:

U.S. source taxable income	$2,000,000
Foreign source taxable income	1,500,000
Accrued Country S income taxes	600,000

a. What is the amount of Jackson's foreign tax credit (assuming the corporate tax rate is 34% and income from all foreign activities fall into a single basket)?
b. Are any foreign tax credit carrybacks or carryovers available? If so, in what years can they be used?

C:16-41 *Foreign Tax Credit Limitation.* Tucson, a U.S. corporation organized in 2005, reports the following items for the period 2005–2007.

	2005	*2006*	*2007*
Foreign tax accrual	$ 100,000	$ 120,000	$ 180,000
Foreign source taxable income	400,000	300,000	500,000
Worldwide taxable income	1,000,000	1,000,000	1,000,000

The foreign source and worldwide taxable income items are determined under U.S. law.
a. What is Tucson's foreign tax credit limitation for the years 2005–2007 (assume a 34% U.S. corporate tax rate and that income from all foreign activities fall into a single basket)?
b. How are Tucson's excess foreign tax credits (if any) treated? Do any carryovers remain after 2007?
c. How would your answers to Parts a and b change if the IRS determines that $100,000 of expenses allocable to U.S.-source income should have been allocable to foreign-source income?
d. What measures should Tucson consider if it expects its current excess foreign tax credit position to persist in the long-run?

C:16-42 *Foreign-Earned Income Exclusion.* Julia, a U.S. citizen, leaves the United States at noon on August 1, 2004 and arrives in Country P at 8:00 a.m. the next day. She immediately establishes in Country P a permanent residence, which she maintains until her return to the United States at 3:00 p.m. on April 5, 2006. Her only trips outside Country P are related to temporary employment in Country B from November 1, 2004, through December 10, 2004, and a U.S. vacation beginning at 5:00 p.m. on June 1, 2005, and ending at 10:00 p.m. on June 30, 2005. Does Julia qualify for the Sec. 911 benefits? If so, what is the amount of her foreign earned income exclusion for the years 2004–2006?

C:16-43 *Foreign-Earned Income Exclusion.* Fred, a U.S. citizen, arrives in Country K on July 15, 2004 and proceeds to a construction site in its oil fields. Once there, he moves into employer-provided housing where he is required to reside. Except for brief periods of local travel and the months of July and August 2005 when he is on vacation in the United States, he remains at the site until his departure on December 1, 2006. He provides no services while in the United States. Fred earns $10,000 per month in salary and allowances while employed overseas. In addition, while in Country K, he receives meals and lodging valued at $1,750 per month. What is the amount of Fred's Sec. 911 exclusions for the years 2004–2006?

C:16-44 *Foreign-Earned Income Exclusion.* Dillon, a U.S. citizen, resides in Country K for all of 2006. Dillon is married, files a joint return and claims two personal exemptions. The following items pertain to his 2006 activities:

Salary and allowances (other than for housing)[a]	$175,000
Housing allowance	28,000
Employment-related expenses[b]	7,500
Housing costs	30,000
Other itemized deductions	4,000
Country K income taxes	12,000

[a]All of Dillon's salary and allowances are attributable to services performed in Country K.
[b]Dillon claims the employment-related expenses as itemized deductions.

What is Dillon's net U.S. tax liability for 2006 (assume that Dillon excludes his earned income and housing cost amount)?

C:16-45 *Tax Calculation for a Nonresident Alien.* Tien is a citizen of Country C. During the current year (2007), she is a nonresident alien for U.S. tax purposes and earns the following amounts:

Dividend received from a U.S. corporation	$ 2,500
Rentals from leasing a U.S. building	13,000
Interest received from a foreign corporation	5,000

Tien does not conduct a U.S. trade or business. Her interest and depreciation expenses from leasing the building under a net lease arrangement total $7,000.

a. Assuming the real estate income is investment related, what is Tien's U.S. tax liability? How is the tax collected?
b. How does your answer to Part a change if Tien makes an election to treat the real estate activity as a U.S. trade or business?

C:16-46 *Taxation of a Nonresident Alien.* Pierre, a single nonresident alien, conducts a U.S. trade or business for 80 days during the current year. Pierre reports the following income items from his U.S. activities. Indicate how each of these items will be taxed and how the tax will be collected.

a. $25,000 of dividends earned on a U.S. portfolio stock investment unrelated to Pierre's trade or business.
b. $75,000 of sales commissions Pierre earned as an employee of a foreign corporation. Pierre generated $50,000 from sales in the United States and $25,000 from sales outside the United States.
c. A $10,000 capital gain on the sale of stock in a U.S. corporation realized by Pierre while in the United States.
d. $3,000 of interest earned on a bank account in Pierre's home country and $1,800 of interest earned on a bank account located in Jacksonville, Florida.

C:16-47 *Deemed Paid Foreign Tax Credit.* Paper, a U.S. corporation, owns 40% of the stock in Sud, a foreign corporation. Sud reports post-1986 earnings and profits of $200,000 (before the payment of any current dividends) and post-1986 foreign income taxes of $50,000. In the current year, Sud pays a total of $90,000 in dividends to all its shareholders. It withholds from the gross dividends paid to nonresident shareholders a 15% Country T income tax.

a. What gross income amount does Paper report upon receiving the dividend?
b. To what extent is Paper's U.S. tax liability increased as a result of the dividend (assume a 34% U.S. corporate tax rate)?
c. How would your answer to Parts a and b change if the post-1986 foreign income taxes instead had been $80,000?

C:16-48 *Deemed Paid Foreign Tax Credit.* Duke, a U.S. corporation, owns all the stock in Taiwan, a foreign corporation. In the current year, Taiwan pays to Duke a $125,000 dividend from which $12,500 in foreign taxes are withheld. Taiwan's post-1986 operating results indicate $1 million of earnings and profits (before payment of the dividend) and $300,000 of foreign income taxes. Assume Duke has no other foreign source income and its U.S. taxable income (excluding the dividend) is $1 million.

a. What is the amount of Duke's deemed paid foreign tax credit?
b. To what extent is Duke's U.S. tax liability increased as a result of the dividend (assume a 34% U.S. corporate tax rate)?
c. How would your answers to Parts a and b change if the $125,000 dividend were instead paid to U.S. citizen Donna (instead of to Duke), whose marginal tax rate is 35%? Assume the foreign-source dividend does not qualify for the 15% reduced tax rate.

C:16-49 *Translation of a Dividend.* Dayton, a U.S. corporation, owns all the stock in Fiero, a foreign corporation organized in early 2007. During 2007, Fiero earns 400,000 pirogs of pretax profits and accrues 100,000 pirogs of Country Z income taxes. On August 25, 2007, Fiero pays to Dayton a 150,000 pirog dividend on which 7,500 pirogs in Country Z taxes are withheld. On March 1, 2008, Fiero pays 100% of its Country Z income taxes for 2007. Assume Dayton has no other foreign source income, and its U.S. taxable income (excluding the dividend) is $1 million. The pirog-U.S. dollar exchange rate on various dates in 2007 and 2008 are as follows:

January 1, 2007	9.0 pirogs = $1 (U.S.)
August 25, 2007	10.0 pirogs = $1 (U.S.)
2007 average	9.5 pirogs = $1 (U.S.)
March 1, 2008	11.0 pirogs = $1 (U.S.)

a. For U.S. tax reporting purposes, what are Dayton's dividend and deemed paid foreign tax credit amounts in U.S. dollars?

b. What is Dayton's net U.S. tax liability as a result of the dividend?

C:16-50 *Worldwide Tax Rates.* Young Corporation conducts a business in both the United States and a foreign country. In each of the following scenarios, what is Young's worldwide (combined U.S. and foreign) tax rate relative to the branch income it earns in the foreign country? Assume that Young wants to claim the maximum foreign tax credit possible.

Scenario	*U.S. Tax Rate*	*Foreign Tax Rate*
1	34%	0%
2	34%	15%
3	34%	34%
4	34%	40%

What incentive exists for the foreign country to increase its tax rates if the United States taxes foreign income when earned? What incentive exists for a foreign country to lower its tax rates if a foreign subsidiary earns income in one year but is taxed in a later year when the income is repatriated to the United States?

C:16-51 *Section 902 Dividend Look Through Rules.* Hamilton, a U.S. corporation, reports the following results from its current year activities:

U.S.-source taxable income	$1,000,000
Foreign-source taxable income from manufacturing branch in Country M	1,000,000
Foreign taxes paid on branch income	390,000
Gross U.S. income tax liability	799,000

Hamilton owns 20% of the stock in Beauvais, a foreign corporation. Beauvais pays a $350,000 dividend to Hamilton on April 20 of the current year. Beauvais' pretax profits from post-1986 tax years are $6 million, and its Country X taxes from post-1986 tax years are $1.2 million. Beauvais' E&P under U.S. rules is $4 million, $3.6 million of which was derived from foreign manufacturing and $400,000 of which was earned on foreign securities. All of the foregoing figures were recorded before payment of the dividend.

a. For foreign tax credit purposes, into which of Hamilton's limitation baskets should the dividend from Beauvais be placed and in what amounts?

b. Calculate Hamilton's current year foreign tax credit.

c. How should any excess credits be treated?

C:16-52 *Definition of a CFC.* In each of the following scenarios, determine whether a foreign corporation with a single class of stock outstanding, is a controlled foreign corporation.

a. The foreign corporation's stock is owned equally by Alpha, a U.S. corporation, and Bart, a U.S. citizen, who owns no Alpha stock.

b. Assume the same facts as in Part a except Bart is a nonresident alien.

c. The foreign corporation's stock is owned 7% by Art, 49% by Phong, 29% by Colleen, and 15% by Danielle. Art, Colleen, and Danielle are U.S. citizens, and Phong is a nonresident alien. All four individuals are unrelated.

d. Assume the same facts as in Part c except Danielle is Art's daughter.

C:16-53 *Definition of Foreign Base Company Income.* Manila Corporation is organized in Country J. All of Manila's stock is owned by Simpson, a U.S. corporation. Indicate which of the following transactions generate Subpart F income.

a. Manila purchases a product from Simpson and sells it to unrelated parties in Countries J and X.

b. Manila receives a dividend from Manila-Sub, a foreign corporation organized and operating exclusively in Country J. All of Manila-Sub's stock has been owned by Manila since its incorporation.

c. Manila purchases raw materials locally, manufactures products in Country J, and sells the products to an unrelated purchaser for use in Country Z.

d. Manila services machinery manufactured by an unrelated Country J corporation. Revenues from servicing this machinery outside of Country J constitute 80% of Manila's gross income.
e. Manila purchases a product from a related U.S. corporation and sells the product to unrelated persons in Country Z.

C:16-54 *Definition of Foreign Base Company Income.* Apache, a U.S. corporation, owns 80% of the stock in Burrito, incorporated in Country Y. Burrito reports the following results for the current year:

	Gross Income	*Deductions*
Foreign base company sales income	$300,000	$120,000
Foreign base company services income	150,000	90,000
Dividend from Kane, a 70%-owned Country Y corporation	70,000	–0–
Rental income earned in Country Y	280,000	220,000

Kane conducts substantially all its business in Country Y.
a. What amount of income must Apache recognize as a result of Burrito's activities?
b. How would your answer to Part a change if Kane were instead a 70%-owned Country M corporation?
c. How would your answer to Part b change if foreign base company sales income before deductions were instead $500,000?

C:16-55 *Transfer Pricing Rules.* Arrow, a U.S. corporation, annually sells one million starter motors to Bentley, a wholly owned foreign subsidiary organized in Country K. Bentley sells the starters as replacement parts through auto dealers in Country K. The statutory Country K tax rate is 20%.
a. What is the value of Arrow's annual U.S. tax deferral if the starters cost Arrow $30 to produce, are sold to Bentley for $50, and are re-sold to the auto dealers for $70? Assume Bentley's operating expenses are $4 million.
b. What additional benefit would accrue to Arrow annually if it reduced the sale price of each starter from $50 to $30? What mechanisms are likely to be used by U.S. tax authorities to address this situation?
c. How would your answer to Part a change if Bentley sold one-half of the starters to auto dealers in Country M under the same terms as it sold them to auto dealers in Country K?

C:16-56 *Sale of CFC Stock.* On April 1, 2005, Irvan, a U.S. corporation, acquired for $300,000 all the stock in DeLeon, a foreign corporation. At the close of business on September 30, 2007, Irvan sells the DeLeon stock for $825,000. Irvan reports $25,000 of Subpart F income as a result of DeLeon's 2005–2007 activities. DeLeon reports E&P balances for the period 2005–2007 as follows:

Year	*E&P*
2005	$120,000
2006	110,000
2007	144,000

a. What are the amount and character of Irvan's gain on the sale of the DeLeon stock?
b. Can Irvan use any of DeLeon foreign taxes to reduce its U.S. tax liability on the stock gain?

COMPREHENSIVE PROBLEM

C:16-57 Allen Blay owns 100% of the stock in AB Corporation, organized ten years ago under the laws of California. AB operates a foreign branch in Country A. In the current year, AB reports $500,000 of taxable income from U.S. activities. The branch reports a 400,000 pirog loss, which translates into a $60,000 (U.S.) loss. Neither the branch nor the U.S. corporation paid Country A income taxes in the current year.

AB owns 50% of FC1, incorporated in Country B. Bob Haynes, a resident of Country B, owns the remaining FC1 stock. In the current year, FC1 generated 200,000 kira of Country B taxable income. The Country B corporate income tax rate is 25%. On December 31, FC1 remitted 50,000 kira of current year profits to AB. The kira-U.S. dollar exchange rate on December 31 was 1.25 kira = $1.00 (U.S.). Amounts repatriated to the United States are subject to a 15% Country B withholding tax. The United States-Country B tax treaty reduces this rate to 10%.

AB owns 100% of the stock in FC2, incorporated in Country C. FC2 purchases electronic testing equipment from AB and employs a local sales force to distribute the equipment throughout the region. Forty percent of the FC2 sales are made to customers in Country C. The remaining sales are made to customers in Country D. Total pre-tax profits from FC2's sales were 275,000 tesos in the current year. FC2 remitted none of its profits to AB. FC2 earned an additional 200,000 tesos of pre-tax profits from manufacturing electronic testing equipment from parts produced by Country C companies and from selling this equipment in Countries C and D. FC2 paid 60,000 tesos of Country C income taxes on its current year activities. The teso-U.S. dollar exchange rate on December 31 was 1.5 tesos = $1.00 (U.S.). FC2 remitted no profits to the United States. The profit margins on sales of electronic testing equipment in the Country C and D markets are substantially higher than those in the United States.

In June of the current year, AB assigned Brad Gould to work for FC2. Brad relocated from Sunnyvale, California, to Country C under a three-year employment contract.

Required: Explain the U.S. tax consequences of each of AB's overseas activities.

TAX STRATEGY PROBLEM

C:16-58 Miami-based Florida Corporation manufactures electronic games that it has sold overseas for the past two years. Its foreign operations are conducted primarily through two distributors in South America who divide up the South American market and handle sales activities within their assigned areas. Florida has been shipping Spanish and Portuguese versions of its U.S. video games directly from Miami to its two South American distributors and billing the distributors for the shipments. All South American advertising, distribution, and billing activities are the responsibility of the two distributors.

In talking with Florida's chief financial officer (CFO), you learn that the company has been paying U.S. corporate income taxes at a 34% rate on its $2 million of profits generated from sales to the two distributors. The company has paid no foreign taxes on this profit because the sales to the two South American distributors have occurred in the United States. The CFO believes that the company can avoid foreign taxation because it has not set up a permanent establishment in any foreign country. The CFO indicates that she would like to reduce or defer the U.S. tax burden on part or all of these profits by setting up a South American subsidiary to distribute the games throughout South America. The subsidiary would be located in a South American country where the income tax rate is substantially less than the 34% U.S. corporate tax rate. She has found two countries that offer favorable business climates in which to establish an overseas presence. The maximum income tax rate in each country is 15%.

The CFO believes she can shift all or a large portion of the foreign sales profits to the country in which the subsidiary is established. By shifting part or all of the profits on the overseas sales to this country, the CFO hopes to defer the 34% U.S. corporate income tax until the profits are repatriated to the United States. Florida also hopes to obtain a tax holiday that would permit deferral or exemption of foreign income taxes as an incentive for investing in the foreign country. Ideally, the effective foreign tax rate would be 15% or lower.

Required: Florida's CFO would like you to advise her on alternative ways to conduct the foreign sales so as to reduce and/or defer the the company's worldwide tax liability. Compare the after-tax earnings that accrue to a foreign branch and a foreign subsidiary over a five-year period. What alternative business forms can Florida use to conduct its overseas activities? For each alternative, identify the U.S. tax treatment, determine the available tax savings, and indicate whether such savings reflect a tax deferral or a permanent exclusion from U.S. income taxation. In addition, identify whether Florida must establish a foreign office or manufacturing facility in a foreign country to obtain tax reductions or deferrals.

TAX FORM/RETURN PREPARATION PROBLEMS

C:16-59 Stephen R. and Rachel K. Bates, both U.S. citizens, resided in Country K for the entire current year except when Stephen was temporarily assigned to his employer's home office in the United States. They file a joint return and use the calendar year as their tax year. Their taxpayer identification number is 123-45-6789. The Bateses report the following current-year income and expense items:

Salary and allowances: United States	$ 20,000
Country K	150,000
Dividends: From U.S. corporation	2,000
From Country K corporation	15,000
Unreimbursed foreign business expenses (directly allocable to Country K earned income and deductible as a miscellaneous itemized deduction)	5,000
Charitable contributions paid to U.S. charities (not directly allocable to any income item)	8,000
Country K income taxes paid on April 1 of current year (in dollars)	12,500
Personal and dependency exemptions	2

Last year, the Bateses elected to accrue their foreign income taxes for foreign tax credit purposes. No foreign tax credit carryovers to the current year are available. Stephen Bates estimates the family will owe 75,000 tesos in Country K income taxes for this year on the Country K salary and dividends. The average annual exchange rate for the current year is 4 tesos to $1 (U.S.). The teso-U.S. dollar exchange rate did not change between year-end and the date the Bates paid their Country K taxes. No Country K taxes were withheld on the foreign corporation dividend.

Complete the two Form 1116s the Bateses must file with their income tax return to claim a credit for the foreign taxes paid on the salary and dividends. Use 2006 tax forms and ignore the implications of the Sec. 911 earned income exclusion, itemized deduction and personal exemption phase-outs, and alternative minimum tax provisions.

C:16-60 John Lawrence Bailey (Social Security number 234-56-7890) is employed in Country T by American Conglomerate Corporation. Bailey has resided with his wife and three children in Country T for seven years. He made one five-day business trip back to the United States in the current year, and $2,000 of his salary (but none of the allowances) is allocable to the U.S. business trip. Bailey reports the following tax-related information for the current year:

Income:	
Base salary	$100,000
Overseas premium in addition to base salary	15,000
Cost-of-living allowance	37,500
Housing allowance	30,000
Education allowance	16,000
Home leave travel allowance	11,000
Income tax reimbursement from employer for preceding tax year	25,000
Expenditures:	
Tuition at U.S. school	12,000
Housing expenses (rental of home and related expenses)	32,500
Itemized deductions (including $4,000 of unreimbursed employee expenses)	10,000
Foreign income taxes	12,000

Complete a 2006 Form 2555 for the Baileys' current tax year. Assume Mr. Bailey established foreign residency in 2002, and all prior tax returns were filed with a Form 2555 claiming that Mr. Bailey was a bona fide foreign resident.

CASE STUDY PROBLEMS

C:16-61 You have performed tax services for Mark Pruett, a U.S. citizen who is being transferred abroad by his employer. Mark's 2006 salary and allowances in Country M will be $210,000, which is substantially above his 2005 salary. The salary differential is due to the higher cost of living in Country M and Mark's added responsibilities. Of the allowances, $30,000 is for housing although Mark's 2006 housing costs are expected to be $40,000. The Country M income tax rate is 40%. Mark's employer conducts business at a second location in Country T, where Mark probably will be transferred in three or four years. The Country T income tax rate is 20%.

The transfer date is February 1. Mark's wife and three-year-old daughter will accompany him. Mark expects to return to the United States for one week of training each year starting in September 2006. Mark takes four weeks of vacation each year. Because Mark still has family in the United States, he may spend substantial vacation time in the United States.

Required: Your tax manager has asked you to draft for her review a memorandum explaining the tax consequences of the relocation, whether Mark is entitled to the foreign earned income exclusion, and what records Mark must maintain to file his tax return for the year of transfer.

C:16-62 Ralph Sampson was hired last year by a small international trading company. You have prepared Ralph's tax returns for a number of years while he worked in the U.S. offices of a large international bank. You continue to perform tax services for Ralph while he is overseas to manage the trading company's office in Country T (a nontreaty country). Ralph has been assigned abroad since November 1, 2005, and has continuously resided in a company-provided apartment located in Country T's capital. His wife and child have maintained their old residence in the United States to enable Mrs. Sampson to continue her career as a university professor and their son to finish high school. During 2005, Ralph was in Country T and other foreign countries for all of November and December. During 2006, Ralph was in the United States for 93 days (spread out evenly throughout the four quarters of that year) and in Country T and other foreign countries for the remainder of the year. Ralph wants you to file an amended 2005 tax return and an initial 2006 tax return claiming on each return the maximum possible foreign earned income exclusion. (The 2005 return originally was filed without claiming the foreign earned income exclusion because Ralph had not yet qualified for the exclusion when the return was due.) Ralph knows that he does not meet the physical presence test, but he has assured you that he meets the bona fide residence test. However, because of his heavy 2006 travel schedule, he has not yet been able to document that he is a Country T resident.

In June 2007, the Sampsons' son will graduate from high school. Mrs. Sampson plans to join her son overseas and obtain a teaching position in an American school for U.S. expatriates. The Sampsons' son will spend 2½ months of summer with his parents overseas but will return to the United States to attend the University of Tennessee. He will join his parents for an additional four weeks in December and January during the university's holiday break.

Required: Should you file the Sampson's amended 2005 tax return and new 2006 income tax return claiming the maximum foreign-earned income exclusion for which Ralph has asked? What information should you ask Ralph to provide before you prepare his return? What ethical issues are raised by your filing the return based on Ralph's promise to obtain the requisite information? When will Mrs. Sampson first be eligible for the foreign earned income exclusion? Under which of the two tests will she likely qualify after she begins her Country T teaching job in June 2007?

TAX RESEARCH PROBLEMS

C:16-63 Spike "Spitball" Weaver, a hard-throwing pitcher, was approaching the end of his major league baseball career. After becoming a free agent at the end of the 2006 baseball season, he signed a lucrative three-year contract (which specified a substantial signing bonus) to play for the Tokyo Bombers in the fledgling World Baseball League starting in 2007. The team's management paid 50% of the bonus in 2006 and will pay the remaining 50% during 2007–2009. This league includes 12 teams, only four of which are located in the United States. Although Spike's salary is paid over a 12-month period, he resides in Japan only for the seven-month regular season, the preseason training period, and the postseason playoffs (if his team makes the playoffs). He spends the remainder of his time at his home in Fitzgerald, Georgia. The tax manager for whom you regularly work has asked you to prepare a memorandum to the file indicating what factors should be considered in allocating Spike's bonus and salary according to work performed at the U.S. and non-U.S. locations.

She suggests that at a minimum you consider

- Reg. Sec. 1.861-4
- Rev. Rul. 76-66, 1976-1 C.B. 189
- Rev. Rul. 87-38, 1987-1 C.B. 176
- *Peter Stemkowski v. CIR*, 50 AFTR 2d 82-5739, 82-2 USTC ¶9589 (2nd Cir., 1982)

C:16-64 Determine whether each of the taxes listed below may be credited against a U.S. income tax liability.

a. Saudi Arabian tax on companies producing petroleum
b. French Company Income Tax

c. Ontario (Canada) Corporations Tax
d. Japan Corporation Tax

A partial list of research sources includes:

- Research Institute of America (RIA), *United States Tax Reporter,* ¶9015.03
- Commerce Clearing House (CCH), *Standard Federal Tax Reporter,* ¶27,826.318
- Bureau of National Affairs (BNA), *Tax Management Portfolios,* individual country portfolios on Saudi Arabia, France, Canada, and Japan

For additional authority, the researcher might consult the tax treaties that the United States has concluded with each of the four countries.

C:16-65 MedTec incorporated in 2000 under the laws of Georgia. It manufactures products for doctors and hospitals in the United States. Because of lower labor costs outside the United States, MedTec establishes in Country X a foreign subsidiary that will manufacture some of its products for shipment back to the United States as well as to other foreign countries. Country X tax rates are lower than U.S. tax rates. In addition, Country X has provided special tax incentives that lead you to believe the subsidiary will pay local income taxes at a 10% rate for the first five years, and at a 25% rate for subsequent years. Only a small portion, if any, of the foreign earnings will be taxed to MedTec under Subpart F. According to financial projections, the foreign subsidiary will generate $500,000 of pre-tax profits each year. Because of MedTec's need for capital to expand its foreign operations, none of the foreign profits will be repatriated to the United States in the first ten years of operations.

Prepare a memorandum for your boss that outlines the proper financial accounting treatment of MedTec's U.S. income taxes with respect to its investment in the Country X subsidiary.

A partial list of research sources is:

- Financial Accounting Standards Board, *SFAS No. 109*
- Accounting Principles Board, *APB Opinion Nos. 23 and 24*
- IRC Sec. 951

C:16-66 AmeriCorp, a U.S. corporation based in Houston, manufactures telecommunications equipment. It sells the equipment to retailers throughout the world. To promote its Latin American sales, AmeriCorp conducts its business through three entities: TelMexico, a *sociedad anonima* organized under Mexican law and 100% owned by AmeriCorp; TelBrazilco, a *sociedade limitada*, organized under Brazilian law and 51% owned by AmeriCorp; and TelCaymanco, an ordinary nonresident company organized under Cayman Islands law and 100% owned by TelBrazilco. Foreign investors own the remaining 49% of TelBrazilco voting stock.

TelMexico routinely purchases telecommunications equipment from AmeriCorp and sells the equipment to independent retailers throughout Central America. This entity derives 20% of its revenues from equipment sales outside of Mexico. TelBrazilco manufactures telecommunications equipment in Brazil and sells the equipment to independent retailers throughout South America. This entity derives 65% of its income from equipment sales outside of Brazil. TelCaymanco purchases telecommunications equipment exclusively from TelBrazilco and sells the equipment to independent retailers throughout Europe. This entity derives 99% of its revenues from equipment sales outside the Cayman Islands. Periodically, TelMexico pays dividends to AmeriCorp, and TelCaymanco pays dividends to TelBrazilco.

AmeriCorp's chief financial officer has approached you with the following questions:

1. What are the tax implications of this organizational structure? Specifically, are the entities controlled foreign corporations, and do their activities generate Subpart F income?
2. Can AmeriCorp use the check-the-box regulations to change the tax treatment of any foreign entity?
3. What tax consequences would ensue if AmeriCorp elected to have,
   a. TelCaymanco and TelBrazilco taxed as corporations (i.e., associations)?
   b. TelBrazilco taxed as a corporation (TelCaymanco would be disregarded as a taxable entity)?

Write a memorandum that addresses these questions. At a minimum, consult the following authorities:

- Reg. Secs. 301.7701-2 and 301.7701-3

APPENDIX A

TAX RESEARCH WORKING PAPER FILE

INDEX TO TAX RESEARCH FILE*

*Most accounting firms maintain a **client file** for each of their clients. Typically, this file contains copies of client letters, memoranda-to-the-file, relevant primary and secondary authorities, and billing information. In our case, the client file for Mercy Hospital would include copies of the following: (1) the September 12 letter to Elizabeth Feghali, (2) the September 9 memorandum-to-the-file, (3) Sec. 119, (4) Reg. Sec. 1.119-1, (5) the *Kowalski* opinion, (6) the *Standard Federal Tax Reporter* annotation, and (7) pertinent billing information.

TAX RESEARCH FILE

As mentioned in Chapter C:1 the tax research process entails six steps.

1. Determine the facts
2. Identify the issues
3. Locate applicable authorities
4. Evaluate these authorities
5. Analyze the facts in terms of applicable authorities
6. Communicate conclusions and recommendations to others.

Let us walk through each of these steps.

Determine the Facts Assume that we have determined the facts to be as follows:

> *Mercy Hospital maintains a cafeteria on its premises. In addition, it rents space to MacDougal's, a privately owned sandwich shop. The cafeteria closes at 8:00 p.m. MacDougal's is open 24 hours. Mercy provides meal vouchers to each of its 240 medical employees to enable them to remain on call in case of emergency. The vouchers are redeemable either at the cafeteria or at MacDougal's. Although the employees are not required to remain on or near the premises during meal hours, they generally do. Elizabeth Fegali, Mercy's Chief Administrator, has approached you with the following question: Is the value of a meal voucher includible in the employees' gross income?*

At this juncture, be sure you understand the facts before proceeding further. Remember, researching the wrong facts could produce the wrong results.

Identify the Issues Identifying the issues presupposes a minimum level of proficiency in tax accounting. This proficiency will come with time, effort, and perseverence. The central issue raised by the facts is the taxability of the meal vouchers. A resolution of this issue will hinge on the resolution of other issues raised in the course of the research.

Locate Applicable Authorities For some students, this step is the most difficult in the research process. It raises the perplexing question, "Where do I begin to look?" The answer depends on the tax resources at one's disposal, as well as one's research preferences. Four rules of thumb apply:

1. *Adopt an approach with which you are comfortable, and that you are confident will produce reliable results.*
2. *Always consult the IRC and other primary authorities.*
3. *Be as thorough as possible, taking into consideration time and billing constraints.*
4. *Make sure that the authorities you consult are current.*

One approach is to conduct a topical search. Begin by consulting the index to the Internal Revenue Code (IRC). Then read the relevant IRC section(s). If the language of the IRC is vague or ambiguous, turn to the Treasury Regulations. Read the relevant regulation section that elaborates or expounds on the IRC provision. If the language of the regulation is confusing or unclear, go to a commercial tax service. Read the relevant tax service paragraphs that explain or analyze the statutory and regulatory provisions. For references to other authorities, browse through the footnotes and annotations of the service. Then, consult these authorities directly. Finally, check the currency of the authorities consulted, with the aid of a citator or status (finding) list.

If a pertinent court decision or IRS ruling has been called to your attention, consult this authority directly. Alternatively, browse through the status (finding) list of a tax service for references to tax service paragraphs that discuss this authority. Better still, consult a citator or status list for references to court opinions or rulings that cite the authority. If you subscribe to a computerized tax service, conduct a keyword, citation, contents, or topical search. (For a discussion of these types of searches, see the computerized research supplement available for download at *www.prenhall.com/phtax*.) Then, hyperlink to the authorities cited within the text of the documents retrieved. So numerous are the approaches to tax research that one is virtually free to pick and choose. All that is required of the researcher is a basic level of skill and some imagination.

Let us adopt a topical approach to the issue of the meal vouchers. If we consult an index to the IRC, we are likely to find the heading "Meals and Lodging." Below this heading are likely to be several subheadings, some pertaining to deductions, others to exclusions. Because the voucher issue pertains to an exclusion, let us browse through these subheadings. In so doing, we will notice that most of these subheadings refer to Sec. 119. If we look up this IRC section, we will see the following passage:

Sec. 119. Meals or lodging furnished for the convenience of the employer.

> (a) **Meals and lodging furnished to employee, his spouse, and his dependents, pursuant to employment.**
> There shall be excluded from gross income of an employee the value of any meals or lodging furnished to him . . . by, or on behalf of his employer for the convenience of the employer, but only if—
>
> (1) **in the case of meals, the meals are furnished on the business premises of the employer . . .**
>
> (b) **Special rules.** For purposes of subsection (a)—
> (4) **Meals furnished to employees on business premises where meals of most employees are otherwise excludable.** All meals furnished on the business premises of an employer to such employer's employees shall be treated as furnished for the convenience of the employer if . . . more than half of the employees to whom such meals are furnished on such premises are furnished such meals for the convenience of the employer.

Section 119 appears to be applicable. It deals with meals furnished to an employee on the business premises of the employer. Our case deals with meal vouchers furnished to employees for redemption at employer-maintained and employer-rented-out facilities. But here, additional issues arise. For purposes of Sec. 119, are meal vouchers the same as "meals"? (Do not assume they are.) Are employer-maintained and employer-rented-out facilities the same as "the business premises of the employer"? (Again, do not assume they are.) And what does the IRC mean by "for the convenience of the employer"? Because the IRC offers no guidance in this respect, let us turn to the Treasury Regulations.

The applicable regulation is Reg. Sec. 1.119-1. How do we know this? Because Treasury Regulation section numbers track the IRC section numbers. Regulation Sec. 1.119-1 is the only regulation under Sec. 119. If we browse through this regulation, we will find the following provision:

> (a) **Meals . . .**
> (2) **Meals furnished without a charge**
> (i) Meals furnished by an employer without charge to the employee will be regarded as furnished for the convenience of the employer if such meals are furnished for a substantial noncompensatory business reason of the employer . . .
> (ii) (a) Meals will be regarded as furnished for a substantial noncompensatory business reason of the employer when the meals are furnished to the employee during his working hours to have the employee available for emergency call during his meal period . . .
>
> (c) **Business premises of the employer.**
> (1) **In general.** For purposes of this section, the term "business premises of the employer" generally means the place of employment of the employee . . .

Based on a reading of this provision, we might conclude that the hospital meals are furnished "for the convenience of the employer." Why? Because they are furnished for a "substantial noncompensatory business reason of the employer," namely, to have the employees available for emergency call during their meal periods. They also are furnished during the employees' working hours. Moreover, under Sec. 119(b)(4), if more than half the employees satisfy the "for the convenience of the employer" test, all employees will be regarded as satisfying the test. But are the meals furnished on "the business premises of the employer"? Under the regulation, the answer would depend. If the meals are furnished in the hospital cafeteria, they probably are furnished on "the business premises of the employer." The hospital is the place of employment of the medical employees. The cafeteria is part of the hospital. On the other hand, if the meals are furnished at MacDougal's, they probably are not furnished on "the business premises of the employer." MacDougal's is not the place of employment of the medical employees. Nor is it a part of the hospital. Thus, Reg. Sec. 1.119-1 is enlightening with respect to two statutory terms: "for the convenience of the employer" and "the business premises of the employer." However, it is obscure with respect to the third term, "meals." Because of this obscurity, let us turn to a tax service.

Although the index to CCH's *Standard Federal Tax Reporter* does not list "meal vouchers," it does list "cash allowances in lieu of meals" as a subtopic under Meals and Lodging. Are meal vouchers the same as cash meal allowances?—perhaps so; let us see. Next to the heading "cash allowances in lieu of meals" is a reference to CCH ¶7222.59. If we look up this reference, we will find the following annotation:

> **¶7222.59 Meal allowances.**—Cash meal allowances received by an employee (state trooper) from his employer were not excludible from income. *R.J. Kowalski,* SCt, 77-2 USTC ¶9748, 434 US 77.[1]

Here we discover that, in the *Kowalski* case, the U.S. Supreme Court decided that cash meal allowances received by an employee were not excludible from the employee's income. Is the *Kowalski* case similar to our case? It might be. Let us find out. If we turn to paragraph 9748 of the second 1977 volume of *United States Tax Cases,* we will find the text of the *Kowalski* opinion. A synopsis of this opinion is present below.

In the mid-1970s, the State of New Jersey provided cash meal allowances to its state troopers. The state did not require the troopers to use the allowances exclusively for meals. Nor did it require them to consume their meals on its business premises. One trooper, Robert J. Kowalski, failed to report a portion of his allowance on his tax return. The IRS assessed a deficiency, and Kowalski took the IRS to court. In court, Kowalski argued that the meal allowances were excludible, because they were furnished "for the convenience of the employer." The IRS contended that the allowances were taxable because they amounted to compensation. The Supreme Court took up the case and sided with the IRS. The Court held that the Sec. 119 income exclusion does not apply to cash payments; it applies only to meals in kind.[2]

For the sake of illustration, let us assume that Sec. 119, Reg. Sec. 1.119-1, and the *Kowalski* case are the *only* authorities "on point." How should we evaluate them?

Evaluate Authorities Section 119 is the key authority applicable to our case. It supplies the operative rule for resolving the issue of the meal vouchers. It is vague, however, with respect to three terms: "meals," "business premises of the employer," and "for the convenience of the employer." The principal judicial authority is the *Kowalski* case. It provides an official interpretation of the term "meals." Because the U.S. Supreme Court decided *Kowalski*, the case should be assigned considerable weight. The relevant administrative authority is Reg. Sec. 1.119-1. It expounds on the terms "business premises of the employer" and "for the convenience of the employer." Because neither the IRC nor *Kowalski* explain these terms, Reg. Sec. 1.119-1 should be accorded great weight. But what if *Kowalski* had conflicted with Reg. Sec. 1.119-1? Which should be considered more authoritative? As a general rule, high court decisions "trump" the Treasury Regulations (and all IRS pronouncements for that matter). The more recent the decision, the greater its precedential weight. Had there been no Supreme Court decision and a division of appellate authority, equal weight should have been assigned to each of the appellate court decisions.

Analyze the Facts in Terms of Applicable Authorities Analyzing the facts in terms of applicable authorities involves applying the abstraction of the law to the concreteness of the facts. It entails expressing the generalities of the law in terms of the specifics of the facts. In this process, every legal condition must be satisfied for the result implied by the

---

[1] The researcher also might read the main *Standard Federal Tax Reporter* paragraph that discusses meals and lodging furnished by the employer (CCH ¶7222.01). Within this paragraph are likely to be references to other primary authorities.

[2] At this juncture, the researcher should consult a citator to determine whether *Kowalski* is still "good law," and to locate other authorities that cite *Kowalski.*

general rule to ensue. Thus, in our case, the conditions of furnishing "meals," "on the business premises of the employer," and "for the convenience of the employer" must be satisfied for the value of the "meals" to be excluded from the employee's income.

When analyzing the facts in terms of case law, the researcher should always draw an *analogy* between case facts and client facts. Likewise, he or she should always draw a *distinction* between case facts and client facts. Remember, under the rule of precedent, a court deciding the client's case will be bound by the precedent of cases involving *similar* facts and issues. By the same token, it will *not* be bound by the precedent of cases involving *dissimilar* facts and issues.

The most useful vehicle for analyzing client facts is the memorandum-to-the-file (see page A-6). The purpose of this document is threefold: first, it assists the researcher in recollecting transactions long transpired; second, it apprises colleagues and supervisors of the nature of one's research; third, it provides "substantial authority" for the tax treatment of a particular item. Let us analyze the facts of our case by way of a memorandum-to-the-file. Notice the format of this document; it generally tracks the steps in the research process itself.

Communicate Conclusions and Recommendations to Others For three practical reasons, research results always should be communicated to the client *in writing*. First, a written communication can be made after extensive revisions. An oral communication cannot. Second, in a written communication, the researcher can delve into the intricacies of tax law. Often, in an oral communication, he or she cannot. Third, a written communication reinforces an oral understanding. Alternatively, it brings to light an oral misunderstanding.

The written communication usually takes the form of a client letter (see page A-7). The purpose of this letter is two-fold: first, it apprises the client of the results of one's research and, second, it recommends to the client a course of action based on these results. A sample client letter is presented below. Notice the organization of this document; it is similar to that of the memorandum-to-the-file.

Memorandum-to-the-File

Date: December 9, 20X1
From: Rosina Havacek
Re: The taxability of meal vouchers furnished by Mercy Hospital to its medical staff.

Facts
[*State only the facts that are relevant to the Issue(s) and necessary for the Analysis.*] Our client, Mercy Hospital ("Mercy"), provides meal vouchers to its medical employees to enable them to remain on emergency call. The vouchers are redeemable at Mercy's onsite cafeteria and at MacDougal's, a privately owned sandwich shop. MacDougal's rents business space from the hospital. Although Mercy does not require its employees to remain on or near its premises during their meal hours, the employees generally do. Elizabeth Fegali, Mercy's Chief Administrator, has asked us to research whether the value of the meal vouchers is taxable to the employees.

Issues
[*Identify the issue(s) raised by the Facts. Be specific.*] The taxability of the meal vouchers depends on three issues: first, whether the meals are furnished "for the convenience of the employer"; second, whether they are furnished "on the business premises of the employer"; and third, whether the vouchers are equivalent to cash.

Applicable Law
[*Discuss those legal principles that both strengthen and weaken the client's case. Because the primary authority for tax law is the IRC, begin with the IRC.*] Section 119 provides that the value of meals is excludible from an employee's income if the meals are furnished for the convenience of, and on the business premises of the employer. [*Discuss how administrative and/or judicial authorities expound on statutory terms.*] Under Reg. Sec. 1.119-1, a meal is furnished "for the convenience of the employer" if it is furnished for a "substantial noncompensatory business reason." A "substantial noncompensatory business reason" includes the need to have the employee available for emergency calls during his or her meal period. Under Sec. 119(b)(4), if more than half the employees satisfy the "for the convenience of the employer" test, all employees will be regarded as satisfying the test. Regulation Sec. 1.119-1 defines "business premises of the employer" as the place of employment of the employee.

[*When discussing court cases, present case facts in such a way as to enable the reader to draw an analogy with client facts.*] A Supreme Court case, *Kowalski v. CIR*, 434 U.S. 77, 77-2 USTC ¶9748, discusses what constitutes "meals" for purposes of Sec. 119. In *Kowalski*, the State of New Jersey furnished cash meal allowances to its state troopers to enable them to eat while on duty. It did not require the troopers to use the allowances exclusively for meals. Nor did it require them to consume their meals on its business premises. One trooper, R.J. Kowalski, excluded the value of his allowances from his income. The IRS disputed this treatment, and Kowalski took the IRS to Court. In Court, Kowalski argued that the allowances were excludible because they were furnished "for the convenience of the employer." The IRS contended that the allowances were taxable because they amounted to compensation. The U.S. Supreme Court took up the case and decided for the IRS. The Court held that the Sec. 119 income exlusion does not apply to payments in cash.

Analysis
[*The Analysis should (a) apply Applicable Law to the Facts and (b) address the Issue(s). In this section, every proposition should be supported by either authority, logic, or plausible assumptions.*]

Issue 1: The meals provided by Mercy seem to be furnished "for the convenience of the employer." They are furnished to have employees available for emergency call during their meal breaks. This is a "substantial noncompensatory reason" within the meaning of Reg. Sec. 1.119-1.

Issue 2: Although the hospital cafeteria appears to be the "business premises of the employer," MacDougal's does not appear to be. The hospital is the place of employment of the medical employees. MacDougal's is not.

Issue 3: [*In applying case law to the Facts, indicate how case facts are similar to/dissimilar from client facts. If the analysis does not support a "yes-no" answer, do not give one.*] Based on the foregoing authorities, it is unclear whether the vouchers are equivalent to cash. On the one hand, they are redeemable only in meals. Thus, they resemble meals-in-kind. On the other hand, they are redeemable at more than one institution. Thus, they resemble cash. Nor is it clear whether a court deciding this case would reach the same conclusion as the Supreme Court did in *Kowalski*. In the latter case, the State of New Jersey provided its meal allowances in the form of cash. It did not require its employees to use the allowances exclusively for meals. Nor did it require them to consume their meals on its business premises. In our case, Mercy provides its meal allowances in the form of vouchers. Thus, it indirectly requires its employees to use the allowances exclusively for meals. On the other hand, it does not require them to consume their meals on its business premises.

Conclusion
[*The Conclusion should (a) logically flow from the Analysis, and (b) address the Issue(s).*] Although it appears that the meals acquired by voucher in the hospital cafeteria are furnished "for the convenience of the employer" and "on the business premises of the employer," it is unclear whether the vouchers are equivalent to cash. If they *are* equivalent to cash, *or* if they are redeemed at MacDougal's, their value is likely to be taxable to the employees. On the other hand, if they are not equivalent to cash, *and* they are redeemed only in the hospital cafeteria, their value is likely to be excludible.

Professional Accounting Associates
2701 First City Plaza
Suite 905
Dallas, Texas 75019

December 12, 20X1

Elizabeth Feghali, Chief Administrator
Mercy Hospital
22650 West Haven Drive
Arlington, Texas 75527

Dear Ms. Feghali:

[*Introduction. Set a cordial tone.*] It was great to see you at last Thursday's football game. If not for that last minute fumble, the Longhorns might have taken the Big 12 Conference championship!

[*Issue/Purpose.*] In our meeting of December 6, you asked us to research whether the value of the meal vouchers that Mercy provides to its medical employees is taxable to the employees. [*Short Answer.*] I regret to inform you that if the vouchers are redeemed at MacDougal's, their value is likely to be taxable to the employees. On the other hand, if the vouchers are redeemed in the hospital cafeteria, their value is likely to be excludible from the employee's income. [*The remainder of the letter should elaborate, support, and qualify this answer.*]

[*Steps Taken in Deriving Conclusion.*] In reaching this conclusion, we consulted relevant provisions of the Internal Revenue Code ("IRC"), applicable Treasury Regulations under the IRC, and a pertinent Supreme Court case. In addition, we reviewed the documents on employee benefits that you submitted to us at our earlier meeting.

[*Facts. State only the facts that are relevant to the Issue and necessary for the Analysis.*] The facts as we understand them are as follows: Mercy provides meal vouchers to its medical employees to enable them to eat while on emergency call. The vouchers are redeemable either in the hospital cafeteria or at MacDougal's. MacDougal's is a privately owned institution that rents business space from the hospital. Although Mercy's employees are not required to remain on or near the premises during their meal hours, they generally do.

Applicable Law. State, do not interpret.] Under the IRC, the value of meals is excludible from an employee's income if two conditions are met: first, the meals are furnished "for the convenience of the employer" and second, they are provided "on the business premises of the employer." Although the IRC does not explain what is meant by "for the convenience of the employer," "business premises of the employer," and "meals," other authorities do. Specificly, the Treasury Regulations define "business premises of the employer" to be the place of employment of the employees. The regulations state that providing meals during work hours to have an employee available for emergency calls is "for the convenience of the employer." Moreover, under the IRC, if more than half the employees satisfy the "for the convenience of the employer" test, all the employees will be regarded as satisfying the test. The Supreme Court has interpreted "meals" to mean food-in-kind. The Court has held that cash allowances do not qualify as "meals."

[*Analysis. Express the generalities of Applicable Law in terms of the specifics of the Facts.*] Clearly, the meals furnished by Mercy are "for the convenience of the employer." They are furnished during the employees' work hours to have the employees available for emergency call. Although the meals provided in the hospital cafeteria appear to be furnished "on the business premises of the employer," the meals provided at MacDougal's do not appear to be. The hospital is the place of employment of the medical employees. MacDougal's is not. What is unclear is whether the meal vouchers are equivalent to food-in-kind. On the one hand, they are redeemable at more than one institution and thus resemble cash allowances. On the other hand, they are redeemable only in meals and thus resemble food-in-kind.

[*Conclusion/Recommendation.*] Because of this lack of clarity, we suggest that you modify your employee benefits plan to allow for the provision of meals-in-kind exclusively in the hospital cafeteria. In this way, you will dispel any doubt that Mercy is furnishing "meals," "for the convenience of the employer," "on the premises of the employer."

[*Closing/Follow Up.*] Please call me at 475-2020 if you have any questions concerning this conclusion. May I suggest that we meet next week to discuss the possibility of revising your employee benefits plan.

Very truly yours,
Professional Accounting Associates

By: Rosina Havacek, Junior Associate

APPENDIX B

COMPLETED TAX FORMS

SCHEDULE C (Form 1040)
Department of the Treasury Internal Revenue Service (99)

Profit or Loss From Business

(Sole Proprietorship)

▶ Partnerships, joint ventures, etc., must file Form 1065 or 1065-B.

▶ Attach to Form 1040, 1040NR, or 1041. ▶ See Instructions for Schedule C (Form 1040).

OMB No. 1545-0074
2006
Attachment Sequence No. **09**

Name of proprietor: Andrew Lawrence
Social security number (SSN): 297 63 2110

A Principal business or profession, including product or service (see page C-2 of the instructions): Manufacturing Furniture
B Enter code from pages C-8, 9, & 10 ▶ 337000

C Business name. If no separate business name, leave blank.
D Employer ID number (EIN), if any: 59-2029763

E Business address (including suite or room no.) ▶ 1234 University Avenue
City, town or post office, state, and ZIP code: Gainesville, FL 32611

F Accounting method: (1) ☐ Cash (2) ☒ Accrual (3) ☐ Other (specify) ▶

G Did you "materially participate" in the operation of this business during 2006? If "No," see page C-3 for limit on losses ☒ Yes ☐ No

H If you started or acquired this business during 2006, check here ▶ ☐

Part I Income

Line	Description		Amount
1	Gross receipts or sales. **Caution.** If this income was reported to you on Form W-2 and the "Statutory employee" box on that form was checked, see page C-3 and check here ▶ ☐	1	869,658
2	Returns and allowances	2	29,242
3	Subtract line 2 from line 1	3	840,416
4	Cost of goods sold (from line 42 on page 2)	4	540,204
5	**Gross profit.** Subtract line 4 from line 3	5	300,212
6	Other income, including federal and state gasoline or fuel tax credit or refund (see page C-3)	6	
7	**Gross income.** Add lines 5 and 6 ▶	7	300,212

Part II Expenses. Enter expenses for business use of your home **only** on line 30.

Line	Description		Amount	Line	Description		Amount
8	Advertising	8	13,000	18	Office expense	18	16,000
9	Car and truck expenses (see page C-4)	9	4,000	19	Pension and profit-sharing plans	19	2,000
10	Commissions and fees	10	10,400	20	Rent or lease (see page C-5):		
11	Contract labor (see page C-4)	11		a	Vehicles, machinery, and equipment	20a	36,000
12	Depletion	12		b	Other business property	20b	
13	Depreciation and section 179 expense deduction (not included in Part III) (see page C-4)	13	12,476	21	Repairs and maintenance	21	
				22	Supplies (not included in Part III)	22	
				23	Taxes and licenses	23	9,840
				24	Travel, meals, and entertainment:		
				a	Travel	24a	4,000
14	Employee benefit programs (other than on line 19)	14	4,000	b	Deductible meals and entertainment (see page C-6)	24b	4,000
15	Insurance (other than health)	15		25	Utilities	25	
16	Interest:			26	Wages (less employment credits)	26	52,000
a	Mortgage (paid to banks, etc.)	16a		27	Other expenses (from line 48 on page 2)	27	8,650
b	Other	16b	8,000				
17	Legal and professional services	17					

Line	Description		Amount
28	**Total expenses** before expenses for business use of home. Add lines 8 through 27 in columns ▶	28	184,366
29	Tentative profit (loss). Subtract line 28 from line 7	29	115,846
30	Expenses for business use of your home. Attach **Form 8829**	30	
31	**Net profit or (loss).** Subtract line 30 from line 29. • If a profit, enter on both **Form 1040, line 12,** and **Schedule SE, line 2,** or on **Form 1040NR, line 13** (statutory employees, see page C-6). Estates and trusts, enter on Form 1041, line 3. • If a loss, you **must** go to line 32.	31	115,846

32 If you have a loss, check the box that describes your investment in this activity (see page C-6).
• If you checked 32a, enter the loss on both **Form 1040, line 12,** and **Schedule SE, line 2,** or on **Form 1040NR, line 13** (statutory employees, see page C-6). Estates and trusts, enter on Form 1041, line 3.
• If you checked 32b, you **must** attach **Form 6198.** Your loss may be limited.

32a ☒ All investment is at risk.
32b ☐ Some investment is not at risk.

Schedule C (Form 1040) 2006 — Page 2

Part III Cost of Goods Sold (see page C-7)

Line	Description		Amount
33	Method(s) used to value closing inventory: a [X] Cost b [ ] Lower of cost or market c [ ] Other (attach explanation)		
34	Was there any change in determining quantities, costs, or valuations between opening and closing inventory? If "Yes," attach explanation . . . [ ] Yes [ ] No		
35	Inventory at beginning of year. If different from last year's closing inventory, attach explanation	35	64,000
36	Purchases less cost of items withdrawn for personal use	36	340,800
37	Cost of labor. Do not include any amounts paid to yourself	37	143,204
38	Materials and supplies	38	
39	Other costs	39	97,000
40	Add lines 35 through 39	40	645,004
41	Inventory at end of year	41	104,800
42	**Cost of goods sold.** Subtract line 41 from line 40. Enter the result here and on page 1, line 4	42	540,204

Part IV Information on Your Vehicle.

Complete this part **only** if you are claiming car or truck expenses on line 9 and are not required to file Form 4562 for this business. See the instructions for line 13 on page C-4 to find out if you must file Form 4562.

43 When did you place your vehicle in service for business purposes? (month, day, year) ▶ 3 / 12 / 05

44 Of the total number of miles you drove your vehicle during 2006, enter the number of miles you used your vehicle for:

a Business 17,000 b Commuting (see instructions) 4,500 c Other 12,000

45 Do you (or your spouse) have another vehicle available for personal use? [X] Yes [ ] No

46 Was your vehicle available for personal use during off-duty hours? [X] Yes [ ] No

47a Do you have evidence to support your deduction? [X] Yes [ ] No

b If "Yes," is the evidence written? [X] Yes [ ] No

Part V Other Expenses.

List below business expenses not included on lines 8–26 or line 30.

Expense	Amount
Repairs	4,800
General and administrative	3,000
Miscellaneous	850

Line	Description		Amount
48	**Total other expenses.** Enter here and on page 1, line 27	48	8,650

Schedule C (Form 1040) 2006

FACTS FOR SOLE PROPRIETORSHIP (SCHEDULE C)

Andrew Lawrence is the sole proprietor of a business that operates under the name Andrew Lawrence Furniture (Business Code 337000). The proprietorship is located at 1234 University Ave., Gainesville, FL 32611. Its employer identification number is 59-2029763. Andrew started the business with a $200,000 capital investment on June 1, 2000. The proprietorship uses the calendar year as its tax year (the same as its proprietor) and the accrual method of accounting. The following information pertains to its 2006 activities:

A trial balance is included as part of the accompanying worksheet. Notes accompanying the account balances are presented below.

1. Cost of goods sold is determined as follows:

Inventory at beginning of year	$ 64,000
Plus: Purchases	340,800
Cost of labor	143,204
Additional Sec. 263A adjustment	7,000
Other costs	90,000
Goods available for sale	$645,004
Minus: Inventory at end of year	(104,800)
Cost of goods sold	$540,204

The proprietorship values its inventory using the first-in, first-out method and historical costs. The Sec. 263A rules apply to the proprietorship. No change in valuing inventories occurred between the beginning and end of the tax year.

2. The proprietorship uses MACRS depreciation for tax purposes. The current year tax depreciation is $27,476. Of this amount, $15,000 is included in cost of goods sold and inventory. The AMT depreciation adjustment on post-1986 personal property is $1,514. This amount is reported on Andrew Lawrence's Form 6251 (Alternative Minimum Tax—Individuals), which is not reproduced here.

3. Using its excess funds, the proprietorship has purchased various temporary investments, including a 2% investment in Plaza Corporation stock, 50 shares of Service Corporation stock, and some tax-exempt municipal bonds. The proprietorship has held the Plaza stock for two years and sold it in July for $4,500 more than its $7,000 adjusted basis. Prior to the sale, Plaza paid a $1,000 dividend. The 50 shares of Service stock, which had been purchased during the year, was declared worthless during the year. The proprietorship recovered none of its $2,100 adjusted basis.

4. Employees other than Andrew Lawrence receive limited fringe benefits. One employee also receives a $2,000 contribution to an Individual Retirement Account paid by the proprietorship.

5. Miscellaneous expenses include $150 of expenses related to the production of the dividend income.

6. The proprietorship paid no estimated taxes.

7. Balance sheet information is not provided for the sole proprietorship because it is not reported on the Schedule C. Balance sheet information, however, can be found on page 4 of the C corporation tax return.

Andrew Lawrence, Sole Proprietorship Reconciliation of Book and Taxable Income For Year Ending December 31, 2006

	Book Income		Adjustments		Taxable Income		Schedule	Other Tax	
Account Name	Debit	Credit	Debit	Credit	Debit	Credit	C	Forms	
Sales		$869,658				$869,658	$869,658		
Sales returns & allowances	$ 29,242				$ 29,242		(29,242)		
Cost of sales	540,204				540,204		(540,204)		
Dividends		1,000			1,000	1,000		$ 1,000	(Sch. B)
Tax-exempt interest		18,000	$18,000			0			
Gain on July stock sale		4,500				4,500		4,500	(Sch. D)
Worthless stock loss	2,100				2,100			(2,100)	(Sch. D)
Proprietor's salary[(a)]	36,000			$36,000	0		0	0	
Other salaries	52,000				52,000		(52,000)		
Rentals	36,000				36,000		(36,000)		
Bad debts	4,000				4,000		(4,000)		
Interest:									
Working capital loans	8,000				8,000		(8,000)		
Purchase tax-exempt bonds	2,000			2,000	0				
Employment taxes	8,320				8,320		(8,320)		
Taxes	1,520				1,520		(1,520)		
Repairs	4,800				4,800		(4,800)		
Depreciation[(b)]	12,000		476		12,476		(12,476)		
Charitable contributions	12,000				12,000			(12,000)	(Sch. A)
Travel	4,000				4,000		(4,000)		
Meals and entertainment[(c)]	8,000			4,000	4,000		(4,000)		
Office expenses	16,000				16,000		(16,000)		
Advertising	13,000				13,000		(13,000)		
Transportation expense	10,400				10,400		(10,400)		
General and administrative	3,000				3,000		(3,000)		
Pension plans[(d)]	2,000				2,000		(2,000)		
Employee benefit programs[(e)]	4,000				4,000		(4,000)		
Miscellaneous	1,000				1,000		(850)	(150)	(Form 4952)
Net profit/Taxable income	83,572		23,524		107,096				
Total	$893,158	$893,158	$42,000	$42,000	$875,158	$875,158	$115,846		

[(a)] The $3,000 monthly salary for Andrew Lawrence is treated as a withdrawal from the proprietorship and is not deducted on Schedule C. The salary does not reduce Schedule C income and therefore is taxed as self-employment income.

[(b)] MACRS depreciation is $27,476 − $15,000 = $12,476

[(c)] 50% of the meals and entertainment expense is not deductible for tax purposes.

[(d)] The pension plan expense is the same for book and tax purposes for this business. No pension expenses relate to pensions for the proprietor.

[(e)] The employee benefit expense is the same for book and tax purposes for this business. None relates to proprietor benefits.

Form **1120** Department of the Treasury Internal Revenue Service

U.S. Corporation Income Tax Return

For calendar year 2006 or tax year beginning ...., 2006, ending ...., 20 ....
▶ See separate instructions.

OMB No. 1545-0123 **2006**

A Check if:		Name	B Employer identification number
1 Consolidated return (attach Form 851) ☐	Use IRS label. Otherwise, print or type.	Johns and Lawrence, Inc.	76 3456789
2 Personal holding co. (attach Sch. PH) ☐		Number, street, and room or suite no. If a P.O. box, see instructions.	C Date incorporated
3 Personal service corp. (see instructions) ☐		1234 University Avenue	6/1/2000
4 Schedule M-3 required (attach Sch. M-3) ☐		City or town, state, and ZIP code	D Total assets (see instructions)
		Gainesville, FL 32611	$ 479,324

E Check if: (1) ☐ Initial return (2) ☐ Final return (3) ☐ Name change (4) ☐ Address change

Income	1a	Gross receipts or sales 869,658 b Less returns and allowances 29,242 c Bal ▶	1c	840,416
	2	Cost of goods sold (Schedule A, line 8)	2	540,204
	3	Gross profit. Subtract line 2 from line 1c	3	300,212
	4	Dividends (Schedule C, line 19)	4	1,000
	5	Interest	5	
	6	Gross rents	6	
	7	Gross royalties	7	
	8	Capital gain net income (attach Schedule D (Form 1120)) Not Reproduced	8	2,400
	9	Net gain or (loss) from Form 4797, Part II, line 17 (attach Form 4797)	9	
	10	Other income (see instructions–attach schedule)	10	
	11	**Total income.** Add lines 3 through 10 ▶	11	303,612
Deductions (See instructions for limitations on deductions.)	12	Compensation of officers (Schedule E, line 4)	12	36,000
	13	Salaries and wages (less employment credits)	13	52,000
	14	Repairs and maintenance	14	4,800
	15	Bad debts	15	4,000
	16	Rents	16	36,000
	17	Taxes and licenses	17	16,000
	18	Interest	18	8,000
	19	Charitable contributions	19	7,694
	20	Depreciation from Form 4562 not claimed on Schedule A or elsewhere on return (attach Form 4562)	20	12,476
	21	Depletion	21	
	22	Advertising	22	13,000
	23	Pension, profit-sharing, etc., plans	23	2,000
	24	Employee benefit programs	24	4,000
	25	Domestic production activities deduction (attach Form 8903) Not Reproduced	25	2,056
	26	Other deductions (attach schedule)	26	38,400
	27	**Total deductions.** Add lines 12 through 26 ▶	27	236,426
	28	Taxable income before net operating loss deduction and special deductions. Subtract line 27 from line 11	28	67,186
	29	**Less:** a Net operating loss deduction (see instructions) 29a		
		b Special deductions (Schedule C, line 20) 29b 700	29c	700
Tax and Payments	30	**Taxable income.** Subtract line 29c from line 28 (see instructions)	30	66,486
	31	**Total tax** (Schedule J, line 10)	31	11,622
	32a	2005 overpayment credited to 2006 32a		
	b	2006 estimated tax payments 32b 14,000		
	c	2006 refund applied for on Form 4466 32c ( ) d Bal ▶ 32d 14,000		
	e	Tax deposited with Form 7004 32e		
	f	Credits: (1) Form 2439 (2) Form 4136 32f		
	g	Credit for federal telephone excise tax paid (attach Form 8913) 32g	32h	14,000
	33	Estimated tax penalty (see instructions). Check if Form 2220 is attached ▶ ☐	33	
	34	**Amount owed.** If line 32h is smaller than the total of lines 31 and 33, enter amount owed	34	
	35	**Overpayment.** If line 32h is larger than the total of lines 31 and 33, enter amount overpaid	35	1,864
	36	Enter amount from line 35 you want: **Credited to 2007 estimated tax** ▶ 1,864 **Refunded** ▶	36	

Sign Here

Under penalties of perjury, I declare that I have examined this return, including accompanying schedules and statements, and to the best of my knowledge and belief, it is true, correct, and complete. Declaration of preparer (other than taxpayer) is based on all information of which preparer has any knowledge.

Andrew Lawrence — Signature of officer | 3-15-07 — Date | Vice-President — Title

May the IRS discuss this return with the preparer shown below (see instructions)? ☒ Yes ☐ No

Paid Preparer's Use Only

Preparer's signature	Michael Kramer	Date 3-14-07	Check if self-employed ☒	Preparer's SSN or PTIN 375-49-6339
Firm's name (or yours if self-employed), address, and ZIP code	Michael S. Kramer 1110 McMillian Gainesville, FL 32611		EIN 59 2029763	Phone no. (352) 555-2000

For Privacy Act and Paperwork Reduction Act Notice, see separate instructions. Cat. No. 11450Q Form **1120** (2006)

Form 1120 (2006) Page 2

Schedule A Cost of Goods Sold (see instructions)

Line	Description		Amount
1	Inventory at beginning of year	1	64,000
2	Purchases	2	340,800
3	Cost of labor	3	143,204
4	Additional section 263A costs (attach schedule)	4	7,000
5	Other costs (attach schedule)	5	90,000
6	**Total.** Add lines 1 through 5	6	645,004
7	Inventory at end of year	7	104,800
8	**Cost of goods sold.** Subtract line 7 from line 6. Enter here and on page 1, line 2	8	540,204

9a Check all methods used for valuing closing inventory:

(i) [X] Cost

(ii) [ ] Lower of cost or market

(iii) [ ] Other (Specify method used and attach explanation.) ▶

b Check if there was a writedown of subnormal goods ▶ [ ]

c Check if the LIFO inventory method was adopted this tax year for any goods (if checked, attach Form 970) ▶ [ ]

d If the LIFO inventory method was used for this tax year, enter percentage (or amounts) of closing inventory computed under LIFO 9d

e If property is produced or acquired for resale, do the rules of section 263A apply to the corporation? [X] Yes [ ] No

f Was there any change in determining quantities, cost, or valuations between opening and closing inventory? If "Yes," attach explanation [ ] Yes [X] No

Schedule C Dividends and Special Deductions (see instructions)

Line	Description	(a) Dividends received	(b) %	(c) Special deductions (a) × (b)
1	Dividends from less-than-20%-owned domestic corporations (other than debt-financed stock)	1,000	70	700
2	Dividends from 20%-or-more-owned domestic corporations (other than debt-financed stock)		80	
3	Dividends on debt-financed stock of domestic and foreign corporations		see instructions	
4	Dividends on certain preferred stock of less-than-20%-owned public utilities		42	
5	Dividends on certain preferred stock of 20%-or-more-owned public utilities		48	
6	Dividends from less-than-20%-owned foreign corporations and certain FSCs		70	
7	Dividends from 20%-or-more-owned foreign corporations and certain FSCs		80	
8	Dividends from wholly owned foreign subsidiaries		100	
9	**Total.** Add lines 1 through 8. See instructions for limitation			700
10	Dividends from domestic corporations received by a small business investment company operating under the Small Business Investment Act of 1958		100	
11	Dividends from affiliated group members		100	
12	Dividends from certain FSCs		100	
13	Dividends from foreign corporations not included on lines 3, 6, 7, 8, 11, or 12			
14	Income from controlled foreign corporations under subpart F (attach Form(s) 5471)			
15	Foreign dividend gross-up			
16	IC-DISC and former DISC dividends not included on lines 1, 2, or 3			
17	Other dividends			
18	Deduction for dividends paid on certain preferred stock of public utilities			
19	**Total dividends.** Add lines 1 through 17. Enter here and on page 1, line 4 ▶			
20	**Total special deductions.** Add lines 9, 10, 11, 12, and 18. Enter here and on page 1, line 29b ▶			700

Schedule E Compensation of Officers (see instructions for page 1, line 12)

Note: *Complete Schedule E only if total receipts (line 1a plus lines 4 through 10 on page 1) are $500,000 or more.*

	(a) Name of officer	(b) Social security number	(c) Percent of time devoted to business	Percent of corporation stock owned (d) Common	(e) Preferred	(f) Amount of compensation
1	Stephen Johns	386-05-9174	100 %	50 %	%	18,000
	Andrew Lawrence	297-63-2110	100 %	50 %	%	18,000
			%	%	%	
			%	%	%	
			%	%	%	

Line	Description	Amount
2	Total compensation of officers	36,000
3	Compensation of officers claimed on Schedule A and elsewhere on return	
4	Subtract line 3 from line 2. Enter the result here and on page 1, line 12	36,000

Form **1120** (2006)

Form 1120 (2006) Page **3**

Schedule J Tax Computation (see instructions)

1	Check if the corporation is a member of a controlled group (attach Schedule O (Form 1120)) ▶ ☐		
2	Income tax. Check if a qualified personal service corporation (see instructions) ▶ ☐	2	11,622
3	Alternative minimum tax (attach Form 4626)	3	
4	Add lines 2 and 3	4	11,622
5a	Foreign tax credit (attach Form 1118) — 5a		
b	Qualified electric vehicle credit (attach Form 8834) — 5b		
c	General business credit. Check applicable box(es): ☐ Form 3800 ☐ Form 6478 ☐ Form 8835, Section B ☐ Form 8844 — 5c		
d	Credit for prior year minimum tax (attach Form 8827) — 5d		
e	Bond credits from: ☐ Form 8860 ☐ Form 8912 — 5e		
6	**Total credits.** Add lines 5a through 5e	6	-0-
7	Subtract line 6 from line 4	7	11,622
8	Personal holding company tax (attach Schedule PH (Form 1120))	8	
9	Other taxes. Check if from: ☐ Form 4255 ☐ Form 8611 ☐ Form 8697 ☐ Form 8866 ☐ Form 8902 ☐ Other (attach schedule)	9	
10	**Total tax.** Add lines 7 through 9. Enter here and on page 1, line 31	10	11,622

Schedule K Other Information (see instructions)

		Yes	No
1	Check accounting method: a ☐ Cash b ☒ Accrual c ☐ Other (specify) ▶		
2	See the instructions and enter the:		
a	Business activity code no. ▶ 337,000		
b	Business activity ▶ Manufacturing		
c	Product or service ▶ Furniture		
3	At the end of the tax year, did the corporation own, directly or indirectly, 50% or more of the voting stock of a domestic corporation? (For rules of attribution, see section 267(c).)		X
	If "Yes," attach a schedule showing: **(a)** name and employer identification number (EIN), **(b)** percentage owned, and **(c)** taxable income or (loss) before NOL and special deductions of such corporation for the tax year ending with or within your tax year.		
4	Is the corporation a subsidiary in an affiliated group or a parent-subsidiary controlled group?		X
	If "Yes," enter name and EIN of the parent corporation ▶		
5	At the end of the tax year, did any individual, partnership, corporation, estate, or trust own, directly or indirectly, 50% or more of the corporation's voting stock? (For rules of attribution, see section 267(c).)	X	
	If "Yes," attach a schedule showing name and identifying number. (Do not include any information already entered in **4** above.) Enter percentage owned ▶ 50%*		
6	During this tax year, did the corporation pay dividends (other than stock dividends and distributions in exchange for stock) in excess of the corporation's current and accumulated earnings and profits? (See sections 301 and 316.)	X	
	If "Yes," file **Form 5452,** Corporate Report of Nondividend Distributions.		
	If this is a consolidated return, answer here for the parent corporation and on **Form 851,** Affiliations Schedule, for each subsidiary.		
7	At any time during the tax year, did one foreign person own, directly or indirectly, at least 25% of **(a)** the total voting power of all classes of stock of the corporation entitled to vote or **(b)** the total value of all classes of stock of the corporation?		X
	If "Yes," enter: **(a)** Percentage owned ▶ N/A and **(b)** Owner's country ▶ N/A		
c	The corporation may have to file **Form 5472,** Information Return of a 25% Foreign-Owned U.S. Corporation or a Foreign Corporation Engaged in a U.S. Trade or Business. Enter number of Forms 5472 attached ▶		
8	Check this box if the corporation issued publicly offered debt instruments with original issue discount ▶ ☐		
	If checked, the corporation may have to file **Form 8281,** Information Return for Publicly Offered Original Issue Discount Instruments.		
9	Enter the amount of tax-exempt interest received or accrued during the tax year ▶ $ 18,000		
10	Enter the number of shareholders at the end of the tax year (if 100 or fewer) ▶ 2		
11	If the corporation has an NOL for the tax year and is electing to forego the carryback period, check here ▶ ☐		
	If the corporation is filing a consolidated return, the statement required by Temporary Regulations section 1.1502-21T(b)(3) must be attached or the election will not be valid.		
12	Enter the available NOL carryover from prior tax years (Do not reduce it by any deduction on line 29a.) ▶ $ None		
13	Are the corporation's total receipts (line 1a plus lines 4 through 10 on page 1) for the tax year **and** its total assets at the end of the tax year less than $250,000?		X
	If "Yes," the corporation is not required to complete Schedules L, M-1, and M-2 on page 4. Instead, enter the total amount of cash distributions and the book value of property distributions (other than cash) made during the tax year. ▶ $		

Note: If the corporation, at any time during the tax year, had assets or operated a business in a foreign country or U.S. possession, it may be required to attach **Schedule N (Form 1120),** *Foreign Operations of U.S. Corporations, to this return. See Schedule N for details.*

*See Schedule E

Form 1120 (2006) Page 4

Schedule L Balance Sheets per Books

Assets	Beginning of tax year (a)	(b)	End of tax year (c)	(d)
1 Cash		60,000		72,600
2a Trade notes and accounts receivable	25,000		24,000	
b Less allowance for bad debts	(1,000)	24,000	(1,000)	23,000
3 Inventories		64,000		104,800
4 U.S. government obligations				
5 Tax-exempt securities (see instructions)		200,000		200,000
6 Other current assets (attach schedule)		7,000		
7 Loans to shareholders				
8 Mortgage and real estate loans				
9 Other investments (attach schedule)				
10a Buildings and other depreciable assets	151,600		151,600	
b Less accumulated depreciation	(45,200)	106,400	(72,676)	78,924
11a Depletable assets				
b Less accumulated depletion	( )		( )	
12 Land (net of any amortization)				
13a Intangible assets (amortizable only)				
b Less accumulated amortization	( )		( )	
14 Other assets (attach schedule)				
15 Total assets		461,400		479,324
Liabilities and Shareholders' Equity				
16 Accounts payable		26,000		19,000
17 Mortgages, notes, bonds payable in less than 1 year		4,000		4,000
18 Other current liabilities (attach schedule)		3,600		3,600
19 Loans from shareholders				
20 Mortgages, notes, bonds payable in 1 year or more		130,000		119,724
21 Other liabilities (attach schedule)				
22 Capital stock: a Preferred stock				
b Common stock	200,000	200,000	200,000	200,000
23 Additional paid-in capital				
24 Retained earnings–Appropriated (attach schedule)				
25 Retained earnings–Unappropriated		97,800		133,000
26 Adjustments to shareholders' equity (attach schedule)				
27 Less cost of treasury stock		( )		( )
28 Total liabilities and shareholders' equity		461,400		479,324

Schedule M-1 Reconciliation of Income (Loss) per Books With Income per Return

Note: Schedule M-3 required instead of Schedule M-1 if total assets are $10 million or more–see instructions

1 Net income (loss) per books	63,412	7 Income recorded on books this year not included on this return (itemize): Tax-exempt interest $ 18,000	18,000
2 Federal income tax per books	14,000		
3 Excess of capital losses over capital gains			
4 Income subject to tax not recorded on books this year (itemize):		8 Deductions on this return not charged against book income this year (itemize):	
5 Expenses recorded on books this year not deducted on this return (itemize):		a Depreciation $ 476	
a Depreciation $ 4,306		b Charitable contributions $	
b Charitable contributions $ 4,000		U.S. prod. act. ded. $2,056	
c Travel and entertainment $			2,532
Nondeductable interest* $2,000	10,306	9 Add lines 7 and 8	20,532
6 Add lines 1 through 5	87,718	10 Income (page 1, line 28)– line 6 less line 9	67,186

Schedule M-2 Analysis of Unappropriated Retained Earnings per Books (Line 25, Schedule L)

1 Balance at beginning of year	97,800	5 Distributions: a Cash	28,212
2 Net income (loss) per books	63,412	b Stock	
3 Other increases (itemize):		c Property	
		6 Other decreases (itemize):	
		7 Add lines 5 and 6	28,212
4 Add lines 1, 2, and 3	161,212	8 Balance at end of year (line 4 less line 7)	133,000

*On loans to acquire municipal bonds.

Form **1120** (2006)

FACTS FOR C CORPORATION (FORM 1120)

The same basic facts presented for the Andrew Lawrence proprietorship are used for the C corporation except for the following:

1. Andrew Lawrence and Stephen Johns are the two 50% shareholders of Johns and Lawrence, Inc., a furniture manufacturer (Business Code 337000). Johns and Lawrence is located at 1234 University Ave., Gainesville, FL 32611. Its employer identification number is 76-3456789. The following information pertains to the 2006 corporate tax return:

Compensation of Officers

Name	S.S. No.	Share	Title	Compensation
Stephen Johns	386-05-9174	1,000	President	$18,000
Andrew Lawrence	297-63-2110	1,000	V.P.	18,000
Total		2,000		$36,000

The coporation paid all salaries owed to the shareholders in 2006. The coporation paid none of the interest or rentals to the shareholders.

2. The book income for the corporation appears in the attached worksheet, which reconciles the corporation's book income and its taxable income.

3. The company was incorporated on June 1, 2000. Each of the two officers hold one-half the stock, which they acquired on that date for a total cash and property contribution of $200,000. No change in the stockholdings has occurred since incorporation. Johns and Lawrence each devote 100% of their time to the business. The corporation provides no expense allowances. The corporation, however, reimburses properly substantiated expenses. Both officers are U.S. citizens. Johns and Lawrence is not a member of a controlled group.

4. Addresses for the officers are: Andrew Lawrence, 436 N.W. 24th Ave., Gainesville, FL 32607; Stephen Johns, 1250 N.E. 12th Ave., Gainesville, FL 32601.

5. The corporation paid estimated taxes of $14,000 for tax year 2006.

6. Other deductions include:

Travel	$ 4,000
Meals and entertainment	8,000
Minus: 50% disallowance	(4,000)
Office expenses	16,000
Transportation	10,400
General and administrative	3,000
Miscellaneous	1,000
Total	$38,400

7. The charitable contributions deduction limitation is $7,694 (see footnote b in Reconciliation worksheet on next page). The remaining $4,306 ($12,000 − $7,694) carries over to 2007 and the four succeeding tax years.

8. Qualified production activities income (QPAI) equals $80,000. Employer's W-2 wages equal $88,000.

9. The $28,212 of withdrawals made by the two owners are dividends out of the corporation's earnings and profits. They are reported as gross income on the shareholders' individual tax returns.

10. The beginning-of-the-year balance sheets for all entity forms are the same, which permits a direct comparison of the 2006 tax differences. Actually, the corporation would have reported tax differences in all prior years (2000 through 2005), which would have been included in the January 1, 2006 balance sheet. If these differences were so included, the direct comparisons would be much more difficult.

Johns and Lawrence, Inc. (C Corporation) Book Income to Taxable Income Reconciliation For Year Ending December 31, 2006

	Book Income		Adjustments		Taxable Income	
Account Name	Debit	Credit	Debit	Credit	Debit	Credit
Sales		$869,658				$869,658
Sales returns & allowances	$ 29,242				$ 29,242	
Cost of sales	540,204				540,204	
Dividends		1,000				1,000
Tax-exempt interest		18,000	$18,000			0
Gain on stock sale		4,500				4,500
Worthless stock loss	2,100				2,100	
Officers' salaries	36,000				36,000	
Other salaries	52,000				52,000	
Rentals	36,000				36,000	
Bad debts	4,000				4,000	
Interest:						
Working capital loans	8,000				8,000	
Purchase tax-exempt bonds	2,000			$ 2,000	0	
Employment taxes	14,480				14,480	
Taxes	1,520				1,520	
Repairs	4,800				4,800	
Depreciation[(a)]	12,000		476		12,476	
Charitable contributions[(b)]	12,000			4,306	7,694	
Travel	4,000				4,000	
Meals and entertainment[(c)]	8,000			4,000	4,000	
Office expenses	16,000				16,000	
Advertising	13,000				13,000	
Transportation expense	10,400				10,400	
General and administrative	3,000				3,000	
Pension plans	2,000				2,000	
Employee benefit programs	4,000				4,000	
Miscellaneous	1,000				1,000	
U.S. prod. act. ded.	0		2,056		2,056	
Federal income taxes	14,000			14,000	0	
Taxable income before spec. deds.			18,476	24,306	69,242	
Div. rec. ded. (10%-owned)[(e)]			700		700	
NOL deduction					0	
Net profit/Taxable income	63,412		3,074		66,486	
Total	$893,158	$893,158	$24,306	$24,306	$875,158	$875,158

[(a)] MACRS depreciation is $27,476 − $15,000 = $12,476

[(b)] Charitable contribution deduction limitation:

Total income (Form 1120, page 1, line 11)	$303,612
Minus: Deductions other than char. cont. & DRD	(226,676)
Charitable contribution base	$ 76,936
Times: 10%	0.10
Charitable contribution deduction	$ 7,694

[(c)] $8,000 × 0.50 disallowance rate = $4,000 disallowed expenses

[(d)]

Total income (Form 1120, page 1, line 11)	$303,612
Minus: Deductions other than the U.S. prod. act. ded.	(235,070)
Taxable income before the U.S. prod. act. ded.	$ 68,542
Times: 3%	0.03
U.S. prod. act. ded.	$ 2,056

[(e)] Dividends-received deduction: $1,000 × 0.70 = $700.

Form **7004** (Rev. December 2006) Department of the Treasury Internal Revenue Service

Application for Automatic 6-Month Extension of Time To File Certain Business Income Tax, Information, and Other Returns

OMB No. 1545-0233

▶ File a separate application for each return.

Type or Print

File by the due date for the return for which an extension is requested. See instructions.

Name: Palmer Corporation

Identifying number: 38-1505286

Number, street, and room or suite no. (If P.O. box, see instructions.): 1631 W. University Avenue

City, town, state, and ZIP code (If a foreign address, enter city, province or state, and country (follow the country's practice for entering postal code)): Gainesville, FL 32601

Note. See instructions before completing this form.

1 Enter the form code for the return that this application is for (see below) 1 2

2 If the foreign corporation does not have an office or place of business in the United States, check here . . . ▶ ☐

3 If the organization is a corporation or partnership that qualifies under Regulations section 1.6081-5, check here . ▶ ☐

4a The application is for calendar year 20 ____, or tax year beginning Oct. 1, 20 06, and ending Sept. 30, 20 07

b **Short tax year.** If this tax year is less than 12 months, check the reason:
☐ Initial return ☐ Final return ☐ Change in accounting period ☐ Consolidated return to be filed

5 If the organization is a corporation and is the common parent of a group that intends to file a consolidated return, check here ▶ . . . . ☐
If checked, attach a schedule, listing the name, address, and Employer Identification Number (EIN) for each member covered by this application.

6	Tentative total tax	6	72,000
7	**Total** payments and credits (see instructions)	7	68,000
8	**Balance due.** Subtract line 7 from line 6. **Generally, you must deposit this amount using the Electronic Federal Tax Payment System (EFTPS), a Federal Tax Deposit (FTD) Coupon, or Electronic Funds Withdrawal (EFW)** (see instructions for exceptions)	8	4,000

Application Is For:	Form Code	Application Is For:	Form Code
Form 706-GS(D)	01	Form 1120-H	17
Form 706-GS(T)	02	Form 1120-L	18
Form 990-C (2005 fiscal year filers only)	03	Form 1120-ND	19
Form 1041 (estate)	04	Form 1120-ND (section 4951 taxes)	20
Form 1041 (trust)	05	Form 1120-PC	21
Form 1041-N	06	Form 1120-POL	22
Form 1041-QFT	07	Form 1120-REIT	23
Form 1042	08	Form 1120-RIC	24
Form 1065	09	Form 1120-S	25
Form 1065-B	10	Form 1120-SF	26
Form 1066	11	Form 3520-A	27
Form 1120	12	Form 8612	28
Form 1120 (sub T) (2005 fiscal year filers only)	13	Form 8613	29
Form 1120-A	14	Form 8725	30
Form 1120-C	34	Form 8804	31
Form 1120-F	15	Form 8831	32
Form 1120-FSC	16	Form 8876	33

For Paperwork Reduction Act Notice, see instructions. Cat. No. 13804A Form **7004** (Rev. 12-2006)

Form **2220**

Department of the Treasury
Internal Revenue Service

Underpayment of Estimated Tax by Corporations

► See separate instructions.

► Attach to the corporation's tax return.

OMB No. 1545-0142

2006

Name: Globe Corporation

Employer identification number: 38 1505087

Note: *Generally, the corporation is not required to file Form 2220 (see Part II below for exceptions) because the IRS will figure any penalty owed and bill the corporation. However, the corporation may still use Form 2220 to figure the penalty. If so, enter the amount from page 2, line 34 on the estimated tax penalty line of the corporation's income tax return, but* **do not** *attach Form 2220.*

Part I Required Annual Payment

1	Total tax (see instructions)			1	100,000
2a	Personal holding company tax (Schedule PH (Form 1120), line 26) included on line 1	2a			
b	Look-back interest included on line 1 under section 460(b)(2) for completed long-term contracts or section 167(g) for depreciation under the income forecast method	2b			
c	Credit for Federal tax paid on fuels (see instructions)	2c			
d	**Total.** Add lines 2a through 2c			2d	
3	Subtract line 2d from line 1. If the result is less than $500, **do not** complete or file this form. The corporation does not owe the penalty			3	100,000
4	Enter the tax shown on the corporation's 2005 income tax return (see instructions). **Caution:** ***If the tax is zero or the tax year was for less than 12 months, skip this line and enter the amount from line 3 on line 5***			4	125,000
5	**Required annual payment.** Enter the **smaller** of line 3 or line 4. If the corporation is required to skip line 4, enter the amount from line 3			5	100,000

Part II Reasons for Filing– Check the boxes below that apply. If any boxes are checked, the corporation **must** file Form 2220 even if it does not owe a penalty (see instructions).

6 ☐ The corporation is using the adjusted seasonal installment method.

7 ☐ The corporation is using the annualized income installment method.

8 ☐ The corporation is a "large corporation" figuring its first required installment based on the prior year's tax.

Part III Figuring the Underpayment

			(a)	(b)	(c)	(d)
9	**Installment due dates.** Enter in columns (a) through (d) the 15th day of the 4th (***Form 990-PF filers:*** Use 5th month), 6th, 9th, and 12th months of the corporation's tax year	9	4-17-06	6-15-06	9-15-06	12-15-06
10	**Required installments.** If the box on line 6 and/or line 7 above is checked, enter the amounts from Schedule A, line 38. If the box on line 8 (but not 6 or 7) is checked, see instructions for the amounts to enter. If none of these boxes are checked, enter 25% of line 5 above in each column. Special rules apply to corporations with assets of $1 billion or more (see instructions).	10	25,000	25,000	25,000	25,000
11	Estimated tax paid or credited for each period (see instructions). For column (a) only, enter the amount from line 11 on line 15	11	16,000	16,000	16,000	16,000
	Complete lines 12 through 18 of one column before going to the next column.					
12	Enter amount, if any, from line 18 of the preceding column	12		-0-	-0-	-0-
13	Add lines 11 and 12	13		16,000	16,000	16,000
* 14	Add amounts on lines 16 and 17 of the preceding column	14		9,000	18,000	27,000
15	Subtract line 14 from line 13. If zero or less, enter -0-	15	16,000	7,000	-0-	-0-
16	If the amount on line 15 is zero, subtract line 13 from line 14. Otherwise, enter -0-	16		-0-	2,000	11,000
** 17	**Underpayment.** If line 15 is less than or equal to line 10, subtract line 15 from line 10. Then go to line 12 of the next column. Otherwise, go to line 18	17	9,000	18,000	27,000	36,000
18	**Overpayment.** If line 10 is less than line 15, subtract line 10 from line 15. Then go to line 12 of the next column	18				

Go to Part IV on page 2 to figure the penalty. Do not go to Part IV if there are no entries on line 17–no penalty is owed.

For Paperwork Reduction Act Notice, see separate instructions. Cat. No. 11746L Form **2220** (2006)

*This amount is from line 17 only from the preceding column.

**Also add the amount on line 16 to "force" the correct cumulative underpayment on line 17.

Form 2220 (2006) Page 2

Part IV Figuring the Penalty

		(a)	(b)	(c)	(d)
19 Enter the date of payment or the 15th day of the 3rd month after the close of the tax year, whichever is earlier (see instructions). *(Form 990-PF and Form 990-T filers:* Use 5th month instead of 3rd month.)	19	6-15-06	9-15-06	12-15-06	3-15-07
20 Number of days from due date of installment on line 9 to the date shown on line 19	20	59	92	91	90
21 Number of days on line 20 after 4/15/2006 and before 7/1/2006	21	59	15		
22 Underpayment on line 17 × $\frac{\text{Number of days on line 21}}{365}$ × 7%	22	$ 102	$ 52	$	$
23 Number of days on line 20 after 6/30/2006 and before 4/1/2007	23		77	91	90
24 Underpayment on line 17 × $\frac{\text{Number of days on line 23}}{365}$ × 8%	24	$	$ 304	$ 539	$ 710
25 Number of days on line 20 after 3/31/2007 and before 7/1/2007	25				
26 Underpayment on line 17 × $\frac{\text{Number of days on line 25}}{365}$ × *%	26	$	$	$	$
27 Number of days on line 20 after 6/30/2007 and before 10/1/2007	27				
28 Underpayment on line 17 × $\frac{\text{Number of days on line 27}}{365}$ × *%	28	$	$	$	$
29 Number of days on line 20 after 9/30/2007 and before 1/1/2008	29				
30 Underpayment on line 17 × $\frac{\text{Number of days on line 29}}{365}$ × *%	30	$	$	$	$
31 Number of days on line 20 after 12/31/2007 and before 2/16/2008	31				
32 Underpayment on line 17 × $\frac{\text{Number of days on line 31}}{366}$ × *%	32	$	$	$	$
33 Add lines 22, 24, 26, 28, 30, and 32	33	$ 102	$ 356	$ 539	$ 710

34 Penalty. Add columns (a) through (d) of line 33. Enter the total here and on Form 1120, line 33; Form 1120-A, line 29; or the comparable line for other income tax returns **34** $ 1,707

***For underpayments paid after March 31, 2007:** For lines 26, 28, 30, and 32, use the penalty interest rate for each calendar quarter, which the IRS will determine during the first month in the preceding quarter. These rates are published quarterly in an IRS News Release and in a revenue ruling in the Internal Revenue Bulletin. To obtain this information on the Internet, access the IRS website at **www.irs.gov.** You can also call 1-800-829-4933 to get interest rate information.

Form **2220** (2006)

SCHEDULE M-3 (Form 1120)

Department of the Treasury
Internal Revenue Service

Net Income (Loss) Reconciliation for Corporations With Total Assets of $10 Million or More

► Attach to Form 1120 or 1120-C.
► See separate instructions.

OMB No. 1545-0123

2006

Name of corporation (common parent, if consolidated return): Valley Corporation

Employer identification number

Check applicable box(es): (1) ☐ Non-Consolidated return (2) ☐ Consolidated return (Form 1120 only)
(3) ☐ Mixed 1120/L/PC group (4) ☐ Dormant subsidiaries schedule attached

Part I Financial Information and Net Income (Loss) Reconciliation (see instructions)

1a Did the corporation file SEC Form 10-K for its income statement period ending with or within this tax year?
☐ **Yes.** Skip lines 1b and 1c and complete lines 2a through 11 with respect to that SEC Form 10-K.
☒ **No.** Go to line 1b.

b Did the corporation prepare a certified audited income statement for that period?
☐ **Yes.** Skip line 1c and complete lines 2a through 11 with respect to that income statement.
☒ **No.** Go to line 1c.

c Did the corporation prepare an income statement for that period?
☒ **Yes.** Complete lines 2a through 11 with respect to that income statement.
☐ **No.** Skip lines 2a through 3c and enter the corporation's net income (loss) per its books and records on line 4.

2a Enter the income statement period: Beginning 1 / 1 / 06 Ending 12 / 31 / 06

b Has the corporation's income statement been restated for the income statement period on line 2a?
☐ **Yes.** (If "Yes," attach an explanation and the amount of each item restated.)
☒ **No.**

c Has the corporation's income statement been restated for any of the five income statement periods preceding the period on line 2a?
☐ **Yes.** (If "Yes," attach an explanation and the amount of each item restated.)
☒ **No.**

3a Is any of the corporation's voting common stock publicly traded?
☐ **Yes.**
☒ **No.** If "No," go to line 4.

b Enter the symbol of the corporation's primary U.S. publicly traded voting common stock . . . . ☐☐☐☐☐

c Enter the nine-digit CUSIP number of the corporation's primary publicly traded voting common stock . . . . ☐☐☐☐☐☐☐☐☐

4	Worldwide consolidated net income (loss) from income statement source identified in Part I, line 1	4	
5a	Net income from nonincludible foreign entities (attach schedule)	5a	(295,118)
b	Net loss from nonincludible foreign entities (attach schedule and enter as a positive amount)	5b	
6a	Net income from nonincludible U.S. entities (attach schedule)	6a	( )
b	Net loss from nonincludible U.S. entities (attach schedule and enter as a positive amount)	6b	
7a	Net income of other includible entities (attach schedule)	7a	
b	Net loss of other includible entities (attach schedule)	7b	( )
8	Adjustment to eliminations of transactions between includible entities and nonincludible entities (attach schedule)	8	
9	Adjustment to reconcile income statement period to tax year (attach schedule)	9	
10a	Intercompany dividend adjustments to reconcile to line 11 (attach schedule)	10a	
b	Other statutory accounting adjustments to reconcile to line 11 (attach schedule)	10b	
c	Other adjustments to reconcile to amount on line 11 (attach schedule)	10c	
11	**Net income (loss) per income statement of includible corporations.** Combine lines 4 through 10	11	295,118

For Privacy Act and Paperwork Reduction Act Notice, see the Instructions for Forms 1120 and 1120-A. Cat. No. 37961C **Schedule M-3 (Form 1120) 2006**

Schedule M-3 (Form 1120) 2006 Page **2**

Name of corporation (common parent, if consolidated return)	Employer identification number
Valley Corporation	

Check applicable box(es): (1) ☐ Consolidated group (2) ☐ Parent corp (3) ☐ Consolidated eliminations (4) ☐ Subsidiary corp (5) ☐ Mixed 1120/L/PC group

Check if a sub-consolidated: (6) ☐ 1120 group (7) ☐ 1120 eliminations

Name of subsidiary (if consolidated return)	Employer identification number

Part II **Reconciliation of Net Income (Loss) per Income Statement of Includible Corporations With Taxable Income per Return** (see instructions)

	Income (Loss) Items (Attach schedules for lines 1 through 8)	(a) Income (Loss) per Income Statement	(b) Temporary Difference	(c) Permanent Difference	(d) Income (Loss) per Tax Return
1	Income (loss) from equity method foreign corporations				
2	Gross foreign dividends not previously taxed				
3	Subpart F, QEF, and similar income inclusions				
4	Section 78 gross-up				
5	Gross foreign distributions previously taxed				
6	Income (loss) from equity method U.S. corporations				
7	U.S. dividends not eliminated in tax consolidation				
8	Minority interest for includible corporations				
9	Income (loss) from U.S. partnerships (attach schedule)				
10	Income (loss) from foreign partnerships (attach schedule)				
11	Income (loss) from other pass-through entities (attach schedule)				
12	Items relating to reportable transactions (attach details)				
13	Interest income				
14	Total accrual to cash adjustment				
15	Hedging transactions				
16	Mark-to-market income (loss)				
17	Cost of goods sold (attach Form 8916-A)				
18	Sale versus lease (for sellers and/or lessors)				
19	Section 481(a) adjustments				
20	Unearned/deferred revenue Prepaid rent	– 0 –	8,000		8,000
21	Income recognition from long-term contracts				
22	Original issue discount and other imputed interest				
23a	Income statement gain/loss on sale, exchange, abandonment, worthlessness, or other disposition of assets other than inventory and pass-through entities	(12,000)			
b	Gross capital gains from Schedule D, excluding amounts from pass-through entities				
c	Gross capital losses from Schedule D, excluding amounts from pass-through entities, abandonment losses, and worthless stock losses				
d	Net gain/loss reported on Form 4797, line 17, excluding amounts from pass-through entities, abandonment losses, and worthless stock losses				
e	Abandonment losses				
f	Worthless stock losses (attach details)				
g	Other gain/loss on disposition of assets other than inventory				
24	Capital loss limitation and carryforward used		12,000		– 0 –
25	Other income (loss) items with differences (attach schedule)*	3,000		(3,000)	– 0 –
26	**Total income (loss) items.** Combine lines 1 through 25	(9,000)	20,000	(3,000)	8,000
27	**Total expense/deduction items** (from Part III, line 36)	(230,882)	(110,000)	144,712	(196,170)
28	Other items with no differences**	535,000			535,000
29a	1120 subgroup reconciliation totals. Add lines 26 through 28	295,118	(90,000)	141,712	346,830
b	PC insurance subgroup reconciliation totals				
c	Life insurance subgroup reconciliation totals				
30	**Reconciliation totals.** Combine lines 29a through 29c	295,118	(90,000)	141,712	346,830

Note. Line 30, column (a), must equal the amount on Part I, line 11, and column (d) must equal Form 1120, page 1, line 28.

Schedule M-3 (Form 1120) 2006

* Tax-exempt interest $3,000

** Gross profit $900,000, plus dividends received $10,000, minus business interest $75,000, and minus operating expenses $300,000

Schedule M-3 (Form 1120) 2006 Page **3**

Name of corporation (common parent, if consolidated return)	**Employer identification number**
Valley Corporation	

Check applicable box(es): **(1)** ☐ Consolidated group **(2)** ☐ Parent corp **(3)** ☐ Consolidated eliminations **(4)** ☐ Subsidiary corp **(5)** ☐ Mixed 1120/L/PC group

Check if a sub-consolidated: **(6)** ☐ 1120 group **(7)** ☐ 1120 eliminations

Name of subsidiary (if consolidated return)	**Employer identification number**

Part III Reconciliation of Net Income (Loss) per Income Statement of Includible Corporations With Taxable Income per Return–Expense/Deduction Items (see instructions)

	Expense/Deduction Items	(a) Expense per Income Statement	(b) Temporary Difference	(c) Permanent Difference	(d) Deduction per Tax Return
1	U.S. current income tax expense	115,542		115,542	
2	U.S. deferred income tax expense	27,540		(27,540)	
3	State and local current income tax expense				
4	State and local deferred income tax expense				
5	Foreign current income tax expense (other than foreign withholding taxes)				
6	Foreign deferred income tax expense				
7	Foreign withholding taxes				
8	Interest expense				
9	Stock option expense				
10	Other equity-based compensation				
11	Meals and entertainment				
12	Fines and penalties				
13	Judgments, damages, awards, and similar costs				
14	Parachute payments				
15	Compensation with section 162(m) limitation				
16	Pension and profit-sharing				
17	Other post-retirement benefits				
18	Deferred compensation				
19	Charitable contribution of cash and tangible property				
20	Charitable contribution of intangible property				
21	Charitable contribution limitation/carryforward				
22	Domestic production activities deduction			10,170	10,170
23	Current year acquisition or reorganization investment banking fees				
24	Current year acquisition or reorganization legal and accounting fees				
25	Current year acquisition/reorganization other costs				
26	Amortization/impairment of goodwill				
27	Amortization of acquisition, reorganization, and start-up costs				
28	Other amortization or impairment write-offs				
29	Section 198 environmental remediation costs				
30	Depletion				
31	Depreciation	60,000	110,000		170,000
32	Bad debt expense	25,000		(9,000)	16,000
33	Corporate owned life insurance premiums	2,800		(2,800)	– 0 –
34	Purchase versus lease (for purchasers and/or lessees)				
35	Other expense/deduction items with differences (attach schedule)				
36	**Total expense/deduction items.** Combine lines 1 through 35. Enter here and on Part II, line 27	230,882	110,000	(144,712)	196,170

Schedule M-3 (Form 1120) 2006

Form **4626** | **Alternative Minimum Tax—Corporations** | OMB No. 1545-0175

Department of the Treasury
Internal Revenue Service

▶ See separate instructions.
▶ Attach to the corporation's tax return.

2006

Name: Glidden Corporation

Employer identification number: 38 : 1505786

Note: *See the instructions to find out if the corporation is a small corporation exempt from the alternative minimum tax (AMT) under section 55(e).*

1	Taxable income or (loss) before net operating loss deduction	1	128,278
2	**Adjustments and preferences:**		
a	Depreciation of post-1986 property	2a	7,500
b	Amortization of certified pollution control facilities	2b	
c	Amortization of mining exploration and development costs	2c	
d	Amortization of circulation expenditures (personal holding companies only)	2d	
e	Adjusted gain or loss	2e	(6,918)
f	Long-term contracts	2f	
g	Merchant marine capital construction funds	2g	
h	Section 833(b) deduction (Blue Cross, Blue Shield, and similar type organizations only)	2h	
i	Tax shelter farm activities (personal service corporations only)	2i	
j	Passive activities (closely held corporations and personal service corporations only)	2j	
k	Loss limitations	2k	
l	Depletion	2l	
m	Tax-exempt interest income from specified private activity bonds	2m	
n	Intangible drilling costs	2n	
o	Other adjustments and preferences	2o	
3	Pre-adjustment alternative minimum taxable income (AMTI). Combine lines 1 through 2o	3	128,860
4	**Adjusted current earnings (ACE) adjustment:**		
a	ACE from line 10 of the ACE worksheet in the instructions — 4a: 312,360		
b	Subtract line 3 from line 4a. If line 3 exceeds line 4a, enter the difference as a negative amount (see instructions) — 4b: 183,500		
c	Multiply line 4b by 75% (.75). Enter the result as a positive amount — 4c: 137,625		
d	Enter the excess, if any, of the corporation's total increases in AMTI from prior year ACE adjustments over its total reductions in AMTI from prior year ACE adjustments (see instructions). **Note:** *You **must** enter an amount on line 4d (even if line 4b is positive)* — 4d: 311,296		
e	ACE adjustment. • If line 4b is zero or more, enter the amount from line 4c • If line 4b is less than zero, enter the **smaller** of line 4c or line 4d as a negative amount	4e	137,625
5	Combine lines 3 and 4e. If zero or less, stop here; the corporation does not owe any AMT	5	266,485
6	Alternative tax net operating loss deduction (see instructions)	6	— 0 —
7	**Alternative minimum taxable income.** Subtract line 6 from line 5. If the corporation held a residual interest in a REMIC, see instructions	7	266,485
8	**Exemption phase-out** (if line 7 is $310,000 or more, skip lines 8a and 8b and enter -0- on line 8c):		
a	Subtract $150,000 from line 7 (if completing this line for a member of a controlled group, see instructions). If zero or less, enter -0- — 8a: 116,485		
b	Multiply line 8a by 25% (.25) — 8b: 29,121		
c	Exemption. Subtract line 8b from $40,000 (if completing this line for a member of a controlled group, see instructions). If zero or less, enter -0-	8c	10,879
9	Subtract line 8c from line 7. If zero or less, enter -0-	9	255,606
10	Multiply line 9 by 20% (.20)	10	51,121
11	Alternative minimum tax foreign tax credit (AMTFTC) (see instructions)	11	— 0 —
12	Tentative minimum tax. Subtract line 11 from line 10	12	51,121
13	Regular tax liability before applying all credits except the foreign tax credit and the American Samoa economic development credit	13	33,278
14	**Alternative minimum tax.** Subtract line 13 from line 12. If zero or less, enter -0-. Enter here and on Form 1120, Schedule J, line 3, or the appropriate line of the corporation's income tax return	14	17,843

For Paperwork Reduction Act Notice, see the instructions. Cat. No. 12955I Form **4626** (2006)

Adjusted Current Earnings (ACE) Worksheet

See ACE Worksheet Instruction (which begin on page 8).

1	Pre-adjustment AMTI . Enter the amount from line 3 of Form 4626				1	128,860
2	ACE depreciation adjustment:					
a	AMT depreciation		2a	32,500		
b	ACE depreciation:					
	(1) Post-1993 property	2b(1) 32,500				
	(2) Post-1989, pre-1994 property	2b(2)				
	(3) Pre-1990 MACRS property	2b(3)				
	(4) Pre-1990 original ACRS property	2b(4)				
	(5) Property described in sections 168(f)(1) through (4)	2b(5)				
	(6) Other property	2(b6)				
	(7) Total ACE depreciation. Add lines 2b(1) through 2b(6)		2b(7)	32,500		
c	ACE depreciation adjustment. Subtract line 2b(7) from line 2a				2c	– 0 –
3	Inclusion in ACE of items included in earnings and profits (E&P):					
a	Tax-exempt interest income		3a	15,000		
b	Death benefits from life insurance contracts		3b	100,000		
c	All other distributions from life insurance contracts (including surrenders)		3c			
d	Inside buildup of undistributed income in life insurance contracts		3d			
e	Other items (see Regulations sections 1.56(g)-1(c)(6)(iii) through (ix) for a partial list)		3e			
f	Total increase to ACE from inclusion in ACE of items included in E&P. Add lines 3a through 3e				3f	115,000
4	Disallowance of items not deductible from E&P:					
a	Certain dividends received		4a	14,000		
b	Dividends paid on certain prefered stock of public utilities that are deductible under section 247		4b			
c	Dividends paid to an ESOP that are deductible under section 404(k)		4c			
d	Nonpatronage dividends that are paid and deductible under section 1382(c)		4d			
e	Other items (see Regulations sections 1.56(g)-1(d)(3)(i) and (ii) for a partial list)		4e			
f	Total increase to ACE because of disallowance of items not deductible from E&P. Add lines 4a through 4e				4f	14,000
5	Other adjustments based on rules for figuring E&P:					
a	Intangible drilling costs		5a			
b	Circulation expenditures		5b			
c	Organizational expenditures		5c	2,500		
d	LIFO inventory adjustments		5d			
e	Installment sales		5e	52,000		
f	Total other E&P adjustments. Combine lines 5a through 5e				5f	54,500
6	Disallowance of loss on exchange of debt pools				6	
7	Acquisition expenses of life insurance companies for qualified foreign contracts				7	
8	Depletion				8	
9	Basis adjustments in determining gain or loss from sale or exchange of pre-1994 property				9	
10	**Adjusted current earnings.** Combine lines 1, 2c, 3f, 4f, and 5f through 9. Enter the result here and on line 4a of Form 4626				10	312,360

Form **1120** | Department of the Treasury Internal Revenue Service

U.S. Corporation Income Tax Return

For calendar year 2006 or tax year beginning ...., 2006, ending ...., 20 ....
► See separate instructions.

OMB No. 1545-0123 | **2006**

A Check if:
1 Consolidated return (attach Form 851) [X]
2 Personal holding co. (attach Sch. PH) [ ]
3 Personal service corp. (see instructions) [ ]
4 Schedule M-3 required (attach Sch. M-3) [ ]

Use IRS label. Otherwise, print or type.
Name: Alpha Manufacturing Corp. and Subsidaries
Number, street, and room or suite no. If a P.O. box, see instructions.: 820 N.W. 1st Place
City or town, state, and ZIP code: Gainesville, FL 32601

B Employer identification number: 38 0000001
C Date incorporated: 9/15/96
D Total assets (see instructions): $ 3,976,492

E Check if: (1) [ ] Initial return (2) [ ] Final return (3) [ ] Name change (4) [ ] Address change

Income	1a	Gross receipts or sales 6,147,000 b Less returns and allowances – 0 – c Bal ►	1c	6,147,000
	2	Cost of goods sold (Schedule A, line 8)	2	2,301,000
	3	Gross profit. Subtract line 2 from line 1c	3	3,846,000
	4	Dividends (Schedule C, line 19)	4	40,000
	5	Interest	5	156,000
	6	Gross rents	6	195,000
	7	Gross royalties	7	
	8	Capital gain net income (attach Schedule D (Form 1120))	8	67,939
	9	Net gain or (loss) from Form 4797, Part II, line 17 (attach Form 4797)	9	37,080
	10	Other income (see instructions–attach schedule)	10	10,000
	11	**Total income.** Add lines 3 through 10 ►	11	4,352,019
Deductions (See instructions for limitations on deductions.)	12	Compensation of officers (Schedule E, line 4)	12	165,000
	13	Salaries and wages (less employment credits)	13	1,356,000
	14	Repairs and maintenance	14	83,000
	15	Bad debts	15	48,500
	16	Rents	16	179,000
	17	Taxes and licenses	17	138,000
	18	Interest	18	58,000
	19	Charitable contributions	19	15,000
	20	Depreciation from Form 4562 not claimed on Schedule A or elsewhere on return (attach Form 4562)	20	168,693
	21	Depletion	21	
	22	Advertising	22	269,140
	23	Pension, profit-sharing, etc., plans	23	140,000
	24	Employee benefit programs	24	105,000
	25	Domestic production activities deduction (attach Form 8903)	25	9,320
	26	Other deductions (attach schedule)	26	1,284,000
	27	**Total deductions.** Add lines 12 through 26 ►	27	4,018,653
	28	Taxable income before net operating loss deduction and special deductions. Subtract line 27 from line 11	28	333,366
	29	**Less:** a Net operating loss deduction (see instructions) 29a		
		b Special deductions (Schedule C, line 20) 29b 32,000	29c	32,000
Tax and Payments	30	**Taxable income.** Subtract line 29c from line 28 (see instructions)	30	301,366
	31	**Total tax** (Schedule J, line 10)	31	100,783
	32a	2005 overpayment credited to 2006 32a		
	b	2006 estimated tax payments 32b 146,000		
	c	2006 refund applied for on Form 4466 32c ( ) d Bal ► 32d 146,000		
	e	Tax deposited with Form 7004 32e		
	f	Credits: (1) Form 2439 ____ (2) Form 4136 ____ 32f		
	g	Credit for federal telephone excise tax paid (attach Form 8913) 32g	32h	146,000
	33	Estimated tax penalty (see instructions). Check if Form 2220 is attached ► [ ]	33	
	34	**Amount owed.** If line 32h is smaller than the total of lines 31 and 33, enter amount owed	34	
	35	**Overpayment.** If line 32h is larger than the total of lines 31 and 33, enter amount overpaid	35	45,217
	36	Enter amount from line 35 you want: **Credited to 2007 estimated tax** ► 26,000 **Refunded** ►	36	19,217

Sign Here
Under penalties of perjury, I declare that I have examined this return, including accompanying schedules and statements, and to the best of my knowledge and belief, it is true, correct, and complete. Declaration of preparer (other than taxpayer) is based on all information of which preparer has any knowledge.

Signature of officer: U. R. Stuck | Date: 3-15-07 | Title: President

May the IRS discuss this return with the preparer shown below (see instructions)? [ ] Yes [ ] No

Paid Preparer's Use Only
Preparer's signature: John A. Kramer | Date: 3-14-07 | Check if self-employed [X] | Preparer's SSN or PTIN: 241693967
Firm's name (or yours if self-employed), address, and ZIP code: Kramer and Associates, 4710 N.W. 68th Terrace Gainesville, FL | EIN 01 0000001 | Phone no. (352) 555-5555

Form 1120—Consolidated Taxable Income Computation

Line	Title	Consolidated	Adjustments and Eliminations	1 Alpha Mfg. Corp.	2 Beta Corp.	3 Charlie Corp.	4 Delta Corp.	5 Echo Corp.
1	Gross receipts	$6,147,000	($109,000)[1]	$1,566,000	$2,680,000	$676,000		$1,249,000
	Returns/Allowances		85,000[2]					
2	Cost goods/Operations	(2,301,000)		(783,000)	(1,390,000)	(128,000)		–0–
3	Gross profit	$3,846,000	($24,000)	$ 783,000	$1,290,000	$548,000	$ –0–	$1,249,000
4	Dividends (Sch. C)	40,000	(170,000)[3]	210,000				
5	Interest	156,000[5]		46,000	89,000			21,000
6	Gross rents	195,000					$195,000	
7	Gross royalties							
8	Capital gain net income (Sch. D)	67,939		67,939				
9	Net gain or loss from		(14,600)					
	Form 4797	37,080	2,920[6]	52,760	(4,000)			
10	Other income	10,000[4]		10,000				
11	Total income	$4,352,019	($205,680)	$1,169,699	$1,375,000	$548,000	$195,000	$1,270,000
12	Compensation of officers	$ 165,000		$ 165,000				
13	Salaries and wages	1,356,000		138,000	$ 240,000	$377,000	$ 36,000	$ 565,000
14	Repairs	83,000		19,000	18,000	7,000	18,000	21,000
15	Bad debts	48,500			36,500	4,000		8,000
16	Rents	179,000		93,000	39,000	11,000		36,000
17	Taxes	138,000[4]		36,000	27,000	10,000	16,000	49,000
18	Interest	58,000		27,000			29,000[5]	2,000
19	Contributions	15,000[4]		9,000	4,000			2,000
20	Depreciation	168,693		24,500	62,930	24,370	24,043	32,850
21	Depletion	–0–						
22	Advertising	269,140			223,140	27,000		19,000
23	Pension, profit sharing, etc. plans	140,000		39,000	21,000	35,000		45,000
24	Employee benefit programs	105,000		26,000	16,000	29,000		34,000
25	U.S. prod. act. ded.	9,320[7]			6,350			2,970
26	Other deductions	1,284,000[4]		409,000	401,000	72,000	49,000	353,000
27	Total deductions	$4,018,653	$ –0–	$ 985,500	$1,094,920	$596,370	$172,043	$1,169,820

Line	Title	Consolidated	Adjustments and Eliminations	1 Alpha Mfg. Corp.	2 Beta Corp.	3 Charlie Corp.	4 Delta Corp.	5 Echo Corp.
28	Taxable income before NOL ded. and special deductions	$333,366	($205,680)	$184,199	$280,080	($48,370)	$22,957	$100,180
29a	NOL deduction							
29b	Special deductions	(32,000)	(32,000)[3]					
30	Taxable income	$301,366	($237,680)					

Explanatory Notes

[1] The deferred intercompany profit on the sale of inventory items (intercompany item) from Alpha to Beta during the current year was $109,000. This amount is eliminated from revenue. The deferred intercompany profit amount is reported when Beta sells the inventory outside the affiliated group or some other corresponding item occurs.

[2] Restoration of $85,000 in deferred intercompany profits arising from the sale of inventory items from Alpha to Beta in the current and prior years. These goods were sold outside the affiliated group in the current year. The increased intercompany profit deferral for the current year is $24,000 ($109,000 − $85,000). This amount is reflected in the reduced gross profit amount.

[3] Intragroup dividends of $100,000 and $70,000 paid by Beta and Echo, respectively, to Alpha are an adjustment to consolidated taxable income because they were included in Alpha's separate tax return. The remaining $40,000 of dividends are from unaffiliated domestic corporations that are more than 20%-owned and eligible for an 80% dividends-received deduction (see Line 29b). The group claims a $32,000 dividends-received deduction.

[4] The supporting schedule of component items is not reproduced here.

[5] Alpha Manufacturing loaned money to Delta Corporation. Delta accrued and paid $12,000 in interest during the year. The individual firms have reported these amounts in their separate expense and income items.

[6] Alpha sells a truck to Beta on June of the current year for $25,000. The truck (a five-year MACRS property) cost $26,000 when purchased new on June 1 two years ago. Alpha did not elect Sec. 179 expensing or bonus depreciation on the truck and thus claimed depreciation of $13,520 [$26,000 × (0.20 + 0.32)] on the truck in the prior two years. Alpha claims depreciation of $2,080 ($26,000 × 0.192 × 5/12) in the current year. Alpha claims a total of $15,600 ($13,520 + $2,080) in depreciation prior to the sale. Alpha's deferred gain (intercompany item) on the sale is $14,600 [$25,000 − ($26,000 − $15,600)]. (See Line 9, Adjustments and Eliminations.) The truck is recorded as two separate MACRS properties on Beta's tax books. Beta depreciates the original $26,000 basis for the truck using the remainder of Alpha's five-year recovery period. Depreciation on this portion of the basis is $2,912 ($26,000 × 0.1920 × 7/12) in the current year. Beta also can depreciate the second MACRS property; that is, the step-up in basis that results from the intercompany sale. Beta elects to depreciate this portion of the basis as a five-year MACRS property and claims an additional $2,920 ($14,600 × 0.2000) of depreciation in the current year. The $2,920 is the portion of the deferred gain (Sec. 1245 income) Alpha reported in the current year.

[7] The consolidated U.S. production activities deduction is computed as $310,686 × 0.03, where $310,686 is consolidated taxable income before that deduction. The deduction is then allocated to the group members based on Reg. Sec. 1.199-7.

Form **1065** Department of the Treasury Internal Revenue Service

U.S. Return of Partnership Income

For calendar year 2006, or tax year beginning ...., 2006, ending ...., 20.....
▶ See separate instructions.

OMB No. 1545-0099 **2006**

A Principal business activity: Manufacturing	Use the IRS label. Otherwise, print or type.	Name of partnership: Johns and Lawrence	D Employer identification number: 76 3456789
B Principal product or service: Furniture		Number, street, and room or suite no. If a P.O. box, see the instructions.: 1234 University Avenue	E Date business started: 6-1-2000
C Business code number: 337000		City or town, state, and ZIP code: Gainesville, FL 32611	F Total assets (see the instructions): $ 499,484

G Check applicable boxes: (1) ☐ Initial return (2) ☐ Final return (3) ☐ Name change (4) ☐ Address change (5) ☐ Amended return
H Check accounting method: (1) ☐ Cash (2) ☒ Accrual (3) ☐ Other (specify) ▶
I Number of Schedules K-1. Attach one for each person who was a partner at any time during the tax year ▶
J Check if Schedule M-3 required (attach Schedule M-3) ☐

Caution. *Include **only** trade or business income and expenses on lines 1a through 22 below. See the instructions for more information.*

Section	Line	Description	Sub-line	Sub-amount	Line	Amount
Income	1a	Gross receipts or sales	1a	869,658		
	b	Less returns and allowances	1b	29,242	1c	840,416
	2	Cost of goods sold (Schedule A, line 8)			2	540,204
	3	Gross profit. Subtract line 2 from line 1c			3	300,212
	4	Ordinary income (loss) from other partnerships, estates, and trusts *(attach statement)*			4	
	5	Net farm profit (loss) *(attach Schedule F (Form 1040))*			5	
	6	Net gain (loss) from Form 4797, Part II, line 17 (attach Form 4797)			6	
	7	Other income (loss) *(attach statement)*			7	
	8	**Total income (loss).** Combine lines 3 through 7			8	300,212
Deductions (see the instructions for limitations)	9	Salaries and wages (other than to partners) (less employment credits)			9	52,000
	10	Guaranteed payments to partners			10	36,000
	11	Repairs and maintenance			11	4,800
	12	Bad debts			12	4,000
	13	Rent			13	36,000
	14	Taxes and licenses (8,320 + 1,520)			14	9,840
	15	Interest			15	8,000
	16a	Depreciation *(if required, attach Form 4562)*	16a	27,476		
	b	Less depreciation reported on Schedule A and elsewhere on return	16b	15,000	16c	12,476
	17	Depletion **(Do not deduct oil and gas depletion.)**			17	
	18	Retirement plans, etc.			18	2,000
	19	Employee benefit programs			19	4,000
	20	Other deductions *(attach statement)*			20	51,250
	21	**Total deductions.** Add the amounts shown in the far right column for lines 9 through 20			21	220,366
	22	**Ordinary business income (loss).** Subtract line 21 from line 8			22	
	23	Credit for federal telephone excise tax paid (attach Form 8913)			23	79,846

Sign Here

Under penalties of perjury, I declare that I have examined this return, including accompanying schedules and statements, and to the best of my knowledge and belief, it is true, correct, and complete. Declaration of preparer (other than general partner or limited liability company member manager) is based on all information of which preparer has any knowledge.

▶ *Andrew Lawrence* — Signature of general partner or limited liability company member manager ▶ 4-10-07 Date

May the IRS discuss this return with the preparer shown below (see instructions)? ☐ Yes ☐ No

Paid Preparer's Use Only

Preparer's signature: *Michael S. Kramer*	Date: 4-7-07	Check if self-employed ▶ ☒	Preparer's SSN or PTIN: 375-49-6339
Firm's name (or yours if self-employed), address, and ZIP code ▶ Michael S. Kramer 1110 McMillon Gainesville, FL 37611		EIN ▶ 59 2029763	Phone no. (352) 555-2000

For Privacy Act and Paperwork Reduction Act Notice, see separate instructions. Cat. No. 11390Z Form **1065** (2006)

Form 1065 (2006) Page 2

Schedule A **Cost of Goods Sold** (see the instructions)

1	Inventory at beginning of year	1	64,000
2	Purchases less cost of items withdrawn for personal use	2	340,800
3	Cost of labor	3	143,204
4	Additional section 263A costs *(attach statement)*	4	7,000
5	Other costs *(attach statement)*	5	90,000
6	**Total.** Add lines 1 through 5	6	645,004
7	Inventory at end of year	7	104,800
8	**Cost of goods sold.** Subtract line 7 from line 6. Enter here and on page 1, line 2	8	540,204

9a Check all methods used for valuing closing inventory:

(i) ☒ Cost as described in Regulations section 1.471-3

(ii) ☐ Lower of cost or market as described in Regulations section 1.471-4

(iii) ☐ Other (specify method used and attach explanation) ▶

b Check this box if there was a writedown of "subnormal" goods as described in Regulations section 1.471-2(c) ▶ ☐

c Check this box if the LIFO inventory method was adopted this tax year for any goods *(if checked, attach Form 970)*. ▶ ☐

d Do the rules of section 263A (for property produced or acquired for resale) apply to the partnership? ☒ Yes ☐ No

e Was there any change in determining quantities, cost, or valuations between opening and closing inventory? ☐ Yes ☒ No
If "Yes," attach explanation.

Schedule B **Other Information**

		Yes	No
1	What type of entity is filing this return? Check the applicable box: a ☐ Domestic general partnership b ☐ Domestic limited partnership c ☐ Domestic limited liability company d ☐ Domestic limited liability partnership e ☐ Foreign partnership f ☐ Other ▶		
2	Are any partners in this partnership also partnerships?		X
3	During the partnership's tax year, did the partnership own any interest in another partnership or in any foreign entity that was disregarded as an entity separate from its owner under Regulations sections 301.7701-2 and 301.7701-3? If yes, see instructions for required attachment		X
4	Did the partnership file Form 8893, Election of Partnership Level Tax Treatment, or an election statement under section 6231(a)(1)(B)(ii) for partnership-level tax treatment, that is in effect for this tax year? See Form 8893 for more details		X
5	Does this partnership meet all three of the following requirements? a The partnership's total receipts for the tax year were less than $250,000; b The partnership's total assets at the end of the tax year were less than $600,000; and c Schedules K-1 are filed with the return and furnished to the partners on or before the due date (including extensions) for the partnership return. If "Yes," the partnership is not required to complete Schedules L, M-1, and M-2; Item F on page 1 of Form 1065; or Item N on Schedule K-1.		X
6	Does this partnership have any foreign partners? If "Yes," the partnership may have to file Forms 8804, 8805 and 8813. See the instructions		X
7	Is this partnership a publicly traded partnership as defined in section 469(k)(2)?		X
8	Has this partnership filed, or is it required to file, a return under section 6111 to provide information on any reportable transaction?		X
9	At any time during calendar year 2006, did the partnership have an interest in or a signature or other authority over a financial account in a foreign country (such as a bank account, securities account, or other financial account)? See the instructions for exceptions and filing requirements for Form TD F 90-22.1. If "Yes," enter the name of the foreign country. ▶		X
10	During the tax year, did the partnership receive a distribution from, or was it the grantor of, or transferor to, a foreign trust? If ™Yes,∫ the partnership may have to file Form 3520. See the instructions.		X
11	Was there a distribution of property or a transfer (for example, by sale or death) of a partnership interest during the tax year? If "Yes," you may elect to adjust the basis of the partnership's assets under section 754 by attaching the statement described under *Elections Made By the Partnership* in the instructions		X
12	Enter the number of Forms 8865, Return of U.S. Persons With Respect to Certain Foreign Partnerships, attached to this return ▶		

Designation of Tax Matters Partner (see the instructions)

Enter below the general partner designated as the tax matters partner (TMP) for the tax year of this return: **(Not Required)**

Name of designated TMP ▶ Andrew Lawrence — Identifying number of TMP ▶ 297-63-2110

Address of designated TMP ▶ 436 N.W. 24th Ave.
Gainesville, FL 32607

Form **1065** (2006)

Form 1065 (2006) Page 3

Schedule K Partners' Distributive Share Items

Section	Item	Line	Total amount	
Income (Loss)	1 Ordinary business income (loss) (page 1, line 22)	1	79,846	
	2 Net rental real estate income (loss) *(attach Form 8825)*	2		
	3a Other gross rental income (loss) — 3a			
	b Expenses from other rental activities *(attach statement)* — 3b			
	c Other net rental income (loss). Subtract line 3b from line 3a	3c		
	4 Guaranteed payments	4	36,000	
	5 Interest income	5		
	6 Dividends: a Ordinary dividends	6a	1,000	
	b Qualified dividends — 6b 1,000			
	7 Royalties	7		
	8 Net short-term capital gain (loss) *(attach Schedule D (Form 1065))*	8	(2,100)	
	9a Net long-term capital gain (loss) *(attach Schedule D (Form 1065))*	9a	4,500	
	b Collectibles (28%) gain (loss) — 9b			
	c Unrecaptured section 1250 gain *(attach statement)* — 9c			
	10 Net section 1231 gain (loss) *(attach Form 4797)*	10		
	11 Other income (loss) *(see instructions)* Type ▶	11		
Deductions	12 Section 179 deduction *(attach Form 4562)*	12		
	13a Contributions	13a	12,000	
	b Investment interest expense	13b	150	
	c Section 59(e)(2) expenditures: (1) Type ▶ (2) Amount ▶	13c(2)		
	d Other deductions *(see instructions)* Type ▶	13d	*	
Self-Employment	14a Net earnings (loss) from self-employment	14a	115,846	
	b Gross farming or fishing income	14b		
	c Gross nonfarm income	14c		
Credits	15a Low-income housing credit (section 42(j)(5))	15a		
	b Low-income housing credit (other)	15b		
	c Qualified rehabilitation expenditures (rental real estate) *(attach Form 3468)*	15c		
	d Other rental real estate credits *(see instructions)* Type ▶	15d		
	e Other rental credits *(see instructions)* Type ▶	15e		
	f Other credits *(see instructions)* Type ▶	15f		
Foreign Transactions	16a Name of country or U.S. possession ▶			
	b Gross income from all sources	16b		
	c Gross income sourced at partner level	16c		
	Foreign gross income sourced at partnership level			
	d Passive ▶ e Listed categories *(attach statement)* ▶ f General limitation ▶	16f		
	Deductions allocated and apportioned at partner level			
	g Interest expense ▶ h Other ▶	16h		
	Deductions allocated and apportioned at partnership level to foreign source income			
	i Passive ▶ j Listed categories *(attach statement)* ▶ k General limitation ▶	16k		
	l Total foreign taxes (check one): ▶ Paid ☐ Accrued ☐	16l		
	m Reduction in taxes available for credit *(attach statement)*	16m		
	n Other foreign tax information *(attach statement)*			
Alternative Minimum Tax (AMT) Items	17a Post-1986 depreciation adjustment	17a	1,514	
	b Adjusted gain or loss	17b		
	c Depletion (other than oil and gas)	17c		
	d Oil, gas, and geothermal properties–gross income	17d		
	e Oil, gas, and geothermal properties–deductions	17e		
	f Other AMT items *(attach statement)*	17f		
Other Information	18a Tax-exempt interest income	18a	18,000	
	b Other tax-exempt income	18b		
	c Nondeductible expenses	18c	6,000	**
	19a Distributions of cash and marketable securities	19a	28,212	
	b Distributions of other property	19b		
	20a Investment income	20a	1,000	***
	b Investment expenses	20b		
	c Other items and amounts *(attach statement)*			

Form 1065 (2006)

* Qualified production activities income (QPAI) equals $80,000. Employer's W-2 wages equal $52,000.

** Disallowed meals and entertainment expenses ($4,000) and interest on loan used to purchase tax-exempt bonds ($2,000).

*** If partners elect to tax dividends at ordinary rates under Sec. 163(d)(4)(B).

Form 1065 (2006) Page **4**

Analysis of Net Income (Loss)

1	Net income (loss). Combine Schedule K, lines 1 through 11. From the result, subtract the sum of Schedule K, lines 12 through 13d, and 16l 1	107,096

2 Analysis by partner type:	(i) Corporate	(ii) Individual (active)	(iii) Individual (passive)	(iv) Partnership	(v) Exempt organization	(vi) Nominee/Other
a General partners		107,096				
b Limited partners						

Schedule L Balance Sheets per Books

Assets	Beginning of tax year (a)	(b)	End of tax year (c)	(d)
1 Cash		60,000		92,760
2a Trade notes and accounts receivable	25,100		24,000	
b Less allowance for bad debts	1,000	24,000	1,000	23,000
3 Inventories		64,000		104,800
4 U.S. government obligations				
5 Tax-exempt securities		200,000		200,000
6 Other current assets *(attach statement)*		7,000		-0-
7 Mortgage and real estate loans				
8 Other investments *(attach statement)*				
9a Buildings and other depreciable assets	151,600		151,600	
b Less accumulated depreciation	45,200	106,400	72,760	78,924
10a Depletable assets				
b Less accumulated depletion				
11 Land (net of any amortization)				
12a Intangible assets (amortizable only)				
b Less accumulated amortization				
13 Other assets *(attach statement)*				
14 Total assets		461,400		499,484
Liabilities and Capital				
15 Accounts payable		26,000		19,000
16 Mortgages, notes, bonds payable in less than 1 year		4,000		4,000
17 Other current liabilities *(attach statement)*		3,600		3,600
18 All nonrecourse loans				
19 Mortgages, notes, bonds payable in 1 year or more		130,000		119,724
20 Other liabilities *(attach statement)*				
21 Partners' capital accounts		297,800		353,160
22 Total liabilities and capital		461,400		499,484

Schedule M-1 Reconciliation of Income (Loss) per Books With Income (Loss) per Return

Note. Schedule M-3 may be required instead of Schedule M-1 (see instructions).

1 Net income (loss) per books	83,572	6 Income recorded on books this year not included on Schedule K, lines 1 through 11 (itemize): a Tax-exempt interest $ 18,000	18,000
2 Income included on Schedule K, lines 1, 2, 3c, 5, 6a, 7, 8, 9a, 10, and 11, not recorded on books this year (itemize):			
3 Guaranteed payments (other than health insurance)	36,000	7 Deductions included on Schedule K, lines 1 through 13d, and 16l, not charged against book income this year (itemize): a Depreciation $ 476	476
4 Expenses recorded on books this year not included on Schedule K, lines 1 through 13d, and 16l (itemize): a Depreciation $ b Travel and entertainment $ 4,000 Interest on loans* 2,000	6,000	8 Add lines 6 and 7	18,476
5 Add lines 1 through 4	125,572	9 Income (loss) (Analysis of Net Income (Loss), line 1). Subtract line 8 from line 5	107,096

Schedule M-2 Analysis of Partners' Capital Accounts

1 Balance at beginning of year	297,800	6 Distributions: a Cash	28,212
2 Capital contributed: a Cash		b Property	
b Property		7 Other decreases (itemize):	
3 Net income (loss) per books	83,572		
4 Other increases (itemize):		8 Add lines 6 and 7	28,212
5 Add lines 1 through 4	381,372	9 Balance at end of year. Subtract line 8 from line 5	353,160

*To buy tax-exempt bonds.

651106

☐ Final K-1 ☐ Amended K-1 OMB No. 1545-0099

Schedule K-1 (Form 1065) **2006**

Department of the Treasury
Internal Revenue Service

For calendar year 2006, or tax year beginning ________, 2006 ending ________, 20__

Partner's Share of Income, Deductions, Credits, etc.

► See back of form and separate instructions.

Part I Information About the Partnership

A Partnership's employer identification number
76-3456789

B Partnership's name, address, city, state, and ZIP code
Johns and Lawrence
1234 University Ave.
Gainesville, FL 32611

C IRS Center where partnership filed return
Atlanta, GA

D ☐ Check if this is a publicly traded partnership (PTP)

E ☐ Tax shelter registration number, if any ________

F ☐ Check if Form 8271 is attached

Part II Information About the Partner

G Partner's identifying number
297-63-2110

H Partner's name, address, city, state, and ZIP code
Andrew Lawrence*
436 N.W. 24th Ave.
Gainesville, FL 32607

I ☒ General partner or LLC member-manager ☐ Limited partner or other LLC member

J ☐ Domestic partner ☐ Foreign partner

K What type of entity is this partner? Individual

L Partner's share of profit, loss, and capital:

	Beginning	Ending
Profit	50 %	50 %
Loss	50 %	50 %
Capital	50 %	50 %

M Partner's share of liabilities at year end:

Nonrecourse	$
Qualified nonrecourse financing	$
Recourse	$ 73,162

N Partner's capital account analysis:

Beginning capital account	$ 148,900
Capital contributed during the year	$ -0-
Current year increase (decrease)	$ 41,786
Withdrawals & distributions	$ (14,106)
Ending capital account	$ 176,580

☐ Tax basis ☒ GAAP ☐ Section 704(b) book
☐ Other (explain)

Part III Partner's Share of Current Year Income, Deductions, Credits, and Other Items

1	Ordinary business income (loss)	39,923	15	Credits
2	Net rental real estate income (loss)		
3	Other net rental income (loss)		16	Foreign transactions
4	Guaranteed payments	18,000	
5	Interest income		
6a	Ordinary dividends	500	
6b	Qualified dividends	500	
7	Royalties		
8	Net short-term capital gain (loss)	(1,050)	
9a	Net long-term capital gain (loss)	2,250	17	Alternative minimum tax (AMT) items — A 757
9b	Collectibles (28%) gain (loss)		
9c	Unrecaptured section 1250 gain		
10	Net section 1231 gain (loss)		18	Tax-exempt income and nondeductible expenses — A 9,000; C 3,000
11	Other income (loss)		
12	Section 179 deduction		19	Distributions — A 14,106
13	Other deductions	A 6,000; G 75; U 40,000; V 26,000	20	Other information — A 500**
14	Self-employment earnings (loss)	A 57,923	

*See attached statement for additional information.

For IRS Use Only

For Privacy Act and Paperwork Reduction Act Notice, see Instructions for Form 1065. Cat. No. 11394R Schedule K-1 (Form 1065) 2006

*Schedule K-1 for Stephen Johns is similar to this one and is not reproduced here.

**If partner elects to tax dividends at ordinary rates under Sec. 163(d)(4)(B).

This list identifies the codes used on Schedule K-1 for all partners and provides summarized reporting information for partners who file Form 1040. For detailed reporting and filing information, see the separate Partner's Instructions for Schedule K-1 and the instructions for your income tax return.

1. Ordinary business income (loss). You must first determine whether the income (loss) is passive or nonpassive. Then enter on your return as follows:

	Report on
Passive loss	See the Partner's Instructions
Passive income	Schedule E, line 28, column (g)
Nonpassive loss	Schedule E, line 28, column (h)
Nonpassive income	Schedule E, line 28, column (j)
2. Net rental real estate income (loss)	See the Partner's Instructions
3. Other net rental income (loss)	
Net income	Schedule E, line 28, column (g)
Net loss	See the Partner's Instructions
4. Guaranteed payments	Schedule E, line 28, column (j)
5. Interest income	Form 1040, line 8a
6a. Ordinary dividends	Form 1040, line 9a
6b. Qualified dividends	Form 1040, line 9b
7. Royalties	Schedule E, line 4
8. Net short-term capital gain (loss)	Schedule D, line 5, column (f)
9a. Net long-term capital gain (loss)	Schedule D, line 12, column (f)
9b. Collectibles (28%) gain (loss)	28% Rate Gain Worksheet, line 4 (Schedule D Instructions)
9c. Unrecaptured section 1250 gain	See the Partner's Instructions
10. Net section 1231 gain (loss)	See the Partner's Instructions
11. Other income (loss)	
Code	
A Other portfolio income (loss)	See the Partner's Instructions
B Involuntary conversions	See the Partner's Instructions
C Sec. 1256 contracts & straddles	Form 6781, line 1
D Mining exploration costs recapture	See Pub. 535
E Cancellation of debt	Form 1040, line 21 or Form 982
F Other income (loss)	See the Partner's Instructions
12. Section 179 deduction	See the Partner's Instructions
13. Other deductions	
A Cash contributions (50%)	See the Partner's Instructions (A–F)
B Cash contributions (30%)	
C Noncash contributions (50%)	
D Noncash contributions (30%)	
E Capital gain property to a 50% organization (30%)	
F Capital gain property (20%)	
G Investment interest expense	Form 4952, line 1
H Deductions–royalty income	Schedule E, line 18
I Section 59(e)(2) expenditures	See the Partner's Instructions
J Deductions–portfolio (2% floor)	Schedule A, line 22
K Deductions–portfolio (other)	Schedule A, line 27
L Amounts paid for medical insurance	Schedule A, line 1 or Form 1040, line 29
M Educational assistance benefits	See the Partner's Instructions
N Dependent care benefits	Form 2441, line 12
O Preproductive period expenses	See the Partner's Instructions
P Commercial revitalization deduction from rental real estate activities	See Form 8582 Instructions
Q Pensions and IRAs	See the Partner's Instructions
R Reforestation expense deduction	See the Partner's Instructions
S Domestic production activities information	See Form 8903 instructions
T Qualified production activities income	Form 8903, line 7
U Employer's W-2 wages	Form 8903, line 13
V Other deductions	See the Partner's Instructions

14. Self-employment earnings (loss)

Note. *If you have a section 179 deduction or any partner-level deductions, see the Partner's Instructions before completing Schedule SE.*

A Net earnings (loss) from self-employment	Schedule SE, Section A or B
B Gross farming or fishing income	See the Partner's Instructions
C Gross non-farm income	See the Partner's Instructions
15. Credits	
A Low-income housing credit (section 42(j)(5))	See the Partner's Instructions (A–E)
B Low-income housing credit (other)	
C Qualified rehabilitation expenditures (rental real estate)	
D Other rental real estate credits	
E Other rental credits	
F Undistributed capital gains credit	Form 1040, line 70; check box a
G Credit for alcohol used as fuel	See the Partner's Instructions
H Work opportunity credit	See the Partner's Instructions (H–J)
I Welfare-to-work credit	
J Disabled access credit	

Code	*Report on*
K Empowerment zone and renewal community employment credit	Form 8844, line 3
L Credit for increasing research activities	See the Partner's Instructions (L–N)
M New markets credit	
N Credit for employer social security and Medicare taxes	
O Backup withholding	Form 1040, line 64
P Other credits	See the Partner's Instructions
16. Foreign transactions	
A Name of country or U.S. possession	Form 1116, Part I (A–C)
B Gross income from all sources	
C Gross income sourced at partner level	
Foreign gross income sourced at partnership level	
D Passive	Form 1116, Part I (D–F)
E Listed categories	
F General limitation	
Deductions allocated and apportioned at partner level	
G Interest expense	Form 1116, Part I
H Other	Form 1116, Part I
Deductions allocated and apportioned at partnership level to foreign source income	
I Passive	Form 1116, Part I (I–K)
J Listed categories	
K General limitation	
Other information	
L Total foreign taxes paid	Form 1116, Part II
M Total foreign taxes accrued	Form 1116, Part II
N Reduction in taxes available for credit	Form 1116, line 12
O Foreign trading gross receipts	Form 8873
P Extraterritorial income exclusion	Form 8873
Q Other foreign transactions	See the Partner's Instructions
17. Alternative minimum tax (AMT) items	
A Post-1986 depreciation adjustment	See the Partner's Instructions and the Instructions for Form 6251 (A–F)
B Adjusted gain or loss	
C Depletion (other than oil & gas)	
D Oil, gas, & geothermal–gross income	
E Oil, gas, & geothermal–deductions	
F Other AMT items	
18. Tax-exempt income and nondeductible expenses	
A Tax-exempt interest income	Form 1040, line 8b
B Other tax-exempt income	See the Partner's Instructions
C Nondeductible expenses	See the Partner's Instructions
19. Distributions	
A Cash and marketable securities	See the Partner's Instructions
B Other property	See the Partner's Instructions
20. Other information	
A Investment income	Form 4952, line 4a
B Investment expenses	Form 4952, line 5
C Fuel tax credit information	Form 4136
D Qualified rehabilitation expenditures (other than rental real estate)	See the Partner's Instructions
E Basis of energy property	See the Partner's Instructions
F Recapture of low-income housing credit (section 42(j)(5))	Form 8611, line 8
G Recapture of low-income housing credit (other)	Form 8611, line 8
H Recapture of investment credit	Form 4255
I Recapture of other credits	See the Partner's Instructions
J Look-back interest–completed long-term contracts	Form 8697
K Look-back interest–income forecast method	Form 8866
L Dispositions of property with section 179 deductions	See the Partner's Instructions (L–W)
M Recapture of section 179 deduction	
N Interest expense for corporate partners	
O Section 453(l)(3) information	
P Section 453A(c) information	
Q Section 1260(b) information	
R Interest allocable to production expenditures	
S CCF nonqualified withdrawals	
T Information needed to figure depletion–oil and gas	
U Amortization of reforestation costs	
V Unrelated business taxable income	
W Other information	

FACTS FOR GENERAL PARTNERSHIP (FORM 1065)

The same basic facts presented for the Andrew Lawrence proprietorship are used for the partnership except for the following:

1. Johns and Lawrence is instead a general partnership. Andrew Lawrence and Stephen Johns are both general partners and have equal capital and profits interests. The partners formed the partnership on June 1, 2000. Johns and Lawrence each exchanged their $100,000 of property for a 50% interest in capital and profits.
2. The book income for Johns and Lawrence is presented in the attached worksheet, which reconciles book income and partnership taxable income.
3. The $18,000 salaries paid to each partner are stipulated in the partnership agreement and are treated as guaranteed payments.
4. The partnership pays federal and state employment taxes on the wages paid to employees other than the partners Johns and Lawrence. The employment tax expense is $52,000 × 0.16 = $8,320. The guaranteed payments made to Johns and Lawrence are treated as self-employment income by the two partners.
5. The partnership paid no estimated federal income taxes.
6. The partnership distributed $14,106 to each of the two partners.
7. Other deductions include:

Travel	$ 4,000
Meals and entertainment	8,000
Minus: 50% disallowance	(4,000)
Office expenses	16,000
Transportation	10,400
General and administrative	3,000
Advertising	13,000
Miscellaneous*	850
Total	$51,250

*$150 of the miscellaneous expenses are related to the production of the dividend income and are separately stated.

8. The following schedule reconciles net income for the C corporation and the partnership:

Net income per books for C corporation	$63,412
Plus: Federal income taxes	14,000
Employment tax adjustment ($14,480 − $8,320)	6,160
Net income per books for partnership	$83,572

9. Total paid-in capital and accumulated profits were divided equally between the two partners in accordance with the actual contributions and allocation of partnership profits in the partnership agreement. Actual business operations may provide for an unequal allocation.
10. Qualified production activities income (QPAI) equals $80,000. Employer's W-2 wages $52,000.
11. The balance sheet for Johns and Lawrence appears on page 4 of Form 1065.

Johns and Lawrence General Partnership Reconciliation of Book and Taxable Income For Year Ending December 31, 2006

	Book Income		Adjustments		Taxable Income		Form 1065 Schedule K	
Account Name	Debit	Credit	Debit	Credit	Debit	Credit	Ordinary Income	Separately Stated Items
Sales		$869,658				$869,658	$869,658	
Sales returns & allowances	$ 29,242				$ 29,242		(29,242)	
Cost of sales	540,204				540,204		(540,204)	
Dividends		1,000				1,000		$ 1,000
Tax-exempt interest		18,000	$18,000			0		18,000
Gain on stock sale		4,500				4,500		4,500
Worthless stock loss	2,100				2,100			(2,100)
Guaranteed payments[a]	36,000			$36,000	0		(36,000)	
Other salaries	52,000				52,000		(52,000)	
Rentals	36,000				36,000		(36,000)	
Bad debts	4,000				4,000		(4,000)	
Interest:								
Working capital loans	8,000				8,000		(8,000)	
Purchase tax-exempt bonds	2,000			2,000	0			(2,000)
Employment taxes	8,320				8,320		(8,320)	
Taxes	1,520				1,520		(1,520)	
Repairs	4,800				4,800		(4,800)	
Depreciation[b]	12,000		476		12,476		(12,476)	
Charitable contributions	12,000				12,000			(12,000)
Travel	4,000				4,000		(4,000)	
Meals and entertainment[c]	8,000			4,000	4,000		(4,000)	
Meals and ent. nondeductible								(4,000)
Office expenses	16,000				16,000		(16,000)	
Advertising	13,000				13,000		(13,000)	
Transportation expense	10,400				10,400		(10,400)	
General and administrative	3,000				3,000		(3,000)	
Pension plans[d]	2,000				2,000		(2,000)	
Employee benefit programs[e]	4,000				4,000		(4,000)	
Miscellaneous	1,000				1,000		(850)	(150)
Net profit/Taxable income	83,572		$23,524		107,096			
Total	$893,158	$893,158	$42,000	$42,000	$875,158	$875,158	$ 79,846	

[a] Guaranteed payments have no net effect on taxable income. The guaranteed payments both reduce ordinary income and increase separately stated income items that are taxable.

[b] MACRS depreciation is $27,476 − $15,000 = $12,476

[c] 50% of the meals and entertainment expense is not deductible for tax purposes but must be separately stated on Schedules K and K-1.

[d] The pension plan expense is the same for book and tax purposes for this partnership. No pension expenses relate to pensions for the partners.

[e] The employee benefit expense is the same for book and tax purposes for this partnership. None relates to partner benefits.

Form **1120S**
Department of the Treasury
Internal Revenue Service

U.S. Income Tax Return for an S Corporation

▶ **Do not file this form unless the corporation has filed Form 2553 to elect to be an S corporation.**
▶ **See separate instructions.**

OMB No. 1545-0130
2006

For calendar year 2006 or tax year beginning , 2006, ending , 20

A Effective date of S election: 6-13-2000	Use IRS label. Otherwise, print or type. Name: Johns and Lawrence, Inc.	**C Employer identification number**: 76 : 3456789
B Business activity code number (see instructions): 337000	Number, street, and room or suite no. If a P.O. box, see instructions.: 1234 University Avenue	**D** Date incorporated: 6-1-2000
	City or town, state, and ZIP code: Gainsville, FL 32611	**E** Total assets *(see instructions)*: $ 498,324

F Check if: **(1)** ☐ Initial return **(2)** ☐ Final return **(3)** ☐ Name change **(4)** ☐ Address change **(5)** ☐ Amended return

G Enter the number of shareholders in the corporation at the end of the tax year ▶ 2

H Check if Schedule M-3 is required *(attach Schedule M-3)* ▶ ☐

Caution. *Include **only** trade or business income and expenses on lines 1a through 21. See the instructions for more information.*

Income

Line	Description		Amount
1a	Gross receipts or sales 869,658 **b** Less returns and allowances 29,242 **c** Bal ▶	1c	840,416
2	Cost of goods sold (Schedule A, line 8)	2	540,204
3	Gross profit. Subtract line 2 from line 1c	3	300,212
4	Net gain (loss) from Form 4797, Part II, line 17 *(attach Form 4797)*	4	
5	Other income (loss) *(see instructions–attach statement)*	5	
6	**Total income (loss).** Add lines 3 through 5 ▶	6	300,212

Deductions (see instructions for limitations)

Line	Description		Amount
7	Compensation of officers	7	36,000
8	Salaries and wages (less employment credits)	8	52,000
9	Repairs and maintenance	9	4,800
10	Bad debts	10	4,000
11	Rents	11	36,000
12	Taxes and licenses	12	16,000
13	Interest	13	8,000
14	Depreciation not claimed on Schedule A or elsewhere on return *(attach Form 4562)*	14	12,476
15	Depletion **(Do not deduct oil and gas depletion.)**	15	
16	Advertising	16	13,000
17	Pension, profit-sharing, etc., plans	17	2,000
18	Employee benefit programs	18	4,000
19	Other deductions *(attach statement)*	19	38,250
20	**Total deductions.** Add lines 7 through 19 ▶	20	226,526
21	**Ordinary business income (loss).** Subtract line 20 from line 6	21	73,686

Tax and Payments

Line	Description				Amount
22a	Excess net passive income or LIFO recapture tax *(see instructions)*	22a			
b	Tax from Schedule D (Form 1120S)	22b			
c	Add lines 22a and 22b *(see instructions for additional taxes)*			22c	NONE
23a	2006 estimated tax payments and 2005 overpayment credited to 2006	23a			
b	Tax deposited with Form 7004	23b			
c	Credit for federal tax paid on fuels *(attach Form 4136)*	23c			
d	Credit for federal telephone excise tax paid *(attach Form 8913)*	23d			
e	Add lines 23a through 23d			23e	NONE
24	Estimated tax penalty *(see instructions).* Check if Form 2220 is attached ▶ ☐			24	
25	**Amount owed.** If line 23e is smaller than the total of lines 22c and 24, enter amount owed			25	NONE
26	**Overpayment.** If line 23e is larger than the total of lines 22c and 24, enter amount overpaid			26	
27	Enter amount from line 26 **Credited to 2007 estimated tax** ▶	**Refunded** ▶		27	

Sign Here

Under penalties of perjury, I declare that I have examined this return, including accompanying schedules and statements, and to the best of my knowledge and belief, it is true, correct, and complete. Declaration of preparer (other than taxpayer) is based on all information of which preparer has any knowledge.

Andrew Lawrence — Signature of officer | 3-15-07 — Date | Vice-President — Title

May the IRS discuss this return with the preparer shown below (see instructions)? ☒ Yes ☐ No

Paid Preparer's Use Only

Preparer's signature ▶ Michael Kramer	Date 3-14-07	Check if self-employed ☒	Preparer's SSN or PTIN 375-49-6339
Firm's name (or yours if self-employed), address, and ZIP code ▶ Michael S. Kramer 1110 McMillon, Gainesville, FL 32611		EIN 59 : 2029763	Phone no. (352) 555-2000

Form 1120S (2006) Page 2

Schedule A **Cost of Goods Sold** (see instructions)

1	Inventory at beginning of year	1	64,000
2	Purchases	2	340,800
3	Cost of labor	3	143,204
4	Additional section 263A costs *(attach statement)*	4	7,000
5	Other costs *(attach statement)*	5	90,000
6	**Total.** Add lines 1 through 5	6	645,004
7	Inventory at end of year	7	104,800
8	**Cost of goods sold.** Subtract line 7 from line 6. Enter here and on page 1, line 2	8	540,204

9a Check all methods used for valuing closing inventory: *(i)* ☒ Cost as described in Regulations section 1.471-3
(ii) ☐ Lower of cost or market as described in Regulations section 1.471-4
(iii) ☐ Other (Specify method used and attach explanation.) ▶

b Check if there was a writedown of subnormal goods as described in Regulations section 1.471-2(c) ▶ ☐

c Check if the LIFO inventory method was adopted this tax year for any goods (if checked, attach Form 970) ▶ ☐

d If the LIFO inventory method was used for this tax year, enter percentage (or amounts) of closing inventory computed under LIFO | 9d |

e If property is produced or acquired for resale, do the rules of section 263A apply to the corporation? ☒ Yes ☐ No

f Was there any change in determining quantities, cost, or valuations between opening and closing inventory? ☐ Yes ☒ No
If "Yes," attach explanation.

Schedule B **Other Information** (see instructions)

		Yes	No
1	Check accounting method: a ☐ Cash b ☒ Accrual c ☐ Other (specify) ▶		
2	See the instructions and enter the: a Business activity ▶ Manufacturing b Product or service ▶ Furniture		
3	At the end of the tax year, did the corporation own, directly or indirectly, 50% or more of the voting stock of a domestic corporation? (For rules of attribution, see section 267(c).) If "Yes," attach a statement showing: **(a)** name and employer identification number (EIN), **(b)** percentage owned, and **(c)** if 100% owned, was a QSub election made?		X
4	Was the corporation a member of a controlled group subject to the provisions of section 1561?		X
5	Has this corporation filed, or is it required to file, a return under section 6111 to provide information on any reportable transaction?		
6	Check this box if the corporation issued publicly offered debt instruments with original issue discount ▶ ☐ If checked, the corporation may have to file **Form 8281,** Information Return for Publicly Offered Original Issue Discount Instruments.		
7	If the corporation: **(a)** was a C corporation before it elected to be an S corporation **or** the corporation acquired an asset with a basis determined by reference to its basis (or the basis of any other property) in the hands of a C corporation **and (b)** has net unrealized built-in gain (defined in section 1374(d)(1)) in excess of the net recognized built-in gain from prior years, enter the net unrealized built-in gain reduced by net recognized built-in gain from prior years ▶ $		
8	Enter the accumulated earnings and profits of the corporation at the end of the tax year. $		
9	Are the corporation's total receipts *(see instructions)* for the tax year **and** its total assets at the end of the tax year less than $250,000? If "Yes," the corporation is not required to complete Schedules L and M-1.		X

Note: *If the corporation, at any time during the tax year, had assets or operated a business in a foreign country or U.S. possession, it may be required to attach* **Schedule N (Form 1120),** *Foreign Operations of U.S. Corporations, to this return. See Schedule N for details.*

Schedule K **Shareholders' Pro Rata Share Items**

					Total amount
Income (Loss)	1 Ordinary business income (loss) (page 1, line 21)			1	73,686
	2 Net rental real estate income (loss) *(attach Form 8825)*			2	
	3a Other gross rental income (loss)	3a			
	b Expenses from other rental activities *(attach statement)*	3b			
	c Other net rental income (loss). Subtract line 3b from line 3a			3c	
	4 Interest income			4	
	5 Dividends: a Ordinary dividends			5a	1,000
	b Qualified dividends	5b	1,000		
	6 Royalties			6	
	7 Net short-term capital gain (loss) *(attach Schedule D (Form 1120S))*			7	(2,100)
	8a Net long-term capital gain (loss) *(attach Schedule D (Form 1120S))*			8a	4,500
	b Collectibles (28%) gain (loss)	8b			
	c Unrecaptured section 1250 gain *(attach statement)*	8c			
	9 Net section 1231 gain (loss) *(attach Form 4797)*			9	
	10 Other income (loss) *(see instructions)* Type ▶			10	

Form **1120S** (2006)

Form 1120S (2006) Page **3**

Section	Shareholders' Pro Rata Share Items (continued)	Line	Total amount	
Deductions	11 Section 179 deduction *(attach Form 4562)*	11	12,000	
	12a Contributions	12a	150	
	b Investment interest expense	12b		
	c Section 59(e)(2) expenditures **(1)** Type ▶ **(2)** Amount ▶	12c(2)	*	
	d Other deductions *(see instructions)* Type ▶	12d		
Credits	13a Low-income housing credit (section 42(j)(5))	13a		
	b Low-income housing credit (other)	13b		
	c Qualified rehabilitation expenditures (rental real estate) *(attach Form 3468)*	13c		
	d Other rental real estate credits *(see instructions)* Type ▶	13d		
	e Other rental credits (see instructions) Type ▶	13e		
	f Credit for alcohol used as fuel *(attach Form 6478)*	13f		
	g Other credits *(see instructions)* Type ▶	13g		
Foreign Transactions	14a Name of country or U.S. possession ▶			
	b Gross income from all sources	14b		
	c Gross income sourced at shareholder level	14c		
	Foreign gross income sourced at corporate level			
	d Passive	14d		
	e Listed categories *(attach statement)*	14e		
	f General limitation	14f		
	Deductions allocated and apportioned at shareholder level			
	g Interest expense	14g		
	h Other	14h		
	Deductions allocated and apportioned at corporate level to foreign source income			
	i Passive	14i		
	j Listed categories *(attach statement)*	14j		
	k General limitation	14k		
	Other information			
	l Total foreign taxes (check one): ▶ ☐ Paid ☐ Accrued	14l		
	m Reduction in taxes available for credit *(attach statement)*	14m		
	n Other foreign tax information *(attach statement)*			
Alternative Minimum Tax (AMT) Items	15a Post-1986 depreciation adjustment	15a	1,514	
	b Adjusted gain or loss	15b		
	c Depletion (other than oil and gas)	15c		
	d Oil, gas, and geothermal properties–gross income	15d		
	e Oil, gas, and geothermal properties–deductions	15e		
	f Other AMT items *(attach statement)*	15f		
Items Affecting Shareholder Basis	16a Tax-exempt interest income	16a	18,000	
	b Other tax-exempt income	16b		
	c Nondeductible expenses	16c	6,000	**
	d Property distributions	16d	28,212	
	e Repayment of loans from shareholders	16e		
Other Information	17a Investment income	17a	1,000	***
	b Investment expenses	17b		
	c Dividend distributions paid from accumulated earnings and profits	17c		
	d Other items and amounts *(attach statement)*			
Reconciliation	18 **Income/loss reconciliation.** Combine the amounts on lines 1 through 10 in the far right column. From the result, subtract the sum of the amounts on lines 11 through 12d and 14l	18	64,936	

Form **1120S** (2006)

*Qualified production activities income (QPAI) equals $80,000. Employer's W-2 wages equal $88,000.

**Disallowed meals and entertainment expenses ($4,000) and interest on loan used to purchase tax-exempt bonds ($2,000).

***If partners elect to tax dividends at ordinary rates under Sec. 163(d)(4)(B).

Form 1120S (2006) Page 4

Schedule L — Balance Sheets per Books

Assets	Beginning of tax year (a)	(b)	End of tax year (c)	(d)
1 Cash		60,000		86,600
2a Trade notes and accounts receivable	25,000		24,000	
b Less allowance for bad debts	(1,000)	24,000	(1,000)	23,000
3 Inventories		64,000		104,800
4 U.S. government obligations				
5 Tax-exempt securities *(see instructions)*		200,000		200,000
6 Other current assets *(attach statement)*		7,000		
7 Loans to shareholders				
8 Mortgage and real estate loans				
9 Other investments *(attach statement)*				
10a Buildings and other depreciable assets	151,600		151,600	
b Less accumulated depreciation	(45,200)	106,400	(72,676)	78,924
11a Depletable assets				
b Less accumulated depletion	( )		( )	
12 Land (net of any amortization)				
13a Intangible assets (amortizable only)				
b Less accumulated amortization	( )		( )	
14 Other assets *(attach statement)*				
15 Total assets		461,400		493,324
Liabilities and Shareholders' Equity				
16 Accounts payable		26,000		19,000
17 Mortgages, notes, bonds payable in less than 1 year		4,000		4,000
18 Other current liabilities *(attach statement)*		3,600		3,600
19 Loans from shareholders				
20 Mortgages, notes, bonds payable in 1 year or more		130,000		119,724
21 Other liabilities *(attach statement)*				
22 Capital stock		200,000		200,000
23 Additional paid-in capital				
24 Retained earnings		97,800		147,000
25 Adjustments to shareholders' equity *(attach statement)*				
26 Less cost of treasury stock		( )		( )
27 Total liabilities and shareholders' equity		461,400		493,324

Schedule M-1 — Reconciliation of Income (Loss) per Books With Income (Loss) per Return

Note: Schedule M-3 required instead of Schedule M-1 if total assets are $10 million or more–see instructions

1 Net income (loss) per books	77,412	5 Income recorded on books this year not included on Schedule K, lines 1 through 10 (itemize): a Tax-exempt interest $ 18,000	18,000
2 Income included on Schedule K, lines 1, 2, 3c, 4, 5a, 6, 7, 8a, 9, and 10, not recorded on books this year (itemize):			
3 Expenses recorded on books this year not included on Schedule K, lines 1 through 12 and 14l (itemize): a Depreciation $ b Travel and entertainment $ 4,000 Interest on loans* $2,000	6,000	6 Deductions included on Schedule K, lines 1 through 12 and 14l, not charged against book income this year (itemize): a Depreciation $ 476	476
4 Add lines 1 through 3	83,412	7 Add lines 5 and 6	18,476
		8 Income (loss) (Schedule K, line 18). Line 4 less line 7	64,936

Schedule M-2 — Analysis of Accumulated Adjustments Account, Other Adjustments Account, and Shareholders' Undistributed Taxable Income Previously Taxed (see instructions)

	(a) Accumulated adjustments account	(b) Other adjustments account	(c) Shareholders' undistributed taxable income previously taxed
1 Balance at beginning of tax year	86,100	11,700	
2 Ordinary income from page 1, line 21	73,686		
3 Other additions	5,500**	18,000	
4 Loss from page 1, line 21	( )		
5 Other reductions	(18,250***)	(2,000)	
6 Combine lines 1 through 5	147,036		
7 Distributions other than dividend distributions	28,212		
8 Balance at end of tax year. Subtract line 7 from line 6	118,824	27,700	

Form **1120S** (2006)

* For municipal bonds

** $1,000 + $4,500 = $5,500

*** $12,000 + $4,000 + $150 + $2,100 = $18,250

671106

☐ Final K-1 ☐ Amended K-1 OMB No. 1545-0130

Schedule K-1 (Form 1120S) **2006**

Department of the Treasury
Internal Revenue Service

For calendar year 2006, or tax year beginning ________, 2006 ending ________, 20__

Shareholder's Share of Income, Deductions, Credits, etc.

▶ See back of form and separate instructions.

Part I Information About the Corporation

A Corporation's employer identification number
76-3456789

B Corporation's name, address, city, state, and ZIP code
Johns and Lawrence, Inc.
1234 University Ave.
Gainesville, FL 32611

C IRS Center where corporation filed return
Atlanta, GA

D ☐ Tax shelter registration number, if any ________

E ☐ Check if Form 8271 is attached

Part II Information About the Shareholder

F Shareholder's identifying number
297-63-2110

G Shareholder's name, address, city, state and ZIP code
Andrew Lawrence
436 N.W. 24th Ave.
Gainesville, FL 32607

H Shareholder's percentage of stock ownership for tax year . . . . 50% %

For IRS Use Only

Part III Shareholder's Share of Current Year Income, Deductions, Credits, and Other Items

Line	Item	Amount	Line	Item	Amount
1	Ordinary business income (loss)	36,843	13	Credits	
2	Net rental real estate income (loss)				
3	Other net rental income (loss)				
4	Interest income				
5a	Ordinary dividends	500			
5b	Qualified dividends	500	14	Foreign transactions	
6	Royalties				
7	Net short-term capital gain (loss)	(1,050)			
8a	Net long-term capital gain (loss)	2,250			
8b	Collectibles (28%) gain (loss)				
8c	Unrecaptured section 1250 gain				
9	Net section 1231 gain (loss)				
10	Other income (loss)		15	Alternative minimum tax (AMT) items	
			A		757
11	Section 179 deduction		16	Items affecting shareholder basis	
			A		9,000
12	Other deductions				
A		6,000	C		3,000
G		75	D		14,106
Q		40,000			
R		44,000			
			17	Other information	
			A		500 **

* See attached statement for additional information.

For Privacy Act and Paperwork Reduction Act Notice, see Instructions for Form 1120S. Cat. No. 11520D **Schedule K-1 (Form 1120S) 2006**

*Schedule K-1 for Stephen Johns is similar to this one and is not reproduced here.

**If partner elects to tax dividends at ordinary rates under Sec. 163(d)(4)(B).

This list identifies the codes used on Schedule K-1 for all shareholders and provides summarized reporting information for shareholders who file Form 1040. For detailed reporting and filing information, see the separate Shareholder's Instructions for Schedule K-1 and the instructions for your income tax return.

1. Ordinary business income (loss). You must first determine whether the income (loss) is passive or nonpassive. Then enter on your return as follows:

	Report on
Passive loss	See the Shareholder's Instructions
Passive income	Schedule E, line 28, column (g)
Nonpassive loss	Schedule E, line 28, column (h)
Nonpassive income	Schedule E, line 28, column (j)

2. Net rental real estate income (loss)	See the Shareholder's Instructions
3. Other net rental income (loss)	
Net income	Schedule E, line 28, column (g)
Net loss	See the Shareholder's Instructions
4. Interest income	Form 1040, line 8a
5a. Ordinary dividends	Form 1040, line 9a
5b. Qualified dividends	Form 1040, line 9b
6. Royalties	Schedule E, line 4
7. Net short-term capital gain (loss)	Schedule D, line 5, column (f)
8a. Net long-term capital gain (loss)	Schedule D, line 12, column (f)
8b. Collectibles (28%) gain (loss)	28% Rate Gain Worksheet, line 4 (Schedule D instructions)
8c. Unrecaptured section 1250 gain	See the Shareholder's Instructions
9. Net section 1231 gain (loss)	See the Shareholder's Instructions

10. Other income (loss)

Code	
A Other portfolio income (loss)	See the Shareholder's Instructions
B Involuntary conversions	See the Shareholder's Instructions
C Sec. 1256 contracts & straddles	Form 6781, line 1
D Mining exploration costs recapture	See Pub. 535
E Other income (loss)	See the Shareholder's Instructions

11. Section 179 deduction	See the Shareholder's Instructions

12. Other deductions

A Cash contributions (50%)	See the Shareholder's Instructions (A–F)
B Cash contributions (30%)	
C Noncash contributions (50%)	
D Noncash contributions (30%)	
E Capital gain property to a 50% organization (30%)	
F Capital gain property (20%)	
G Investment interest expense	Form 4952, line 1
H Deductions—royalty income	Schedule E, line 18
I Section 59(e)(2) expenditures	See the Shareholder's Instructions
J Deductions—portfolio (2% floor)	Schedule A, line 22
K Deductions—portfolio (other)	Schedule A, line 27
L Preproductive period expenses	See the Shareholder's Instructions
M Commercial revitalization deduction from rental real estate activities	See Form 8582 Instructions
N Reforestation expense deduction	See the Shareholder's Instructions
O Domestic production activities information	See Form 8903 Instructions
P Qualified production activities income	Form 8903, line 7
Q Employer's W-2 wages	Form 8903, line 13
R Other deductions	See the Shareholder's Instructions

13. Credits

A Low-income housing credit (section 42(j)(5))	See the Shareholder's Instructions (A–E)
B Low-income housing credit (other)	
C Qualified rehabilitation expenditures (rental real estate)	
D Other rental real estate credits	
E Other rental credits	
F Undistributed capital gains credit	Form 1040, line 70, check box a
G Credit for alcohol used as fuel	See the Shareholder's Instructions (G–J)
H Work opportunity credit	
I Welfare-to-work credit	
J Disabled access credit	
K Empowerment zone and renewal community employment credit	Form 8844, line 3
L Credit for increasing research activities	See the Shareholder's Instructions (L–N)
M New markets credit	
N Credit for employer social security and Medicare taxes	
O Backup withholding	Form 1040, line 64
P Other credits	See the Shareholder's Instructions

14. Foreign transactions

Code	*Report on*
A Name of country or U.S. possession	Form 1116, Part I (A–C)
B Gross income from all sources	
C Gross income sourced at shareholder level	
Foreign gross income sourced at corporate level	
D Passive	Form 1116, Part I (D–F)
E Listed categories	
F General limitation	
Deductions allocated and apportioned at shareholder level	
G Interest expense	Form 1116, Part I
H Other	Form 1116, Part I
Deductions allocated and apportioned at corporate level to foreign source income	
I Passive	Form 1116, Part I (I–K)
J Listed categories	
K General limitation	
Other information	
L Total foreign taxes paid	Form 1116, Part II
M Total foreign taxes accrued	Form 1116, Part II
N Reduction in taxes available for credit	Form 1116, line 12
O Foreign trading gross receipts	Form 8873
P Extraterritorial income exclusion	Form 8873
Q Other foreign transactions	See the Shareholder's Instructions

15. Alternative minimum tax (AMT) items

A Post-1986 depreciation adjustment	See the Shareholder's Instructions and the Instructions for Form 6251 (A–F)
B Adjusted gain or loss	
C Depletion (other than oil & gas)	
D Oil, gas, & geothermal–gross income	
E Oil, gas, & geothermal–deductions	
F Other AMT items	

16. Items affecting shareholder basis

A Tax-exempt interest income	Form 1040, line 8b
B Other tax-exempt income	See the Shareholder's Instructions (B–E)
C Nondeductible expenses	
D Property distributions	
E Repayment of loans from shareholders	

17. Other information

A Investment income	Form 4952, line 4a
B Investment expenses	Form 4952, line 5
C Qualified rehabilitation expenditures (other than rental real estate)	See the Shareholder's Instructions
D Basis of energy property	See the Shareholder's Instructions
E Recapture of low-income housing credit (section 42(j)(5))	Form 8611, line 8
F Recapture of low-income housing credit (other)	Form 8611, line 8
G Recapture of investment credit	See Form 4255
H Recapture of other credits	See the Shareholder's Instructions
I Look-back interest–completed long-term contracts	See Form 8697
J Look-back interest–income forecast method	See Form 8866
K Dispositions of property with section 179 deductions	See the Shareholder's Instructions (K–T)
L Recapture of section 179 deduction	
M Section 453(l)(3) information	
N Section 453A(c) information	
O Section 1260(b) information	
P Interest allocable to production expenditures	
Q CCF nonqualified withdrawals	
R Information needed to figure depletion–oil and gas	
S Amortization of reforestation costs	
T Other information	

FACTS FOR S CORPORATION (FORM 1120S)

The same basic facts presented for the Andrew Lawrence proprietorship are used for the S corporation except for the following:

1. Johns and Lawrence, Inc. made an S corporation election on June 13, 2000. The election was effective for its initial tax year.
2. The book income for Johns and Lawrence is presented in the attached worksheet, which reconciles book income and S corporation taxable income.
3. The $18,000 salaries paid to each employee are subject to the same employment tax requirements as when paid by the C corporation. The total employment taxes ($14,480) are the same as for the C corporation.
4. The S corporation paid no estimated federal income taxes.
5. The corporation distributed $14,106 to each of the two shareholders.
6. Other deductions include:

Travel	$ 4,000
Meals and entertainment	8,000
Minus: 50% disallowance	(4,000)
Office expenses	16,000
Transportation	10,400
General and administrative	3,000
Miscellaneous*	850
Total	$38,250

*$150 of the miscellaneous expenses are related to the production of the dividend income and are separately stated.

7. The following schedule reconciles net income for the C corporation and the S corporation:

Net income per books for C corporation	$63,412
Plus: Federal income taxes	14,000
Net income per books for S corporation	$77,412

The S corporation return can be tied back to the partnership return. The only difference between the two returns is that the S corporation pays an additional $6,160 in employment taxes with respect to the shareholder-employee salaries, as compared to the partnership's guaranteed payments. This dollar difference is reflected in the net income numbers, the ordinary income numbers, capital account balances, and total asset amounts.

8. Qualifed production activities income (QPAI) equals $80,000. Employer's W-2 wages equal $88,000.
9. The balance sheet for Johns and Lawrence appears on page 4 of Form 1120S.

Johns and Lawrence, Inc. (S Corporation) Reconciliation of Book and Taxable Income For Year Ending December 31, 2006

	Book Income		Adjustments		Taxable Income		Form 1120S Schedule K	
Account Name	Debit	Credit	Debit	Credit	Debit	Credit	Ordinary Income	Separately Stated Items
Sales		$869,658				$869,658	$869,658	
Sales returns & allowances	$ 29,242				$ 29,242		(29,242)	
Cost of sales	540,204				540,204		(540,204)	
Dividends		1,000				1,000		1,000
Tax-exempt interest		18,000	$18,000			0		$18,000
Gain on stock sale		4,500				4,500		4,500
Worthless stock loss	2,100				2,100			(2,100)
Officers salaries[a]	36,000				36,000		(36,000)	
Other salaries	52,000				52,000		(52,000)	
Rentals	36,000				36,000		(36,000)	
Bad debts	4,000				4,000		(4,000)	
Interest:								
Working capital loans	8,000				8,000		(8,000)	
Purchase tax-exempt bonds	2,000			$ 2,000	0			(2,000)
Employment taxes	14,480				14,480		(14,480)	
Taxes	1,520				1,520		(1,520)	
Repairs	4,800				4,800		(4,800)	
Depreciation[b]	12,000		476		12,476		(12,476)	
Charitable contributions	12,000				12,000			(12,000)
Travel	4,000				4,000		(4,000)	
Meals and entertainment[c]	8,000			4,000	4,000		(4,000)	
Meals and ent. nondeductible								(4,000)
Office expenses	16,000				16,000		(16,000)	
Advertising	13,000				13,000		(13,000)	
Transportation expense	10,400				10,400		(10,400)	
General and administrative	3,000				3,000		(3,000)	
Pension plans[d]	2,000				2,000		(2,000)	
Employee benefit programs[e]	4,000				4,000		(4,000)	
Miscellaneous	1,000				1,000		(850)	(150)
Net profit/Taxable income	77,412			12,476	64,936			
Total	$893,158	$893,158	$18,476	$18,476	$875,158	$875,158	$ 73,686	

[a] Salaries for the S corporation's shareholder-employees are deductible by the S corporation and are subject to the same employee taxes imposed on nonshareholder-employees.

[b] MACRS is depreciation is $27,476 − $15,000 = $12,476

[c] 50% of the meals and entertainment expense is not deductible for tax purposes but must be separately stated on the Schedules K and K-1.

[d] The pension plan expense is the same for book and tax purposes for this corporation. No pension expenses relate to pensions for the shareholder-employees.

[e] The employee benefit expense is the same for book and tax purposes for this corporation. None relates to shareholder-employee benefits.

Form **709** Department of the Treasury Internal Revenue Service

United States Gift (and Generation-Skipping Transfer) Tax Return

(For gifts made during calendar year 2006)

▶ **See separate instructions.**

OMB No. 1545-0020

2006

Part 1–General Information

1 Donor's first name and middle initial	2 Donor's last name	3 **Donor's social security number**
Wilma	Brown	123 45 6789
4 Address (number, street, and apartment number)		5 Legal residence (domicile) (county and state)
2 Main Street		Whitefield, GA
6 City, state, and ZIP code		7 Citizenship
Dalton, GA 35901		U.S.A.

		Yes	No
8	If the donor died during the year, check here ▶ ☐ and enter date of death ______, ______		
9	If you extended the time to file this Form 709, check here ▶ ☐		
10	Enter the total number of donees listed on Schedule A. Count each person only once. ▶ 5		
11a	Have you (the donor) previously filed a Form 709 (or 709-A) for any other year? If "No," skip line 11b	X	
11b	If the answer to line 11a is "Yes," has your address changed since you last filed Form 709 (or 709-A)?		X
12	**Gifts by husband or wife to third parties.** Do you consent to have the gifts (including generation-skipping transfers) made by you and by your spouse to third parties during the calendar year considered as made one-half by each of you? (See instructions.) (If the answer is "Yes," the following information must be furnished and your spouse must sign the consent shown below. **If the answer is "No," skip lines 13–18 and go to Schedule A.**)	X	
13	Name of consenting spouse Hugh Brown — 14 SSN 987-65-4321		
15	Were you married to one another during the entire calendar year? (see instructions)	X	
16	If 15 is "No," check whether ☐ married ☐ divorced or ☐ widowed/deceased, and give date (see instructions) ▶		
17	Will a gift tax return for this year be filed by your spouse? (If "Yes," mail both returns in the same envelope.)	X	

18 **Consent of Spouse.** I consent to have the gifts (and generation-skipping transfers) made by me and by my spouse to third parties during the calendar year considered as made one-half by each of us. We are both aware of the joint and several liability for tax created by the execution of this consent.

Consenting spouse's signature ▶ *Hugh Brown* **Date** ▶ 3-2-2007

Part 2–Tax Computation

		Line	Amount	
1	Enter the amount from Schedule A, Part 4, line 11	1	340,598	
2	Enter the amount from Schedule B, line 3	2	500,000	
3	Total taxable gifts. Add lines 1 and 2	3	840,598	
4	Tax computed on amount on line 3 (see *Table for Computing Gift Tax* in separate instructions)	4	283,633	
5	Tax computed on amount on line 2 (see *Table for Computing Gift Tax* in separate instructions)	5	155,800	
6	Balance. Subtract line 5 from line 4	6	127,833	
7	Maximum unified credit (nonresident aliens, see instructions)	7	345,800	00
8	Enter the unified credit against tax allowable for all prior periods (from Sch. B, line 1, col. C)	8	68,000	
9	Balance. Subtract line 8 from line 7	9	277,800	
10	Enter 20% (.20) of the amount allowed as a specific exemption for gifts made after September 8, 1976, and before January 1, 1977 (see instructions)	10	-0-	
11	Balance. Subtract line 10 from line 9	11	277,800	
12	Unified credit. Enter the smaller of line 6 or line 11	12	127,833	
13	Credit for foreign gift taxes (see instructions)	13	-0-	
14	Total credits. Add lines 12 and 13	14	127,833	
15	Balance. Subtract line 14 from line 6. Do not enter less than zero	15	-0-	
16	Generation-skipping transfer taxes (from Schedule C, Part 3, col. H, Total)	16	-0-	
17	Total tax. Add lines 15 and 16	17	-0-	
18	Gift and generation-skipping transfer taxes prepaid with extension of time to file	18	-0-	
19	If line 18 is less than line 17, enter **balance due** (see instructions)	19	-0-	
20	If line 18 is greater than line 17, enter **amount to be refunded**	20		

Attach check or money order here.

Sign Here

Under penalties of perjury, I declare that I have examined this return, including any accompanying schedules and statements, and to the best of my knowledge and belief, it is true, correct, and complete. Declaration of preparer (other than donor) is based on all information of which preparer has any knowledge.

▶ *Wilma Brown* — Signature of donor — Date 3-2-2007

Paid Preparer's Use Only

Preparer's signature ▶ *Sally Preparer* — Date 3-2-2007 — Check if self-employed ▶ ☒

Firm's name (or yours if self-employed), address, and ZIP code ▶ Sally Preparer, 110 Last Bank Tower Dalton, GA 35901 — Phone no. ▶ (706) 934-5000

For Disclosure, Privacy Act, and Paperwork Reduction Act Notice, see page 12 of the separate instructions for this form. Cat. No. 16783M Form **709** (2006)

Note: Page 4, which is not pertinent to the tax consequences, is omitted because the donor made no generation skipping transfers.

Form 709 (2006) Page 2

SCHEDULE A Computation of Taxable Gifts (Including transfers in trust) (see instructions)

A Does the value of any item listed on Schedule A reflect any valuation discount? If "Yes," attach explanation . . . . Yes ☐ No ☒

B ☐ ◄ Check here if you elect under section 529(c)(2)(B) to treat any transfers made this year to a qualified tuition program as made ratably over a 5-year period beginning this year. See instructions. Attach explanation.

Part 1–Gifts Subject Only to Gift Tax. Gifts less political organization, medical, and educational exclusions. See instructions.

A Item number	B • Donee's name and address • Relationship to donor (if any) • Description of gift • If the gift was of securities, give CUSIP no. • If closely held entity, give EIN	C	D Donor's adjusted basis of gift	E Date of gift	F Value at date of gift	G For split gifts, enter ½ of column F	H Net transfer (subtract col. G from col. F)
1 2-4	} Schedule Attached		593,000		729,196	64,598	664,598
Gifts made by spouse– *complete **only** if you are splitting gifts with your spouse and he/she also made gifts.*							
5	State University, stock		32,000*	2006	80,000	40,000	40,000
6	Betsy Brown, land		112,000*	2006	600,000	300,000	300,000

Total of Part 1. Add amounts from Part 1, column H . . . . ► 1,004,598

Part 2–Direct Skips. Gifts that are direct skips and are subject to both gift tax and generation-skipping transfer tax. You must list the gifts in chronological order.

A Item number	B • Donee's name and address • Relationship to donor (if any) • Description of gift • If the gift was of securities, give CUSIP no. • If closely held entity, give EIN	C 2632(b) election out	D Donor's adjusted basis of gift	E Date of gift	F Value at date of gift	G For split gifts, enter ½ of column F	H Net transfer (subtract col. G from col. F)
1							
Gifts made by spouse– *complete **only** if you are splitting gifts with your spouse and he/she also made gifts.*							

Total of Part 2. Add amounts from Part 2, column H . . . . ►

Part 3–Indirect Skips. Gifts to trusts that are currently subject to gift tax and may later be subject to generation-skipping transfer tax. You must list these gifts in chronological order.

A Item number	B • Donee's name and address • Relationship to donor (if any) • Description of gift • If the gift was of securities, give CUSIP no. • If closely held entity, give EIN	C 2632(c) election	D Donor's adjusted basis of gift	E Date of gift	F Value at date of gift	G For split gifts, enter ½ of column F	H Net transfer (subtract col. G from col. F)
1							
Gifts made by spouse–*complete **only** if you are splitting gifts with your spouse and he/she also made gifts.*							

Total of Part 3. Add amounts from Part 3, column H . . . . ►

(If more space is needed, attach additional sheets of same size.) Form **709** (2006)

*Assumed amounts not listed in the facts.

Form 709 (2006) Page **3**

Part 4–Taxable Gift Reconciliation

1	Total value of gifts of donor. Add totals from column H of Parts 1, 2, and 3	1	1,004,598	
2	Total annual exclusions for gifts listed on line 1 (see instructions)	2	48,000	**
3	Total included amount of gifts. Subtract line 2 from line 1	3	956,598	
	Deductions (see instructions)			
4	Gifts of interests to spouse for which a marital deduction will be claimed, based on item numbers 4 of Schedule A — 4: 600,000			
5	Exclusions attributable to gifts on line 4 — 5: 12,000			
6	Marital deduction. Subtract line 5 from line 4 — 6: 588,000			
7	Charitable deduction, based on item nos. 5 less exclusions — 7: 28,000			
8	Total deductions. Add lines 6 and 7	8	616,000	
9	Subtract line 8 from line 3	9	340,598	
10	Generation-skipping transfer taxes payable with this Form 709 (from Schedule C, Part 3, col. H, Total)	10		
11	**Taxable gifts.** Add lines 9 and 10. Enter here and on page 1, Part 2–Tax Computation, line 1	11	340,598	

Terminable Interest (QTIP) Marital Deduction. (See instructions for Schedule A, Part 4, line 4.)

If a trust (or other property) meets the requirements of qualified terminable interest property under section 2523(f), and:

a. The trust (or other property) is listed on Schedule A, and

b. The value of the trust (or other property) is entered in whole or in part as a deduction on Schedule A, Part 4, line 4, then the donor shall be deemed to have made an election to have such trust (or other property) treated as qualified terminable interest property under section 2523(f).

If less than the entire value of the trust (or other property) that the donor has included in Parts 1 and 3 of Schedule A is entered as a deduction on line 4, the donor shall be considered to have made an election only as to a fraction of the trust (or other property). The numerator of this fraction is equal to the amount of the trust (or other property) deducted on Schedule A, Part 4, line 6. The denominator is equal to the total value of the trust (or other property) listed in Parts 1 and 3 of Schedule A.

If you make the QTIP election, the terminable interest property involved will be included in your spouse's gross estate upon his or her death (section 2044). See instructions for line 4 of Schedule A. If your spouse disposes (by gift or otherwise) of all or part of the qualifying life income interest, he or she will be considered to have made a transfer of the entire property that is subject to the gift tax. See *Transfer of Certain Life Estates Received From Spouse* on page 4 of the instructions.

12 Election Out of QTIP Treatment of Annuities

☐ ◀ Check here if you elect under section 2523(f)(6) **not** to treat as qualified terminable interest property any joint and survivor annuities that are reported on Schedule A and would otherwise be treated as qualified terminable interest property under section 2523(f). See instructions. Enter the item numbers from Schedule A for the annuities for which you are making this election ▶ ______

SCHEDULE B **Gifts From Prior Periods**

If you answered "Yes" on line 11a of page 1, Part 1, see the instructions for completing Schedule B. If you answered "No," skip to the Tax Computation on page 1 (or Schedule C, if applicable).

A Calendar year or calendar quarter (see instructions)	B Internal Revenue office where prior return was filed	C Amount of unified credit against gift tax for periods after December 31, 1976	D Amount of specific exemption for prior periods ending before January 1, 1977	E Amount of taxable gifts
1975	Atlanta, GA	-0-	-0-	300,000
1988	Atlanta, GA	68,000		200,000
1 Totals for prior periods	1	68,000		500,000

2	Amount, if any, by which total specific exemption, line 1, column D, is more than $30,000	2	-0-
3	Total amount of taxable gifts for prior periods. Add amount on line 1, column E and amount, if any, on line 2. Enter here and on page 1, Part 2–Tax Computation, line 2	3	500,000

(If more space is needed, attach additional sheets of same size.) Form **709** (2006)

**$12,000 each for Billy, Betsy, State University, and Hugh.

Form 709 (2006), Schedule A, Part 1

A	B	C	D	E	F	G	H
1	Billy Brown, cash		$ 80,000	2006	$ 80,000	$40,000	$ 40,000
2	Betsy Brown, jewelry		18,000*	2006	28,000	14,000	14,000
3	Ruth Cain, remainder interest in vacation cabin (0.21196 x 100,000)		15,000*	2006	21,196	10,598	10,598
4	Trust at First Bank, income to Hugh Brown for life. Remainder to Jeff Bass (QTIP trust)		480,000*	2006	600,000		600,000
			$593,000		$729,196	$64,598	$664,598

*Assumed amounts not listed in the facts.

Form **706** (Rev. October 2006)

Department of the Treasury Internal Revenue Service

United States Estate (and Generation-Skipping Transfer) Tax Return

Estate of a citizen or resident of the United States (see separate instructions). To be filed for decedents dying after December 31, 2005, and before January 1, 2007.

OMB No. 1545-0015

Part 1–Decedent and Executor

1a Decedent's first name and middle initial (and maiden name, if any): Herman	1b Decedent's last name: Estes	2 Decedent's Social Security No.: 999 11 4444
3a County, state, and ZIP code, or foreign country, of legal residence (domicile) at time of death: Montgomery, OH 45347	3b Year domicile established: 1937 / 4 Date of birth: 1920	5 Date of death: 10-13-2006
6a Name of executor (see page 4 of the instructions): John Johnson	6b Executor's address (number and street including apartment or suite no. or rural route; city, town, or post office; state; and ZIP code) and phone no.: 10 Main Place, Dayton, OH 45347	Phone no. ( )
6c Executor's social security number (see page 4 of the instructions): 998 12 5732		
7a Name and location of court where will was probated or estate administered		7b Case number

8 If decedent died testate, check here ▶ [X] and attach a certified copy of the will. 9 If you extended the time to file this Form 706, check here ▶ ☐

10 If Schedule R-1 is attached, check here ▶ ☐

Part 2–Tax Computation

1	Total gross estate less exclusion (from Part 5–Recapitulation, page 3, item 12)	1	2,947,150
2	Tentative total allowable deductions (from Part 5–Recapitulation, page 3, item 22)	2	1,176,700
3a	Tentative taxable estate (before state death tax deduction) (subtract line 2 from line 1)	3a	1,770,450
b	State death tax deduction	3b	-0-
c	Taxable estate (subtract line 3b from line 3a)	3c	1,770,450
4	Adjusted taxable gifts (total taxable gifts (within the meaning of section 2503) made by the decedent after December 31, 1976, other than gifts that are includible in decedent's gross estate (section 2001(b)))	4	1,700,000
5	Add lines 3c and 4	5	3,470,450
6	Tentative tax on the amount on line 5 from Table A on page 4 of the instructions	6	1,457,207
7	Total gift tax paid or payable with respect to gifts made by the decedent after December 31, 1976. Include gift taxes by the decedent's spouse for such spouse's share of split gifts (section 2513) only if the decedent was the donor of these gifts and they are includible in the decedent's gross estate (see instructions)	7	315,900
8	Gross estate tax (subtract line 7 from line 6)	8	1,141,307
9	Maximum unified credit (applicable credit amount) against estate tax — 9: 780,800		
10	Adjustment to unified credit (applicable credit amount). (This adjustment may not exceed $6,000. See page 6 of the instructions.) — 10: -0-		
11	Allowable unified credit (applicable credit amount) (subtract line 10 from line 9)	11	780,800
12	Subtract line 11 from line 8 (but do not enter less than zero)	12	360,507
13	Credit for foreign death taxes (from Schedule(s) P). (Attach Form(s) 706-CE.) — 13:		
14	Credit for tax on prior transfers (from Schedule Q) — 14:		
15	Total credits (add lines 13 and 14)	15	
16	Net estate tax (subtract line 15 from line 12)	16	360,507
17	Generation-skipping transfer (GST) taxes payable (from Schedule R, Part 2, line 10)	17	
18	Total transfer taxes (add lines 16 and 17)	18	360,507
19	Prior payments. Explain in an attached statement	19	
20	Balance due (or overpayment) (subtract line 19 from line 18)	20	360,507

Under penalties of perjury, I declare that I have examined this return, including accompanying schedules and statements, and to the best of my knowledge and belief, it is true, correct, and complete. Declaration of preparer other than the executor is based on all information of which preparer has any knowledge.

John Johnson — Signature(s) of executor(s) — Date: 5-14-07

Mary Wilson CPA — Signature of preparer other than executor — 100 Tower Bldg., Austin TX 78703 — Address (and ZIP code) — Date: 5-12-07

For Privacy Act and Paperwork Reduction Act Notice, see page 28 of the separate instructions for this form. Cat. No. 20548R Form **706** (Rev. 10-2006)

Note: Pages not pertinent to the tax consequences are omitted.

Form 706 (Rev. 10-2006)

Estate of: Herman Estes

Part 3–Elections by the Executor

Please check the "Yes" or "No" box for each question (see instructions beginning on page 6).

Note. Some of these elections require the posting of bonds or liens.

			Yes	No
1	Do you elect alternate valuation?	1		X
2	Do you elect special-use valuation? If "Yes," you must complete and attach Schedule A–1.	2		X
3	Do you elect to pay the taxes in installments as described in section 6166? If "Yes," you must attach the additional information described on pages 9 and 10 of the instructions. **Note. By electing section 6166, you agree to provide security for estate tax deferred under section 6166 and interest in the form of a surety bond or a section 6324A special lien.**	3		X
4	Do you elect to postpone the part of the taxes attributable to a reversionary or remainder interest as described in section 6163?	4		X

Part 4–General Information

(**Note.** Please attach the necessary supplemental documents. **You must attach the death certificate.**) (see instructions on page 11)

Authorization to receive confidential tax information under Regs. sec. 601.504(b)(2)(i); to act as the estate's representative before the IRS; and to make written or oral presentations on behalf of the estate if return prepared by an attorney, accountant, or enrolled agent for the executor:

Name of representative (print or type)	State	Address (number, street, and room or suite no., city, state, and ZIP code)
Mary Wilson	TX	100 Tower Bldg., Austin, TX 78703

I declare that I am the ☐ attorney/ ☐ certified public accountant/ ☐ enrolled agent (you must check the applicable box) for the executor and prepared this return for the executor. I am not under suspension or disbarment from practice before the Internal Revenue Service and am qualified to practice in the state shown above.

Signature	CAF number	Date	Telephone number
Mary Wilson, CPA		5-12-07	512-474-4447

1 Death certificate number and issuing authority (attach a copy of the death certificate to this return).
1246, County Coroner

2 Decedent's business or occupation. If retired, check here ▶ ☒ and state decedent's former business or occupation.
Executive

3 Marital status of the decedent at time of death:

☒ Married
☐ Widow or widower—Name, SSN, and date of death of deceased spouse ▶
☐ Single
☐ Legally separated
☐ Divorced—Date divorce decree became final ▶

4a Surviving spouse's name	4b Social security number	4c Amount received (see page 11 of the instructions)
Ann Estes	555 77 9999	1,050,000

5 Individuals (other than the surviving spouse), trusts, or other estates who receive benefits from the estate (do not include charitable beneficiaries shown in Schedule O) (see instructions).

Name of individual, trust, or estate receiving $5,000 or more	Identifying number	Relationship to decedent	Amount (see instructions)
Johnny Estes	555-61-4107	Son	661,021
Billy Estes	556-63-4437	Son	461,022
Daughter, Dorothy Estes, received the corpus in the special power of appointment trust created by Amelia Estes.			
All unascertainable beneficiaries and those who receive less than $5,000 ▶			
Total			1,122,043

Please check the "Yes" or "No" box for each question.

		Yes	No
6	Does the gross estate contain any section 2044 property (qualified terminable interest property (QTIP) from a prior gift or estate) (see page 11 of the instructions)?		X
7a	Have federal gift tax returns ever been filed? If ™Yes,⌋ please attach copies of the returns, if available, and furnish the following information:	X	

7b Period(s) covered	7c Internal Revenue office(s) where filed
1974, 1978, 2004	Cincinnati, OH

(continued on next page)

Form 706 (Rev. 10-2006)

Part 4–General Information *(continued)*

If you answer "Yes" to any of questions 8–16, you must attach additional information as described in the instructions.	Yes	No
8a Was there any insurance on the decedent's life that is not included on the return as part of the gross estate?		X
b Did the decedent own any insurance on the life of another that is not included in the gross estate?		X
9 Did the decedent at the time of death own any property as a joint tenant with right of survivorship in which **(a)** one or more of the other joint tenants was someone other than the decedent's spouse, and **(b)** less than the full value of the property is included on the return as part of the gross estate? If "Yes," you must complete and attach Schedule E		X
10 Did the decedent, at the time of death, own any interest in a partnership or unincorporated business or any stock in an inactive or closely held corporation?		X
11 Did the decedent make any transfer described in section 2035, 2036, 2037, or 2038 (see the instructions for Schedule G beginning on page 13 of the separate instructions)? If "Yes," you must complete and attach Schedule G	X	
12a Were there in existence at the time of the decedent's death any trusts created by the decedent during his or her lifetime?		X
b Were there in existence at the time of the decedent's death any trusts not created by the decedent under which the decedent possessed any power, beneficial interest, or trusteeship?	X	
c Was the decedent receiving income from a trust created after October 22, 1986 by a parent or grandparent?	X	
If "Yes," was there a GST taxable termination (under section 2612) upon the death of the decedent?		X
d If there was a GST taxable termination (under section 2612), attach a statement to explain. Provide a copy of the trust or will creating the trust, and give the name, address, and phone number of the current trustee(s).		
e Did decedent at any time during his or her lifetime transfer or sell an interest in a partnership, limited liability company, or closely held corporation to a trust described in question 12a or 12b?		X
If "Yes," provide the EIN number to this transferred/sold item. ▶		
13 Did the decedent ever possess, exercise, or release any general power of appointment? If "Yes," you must complete and attach Schedule H		X
14 Was the marital deduction computed under the transitional rule of Public Law 97-34, section 403(e)(3) (Economic Recovery Tax Act of 1981)?		X
If "Yes," attach a separate computation of the marital deduction, enter the amount on item 20 of the Recapitulation, and note on item 20 "computation attached."		
15 Was the decedent, immediately before death, receiving an annuity described in the "General" paragraph of the instructions for Schedule I or a private annuity? If "Yes," you must complete and attach Schedule I	X	
16 Was the decedent ever the beneficiary of a trust for which a deduction was claimed by the estate of a pre-deceased spouse under section 2056(b)(7) and which is not reported on this return? If "Yes," attach an explanation		X

Part 5–Recapitulation

Item number	Gross estate		Alternate value	Value at date of death
1	Schedule A–Real Estate	1		325,000
2	Schedule B–Stocks and Bonds	2		1,600,000
3	Schedule C–Mortgages, Notes, and Cash	3		94,250
4	Schedule D–Insurance on the Decedent's Life (attach Form(s) 712)	4		200,000
5	Schedule E–Jointly Owned Property (attach Form(s) 712 for life insurance)	5		200,000
6	Schedule F–Other Miscellaneous Property (attach Form(s) 712 for life insurance)	6		-0-
7	Schedule G–Transfers During Decedent's Life (att. Form(s) 712 for life insurance)	7		287,900
8	Schedule H–Powers of Appointment	8		-0-
9	Schedule I–Annuities	9		240,000
10	Total gross estate (add items 1 through 9)	10		2,947,150
11	Schedule U–Qualified Conservation Easement Exclusion	11		
12	Total gross estate less exclusion (subtract item 11 from item 10). Enter here and on line 1 of Part 2–Tax Computation	12		2,947,150

Item number	Deductions		Amount
13	Schedule J–Funeral Expenses and Expenses Incurred in Administering Property Subject to Claims	13	85,000
14	Schedule K–Debts of the Decedent	14	31,700
15	Schedule K–Mortgages and Liens	15	-0-
16	Total of items 13 through 15	16	116,700
17	Allowable amount of deductions from item 16 (see the instructions for item 17 of the Recapitulation)	17	116,700
18	Schedule L–Net Losses During Administration	18	-0-
19	Schedule L–Expenses Incurred in Administering Property Not Subject to Claims	19	-0-
20	Schedule M–Bequests, etc., to Surviving Spouse	20	1,050,000
21	Schedule O–Charitable, Public, and Similar Gifts and Bequests	21	10,000
22	Tentative total allowable deductions (add items 17 through 21). Enter here and on line 2 of the Tax Computation	22	1,176,700

Form 706 (Rev. 10-2006)

Estate of: Herman Estes

SCHEDULE A—Real Estate

- For jointly owned property that must be disclosed on Schedule E, see the instructions on the reverse side of Schedule E.
- Real estate that is part of a sole proprietorship should be shown on Schedule F.
- Real estate that is included in the gross estate under section 2035, 2036, 2037, or 2038 should be shown on Schedule G.
- Real estate that is included in the gross estate under section 2041 should be shown on Schedule H.
- If you elect section 2032A valuation, you must complete Schedule A and Schedule A-1.

Item number	Description	Alternate valuation date	Alternate value	Value at date of death
1	Personal residence, house and lot, located at 105 Elm Court, Dayton, OH			325,000
	Total from continuation schedules or additional sheets attached to this schedule			
	TOTAL. (Also enter on Part 5–Recapitulation, page 3, at item 1.)			325,000

(If more space is needed, attach the continuation schedule from the end of this package or additional sheets of the same size.)
(See the instructions on the reverse side.)

Form 706 (Rev. 10-2006)

Estate of: Herman Estes

SCHEDULE B—Stocks and Bonds

(For jointly owned property that must be disclosed on Schedule E, see the instructions for Schedule E.)

Item number	Description, including face amount of bonds or number of shares and par value for identification. Give CUSIP number. If trust, partnership, or closely held entity, give EIN	CUSIP number or EIN, where applicable	Unit value	Alternate valuation date	Alternate value	Value at date of death
1	Stock in Ajax Corporation 1,000 shares, $10 per share par value		1,600			1,600,000
	Total from continuation schedules (or additional sheets) attached to this schedule . .					
	TOTAL. (Also enter on Part 5–Recapitulation, page 3, at item 2.)					1,600,000

(If more space is needed, attach the continuation schedule from the end of this package or additional sheets of the same size.)
(The instructions to Schedule B are in the separate instructions.)

Form 706 (Rev. 10-2006)

Estate of: Herman Estes

SCHEDULE C—Mortgages, Notes, and Cash

(For jointly owned property that must be disclosed on Schedule E, see the instructions for Schedule E.)

Item number	Description	Alternate valuation date	Alternate value	Value at date of death
1	Checking account			19,250
2	Savings account (includes accrued interest through date of death)			75,000
	Total from continuation schedules (or additional sheets) attached to this schedule .			
	TOTAL. (Also enter on Part 5–Recapitulation, page 3, at item 3.)			94,250

(If more space is needed, attach the continuation schedule from the end of this package or additional sheets of the same size.)
(See the instructions on the reverse side.)

Form 706 (Rev. 10-2006)

Estate of: Herman Estes

SCHEDULE D—Insurance on the Decedent's Life

You must list all policies on the life of the decedent and attach a Form 712 for each policy.

Item number	Description	Alternate valuation date	Alternate value	Value at date of death
1	Life insurance policy No. 123-A issued by the Life Insurance Company of Ohio. Beneficiary — Johnny Estes			200,000
	Total from continuation schedules (or additional sheets) attached to this schedule .			
	TOTAL. (Also enter on Part 5–Recapitulation, page 3, at item 4.)			200,000

(If more space is needed, attach the continuation schedule from the end of this package or additional sheets of the same size.)

(See the instructions on the reverse side.)

Form 706 (Rev. 10-2006)

Estate of: Herman Estes

SCHEDULE E—Jointly Owned Property

(If you elect section 2032A valuation, you must complete Schedule E and Schedule A-1.)

PART 1. Qualified Joint Interests–Interests Held by the Decedent and His or Her Spouse as the Only Joint Tenants (Section 2040(b)(2))

Item number	Description. For securities, give CUSIP number. If trust, partnership, or closely held entity, give EIN	CUSIP number or EIN, where applicable	Alternate valuation date	Alternate value	Value at date of death
1	Land				400,000
	Total from continuation schedules (or additional sheets) attached to this schedule				
1a	Totals		1a		400,000
1b	Amounts included in gross estate (one-half of line **1a**)		1b		200,000

PART 2. All Other Joint Interests

2a State the name and address of each surviving co-tenant. If there are more than three surviving co-tenants, list the additional co-tenants on an attached sheet.

	Name	Address (number and street, city, state, and ZIP code)
A.		
B.		
C.		

Item number	Enter letter for co-tenant	Description (including alternate valuation date if any). For securities, give CUSIP number. If trust, partnership, or closely held entity, give EIN	CUSIP number or EIN, where applicable	Percentage includible	Includible alternate value	Includible value at date of death
1						
		Total from continuation schedules (or additional sheets) attached to this schedule				
2b		Total other joint interests		2b		
3		**Total includible joint interests** (add lines 1b and 2b). Also enter on Part 5–Recapitulation, page 3, at item 5		3		200,000

(If more space is needed, attach the continuation schedule from the end of this package or additional sheets of the same size.)
(See the instructions on the reverse side.)

Form 706 (Rev. 10-2006)

Estate of: Herman Estes

SCHEDULE G—Transfers During Decedent's Life

(If you elect section 2032A valuation, you must complete Schedule G and Schedule A-1.)

Item number	Description. For securities, give CUSIP number. If trust, partnership, or closely held entity, give EIN	Alternate valuation date	Alternate value	Value at date of death
A.	Gift tax paid or payable by the decedent or the estate for all gifts made by the decedent or his or her spouse within 3 years before the decedent's death (section 2035(b))	X X X X X		287,900
B.	Transfers includible under section 2035(a), 2036, 2037, or 2038:			
1				
	Total from continuation schedules (or additional sheets) attached to this schedule .			
	TOTAL. (Also enter on Part 5–Recapitulation, page 3, at item 7.)			287,900

SCHEDULE H—Powers of Appointment

(Include "5 and 5 lapsing" powers (section 2041(b)(2)) held by the decedent.)

(If you elect section 2032A valuation, you must complete Schedule H and Schedule A-1.)

Item number	Description	Alternate valuation date	Alternate value	Value at date of death
1				
	Total from continuation schedules (or additional sheets) attached to this schedule .			
	TOTAL. (Also enter on Part 5–Recapitulation, page 3, at item 8.)			

(If more space is needed, attach the continuation schedule from the end of this package or additional sheets of the same size.)
(The instructions to Schedules G and H are in the separate instructions.)

Form 706 (Rev. 10-2006)

Estate of: Herman Estes

SCHEDULE I—Annuities

Note. Generally, no exclusion is allowed for the estates of decedents dying after December 31, 1984 (see page 16 of the instructions).

	Yes	No
A Are you excluding from the decedent's gross estate the value of a lump-sum distribution described in section 2039(f)(2) (as in effect before its repeal by the Deficit Reduction Act of 1984)? . . . . If "Yes," you must attach the information required by the instructions.		X

Item number	Description. Show the entire value of the annuity before any exclusions	Alternate valuation date	Includible alternate value	Includible value at date of death
1	Qualified pension plan issued by Buckeye Corporation; beneficiary — Ann Estes, spouse			240,000
	Total from continuation schedules (or additional sheets) attached to this schedule .			
	TOTAL. (Also enter on Part 5–Recapitulation, page 3, at item 9.)			240,000

(If more space is needed, attach the continuation schedule from the end of this package or additional sheets of the same size.)

(The instructions to Schedule I are in the separate instructions.)

Form 706 (Rev. 10-2006)

Estate of: Herman Estes

SCHEDULE J—Funeral Expenses and Expenses Incurred in Administering Property Subject to Claims

Note. Do not list on this schedule expenses of administering property not subject to claims. For those expenses, see the instructions for Schedule L.

If executors' commissions, attorney fees, etc., are claimed and allowed as a deduction for estate tax purposes, they are not allowable as a deduction in computing the taxable income of the estate for federal income tax purposes. They are allowable as an income tax deduction on Form 1041 if a waiver is filed to waive the deduction on Form 706 (see the Form 1041 instructions).

Item number	Description	Expense amount	Total amount
	A. Funeral expenses:		
1		15,000	
	Total funeral expenses . . . . ▶		15,000
	B. Administration expenses:		
	1 Executors' commissions–amount estimated/agreed upon/paid. (Strike out the words that do not apply.)		70,000
	2 Attorney fees–amount estimated/agreed upon/paid. (Strike out the words that do not apply.)		
	3 Accountant fees–amount estimated/agreed upon/paid. (Strike out the words that do not apply.)		
	4 Miscellaneous expenses:	Expense amount	
	Total miscellaneous expenses from continuation schedules (or additional sheets) attached to this schedule		
	Total miscellaneous expenses . . . . ▶		

TOTAL. (Also enter on Part 5–Recapitulation, page 3, at item 13.) . . . . ▶ 85,000

(If more space is needed, attach the continuation schedule from the end of this package or additional sheets of the same size.)
(See the instructions on the reverse side.)

Form 706 (Rev. 10-2006)

Estate of: Herman Estes

SCHEDULE K—Debts of the Decedent, and Mortgages and Liens

Item number	Debts of the Decedent—Creditor and nature of claim, and allowable death taxes	Amount unpaid to date	Amount in contest	Amount claimed as a deduction
1	Bank loan (including $200 interest accrued through date of death)	25,200		25,200
2	American Express, Visa, and Master Card credit card debts	6,500		6,500
	Total from continuation schedules (or additional sheets) attached to this schedule			
	TOTAL. (Also enter on Part 5–Recapitulation, page 3, at item 14.)			31,700

Item number	Mortgages and Liens—Description	Amount
1		
	Total from continuation schedules (or additional sheets) attached to this schedule	
	TOTAL. (Also enter on Part 5–Recapitulation, page 3, at item 15.)	

(If more space is needed, attach the continuation schedule from the end of this package or additional sheets of the same size.)
(The instructions to Schedule K are in the separate instructions.)

Form 706 (Rev. 10-2006)

Estate of: Herman Estes

SCHEDULE M—Bequests, etc., to Surviving Spouse

Election To Deduct Qualified Terminable Interest Property Under Section 2056(b)(7). If a trust (or other property) meets the requirements of qualified terminable interest property under section 2056(b)(7), and

a. The trust or other property is listed on Schedule M and

b. The value of the trust (or other property) is entered in whole or in part as a deduction on Schedule M,

then unless the executor specifically identifies the trust (all or a fractional portion or percentage) or other property to be excluded from the election, the executor shall be deemed to have made an election to have such trust (or other property) treated as qualified terminable interest property under section 2056(b)(7).

If less than the entire value of the trust (or other property) that the executor has included in the gross estate is entered as a deduction on Schedule M, the executor shall be considered to have made an election only as to a fraction of the trust (or other property). The numerator of this fraction is equal to the amount of the trust (or other property) deducted on Schedule M. The denominator is equal to the total value of the trust (or other property).

Election To Deduct Qualified Domestic Trust Property Under Section 2056A. If a trust meets the requirements of a qualified domestic trust under section 2056A(a) and this return is filed no later than 1 year after the time prescribed by law (including extensions) for filing the return, and

a. The entire value of a trust or trust property is listed on Schedule M and

b. The entire value of the trust or trust property is entered as a deduction on Schedule M,

then unless the executor specifically identifies the trust to be excluded from the election, the executor shall be deemed to have made an election to have the entire trust treated as qualified domestic trust property.

			Yes	No
1	Did any property pass to the surviving spouse as a result of a qualified disclaimer? If "Yes," attach a copy of the written disclaimer required by section 2518(b).	1		X
2a	In what country was the surviving spouse born? United States			
b	What is the surviving spouse's date of birth? 3-12-1943			
c	Is the surviving spouse a U.S. citizen?	2c	X	
d	If the surviving spouse is a naturalized citizen, when did the surviving spouse acquire citizenship? N/A			
e	If the surviving spouse is not a U.S. citizen, of what country is the surviving spouse a citizen? N/A			
3	**Election Out of QTIP Treatment of Annuities.** Do you elect under section 2056(b)(7)(C)(ii) not to treat as qualified terminable interest property any joint and survivor annuities that are included in the gross estate and would otherwise be treated as qualified terminable interest property under section 2056(b)(7)(C)? (see instructions)	3		X

Item number	Description of property interests passing to surviving spouse. For securities, give CUSIP number. If trust, partnership, or closely held entity, give EIN	Amount
	QTIP property:	
A1	Trust with First Bank as trustee	200,000
	All other property:	
B1	Residence	325,000
	Savings account	75,000
	Cash from checking account	10,000
	Land held in joint tenancy	200,000
	Qualified pension plan	240,000
	Total from continuation schedules (or additional sheets) attached to this schedule	

4	**Total** amount of property interests listed on Schedule M	4	1,050,000
5a	Federal estate taxes payable out of property interests listed on Schedule M	5a	
b	Other death taxes payable out of property interests listed on Schedule M	5b	
c	Federal and state GST taxes payable out of property interests listed on Schedule M	5c	
d	Add items 5a, 5b, and 5c	5d	-0-
6	Net amount of property interests listed on Schedule M (subtract 5d from 4). Also enter on Part 5–Recapitulation, page 3, at item 20	6	1,050,000

(If more space is needed, attach the continuation schedule from the end of this package or additional sheets of the same size.) (See the instructions on the reverse side.)

Form 706 (Rev. 10-2006)

Estate of: Herman Estes

SCHEDULE O—Charitable, Public, and Similar Gifts and Bequests

		Yes	No
1a	If the transfer was made by will, has any action been instituted to have interpreted or to contest the will or any of its provisions affecting the charitable deductions claimed in this schedule? If "Yes," full details must be submitted with this schedule.		X
b	According to the information and belief of the person or persons filing this return, is any such action planned? If "Yes," full details must be submitted with this schedule.		X
2	Did any property pass to charity as the result of a qualified disclaimer? If "Yes," attach a copy of the written disclaimer required by section 2518(b).		X

Item number	Name and address of beneficiary	Character of institution	Amount
1	American Cancer Society	Charity	10,000

	Total from continuation schedules (or additional sheets) attached to this schedule		10,000
3	Total	3	
4a	Federal estate tax payable out of property interests listed above	4a	
b	Other death taxes payable out of property interests listed above	4b	
c	Federal and state GST taxes payable out of property interests listed above	4c	
d	Add items 4a, 4b, and 4c	4d	-0-
5	Net value of property interests listed above (subtract 4d from 3). Also enter on Part 5–Recapitulation, page 3, at item 21	5	10,000

(If more space is needed, attach the continuation schedule from the end of this package or additional sheets of the same size.)
(The instructions to Schedule O are in the separate instructions.)

Form **1041** Department of the Treasury– Internal Revenue Service
U.S. Income Tax Return for Estates and Trusts **2006** OMB No. 1545-0092

A Type of entity (see instr.):	For calendar year 2006 or fiscal year beginning , 2006, and ending , 20	
☐ Decedent's estate	Name of estate or trust (If a grantor type trust, see page 12 of the instructions.)	C Employer identification number
☒ Simple trust	Bob Adams Trust (Simple Trust)	74 : 1237211
☐ Complex trust	Name and title of fiduciary	D Date entity created
☐ Qualified disability trust	First Bank	1993
☐ ESBT (S portion only)	Number, street, and room or suite no. (If a P.O. box, see page 12 of the instructions.)	E Nonexempt charitable and split-interest trusts, check applicable boxes (see page 13 of the instr.):
☐ Grantor type trust		
☐ Bankruptcy estate–Ch. 7	Post Office Box 100	☐ Described in section 4947(a)(1)
☐ Bankruptcy estate–Ch. 11	City or town, state, and ZIP code	☐ Not a private foundation
☐ Pooled income fund	Nashville, TN 37203	☐ Described in section 4947(a)(2)

B Number of Schedules K-1 attached (see instructions) ▶ 1
F Check applicable boxes: ☐ Initial return ☐ Final return ☐ Amended return ☐ Change in trust's name ☐ Change in fiduciary ☐ Change in fiduciary's name ☐ Change in fiduciary's address
G Pooled mortgage account (see page 14 of the instructions): ☐ Bought ☐ Sold Date:

Income	1	Interest income	1	
	2a	Total ordinary dividends	2a	30,000
	b	Qualified dividends allocable to: (1) Beneficiaries 30,000 (2) Estate or trust -0-		
	3	Business income or (loss). Attach Schedule C or C-EZ (Form 1040)	3	
	4	Capital gain or (loss). Attach Schedule D (Form 1041)	4	12,000
	5	Rents, royalties, partnerships, other estates and trusts, etc. Attach Schedule E (Form 1040) (see below)	5	4,000
	6	Farm income or (loss). Attach Schedule F (Form 1040)	6	
	7	Ordinary gain or (loss). Attach Form 4797	7	
	8	Other income. List type and amount	8	
	9	**Total income.** Combine lines 1, 2a, and 3 through 8 ▶	9	46,000
Deductions	10	Interest. Check if Form 4952 is attached ▶ ☐	10	
	11	Taxes	11	
	12	Fiduciary fees ($1,200 – $360)	12	840
	13	Charitable deduction (from Schedule A, line 7)	13	
	14	Attorney, accountant, and return preparer fees	14	500
	15a	Other deductions **not** subject to the 2% floor (attach schedule)	15a	
	b	Allowable miscellaneous itemized deductions subject to the 2% floor	15b	
	16	Add lines 10 through 15b ▶	16	1,340
	17	Adjusted total income or (loss). Subtract line 16 from line 9 [17 44,660]		
	18	Income distribution deduction (from Schedule B, line 15). Attach Schedules K-1 (Form 1041)	18	32,660
	19	Estate tax deduction including certain generation-skipping taxes (attach computation)	19	
	20	Exemption	20	300
	21	Add lines 18 through 20 ▶	21	32,960
Tax and Payments	22	Taxable income. Subtract line 21 from line 17. If a loss, see page 20 of the instructions	22	11,700
	23	**Total tax** (from Schedule G, line 7)	23	1,550
	24	**Payments: a** 2006 estimated tax payments and amount applied from 2005 return	24a	2,600
	b	Estimated tax payments allocated to beneficiaries (from Form 1041-T)	24b	
	c	Subtract line 24b from line 24a	24c	2,600
	d	Tax paid with Form 7004 (see page 20 of the instructions)	24d	
	e	Federal income tax withheld. If any is from Form(s) 1099, check ▶ ☐	24e	
	f	Credit for federal telephone excise tax paid. Attach Form 8913	24f	
		Other payments: g Form 2439 ; h Form 4136 ; Total ▶	24i	
	25	**Total payments.** Add lines 24c through 24f, and 24i ▶	25	2,600
	26	Estimated tax penalty (see page 20 of the instructions)	26	
	27	**Tax due.** If line 25 is smaller than the total of lines 23 and 26, enter amount owed	27	
	28	**Overpayment.** If line 25 is larger than the total of lines 23 and 26, enter amount overpaid	28	1,050
	29	Amount of line 28 to be: **a Credited to 2007 estimated tax** ▶ 1,050 ; **b Refunded** ▶	29	

Sign Here Under penalties of perjury, I declare that I have examined this return, including accompanying schedules and statements, and to the best of my knowledge and belief, it is true, correct, and complete. Declaration of preparer (other than taxpayer) is based on all information of which preparer has any knowledge.

Tom Trusty — Signature of fiduciary or officer representing fiduciary | Date 3-15-07 | ▶ 38 : 1505087 EIN of fiduciary if a financial institution | May the IRS discuss this return with the preparer shown below (see instr.)? ☒ Yes ☐ No

Paid Preparer's Use Only

Preparer's signature	Karen Certified	Date 3-14-07	Check if self-employed ☒	Preparer's SSN or PTIN 444-17-1313
Firm's name (or yours if self-employed), address, and ZIP code	Karen Certified One Opryland Place, Nashville TN 37204		EIN	Phone no. (615) 372-1800

For Privacy Act and Paperwork Reduction Act Notice, see the separate instructions. Cat. No. 11370H Form **1041** (2006)

Line 5: Net rental income = Rental income ($5,000) – Realtor's commissions ($1,000) = Net rental income ($4,000)

Note: Pages concerning the AMT are omitted because the trust does not owe the AMT.

Form 1041 (2006) Page 2

Schedule A **Charitable Deduction.** Do not complete for a simple trust or a pooled income fund.

1	Amounts paid or permanently set aside for charitable purposes from gross income (see page 21)	1	
2	Tax-exempt income allocable to charitable contributions (see page 21 of the instructions)	2	
3	Subtract line 2 from line 1	3	
4	Capital gains for the tax year allocated to corpus and paid or permanently set aside for charitable purposes	4	
5	Add lines 3 and 4	5	
6	Section 1202 exclusion allocable to capital gains paid or permanently set aside for charitable purposes (see page 21 of the instructions)	6	
7	**Charitable deduction.** Subtract line 6 from line 5. Enter here and on page 1, line 13	7	

Schedule B **Income Distribution Deduction**

1	Adjusted total income (see page 22 of the instructions)	1	44,660
2	Adjusted tax-exempt interest ($15,000 – $360)	2	14,640
3	Total net gain from Schedule D (Form 1041), line 15, column (1) (see page 22 of the instructions)	3	
4	Enter amount from Schedule A, line 4 (minus any allocable section 1202 exclusion)	4	
5	Capital gains for the tax year included on Schedule A, line 1 (see page 22 of the instructions)	5	
6	Enter any gain from page 1, line 4, as a negative number. If page 1, line 4, is a loss, enter the loss as a positive number	6	(12,000)
7	**Distributable net income (DNI).** Combine lines 1 through 6. If zero or less, enter -0-	7	47,300
8	If a complex trust, enter accounting income for the tax year as determined under the governing instrument and applicable local law (8)		
9	Income required to be distributed currently	9	48,500
10	Other amounts paid, credited, or otherwise required to be distributed	10	-0-
11	Total distributions. Add lines 9 and 10. If greater than line 8, see page 22 of the instructions	11	48,500
12	Enter the amount of tax-exempt income included on line 11	12	14,640
13	Tentative income distribution deduction. Subtract line 12 from line 11	13	33,860
14	Tentative income distribution deduction. Subtract line 2 from line 7. If zero or less, enter -0-	14	32,660
15	**Income distribution deduction.** Enter the smaller of line 13 or line 14 here and on page 1, line 18	15	32,660

Schedule G **Tax Computation** (see page 23 of the instructions)

1	**Tax:** a Tax on taxable income (see page 23 of the instructions)	1a	1,550		
	b Tax on lump-sum distributions. Attach Form 4972	1b			
	c Alternative minimum tax (from Schedule I, line 56)	1c			
	d **Total.** Add lines 1a through 1c ▶			1d	1,550
2a	Foreign tax credit. Attach Form 1116	2a			
b	Other nonbusiness credits (attach schedule)	2b			
c	General business credit. Enter here and check which forms are attached: ☐ Form 3800 ☐ Forms (specify) ▶	2c			
d	Credit for prior year minimum tax. Attach Form 8801	2d			
3	**Total credits.** Add lines 2a through 2d ▶			3	
4	Subtract line 3 from line 1d. If zero or less, enter -0-.			4	1,550
5	Recapture taxes. Check if from: ☐ Form 4255 ☐ Form 8611			5	
6	Household employment taxes. Attach Schedule H (Form 1040)			6	
7	**Total tax.** Add lines 4 through 6. Enter here and on page 1, line 23 ▶			7	1,550

Other Information

		Yes	No
1	Did the estate or trust receive tax-exempt income? If "Yes," attach a computation of the allocation of expenses. Enter the amount of tax-exempt interest income and exempt-interest dividends ▶ $ 15,000 (see below)	X	
2	Did the estate or trust receive all or any part of the earnings (salary, wages, and other compensation) of any individual by reason of a contract assignment or similar arrangement?		X
3	At any time during calendar year 2006, did the estate or trust have an interest in or a signature or other authority over a bank, securities, or other financial account in a foreign country? See page 25 of the instructions for exceptions and filing requirements for Form TD F 90-22.1. If "Yes," enter the name of the foreign country ▶		X
4	During the tax year, did the estate or trust receive a distribution from, or was it the grantor of, or transferor to, a foreign trust? If "Yes," the estate or trust may have to file Form 3520. See page 25 of the instructions		X
5	Did the estate or trust receive, or pay, any qualified residence interest on seller-provided financing? If "Yes," see page 25 for required attachment		X
6	If this is an estate or a complex trust making the section 663(b) election, check here (see page 25) ▶ ☐		
7	To make a section 643(e)(3) election, attach Schedule D (Form 1041), and check here (see page 25) ▶ ☐		
8	If the decedent's estate has been open for more than 2 years, attach an explanation for the delay in closing the estate, and check here ▶ ☐		
9	Are any present or future trust beneficiaries skip persons? See page 25 of the instructions		X

Form **1041** (2006)

Line 2: Allocation of expenses: $\frac{\$15,000}{\$50,000} \times \$1,200 = \$360$ of trustees fee allocated to tax-exempt income

SCHEDULE D (Form 1041)

Department of the Treasury Internal Revenue Service

Capital Gains and Losses

► Attach to Form 1041, Form 5227, or Form 990-T. See the separate instructions for Form 1041 (also for Form 5227 or Form 990-T, if applicable).

OMB No. 1545-0092

2006

Name of estate or trust: Bob Adams Trust

Employer identification number: 74 ⋮ 1237211

Note: *Form 5227 filers need to complete **only** Parts I and II.*

Part I Short-Term Capital Gains and Losses–Assets Held One Year or Less

	(a) Description of property (Example: 100 shares 7% preferred of "Z" Co.)	(b) Date acquired (mo., day, yr.)	(c) Date sold (mo., day, yr.)	(d) Sales price	(e) Cost or other basis (see page 35)	(f) Gain or (Loss) for the entire year (col. (d) less col. (e))
1						

2	Short-term capital gain or (loss) from Forms 4684, 6252, 6781, and 8824	2	
3	Net short-term gain or (loss) from partnerships, S corporations, and other estates or trusts .	3	
4	Short-term capital loss carryover. Enter the amount, if any, from line 9 of the 2005 Capital Loss Carryover Worksheet	4	( )
5	**Net short-term gain or (loss).** Combine lines 1 through 4 in column (f). Enter here and on line 13, column (3) below . . . . ►	5	

Part II Long-Term Capital Gains and Losses–Assets Held More Than One Year

	(a) Description of property (Example: 100 shares 7% preferred of "Z" Co.)	(b) Date acquired (mo., day, yr.)	(c) Date sold (mo., day, yr.)	(d) Sales price	(e) Cost or other basis (see page 35)	(f) Gain or (Loss) for the entire year (col. (d) less col. (e))
6	1,000 shares of ABC Corp.	2002	Oct. 2006	15,000	3,000	12,000

7	Long-term capital gain or (loss) from Forms 2439, 4684, 6252, 6781, and 8824	7	
8	Net long-term gain or (loss) from partnerships, S corporations, and other estates or trusts .	8	
9	Capital gain distributions	9	
10	Gain from Form 4797, Part I	10	
11	Long-term capital loss carryover. Enter the amount, if any, from line 14 of the 2005 Capital Loss Carryover Worksheet	11	( )
12	**Net long-term gain or (loss).** Combine lines 6 through 11 in column (f). Enter here and on line 14a, column (3) below . . . . ►	12	12,000

Part III Summary of Parts I and II

Caution: *Read the instructions **before** completing this part.*

			(1) Beneficiaries' (see page 36)	(2) Estate's or trust's	(3) Total
13	**Net short-term gain or (loss)**	13			
14	**Net long-term gain or (loss):**				
a	Total for year	14a		12,000	12,000
b	Unrecaptured section 1250 gain (see line 18 of the worksheet on page 36)	14b			
c	28% rate gain	14c			
15	**Total net gain or (loss).** Combine lines 13 and 14a . ►	15		12,000	12,000

Note: *If line 15, column (3), is a net gain, enter the gain on Form 1041, line 4. If lines 14a and 15, column (2), are net gains, go to Part V, and **do not** complete Part IV. If line 15, column (3), is a net loss, complete Part IV and the **Capital Loss Carryover Worksheet,** as necessary.*

Schedule D (Form 1041) 2006 Page **2**

Part IV Capital Loss Limitation

16 Enter here and enter as a (loss) on Form 1041, line 4, the **smaller** of:			
a The loss on line 15, column (3) **or**			
b $3,000	16	(	)

*If the loss on line 15, column (3), is more than $3,000, **or** if Form 1041, page 1, line 22, is a loss, complete the **Capital Loss Carryover Worksheet** on page 39 of the instructions to determine your capital loss carryover.*

Part V Tax Computation Using Maximum Capital Gains Rates

(Complete this part **only** if both lines 14a and 15 in column (2) are gains, or an amount is entered in Part I or Part II and there is an entry on Form 1041, line 2b(2), **and** Form 1041, line 22 is more than zero.)

Note: *If line 14b, column (2) or line 14c, column (2) is more than zero, complete the worksheet on page 38 of the instructions and skip Part V. Otherwise, go to line 17.*

17	Enter taxable income from Form 1041, line 22			17	11,700		
18	Enter the **smaller** of line 14a or 15 in column (2) but not less than zero	18	12,000				
19	Enter the estate's or trust's qualified dividends from Form 1041, line 2b(2)	19	-0-				
20	Add lines 18 and 19	20	12,000				
21	If the estate or trust is filing Form 4952, enter the amount from line 4g; otherwise, enter -0- ▶	21	-0-				
22	Subtract line 21 from line 20. If zero or less, enter -0-			22	12,000		
23	Subtract line 22 from line 17. If zero or less, enter -0-			23	-0-		
24	Enter the **smaller** of the amount on line 17 or $2,050			24	2,050		
25	Is the amount on line 23 equal to or more than the amount on line 24? ☐ **Yes.** Skip lines 25 through 27; go to line 28 and check the "No" box. ☒ **No.** Enter the amount from line 23			25	-0-		
26	Subtract line 25 from line 24			26	2,050		
27	Multiply line 26 by 5% (.05)					27	103
28	Are the amounts on lines 22 and 26 the same? ☐ **Yes.** Skip lines 28 through 31; go to line 32. ☒ **No.** Enter the **smaller** of line 17 or line 22			28	11,700		
29	Enter the amount from line 26 (If line 26 is blank, enter -0-).			29	2,050		
30	Subtract line 29 from line 28			30	9,650		
31	Multiply line 30 by 15% (.15)					31	1,447
32	Figure the tax on the amount on line 23. Use the 2006 Tax Rate Schedule on page 23 of the instructions					32	-0-
33	Add lines 27, 31, and 32					33	1,550
34	Figure the tax on the amount on line 17. Use the 2006 Tax Rate Schedule on page 23 of the instructions					34	3,174
35	**Tax on all taxable income.** Enter the **smaller** of line 33 or line 34 here and on line 1a of Schedule G, Form 1041					35	1,550

Schedule D (Form 1041) 2006

661106

☐ Final K-1 ☐ Amended K-1 OMB No. 1545-0092

Schedule K-1 (Form 1041) **2006**

Department of the Treasury
Internal Revenue Service

For calendar year 2006,
or tax year beginning ____________, 2006
and ending ____________, 20____

Beneficiary's Share of Income, Deductions, Credits, etc.

▶ See back of form and instructions.

Part I Information About the Estate or Trust

A Estate's or trust's employer identification number
74-1237211

B Estate's or trust's name
Bob Adams Trust

C Fiduciary's name, address, city, state, and ZIP code
First Bank
Post OfficeBox 100
Nashville, TN 37203

D ☐ Check if Form 1041-T was filed and enter the date it was filed ____/____/____

E ☐ Check if this is the final Form 1041 for the estate or trust

F ☐ Tax shelter registration number, if any ____________

G ☐ Check if Form 8271 is attached

Part II Information About the Beneficiary

H Beneficiary's identifying number
389-16-4001

I Beneficiary's name, address, city, state, and ZIP code
Bob Adams
3 Andrew Jackson Highway
Nashville, TN 37211

J ☒ Domestic beneficiary ☐ Foreign beneficiary

Part III Beneficiary's Share of Current Year Income, Deductions, Credits, and Other Items

No.	Item	Amount	No.	Item	Amount
1	Interest income		11	Final year deductions	
2a	Ordinary dividends	30,000			
2b	Qualified dividends	30,000			
3	Net short-term capital gain				
4a	Net long-term capital gain				
4b	28% rate gain		12	Alternative minimum tax adjustment	
4c	Unrecaptured section 1250 gain				
5	Other portfolio and nonbusiness income				
6	Ordinary business income				
7	Net rental real estate income	2,660*	13	Credits and credit recapture	
8	Other rental income				
9	Directly apportioned deductions				
			14	Other information	
10	Estate tax deduction		A		14,640

*See attached statement for additional information.

Note: A statement must be attached showing the beneficiary's share of income and directly apportioned deductions from each business, rental real estate, and other rental activity.

For IRS Use Only

For Paperwork Reduction Act Notice, see the Instructions for Form 1041. Cat. No. 11380D **Schedule K-1 (Form 1041) 2006**

*5,000 – ($1,000 + $840 + $500) = $2,660

This list identifies the codes used on Schedule K-1 for beneficiaries and provides summarized reporting information for beneficiaries who file Form 1040. For detailed reporting and filing information, see the Instructions for Beneficiary Filing Form 1040 and the instructions for your income tax return.

	Report on
1. Interest income	Form 1040, line 8a
2a. Ordinary dividends	Form 1040, line 9a
2b. Qualified dividends	Form 1040, line 9b
3. Net short-term capital gain	Schedule D, line 5, column (f)
4a. Net long-term capital gain	Schedule D, line 12, column (f)
4b. 28% rate gain	Line 4 of the worksheet for Schedule D, line 18
4c. Unrecaptured section 1250 gain	Line 11 of the worksheet for Schedule D, line 19
5. Other portfolio and nonbusiness income	Schedule E, line 33, column (f)
6. Ordinary business Income	Schedule E, line 33, column (d) or (f)
7. Net rental real estate income	Schedule E, line 33, column (d) or (f)
8. Other rental income	Schedule E, line 33, column (d) or (f)
9. Directly apportioned deductions	
Code	
A Depreciation	Form 8582 or Schedule E, line 33, column (c) or (e)
B Depletion	Form 8582 or Schedule E, line 33, column (c) or (e)
C Amortization	Form 8582 or Schedule E, line 33, column (c) or (e)
10. Estate tax deduction	Schedule A, line 27
11. Final year deductions	
A Excess deductions	Schedule A, line 22
B Short-term capital loss carryover	Schedule D, line 5, column (f)
C Long-term capital loss carryover	Schedule D, line 12, column (f); line 5 of the wksht. for Sch. D, line 18; and line 16 of the wksht. for Sch. D, line 19
D Net operating loss carryover – regular tax	Form 1040, line 21
E Net operating loss carryover – minimum tax	Form 6251, line 27

12. Alternative minimum tax items	
Code	*Report on*
A Adjustment for minimum tax purposes	Form 6251, line 14
B AMT adjustment attributable to qualified dividends	See the beneficiary's instructions and the Instructions for Form 6251
C AMT adjustment attributable to net short-term capital gain	
D AMT adjustment attributable to net long-term capital gain	
E AMT adjustment attributable to unrecaptured section 1250 gain	
F AMT adjustment attributable to 28% rate gain	
G Accelerated depreciation	
H Depletion	
I Amortization	
J Exclusion items	2007 Form 8801
13. Credits and credit recapture	
A Credit for estimated taxes	Form 1040, line 65
B Credit for backup withholding	Form 1040, line 64
C Low-income housing credit	Form 3800, line 1e
D Qualified rehabilitation expenditures	See the beneficiary's instructions
E Basis of other investment credit property	See the beneficiary's instructions
F Work opportunity credit	Form 3800, line 1b
G Welfare-to-work credit	Form 3800, line 1c
H Alcohol fuel credit	Form 6478, line 5 (also see the beneficiary's instructions)
I Credit for increasing research activities	Form 3800, line 1d
J Renewable electricity, refined coal, and Indian coal production credit	See the beneficiary's instructions
K Empowerment zone and renewal community employment credit	Form 8844, line 3
L Indian employment credit	Form 3800, line 1i
M Orphan drug credit	Form 3800, line 1k
N Credit for employer provided child care and facilities	Form 3800, line 1n
O Biodiesel and renewable diesel fuels credit	Form 8864, line 9 (also see the beneficiary's instructions)
P Nonconventional source fuel credit	Form 3800, line 1s
Q Clean renewable energy bond and Gulf tax credit bond credits	See the beneficiary's instructions and Form 8912
R Credits for employers affected by Hurricane Katrina, Rita, or Wilma	Form 3800, line 1aa (also see the beneficiary's instructions)
S Energy efficient appliance credit	Form 3800, line 1u
T Recapture of credits	See the beneficiary's instructions
14. Other information	
A Tax-exempt interest	Form 1040, line 8b
B Foreign taxes	Form 1040, line 47 or Sch. A, line 8
C Qualified production activities income	Form 8903, line 7
D Form W-2 wages	Form 8903, line 13
E Net investment income	Form 4952, line 4a
F Gross farm and fishing income	Schedule E, line 42
G Foreign trading gross receipts (IRC 942(a))	See the instructions for Form 8873
H Other information	See the beneficiary's instructions

Note. If you are a beneficiary who does not file a Form 1040, see instructions for the type of income tax return you are filing.

Form **1041** Department of the Treasury– Internal Revenue Service

U.S. Income Tax Return for Estates and Trusts 2006

OMB No. 1545-0092

A Type of entity (see instr.):
- ☐ Decedent's estate
- ☐ Simple trust
- ☒ Complex trust
- ☐ Qualified disability trust
- ☐ ESBT (S portion only)
- ☐ Grantor type trust
- ☐ Bankruptcy estate±Ch. 7
- ☐ Bankruptcy estate±Ch. 11
- ☐ Pooled income fund

B Number of Schedules K-1 attached (see instructions) ▶ 2

For calendar year 2006 or fiscal year beginning , 2006, and ending , 20

Name of estate or trust (If a grantor type trust, see page 12 of the instructions.): Cathy and Karen Stephens Trust (Complex Trust)

Name and title of fiduciary: Merchants Bank

Number, street, and room or suite no. (If a P.O. box, see page 12 of the instructions.): 3000 Sun Plaza I

City or town, state, and ZIP code: Tampa, FL 32843

C Employer identification number: 74 : 5727422

D Date entity created: 3-12-94

E Nonexempt charitable and split-interest trusts, check applicable boxes (see page 13 of the instr.):
- ☐ Described in section 4947(a)(1)
- ☐ Not a private foundation
- ☐ Described in section 4947(a)(2)

F Check applicable boxes: ☐ Initial return ☐ Final return ☐ Amended return ☐ Change in trust's name ☐ Change in fiduciary ☐ Change in fiduciary's name ☐ Change in fiduciary's address

G Pooled mortgage account (see page 14 of the instructions): ☐ Bought ☐ Sold Date:

Income

Line	Description		Amount
1	Interest income	1	
2a	Total ordinary dividends	2a	30,000
b	Qualified dividends allocable to: (1) Beneficiaries 13,319 (2) Estate or trust 16,681		
3	Business income or (loss). Attach Schedule C or C-EZ (Form 1040)	3	
4	Capital gain or (loss). Attach Schedule D (Form 1041)	4	12,000
5	Rents, royalties, partnerships, other estates and trusts, etc. Attach Schedule E (Form 1040) [see below]	5	4,000
6	Farm income or (loss). Attach Schedule F (Form 1040)	6	
7	Ordinary gain or (loss). Attach Form 4797	7	
8	Other income. List type and amount	8	
9	**Total income.** Combine lines 1, 2a, and 3 through 8 ▶	9	46,000

Deductions

Line	Description		Amount
10	Interest. Check if Form 4952 is attached ▶ ☐	10	
11	Taxes	11	
12	Fiduciary fees ($1,200 – $360)	12	840
13	Charitable deduction (from Schedule A, line 7)	13	
14	Attorney, accountant, and return preparer fees	14	500
15a	Other deductions **not** subject to the 2% floor (attach schedule)	15a	
b	Allowable miscellaneous itemized deductions subject to the 2% floor	15b	
16	Add lines 10 through 15b ▶	16	1,340
17	Adjusted total income or (loss). Subtract line 16 from line 9 [17: 44,660]		
18	Income distribution deduction (from Schedule B, line 15). Attach Schedules K-1 (Form 1041)	18	14,500
19	Estate tax deduction including certain generation-skipping taxes (attach computation)	19	
20	Exemption	20	100
21	Add lines 18 through 20 ▶	21	14,600

Tax and Payments

Line	Description		Amount
22	Taxable income. Subtract line 21 from line 17. If a loss, see page 20 of the instructions	22	30,060
23	**Total tax** (from Schedule G, line 7)	23	4,443
24	**Payments: a** 2006 estimated tax payments and amount applied from 2005 return	24a	8,600
b	Estimated tax payments allocated to beneficiaries (from Form 1041-T)	24b	
c	Subtract line 24b from line 24a	24c	8,600
d	Tax paid with Form 7004 (see page 20 of the instructions)	24d	
e	Federal income tax withheld. If any is from Form(s) 1099, check ▶ ☐	24e	
f	Credit for federal telephone excise tax paid. Attach Form 8913	24f	
	Other payments: g Form 2439 ; h Form 4136 ; Total ▶	24i	
25	**Total payments.** Add lines 24c through 24f, and 24i ▶	25	8,600
26	Estimated tax penalty (see page 20 of the instructions)	26	
27	**Tax due.** If line 25 is smaller than the total of lines 23 and 26, enter amount owed	27	
28	**Overpayment.** If line 25 is larger than the total of lines 23 and 26, enter amount overpaid	28	4,157
29	Amount of line 28 to be: **a Credited to 2007 estimated tax** ▶ 4,157 ; **b Refunded** ▶	29	

Sign Here

Under penalties of perjury, I declare that I have examined this return, including accompanying schedules and statements, and to the best of my knowledge and belief, it is true, correct, and complete. Declaration of preparer (other than taxpayer) is based on all information of which preparer has any knowledge.

Fred Fidus — Signature of fiduciary or officer representing fiduciary | Date: 3-20-07 | ▶ 38 : 4371419 — EIN of fiduciary if a financial institution

May the IRS discuss this return with the preparer shown below (see instr.)? ☒ Yes ☐ No

Paid Preparer's Use Only

Preparer's signature: Sarah Public | Date: 3-15-07 | Check if self-employed ☒ | Preparer's SSN or PTIN: 127-84-3878

Firm's name (or yours if self-employed), address, and ZIP code: Sarah Public 200 Sun Plaza III, Tampa, FL 32843 | EIN | Phone no. (863) 437-1000

For Privacy Act and Paperwork Reduction Act Notice, see the separate instructions. Cat. No. 11370H Form **1041** (2006)

Line 4: Net Rental income

Rental income ($5,000) – Rental expenses ($1,000) = Net rental income ($4,000)

Note: Pages concerning the AMT are omitted because the trust does not owe the AMT.

Form 1041 (2006) Page 2

Schedule A **Charitable Deduction.** Do not complete for a simple trust or a pooled income fund.

1	Amounts paid or permanently set aside for charitable purposes from gross income (see page 21)	1	
2	Tax-exempt income allocable to charitable contributions (see page 21 of the instructions)	2	
3	Subtract line 2 from line 1	3	
4	Capital gains for the tax year allocated to corpus and paid or permanently set aside for charitable purposes	4	
5	Add lines 3 and 4	5	
6	Section 1202 exclusion allocable to capital gains paid or permanently set aside for charitable purposes (see page 21 of the instructions)	6	
7	**Charitable deduction.** Subtract line 6 from line 5. Enter here and on page 1, line 13	7	

Schedule B **Income Distribution Deduction**

1	Adjusted total income (see page 22 of the instructions)	1	44,660
2	Adjusted tax-exempt interest . ($15,000 – $360)	2	14,640
3	Total net gain from Schedule D (Form 1041), line 15, column (1) (see page 22 of the instructions)	3	
4	Enter amount from Schedule A, line 4 (minus any allocable section 1202 exclusion)	4	
5	Capital gains for the tax year included on Schedule A, line 1 (see page 22 of the instructions)	5	
6	Enter any gain from page 1, line 4, as a negative number. If page 1, line 4, is a loss, enter the loss as a positive number	6	(12,000)
7	**Distributable net income (DNI).** Combine lines 1 through 6. If zero or less, enter -0-	7	47,300
8	If a complex trust, enter accounting income for the tax year as determined under the governing instrument and applicable local law — 8: 48,500		
9	Income required to be distributed currently	9	-0-
10	Other amounts paid, credited, or otherwise required to be distributed	10	21,000
11	Total distributions. Add lines 9 and 10. If greater than line 8, see page 22 of the instructions	11	21,000
12	Enter the amount of tax-exempt income included on line 11	12	6,500
13	Tentative income distribution deduction. Subtract line 12 from line 11	13	14,500
14	Tentative income distribution deduction. Subtract line 2 from line 7. If zero or less, enter -0-	14	32,660
15	**Income distribution deduction.** Enter the smaller of line 13 or line 14 here and on page 1, line 18	15	14,500

Schedule G **Tax Computation** (see page 23 of the instructions)

1 Tax: a	Tax on taxable income (see page 23 of the instructions)	1a	4,443		
b	Tax on lump-sum distributions. Attach Form 4972	1b			
c	Alternative minimum tax (from Schedule I, line 56)	1c			
d	**Total.** Add lines 1a through 1c ▶			1d	4,443
2a	Foreign tax credit. Attach Form 1116	2a			
b	Other nonbusiness credits (attach schedule)	2b			
c	General business credit. Enter here and check which forms are attached: ☐ Form 3800 ☐ Forms (specify) ▶	2c			
d	Credit for prior year minimum tax. Attach Form 8801	2d			
3	**Total credits.** Add lines 2a through 2d ▶			3	
4	Subtract line 3 from line 1d. If zero or less, enter -0-			4	4,443
5	Recapture taxes. Check if from: ☐ Form 4255 ☐ Form 8611			5	
6	Household employment taxes. Attach Schedule H (Form 1040)			6	
7	**Total tax.** Add lines 4 through 6. Enter here and on page 1, line 23 ▶			7	4,443

Other Information

		Yes	No
1	Did the estate or trust receive tax-exempt income? If "Yes," attach a computation of the allocation of expenses. Enter the amount of tax-exempt interest income and exempt-interest dividends ▶ $ 15,000; (see below)	X	
2	Did the estate or trust receive all or any part of the earnings (salary, wages, and other compensation) of any individual by reason of a contract assignment or similar arrangement?		X
3	At any time during calendar year 2006, did the estate or trust have an interest in or a signature or other authority over a bank, securities, or other financial account in a foreign country? See page 25 of the instructions for exceptions and filing requirements for Form TD F 90-22.1. If "Yes," enter the name of the foreign country ▶		X
4	During the tax year, did the estate or trust receive a distribution from, or was it the grantor of, or transferor to, a foreign trust? If "Yes," the estate or trust may have to file Form 3520. See page 25 of the instructions		X
5	Did the estate or trust receive, or pay, any qualified residence interest on seller-provided financing? If "Yes," see page 25 for required attachment		X
6	If this is an estate or a complex trust making the section 663(b) election, check here (see page 25) ▶ ☐		
7	To make a section 643(e)(3) election, attach Schedule D (Form 1041), and check here (see page 25) ▶ ☐		
8	If the decedent's estate has been open for more than 2 years, attach an explanation for the delay in closing the estate, and check here ▶ ☐		
9	Are any present or future trust beneficiaries skip persons? See page 25 of the instructions		X

Form **1041** (2006)

Line 2: Allocation of expenses: $\frac{\$15,000}{\$50,000} \times \$1,200 = \$360$ of trustee's fee allocated to tax-exempt income

SCHEDULE D (Form 1041)

Department of the Treasury
Internal Revenue Service

Capital Gains and Losses

► Attach to Form 1041, Form 5227, or Form 990-T. See the separate instructions for Form 1041 (also for Form 5227 or Form 990-T, if applicable).

OMB No. 1545-0092

2006

Name of estate or trust: Cathy and Karen Stephens Trust

Employer identification number: 74 5724722

Note: *Form 5227 filers need to complete **only** Parts I and II.*

Part I Short-Term Capital Gains and Losses—Assets Held One Year or Less

(a) Description of property (Example: 100 shares 7% preferred of "Z" Co.)	(b) Date acquired (mo., day, yr.)	(c) Date sold (mo., day, yr.)	(d) Sales price	(e) Cost or other basis (see page 35)	(f) Gain or (Loss) for the entire year (col. (d) less col. (e))
1					

Line	Description	Box	Amount
2	Short-term capital gain or (loss) from Forms 4684, 6252, 6781, and 8824	2	
3	Net short-term gain or (loss) from partnerships, S corporations, and other estates or trusts	3	
4	Short-term capital loss carryover. Enter the amount, if any, from line 9 of the 2005 Capital Loss Carryover Worksheet	4	( )
5	**Net short-term gain or (loss).** Combine lines 1 through 4 in column (f). Enter here and on line 13, column (3) below ►	5	

Part II Long-Term Capital Gains and Losses—Assets Held More Than One Year

(a) Description of property (Example: 100 shares 7% preferred of "Z" Co.)	(b) Date acquired (mo., day, yr.)	(c) Date sold (mo., day, yr.)	(d) Sales price	(e) Cost or other basis (see page 35)	(f) Gain or (Loss) for the entire year (col. (d) less col. (e))
6 1,000 shares of ABC Corporation stock	2002	Oct. 2006	15,000	3,000	12,000

Line	Description	Box	Amount
7	Long-term capital gain or (loss) from Forms 2439, 4684, 6252, 6781, and 8824	7	
8	Net long-term gain or (loss) from partnerships, S corporations, and other estates or trusts	8	
9	Capital gain distributions	9	
10	Gain from Form 4797, Part I	10	
11	Long-term capital loss carryover. Enter the amount, if any, from line 14 of the 2005 Capital Loss Carryover Worksheet	11	( )
12	**Net long-term gain or (loss).** Combine lines 6 through 11 in column (f). Enter here and on line 14a, column (3) below ►	12	12,000

Part III Summary of Parts I and II

Caution: *Read the instructions **before** completing this part.*

		(1) Beneficiaries' (see page 36)	(2) Estate's or trust's	(3) Total
13 **Net short-term gain or (loss)**	13			
14 **Net long-term gain or (loss):**				
a Total for year	14a		12,000	12,000
b Unrecaptured section 1250 gain (see line 18 of the worksheet on page 36)	14b			
c 28% rate gain	14c			
15 **Total net gain or (loss).** Combine lines 13 and 14a ►	15		12,000	12,000

Note: *If line 15, column (3), is a net gain, enter the gain on Form 1041, line 4. If lines 14a and 15, column (2), are net gains, go to Part V, and **do not** complete Part IV. If line 15, column (3), is a net loss, complete Part IV and the **Capital Loss Carryover Worksheet,** as necessary.*

Part IV **Capital Loss Limitation**

16 Enter here and enter as a (loss) on Form 1041, line 4, the **smaller** of:
a The loss on line 15, column (3) **or**
b $3,000 . . . . 16 ( )

If the loss on line 15, column (3), is more than $3,000, ***or*** *if Form 1041, page 1, line 22, is a loss, complete the* ***Capital Loss Carryover Worksheet*** *on page 39 of the instructions to determine your capital loss carryover.*

Part V **Tax Computation Using Maximum Capital Gains Rates** (Complete this part **only** if both lines 14a and 15 in column (2) are gains, or an amount is entered in Part I or Part II and there is an entry on Form 1041, line 2b(2), **and** Form 1041, line 22 is more than zero.)

Note: *If line 14b, column (2) or line 14c, column (2) is more than zero, complete the worksheet on page 38 of the instructions and skip Part V. Otherwise, go to line 17.*

17	Enter taxable income from Form 1041, line 22		17	30,060	
18	Enter the **smaller** of line 14a or 15 in column (2) but not less than zero	18	12,000		
19	Enter the estate's or trust's qualified dividends from Form 1041, line 2b(2)	19	16,681		
20	Add lines 18 and 19	20	28,681		
21	If the estate or trust is filing Form 4952, enter the amount from line 4g; otherwise, enter -0- ▶	21	-0-		
22	Subtract line 21 from line 20. If zero or less, enter -0-		22	28,681	
23	Subtract line 22 from line 17. If zero or less, enter -0-		23	1,379	
24	Enter the **smaller** of the amount on line 17 or $2,050		24	2,050	
25	Is the amount on line 23 equal to or more than the amount on line 24? ☐ **Yes.** Skip lines 25 through 27; go to line 28 and check the "No" box. ☒ **No.** Enter the amount from line 23		25	1,379	
26	Subtract line 25 from line 24		26	671	
27	Multiply line 26 by 5% (.05)			27	34
28	Are the amounts on lines 22 and 26 the same? ☐ **Yes.** Skip lines 28 through 31; go to line 32. ☒ **No.** Enter the **smaller** of line 17 or line 22		28	28,681	
29	Enter the amount from line 26 (If line 26 is blank, enter -0-)		29	671	
30	Subtract line 29 from line 28		30	28,010	
31	Multiply line 30 by 15% (.15)			31	4,202
32	Figure the tax on the amount on line 23. Use the 2006 Tax Rate Schedule on page 23 of the instructions			32	207
33	Add lines 27, 31, and 32			33	4,443
34	Figure the tax on the amount on line 17. Use the 2006 Tax Rate Schedule on page 23 of the instructions			34	9,600
35	**Tax on all taxable income.** Enter the **smaller** of line 33 or line 34 here and on line 1a of Schedule G, Form 1041			35	4,443

661106

☐ Final K-1 ☐ Amended K-1 OMB No. 1545-0092

Schedule K-1 (Form 1041) **2006**

Department of the Treasury
Internal Revenue Service

For calendar year 2006,
or tax year beginning ________, 2006
and ending ________, 20 ____

Beneficiary's Share of Income, Deductions, Credits, etc.

► See back of form and instructions.

Part I Information About the Estate or Trust

A Estate's or trust's employer identification number
74-5727422

B Estate's or trust's name
Cathy and Karen Stephens Trust

C Fiduciary's name, address, city, state, and ZIP code
Merchants Bank
3000 Sun Plaza I
Tampa, FL 32843

D ☐ Check if Form 1041-T was filed and enter the date it was filed ___/___/___

E ☐ Check if this is the final Form 1041 for the estate or trust

F ☐ Tax shelter registration number, if any ________

G ☐ Check if Form 8271 is attached

Part II Information About the Beneficiary

H Beneficiary's identifying number
411-36-4761

I Beneficiary's name, address, city, state, and ZIP code
Cathy Stephens
13 Sunny Shores
Miami Beach, FL 33131

J ☒ Domestic beneficiary ☐ Foreign beneficiary

Part III Beneficiary's Share of Current Year Income, Deductions, Credits, and Other Items

1	Interest income	
2a	Ordinary dividends	8,879
2b	Qualified dividends	8,879
3	Net short-term capital gain	
4a	Net long-term capital gain	
4b	28% rate gain	
4c	Unrecaptured section 1250 gain	
5	Other portfolio and nonbusiness income	
6	Ordinary business income	
7	Net rental real estate income	788
8	Other rental income	
9	Directly apportioned deductions	
10	Estate tax deduction	
11	Final year deductions	
12	Alternative minimum tax adjustment	
13	Credits and credit recapture	
14	Other information	A 4,333

*See attached statement for additional information.

Note: A statement must be attached showing the beneficiary's share of income and directly apportioned deductions from each business, rental real estate, and other rental activity.

For IRS Use Only

For Paperwork Reduction Act Notice, see the Instructions for Form 1041. Cat. No. 11380D **Schedule K-1 (Form 1041) 2006**

661106

☐ Final K-1 ☐ Amended K-1 OMB No. 1545-0092

Schedule K-1 (Form 1041) **2006**

Department of the Treasury
Internal Revenue Service

For calendar year 2006,
or tax year beginning ______________, 2006
and ending ______________, 20____

Beneficiary's Share of Income, Deductions, Credits, etc.

▶ See back of form and instructions.

Part I Information About the Estate or Trust

A Estate's or trust's employer identification number
74-5727422

B Estate's or trust's name
Cathy and Karen Stephens Trust

C Fiduciary's name, address, city, state, and ZIP code
Merchants Bank
3000 Sun Plaza I
Tampa, FL 32843

D ☐ Check if Form 1041-T was filed and enter the date it was filed ____/____/____

E ☐ Check if this is the final Form 1041 for the estate or trust

F ☐ Tax shelter registration number, if any ______________

G ☐ Check if Form 8271 is attached

Part II Information About the Beneficiary

H Beneficiary's identifying number
456-78-1230

I Beneficiary's name, address, city, state, and ZIP code
Karen Stephens
1472 Ski Run
Vail, CO 74820

J ☒ Domestic beneficiary ☐ Foreign beneficiary

Part III Beneficiary's Share of Current Year Income, Deductions, Credits, and Other Items

No.	Item	Amount	No.	Item
1	Interest income		11	Final year deductions
2a	Ordinary dividends	4,440		
2b	Qualified dividends	4,440		
3	Net short-term capital gain			
4a	Net long-term capital gain			
4b	28% rate gain		12	Alternative minimum tax adjustment
4c	Unrecaptured section 1250 gain			
5	Other portfolio and nonbusiness income			
6	Ordinary business income			
7	Net rental real estate income	393		
8	Other rental income		13	Credits and credit recapture
9	Directly apportioned deductions			
			14	Other information
			A	2,167
10	Estate tax deduction			

*See attached statement for additional information.

Note: A statement must be attached showing the beneficiary's share of income and directly apportioned deductions from each business, rental real estate, and other rental activity.

For IRS Use Only

For Paperwork Reduction Act Notice, see the Instructions for Form 1041. Cat. No. 11380D **Schedule K-1 (Form 1041) 2006**

Schedule K-1 (Form 1041) 2006 Page **2**

This list identifies the codes used on Schedule K-1 for beneficiaries and provides summarized reporting information for beneficiaries who file Form 1040. For detailed reporting and filing information, see the Instructions for Beneficiary Filing Form 1040 and the instructions for your income tax return.

	Report on
1. Interest income	Form 1040, line 8a
2a. Ordinary dividends	Form 1040, line 9a
2b. Qualified dividends	Form 1040, line 9b
3. Net short-term capital gain	Schedule D, line 5, column (f)
4a. Net long-term capital gain	Schedule D, line 12, column (f)
4b. 28% rate gain	Line 4 of the worksheet for Schedule D, line 18
4c. Unrecaptured section 1250 gain	Line 11 of the worksheet for Schedule D, line 19
5. Other portfolio and nonbusiness income	Schedule E, line 33, column (f)
6. Ordinary business Income	Schedule E, line 33, column (d) or (f)
7. Net rental real estate income	Schedule E, line 33, column (d) or (f)
8. Other rental income	Schedule E, line 33, column (d) or (f)
9. Directly apportioned deductions	
Code	
A Depreciation	Form 8582 or Schedule E, line 33, column (c) or (e)
B Depletion	Form 8582 or Schedule E, line 33, column (c) or (e)
C Amortization	Form 8582 or Schedule E, line 33, column (c) or (e)
10. Estate tax deduction	Schedule A, line 27
11. Final year deductions	
A Excess deductions	Schedule A, line 22
B Short-term capital loss carryover	Schedule D, line 5, column (f)
C Long-term capital loss carryover	Schedule D, line 12, column (f); line 5 of the wksht. for Sch. D, line 18; and line 16 of the wksht. for Sch. D, line 19
D Net operating loss carryover – regular tax	Form 1040, line 21
E Net operating loss carryover – minimum tax	Form 6251, line 27

12. Alternative minimum tax items	
Code	*Report on*
A Adjustment for minimum tax purposes	Form 6251, line 14
B AMT adjustment attributable to qualified dividends	See the beneficiary's instructions and the Instructions for Form 6251
C AMT adjustment attributable to net short-term capital gain	(same)
D AMT adjustment attributable to net long-term capital gain	(same)
E AMT adjustment attributable to unrecaptured section 1250 gain	(same)
F AMT adjustment attributable to 28% rate gain	(same)
G Accelerated depreciation	(same)
H Depletion	(same)
I Amortization	(same)
J Exclusion items	2007 Form 8801
13. Credits and credit recapture	
A Credit for estimated taxes	Form 1040, line 65
B Credit for backup withholding	Form 1040, line 64
C Low-income housing credit	Form 3800, line 1e
D Qualified rehabilitation expenditures	See the beneficiary's instructions
E Basis of other investment credit property	See the beneficiary's instructions
F Work opportunity credit	Form 3800, line 1b
G Welfare-to-work credit	Form 3800, line 1c
H Alcohol fuel credit	Form 6478, line 5 (also see the beneficiary's instructions)
I Credit for increasing research activities	Form 3800, line 1d
J Renewable electricity, refined coal, and Indian coal production credit	See the beneficiary's instructions
K Empowerment zone and renewal community employment credit	Form 8844, line 3
L Indian employment credit	Form 3800, line 1i
M Orphan drug credit	Form 3800, line 1k
N Credit for employer provided child care and facilities	Form 3800, line 1n
O Biodiesel and renewable diesel fuels credit	Form 8864, line 9 (also see the beneficiary's instructions)
P Nonconventional source fuel credit	Form 3800, line 1s
Q Clean renewable energy bond and Gulf tax credit bond credits	See the beneficiary's instructions and Form 8912
R Credits for employers affected by Hurricane Katrina, Rita, or Wilma	Form 3800, line 1aa (also see the beneficiary's instructions)
S Energy efficient appliance credit	Form 3800, line 1u
T Recapture of credits	See the beneficiary's instructions
14. Other information	
A Tax-exempt interest	Form 1040, line 8b
B Foreign taxes	Form 1040, line 47 or Sch. A, line 8
C Qualified production activities income	Form 8903, line 7
D Form W-2 wages	Form 8903, line 13
E Net investment income	Form 4952, line 4a
F Gross farm and fishing income	Schedule E, line 42
G Foreign trading gross receipts (IRC 942(a))	See the instructions for Form 8873
H Other information	See the beneficiary's instructions

Note. If you are a beneficiary who does not file a Form 1040, see instructions for the type of income tax return you are filing.

Form **1116** — Department of the Treasury, Internal Revenue Service (99)

Foreign Tax Credit

(Individual, Estate, or Trust)

▶ **Attach to Form 1040, 1040NR, 1041, or 990-T.**

▶ **See separate instructions.**

OMB No. 1545-0121 — **2006** — Attachment Sequence No. **19**

Name: Andrew Roberts — **Identifying number** as shown on page 1 of your tax return: 123-45-6789

Use a separate Form 1116 for each category of income listed below. See **Categories of Income** on page 3 of the instructions. Check only one box on each Form 1116. Report all amounts in U.S. dollars except where specified in Part II below.

- a ☒ Passive income
- b ☐ High withholding tax interest
- c ☐ Financial services income
- d ☐ Shipping income
- e ☐ Dividends from a DISC or former DISC
- f ☐ Certain distributions from a foreign sales corporation (FSC) or former FSC
- g ☐ Lump-sum distributions
- h ☐ Section 901(j) income
- i ☐ Certain income re-sourced by treaty
- j ☐ General limitation income

k Resident of (name of country) ▶ United States

Note: *If you paid taxes to only one foreign country or U.S. possession, use column A in Part I and line A in Part II. If you paid taxes to* ***more than one*** *foreign country or U.S. possession, use a separate column and line for each country or possession.*

Part I Taxable Income or Loss From Sources Outside the United States (for Category Checked Above)

	Foreign Country or U.S. Possession A	B	C		Total (Add cols. A, B, and C.)
I **Enter the name of the foreign country or U.S. possession** ▶	Canada				
1a Gross income from sources within country shown above and of the type checked above (see page 13 of the instructions): Dividends	18,936			1a	18,936
b Check if line 1a is compensation for personal services as an employee, your total compensation from all sources is $250,000 or more, and you used an alternative basis to determine its source (see instructions) ▶ ☐					
Deductions and losses (*Caution:* *See pages 13 and 14 of the instructions*):					
2 Expenses **definitely related** to the income on line 1a (attach statement)					
3 Pro rata share of other deductions **not definitely related:**					
a Certain itemized deductions or standard deduction (see instructions)					
b Other deductions (attach statement)					
c Add lines 3a and 3b					
d Gross foreign source income (see instructions)					
e Gross income from all sources (see instructions)					
f Divide line 3d by line 3e (see instructions)					
g Multiply line 3c by line 3f					
4 Pro rata share of interest expense (see instructions):					
a Home mortgage interest (use worksheet on page 13 of the instructions)					
b Other interest expense					
5 Losses from foreign sources					
6 Add lines 2, 3g, 4a, 4b, and 5	-0-			6	-0-
7 Subtract line 6 from line 1a. Enter the result here and on line 14, page 2 ▶				7	18,936

Part II Foreign Taxes Paid or Accrued (see page 14 of the instructions)

Credit is claimed for taxes (you must check one): (m) ☒ Paid (n) ☐ Accrued

Country	(o) Date paid or accrued	In foreign currency — Taxes withheld at source on: (p) Dividends	(q) Rents and royalties	(r) Interest	(s) Other foreign taxes paid or accrued	In U.S. dollars — Taxes withheld at source on: (t) Dividends	(u) Rents and royalties	(v) Interest	(w) Other foreign taxes paid or accrued	(x) Total foreign taxes paid or accrued (add cols. (t) through (w))
A	12-31-06	4,500*				2,840				2,840
B										
C										

8 Add lines A through C, column (x). Enter the total here and on line 9, page 2 ▶ 8 **2,840**

For Paperwork Reduction Act Notice, see page 18 of the instructions. Cat. No. 11440U Form **1116** (2006)

*Canadian dollars

Form 1116 (2006) Page **2**

Part III Figuring the Credit

Line	Description		Amount		Amount
9	Enter the amount from line 8. These are your total foreign taxes paid or accrued for the category of income checked above Part I	9	2,840		
10	Carryback or carryover (attach detailed computation)	10			
11	Add lines 9 and 10	11	2,840		
12	Reduction in foreign taxes (see page 15 of the instructions)	12	-0-		
13	Subtract line 12 from line 11. This is the total amount of foreign taxes available for credit			13	2,840
14	Enter the amount from line 7. This is your taxable income or (loss) from sources outside the United States (before adjustments) for the category of income checked above Part I (see page 15 of the instructions)	14	18,936		
15	Adjustments to line 14 (see pages 15 and 16 of the instructions)	15			
16	Combine the amounts on lines 14 and 15. This is your net foreign source taxable income. (If the result is zero or less, you have no foreign tax credit for the category of income you checked above Part I. Skip lines 17 through 21. However, if you are filing more than one Form 1116, you must complete line 19.)	16	18,936		
17	**Individuals:** Enter the amount from Form 1040, line 41 (minus any amount on Form 8914, line 6). If you are a nonresident alien, enter the amount from Form 1040NR, line 38 (minus any amount on Form 8914, line 6). **Estates and trusts:** Enter your taxable income without the deduction for your exemption	17	86,000		
	Caution: *If you figured your tax using the lower rates on qualified dividends or capital gains, see page 16 of the instructions.*				
18	Divide line 16 by line 17. If line 16 is more than line 17, enter "1"			18	0.22019
19	**Individuals:** Enter the amount from Form 1040, line 44. If you are a nonresident alien, enter the amount from Form 1040NR, line 41. **Estates and trusts:** Enter the amount from Form 1041, Schedule G, line 1a, or the total of Form 990-T, lines 36 and 37			19	12,965*
	Caution: *If you are completing line 19 for separate category **g** (lump-sum distributions), see page 18 of the instructions.*				
20	Multiply line 19 by line 18 (maximum amount of credit)			20	2,855
21	Enter the **smaller** of line 13 or line 20. If this is the only Form 1116 you are filing, skip lines 22 through 30 and enter this amount on line 31. Otherwise, complete the appropriate line in Part IV (see page 18 of the instructions) ▶			21	2,855

Part IV Summary of Credits From Separate Parts III (see page 18 of the instructions)

Line	Description		Amount		Amount
22	Credit for taxes on passive income	22			
23	Credit for taxes on high withholding tax interest	23			
24	Credit for taxes on financial services income	24			
25	Credit for taxes on shipping income	25			
26	Credit for taxes on dividends from a DISC or former DISC and certain distributions from a FSC or former FSC	26			
27	Credit for taxes on lump-sum distributions	27			
28	Credit for taxes on certain income re-sourced by treaty	28			
29	Credit for taxes on general limitation income	29			
30	Add lines 22 through 29			30	
31	Enter the **smaller** of line 19 or line 30			31	2,855
32	Reduction of credit for international boycott operations. See instructions for line 12 on page 15			32	
33	Subtract line 32 from line 31. This is your **foreign tax credit.** Enter here and on Form 1040, line 47; Form 1040NR, line 44; Form 1041, Schedule G, line 2a; or Form 990-T, line 40a ▶			33	2,855

Form **1116** (2006)

*Tax on $86,000 – (2 x $3,300) = $79,400 taxable income

Form **2555** Department of the Treasury Internal Revenue Service (99)

Foreign Earned Income

▶ See separate instructions. ▶ Attach to Form 1040.

OMB No. 1545-0074 **2006** Attachment Sequence No. 34

For Use by U.S. Citizens and Resident Aliens Only

Name shown on Form 1040: Lawrence E. Smith | Your social security number: 234 56 7890

Part I General Information

1 Your foreign address (including country): 123 Rue de Harve 75011 Paris France
2 Your occupation: Financial Vice-President

3 Employer's name ▶ Very Public Corporation
4a Employer's U.S. address ▶ 90 Fifty Avenue, New York, NY 10011
b Employer's foreign address ▶ 11 Rue de Nanettes/5 e'Etage, 75011 Paris France
5 Employer is (check any that apply): a ☐ A foreign entity b ☒ A U.S. company c ☐ Self d ☐ A foreign affiliate of a U.S. company e ☐ Other (specify) ▶
6a If, after 1981, you filed Form 2555 or Form 2555-EZ, enter the last year you filed the form. ▶ 2005
b If you did not file Form 2555 or 2555-EZ after 1981 to claim either of the exclusions, check here ▶ ☐ and go to line 7.
c Have you ever revoked either of the exclusions? ☐ Yes ☒ No
d If you answered "Yes," enter the type of exclusion and the tax year for which the revocation was effective. ▶
7 Of what country are you a citizen/national? ▶ United States
8a Did you maintain a separate foreign residence for your family because of adverse living conditions at your tax home? See **Second foreign household** on page 3 of the instructions ☐ Yes ☒ No
b If "Yes," enter city and country of the separate foreign residence. Also, enter the number of days during your tax year that you maintained a second household at that address. ▶ N/A
9 List your tax home(s) during your tax year and date(s) established. ▶ 123 Rue de Harve, 75011 Paris France July 10, 2005

Next, complete either Part II or Part III. If an item does not apply, enter "NA." If you do not give the information asked for, any exclusion or deduction you claim may be disallowed.

Part II Taxpayers Qualifying Under Bona Fide Residence Test (see page 2 of the instructions)

10 Date bona fide residence began ▶ July 10, 2005, and ended ▶ Presently a resident
11 Kind of living quarters in foreign country ▶ a ☐ Purchased house b ☒ Rented house or apartment c ☐ Rented room d ☐ Quarters furnished by employer
12a Did any of your family live with you abroad during any part of the tax year? ☒ Yes ☐ No
b If "Yes," who and for what period? ▶ Wife and two children for entire year
13a Have you submitted a statement to the authorities of the foreign country where you claim bona fide residence that you are not a resident of that country? See instructions ☐ Yes ☒ No
b Are you required to pay income tax to the country where you claim bona fide residence? See instructions ☒ Yes ☐ No
If you answered "Yes" to 13a and "No" to 13b, you do not qualify as a bona fide resident. Do not complete the rest of this part.
14 If you were present in the United States or its possessions during the tax year, complete columns **(a)–(d)** below. **Do not** include the income from column **(d)** in Part IV, but report it on Form 1040.

(a) Date arrived in U.S.	(b) Date left U.S.	(c) Number of days in U.S. on business	(d) Income earned in U.S. on business (attach computation)	(a) Date arrived in U.S.	(b) Date left U.S.	(c) Number of days in U.S. on business	(d) Income earned in U.S. on business (attach computation)
2-19-06	2-23-06	5	1,200				

15a List any contractual terms or other conditions relating to the length of your employment abroad. ▶ Indefinite
b Enter the type of visa under which you entered the foreign country. ▶ Resident
c Did your visa limit the length of your stay or employment in a foreign country? If "Yes," attach explanation ☐ Yes ☒ No
d Did you maintain a home in the United States while living abroad? ☒ Yes ☐ No
e If "Yes," enter address of your home, whether it was rented, the names of the occupants, and their relationship to you. ▶ 4710 N.W. 68th Terrace, Gainesville, FL 32601 (rented to unrelated party)

Form 2555 (2006) Page **2**

Part III Taxpayers Qualifying Under Physical Presence Test (see page 2 of the instructions)

16 The physical presence test is based on the 12-month period from ▶ N/A through ▶

17 Enter your principal country of employment during your tax year. ▶

18 If you traveled abroad during the 12-month period entered on line 16, complete columns **(a)–(f)** below. Exclude travel between foreign countries that did not involve travel on or over international waters, or in or over the United States, for 24 hours or more. If you have no travel to report during the period, enter "Physically present in a foreign country or countries for the entire 12-month period." **Do not** include the income from column **(f)** below in Part IV, but report it on Form 1040.

(a) Name of country (including U.S.)	**(b)** Date arrived	**(c)** Date left	**(d)** Full days present in country	**(e)** Number of days in U.S. on business	**(f)** Income earned in U.S. on business (attach computation)

Part IV All Taxpayers

Note: *Enter on lines 19 through 23 all income, including noncash income, you earned and actually or constructively received during your 2006 tax year for services you performed in a foreign country. If any of the foreign earned income received this tax year was earned in a prior tax year, or will be earned in a later tax year (such as a bonus), see the instructions.* ***Do not*** *include income from line 14, column* ***(d)****, or line 18, column* ***(f)****. Report amounts in U.S. dollars, using the exchange rates in effect when you actually or constructively received the income.*

If you are a cash basis taxpayer, report on Form 1040 all income you received in 2006, no matter when you performed the service.

	2006 Foreign Earned Income				**Amount (in U.S. dollars)**
19	Total wages, salaries, bonuses, commissions, etc.			19	60,000
20	Allowable share of income for personal services performed (see instructions):				
a	In a business (including farming) or profession			20a	
b	In a partnership. List partnership's name and address and type of income. ▶			20b	
21	Noncash income (market value of property or facilities furnished by employer–attach statement showing how it was determined):				
a	Home (lodging)			21a	
b	Meals			21b	
c	Car			21c	
d	Other property or facilities. List type and amount. ▶			21d	
22	Allowances, reimbursements, or expenses paid on your behalf for services you performed:				
a	Cost of living and overseas differential	22a	27,000		
b	Family	22b			
c	Education	22c	8,000		
d	Home leave	22d	6,400		
e	Quarters	22e	21,300		
f	For any other purpose. List type and amount. ▶ Less U.S. Source Income	22f	(1,200)		
g	Add lines 22a through 22f			22g	61,500
23	Other foreign earned income. List type and amount. ▶			23	
24	Add lines 19 through 21d, line 22g, and line 23			24	121,500
25	Total amount of meals and lodging included on line 24 that is excludable (see instructions)			25	
26	Subtract line 25 from line 24. Enter the result here and on line 27 on page 3. This is your **2006 foreign earned income** ▶			26	121,500

Form 2555 (2006) Page **3**

Part V **All Taxpayers**

27	Enter the amount from line 26	27	121,500

Are you claiming the housing exclusion or housing deduction?
☒ **Yes.** Complete Part VI.
☐ **No.** Go to Part VII.

Part VI **Taxpayers Claiming the Housing Exclusion and/or Deduction**

28	Qualified housing expenses for the tax year (see instructions)	28	21,300
29a	Enter location where housing expenses incurred (see instructions) ▶		
b	Enter limit on housing expenses (see instructions)	29b	
30	Enter the **smaller** of line 28 or line 29b	30	
31	Number of days in your qualifying period that fall within your 2006 tax year (see instructions) — 31 — 365 days		
32	Multiply $36.12 by the number of days on line 31. If 365 is entered on line 31, enter $13,184.00 here	32	13,184
33	Subtract line 32 from line 30. If the result is zero or less, do not complete the rest of this part or any of Part IX	33	8,116
34	Enter employer-provided amounts (see instructions) — 34 — 8,116		
35	Divide line 34 by line 27. Enter the result as a decimal (rounded to at least three places), but do not enter more than "1.000"	35	× 1. 00
36	**Housing exclusion.** Multiply line 33 by line 35. Enter the result but do not enter more than the amount on line 34. Also, complete Part VIII ▶	36	8,116

Note: *The housing deduction is figured in Part IX. If you choose to claim the foreign earned income exclusion, complete Parts VII and VIII before Part IX.*

Part VII **Taxpayers Claiming the Foreign Earned Income Exclusion**

37	Maximum foreign earned income exclusion	37	$82,400 00
38	• If you completed Part VI, enter the number from line 31. • All others, enter the number of days in your qualifying period that fall within your 2006 tax year (see the instructions for line 31). — 38 — 365 days		
39	• If line 38 and the number of days in your 2006 tax year (usually 365) are the same, enter "1.000." • Otherwise, divide line 38 by the number of days in your 2006 tax year and enter the result as a decimal (rounded to at least three places).	39	× 1. 00
40	Multiply line 37 by line 39	40	82,400
41	Subtract line 36 from line 27	41	112,391
42	**Foreign earned income exclusion.** Enter the **smaller** of line 40 or line 41. Also, complete Part VIII ▶	42	82,400

Part VIII **Taxpayers Claiming the Housing Exclusion, Foreign Earned Income Exclusion, or Both**

43	Add lines 36 and 42	43	90,516
44	Deductions allowed in figuring your adjusted gross income (Form 1040, line 37) that are allocable to the excluded income. See instructions and attach computation	44	
45	Subtract line 44 from line 43. Enter the result here and in parentheses on **Form 1040, line 21.** Next to the amount enter "Form 2555." On Form 1040, subtract this amount from your income to arrive at total income on Form 1040, line 22 ▶	45	90,516

Part IX **Taxpayers Claiming the Housing Deduction–** Complete this part only if **(a)** line 33 is more than line 36 and **(b)** line 27 is more than line 43.

46	Subtract line 36 from line 33	46	
47	Subtract line 43 from line 27	47	
48	Enter the **smaller** of line 46 or line 47	48	

Note: *If line 47 is* ***more than*** *line 48 and you could not deduct all of your 2005 housing deduction because of the 2005 limit, use the worksheet on page 4 of the instructions to figure the amount to enter on line 49. Otherwise, go to line 50.*

49	Housing deduction carryover from 2005 (from worksheet on page 4 of the instructions)	49	
50	**Housing deduction.** Add lines 48 and 49. Enter the total here and on Form 1040 to the left of line 36. Next to the amount on Form 1040, enter "Form 2555." Add it to the total adjustments reported on that line ▶	50	N/A

Form **2555** (2006)

APPENDIX C

MACRS TABLES

MACRS, ADS and ACRS Depreciation Methods Summary

System	Characteristics	Depreciation Method: MACRS	Depreciation Method: ADS	Table No.[a] MACRS	Table No.[a] ADS
MACRS & ADS	Personal Property:				
	1. Accounting convention	Half-year or mid-quarter	Half-year or mid-quarter[b]		
	2. Life and method				
	a. 3-year, 5-year, 7-year, 10-year	200% DB or elect straight-line	150% DB or elect straight-line	1, 2, 3, 4, 5	10, 11[c]
	b. 15-year, 20-year	150% DB or elect straight-line	150% DB or elect straight-line[d]	1, 2, 3, 4, 5	
	3. Luxury Automobile Limitations			6	
	Real property:				
	1. Accounting convention	Mid-month	Mid-month		
	2. Life and method				
	a. Residential rental property	27.5 years, straight-line	40 years straight-line	7	12
	b. Nonresidential real property	39 years, straight-line[e]	40 years straight-line	9	12
	Characteristics	**ACRS**			
ACRS[f]	Personal Property				
	1. Accounting convention	Half-year			
	2. Life and method				
	a. 3-year, 5-year, 10-year, 15-year	150% DB or elect straight-line			
	Real Property				
	1. Accounting convention	First of month or mid-month			
	2. Life				
	a. 15-year property	Placed in service after 12/31/80 and before 3/16/84			
	b. 18-year property	Placed in service after 3/15/84 and before 5/9/85			
	c. 19-year property	Placed in service after 5/8/85 and before 1/1/87			
	3. Method				
	a. All but low-income housing	175% DB or elect straight-line			
	b. Low-income housing property	200% DB or elect straight-line			

[a] All depreciation tables in this appendix are based upon tables contained in Rev. Proc. 87-57, as amended.

[b] General and ADS tables are available for property lives from 2.5–50.0 years using the straight-line method. These tables are contained in Rev. Proc. 87-57 and are only partially reproduced here.

[c] The mid-quarter tables are available in Rev. Proc. 87-57, but are not reproduced here.

[d] Special recovery periods are assigned certain MACRS properties under the alternative depreciation system.

[e] A 31.5-year recovery period applied to nonresidential real property placed in service under the MACRS rules prior to May 13, 1993 (see Table 8).

[f] ACRS was effective for years 1981–1986. ACRS tables are no longer reproduced in this textbook.

▼ **TABLE 1**

General Depreciation System—MACRS
Personal Property Placed in Service after 12/31/86
Applicable Convention: Half-year
Applicable Depreciation Method: 200 or 150 Percent Declining Balance Switching to Straight Line

If the Recovery Year Is:	And the Recovery Period Is: 3-Year	5-Year	7-Year	10-Year	15-Year	20-Year
	The Depreciation Rate Is:					
1	33.33	20.00	14.29	10.00	5.00	3.750
2	44.45	32.00	24.49	18.00	9.50	7.219
3	14.81	19.20	17.49	14.40	8.55	6.677
4	7.41	11.52	12.49	11.52	7.70	6.177
5		11.52	8.93	9.22	6.93	5.713
6		5.76	8.92	7.37	6.23	5.285
7			8.93	6.55	5.90	4.888
8			4.46	6.55	5.90	4.522
9				6.56	5.91	4.462
10				6.55	5.90	4.461
11				3.28	5.91	4.462
12					5.90	4.461
13					5.91	4.462
14					5.90	4.461
15					5.91	4.462
16					2.95	4.461
17						4.462
18						4.461
19						4.462
20						4.461
21						2.231

▼ TABLE 2

General Depreciation System—MACRS
Personal Property Placed in Service after 12/31/86
Applicable Convention: Mid-quarter (Property Placed in Service in First Quarter)
Applicable Depreciation Method: 200 or 150 Percent Declining Balance Switching to Straight Line

If the Recovery Year Is:	And the Recovery Period Is: 3-Year	5-Year	7-Year	10-Year	15-Year	20-Year
	The Depreciation Rate Is:					
1	58.33	35.00	25.00	17.50	8.75	6.563
2	27.78	26.00	21.43	16.50	9.13	7.000
3	12.35	15.60	15.31	13.20	8.21	6.482
4	1.54	11.01	10.93	10.56	7.39	5.996
5		11.01	8.75	8.45	6.65	5.546
6		1.38	8.74	6.76	5.99	5.130
7			8.75	6.55	5.90	4.746
8			1.09	6.55	5.91	4.459
9				6.56	5.90	4.459
10				6.55	5.91	4.459
11				0.82	5.90	4.459
12					5.91	4.460
13					5.90	4.459
14					5.91	4.460
15					5.90	4.459
16					0.74	4.460
17						4.459
18						4.460
19						4.459
20						4.460
21						0.557

▼ **TABLE 3**

General Depreciation System—MACRS
Personal Property Placed in Service after 12/31/86
Applicable Convention: Mid-quarter (Property Placed in Service in Second Quarter)
Applicable Depreciation Method: 200 or 150 Percent Declining Balance Switching to Straight Line

If the Recovery Year Is:	And the Recovery Period Is: 3-Year	5-Year	7-Year	10-Year	15-Year	20-Year
	The Depreciation Rate Is:					
1	41.67	25.00	17.85	12.50	6.25	4.688
2	38.89	30.00	23.47	17.50	9.38	7.148
3	14.14	18.00	16.76	14.00	8.44	6.612
4	5.30	11.37	11.97	11.20	7.59	6.116
5		11.37	8.87	8.96	6.83	5.658
6		4.26	8.87	7.17	6.15	5.233
7			8.87	6.55	5.91	4.841
8			3.33	6.55	5.90	4.478
9				6.56	5.91	4.463
10				6.55	5.90	4.463
11				2.46	5.91	4.463
12					5.90	4.463
13					5.91	4.463
14					5.90	4.463
15					5.91	4.462
16					2.21	4.463
17						4.462
18						4.463
19						4.462
20						4.463
21						1.673

▼ **TABLE 4**

General Depreciation System—MACRS
Personal Property Placed in Service after 12/31/86
Applicable Convention: Mid-quarter (Property Placed in Service in Third Quarter)
Applicable Depreciation Method: 200 or 150 Percent Declining Balance Switching to Straight Line

If the Recovery Year Is:	And the Recovery Period Is: 3-Year	5-Year	7-Year	10-Year	15-Year	20-Year
	The Depreciation Rate Is:					
1	25.00	15.00	10.71	7.50	3.75	2.813
2	50.00	34.00	25.51	18.50	9.63	7.289
3	16.67	20.40	18.22	14.80	8.66	6.742
4	8.33	12.24	13.02	11.84	7.80	6.237
5		11.30	9.30	9.47	7.02	5.769
6		7.06	8.85	7.58	6.31	5.336
7			8.86	6.55	5.90	4.936
8			5.53	6.55	5.90	4.566
9				6.56	5.91	4.460
10				6.55	5.90	4.460
11				4.10	5.91	4.460
12					5.90	4.460
13					5.91	4.461
14					5.90	4.460
15					5.91	4.461
16					3.69	4.460
17						4.461
18						4.460
19						4.461
20						4.460
21						2.788

▼ **TABLE 5**

General Depreciation System—MACRS
Personal Property Placed in Service after 12/31/86
Applicable Convention: Mid-quarter (Property Placed in Service in Fourth Quarter)
Applicable Depreciation Method: 200 or 150 Percent Declining Balance Switching to Straight Line

If the Recovery Year Is:	And the Recovery Period Is: 3-Year	5-Year	7-Year	10-Year	15-Year	20-Year
	The Depreciation Rate Is:					
1	8.33	5.00	3.57	2.50	1.25	0.938
2	61.11	38.00	27.55	19.50	9.88	7.430
3	20.37	22.80	19.68	15.60	8.89	6.872
4	10.19	13.68	14.06	12.48	8.00	6.357
5		10.94	10.04	9.98	7.20	5.880
6		9.58	8.73	7.99	6.48	5.439
7			8.73	6.55	5.90	5.031
8			7.64	6.55	5.90	4.654
9				6.56	5.90	4.458
10				6.55	5.91	4.458
11				5.74	5.90	4.458
12					5.91	4.458
13					5.90	4.458
14					5.91	4.458
15					5.90	4.458
16					5.17	4.458
17						4.458
18						4.459
19						4.458
20						4.459
21						3.901

▼ **TABLE 6**

Luxury Automobile Limitations

	Year Automobile is Placed in Service[a]: 2007	2006	2005	2004[b]	2004[c]
Year 1	3,060	2,960	2,960	10,610	2,960
Year 2	4,900	4,800	4,700	4,800	4,800
Year 3	2,850	2,850	2,850	2,850	2,850
Year 4 and Each Succeeding Year	1,775	1,775	1,675	1,675	1,675

[a]For years prior to 2004, see Revenue Procedure for appropriate year.
[b]Luxury automobiles placed in service in 2004 and 50% or 30% bonus depreciation elected.
[c]Luxury automobiles placed in service in 2004 and bonus depreciation not elected.

▼ TABLE 6 (continued)
Trucks and Vans Limitations

	Year Truck or Van is Placed in Service: 2007	2006 & 2005	2004[a]	2004[b]
Year 1	3,260	3,260	10,910	3,260
Year 2	5,200	5,200	5,300	5,300
Year 3	3,050	3,150	3,150	3,150
Year 4 and Succeeding Years	1,875	1,875	1,875	1,875

[a]For trucks and vans placed in service in 2004 and bonus depreciation is elected.
[b]For trucks and vans placed in service in 2004 and bonus depreciation not elected.

▼ TABLE 7
General Depreciation System—MACRS
Residential Rental Real Property Placed in Service after 12/31/86
Applicable Recovery Period: 27.5 Years
Applicable Convention: Mid-month
Applicable Depreciation Method: Straight Line

If the Recovery Year Is:	And the Month in the First Recovery Year the Property Is Placed in Service Is: 1	2	3	4	5	6	7	8	9	10	11	12
	The Depreciation Rate Is:											
1	3.485	3.182	2.879	2.576	2.273	1.970	1.667	1.364	1.061	0.758	0.455	0.152
2	3.636	3.636	3.636	3.636	3.636	3.636	3.636	3.636	3.636	3.636	3.636	3.636
3	3.636	3.636	3.636	3.636	3.636	3.636	3.636	3.636	3.636	3.636	3.636	3.636
4	3.636	3.636	3.636	3.636	3.636	3.636	3.636	3.636	3.636	3.636	3.636	3.636
5	3.636	3.636	3.636	3.636	3.636	3.636	3.636	3.636	3.636	3.636	3.636	3.636
6	3.636	3.636	3.636	3.636	3.636	3.636	3.636	3.636	3.636	3.636	3.636	3.636
7	3.636	3.636	3.636	3.636	3.636	3.636	3.636	3.636	3.636	3.636	3.636	3.636
8	3.636	3.636	3.636	3.636	3.636	3.636	3.636	3.636	3.636	3.636	3.636	3.636
9	3.636	3.636	3.636	3.636	3.636	3.636	3.636	3.636	3.636	3.636	3.636	3.636
10	3.637	3.637	3.637	3.637	3.637	3.637	3.636	3.636	3.636	3.636	3.636	3.636
11	3.636	3.636	3.636	3.636	3.636	3.636	3.637	3.637	3.637	3.637	3.637	3.637
12	3.637	3.637	3.637	3.637	3.637	3.637	3.636	3.636	3.636	3.636	3.636	3.636
13	3.636	3.636	3.636	3.636	3.636	3.636	3.637	3.637	3.637	3.637	3.637	3.637
14	3.637	3.637	3.637	3.637	3.637	3.637	3.636	3.636	3.636	3.636	3.636	3.636
15	3.636	3.636	3.636	3.636	3.636	3.636	3.637	3.637	3.637	3.637	3.637	3.637
16	3.637	3.637	3.637	3.637	3.637	3.637	3.636	3.636	3.636	3.636	3.636	3.636
17	3.636	3.636	3.636	3.636	3.636	3.636	3.637	3.637	3.637	3.637	3.637	3.637
18	3.637	3.637	3.637	3.637	3.637	3.637	3.636	3.636	3.636	3.636	3.636	3.636
19	3.636	3.636	3.636	3.636	3.636	3.636	3.637	3.637	3.637	3.637	3.637	3.637
20	3.637	3.637	3.637	3.637	3.637	3.637	3.636	3.636	3.636	3.636	3.636	3.636
21	3.636	3.636	3.636	3.636	3.636	3.636	3.637	3.637	3.637	3.637	3.637	3.637
22	3.637	3.637	3.637	3.637	3.637	3.637	3.636	3.636	3.636	3.636	3.636	3.636
23	3.636	3.636	3.636	3.636	3.636	3.636	3.637	3.637	3.637	3.637	3.637	3.637
24	3.637	3.637	3.637	3.637	3.637	3.637	3.636	3.636	3.636	3.636	3.636	3.636
25	3.636	3.636	3.636	3.636	3.636	3.636	3.637	3.637	3.637	3.637	3.637	3.637
26	3.637	3.637	3.637	3.637	3.637	3.637	3.636	3.636	3.636	3.636	3.636	3.636
27	3.636	3.636	3.636	3.636	3.636	3.636	3.637	3.637	3.637	3.637	3.637	3.637
28	1.970	2.273	2.576	2.879	3.182	3.485	3.636	3.636	3.636	3.636	3.636	3.636
29	0.000	0.000	0.000	0.000	0.000	0.000	0.152	0.455	0.758	1.061	1.364	1.667

▼ TABLE 8

General Depreciation System—MACRS
Nonresidential Real Property Placed in Service after 12/31/86 and before 5/13/93
Applicable Recovery Period: 31.5 Years
Applicable Convention: Mid-month
Applicable Depreciation Method: Straight Line

If the Recovery Year Is:	And the Month in the First Recovery Year the Property Is Placed in Service Is: 1	2	3	4	5	6	7	8	9	10	11	12
	The Depreciation Rate Is:											
1	3.042	2.778	2.513	2.249	1.984	1.720	1.455	1.190	0.926	0.661	0.397	0.132
2	3.175	3.175	3.175	3.175	3.175	3.175	3.175	3.175	3.175	3.175	3.175	3.175
3	3.175	3.175	3.175	3.175	3.175	3.175	3.175	3.175	3.175	3.175	3.175	3.175
4	3.175	3.175	3.175	3.175	3.175	3.175	3.175	3.175	3.175	3.175	3.175	3.175
5	3.175	3.175	3.175	3.175	3.175	3.175	3.175	3.175	3.175	3.175	3.175	3.175
6	3.175	3.175	3.175	3.175	3.175	3.175	3.175	3.175	3.175	3.175	3.175	3.175
7	3.175	3.175	3.175	3.175	3.175	3.175	3.175	3.175	3.175	3.175	3.175	3.175
8	3.175	3.174	3.175	3.174	3.175	3.174	3.175	3.175	3.175	3.175	3.175	3.175
9	3.174	3.175	3.174	3.175	3.174	3.175	3.174	3.175	3.174	3.175	3.174	3.175
10	3.175	3.174	3.175	3.174	3.175	3.174	3.175	3.174	3.175	3.174	3.175	3.174
11	3.174	3.175	3.174	3.175	3.174	3.175	3.174	3.175	3.174	3.175	3.174	3.175
12	3.175	3.174	3.175	3.174	3.175	3.174	3.175	3.174	3.175	3.174	3.175	3.174
13	3.174	3.175	3.174	3.175	3.174	3.175	3.174	3.175	3.174	3.175	3.174	3.175
14	3.175	3.174	3.175	3.174	3.175	3.174	3.175	3.174	3.175	3.174	3.175	3.174
15	3.174	3.175	3.174	3.175	3.174	3.175	3.174	3.175	3.174	3.175	3.174	3.175
16	3.175	3.174	3.175	3.174	3.175	3.174	3.175	3.174	3.175	3.174	3.175	3.174
17	3.174	3.175	3.174	3.175	3.174	3.175	3.174	3.175	3.174	3.175	3.174	3.175
18	3.175	3.174	3.175	3.174	3.175	3.174	3.175	3.174	3.175	3.174	3.175	3.174
19	3.174	3.175	3.174	3.175	3.174	3.175	3.174	3.175	3.174	3.175	3.174	3.175
20	3.175	3.174	3.175	3.174	3.175	3.174	3.175	3.174	3.175	3.174	3.175	3.174
21	3.174	3.175	3.174	3.175	3.174	3.175	3.174	3.175	3.174	3.175	3.174	3.175
22	3.175	3.174	3.175	3.174	3.175	3.174	3.175	3.174	3.175	3.174	3.175	3.174
23	3.174	3.175	3.174	3.175	3.174	3.175	3.174	3.175	3.174	3.175	3.174	3.175
24	3.175	3.174	3.175	3.174	3.175	3.174	3.175	3.174	3.175	3.174	3.175	3.174
25	3.174	3.175	3.174	3.175	3.174	3.175	3.174	3.175	3.174	3.175	3.174	3.175
26	3.175	3.174	3.175	3.174	3.175	3.174	3.175	3.174	3.175	3.174	3.175	3.174
27	3.174	3.175	3.174	3.175	3.174	3.175	3.174	3.175	3.174	3.175	3.174	3.175
28	3.175	3.174	3.175	3.174	3.175	3.174	3.175	3.174	3.175	3.174	3.175	3.174
29	3.174	3.175	3.174	3.175	3.174	3.175	3.174	3.175	3.174	3.175	3.174	3.175
30	3.175	3.174	3.175	3.174	3.175	3.174	3.175	3.174	3.175	3.174	3.175	3.174
31	3.174	3.175	3.174	3.175	3.174	3.175	3.174	3.175	3.174	3.175	3.174	3.175
32	1.720	1.984	2.249	2.513	2.778	3.042	3.175	3.174	3.175	3.174	3.175	3.174
33	0.000	0.000	0.000	0.000	0.000	0.000	0.132	0.397	0.661	0.926	1.190	1.455

▼ TABLE 9

General Depreciation System—MACRS
Nonresidential Real Property Placed in Service after 5/12/93
Applicable Recovery Period: 39 years
Applicable Depreciation Method: Straight Line

If the Recovery Year Is:	And the Month in the First Recovery Year the Property Is Placed in Service Is: 1	2	3	4	5	6	7	8	9	10	11	12
	The Depreciation Rate Is:											
1	2.461	2.247	2.033	1.819	1.605	1.391	1.177	0.963	0.749	0.535	0.321	0.107
2-39	2.564	2.564	2.564	2.564	2.564	2.564	2.564	2.564	2.564	2.564	2.564	2.564
40	0.107	0.321	0.535	0.749	0.963	1.177	1.391	1.605	1.819	2.033	2.247	2.461

▼ TABLE 10

Alternative Depreciation System—MACRS (Partial Table)
Property Placed in Service after 12/31/86
Applicable Convention: Half-year
Applicable Depreciation Method: 150 Percent Declining Balance Switching to Straight Line

If the Recovery Year Is:	And the Recovery Period Is: 3	4	5	7	10	12
	The Depreciation Rate Is:					
1	25.00	18.75	15.00	10.71	7.50	6.25
2	37.50	30.47	25.50	19.13	13.88	11.72
3	25.00	20.31	17.85	15.03	11.79	10.25
4	12.50	20.31	16.66	12.25	10.02	8.97
5		10.16	16.66	12.25	8.74	7.85
6			8.33	12.25	8.74	7.33
7				12.25	8.74	7.33
8				6.13	8.74	7.33
9					8.74	7.33
10					8.74	7.33
11					4.37	7.32
12						7.33
13						3.66

▼ **TABLE 11**

Alternative Depreciation System—MACRS (Partial Table)
Property Placed in Service after 12/31/86
Applicable Convention: Half-year
Applicable Depreciation Method: Straight Line

If the Recovery Year Is:	And the Recovery Period Is: 3	4	5	7	10	12
	The Depreciation Rate Is:					
1	16.67	12.50	10.00	7.14	5.00	4.17
2	33.33	25.00	20.00	14.29	10.00	8.33
3	33.33	25.00	20.00	14.29	10.00	8.33
4	16.67	25.00	20.00	14.28	10.00	8.33
5		12.50	20.00	14.29	10.00	8.33
6			10.00	14.28	10.00	8.33
7				14.29	10.00	8.34
8				7.14	10.00	8.33
9					10.00	8.34
10					10.00	8.33
11					5.00	8.34
12						8.33
13						4.17

▼ **TABLE 12**

Alternative Depreciation System—MACRS
Real Property Placed into Service after 12/31/86
Applicable Recovery Period: 40 years
Applicable Convention: Mid-month
Applicable Depreciation Method: Straight Line

If the Recovery Year Is:	And the Month in the First Recovery Year the Property Is Placed in Service Is: 1	2	3	4	5	6	7	8	9	10	11	12
	The Depreciation Rate Is:											
1	2.396	2.188	1.979	1.771	1.563	1.354	1.146	0.938	0.729	0.521	0.313	0.104
2 to 40	2.500	2.500	2.500	2.500	2.500	2.500	2.500	2.500	2.500	2.500	2.500	2.500
41	0.104	0.312	0.521	0.729	0.937	1.146	1.354	1.562	1.771	1.979	2.187	2.396

▼ TABLE 13
Lease Inclusion Dollar Amounts for Automobiles (Other Than for Trucks, Vans, or Electronic Automobiles) With a Lease Term Beginning in Calendar Year 2006[a]

Fair Market Value of Passenger Automobile		Tax Year During Lease				
Over	Not Over	1st	2nd	3rd	4th	5th and Later
$15,200	$15,500	4	6	10	10	10
15,500	15,800	6	10	16	18	18
15,800	16,100	8	15	22	25	28
16,100	16,400	9	19	29	33	36
16,400	16,700	11	24	35	40	45
16,700	17,000	13	28	42	48	53
17,000	17,500	16	34	50	58	66
17,500	18,000	19	41	61	71	80
18,000	18,500	23	48	71	84	95
18,500	19,000	26	55	82	96	110
19,000	19,500	29	62	93	109	125
19,500	20,000	32	70	103	122	139
20,000	20,500	36	76	114	135	154
20,500	21,000	39	84	124	148	168
21,000	21,500	42	91	135	160	184
21,500	22,000	45	98	146	173	198
22,000	23,000	50	109	162	192	220
23,000	24,000	57	123	183	218	250
24,000	25,000	63	138	204	243	279
25,000	26,000	70	152	225	269	309
26,000	27,000	76	166	247	294	339
27,000	28,000	83	181	268	319	368
28,000	29,000	90	195	289	345	397
29,000	30,000	96	209	311	371	426
30,000	31,000	103	223	332	397	455
31,000	32,000	109	238	353	422	485
32,000	33,000	116	252	374	448	515
33,000	34,000	122	267	395	473	545
34,000	35,000	129	281	417	498	574
35,000	36,000	135	295	439	523	604
36,000	37,000	142	309	460	549	633
37,000	38,000	148	324	481	575	662
38,000	39,000	155	338	502	601	691
39,000	40,000	161	353	523	626	721
40,000	41,000	168	367	545	651	750
41,000	42,000	175	381	566	677	780
42,000	43,000	181	396	587	702	810
43,000	44,000	188	410	608	728	839
44,000	45,000	194	424	630	753	869
45,000	46,000	201	438	651	779	898
46,000	47,000	207	453	672	805	927
47,000	48,000	214	467	694	830	956
48,000	49,000	220	482	715	855	986
49,000	50,000	227	496	736	881	1,016
50,000	51,000	233	510	758	906	1,045
51,000	52,000	240	525	778	932	1,075
52,000	53,000	246	539	800	958	1,104
53,000	54,000	253	553	821	984	1,133

[a]Per *Rev. Proc.* 2006-18. The table for 2007 had not been released at the date of the printing.

▼ TABLE 13[a] (continued)

Fair Market Value of Passenger Automobile		Tax Year During Lease				
Over	Not Over	1st	2nd	3rd	4th	5th and Later
54,000	55,000	259	568	842	1,009	1,163
55,000	56,000	266	582	864	1,034	1,192
56,000	57,000	273	596	885	1,060	1,221
57,000	58,000	279	611	906	1,085	1,251
58,000	59,000	286	625	927	1,111	1,281
59,000	60,000	292	639	949	1,136	1,311
60,000	62,000	302	661	981	1,174	1,354
62,000	64,000	315	690	1,023	1,225	1,413
64,000	66,000	328	718	1,066	1,276	1,473
66,000	68,000	341	747	1,108	1,328	1,531
68,000	70,000	354	776	1,151	1,378	1,590
70,000	72,000	367	804	1,194	1,429	1,649
72,000	74,000	380	833	1,236	1,481	1,707
74,000	76,000	393	862	1,278	1,532	1,767
76,000	78,000	407	890	1,321	1,583	1,825
78,000	80,000	420	919	1,363	1,634	1,884
80,000	85,000	443	969	1,438	1,723	1,987
85,000	90,000	475	1,041	1,544	1,851	2,135
90,000	95,000	508	1,112	1,651	1,978	2,282
95,000	100,000	541	1,184	1,757	2,106	2,429
100,000	110,000	590	1,291	1,917	2,297	2,650
110,000	120,000	655	1,435	2,130	2,552	2,944
120,000	130,000	720	1,579	2,342	2,807	3,239
130,000	140,000	786	1,722	2,555	3,062	3,534
140,000	150,000	851	1,865	2,768	3,317	3,829
150,000	160,000	916	2,009	2,980	3,573	4,123
160,000	170,000	982	2,152	3,193	3,828	4,417
170,000	180,000	1,047	2,295	3,406	4,083	4,712
180,000	190,000	1,112	2,439	3,619	4,337	5,007
190,000	200,000	1,178	2,582	3,832	4,592	5,301
200,000	210,000	1,243	2,726	4,044	4,848	5,595
210,000	220,000	1,309	2,869	4,257	5,103	5,890
220,000	230,000	1,374	3,012	4,470	5,358	6,185
230,000	240,000	1,439	3,156	4,682	5,613	6,480
240,000	and up	1,505	3,299	4,895	5,868	6,774

[a]Per *Rev. Proc.* 2006-18. The table for 2007 had not been released at the date of the printing.

▼ TABLE 14

Lease Inclusion Dollar Amounts for Trucks and Vans With a Lease Term Beginning in Calendar Year 2006[a]

Fair Market Value of Truck or Van		Tax Year During Lease				
Over	**Not Over**	**1st**	**2nd**	**3rd**	**4th**	**5th and Later**
$16,700	$ 17,000	4	8	12	14	16
17,000	17,500	6	14	20	24	29
17,500	18,000	9	21	31	37	43
18,000	18,500	13	28	42	49	58
18,500	19,000	16	36	52	62	72
19,000	19,500	19	43	63	75	87
19,500	20,000	23	50	73	88	102
20,000	20,500	26	57	84	101	116
20,500	21,000	29	64	95	113	131
21,000	21,500	32	72	105	126	146
21,500	22,000	36	78	116	139	161
22,000	23,000	41	89	132	158	183
23,000	24,000	47	104	153	183	213
24,000	25,000	54	118	174	209	242
25,000	26,000	60	132	196	235	271
26,000	27,000	67	146	217	261	300
27,000	28,000	73	161	238	286	330
28,000	29,000	80	175	260	311	359
29,000	30,000	86	190	281	336	389
30,000	31,000	93	204	302	362	418
31,000	32,000	99	219	323	388	447
32,000	33,000	106	233	344	413	478
33,000	34,000	112	247	366	439	506
34,000	35,000	119	261	387	465	536
35,000	36,000	125	276	408	490	566
36,000	37,000	132	290	430	515	595
37,000	38,000	139	304	451	541	624
38,000	39,000	145	319	472	566	654
39,000	40,000	152	333	493	592	684
40,000	41,000	158	347	515	618	712
41,000	42,000	165	362	536	642	743
42,000	43,000	171	376	557	669	772
43,000	44,000	178	390	579	694	801
44,000	45,000	184	405	600	719	831
45,000	46,000	191	419	621	745	860
46,000	47,000	197	434	642	770	890
47,000	48,000	204	448	663	796	919
48,000	49,000	210	462	685	822	948
49,000	50,000	217	476	707	847	977
50,000	51,000	224	490	728	872	1,008
51,000	52,000	230	505	749	898	1,037
52,000	53,000	237	519	770	924	1,066
53,000	54,000	243	534	791	949	1,096
54,000	55,000	250	548	813	974	1,125
55,000	56,000	256	563	833	1,000	1,155
56,000	57,000	263	577	855	1,025	1,184
57,000	58,000	269	591	877	1,051	1,213
58,000	59,000	276	605	898	1,077	1,243
59,000	60,000	282	620	919	1,102	1,272

[a]Per *Rev. Proc.* 2006-18. The table for 2007 had not been released at the date of the printing.

▼ TABLE 14[a] (continued)

Fair Market Value of Automobiles		Tax Year During Lease				
Over	Not Over	1st	2nd	3rd	4th	5th and Later
60,000	62,000	292	641	951	1,141	1,316
62,000	64,000	305	670	994	1,191	1,375
64,000	66,000	318	699	1,036	1,242	1,435
66,000	68,000	331	728	1,078	1,293	1,494
68,000	70,000	344	756	1,121	1,345	1,552
70,000	72,000	358	784	1,164	1,395	1,612
72,000	74,000	371	813	1,206	1,447	1,670
74,000	76,000	384	842	1,249	1,497	1,729
76,000	78,000	397	871	1,291	1,548	1,788
78,000	80,000	410	899	1,334	1,600	1,846
80,000	85,000	433	949	1,409	1,688	1,950
85,000	90,000	465	1,021	1,515	1,816	2,098
90,000	95,000	498	1,093	1,621	1,944	2,244
95,000	100,000	531	1,164	1,728	2,071	2,392
100,000	110,000	580	1,272	1,887	2,263	2,612
110,000	120,000	645	1,416	2,099	2,518	2,901
120,000	130,000	711	1,559	2,312	2,773	3,202
130,000	140,000	776	1,702	2,525	3,028	3,497
140,000	150,000	841	1,846	2,738	3,283	3,791
150,000	160,000	907	1,989	2,950	3,539	4,085
160,000	170,000	972	2,132	3,164	3,793	4,380
170,000	180,000	1,037	2,276	3,376	4,049	4,674
180,000	190,000	1,103	2,419	3,589	4,303	4,969
190,000	200,000	1,168	2,563	3,801	4,559	5,263
200,000	210,000	1,233	2,706	4,015	4,813	5,558
210,000	220,000	1,299	2,849	4,227	5,069	5,853
220,000	230,000	1,364	2,993	4,440	5,324	6,147
230,000	240,000	1,430	3,136	4,652	5,580	6,441
240,000	and up	1,495	3,279	4,866	5,834	6,736

[a]Per *Rev. Proc.* 2006-18. The table for 2007 had not been released at the date of the printing.

APPENDIX D

GLOSSARY

Accounting method The rules used to determine the tax year in which income and expenses are reported for tax purposes. Generally, the same accounting method must be used for tax purposes as is used for keeping books and records. The accounting treatment used for any item of income or expense and for specific items (e.g., installment sales and contracts) is included in this term.

Accounting period See Tax year.

Accumulated adjustments account (AAA) Account that must be kept by S corporations. The cumulative total of the ordinary income or loss and separately stated items for the most recent S corporation election period.

Accumulated earnings and profits The sum of the undistributed current earnings and profits balances (and deficits) from previous years reduced by any distributions that have been made out of accumulated earnings and profits.

Accumulated earnings credit Deduction that reduces the accumulated taxable income amount. It does not offset the accumulated earnings tax on a dollar-for-dollar basis. Different rules apply for operating companies, service companies, and holding or investment companies.

Accumulated earnings tax Penalty tax on corporations other than those subject to the personal holding company tax among others. It is levied on a corporation's current year addition to its accumulated earnings balance exceeding the amount needed for reasonable business purposes and not distributed to the shareholders. This tax is intended to discourage companies from retaining excessive amounts of earnings if the funds are invested in activities unrelated to business needs. The tax is 15% of accumulated taxable income.

Accumulated taxable income The tax base for the accumulated earnings tax, which is determined by taking the corporation's taxable income and increasing (decreasing) it by positive (negative) adjustments and decreasing it by the accumulated earnings credit and available dividends-paid deductions.

Accumulation distribution rules (throwback rules) Exception to the general rule that distributable net income (DNI) serves as a ceiling on the amount taxable to a beneficiary. Under the general rule, the beneficiary excludes the portion of any distribution exceeding DNI from his gross income. Accumulation distributions made by a trust are taxable to the beneficiaries in the year received.

ACE See Adjusted current earnings.

Acquiescence policy IRS policy of announcing whether it agrees or disagrees with a court decision decided in favor of the taxpayer. Such statements are not issued for every case.

Acquisitive reorganization A transaction in which the acquiring corporation obtains all or part of the stock or assets of a target corporation.

Adjusted current earnings (ACE) Alternative minimum taxable income for the tax year plus or minus a series of special adjusted current earnings adjustments specified in Sec. 56(g)(4) (special depreciation calculation, special E&P rules, etc.).

Adjusted current earnings adjustment 75% of the excess (if any) of the adjusted current earnings of the corporation over the preadjustment AMTI. A downward adjustment is provided for 75% of the excess (if any) of preadjustment AMTI over the adjusted current earnings of the corporation.

Adjusted grossed-up basis For Sec. 338 purposes, the sum of (1) the basis of a purchasing corporation's stock interest in a target corporation plus (2) an adjustment for the target corporation's liabilities on the day following the acquisition date plus or minus (3) other relevant items.

Adjusted income from rents (AIR) This amount equals the corporation's gross income from rents reduced by the deductions claimed for amortization or depreciation, property taxes, interest, and rent.

Adjusted ordinary gross income (AOGI) A corporation's adjusted ordinary gross income is its ordinary gross income reduced by (1) certain expenses incurred in connection with gross income from rents, mineral, oil and gas royalties, and working interests in oil or gas wells, (2) interest received by dealers on certain U.S. obligations, (3) interest received from condemnation awards, judgments, or tax refunds, and (4) rents from certain tangible personal property manufactured or produced by the corporation.

Adjusted taxable gift Taxable gifts made after 1976 that are valued at their date-of-gift value. These gifts affect the size of the transfer tax base at death.

Administrative pronouncement Treasury Department or IRS statement that interprets provisions of the IRC. Such pronouncements may be in the form of Treasury regulations, revenue rulings, or revenue procedures.

Advance ruling See Letter ruling.

Affiliated group A group consisting of a parent corporation and at least one subsidiary corporation.

Aggregate Deemed Sale Price (ADSP) Price at which old target is deemed to have sold all of its assets pursuant to a Sec. 338 deemed sale election.

AIR See Adjusted income from rents.

Alien An individual who is not a U.S. citizen.

Alternate valuation date The alternate valuation date is the earlier of six months after the date of death or the date the property is sold, exchanged, distributed, etc. by the estate. Unless this option is elected, the gross estate is valued at its FMV on the date of the decedent's death.

Alternative minimum tax (AMT) Tax that applies to individuals, corporations, and estates and trusts if it exceeds the taxpayer's regular tax. Most taxpayers are not subject to this tax, including corporations meeting the small corporation exception. This tax equals the amount by which the tentative minimum tax exceeds the regular tax.

Alternative minimum taxable income (AMTI) The taxpayer's taxable income (1) increased by tax preference items and (2) adjusted for income, gain, deduction, and loss items that have to be recomputed under the AMT system.

AMT See Alternative minimum tax.

AMTI See Alternative minimum taxable income.

Annotated tax service A multivolume tax commentary organized by IRC section number. The IRC-arranged subdivisions contain the IRC provision, related Treasury Regulations, publisher-provided commentary and explanations, and annotations that summarize related cases and IRS pronouncements. The service has a topical index to assist research.

Announcement Information release issued by the IRS to provide a technical explanation of a current tax issue. Announcements are aimed at tax practitioners rather than the general public.

Annual exclusion An exemption intended to relieve a donor from keeping an account of and reporting the numerous small gifts (e.g., wedding and Christmas gifts) made throughout the year. This exclusion currently is $12,000 per donee.

AOGI See Adjusted ordinary gross income.

Appeals coordinated issue Issue over which the appeals officer must obtain a concurrence of guidance from the regional director of appeals to render a decision.

Applicable exclusion amount Portion of the estate and gift tax base that is completely free of transfer taxes because of the unified credit (previously called the exemption equivalent).

Assignment of income doctrine A judicial requirement that income be taxed to the person that earns it.

At-risk basis Essentially the same amount as the regular partnership basis with the exception that liabilities increase the at-risk basis only if the partner is at-risk for such an amount.

At-risk rules These rules limit the partner's loss deductions to his or her at-risk basis.

Bardahl formula Mathematical formula for determining the amount of working capital that a business reasonably needs for accumulated earnings tax purposes. For a manufacturing company, the formula is based on the business's operating cycle.

Boot Property that may not be received tax-free in certain nontaxable transactions (i.e., any money, debt obligations, and so on).

Bootstrap acquisition An acquisition where an investor purchases part of a corporation's stock and then has the corporation redeem the remainder of the seller's stock.

Branch profits tax Special tax levied by the U.S. government on the branch activities of a foreign corporation doing business in the United States.

Brother-sister controlled group Under the narrow 50%-80% definition, this type of controlled group exists if (1) five or fewer individuals, estates, or trusts own at least 80% of the voting stock or 80% of the value of each corporation and (2) the shareholders have common ownership of more than 50% of the voting power or 50% of the value of all classes of stock. Under the broad 50%-only definition, the five or fewer shareholders need to meet only the 50% test.

Built-in deduction A deduction that accrues in a separate return limitation year but which is recognized for tax purposes in a consolidated return year.

Built-in gain A gain that accrued prior to the conversion of a C corporation to an S corporation.

Built-in gains (Sec. 1374) tax Tax on built-in gains recognized by the S corporation during the ten-year period beginning on the date the S corporation election took effect.

Built-in loss A loss that accrued prior to the conversion of a C corporation to an S corporation.

Business purpose A judicial doctrine established by the U.S. Supreme Court that a transaction cannot be solely motivated by a tax avoidance purpose. Transactions that serve no business purpose usually are ignored by the IRS and the courts.

Capital gain property For charitable contribution deduction purposes, property upon which a long-term capital gain would be recognized if that property were sold at its FMV.

Capital interest An interest in the assets owned by a partnership.

C corporation Form of business entity taxed as a separate taxpaying entity. Its income is subject to an initial tax at the corporate level. Its shareholders are subject to a second tax if the corporation pays dividends from its earnings and profits. This type of corporation is sometimes referred to as a regular corporation.

Certiorari An appeal from a lower court (i.e., a federal court of appeals) that the U.S. Supreme Court agrees to hear. Such appeals, which are made as a writ of certiorari, generally are not granted unless (1) a constitutional issue needs to be decided or (2) a conflict among the lower court decisions must be clarified.

CFC See Controlled foreign corporation.

Charitable contribution deduction Contributions of money or property made to qualified organizations (i.e., public charities and private nonoperating foundations). For income tax purposes, the amount of the deduction depends on (1) the type of charity receiving the contribution, (2) the type of property contributed, and (3) other limitations mandated by the tax law. Charitable contributions also are deductible under the unified transfer tax (i.e., gift tax and estate tax rules).

Charitable remainder annuity trust This type of trust makes distributions to individuals for a certain time period or for life. The annual distributions are a uniform percentage (5% or higher) of the value of the trust property as valued on the date of transfer.

Charitable remainder unitrust This type of trust makes annual distributions for either a specified time period or for life. The distributions are a uniform percentage (5% or higher) of the value of the property as revalued annually.

Check-the-box regulations Treasury Regulations that permit certain entities (e.g., partnerships and limited liability companies) to select an income tax status different from their basic classification.

Clifford trust A trust that normally is held for a ten-year period after which the principal reverts to the grantor. The trust accounting income generally is not taxed to the grantor.

Closed-fact or tax compliance situation Situation or transaction in which the facts have already occurred. In such situations, the tax advisor's task is to analyze the facts to determine the appropriate tax treatment.

Closed transaction Situation where the property in question (e.g., property distributed in a corporate liquidation) can be valued with reasonable certainty. The gain or loss reported on the transaction is determinable at the time the transaction occurs. See Open transaction doctrine.

Closely held corporation A corporation owned by either a single individual or a small group of individuals who may or may not be family members.

Closely held C corporation For purposes of the at-risk rules, a C corporation in which more than 50% of the stock is owned by five or fewer individuals at any time during the last half of the corporation's tax year.

Combined controlled group A group of three or more corporations that are members of a parent-subsidiary or brother-sister controlled group. In addition, at least one of the corporations must be the parent corporation of the parent-subsidiary controlled group and a member of a brother-sister controlled group.

Combined taxable income The total amount of the separate taxable incomes of the individual group members of an affiliated group that is filing a consolidated tax return.

Common law state All states other than the community property states are common law states. In such states, all assets acquired during the marriage are the property of the acquiring spouse.

Community property law Law in community property states mandating that all property acquired after marriage generally is community property unless acquired by gift or inheritance. Each spouse owns a one-half interest in community property.

Community property state The eight traditional community property states (Louisiana, Texas, New Mexico, Arizona, California, Washington, Idaho, and Nevada) and Wisconsin (which adopted a similar law). These states do not follow the common law concept of property ownership.

Complex trust Trust that is not required to distribute all of its income currently.

Congressional intent What Congress *intended* by a particular statutory term, phrase, or provision as gleaned from House and Senate committee reports, records of committee hearings, and transcripts of floor debates.

Consent dividend Hypothetical dividend generally deemed paid to a personal holding company's shareholders on the last day of the corporation's tax year. Also may be paid to avoid the personal holding company tax or accumulated earnings tax.

Consolidated return year A tax year for which a consolidated return is filed or is required to be filed by an affiliated group.

Consolidated taxable income The taxable income reported on a consolidated return filed by a group of affiliated corporations. The calculation of this amount is determined by establishing each member's separate taxable income and then following a series of steps that result in a consolidated amount.

Consolidated tax return A single tax return filed by a group of related corporations (i.e., affiliated group).

Consolidation A form of tax-free reorganization involving two or more corporations whose assets are acquired by a new corporation. The stock, securities, and other consideration transferred by the acquiring corporation is then distributed by each target corporation to its shareholders and security holders in exchange for their stock and securities.

Constructive dividend The manner in which the IRS or the courts might recharacterize an excessive corporate payment to a shareholder to reflect the true economic benefit conferred upon the shareholder. As a result of the recharcterization, the IRS or the courts usually recast a corporate-shareholder transaction as an E&P distribution, deny the corporation an offsetting deduction, and treat all or a portion of the income recognized by the shareholder as a dividend.

Continuity of interest doctrine The judicial requirement that shareholders who transfer property to a transferee corporation continue their ownership in the property through holding the transferee corporation's stock to defer recognition of their gains.

Controlled foreign corporation (CFC) Foreign corporation that is directly or indirectly controlled by U.S. shareholders at any time during the taxable year, provided that such U.S. shareholders control more than 50% of its voting power or more than 50% of the value of the outstanding stock.

Controlled group Two or more separately incorporated businesses owned by a related group of individuals or entities. Such groups include parent-subsidiary groups, brother-sister groups, or combined groups.

Corporation A separate taxpaying entity (such as an association, joint stock company, or insurance company) that must file a tax return every year, even when it had no income or loss for the year.

Corresponding item The buyer's income, gain, deduction, or loss from an intercompany transaction, or from property acquired in an intercompany transaction. Corresponding items cause intercompany items to be recognized. See Intercompany item.

Crummey trust Technique that allows a donor to set up a discretionary trust and obtain an annual exclusion. Such a trust arrangement allows the beneficiary to demand an annual distribution of the lesser of the annual exclusion ($12,000 in 2007) or the amount transferred to the trust that year.

C short year That portion of an S termination year that begins on the day on which the termination is effective and continues through to the last day of the corporation's tax year.

Current distribution See Nonliquidating distribution.

Current earnings and profits Earnings and profits calculated annually by (1) adjusting the corporation's taxable income (or net operating loss) for items that must be recomputed, (2) adding back any excluded income items, income deferrals, and deductions not allowed in computing earnings and profits, and (3) subtracting any expenses and losses not deductible in computing the corporation's taxable income.

Curtesy A widower's interest in his deceased wife's property.

Deductions in respect of a decedent (DRD) Deduction accrued prior to death but not includible on decedent's final tax return because of the decedent's method of accounting.

Deemed paid credit An indirect foreign tax credit available to a domestic corporation owning at least 10% of the voting stock of a foreign corporation when the foreign corporation pays or accrues creditable foreign taxes.

Deemed sale election Election under Sec. 338 permitting an acquiring corporation that acquires a controlling interest in a target corporation's stock to step-up or step-down the basis of the target corporation's assets to their adjusted grossed-up basis via a deemed sale and purchase of its assets.

Deferral privilege A tax exemption provided U.S. taxpayers who own stock of a foreign corporation. The foreign corporation's earnings generally are not taxed in the United States until repatriated unless an exception such as the Subpart F rules applies.

Deferred tax asset A book balance sheet item that results from temporary differences that produce tax deductions in the future when the differences reverse. The amount is the applicable tax rate times the temporary difference.

Deferred tax liability A book balance sheet item that results from temporary differences that produce taxable income in the future when the differences reverse. The amount is the applicable tax rate times the temporary difference.

Deficiency dividend This type of dividend substitutes an income tax levy on the dividend payment at the shareholder level for the payment of the personal holding company tax.

DIF See Discriminant Function Program.

Discriminant Function Program (DIF) Program used by the IRS to select individual returns for audit. This system is intended to identify those tax returns that are most likely to contain errors.

Dissolution A legal term implying that a corporation has surrendered the charter it originally received from the state.

Distributable net income (DNI) Maximum amount of distributions taxed to the beneficiaries and deducted by a trust or estate.

Distributive share The portion of partnership taxable and nontaxable income, losses, credits, and so on that the partner must report for tax purposes.

Dividend A distribution of property made by a corporation out of its earnings and profits.

Dividends-paid deduction Distributions made out of a corporation's earnings and profits are eligible for this deduction for personal holding company tax and accumulated earnings tax purposes. The deduction is equal to the amount of money plus the adjusted basis of the nonmoney property distributed.

Dividends-received deduction This deduction attempts to mitigate the triple taxation that would occur if one corporation paid dividends to a corporate shareholder who, in turn, distributed such amounts to its individual shareholders. Certain restrictions and limitations apply to this deduction.

Divisive reorganization Transaction in which part of a transferor corporation's assets are transferred to a second, newly created corporation controlled by either the transferee or its shareholders.

DNI See Distributable net income.

Domestic corporation Corporation incorporated in one of the 50 states or under federal law.

Dower A widow's interest in her deceased husband's property.

DRD See Deductions in respect of a decedent.

E&P See Earnings and profits.

E&P adjusted basis Adjusted basis obtained by using special calculations required under the E&P rules (e.g., calculation using straight-line depreciation under the alternative depreciation system).

E&P gain The difference between an asset's FMV an its E&P adjusted basis, which may differ from an asset's tax gain.

Earnings and profits A measure of the corporation's ability to pay a dividend from its current and accumulated earnings without an impairment of capital.

Effective tax rate Total book income tax expense divided by pretax book income. In footnotes to the financial statements, firms reconcile the effective tax rate to the statutory tax rate.

Electing large partnership A partnership having at least 100 partners for the preceding tax year (excluding service partners). Electing large partnerships have a simplified reporting procedure that reduces the number of income, gain, loss, deductions, and credit items passing through to the partners.

Estate A legal entity that comes into being only upon the death of the person whose assets are being administered. The estate continues in existence until the duties of the executor have been completed.

Excess loss account A negative investment account of a member of an affiliated group that files a consolidated tax return which attaches to an investment in a lower-tier subsidiary corporation.

Excess net passive income An amount equal to the S corporation's net passive income multiplied by the fraction consisting of its passive investment income less 25% of its gross receipts divided by its passive investment income. It is limited to the corporation's taxable income.

Excess net passive income (Sec. 1375) tax Tax levied when (1) an S corporation has passive investment income for the taxable year that exceeds 25% of its gross receipts and (2) at the close of the tax year the S corporation has earnings and profits from C corporation tax years.

Exemption equivalent That portion of the tax base that is completely free of transfer taxes because of the unified credit. (Now called the applicable exclusion amount.)

Failure-to-file penalty Penalty imposed for the failure to file a timely return. The penalty is assessed at 5% per month (or fraction thereof) on the amount of the net tax due. The maximum penalty for failing to file is 25%. The minimum penalty is the lesser of $100 or 100% of the tax due.

Failure-to-pay penalty Penalty imposed at 0.5% per month (or fraction thereof) on the amount of tax shown on the return less any tax payments made before the beginning of the month for which the penalty is being calculated. The maximum penalty is 25%.

Fair market value (FMV) The amount that would be realized from the sale of a property at a price that is agreeable to both the buyer and the seller when neither party is obligated to participate in the transaction.

Fiduciary A person or other entity (e.g., a guardian, executor, trustee, or administrator) who holds and manages property for someone else.

Fiduciary taxation The special tax rules that apply to fiduciaries (e.g., trusts and estates).

FMV See Fair market value.

Foreign branch An office or other establishment of a domestic entity that operates in a foreign country.

Foreign corporation A corporation that is incorporated under the laws of a country other than the United States.

Foreign tax credit Tax credit given to mitigate the possibility of double taxation faced by U.S. citizens, residents, and corporations earning foreign income.

Forum shopping The ability to consider differing precedents in choosing the forum for litigation.

Future interest Such interests include reversions, remainders, and other interests that may not be used, owned, or enjoyed until some future date.

General partner Partner or partners with (1) the authority to make management decisions and commitments for the partnership and (2) unlimited liability for all partnership debts.

General partnership A partnership with two or more partners where no partner is a limited partner.

General power of appointment Power of appointment under which the holder can appoint the property to himself, his estate, his creditors, or the creditors of his estate. Such power may be exercisable during the decedent's life, by his will, or both.

Generation-skipping transfer A disposition that (1) provides interests for more than one generation of beneficiaries who are in a younger generation than the transferor or (2) provides an interest solely for a person two or more generations younger than the transferor.

Gift tax A wealth transfer tax that applies if the property transfer occurs during a person's lifetime.

Grantor The transferor who creates a trust.

Grantor trust Trust governed by Secs. 671 through 679. The income from such trusts is taxed to the grantor even if some or all of the income has been distributed.

Gross estate The gross estate includes items to which the decedent held title at death as well as certain incomplete transfers made by the decedent prior to death.

Guaranteed minimum Minimum amount of payment guaranteed to a partner. This amount is important if the partner's distributive share is less than his guaranteed minimum. See also Guaranteed payment.

Guaranteed payment Minimum amount of payment guaranteed to a partner in the form of a salary-like payment made for services provided to the partnership and interest-like payments for the use of invested capital. Guaranteed payments, which may be in the form of a guaranteed minimum amount or a set amount, are taxed as ordinary income. See also Guaranteed minimum.

Headnote An editorial summary of a particular point of case law that appears immediately before the text of a judicial opinion.

Hedge agreement An obligation on the part of a shareholder-employee to repay to the corporation any portion of salary disallowed by the IRS as a deduction. It also is used in connection with other corporate payments to shareholder-employees (e.g., travel and entertainment expenses).

Housing cost amount A special deduction or exclusion equal to the housing expenses incurred by a taxpayer eligible for the Sec. 911 earned income exclusion minus the base housing amount.

Income beneficiary Entity or individual that receives the income from a trust.

Income in respect of a decedent (IRD) Amount to which the decedent was entitled as gross income but which were not properly includible in computing his taxable income for the tax year ending with his date of death or for a previous tax year under the method of accounting employed by the decedent.

Income tax expense A subtraction item in the book income statement that represents a firm's current and deferred tax expense for the year. It is the total tax expense and sometimes is called the total tax provision.

Information release An administrative pronouncement concerning an issue that the IRS thinks the general public will be interested in. Such releases are issued in lay terms and widely published.

Innocent spouse relief This provision exempts a spouse from penalty and liability for tax if such spouse meets certain requirements.

Intercompany item The seller's income, gain, deduction, or loss from an intercompany transaction. Intercompany items are recognized when a corresponding item is incurred. See Corresponding item.

Intercompany transaction Transaction that takes place during a consolidated return year between corporations that are members of the same group immediately after the transaction.

Interpretative regulations Treasury Regulations that serve to interpret the provisions of the Internal Revenue Code. Interpretative regulations are less authoritative than legislative regulations.

Inter vivos trust Transfer to a trust that is made during the grantor's lifetime.

Inversion A transaction in which a U.S. corporation reorganizes as a foreign entity for the purpose of removing foreign-source income not associated with a U.S. business from U.S. taxing jurisdiction.

IRD See Income in respect of a decedent.

Irrevocable trust Trust under which the grantor cannot require the trustee to return the trust's assets.

Joint and several liability The potential liability for the full amount of tax due. If one joint filer is unable to pay any or all of the tax, the other joint filer is liable for the deficiency. Also see Proportional liability.

Joint tenancy A popular form of property ownership that serves as a substitute for a will. Each joint tenant is deemed to have an equal interest in the property.

Judicial decisions Decision rendered by a court deciding the case that is presented to it by a plaintiff and defendant. These decisions are important sources of the tax law and can come from trial courts and appellate courts.

Legislative reenactment doctrine Rule holding that Congress's failure to change the wording in the IRC over an extended period signifies that Congress has approved the treatment provided in Treasury Regulations.

Legislative regulations Treasury Regulations that are treated as law because Congress has delegated its rulemaking authority to the Treasury Department. Such regulations may be overturned by the courts on the grounds that they exceed the scope of the delegated authority or are unreasonable.

Letter ruling A letter ruling originates from the IRS at the taxpayer's request. It describes how the IRS will treat a proposed transaction. It is binding only on the person requesting the ruling provided the transaction is completed as proposed in the ruling. Letter rulings that are of general interest are published as revenue rulings.

Life estate A property transfer in trust that results in the transferor reserving the right to income for life. Another individual is named to receive the property upon the transferor's death.

LIFO recapture tax A tax imposed on a C corporation that uses the LIFO inventory method and which elects S corporation treatment. The tax is imposed in the final C corporation tax year and is paid over a four-year period.

Limited liability company (LLC) A business entity that combines the legal and tax benefits of partnerships and S corporations. These entities are taxed as partnerships for federal tax purposes unless they elect to be taxed as corporations under the check-the-box regulations.

Limited liability partnership (LLP) Similar to a limited liability company, but formed under a separate state statute that generally applies to service companies.

Limited partner Partner who has no right to be active in the management of the partnership and whose liability is limited to his original investment plus any additional amounts he or she is obligated to contribute.

Limited partnership A partnership where one or more of the partners is designated as a limited partner and at least one partner is a general partner.

Liquidating distribution A distribution that (1) liquidates a partner's entire partnership interest due to retirement, death, or other business reason or (2) partially or totally liquidates a shareholder's stock interest in a corporation following the adoption of a plan at liquidation.

Loss corporation A corporation entitled to use a net operating loss carryover or having a net operating loss for the taxable year in which an ownership change occurs.

Majority partners The one or more partners in a partnership who have an aggregate interest in partnership profits and capital exceeding 50%.

Mandatory basis adjustment Required basis adjustment if the partnership has a substantial built-in loss at the time a partner sells his or her partnership interest or if the partnership has a decreasing basis adjustment at the time of a liquidating distribution.

Marital deduction Deduction allowed for tax-free inter-spousal transfers other than those for gifts of certain terminable interests.

Memorandum (memo) decision Decision issued by the Tax Court dealing with a factual variation on a matter where the law already has been decided in an earlier case.

Merger A tax-free reorganization one form of which has the acquiring corporation transfer its stock, securities, and other consideration to the target corporation in exchange for its assets and liabilities. The target corporation then distributes the consideration it receives to its shareholders and security holders in exchange for their stock and securities.

Minimum tax credit (MTC) A tax credit allowed for the amount of alternative minimum tax that arose because of deferral and permanent adjustments and preference items. This credit carries over to offset regular tax liabilities in subsequent years.

MTC See Minimum tax credit.

National Research Program (NRP) An IRS program designed to develop new statistical models for identifying returns most likely to contain errors. The models are based on pre-existing audit data as well as data compiled in ordinary audits.

Negligence The IRC defines negligence as (1) any failure to reasonably attempt to comply with the IRC and (2) "careless, reckless, or intentional disregard" of the rules and regulations.

Negligence penalty Penalty assessed if the IRS finds that the taxpayer has filed an incorrect return because of negligence. Generally, this penalty is 20% of the underpayment attributable to negligence.

Net accounting income The excess of accounting income over expenses for a fiduciary (i.e., an estate or trust). Excluded are any items credited to or charged against capital.

Net gift A gift upon which the donee pays the gift tax as a condition of receiving the gift.

Net operating loss (NOL) A net operating loss occurs when business expenses exceed business income for any taxable year. Such losses may be carried back two years or carried forward 20 years to a year in which the taxpayer has taxable income. The loss is carried back first and must be deducted from years in chronological order unless the taxpayer makes a special election to forgo the carryback.

New loss corporation Any corporation permitted to use a net operating loss carryover after an ownership change occurs.

Ninety (90)-day letter Officially called a Statutory Notice of Deficiency, this letter is sent when (1) the taxpayer does not file a protest letter within 30 days of receipt of the 30-day letter or (2) the taxpayer has met with an appeals officer but no agreement was reached. The letter notifies the taxpayer of the amount of the deficiency, how that amount was determined, and that a deficiency will be assessed if a petition is not filed with the Tax Court within 90 days. The taxpayer also is advised of the alternatives available to him.

NOL See Net operating loss.

Nonliquidating (current) distribution Distribution that (1) reduces, but does not eliminate, a partner's partnership interest or (2) is made with respect to a shareholder's stock interest in a corporation at a time when no plan of liquidation has been adopted and may or may not reduce the shareholder's interest in the corporation.

Nonrecourse loan Loan for which the borrower has no personal liability. Usually, the lender can look only to the secured property for satisfaction.

Nonresident alien Individual whose residence is not the United States and who is not a U.S. citizen.

Notice An interpretation by the IRS that provides quidance concerning how to interpret a statute, perhaps one recently enacted.

OGI See Ordinary gross income.

Old loss corporation Any corporation allowed to use a net operating loss carryover, or that has a net operating loss for the tax year in which an ownership change occurs, and that undergoes the requisite stock ownership change.

Open-fact or tax-planning situation Situation or transaction in which the facts have not yet occurred. In such situations, the tax advisor's task is to plan for the facts or shape them so as to produce a favorable tax result.

Open transaction doctrine Valuation technique for property that can be valued only on the basis of uncertain future payments. This doctrine determines the shareholder's gain or loss when the asset is sold, collected, or able to be valued. Assets that cannot be valued are assigned a value of zero.

Optional basis adjustment An elective technique that adjusts the basis for the underlying partnership assets up or down as a result of (1) distributions from the partnership to its partners, (2) sales of partnership interests by existing partners, or (3) transfers of the interest following the death of a partner.

Ordinary gross income (OGI) A corporation's ordinary gross income is its gross income reduced by capital gains and Sec. 1231 gains.

Ordinary income property For charitable contribution deduction purposes, any property that would result in the recognition of ordinary income if it were sold. Such property includes inventory, works of art or manuscripts created by the taxpayer, capital assets that have been held for one year or less, and Sec. 1231 property that results in ordinary income due to depreciation recapture.

Other intercompany transactions An intercompany transaction that is not a deferred intercompany transaction. See Intercompany transaction.

Parent-subsidiary controlled group To qualify as such, a common parent must own at least 80% of the voting stock or at least 80% of the value of at least one subsidiary corporation and at least 80% of each other component member of the controlled group must be owned by other members of the controlled group.

Partial liquidation Occurs when a corporation discontinues one line of business, distributes the assets related to that business to its shareholders, and continues at least one other line of business.

Partner A member of a partnership. The member may be an individual, trust, estate, or corporation. Also see General partner and Limited partner.

Partnership Syndicate, group, pool, joint venture, or other unincorporated organization that carries on a business or financial operation or venture and that has at least two partners.

Partnership agreement Agreement that governs the relationship between the partners and the partnership.

Partnership item Virtually all items reported by the partnership for the tax year, including tax preference items, credit recapture items, guaranteed payments, and at-risk amounts.

Partnership ordinary income The positive sum of all partnership items of income, gain, loss, or deduction that do not have to be separately stated.

Partnership ordinary loss The negative sum of all partnership items of income, gain, loss, or deduction that do not have to be separately stated.

Partnership taxable income The sum of all taxable items among the separately stated items plus the partnership ordinary income or ordinary loss.

Party to a reorganization Such parties include corporations that result from a reorganization and the corporations involved in a reorganization where one corporation acquires the stock or assets of the other corporation.

Passive activity limitation Separate limitation on the amount of losses and credits that can be claimed with respect to a passive activity.

Passive foreign investment company (PFIC) A foreign corporation having passive income as 75% or more of its gross income for the tax year, or at least 50% of the average value of its assets during the tax year producing or held for producing passive income.

Passive income Income from an activity that does not require the taxpayer's material involvement or participation. Thus, income from tax shelters and rental activities generally fall into this category.

Passive loss Loss generated from a passive activity. Such losses are computed separately. They may be used to offset income from other passive activities but may not be used to offset either active income or portfolio income.

Permanent difference Items reported in taxable income but not book income or vice versa. Such differences include book income items that are nontaxable in the current year and will never be taxable and book expense items that are nondeductible in computing taxable income for the current year and will never be deductible.

Personal holding company (PHC) A closely held corporation (1) that is owned by five or fewer shareholders who own more than 50% of the corporation's outstanding stock at any time during the last half of its tax year and (2) whose PHC income equals at least 60% of the corporation's adjusted ordinary gross income for the tax year. Certain corporations (e.g., S corporations) are exempt from this definition.

Personal holding company income (PHCI) Twelve categories of income including the following: dividends; interest; annuities; royalties (other than minerals, oil and gas, computer software, and copyright royalties); adjusted income from rents; adjusted income from mineral, oil and gas royalties, or working interests in oil and gas wells; computer software royalties; copyright royalties; produced film rents; income from personal service contracts involving a 25% or more shareholder; rental income from corporate property used by a 25% or more shareholder; and distributions from estates and trusts.

Personal holding company (PHC) tax This tax equals 15% of the undistributed personal holding company income and, if applicable, is assessed in addition to the regular corporate income tax and the AMT.

Personal service corporation Corporation whose principal activity is the performance of personal services.

PHC See Personal holding company.

PHCI See Personal holding company income.

Plan of liquidation A written document detailing the steps to be undertaken while carrying out the complete liquidation of a corporation.

Plan of reorganization A consummated transaction that is specifically defined as a reorganization.

Pooled income fund A fund in which individuals receive an income interest for life and a charitable contribution deduction equal to the remainder interest for amounts contributed to the fund. The various individual beneficiaries receive annual distributions of income based upon their proportionate share of the fund's earnings.

Post-termination transition period The period of time following the termination of the S corporation election during which (1) loss and deduction carryovers can be deducted or (2) distributions of S corporation previously taxed earnings can be made tax-free.

Power of appointment The power to designate the eventual owner of a property. Such appointments may be general or specific. Also see General power of appointment.

Preadjustment AMTI Alternative minimum taxable income determined without the adjusted current earnings adjustment and the alternative tax NOL deduction.

Preferential dividend Dividends are preferential if (1) the amount distributed to a shareholder exceeds his ratable share of the distribution as determined by the number of shares owned or (2) the distribution amount for a class of stock is more or less than its rightful amount.

Preferred stock bailout A tax treatment mandated by Sec. 306 that prevents shareholders who receive nontaxable preferred stock dividends from receiving capital gain treatment upon the sale or redemption of the preferred stock.

Present interest An unrestricted right to the immediate use, possession, or enjoyment of property or the income from property (e.g., a life estate or term certain).

Previously taxed income (PTI) Income earned in a pre-1983 S corporation tax year and that was taxed to the shareholder. A money distribution of PTI can be distributed tax-free once all of a corporation's AAA balance has been distributed. See Accumulated adjustments account.

Primary citation The highest level official reporter that reports a particular case.

Principal partner Partner who owns at least a 5% interest in the partnership's capital or profits.

Private Letter Ruling See Letter ruling.

Probate estate Properties that (1) pass subject to the will or under an intestacy statute and (2) are subject to court administration are part of the probate estate.

Profits interest Interest in the partnership's future earnings.

Property Cash, tangible property (e.g., buildings and land), and intangible property (e.g., franchise rights, trademarks, and leases).

Proportional liability The liability for one's pro rata share of the amount of tax due. If one joint filer is unable to pay any or all the tax, the other joint filer is liable only for the portion of the tax attributable to his or her separate taxable items. Also see Joint and several liability.

Protest letter If the additional tax in question is more than $10,000 and the IRS audit was a field audit, the taxpayer must file a protest letter within 30 days. If no such letter is sent, the IRS will follow-up with a 90-day letter. Also see Ninety (90)-day letter.

Publicly traded partnership A partnership that is actively traded on an established securities exchange or is traded in a secondary market or the equivalent thereof. Such partnerships formed after December 17, 1987 are taxed as corporations unless they earn predominantly passive income; publicly traded partnerships that existed before that date will be treated as partnerships if they agree to pay a special excise tax on their gross income.

QTIP See Qualified terminable interest property.

Qualified disclaimer Disclaimer made by a person named to receive property under a decedent's will who wishes to renounce the property and any of its benefits. Such a disclaimer must be in written form and be irrevocable. In addition, it must be made no later than nine months after the later of the day the transfer is made or the day the recipient becomes 21 years old. The property must pass to either the decedent's spouse or another person not named by the person making the disclaimer.

Qualified joint interest If spouses are the only joint owners of a property, that property is classified as a qualified joint interest.

Qualified Subchapter S Subsidiary (QSub) An S corporation that is 100%-owned by another S corporation. The income earned by a QSub is treated and reported as if earned by its parent corporation.

Qualified Subchapter S trusts (QSSTs) A domestic trust that owns stock in one or more S corporations and distributes (or is required to distribute) all of its income to its sole income beneficiary. The beneficiary must make an irrevocable election to be treated as the owner of the trust consisting of the S corporation stock. A separate QSST election must be made for each corporation's stock owned by the trust.

Qualified terminable interest property (QTIP) QTIP property is property for which a special election has been made that makes it eligible for the marital deduction. Such property must be transferred by the donor-spouse to a donee-spouse who has a qualifying interest for life. In other words, the donor does not have to grant full control over the property to his spouse.

Reasonable business needs For accumulated earnings tax purposes, the amount that a prudent business person would consider appropriate for the business's bona fide present and future needs, Sec. 303 (death tax) redemption needs, and excess business holding redemption needs.

Recapitalization A nontaxable change in the capital structure of an existing corporation for a bona fide business purpose.

Recourse loan Loan for which the borrower remains liable until repayment is complete. If the loan is secured, the lender can be repaid by selling the security. Any difference in the sale amount and the loan amount must be paid by the borrower.

Regular corporation See C corporation.

Regular decision Tax Court decision issued on a particular issue for the first time.

Regular tax A corporation's tax liability for income tax purposes reduced by foreign tax credits allowable for income tax purposes.

Remainder interest The portion of an interest in property retained by a transferor who is not transferring his entire interest in the property.

Remainderman The person entitled to the remainder interest.

Reorganization A corporate acquistion or division that meets specific requirements to qualify as nontaxable transaction. Reorganizations are classified as Type A, B, C, D, E, F, or G.

Resident alien An individual whose residence is the United States but who is not a U.S. citizen.

Revenue procedure Issued by the national office of the IRS and reflects the IRS's position on procedural aspects of tax practice issues. Revenue procedures are published in the Cumulative Bulletin.

Revenue ruling Issued by the national office of the IRS and reflects the IRS's interpretation of a narrow tax issue. Revenue rulings, which are published in the Cumulative Bulletin, have less weight than Treasury Regulations.

Reverse triangular merger Type of nontaxable transaction in which a subsidiary corporation is merged into a target corporation, and the target corporation stays alive as a subsidiary of the parent corporation.

Reversionary interest An interest in property that might revert back to the transferor under the terms of the transfer. If the amount of reversionary interest is 5% or less, it is not included in the gross estate.

Revocable trust Trust under which the grantor may demand that the assets be returned.

Rule against perpetuities The requirement that no property interet vest more than 21 years, plus the gestation period, after some life or lives in being at the time the interest is created.

S corporation Election that can be made by small business corporations that allows them to be taxed like partnerships rather than like C corporations. Small business corporations are those that meet the 100-shareholder limitation, the type of shareholder restrictions, and the one class of stock restriction.

Secondary citation Citation to a secondary source (i.e., an unofficial reporter) for a particular case.

Section 306 stock Preferred stock received as a stock dividend or a part of a nontaxable reorganization. Sec. 306 stock is subject to the special preferred stock bailout rules when sold or redeemed. See Preferred stock bailouts.

Section 382 loss limitation rules Limitation that principally prevents trafficking in NOLs. Applies to corporate acquisitions, stock redemptions, and reorganizations when a more than 50 percentage point change in ownership occurs. The NOL that can be used in a tax year is limited to the value of the loss corporation's stock times a federal long-term tax exempt rate.

Section 444 election Personal service corporations, partnerships, and S corporations that are unable to otherwise elect a fiscal year instead of their required tax year, under Sec. 444 can elect a fiscal year as their taxable year.

Section 482 rules The IRS has the power under Sec. 482 to distribute, apportion, or allocate income, deductions, credits, or allowances between or among controlled entities to prevent tax evasion and to clearly reflect the income of the entities.

Section 2503(c) trust Trust created for children under age 21 that need not distribute all of its income annually. The undistributed interest passes to the beneficiary when he or she attains age 21 or to his or her estate should he or she die before age 21.

Security A security includes (1) shares of stock in a corporation; (2) a right to subscribe for, or the right to receive, a share of stock in a corporation; and (3) a bond, debenture, note, or other evidence of indebtedness issued by a corporation with interest coupons or in registered form.

Separate return limitation year Any separate return year except (1) a separate return year of the group member designated as the parent corporation for the consolidated return year to which the tax attribute is carried or (2) a separate return year of any corporation that was a group member for every day of the loss year.

Separate return limitation year (SRLY) rules Limitation on the amount of net operating loss and other deduction and loss amounts from a separate return year that can be used by an affiliated group in a consolidated return year to the member's contribution to consolidated taxable income.

Separate return year A tax year for which a corporation files a separate return or joins in the filing of a consolidated return with a different affiliated group.

Separate share rule Rule permitting a trust with several beneficiaries to treat each beneficiary as having a separate trust interest for purposes of determining the amount of the distribution deduction and the beneficiary's gross income.

Separate taxable income The taxable income of an individual corporate member of an affiliated group filing a consolidated tax return. This amount is used to calculate the group's combined taxable income.

Short-period tax return A tax return covering a period of less than 12 months. Short period returns are commonly filed in the first or final tax year or when a change in tax year is made.

Short-term trust Trust whose period is long enough for the grantor to escape being taxed on the trust's accounting income. A *Clifford* trust is a short-term trust.

Simple trust Trust that must distribute all of its income currently and is not empowered to make a charitable contribution.

Small business trust A type of trust that can own stock in a small business corporation that has made an S election to be taxed as an S corporation.

Small cases procedure A Tax Court procedure for adjudicating tax-related claims of $50,000 or less. Small cases procedure decisions are not appealable and have no precedential value.

Sole proprietorship Form of business owned by an individual who reports all items of income and expense on Schedule C (or Schedule C-EZ) of his individual return.

Special agents The IRS agents responsible for criminal fraud investigations.

Spin-off A nontaxable distribution in which a parent corporation distributes the stock and securities of a subsidiary to its shareholders without receiving anything in exchange.

Split-interest transfer A transfer made for both private (i.e., an individual) and public (i.e., a charitable organization) purposes.

Split-off A nontaxable distribution in which a parent corporation distributes a subsidiary's stock and securities to some or all of its shareholders in exchange for part or all of their stock and securities in the parent corporation.

Split-up A nontaxable distribution in which a parent corporation distributes the stock or securities of two or more subsidiaries to its shareholders in exchange for all of their stock and securities in the parent corporation. The parent corporation then goes out of existence.

Sprinkling trust A discretionary trust with several beneficiaries.

SRTP See Statements on Responsibilities in Tax Practice.

S short year That portion of an S termination year that begins on the first day of the tax year and ends on the day preceding the day on which the termination is effective.

Statements on Standards for Tax Services (SSTS) Ethical standards of practice and compliance set by the Tax Division of the American Institute of Certified Public Accountants. The AICPA enforces these standards, and thus they have a great deal of influence on ethics in tax practice.

Statute of limitations A period of time as provided by law after which a taxpayer's return may not be changed either by the IRS or the taxpayer. The limitations period is generally three years from the later of the date the tax return is filed or its due date. A fraudulent return has no statute of limitations.

Step transaction doctrine A judicial doctrine that the IRS can use to collapse a multistep transaction into a single transaction (either taxable or tax-free) to prevent the taxpayers from arranging a series of business transactions to obtain a tax result that is not available if only a single transaction is used.

S termination year A tax year in which a termination event occurs on any day other than the first day of the tax year. It is divided into an S short year and a C short year.

Stock dividend A dividend paid in the form of stock in the corporation issuing the dividend.

Stock redemption The acquisition by a corporation of its own stock in exchange for property. Such stock may be cancelled, retired, or held as treasury stock.

Stock rights Rights issued by a corporation to its shareholders or creditors that permit the purchase of an additional share(s) of stock at a designated exercise price with the surrender of one or more of the stock rights.

Subpart F income A series of income categories deemed distributed to the U.S. shareholders of a controlled foreign corporation on the last day of its tax year. Subpart F income includes income from insurance of U.S. and foreign risks, foreign base company income, boycott-related income, bribes, and income from countries where for political reasons, etc. the deferral privilege is denied.

Substantially appreciated inventory This type of inventory includes (1) items held for sale in the normal course of partnership business, (2) other property that would not be considered a capital asset or Sec. 1231 property if it were sold by the partnership, and (3) any other property held by the partnership that would fall into the above classification if it were held by the selling or distributee partner.

Target corporation The corporation that transfers its assets as part of a taxable or nontaxable acquisition. Also may be known as the acquired or transferor company.

Tax attributes Corporations have various tax items, such as earnings and profits, deduction and credit carryovers, and depreciation recapture potential, that are called tax attributes. The tax attributes of a target or liquidating corporation are assumed by the acquiring or parent corporation, respectively, in acquisitive reorganizations and tax-free liquidations.

Tax matters partner Partner who is designated by the partnership or who is the general partner having the largest profits interests at the close of the partnership's tax year.

Taxpayer Compliance Measurement Program (TCMP) A stratified random sample used to select tax returns for audit. The program is intended to test the extent to which taxpayers are in compliance with the law.

Tax preference items Designated items, such as accelerated depreciation claimed on pre-1987 real property, that increase taxable income to arrive at AMTI. Unlike AMT adjustments, tax preference items do not reverse in later years and reduce AMTI.

Tax research The process of solving a specific tax-related question on the basis of both tax law sources and the specific circumstances surrounding the particular situation.

Tax services Multivolume commentaries on the tax law. Generally, these commentaries contain copies of the Internal Revenue Code and the Treasury Regulations. Also included are editorial comments prepared by the publisher of the tax service, current matters, and a cross-reference to various government promulgations and judicial decisions.

Tax treaties Bilateral agreements entered into between two nations that address tax and other matters. Treaties provide for modifications to the basic tax laws involving residents of the two countries (e.g., reductions in the withholding rates).

Tax year The period of time (usually 12 months) selected by taxpayers to compute their taxable income. The tax year may be a calendar year or a fiscal year. The election is made on the taxpayer's first return and cannot be changed without IRS approval. The tax year may be less than 12 months if it is the taxpayer's first or final return or if the taxpayer is changing accounting periods.

TCMP See Taxpayer Compliance Measurement Program.

Technical advice memorandum Such memoranda are administrative interpretations issued by the national office of the IRS in the form of a letter ruling. Taxpayers may request them if they need guidance about the tax treatment of complicated technical matters being audited.

Temporary differences Items that are included in book income in the current year but that were included in taxable income in the past or will be included in the future. Book income items that are nontaxable in the current year even though they were taxed in the past or will be taxed in the future and book expenses that are not currently deductible even though that status was different in the past or will be different in the future are categorized as temporary differences.

Temporary regulations Regulations issued by the Treasury Department relating to an IRC provision. Such regulations are effective for a limited period of time, usually three years.

Issuance of temporary regulations is not preceded by a public hearing on their substance. Temporary regulations have the same precedential value as final regulations.

Tentative minimum tax (TMT) Tax calculated by (1) multiplying 20% times the corporation's alternative minimum taxable income less a statutory exemption amount and (2) deducting allowable foreign tax credits.

Term certain interest A person holding such an interest has a right to receive income from property for a specified term but does not own or hold title to such property. The property reverts to the grantor at the end of the term.

Terminable interest A property interest that ends when some event occurs (or fails to occur) or when a specified amount of time passes.

Testamentary Of, pertaining to, or of the nature of a testament or will.

Testamentary transfers A transferor's control or enjoyment of a property ceases at death.

Testamentary trust Trust created under the direction of a decedent's will and funded by the decedent's estate.

Thirty (30)-day letter A report sent to the taxpayer if the taxpayer does not sign Form 870 (Waiver of Statutory Notice) concerning any additional taxes assessed. The letter details the proposed changes and advises the taxpayer of his or her right to pursue the matter with the Appeals Office. The taxpayer then has 30 days in which to request a conference.

Throwback dividends For accumulated earnings tax and personal holding company tax purposes, these are distributions made out of current or accumulated earnings and profits in the first two and one-half months after the close of the tax year.

Tier-1 beneficiary Beneficiary to whom a distribution must be made.

Tier-2 beneficiary Beneficiary who receives a discretionary distribution.

TMT See Tentative minimum tax.

Topical tax service A multivolume tax commentary organized by topic. Topics might include, for example, deferred compensation, Type A reorganizations, or S corporations. These volumes are an excellent place to begin research in an unfamiliar area.

Transferor corporation The corporation that transfers its assets as part of a reorganization. Also may be known as acquired or target corporation.

Triangular merger A type of merger transaction where the parent corporation uses a subsidiary corporation to serve as the acquiring corporation.

Triangular reorganization A type of reorganization (i.e., Type A, B, or C) where the parent corporation uses a subsidiary corporation to serve as the acquiring corporation. Also see Triangular merger.

Trust An arrangement created either by will or by an inter vivos declaration whereby trustees take title to property for the purpose of protecting it or conserving it for the beneficiaries.

Trustee An individual or institution that administers a trust for the benefit of a beneficiary.

Trustor The grantor or transferor of a trust.

Type A reorganization Type of corporate reorganization that meets the requirements of state or federal law. It may take the form of a consolidation, merger, triangular merger, or reverse triangular merger.

Type B reorganization Reorganization characterized by a stock-for-stock exchange. The target corporation remains in existence as a subsidiary of the acquiring corporation.

Type C reorganization A transaction that requires the acquiring corporation to obtain substantially all the target corporation's assets in exchange for its voting stock and a limited amount of other consideration. The target corporation generally is liquidated.

Type D reorganization This type of reorganization may be either acquisitive or divisive. In the former, substantially all the transferor corporation's assets (and possibly some or all of its liabilities) are acquired by a controlled corporation. The target corporation is liquidated. The latter involves the acquisition of the part or all of the transferor corporation's assets (and liabilities) by a controlled subsidiary corporation(s). The transferor corporation may either remain in existence or be liquidated.

Type E reorganization This type of reorganization changes the capital structure of a corporation. The corporation remains in existence.

Type F reorganization The old corporation's assets or stock are transferred to a single newly formed corporation in this type of transaction. The "old" corporation is liquidated.

Type G reorganization This type of reorganization may be either acquisitive or divisive. In either case, part or all the target or transferor corporation's assets (and possibly some or all of its liabilities) are transferred to another corporation as part of a bankruptcy proceeding. The target or transferor corporation may either remain in existence or be liquidated.

Unauthorized practice of law The engagement of nonlawyers in professional activities traditionally relegated to the legal profession. Such activities include preparing legal documents, formalizing business entities, and representing clients in criminal investigations.

Unified credit The unified credit enables a tax base of a certain size (i.e., the exemption equivalent or applicable exclusion amount) to be completely free of transfer taxes. It may be subtracted only once against all of a person's transfers—throughout one's lifetime and at death. See Exemption equivalent and Applicable exclusion amount.

Unified rate schedule Progressive rate schedule for estate and gift taxes. These rates are effective for gifts made after 1976 and deaths occurring after 1976.

Unrealized receivable Right to payment for goods and services that has not been included in the owner's income because of its method of accounting.

Unreported decisions District court decisions that are not reported in official reporters. Such decisions may be reported in secondary reporters that report only tax-related cases.

U.S. production activities deduction A deduction equal to a percentage times the lesser of (1) qualified production activities income for the year or (2) taxable income before the U.S. production activities deduction. The phased-in percentages are 3% for 2005 and 2006, 6% for 2007–2009, and 9% for 2010 and thereafter. The deduction, however, cannot exceed 50% of the corporation's W-2 wages for the year..

U.S. shareholder For controlled foreign corporation purposes, a U.S. person who owns at least 10% of the foreign corporation's voting stock.

Valuation allowance A contra-type account that represents the portion of a deferred tax asset that likely will not be realized.

Voting trust An arrangement whereby the stock owned by a number of shareholders is placed under the control of a trustee for purposes of exercising the voting rights possessed by the stock. This practice increases the voting power of the minority shareholders.

Wealth transfer taxes Estate taxes (i.e., the tax on dispositions of property that occur as a result of the transferor's death) and gift taxes (i.e., the tax on lifetime transfers) are wealth transfer taxes.

Writ of certiorari See Certiorari.

APPENDIX E

• AICPA STATEMENTS ON STANDARDS FOR TAX SERVICES NOS. 1–8 (AUGUST 2000)

• INTERPRETATION NO. 1–2 FOR SSTS NO. 1 (OCTOBER 2003)

PREFACE

1. Practice standards are the hallmark of calling one's self a professional. Members should fulfill their responsibilities as professionals by instituting and maintaining standards against which their professional performance can be measured. Compliance with professional standards of tax practice also confirms the public's awareness of the professionalism that is associated with CPAs as well as the AICPA.

2. This publication sets forth ethical tax practice standards for members of the AICPA: Statements on Standards for Tax Services (SSTSs or Statements). Although other standards of tax practice exist, most notably Treasury Department Circular No. 230 and penalty provisions of the Internal Revenue Code (IRC), those standards are limited in that (1) Circular No. 230 does not provide the depth of guidance contained in these Statements, (2) the IRC penalty provisions apply only to income-tax return preparation, and (3) both Circular No. 230 and the penalty provisions apply only to federal tax practice.

3. The SSTSs have been written in as simple and objective a manner as possible. However, by their nature, ethical standards provide for an appropriate range of behavior that recognizes the need for interpretations to meet a broad range of personal and professional situations. The SSTSs recognize this need by, in some sections, providing relatively subjective rules and by leaving certain terms undefined. These terms and concepts are generally rooted in tax concepts, and therefore should be readily understood by tax practitioners. It is, therefore, recognized that the enforcement of these rules, as part of the AICPA's Code of Professional Conduct Rule 201, General Standards, and Rule 202, Compliance With Standards, will be undertaken with flexibility in mind and handled on a case-by-case basis. Members are expected to comply with them.

HISTORY

4. The SSTSs have their origin in the Statements on Responsibilities in Tax Practice (SRTPs), which provided a body of advisory opinions on good tax practice. The guidelines as originally set forth in the SRTPs had come to play a much more important role than most members realized. The courts, Internal Revenue Service, state accountancy boards, and other professional organizations recognized and relied on the SRTPs as the appropriate articulation of professional conduct in a CPA's tax practice. The SRTPs, in and of themselves, had become de facto enforceable standards of professional practice, because state disciplinary organizations and malpractice cases in effect regularly held CPAs accountable for failure to follow the SRTPs when their professional practice conduct failed to meet the prescribed guidelines of conduct.

5. The AICPA's Tax Executive Committee concluded that appropriate action entailed issuance of tax practice standards that would become a part of the Institute's Code of Professional Conduct. At its July 1999 meeting, the AICPA Board of Directors approved support of the executive committee's initiative and placed the matter on the agenda of the October 1999 meeting of the Institute's governing Council. On October 19, 1999, Council approved designating the Tax Executive Committee as a standard-setting body, thus authorizing that committee to promulgate standards of tax practice. These SSTSs, largely mirroring the SRTPs, are the result.

6. The SRTPs were originally issued between 1964 and 1977. The first nine SRTPs and the Introduction were codified in 1976; the tenth SRTP was issued in 1977. The original SRTPs concerning the CPA's responsibility to sign the return (SRTPs No. 1, *Signature of Preparers*, and No. 2, *Signature of Reviewer: Assumption of Preparer's Responsibility*) were withdrawn in 1982 after Treasury Department regulations were issued adopt-

ing substantially the same standards for all tax return preparers. The sixth and seventh SRTPs, concerning the responsibility of a CPA who becomes aware of an error, were revised in 1991. The first Interpretation of the SRTPs, Interpretation 1-1, "Realistic Possibility Standard," was approved in December 1990. The SSTSs and Interpretation supersede and replace the SRTPs and their Interpretation 1-1 effective October 31, 2000. Although the number and names of the SSTSs, and the substance of the rules contained in each of them, remain the same as in the SRTPs, the language has been edited to both clarify and reflect the enforceable nature of the SSTSs. In addition, because the applicability of these standards is not limited to federal income-tax practice, the language has been changed to mirror the broader scope.

ONGOING PROCESS

7. The following Statements on Standards for Tax Services and Interpretation 1-1 to Statement No. 1, "Realistic Possibility Standard," reflect the AICPA's standards of tax practice and delineate members' responsibilities to taxpayers, the public, the government, and the profession. The Statements are intended to be part of an ongoing process that may require changes to and interpretations of current SSTSs in recognition of the accelerating rate of change in tax laws and the continued importance of tax practice to members.

8. The Tax Executive Committee promulgates SSTSs. Even though the 1999–2000 Tax Executive Committee approved this version, acknowledgment is also due to the many members whose efforts over the years went into the development of the original statements.

STATEMENT ON STANDARDS FOR TAX SERVICES NO. 1, TAX RETURN POSITIONS

INTRODUCTION

1. This Statement sets forth the applicable standards for members when recommending tax return positions and preparing or signing tax returns (including amended returns, claims for refund, and information returns) filed with any taxing authority. For purposes of these standards, a *tax return position* is (*a*) a position reflected on the tax return as to which the taxpayer has been specifically advised by a member or (*b*) a position about which a member has knowledge of all material facts and, on the basis of those facts, has concluded whether the position is appropriate. For purposes of these standards, a *taxpayer* is a client, a member's employer, or any other third-party recipient of tax services.

STATEMENT

2. The following standards apply to a member when providing professional services that involve tax return positions:

a. A member should not recommend that a tax return position be taken with respect to any item unless the member has a good-faith belief that the position has a realistic possibility of being sustained administratively or judicially on its merits if challenged.

b. A member should not prepare or sign a return that the member is aware takes a position that the member may not recommend under the standard expressed in paragraph *2a*.

c. Notwithstanding paragraph *2a*, a member may recommend a tax return position that the member concludes is not frivolous as long as the member advises the taxpayer to appropriately disclose. Notwithstanding paragraph *2b*, the member may prepare or sign a return that reflects a position that the member concludes is not frivolous as long as the position is appropriately disclosed.

d. When recommending tax return positions and when preparing or signing a return on which a tax return position is taken, a member should, when relevant, advise the taxpayer regarding potential penalty consequences of such tax return position and the opportunity, if any, to avoid such penalties through disclosure.

3. A member should not recommend a tax return position or prepare or sign a return reflecting a position that the member knows—

a. Exploits the audit selection process of a taxing authority.

b. Serves as a mere arguing position advanced solely to obtain leverage in the bargaining process of settlement negotiation with a taxing authority.

4. When recommending a tax return position, a member has both the right and responsibility to be an advocate for the taxpayer with respect to any position satisfying the aforementioned standards.

EXPLANATION

5. Our self-assessment tax system can function effectively only if taxpayers file tax returns that are true, correct, and complete. A tax return is primarily a taxpayer's representation of facts, and the taxpayer has the final responsibility for positions taken on the return.

6. In addition to a duty to the taxpayer, a member has a duty to the tax system. However, it is well established that the taxpayer has no obligation to pay more taxes than are legally owed, and a member has a duty to the taxpayer to assist in achieving that result. The standards contained in paragraphs 2, 3, and 4 recognize the members' responsibilities to both taxpayers and to the tax system.

7. In order to meet the standards contained in paragraph 2, a member should in good faith believe that the tax return position is warranted in existing law or can be supported by a good-faith argument for an extension, modification, or reversal of existing law. For example, in reaching such a conclusion, a member may consider a well-reasoned construction of the applicable statute, well-reasoned articles or treatises, or pronouncements issued by the applicable taxing authority, regardless of whether such sources would be treated as *authority* under Internal Revenue

Code section 6662 and the regulations thereunder. A position would not fail to meet these standards merely because it is later abandoned for practical or procedural considerations during an administrative hearing or in the litigation process.

8. If a member has a good-faith belief that more than one tax return position meets the standards set forth in paragraph 2, a member's advice concerning alternative acceptable positions may include a discussion of the likelihood that each such position might or might not cause the taxpayer's tax return to be examined and whether the position would be challenged in an examination. In such circumstances, such advice is not a violation of paragraph *3a*.

9. In some cases, a member may conclude that a tax return position is not warranted under the standard set forth in paragraph *2a*. A taxpayer may, however, still wish to take such a position. Under such circumstances, the taxpayer should have the opportunity to take such a position, and the member may prepare and sign the return provided the position is appropriately disclosed on the return or claim for refund and the position is not frivolous. A frivolous position is one that is knowingly advanced in bad faith and is patently improper.

10. A member's determination of whether information is appropriately disclosed by the taxpayer should be based on the facts and circumstances of the particular case and the authorities regarding disclosure in the applicable taxing jurisdiction. If a member recommending a position, but not engaged to prepare or sign the related tax return, advises the taxpayer concerning appropriate disclosure of the position, then the member shall be deemed to meet these standards.

11. If particular facts and circumstances lead a member to believe that a taxpayer penalty might be asserted, the member should so advise the taxpayer and should discuss with the taxpayer the opportunity to avoid such penalty by disclosing the position on the tax return. Although a member should advise the taxpayer with respect to disclosure, it is the taxpayer's responsibility to decide whether and how to disclose.

12. For purposes of this Statement, preparation of a tax return includes giving advice on events that have occurred at the time the advice is given if the advice is directly relevant to determining the existence, character, or amount of a schedule, entry, or other portion of a tax return.

INTERPRETATION NO. 1-1, "REALISTIC POSSIBILITY STANDARD" OF STATEMENT ON STANDARDS FOR TAX SERVICES NO. 1, TAX RETURN POSITIONS

BACKGROUND

1. Statement on Standards for Tax Services (SSTS) No. 1, *Tax Return Positions,* contains the standards a member should follow in recommending tax return positions and in preparing or signing tax returns. In general, a member should have a good-faith belief that the tax return position being recommended has a realistic possibility of being sustained administratively or judicially on its merits, if challenged. The standard contained in SSTS No. 1, paragraph *2a*, is referred to here as the realistic possibility standard. If a member concludes that a tax return position does not meet the realistic possibility standard:

a. The member may still recommend the position to the taxpayer if the position is not frivolous, and the member recommends appropriate disclosure of the position; or

b. The member may still prepare or sign a tax return containing the position, if the position is not frivolous, and the position is appropriately disclosed.

2. A *frivolous position* is one that is knowingly advanced in bad faith and is patently improper (see SSTS No. 1, paragraph 9). A member's determination of whether information is appropriately disclosed on a tax return or claim for refund is based on the facts and circumstances of the particular case and the authorities regarding disclosure in the applicable jurisdiction (see SSTS No. 1, paragraph 10).

3. If a member believes there is a possibility that a tax return position might result in penalties being asserted against a taxpayer, the member should so advise the taxpayer and should discuss with the taxpayer the opportunity, if any, of avoiding such penalties through disclosure (see SSTS No. 1, paragraph 11). Such advice may be given orally.

GENERAL INTERPRETATION

4. To meet the realistic possibility standard, a member should have a good-faith belief that the position is warranted by existing law or can be supported by a good-faith argument for an extension, modification, or reversal of the existing law through the administrative or judicial process. Such a belief should be based on reasonable interpretations of the tax law. A member should not take into account the likelihood of audit or detection when determining whether this standard has been met (see SSTS No. 1, paragraphs *3a* and 8).

5. The realistic possibility standard is less stringent than the substantial authority standard and the more likely than not standard that apply under the Internal Revenue Code (IRC) to substantial understatements of liability by taxpayers. The realistic possibility standard is stricter than the reasonable basis standard that is in the IRC.

6. In determining whether a tax return position meets the realistic possibility standard, a member may rely on authorities in addition to those evaluated when determining whether substantial authority exists under IRC section 6662. Accordingly, a member may rely on well-reasoned treatises, articles in recognized professional tax publications, and other reference tools and sources of tax analyses commonly used by tax advisers and preparers of returns.

7. In determining whether a realistic possibility exists, a member should do all of the following:

- Establish relevant background facts
- Distill the appropriate questions from those facts
- Search for authoritative answers to those questions

- Resolve the questions by weighing the authorities uncovered by that search
- Arrive at a conclusion supported by the authorities

8. A member should consider the weight of each authority to conclude whether a position meets the realistic possibility standard. In determining the weight of an authority, a member should consider its persuasiveness, relevance, and source. Thus, the type of authority is a significant factor. Other important factors include whether the facts stated by the authority are distinguishable from those of the taxpayer and whether the authority contains an analysis of the issue or merely states a conclusion.

9. The realistic possibility standard may be met despite the absence of certain types of authority. For example, a member may conclude that the realistic possibility standard has been met when the position is supported only by a well-reasoned construction of the applicable statutory provision.

10. In determining whether the realistic possibility standard has been met, the extent of research required is left to the professional judgment of the member with respect to all the facts and circumstances known to the member. A member may conclude that more than one position meets the realistic possibility standard.

SPECIFIC ILLUSTRATIONS

11. The following illustrations deal with general fact patterns. Accordingly, the application of the guidance discussed in the General Interpretation section to variations in such general facts or to particular facts or circumstances may lead to different conclusions. In each illustration there is no authority other than that indicated.

12. *Illustration 1.* A taxpayer has engaged in a transaction that is adversely affected by a new statutory provision. Prior law supports a position favorable to the taxpayer. The taxpayer believes, and the member concurs, that the new statute is inequitable as applied to the taxpayer's situation. The statute is constitutional, clearly drafted, and unambiguous. The legislative history discussing the new statute contains general comments that do not specifically address the taxpayer's situation.

13. *Conclusion.* The member should recommend the return position supported by the new statute. A position contrary to a constitutional, clear, and unambiguous statute would ordinarily be considered a frivolous position.

14. *Illustration 2.* The facts are the same as in illustration 1 except that the legislative history discussing the new statute specifically addresses the taxpayer's situation and supports a position favorable to the taxpayer.

15. *Conclusion.* In a case where the statute is clearly and unambiguously against the taxpayer's position but a contrary position exists based on legislative history specifically addressing the taxpayer's situation, a return position based either on the statutory language or on the legislative history satisfies the realistic possibility standard.

16. *Illustration 3.* The facts are the same as in illustration 1 except that the legislative history can be interpreted to provide some evidence or authority in support of the taxpayer's position; however, the legislative history does not specifically address the situation.

17. *Conclusion.* In a case where the statute is clear and unambiguous, a contrary position based on an interpretation of the legislative history that does not explicitly address the taxpayer's situation does not meet the realistic possibility standard. However, because the legislative history provides some support or evidence for the taxpayer's position, such a return position is not frivolous. A member may recommend the position to the taxpayer if the member also recommends appropriate disclosure.

18. *Illustration 4.* A taxpayer is faced with an issue involving the interpretation of a new statute. Following its passage, the statute was widely recognized to contain a drafting error, and a technical correction proposal has been introduced. The taxing authority issues a pronouncement indicating how it will administer the provision. The pronouncement interprets the statute in accordance with the proposed technical correction.

19. *Conclusion.* Return positions based on either the existing statutory language or the taxing authority pronouncement satisfy the realistic possibility standard.

20. *Illustration 5.* The facts are the same as in illustration 4 except that no taxing authority pronouncement has been issued.

21. *Conclusion.* In the absence of a taxing authority pronouncement interpreting the statute in accordance with the technical correction, only a return position based on the existing statutory language will meet the realistic possibility standard. A return position based on the proposed technical correction may be recommended if it is appropriately disclosed, since it is not frivolous.

22. *Illustration 6.* A taxpayer is seeking advice from a member regarding a recently amended statute. The member has reviewed the statute, the legislative history that specifically addresses the issue, and a recently published notice issued by the taxing authority. The member has concluded in good faith that, based on the statute and the legislative history, the taxing authority's position as stated in the notice does not reflect legislative intent.

23. *Conclusion.* The member may recommend the position supported by the statute and the legislative history because it meets the realistic possibility standard.

24. *Illustration 7.* The facts are the same as in illustration 6 except that the taxing authority pronouncement is a temporary regulation.

25. *Conclusion.* In determining whether the position meets the realistic possibility standard, a member should determine the weight to be given the regulation by analyzing factors such as whether the regulation is legislative or interpretative, or if it is inconsistent with the statute. If a member concludes that the position does not meet the realistic possibility standard, because it is not frivolous, the position may nevertheless be recommended if the member also recommends appropriate disclosure.

26. *Illustration 8.* A tax form published by a taxing authority is incorrect, but completion of the form as published provides a benefit to the taxpayer. The member knows that the taxing authority has published an announcement acknowledging the error.

27. *Conclusion.* In these circumstances, a return position in accordance with the published form is a frivolous position.

28. *Illustration 9.* A taxpayer wants to take a position that a member has concluded is frivolous. The taxpayer maintains that even if the taxing authority examines the return, the issue will not be raised.

29. *Conclusion.* The member should not consider the likelihood of audit or detection when determining whether the realistic possibility standard has been met. The member should not prepare or sign a return that contains a frivolous position even if it is disclosed.

30. *Illustration 10.* A statute is passed requiring the capitalization of certain expenditures. The taxpayer believes, and the member concurs, that to comply fully, the taxpayer will need to acquire new computer hardware and software and implement a number of new accounting procedures. The taxpayer and member agree that the costs of full compliance will be significantly greater than the resulting increase in tax due under the new provision. Because of these cost considerations, the taxpayer makes no effort to comply. The taxpayer wants the member to prepare and sign a return on which the new requirement is simply ignored.

31. *Conclusion.* The return position desired by the taxpayer is frivolous, and the member should neither prepare nor sign the return.

32. *Illustration 11.* The facts are the same as in illustration 10 except that a taxpayer has made a good-faith effort to comply with the law by calculating an estimate of expenditures to be capitalized under the new provision.

33. *Conclusion.* In this situation, the realistic possibility standard has been met. When using estimates in the preparation of a return, a member should refer to SSTS No. 4, *Use of Estimates.*

34. *Illustration 12.* On a given issue, a member has located and weighed two authorities concerning the treatment of a particular expenditure. A taxing authority has issued an administrative ruling that required the expenditure to be capitalized and amortized over several years. On the other hand, a court opinion permitted the current deduction of the expenditure. The member has concluded that these are the relevant authorities, considered the source of both authorities, and concluded that both are persuasive and relevant.

35. *Conclusion.* The realistic possibility standard is met by either position.

36. *Illustration 13.* A tax statute is silent on the treatment of an item under the statute. However, the legislative history explaining the statute directs the taxing authority to issue regulations that will require a specific treatment of the item. No regulations have been issued at the time the member must recommend a position on the tax treatment of the item.

37. *Conclusion.* The member may recommend the position supported by the legislative history because it meets the realistic possibility standard.

38. *Illustration 14.* A taxpayer wants to take a position that a member concludes meets the realistic possibility standard based on an assumption regarding an underlying nontax legal issue. The member recommends that the taxpayer seek advice from its legal counsel, and the taxpayer's attorney gives an opinion on the nontax legal issue.

39. *Conclusion.* A member may in general rely on a legal opinion on a nontax legal issue. A member should, however, use professional judgment when relying on a legal opinion. If, on its face, the opinion of the taxpayer's attorney appears to be unreasonable, unsubstantiated, or unwarranted, a member should consult his or her attorney before relying on the opinion.

40. *Illustration 15.* A taxpayer has obtained from its attorney an opinion on the tax treatment of an item and requests that a member rely on the opinion.

41. *Conclusion.* The authorities on which a member may rely include well-reasoned sources of tax analysis. If a member is satisfied about the source, relevance, and persuasiveness of the legal opinion, a member may rely on that opinion when determining whether the realistic possibility standard has been met.

STATEMENT ON STANDARDS FOR TAX SERVICES NO. 2, ANSWERS TO QUESTIONS ON RETURNS

INTRODUCTION

1. This Statement sets forth the applicable standards for members when signing the preparer's declaration on a tax return if one or more questions on the return have not been answered. The term *questions* includes requests for information on the return, in the instructions, or in the regulations, whether or not stated in the form of a question.

STATEMENT

2. A member should make a reasonable effort to obtain from the taxpayer the information necessary to provide appropriate answers to all questions on a tax return before signing as preparer.

EXPLANATION

3. It is recognized that the questions on tax returns are not of uniform importance, and often they are not applicable to the particular taxpayer. Nevertheless, there are at least two reasons why a member should be satisfied that a reasonable effort has been made to obtain information to provide appropriate answers to the questions on the return that are applicable to a taxpayer.

a. A question may be of importance in determining taxable income or loss, or the tax liability shown on the return, in which circumstance an omission may detract from the quality of the return.

b. A member often must sign a preparer's declaration stating that the return is true, correct, and complete.

4. Reasonable grounds may exist for omitting an answer to a question applicable to a taxpayer. For example, reasonable grounds may include the following:

a. The information is not readily available and the answer is not significant in terms of taxable income or loss, or the tax liability shown on the return.

b. Genuine uncertainty exists regarding the meaning of the question in relation to the particular return.

c. The answer to the question is voluminous; in such cases, a statement should be made on the return that the data will be supplied upon examination.

5. A member should not omit an answer merely because it might prove disadvantageous to a taxpayer.

6. If reasonable grounds exist for omission of an answer to an applicable question, a taxpayer is not required to provide on the return an explanation of the reason for the omission. In this connection, a member should consider whether the omission of an answer to a question may cause the return to be deemed incomplete.

STATEMENT ON STANDARDS FOR TAX SERVICES NO. 3, CERTAIN PROCEDURAL ASPECTS OF PREPARING RETURNS

INTRODUCTION

1. This Statement sets forth the applicable standards for members concerning the obligation to examine or verify certain supporting data or to consider information related to another taxpayer when preparing a taxpayer's tax return.

STATEMENT

2. In preparing or signing a return, a member may in good faith rely, without verification, on information furnished by the taxpayer or by third parties. However, a member should not ignore the implications of information furnished and should make reasonable inquiries if the information furnished appears to be incorrect, incomplete, or inconsistent either on its face or on the basis of other facts known to a member. Further, a member should refer to the taxpayer's returns for one or more prior years whenever feasible.

3. If the tax law or regulations impose a condition with respect to deductibility or other tax treatment of an item, such as taxpayer maintenance of books and records or substantiating documentation to support the reported deduction or tax treatment, a member should make appropriate inquiries to determine to the member's satisfaction whether such condition has been met.

4. When preparing a tax return, a member should consider information actually known to that member from the tax return of another taxpayer if the information is relevant to that tax return and its consideration is necessary to properly prepare that tax return. In using such information, a member should consider any limitations imposed by any law or rule relating to confidentiality.

EXPLANATION

5. The preparer's declaration on a tax return often states that the information contained therein is true, correct, and complete to the best of the preparer's knowledge and belief based on all information known by the preparer. This type of reference should be understood to include information furnished by the taxpayer or by third parties to a member in connection with the preparation of the return.

6. The preparer's declaration does not require a member to examine or verify supporting data. However, a distinction should be made between (*a*) the need either to determine by inquiry that a specifically required condition, such as maintaining books and records or substantiating documentation, has been satisfied or to obtain information when the material furnished appears to be incorrect or incomplete and (*b*) the need for a member to examine underlying information. In fulfilling his or her obligation to exercise due diligence in preparing a return, a member may rely on information furnished by the taxpayer unless it appears to be incorrect, incomplete, or inconsistent. Although a member has certain responsibilities in exercising due diligence in preparing a return, the taxpayer has the ultimate responsibility for the contents of the return. Thus, if the taxpayer presents unsupported data in the form of lists of tax information, such as dividends and interest received, charitable contributions, and medical expenses, such information may be used in the preparation of a tax return without verification unless it appears to be incorrect, incomplete, or inconsistent either on its face or on the basis of other facts known to a member.

7. Even though there is no requirement to examine underlying documentation, a member should encourage the taxpayer to provide supporting data where appropriate. For example, a member should encourage the taxpayer to submit underlying documents for use in tax return preparation to permit full consideration of income and deductions arising from security transactions and from pass-through entities, such as estates, trusts, partnerships, and S corporations.

8. The source of information provided to a member by a taxpayer for use in preparing the return is often a pass-through entity, such as a limited partnership, in which the taxpayer has an interest but is not involved in management. A member may accept the information provided by the pass-through entity without further inquiry, unless there is reason to believe it is incorrect, incomplete, or inconsistent, either on its face or on the basis of other facts known to the member. In some instances, it may be appropriate for a member to advise the taxpayer to ascertain the nature and amount of possible exposure to tax deficiencies, interest, and penalties, by contact with management of the pass-through entity.

9. A member should make use of a taxpayer's returns for one or more prior years in preparing the current return whenever feasible. Reference to prior returns and discussion of prior-year tax determinations with the taxpayer should provide information to determine the taxpayer's general tax status, avoid the omission or duplication of items, and afford a basis for the treatment of similar or related transactions. As with the examination of information supplied for the current year's return, the extent of comparison of the details of income and deduction between years depends on the particular circumstances.

STATEMENT ON STANDARDS FOR TAX SERVICES NO. 4, USE OF ESTIMATES

INTRODUCTION

1. This Statement sets forth the applicable standards for members when using the taxpayer's estimates in the preparation of a tax return. A member may advise on estimates used in the preparation of a tax return, but the taxpayer has the responsibility to provide the estimated data. Appraisals or valuations are not considered estimates for purposes of this Statement.

STATEMENT

2. Unless prohibited by statute or by rule, a member may use the taxpayer's estimates in the preparation of a tax return if it is not practical to obtain exact data and if the member determines that the estimates are reasonable based on the facts and circumstances known to the member. If the taxpayer's estimates are used, they should be presented in a manner that does not imply greater accuracy than exists.

EXPLANATION

3. Accounting requires the exercise of professional judgment and, in many instances, the use of approximations based on judgment. The application of such accounting judgments, as long as not in conflict with methods set forth by a taxing authority, is acceptable. These judgments are not estimates within the purview of this Statement. For example, a federal income tax regulation provides that if all other conditions for accrual are met, the exact amount of income or expense need not be known or ascertained at year end if the amount can be determined with reasonable accuracy.

4. When the taxpayer's records do not accurately reflect information related to small expenditures, accuracy in recording some data may be difficult to achieve. Therefore, the use of estimates by a taxpayer in determining the amount to be deducted for such items may be appropriate.

5. When records are missing or precise information about a transaction is not available at the time the return must be filed, a member may prepare a tax return using a taxpayer's estimates of the missing data.

6. Estimated amounts should not be presented in a manner that provides a misleading impression about the degree of factual accuracy.

7. Specific disclosure that an estimate is used for an item in the return is not generally required; however, such disclosure should be made in unusual circumstances where nondisclosure might mislead the taxing authority regarding the degree of accuracy of the return as a whole. Some examples of unusual circumstances include the following:

a. A taxpayer has died or is ill at the time the return must be filed.

b. A taxpayer has not received a Schedule K-1 for a pass-through entity at the time the tax return is to be filed.

c. There is litigation pending (for example, a bankruptcy proceeding) that bears on the return.

d. Fire or computer failure has destroyed the relevant records.

STATEMENT ON STANDARDS FOR TAX SERVICES NO. 5, DEPARTURE FROM A POSITION PREVIOUSLY CONCLUDED IN AN ADMINISTRATIVE PROCEEDING OR COURT DECISION

INTRODUCTION

1. This Statement sets forth the applicable standards for members in recommending a tax return position that departs from the position determined in an administrative proceeding or in a court decision with respect to the taxpayer's prior return.

2. For purposes of this Statement, *administrative proceeding* also includes an examination by a taxing authority or an appeals conference relating to a return or a claim for refund.

3. For purposes of this Statement, *court decision* means a decision by any court having jurisdiction over tax matters.

STATEMENT

4. The tax return position with respect to an item as determined in an administrative proceeding or court decision does not restrict a member from recommending a different tax position in a later year's return, unless the taxpayer is bound to a specified treatment in the later year, such as by a formal closing agreement. Therefore, as provided in Statement on Standards for Tax Services (SSTS) No. 1, *Tax Return Positions,* the member may recommend a tax return position or prepare or sign a tax return that departs from the treatment of an item as concluded in an administrative proceeding or court decision with respect to a prior return of the taxpayer.

EXPLANATION

5. If an administrative proceeding or court decision has resulted in a determination concerning a specific tax treatment of an item in a prior year's return, a member will usually recommend this

same tax treatment in subsequent years. However, departures from consistent treatment may be justified under such circumstances as the following:

a. Taxing authorities tend to act consistently in the disposition of an item that was the subject of a prior administrative proceeding but generally are not bound to do so. Similarly, a taxpayer is not bound to follow the tax treatment of an item as consented to in an earlier administrative proceeding.

b. The determination in the administrative proceeding or the court's decision may have been caused by a lack of documentation. Supporting data for the later year may be appropriate.

c. A taxpayer may have yielded in the administrative proceeding for settlement purposes or not appealed the court decision, even though the position met the standards in SSTS No. 1.

d. Court decisions, rulings, or other authorities that are more favorable to a taxpayer's current position may have developed since the prior administrative proceeding was concluded or the prior court decision was rendered.

6. The consent in an earlier administrative proceeding and the existence of an unfavorable court decision are factors that the member should consider in evaluating whether the standards in SSTS No. 1 are met.

STATEMENT ON STANDARDS FOR TAX SERVICES NO. 6, KNOWLEDGE OF ERROR: RETURN PREPARATION

INTRODUCTION

1. This Statement sets forth the applicable standards for a member who becomes aware of an error in a taxpayer's previously filed tax return or of a taxpayer's failure to file a required tax return. As used herein, the term error includes any position, omission, or method of accounting that, at the time the return is filed, fails to meet the standards set out in Statement on Standards for Tax Services (SSTS) No. 1, *Tax Return Positions.* The term *error* also includes a position taken on a prior year's return that no longer meets these standards due to legislation, judicial decisions, or administrative pronouncements having retroactive effect. However, an error does not include an item that has an insignificant effect on the taxpayer's tax liability.

2. This Statement applies whether or not the member prepared or signed the return that contains the error.

STATEMENT

3. A member should inform the taxpayer promptly upon becoming aware of an error in a previously filed return or upon becoming aware of a taxpayer's failure to file a required return. A member should recommend the corrective measures to be taken. Such recommendation may be given orally. The member is not obligated to inform the taxing authority, and a member may not do so without the taxpayer's permission, except when required by law.

4. If a member is requested to prepare the current year's return and the taxpayer has not taken appropriate action to correct an error in a prior year's return, the member should consider whether to withdraw from preparing the return and whether to continue a professional or employment relationship with the taxpayer. If the member does prepare such current year's return, the member should take reasonable steps to ensure that the error is not repeated.

EXPLANATION

5. While performing services for a taxpayer, a member may become aware of an error in a previously filed return or may become aware that the taxpayer failed to file a required return. The member should advise the taxpayer of the error and the measures to be taken. Such recommendation may be given orally. If the member believes that the taxpayer could be charged with fraud or other criminal misconduct, the taxpayer should be advised to consult legal counsel before taking any action.

6. It is the taxpayer's responsibility to decide whether to correct the error. If the taxpayer does not correct an error, a member should consider whether to continue a professional or employment relationship with the taxpayer. While recognizing that the taxpayer may not be required by statute to correct an error by filing an amended return, a member should consider whether a taxpayer's decision not to file an amended return may predict future behavior that might require termination of the relationship. The potential for violating Code of Professional Conduct rule 301 (relating to the member's confidential client relationship), the tax law and regulations, or laws on privileged communications, and other considerations may create a conflict between the member's interests and those of the taxpayer. Therefore, a member should consider consulting with his or her own legal counsel before deciding upon recommendations to the taxpayer and whether to continue a professional or employment relationship with the taxpayer.

7. If a member decides to continue a professional or employment relationship with the taxpayer and is requested to prepare a tax return for a year subsequent to that in which the error occurred, the member should take reasonable steps to ensure that the error is not repeated. If the subsequent year's tax return cannot be prepared without perpetuating the error, the member should consider withdrawal from the return preparation. If a member learns that the taxpayer is using an erroneous method of accounting and it is past the due date to request permission to change to a method meeting the standards of SSTS No. 1, the member may sign a tax return for the current year, providing the tax return includes appropriate disclosure of the use of the erroneous method.

8. Whether an error has no more than an insignificant effect on the taxpayer's tax liability is left to the professional judgment of the member based on all the facts and circumstances known to the member. In judging whether an erroneous method of

accounting has more than an insignificant effect, a member should consider the method's cumulative effect and its effect on the current year's tax return.

9. If a member becomes aware of the error while performing services for a taxpayer that do not involve tax return preparation, the member's responsibility is to advise the taxpayer of the existence of the error and to recommend that the error be discussed with the taxpayer's tax return preparer. Such recommendation may be given orally.

STATEMENT ON STANDARDS FOR TAX SERVICES NO. 7, KNOWLEDGE OF ERROR: ADMINISTRATIVE PROCEEDINGS

INTRODUCTION

1. This Statement sets forth the applicable standards for a member who becomes aware of an error in a return that is the subject of an administrative proceeding, such as an examination by a taxing authority or an appeals conference. The term *administrative proceeding* does not include a criminal proceeding. As used herein, the term *error* includes any position, omission, or method of accounting that, at the time the return is filed, fails to meet the standards set out in Statement on Standards for Tax Services (SSTS) No. 1, *Tax Return Positions.* The term *error* also includes a position taken on a prior year's return that no longer meets these standards due to legislation, judicial decisions, or administrative pronouncements having retroactive effect. However, an error does not include an item that has an insignificant effect on the taxpayer's tax liability.

2. This Statement applies whether or not the member prepared or signed the return that contains the error. Special considerations may apply when a member has been engaged by legal counsel to provide assistance in a matter relating to the counsel's client.

STATEMENT

3. If a member is representing a taxpayer in an administrative proceeding with respect to a return that contains an error of which the member is aware, the member should inform the taxpayer promptly upon becoming aware of the error. The member should recommend the corrective measures to be taken. Such recommendation may be given orally. A member is neither obligated to inform the taxing authority nor allowed to do so without the taxpayer's permission, except where required by law.

4. A member should request the taxpayer's agreement to disclose the error to the taxing authority. Lacking such agreement, the member should consider whether to withdraw from representing the taxpayer in the administrative proceeding and whether to continue a professional or employment relationship with the taxpayer.

EXPLANATION

5. When the member is engaged to represent the taxpayer before a taxing authority in an administrative proceeding with respect to a return containing an error of which the member is aware, the member should advise the taxpayer to disclose the error to the taxing authority. Such recommendation may be given orally. If the member believes that the taxpayer could be charged with fraud or other criminal misconduct, the taxpayer should be advised to consult legal counsel before taking any action.

6. It is the taxpayer's responsibility to decide whether to correct the error. If the taxpayer does not correct an error, a member should consider whether to withdraw from representing the taxpayer in the administrative proceeding and whether to continue a professional or employment relationship with the taxpayer. While recognizing that the taxpayer may not be required by statute to correct an error by filing an amended return, a member should consider whether a taxpayer's decision not to file an amended return may predict future behavior that might require termination of the relationship. Moreover, a member should consider consulting with his or her own legal counsel before deciding on recommendations to the taxpayer and whether to continue a professional or employment relationship with the taxpayer. The potential for violating Code of Professional Conduct rule 301 (relating to the member's confidential client relationship), the tax law and regulations, laws on privileged communications, potential adverse impact on a taxpayer of a member's withdrawal, and other considerations may create a conflict between the member's interests and those of the taxpayer.

7. Once disclosure is agreed on, it should not be delayed to such a degree that the taxpayer or member might be considered to have failed to act in good faith or to have, in effect, provided misleading information. In any event, disclosure should be made before the conclusion of the administrative proceeding.

8. Whether an error has an insignificant effect on the taxpayer's tax liability is left to the professional judgment of the member based on all the facts and circumstances known to the member. In judging whether an erroneous method of accounting has more than an insignificant effect, a member should consider the method's cumulative effect and its effect on the return that is the subject of the administrative proceeding.

STATEMENT ON STANDARDS FOR TAX SERVICES NO. 8, FORM AND CONTENT OF ADVICE TO TAXPAYERS

INTRODUCTION

1. This Statement sets forth the applicable standards for members concerning certain aspects of providing advice to a taxpayer and considers the circumstances in which a member has a responsibility to communicate with a taxpayer when subsequent developments affect advice previously provided. The Statement does not, however, cover a member's responsibilities when the expectation is that the advice rendered is likely to be relied on by parties other than the taxpayer.

STATEMENT

2. A member should use judgment to ensure that tax advice provided to a taxpayer reflects professional competence and appropriately serves the taxpayer's needs. A member is not required to follow a standard format or guidelines in communicating written or oral advice to a taxpayer.

3. A member should assume that tax advice provided to a taxpayer will affect the manner in which the matters or transactions considered would be reported on the taxpayer's tax returns. Thus, for all tax advice given to a taxpayer, a member should follow the standards in Statement on Standards for Tax Services (SSTS) No. 1, *Tax Return Positions.*

4. A member has no obligation to communicate with a taxpayer when subsequent developments affect advice previously provided with respect to significant matters, except while assisting a taxpayer in implementing procedures or plans associated with the advice provided or when a member undertakes this obligation by specific agreement.

EXPLANATION

5. Tax advice is recognized as a valuable service provided by members. The form of advice may be oral or written and the subject matter may range from routine to complex. Because the range of advice is so extensive and because advice should meet the specific needs of a taxpayer, neither a standard format nor guidelines for communicating or documenting advice to the taxpayer can be established to cover all situations.

6. Although oral advice may serve a taxpayer's needs appropriately in routine matters or in well-defined areas, written communications are recommended in important, unusual, or complicated transactions. The member may use professional judgment about whether, subsequently, to document oral advice in writing.

7. In deciding on the form of advice provided to a taxpayer, a member should exercise professional judgment and should consider such factors as the following:

a. The importance of the transaction and amounts involved
b. The specific or general nature of the taxpayer's inquiry
c. The time available for development and submission of the advice
d. The technical complications presented
e. The existence of authorities and precedents
f. The tax sophistication of the taxpayer
g. The need to seek other professional advice

8. A member may assist a taxpayer in implementing procedures or plans associated with the advice offered. When providing such assistance, the member should review and revise such advice as warranted by new developments and factors affecting the transaction.

9. Sometimes a member is requested to provide tax advice but does not assist in implementing the plans adopted. Although such developments as legislative or administrative changes or future judicial interpretations may affect the advice previously provided, a member cannot be expected to communicate subsequent developments that affect such advice unless the member undertakes this obligation by specific agreement with the taxpayer.

10. Taxpayers should be informed that advice reflects professional judgment based on an existing situation and that subsequent developments could affect previous professional advice. Members may use precautionary language to the effect that their advice is based on facts as stated and authorities that are subject to change.

11. In providing tax advice, a member should be cognizant of applicable confidentiality privileges.

Tax Executive Committee (1999–2000)

David A. Lifson, *Chair*	Jeffrey A. Porter
Pamela J. Pecarich, *Vice Chair*	Thomas J. Purcell III
Ward M. Bukofsky	Jeffrey L. Raymon
Joseph Cammarata	Frederick II. Rothman
Stephen R. Corrick	Barry D. Roy
Anna C. Fowler	Jane T. Rubin
Jill Gansler	Douglas P. Stives
Diane P. IIerndon	Philip J. Wiesner
Ronald S. Katch	Claude R. Wilson, Jr.
Allan I. Kruger	Robert A. Zarzar
Susan W. Martin	

SRTP Enforceability Task Force

J. Edward Swails, *Chair*	Michael E. Mares
Alan R. Einhorn	Dan L. Mendelson
John C. Gardner	Daniel A. Noakes
Ronald S. Katch	William C. Potter

AICPA Staff

Gerald W. Padwe	Edward S. Karl
Vice President	*Director*
Taxation	*Taxation*

The AICPA gratefully acknowledges the contributions of William A. Tate, Jean L. Rothbarth, and Leonard Podolin, former chairs of the Responsibilities in Tax Practice Committee; A. M. (Tony) Komlyn and Wilber Van Scoik, former members of the Committee; and Carol B. Ferguson, AICPA Technical Manager.

Note: *Statements on Standards for Tax Services are issued by the Tax Executive Committee, the senior technical body of the Institute designated to promulgate standards of tax practice. Rules 201 and 202 of the Institute's Code of Professional Conduct require compliance with these standards.*

INTERPRETATION NO. 1-2, "TAX PLANNING," OF STATEMENT ON STANDARDS FOR TAX SERVICES NO. 1, TAX RETURN POSITIONS (OCTOBER 2003)

NOTICE TO READERS

The Statements on Standards for Tax Services (SSTSs) and Interpretations, promulgated by the Tax Executive Committee, reflect the AICPA's standards of tax practice and delineate members' responsibilities to taxpayers, the public, the government, and the profession. The Statements are intended to be part of an ongoing process that may require changes to and Interpretations of current SSTSs in recognition of the accelerating rate of change in tax laws and the continued importance of tax practice to members. Interpretation No. 1-2 was approved by the Tax Executive Committee on August 21, 2003; its effective date is December 31, 2003.

The SSTSs have been written in as simple and objective a manner as possible. However, by their nature, ethical standards provide for an appropriate range of behavior that recognizes the need for Interpretations to meet a broad range of personal and professional situations. The SSTSs recognize this need by, in some sections, providing relatively subjective rules and by leaving certain terms undefined. These terms and concepts are generally rooted in tax concepts, and therefore should be readily understood by tax practitioners. It is, therefore, recognized that the enforcement of these rules, as part of the AICPA's Code of Professional Conduct Rule 201, *General Standards*, and Rule 202, *Compliance With Standards*, will be undertaken with flexibility in mind and handled on a case-by-case basis. Members are expected to comply with them.

1 2 3 4 5 6 7 8 9 0 TD 0 9 8 7 6 5 4 3

BACKGROUND

1. Statements on Standards for Tax Services (SSTSs) are enforceable standards that govern the conduct of members of the AICPA in tax practice. A significant area of many members' tax practices involves assisting taxpayers in tax planning. Two of the eight SSTSs issued as of the date of this Interpretation's release directly set forth standards that affect the most common activities in tax planning. Several other SSTSs set forth standards related to specific factual situations that may arise while a member is assisting a taxpayer in tax planning. The two SSTSs that are most typically relevant to tax planning are SSTS No. 1, *Tax Return Positions* (AICPA, *Professional Standards*, vol. 2, TS sec. 100), including Interpretation No. 1-1, "Realistic Possibility Standard" (AICPA, *Professional Standards*, vol. 2, TS sec. 9100), and SSTS No. 8, *Form and Content of Advice to Taxpayers* (AICPA, *Professional Standards*, vol. 2, TS sec. 800).

2. Taxing authorities, courts, the AICPA, and other professional organizations have struggled with defining and regulating *tax shelters* and *abusive transactions*. Crucial to the debate is the dificulty of clearly distinguishing between transactions that are abusive and transactions that are legitimate. At the same time, it must be recognized that taxpayers have a legitimate interest in arranging their affairs so as to pay no more than the taxes they owe. It must be recognized that tax professionals, including members, have a role to play in advancing these efforts.

3. This Interpretation is part of the AICPA's continuing efforts at self-regulation of its members in tax practice. It has its origins in the AICPA's desire to provide adequate guidance to its members when providing services in connection with tax planning. The Interpretation does not change or elevate any level of conduct prescribed by any standard. Its goal is to clarify existing standards. It was determined that there was a compelling need for a comprehensive Interpretation of a member's responsibilities in connection with *tax planning*, with the recognition that such guidance would clarify how those standards would apply across the spectrum of tax planning, including those situations involving *tax shelters*, regardless of how that term is defined.

GENERAL INTERPRETATION

4. The realistic possibility standard (see SSTS No. 1, TS sec. 100.02(1), and Interpretation No. 1-1) applies to a member when providing professional services that involve *tax planning*. A member may still recommend a nonfrivolous position provided that the member recommends appropriate disclosure (see SSTS No. 1, TS sec. 100.02(c)).

5. For purposes of this Interpretation, *tax planning* includes, both with respect to prospective and completed transactions, recommending or expressing an opinion (whether written or oral) on (*a*) a tax return position or (*b*) a specific tax plan developed by the member, the taxpayer, or a third party.

6. When issuing an opinion to reflect the results of the tax planning service, a member should do all of the following:

- Establish the relevant background facts.
- Consider the reasonableness of the assumptions and representations.
- Apply the pertinent authorities to the relevant facts.
- Consider the business purpose and economic substance of the transaction, if relevant to the tax consequences of the transaction.
- Arrive at a conclusion supported by the authorities.

7. In assisting a taxpayer in a tax planning transaction in which the taxpayer has obtained an opinion from a third party, and the taxpayer is looking to the member for an evaluation of the opinion, the member should be satisfied as to the source, relevance, and persuasiveness of the opinion, which would include considering whether the opinion indicates the third party did all of the following:

- Established the relevant background facts
- Considered the reasonableness of the assumptions and representations
- Applied the pertinent authorities to the relevant facts
- Considered the business purpose and economic substance of the transaction, if relevant to the tax consequences of the transaction
- Arrived at a conclusion supported by the authorities

8. In conducting the due diligence necessary to establish the relevant background facts, the member should consider whether it is appropriate to rely on an assumption concerning facts in lieu of either other procedures to support the advice or a representation from the taxpayer or another person. A member should also consider whether the member's tax advice will be communicated to third parties, particularly if those third parties may not be knowledgeable or may not be receiving independent tax advice with respiect to a transaction.

9. In tax planning, members often rely on assumptions and representations. Although such reliance is often necessary, the member must take care to assess whether such assumptions and representations are reasonable. In deciding whether an assumption or representation is reasonable, the member should consider its source and consistency with other information know to the member. For example, depending on the circumstances, it may be reasonable for a member to rely on a representation made by the taxpayer, but not on a representation made by a person who is silling or otherwise promoting the transaction to the taxpayer.

10. When engaged in tax planning, the member should understand the business purpose and economic substance of the transaction when relevant to the tax consequences. If a transaction has been proposed by a party other than the taxpayer, the member should consider whether the assumptions made by the third party are consistent with the facts of the taxpayer's situation. If written advice is to be rendered concerning a transaction, the business purpose for the transaction generally should be described. If the business reasons are relevant to the tax consequences, it is insufficient to merely assume that a transaction is entered into for valid business reasons without specifying what those reasons are.

11. The scope of the engagement should be appropriately determined. A member should be diligent in applying such procedures as are appropriate under the circumstances to understand and evaluate the entire transaction. The specific procedures to be performed in this regard will vary with the circumstances and the scope of the engagement.

SPECIFIC ILLUSTRATIONS

12. The following illustrations address general fact patterns. Accordingly, the application of the guidance discussed in the "General Interpretation" section to variations in such general facts or to particular facts or circumstances may lead to different conclusions. In each illustration, there is no authority other than that indicated.

13. *Illustration 1.* The relevant tax code imposes penalties on substantial underpayments that are not associated with tax shelters as defined in such code unless the associated positions are supported by substantial authority.

14. *Conclusion.* In assisting the taxpayer in tax planning in which any associated underpayment would be substantial, the member should inform the taxpayer of the penalty risks associated with the tax return position recommended with respect to any plan under consideration that satisfies the realistic possibility of success standard, but does not possess sufficient authority to satisfy the substantial authority standard.

15. *Illustration 2.* The relevant tax code imposes penalties on tax shelters, as defined in such code, unless the taxpayer concludes that a position taken on a tax return associated with such a tax shelter is, more likely than not, the correct position.

16. *Conclusion.* In assisting the taxpayer in tax planning, the member should inform the taxpayer of the penalty risks associated with the tax return position recommemded with respect to any plan under consideration that satisfies the realistic possibility of success standard, but does not possess sufficient authority to satisfy the more likely than not standard.

17. *Illustration 3.* The relevant tax regulation provides that the details of (or certain information regarding) a specific transaction are required to be attached to the tax return, regardless of the support for the associated tax return position (for example, even if there is substantial authority or a higher level of comfort for the position). While preparing the taxpayer's return for the year, the member is aware that an attachment is required.

18. *Conclusion.* In general, if the taxpayer agrees to include the attachment required by the regulation, the member may sign the return if the member concludes the associated tax return position satisfies the realistic possibility standard. However, if the taxpayer refuses to include the attachment, the member should not sign the return, unless the member concludes the associated tax return position satisfies the realistic possibility standard and there are reasonable grounds for the taxpayer's position with respect to the attachment. In this regard, the member should consider SSTS No. 2, *Answers to Questions on Returns* (AICPA, *Professional Standards*, vol. 2, TS sec. 200.01 and .05), which provides that the term *questions*, as used in the standard, "includes requests for information on the return, in the instructions, or in the regulations, whether or not stated in the form of a question," and that a "member should not omit an answer merely because it might prove disadvantageous to the taxpayer."

19. *Illustration 4.* The relevant tax regulations provide that the details of certain potentially abusive transactions that are designated as "listed transactions" are required to be disclosed in attachments to tax returns, regardless of the support for the associated tax return position (for example, even if there is substantial authority or a higher level of support for the position). Under the regulations, if a listed transaction is not disclosed as required, the taxpayer will have additional penalty risks. While researching the tax consequences of a proposed transaction, a member concludes that the transaction is a listed transaction.

20. *Conclusion.* Notwithstanding the member's conclusion that the transaction is a listed transaction, the member may still recommend a tax return position with respect to the transaction if he or she concludes that the proposed tax return position satisfies the realistic possibility standard. However, the member should inform the taxpayer of the enhanced disclosure requirements of listed transactions and the additional penalty risks for nondisclosure.

21. *Illustration 5.* The same regulations apply as in Illustration 4. The member first becomes aware that a taxpayer entered into a transaction while preparing the taxpayer's return for the year of the transaction. While researching the tax consequences of the transaction, the member concludes that the taxpayer's transaction is a listed transaction.

22. *Conclusion.* The member should inform the taxpayer of the enhanced disclosure requirement and the additional penalty risks for nondisclosure. If the taxpayer agrees to make the disclosure required by the regulation, the member may sign the return if the member concludes the associated tax return position satisfies the realistic possibility standard. Reasonable grounds for nondisclosure (see the conclusion to Illustration 3) generally are not present for a listed transaction. The member should not sign the return if the transaction is not disclosed. If the member is a nonsigning preparer of the return, the member should recommend that the taxpayer disclose the transaction.

23. *Illustration 6.* The same regulations apply as in Illustration 4. The member first becomes aware that a taxpayer entered into a transaction while preparing the taxpayer's return for the year of the transaction. While researching the tax consequences of the transaction, the member concludes that there is uncertainty about whether the taxpayer's transactions is a listed transaction.

24. *Conclusion.* The member should inform the taxpayer of the enhanced disclosure requirement and the additional penalty risks for nondisclosure. If the taxpayer agrees to make the disclosure required by the relevant regulation, the member may sign the return if the member concludes the associated tax return position satisfies the realistic possibility standard. If the taxpayer does not want to disclose the transaction because of the uncertainty about whether it is a listed transaction, the member may sign the return if the member concludes the associated tax return position satisfies the realistic possibility standard and there are reasonable grounds for the taxpayer's position with regard to nondisclosure. In this regard, the member should consider SSTS No. 2, TS sec. 200.04, which indicates that the degree of uncertainty regarding the meaning of a question on a return may affect whether there are reasonable grounds for not responding to the question.

25. *Illustration 7.* A member advises a taxpayer concerning the tax consequences of a transaction involving a loan from a U.S. bank. In the process of reviewing documents associated with the proposed transaction, the member uncovers a reference to a deposit that a wholly owned foreign subsidiary of the taxpayer will make with an overseas branch of the U.S. bank. The transaction documents appear to indicate that this deposit is linked to the U.S. bank's issuance of the loan.

26. *Conclusion.* The member should consider the effect, if any, of the deposit in advising the taxpayer about the tax consequences of the proposed transaction.

27. *Illustration 8.* Under the relevant tax law, the tax consequences of a leasing transaction depend on whether the property to be leased is reasonably expected to have a residual value of 15 percent of its value at the begining of the lease. The member has relied on a taxpayer's instruction to use a particular assumption concerning the residual value.

28. *Conclusion.* Such reliance on the taxpayer's instructions may be appropriate if the assumption is supported by the expertise of the taxpayer, by the member's review of information provided by the taxpayer or a third party, or through the member's own knowledge or analysis.

29. *Illustration 9.* A member is assisting a taxpayer with evaluating a proposed equipment leasing transaction in which the estimated residual value of the equipment at the end of the lease term is critical to the tax consequences of the lease. The broker arranging the leasing transaction has prepared an analysis that sets out an explicit assumption concerning the equipment's estimated residual value.

30. *Conclusion.* The member should consider whether it is appropriate to rely on the broker's assumption concerning the estimated residual value of the equipment instead of obtaining a representation from the broker concerning estimated residual value or performing other procedures to validate the amount to be used as an estimate of residual value in connection with the member's advice. In considering the appropriateness of the broker's assumption, the member should consider, for example, the factors such as the broker's experience in the area, the broker's methodology, and whether alternative sources of information are reasonably available.

31. *Illustration 10.* The tax consequences of a particular reorganization depend, in part, on the majority shareholder of a corporation not disposing of any stock received in the reorganization pursuant to a prearranged agreement to dispose of the stock.

32. *Conclusion.* The member should consider whether it is appropriate in rendering tax advice to assume that such a disposition will not occur or whether, under the circumstances, it is appropriate to request a written representation of the shareholder's intent concerning disposition as a condition to issuing an opinion on the reorganization.

33. *Illustration 11.* A taxpayer is considering a proposed transaction. The taxpayer and the taxpayer's attorney advise the member that the member is responsible for advising the taxpayer on the tax consequences of the transaction.

34. *Conclusion.* In addition to complying with the requirements of paragraph 6, the member generally should review all relevant draft transaction documents in formulating the member's tax advice relating to the transaction.

35. *Illustration 12.* A member is responsible for advising a taxpayer on the tax consequences of the taxpayer's estate plan.

36. *Conclusion.* Under the circumstances, the member should review the will and all other relevant documents to assess whether there appear to be any tax issues raised by the formulation of implementation of the estate plan.

37. *Illustration 13.* A member is assisting a taxpayer in connection with a proposed transaction that has been recommended by an investment bank. To support its recommendation, the investment bank offers a law firm's opinion on the tax consequences. The member reads the opinion, and notes that it is based on a hypothetical statement of facts rather than the taxpayer's facts.

38. *Conclusion.* The member may rely on the law firm's opinion when determining whether the realistic possibility standard has been satisfied with respect to the tax consequences of the hypothetical transaction if the member is satisfied about the source, relevance, and persuasiveness of the opinion. However, the member should be diligent in taking such steps as are appropriate under the circumstances to understand and evaluate the transaction as it applies to the taxpayer's specific situation by:

- Establishing the relevant background facts
- Considering the reasonableness of the assumptions and representations
- Applying the pertinent authorities to the relevant facts
- Considering the business purpose and economic substance of the transaction, if relevant to the tax consequences of the transaction (Mere reliance on a representation that there is business purpose or economic substance is generally insufficient.)
- Arriving at a conclusion supported by the authorities

39. *Illustration 14.* The facts are the same as in Illustration 13 except the member also notes that the law firm that prepared the opinion is one that has a reputation as being knowledgeable about the tax issues associated with the proposed transaction.

40. *Conclusion.* The conclusion is the same as the conclusion to Illustration 13, notwithstanding the expertise of the law firm.

41. *Illustration 15.* A member is assisting a taxpayer in connection with a proposed transaction that has been recommended by an investment bank. To support that recommendation, the investment bank offers a law firm's opinion about the tax consequences. The member reads the opinion, and notes that (unlike the opinions described in Illustrations 13 and 14), it is carefully tailored to the taxpayer's facts.

42. *Conclusion.* The member may rely on the opinion when determining whether the realistic possibility standard has been met with respect to the taxpayer's participation in the transaction if the member is satisfied about the source, relevance, and persuasiveness of the opinion. In making that determination, the member should consider whether the opinion indicates the law firm did all of the following:

- Established the relevant background facts
- Considered the reasonableness of the assumptions and representations
- Applied the pertinent authorities to the relevant facts
- Considered the business purpose and economic substance of the transaction, if relevant to the tax consequences of the transaction (Mere reliance on a representation that there is business purpose or economic substance is generally insufficient.)
- Arrived at a conclusion supported by the authorities

43. *Illustration 16.* The facts are the same as in Illustration 15, except the member also notes that the law firm that prepared the opinion is one that has a reputation of being knowledgeable about the tax issues associated with the proposed transaction.

44. *Conclusion.* The conclusion is the same as the conclusion to Illustration 15, notwithstanding the expertise of the law firm.

45. *Illustration 17.* A member is assisting a taxpayer with year-end planning in connection with the taxpayer's proposed contribution of stock in a closely held corporation to a charitable organization. The taxpayer instructs the member to calculate the anticipated tax liability assuming a contribution of 10,000 shares to a tax-exempt organization assuming the stock has a fair market value of $100 per share. The member is aware that on the taxpayer's gift tax returns for the prior year, the taxpayer indicated that her stock in the corporation was worth $50 per share.

46. *Conclusion.* The member's calculation of the anticipated tax liability is subject to the general interpretations described in paragraphs 8 and 9. Accordingly, even though this potentially may be a case in which the value of the stock substantially appreciated during the year, the member should consider the reasonableness of the assumption and consistency with other information known to the member in connection with preparing the projection. The member should consider whether to document discussions concerning the increase in value of the stock with the taxpayer.

47. *Illustration 18.* The tax consequences to Target Corporation's shareholders of an acquisition turn in part on Acquiring Corporation's continuance of the trade or business of Target Corporation for some time after the acquisition. The member is preparing a tax opinion addressed to Target's shareholders. A colleague has drafted a tax opinion for the member's review. That opinion makes an explicit assumption that Acquiring will continue Target's business for two years following the acquisition.

48. *Conclusion.* In conducting the due diligence necessary to establish the relevant background facts, the member should consider whether it is appropriate to rely on an assumption concerning facts in lieu of a representation from another person. In this case, the member should make reasonable efforts to obtain a representation from Acquiring Corporation concerning its plan to continue Target's business and further consider whether to request a written representation to that effect.

49. *Illustration 19.* The member receives a telephone call from a taxpayer who is the sole shareholder of a corporation. The taxpayer indicates that he is thinking about exchanging his stock in the corporation for stock in a publicly traded business. During the call, the member explains how the transaction should be structured so it will qualify as a tax-free acquisition.

50. *Conclusion.* Although oral advice may serve a taxpayer's needs appropriately in routine matters or in well-defined areas, written communications are recommended in important, unusual, or complicated transactions. The member should use professional judgment about the need to document oral advice.

51. *Illustration 20.* The member receives a telephone call from a taxpayer who wants to know whether he or she should lease or purchase a car. During the call, the member explains how the arrangement should be structured so as to help achieve the taxpayer's objectives.

52. *Conclusion.* In this situation, the member's response is in conformity with this Interpretation in view of the routine nature

of the inquiry and the well-defined tax issues. However, the member should evaluate whether other considerations, such as avoiding misunderstanding with the taxpayer, suggest that the conversation should be documented.

This Interpretation was adopted by the assenting votes of the eighteen voting members of the nineteen-member Tax Executive Committee.

Note: *Statements on Standards for Tax Services are issued by the Tax Executive Comittee, the senior technical body of the Institute designated to promulgate standards of tax practice. Rules 201 and 202 of the Institute's Code of Professional Conduct require compliance with these standards.*

These Statements on Standards for Tax Services and Interpretation were unanimously adopted by the assenting votes of the twenty voting members of the twenty-one-member Tax Executive Committee.

EXPOSURE DRAFT DECEMBER 30, 2005

PROPOSED STATEMENT ON STANDARDS FOR TAX SERVICES QUALITY CONTROL

INTRODUCTION

1. This Statement sets forth the applicable standards for members concerning the obligation to have a system of quality control for their tax practice (public practice) or function (nonpublic practice). In light of the fact that members practice in various forms, or with various size employers, and therefore cannot take personal responsibility for every aspect of such tax practice or function, there has arisen a need for a Statement on what constitutes an adequate system of quality control in a tax practice or function to enhance compliance with the other aspects of the Statements on Standards for Tax Services (SSTSs). For purposes of this Statement, a *system of quality control* is broadly defined as a process to provide the member with reasonable assurance that the *firm* (public practice) or *employer's* (nonpublic practice) *personnel* (for purposes of this Statement, the term *personnel* includes partners, officers, employees, and other associates of the tax practice or function) comply with applicable professional standards.

STATEMENT

2. In general, a member's firm or employer should establish and maintain for its tax practice or function a system of quality control that includes the five elements of quality control (detailed in paragraph 4 and others that follow) and other matters essential to the effective design, implementation, and maintenance of the system. A member providing tax services is encouraged to practice in a firm or work for an employer that has established and maintains an adequate system of quality control for its tax practice or function. However, it is the responsibility of the member(s) in charge of such tax practice or function to ensure an appropriate system of tax practice quality control is implemented.

3. A system of quality control for a tax practice or function should encompass the organizational structure and the policies adopted and procedures established to provide reasonable assurance that such tax practice or function is in compliance with professional standards. The nature, extent, comprehensiveness, and formality of a tax practice or function's quality control policies and procedures may vary due to considerations such as the size of the tax practice or function, the number of offices, the degree of authority granted to personnel and offices, the knowledge and experience of personnel, the nature of the tax practice

or function, the practice area(s) or area(s) of specialty and appropriate cost-benefit considerations. While this Statement is applicable to all members, including members in industry, it must be recognized that each system of quality control must take into account the unique aspects of the tax practice or function, especially with regard to those members providing tax services to employers.

4. *Elements of Quality Control.* To be effective, any system of tax practice quality control should contain policies and procedures covering the following five elements:

a. Integrity and objectivity
b. Personnel management
c. Acceptance and continuance of clients and engagements (public practice only)
d. Performance of professional services
e. Monitoring and inspection

EXPLANATION

Integrity and Objectivity

5. In a tax practice or function, the member and his or her personnel often act as an advocate for the taxpayer. The member and his or her personnel should seek to advocate with integrity and objectivity the taxpayer's position as long as that position and their efforts are in compliance with the AICPA Code of Professional Conduct, including the SSTSs (see SSTS No. 1, *Tax Return Positions* [AICPA, *Professional Standards,* vol. 2, TS sec. 100.04]) and applicable federal, state, and local laws. In addition, a member in public practice should consider the applicability, if any, of auditor independence issues to his or her practice; see Rule 2-01 of Regulation S-X, Preliminary Note, 17 CFR 210.2-01. In fulfilling this role, the member is encouraged to practice in a firm or work for an employer that has established and maintains policies and procedures to provide reasonable assurance that personnel perform all professional responsibilities with integrity, and maintain objectivity in discharging his or her professional responsibilities. Integrity requires the member and his or her personnel to be honest and candid within the constraints of taxpayer confidentiality. Service and the public trust should not be subordinated to personal gain and advantage. Objectivity is a state of mind and a quality that lends value to a tax practice or function.

6. The member's firm or employer should consider establishing and maintaining policies and procedures to accomplish the following objectives to the extent such objectives are applicable to such tax practice or function:

a. Require that personnel adhere to the AICPA Code of Professional Conduct, including the SSTS, Treasury Department Circular No. 230, and any other applicable laws or standards of relevant tax or regulatory agencies (such as state boards of accountancy and federal, foreign, state, and local tax authorities).
b. Communicate to personnel policies and procedures relating to integrity and objectivity. This includes the need to treat as confidential all information regarding taxpayer matters.
c. Document, where appropriate, compliance with policies and procedures relating to integrity and objectivity.

Personnel Management

7. A tax practice system of quality control depends heavily on the proficiency of the firm or employer's personnel. In making assignments, the nature and extent of supervision to be provided should be considered. Generally, the more able and experienced the personnel assigned to a particular engagement or task, the less direct supervision is needed.

8. Personnel management encompasses hiring, assigning personnel to engagements or tasks, supervision, professional development, and advancement activities. Accordingly, the member's firm or employer should consider establishing and maintaining policies and procedures to provide its tax practice or function with reasonable assurance that:

a. Those personnel hired possess the appropriate characteristics to enable them to perform competently.
b. Work is assigned to personnel having the degree of technical training and proficiency required under the circumstances.
c. Personnel are adequately supervised.
d. Personnel participate in tax, general, and (as appropriate) industry-specific continuing professional education and other professional development activities that enable them to fulfill responsibilities assigned, and satisfy applicable continuing professional education requirements of the AICPA, state boards of accountancy, and other regulatory agencies.
e. The performance of tax professionals and other personnel involved in the tax practice or function is periodically evaluated and their progress reviewed with them.
f. Personnel selected for advancement have the necessary qualifications to fulfill the responsibilities they will be called on to assume.

Acceptance and Continuance of Clients and Engagements (Public Practice Only)

9. In public practice, the member's firm should consider establishing and maintaining policies and procedures for deciding whether to accept or continue a client relationship and whether to perform a specific engagement for that client (see also SSTS No. 6, *Knowledge of Error: Return Preparation* [AICPA, *Professional Standards,* vol. 2, TS sec. 600], and SSTS No. 7, *Knowledge of Error: Administrative Proceedings* [AICPA, *Professional Standards,* vol. 2, TS sec. 700]). Establishing such policies and procedures does not imply that a member vouches for the integrity or reliability of a client, nor does it imply that a member has a duty to any person or entity with respect to the acceptance, rejection, or retention of clients. Prudence suggests that a member be selective in determining his or her client relationships and the professional services he or she will provide. These policies and procedures should also provide reasonable assurance that the tax practice:

a. Undertakes only those engagements that can be completed with professional competence, and *b.* Appropriately considers the risks associated with providing professional services in the particular circumstances.

10. The member's firm should consider establishing and maintaining policies and procedures to accomplish the following objectives to the extent applicable to its tax practice:

a. The evaluation and approval of prospective clients, including (when appropriate) contact with predecessor tax preparers.

b. The documentation of the client's understanding and acceptance of the scope of the member's services, the member's responsibility for tax advice and returns, and the financial aspects of the client's relationship with the member. These understandings should be memorialized through the use of engagement letters or alternative documentation.

c. The review and evaluation of clients periodically or upon the occurrence of specific events to determine whether the relationship should be continued, modified, or terminated.

Performance of Professional Services

11. The member's firm or employer should consider establishing and maintaining policies and procedures to provide reasonable assurance that the tax services performed by its personnel meet applicable professional standards, including the AICPA SSTS, regulatory requirements, and the tax practice's or function's standards of quality. To the extent appropriate and as required by applicable professional standards, these policies and procedures should cover planning, performing, supervising, reviewing, documenting, and communicating the results of all tax services. The extent of the supervision and review appropriate in a given situation depends on many factors, including the complexity of the subject matter, the qualifications of the personnel performing the service, and the extent of the consultation used.

12. The member's firm or employer should consider establishing and maintaining policies and procedures to accomplish the following to the extent such objectives are applicable to its tax practice or function:

a. Planning services, including specific evaluation of risk factors.

b. Providing the appropriate level of supervision to personnel.

c. Maintaining the tax practice or function's standards in the performance of specific services.

d. Reviewing working papers, reports, tax returns, tax opinions or advice, and substantive tax correspondence relevant to the services.

e. Documenting the compliance *aspects* of a tax practice or function, including tax return status and due date maintenance. This includes the establishment of appropriate record retention procedures for a member's tax practice or function.

f. Communicating the results of the service as appropriate.

g. Designating individuals within and without the tax practice or function to serve as authoritative sources, and defining their authority in consultative situations. This includes establishing procedures to resolve differences of opinion.

Monitoring and Inspection

13. To provide reasonable assurance that the firm or employer's tax practice quality control system achieves its objectives, appropriate consideration should be given to the assignment of quality control responsibilities within the tax practice or function, the means by which quality control policies and procedures are communicated, and the extent to which the policies and procedures and compliance therewith should be documented. The size, structure, and nature of the firm's tax practice or employer's tax function should be considered in determining whether documentation of quality control policies and procedures is required and, if so, the extent of such documentation. For example, documentation of quality control policies and procedures would generally be expected to be more extensive in a large tax practice or function than in a small one. Similarly, quality control should be more extensive in a multioffice tax practice or function than in a single location.

14. The member's firm or employer should consider establishing and maintaining policies and procedures to accomplish the following objectives to the extent applicable to its tax practice or function:

a. Documenting compliance with the tax practice or function's policies and procedures, as well as the SSTSs and relevant professional codes and guidelines.

b. Maintaining an appropriate library of reference materials, practice guides, and access to appropriate online materials

c. Providing an effective program of professional development and educational activities.

d. Where appropriate, defining the appropriate scope and content of the tax practice or function's inspection program, reporting inspection findings to the appropriate management levels, and monitoring actions taken or planned.

e. Reviewing the relevance and adequacy of its quality control policies and procedures for each of the other elements of the quality control system.

Administration and Documentation of a Quality Control System

15. Responsibility for the design and maintenance of the various quality control policies and procedures should be assigned to an appropriate individual(s) in the tax practice or function. In making that assignment, consideration should be given to the proficiency of the individual(s), the authority to be delegated, and the extent of supervision to be provided. However, all the tax practice or function's personnel are responsible for complying with the quality control policies and procedures.

16. A member's firm or employer should communicate its tax practice quality control policies and procedures to personnel in a manner that provides reasonable assurance that personnel understand and comply with those policies and procedures. The form and extent of such communications should be sufficiently comprehensive and timely to provide personnel with an understanding of the tax practice quality control policies and procedures applicable to them, including changes to such policies and procedures.

Tax Executive Committee
(2005–2006)

Thomas J. Purcell, III, *Chair*	Andrew M. Mattson
Jeffrey R. Hoops, *Vice Chair*	Kenneth N. Orbach
Evelyn M. Capassakis	W. Val Oveson
Stephen R. Corrick	S. Richard Royster II
Alan R. Einhorn	James W. Sansone
Diane D. Fuller	Joseph F. Scutellaro
John C. Gardner	Patricia Thompson
Janice M. Johnson	Paul H. Wilner
Dean A. Jorgensen	Carol E. Zurcher

Tax Practice Responsibilities Committee
(2005–2006)

Eve Elgin, *Chair*	Sharon S. Lassar
J. Edward Swails, *Immediate Past Chair*	Keith R. Lee
	Jay M. Levine
Timothy J. Burke, Jr.	Susan J. Rosenberg
Arthur J. Kip Delinger, Jr.	Eric E. Santa Maria
Jeffrey Frishman	Mark N. Schneider
Mary Lou Gervie	Gerard H. Schreiber, Jr.

SSTS Quality Control Task Force

Joseph F. Scutellaro, *Chair*	Arthur J. Kip Dellinger, Jr.
Lawrence H. Carlton	David L. Meyer
Conrad M. Davis	Joe B. Marchbein
	J. Edward Swails

AICPA Staff

Thomas P. Ochsenschlager *Vice President—Taxation* *Tax Division*	Edward S. Karl *Director* *Tax Division*
William R. Stromsem *Director* *Tax Division*	Carol B. Ferguson *Technical Manager* *Tax Division*

The AICPA gratefully acknowledges the contributions of Barbara A. Bond, Alan R. Einhorn, John C. Gardner, James W. Sansone, and Patricia Thompson, members of the Tax Executive Committee, and Benson S. Goldstein, AICPA Technical Manager.

APPENDIX F

COMPARISON OF TAX ATTRIBUTES FOR C CORPORATIONS, PARTNERSHIPS, AND S CORPORATIONS

APPENDIX F: COMPARISON OF TAX ATTRIBUTES FOR C CORPORATIONS, PARTNERSHIPS, AND S CORPORATIONS

Tax Attribute	C Corporation	Partnership	S Corporation
I. General Characteristics			
1. Application of the separate entity versus conduit (flow through) concept.	*Entity:* The corporation is treated as a separate taxpaying entity. If the corporation distributes income to shareholders in the form of dividends, the shareholders are subject to a second tax on such amounts. Shareholders also are subject to a second tax if they sell their stock.	*Conduit:* The partners report their distributive share of partnership ordinary income and separately stated items on their tax returns. Most elections, such as depreciation methods, accounting period and methods, are made at the partnership level. Special tax rules apply to electing large partnerships.	*Conduit:* Similar to the partnership form of organization. However, the S corporation may be subject to tax at the corporate level on excess net passive income, or built-in gains under special circumstances.
2. Period of existence.	Continues until dissolution; not effected by stock sales by shareholders.	Termination can occur by agreement, or by death, retirement, or disaffiliation of a partner.	Same as for C corporation.
3. Transferability of interest.	Stock can be transferred easily; corporation may retain right to buy back shares.	Addition of new partner or transfer of partner's interest generally requires approval of other partners.	Same as for C corporation.
4. Liability exposure.	Shareholders generally liable only for capital contributions.	General partners are personally, jointly, and severally liable for partnership obligations. Limited partners usually are liable only for capital contributions.	Same as for C corporation.
5. Management responsibility.	Shareholders may be part of management or may hire outside management.	All general partners participate in management. Limited partners generally do not participate.	Because of limited number of shareholders, shareholders usually are part of management.
II. Election and Restrictions			
1. Restrictions on: a. Type of owners.	No restriction.	No restriction.	Limited to individuals, estates, charitable organizations, and certain kinds of trusts.
b. Number of owners.	No restriction.	No restriction.	Limited to 100 shareholders, where a family counts as one shareholder.
c. Type of entity.	Includes domestic or foreign corporations, unincorporated entities known as associations, and certain kinds of trusts. A publicly traded partnership is taxed as a corporation unless more than 90% of its income is qualifying passive income. Grandfathered publicly traded partnerships can avoid corporate taxation by paying an excise tax. Partnerships, LLCs, and proprietorships can elect to be taxed as a corporation under the check-the-box regulations.	Includes a variety of unincorporated entities including limited liability company and limited liability partnership forms. Certain joint undertakings are excluded from partnership status.	Domestic corporations and unincorporated entities (e.g., associations) are eligible. A partnership, LLC, or proprietorship that elects to be treated as an S corporpation automatically is considered to have elected to be treated as a corporation under the check-the-box regulations.

APPENDIX F: COMPARISON OF TAX ATTRIBUTES FOR C CORPORATIONS, PARTNERSHIPS, AND S CORPORATIONS

Tax Attribute	C Corporation	Partnership	S Corporation
d. Special tax classifications.	No restriction.	No restriction.	S corporation cannot be a former Domestic International Sales Corporation, or have elected the special Puerto Rico and U.S. Possessions tax credit. Certain financial institutions and insurance companies also are ineligible.
e. Investments made by entity.	No restriction.	No restriction.	S corporation can own 80% or more of a C corporation but cannot file a consolidated tax return with the C corporation.
f. Capital structure.	No restriction.	No restriction.	Limited to a single class of stock that is outstanding. Differences in voting rights are disregarded. Special "safe harbor" rules are available for debt issues.
g. Passive interest income.	No restriction.	No restriction.	Passive investment income cannot exceed 25% of gross receipts for three consecutive tax years when the corporation also has Subchapter C E&P at the end of the year.
2. Election and shareholder consent.	No election required.	No election required.	Election can be made during the preceding tax year or first 2½ months of the tax year. Shareholders must consent to the election.
3. Termination of election.	Not applicable.	The partnership can terminate if it does not carry on any business, financial operation, or venture or if a sale or exchange of at least 50% of the profits and capital interests occurs within a 12-month period.	Occurs if one of the requirements is failed after the election is first effective or if the passive investment income test is failed for three consecutive tax years. IRS can waive invalid elections and permit inadvertent terminations not to break the S election.
4. Revocation of election.	Not applicable.	Not applicable.	Election may be revoked only by shareholders owning more than one-half of the stock. Must be made in first 2½ months of tax year or on a prospective basis.
5. New election.	Not applicable.	Not applicable.	Not permitted for five-year period without IRS consent to early reelection.

APPENDIX F: COMPARISON OF TAX ATTRIBUTES FOR C CORPORATIONS, PARTNERSHIPS, AND S CORPORATIONS

Tax Attribute	C Corporation	Partnership	S Corporation
III. Accounting Periods and Elections			
1. Taxable year.	Calendar year or fiscal year is permitted. Personal service corporations are restricted to using a calendar year unless IRS grants approval to use a fiscal year. A special election is available to use a fiscal year resulting in a three-month or less income deferral if the corporation meets a series of minimum distribution requirements.	Generally use tax year of majority or principal partners. Otherwise use of the least aggregate deferral year is required. Can use a fiscal year that has a business purpose for which IRS approval is obtained. An electing partnership may use a fiscal year resulting in a three-month or less income deferral if an additional required payment is made.	Can use a fiscal year that has a business purpose for which IRS approval is obtained. An S corporation may use a fiscal year resulting in a three-month or less income deferral if an additional required payment is made. If neither of the above applies, a calendar year must be used.
2. Accounting methods.	Elected by the corporation. Use of cash method of accounting is restricted for certain personal service corporations and C corporations having $5 million or more annual gross receipts.	Elected by the partnership. Restrictions on the use of the cash method of accounting apply to partnerships having a C corporation as a partner or that are tax shelters.	Elected by the S corporation. Restrictions on the use of the cash method of accounting apply to S corporations that are tax shelters.
IV. Taxability of Profits			
1. Taxability of profits.	Ordinary income and capital gains are taxed to the corporation. Profits are taxed a second time when distributed.	Ordinary income and separately stated income and gain items pass through to the partners at the end of the partnership's tax year whether or not distributed.	Same as partnership.
2. Allocation of profits.	Not applicable.	Based on partnership agreement. Special allocations are permitted.	Based on stock ownership on each day of the tax year. Special allocations are not permitted.
3. Character of income.	Distributed profits (including tax-exempt income) are dividends to extent of earnings and profits (E&P).	Items receiving special treatment (e.g., capital gains or tax-exempt income) pass through separately to the partner and retain same character as when earned by the partnership.	Same as partnership.
4. Maximum tax rate for earnings.	15% on the first $50,000; 25% from $50,000 to $75,000; 34% from $75,000 to $10 million. The rate is 35% for taxable income above $10 million. A 5% surcharge applies to taxable income between $100,000 and $335,000, and a 3% surcharge applies to taxable income between $15 million and $18,333,333. Special rules apply to controlled groups. Personal service corporations are taxed at a flat 35% rate.	Rates of tax applicable to noncorporate partners from 10% through 35% (in 2007) are levied on pass-through income from the partnership. C corporation rates apply to corporate partners.	Same as partnership except for certain special situations where a special corporate tax applies to the S corporation.

APPENDIX F: COMPARISON OF TAX ATTRIBUTES FOR C CORPORATIONS, PARTNERSHIPS, AND S CORPORATIONS

Tax Attribute	C Corporation	Partnership	S Corporation
5. Special tax levies.	Can be subject to accumulated earnings tax, personal holding company tax, and corporate alternative minimum tax.	Not applicable.	Can be subject to built-in gains tax, excess net passive income tax, and LIFO recapture tax.
6. Income splitting between family members.	Only possible when earnings are distributed to shareholder. Dividends received by shareholder under age 18 are taxed at parents' marginal tax rate.	Transfer of partnership interest by gift will permit income splitting. Subject to special rules for transactions involving family members requiring payment of reasonable compensation for capital and services. Income received by partner under age 18 is taxed at parents' marginal tax rate.	Transfer of S corporation interest by gift will permit income splitting. Special rules apply to transactions involving family members requiring payment of reasonable compensation for capital and services. Income received by shareholder under age 18 is taxed at parents' marginal tax rate.
7. Sale of ownership interest.	Gain is taxed as capital gain; 50% of gain may be excluded under Sec. 1202 qualified small business stock rules. Loss is eligible for Sec. 1244 treatment.	Gain may be either ordinary income or capital gain depending on the nature of underlying partnership assets. Losses usually are capital.	Gain is capital in nature but is not eligible for special Sec. 1202 small business stock rules. Loss is eligible for Sec. 1244 treatment.
V. Treatment of Special Income, Gain, Loss, Deduction and Credit Items			
1. Capital gains and losses.	Long-term capital gains are taxed at regular tax rates. Capital losses offset capital gains; excess losses carried back three years and forward five years.	Passed through to partners (according to partnership agreement).	Passed through to shareholders (on a daily basis according to stock ownership).
2. Section 1231 gains and losses.	Eligible for long-term capital gain or ordinary loss treatment. Loss recapture occurs at the corporate level.	Passed through to partners. Loss recapture occurs at the partner level.	Same as partnership.
3. Dividends received from domestic corporation.	Eligible for 70%, 80%, or 100% dividends-received deduction.	Passed through to noncorporate partners, subject to the maximum 15% tax rate if qualified. Corporate partners may be eligible for the dividends-received deduction.	Same as partnership except S corporation cannot have corporate shareholders.
4. U.S. production activities deduction.	Deduction equals a 6% (in 2007) times the lesser of (1) qualified production activities income for the year or (2) taxable income before the U.S. production activities deduction. The deduction, however, cannot exceed 50% of the corporation's W-2 wages for the year.	Passed through to partners. Limitations apply at partner level.	Same as partnership.
5. Organizational expenditures.	Deduct up to $5,000 and amortize balance over 180 months.	Same as C corporation.	Same as partnership.
6. Charitable contributions.	Limited to 10% of taxable income.	Passed through to partners. Limitations apply at partner level.	Same as partnership.
7. Expensing of asset acquisition costs.	Limited to $112,000 in 2007.	Limited to $112,000 in 2007 for the partnership and for each partner.	Same as partnership.

APPENDIX F: COMPARISON OF TAX ATTRIBUTES FOR C CORPORATIONS, PARTNERSHIPS, AND S CORPORATIONS

Tax Attribute	C Corporation	Partnership	S Corporation
8. Expenses owed to related parties.	Regular Sec. 267 rules apply to payments and sales or exchanges made to or by the corporation and certain other related parties (e.g., controlling shareholder and corporation or members of a controlled group).	Regular Sec. 267 rules can apply. Special Sec. 267 rules for passthrough entities apply to payments made by the partnership to a partner.	Same as partnership.
9. Employment-related tax considerations.	An owner-employee may be treated as an employee for Social Security tax and corporate fringe benefit purposes. The corporate qualified pension and profit-sharing benefits available to owner-employees are comparable to the plan benefits for self-employed individuals (partners and sole proprietors).	A partner is not considered an employee of the business. Therefore, the partner must pay self-employment tax on the net self-employment income from the business. Corporate fringe benefit exclusions such as group term life insurance are not available (i.e., the premiums are not deductible by the business and are not excludable from the partner's income). Fringe benefits may be provided as nontaxable distribution or as taxable compensation.	Corporate fringe benefit exclusions generally are not available to S corporation shareholders. Fringe benefits usually are provided as nontaxable distribution or taxable compensation. S corporation shareholders may be treated as employees, however, for Social Security tax payments and qualified pension and profit sharing plan rules.
10. Tax preference items and AMT adjustments.	Subject to the corporate alternative minimum tax at the corporate level.	Passed through to partners and taxed under the alternative minimum tax rules applicable to the partner.	Same as partnership.
VI. Deductibility of Losses and Special Items			
1. Deductibility of losses.	Losses create net operating loss (NOL) that carry back two years or forward 20 years or capital loss that carry back three years or forward five years.	Ordinary losses and separately stated loss and deduction items pass through to the partners at the end of the partnership tax year. May create a personal NOL.	Same as partnership.
2. Allocation of losses.	Not applicable.	Based on partnership agreement. Special allocations are permitted.	Based on stock ownership on each day of the tax year. Special allocations are not permitted.
3. Shareholder and entity loss limitations.	Passive losses may be restricted under the passive activity limitation if the C corporation is closely held.	Limited to partner's basis for the partnership interest. Ratable share of all partnership liabilities is included in basis of partnership interest. Excess losses carry over indefinitely until partnership interest again has a basis. Subject to at-risk, passive activity, and hobby loss restrictions.	Limited to shareholder's basis for the stock interest plus basis of S corporation debts to the shareholder. Excess losses carry over indefinitely until shareholder again has basis for stock or debt. Subject to the at-risk, passive activity, and hobby loss restrictions.
4. Basis adjustments for debt and equity interests.	Not applicable.	Basis in partnership interest reduced by loss and deduction passthrough. Subsequent profits increase basis of partnership interest.	Basis in S corporation stock reduced by loss and deduction passthrough. Once basis of stock has been reduced to zero, any other losses and deductions reduce basis of debt (but not below zero). Subsequent net increases restore basis reductions to debt before increasing basis of stock.

Tax Attribute	C Corporation	Partnership	S Corporation
5. Investment interest deduction limitation.	Not applicable.	Investment interest expenses and income pass through to the partners. Limitation applies at partner level.	Same as partnership.
VII. Distributions			
1. Taxability of nonliquidating distributions to shareholder.	Taxable as dividends if made from current or accumulated E&P. Additional distributions first reduce shareholder's basis for stock, and distributions exceeding stock basis trigger capital gain recognition.	Nontaxable unless money, money equivalents, or marketable securities received by the partner exceeds his or her basis for the partnership interest.	Nontaxable if made from the accumulated adjustment account or shareholder's basis for his or her stock. Taxable if made out of accumulated E&P or after stock basis has been reduced to zero.
2. Taxability of nonliquidating distributions to distributing entity.	Gain (but not loss) recognized as if the corporation had sold the property for its FMV immediately before the distribution.	No gain or loss recognized by the partnership except when a disproportionate distribution of Sec. 751 property occurs.	Gain (but not loss) recognized and passed through to the shareholders as if the corporation had sold the property for its FMV immediately before the distribution. Gain may be taxed to the S corporation under one of the special tax levies.
3. Basis adjustment to owner's investment for distribution.	None unless the distribution exceeds E&P.	Amount of money or adjusted basis of distributed property reduces basis in partnership interest.	Amount of money or FMV of distributed property reduces basis of stock except when distribution is made out of accumulated E&P.
VIII. Other Items			
1. Tax return.	Form 1120 or 1120-A. Schedule M-3 may be required.	Form 1065 (Information Return). Schedule M-3 may be required.	Form 1120S (Information Return). Schedule M-3 may be required.
2. Due date.	March 15 for calendar year C corporations.	April 15 for calendar year partnerships.	March 15 for calendar year S corporations.
3. Extensions of time permitted.	Six months.	Six months.	Six months.
4. Estimated tax payments required.	Yes—April 15, June 15, September 15, and December 15 for calendar year C corporations.	No—Estimated taxes are required of the partners for passed through income, etc.	Yes—Applies to built-in gains tax and excess net passive income tax.
5. Audit rules.	IRS audits corporation independently of its shareholders.	Special audit rules apply requiring audit of partnership and requiring partners to take a position consistent with the partnership tax return.	Special rules require consistent tax treatment for Subchapter S items on the corporation and shareholder returns.

APPENDIX G

RESERVED

APPENDIX H

ACTUARIAL TABLES

TRANSFERS MADE AFTER APRIL 30, 1999
EXCERPT FROM TABLE S
SINGLE LIFE REMAINDER FACTORS

	INTEREST RATE								
AGE	7%	8%	9%	10%	AGE	7%	8%	9%	10%
25	.05570	.04218	.03298	.02656	58	.28061	.24453	.21507	.19080
26	.05845	.04438	.03476	.02802	59	.29269	.25610	.22608	.20123
27	.06140	.04676	.03670	.02962	60	.30500	.26794	.23738	.21196
28	.06451	.04929	.03877	.03133	61	.31757	.28007	.24900	.22304
29	.06780	.05198	.04099	.03318	62	.33044	.29255	.26100	.23451
30	.07127	.05483	.04335	.03515	63	.34363	.30539	.27339	.24641
31	.07491	.05785	.04585	.03725	64	.35711	.31857	.28615	.25870
32	.07875	.06103	.04851	.03948	65	.37087	.33208	.29930	.27140
33	.08279	.06441	.05135	.04188	66	.38496	.34597	.31285	.28456
34	.08705	.06798	.05436	.04444	67	.39941	.36028	.32689	.29823
35	.09155	.07179	.05758	.04718	68	.41419	.37499	.34138	.31240
36	.09628	.07581	.06101	.05012	69	.42927	.39006	.35628	.32703
37	.10126	.08006	.06466	.05325	70	.44456	.40540	.37151	.34204
38	.10652	.08459	.06855	.05662	71	.46000	.42095	.38701	.35736
39	.11206	.08938	.07270	.06023	72	.47554	.43666	.40271	.37293
40	.11791	.09447	.07714	.06411	73	.49114	.45249	.41858	.38872
41	.12409	.09989	.08189	.06828	74	.50686	.46849	.43469	.40479
42	.13061	.10564	.08696	.07277	75	.52276	.48474	.45111	.42123
43	.13747	.11174	.09237	.07758	76	.53888	.50130	.46790	.43811
44	.14469	.11819	.09813	.08272	77	.55523	.51815	.48506	.45543
45	.15223	.12496	.10420	.08817	78	.57177	.53527	.50257	.47317
46	.16011	.13207	.11061	.09395	79	.58840	.55256	.52032	.49122
47	.16830	.13950	.11733	.10004	80	.60497	.56985	.53813	.50939
48	.17682	.14727	.12439	.10646	81	.62135	.58701	.55587	.52754
49	.18568	.15539	.13181	.11322	82	.63748	.60395	.57343	.54557
50	.19490	.16388	.13960	.12037	83	.65334	.62066	.59081	.56346
51	.20448	.17275	.14777	.12789	84	.66904	.63727	.60813	.58134
52	.21438	.18196	.15630	.13577	85	.68467	.65386	.62550	.59934
53	.22461	.19151	.16518	.14400	86	.70010	.67029	.64276	.61728
54	.23516	.20140	.17441	.15260	87	.71511	.68632	.66965	.63489
55	.24604	.21166	.18402	.16157	88	.72968	.70194	.67615	.65213
56	.25725	.22227	.19400	.17093	89	.74381	.71712	.69224	.66900
57	.26879	.23324	.20436	.18069					

Source: Reg. Sec. 20.2031-7(d)(7).

EXCERPT FROM TABLE B
TERM CERTAIN REMAINDER FACTORS

	INTEREST RATE			
YEARS	7.0%	8.0%	9.0%	10.0%
1	.934579	.925926	.917431	.909091
2	.873439	.857339	.841680	.826446
3	.816298	.793832	.772183	.751315
4	.762895	.735030	.708425	.683013
5	.712986	.680583	.649931	.620921
6	.666342	.630170	.596267	.564474
7	.622750	.583490	.547034	.513158
8	.582009	.540269	.501866	.466507
9	.543934	.500249	.460428	.424098
10	.508349	.463193	.422411	.385543
11	.475093	.428883	.387533	.350494
12	.444012	.397114	.355535	.318631
13	.414964	.367698	.326179	.289664
14	.387817	.340461	.299246	.263331
15	.362446	.315242	.274538	.239392
16	.338735	.291890	.251870	.217629
17	.316574	.270269	.231073	.197845
18	.295864	.250249	.211994	.179859
19	.276508	.231712	.194490	.163508
20	.258419	.214548	.178431	.148644
21	.241513	.198656	.163698	.135131
22	.225713	.183941	.150182	.122846
23	.210947	.170315	.137781	.111678
24	.197147	.157699	.126405	.101526
25	.184249	.146018	.115968	.092296

Source: Reg. Secs. 20.7520-1(a)(1) and 20.2031-7(d)(6).

APPENDIX I

INDEX OF CODE SECTIONS

APPENDIX J

INDEX OF TREASURY REGULATIONS

Proposed Regulations

Temporary Regulations

APPENDIX K

INDEX OF GOVERNMENT PROMULGATIONS

APPENDIX L

INDEX OF COURT CASES

APPENDIX M

SUBJECT INDEX

2007
TAX RATE SCHEDULES

ESTATES AND TRUSTS

If taxable income is:	The tax is:
Not over $2,150	15% of taxable income.
Over $2,150 but not over $5,000	$322.50, plus 25% of the excess over $2,150.
Over $5,000 but not over $7,650	$1,035.00, plus 28% of the excess over $5,000.
Over $7,650 but not over $10,450	$1,777.00, plus 33% of the excess over $7,650.
Over $10,450	$2,701.00, plus 35% of the excess over $10,450.

CORPORATIONS

If Taxable Income Is:		The Tax Is:	
Over—	But Not Over—		Of the Amount Over—
$ 0	$ 50,000	15%	$ 0
50,000	75,000	$ 7,500 + 25%	50,000
75,000	100,000	13,750 + 34%	75,000
100,000	335,000	22,250 + 39%	100,000
335,000	10,000,000	113,900 + 34%	335,000
10,000,000	15,000,000	3,400,000 + 35%	10,000,000
15,000,000	18,333,333	5,150,000 + 38%	15,000,000
18,333,333		6,416,667 + 35%	18,333,333

UNIFIED CREDIT AMOUNT FOR ESTATE AND GIFT TAX

Year of Gift/Year of Death	Amount of Credit	Exemption Equivalent
January through June, 1977	$ 30,000 (6,000)*	$ 120,666 (30,000)*
July through December, 1977	30,000	120,666
1978	34,000	134,000
1979	38,000	147,333
1980	42,500	161,563
1981	47,000	175,625
1982	62,800	225,000
1983	79,300	275,000
1984	96,300	325,000
1985	121,800	400,000
1986	155,800	500,000
1987 through 1997	192,800	600,000
1998	202,050	625,000
1999	211,300	650,000
2000	220,550	675,000
2001	220,550	675,000
2002 and 2003	345,800	1,000,000
2004 and 2005	555,800 (345,800)*	1,500,000 (1,000,000)*
2006, 2007, and 2008	780,800 (345,800)*	2,000,000 (1,000,000)*
2009	1,455,800 (345,800)*	3,500,000 (1,000,000)*
2010	** (330,800)*	** (1,000,000)*
2011***	345,800 (345,800)*	1,000,000 (1,000,000)*

* The numbers in parentheses represent the credit and exemption equivalent amounts for the gift tax. The gift tax credit decreases in 2010 because the top gift tax rate drops to 35% for that year. ** The estate tax is scheduled to be repealed in 2010. The gift tax is not being repealed. *** Unless Congress acts otherwise, in 2011, the estate and gift tax rules will revert to what they would have been had Congress not enacted the 2001 Act.